FIGHTING PANTIES!

I love B movies. I love the way they make me think "What the hell is this?! That's crazy!" yet still draw me in so that I watch the whole thing. I really like that feeling, and I like to bring a little of that kind of over-the-top flavor into my own manga. That was the initial idea that gave birth to volume 1 of this alchemy manga. Thank you for picking it up. As you read it, please criticize it by saying to yourself "What kind of alchemy is that?!"

—Hiromu Arakawa, 2002

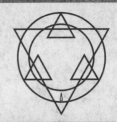

Born in Hokkaido (northern Japan), Hiromu Arakawa first attracted national attention in 1999 with her award-winning manga *Stray Dog*. Her series *Fullmetal Alchemist* debuted in 2001 in Square Enix's monthly manga anthology *Shonen Gangan*.

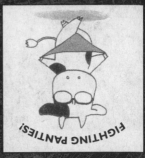

FULLMETAL ALCHEMIST

3-in-1 Edition

VIZ Media Omnibus Edition Volume 1
A compilation of the graphic novel volumes 1–3

Story and Art by Hiromu Arakawa

Translation/Akira Watanabe
English Adaptation/Jake Forbes, Egan Loo
Touch-up Art & Lettering/Wayne Truman
Manga Design/Amy Martin
Omnibus Design/Yukiko Whitley
Manga Editor/Jason Thompson
Omnibus Editor/Alexis Kirsch

FULLMETAL ALCHEMIST vol. 1–3
© 2002 Hiromu Arakawa/SQUARE ENIX.
First published in Japan in 2002 by SQUARE ENIX CO., LTD.
English translation rights arranged with SQUARE ENIX CO., LTD.
and VIZ Media, LLC.

Printed in the U.S.A.

Published by VIZ Media, LLC
P.O. Box 77010
San Francisco, CA 94107

11

Omnibus edition first printing, June 2011
Eleventh printing, October 2017

www.viz.com

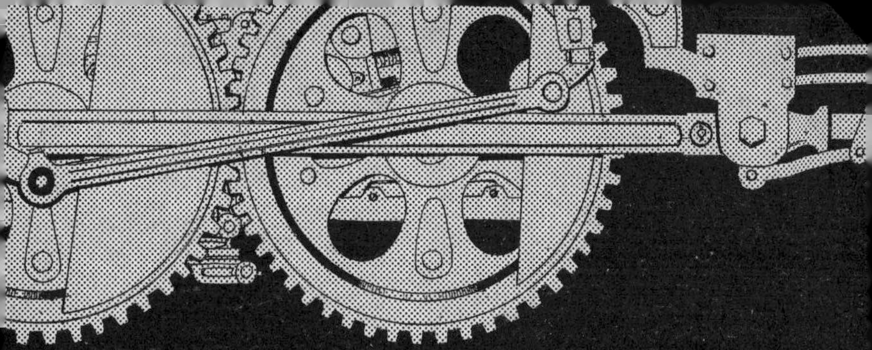

CONTENTS

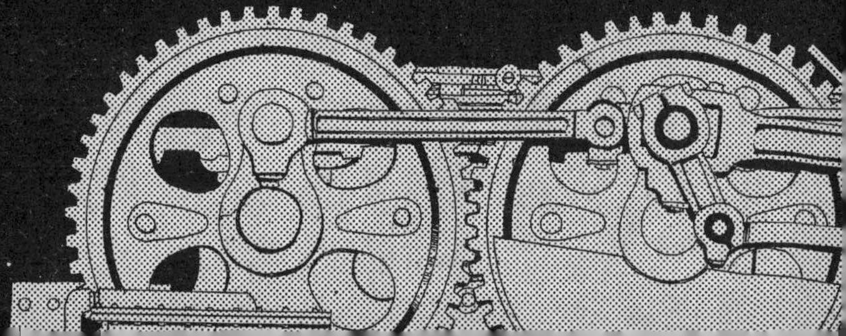

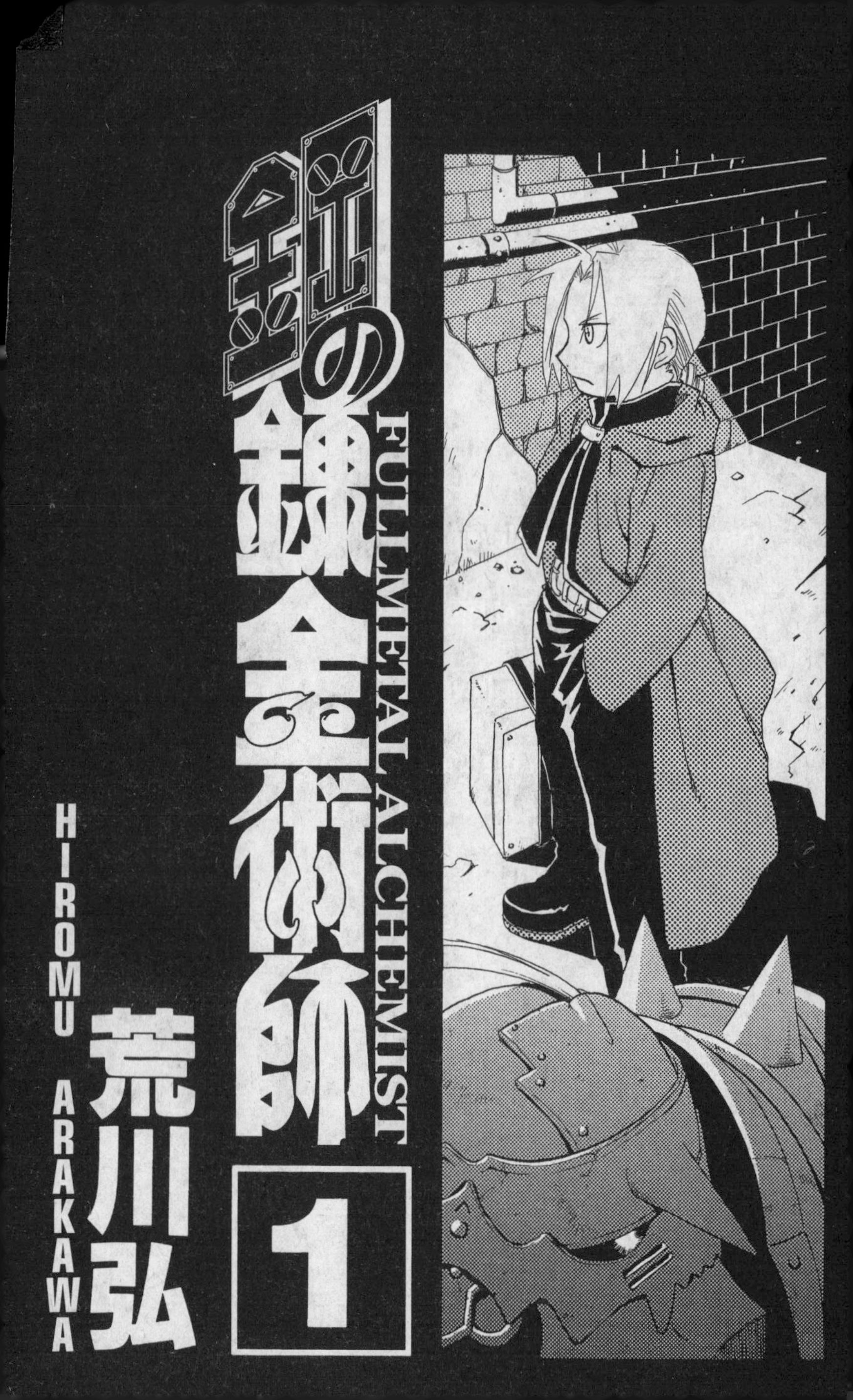

鋼の錬金術師

FULLMETAL ALCHEMIST

1

荒川弘

HIROMU ARAKAWA

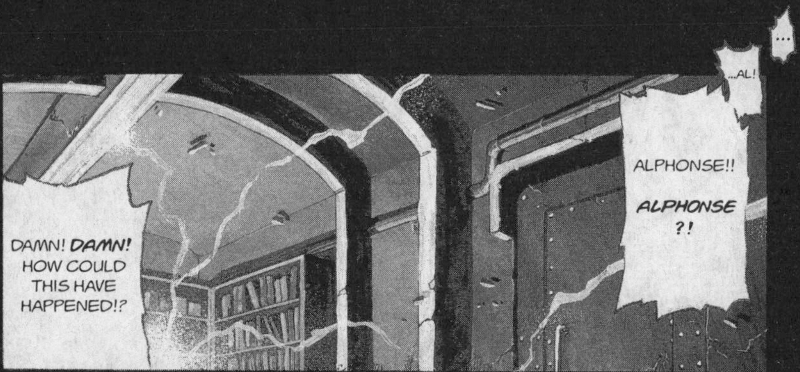
...
...AL!
ALPHONSE!! ALPHONSE ?!
DAMN! DAMN! HOW COULD THIS HAVE HAPPENED!?

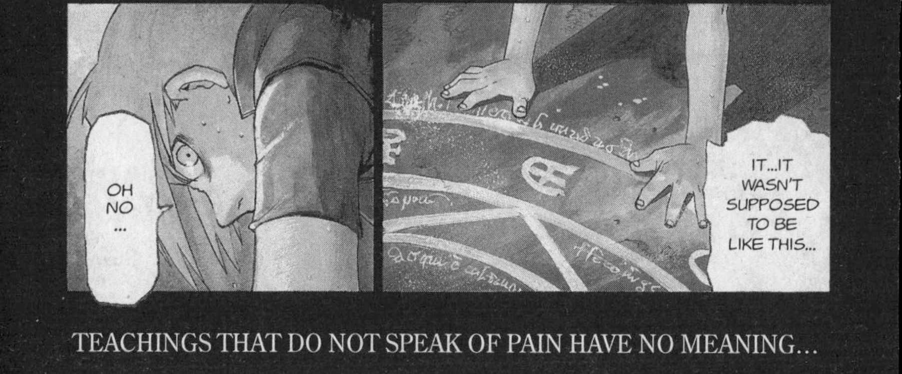
IT...IT WASN'T SUPPOSED TO BE LIKE THIS...
OH NO ...

TEACHINGS THAT DO NOT SPEAK OF PAIN HAVE NO MEANING...

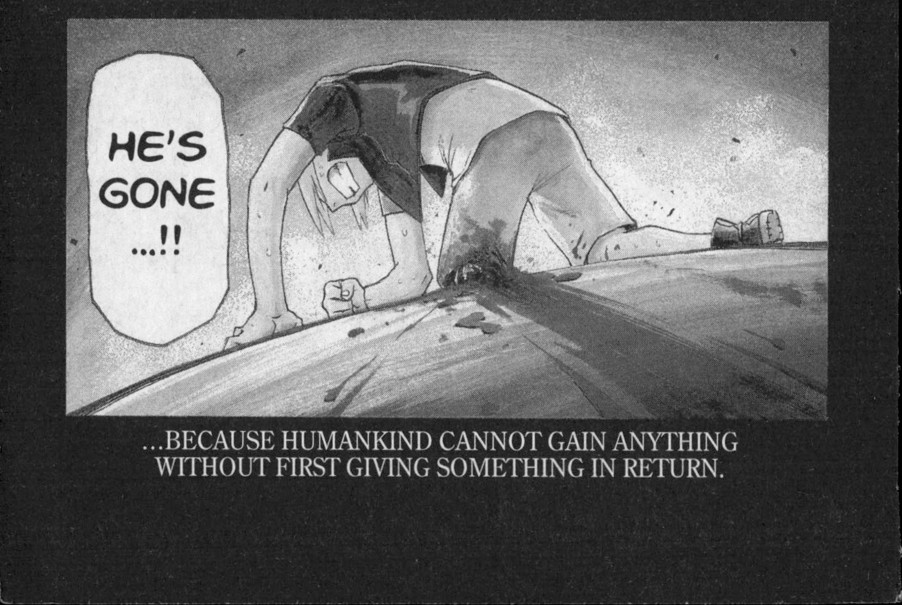
HE'S GONE ...!!

...BECAUSE HUMANKIND CANNOT GAIN ANYTHING WITHOUT FIRST GIVING SOMETHING IN RETURN.

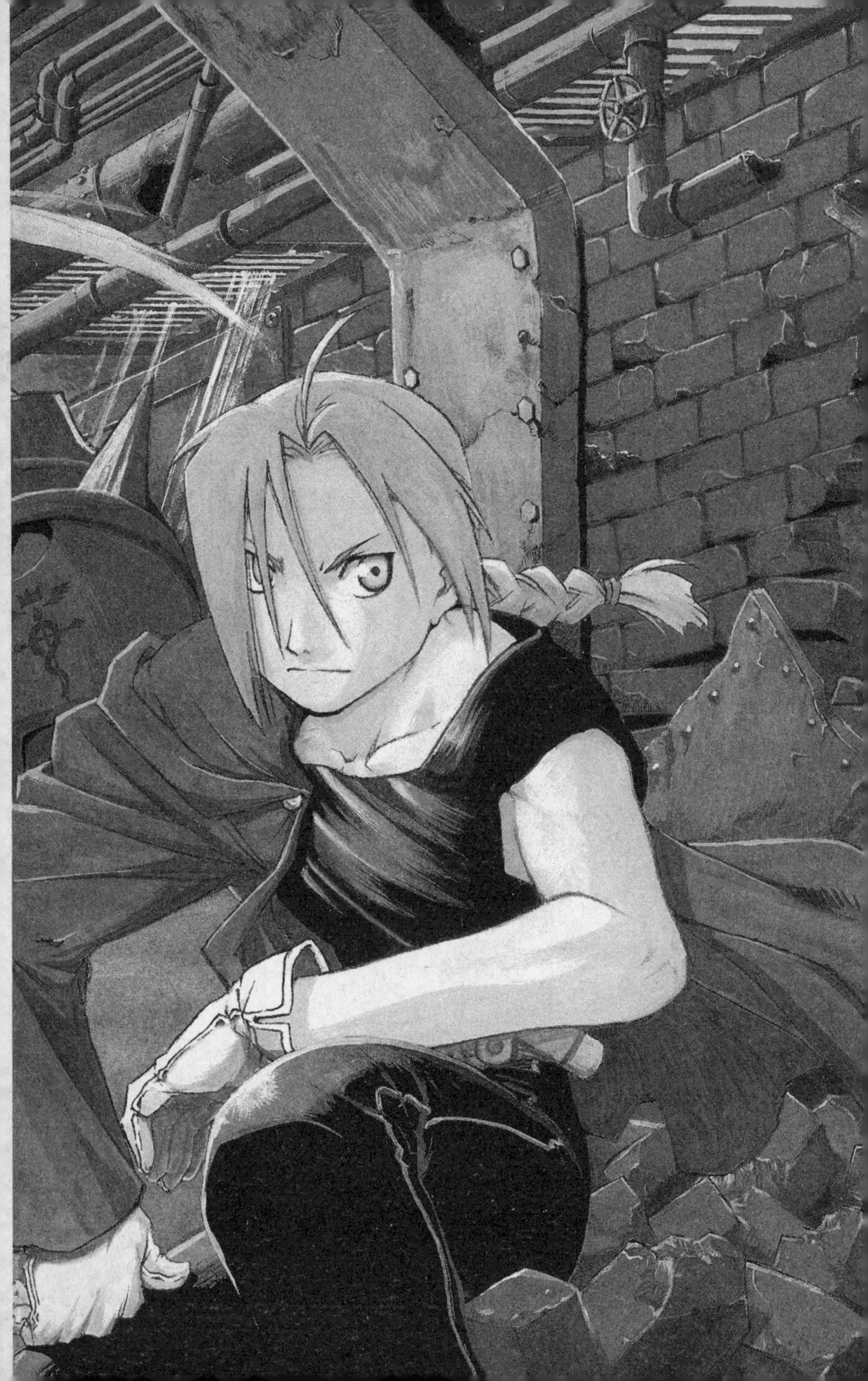

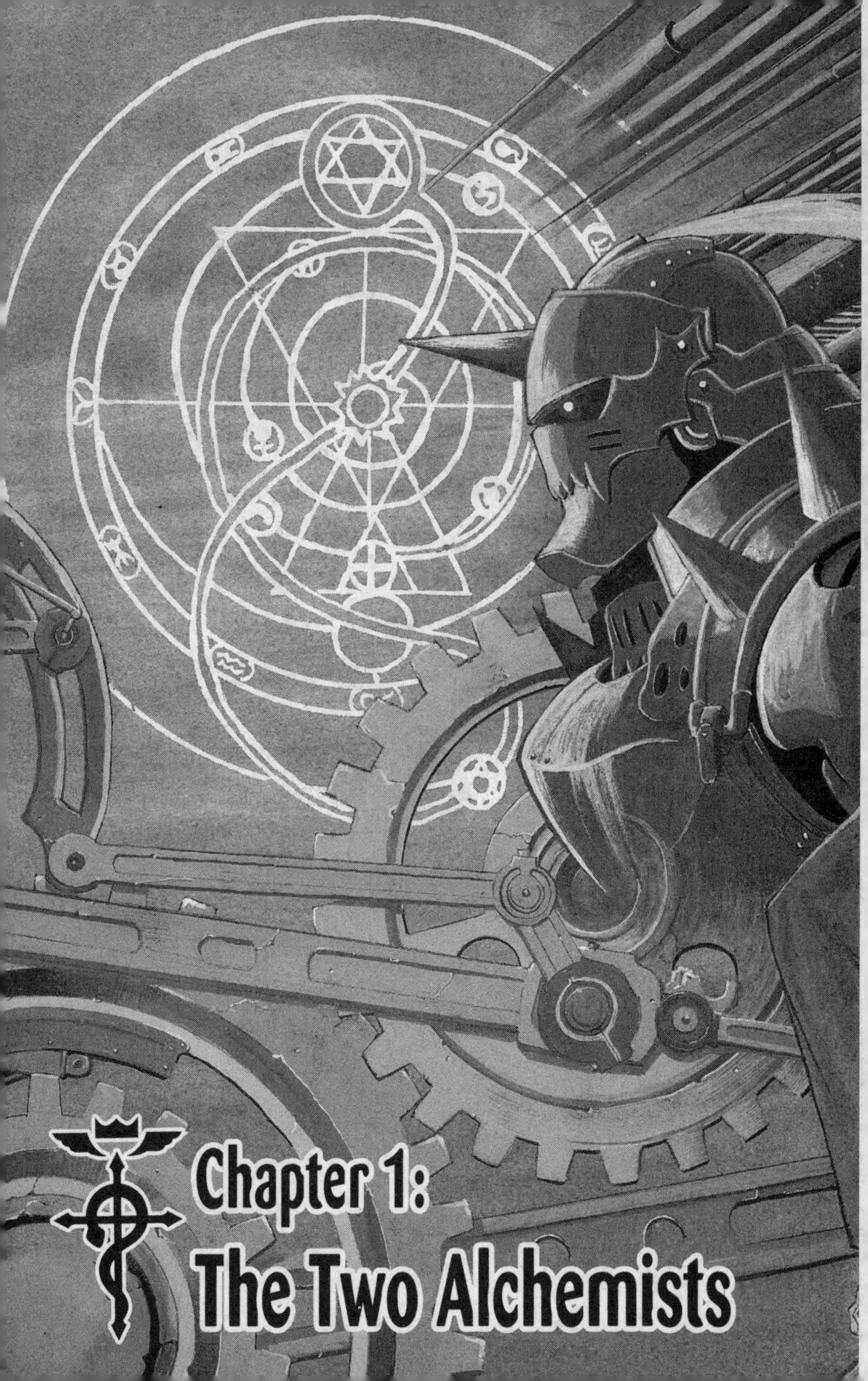

Chapter 1: The Two Alchemists

FULLMETAL
ALCHEMIST

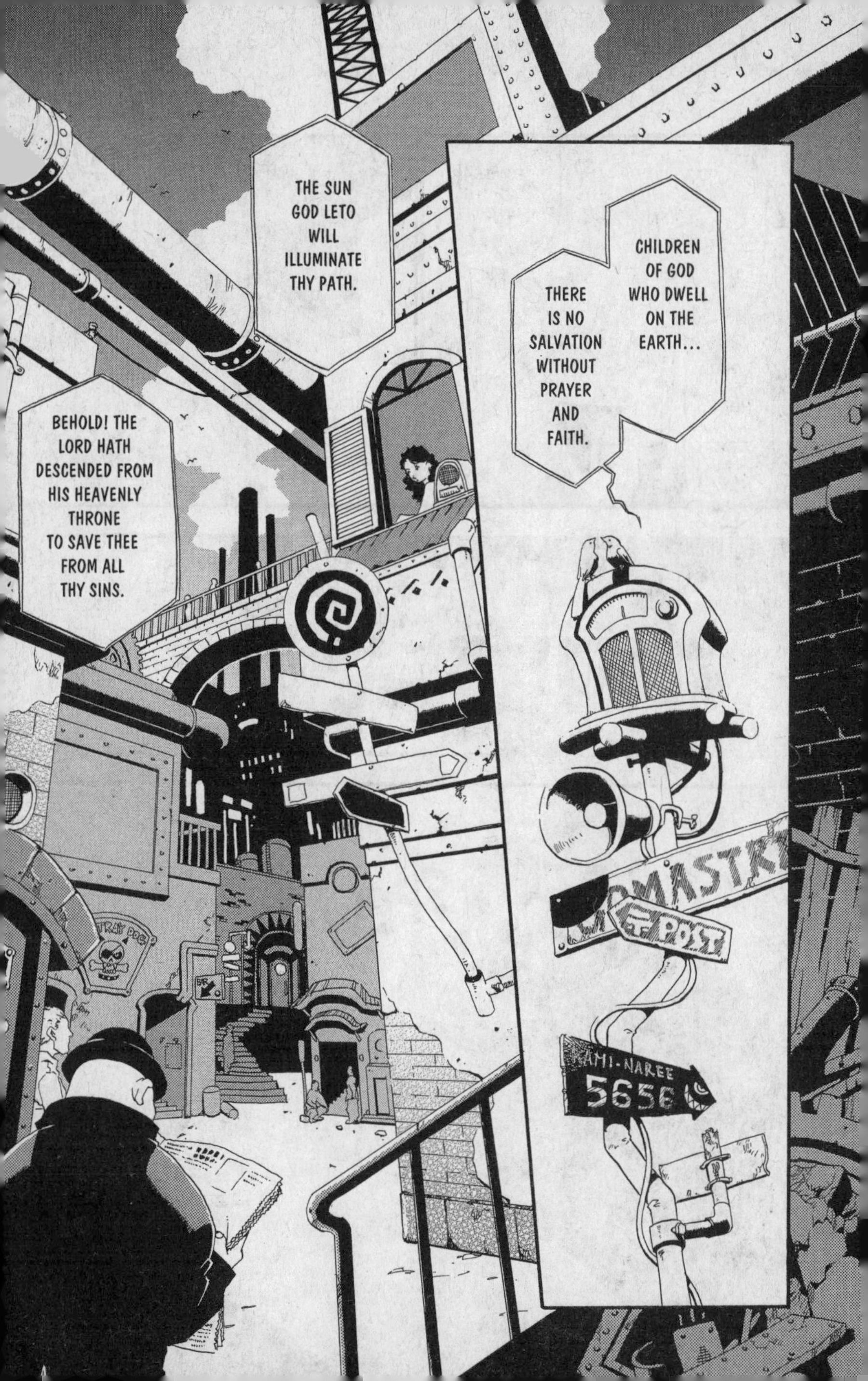

CHILDREN OF GOD WHO DWELL ON THE EARTH...
THERE IS NO SALVATION WITHOUT PRAYER AND FAITH.
THE SUN GOD LETO WILL ILLUMINATE THY PATH.
BEHOLD! THE LORD HATH DESCENDED FROM HIS HEAVENLY THRONE TO SAVE THEE FROM ALL THY SINS.
5656

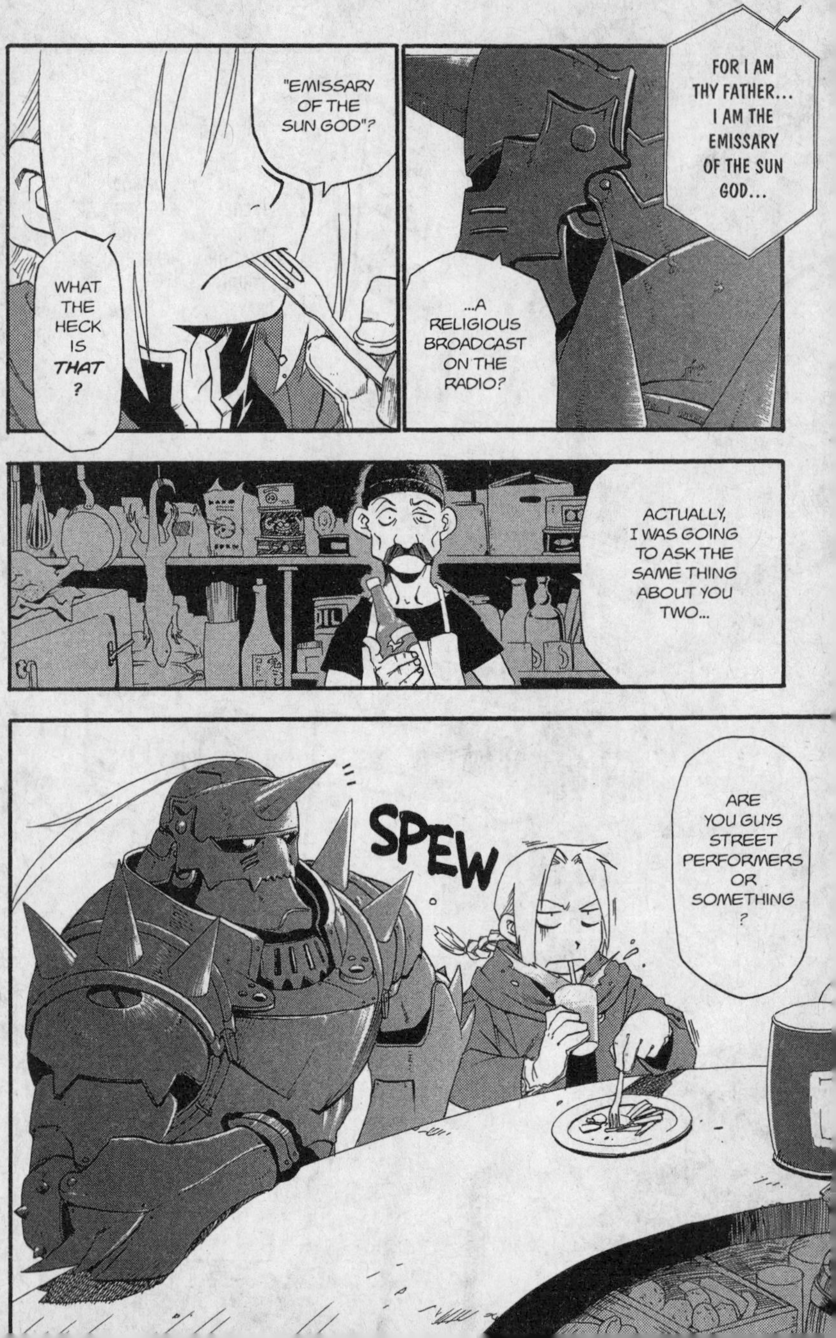
FOR I AM THY FATHER... I AM THE EMISSARY OF THE SUN GOD...
...A RELIGIOUS BROADCAST ON THE RADIO?
"EMISSARY OF THE SUN GOD"?
WHAT THE HECK IS *THAT* ?
ACTUALLY, I WAS GOING TO ASK THE SAME THING ABOUT YOU TWO...
ARE YOU GUYS STREET PERFORMERS OR SOMETHING ?
SPEW

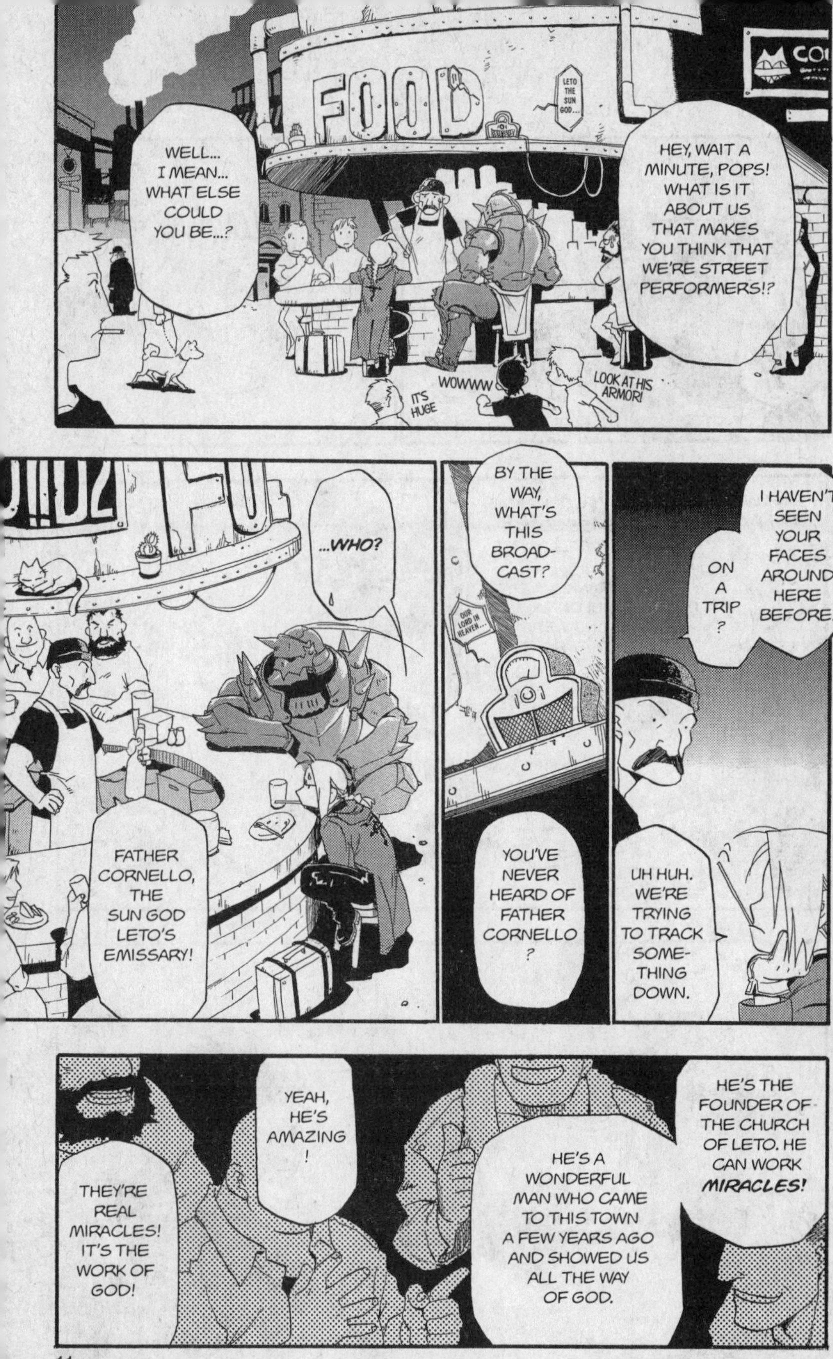
HEY, WAIT A MINUTE, POPS! WHAT IS IT ABOUT US THAT MAKES YOU THINK THAT WE'RE STREET PERFORMERS!?
LETO THE SUN GOD...
WELL... I MEAN... WHAT ELSE COULD YOU BE...?
LOOK AT HIS ARMOR!
WOWWW
IT'S HUGE
I HAVEN'T SEEN YOUR FACES AROUND HERE BEFORE.
ON A TRIP?
UH HUH. WE'RE TRYING TO TRACK SOMETHING DOWN.
BY THE WAY, WHAT'S THIS BROADCAST?
OUR LORD IN HEAVEN...
YOU'VE NEVER HEARD OF FATHER CORNELLO?
...WHO?
FATHER CORNELLO, THE SUN GOD LETO'S EMISSARY!
HE'S THE FOUNDER OF THE CHURCH OF LETO. HE CAN WORK MIRACLES!
HE'S A WONDERFUL MAN WHO CAME TO THIS TOWN A FEW YEARS AGO AND SHOWED US ALL THE WAY OF GOD.
YEAH, HE'S AMAZING!
THEY'RE REAL MIRACLES! IT'S THE WORK OF GOD!

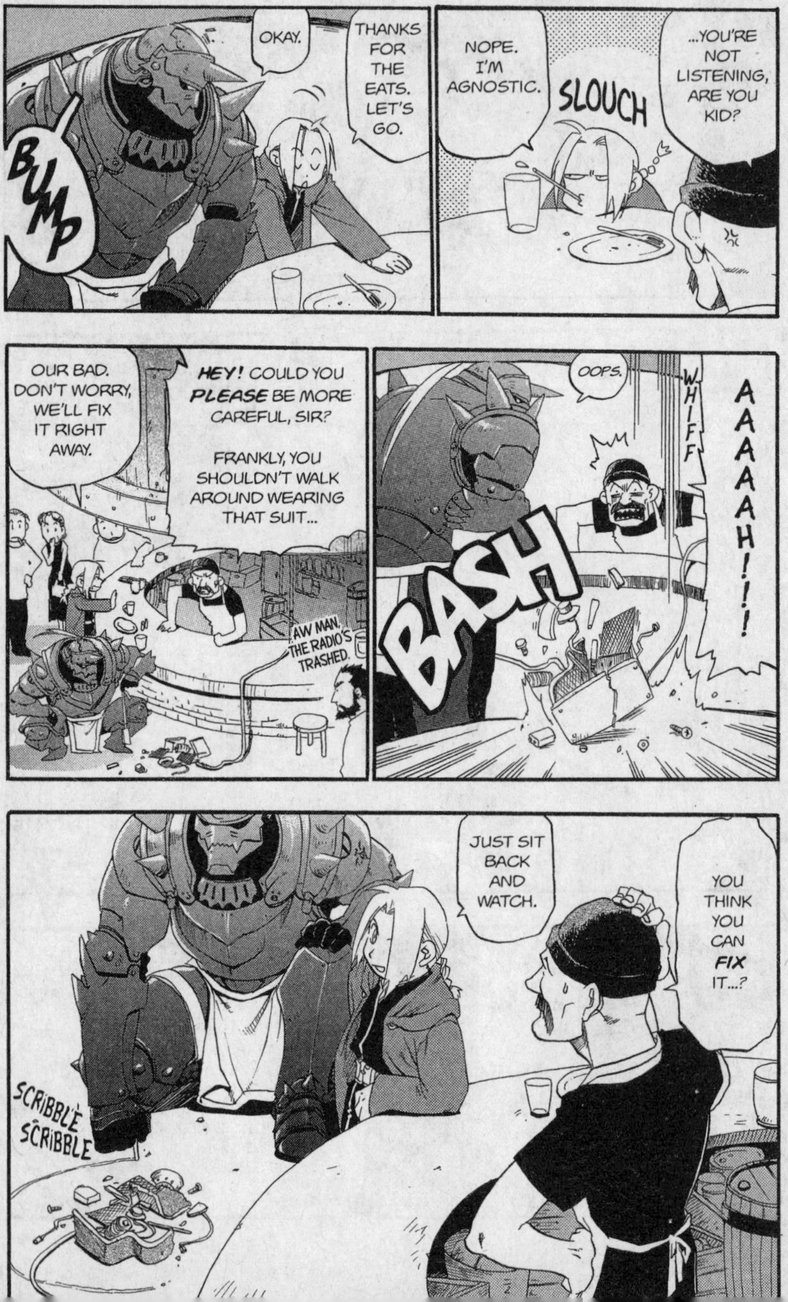

...YOU'RE NOT LISTENING, ARE YOU KID?
SLOUCH
NOPE. I'M AGNOSTIC.
THANKS FOR THE EATS. LET'S GO.
OKAY.
BUMP
OOPS.
WHIFF
AAAAAAH!!!!
BASH
HEY! COULD YOU PLEASE BE MORE CAREFUL, SIR?
FRANKLY, YOU SHOULDN'T WALK AROUND WEARING THAT SUIT...
OUR BAD. DON'T WORRY, WE'LL FIX IT RIGHT AWAY.
AW MAN, THE RADIO'S TRASHED.
YOU THINK YOU CAN FIX IT...?
JUST SIT BACK AND WATCH.
SCRIBBLE SCRIBBLE

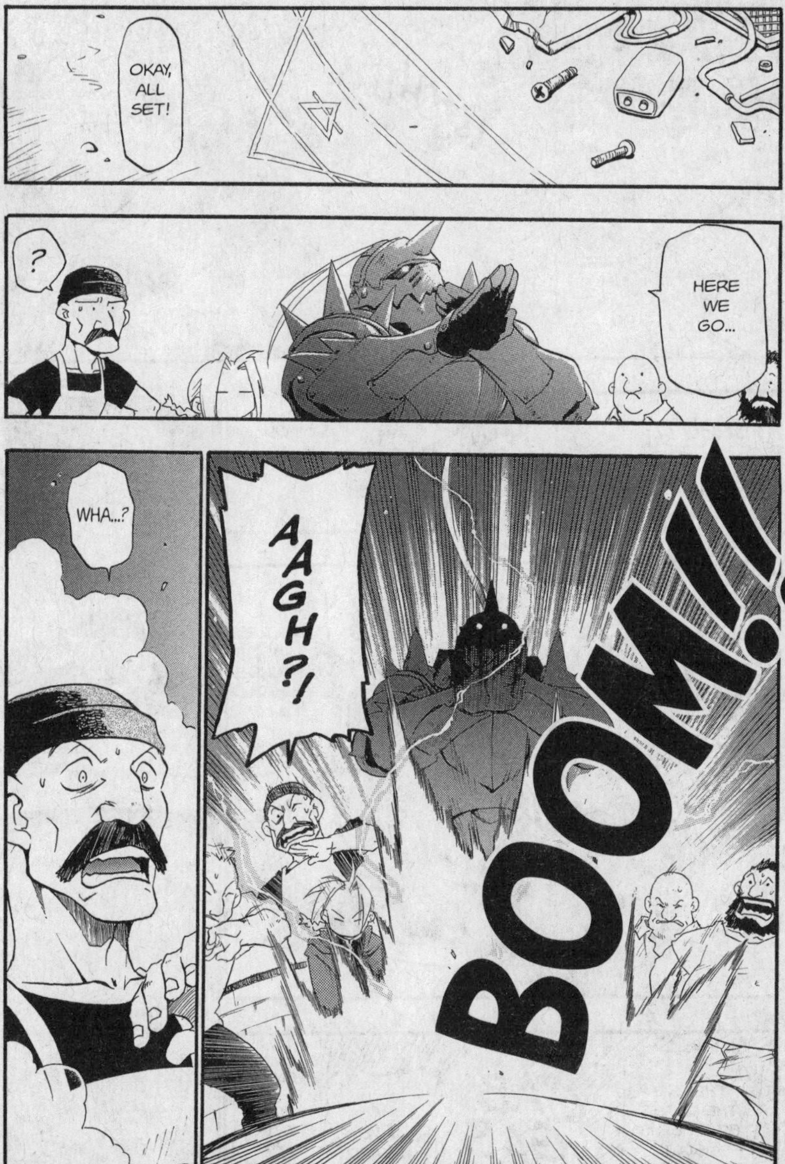
OKAY, ALL SET!
HERE WE GO...
?
BOOM!!!
AAGH?!
WHA...?

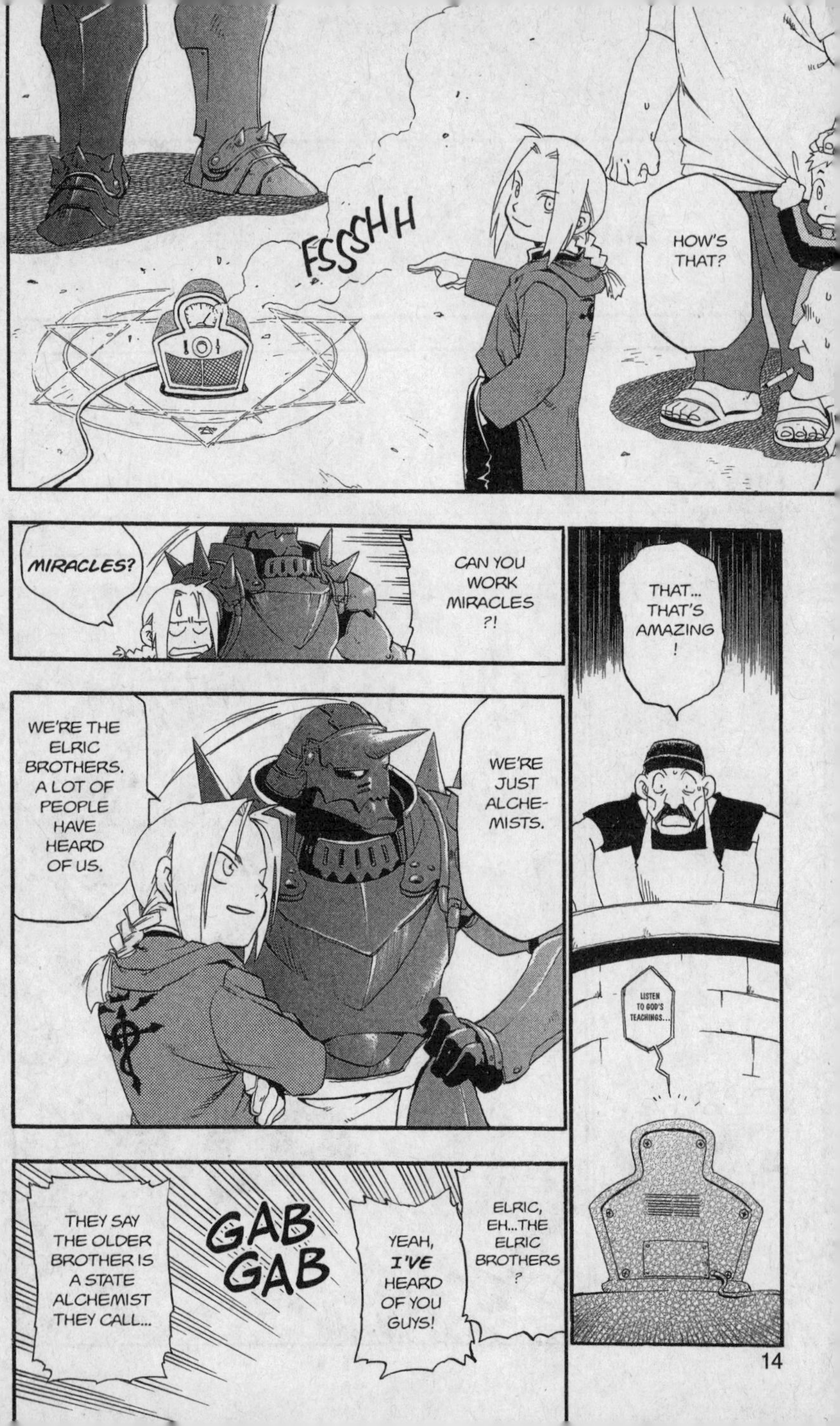
HOW'S THAT?
FSSSHH
THAT... THAT'S AMAZING!
LISTEN TO GOD'S TEACHINGS...
CAN YOU WORK MIRACLES?!
MIRACLES?
WE'RE JUST ALCHEMISTS.
WE'RE THE ELRIC BROTHERS. A LOT OF PEOPLE HAVE HEARD OF US.
ELRIC, EH...THE ELRIC BROTHERS?
YEAH, *I'VE* HEARD OF YOU GUYS!
GAB GAB
THEY SAY THE OLDER BROTHER IS A STATE ALCHEMIST THEY CALL...

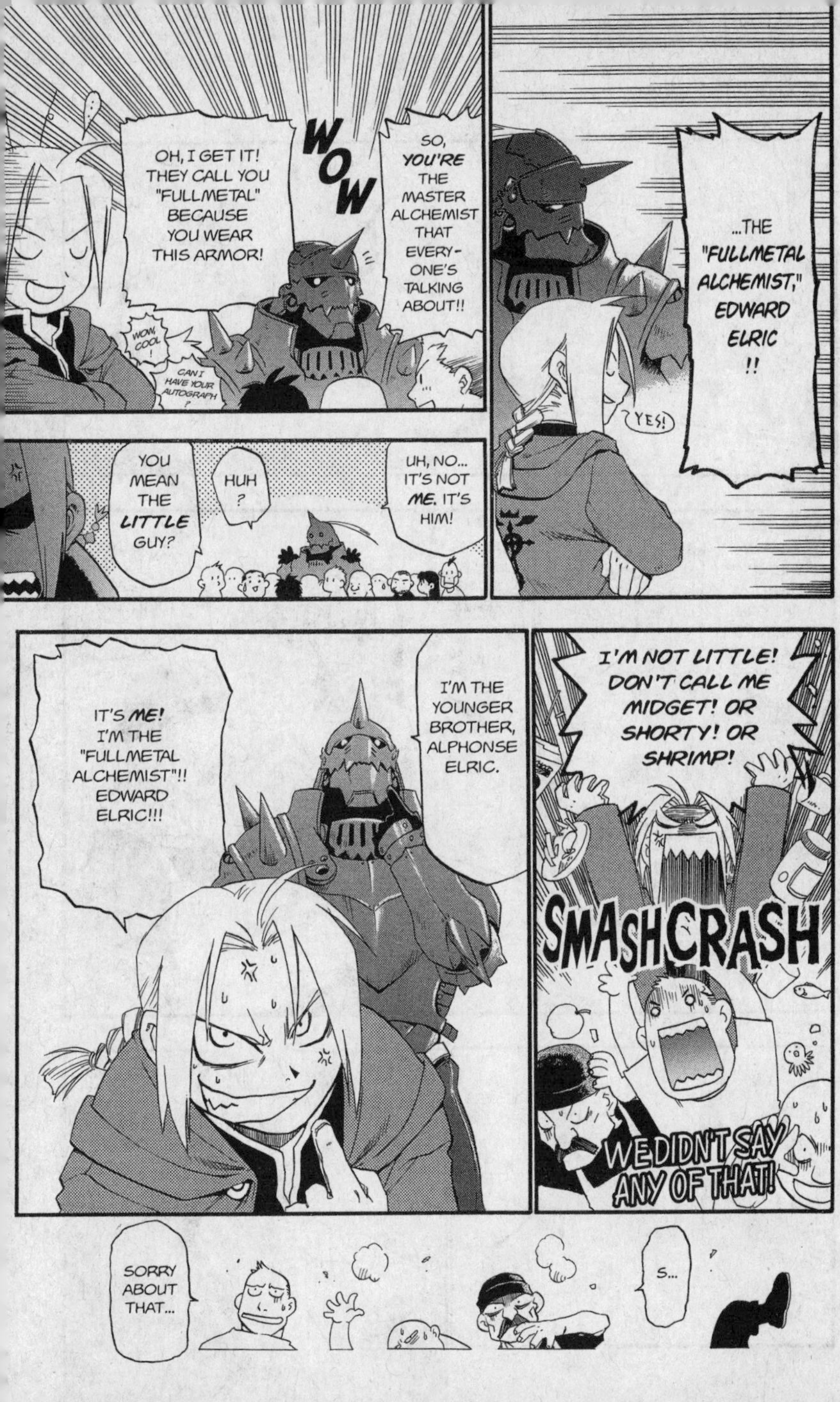
...THE "FULLMETAL ALCHEMIST," EDWARD ELRIC !!
YES!
SO, YOU'RE THE MASTER ALCHEMIST THAT EVERYONE'S TALKING ABOUT!!
WOW
OH, I GET IT! THEY CALL YOU "FULLMETAL" BECAUSE YOU WEAR THIS ARMOR!
WOW, COOL!
CAN I HAVE YOUR AUTOGRAPH?
UH, NO... IT'S NOT ME. IT'S HIM!
HUH?
YOU MEAN THE LITTLE GUY?
I'M NOT LITTLE! DON'T CALL ME MIDGET! OR SHORTY! OR SHRIMP!
SMASH CRASH
WE DIDN'T SAY ANY OF THAT!
I'M THE YOUNGER BROTHER, ALPHONSE ELRIC.
IT'S ME! I'M THE "FULLMETAL ALCHEMIST"!! EDWARD ELRIC!!!
S...
SORRY ABOUT THAT...

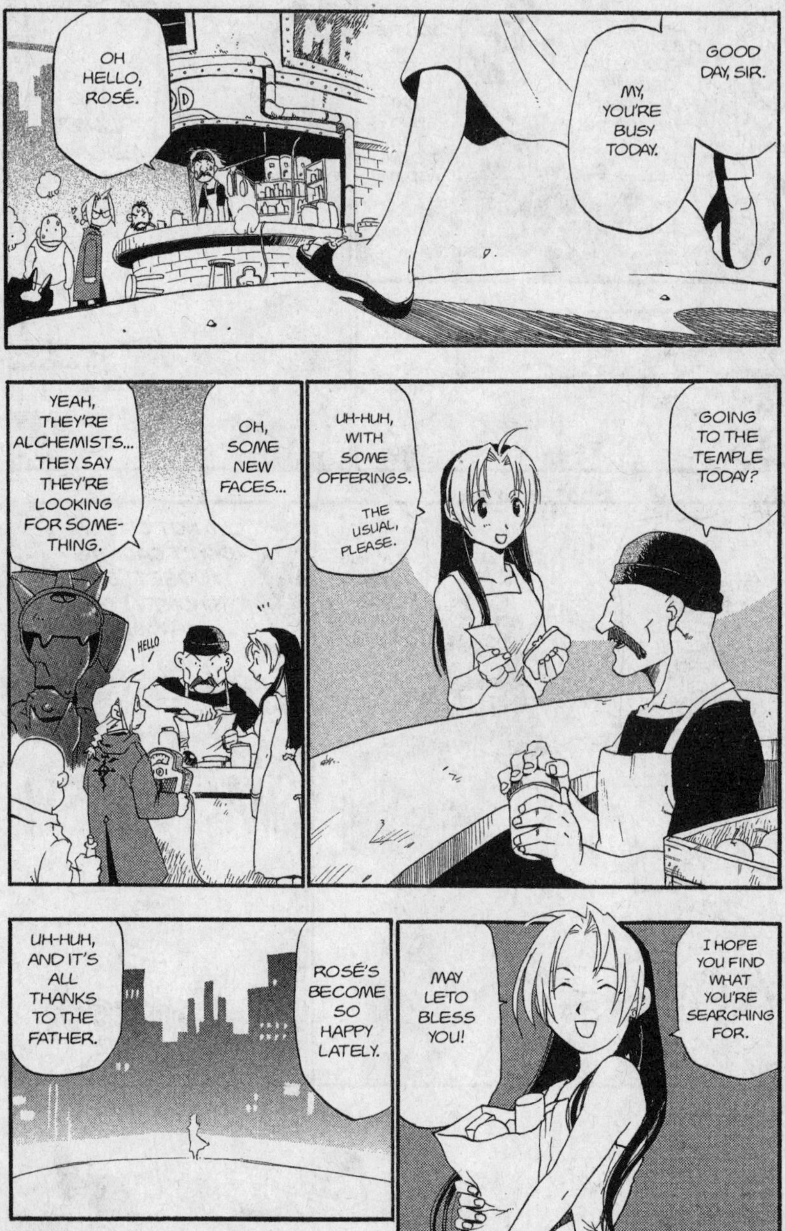
GOOD DAY, SIR.
MY, YOU'RE BUSY TODAY.
OH HELLO, ROSÉ.
GOING TO THE TEMPLE TODAY?
UH-HUH, WITH SOME OFFERINGS.
THE USUAL, PLEASE.
OH, SOME NEW FACES...
YEAH, THEY'RE ALCHEMISTS... THEY SAY THEY'RE LOOKING FOR SOME-THING.
HELLO
I HOPE YOU FIND WHAT YOU'RE SEARCHING FOR.
MAY LETO BLESS YOU!
ROSÉ'S BECOME SO HAPPY LATELY.
UH-HUH, AND IT'S ALL THANKS TO THE FATHER.

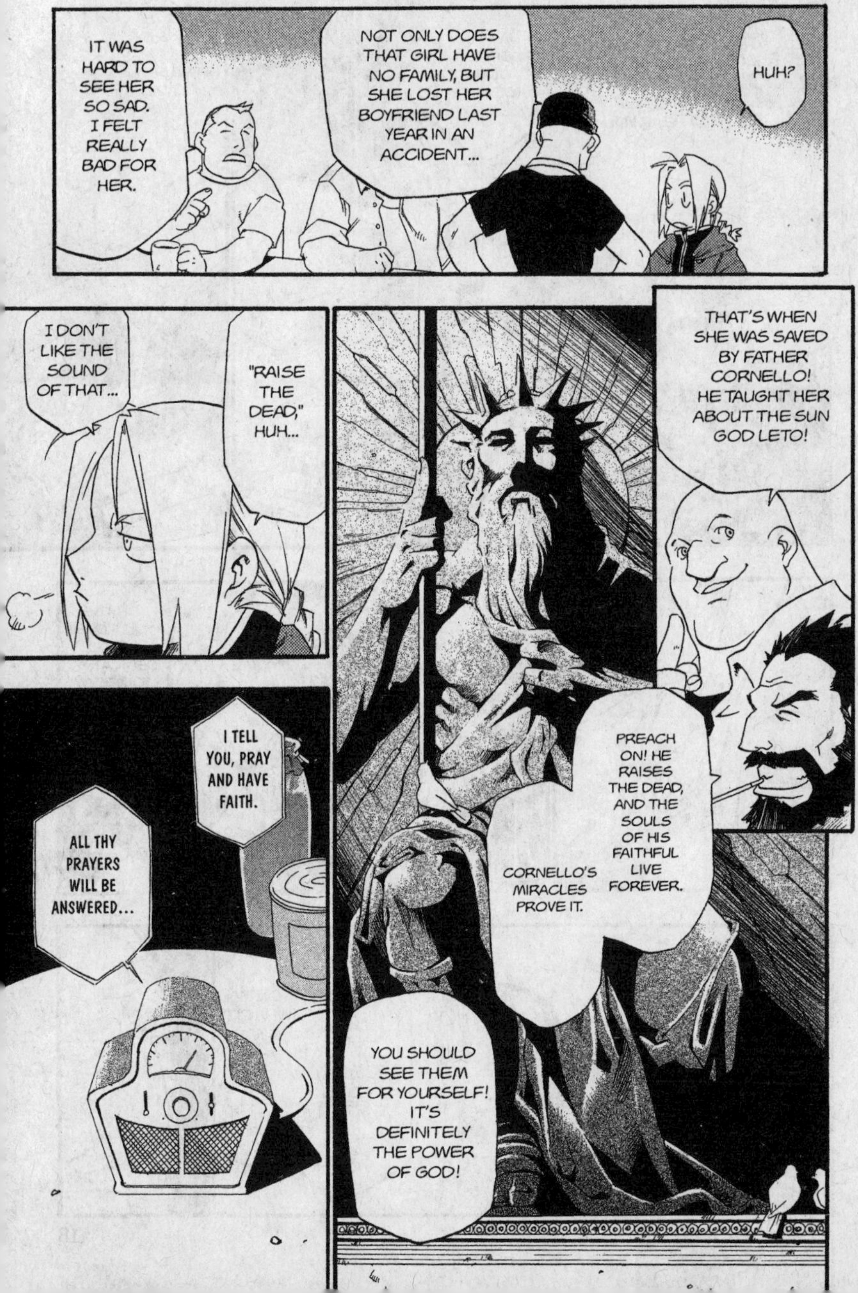
HUH?
NOT ONLY DOES THAT GIRL HAVE NO FAMILY, BUT SHE LOST HER BOYFRIEND LAST YEAR IN AN ACCIDENT...
IT WAS HARD TO SEE HER SO SAD. I FELT REALLY BAD FOR HER.
THAT'S WHEN SHE WAS SAVED BY FATHER CORNELLO! HE TAUGHT HER ABOUT THE SUN GOD LETO!
PREACH ON! HE RAISES THE DEAD, AND THE SOULS OF HIS FAITHFUL LIVE FOREVER.
CORNELLO'S MIRACLES PROVE IT.
YOU SHOULD SEE THEM FOR YOURSELF! IT'S DEFINITELY THE POWER OF GOD!
"RAISE THE DEAD," HUH...
I DON'T LIKE THE SOUND OF THAT...
I TELL YOU, PRAY AND HAVE FAITH.
ALL THY PRAYERS WILL BE ANSWERED...

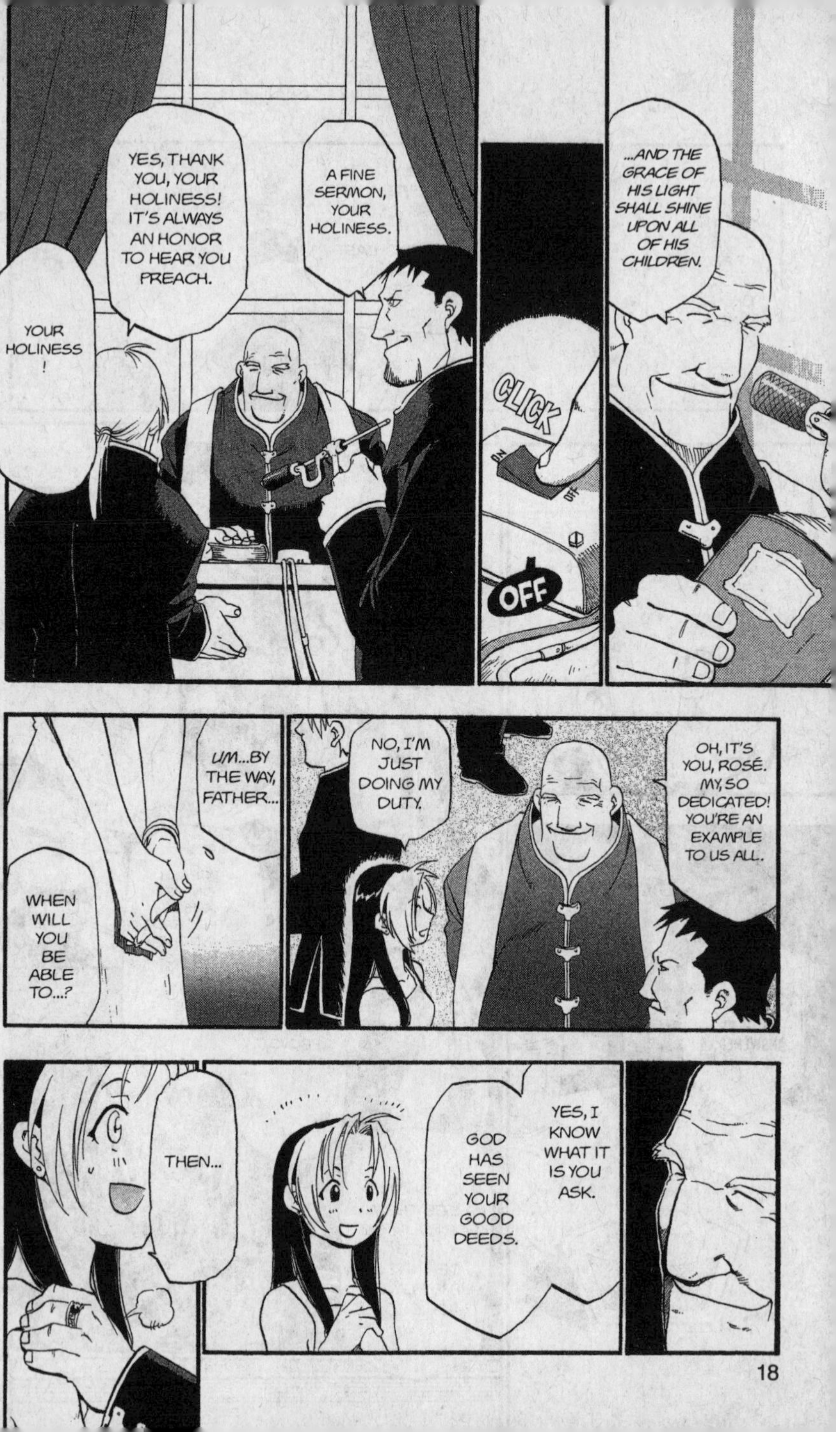
...AND THE GRACE OF HIS LIGHT SHALL SHINE UPON ALL OF HIS CHILDREN.
CLICK
ON
OFF
OFF
A FINE SERMON, YOUR HOLINESS.
YES, THANK YOU, YOUR HOLINESS! IT'S ALWAYS AN HONOR TO HEAR YOU PREACH.
YOUR HOLINESS!
OH, IT'S YOU, ROSÉ. MY, SO DEDICATED! YOU'RE AN EXAMPLE TO US ALL.
NO, I'M JUST DOING MY DUTY.
UM...BY THE WAY, FATHER...
WHEN WILL YOU BE ABLE TO...?
YES, I KNOW WHAT IT IS YOU ASK.
GOD HAS SEEN YOUR GOOD DEEDS.
THEN...

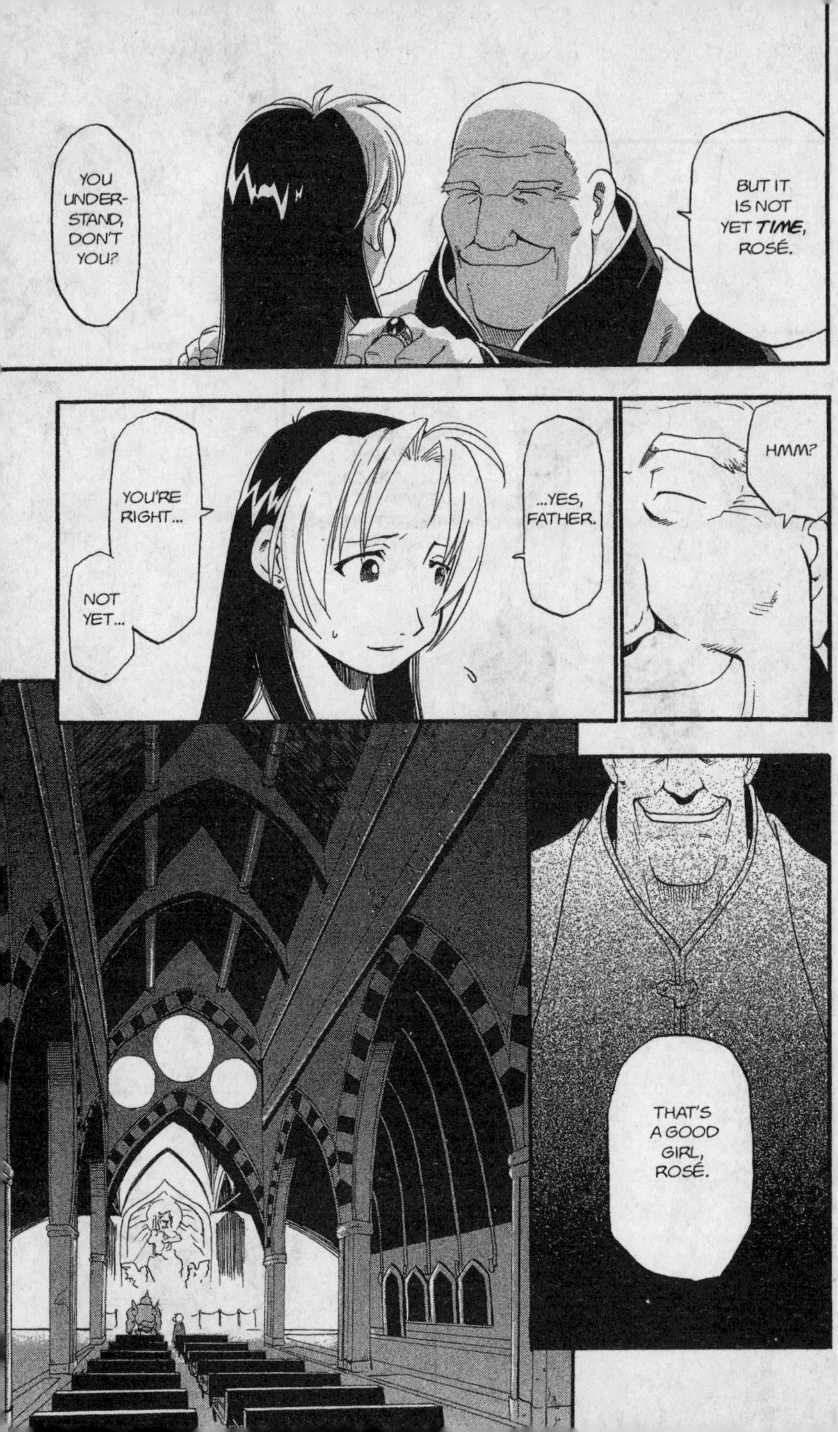
BUT IT IS NOT YET *TIME*, ROSÉ.
YOU UNDER-STAND, DON'T YOU?
HMM?
...YES, FATHER.
YOU'RE RIGHT...
NOT YET...
THAT'S A GOOD GIRL, ROSÉ.

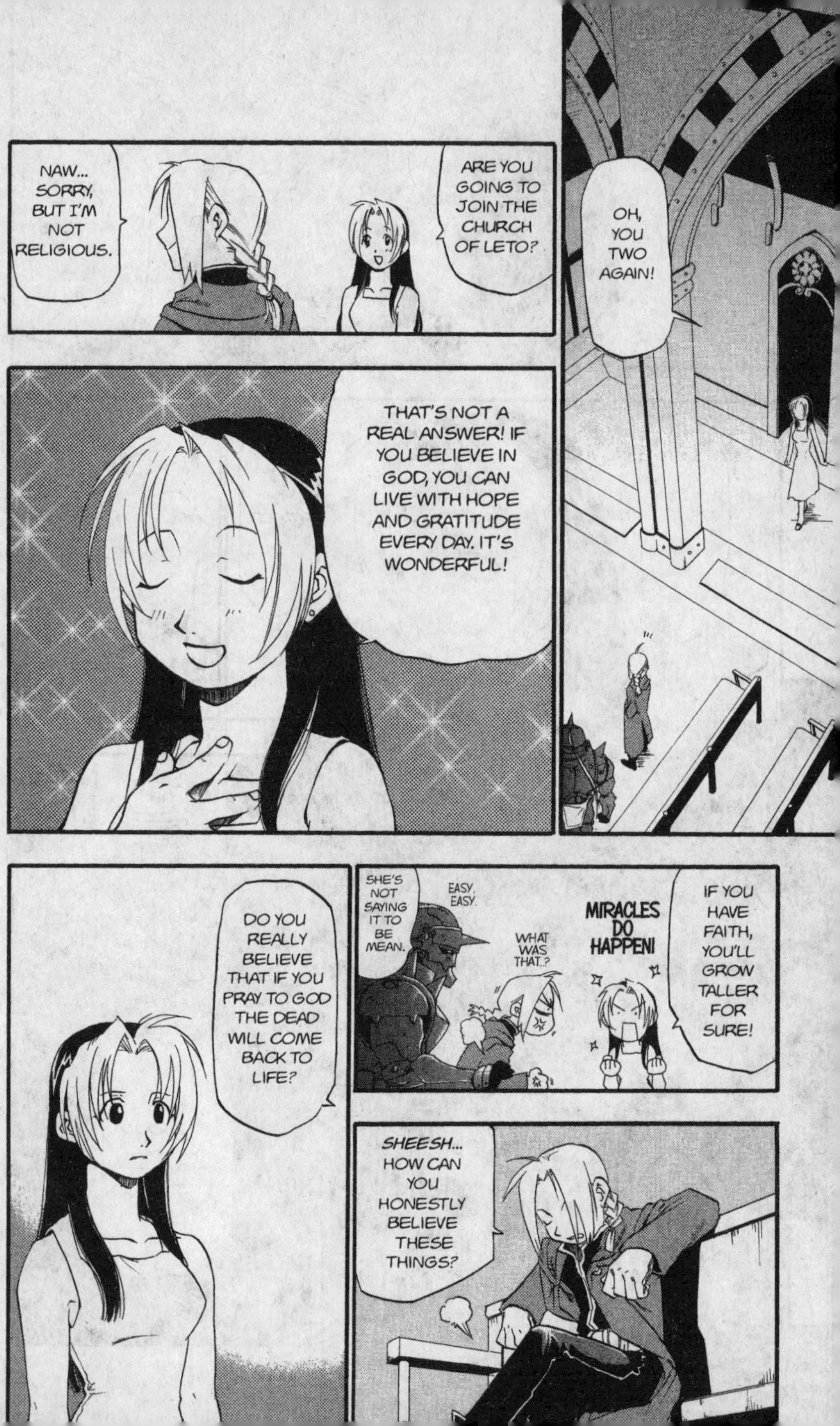
OH, YOU TWO AGAIN!
ARE YOU GOING TO JOIN THE CHURCH OF LETO?
NAW... SORRY, BUT I'M NOT RELIGIOUS.
THAT'S NOT A REAL ANSWER! IF YOU BELIEVE IN GOD, YOU CAN LIVE WITH HOPE AND GRATITUDE EVERY DAY. IT'S WONDERFUL!
IF YOU HAVE FAITH, YOU'LL GROW TALLER FOR SURE!
MIRACLES DO HAPPEN!
WHAT WAS THAT..?
EASY, EASY.
SHE'S NOT SAYING IT TO BE MEAN.
SHEESH... HOW CAN YOU HONESTLY BELIEVE THESE THINGS?
DO YOU REALLY BELIEVE THAT IF YOU PRAY TO GOD THE DEAD WILL COME BACK TO LIFE?

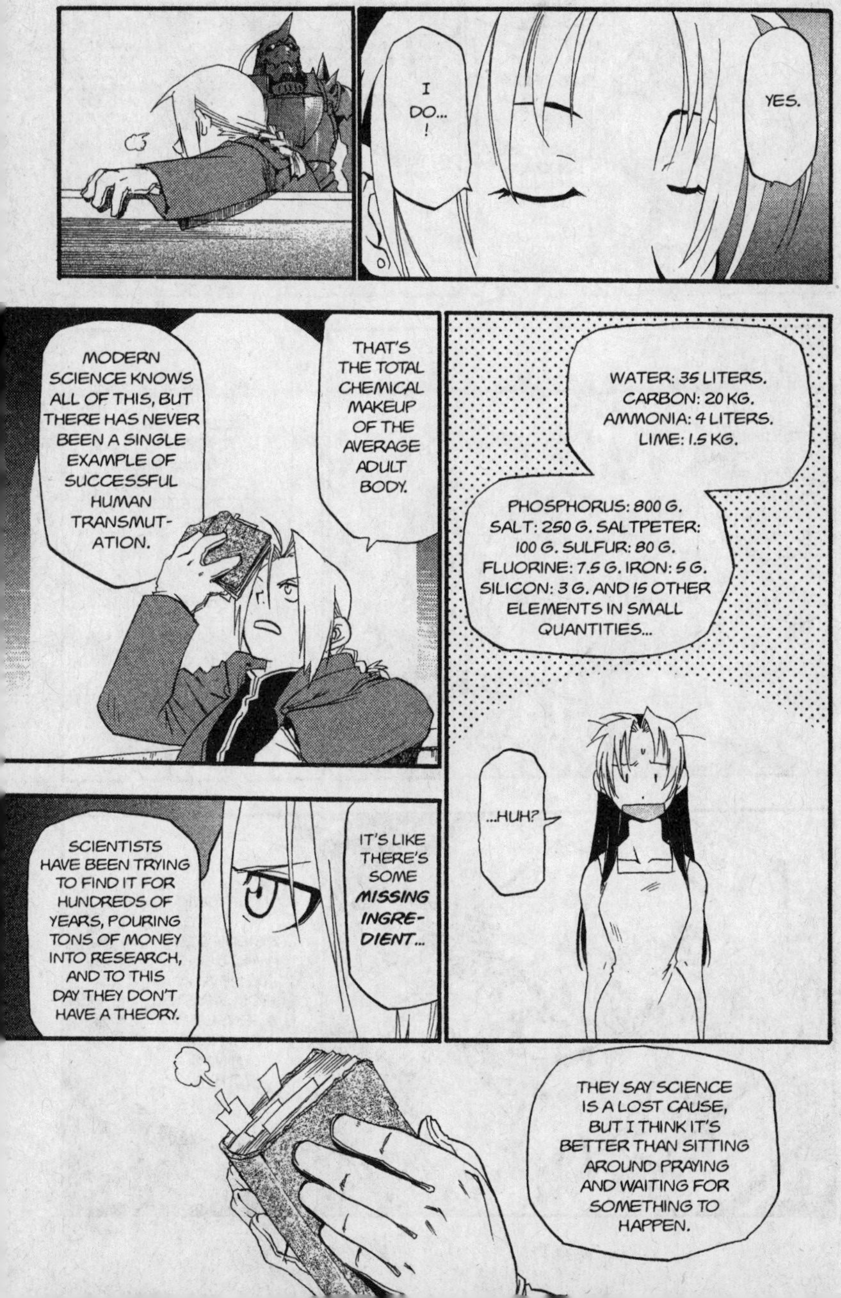
YES.
I DO... !
WATER: 35 LITERS. CARBON: 20 KG. AMMONIA: 4 LITERS. LIME: 1.5 KG.
PHOSPHORUS: 800 G. SALT: 250 G. SALTPETER: 100 G. SULFUR: 80 G. FLUORINE: 7.5 G. IRON: 5 G. SILICON: 3 G. AND 15 OTHER ELEMENTS IN SMALL QUANTITIES...
...HUH?
THAT'S THE TOTAL CHEMICAL MAKEUP OF THE AVERAGE ADULT BODY.
MODERN SCIENCE KNOWS ALL OF THIS, BUT THERE HAS NEVER BEEN A SINGLE EXAMPLE OF SUCCESSFUL HUMAN TRANSMUT-ATION.
IT'S LIKE THERE'S SOME *MISSING INGRE-DIENT*...
SCIENTISTS HAVE BEEN TRYING TO FIND IT FOR HUNDREDS OF YEARS, POURING TONS OF MONEY INTO RESEARCH, AND TO THIS DAY THEY DON'T HAVE A THEORY.
THEY SAY SCIENCE IS A LOST CAUSE, BUT I THINK IT'S BETTER THAN SITTING AROUND PRAYING AND WAITING FOR SOMETHING TO HAPPEN.

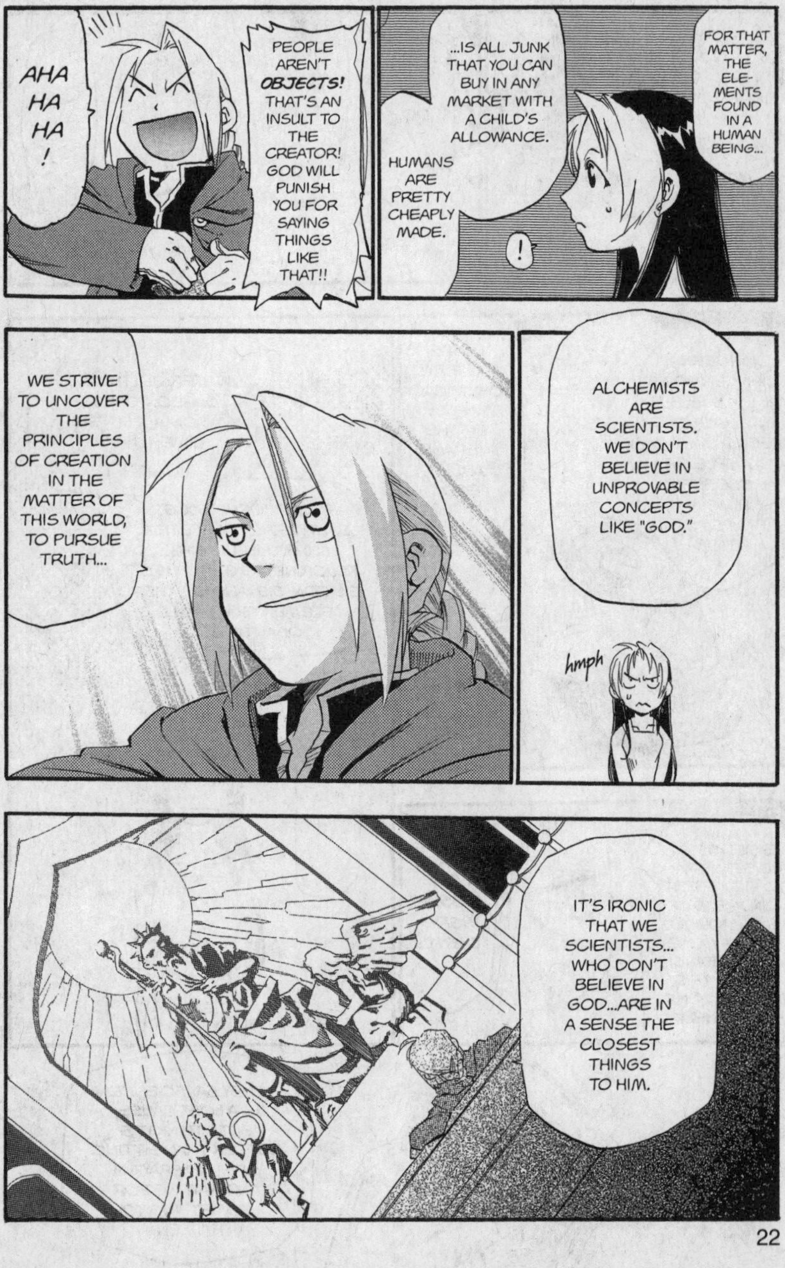
FOR THAT MATTER, THE ELEMENTS FOUND IN A HUMAN BEING...
...IS ALL JUNK THAT YOU CAN BUY IN ANY MARKET WITH A CHILD'S ALLOWANCE.
HUMANS ARE PRETTY CHEAPLY MADE.
!
PEOPLE AREN'T **OBJECTS!** THAT'S AN INSULT TO THE CREATOR! GOD WILL PUNISH YOU FOR SAYING THINGS LIKE THAT!!
AHA HA HA!
ALCHEMISTS ARE SCIENTISTS. WE DON'T BELIEVE IN UNPROVABLE CONCEPTS LIKE "GOD."
hmph
WE STRIVE TO UNCOVER THE PRINCIPLES OF CREATION IN THE MATTER OF THIS WORLD, TO PURSUE TRUTH...
IT'S IRONIC THAT WE SCIENTISTS... WHO DON'T BELIEVE IN GOD...ARE IN A SENSE THE CLOSEST THINGS TO HIM.

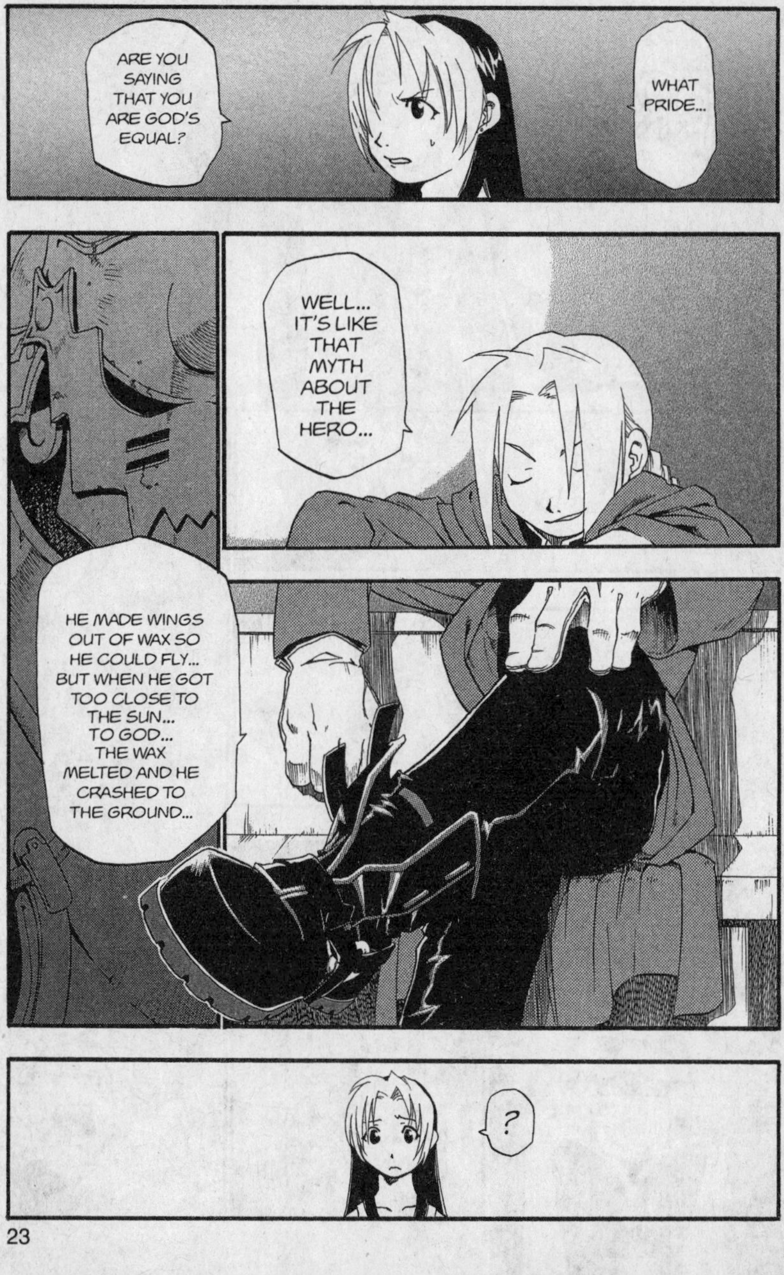
WHAT PRIDE...
ARE YOU SAYING THAT YOU ARE GOD'S EQUAL?
WELL... IT'S LIKE THAT MYTH ABOUT THE HERO...
HE MADE WINGS OUT OF WAX SO HE COULD FLY... BUT WHEN HE GOT TOO CLOSE TO THE SUN... TO GOD... THE WAX MELTED AND HE CRASHED TO THE GROUND...
?

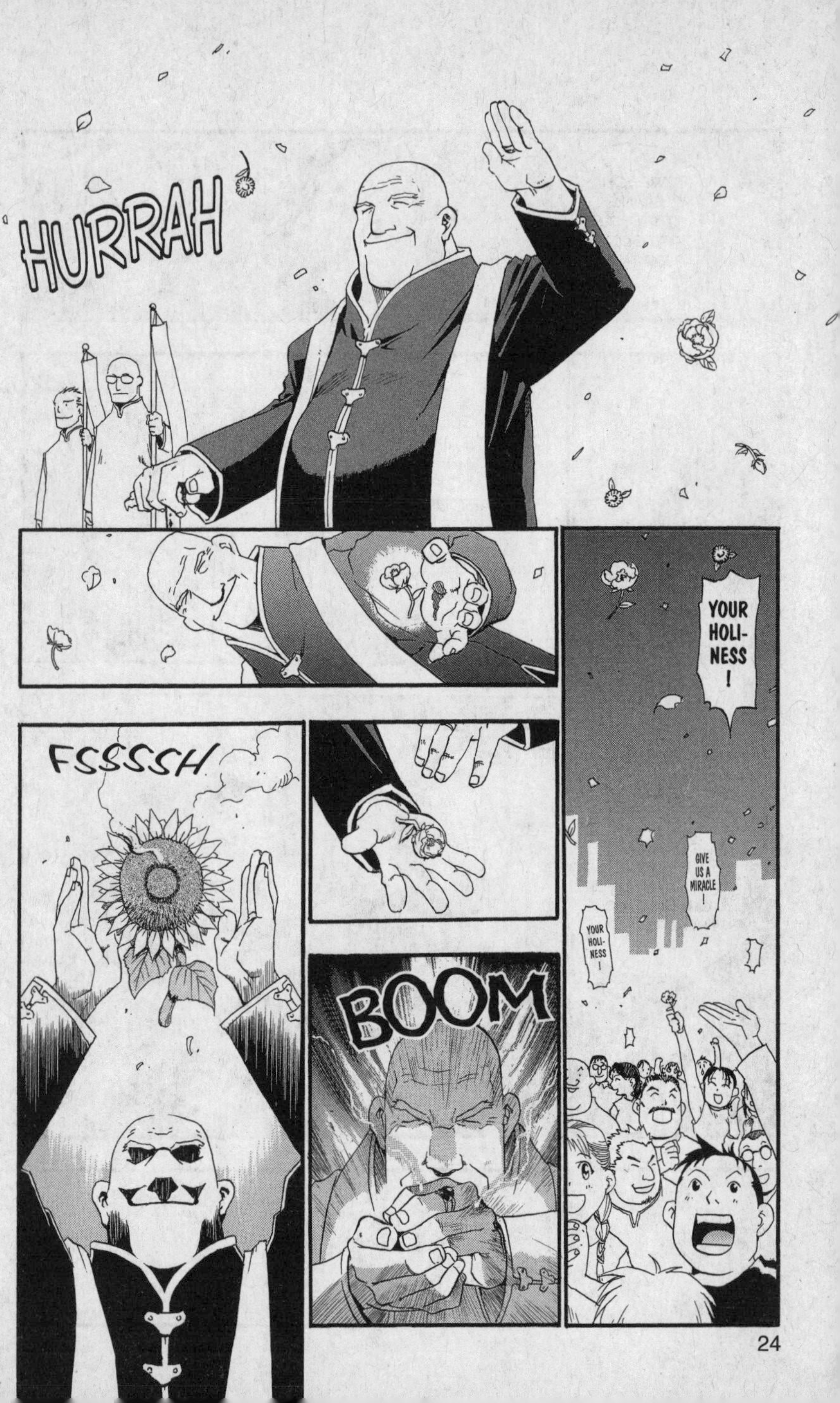
HURRAH
YOUR HOLINESS!
GIVE US A MIRACLE!
YOUR HOLINESS!
BOOM
FSSSH

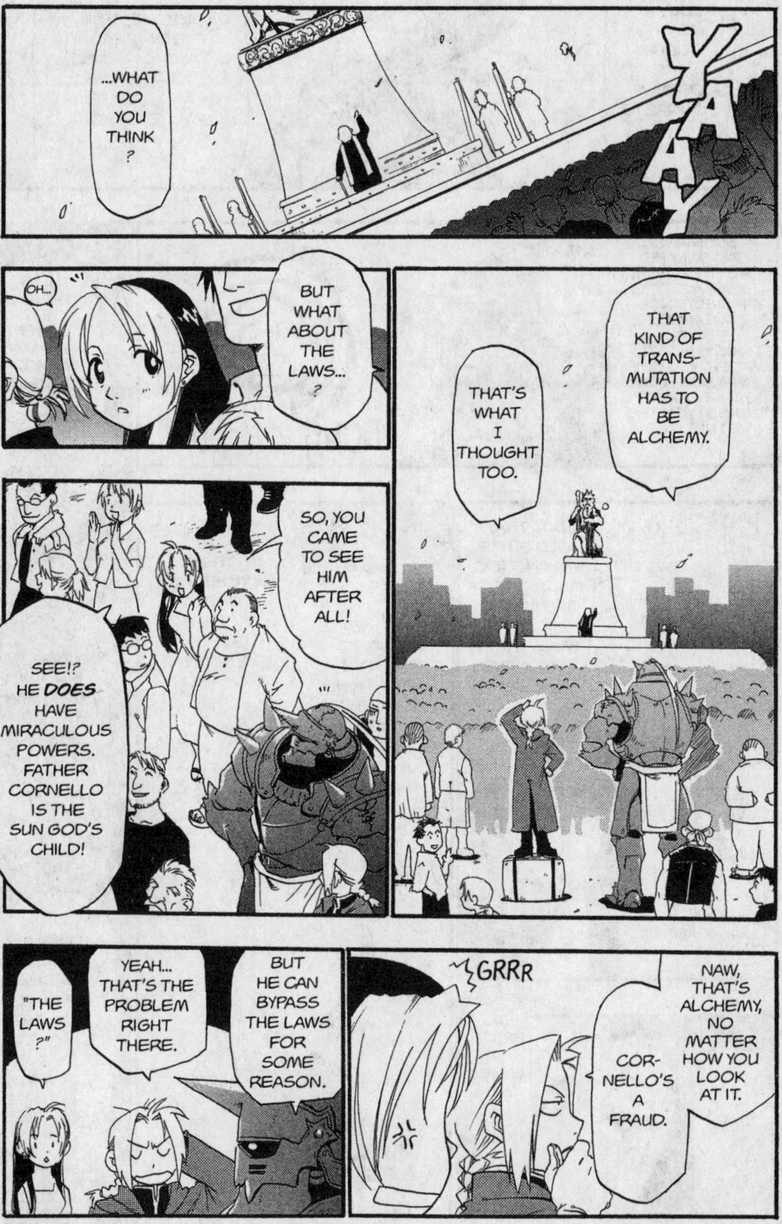
YAAY
...WHAT DO YOU THINK?
THAT KIND OF TRANS-MUTATION HAS TO BE ALCHEMY.
THAT'S WHAT I THOUGHT TOO.
BUT WHAT ABOUT THE LAWS...?
OH...
SO, YOU CAME TO SEE HIM AFTER ALL!
SEE!? HE *DOES* HAVE MIRACULOUS POWERS. FATHER CORNELLO IS THE SUN GOD'S CHILD!
NAW, THAT'S ALCHEMY, NO MATTER HOW YOU LOOK AT IT.
COR-NELLO'S A FRAUD.
GRRR
BUT HE CAN BYPASS THE LAWS FOR SOME REASON.
YEAH... THAT'S THE PROBLEM RIGHT THERE.
"THE LAWS?"

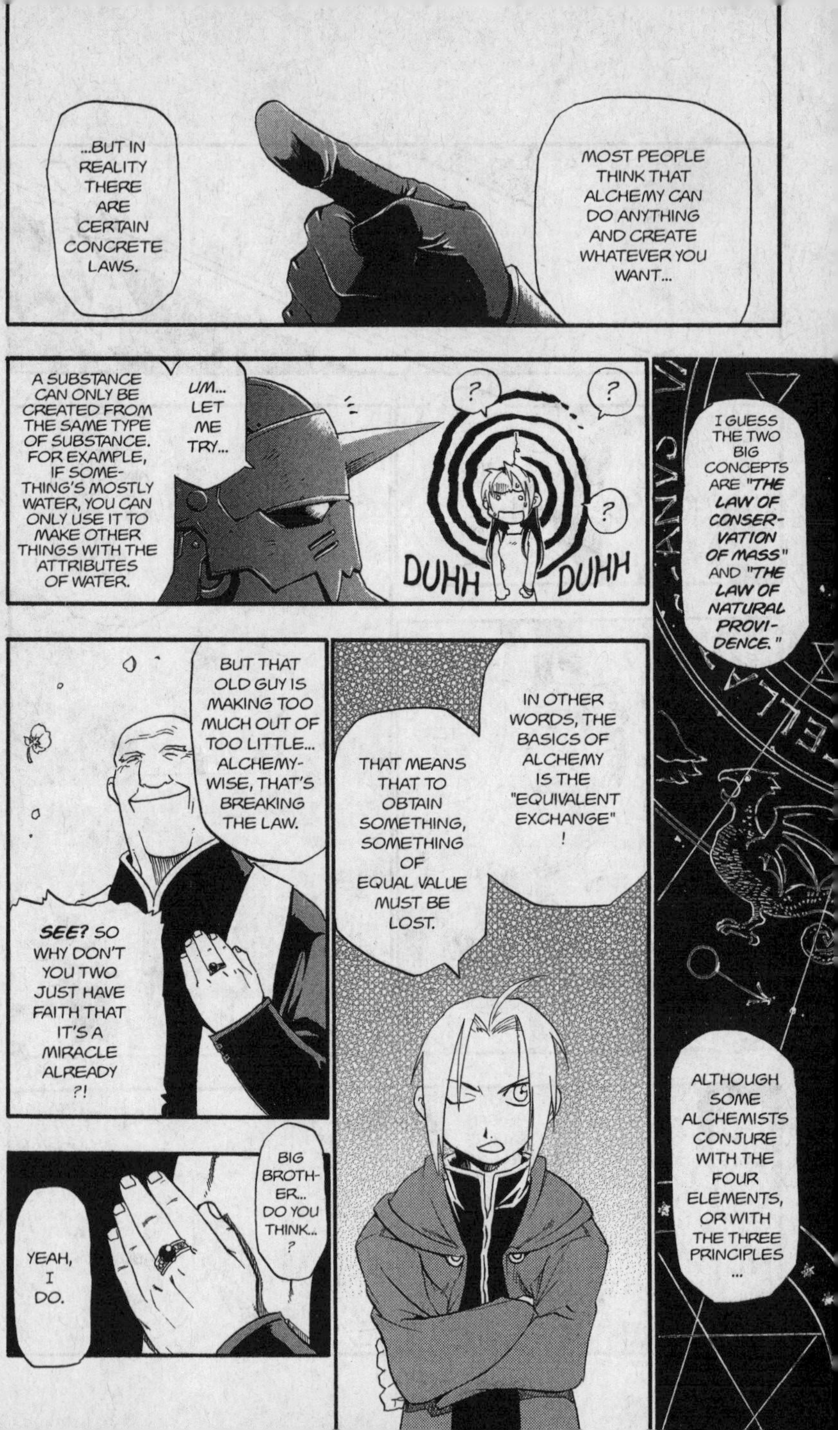
MOST PEOPLE THINK THAT ALCHEMY CAN DO ANYTHING AND CREATE WHATEVER YOU WANT...
...BUT IN REALITY THERE ARE CERTAIN CONCRETE LAWS.
I GUESS THE TWO BIG CONCEPTS ARE "*THE LAW OF CONSERVATION OF MASS*" AND "*THE LAW OF NATURAL PROVIDENCE.*"
ALTHOUGH SOME ALCHEMISTS CONJURE WITH THE FOUR ELEMENTS, OR WITH THE THREE PRINCIPLES ...
?
?
?
DUHH
DUHH
UM... LET ME TRY...
A SUBSTANCE CAN ONLY BE CREATED FROM THE SAME TYPE OF SUBSTANCE. FOR EXAMPLE, IF SOMETHING'S MOSTLY WATER, YOU CAN ONLY USE IT TO MAKE OTHER THINGS WITH THE ATTRIBUTES OF WATER.
IN OTHER WORDS, THE BASICS OF ALCHEMY IS THE "EQUIVALENT EXCHANGE" !
THAT MEANS THAT TO OBTAIN SOMETHING, SOMETHING OF EQUAL VALUE MUST BE LOST.
BUT THAT OLD GUY IS MAKING TOO MUCH OUT OF TOO LITTLE... ALCHEMY-WISE, THAT'S BREAKING THE LAW.
SEE? SO WHY DON'T YOU TWO JUST HAVE FAITH THAT IT'S A MIRACLE ALREADY ?!
BIG BROTHER... DO YOU THINK..?
YEAH, I DO.

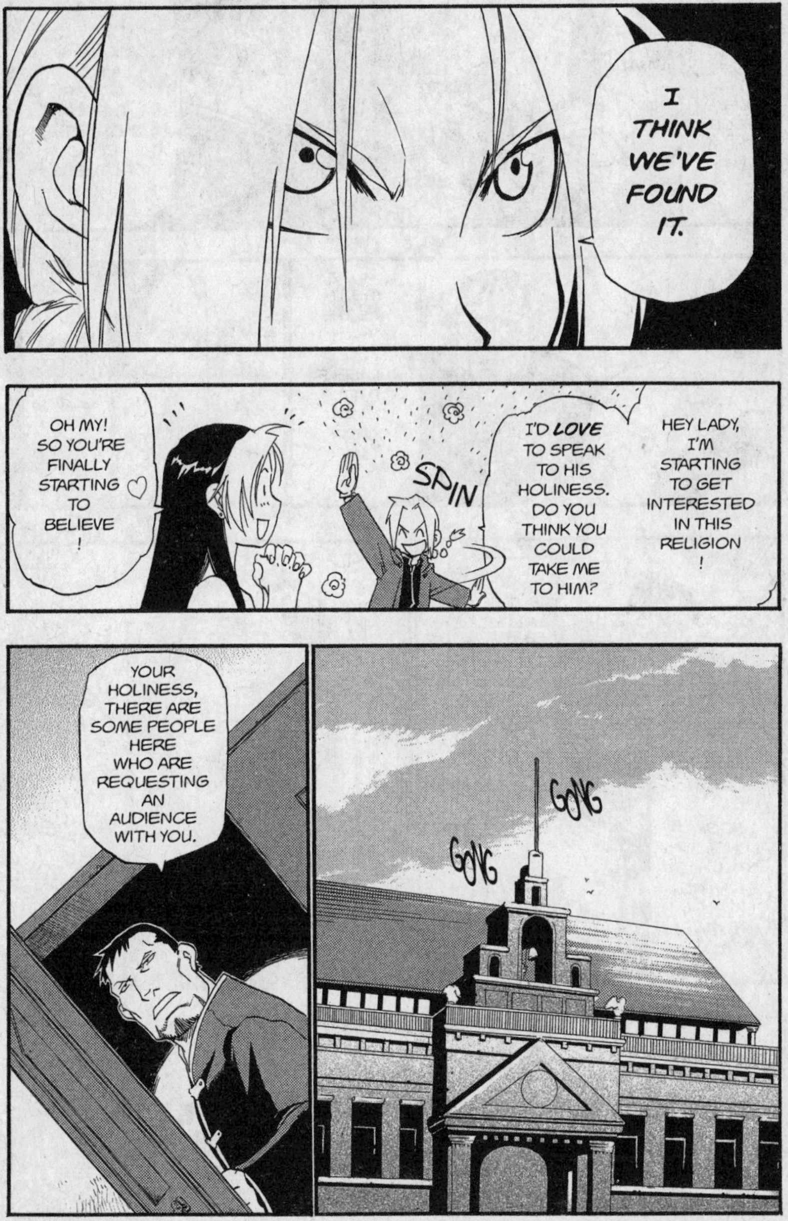
I THINK WE'VE FOUND IT.
HEY LADY, I'M STARTING TO GET INTERESTED IN THIS RELIGION!
I'D **LOVE** TO SPEAK TO HIS HOLINESS. DO YOU THINK YOU COULD TAKE ME TO HIM?
SPIN
OH MY! SO YOU'RE FINALLY STARTING TO BELIEVE!
GONG
GONG
YOUR HOLINESS, THERE ARE SOME PEOPLE HERE WHO ARE REQUESTING AN AUDIENCE WITH YOU.

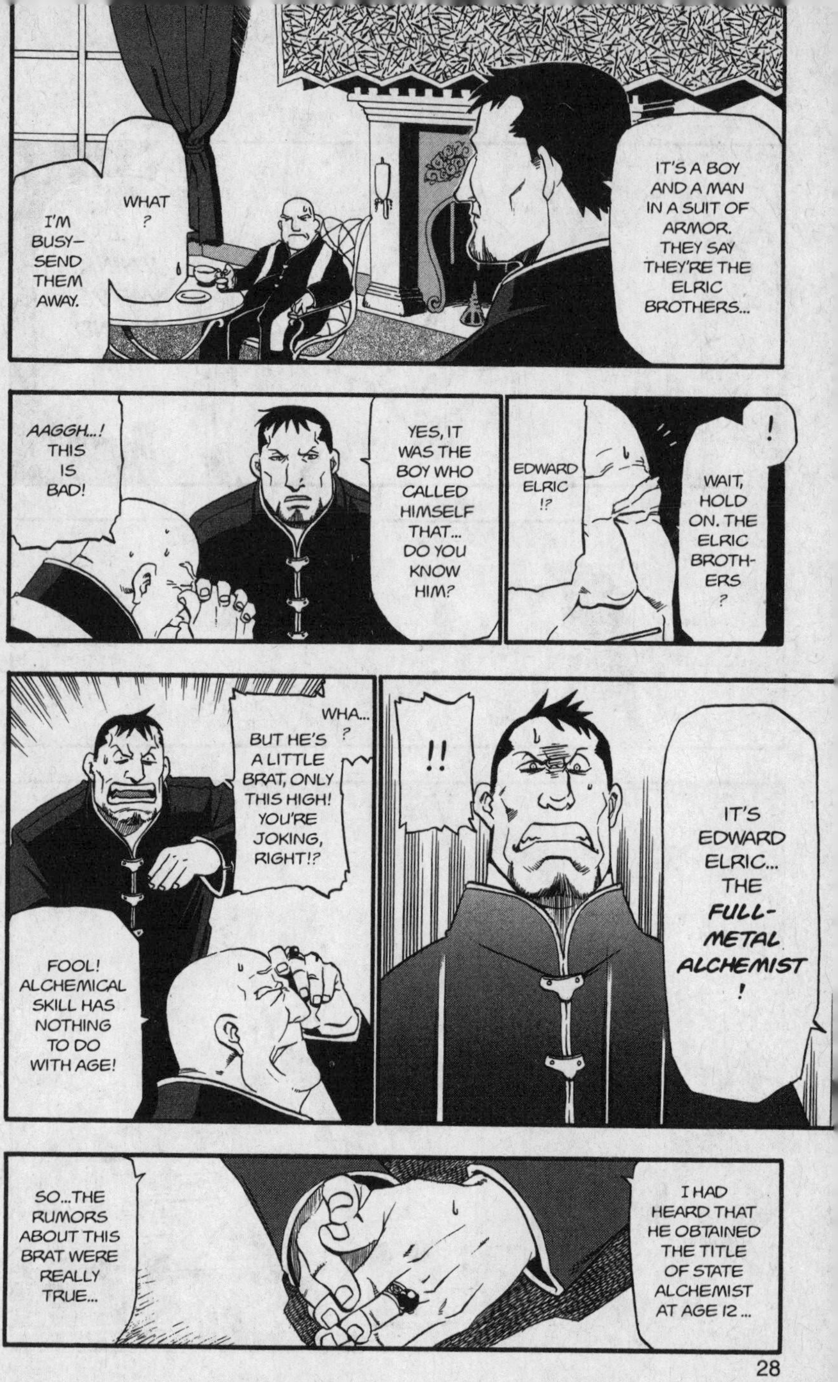
IT'S A BOY AND A MAN IN A SUIT OF ARMOR. THEY SAY THEY'RE THE ELRIC BROTHERS...
WHAT?
I'M BUSY—SEND THEM AWAY.
!
WAIT, HOLD ON. THE ELRIC BROTHERS?
EDWARD ELRIC!?
YES, IT WAS THE BOY WHO CALLED HIMSELF THAT... DO YOU KNOW HIM?
AAGGH...! THIS IS BAD!
IT'S EDWARD ELRIC... THE FULLMETAL ALCHEMIST!
!!
WHA...?
BUT HE'S A LITTLE BRAT, ONLY THIS HIGH! YOU'RE JOKING, RIGHT!?
FOOL! ALCHEMICAL SKILL HAS NOTHING TO DO WITH AGE!
I HAD HEARD THAT HE OBTAINED THE TITLE OF STATE ALCHEMIST AT AGE 12...
SO...THE RUMORS ABOUT THIS BRAT WERE REALLY TRUE...

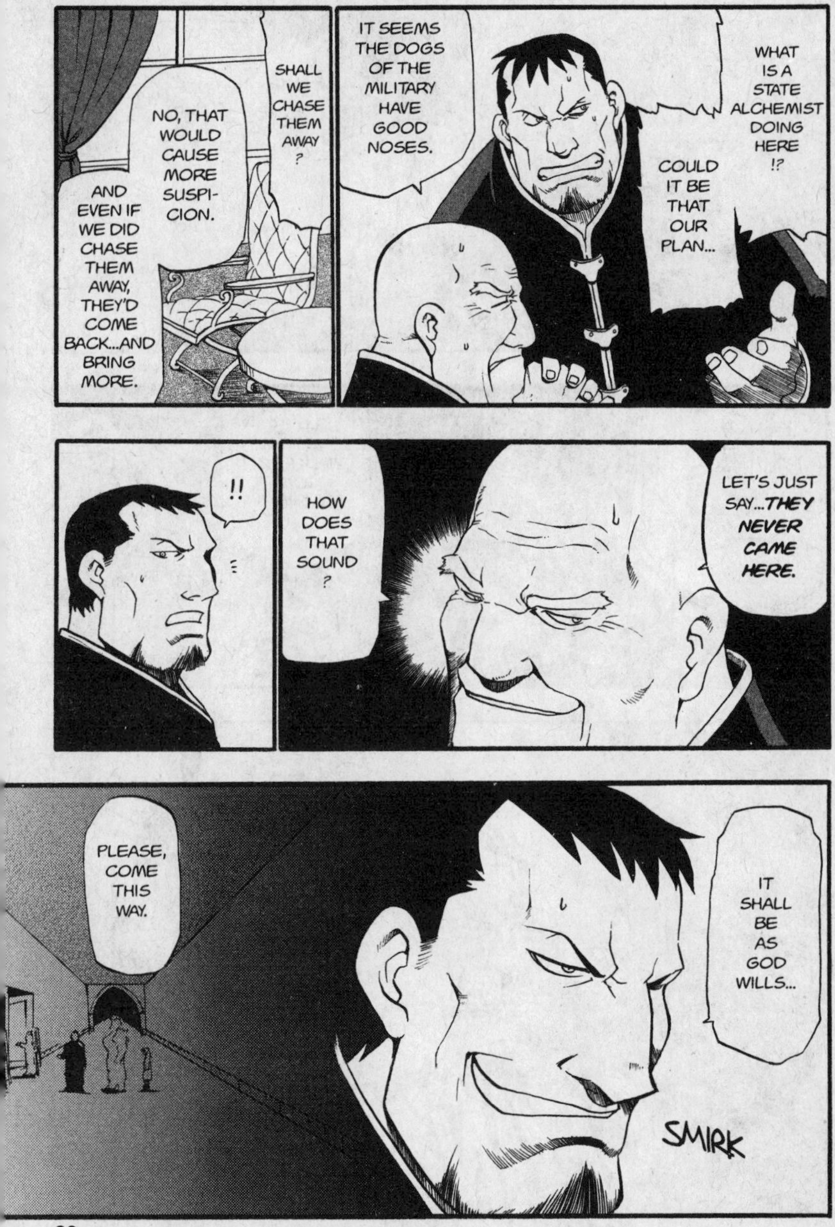
WHAT IS A STATE ALCHEMIST DOING HERE!?
COULD IT BE THAT OUR PLAN...
IT SEEMS THE DOGS OF THE MILITARY HAVE GOOD NOSES.
SHALL WE CHASE THEM AWAY?
NO, THAT WOULD CAUSE MORE SUSPICION.
AND EVEN IF WE DID CHASE THEM AWAY, THEY'D COME BACK...AND BRING MORE.
LET'S JUST SAY...**THEY NEVER CAME HERE.**
HOW DOES THAT SOUND?
!!
IT SHALL BE AS GOD WILLS...
SMIRK
PLEASE, COME THIS WAY.

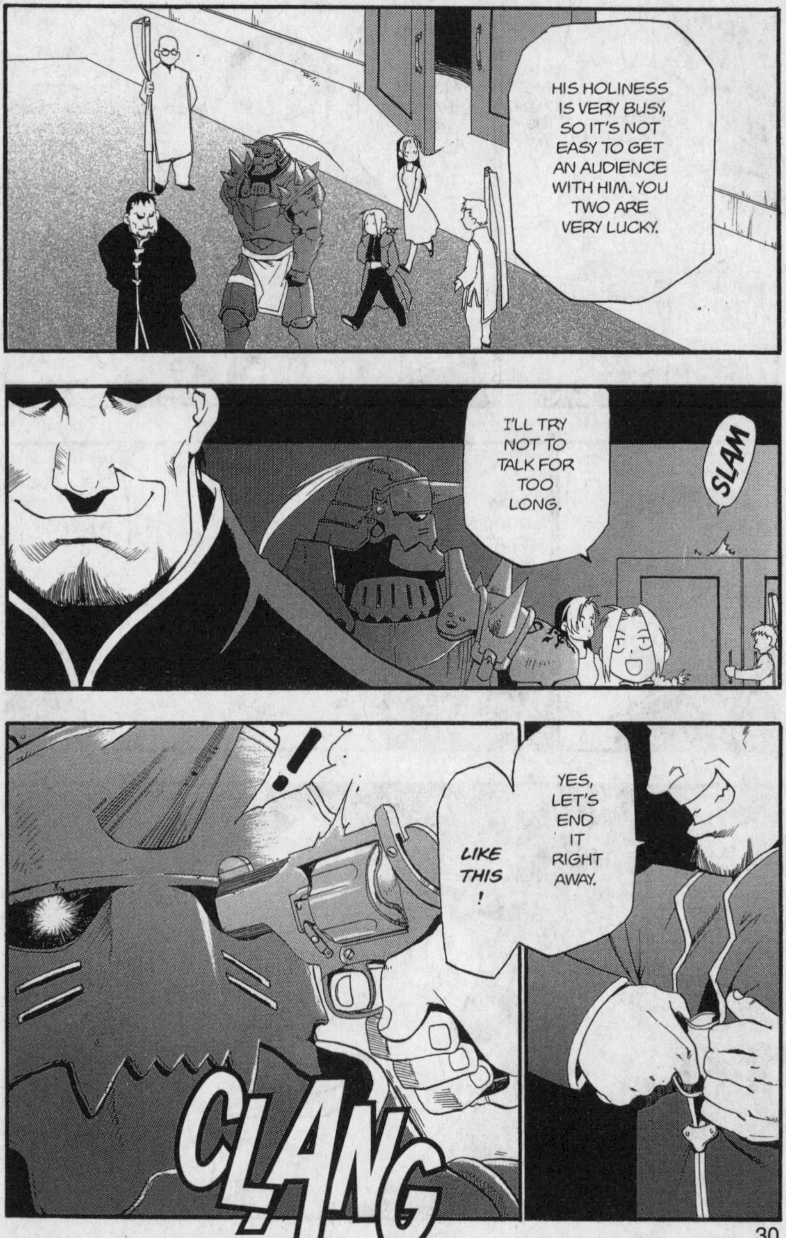
HIS HOLINESS IS VERY BUSY, SO IT'S NOT EASY TO GET AN AUDIENCE WITH HIM. YOU TWO ARE VERY LUCKY.
SLAM
I'LL TRY NOT TO TALK FOR TOO LONG.
YES, LET'S END IT RIGHT AWAY.
LIKE THIS!
!
CLANG

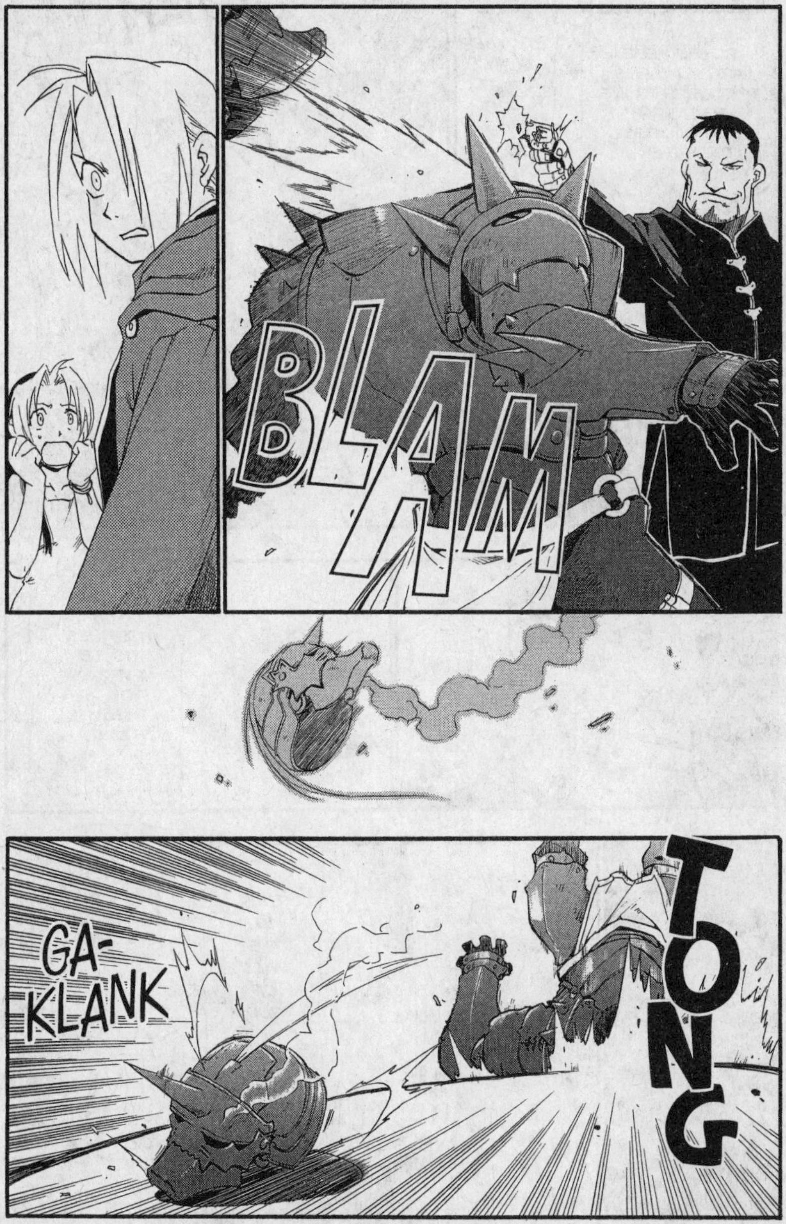
BLAM
TONG
GA-
KLANK

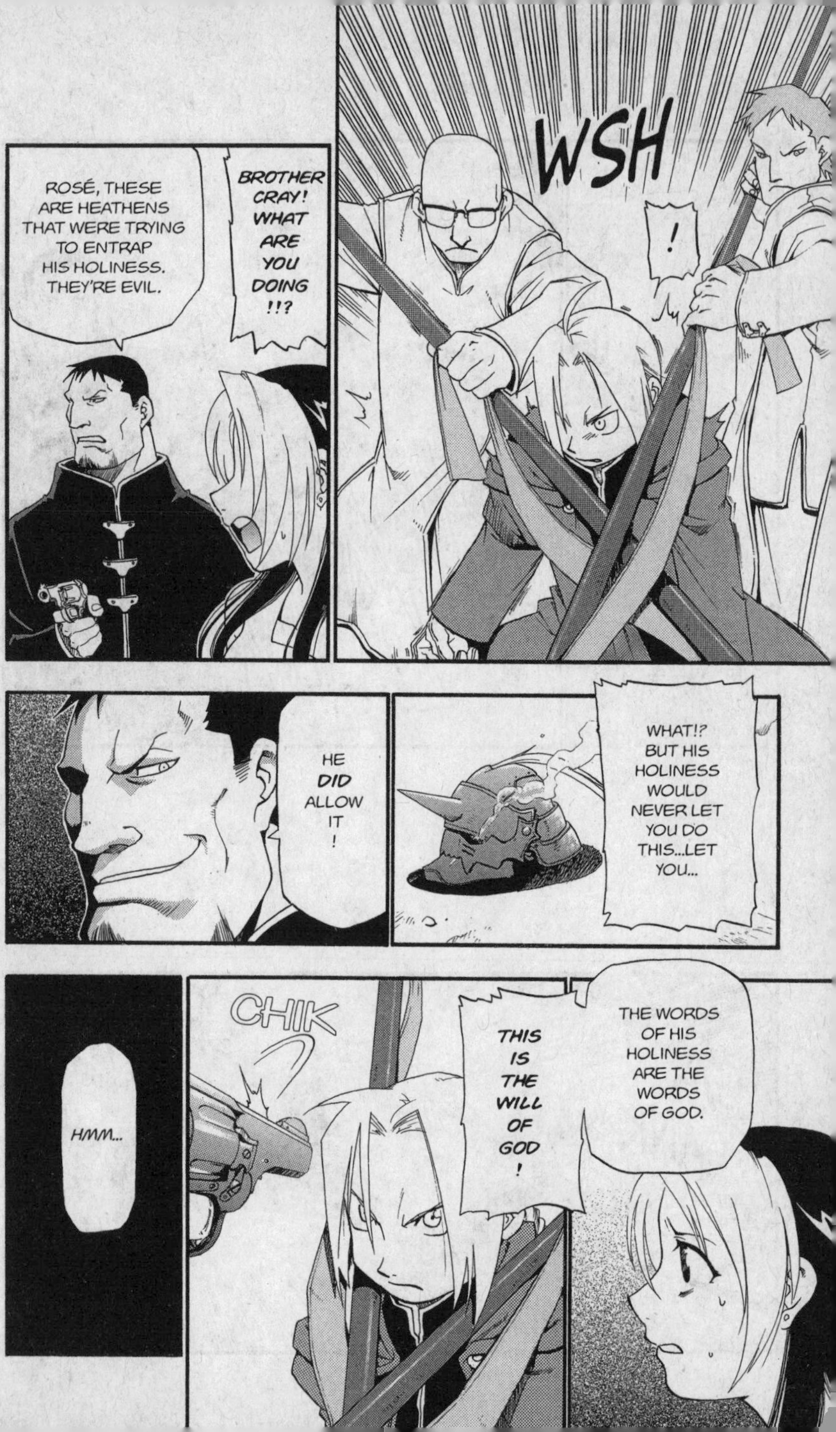
WSH
!
BROTHER CRAY! WHAT ARE YOU DOING!!?
ROSÉ, THESE ARE HEATHENS THAT WERE TRYING TO ENTRAP HIS HOLINESS. THEY'RE EVIL.
WHAT!? BUT HIS HOLINESS WOULD NEVER LET YOU DO THIS...LET YOU...
HE DID ALLOW IT!
THE WORDS OF HIS HOLINESS ARE THE WORDS OF GOD.
THIS IS THE WILL OF GOD!
CHIK
HMM...

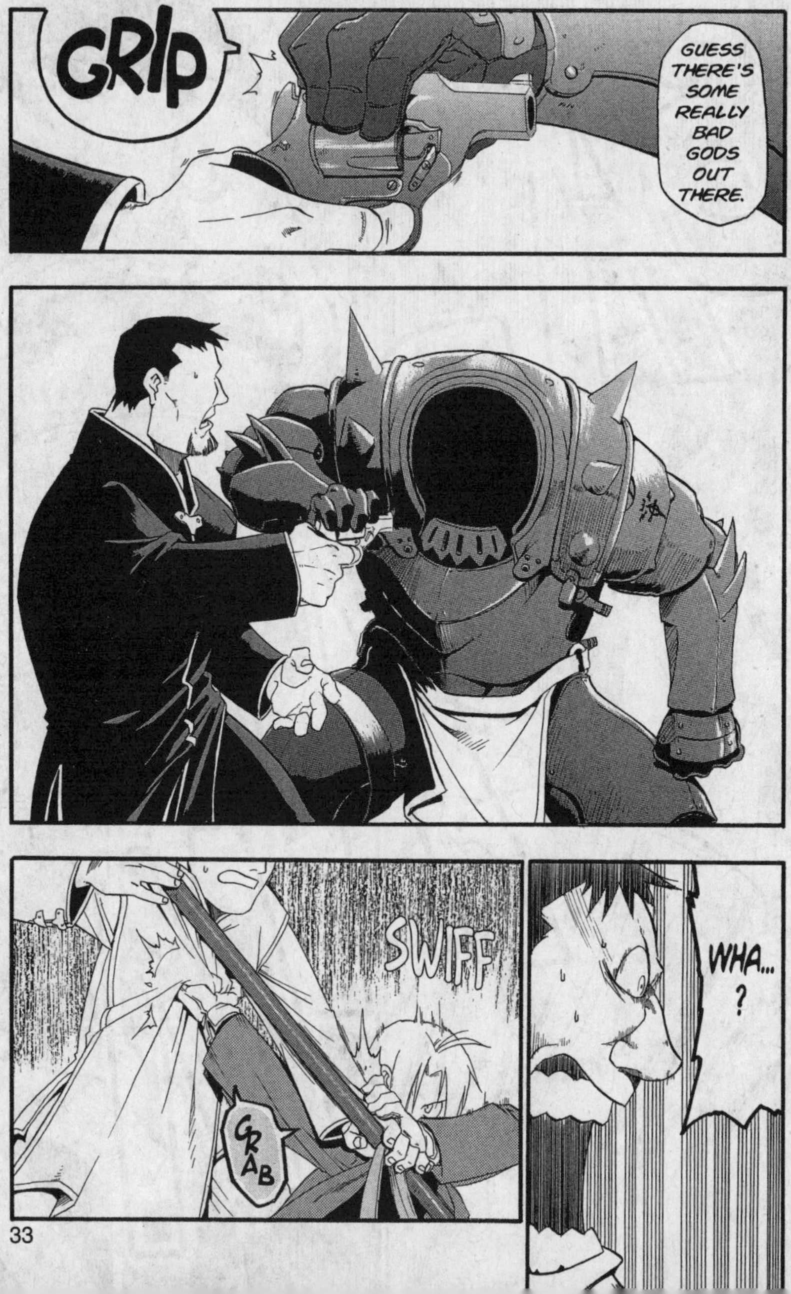
GUESS THERE'S SOME REALLY BAD GODS OUT THERE.
GRIP
WHA... ?
SWIFF
GRAB

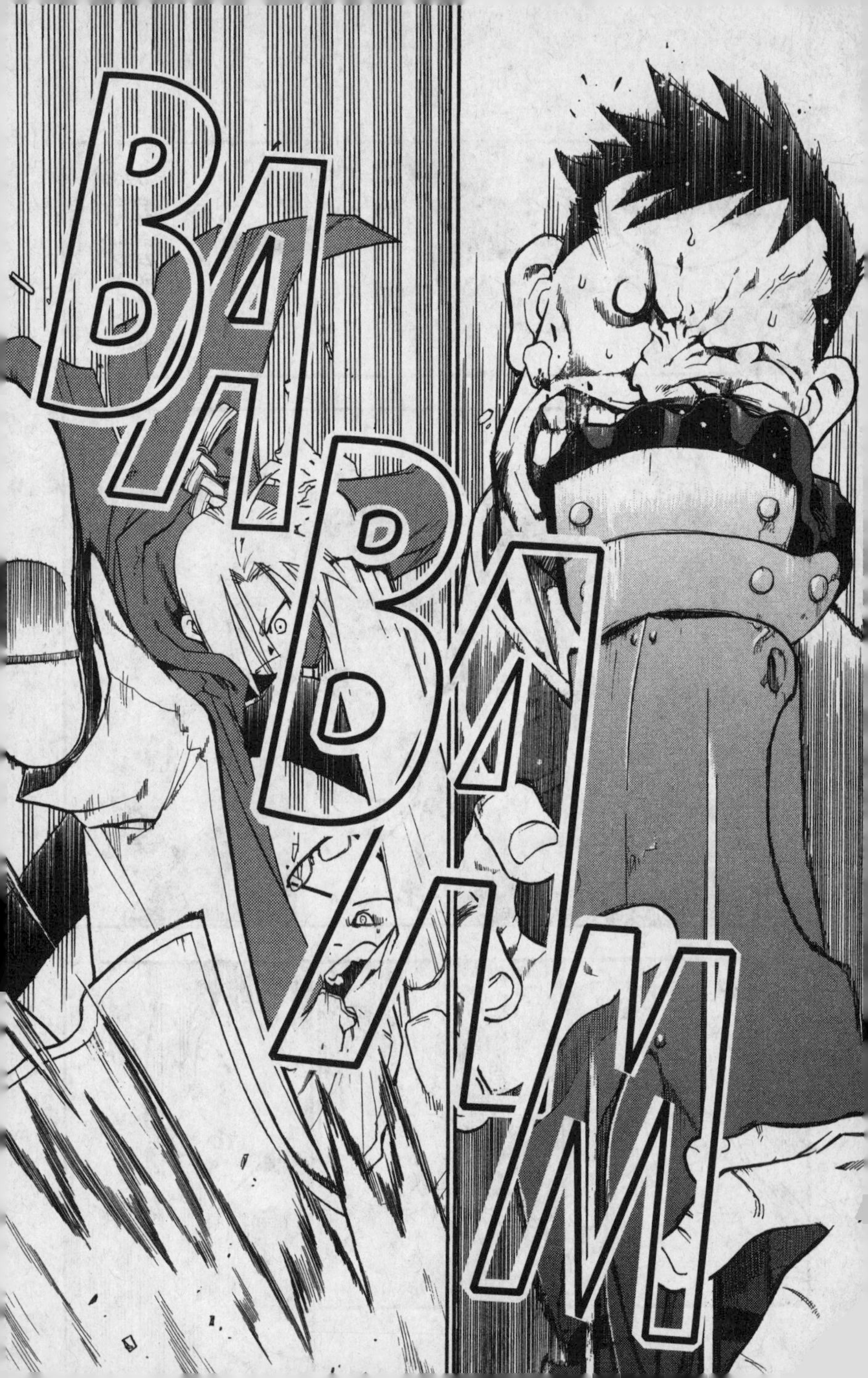
BABAMM

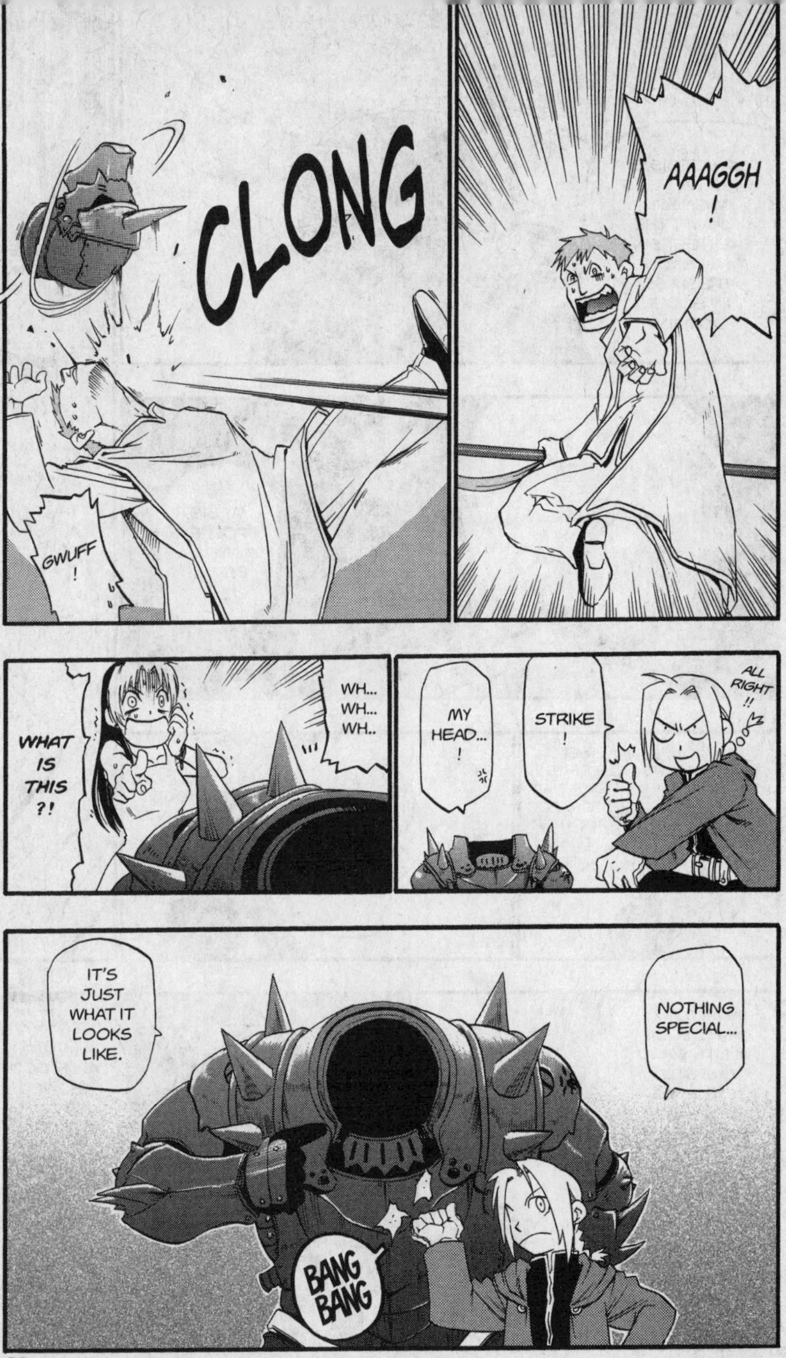
AAAGGH!
CLONG
GWUFF!
ALL RIGHT!!
STRIKE!
MY HEAD...!
WH... WH... WH..
WHAT IS THIS?!
NOTHING SPECIAL...
IT'S JUST WHAT IT LOOKS LIKE.
BANG BANG

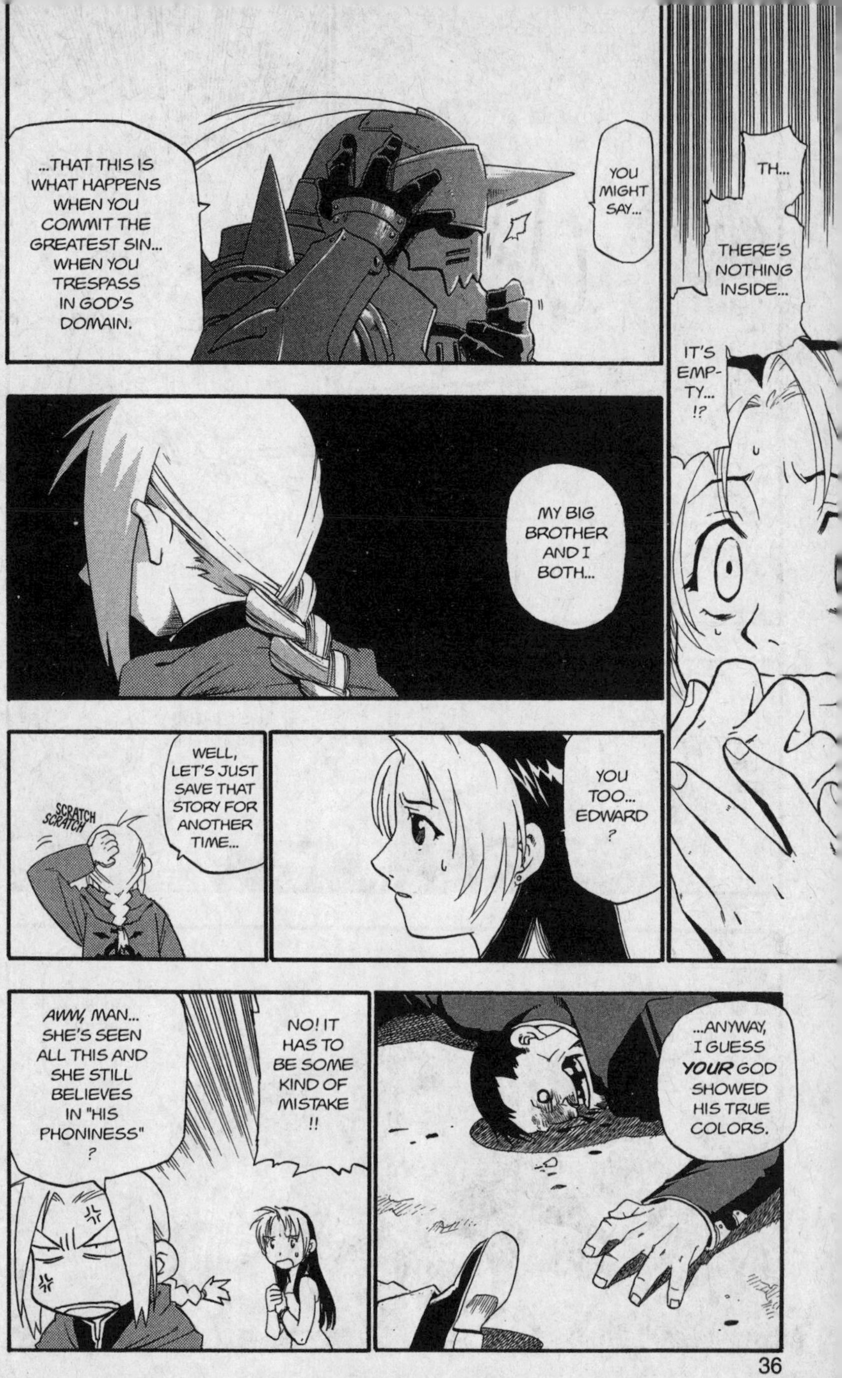
TH...
THERE'S NOTHING INSIDE...
IT'S EMPTY... !?
YOU MIGHT SAY...
...THAT THIS IS WHAT HAPPENS WHEN YOU COMMIT THE GREATEST SIN... WHEN YOU TRESPASS IN GOD'S DOMAIN.
MY BIG BROTHER AND I BOTH...
YOU TOO... EDWARD ?
WELL, LET'S JUST SAVE THAT STORY FOR ANOTHER TIME...
SCRATCH SCRATCH
...ANYWAY, I GUESS *YOUR* GOD SHOWED HIS TRUE COLORS.
NO! IT HAS TO BE SOME KIND OF MISTAKE !!
AWW, MAN... SHE'S SEEN ALL THIS AND SHE STILL BELIEVES IN "HIS PHONINESS" ?

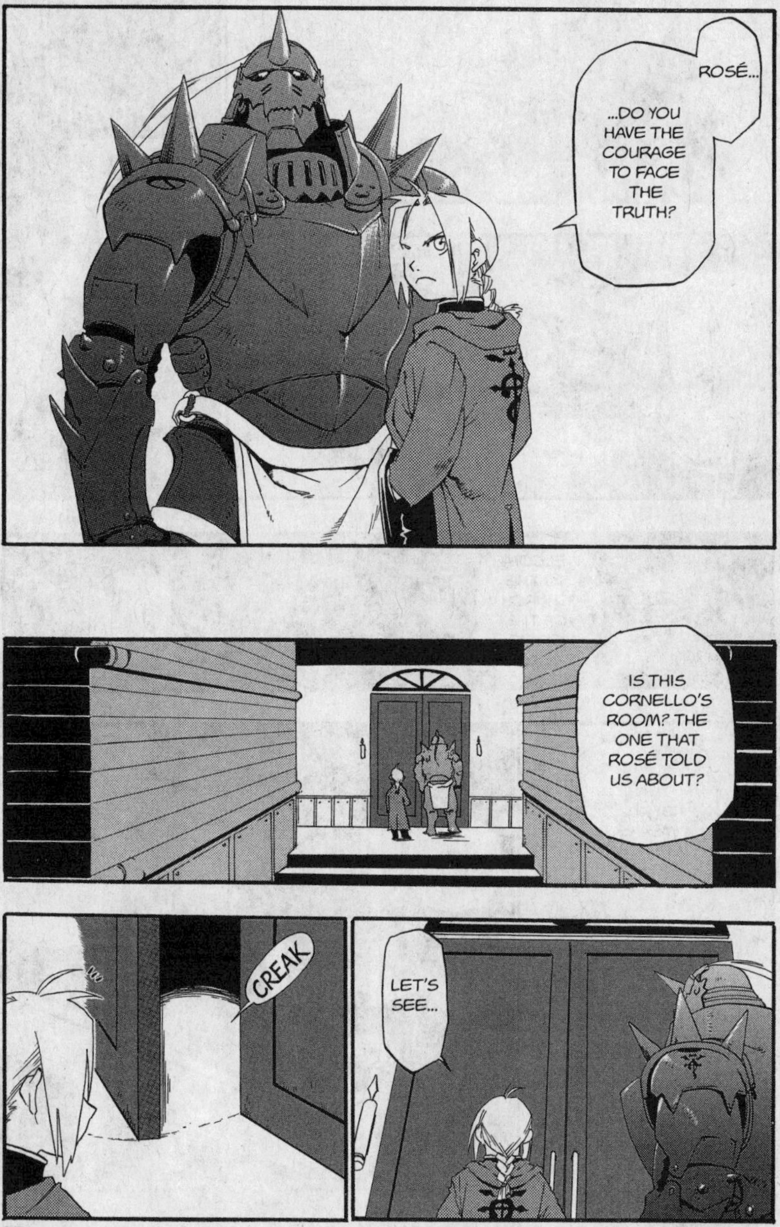
ROSÉ...
...DO YOU HAVE THE COURAGE TO FACE THE TRUTH?
IS THIS CORNELLO'S ROOM? THE ONE THAT ROSÉ TOLD US ABOUT?
LET'S SEE...
CREAK

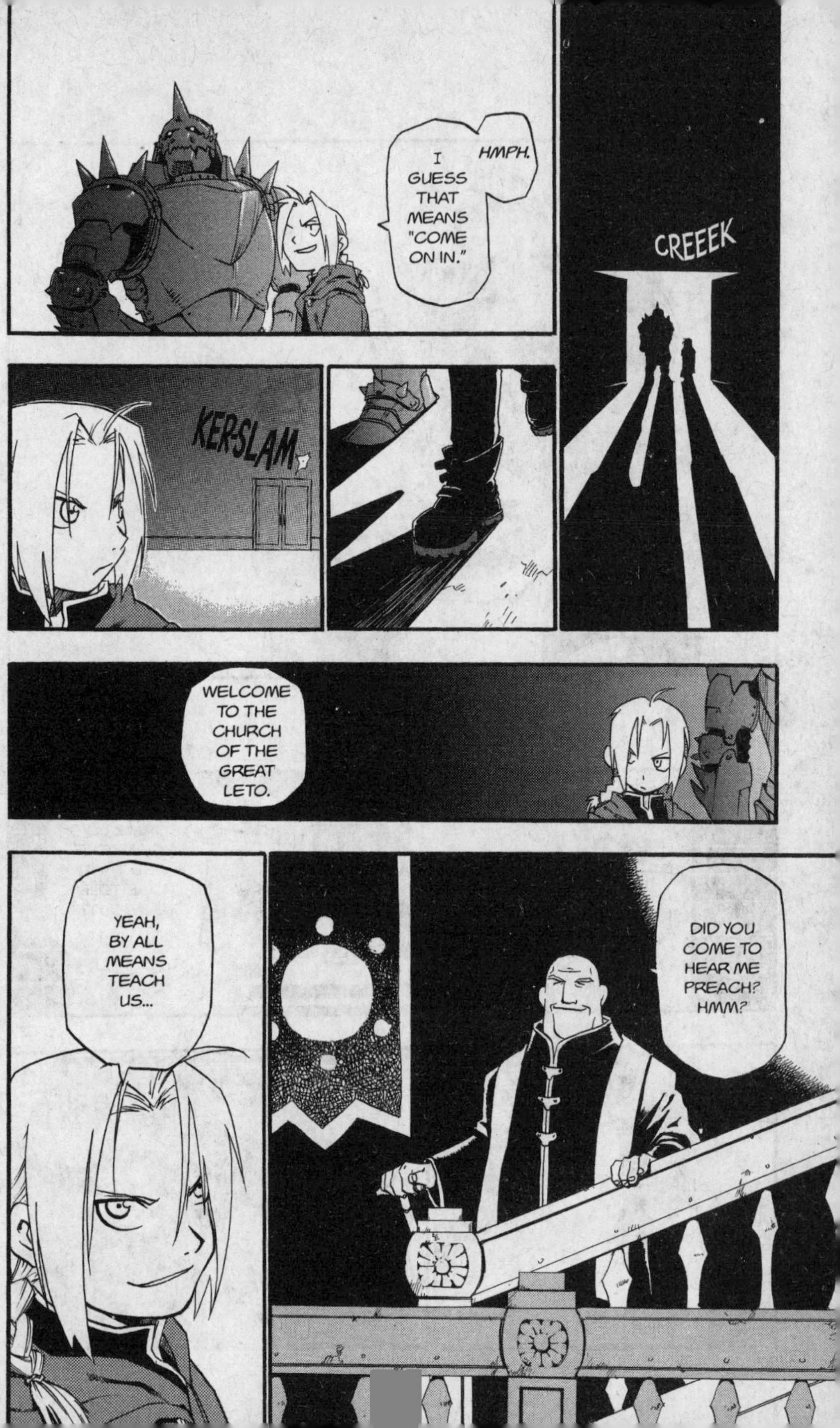
CREEEK
HMPH.
I GUESS THAT MEANS "COME ON IN."
KER-SLAM
WELCOME TO THE CHURCH OF THE GREAT LETO.
DID YOU COME TO HEAR ME PREACH? HMM?
YEAH, BY ALL MEANS TEACH US...

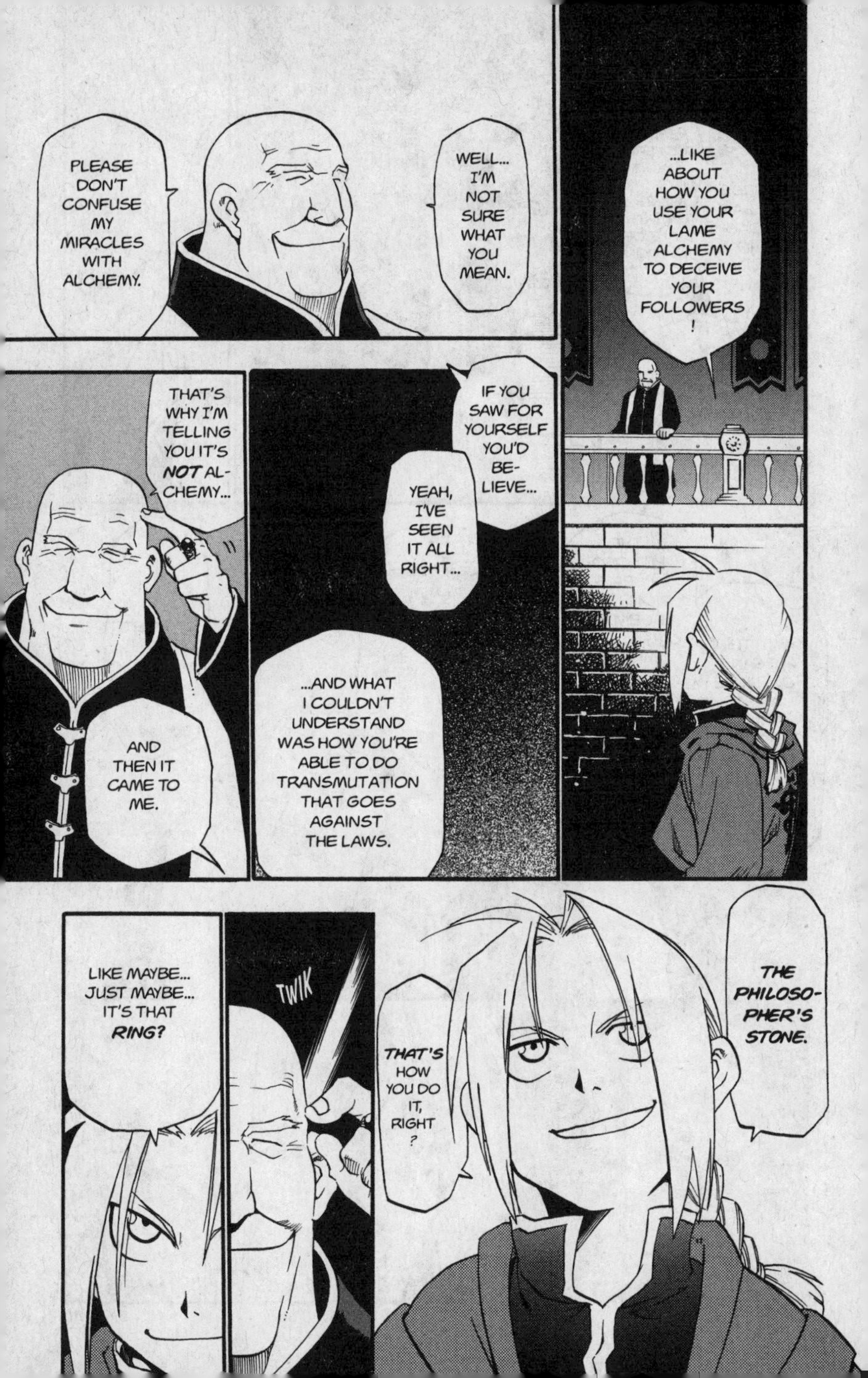

...LIKE ABOUT HOW YOU USE YOUR LAME ALCHEMY TO DECEIVE YOUR FOLLOWERS!
WELL... I'M NOT SURE WHAT YOU MEAN.
PLEASE DON'T CONFUSE MY MIRACLES WITH ALCHEMY.
IF YOU SAW FOR YOURSELF YOU'D BE-LIEVE...
YEAH, I'VE SEEN IT ALL RIGHT...
...AND WHAT I COULDN'T UNDERSTAND WAS HOW YOU'RE ABLE TO DO TRANSMUTATION THAT GOES AGAINST THE LAWS.
THAT'S WHY I'M TELLING YOU IT'S NOT AL-CHEMY...
AND THEN IT CAME TO ME.
THE PHILOSO-PHER'S STONE.
THAT'S HOW YOU DO IT, RIGHT?
TWIK
LIKE MAYBE... JUST MAYBE... IT'S THAT RING?

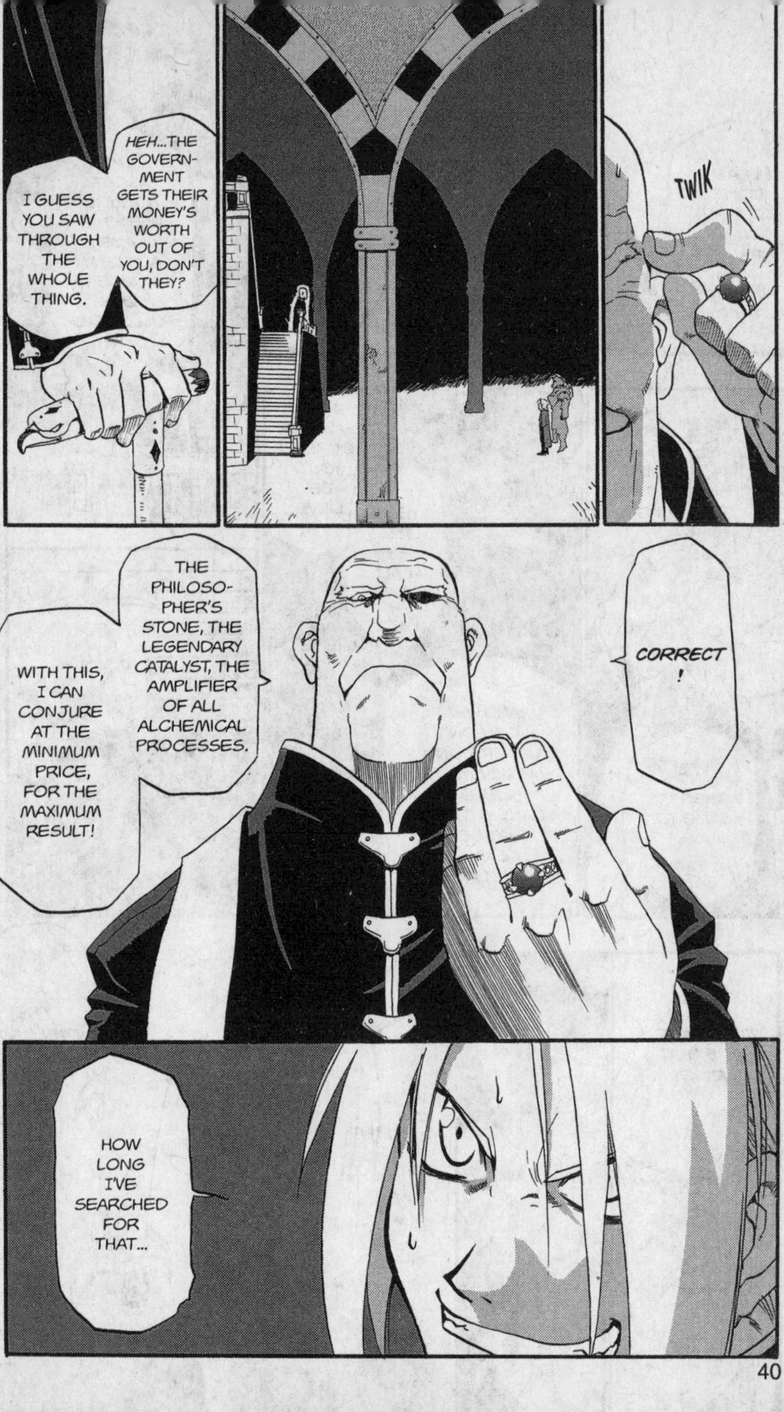
TWIK
HEH...THE GOVERNMENT GETS THEIR MONEY'S WORTH OUT OF YOU, DON'T THEY?
I GUESS YOU SAW THROUGH THE WHOLE THING.
CORRECT!
THE PHILOSOPHER'S STONE, THE LEGENDARY CATALYST, THE AMPLIFIER OF ALL ALCHEMICAL PROCESSES.
WITH THIS, I CAN CONJURE AT THE MINIMUM PRICE, FOR THE MAXIMUM RESULT!
HOW LONG I'VE SEARCHED FOR THAT...

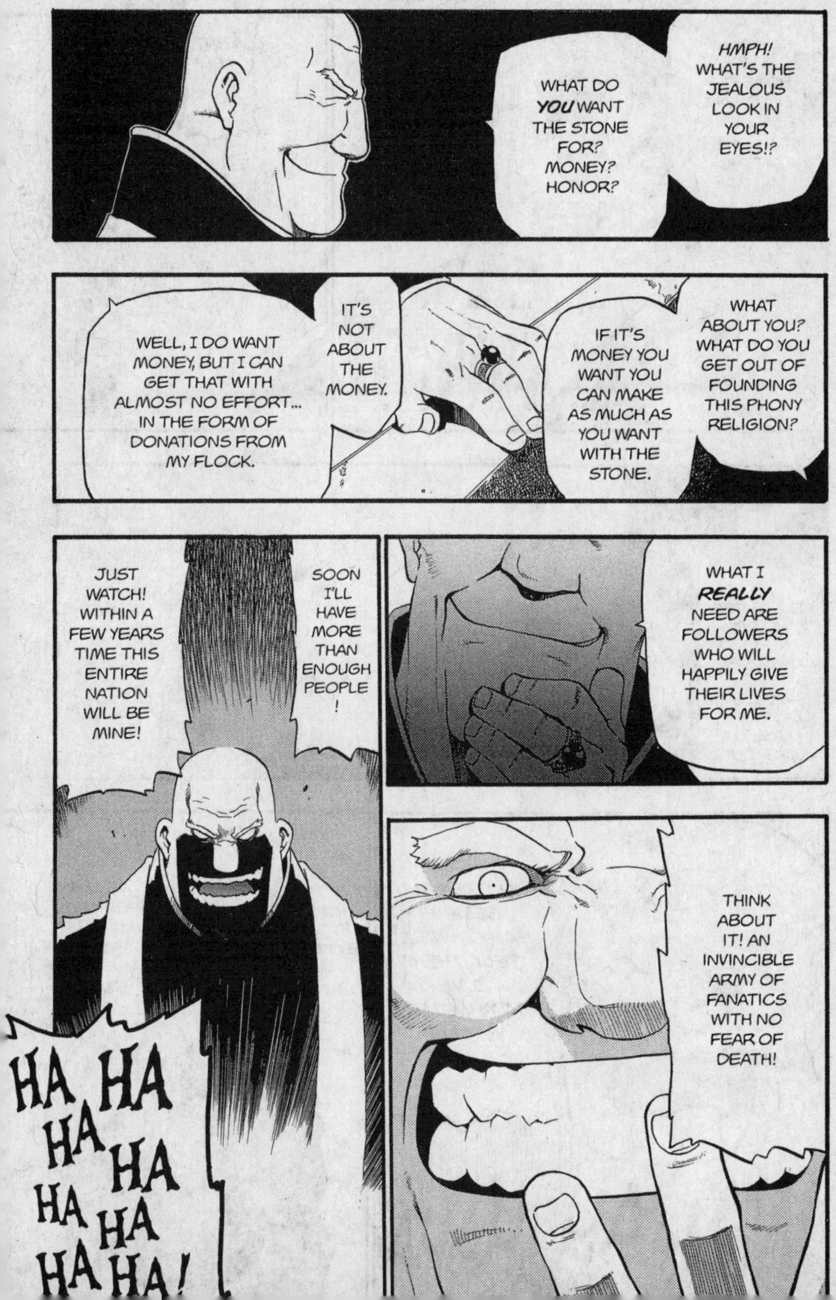
HMPH! WHAT'S THE JEALOUS LOOK IN YOUR EYES!?
WHAT DO YOU WANT THE STONE FOR? MONEY? HONOR?
WHAT ABOUT YOU? WHAT DO YOU GET OUT OF FOUNDING THIS PHONY RELIGION?
IF IT'S MONEY YOU WANT YOU CAN MAKE AS MUCH AS YOU WANT WITH THE STONE.
IT'S NOT ABOUT THE MONEY.
WELL, I DO WANT MONEY, BUT I CAN GET THAT WITH ALMOST NO EFFORT... IN THE FORM OF DONATIONS FROM MY FLOCK.
WHAT I REALLY NEED ARE FOLLOWERS WHO WILL HAPPILY GIVE THEIR LIVES FOR ME.
THINK ABOUT IT! AN INVINCIBLE ARMY OF FANATICS WITH NO FEAR OF DEATH!
SOON I'LL HAVE MORE THAN ENOUGH PEOPLE!
JUST WATCH! WITHIN A FEW YEARS TIME THIS ENTIRE NATION WILL BE MINE!
HA HA HA HA HA HA HA HA HA!

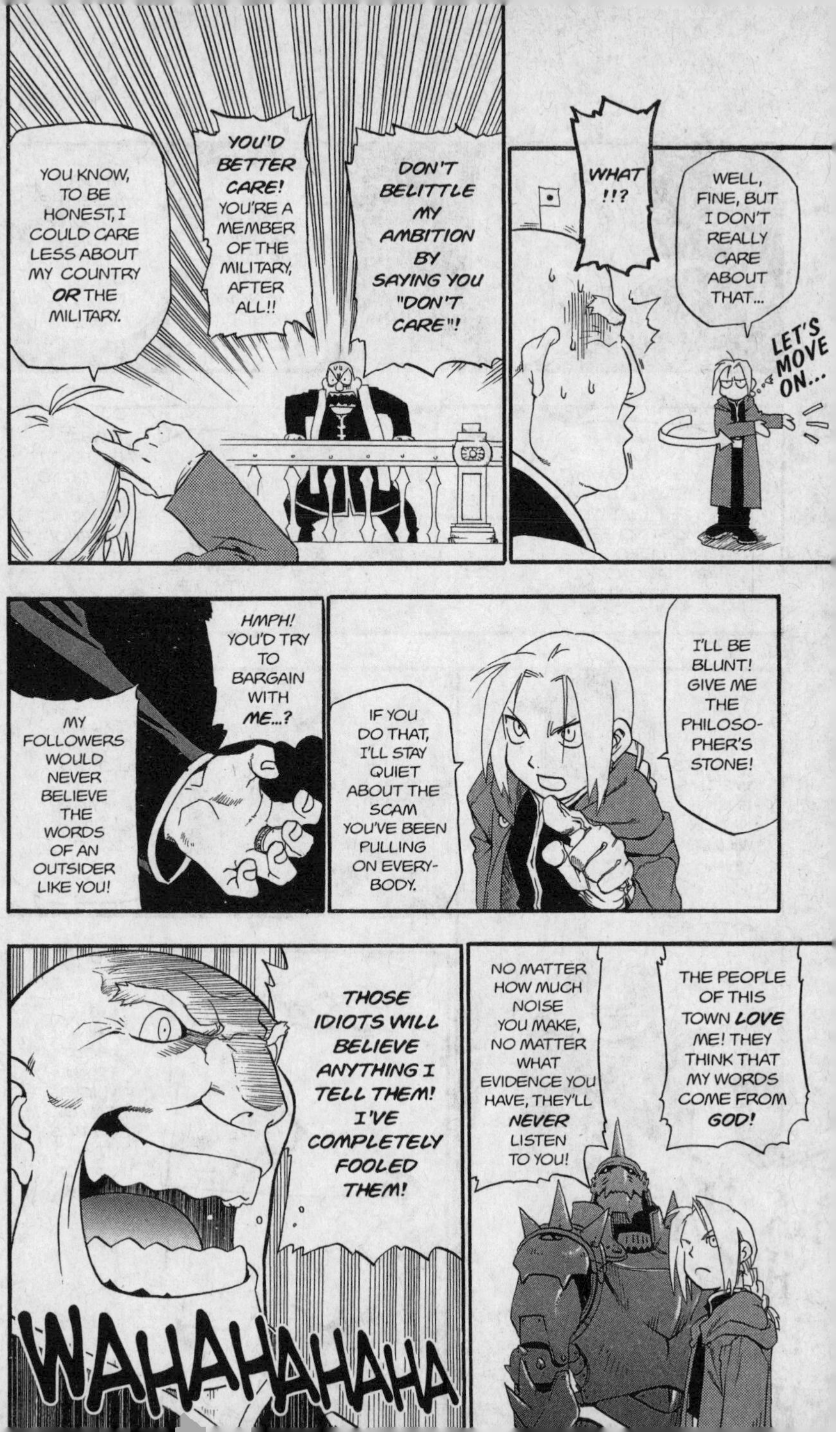

WELL, FINE, BUT I DON'T REALLY CARE ABOUT THAT...
LET'S MOVE ON...
WHAT!!?
DON'T BELITTLE MY AMBITION BY SAYING YOU "DON'T CARE"!
YOU'D BETTER CARE! YOU'RE A MEMBER OF THE MILITARY, AFTER ALL!!
YOU KNOW, TO BE HONEST, I COULD CARE LESS ABOUT MY COUNTRY OR THE MILITARY.
I'LL BE BLUNT! GIVE ME THE PHILOSOPHER'S STONE!
IF YOU DO THAT, I'LL STAY QUIET ABOUT THE SCAM YOU'VE BEEN PULLING ON EVERYBODY.
HMPH! YOU'D TRY TO BARGAIN WITH ME...?
MY FOLLOWERS WOULD NEVER BELIEVE THE WORDS OF AN OUTSIDER LIKE YOU!
THE PEOPLE OF THIS TOWN LOVE ME! THEY THINK THAT MY WORDS COME FROM GOD!
NO MATTER HOW MUCH NOISE YOU MAKE, NO MATTER WHAT EVIDENCE YOU HAVE, THEY'LL NEVER LISTEN TO YOU!
THOSE IDIOTS WILL BELIEVE ANYTHING I TELL THEM! I'VE COMPLETELY FOOLED THEM!
WAHAHAHAHAHA

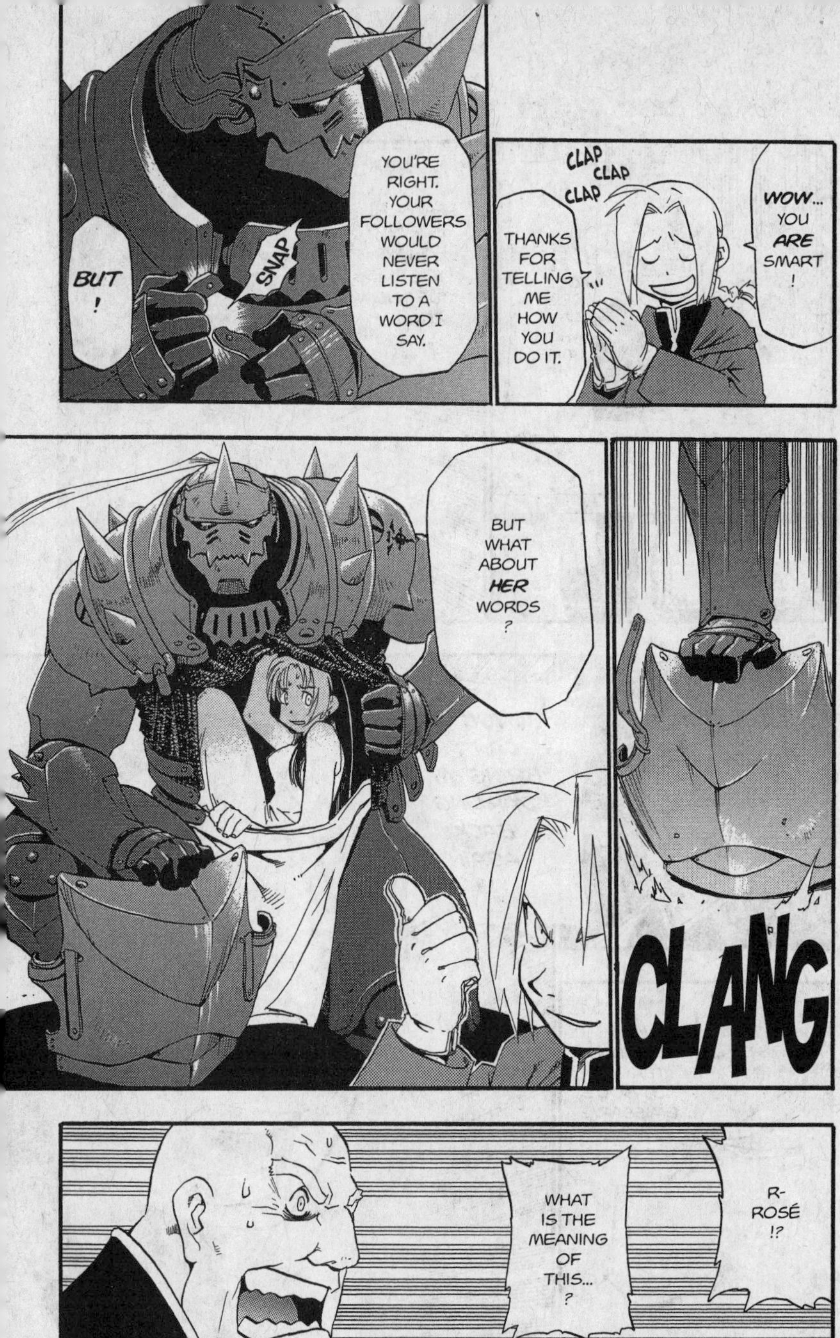
WOW... YOU ARE SMART!
CLAP CLAP CLAP
THANKS FOR TELLING ME HOW YOU DO IT.
YOU'RE RIGHT. YOUR FOLLOWERS WOULD NEVER LISTEN TO A WORD I SAY.
SNAP
BUT!
CLANG
BUT WHAT ABOUT HER WORDS?
R-ROSÉ!?
WHAT IS THE MEANING OF THIS...?

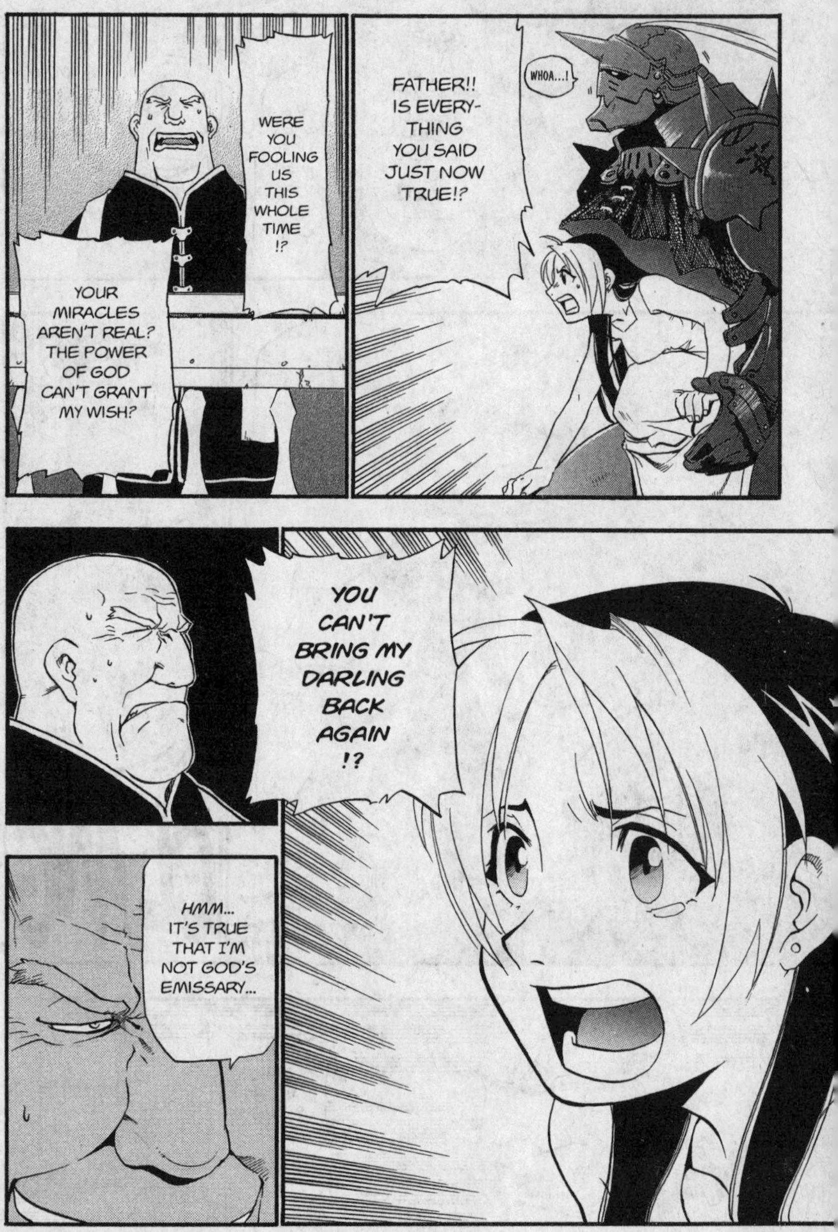
WHOA...!
FATHER!! IS EVERYTHING YOU SAID JUST NOW TRUE!?
WERE YOU FOOLING US THIS WHOLE TIME!?
YOUR MIRACLES AREN'T REAL? THE POWER OF GOD CAN'T GRANT MY WISH?
YOU CAN'T BRING MY DARLING BACK AGAIN!?
HMM... IT'S TRUE THAT I'M NOT GOD'S EMISSARY...

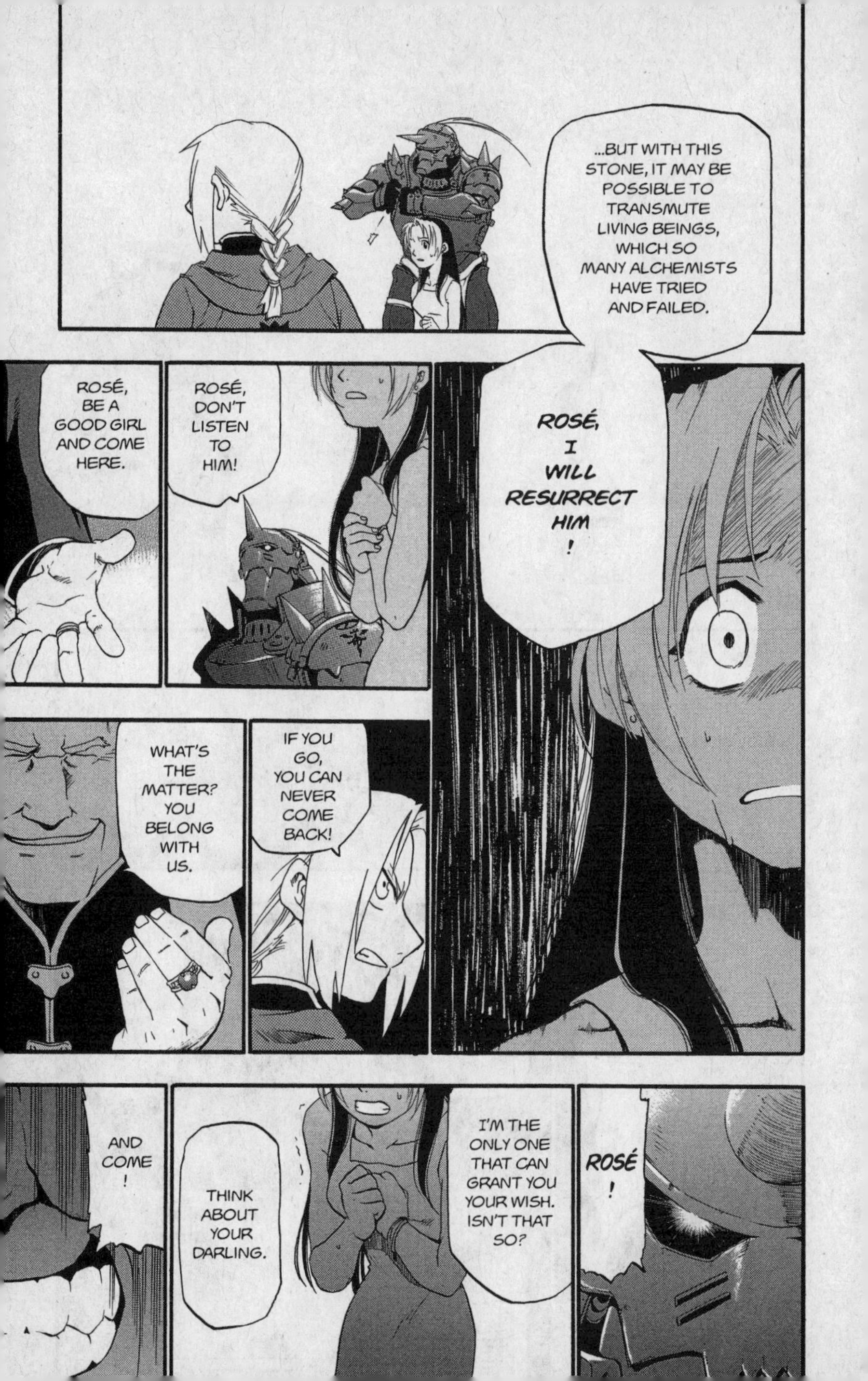
...BUT WITH THIS STONE, IT MAY BE POSSIBLE TO TRANSMUTE LIVING BEINGS, WHICH SO MANY ALCHEMISTS HAVE TRIED AND FAILED.
ROSÉ, I WILL RESURRECT HIM!
ROSÉ, DON'T LISTEN TO HIM!
ROSÉ, BE A GOOD GIRL AND COME HERE.
IF YOU GO, YOU CAN NEVER COME BACK!
WHAT'S THE MATTER? YOU BELONG WITH US.
ROSÉ!
I'M THE ONLY ONE THAT CAN GRANT YOU YOUR WISH. ISN'T THAT SO?
THINK ABOUT YOUR DARLING.
AND COME!

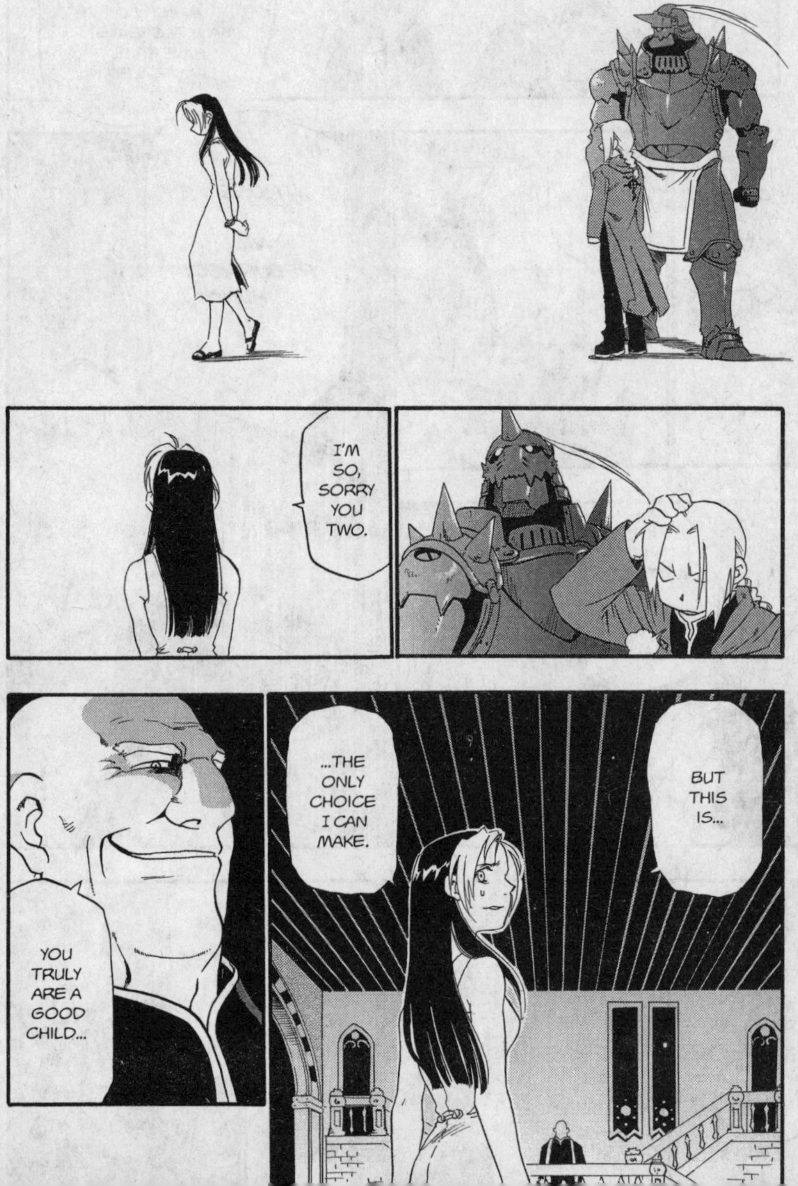
I'M SO, SORRY YOU TWO.
BUT THIS IS...
...THE ONLY CHOICE I CAN MAKE.
YOU TRULY ARE A GOOD CHILD...

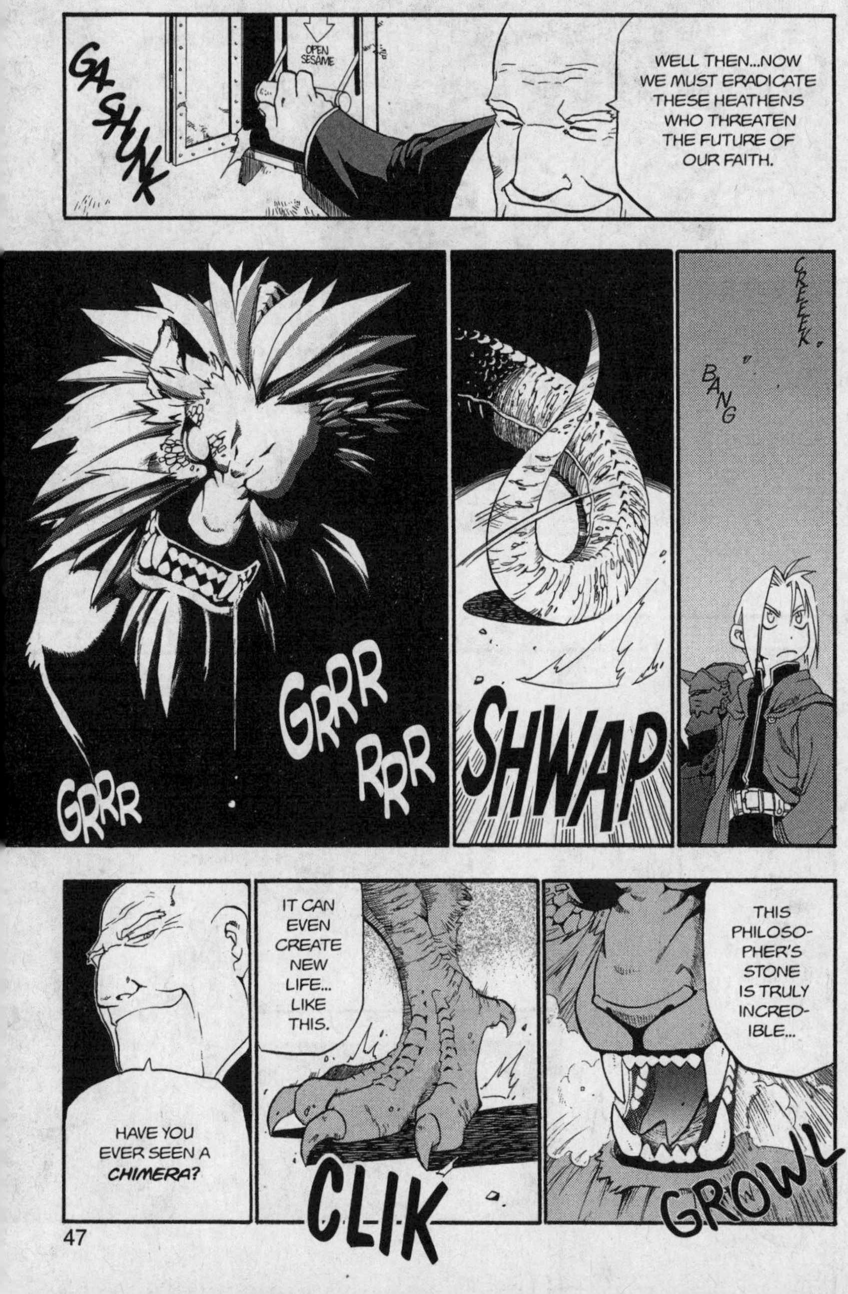
WELL THEN...NOW WE MUST ERADICATE THESE HEATHENS WHO THREATEN THE FUTURE OF OUR FAITH.
OPEN SESAME
GASHUNK
CREEEK
BANG
SHWAP
GRRR RRR
GRRR
THIS PHILOSOPHER'S STONE IS TRULY INCREDIBLE...
GROWL
IT CAN EVEN CREATE NEW LIFE... LIKE THIS.
CLIK
HAVE YOU EVER SEEN A CHIMERA?

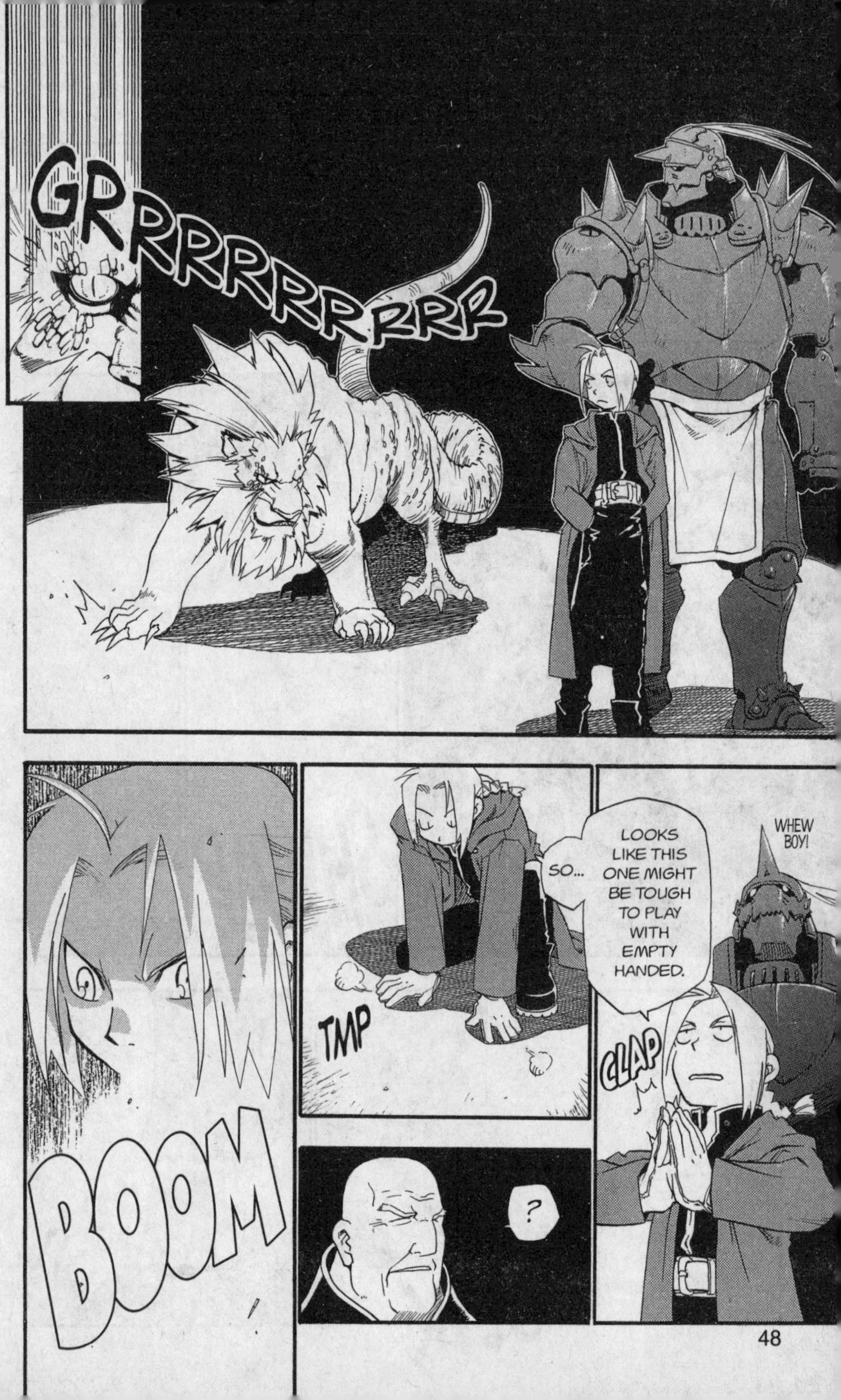
GRRRRRRRRRRR
WHEW BOY!
LOOKS LIKE THIS ONE MIGHT BE TOUGH TO PLAY WITH EMPTY HANDED.
SO...
CLAP
TMP
?
BOOM

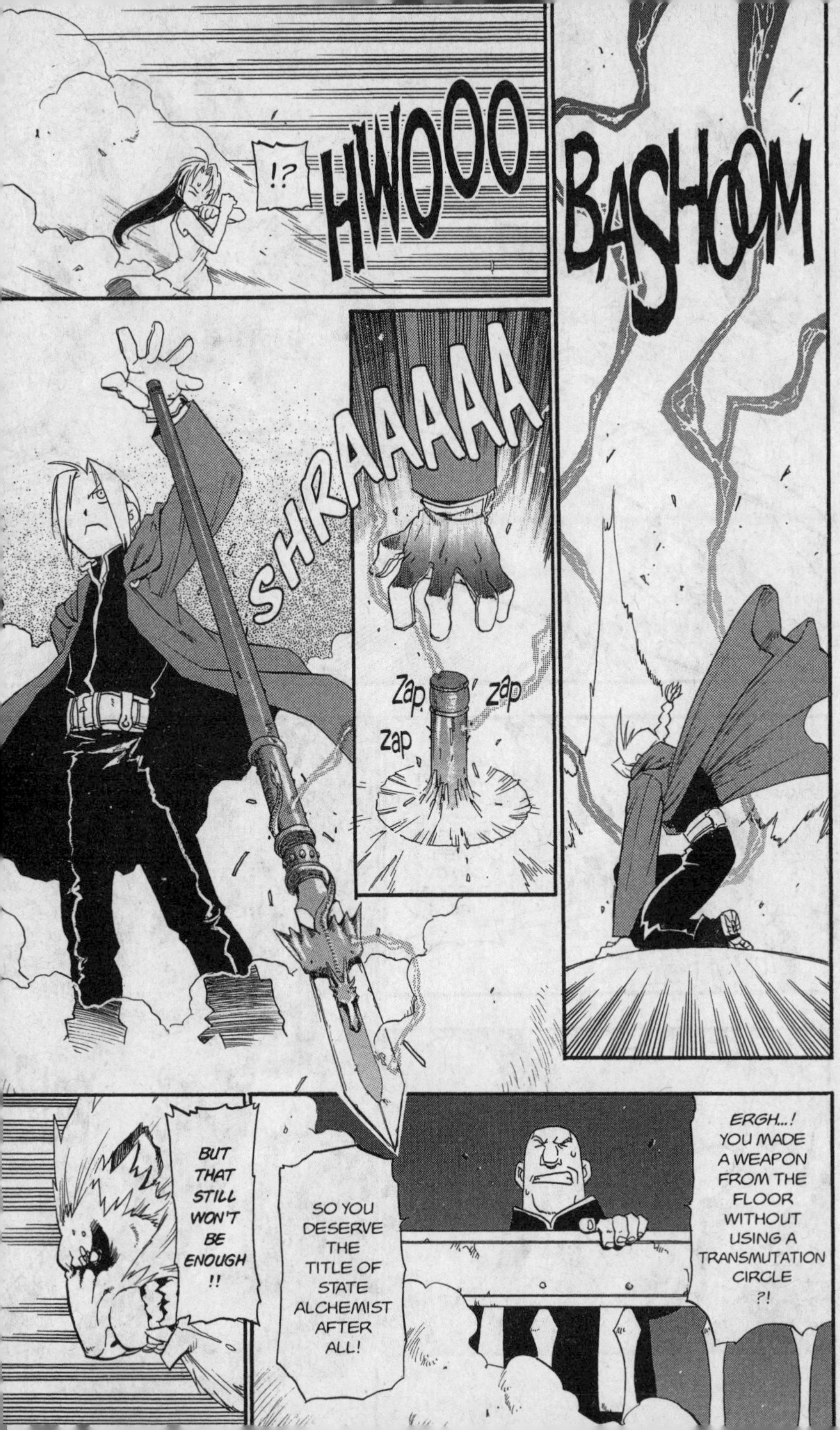
BASHOOM
!?
HWOOO
SHRAAAAA
Zap
zap
zap
ERGH...! YOU MADE A WEAPON FROM THE FLOOR WITHOUT USING A TRANSMUTATION CIRCLE ?!
SO YOU DESERVE THE TITLE OF STATE ALCHEMIST AFTER ALL!
BUT THAT STILL WON'T BE ENOUGH !!

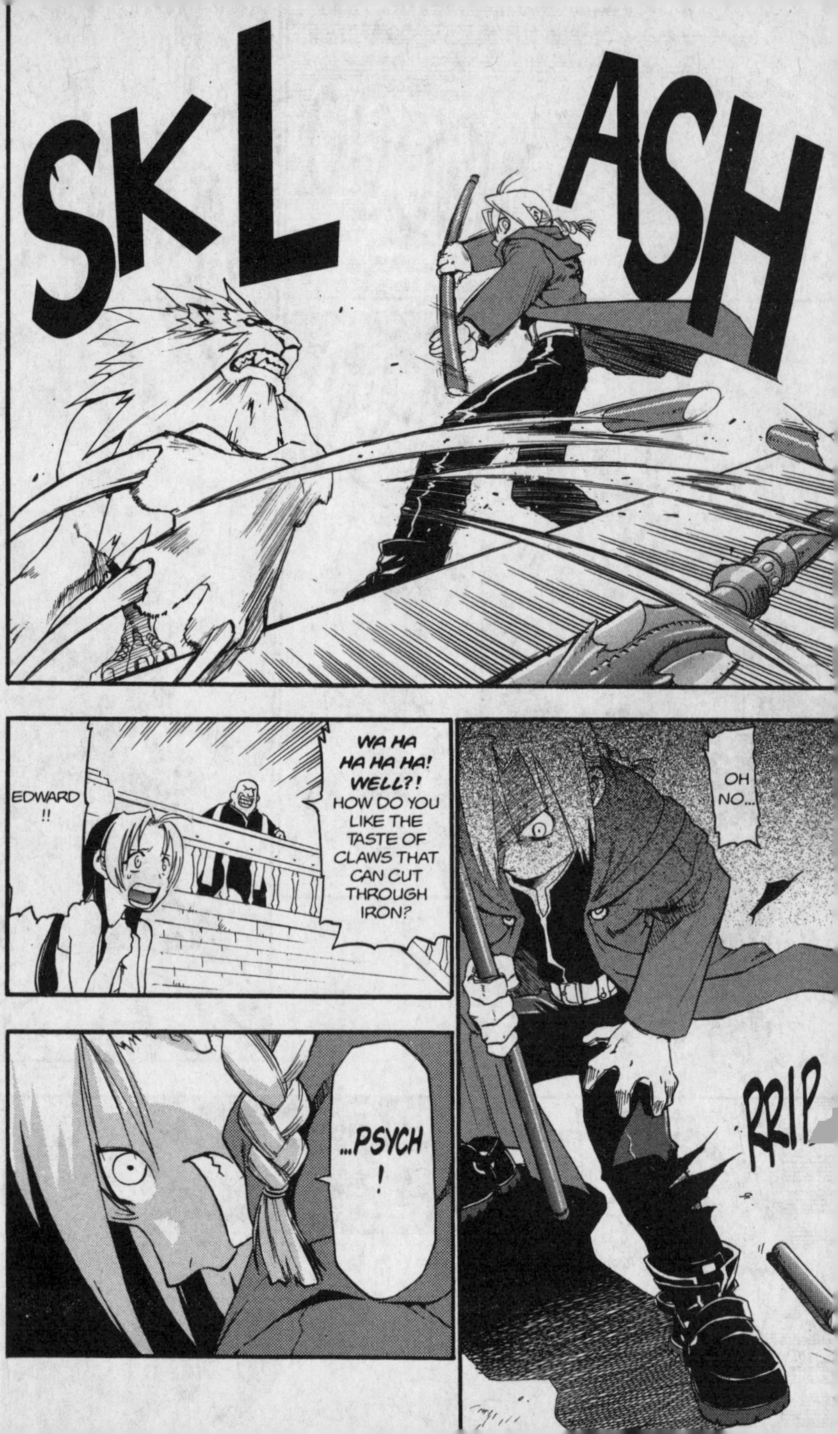
SKLASH
OH NO...
RRIP
WA HA HA HA HA! WELL?! HOW DO YOU LIKE THE TASTE OF CLAWS THAT CAN CUT THROUGH IRON?
EDWARD!!
...PSYCH!

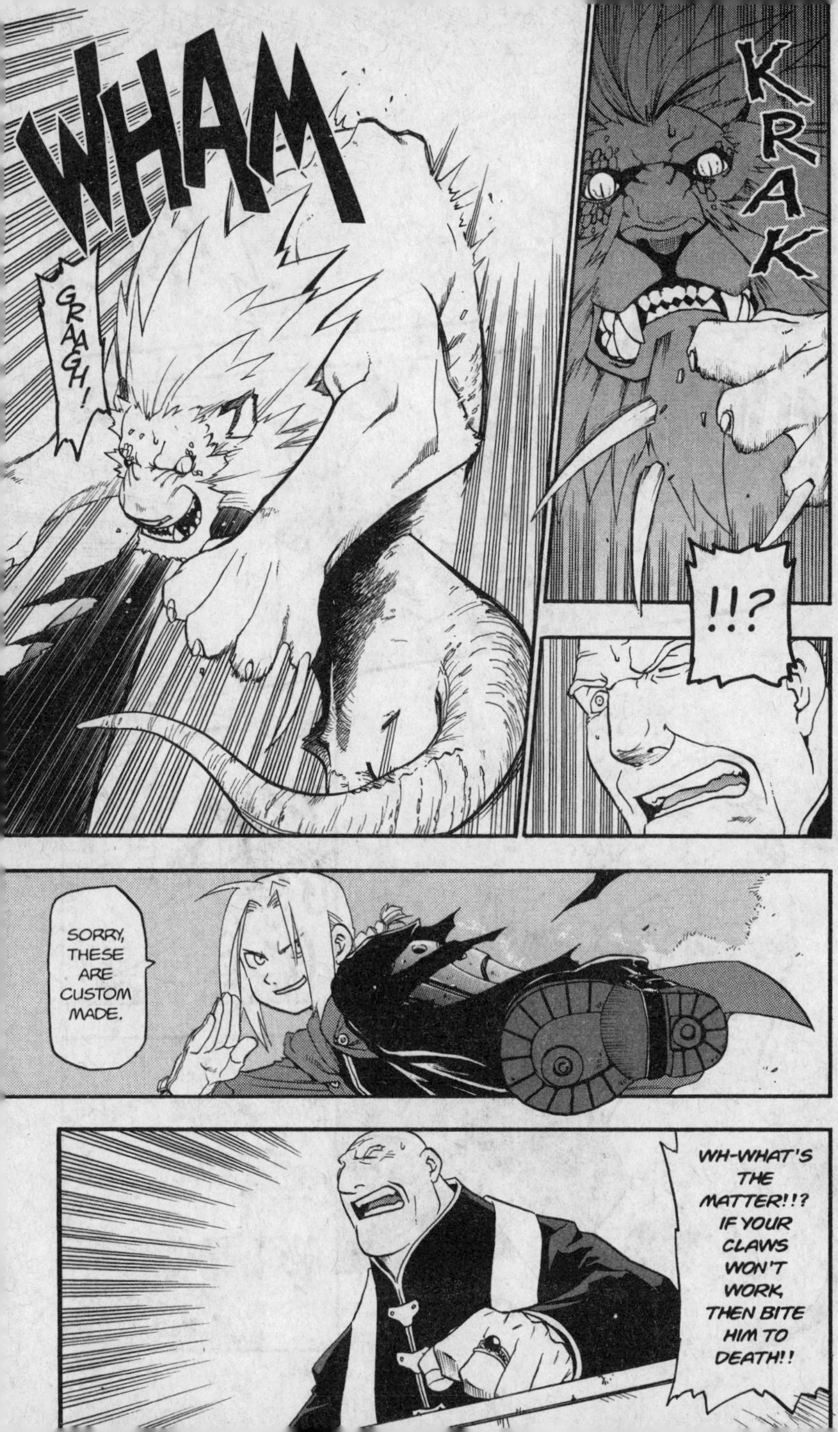
KRAK
!!?
WHAM
GRAAGH!
SORRY, THESE ARE CUSTOM MADE.
WH-WHAT'S THE MATTER!!? IF YOUR CLAWS WON'T WORK, THEN BITE HIM TO DEATH!!

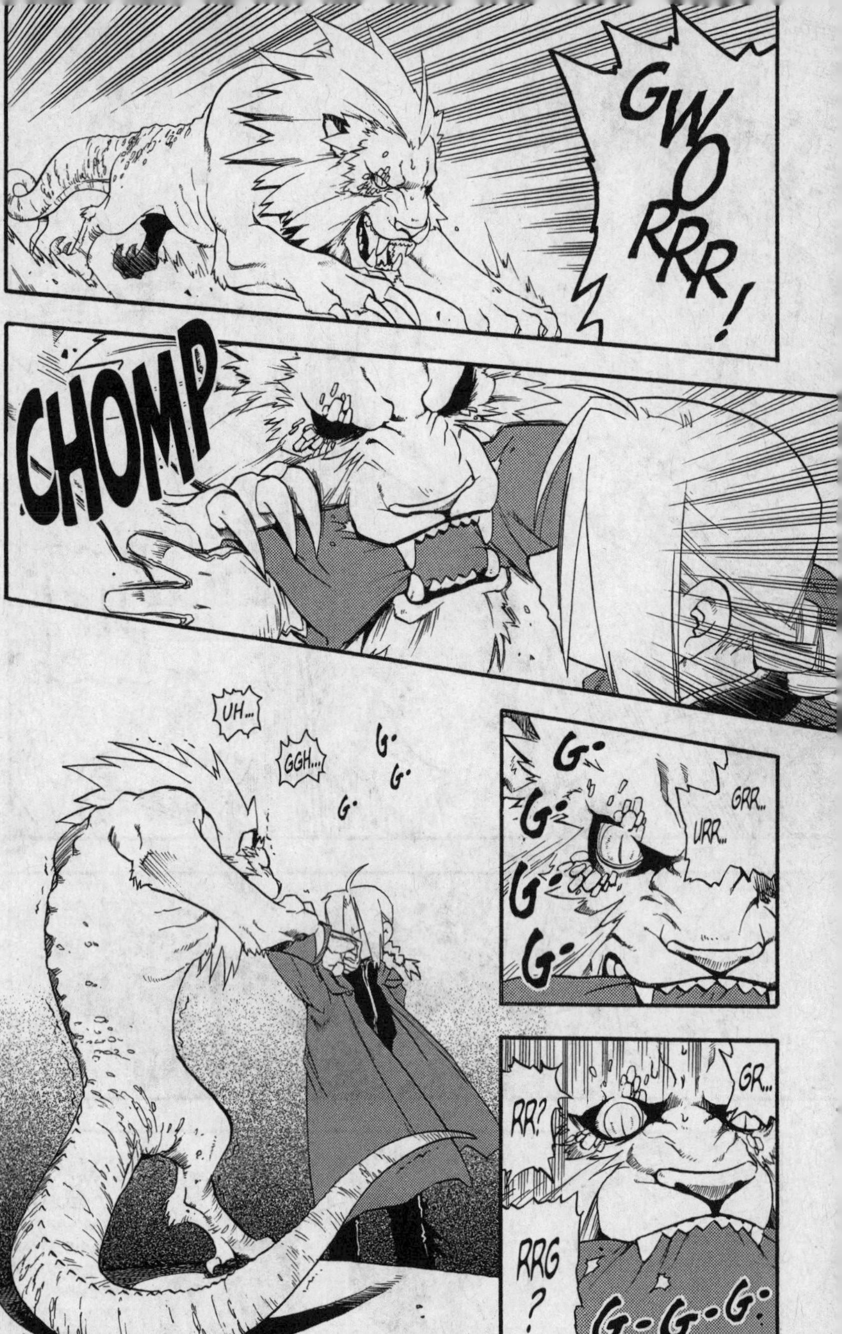
GWORRR!
CHOMP
GRR...
URR...
G- G- G G-
GR...
RR?
RRG ?
G-G-G-G-
UH...
GGH...
G- G- G-

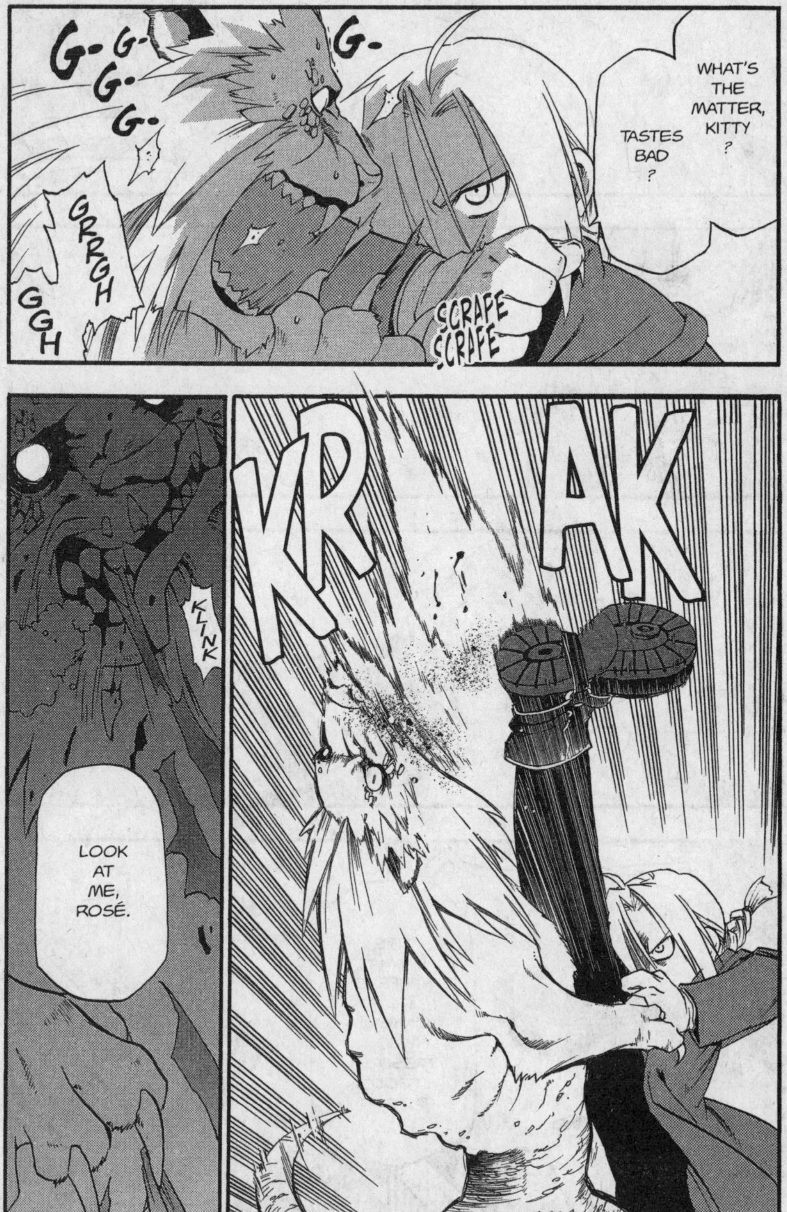
WHAT'S THE MATTER, KITTY?
TASTES BAD?
G-
G-G-
G-
G-
GRRGH
GGH
SCRAPE
SCRAPE
KR AK
KLINK
LOOK AT ME, ROSÉ.

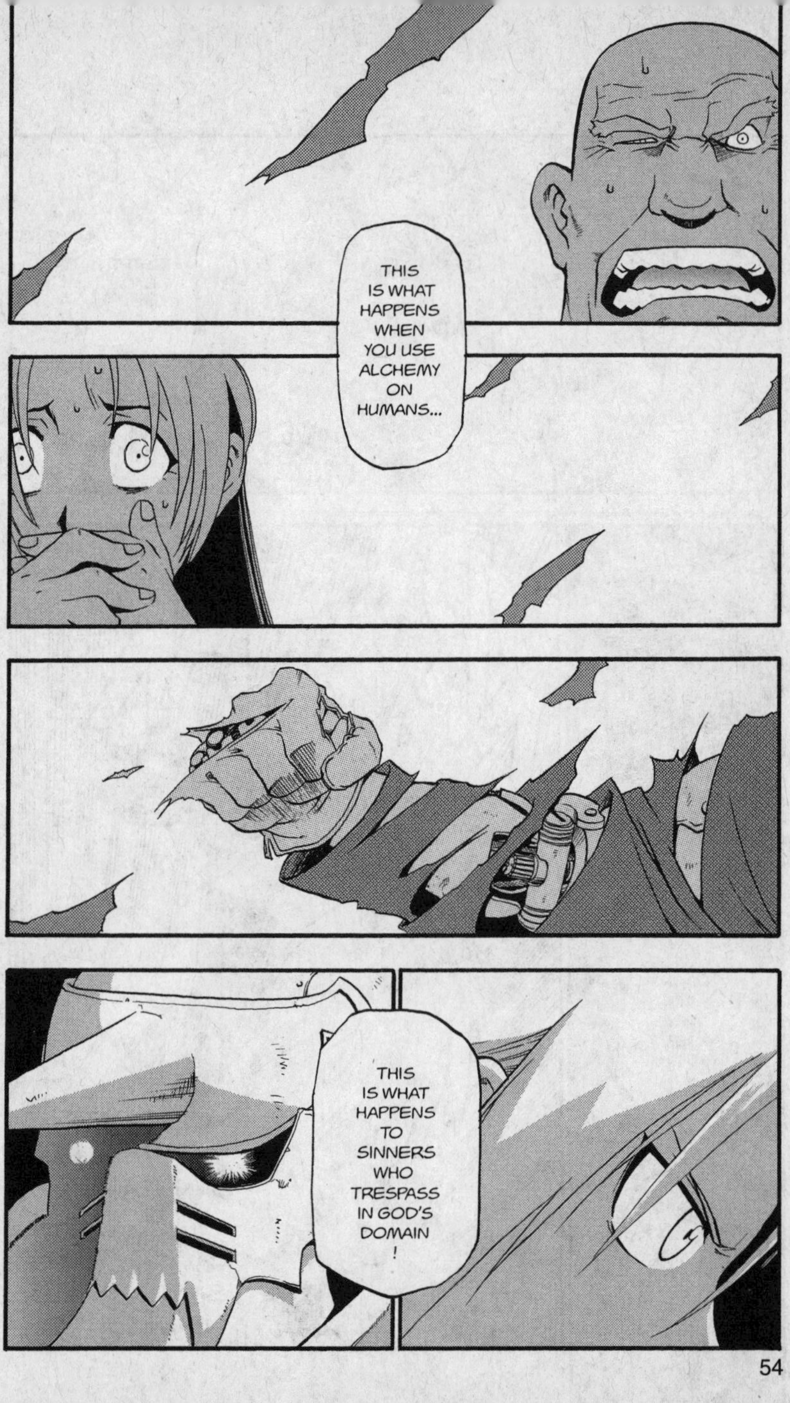
THIS IS WHAT HAPPENS WHEN YOU USE ALCHEMY ON HUMANS...
THIS IS WHAT HAPPENS TO SINNERS WHO TRESPASS IN GOD'S DOMAIN!

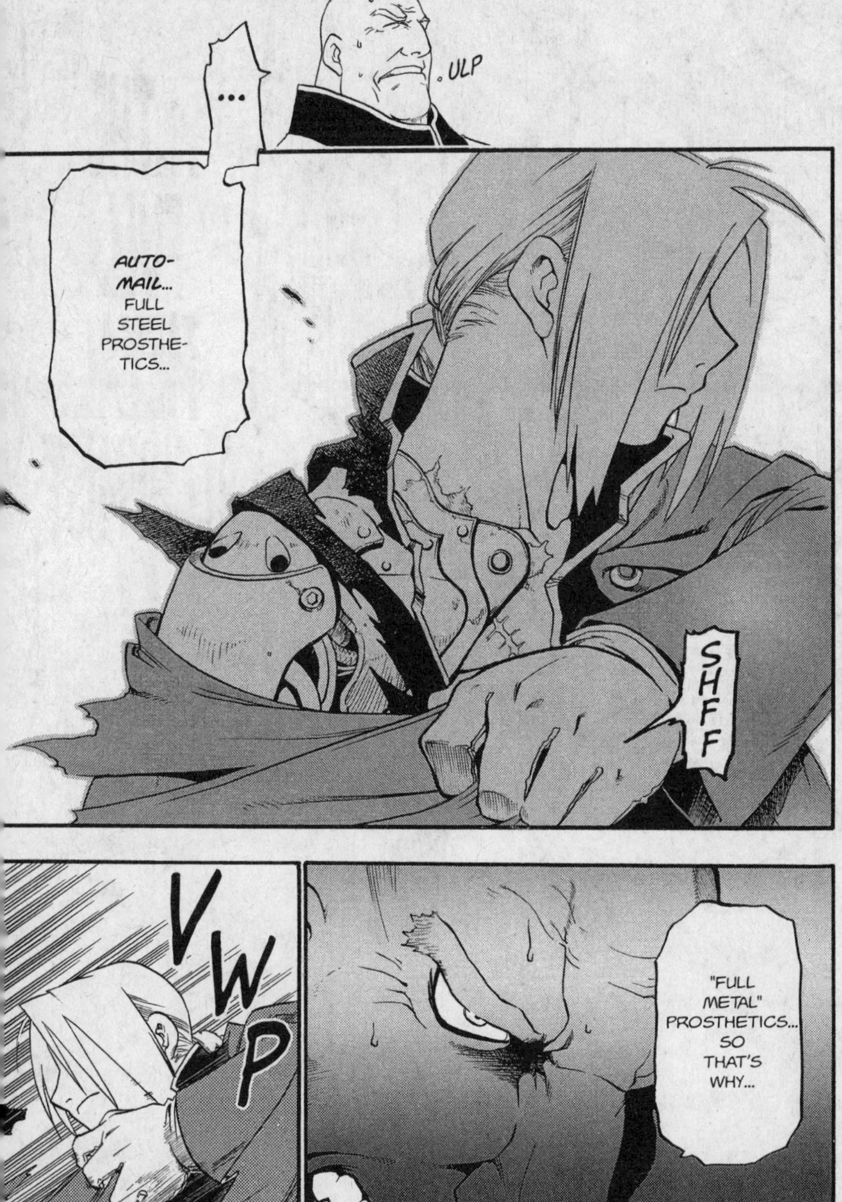
...
ULP
AUTO-MAIL... FULL STEEL PROSTHETICS...
SHFF
"FULL METAL" PROSTHETICS... SO THAT'S WHY...
VWP

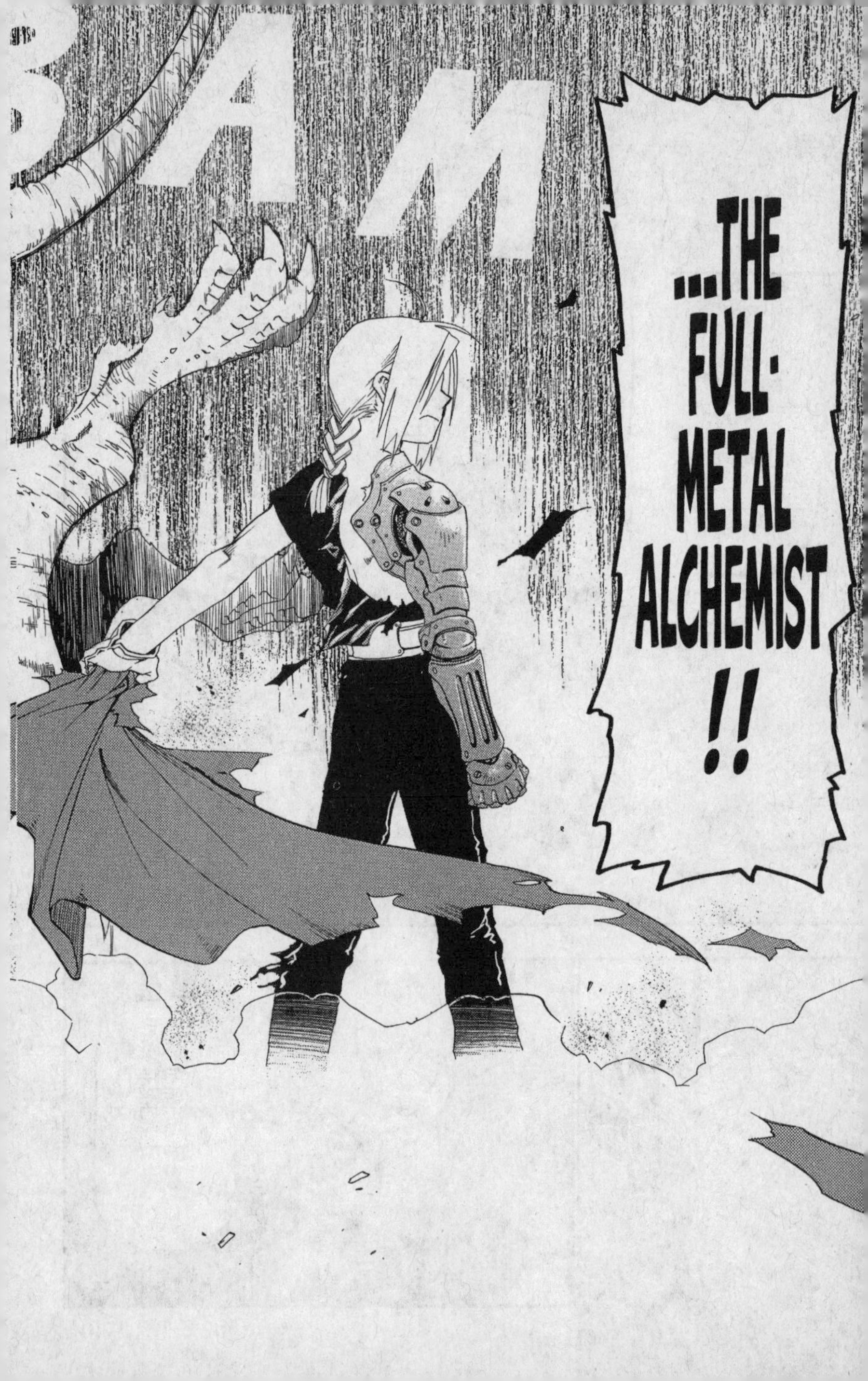
...THE FULL-METAL ALCHEMIST !!

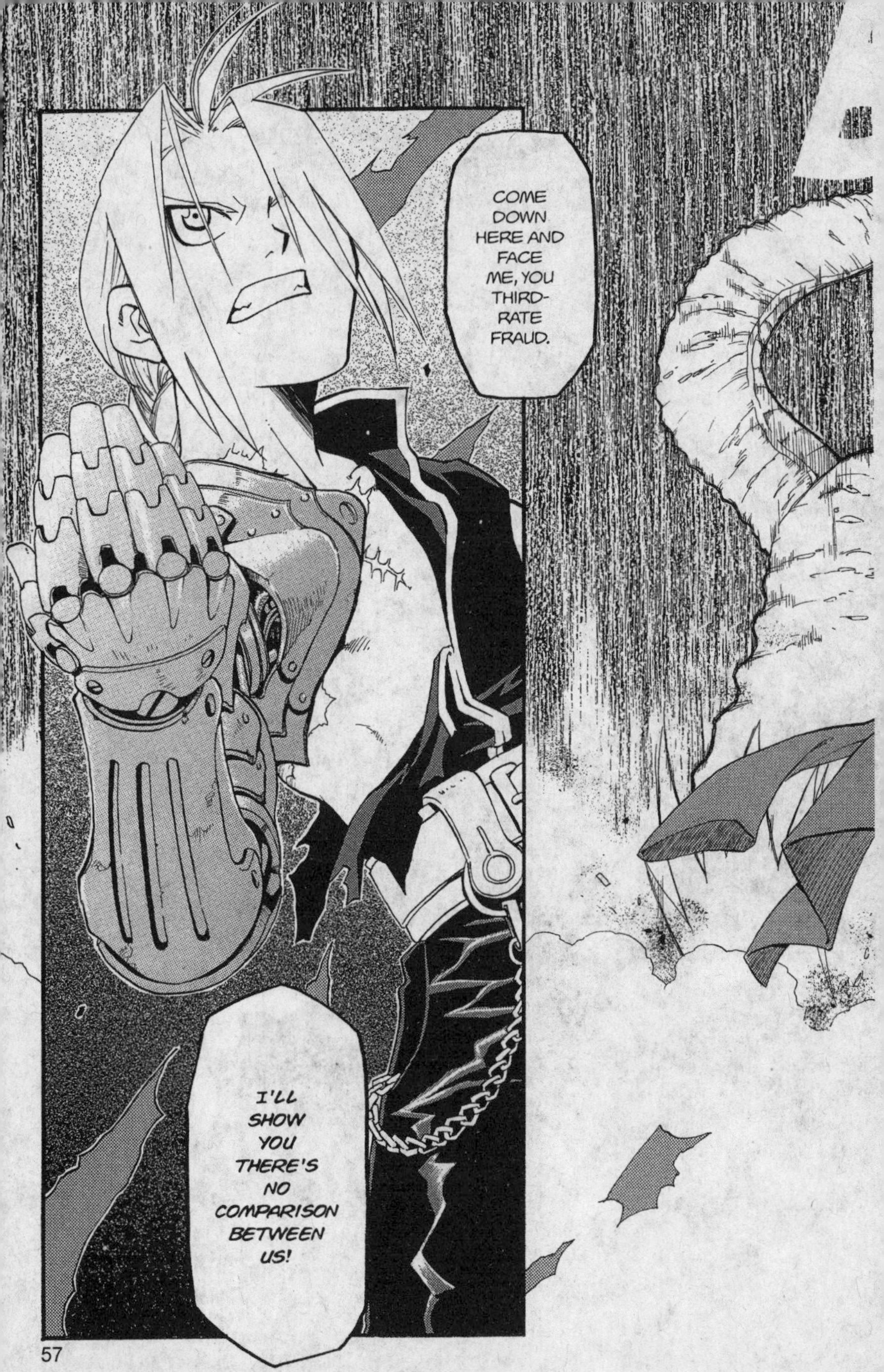
COME DOWN HERE AND FACE ME, YOU THIRD-RATE FRAUD.
I'LL SHOW YOU THERE'S NO COMPARISON BETWEEN US!

FULLMETAL
ALCHEMIST

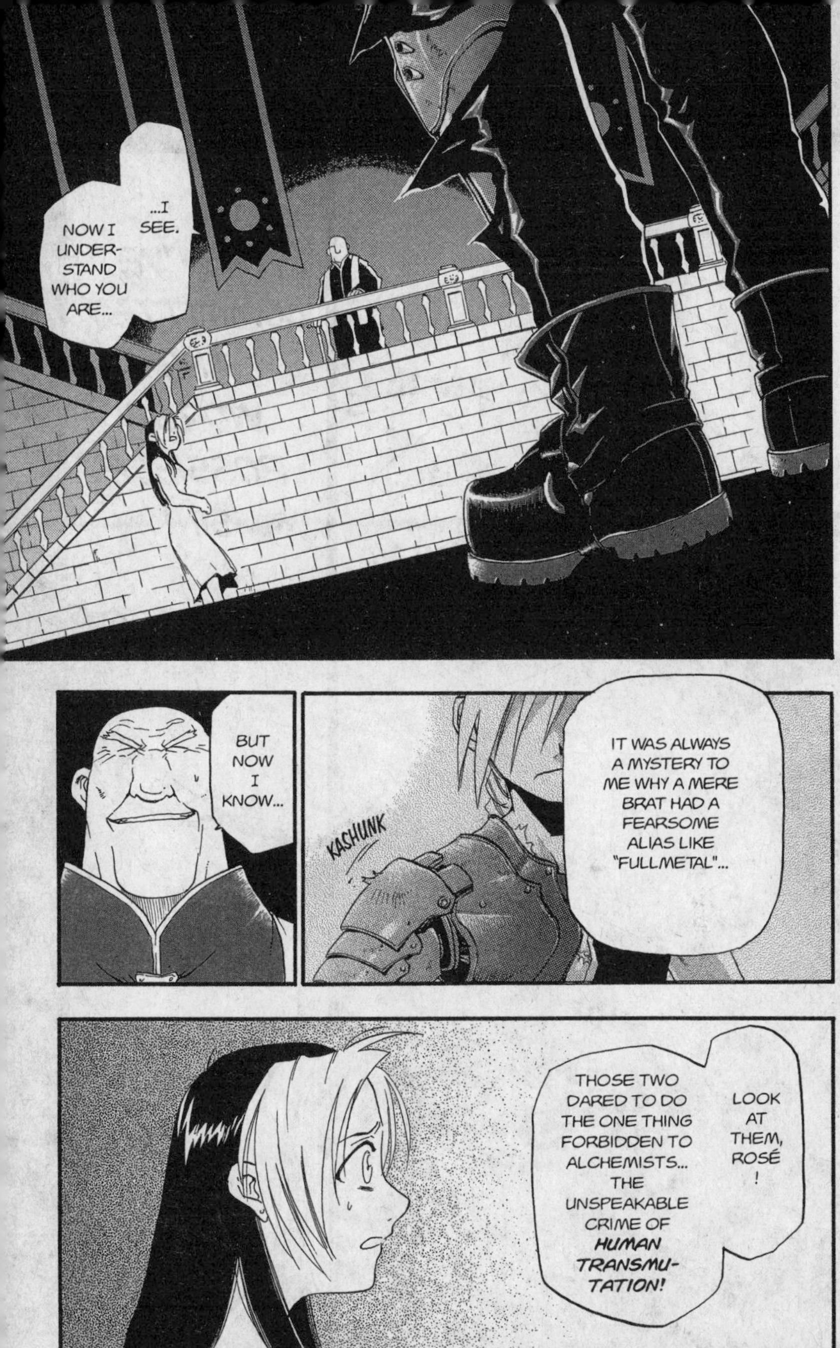
...I SEE.
NOW I UNDERSTAND WHO YOU ARE...
IT WAS ALWAYS A MYSTERY TO ME WHY A MERE BRAT HAD A FEARSOME ALIAS LIKE "FULLMETAL"...
KASHUNK
BUT NOW I KNOW...
LOOK AT THEM, ROSÉ!
THOSE TWO DARED TO DO THE ONE THING FORBIDDEN TO ALCHEMISTS... THE UNSPEAKABLE CRIME OF ***HUMAN TRANSMUTATION!***

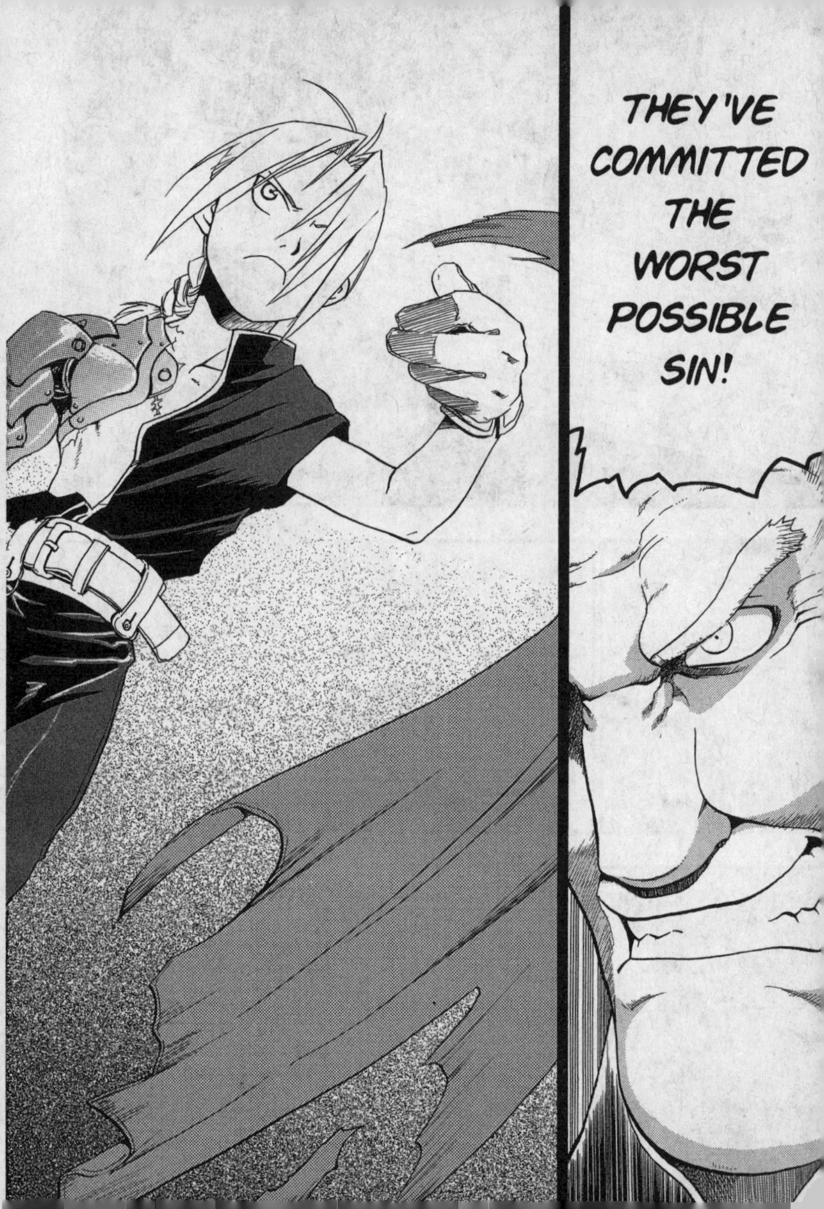
THEY'VE COMMITTED THE WORST POSSIBLE SIN!

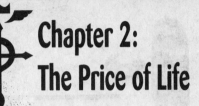

Chapter 2:
The Price of Life

...!

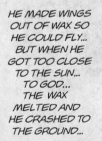

HE MADE WINGS OUT OF WAX SO HE COULD FLY... BUT WHEN HE GOT TOO CLOSE TO THE SUN... TO GOD... THE WAX MELTED AND HE CRASHED TO THE GROUND...

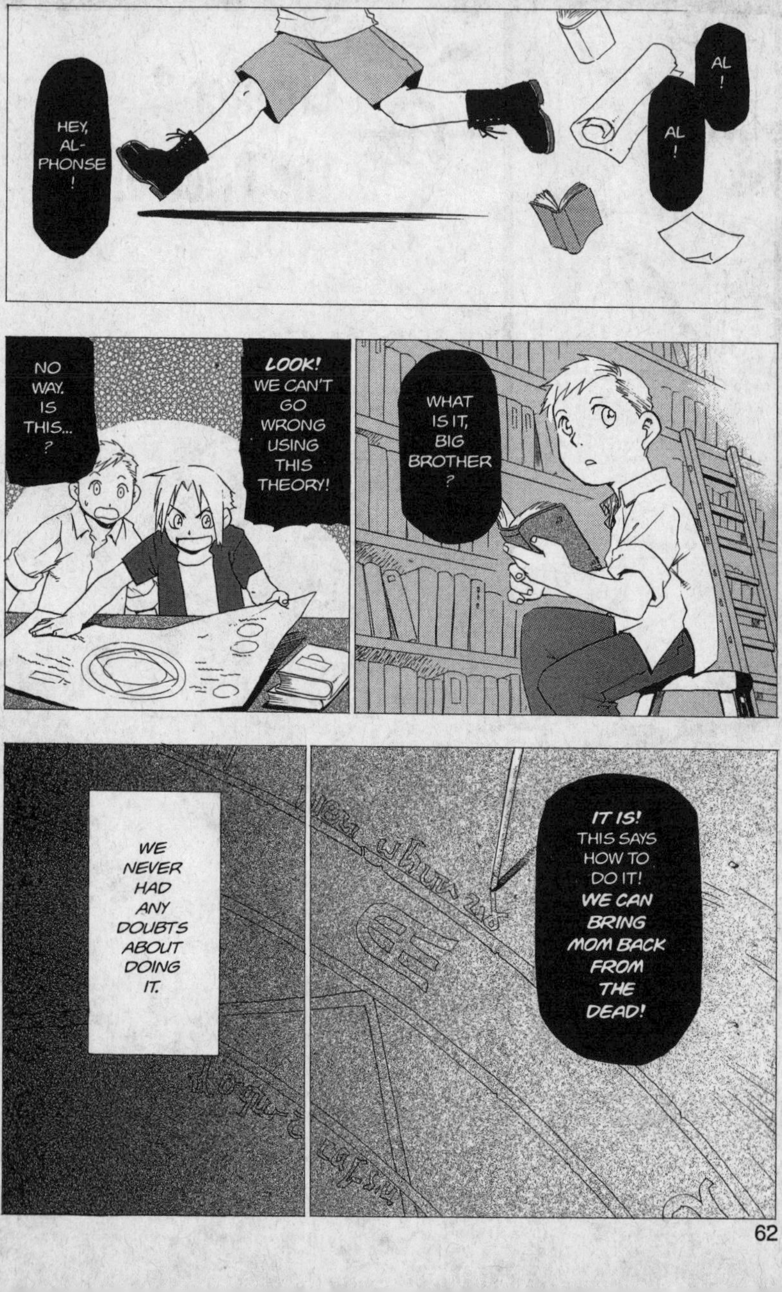
AL!
AL!
HEY, AL-PHONSE!
WHAT IS IT, BIG BROTHER?
LOOK! WE CAN'T GO WRONG USING THIS THEORY!
NO WAY. IS THIS...?
IT IS! THIS SAYS HOW TO DO IT! WE CAN BRING MOM BACK FROM THE DEAD!
WE NEVER HAD ANY DOUBTS ABOUT DOING IT.

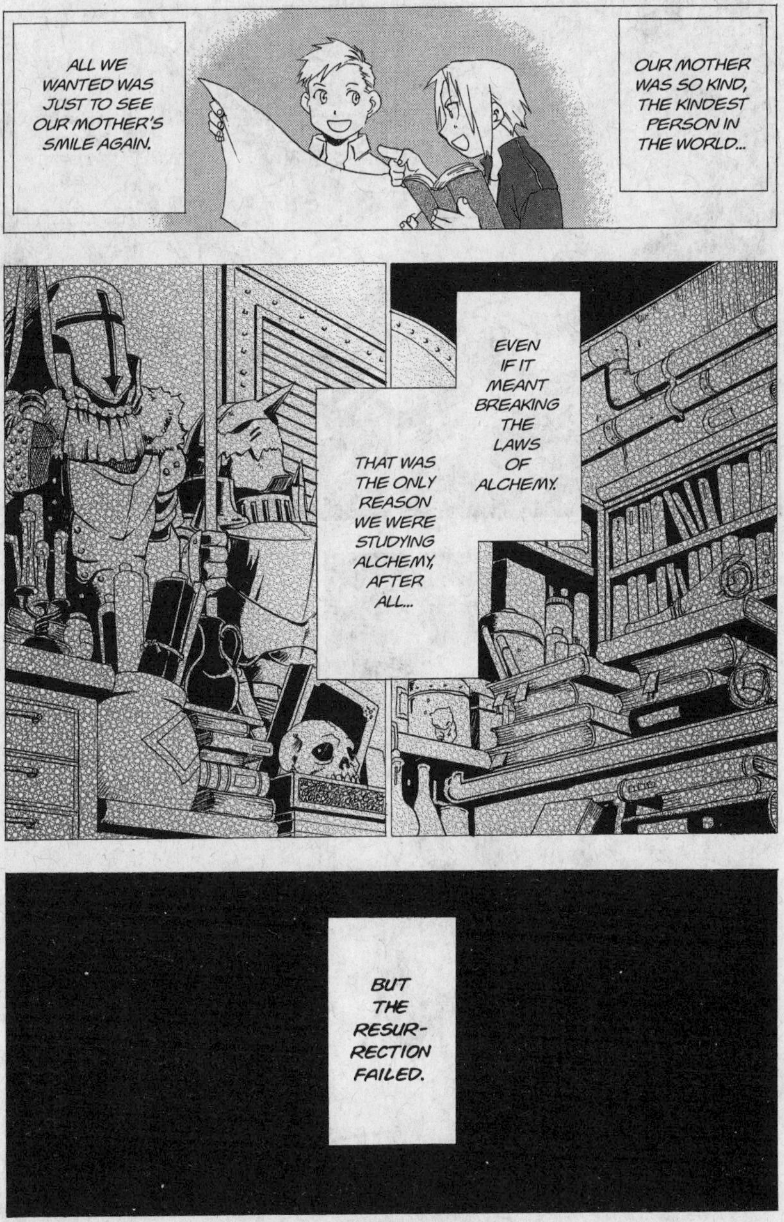
OUR MOTHER WAS SO KIND, THE KINDEST PERSON IN THE WORLD...
ALL WE WANTED WAS JUST TO SEE OUR MOTHER'S SMILE AGAIN.
EVEN IF IT MEANT BREAKING THE LAWS OF ALCHEMY.
THAT WAS THE ONLY REASON WE WERE STUDYING ALCHEMY, AFTER ALL...
BUT THE RESUR- RECTION FAILED.

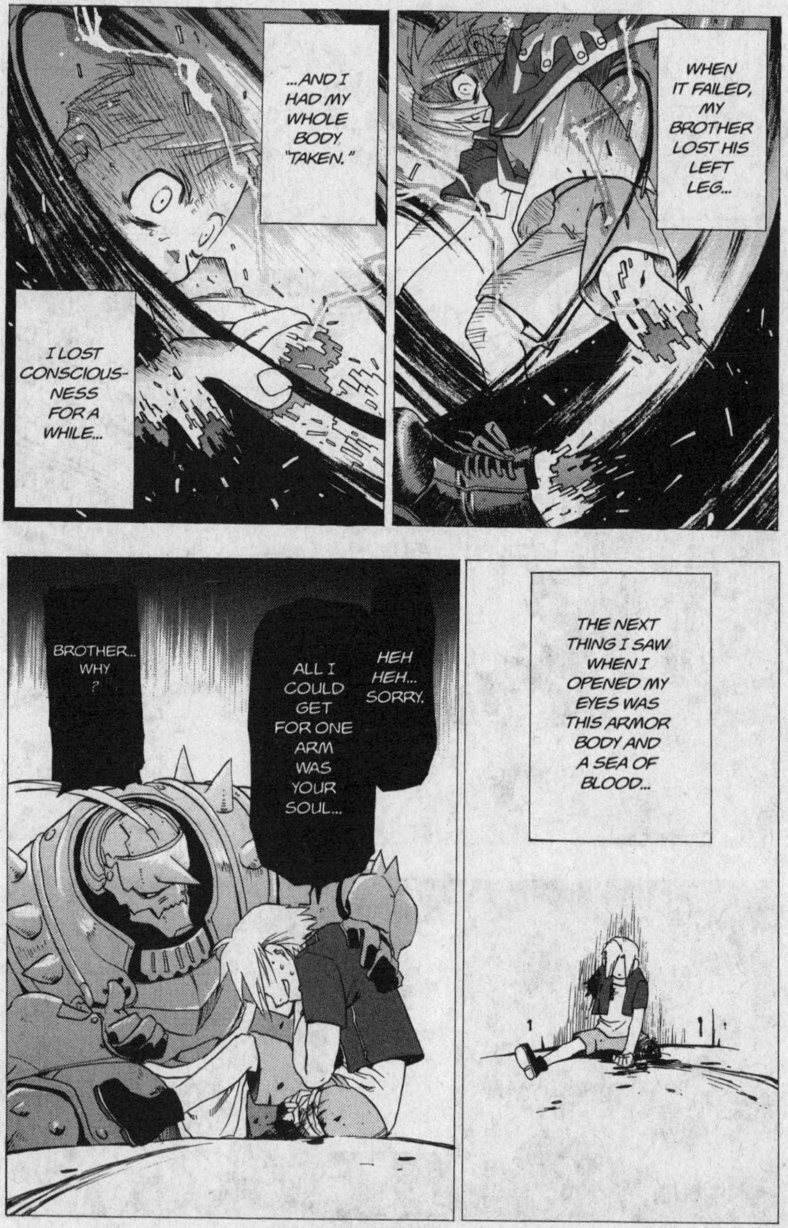
WHEN IT FAILED, MY BROTHER LOST HIS LEFT LEG...
...AND I HAD MY WHOLE BODY "TAKEN."
I LOST CONSCIOUS-NESS FOR A WHILE...
THE NEXT THING I SAW WHEN I OPENED MY EYES WAS THIS ARMOR BODY AND A SEA OF BLOOD...
HEH HEH... SORRY.
ALL I COULD GET FOR ONE ARM WAS YOUR SOUL...
BROTHER... WHY?

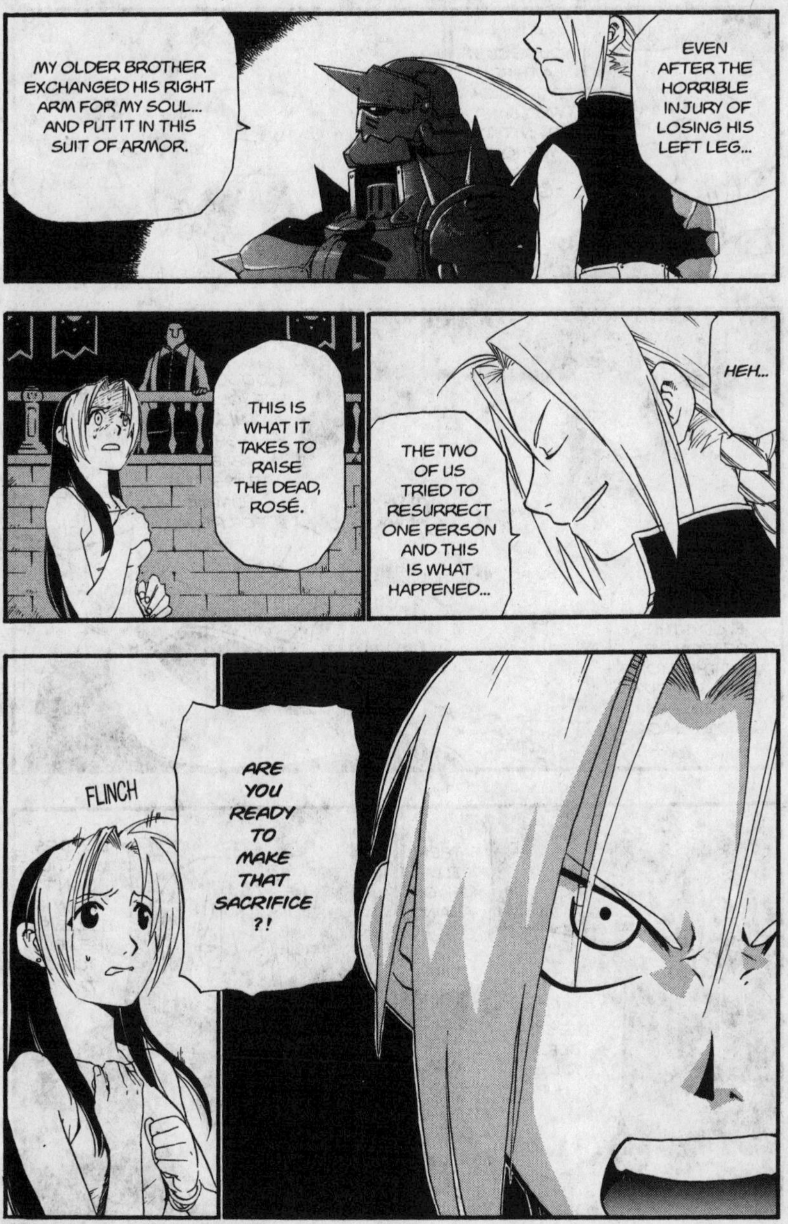
EVEN AFTER THE HORRIBLE INJURY OF LOSING HIS LEFT LEG...
MY OLDER BROTHER EXCHANGED HIS RIGHT ARM FOR MY SOUL... AND PUT IT IN THIS SUIT OF ARMOR.
HEH...
THE TWO OF US TRIED TO RESURRECT ONE PERSON AND THIS IS WHAT HAPPENED...
THIS IS WHAT IT TAKES TO RAISE THE DEAD, ROSÉ.
ARE YOU READY TO MAKE THAT SACRIFICE?!
FLINCH

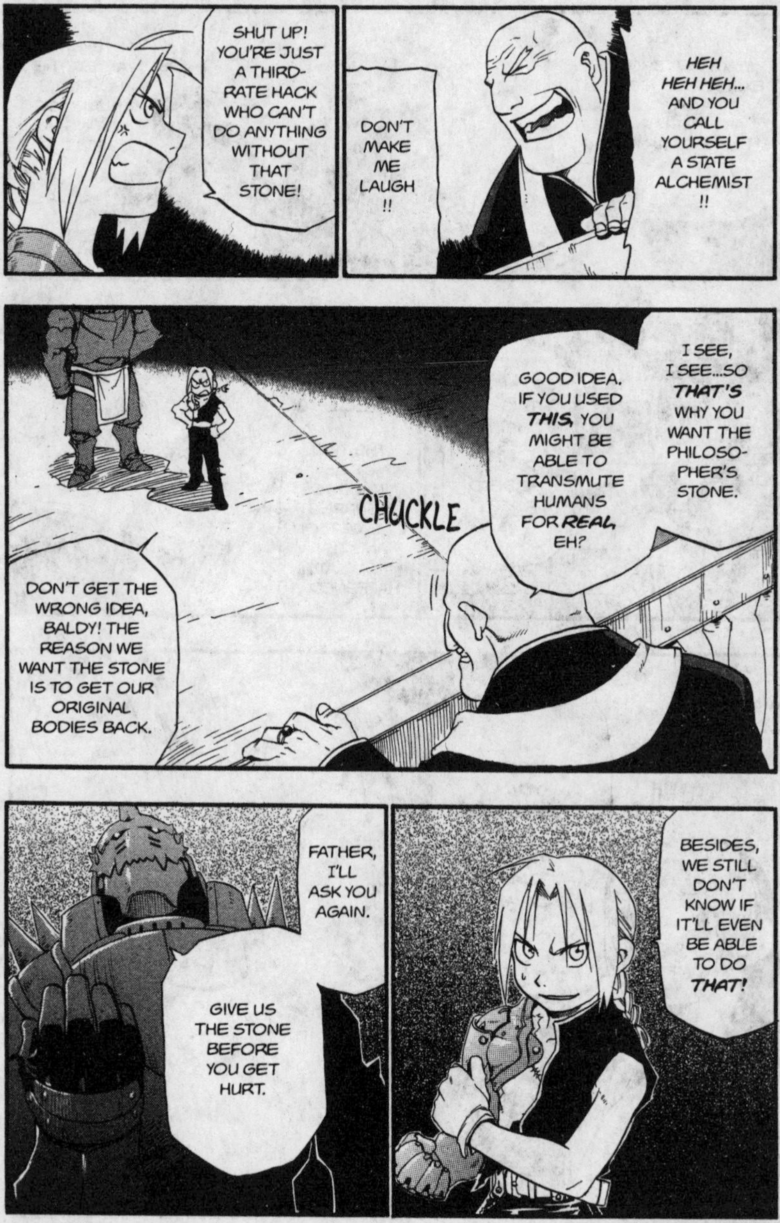
HEH HEH HEH... AND YOU CALL YOURSELF A STATE ALCHEMIST !!
DON'T MAKE ME LAUGH !!
SHUT UP! YOU'RE JUST A THIRD-RATE HACK WHO CAN'T DO ANYTHING WITHOUT THAT STONE!
I SEE, I SEE...SO THAT'S WHY YOU WANT THE PHILOSOPHER'S STONE.
GOOD IDEA. IF YOU USED THIS, YOU MIGHT BE ABLE TO TRANSMUTE HUMANS FOR REAL, EH?
CHUCKLE
DON'T GET THE WRONG IDEA, BALDY! THE REASON WE WANT THE STONE IS TO GET OUR ORIGINAL BODIES BACK.
BESIDES, WE STILL DON'T KNOW IF IT'LL EVEN BE ABLE TO DO THAT!
FATHER, I'LL ASK YOU AGAIN.
GIVE US THE STONE BEFORE YOU GET HURT.

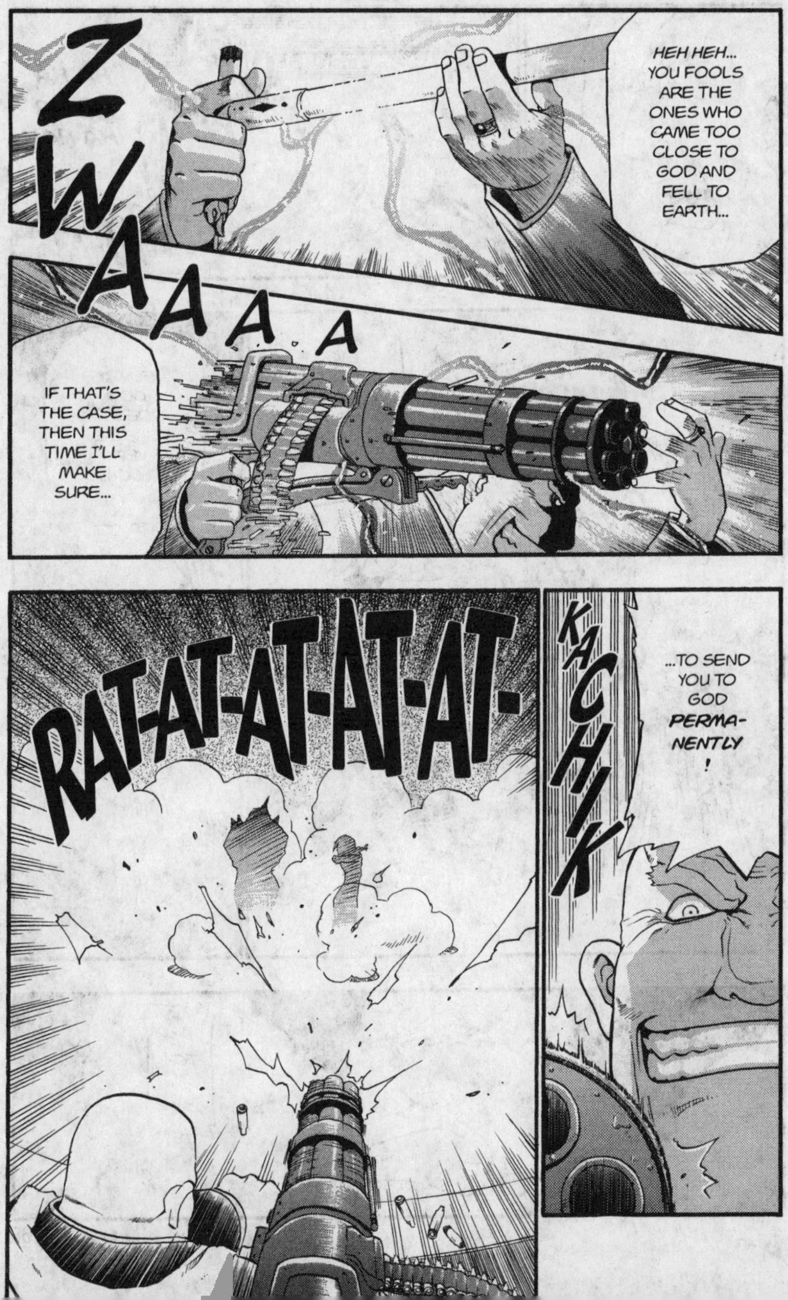
HEH HEH... YOU FOOLS ARE THE ONES WHO CAME TOO CLOSE TO GOD AND FELL TO EARTH...
ZWAAAAA
IF THAT'S THE CASE, THEN THIS TIME I'LL MAKE SURE...
KACHIK
...TO SEND YOU TO GOD PERMANENTLY!
RAT-AT-AT-AT-AT-

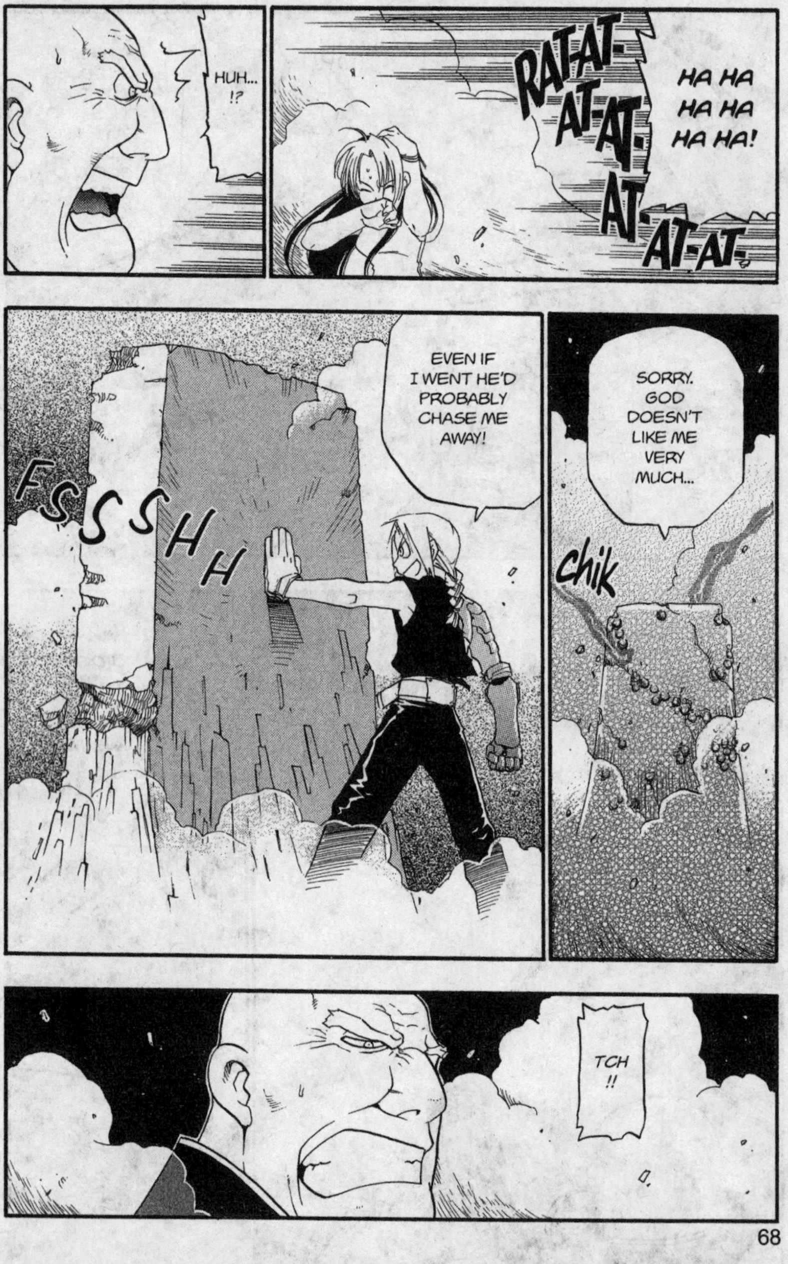
HA HA HA HA HA HA!
RAT-AT-AT-AT-AT-AT-AT-AT-
HUH... !?
SORRY. GOD DOESN'T LIKE ME VERY MUCH...
Chik
EVEN IF I WENT HE'D PROBABLY CHASE ME AWAY!
FSSSHH
TCH !!

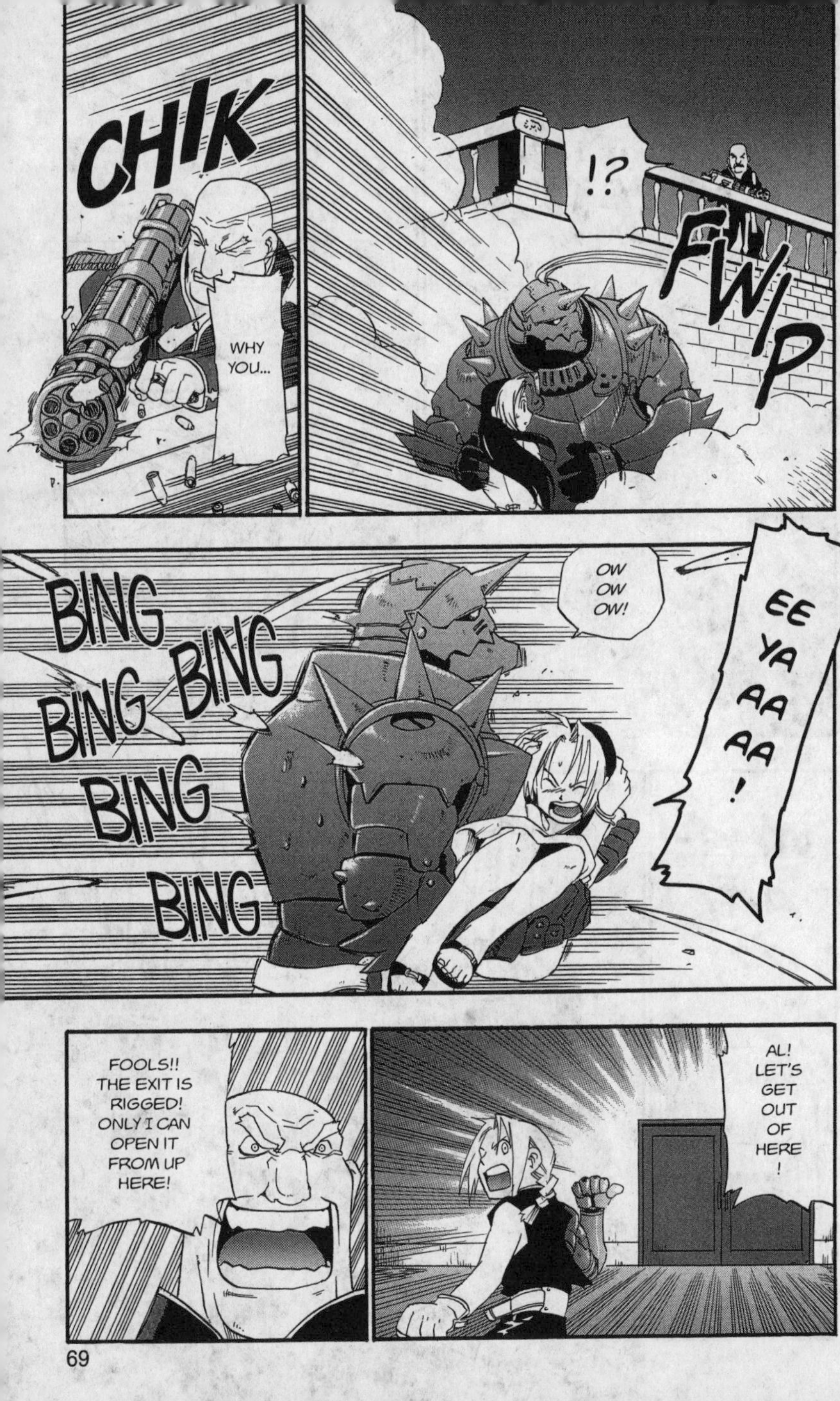
!?
FWIP
CHIK
WHY YOU...
EE YA AA AA !
OW OW OW!
BING BING BING BING BING
AL! LET'S GET OUT OF HERE !
FOOLS!! THE EXIT IS RIGGED! ONLY I CAN OPEN IT FROM UP HERE!

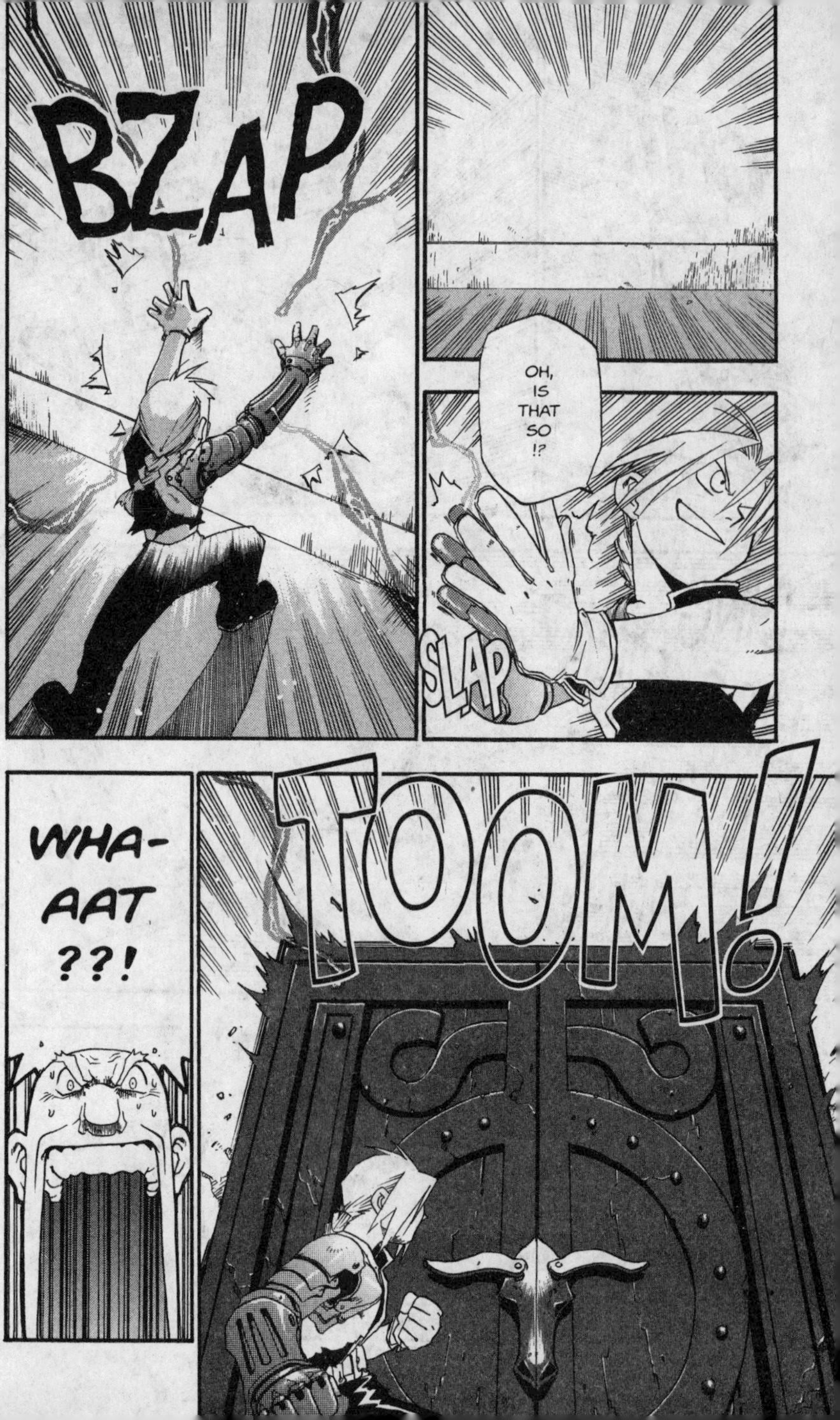
OH, IS THAT SO!?
SLAP
BZAP
TOOM!
WHA-AAT??!

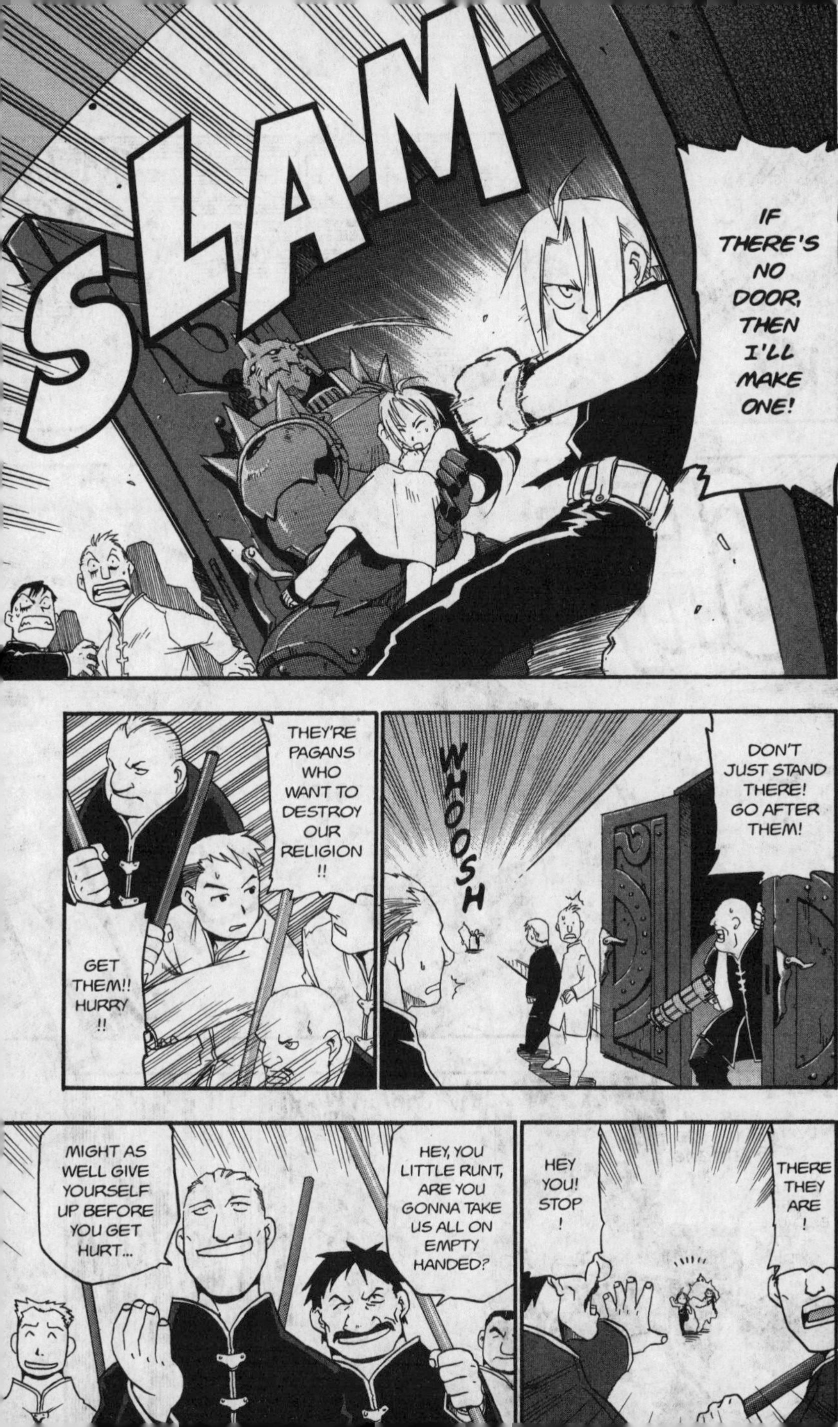
IF THERE'S NO DOOR, THEN I'LL MAKE ONE!
SLAM
DON'T JUST STAND THERE! GO AFTER THEM!
WHOOSH
THEY'RE PAGANS WHO WANT TO DESTROY OUR RELIGION !!
GET THEM!! HURRY !!
THERE THEY ARE !
HEY YOU! STOP !
HEY, YOU LITTLE RUNT, ARE YOU GONNA TAKE US ALL ON EMPTY HANDED?
MIGHT AS WELL GIVE YOURSELF UP BEFORE YOU GET HURT...

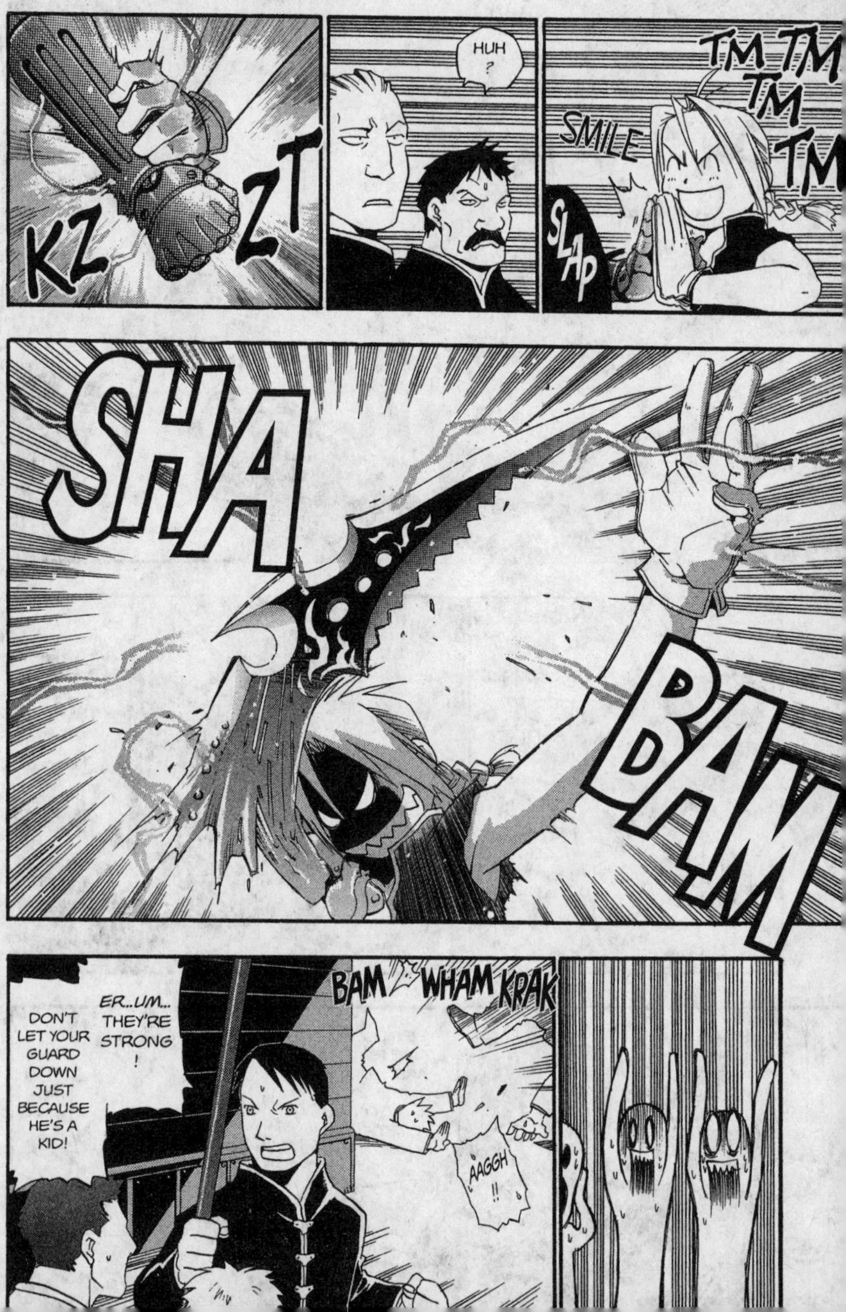
TM TM TM TM TM
SMILE
SLAP
HUH ?
KZZT
SHA
BAM
BAM WHAM KRAK
ER..UM... THEY'RE STRONG!
DON'T LET YOUR GUARD DOWN JUST BECAUSE HE'S A KID!
AAGGH!!

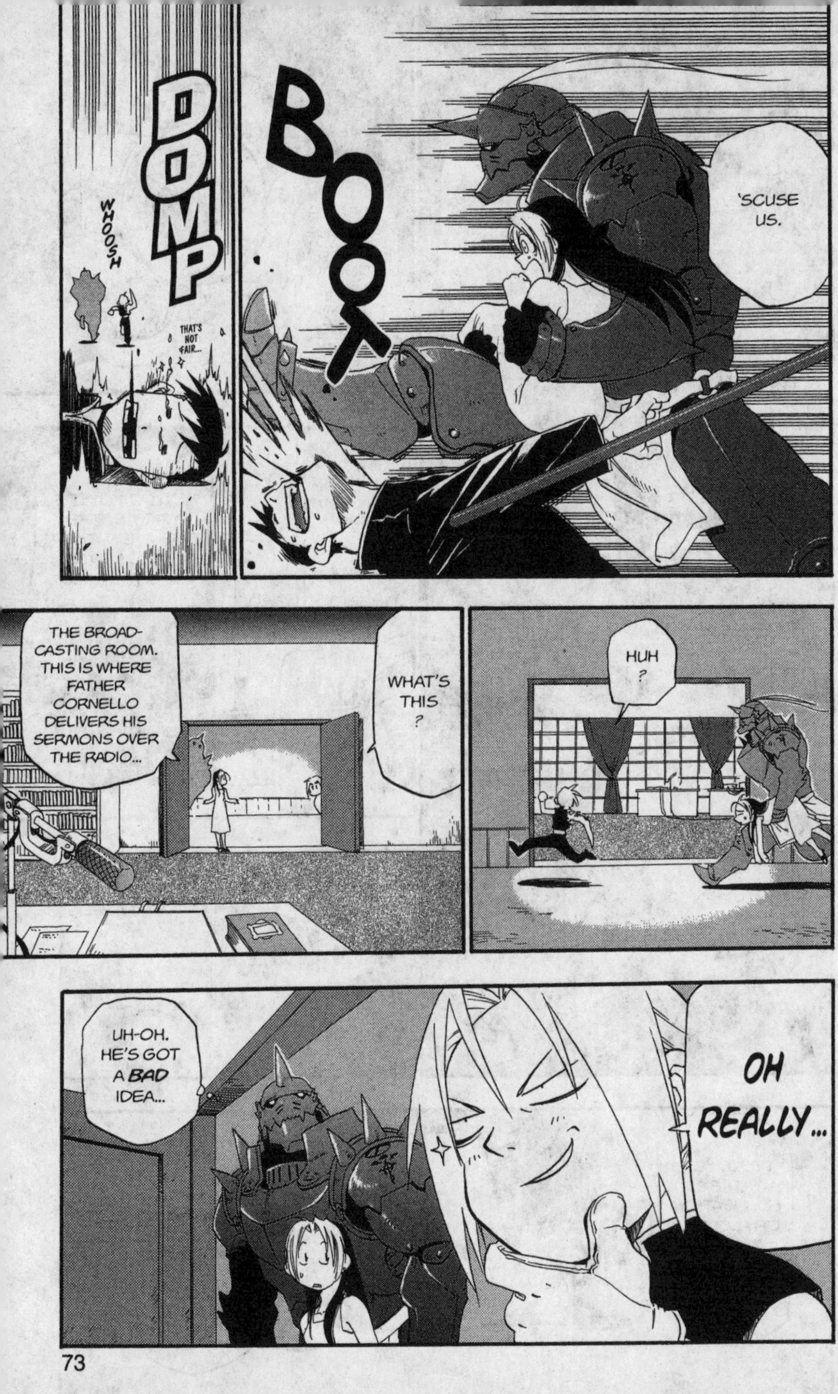
'SCUSE US.
BOOT
DOMP
WHOOSH
THAT'S NOT FAIR...
HUH ?
WHAT'S THIS ?
THE BROAD-CASTING ROOM. THIS IS WHERE FATHER CORNELLO DELIVERS HIS SERMONS OVER THE RADIO...
OH REALLY...
UH-OH. HE'S GOT A BAD IDEA...

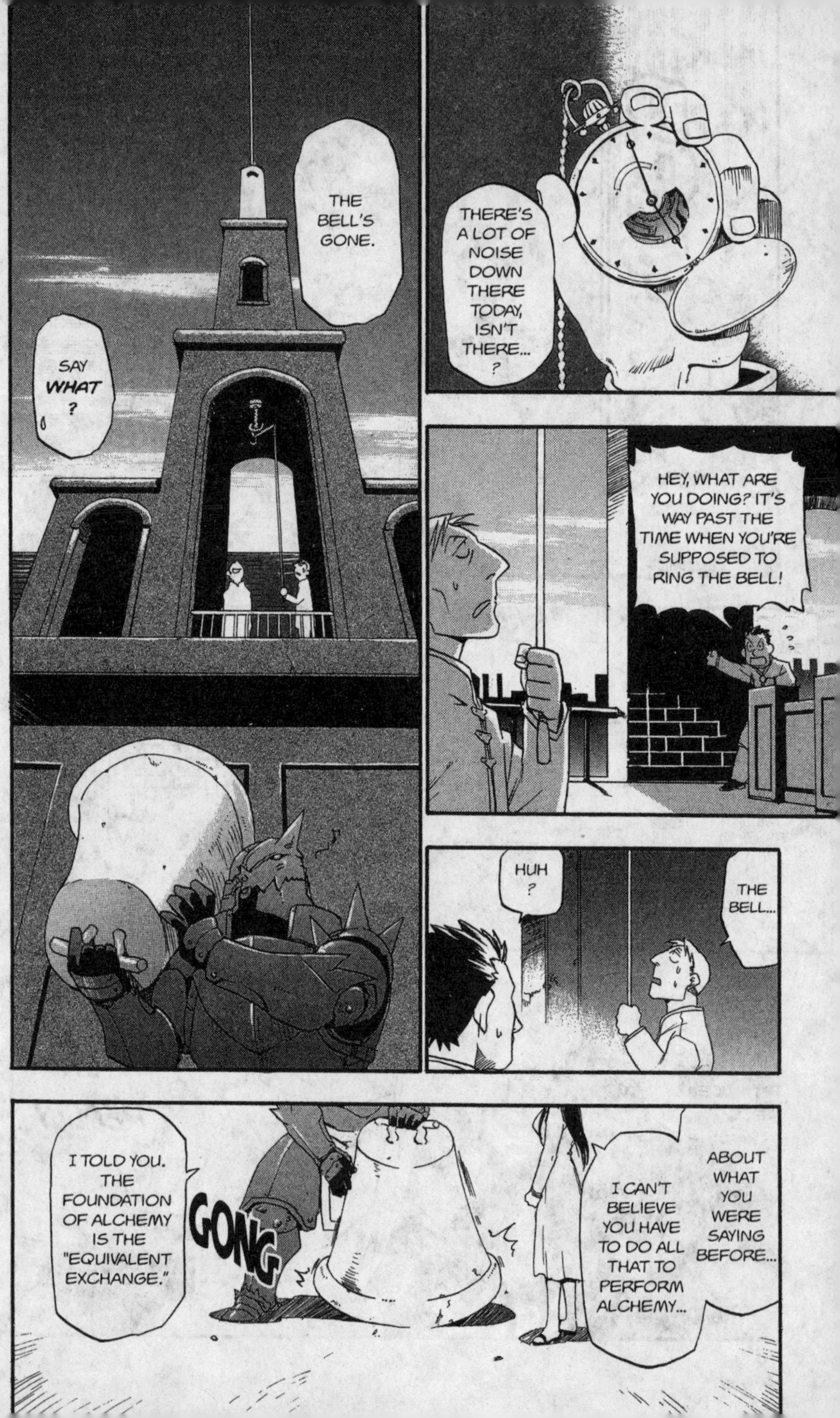
THERE'S A LOT OF NOISE DOWN THERE TODAY, ISN'T THERE...?
HEY, WHAT ARE YOU DOING? IT'S WAY PAST THE TIME WHEN YOU'RE SUPPOSED TO RING THE BELL!
THE BELL...
HUH?
THE BELL'S GONE.
SAY WHAT?
ABOUT WHAT YOU WERE SAYING BEFORE...
I CAN'T BELIEVE YOU HAVE TO DO ALL THAT TO PERFORM ALCHEMY...
GONG
I TOLD YOU. THE FOUNDATION OF ALCHEMY IS THE "EQUIVALENT EXCHANGE."

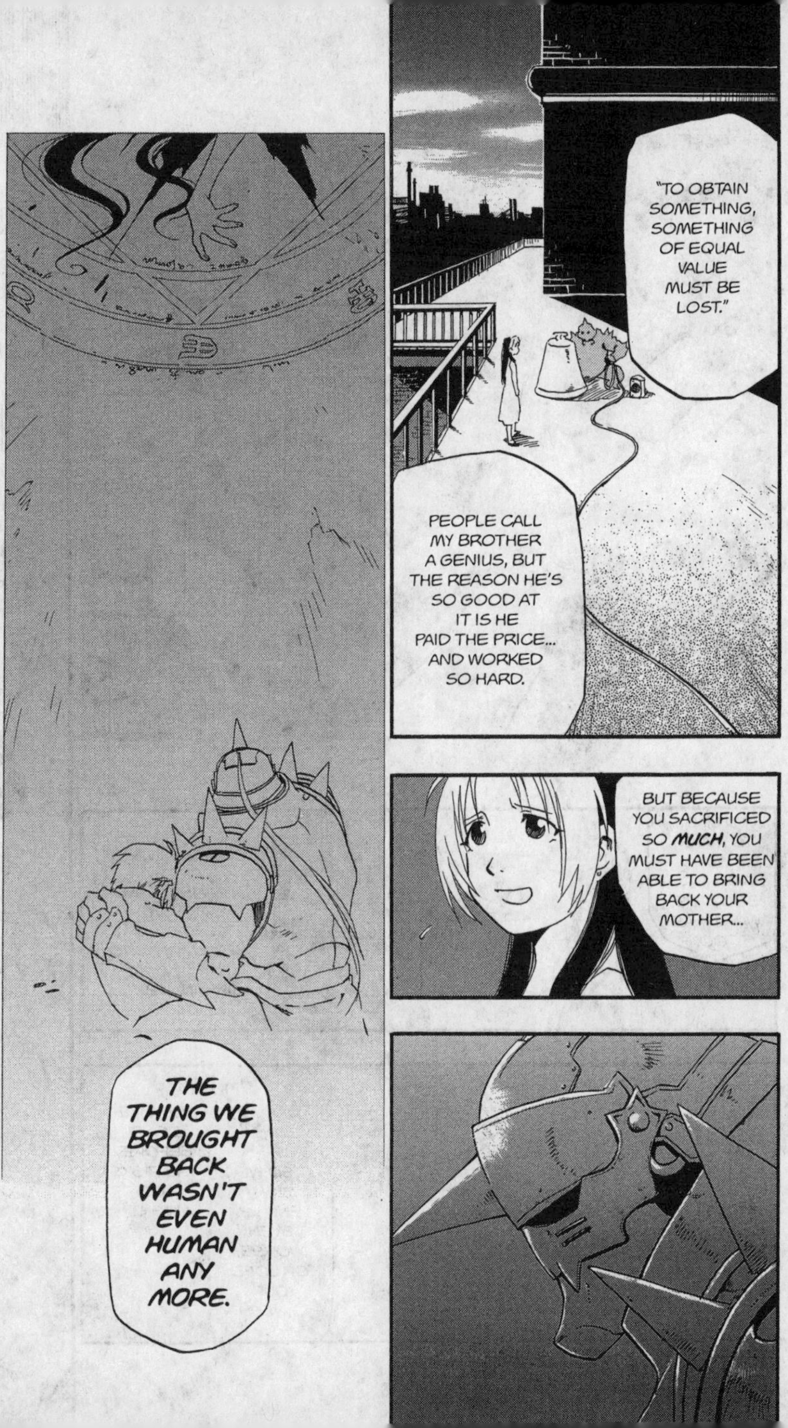
"TO OBTAIN SOMETHING, SOMETHING OF EQUAL VALUE MUST BE LOST."
PEOPLE CALL MY BROTHER A GENIUS, BUT THE REASON HE'S SO GOOD AT IT IS HE PAID THE PRICE... AND WORKED SO HARD.
BUT BECAUSE YOU SACRIFICED SO MUCH, YOU MUST HAVE BEEN ABLE TO BRING BACK YOUR MOTHER...
THE THING WE BROUGHT BACK WASN'T EVEN HUMAN ANY MORE.

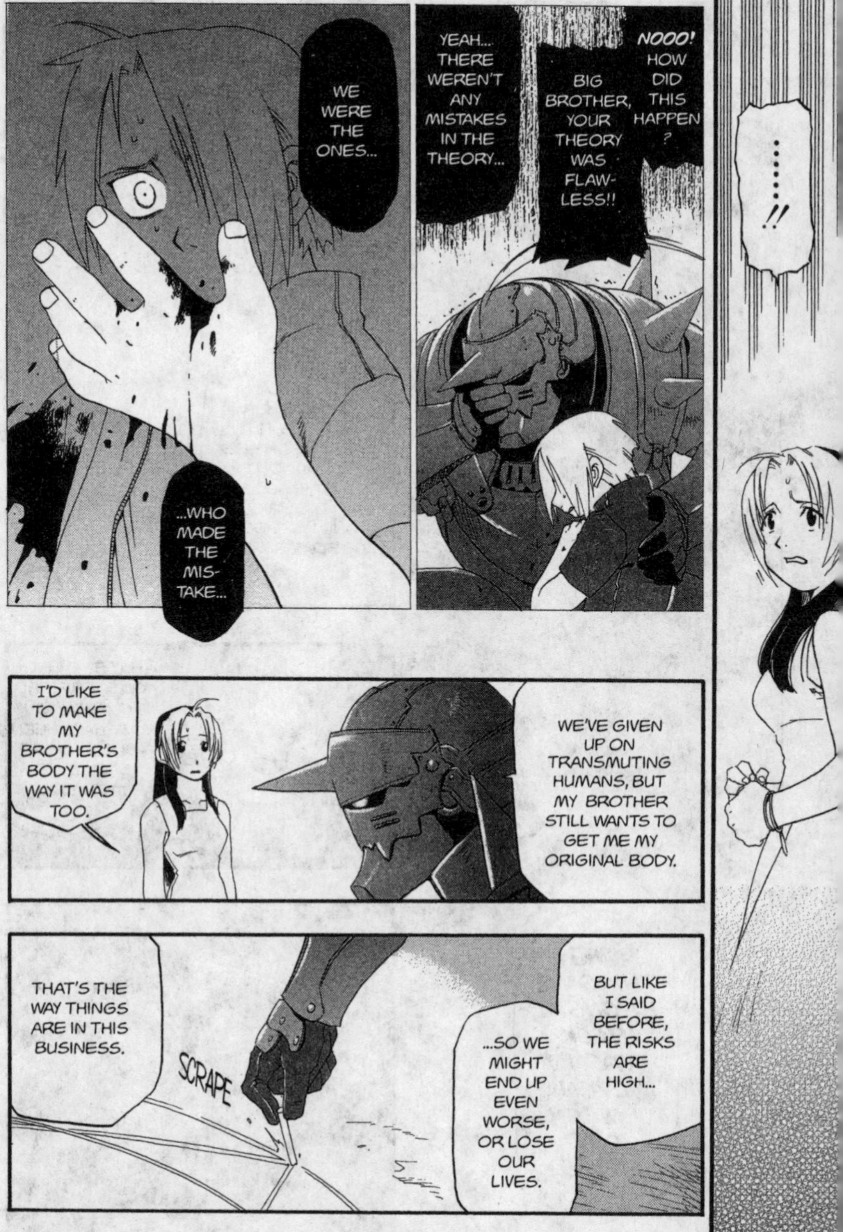
......!!
NOOO! HOW DID THIS HAPPEN?
BIG BROTHER, YOUR THEORY WAS FLAW-LESS!!
YEAH... THERE WEREN'T ANY MISTAKES IN THE THEORY...
WE WERE THE ONES...
...WHO MADE THE MIS-TAKE...
WE'VE GIVEN UP ON TRANSMUTING HUMANS, BUT MY BROTHER STILL WANTS TO GET ME MY ORIGINAL BODY.
I'D LIKE TO MAKE MY BROTHER'S BODY THE WAY IT WAS TOO.
BUT LIKE I SAID BEFORE, THE RISKS ARE HIGH...
...SO WE MIGHT END UP EVEN WORSE, OR LOSE OUR LIVES.
SCRAPE
THAT'S THE WAY THINGS ARE IN THIS BUSINESS.

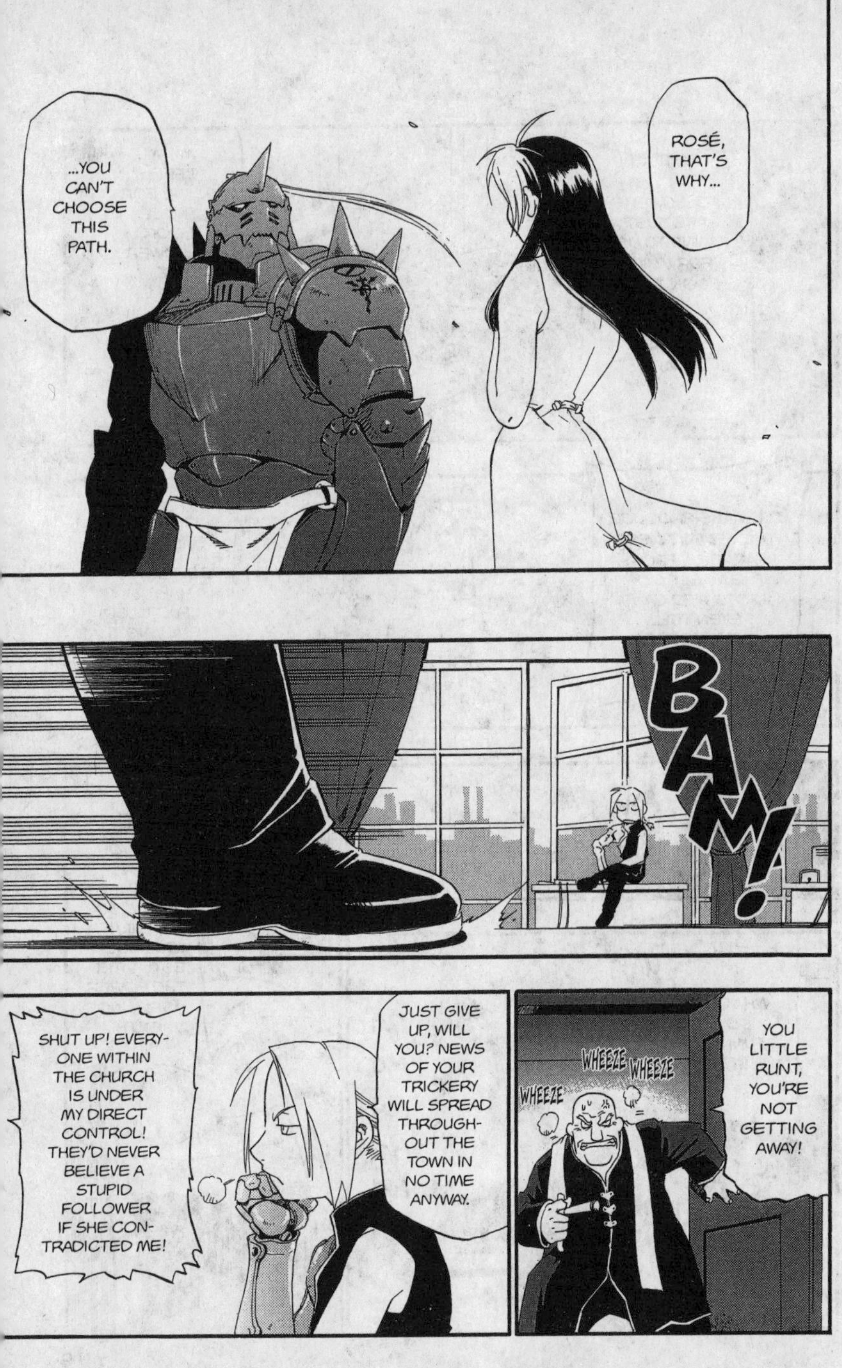
ROSÉ, THAT'S WHY...
...YOU CAN'T CHOOSE THIS PATH.
BAM!
WHEEZE WHEEZE
WHEEZE
YOU LITTLE RUNT, YOU'RE NOT GETTING AWAY!
JUST GIVE UP, WILL YOU? NEWS OF YOUR TRICKERY WILL SPREAD THROUGH-OUT THE TOWN IN NO TIME ANYWAY.
SHUT UP! EVERY-ONE WITHIN THE CHURCH IS UNDER MY DIRECT CONTROL! THEY'D NEVER BELIEVE A STUPID FOLLOWER IF SHE CON-TRADICTED ME!

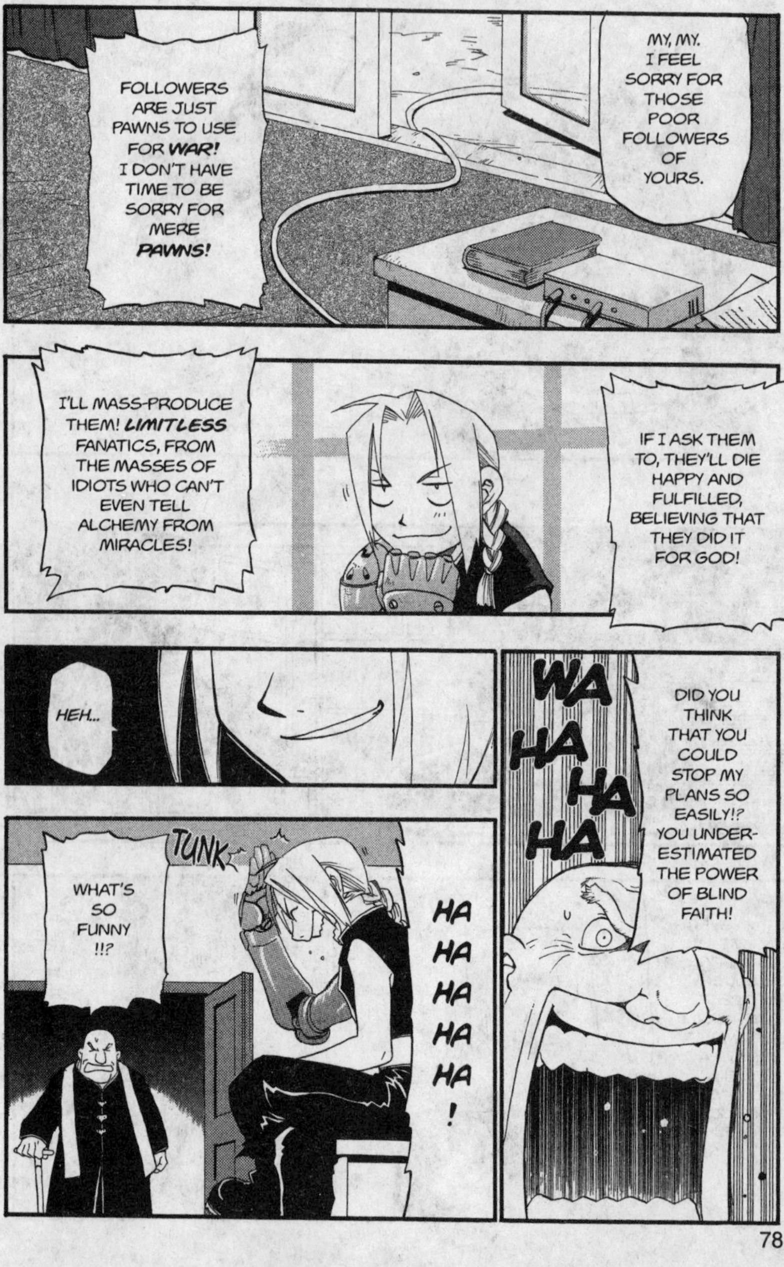
MY, MY. I FEEL SORRY FOR THOSE POOR FOLLOWERS OF YOURS.
FOLLOWERS ARE JUST PAWNS TO USE FOR WAR! I DON'T HAVE TIME TO BE SORRY FOR MERE PAWNS!
IF I ASK THEM TO, THEY'LL DIE HAPPY AND FULFILLED, BELIEVING THAT THEY DID IT FOR GOD!
I'LL MASS-PRODUCE THEM! LIMITLESS FANATICS, FROM THE MASSES OF IDIOTS WHO CAN'T EVEN TELL ALCHEMY FROM MIRACLES!
DID YOU THINK THAT YOU COULD STOP MY PLANS SO EASILY!? YOU UNDER-ESTIMATED THE POWER OF BLIND FAITH!
WA HA HA HA HA
HEH...
TUNK
HA HA HA HA HA HA !
WHAT'S SO FUNNY !!?

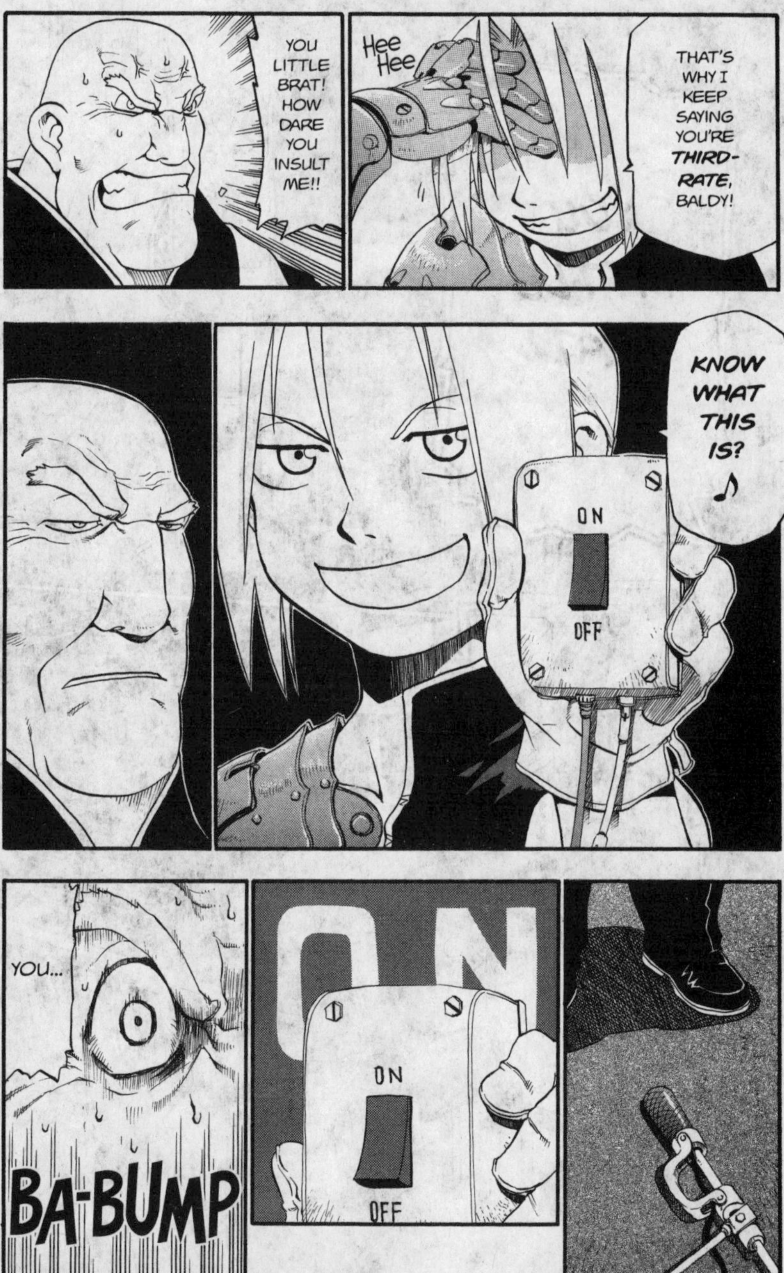
Hee Hee
THAT'S WHY I KEEP SAYING YOU'RE THIRD-RATE, BALDY!
YOU LITTLE BRAT! HOW DARE YOU INSULT ME!!
KNOW WHAT THIS IS? ♪
ON
OFF
ON
ON
OFF
YOU...
BA-BUMP

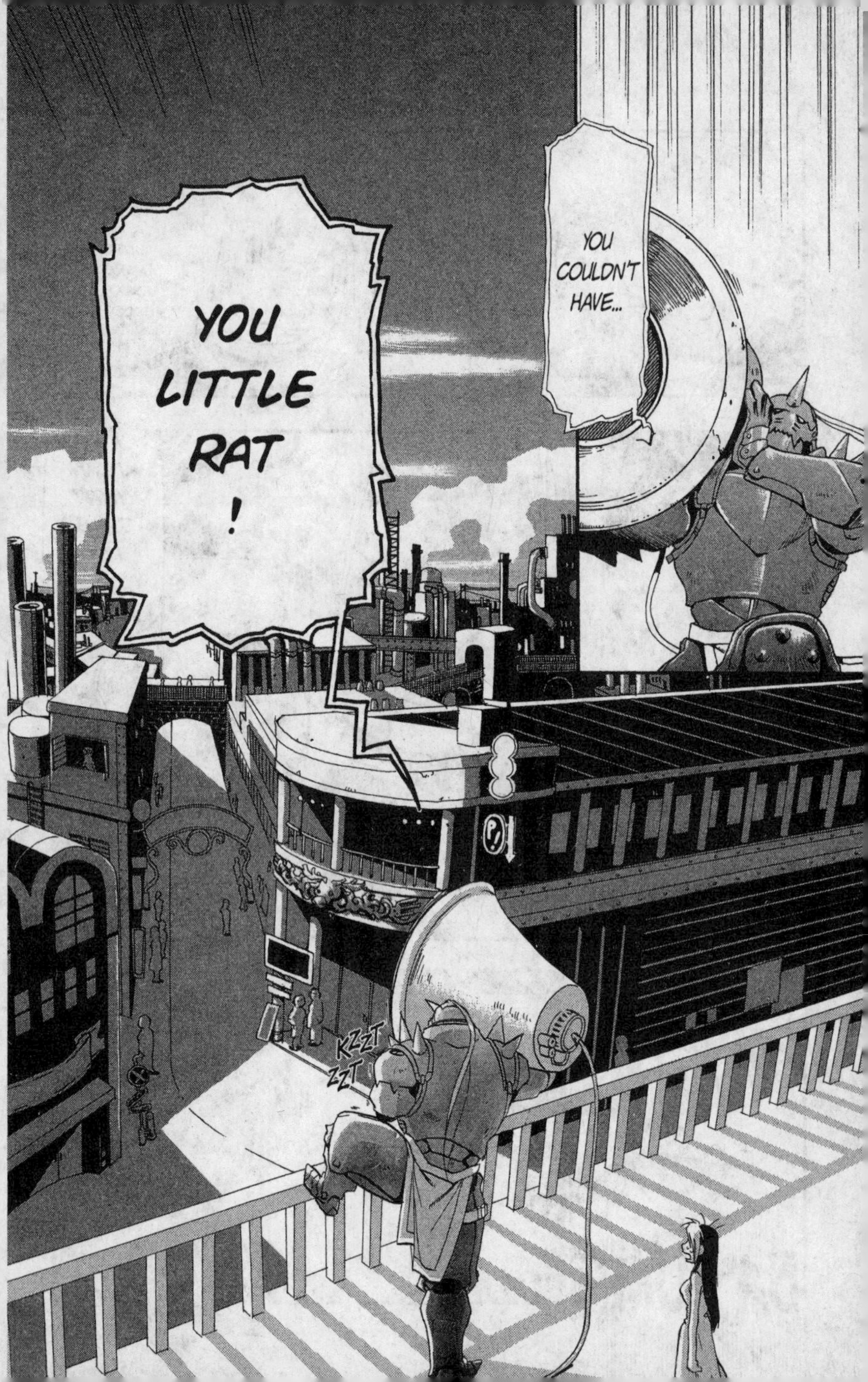
YOU COULDN'T HAVE...
YOU LITTLE RAT!
KZZT ZZT

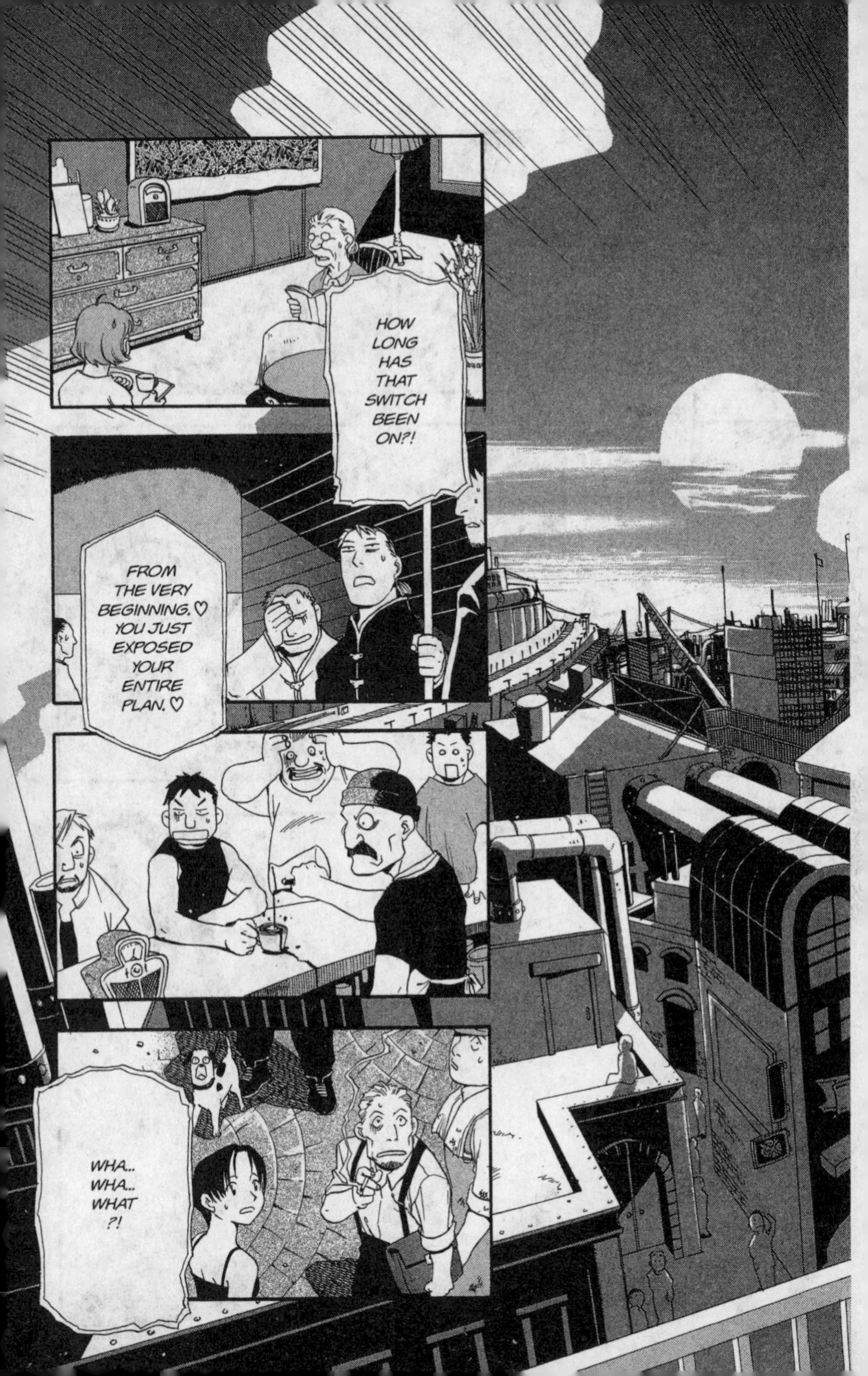
HOW LONG HAS THAT SWITCH BEEN ON?!
FROM THE VERY BEGINNING. ♡ YOU JUST EXPOSED YOUR ENTIRE PLAN. ♡
WHA... WHA... WHAT ?!

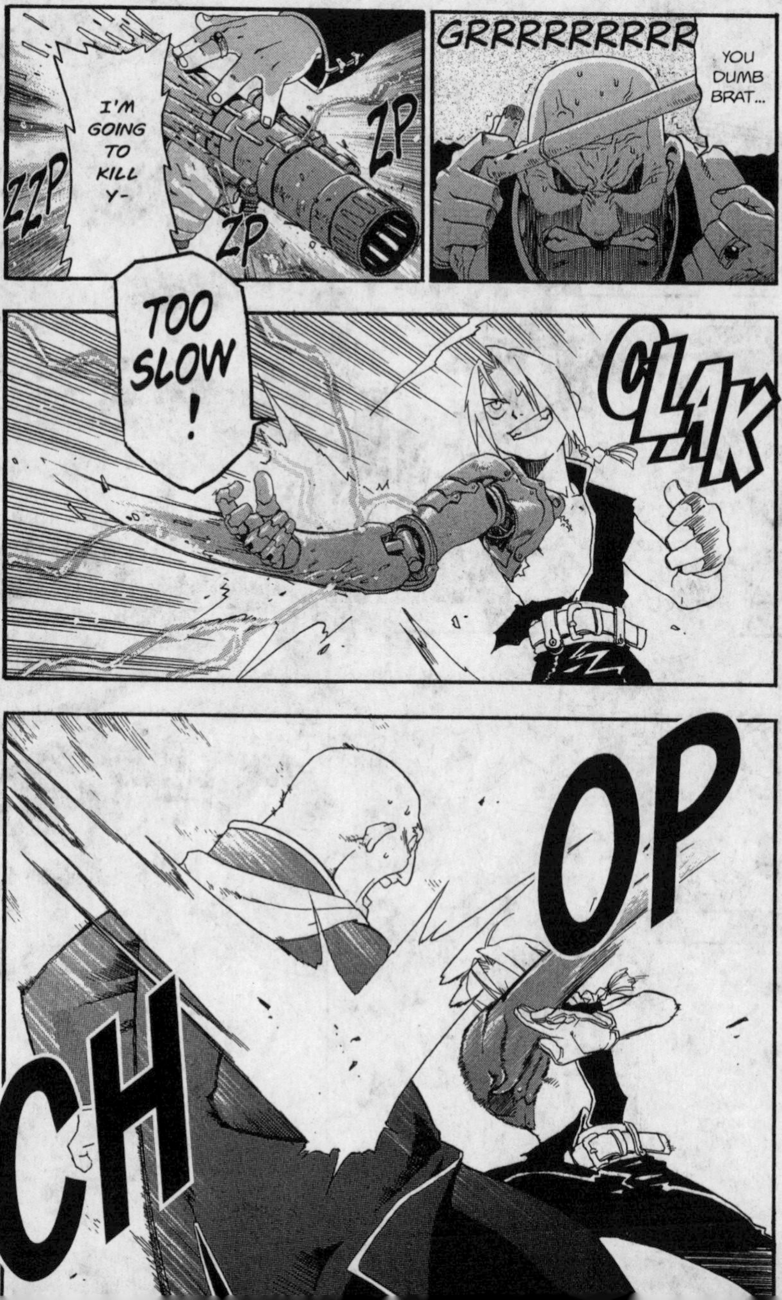
GRRRRRRRRR
YOU DUMB BRAT...
I'M GOING TO KILL Y-
ZP
ZZP
ZP
CLAK
TOO SLOW!
OP
CH

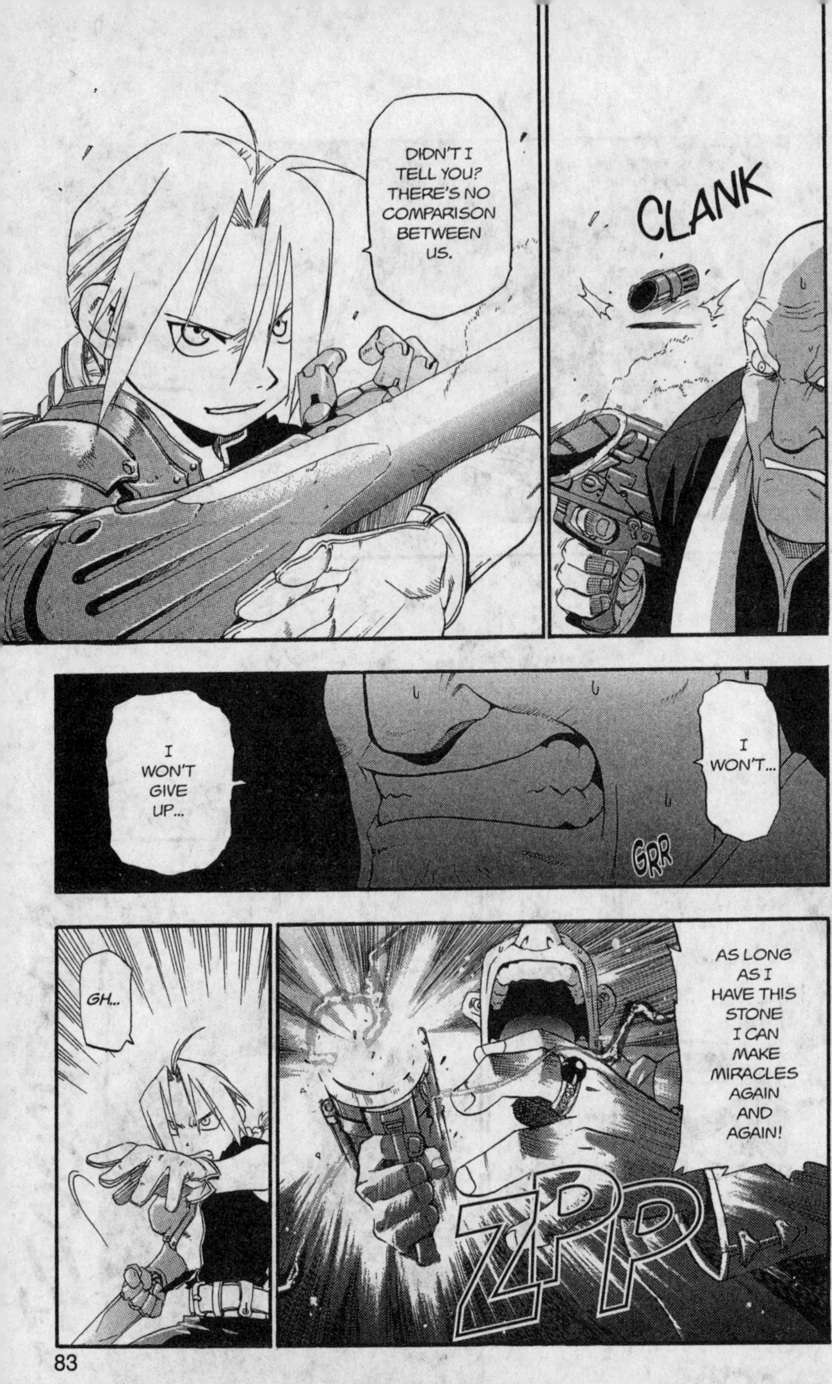
CLANK
DIDN'T I TELL YOU? THERE'S NO COMPARISON BETWEEN US.
I WON'T...
GRR
I WON'T GIVE UP...
AS LONG AS I HAVE THIS STONE I CAN MAKE MIRACLES AGAIN AND AGAIN!
ZPP
GH...

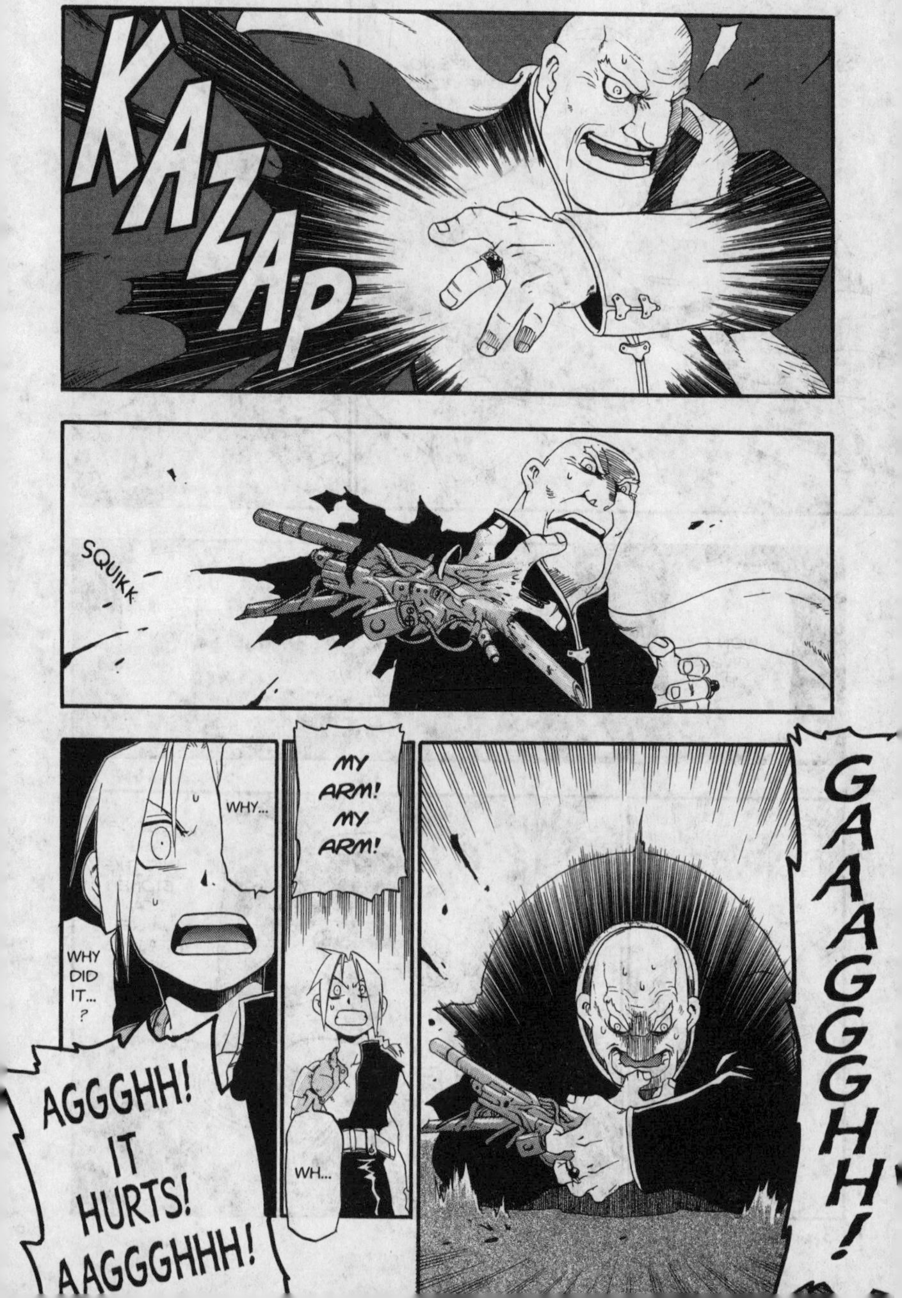
KAZAP
SQUIKK
GAAAGGGH!
MY ARM! MY ARM!
WH...
WHY...
WHY DID IT...?
AGGGHH! IT HURTS! AAGGGHHH!

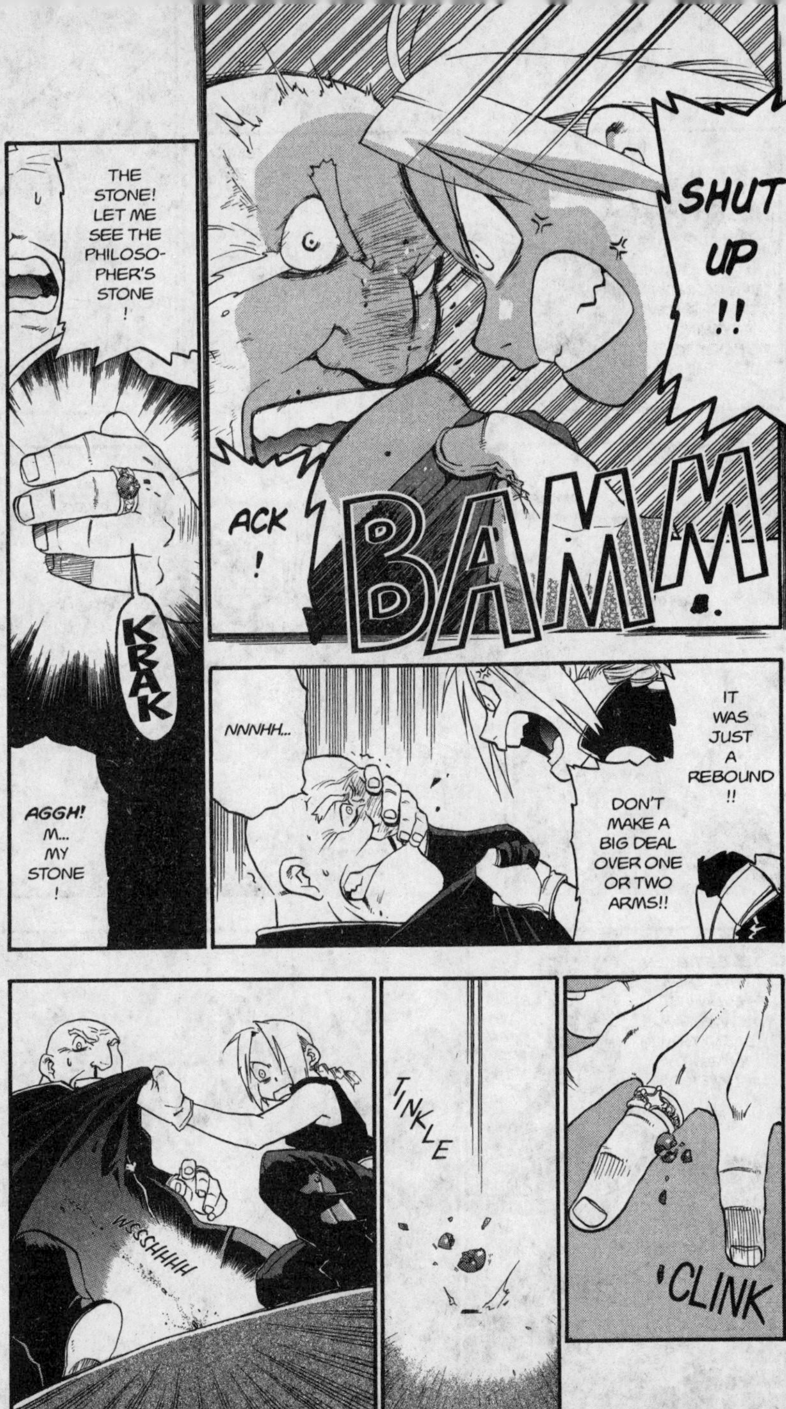
SHUT UP !!
ACK !
BAMM
IT WAS JUST A REBOUND !!
NNNHH...
DON'T MAKE A BIG DEAL OVER ONE OR TWO ARMS!!
THE STONE! LET ME SEE THE PHILOSOPHER'S STONE !
KRAK
AGGH! M... MY STONE !
CLINK
TINKLE
WSSSHHHH

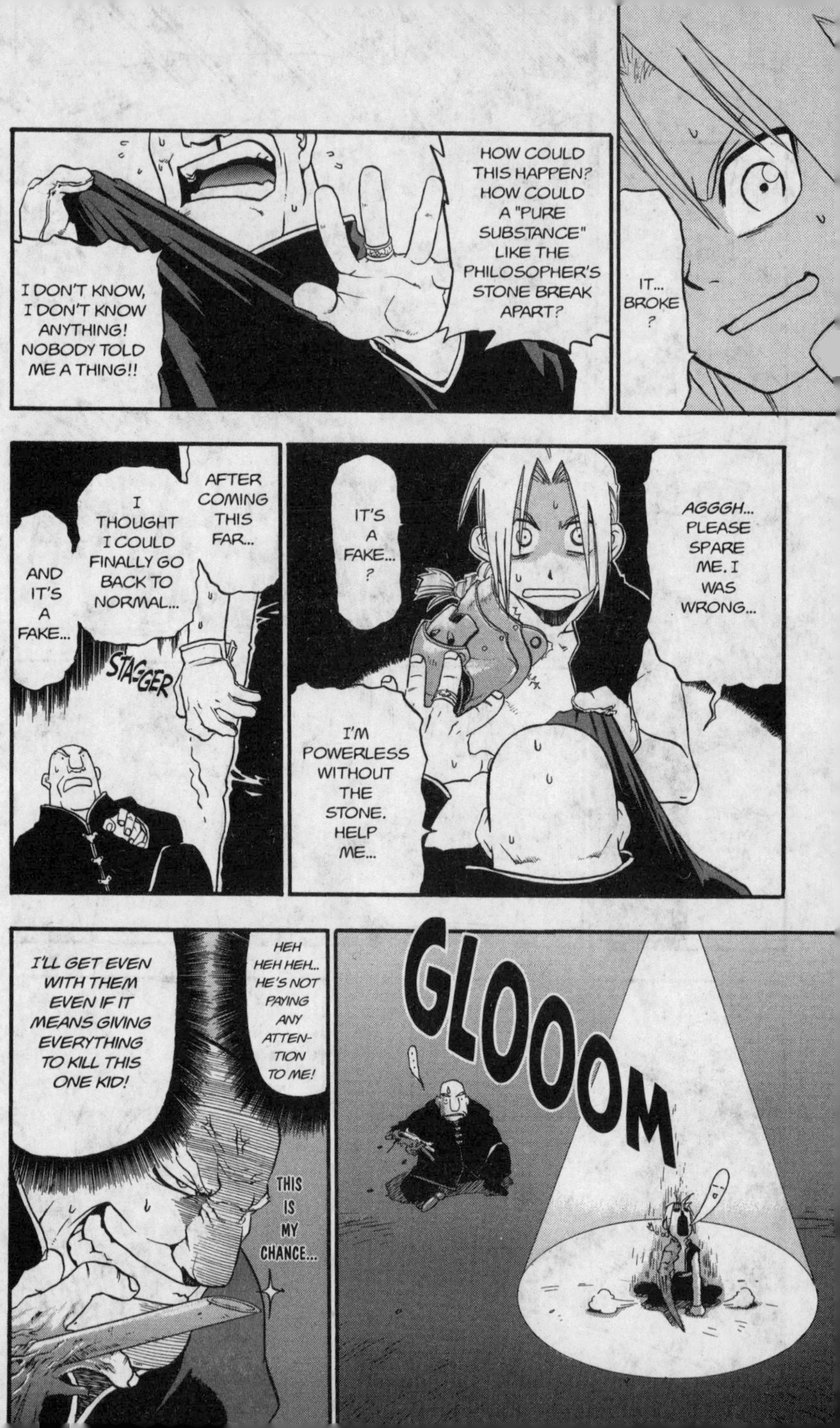
IT... BROKE?
HOW COULD THIS HAPPEN? HOW COULD A "PURE SUBSTANCE" LIKE THE PHILOSOPHER'S STONE BREAK APART?
I DON'T KNOW, I DON'T KNOW ANYTHING! NOBODY TOLD ME A THING!!
AGGGH... PLEASE SPARE ME. I WAS WRONG...
IT'S A FAKE...?
I'M POWERLESS WITHOUT THE STONE. HELP ME...
AFTER COMING THIS FAR...
I THOUGHT I COULD FINALLY GO BACK TO NORMAL...
AND IT'S A FAKE...
STAGGER
GLOOOM
HEH HEH HEH... HE'S NOT PAYING ANY ATTEN-TION TO ME!
I'LL GET EVEN WITH THEM EVEN IF IT MEANS GIVING EVERYTHING TO KILL THIS ONE KID!
THIS IS MY CHANCE...

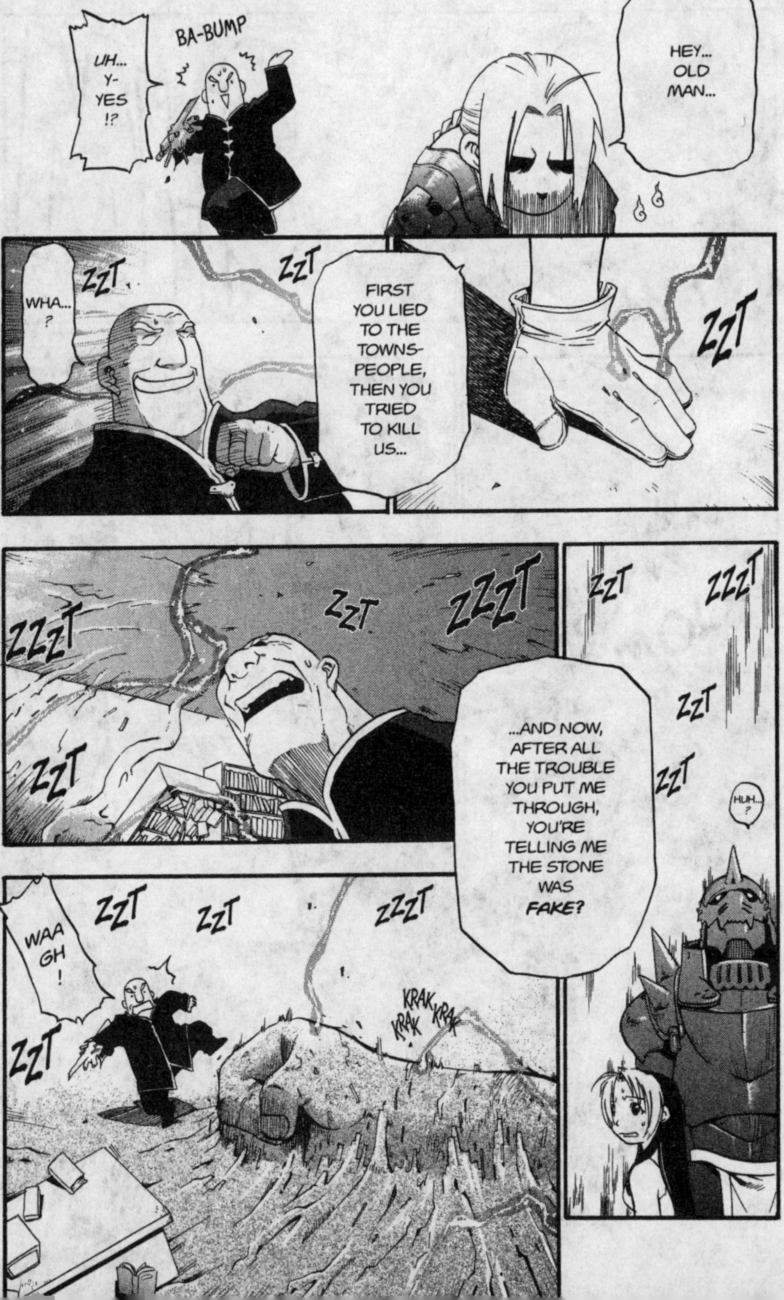

HEY... OLD MAN...
BA-BUMP
UH... Y-YES!?
ZZT
ZZT
FIRST YOU LIED TO THE TOWNS-PEOPLE, THEN YOU TRIED TO KILL US...
ZZT
WHA...?
ZZT
ZZZT
ZZT
ZZT
...AND NOW, AFTER ALL THE TROUBLE YOU PUT ME THROUGH, YOU'RE TELLING ME THE STONE WAS **FAKE?**
HUH...?
ZZZT
ZZT
ZZZT
ZZT
ZZZT
ZZT
ZZT
WAAGH!
KRAK KRAK KRAK
ZZT

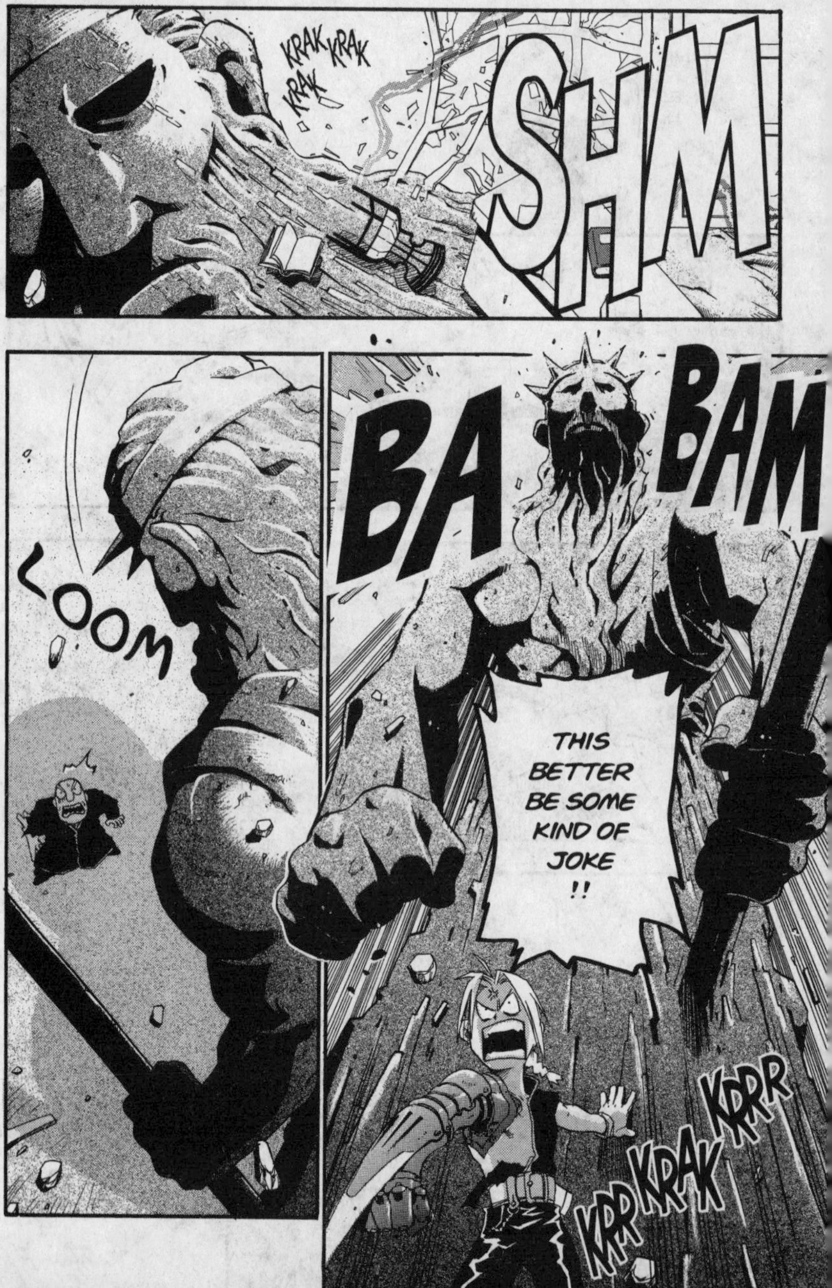
SHM
KRAK KRAK KRAK
BA BAM
THIS BETTER BE SOME KIND OF JOKE !!
KRR KRAK KRR
LOOM

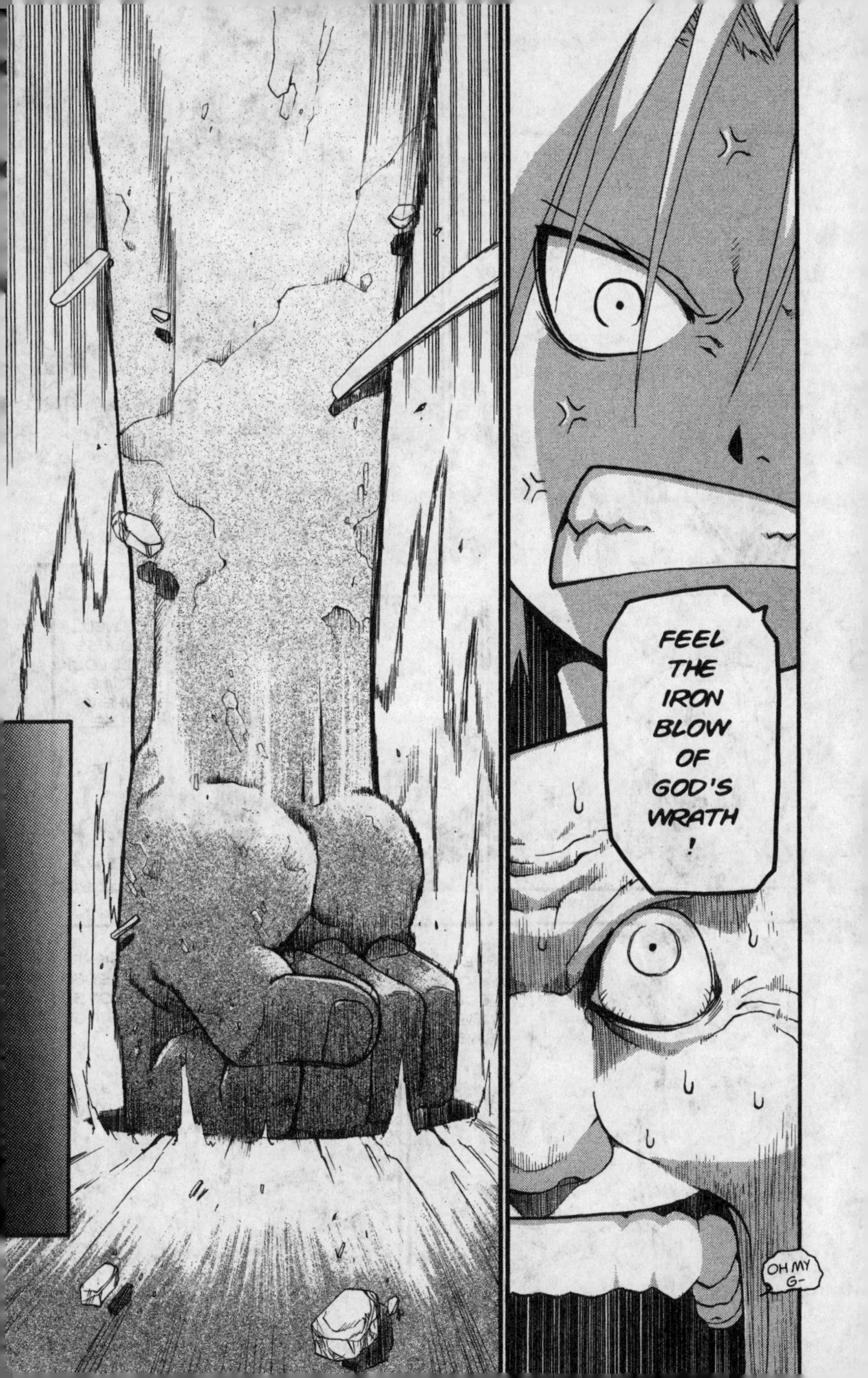
FEEL THE IRON BLOW OF GOD'S WRATH!
OH MY G-

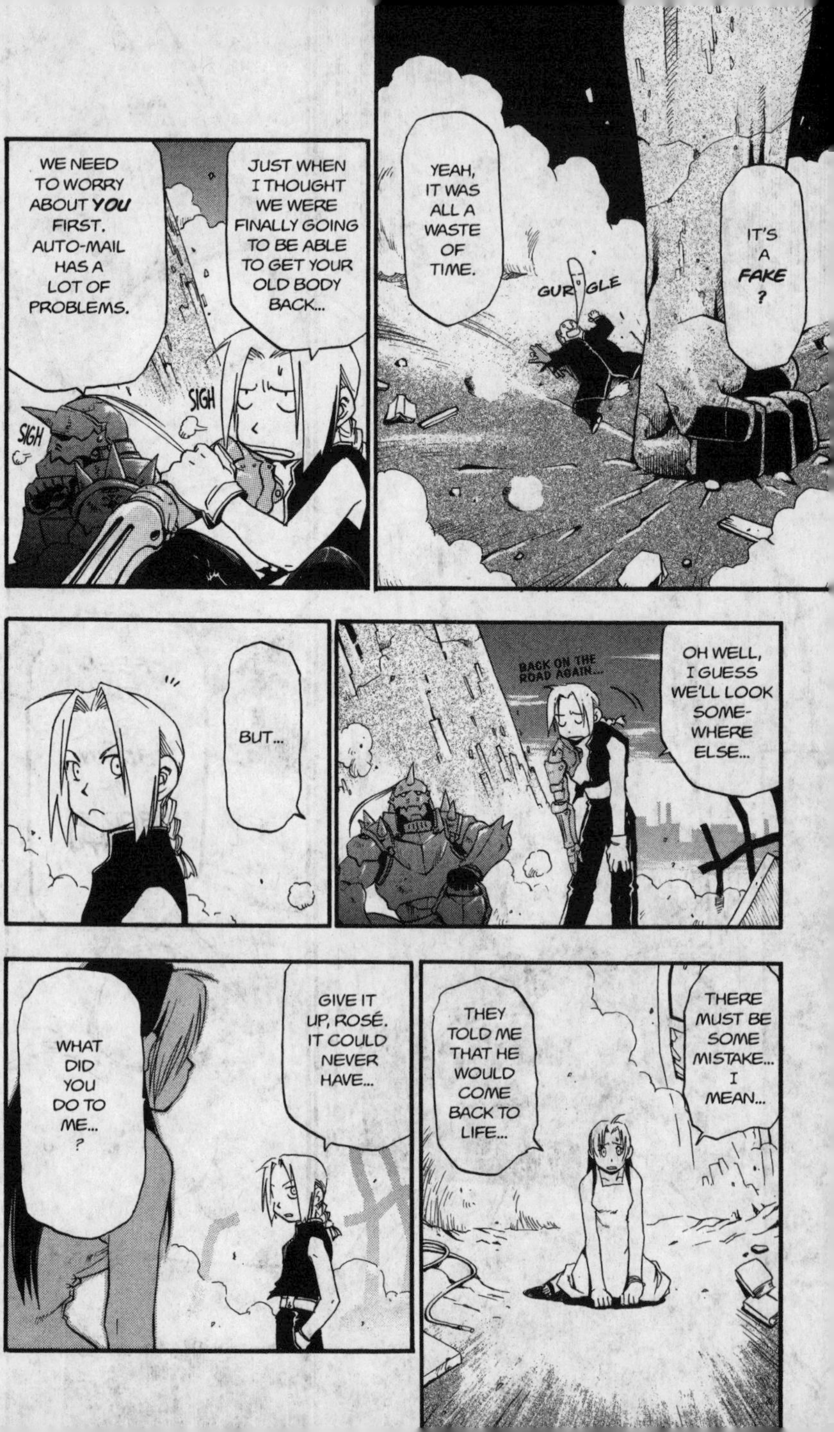
IT'S A FAKE?
GUR GLE
YEAH, IT WAS ALL A WASTE OF TIME.
JUST WHEN I THOUGHT WE WERE FINALLY GOING TO BE ABLE TO GET YOUR OLD BODY BACK...
SIGH
WE NEED TO WORRY ABOUT ***YOU*** FIRST. AUTO-MAIL HAS A LOT OF PROBLEMS.
SIGH
OH WELL, I GUESS WE'LL LOOK SOME-WHERE ELSE...
BACK ON THE ROAD AGAIN...
BUT...
THERE MUST BE SOME MISTAKE... I MEAN...
THEY TOLD ME THAT HE WOULD COME BACK TO LIFE...
GIVE IT UP, ROSÉ. IT COULD NEVER HAVE...
WHAT DID YOU DO TO ME...?

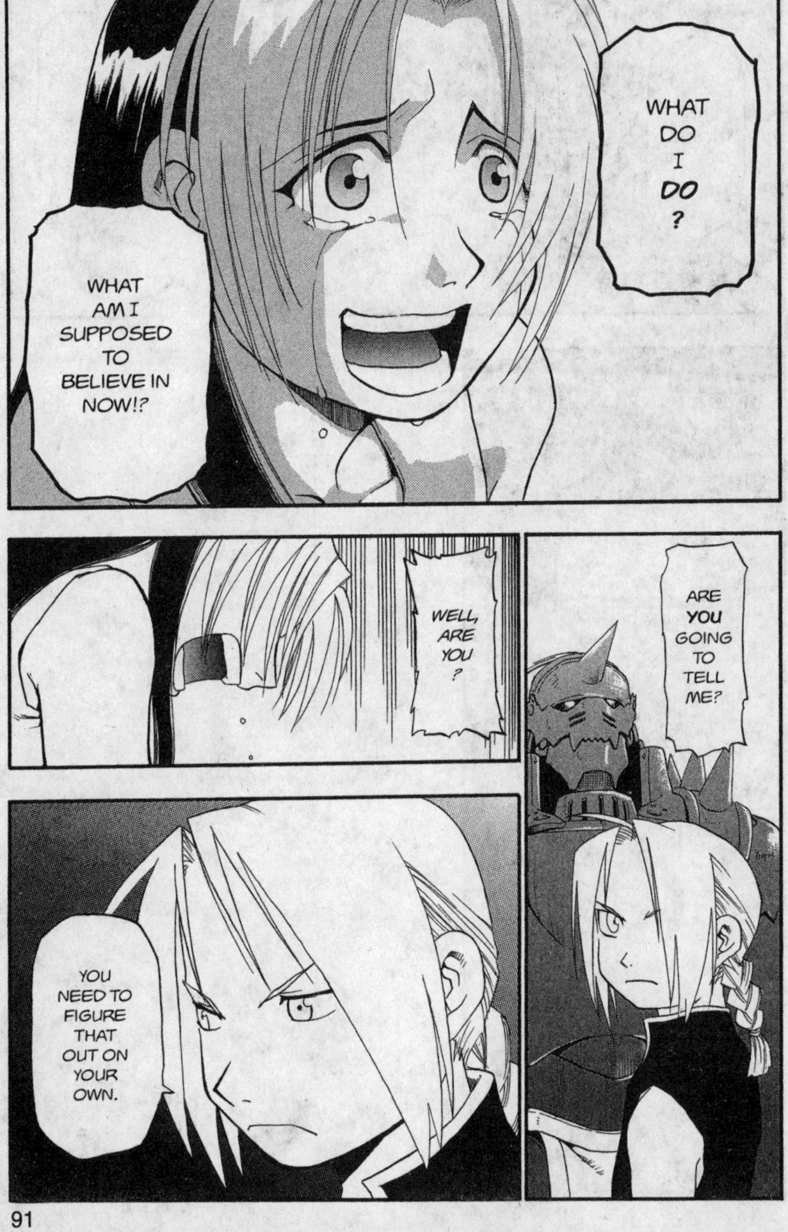
WHAT DO I DO?
WHAT AM I SUPPOSED TO BELIEVE IN NOW!?
ARE YOU GOING TO TELL ME?
WELL, ARE YOU?
YOU NEED TO FIGURE THAT OUT ON YOUR OWN.

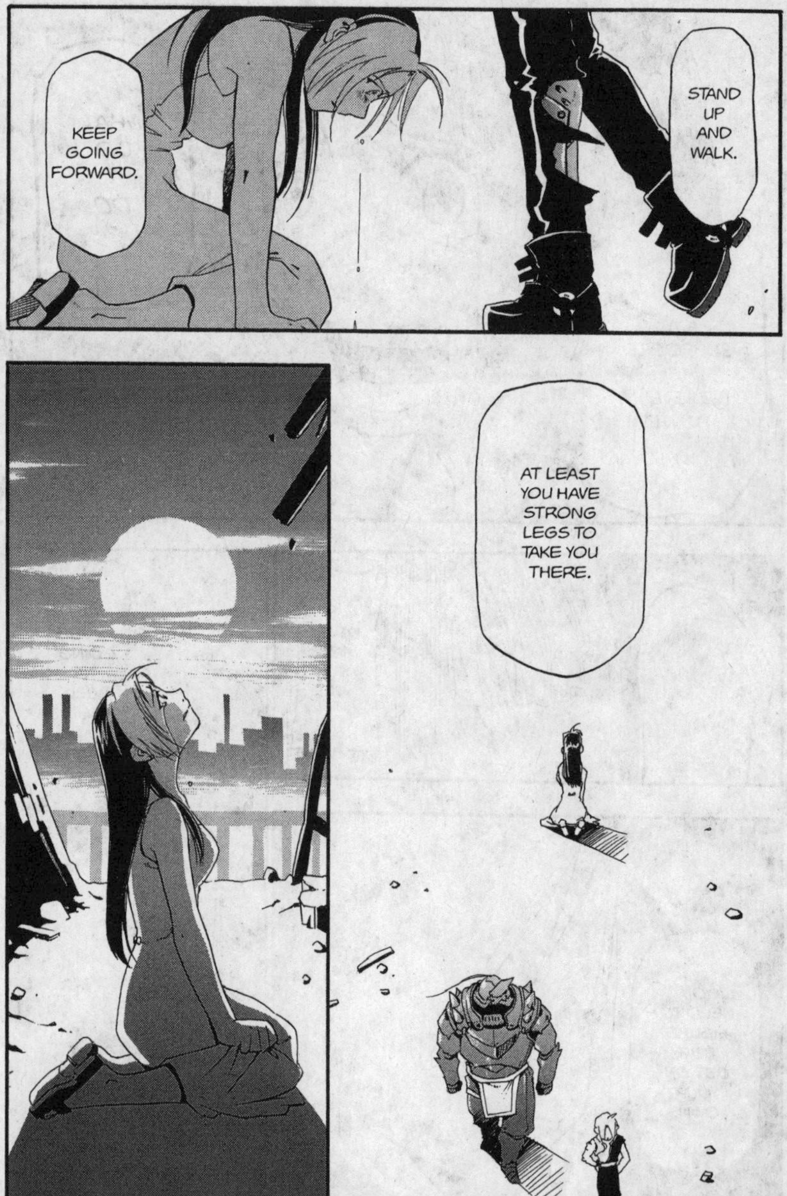
STAND UP AND WALK.
KEEP GOING FORWARD.
AT LEAST YOU HAVE STRONG LEGS TO TAKE YOU THERE.

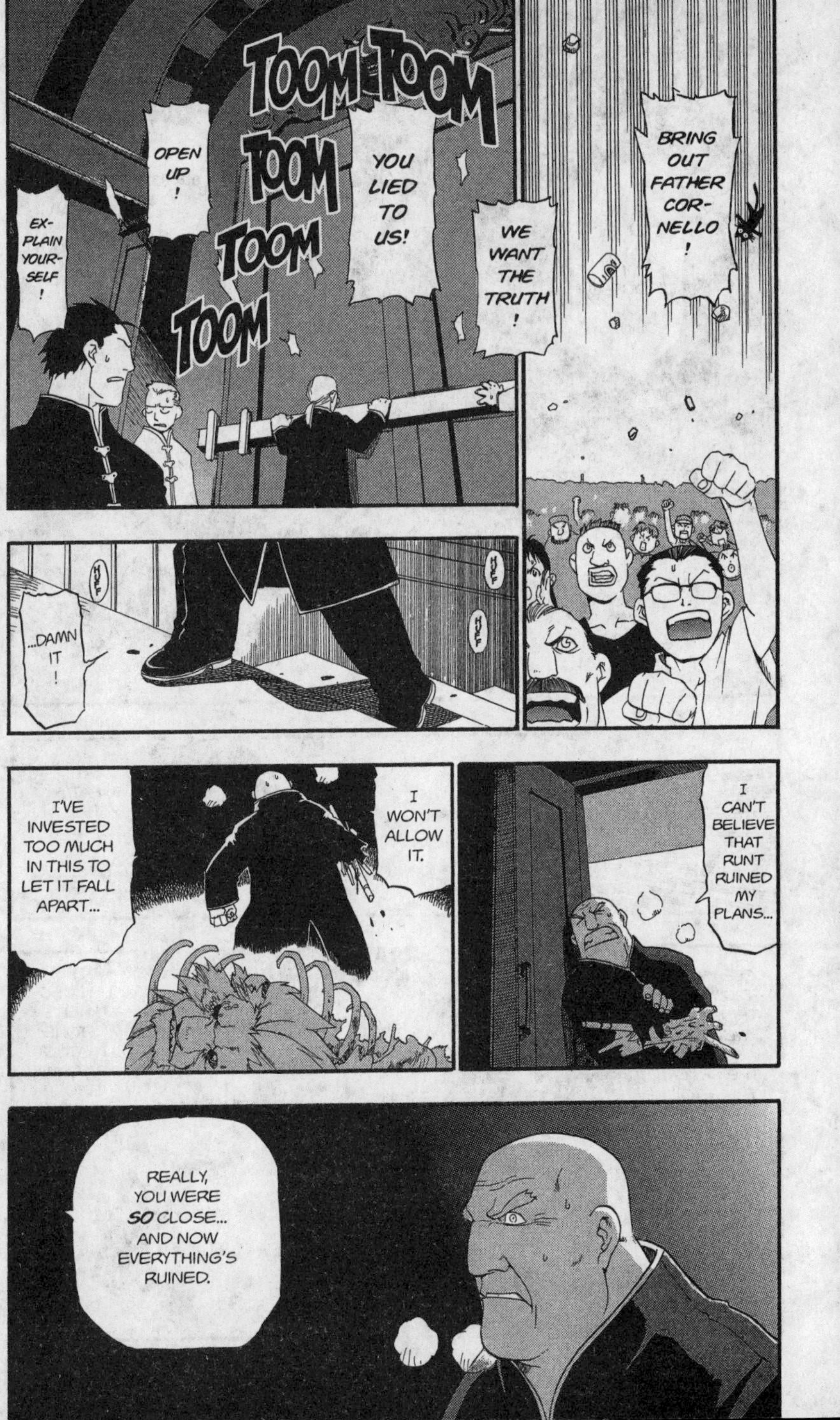
BRING OUT FATHER COR-NELLO!
WE WANT THE TRUTH!
YOU LIED TO US!
TOOM TOOM
TOOM
TOOM
TOOM
OPEN UP!
EX-PLAIN YOUR-SELF!
HUFF
HUFF
...DAMN IT!
I CAN'T BELIEVE THAT RUNT RUINED MY PLANS...
I WON'T ALLOW IT.
I'VE INVESTED TOO MUCH IN THIS TO LET IT FALL APART...
REALLY, YOU WERE *SO* CLOSE... AND NOW EVERYTHING'S RUINED.

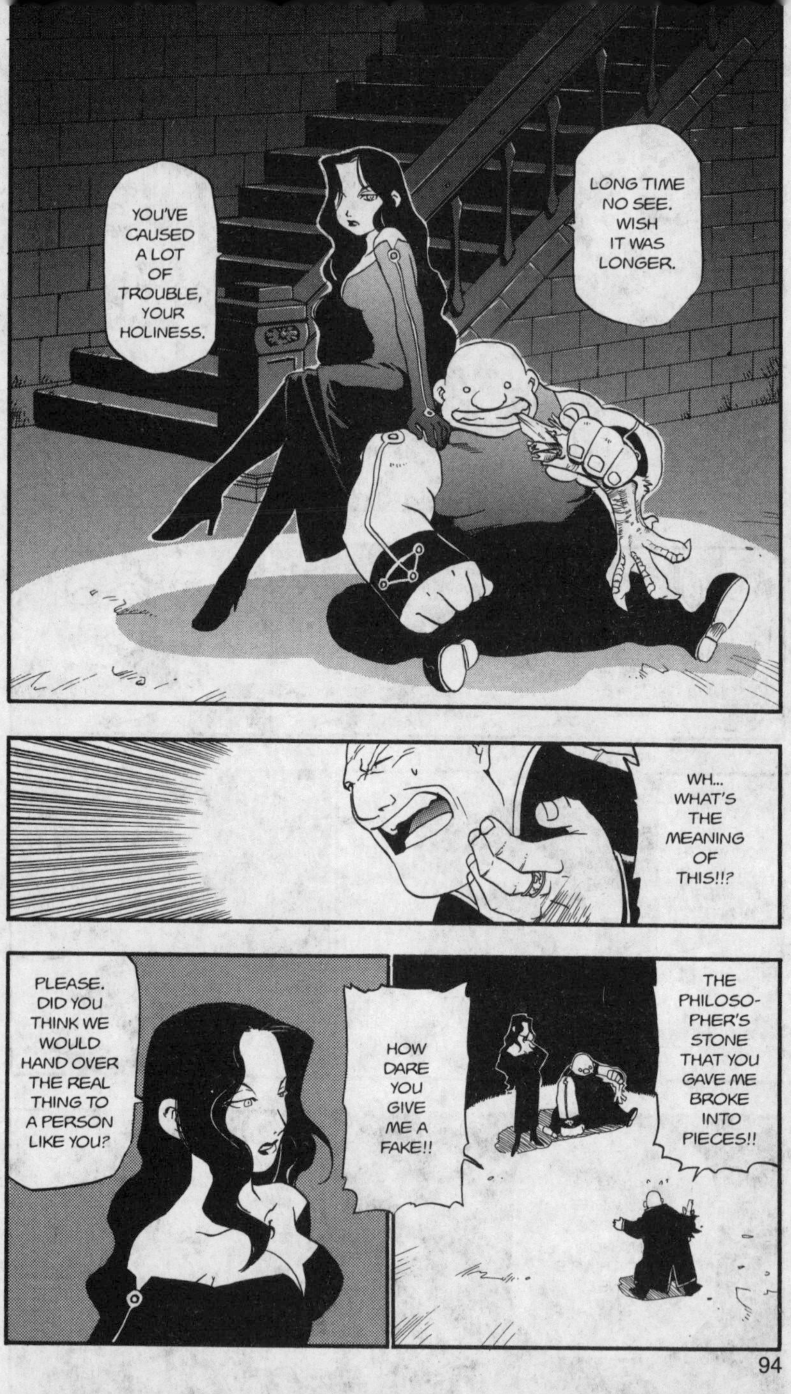
LONG TIME NO SEE. WISH IT WAS LONGER.
YOU'VE CAUSED A LOT OF TROUBLE, YOUR HOLINESS.
WH... WHAT'S THE MEANING OF THIS!!?
THE PHILOSO-PHER'S STONE THAT YOU GAVE ME BROKE INTO PIECES!!
HOW DARE YOU GIVE ME A FAKE!!
PLEASE. DID YOU THINK WE WOULD HAND OVER THE REAL THING TO A PERSON LIKE YOU?

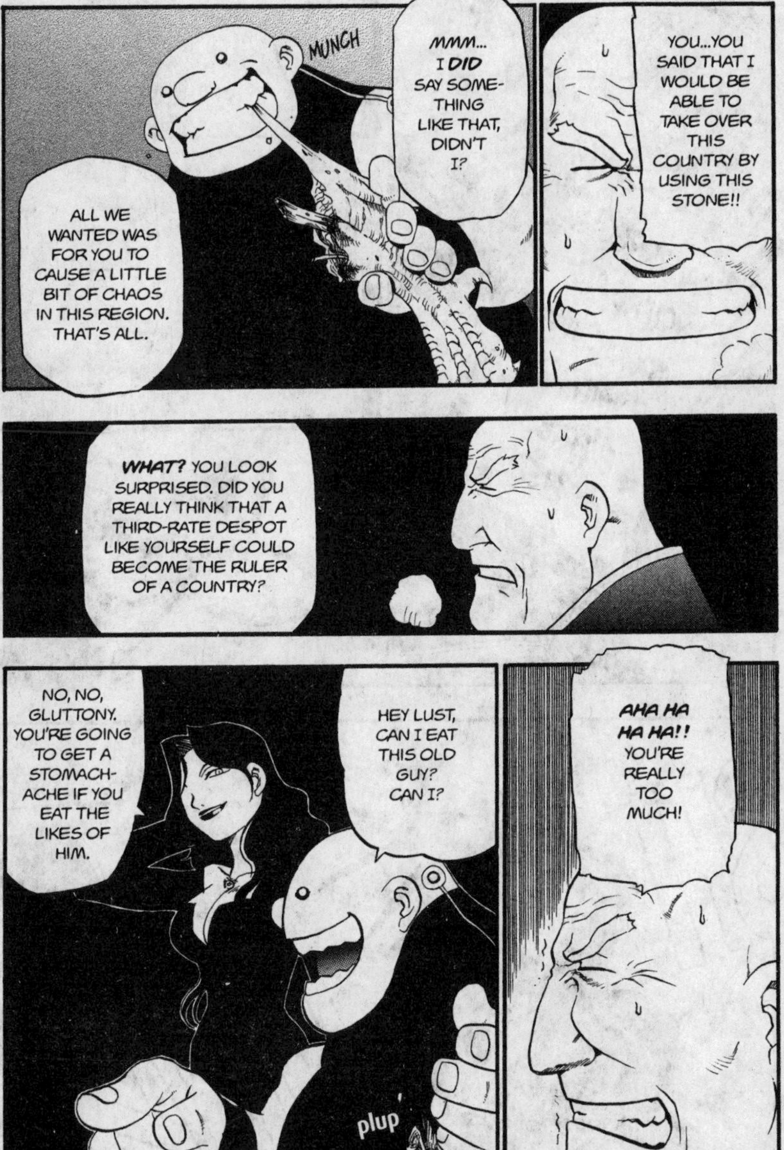
YOU...YOU SAID THAT I WOULD BE ABLE TO TAKE OVER THIS COUNTRY BY USING THIS STONE!!
MMM... I **DID** SAY SOME-THING LIKE THAT, DIDN'T I?
MUNCH
ALL WE WANTED WAS FOR YOU TO CAUSE A LITTLE BIT OF CHAOS IN THIS REGION. THAT'S ALL.
WHAT? YOU LOOK SURPRISED. DID YOU REALLY THINK THAT A THIRD-RATE DESPOT LIKE YOURSELF COULD BECOME THE RULER OF A COUNTRY?
AHA HA HA HA!! YOU'RE REALLY TOO MUCH!
HEY LUST, CAN I EAT THIS OLD GUY? CAN I?
NO, NO, GLUTTONY. YOU'RE GOING TO GET A STOMACH-ACHE IF YOU EAT THE LIKES OF HIM.
plup

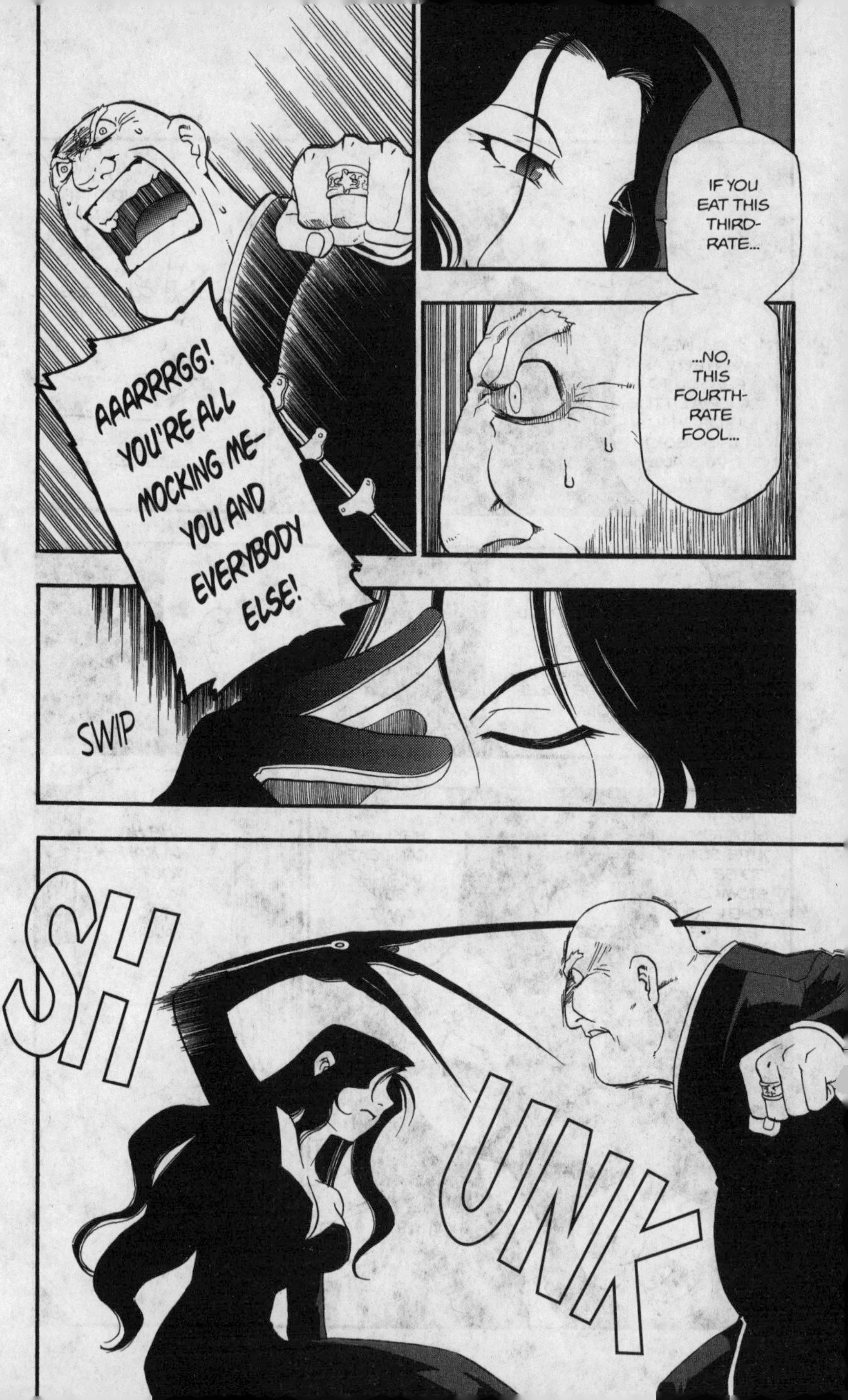
IF YOU EAT THIS THIRD-RATE...
...NO, THIS FOURTH-RATE FOOL...
AAARRRGG! YOU'RE ALL MOCKING ME- YOU AND EVERYBODY ELSE!
SWIP
SHUNK

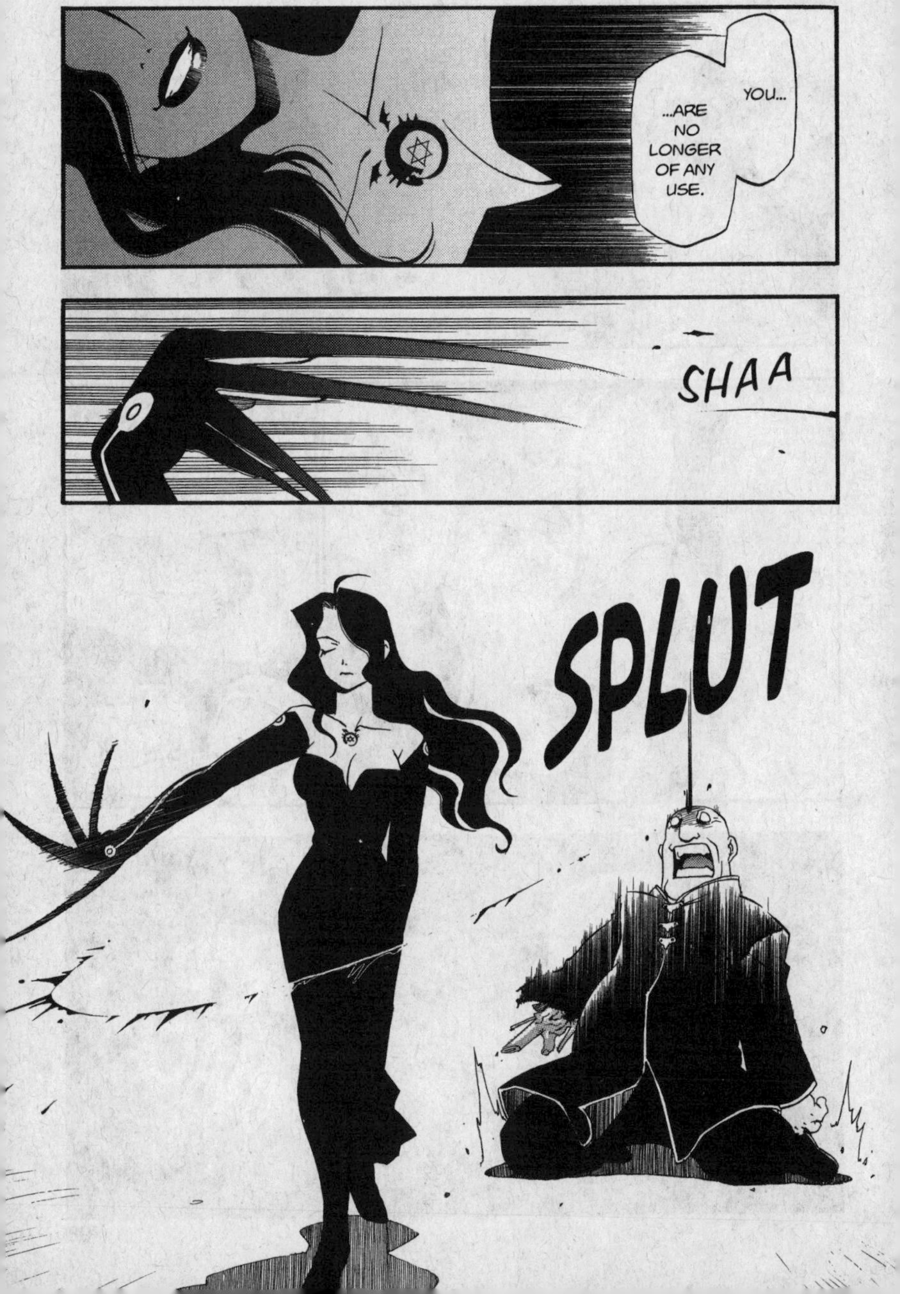
YOU...
...ARE NO LONGER OF ANY USE.
SHAA
SPLUT

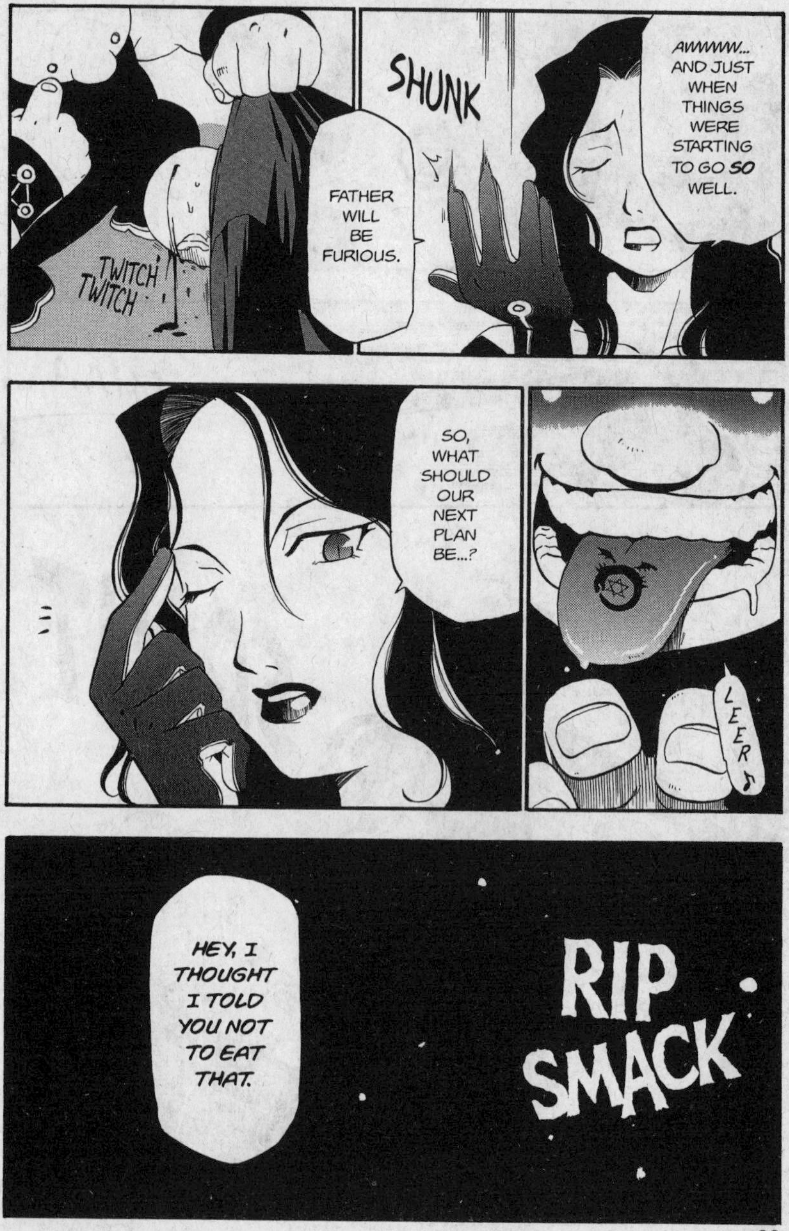
SHUNK
AWWWW... AND JUST WHEN THINGS WERE STARTING TO GO *SO* WELL.
FATHER WILL BE FURIOUS.
TWITCH TWITCH
LEER♪
SO, WHAT SHOULD OUR NEXT PLAN BE...?
RIP
SMACK
HEY, I THOUGHT I TOLD YOU NOT TO EAT THAT.

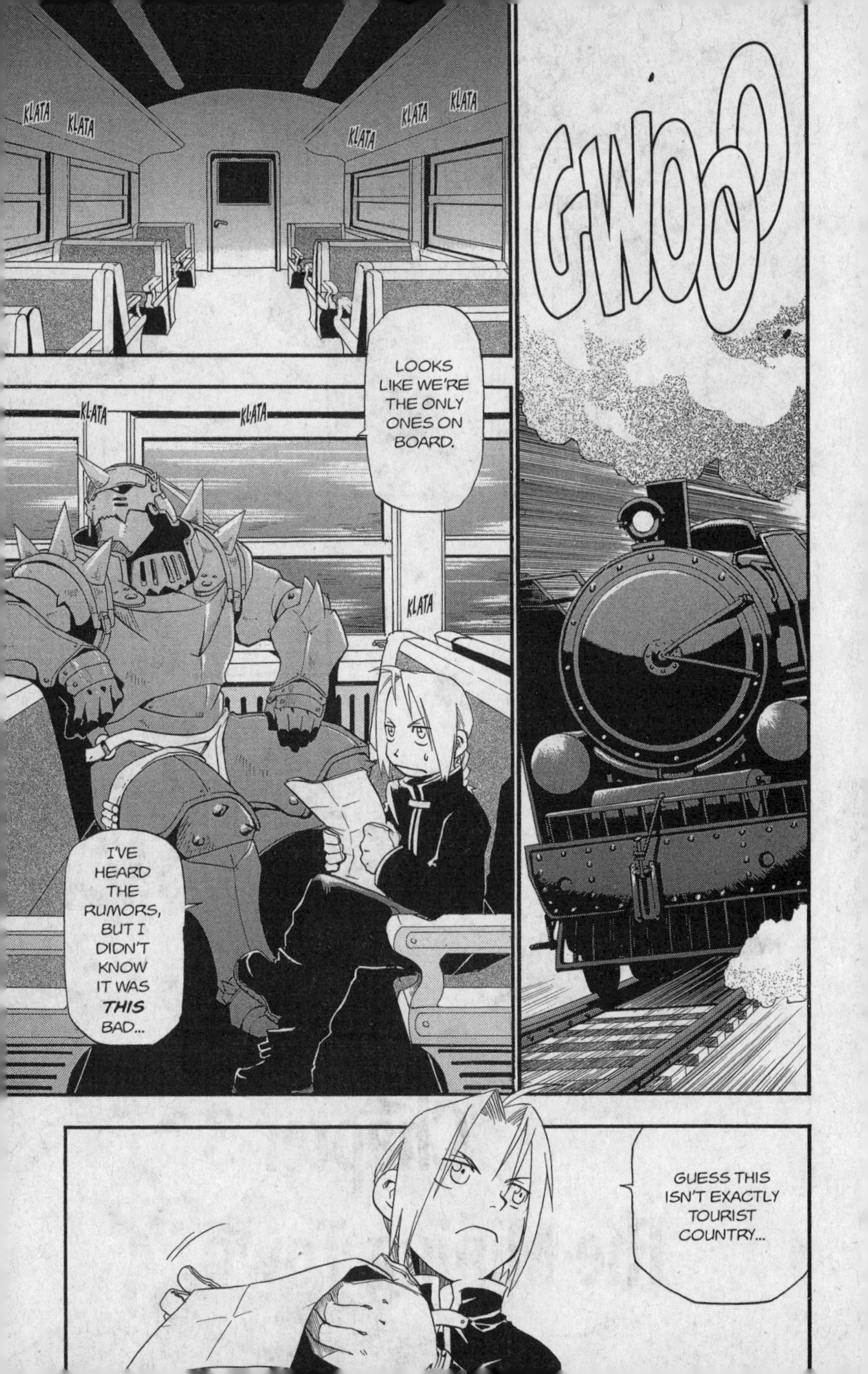

GWOOOO
KLATA
KLATA
KLATA
KLATA
KLATA
KLATA
KLATA
LOOKS LIKE WE'RE THE ONLY ONES ON BOARD.
KLATA
I'VE HEARD THE RUMORS, BUT I DIDN'T KNOW IT WAS **THIS** BAD...
GUESS THIS ISN'T EXACTLY TOURIST COUNTRY...

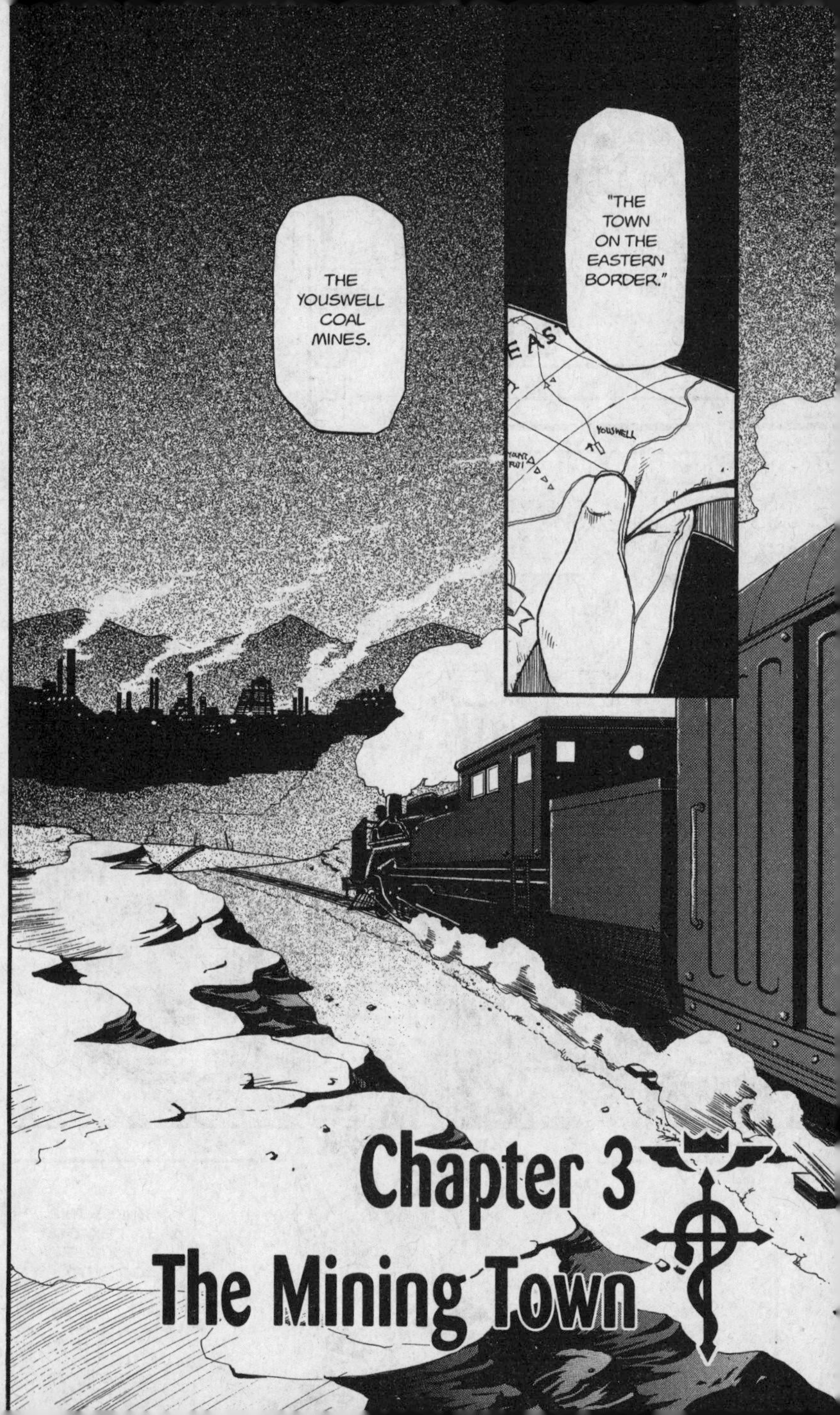
"THE TOWN ON THE EASTERN BORDER."
EAST
YOUSWELL
THE YOUSWELL COAL MINES.
Chapter 3
The Mining Town

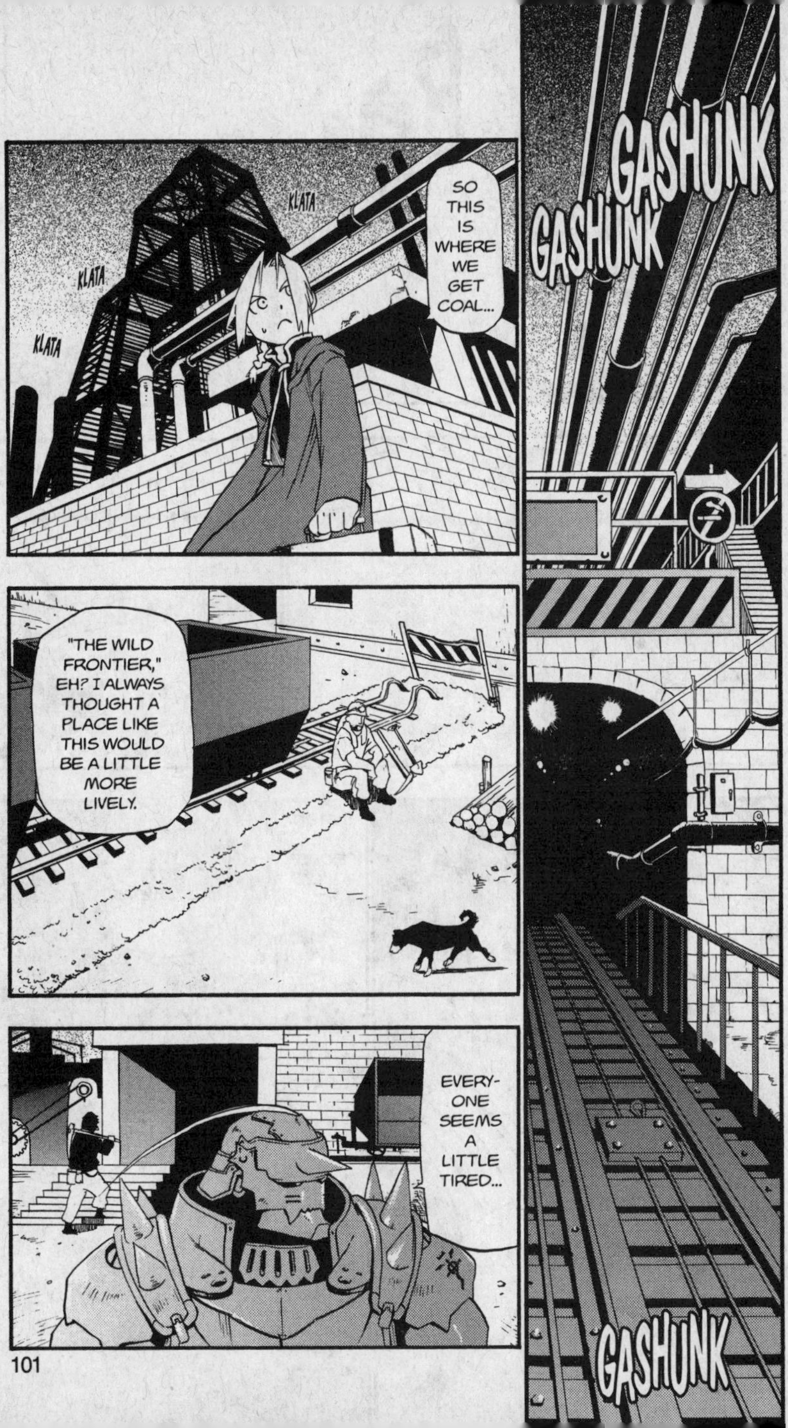
GASHUNK
GASHUNK
GASHUNK
KLATA
KLATA
KLATA
SO THIS IS WHERE WE GET COAL...
"THE WILD FRONTIER," EH? I ALWAYS THOUGHT A PLACE LIKE THIS WOULD BE A LITTLE MORE LIVELY.
EVERY-ONE SEEMS A LITTLE TIRED...

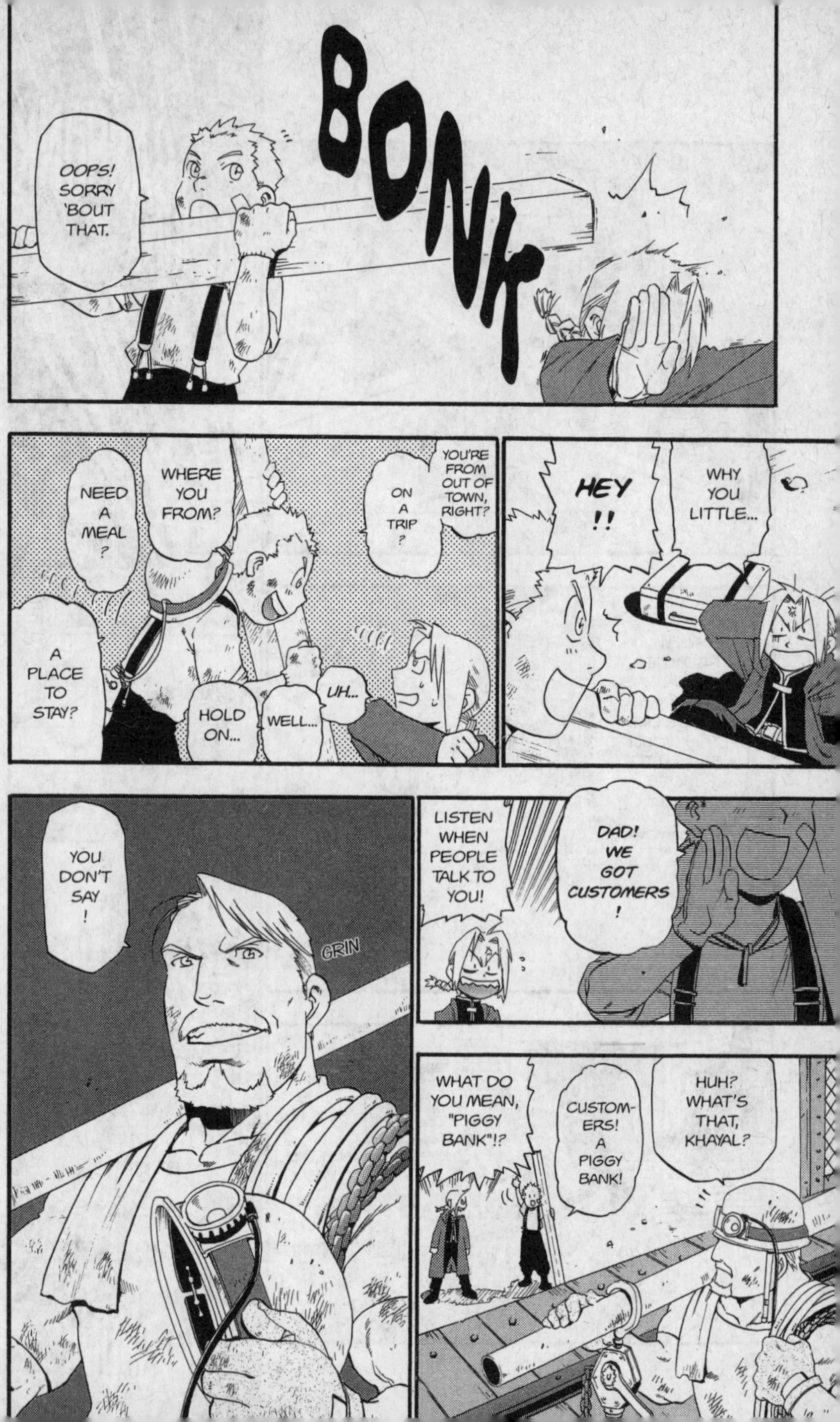
BONK
OOPS! SORRY 'BOUT THAT.
WHY YOU LITTLE...
HEY!!
YOU'RE FROM OUT OF TOWN, RIGHT?
ON A TRIP?
WHERE YOU FROM?
NEED A MEAL?
UH...
WELL...
HOLD ON...
A PLACE TO STAY?
DAD! WE GOT CUSTOMERS!
LISTEN WHEN PEOPLE TALK TO YOU!
HUH? WHAT'S THAT, KHAYAL?
CUSTOM-ERS! A PIGGY BANK!
WHAT DO YOU MEAN, "PIGGY BANK"!?
YOU DON'T SAY!
GRIN

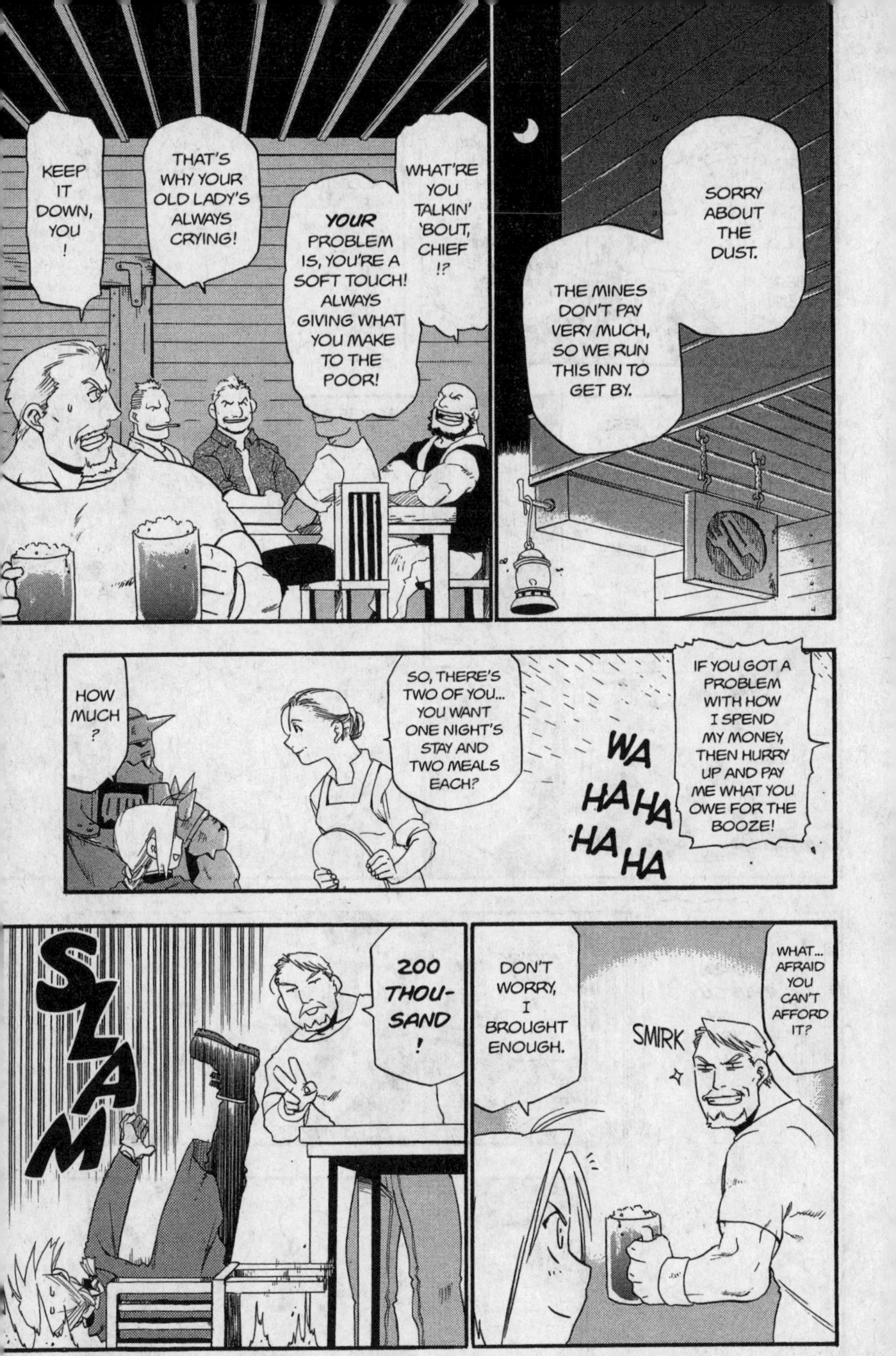
SORRY ABOUT THE DUST.
THE MINES DON'T PAY VERY MUCH, SO WE RUN THIS INN TO GET BY.
WHAT'RE YOU TALKIN' 'BOUT, CHIEF!?
YOUR PROBLEM IS, YOU'RE A SOFT TOUCH! ALWAYS GIVING WHAT YOU MAKE TO THE POOR!
THAT'S WHY YOUR OLD LADY'S ALWAYS CRYING!
KEEP IT DOWN, YOU!
IF YOU GOT A PROBLEM WITH HOW I SPEND MY MONEY, THEN HURRY UP AND PAY ME WHAT YOU OWE FOR THE BOOZE!
WA HAHA HAHA HA
SO, THERE'S TWO OF YOU... YOU WANT ONE NIGHT'S STAY AND TWO MEALS EACH?
HOW MUCH?
WHAT... AFRAID YOU CAN'T AFFORD IT?
SMIRK
DON'T WORRY, I BROUGHT ENOUGH.
200 THOUSAND!
SLAM

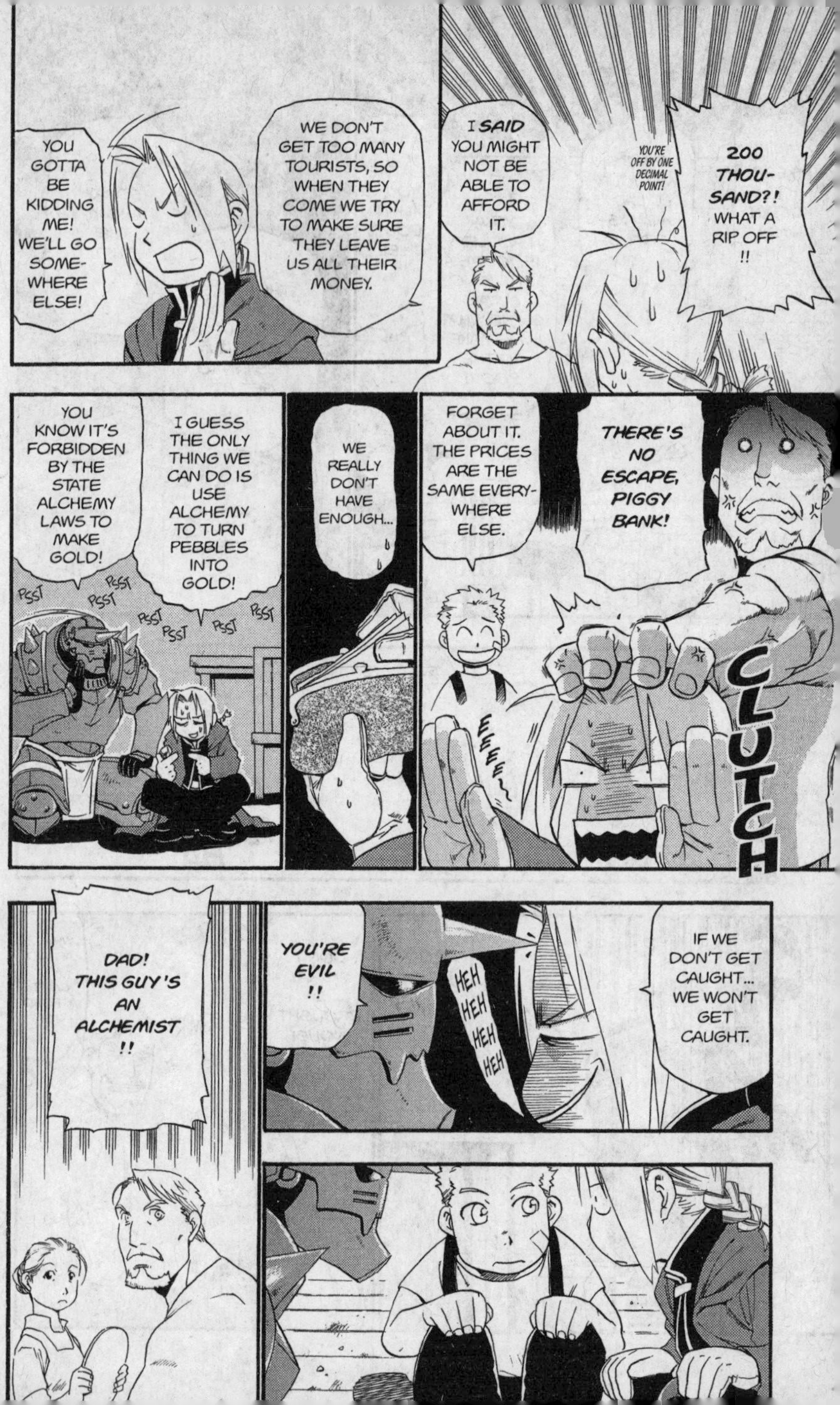
200 THOUSAND?! WHAT A RIP OFF !!
YOU'RE OFF BY ONE DECIMAL POINT!
I SAID YOU MIGHT NOT BE ABLE TO AFFORD IT.
WE DON'T GET TOO MANY TOURISTS, SO WHEN THEY COME WE TRY TO MAKE SURE THEY LEAVE US ALL THEIR MONEY.
YOU GOTTA BE KIDDING ME! WE'LL GO SOMEWHERE ELSE!
THERE'S NO ESCAPE, PIGGY BANK!
FORGET ABOUT IT. THE PRICES ARE THE SAME EVERYWHERE ELSE.
CLUTCH
EEEE
WE REALLY DON'T HAVE ENOUGH...
I GUESS THE ONLY THING WE CAN DO IS USE ALCHEMY TO TURN PEBBLES INTO GOLD!
YOU KNOW IT'S FORBIDDEN BY THE STATE ALCHEMY LAWS TO MAKE GOLD!
PSST PSST PSST PSST PSST PSST PSST
IF WE DON'T GET CAUGHT... WE WON'T GET CAUGHT.
HEH HEH HEH HEH
YOU'RE EVIL !!
DAD! THIS GUY'S AN ALCHEMIST !!

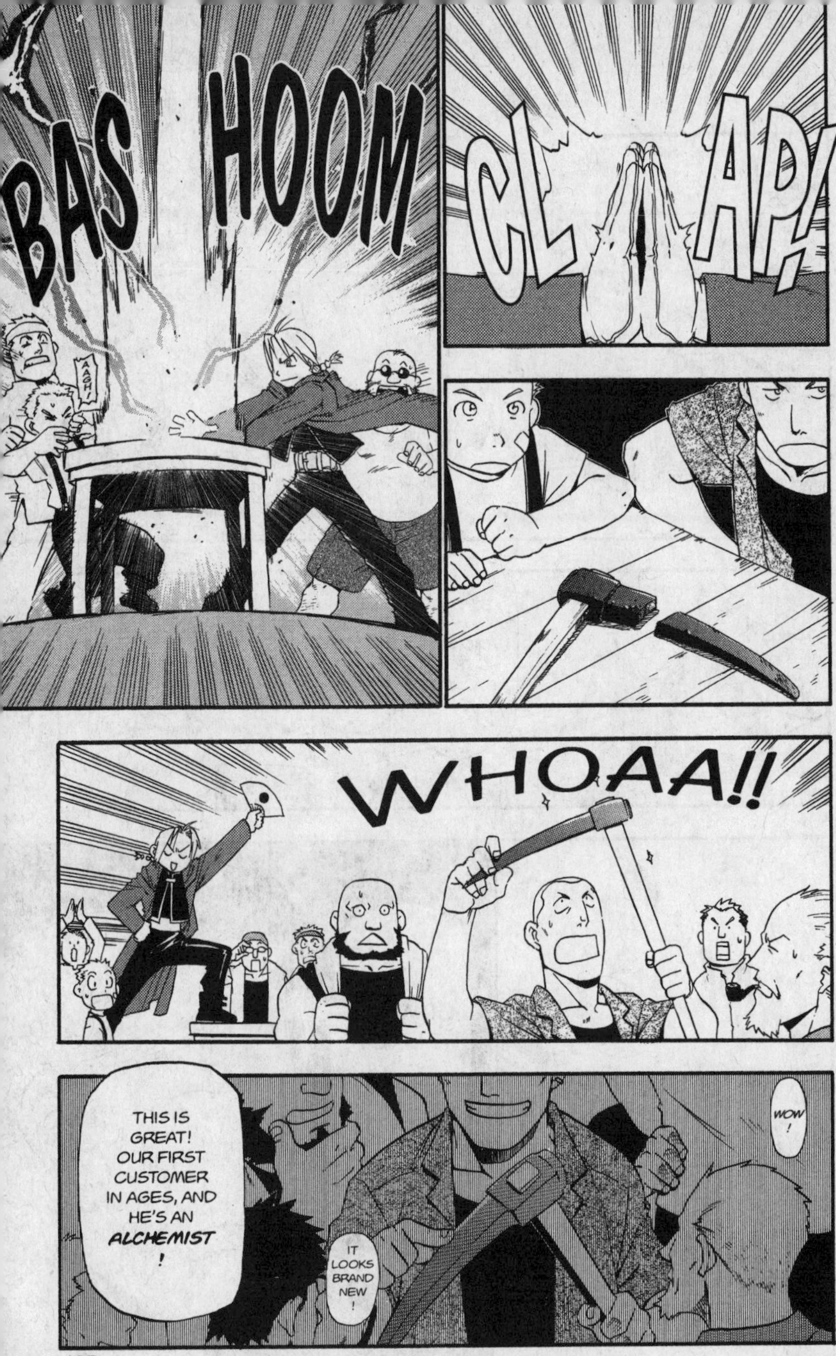
CLAP!
BASHOOM
AAGH!
WHOAA!!
WOW!
THIS IS GREAT! OUR FIRST CUSTOMER IN AGES, AND HE'S AN ALCHEMIST!
IT LOOKS BRAND NEW!

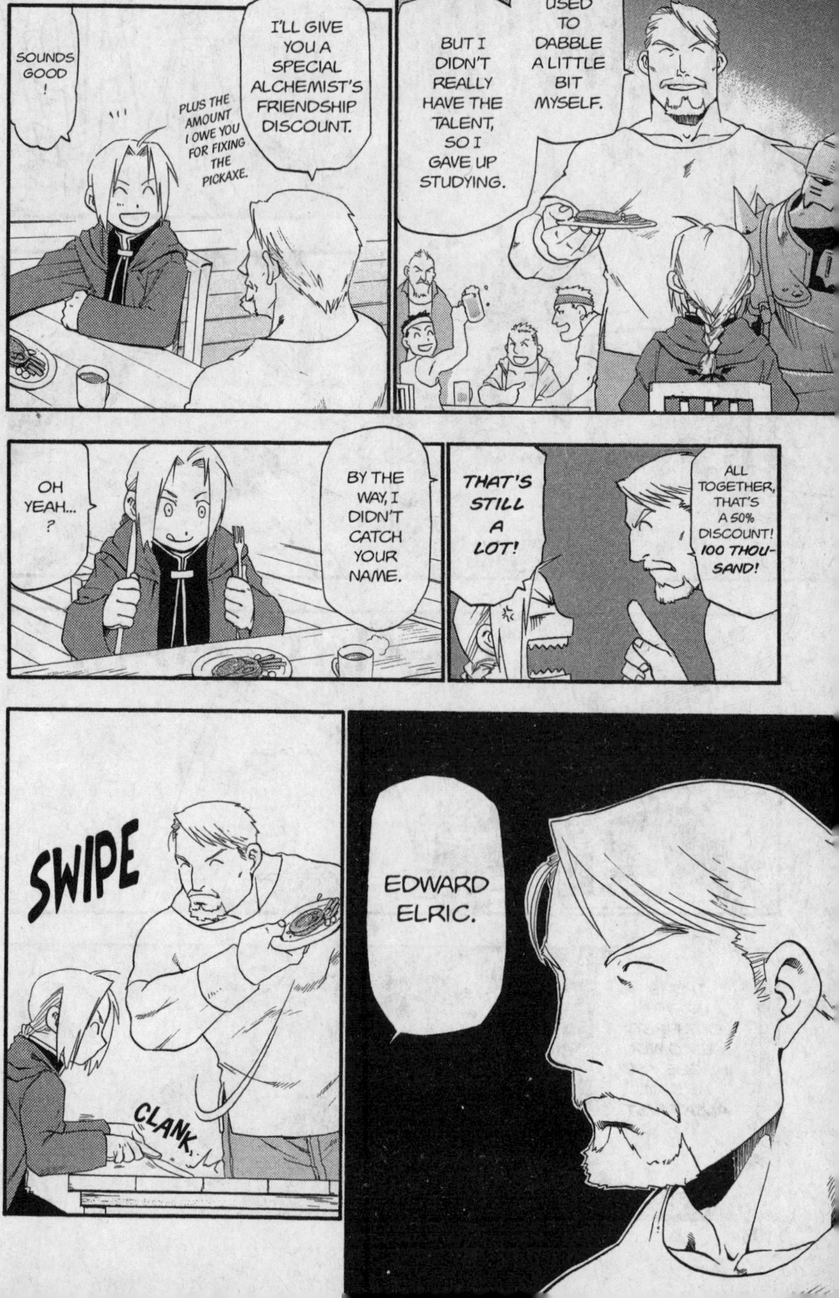
I USED TO DABBLE A LITTLE BIT MYSELF.
BUT I DIDN'T REALLY HAVE THE TALENT, SO I GAVE UP STUDYING.
I'LL GIVE YOU A SPECIAL ALCHEMIST'S FRIENDSHIP DISCOUNT.
PLUS THE AMOUNT I OWE YOU FOR FIXING THE PICKAXE.
SOUNDS GOOD!
ALL TOGETHER, THAT'S A 50% DISCOUNT! 100 THOUSAND!
THAT'S STILL A LOT!
BY THE WAY, I DIDN'T CATCH YOUR NAME.
OH YEAH...?
EDWARD ELRIC.
SWIPE
CLANK

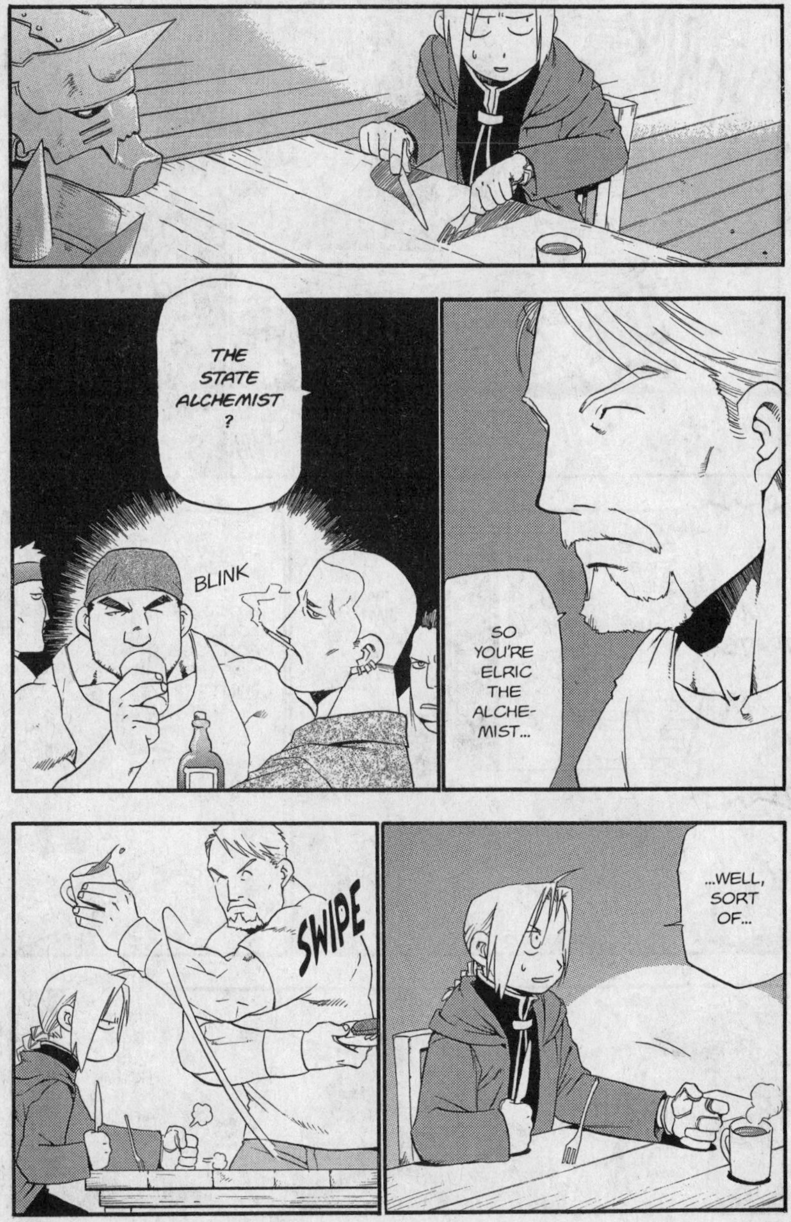
SO YOU'RE ELRIC THE ALCHEMIST...
THE STATE ALCHEMIST?
BLINK
...WELL, SORT OF...
SWIPE

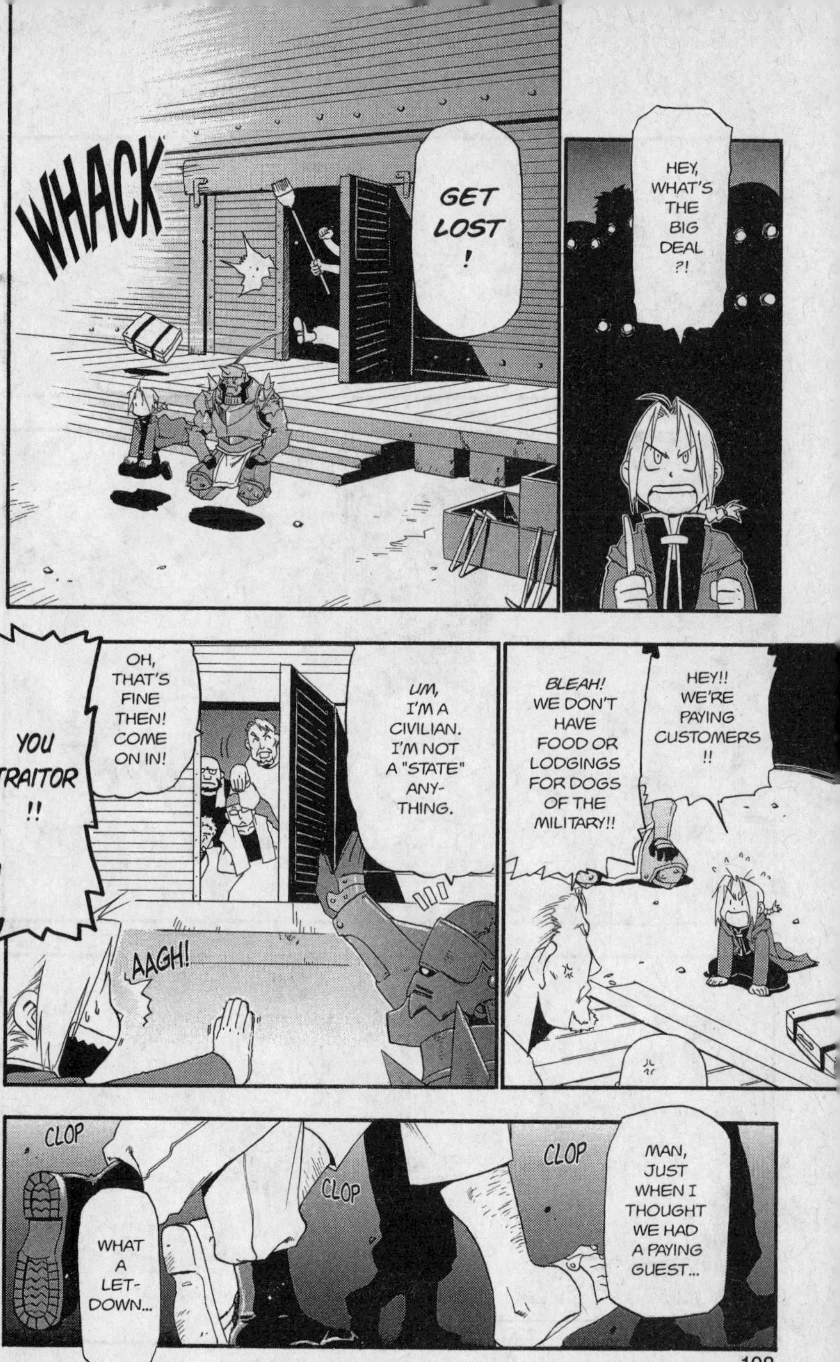
HEY, WHAT'S THE BIG DEAL ?!
GET LOST !
WHACK
HEY!! WE'RE PAYING CUSTOMERS !!
BLEAH! WE DON'T HAVE FOOD OR LODGINGS FOR DOGS OF THE MILITARY!!
UM, I'M A CIVILIAN. I'M NOT A "STATE" ANY- THING.
OH, THAT'S FINE THEN! COME ON IN!
YOU TRAITOR !!
AAGH!
MAN, JUST WHEN I THOUGHT WE HAD A PAYING GUEST...
CLOP
CLOP
CLOP
WHAT A LET- DOWN...

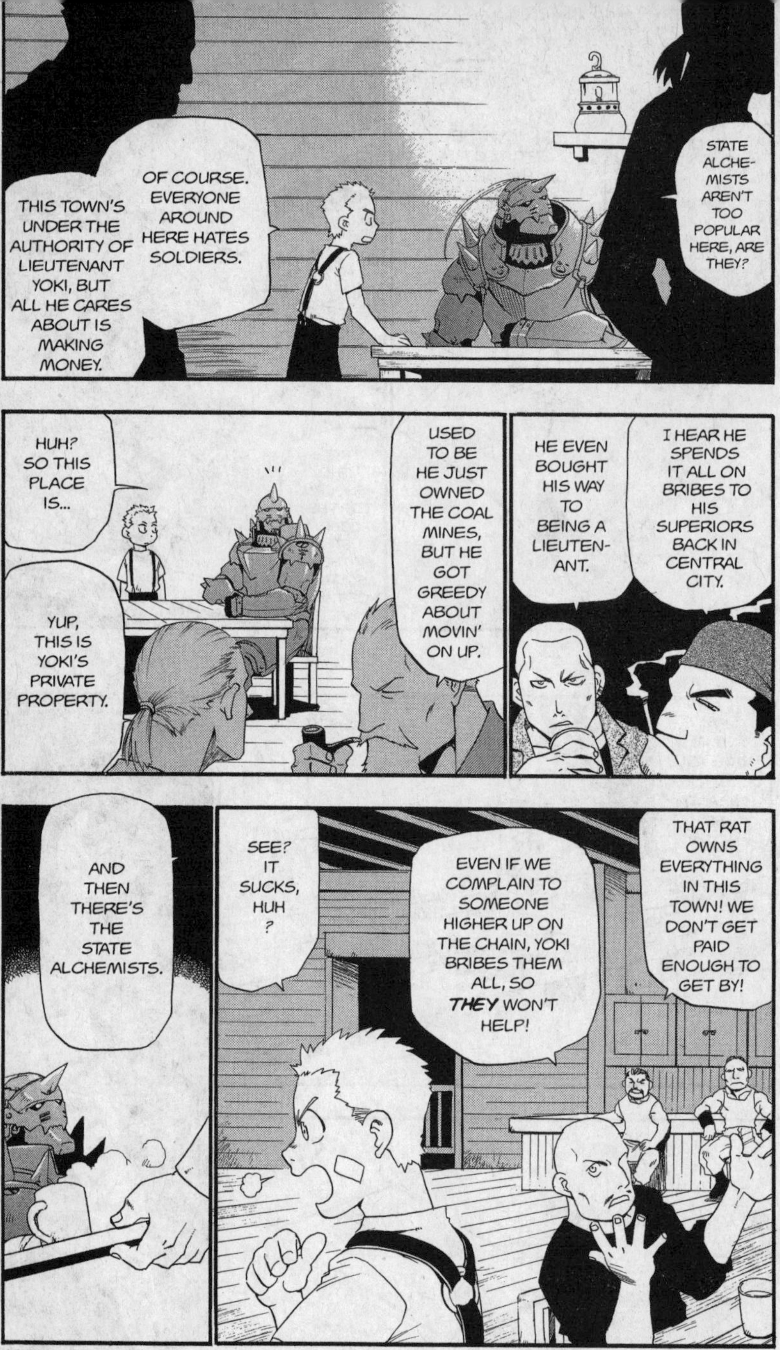
STATE ALCHEMISTS AREN'T TOO POPULAR HERE, ARE THEY?
OF COURSE. EVERYONE AROUND HERE HATES SOLDIERS.
THIS TOWN'S UNDER THE AUTHORITY OF LIEUTENANT YOKI, BUT ALL HE CARES ABOUT IS MAKING MONEY.
I HEAR HE SPENDS IT ALL ON BRIBES TO HIS SUPERIORS BACK IN CENTRAL CITY.
HE EVEN BOUGHT HIS WAY TO BEING A LIEUTENANT.
USED TO BE HE JUST OWNED THE COAL MINES, BUT HE GOT GREEDY ABOUT MOVIN' ON UP.
HUH? SO THIS PLACE IS...
YUP, THIS IS YOKI'S PRIVATE PROPERTY.
THAT RAT OWNS EVERYTHING IN THIS TOWN! WE DON'T GET PAID ENOUGH TO GET BY!
EVEN IF WE COMPLAIN TO SOMEONE HIGHER UP ON THE CHAIN, YOKI BRIBES THEM ALL, SO *THEY* WON'T HELP!
SEE? IT SUCKS, HUH?
AND THEN THERE'S THE STATE ALCHEMISTS.

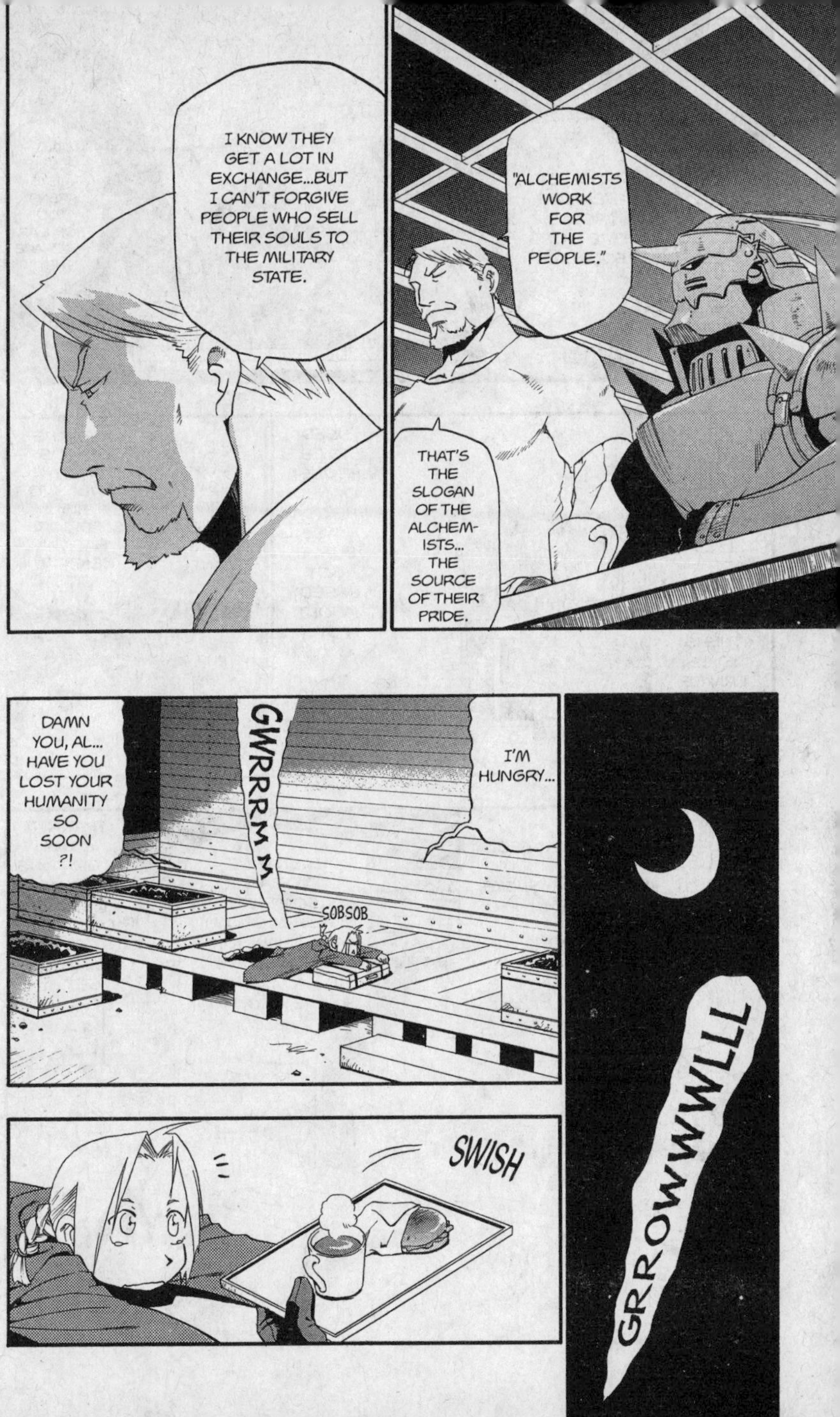
"ALCHEMISTS WORK FOR THE PEOPLE."
THAT'S THE SLOGAN OF THE ALCHEMISTS... THE SOURCE OF THEIR PRIDE.
I KNOW THEY GET A LOT IN EXCHANGE...BUT I CAN'T FORGIVE PEOPLE WHO SELL THEIR SOULS TO THE MILITARY STATE.
GRROWWWLLL
I'M HUNGRY...
GWRRRMM M
SOBSOB
DAMN YOU, AL... HAVE YOU LOST YOUR HUMANITY SO SOON ?!
SWISH

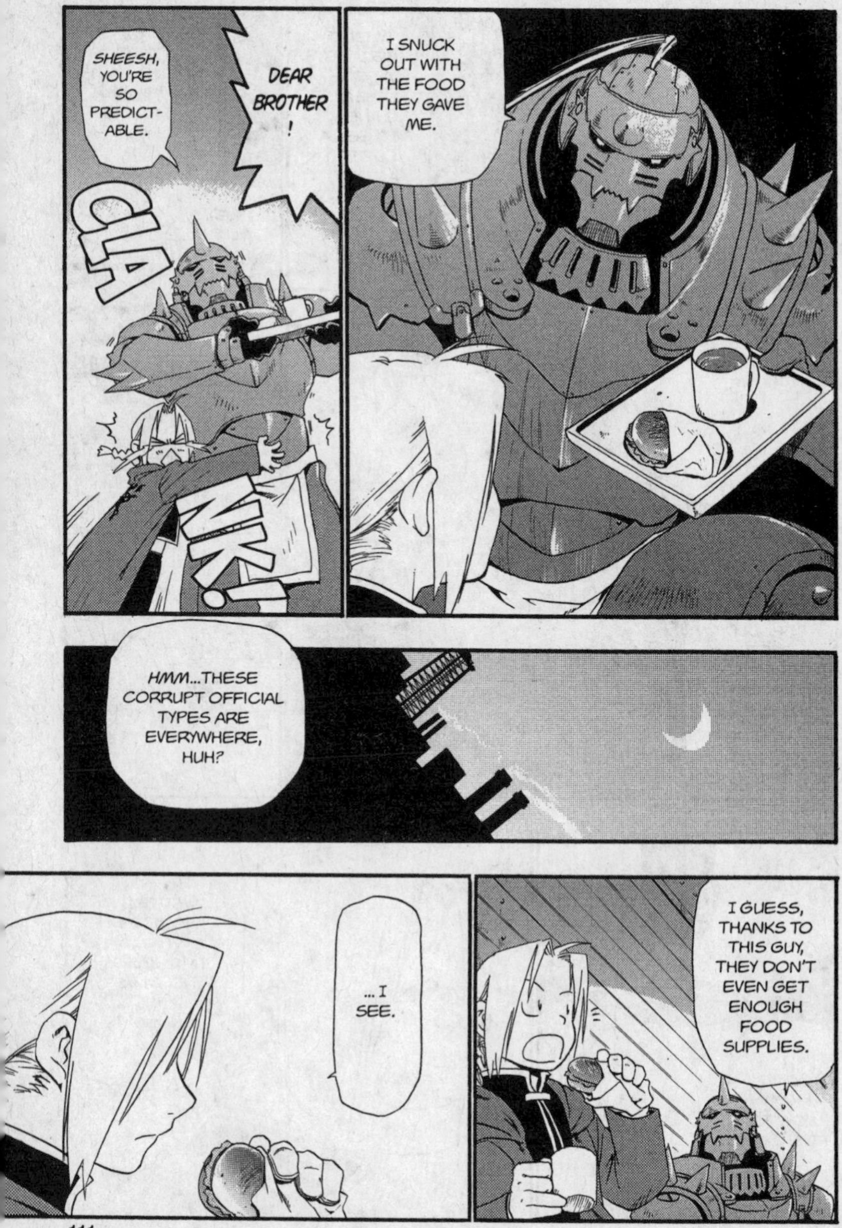
I SNUCK OUT WITH THE FOOD THEY GAVE ME.
DEAR BROTHER!
SHEESH, YOU'RE SO PREDICT-ABLE.
CLANK!
HMM...THESE CORRUPT OFFICIAL TYPES ARE EVERYWHERE, HUH?
I GUESS, THANKS TO THIS GUY, THEY DON'T EVEN GET ENOUGH FOOD SUPPLIES.
...I SEE.

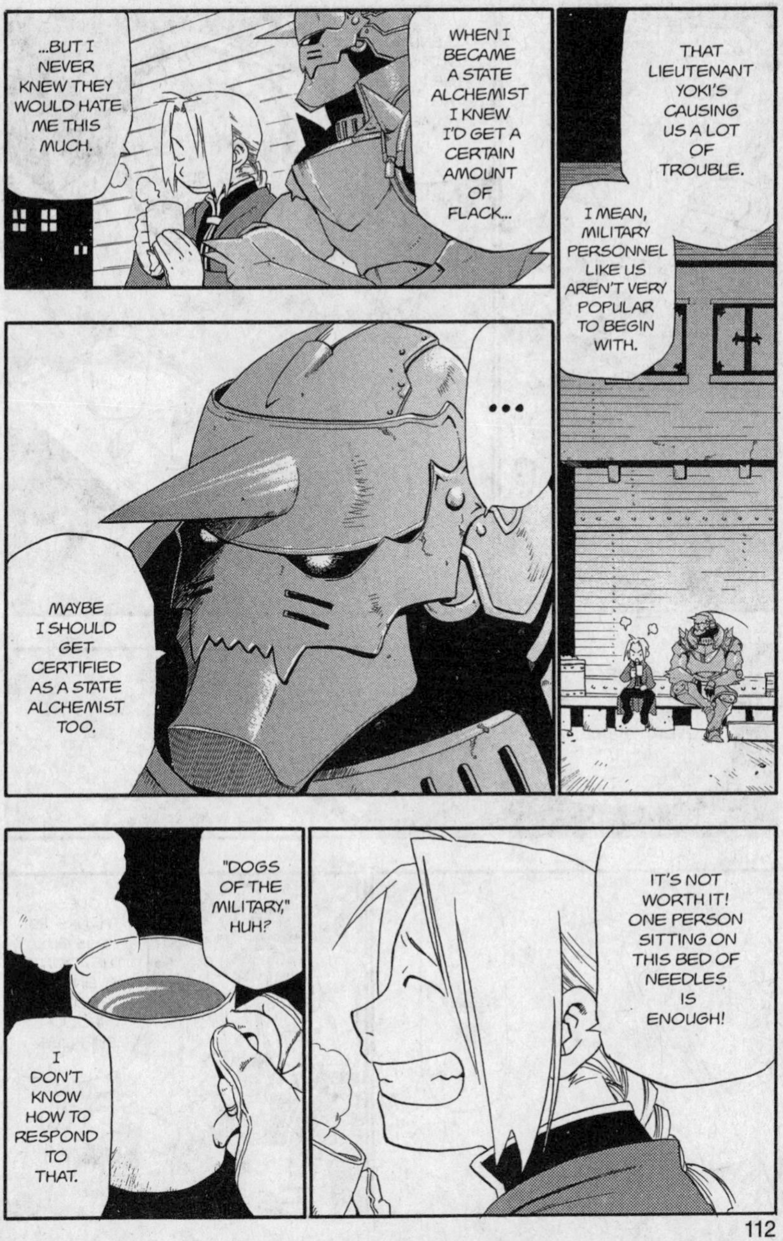
THAT LIEUTENANT YOKI'S CAUSING US A LOT OF TROUBLE.
I MEAN, MILITARY PERSONNEL LIKE US AREN'T VERY POPULAR TO BEGIN WITH.
WHEN I BECAME A STATE ALCHEMIST I KNEW I'D GET A CERTAIN AMOUNT OF FLACK...
...BUT I NEVER KNEW THEY WOULD HATE ME THIS MUCH.
...
MAYBE I SHOULD GET CERTIFIED AS A STATE ALCHEMIST TOO.
IT'S NOT WORTH IT! ONE PERSON SITTING ON THIS BED OF NEEDLES IS ENOUGH!
"DOGS OF THE MILITARY," HUH?
I DON'T KNOW HOW TO RESPOND TO THAT.

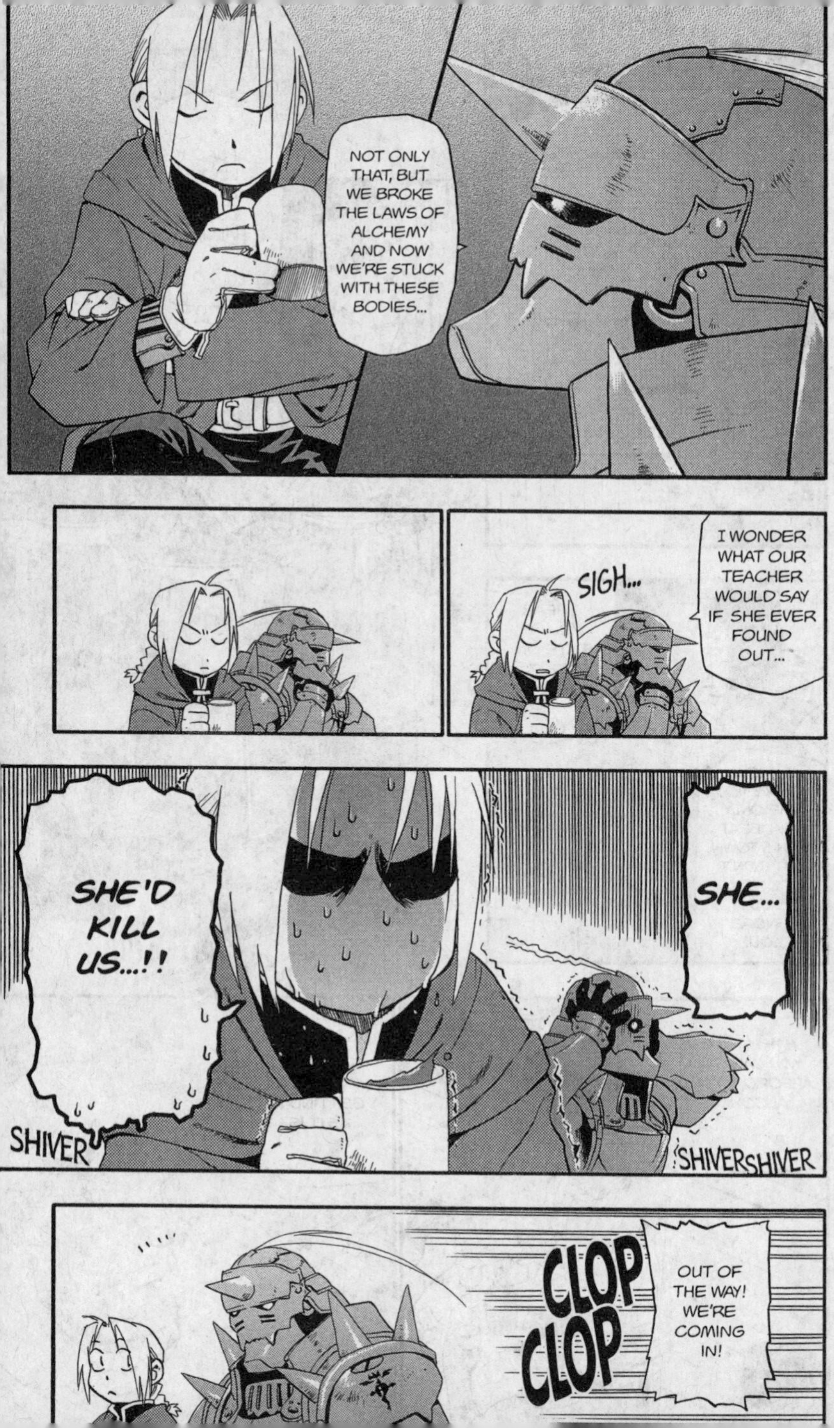
NOT ONLY THAT, BUT WE BROKE THE LAWS OF ALCHEMY AND NOW WE'RE STUCK WITH THESE BODIES...
SIGH...
I WONDER WHAT OUR TEACHER WOULD SAY IF SHE EVER FOUND OUT...
SHE...
SHIVERSHIVER
SHE'D KILL US...!!
SHIVER
OUT OF THE WAY! WE'RE COMING IN!
CLOP CLOP

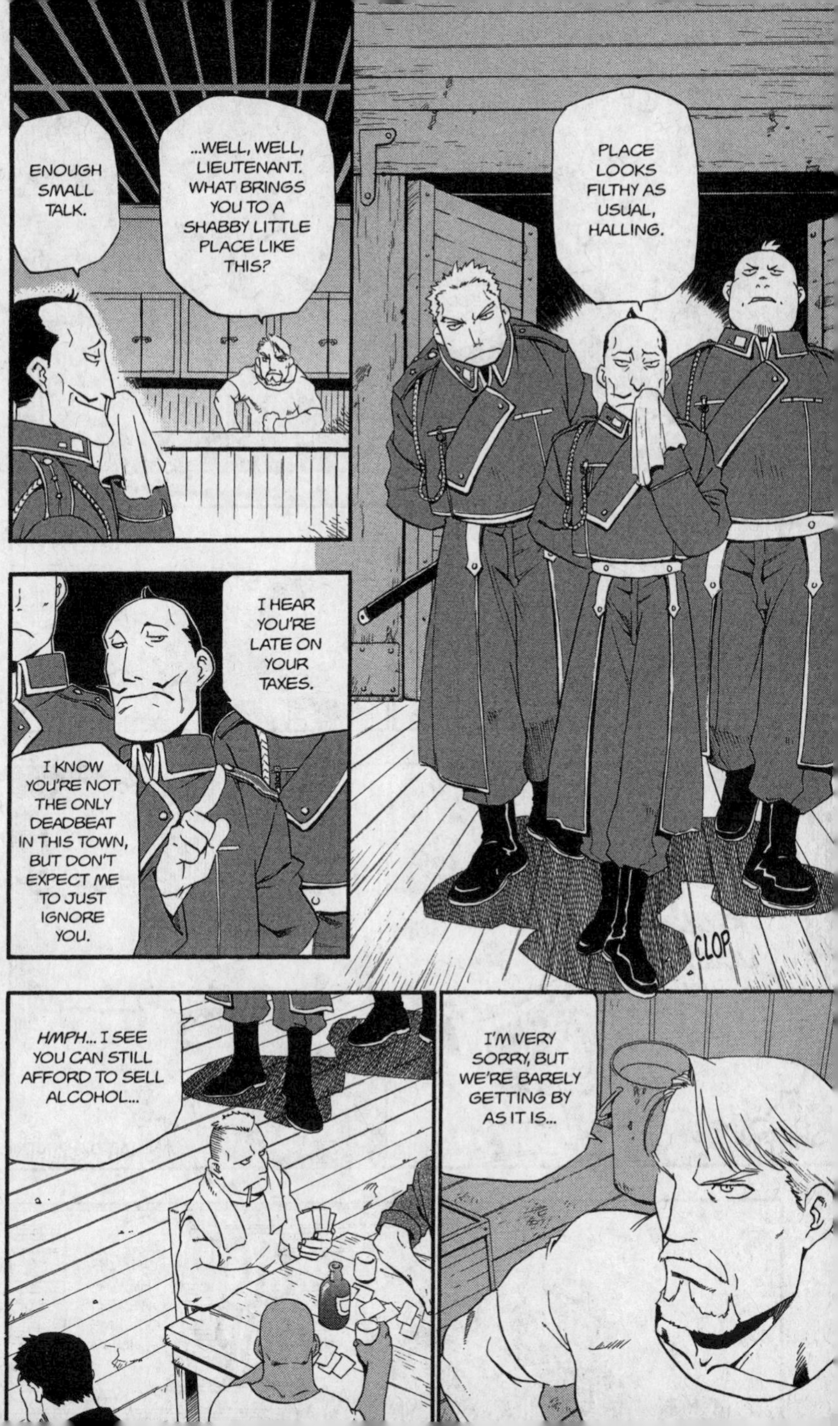
PLACE LOOKS FILTHY AS USUAL, HALLING.
CLOP
...WELL, WELL, LIEUTENANT. WHAT BRINGS YOU TO A SHABBY LITTLE PLACE LIKE THIS?
ENOUGH SMALL TALK.
I HEAR YOU'RE LATE ON YOUR TAXES.
I KNOW YOU'RE NOT THE ONLY DEADBEAT IN THIS TOWN, BUT DON'T EXPECT ME TO JUST IGNORE YOU.
I'M VERY SORRY, BUT WE'RE BARELY GETTING BY AS IT IS...
HMPH... I SEE YOU CAN STILL AFFORD TO SELL ALCOHOL...

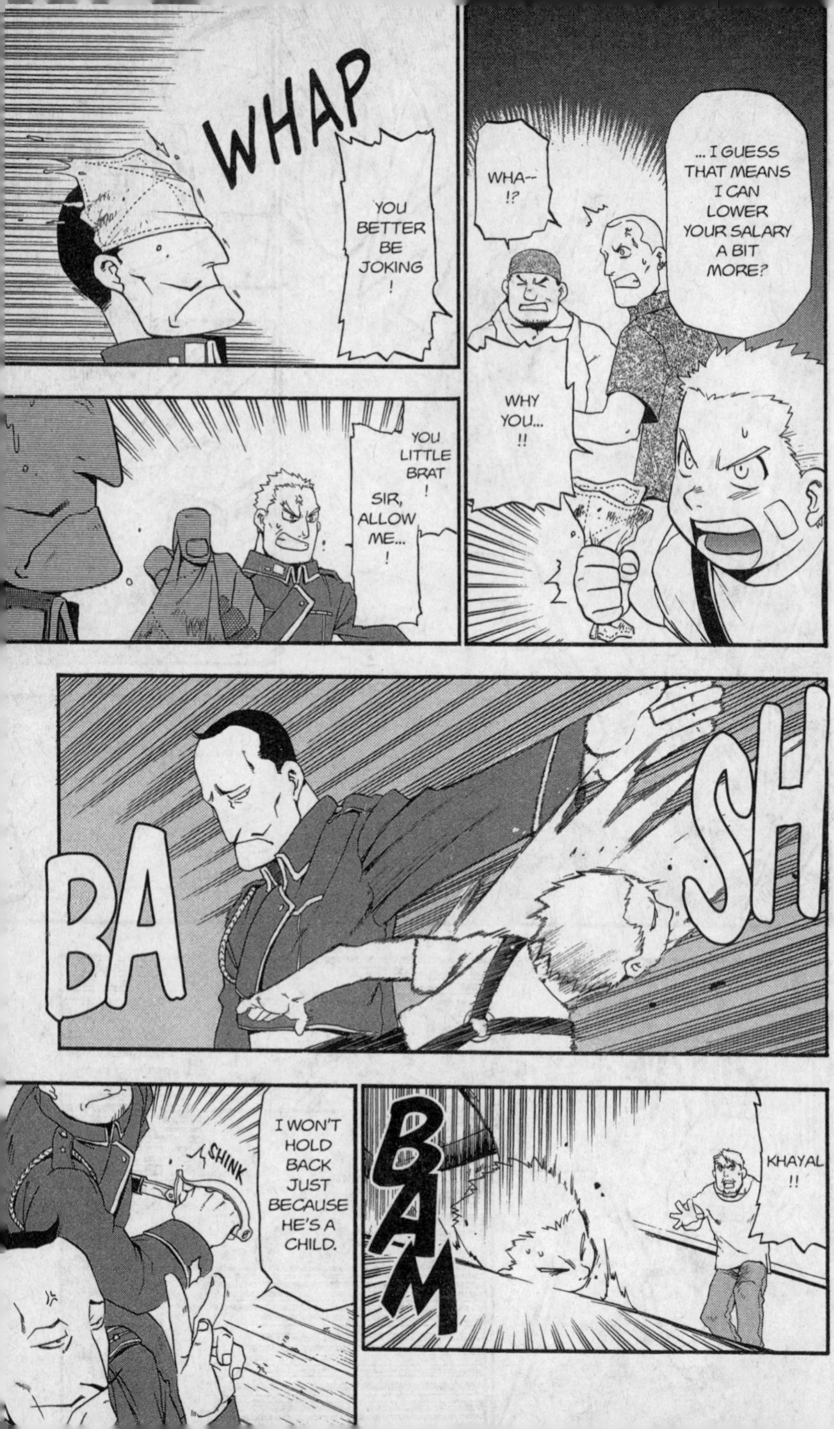
...I GUESS THAT MEANS I CAN LOWER YOUR SALARY A BIT MORE?
WHA-- !?
WHY YOU... !!
WHAP
YOU BETTER BE JOKING !
YOU LITTLE BRAT !
SIR, ALLOW ME... !
BASH
KHAYAL !!
BAM
I WON'T HOLD BACK JUST BECAUSE HE'S A CHILD.
SHINK

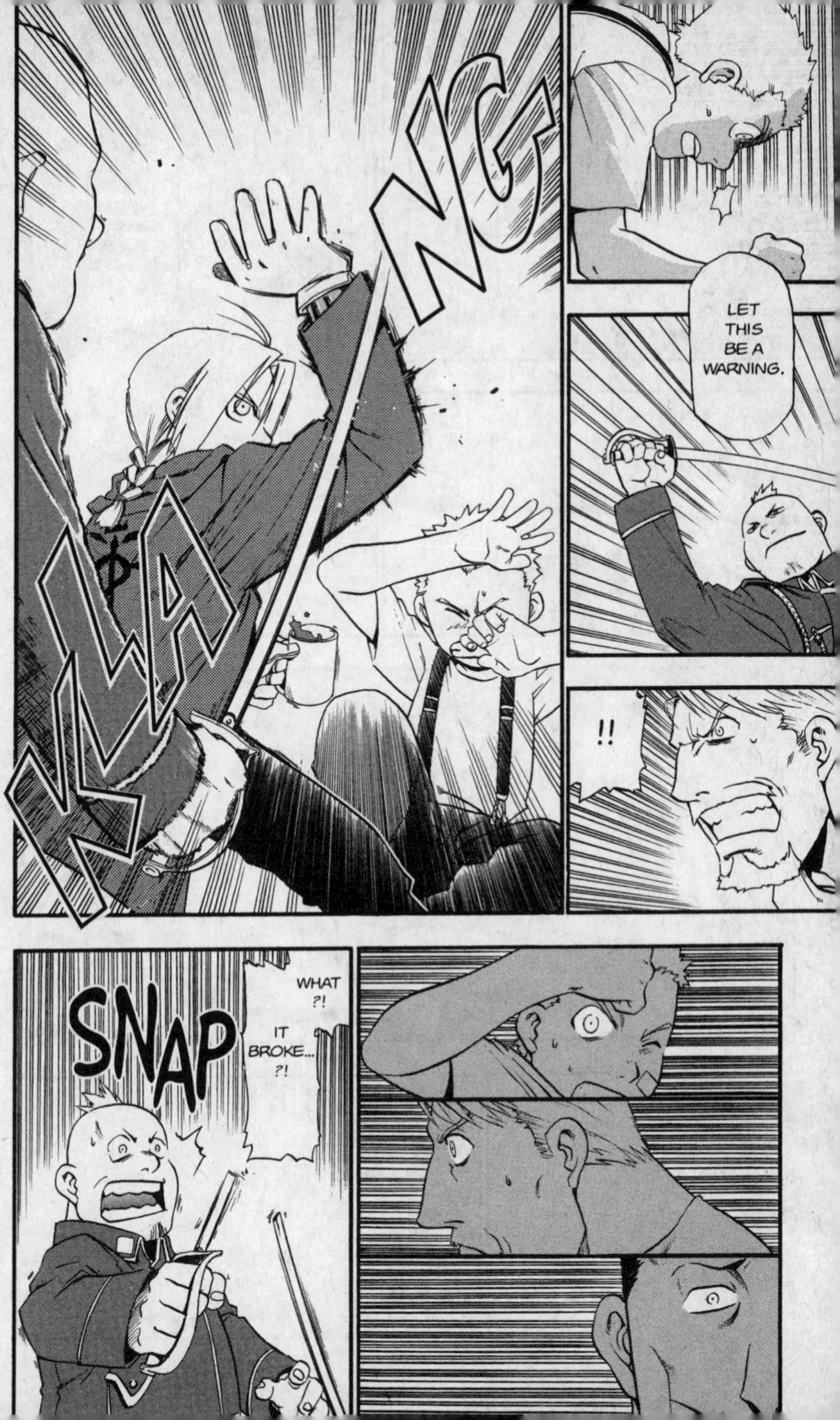
LET THIS BE A WARNING.
!!
KLANG
WHAT?!
IT BROKE...?!
SNAP

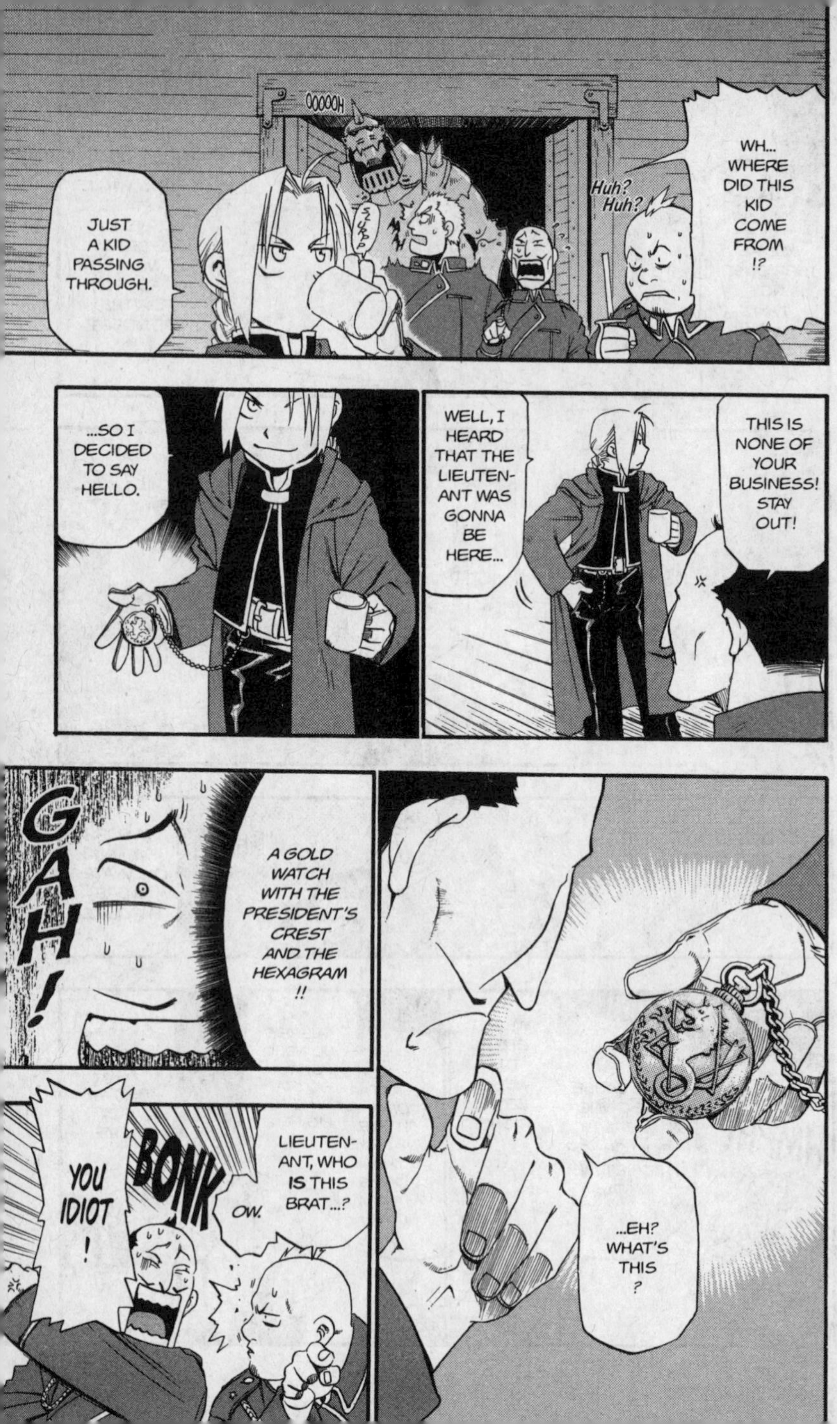
WH... WHERE DID THIS KID COME FROM !?
Huh? Huh?
SLURP
JUST A KID PASSING THROUGH.
THIS IS NONE OF YOUR BUSINESS! STAY OUT!
WELL, I HEARD THAT THE LIEUTEN-ANT WAS GONNA BE HERE...
...SO I DECIDED TO SAY HELLO.
...EH? WHAT'S THIS ?
A GOLD WATCH WITH THE PRESIDENT'S CREST AND THE HEXAGRAM !!
GAH!
LIEUTEN-ANT, WHO IS THIS BRAT...?
OW.
BONK
YOU IDIOT !

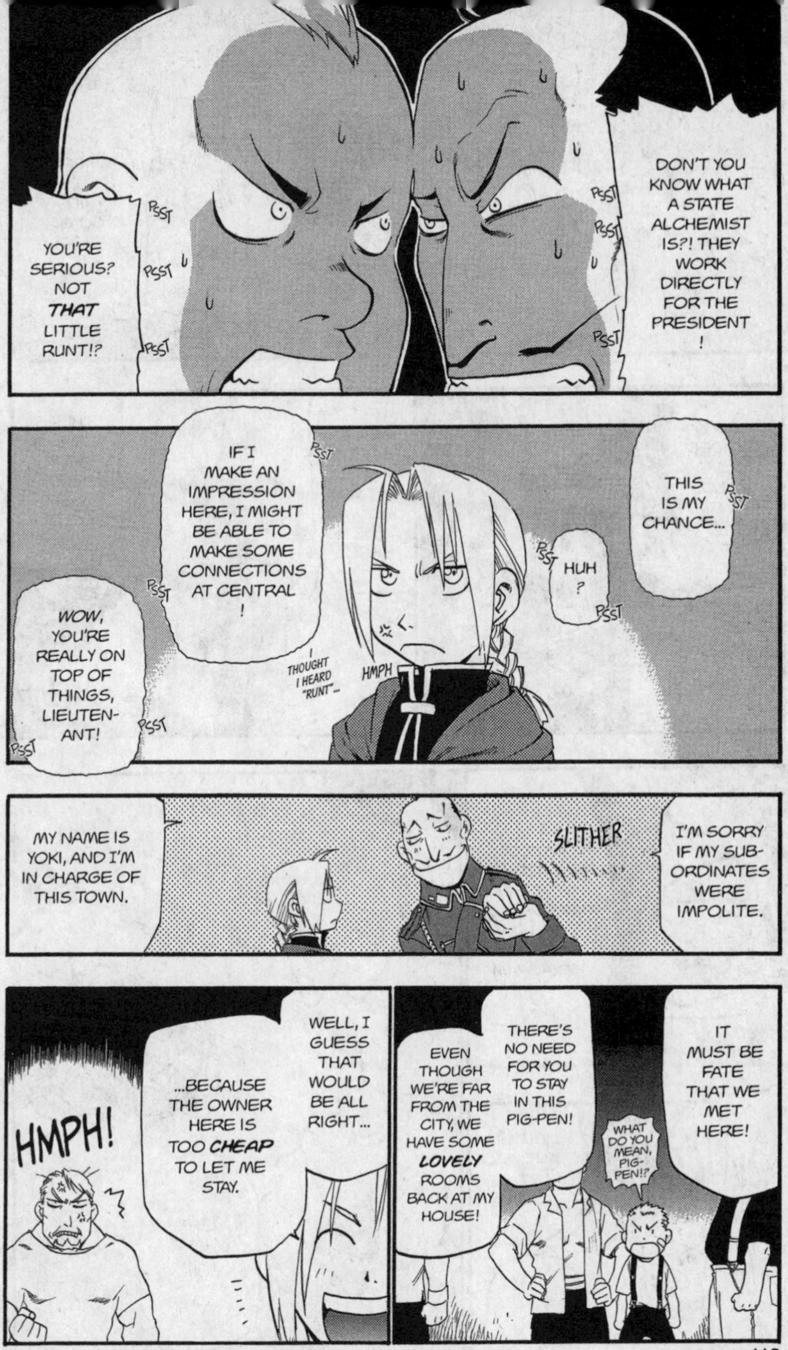
DON'T YOU KNOW WHAT A STATE ALCHEMIST IS?! THEY WORK DIRECTLY FOR THE PRESIDENT!
PSST PSST PSST
YOU'RE SERIOUS? NOT *THAT* LITTLE RUNT!?
PSST PSST PSST
THIS IS MY CHANCE...
PSST
HUH?
PSST PSST
IF I MAKE AN IMPRESSION HERE, I MIGHT BE ABLE TO MAKE SOME CONNECTIONS AT CENTRAL!
PSST PSST
I THOUGHT I HEARD "RUNT"...
HMPH
WOW, YOU'RE REALLY ON TOP OF THINGS, LIEUTENANT!
PSST PSST
I'M SORRY IF MY SUBORDINATES WERE IMPOLITE.
SLITHER
MY NAME IS YOKI, AND I'M IN CHARGE OF THIS TOWN.
IT MUST BE FATE THAT WE MET HERE!
THERE'S NO NEED FOR YOU TO STAY IN THIS PIG-PEN!
EVEN THOUGH WE'RE FAR FROM THE CITY, WE HAVE SOME ***LOVELY*** ROOMS BACK AT MY HOUSE!
WHAT DO YOU MEAN, PIG-PEN!?
WELL, I GUESS THAT WOULD BE ALL RIGHT...
...BECAUSE THE OWNER HERE IS TOO ***CHEAP*** TO LET ME STAY.
HMPH!

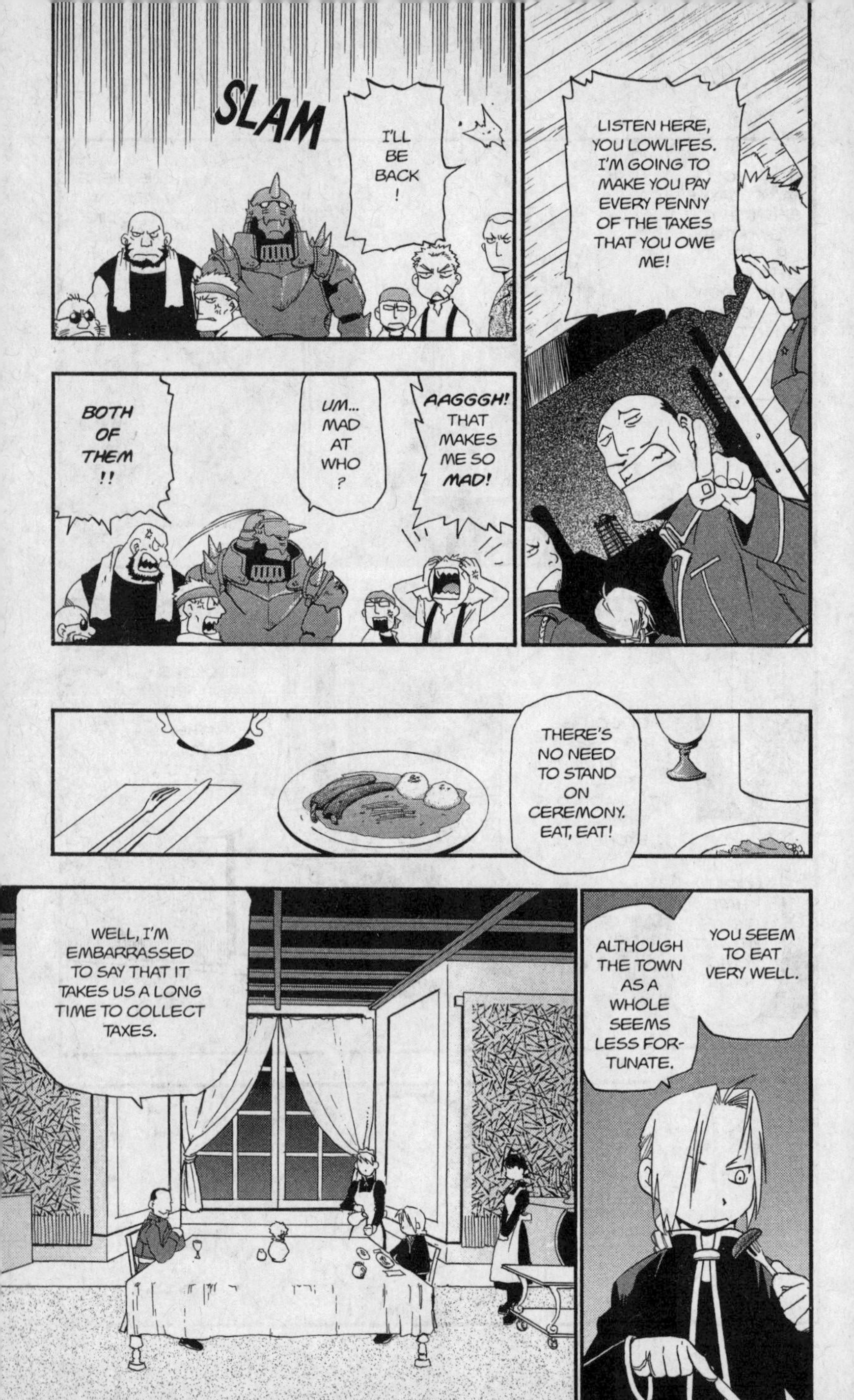
LISTEN HERE, YOU LOWLIFES. I'M GOING TO MAKE YOU PAY EVERY PENNY OF THE TAXES THAT YOU OWE ME!
I'LL BE BACK!
SLAM
AAGGGH! THAT MAKES ME SO MAD!
UM... MAD AT WHO?
BOTH OF THEM!!
THERE'S NO NEED TO STAND ON CEREMONY. EAT, EAT!
YOU SEEM TO EAT VERY WELL.
ALTHOUGH THE TOWN AS A WHOLE SEEMS LESS FOR-TUNATE.
WELL, I'M EMBARRASSED TO SAY THAT IT TAKES US A LONG TIME TO COLLECT TAXES.

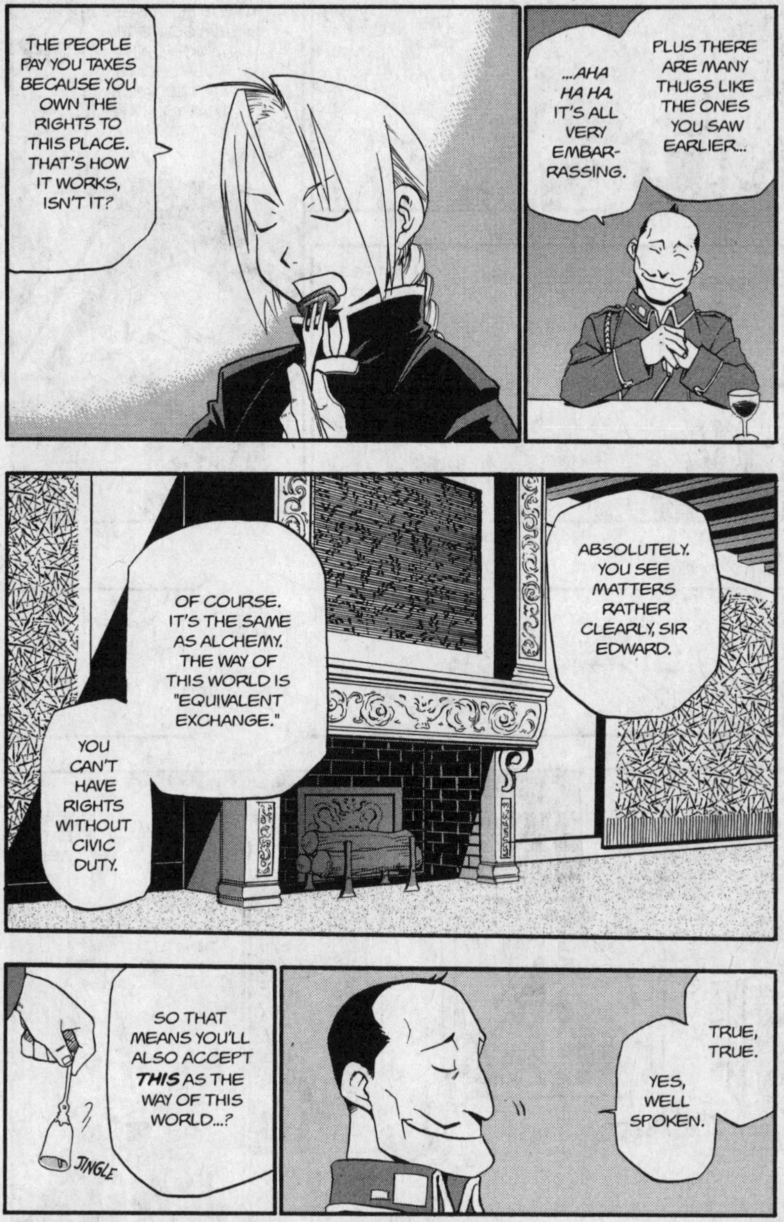
PLUS THERE ARE MANY THUGS LIKE THE ONES YOU SAW EARLIER...
...AHA HA HA. IT'S ALL VERY EMBAR-RASSING.
THE PEOPLE PAY YOU TAXES BECAUSE YOU OWN THE RIGHTS TO THIS PLACE. THAT'S HOW IT WORKS, ISN'T IT?
ABSOLUTELY. YOU SEE MATTERS RATHER CLEARLY, SIR EDWARD.
OF COURSE. IT'S THE SAME AS ALCHEMY. THE WAY OF THIS WORLD IS "EQUIVALENT EXCHANGE."
YOU CAN'T HAVE RIGHTS WITHOUT CIVIC DUTY.
TRUE, TRUE.
YES, WELL SPOKEN.
SO THAT MEANS YOU'LL ALSO ACCEPT ***THIS*** AS THE WAY OF THIS WORLD...?
JINGLE

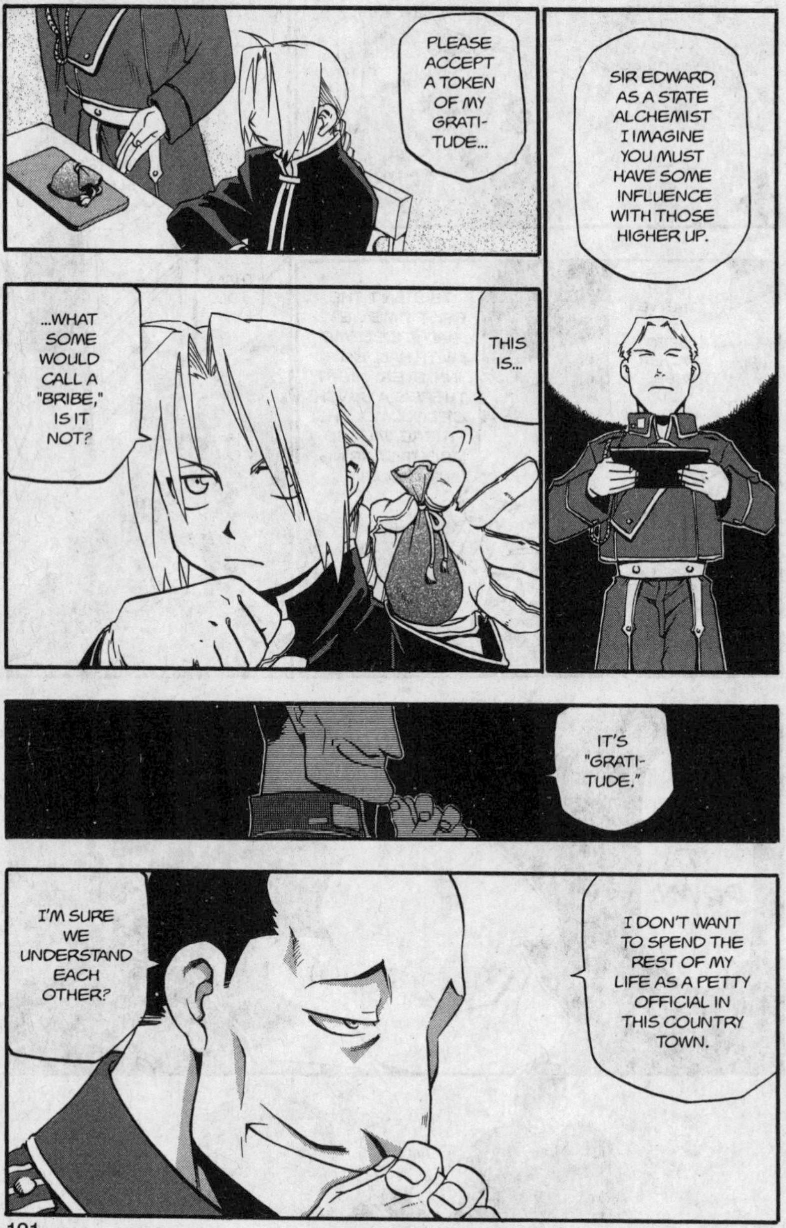
SIR EDWARD, AS A STATE ALCHEMIST I IMAGINE YOU MUST HAVE SOME INFLUENCE WITH THOSE HIGHER UP.
PLEASE ACCEPT A TOKEN OF MY GRATITUDE...
THIS IS...
...WHAT SOME WOULD CALL A "BRIBE," IS IT NOT?
IT'S "GRATITUDE."
I DON'T WANT TO SPEND THE REST OF MY LIFE AS A PETTY OFFICIAL IN THIS COUNTRY TOWN.
I'M SURE WE UNDERSTAND EACH OTHER?

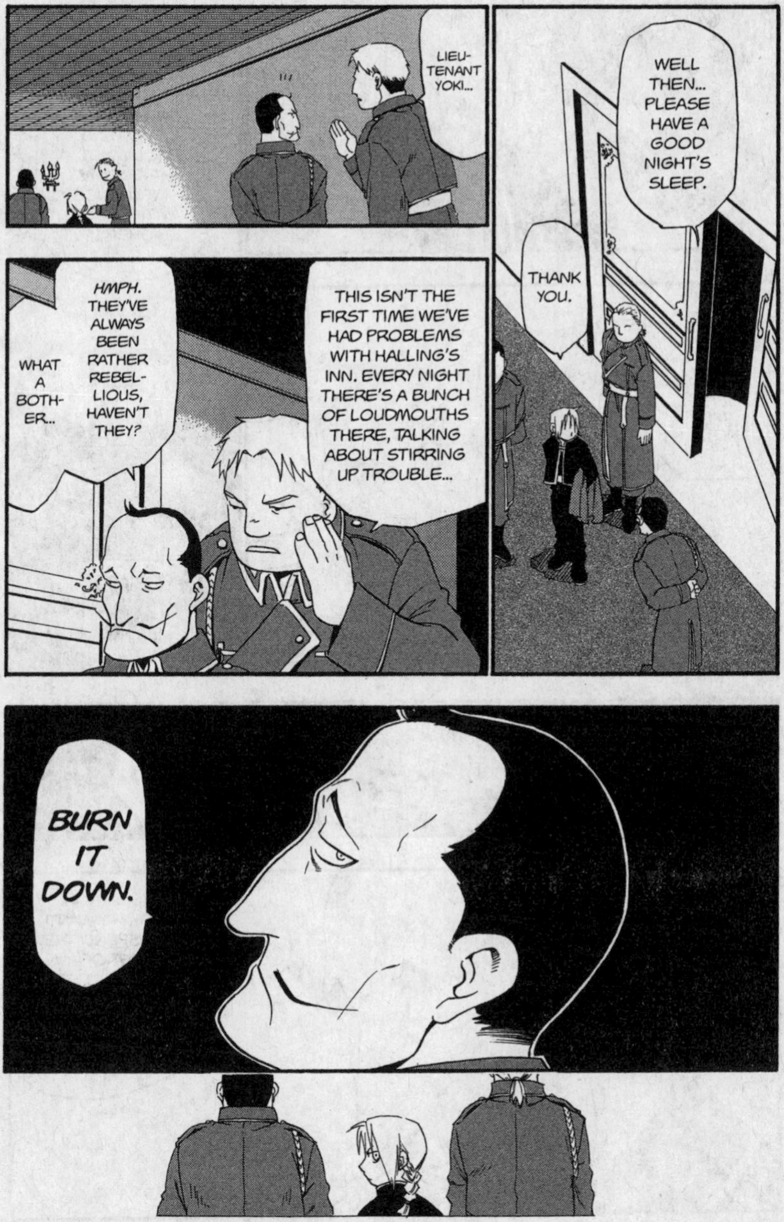
WELL THEN... PLEASE HAVE A GOOD NIGHT'S SLEEP.
THANK YOU.
LIEU-TENANT YOKI...
THIS ISN'T THE FIRST TIME WE'VE HAD PROBLEMS WITH HALLING'S INN. EVERY NIGHT THERE'S A BUNCH OF LOUDMOUTHS THERE, TALKING ABOUT STIRRING UP TROUBLE...
HMPH. THEY'VE ALWAYS BEEN RATHER REBEL-LIOUS, HAVEN'T THEY?
WHAT A BOTH-ER...
BURN IT DOWN.

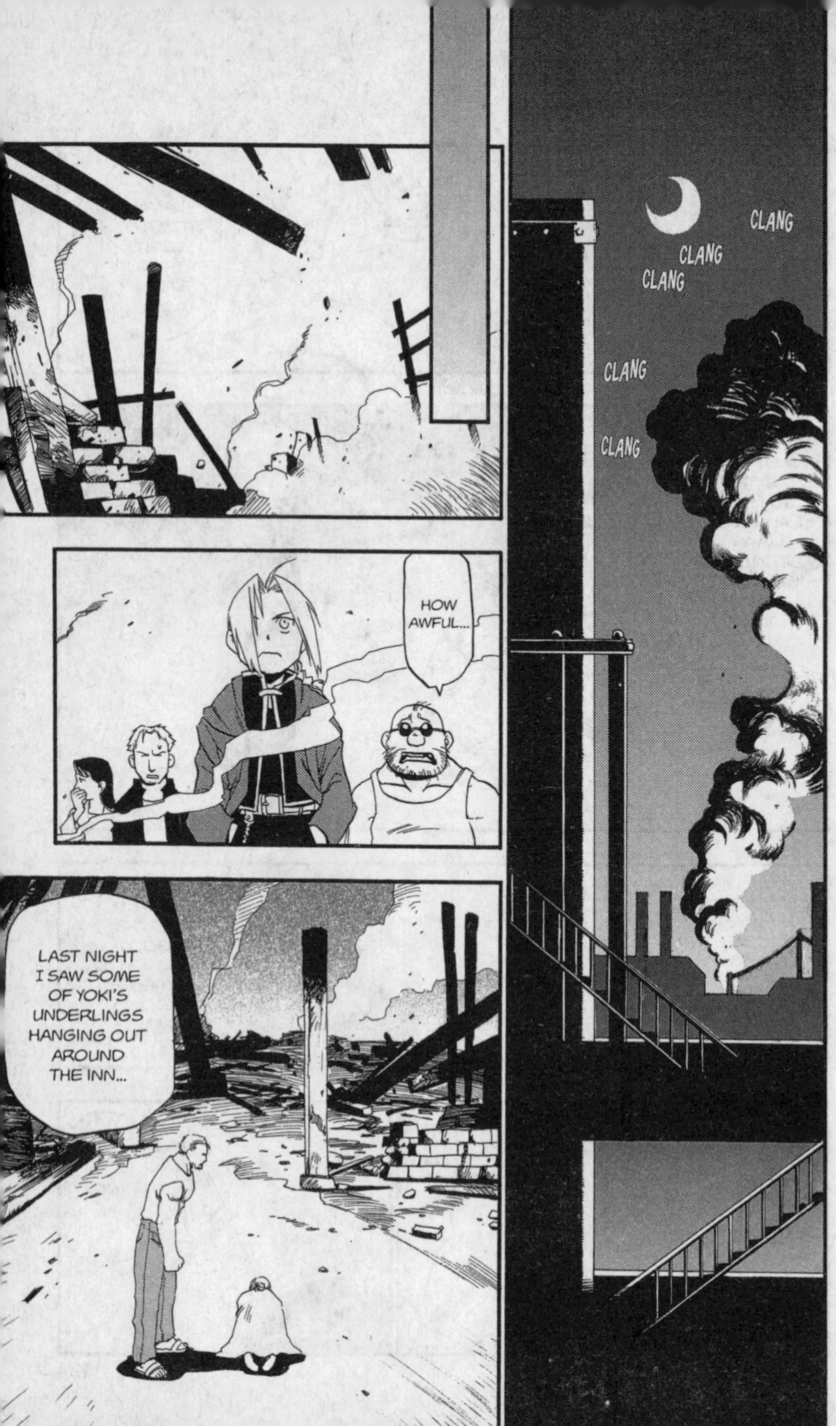
CLANG
CLANG
CLANG
CLANG
CLANG
HOW AWFUL...
LAST NIGHT I SAW SOME OF YOKI'S UNDERLINGS HANGING OUT AROUND THE INN...

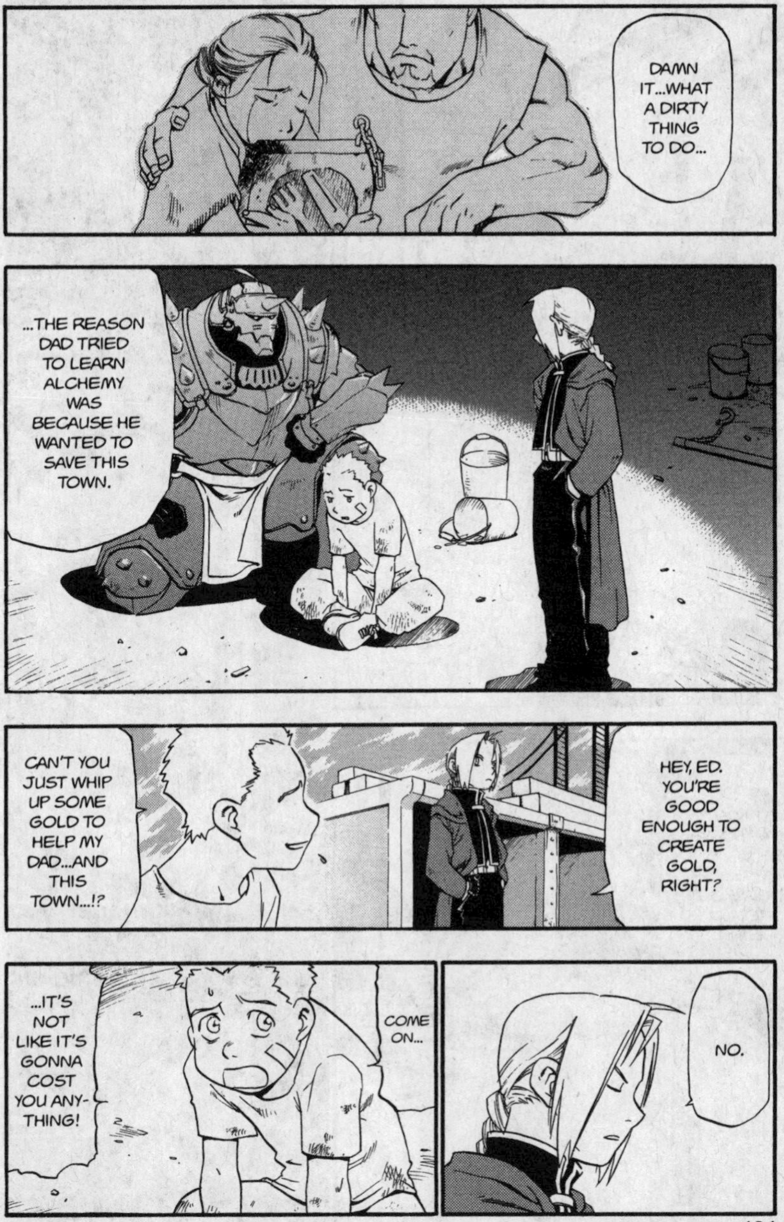
DAMN IT...WHAT A DIRTY THING TO DO...
...THE REASON DAD TRIED TO LEARN ALCHEMY WAS BECAUSE HE WANTED TO SAVE THIS TOWN.
HEY, ED. YOU'RE GOOD ENOUGH TO CREATE GOLD, RIGHT?
CAN'T YOU JUST WHIP UP SOME GOLD TO HELP MY DAD...AND THIS TOWN...!?
NO.
COME ON...
...IT'S NOT LIKE IT'S GONNA COST YOU ANY-THING!

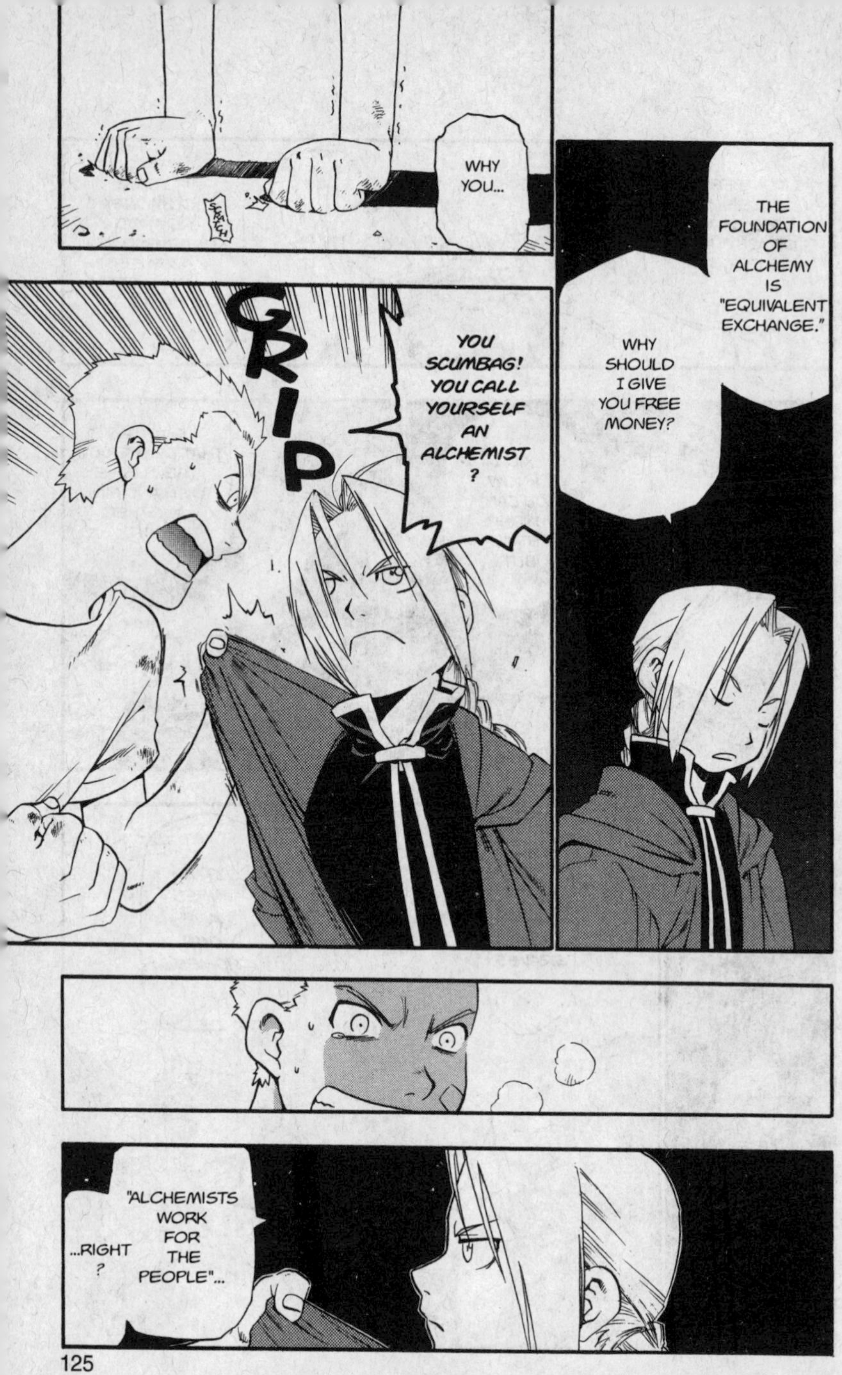
SCRATCH
WHY YOU...
THE FOUNDATION OF ALCHEMY IS "EQUIVALENT EXCHANGE."
WHY SHOULD I GIVE YOU FREE MONEY?
GRIP
YOU SCUMBAG! YOU CALL YOURSELF AN ALCHEMIST?
"ALCHEMISTS WORK FOR THE PEOPLE"...
...RIGHT?

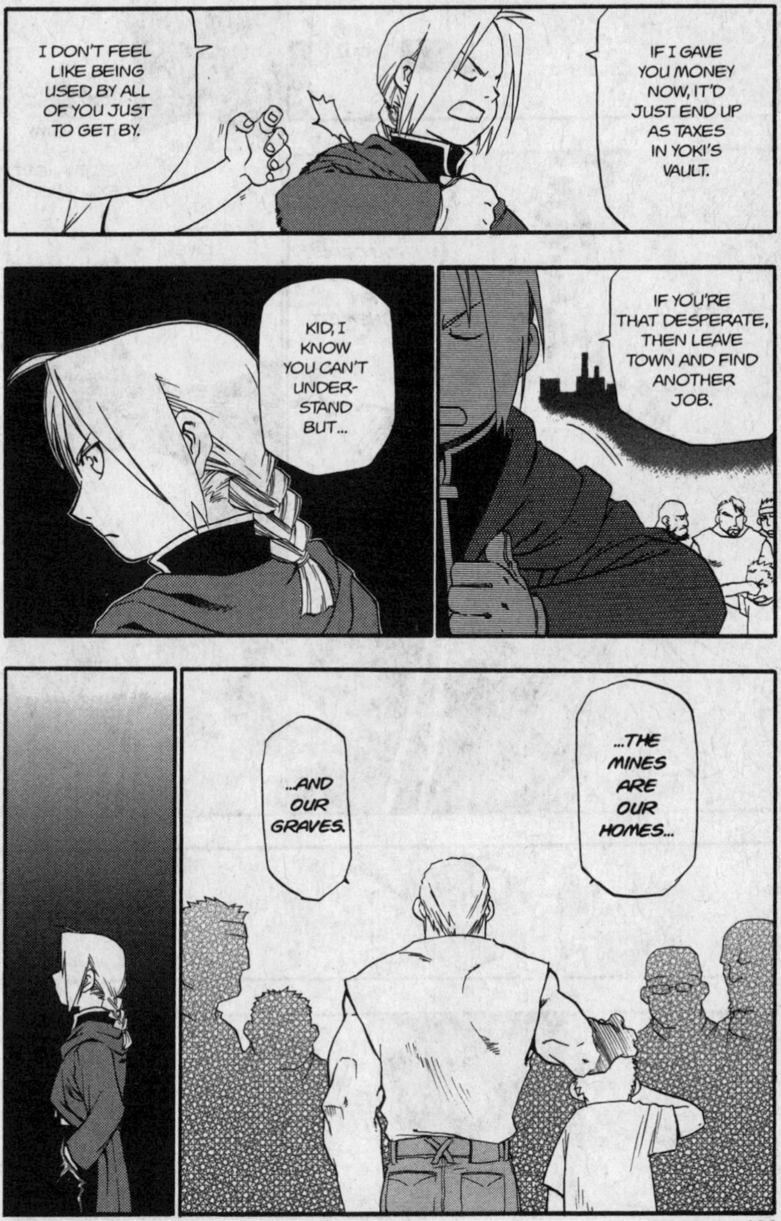
IF I GAVE YOU MONEY NOW, IT'D JUST END UP AS TAXES IN YOKI'S VAULT.
I DON'T FEEL LIKE BEING USED BY ALL OF YOU JUST TO GET BY.
IF YOU'RE THAT DESPERATE, THEN LEAVE TOWN AND FIND ANOTHER JOB.
KID, I KNOW YOU CAN'T UNDER-STAND BUT...
...THE MINES ARE OUR HOMES...
...AND OUR GRAVES.

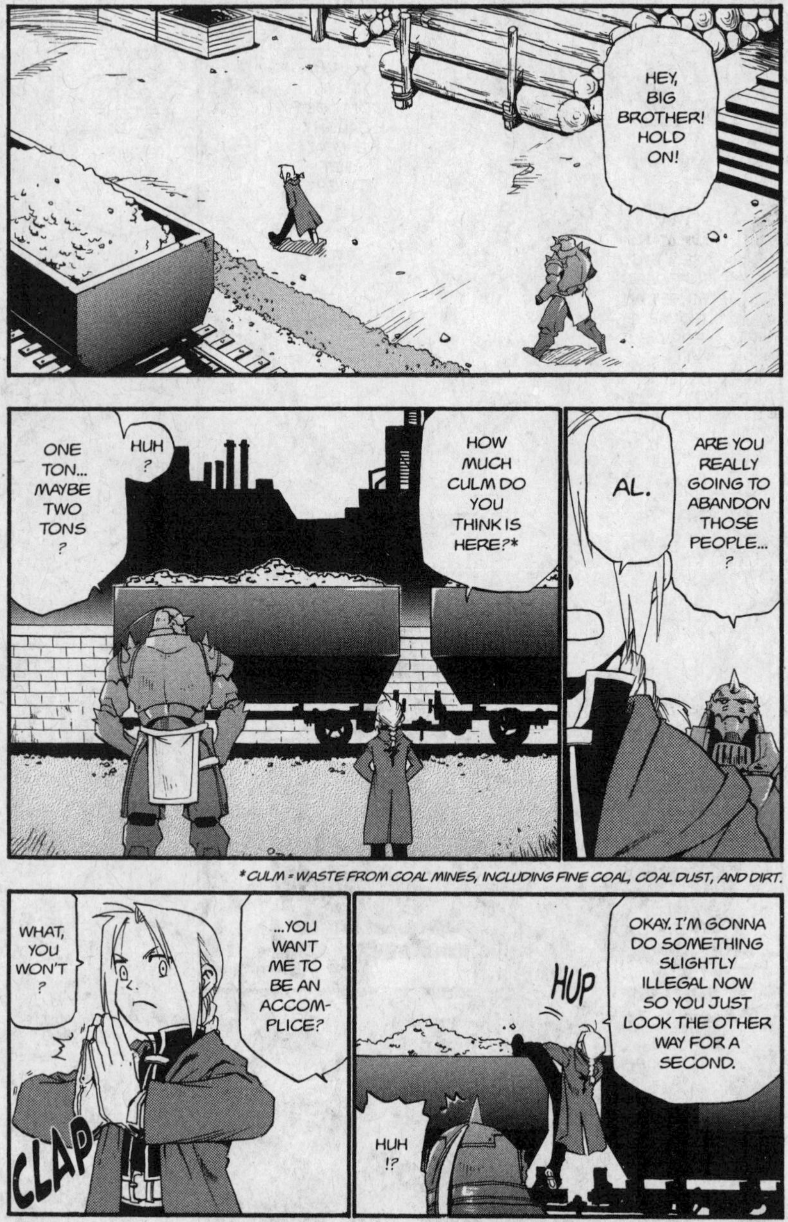
HEY, BIG BROTHER! HOLD ON!
ARE YOU REALLY GOING TO ABANDON THOSE PEOPLE...?
AL.
HOW MUCH CULM DO YOU THINK IS HERE?*
HUH?
ONE TON... MAYBE TWO TONS?
OKAY. I'M GONNA DO SOMETHING SLIGHTLY ILLEGAL NOW SO YOU JUST LOOK THE OTHER WAY FOR A SECOND.
HUP
HUH!?
...YOU WANT ME TO BE AN ACCOMPLICE?
WHAT, YOU WON'T?
CLAP

*CULM = WASTE FROM COAL MINES, INCLUDING FINE COAL, COAL DUST, AND DIRT.

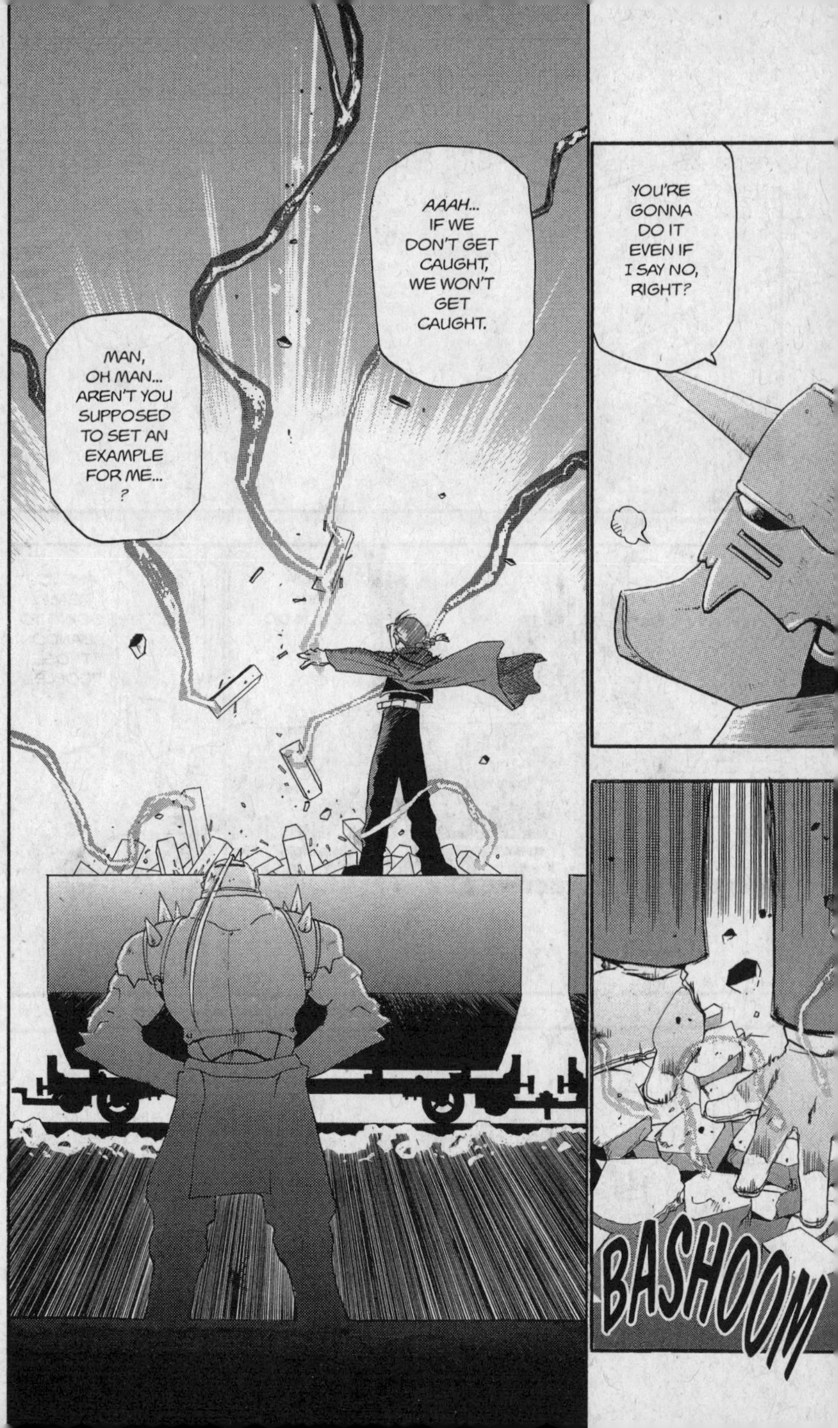
YOU'RE GONNA DO IT EVEN IF I SAY NO, RIGHT?
BASHOOM
AAAH... IF WE DON'T GET CAUGHT, WE WON'T GET CAUGHT.
MAN, OH MAN... AREN'T YOU SUPPOSED TO SET AN EXAMPLE FOR ME... ?

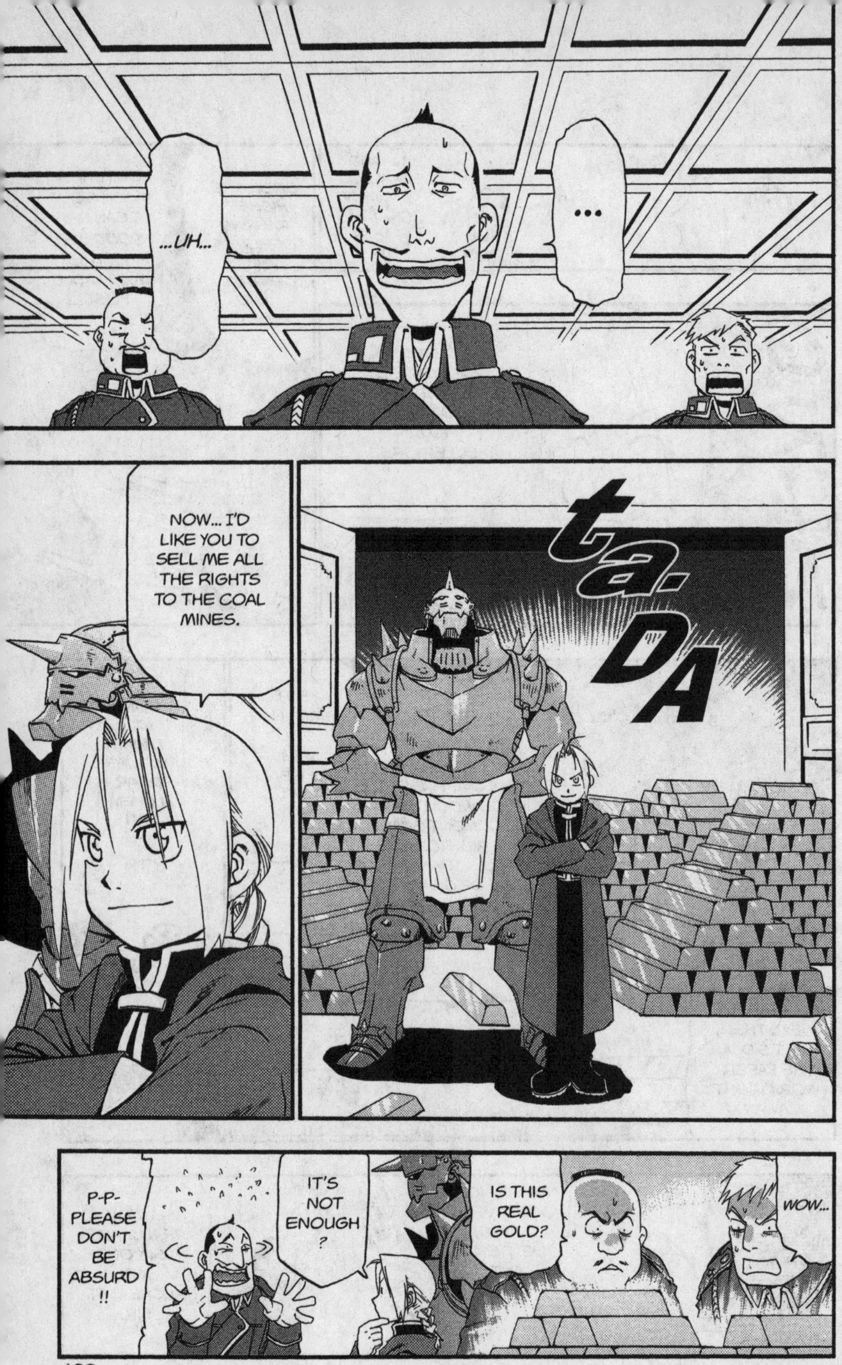
...
...UH...
ta. DA
NOW... I'D LIKE YOU TO SELL ME ALL THE RIGHTS TO THE COAL MINES.
WOW...
IS THIS REAL GOLD?
IT'S NOT ENOUGH?
P-P-PLEASE DON'T BE ABSURD!!

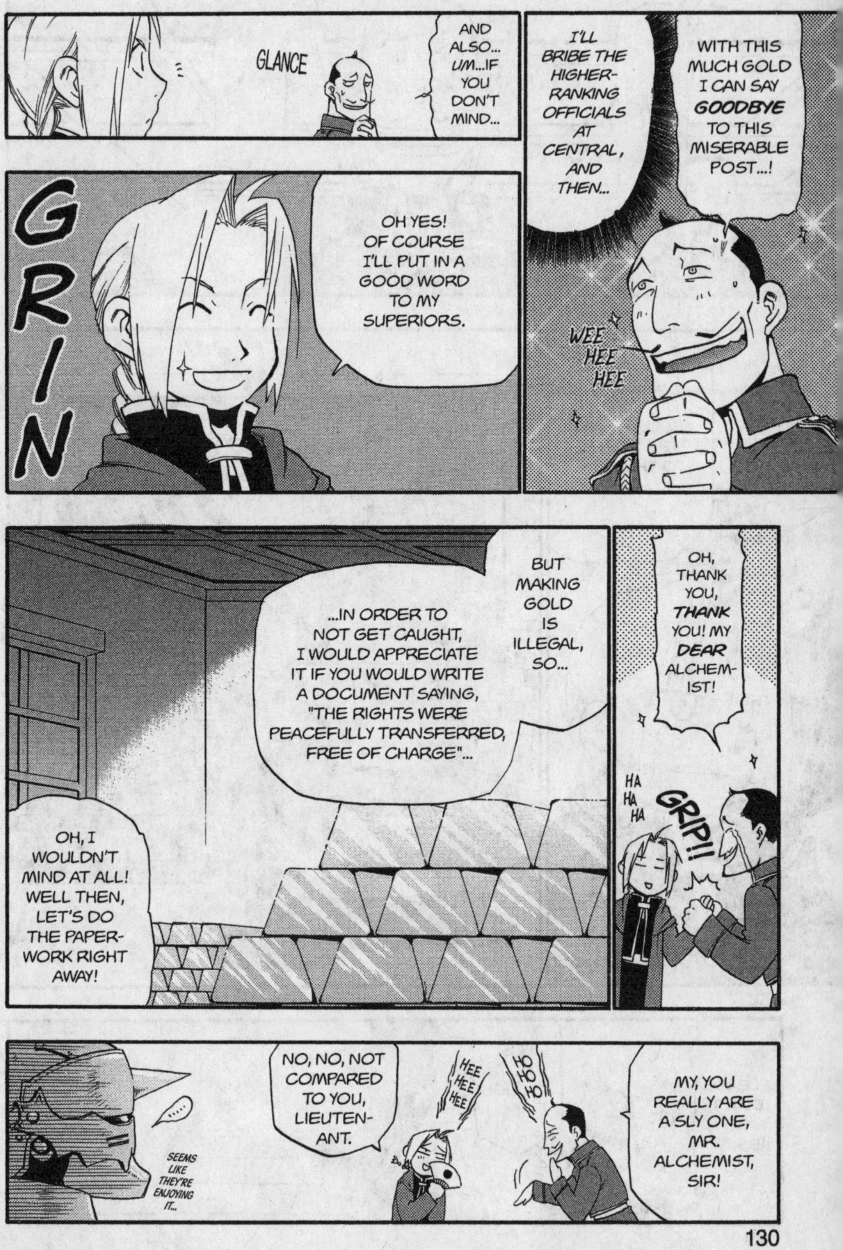
WITH THIS MUCH GOLD I CAN SAY **GOODBYE** TO THIS MISERABLE POST...!
I'LL BRIBE THE HIGHER-RANKING OFFICIALS AT CENTRAL, AND THEN...
WEE HEE HEE
GLANCE
AND ALSO... UM...IF YOU DON'T MIND...
GRIN
OH YES! OF COURSE I'LL PUT IN A GOOD WORD TO MY SUPERIORS.
OH, THANK YOU, **THANK** YOU! MY **DEAR** ALCHEMIST!
HA HA HA
GRIP!!
BUT MAKING GOLD IS ILLEGAL, SO...
...IN ORDER TO NOT GET CAUGHT, I WOULD APPRECIATE IT IF YOU WOULD WRITE A DOCUMENT SAYING, "THE RIGHTS WERE PEACEFULLY TRANSFERRED, FREE OF CHARGE"...
OH, I WOULDN'T MIND AT ALL! WELL THEN, LET'S DO THE PAPER-WORK RIGHT AWAY!
MY, YOU REALLY ARE A SLY ONE, MR. ALCHEMIST, SIR!
HO HO HO
HEE HEE HEE
NO, NO, NOT COMPARED TO YOU, LIEUTEN-ANT.
.....
SEEMS LIKE THEY'RE ENJOYING IT...

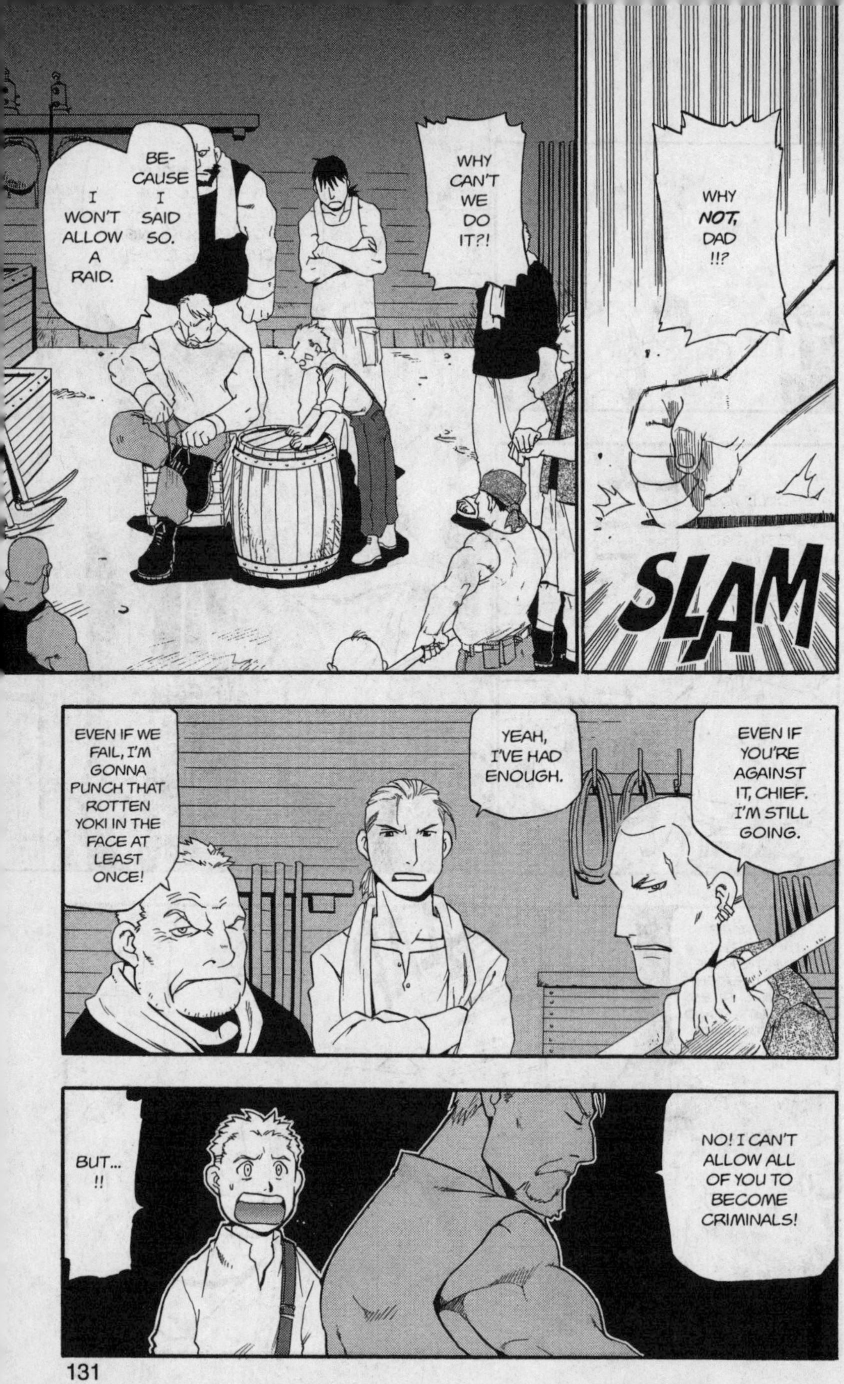
WHY NOT, DAD!!?
SLAM
WHY CAN'T WE DO IT?!
BE-CAUSE I SAID SO.
I WON'T ALLOW A RAID.
EVEN IF YOU'RE AGAINST IT, CHIEF. I'M STILL GOING.
YEAH, I'VE HAD ENOUGH.
EVEN IF WE FAIL, I'M GONNA PUNCH THAT ROTTEN YOKI IN THE FACE AT LEAST ONCE!
NO! I CAN'T ALLOW ALL OF YOU TO BECOME CRIMINALS!
BUT... !!

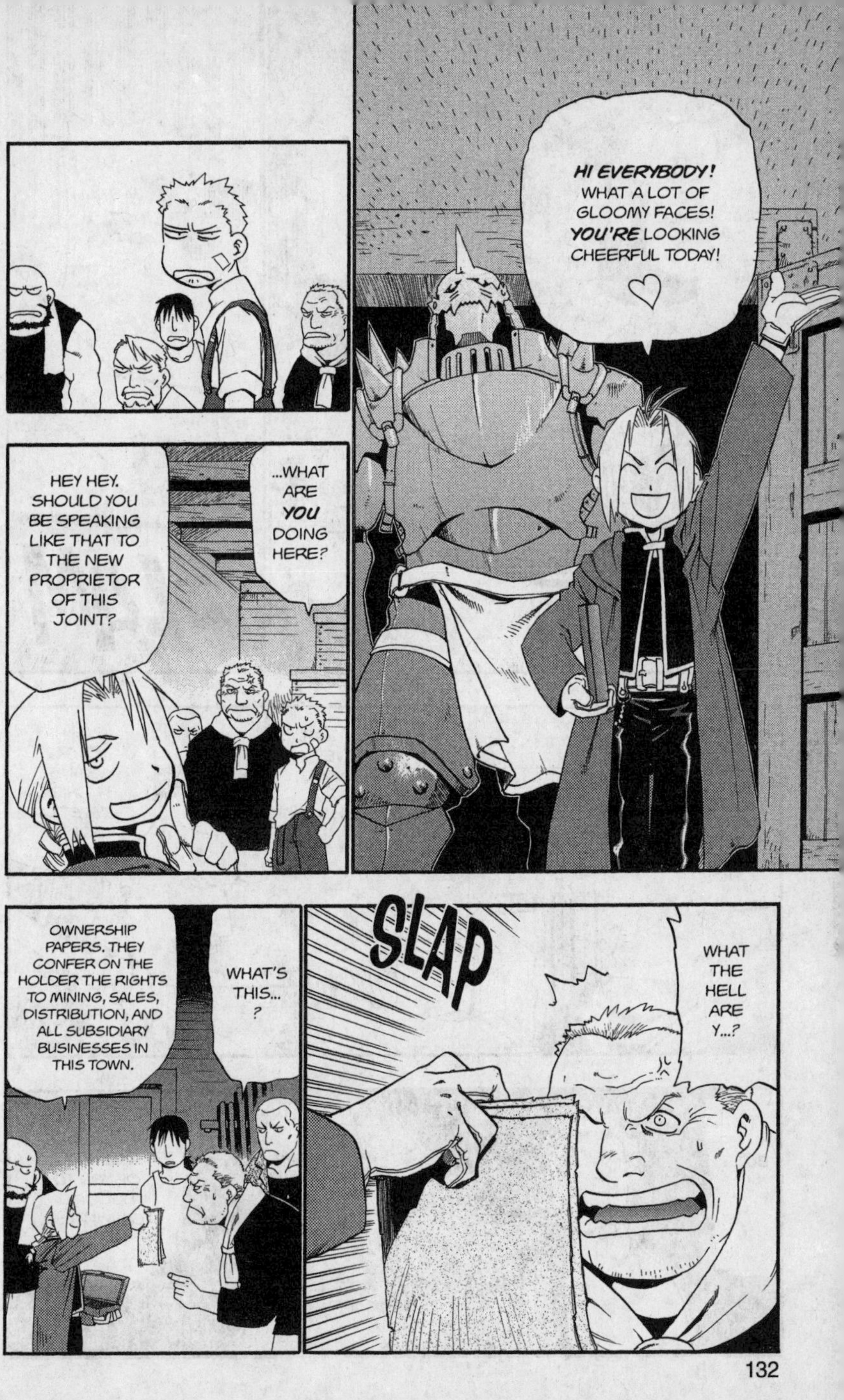
HI EVERYBODY! WHAT A LOT OF GLOOMY FACES! YOU'RE LOOKING CHEERFUL TODAY! ♡
...WHAT ARE YOU DOING HERE?
HEY HEY. SHOULD YOU BE SPEAKING LIKE THAT TO THE NEW PROPRIETOR OF THIS JOINT?
SLAP
WHAT THE HELL ARE Y...?
WHAT'S THIS...?
OWNERSHIP PAPERS. THEY CONFER ON THE HOLDER THE RIGHTS TO MINING, SALES, DISTRIBUTION, AND ALL SUBSIDIARY BUSINESSES IN THIS TOWN.

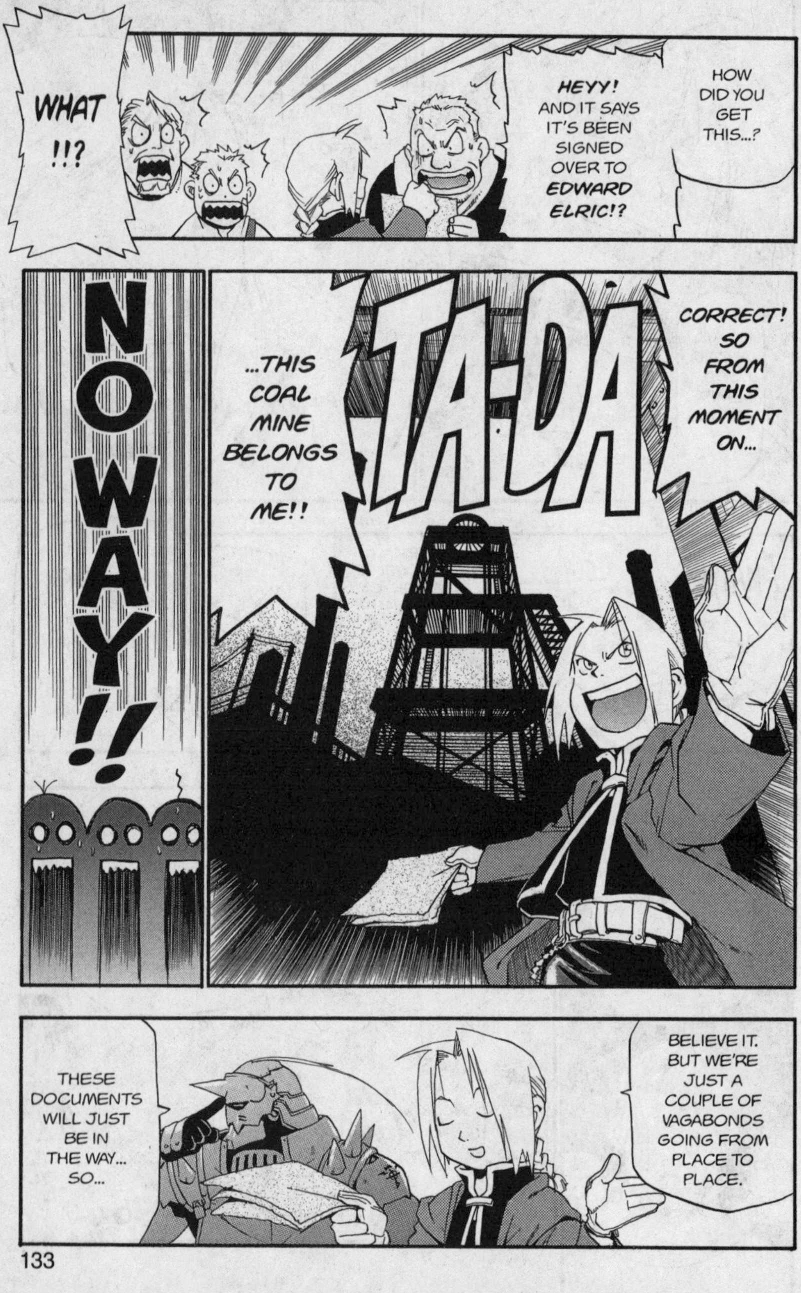
HOW DID YOU GET THIS...?
HEYY! AND IT SAYS IT'S BEEN SIGNED OVER TO EDWARD ELRIC!?
WHAT !!?
CORRECT! SO FROM THIS MOMENT ON...
TA-DA
...THIS COAL MINE BELONGS TO ME!!
NO WAY!!
BELIEVE IT. BUT WE'RE JUST A COUPLE OF VAGABONDS GOING FROM PLACE TO PLACE.
THESE DOCUMENTS WILL JUST BE IN THE WAY... SO...

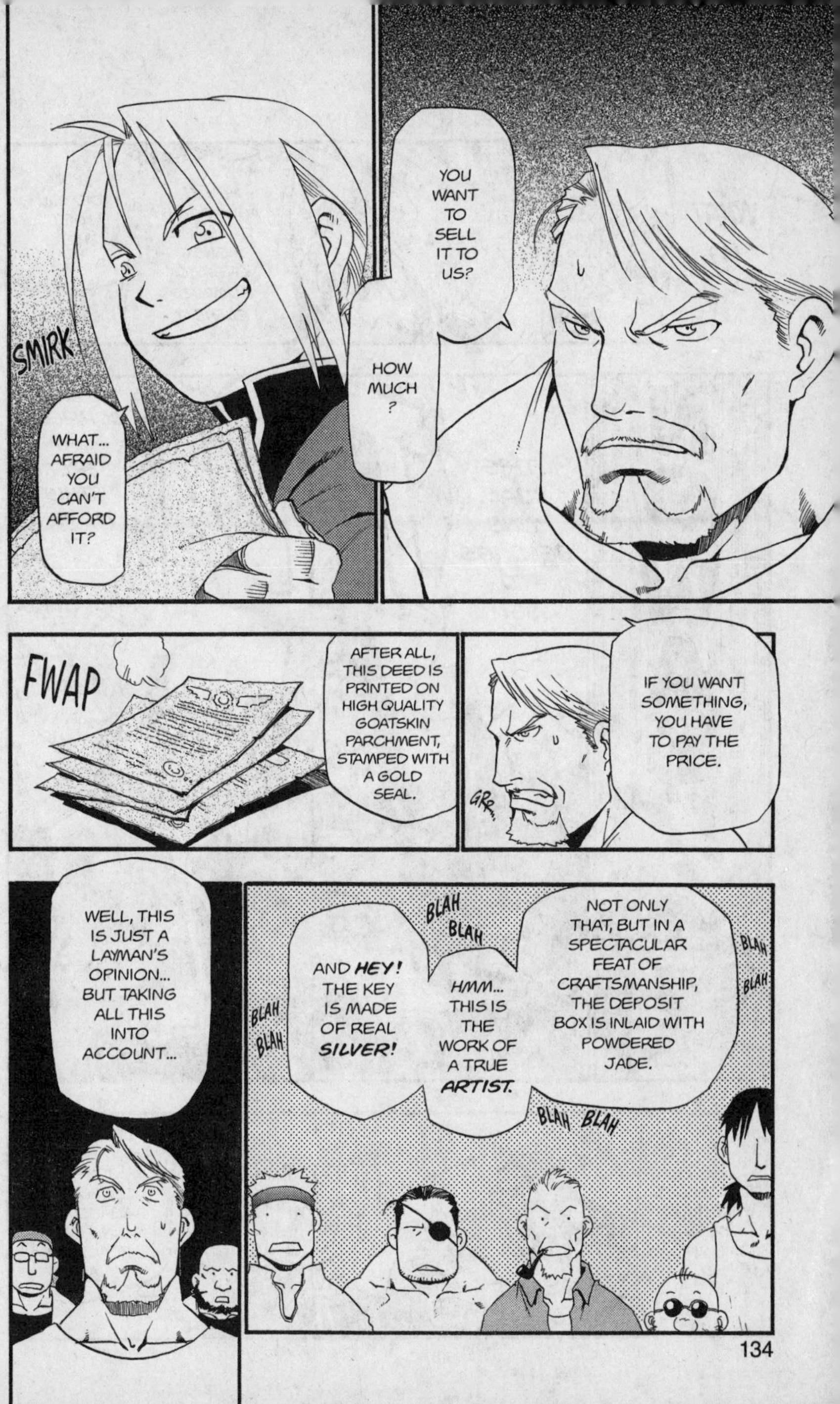
YOU WANT TO SELL IT TO US?
HOW MUCH?
SMIRK
WHAT... AFRAID YOU CAN'T AFFORD IT?
GRR
IF YOU WANT SOMETHING, YOU HAVE TO PAY THE PRICE.
AFTER ALL, THIS DEED IS PRINTED ON HIGH QUALITY GOATSKIN PARCHMENT, STAMPED WITH A GOLD SEAL.
FWAP
BLAH BLAH
NOT ONLY THAT, BUT IN A SPECTACULAR FEAT OF CRAFTSMANSHIP, THE DEPOSIT BOX IS INLAID WITH POWDERED JADE.
BLAH BLAH
HMM... THIS IS THE WORK OF A TRUE ARTIST.
AND HEY! THE KEY IS MADE OF REAL SILVER!
BLAH BLAH
BLAH BLAH
WELL, THIS IS JUST A LAYMAN'S OPINION... BUT TAKING ALL THIS INTO ACCOUNT...

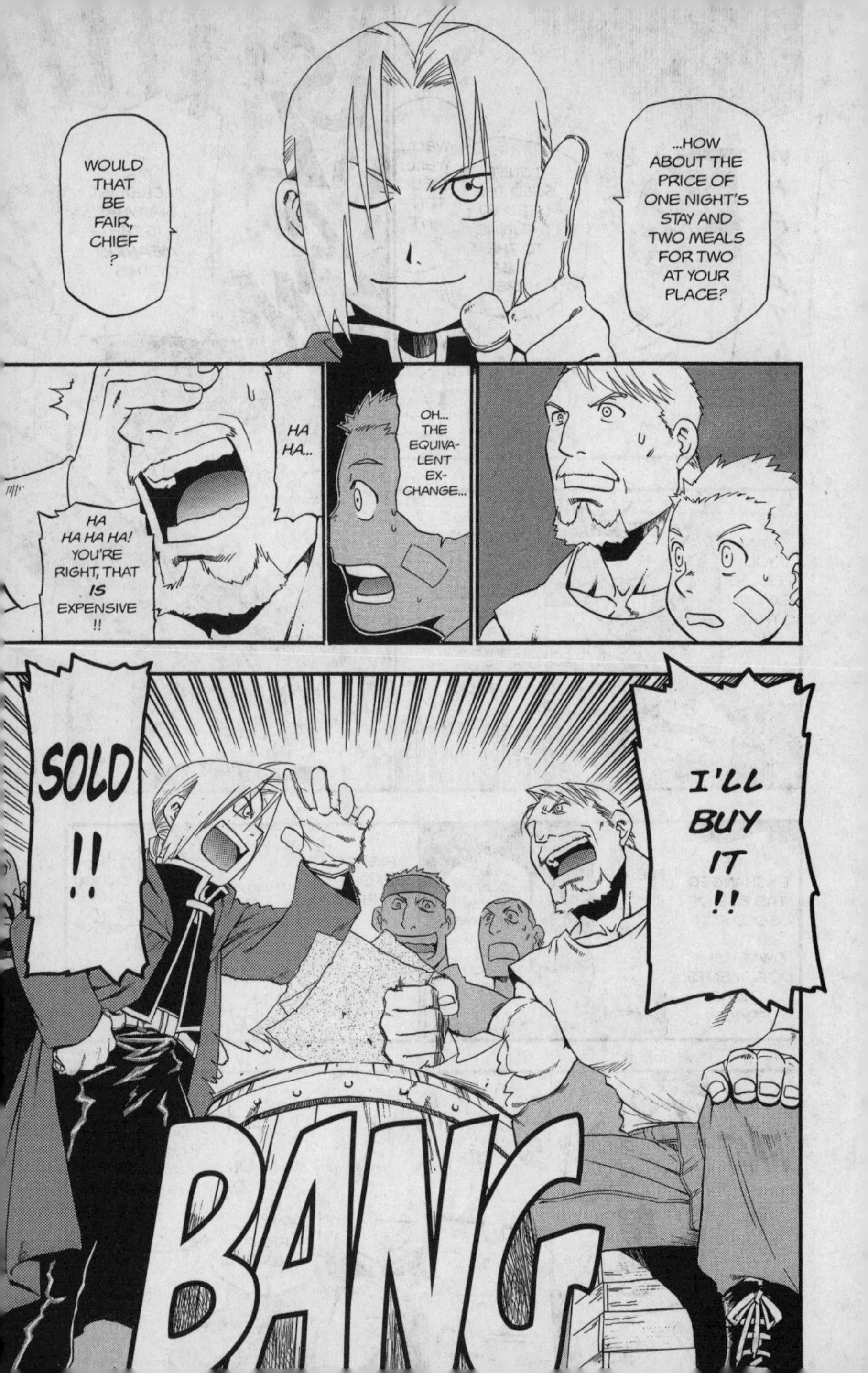
...HOW ABOUT THE PRICE OF ONE NIGHT'S STAY AND TWO MEALS FOR TWO AT YOUR PLACE?
WOULD THAT BE FAIR, CHIEF?
OH... THE EQUIVALENT EXCHANGE...
HA HA...
HA HA HA HA! YOU'RE RIGHT, THAT IS EXPENSIVE!!
I'LL BUY IT!!
SOLD!!
BANG

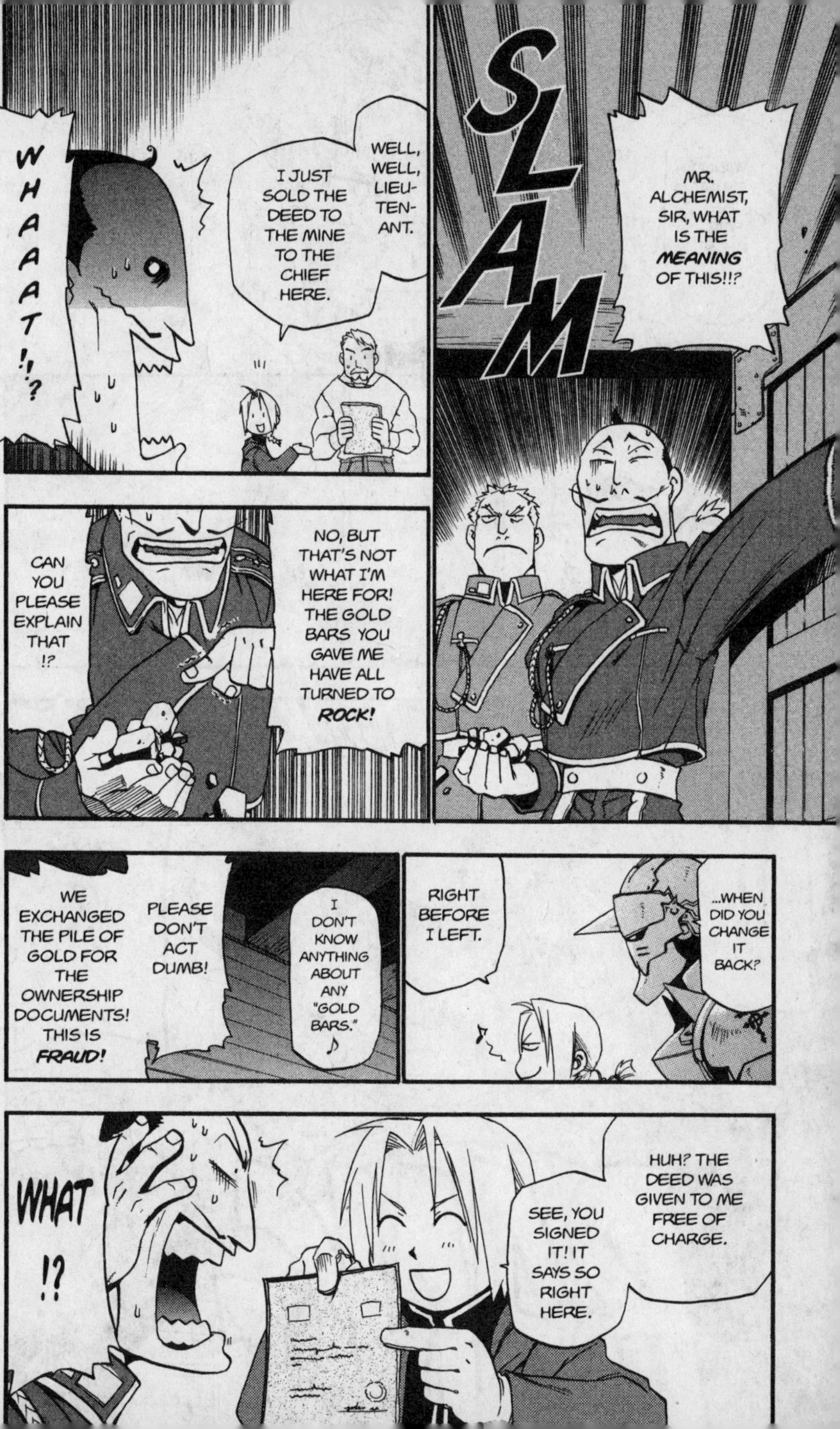
SLAM
MR. ALCHEMIST, SIR, WHAT IS THE MEANING OF THIS!!?
WELL, WELL, LIEUTENANT.
I JUST SOLD THE DEED TO THE MINE TO THE CHIEF HERE.
WHAAAAT!!?
NO, BUT THAT'S NOT WHAT I'M HERE FOR! THE GOLD BARS YOU GAVE ME HAVE ALL TURNED TO ROCK!
CAN YOU PLEASE EXPLAIN THAT!?
...WHEN DID YOU CHANGE IT BACK?
RIGHT BEFORE I LEFT.
I DON'T KNOW ANYTHING ABOUT ANY "GOLD BARS." ♪
PLEASE DON'T ACT DUMB!
WE EXCHANGED THE PILE OF GOLD FOR THE OWNERSHIP DOCUMENTS! THIS IS FRAUD!
HUH? THE DEED WAS GIVEN TO ME FREE OF CHARGE.
SEE, YOU SIGNED IT! IT SAYS SO RIGHT HERE.
WHAT!?

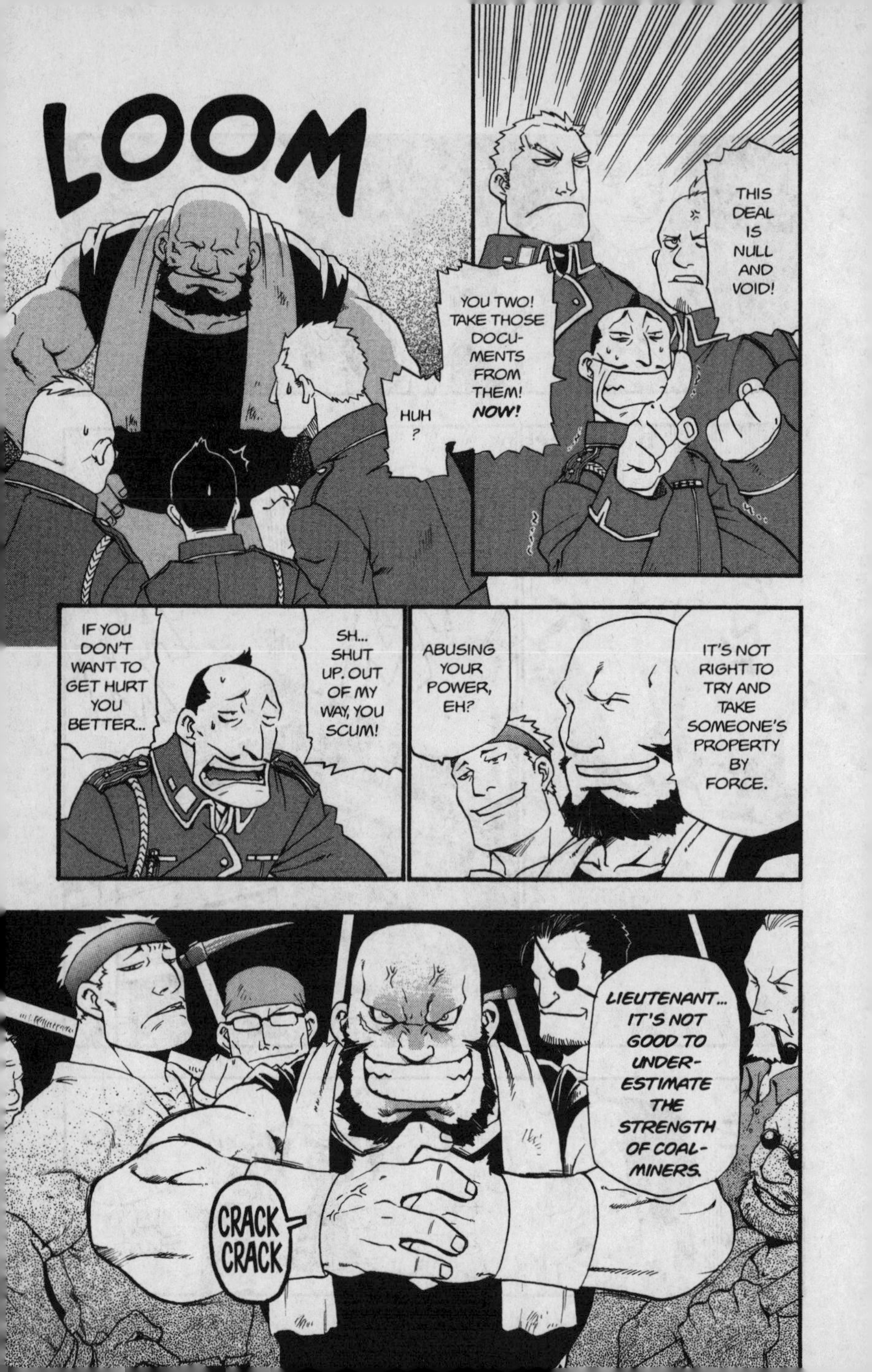
THIS DEAL IS NULL AND VOID!
YOU TWO! TAKE THOSE DOCU-MENTS FROM THEM! NOW!
LOOM
HUH ?
IT'S NOT RIGHT TO TRY AND TAKE SOMEONE'S PROPERTY BY FORCE.
ABUSING YOUR POWER, EH?
SH... SHUT UP. OUT OF MY WAY, YOU SCUM!
IF YOU DON'T WANT TO GET HURT YOU BETTER...
LIEUTENANT... IT'S NOT GOOD TO UNDER-ESTIMATE THE STRENGTH OF COAL-MINERS.
CRACK CRACK

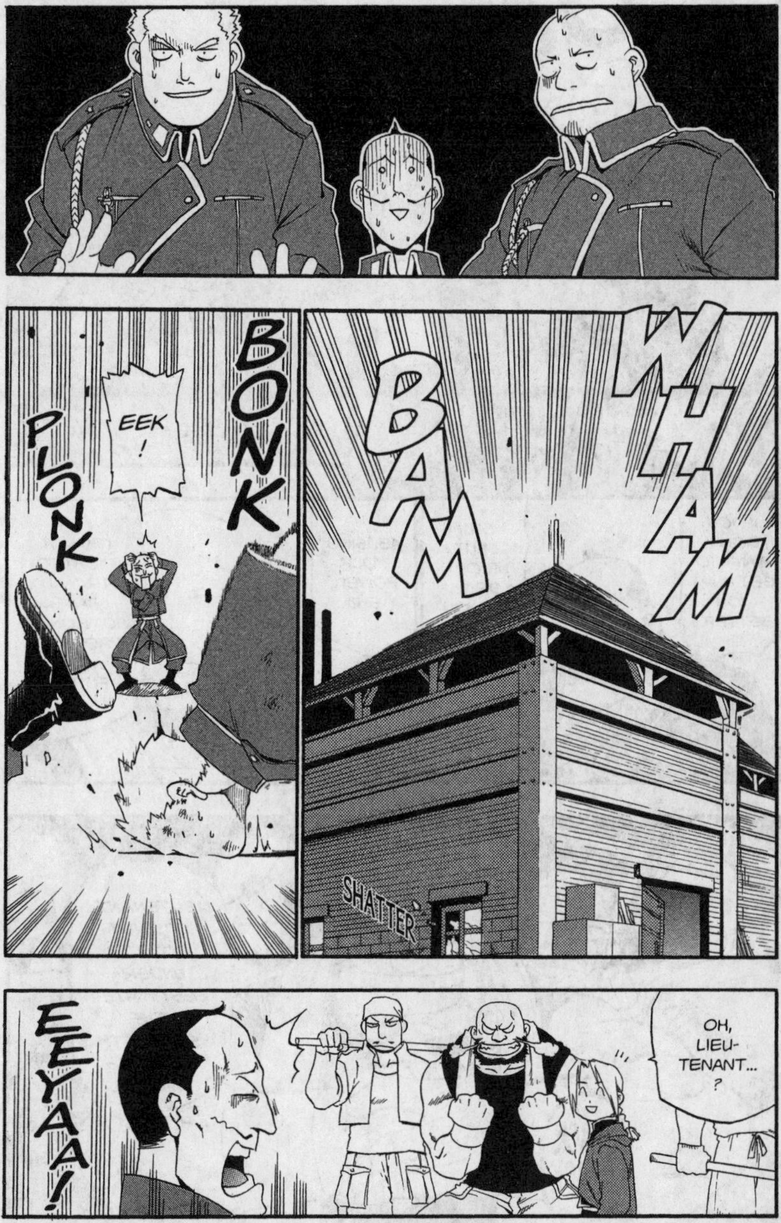
WHAM
BAM
SHATTER
BONK
EEK!
PLONK
OH, LIEU-TENANT...?
EEYAAA!

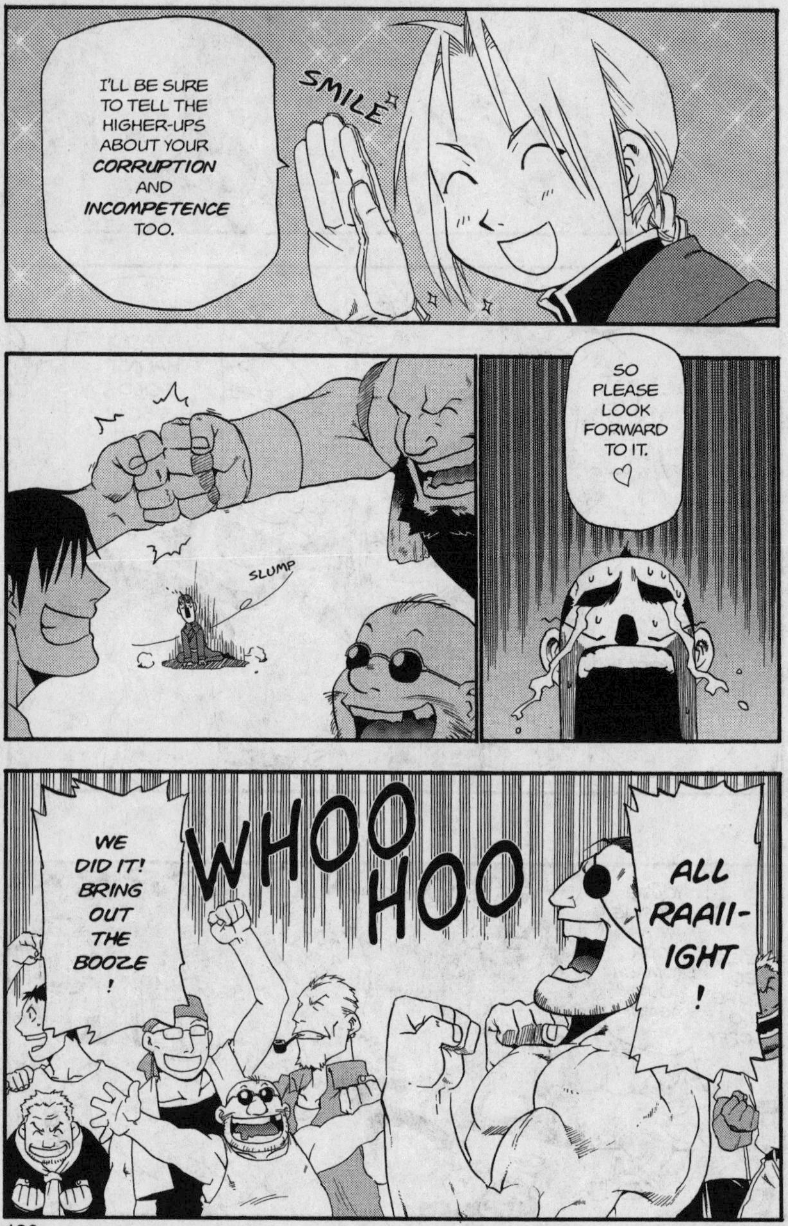
I'LL BE SURE TO TELL THE HIGHER-UPS ABOUT YOUR **CORRUPTION** AND **INCOMPETENCE** TOO.
SMILE
SO PLEASE LOOK FORWARD TO IT. ♡
SLUMP
ALL RAAII-IGHT!
WHOO HOO
WE DID IT! BRING OUT THE BOOZE!

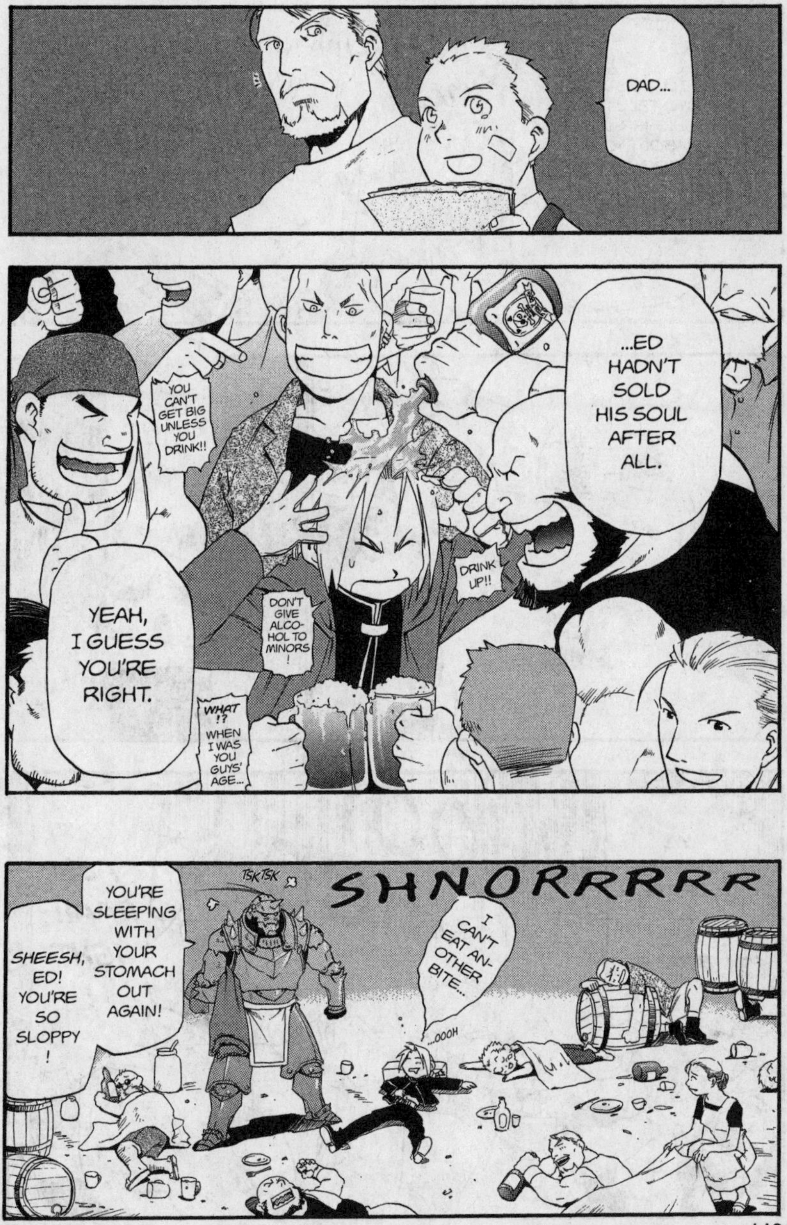
DAD...
...ED HADN'T SOLD HIS SOUL AFTER ALL.
DRINK UP!!
YOU CAN'T GET BIG UNLESS YOU DRINK!!
DON'T GIVE ALCOHOL TO MINORS!
YEAH, I GUESS YOU'RE RIGHT.
WHAT!? WHEN I WAS YOU GUYS' AGE...
SHNORRRRRR
I CAN'T EAT AN-OTHER BITE...
...OOOH
TSK TSK
YOU'RE SLEEPING WITH YOUR STOMACH OUT AGAIN!
SHEESH, ED! YOU'RE SO SLOPPY!

Chapter 4 Battle on the Train

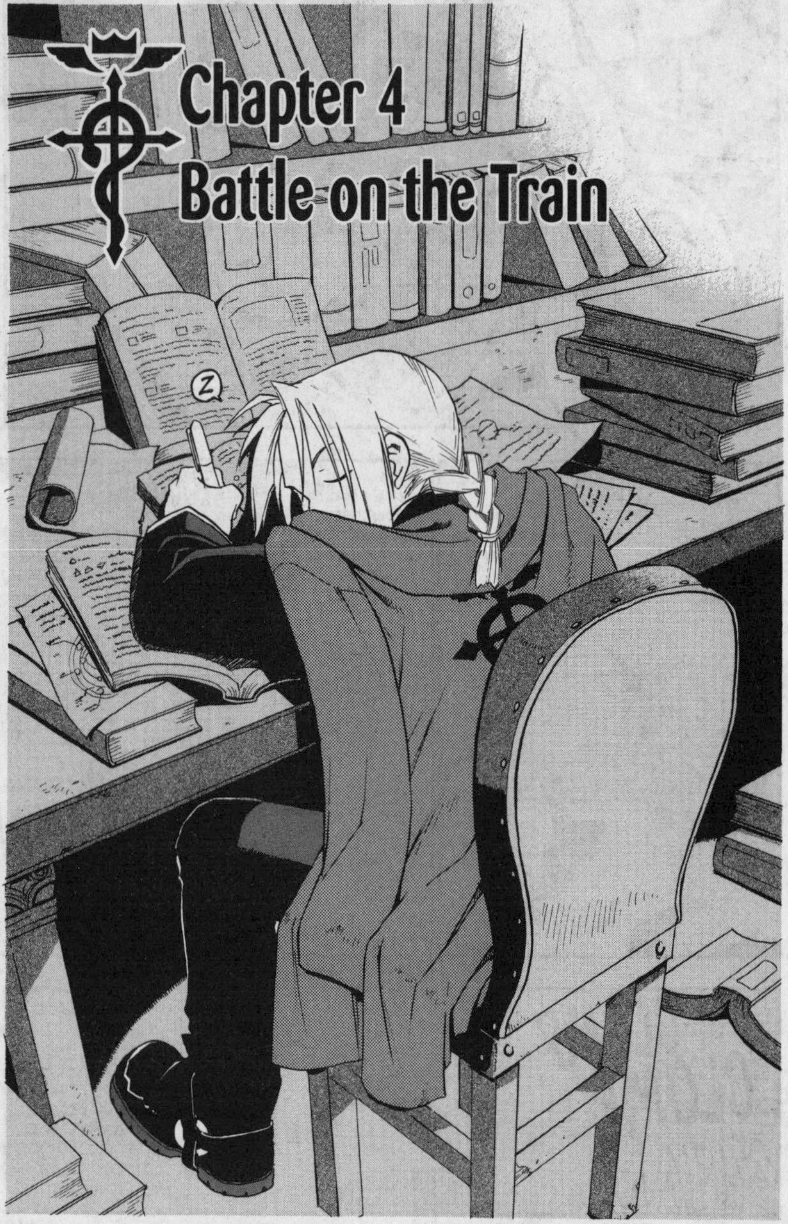
Z

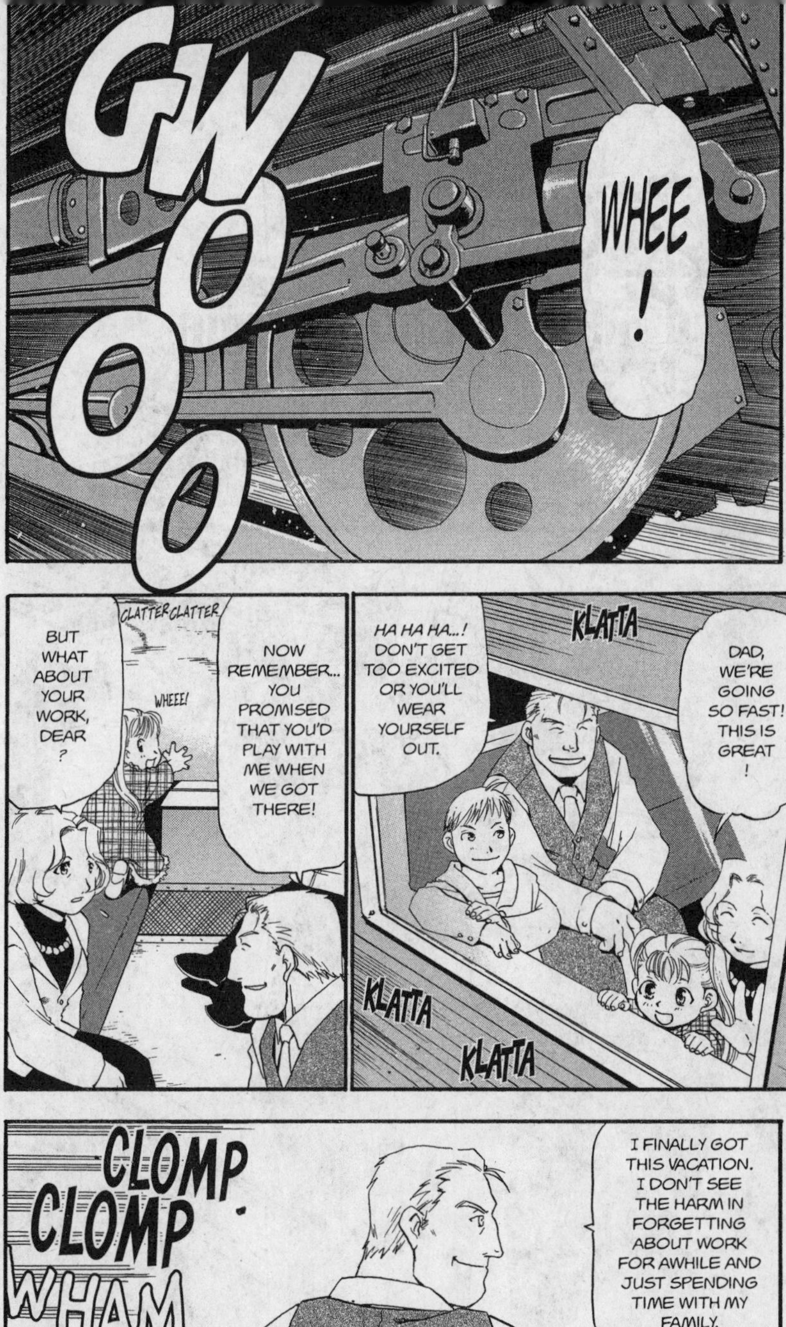
WHEE!
GWOOOO
KLATTA
DAD, WE'RE GOING SO FAST! THIS IS GREAT!
HA HA HA...! DON'T GET TOO EXCITED OR YOU'LL WEAR YOURSELF OUT.
KLATTA
KLATTA
CLATTER CLATTER
NOW REMEMBER... YOU PROMISED THAT YOU'D PLAY WITH ME WHEN WE GOT THERE!
WHEEE!
BUT WHAT ABOUT YOUR WORK, DEAR?
I FINALLY GOT THIS VACATION. I DON'T SEE THE HARM IN FORGETTING ABOUT WORK FOR AWHILE AND JUST SPENDING TIME WITH MY FAMILY.
CLOMP
CLOMP
WHAM

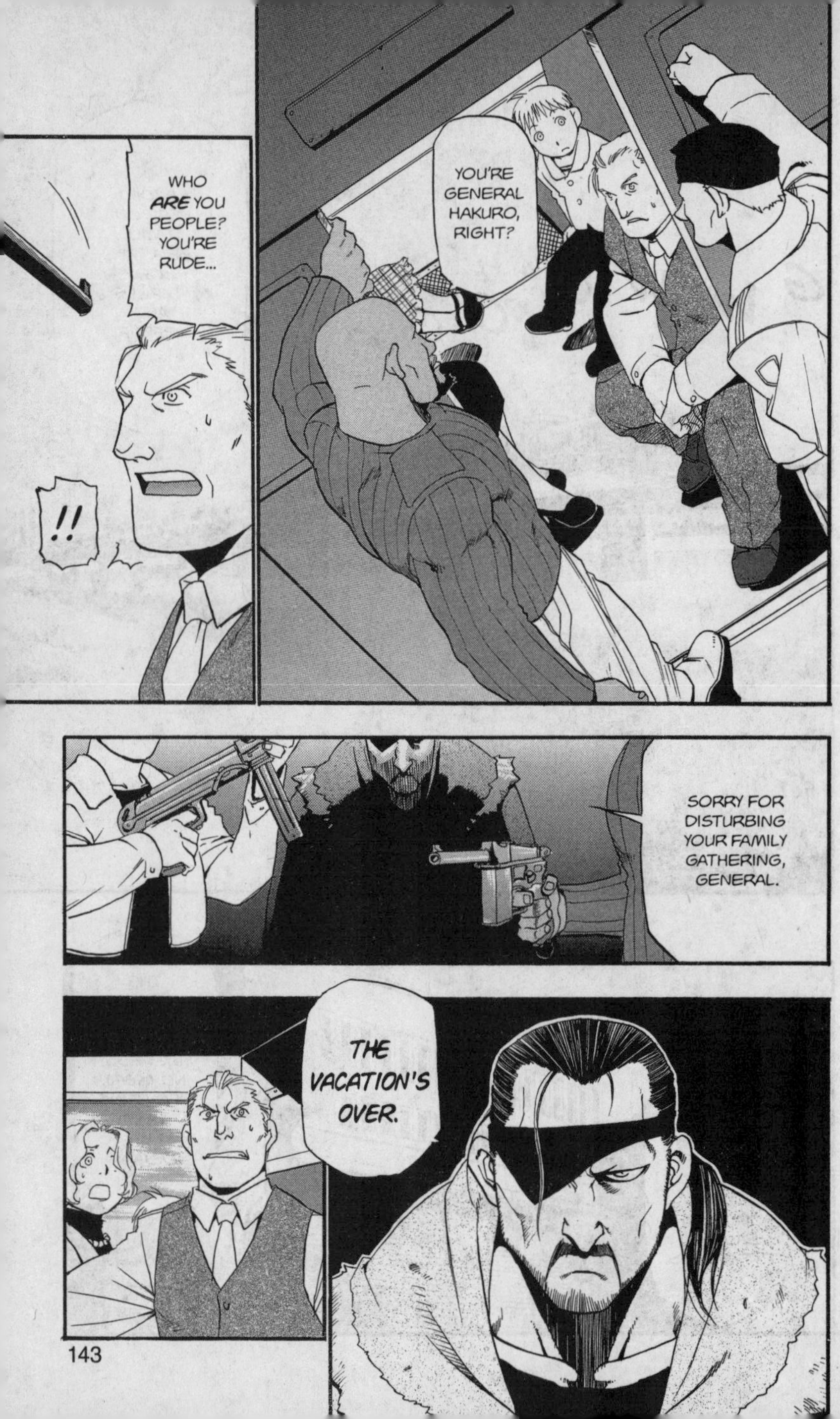
YOU'RE GENERAL HAKURO, RIGHT?
WHO ***ARE*** YOU PEOPLE? YOU'RE RUDE...
!!
SORRY FOR DISTURBING YOUR FAMILY GATHERING, GENERAL.
THE VACATION'S OVER.

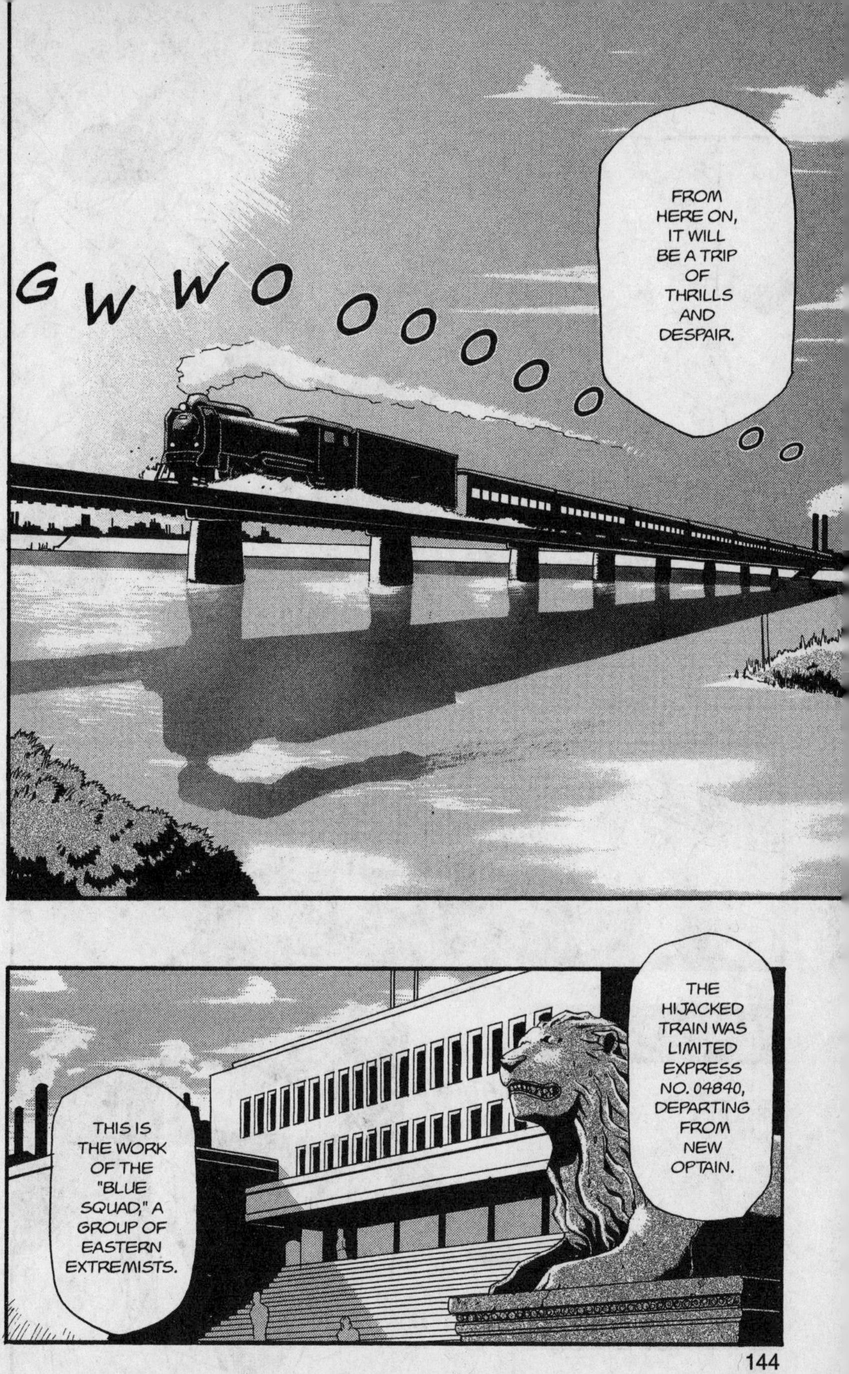

GWWOOOOOOOO
FROM HERE ON, IT WILL BE A TRIP OF THRILLS AND DESPAIR.
THE HIJACKED TRAIN WAS LIMITED EXPRESS NO. 04840, DEPARTING FROM NEW OPTAIN.
THIS IS THE WORK OF THE "BLUE SQUAD," A GROUP OF EASTERN EXTREMISTS.

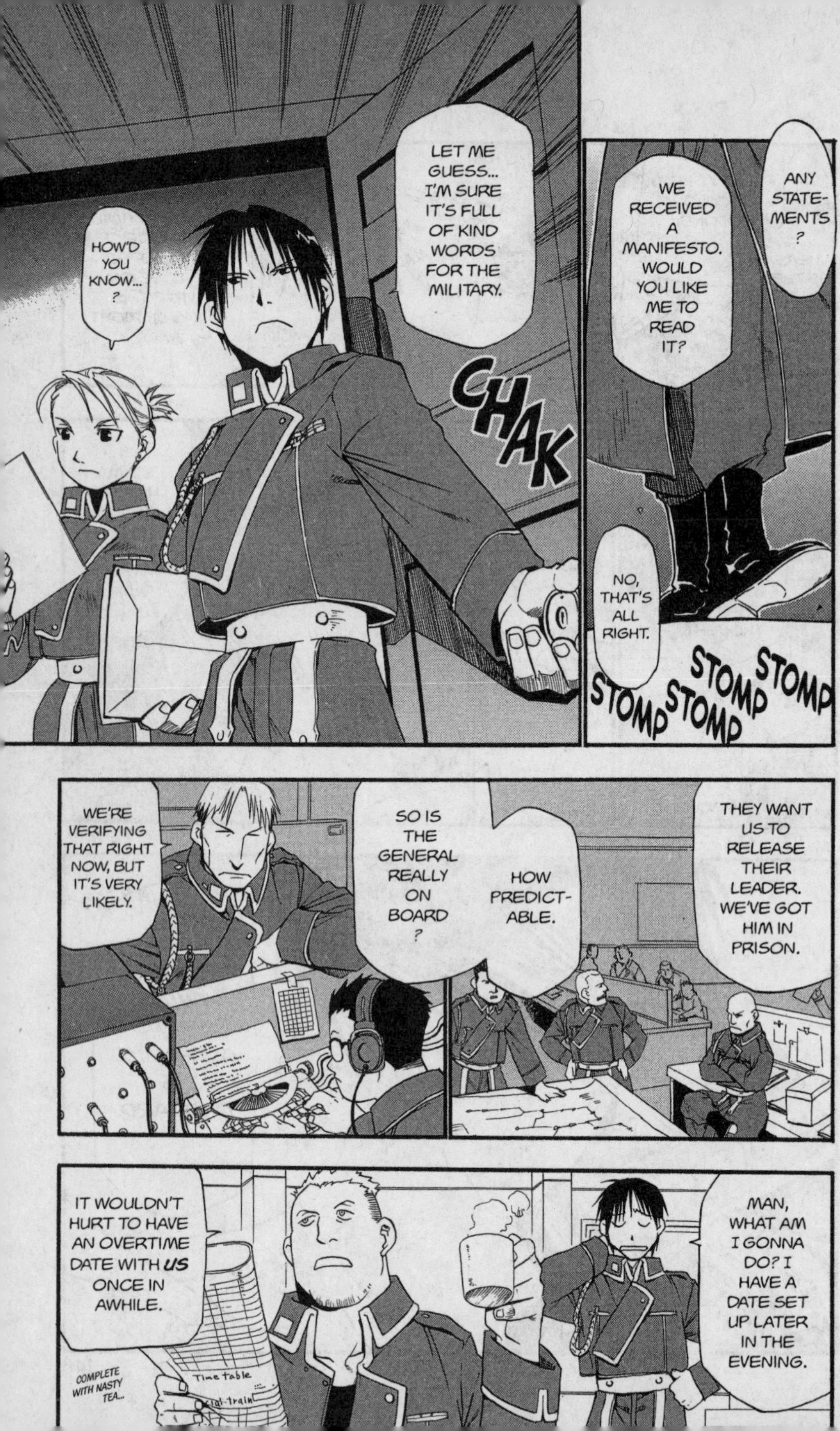
ANY STATEMENTS?
WE RECEIVED A MANIFESTO. WOULD YOU LIKE ME TO READ IT?
NO, THAT'S ALL RIGHT.
STOMP STOMP STOMP STOMP
LET ME GUESS... I'M SURE IT'S FULL OF KIND WORDS FOR THE MILITARY.
CHAK
HOW'D YOU KNOW...?
THEY WANT US TO RELEASE THEIR LEADER. WE'VE GOT HIM IN PRISON.
HOW PREDICTABLE.
SO IS THE GENERAL REALLY ON BOARD?
WE'RE VERIFYING THAT RIGHT NOW, BUT IT'S VERY LIKELY.
MAN, WHAT AM I GONNA DO? I HAVE A DATE SET UP LATER IN THE EVENING.
IT WOULDN'T HURT TO HAVE AN OVERTIME DATE WITH ***US*** ONCE IN AWHILE.
COMPLETE WITH NASTY TEA...
Time table

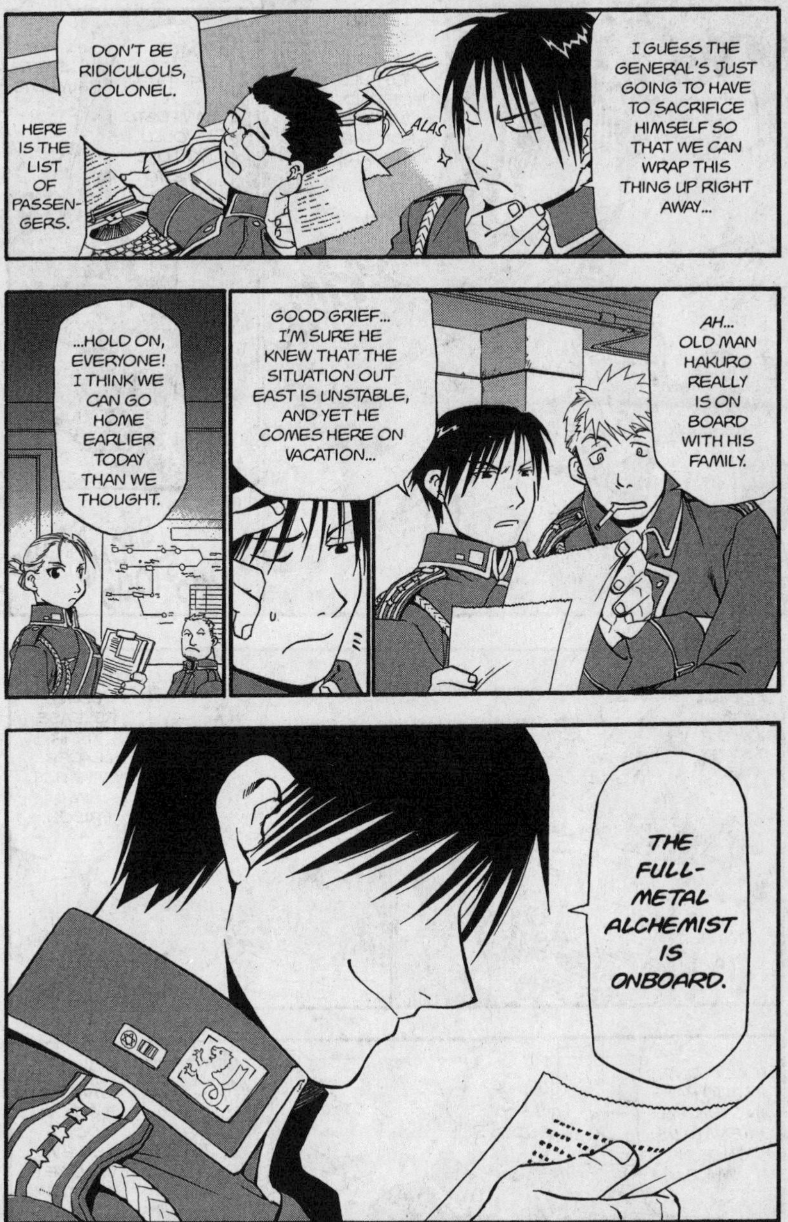
I GUESS THE GENERAL'S JUST GOING TO HAVE TO SACRIFICE HIMSELF SO THAT WE CAN WRAP THIS THING UP RIGHT AWAY...
ALAS
DON'T BE RIDICULOUS, COLONEL.
HERE IS THE LIST OF PASSEN-GERS.
AH... OLD MAN HAKURO REALLY IS ON BOARD WITH HIS FAMILY.
GOOD GRIEF... I'M SURE HE KNEW THAT THE SITUATION OUT EAST IS UNSTABLE, AND YET HE COMES HERE ON VACATION...
...HOLD ON, EVERYONE! I THINK WE CAN GO HOME EARLIER TODAY THAN WE THOUGHT.
THE FULL-METAL ALCHEMIST IS ONBOARD.

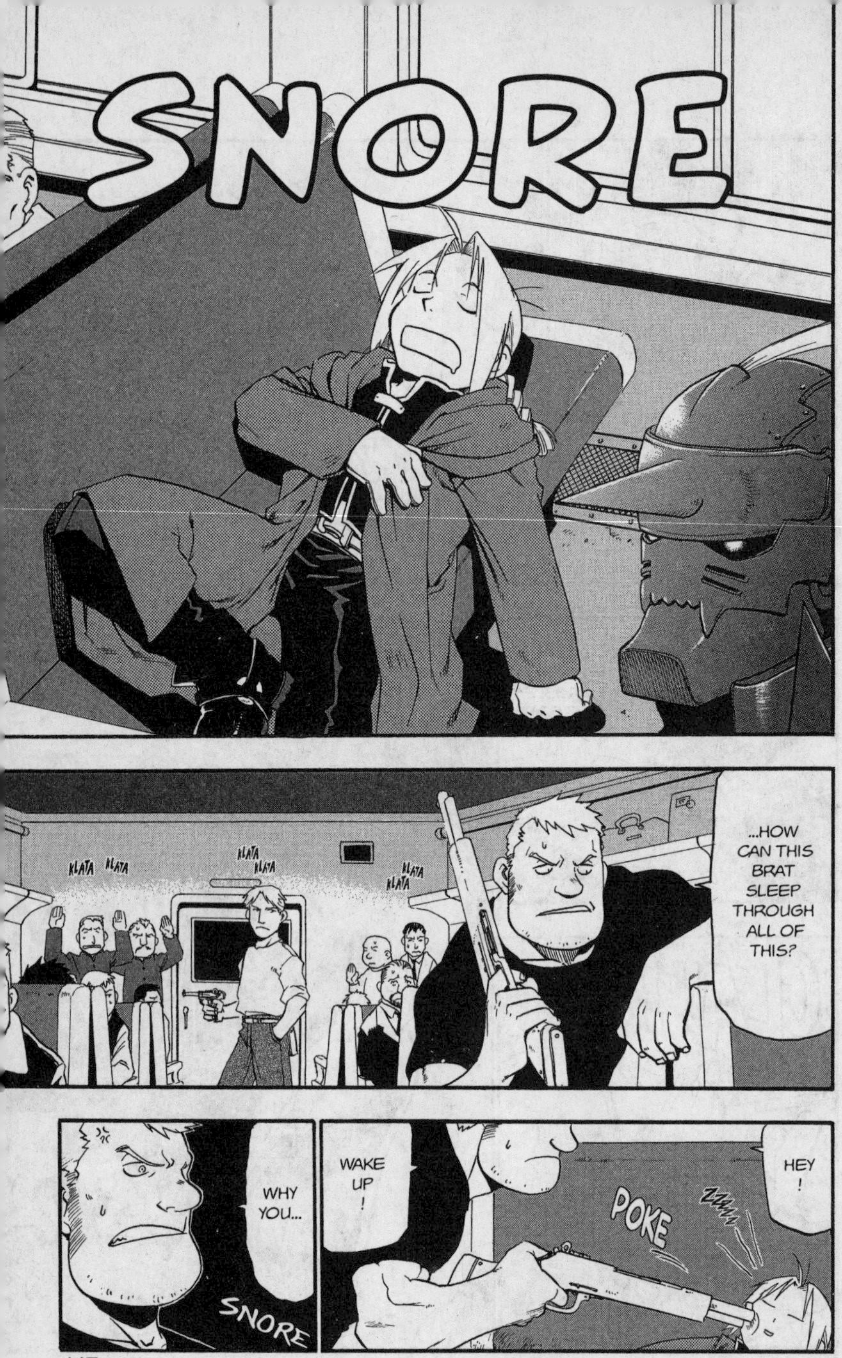
SNORE
...HOW CAN THIS BRAT SLEEP THROUGH ALL OF THIS?
KLATA KLATA
KLATA KLATA
KLATA KLATA
HEY!
POKE
WAKE UP!
WHY YOU...
SNORE

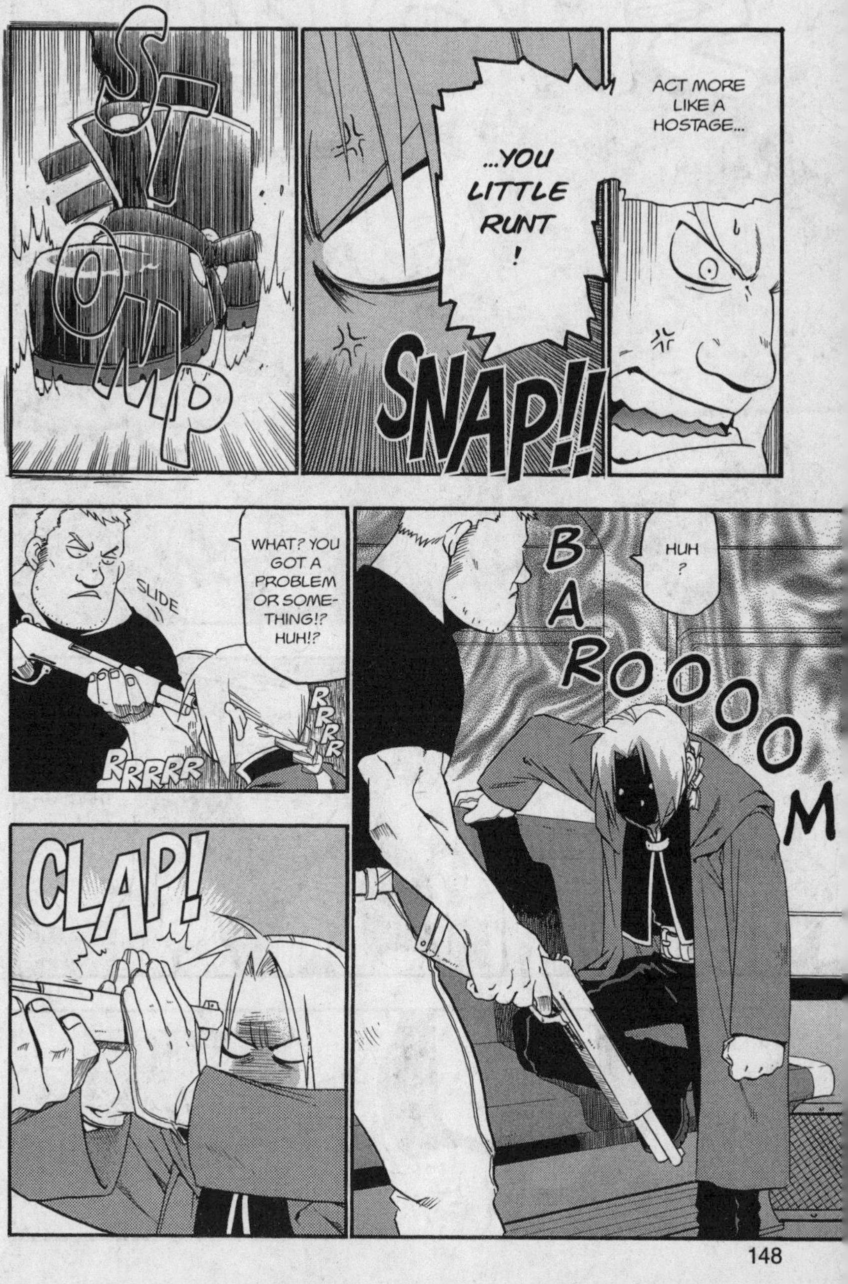
ACT MORE LIKE A HOSTAGE...
...YOU LITTLE RUNT !
SNAP!!
STOMP
HUH ?
BAROOOOOM
WHAT? YOU GOT A PROBLEM OR SOME-THING!? HUH!?
SLIDE
RRRR
RRRRR
CLAP!

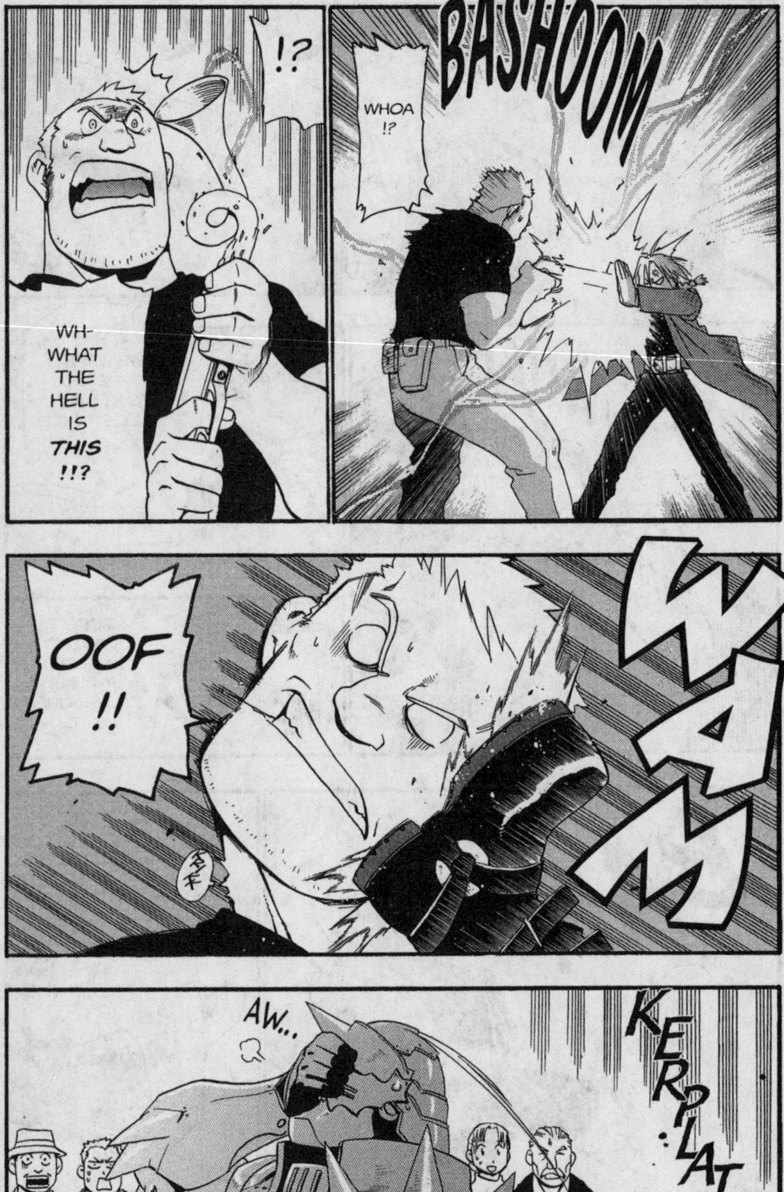
BASHOOM
WHOA !?
!?
WH- WHAT THE HELL IS THIS !!?
WAM
OOF !!
KERPLAT
AW...

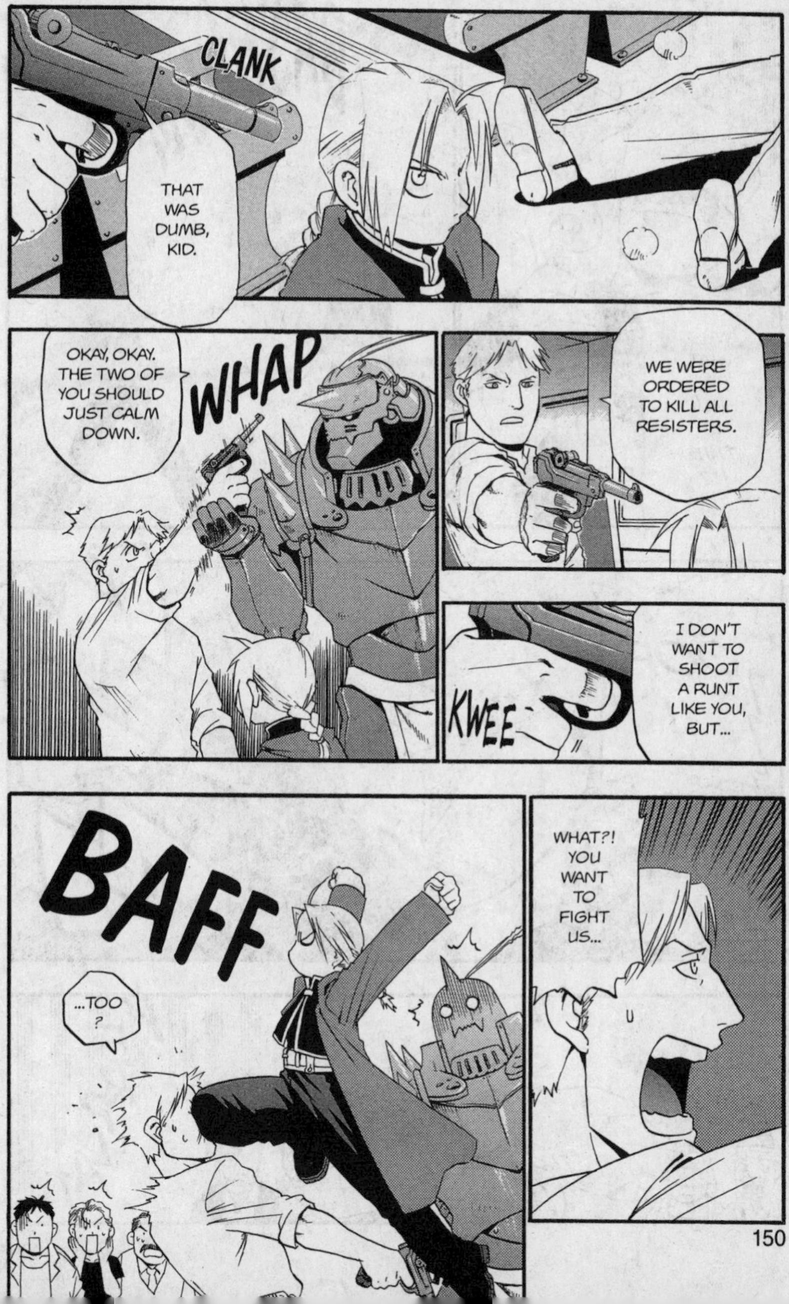
CLANK
THAT WAS DUMB, KID.
WE WERE ORDERED TO KILL ALL RESISTERS.
I DON'T WANT TO SHOOT A RUNT LIKE YOU, BUT...
KWEE
OKAY, OKAY. THE TWO OF YOU SHOULD JUST CALM DOWN.
WHAP
WHAT?! YOU WANT TO FIGHT US...
BAFF
...TOO ?

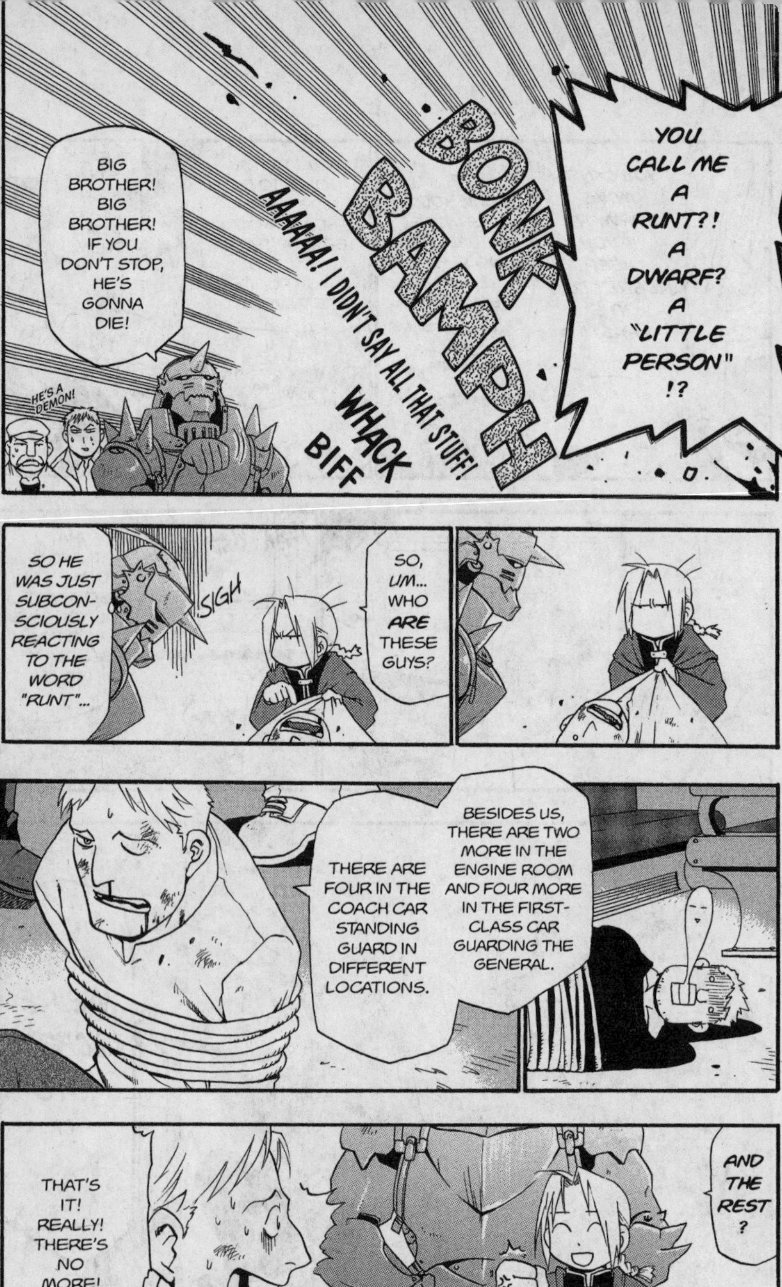
YOU CALL ME A RUNT?! A DWARF? A "LITTLE PERSON"!?
BONK
BAMPH
AAAAAA! I DIDN'T SAY ALL THAT STUFF!
WHACK
BIFF
BIG BROTHER! BIG BROTHER! IF YOU DON'T STOP, HE'S GONNA DIE!
HE'S A DEMON!
SO, UM... WHO ARE THESE GUYS?
SIGH
SO HE WAS JUST SUBCONSCIOUSLY REACTING TO THE WORD "RUNT"...
THERE ARE FOUR IN THE COACH CAR STANDING GUARD IN DIFFERENT LOCATIONS.
BESIDES US, THERE ARE TWO MORE IN THE ENGINE ROOM AND FOUR MORE IN THE FIRST-CLASS CAR GUARDING THE GENERAL.
AND THE REST?
THAT'S IT! REALLY! THERE'S NO MORE!

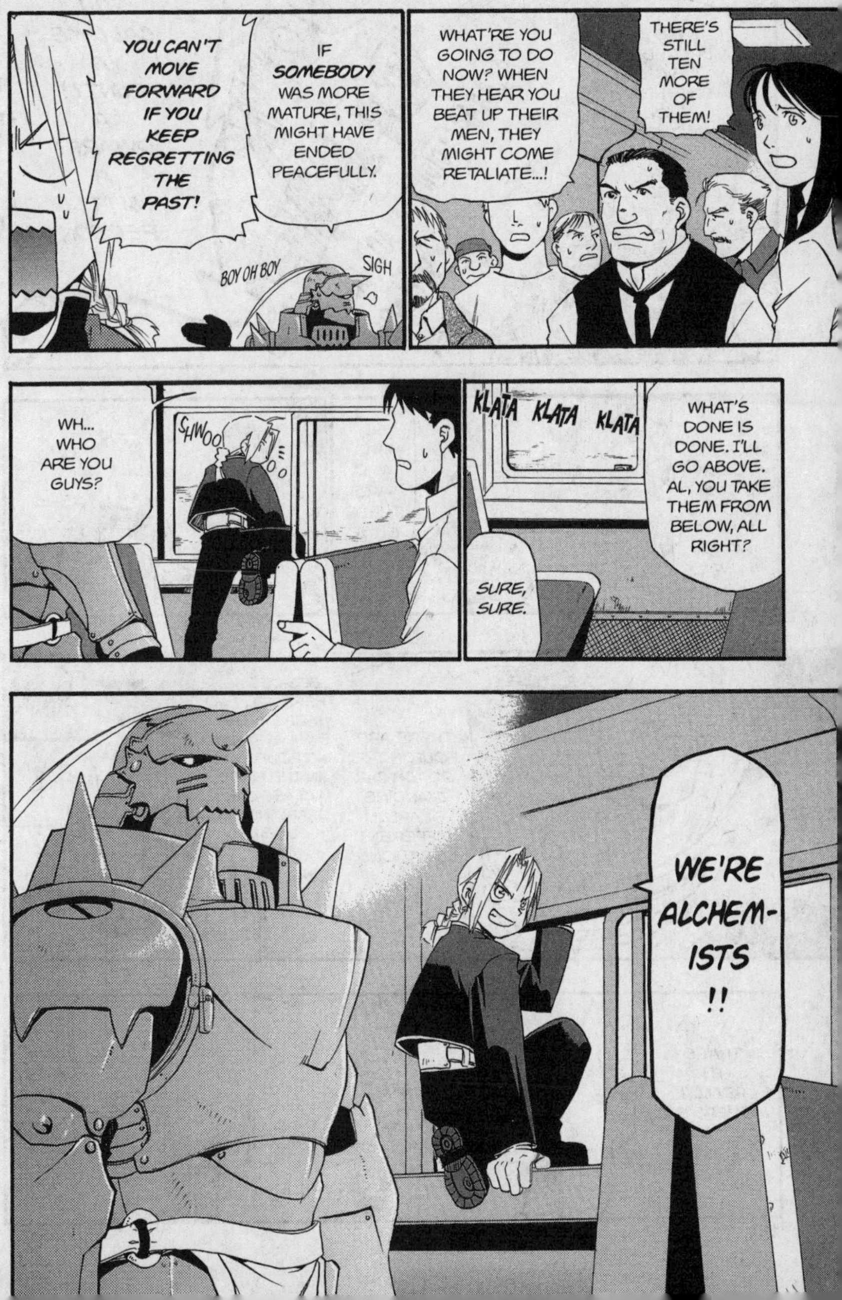
THERE'S STILL TEN MORE OF THEM!
WHAT'RE YOU GOING TO DO NOW? WHEN THEY HEAR YOU BEAT UP THEIR MEN, THEY MIGHT COME RETALIATE...!
IF SOMEBODY WAS MORE MATURE, THIS MIGHT HAVE ENDED PEACEFULLY.
YOU CAN'T MOVE FORWARD IF YOU KEEP REGRETTING THE PAST!
SIGH
BOY OH BOY
WHAT'S DONE IS DONE. I'LL GO ABOVE. AL, YOU TAKE THEM FROM BELOW, ALL RIGHT?
KLATA KLATA KLATA
SURE, SURE.
WH... WHO ARE YOU GUYS?
SHWOO
WE'RE ALCHEM-ISTS!!

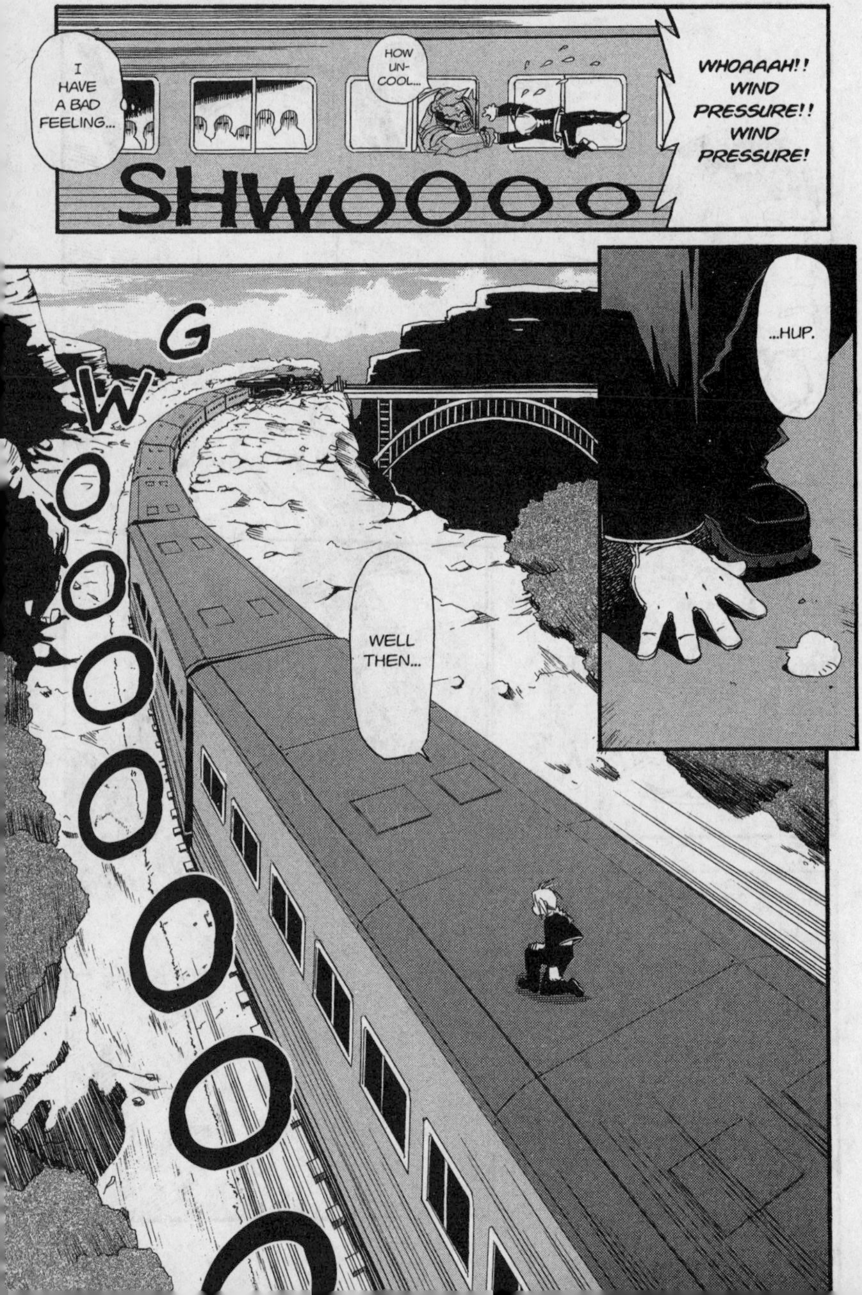
WHOAAAH!! WIND PRESSURE!! WIND PRESSURE!
HOW UN-COOL...
I HAVE A BAD FEELING...
SHWOOOO
...HUP.
WELL THEN...
GWOOOOOOO

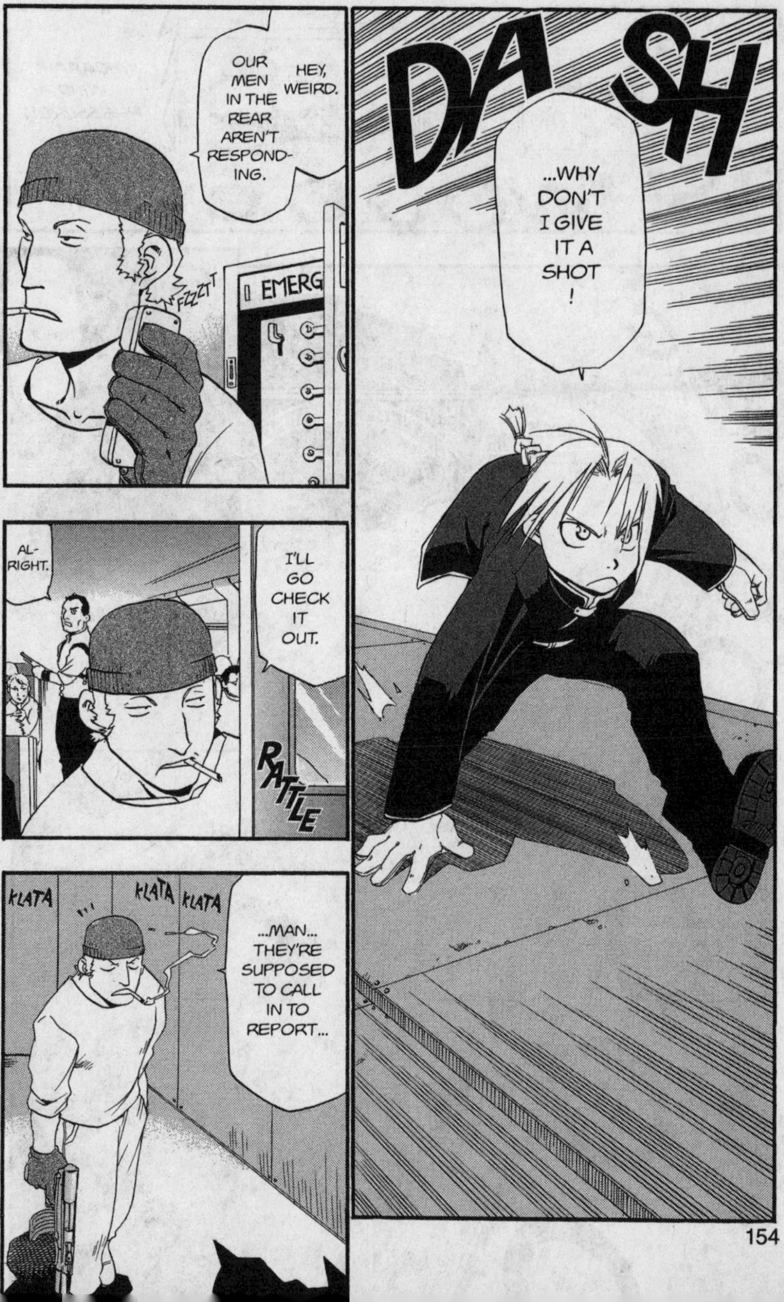
DASH
...WHY DON'T I GIVE IT A SHOT !
HEY, WEIRD.
OUR MEN IN THE REAR AREN'T RESPOND-ING.
FZZZZT
EMERG
I'LL GO CHECK IT OUT.
AL-RIGHT.
RATTLE
KLATA KLATA
KLATA
...MAN... THEY'RE SUPPOSED TO CALL IN TO REPORT...

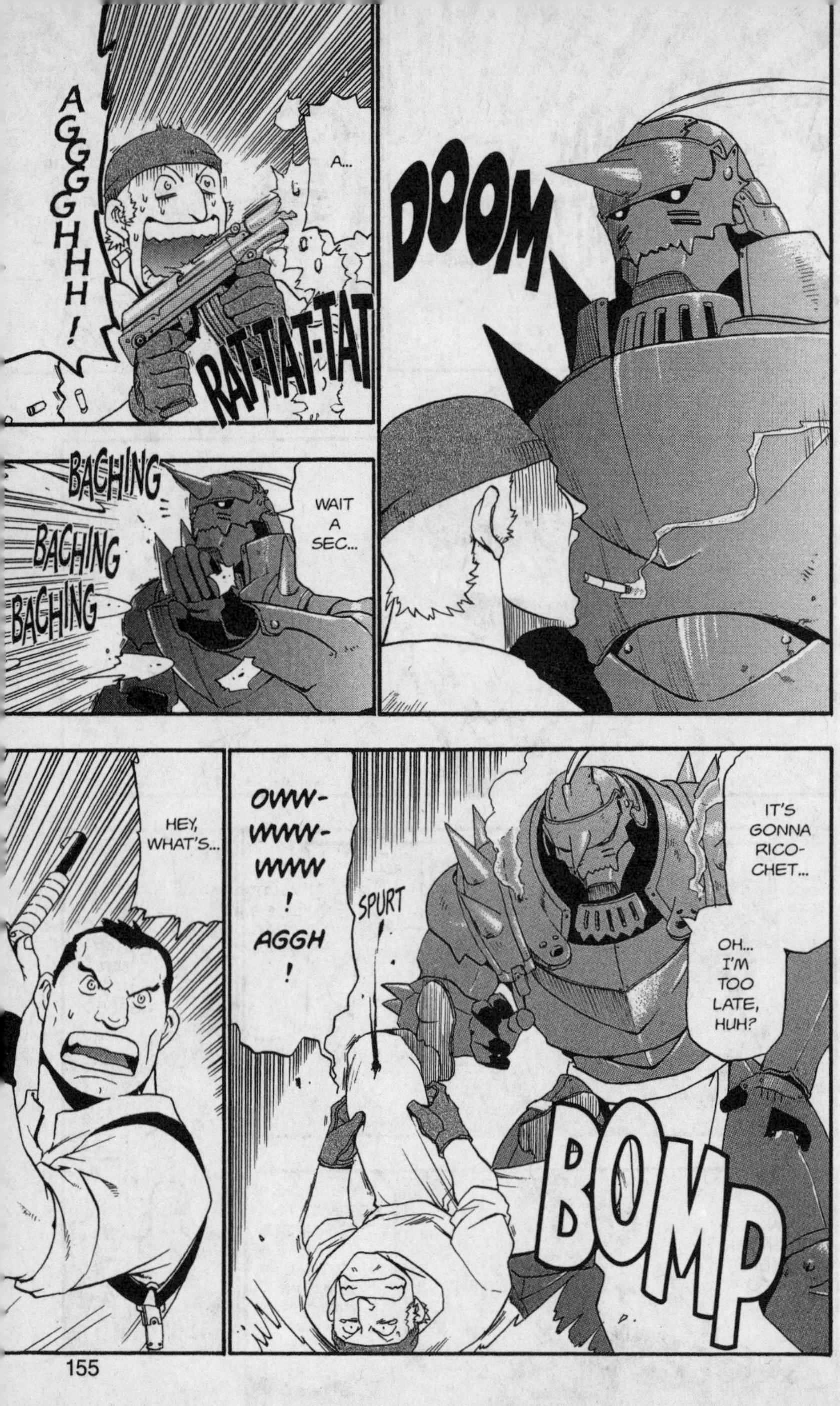
DOOM
A...
AGGGHHH!
RAT-TAT-TAT
WAIT A SEC...
BACHING
BACHING
BACHING
IT'S GONNA RICO-CHET...
OH... I'M TOO LATE, HUH?
OWW-WWW-WWW! AGGH!
SPURT!
BOMP
HEY, WHAT'S...

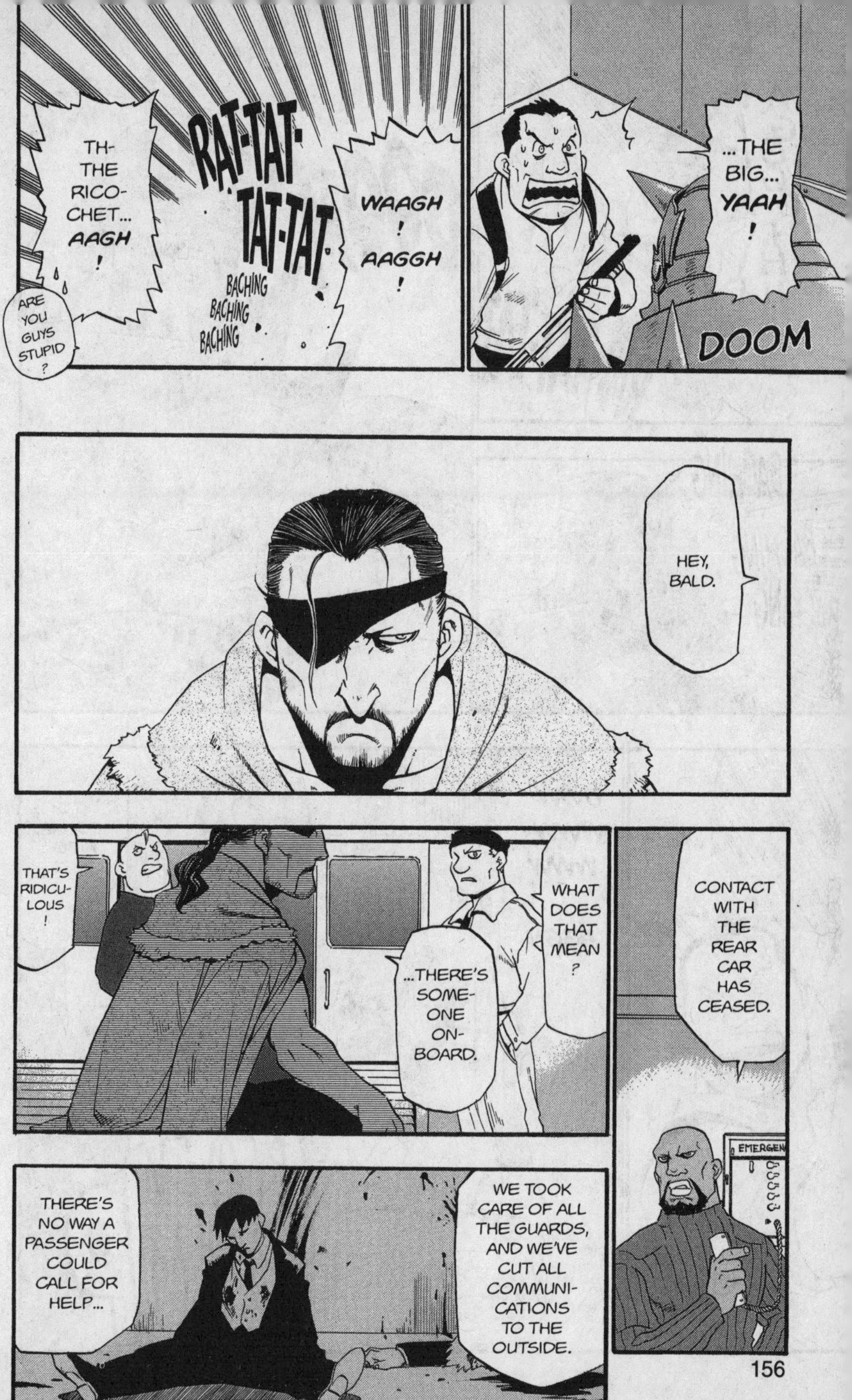
...THE BIG... YAAH!
DOOM
WAAGH! AAGGH!
RAT-TAT-TAT-TAT-TAT
BACHING BACHING BACHING
TH-THE RICOCHET... AAGH!
ARE YOU GUYS STUPID?
HEY, BALD.
CONTACT WITH THE REAR CAR HAS CEASED.
WHAT DOES THAT MEAN?
...THERE'S SOMEONE ONBOARD.
THAT'S RIDICULOUS!
WE TOOK CARE OF ALL THE GUARDS, AND WE'VE CUT ALL COMMUNICATIONS TO THE OUTSIDE.
THERE'S NO WAY A PASSENGER COULD CALL FOR HELP...

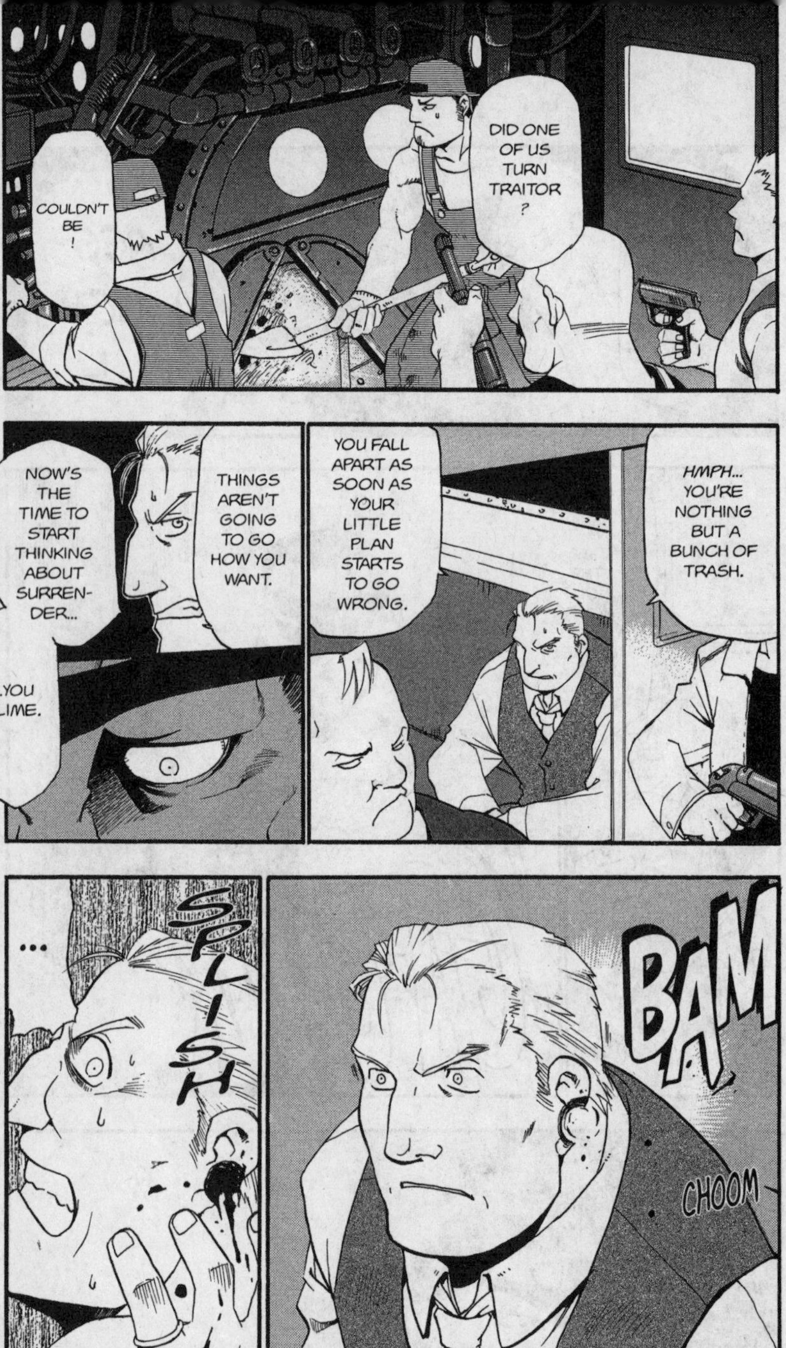
DID ONE OF US TURN TRAITOR?
COULDN'T BE!
HMPH... YOU'RE NOTHING BUT A BUNCH OF TRASH.
YOU FALL APART AS SOON AS YOUR LITTLE PLAN STARTS TO GO WRONG.
THINGS AREN'T GOING TO GO HOW YOU WANT.
NOW'S THE TIME TO START THINKING ABOUT SURRENDER...
...YOU SLIME.
BAM
CHOOM
SPLISH
...

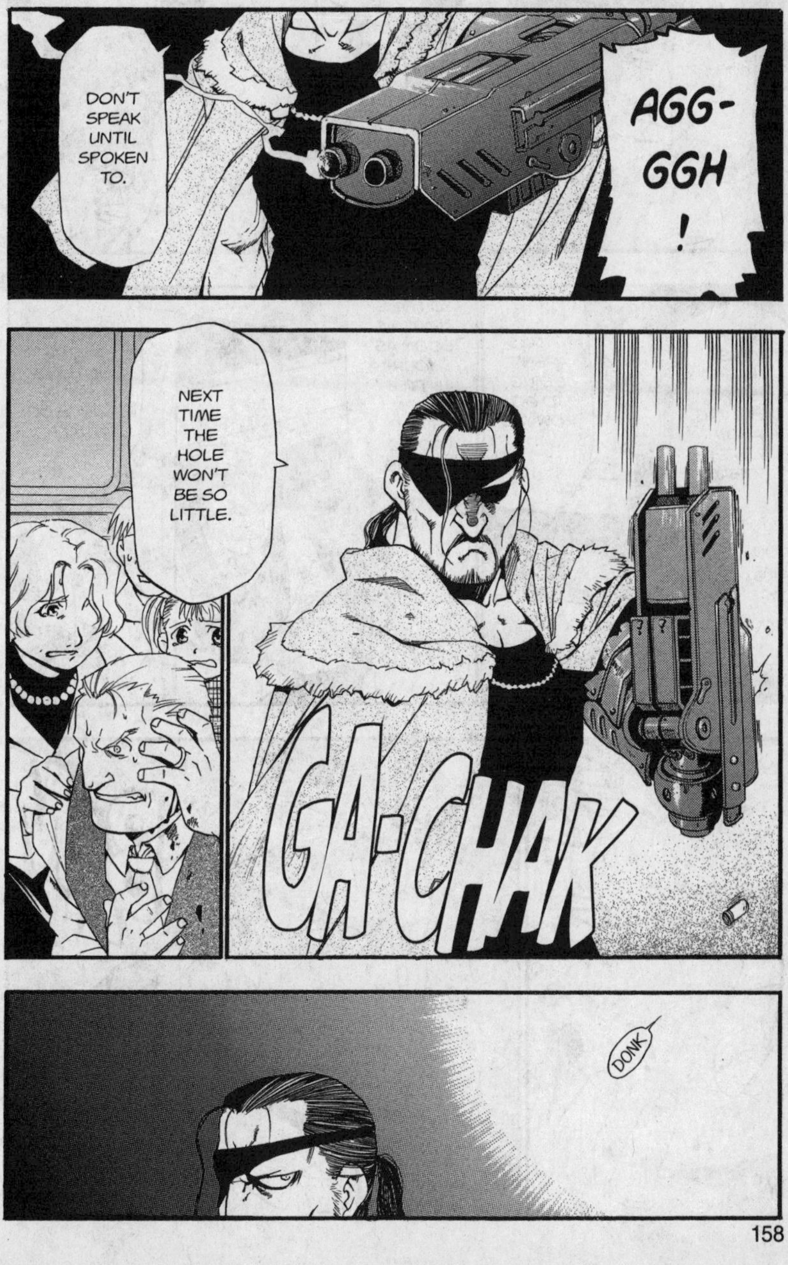
AGG-GGH!
DON'T SPEAK UNTIL SPOKEN TO.
NEXT TIME THE HOLE WON'T BE SO LITTLE.
GA-CHAK
DONK

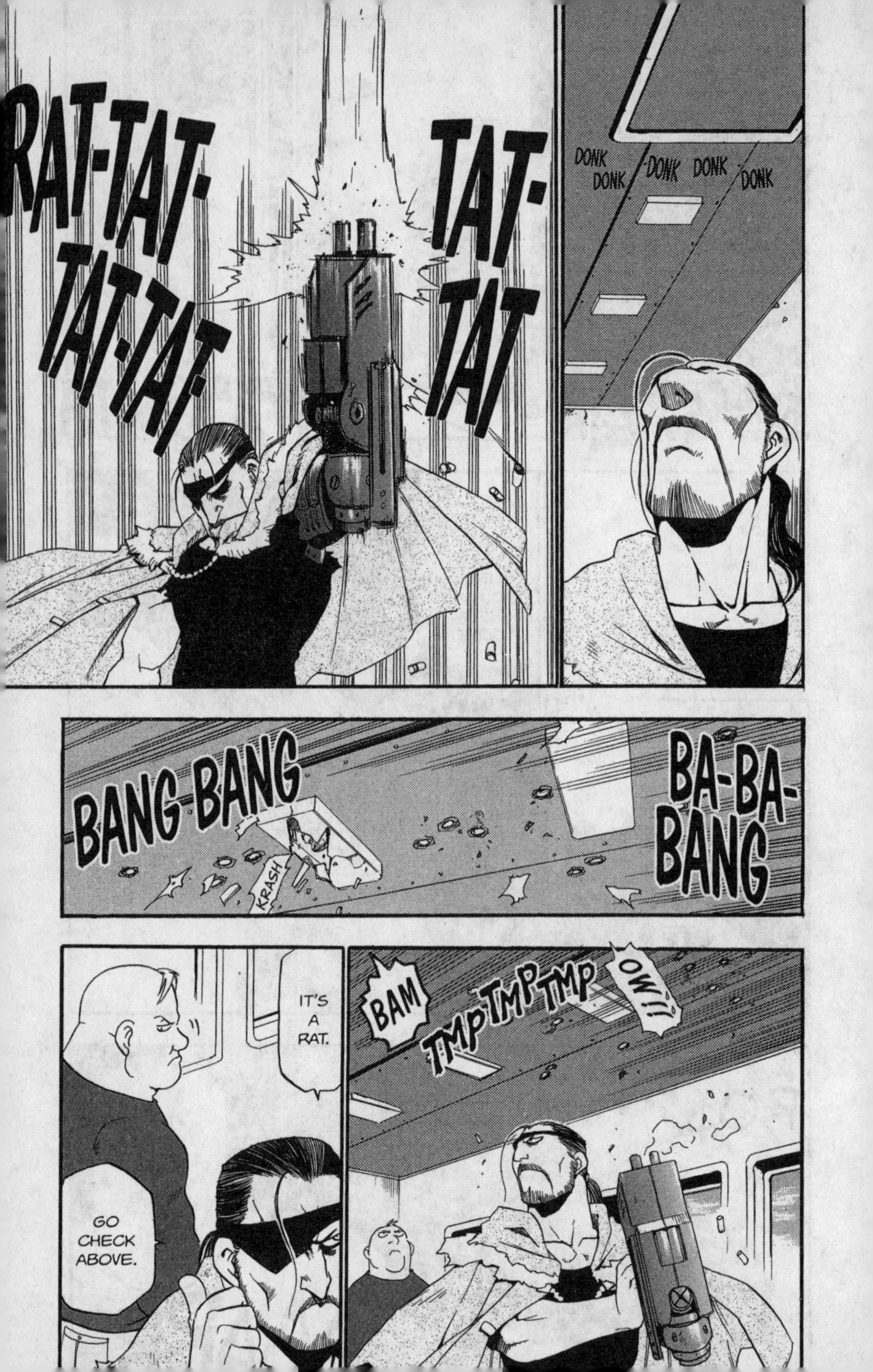
DONK
DONK DONK
DONK
DONK
RAT-TAT-TAT-TAT-TAT-
TAT-TAT
BA-BA-BANG
BANG BANG
KRASH
OW!!
TMP TMP TMP
BAM
IT'S A RAT.
GO CHECK ABOVE.

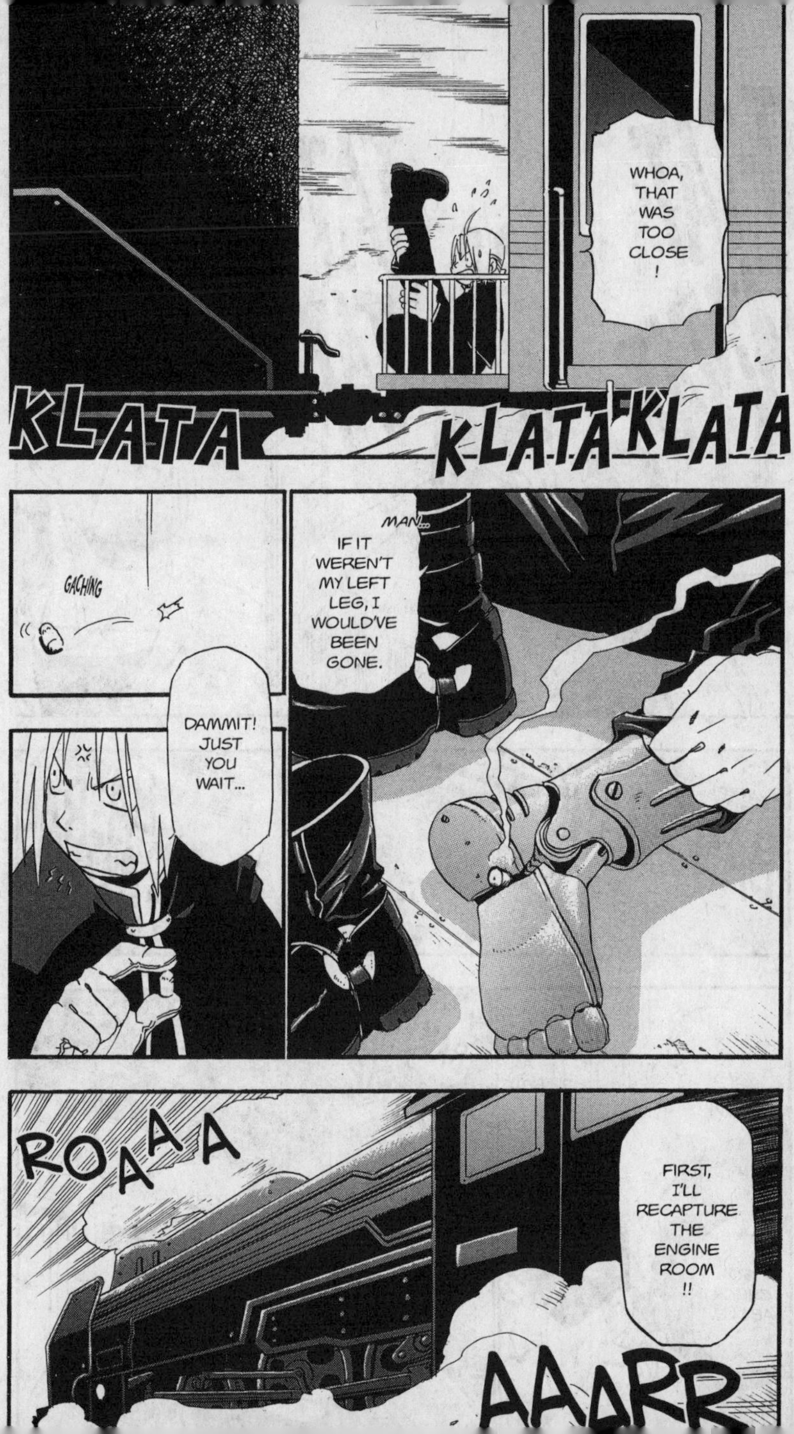
WHOA, THAT WAS TOO CLOSE !
KLATA
KLATA KLATA
MAN...
IF IT WEREN'T MY LEFT LEG, I WOULD'VE BEEN GONE.
GACHING
DAMMIT! JUST YOU WAIT...
FIRST, I'LL RECAPTURE THE ENGINE ROOM !!
ROAAA
AAARR

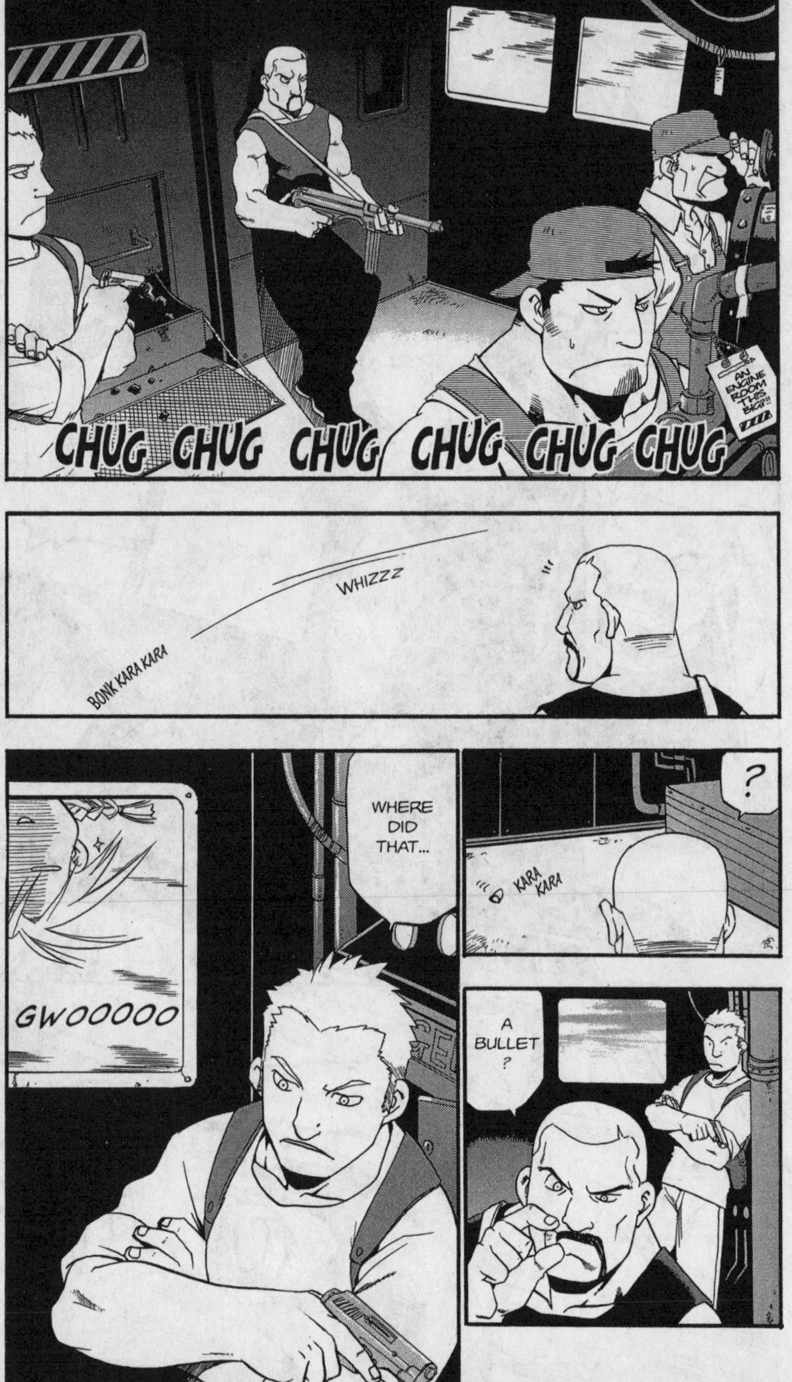
AN ENGINE ROOM THIS BIG?!!
CHUG CHUG CHUG CHUG CHUG CHUG
WHIZZZ
BONK KARA KARA
?
KARA KARA
A BULLET ?
WHERE DID THAT...
GWOOOOO

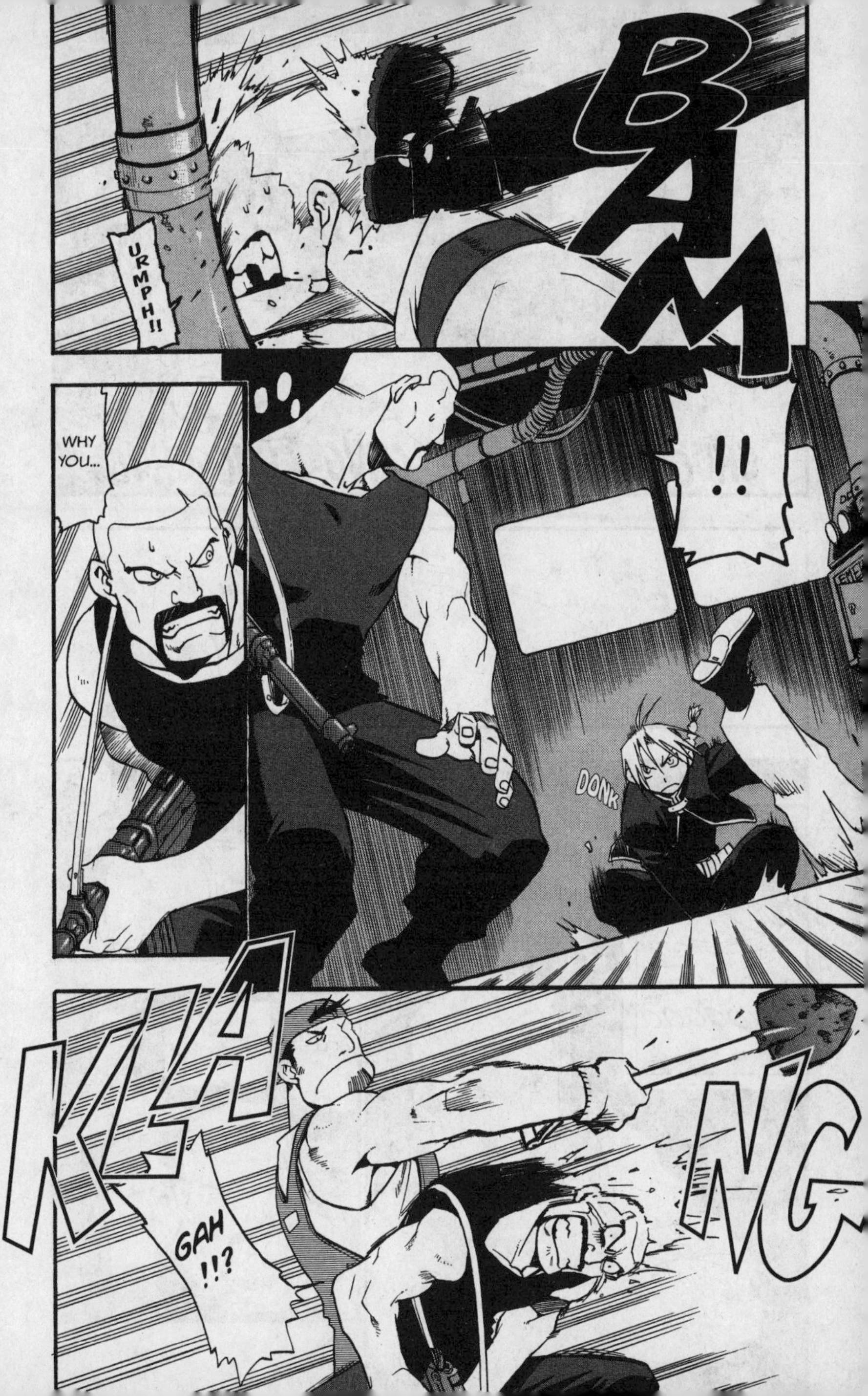
BAM
URMPH!!
!!
DONK
WHY YOU...
KLANG
GAH !!?

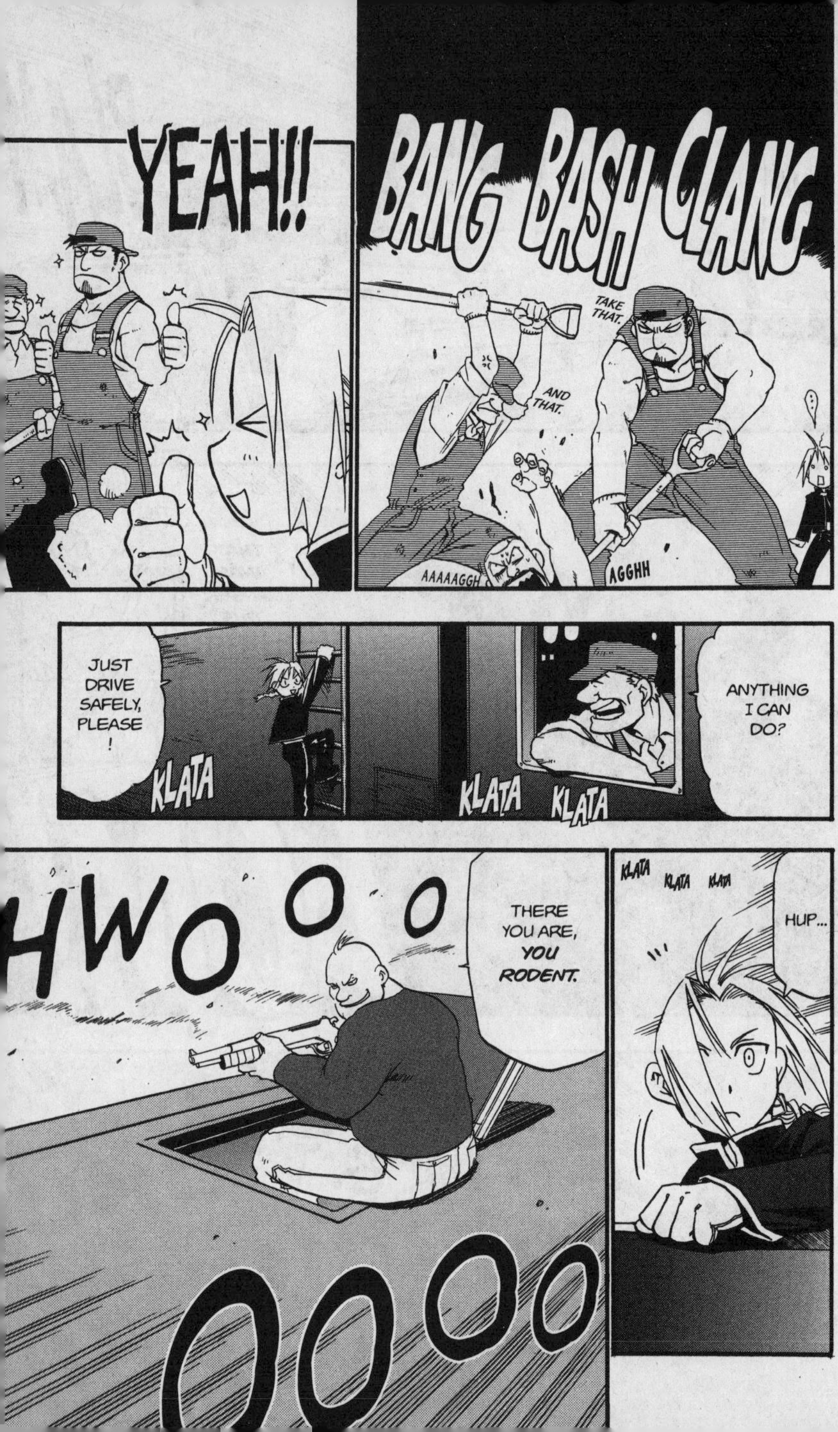
BANG BASH CLANG
TAKE THAT.
AND THAT.
AGGHH
AAAAAGGH
YEAH!!
ANYTHING I CAN DO?
KLATA KLATA
JUST DRIVE SAFELY, PLEASE!
KLATA
KLATA KLATA KLATA
HUP...
HWOOOOOOO
THERE YOU ARE, YOU RODENT.

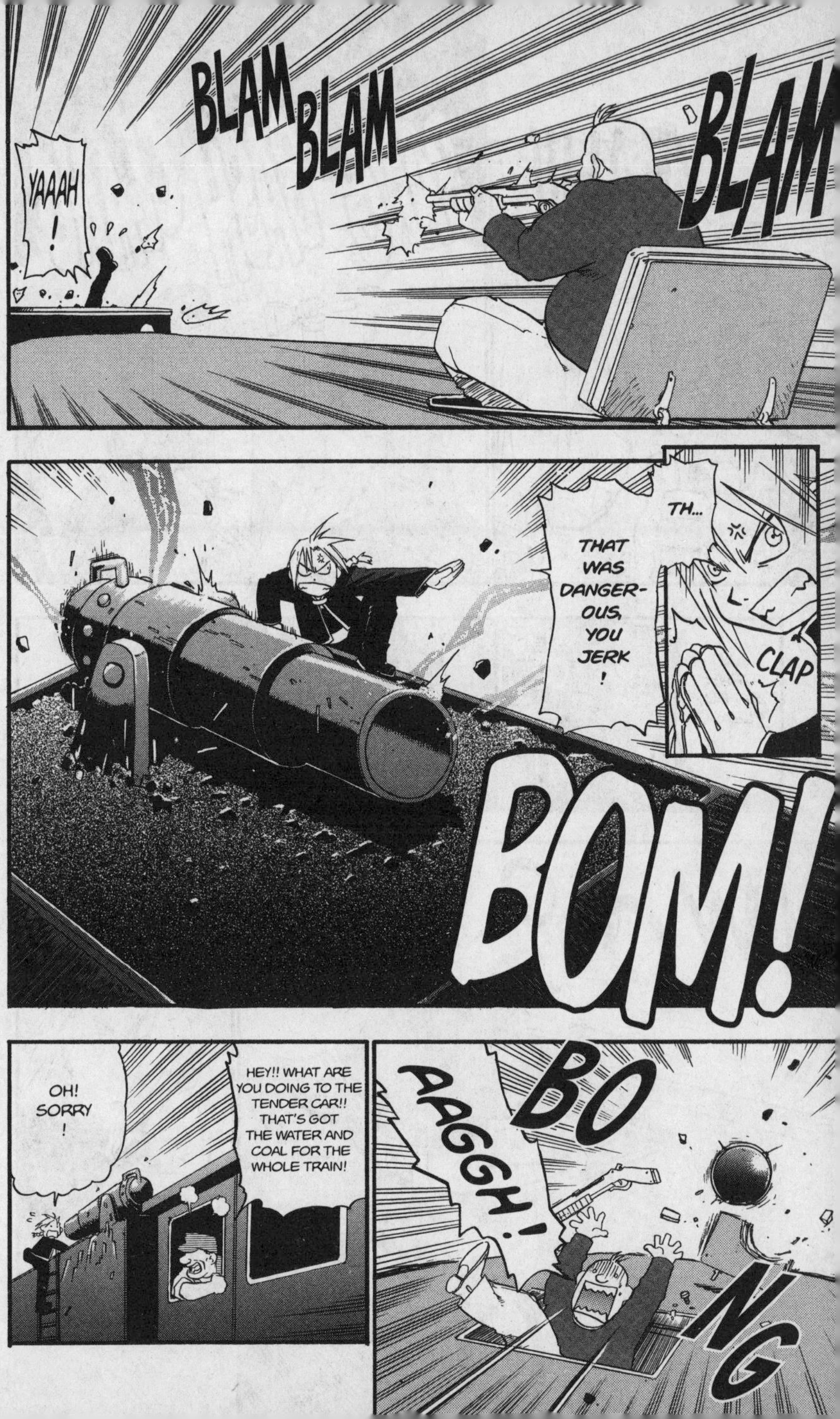
BLAM
BLAM
BLAM
YAAAH!
TH...
THAT WAS DANGEROUS, YOU JERK!
CLAP
BOM!
BOING
AAGGH!
HEY!! WHAT ARE YOU DOING TO THE TENDER CAR!! THAT'S GOT THE WATER AND COAL FOR THE WHOLE TRAIN!
OH! SORRY!

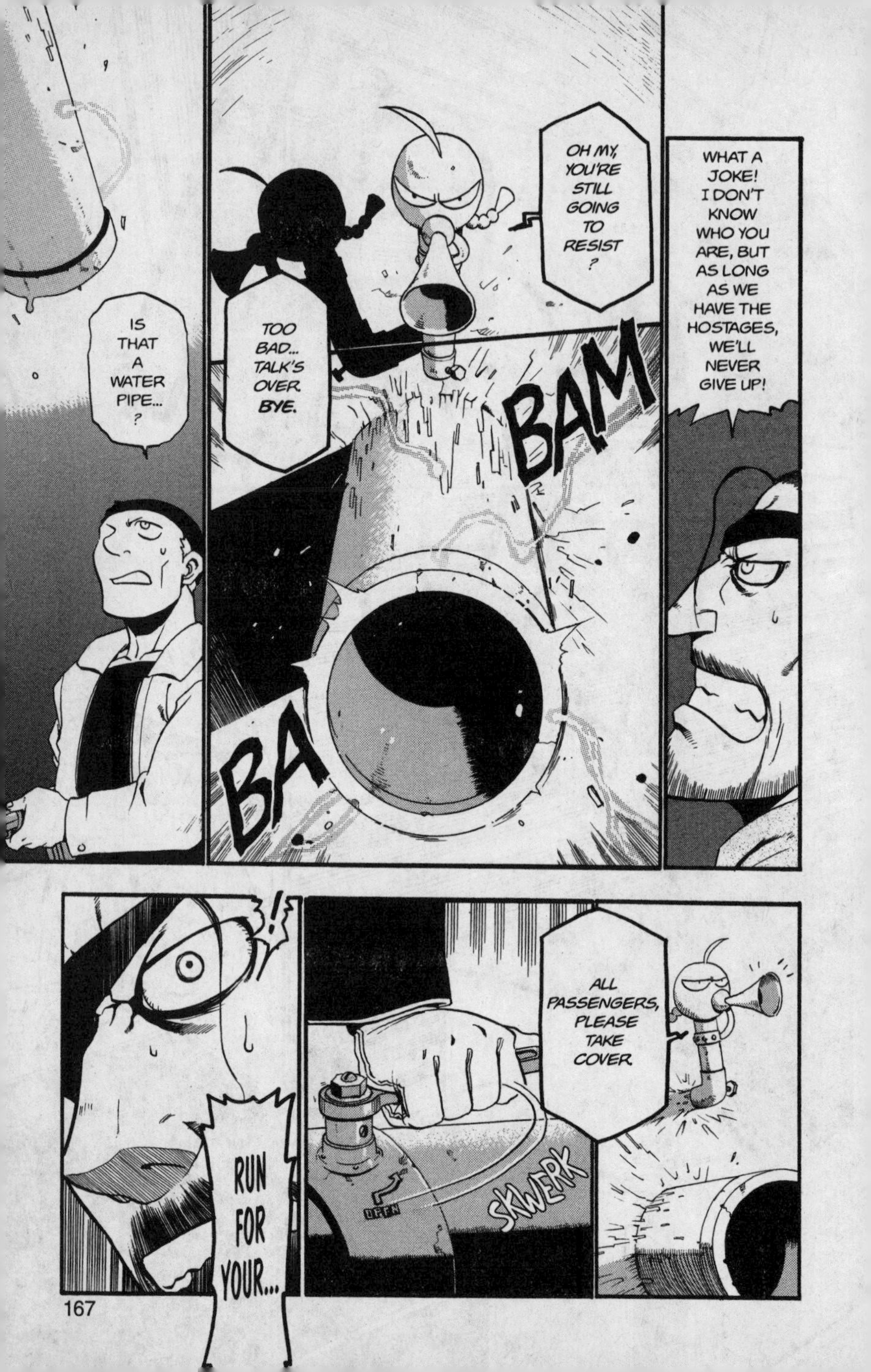
WHAT A JOKE! I DON'T KNOW WHO YOU ARE, BUT AS LONG AS WE HAVE THE HOSTAGES, WE'LL NEVER GIVE UP!
OH MY, YOU'RE STILL GOING TO RESIST?
TOO BAD... TALK'S OVER. BYE.
BAM
BA
IS THAT A WATER PIPE...?
ALL PASSENGERS, PLEASE TAKE COVER.
SKWERK
!
RUN FOR YOUR...

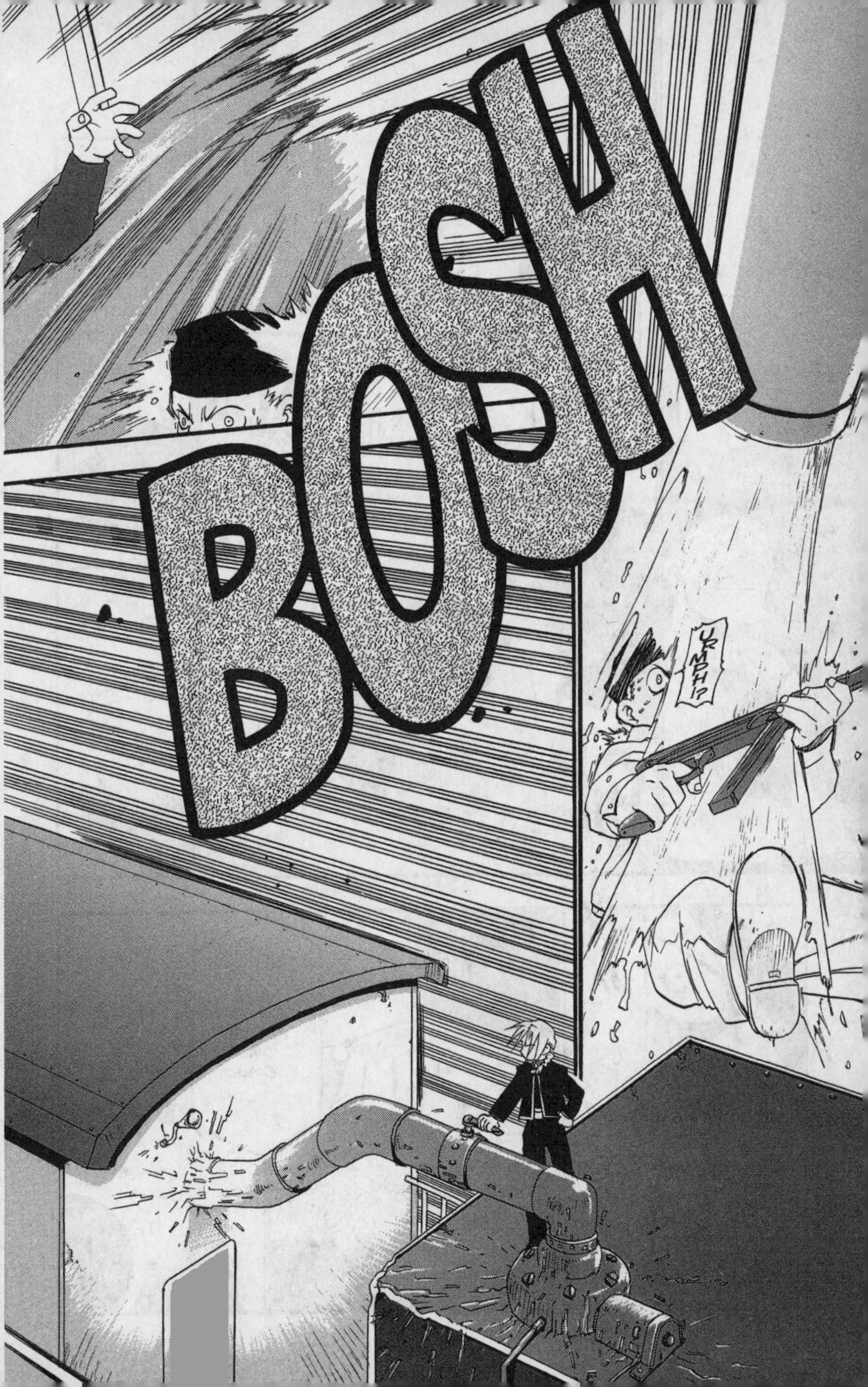
BOSH
URMPH!?

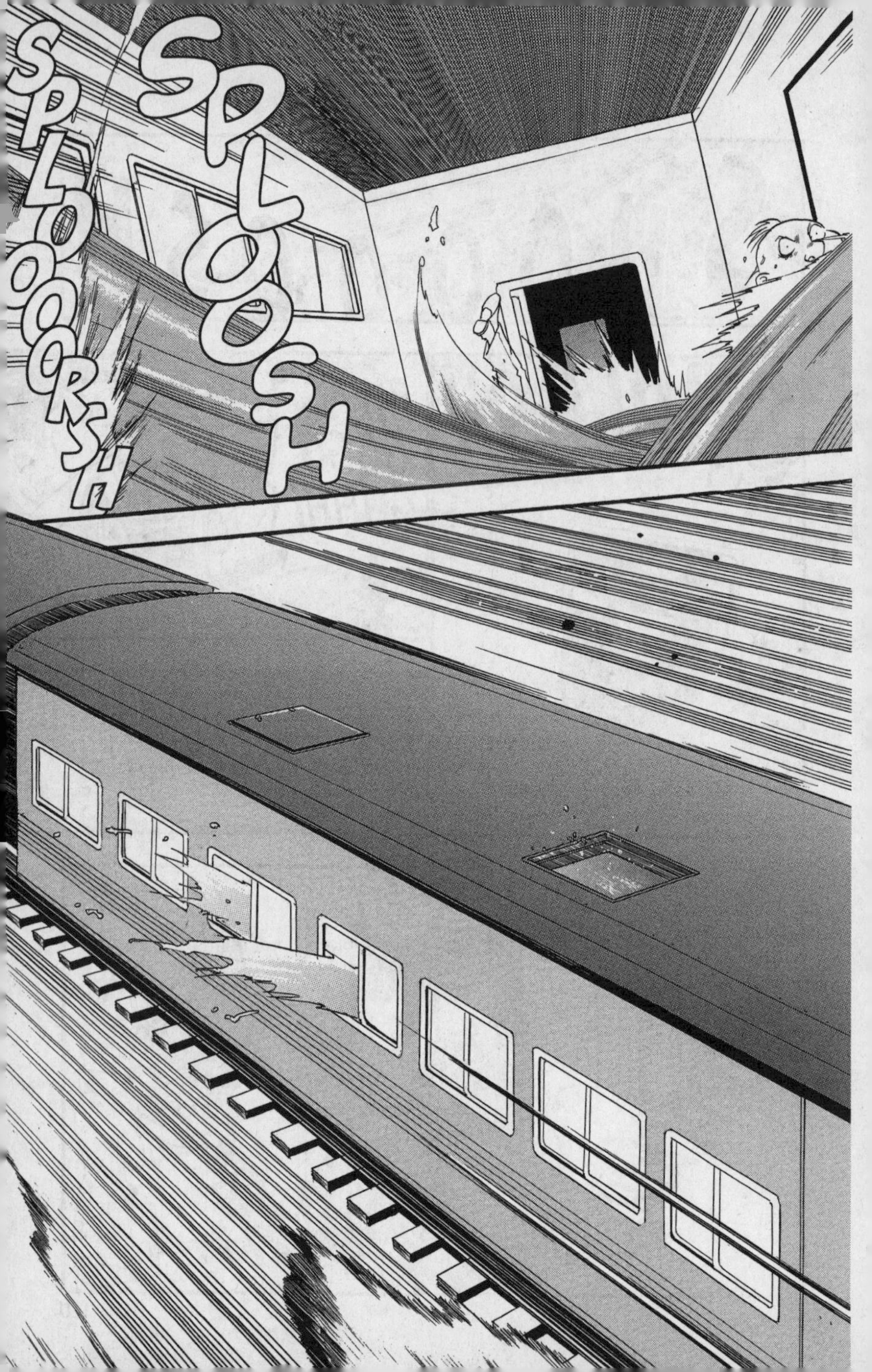
SPLOOSH
SPLOOOORSH

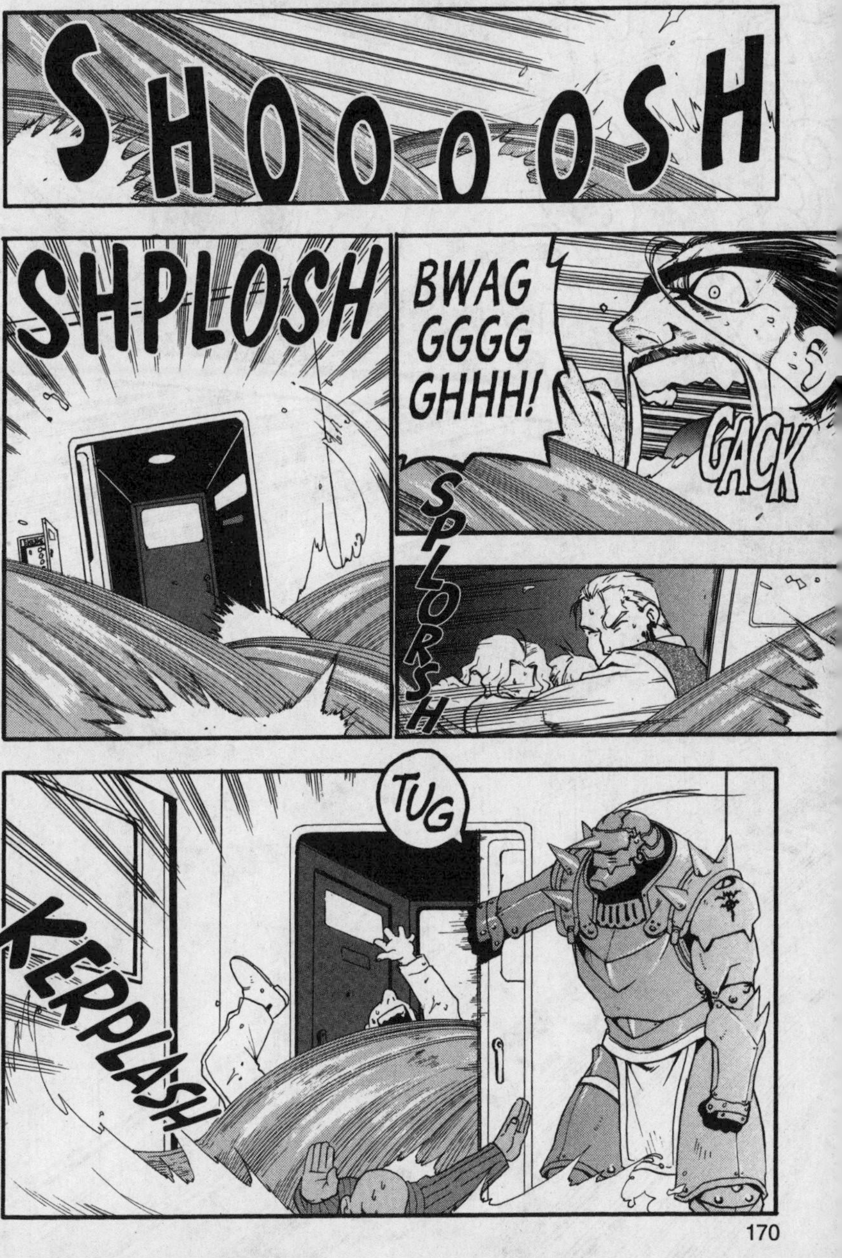
SHOOOOSH
BWAG GGGG GHHH!
GACK
SPLORSH
SHPLOSH
TUG
KERPLASH

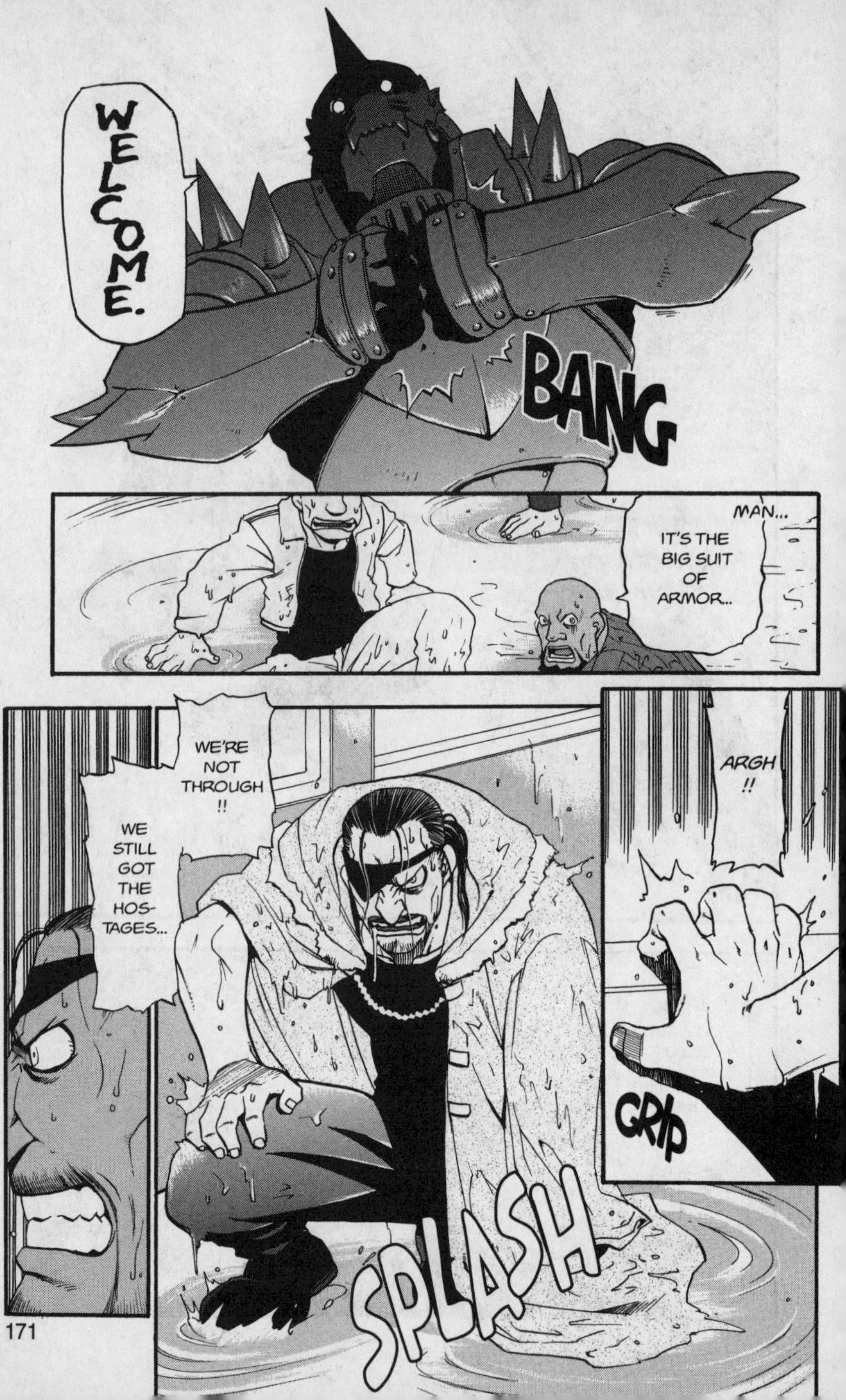
WELCOME.
BANG
MAN... IT'S THE BIG SUIT OF ARMOR...
ARGH!!
GRIP
WE'RE NOT THROUGH!!
WE STILL GOT THE HOSTAGES...
SPLASH

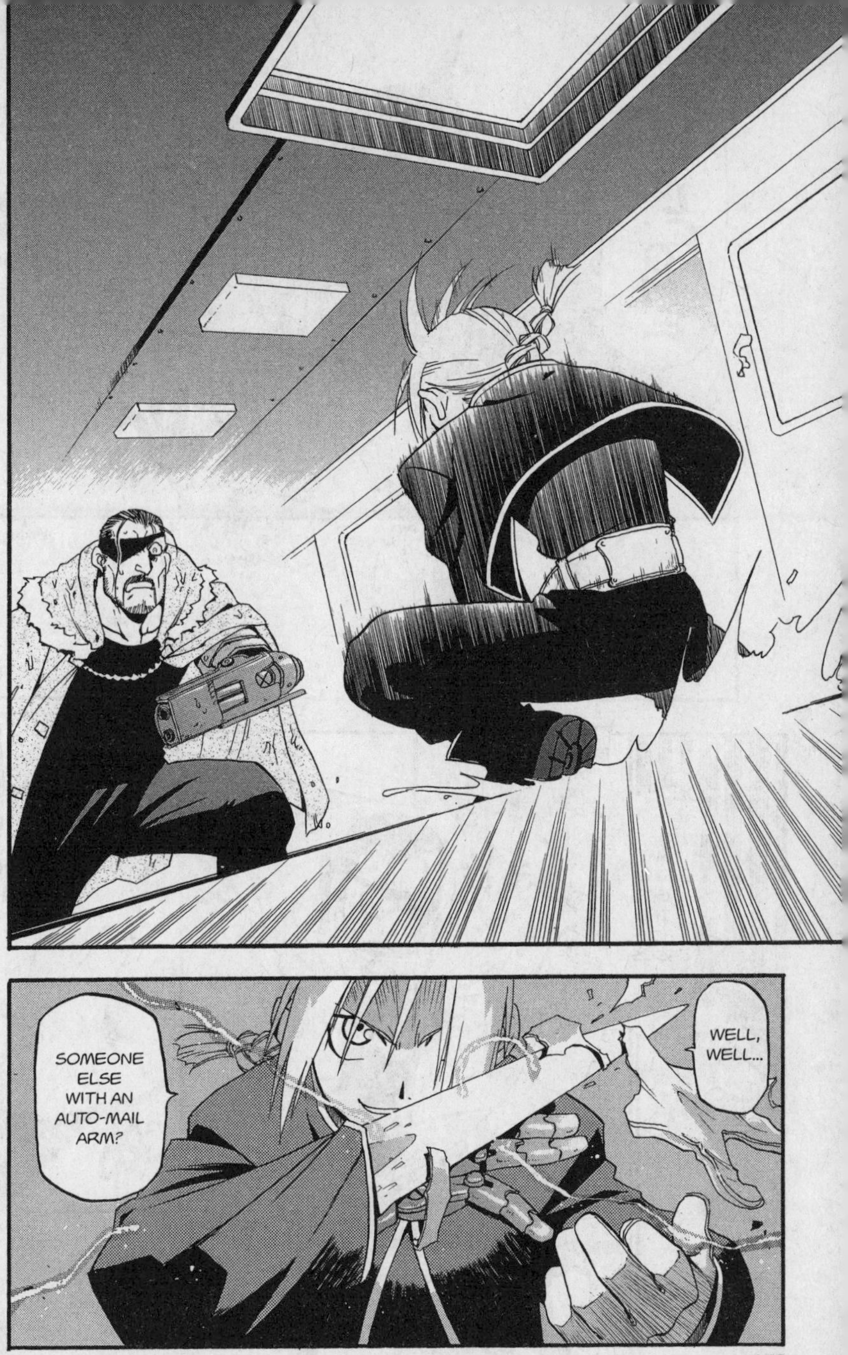
WELL, WELL...
SOMEONE ELSE WITH AN AUTO-MAIL ARM?

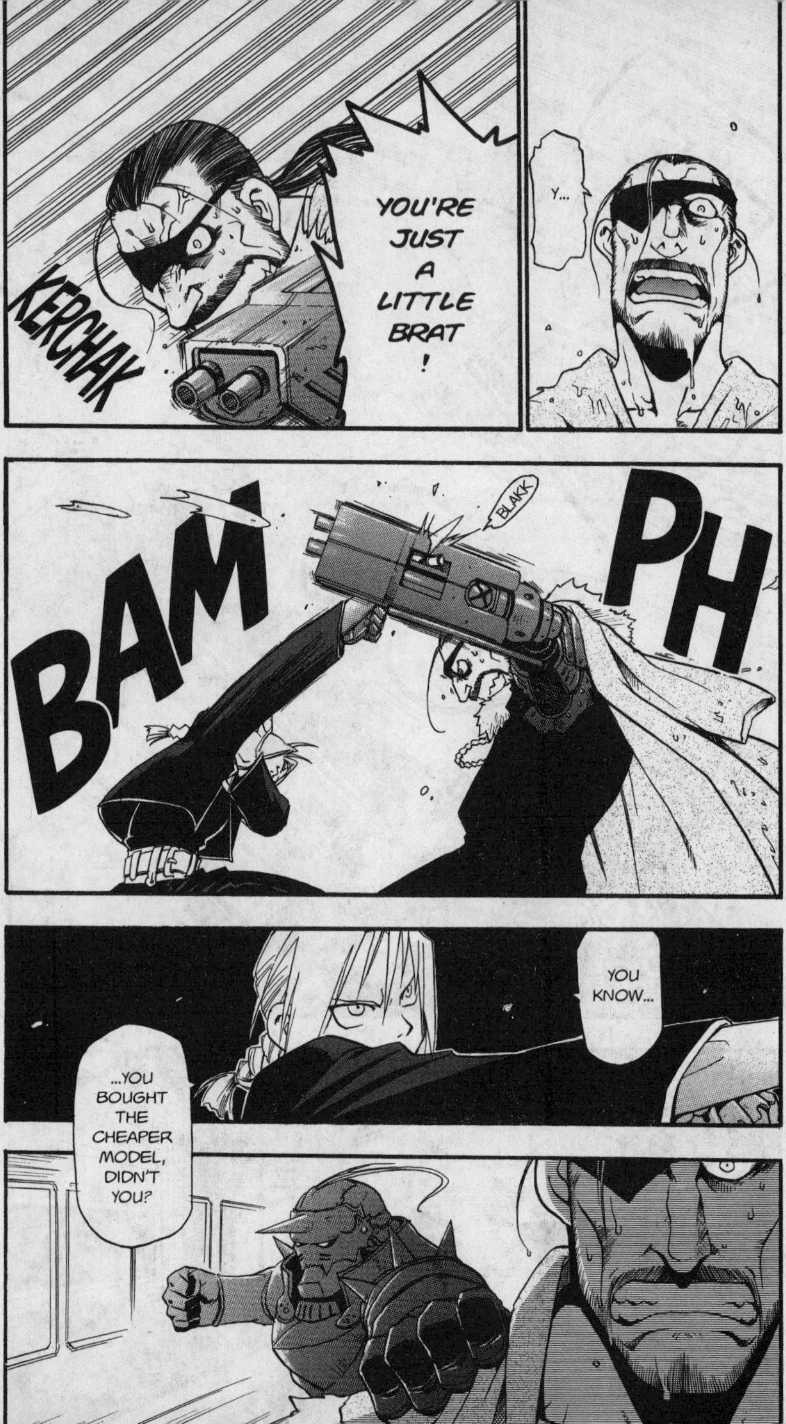

Y...
KERCHAK
YOU'RE JUST A LITTLE BRAT!
PH
BLAKK
BAM
YOU KNOW...
...YOU BOUGHT THE CHEAPER MODEL, DIDN'T YOU?

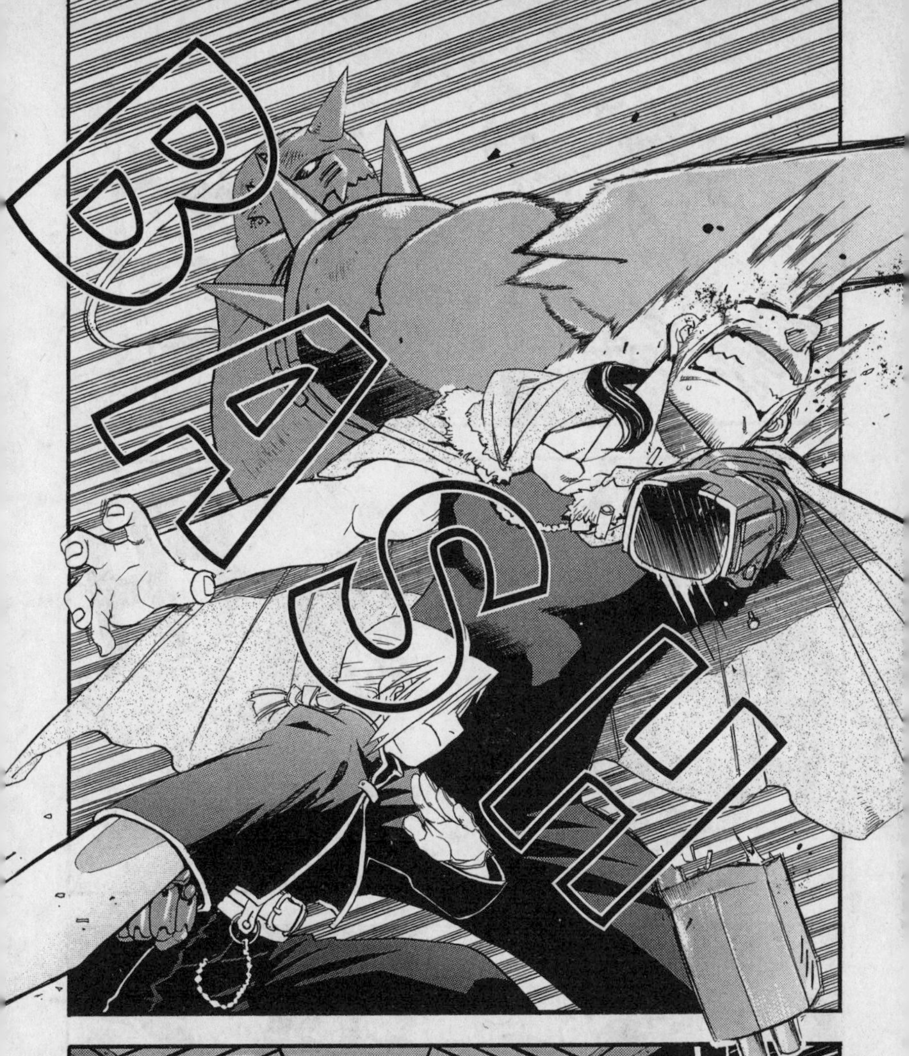
BASH

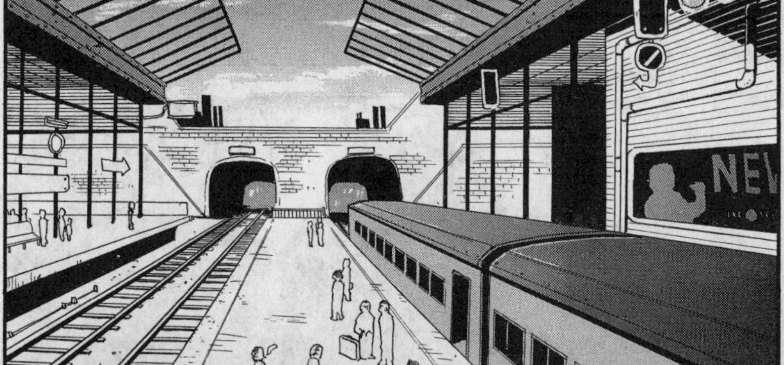

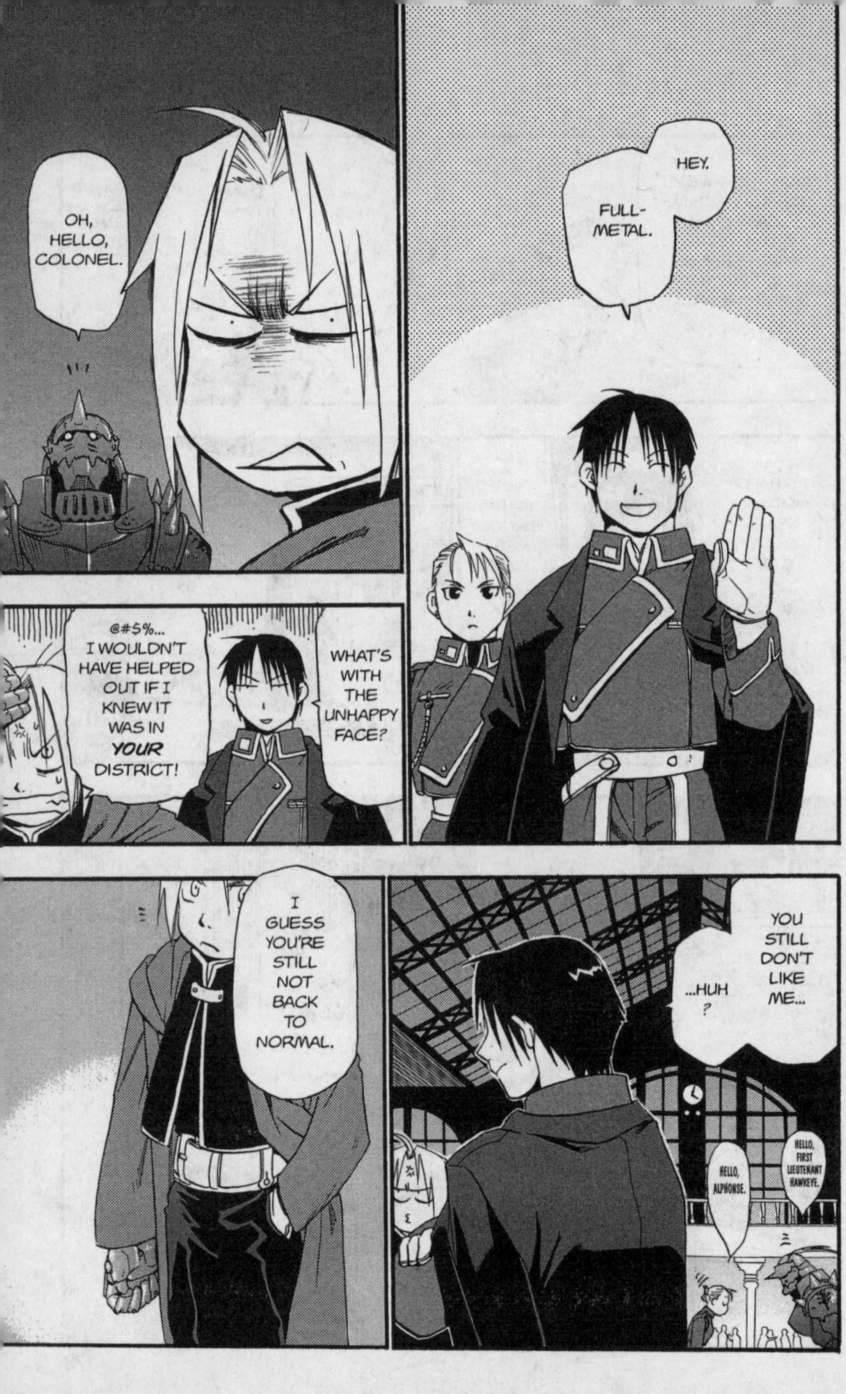
HEY.
FULL-METAL.
OH, HELLO, COLONEL.
WHAT'S WITH THE UNHAPPY FACE?
@#$%... I WOULDN'T HAVE HELPED OUT IF I KNEW IT WAS IN **YOUR** DISTRICT!
YOU STILL DON'T LIKE ME...
...HUH?
HELLO, FIRST LIEUTENANT HAWKEYE.
HELLO, ALPHONSE.
I GUESS YOU'RE STILL NOT BACK TO NORMAL.

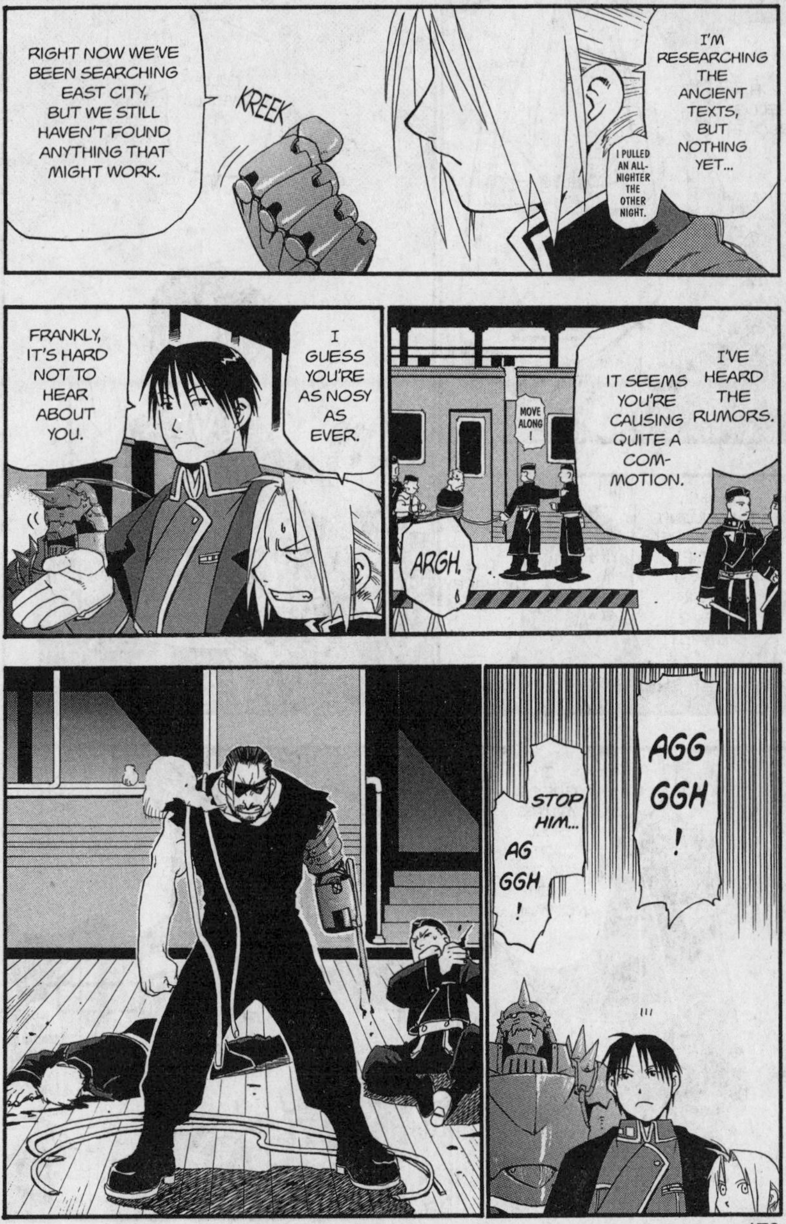
I'M RESEARCHING THE ANCIENT TEXTS, BUT NOTHING YET...
I PULLED AN ALL-NIGHTER THE OTHER NIGHT.
KREEK
RIGHT NOW WE'VE BEEN SEARCHING EAST CITY, BUT WE STILL HAVEN'T FOUND ANYTHING THAT MIGHT WORK.
I'VE HEARD THE RUMORS.
IT SEEMS YOU'RE CAUSING QUITE A COM-MOTION.
MOVE ALONG!
ARGH.
I GUESS YOU'RE AS NOSY AS EVER.
FRANKLY, IT'S HARD NOT TO HEAR ABOUT YOU.
AGG GGH!
STOP HIM...
AG GGH!

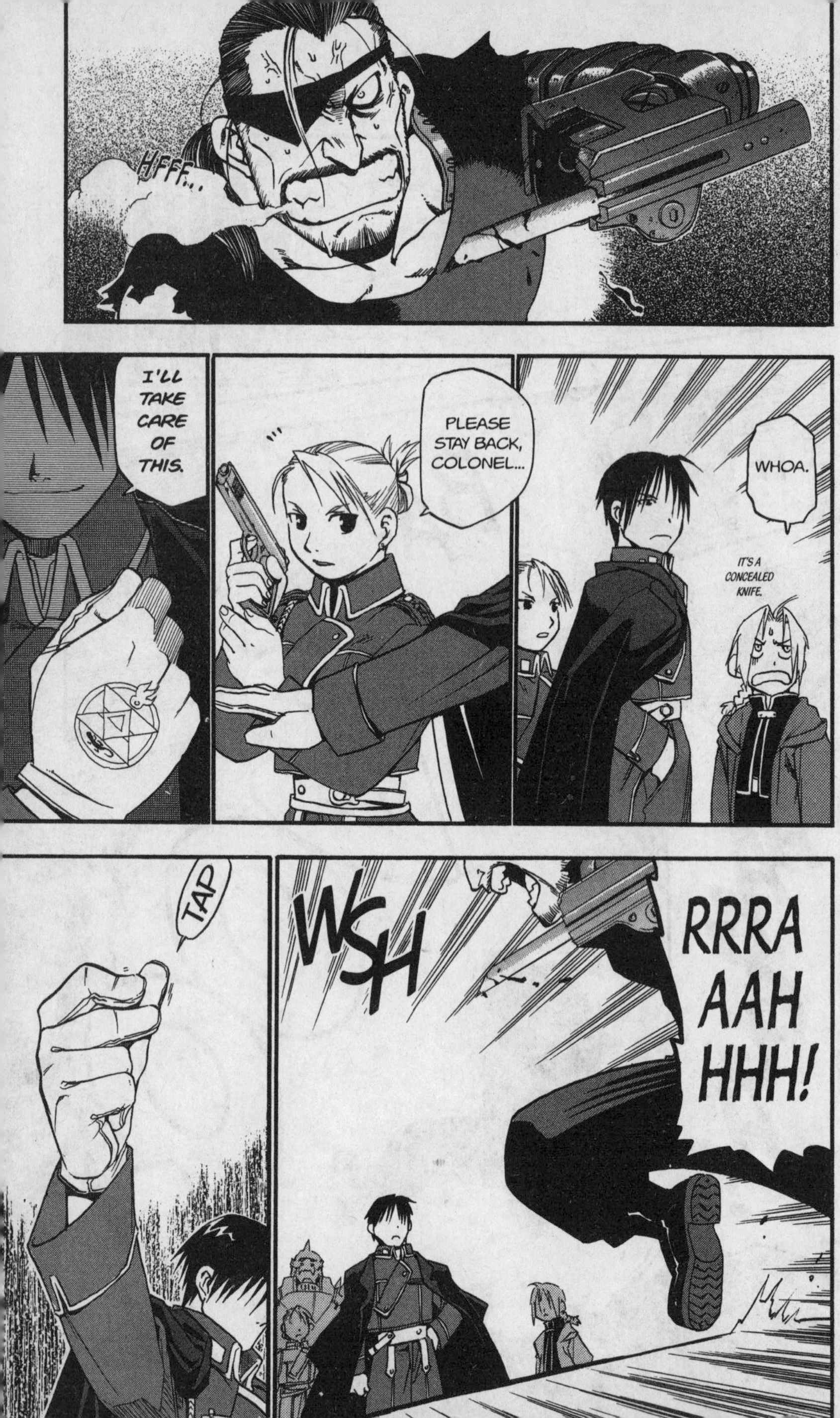
HFFF...
WHOA.
IT'S A CONCEALED KNIFE.
PLEASE STAY BACK, COLONEL...
I'LL TAKE CARE OF THIS.
RRRAAAHHHH!
WSH
TAP

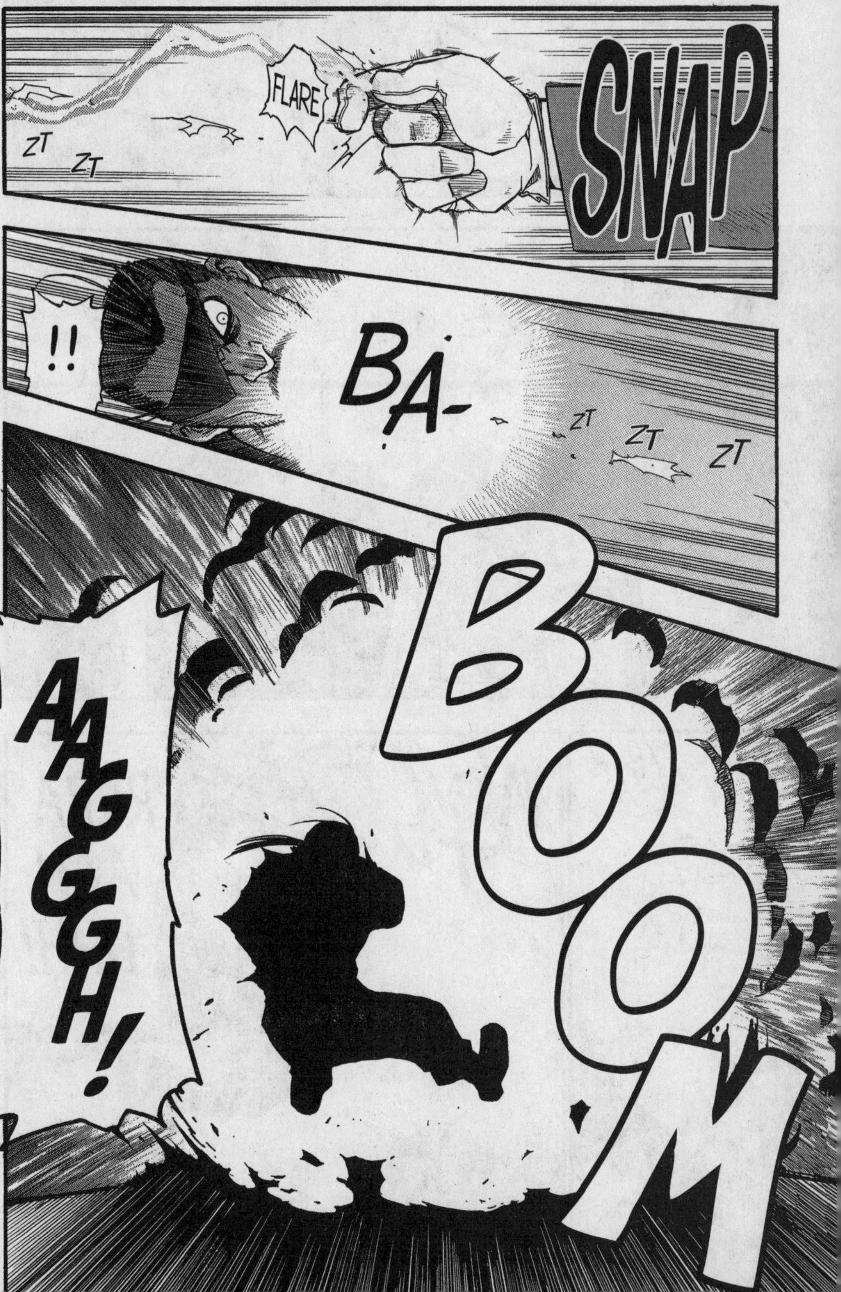
SNAP
FLARE
ZT
ZT
BA-
ZT
ZT
ZT
!!
BOOOM
AAGGGH!

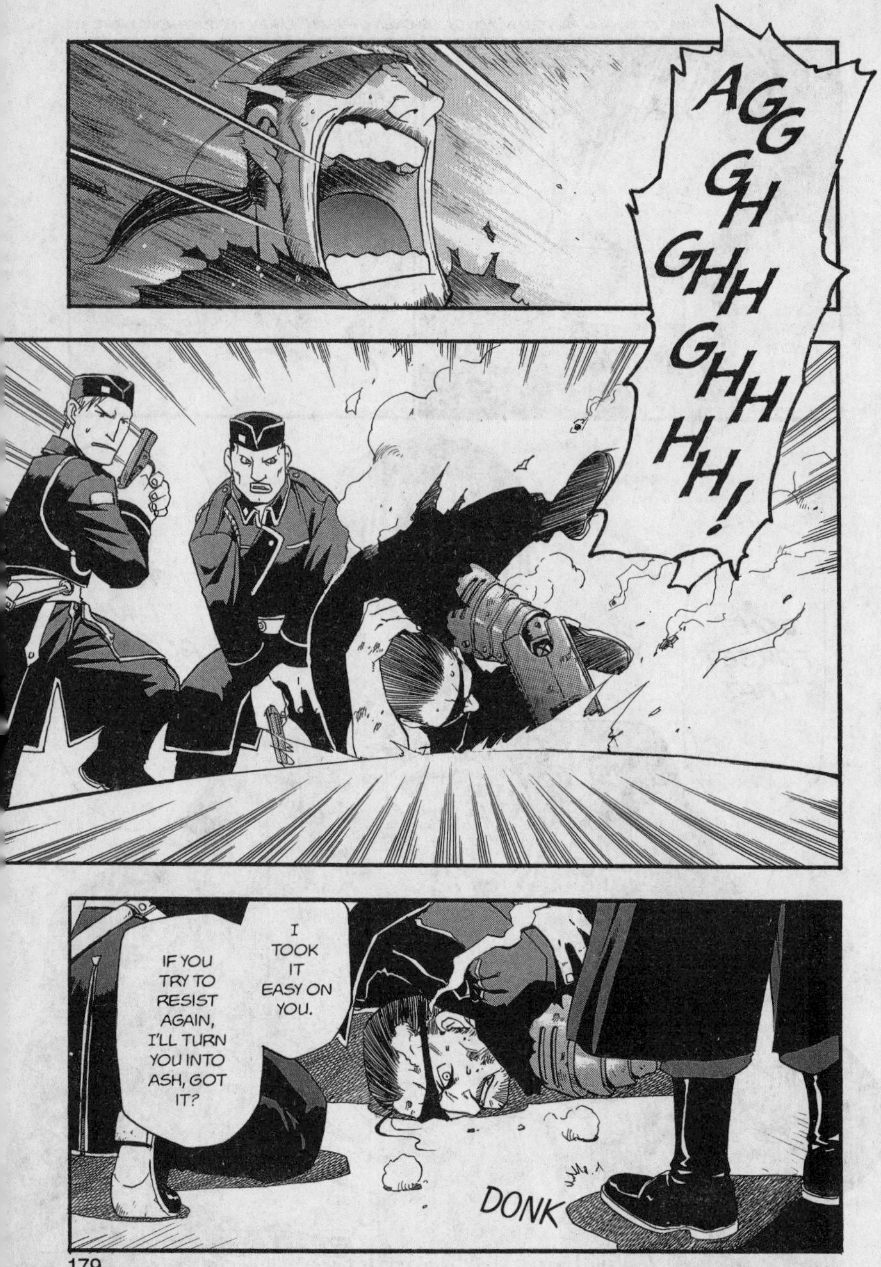
AGGGHGHHGHHHHH!
I TOOK IT EASY ON YOU.
IF YOU TRY TO RESIST AGAIN, I'LL TURN YOU INTO ASH, GOT IT?
DONK

THIS MANGA WAS ORIGINALLY PRINTED IN MONTHLY **SHONEN GANGAN**, AUGUST THROUGH NOVEMBER 2001.

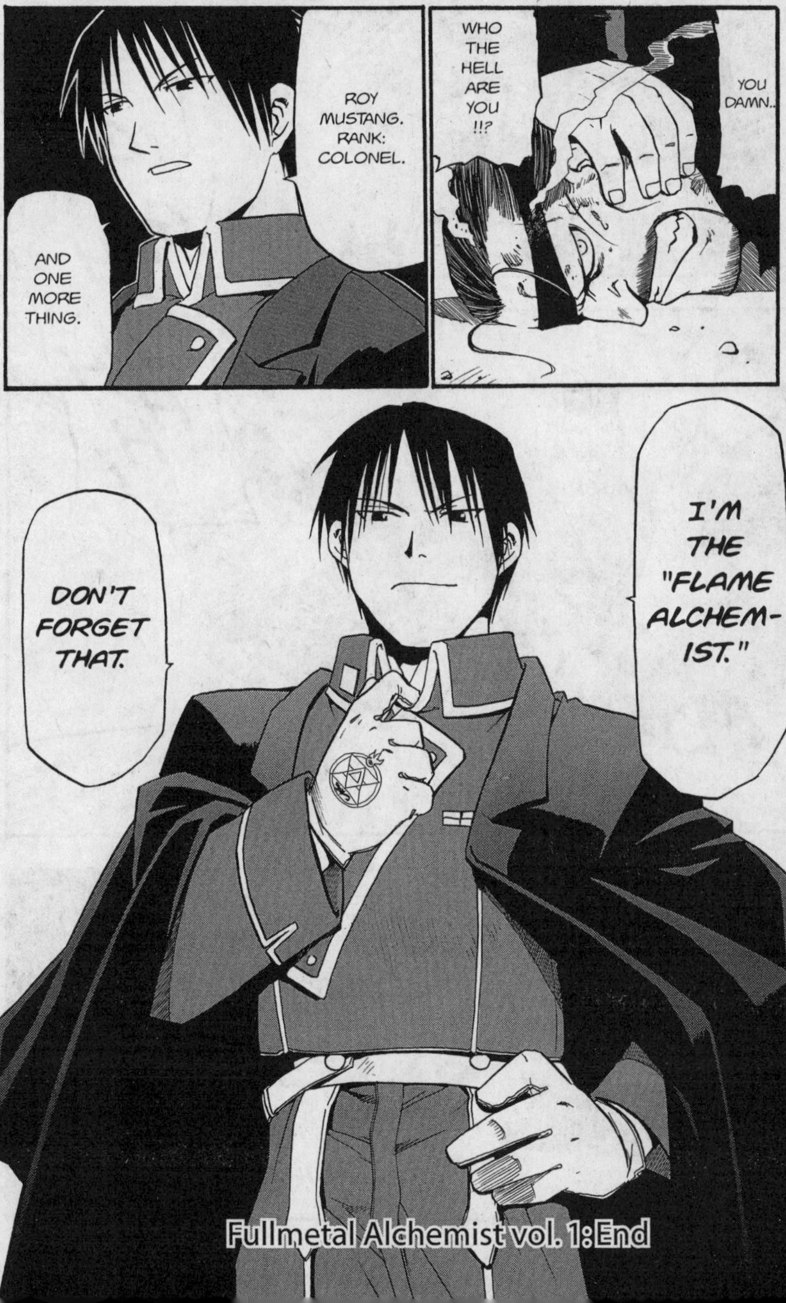
YOU DAMN..
WHO THE HELL ARE YOU !!?
ROY MUSTANG. RANK: COLONEL.
AND ONE MORE THING.
I'M THE "FLAME ALCHEMIST."
DON'T FORGET THAT.
Fullmetal Alchemist vol. 1: End

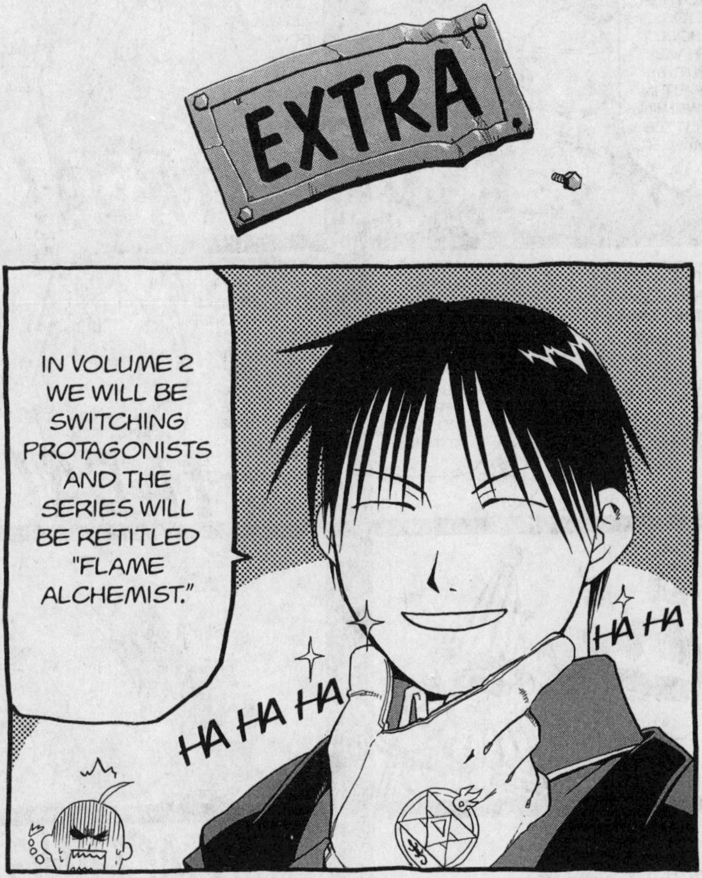
EXTRA
IN VOLUME 2 WE WILL BE SWITCHING PROTAGONISTS AND THE SERIES WILL BE RETITLED "FLAME ALCHEMIST."
HA HA
HA HA HA

That's not true.

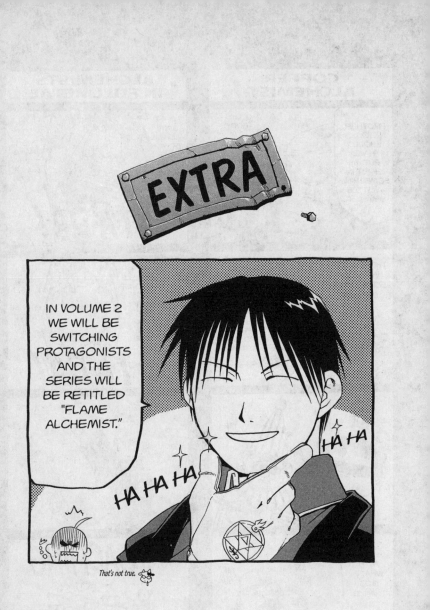

ALCHEMISTS IN FULLMETAL

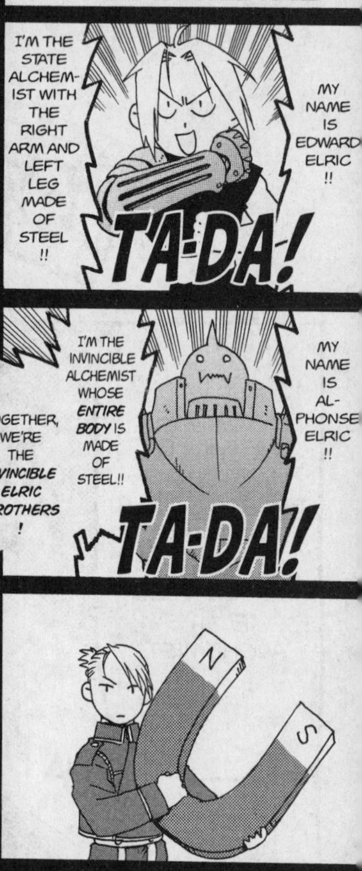
MY NAME IS EDWARD ELRIC!!
I'M THE STATE ALCHEMIST WITH THE RIGHT ARM AND LEFT LEG MADE OF STEEL!!
TA-DA!
MY NAME IS ALPHONSE ELRIC!!
I'M THE INVINCIBLE ALCHEMIST WHOSE ENTIRE BODY IS MADE OF STEEL!!
TOGETHER, WE'RE THE INVINCIBLE ELRIC BROTHERS!
TA-DA!
N
S
GACHING

COPPER ALCHEMIST

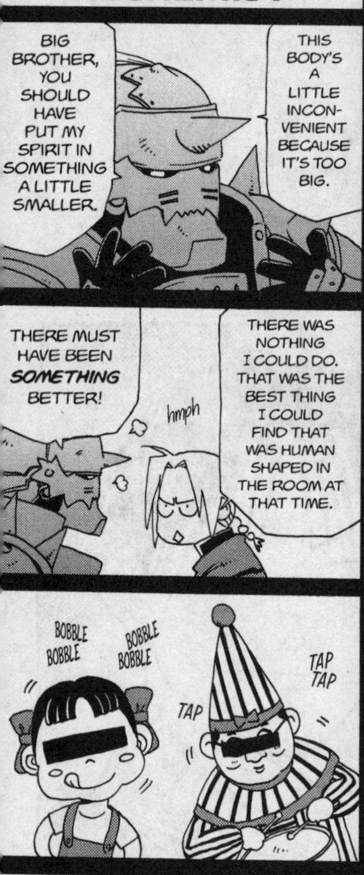
THIS BODY'S A LITTLE INCONVENIENT BECAUSE IT'S TOO BIG.
BIG BROTHER, YOU SHOULD HAVE PUT MY SPIRIT IN SOMETHING A LITTLE SMALLER.
THERE WAS NOTHING I COULD DO. THAT WAS THE BEST THING I COULD FIND THAT WAS HUMAN SHAPED IN THE ROOM AT THAT TIME.
hmph
THERE MUST HAVE BEEN SOMETHING BETTER!
TAP TAP
TAP
BOBBLE BOBBLE
BOBBLE BOBBLE
TAP TAP TAP
BOBBLE BOBBLE
BOBBLE BOBBLE
I'M GOOD WITH WHAT I GOT. THANKS.

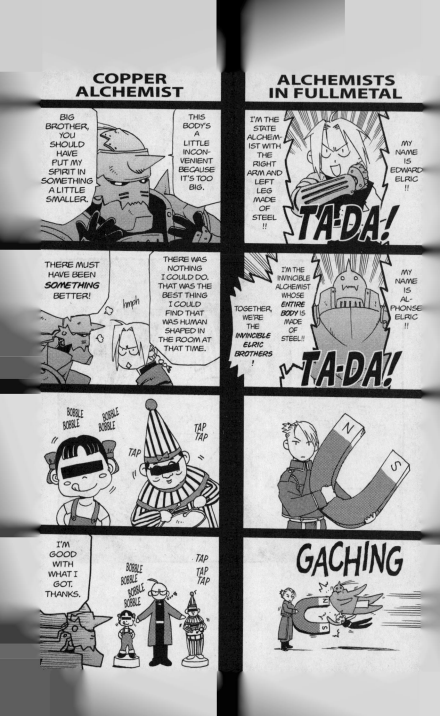

FULLMETAL ALCHEMIST-- COMPLETE

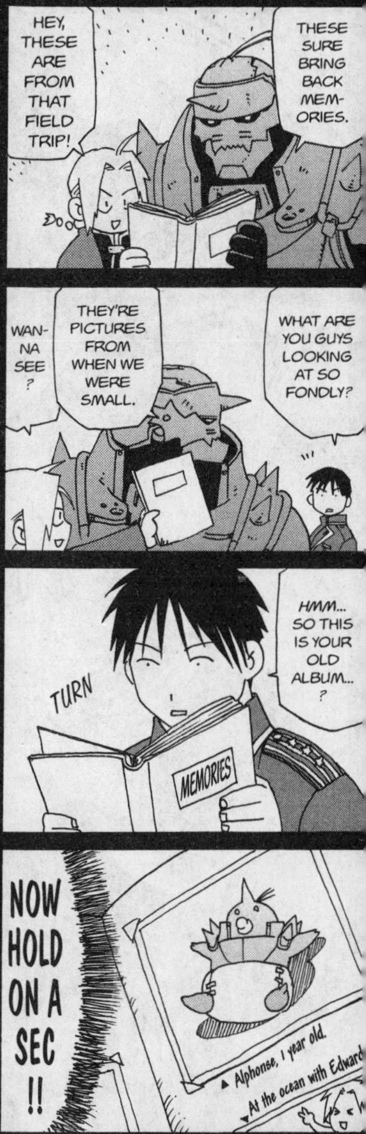

THESE SURE BRING BACK MEMORIES.
HEY, THESE ARE FROM THAT FIELD TRIP!
WHAT ARE YOU GUYS LOOKING AT SO FONDLY?
THEY'RE PICTURES FROM WHEN WE WERE SMALL.
WANNA SEE?
HMM... SO THIS IS YOUR OLD ALBUM...?
TURN
MEMORIES
NOW HOLD ON A SEC!!
Alphonse, 1 year old.
At the ocean with Edward

FULLMETAL ALCHEMIST I SPECIAL THANKS TO...

KEISUI TAKAEDA-SAN
SANKICHI HINODEYA-SAN
JUN MORIYASU-SAN
YOICHI KAMITONO-ANII
KEI GINKO-SAN
RENJURO KINDAICHI-SENSEI

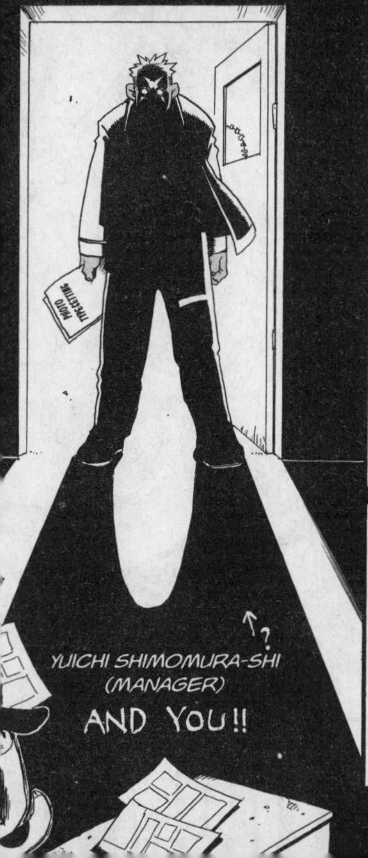

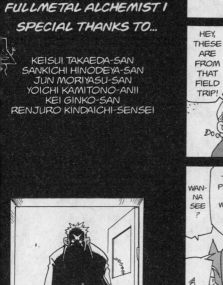

PHOTO TYPESETTING
YUICHI SHIMOMURA-SHI (MANAGER)
AND YOU!!

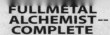

A real live alchemist is captured

In Memoriam

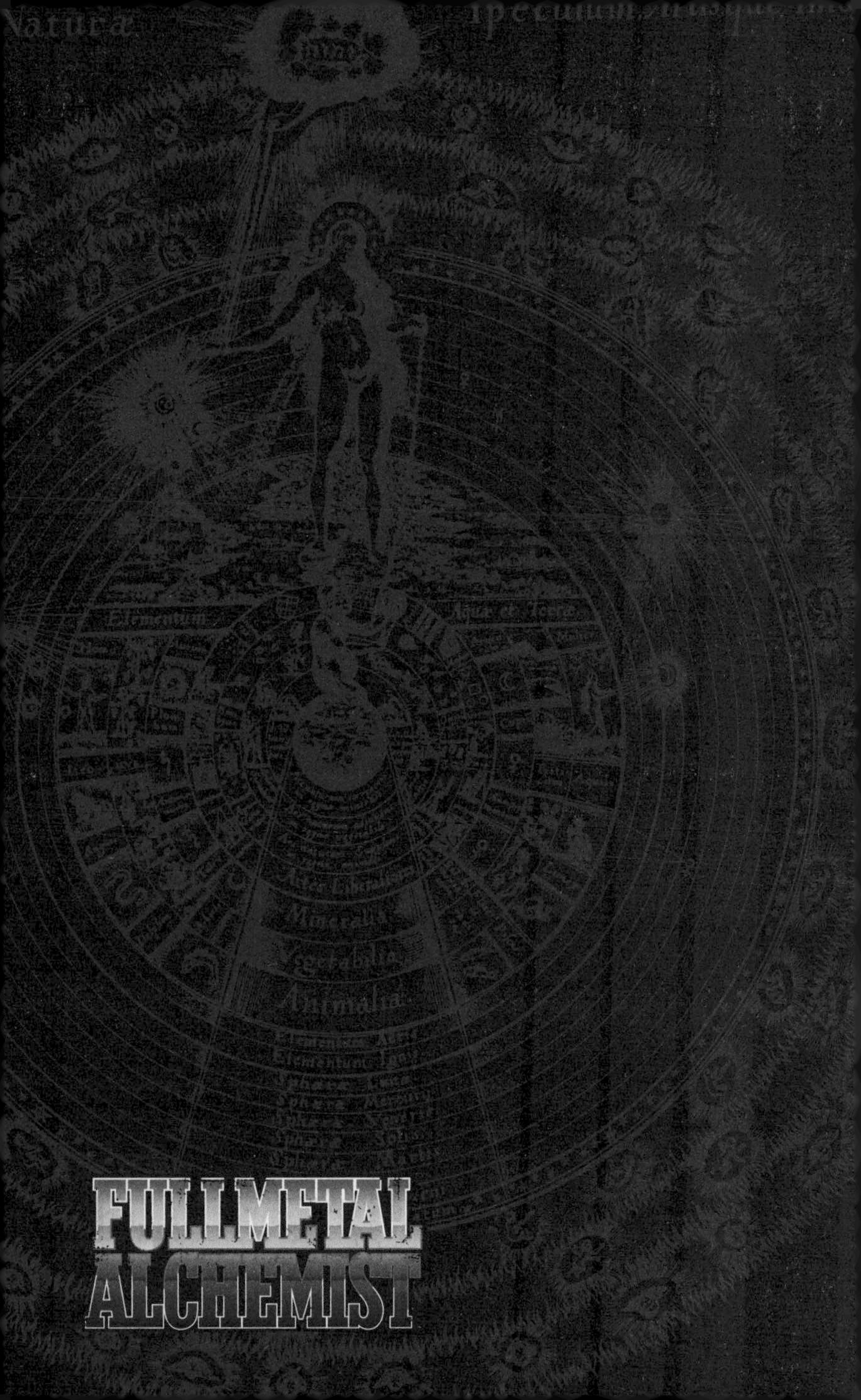
Natura
FULLMETAL ALCHEMIST

Like a piece of beef
that can't respond...

It's been a few years since I left home, saying, "I won't come back here until I can make a living drawing manga." I got my wish, but now I'm so busy that I don't have time to go home. I feel happy and sad at the same time.

—Hiromu Arakawa, 2002

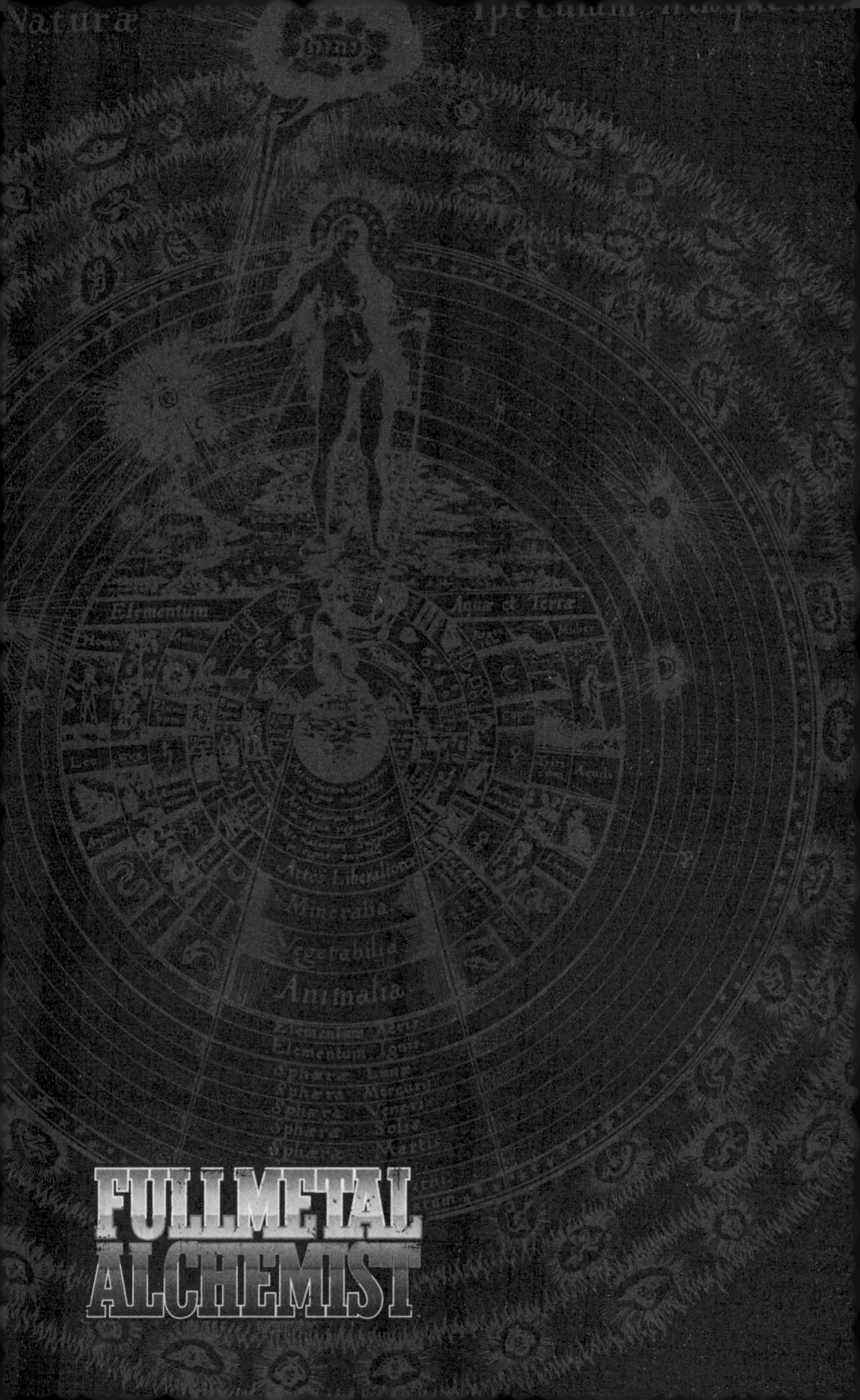
Natura
Elementum
Artes Liberalium
Mineralia
Vegetabilia
Animalia
FULLMETAL
ALCHEMIST

鋼の錬金術師

FULLMETAL ALCHEMIST

2

荒川弘

HIROMU ARAKAWA

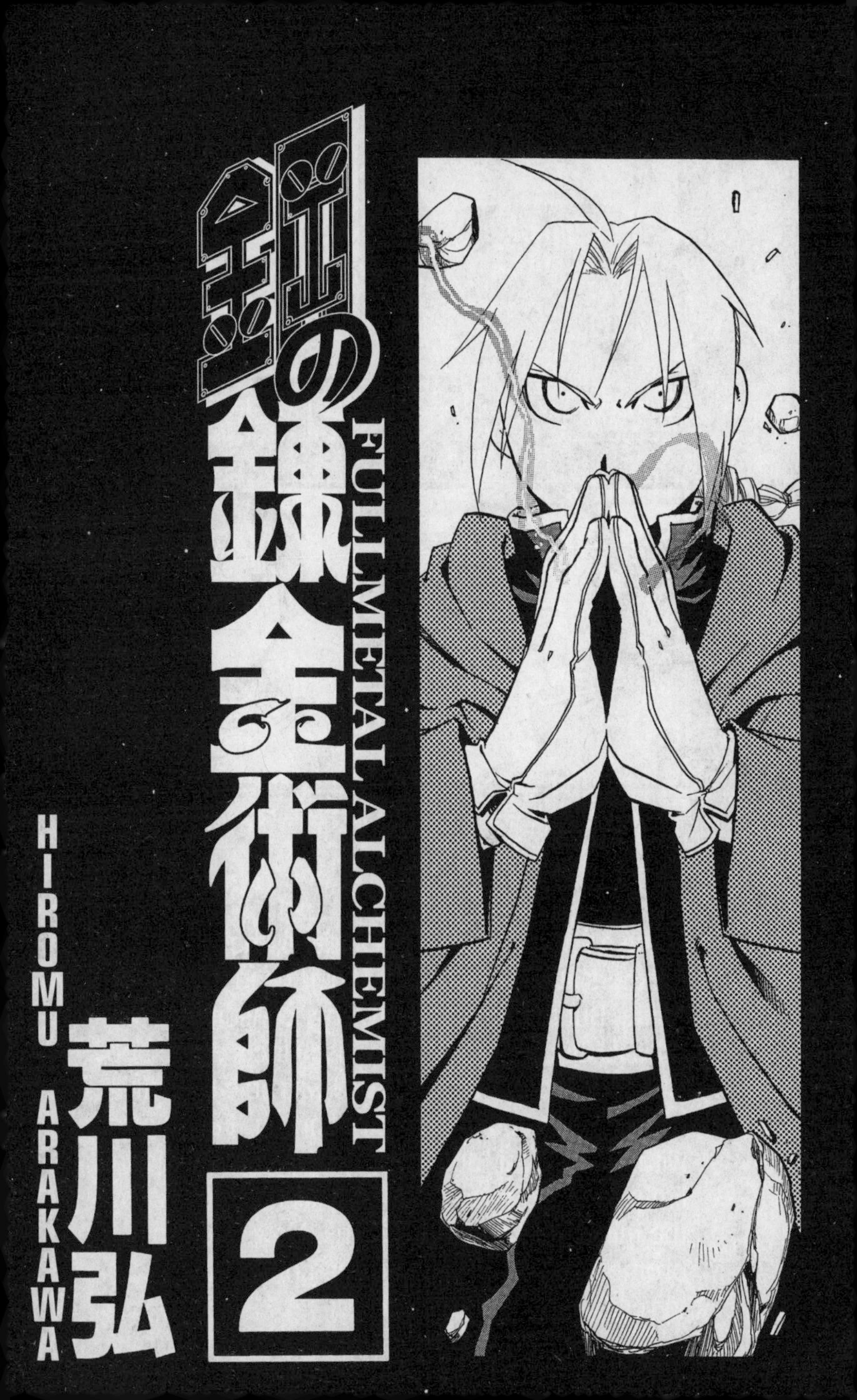

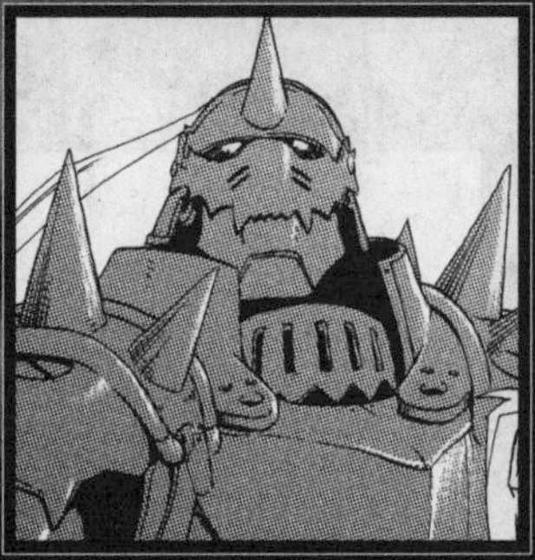

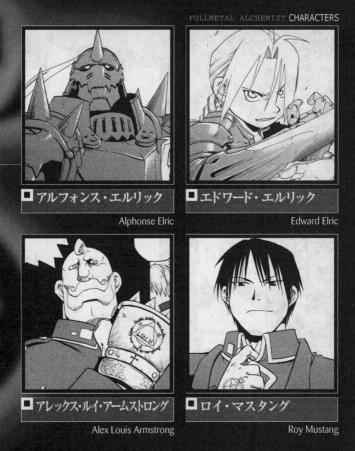

アルフォンス・エルリック

Alphonse Elric

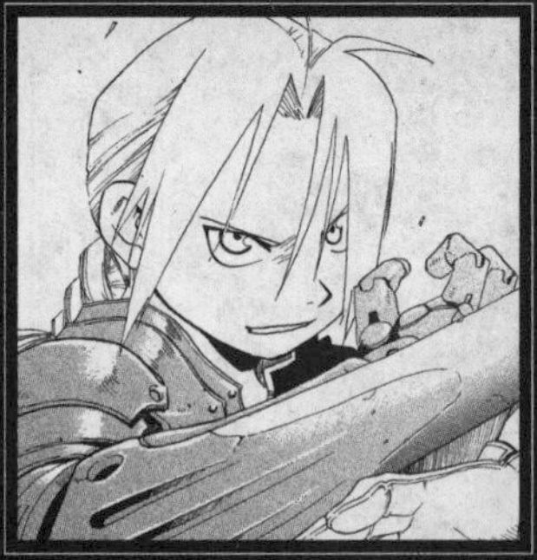

エドワード・エルリック

Edward Elric

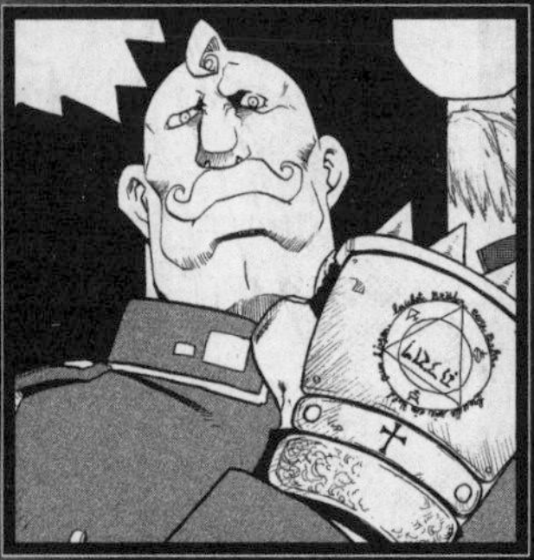

アレックス・ルイ・アームストロング

Alex Louis Armstrong

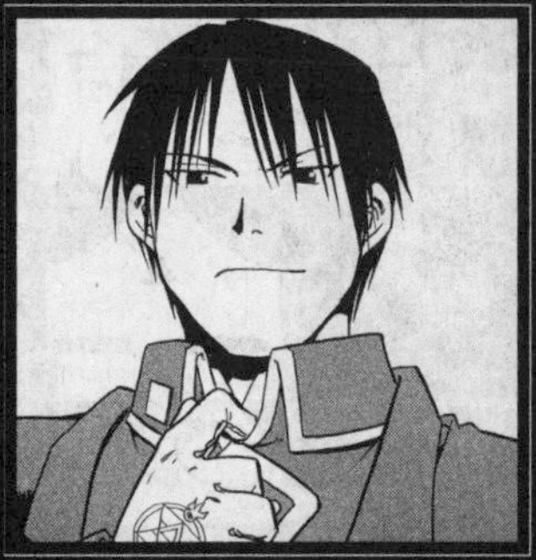

ロイ・マスタング

Roy Mustang

Using a forbidden alchemical ritual, the Elric brothers attempted to bring their dead mother back to life. But the ritual went wrong, consuming Edward Elric's leg and Alphonse Elric's entire body. At the cost of his arm, Edward was able to graft his brother's soul into a suit of armor. Equipped with mechanical "auto-mail" to replace his missing limbs, Edward becomes a state alchemist, serving the military on deadly missions. Now, the two brothers roam the world in search of a way to regain what they have lost...

鋼の錬金術師
FULLMETAL ALCHEMIST

▊CHARACTERS
FULLMETAL ALCHEMIST

□ ショウ・タッカー

Shou Tucker

□ 傷の男（スカー）

Scar

□ グラトニー

Gluttony

□ ラスト

Lust

▊OUTLINE
FULLMETAL ALCHEMIST

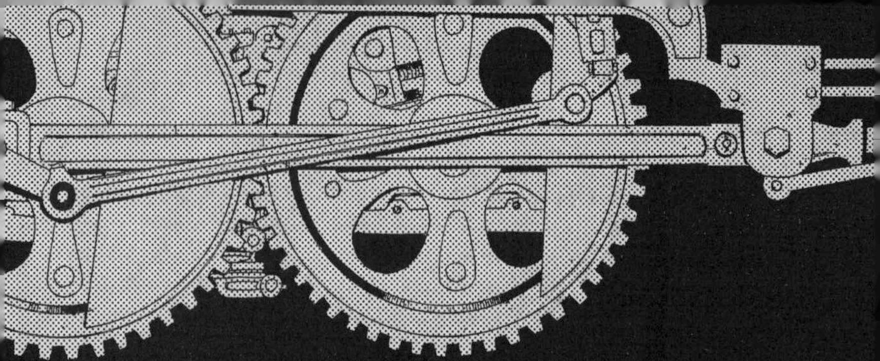

CONTENTS

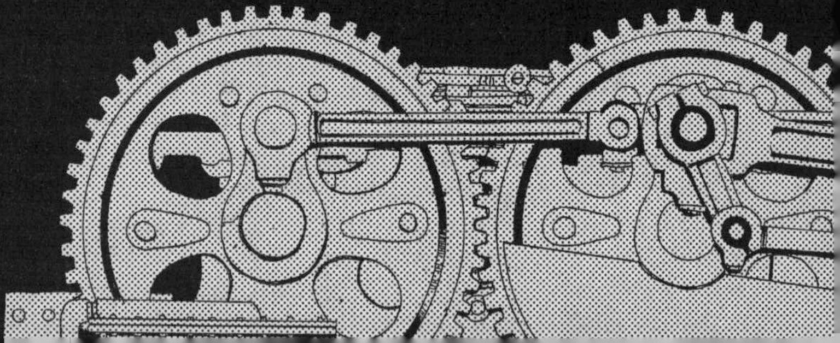

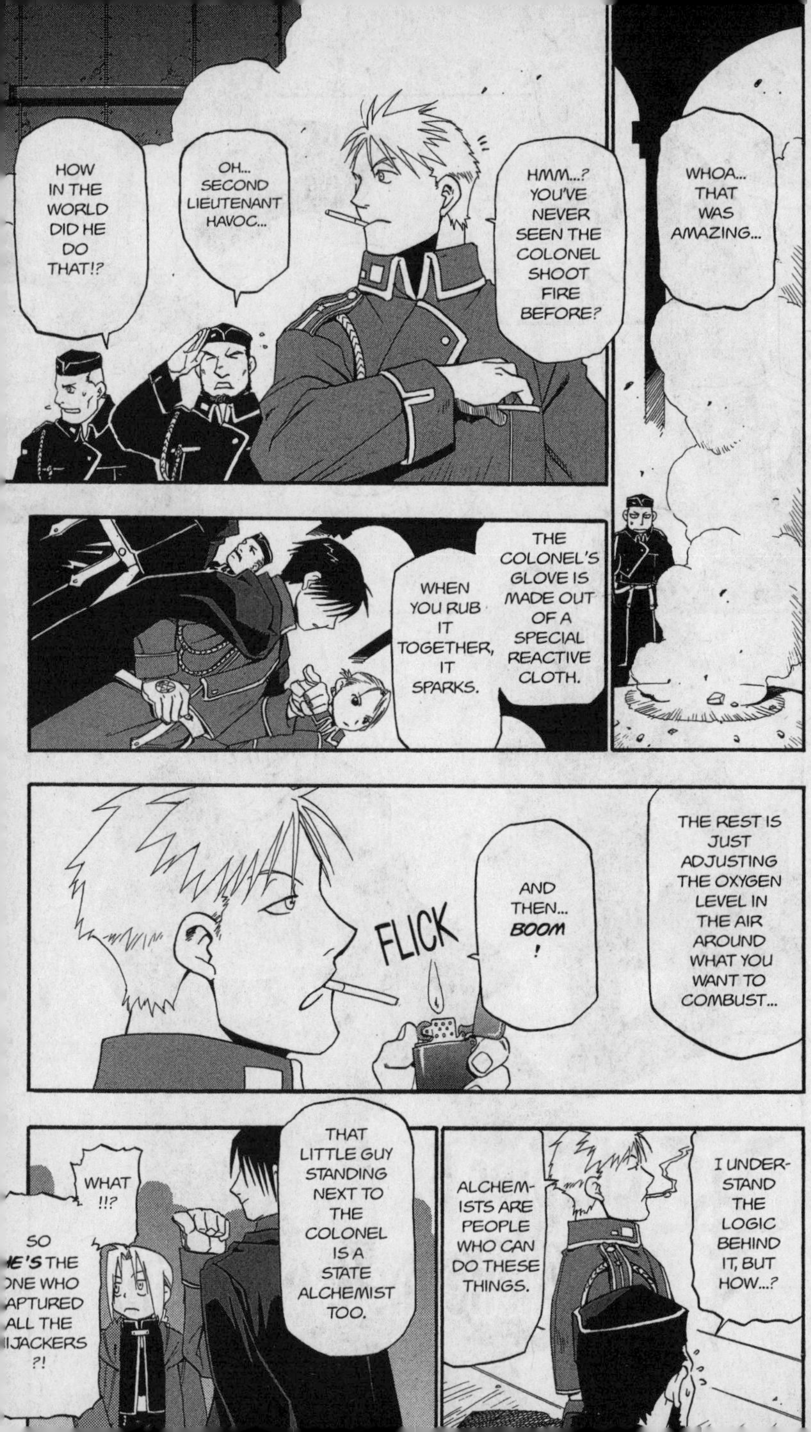
WHOA... THAT WAS AMAZING...
HMM...? YOU'VE NEVER SEEN THE COLONEL SHOOT FIRE BEFORE?
OH... SECOND LIEUTENANT HAVOC...
HOW IN THE WORLD DID HE DO THAT!?
THE COLONEL'S GLOVE IS MADE OUT OF A SPECIAL REACTIVE CLOTH.
WHEN YOU RUB IT TOGETHER, IT SPARKS.
THE REST IS JUST ADJUSTING THE OXYGEN LEVEL IN THE AIR AROUND WHAT YOU WANT TO COMBUST...
AND THEN... BOOM!
FLICK
I UNDER-STAND THE LOGIC BEHIND IT, BUT HOW...?
ALCHEM-ISTS ARE PEOPLE WHO CAN DO THESE THINGS.
THAT LITTLE GUY STANDING NEXT TO THE COLONEL IS A STATE ALCHEMIST TOO.
WHAT !!?
SO E'S THE ONE WHO APTURED ALL THE IJACKERS ?!

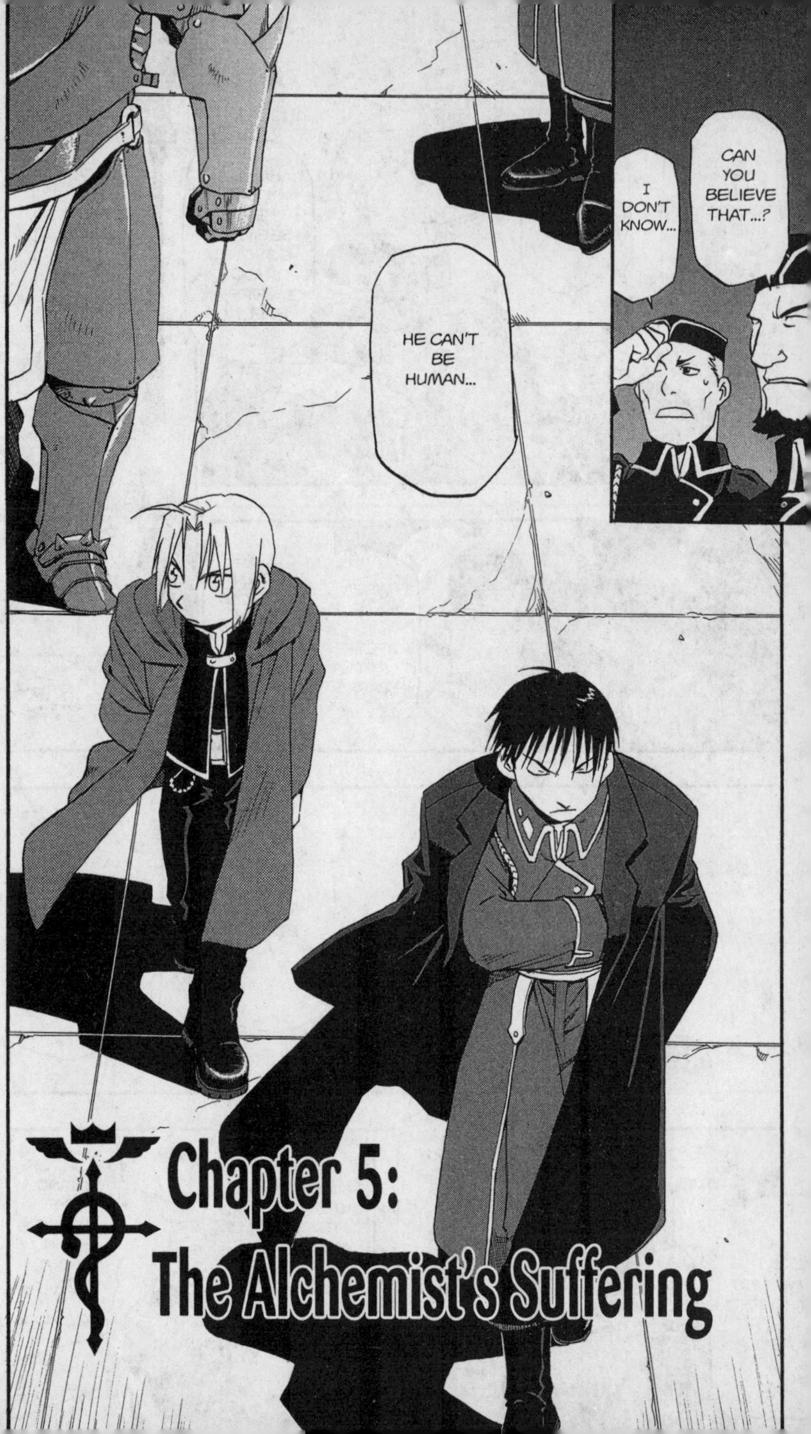
CAN YOU BELIEVE THAT...?
I DON'T KNOW...
HE CAN'T BE HUMAN...

Chapter 5: The Alchemist's Suffering

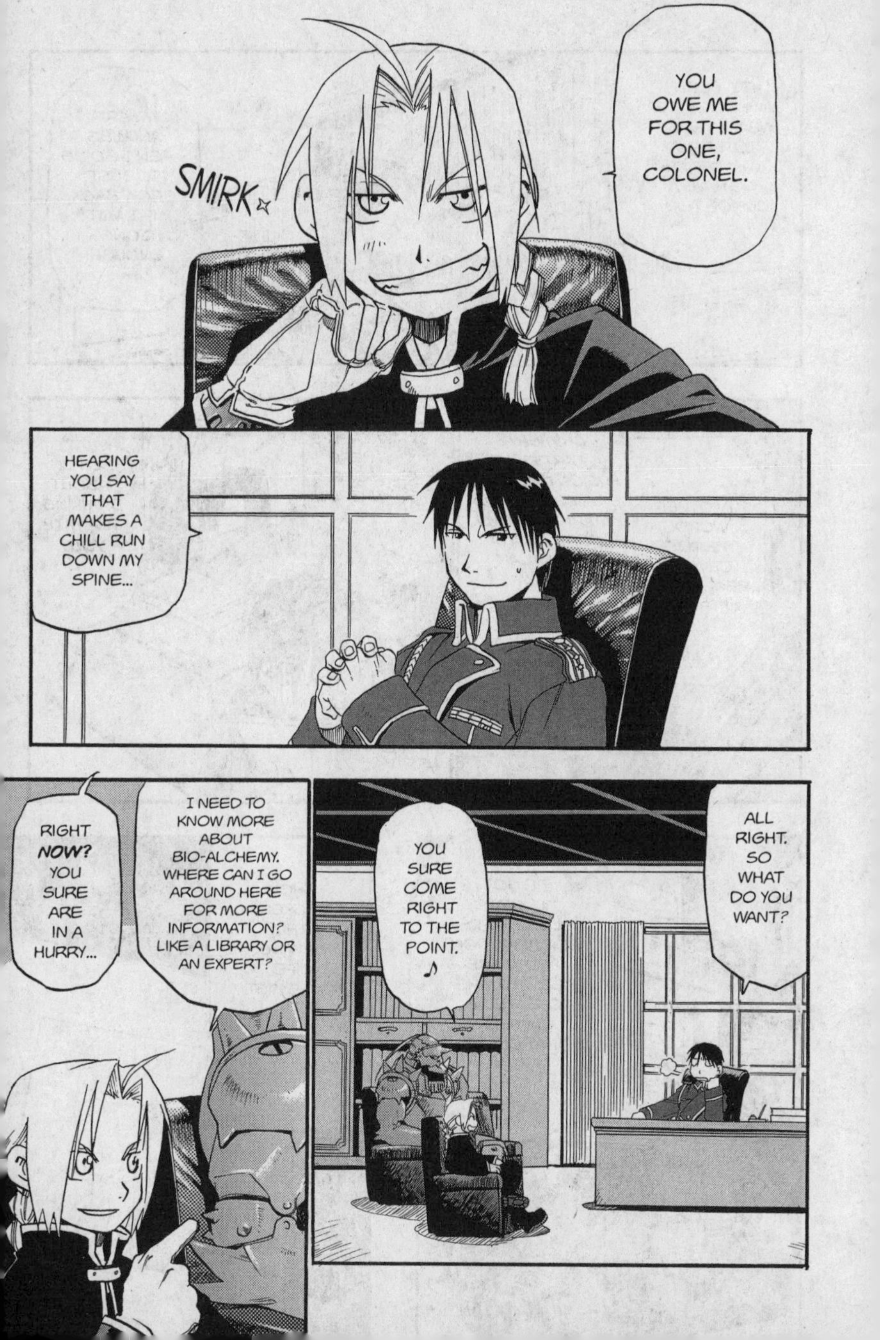
YOU OWE ME FOR THIS ONE, COLONEL.
SMIRK
HEARING YOU SAY THAT MAKES A CHILL RUN DOWN MY SPINE...
ALL RIGHT. SO WHAT DO YOU WANT?
YOU SURE COME RIGHT TO THE POINT. ♪
I NEED TO KNOW MORE ABOUT BIO-ALCHEMY. WHERE CAN I GO AROUND HERE FOR MORE INFORMATION? LIKE A LIBRARY OR AN EXPERT?
RIGHT ***NOW?*** YOU SURE ARE IN A HURRY...

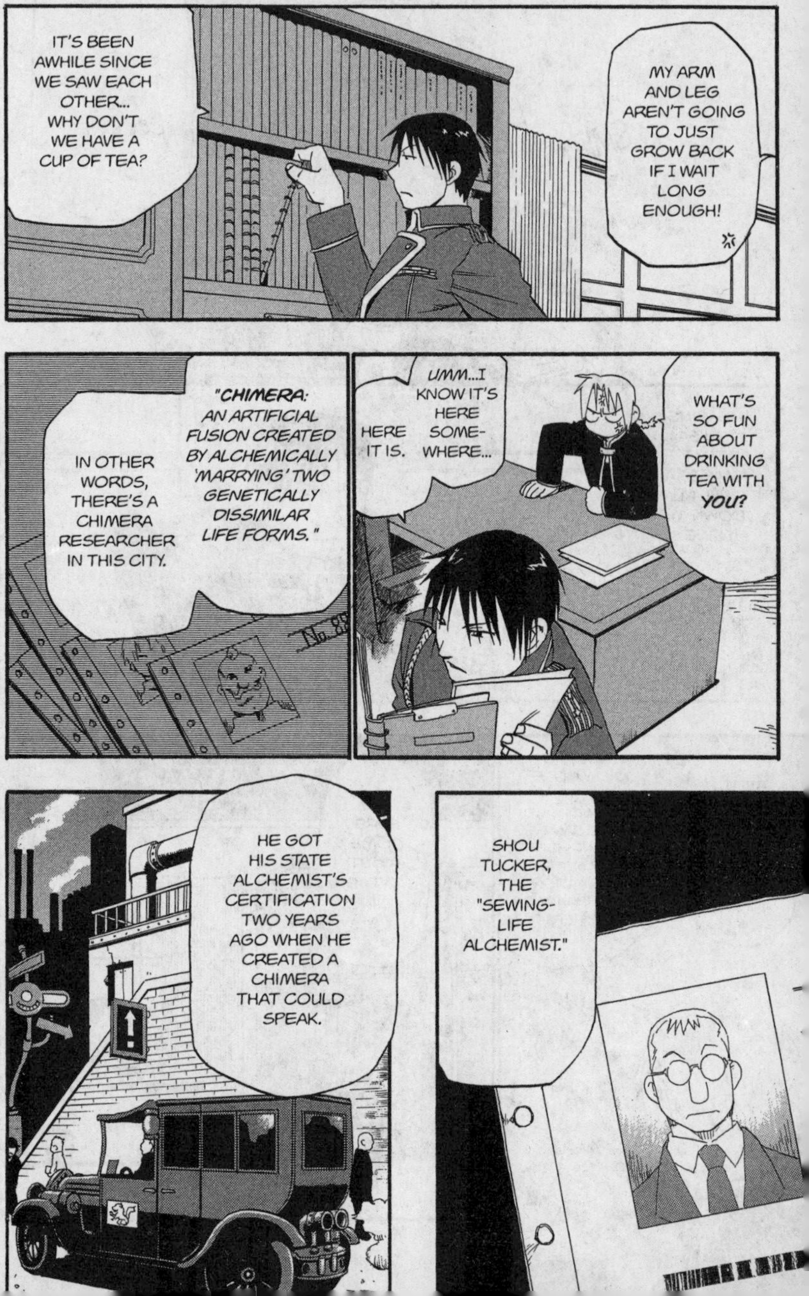
IT'S BEEN AWHILE SINCE WE SAW EACH OTHER... WHY DON'T WE HAVE A CUP OF TEA?
MY ARM AND LEG AREN'T GOING TO JUST GROW BACK IF I WAIT LONG ENOUGH!
WHAT'S SO FUN ABOUT DRINKING TEA WITH *YOU*?
UMM...I KNOW IT'S HERE SOME- WHERE...
HERE IT IS.
"*CHIMERA*: AN ARTIFICIAL FUSION CREATED BY ALCHEMICALLY 'MARRYING' TWO GENETICALLY DISSIMILAR LIFE FORMS."
IN OTHER WORDS, THERE'S A CHIMERA RESEARCHER IN THIS CITY.
SHOU TUCKER, THE "SEWING- LIFE ALCHEMIST."
HE GOT HIS STATE ALCHEMIST'S CERTIFICATION TWO YEARS AGO WHEN HE CREATED A CHIMERA THAT COULD SPEAK.

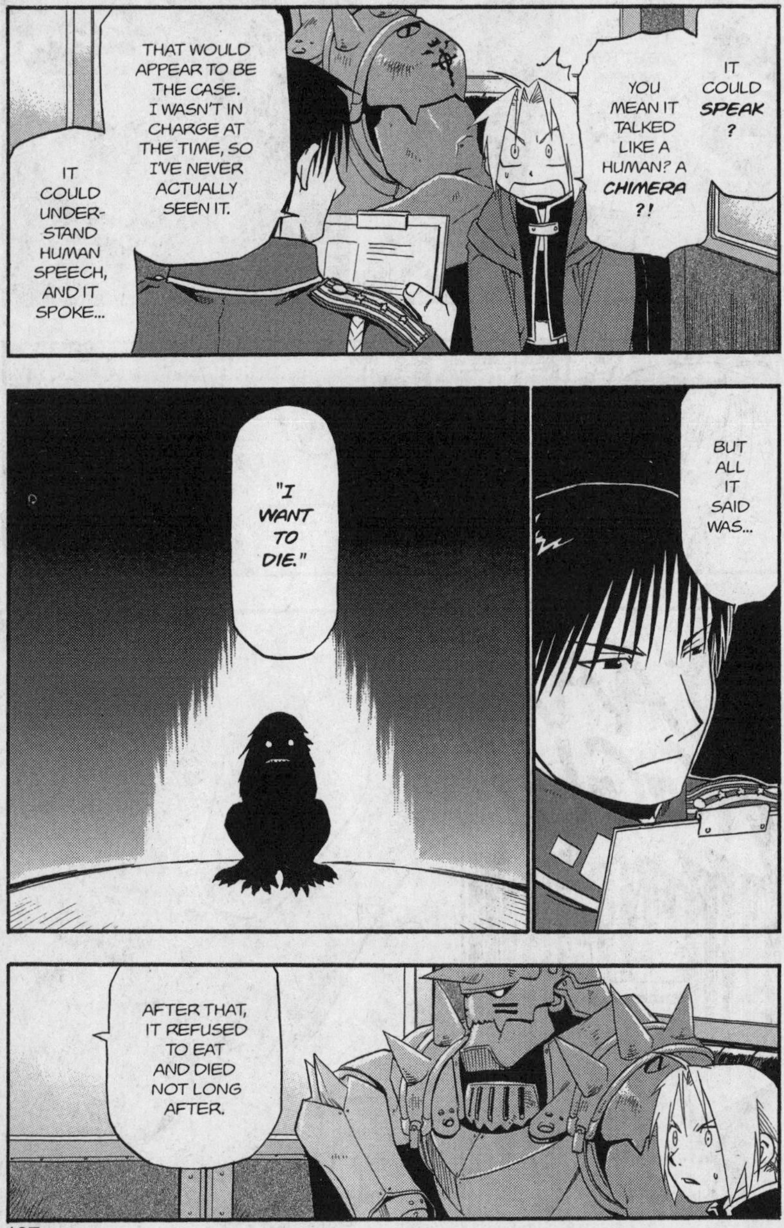
IT COULD SPEAK?
YOU MEAN IT TALKED LIKE A HUMAN? A CHIMERA?!
THAT WOULD APPEAR TO BE THE CASE. I WASN'T IN CHARGE AT THE TIME, SO I'VE NEVER ACTUALLY SEEN IT.
IT COULD UNDER-STAND HUMAN SPEECH, AND IT SPOKE...
BUT ALL IT SAID WAS...
"I WANT TO DIE."
AFTER THAT, IT REFUSED TO EAT AND DIED NOT LONG AFTER.

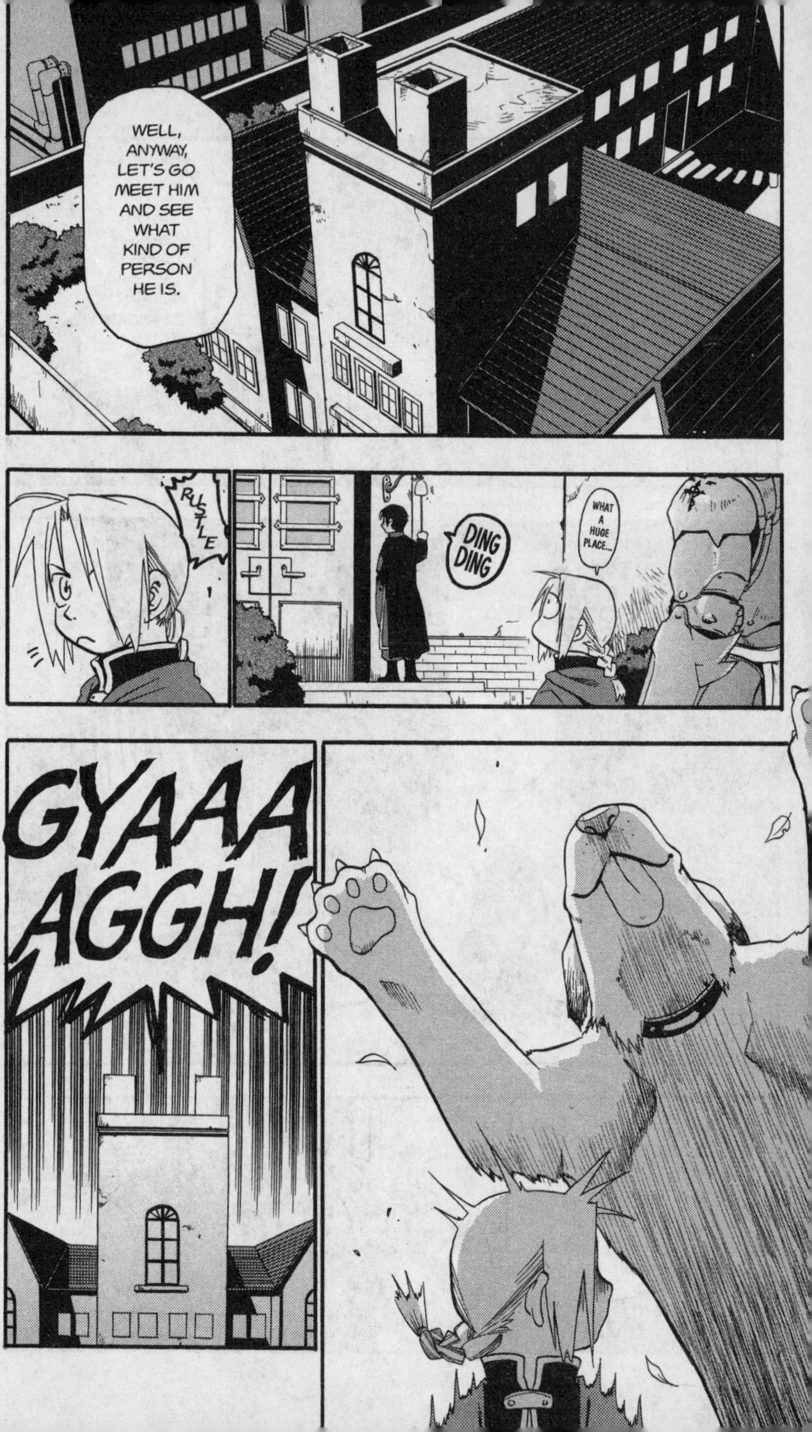
WELL, ANYWAY, LET'S GO MEET HIM AND SEE WHAT KIND OF PERSON HE IS.
WHAT A HUGE PLACE...
DING DING
RUSTLE
GYAAAAGGH!

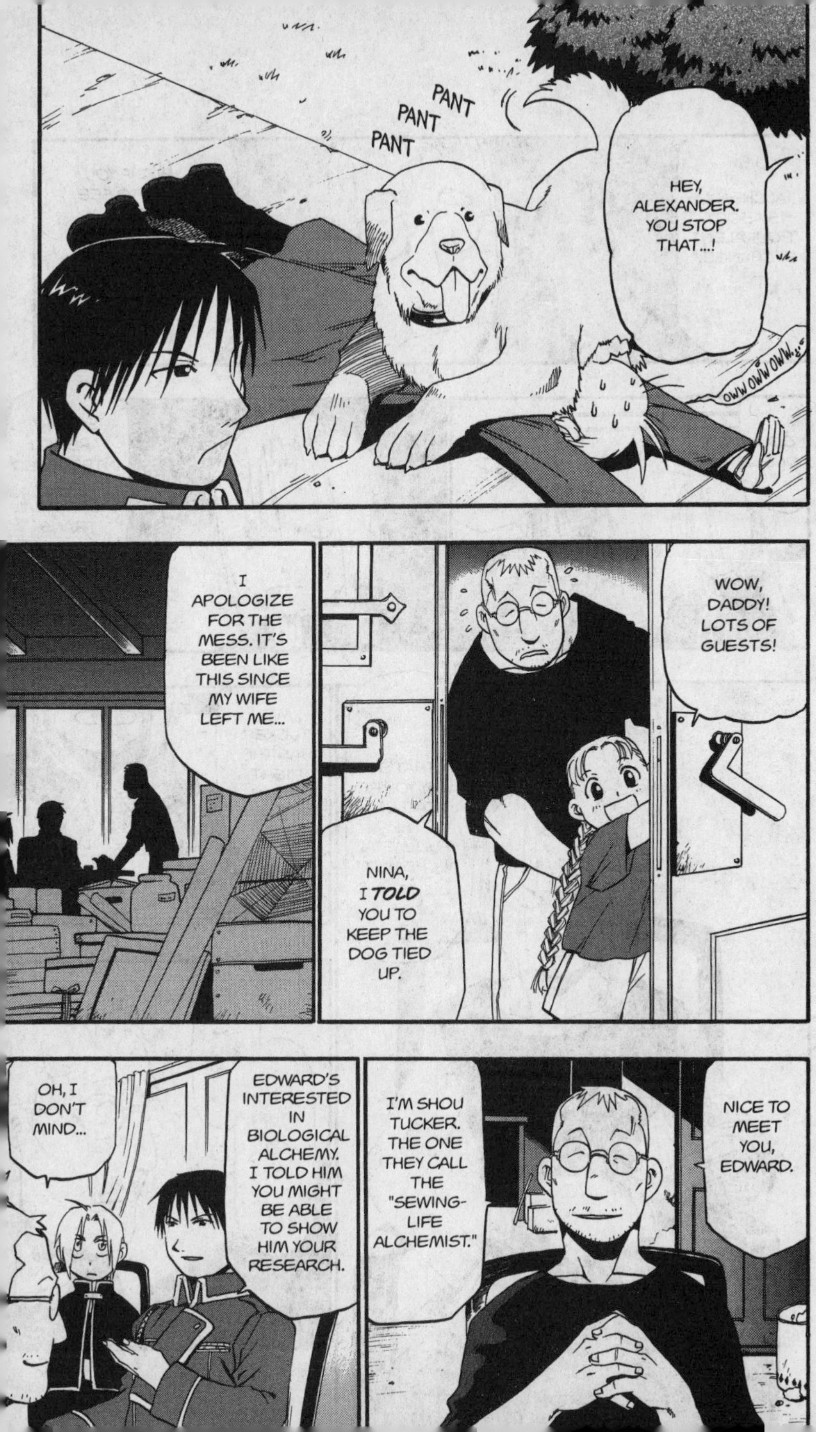
PANT PANT PANT
HEY, ALEXANDER. YOU STOP THAT...!
OWW OWW OWW...
WOW, DADDY! LOTS OF GUESTS!
NINA, I TOLD YOU TO KEEP THE DOG TIED UP.
I APOLOGIZE FOR THE MESS. IT'S BEEN LIKE THIS SINCE MY WIFE LEFT ME...
NICE TO MEET YOU, EDWARD.
I'M SHOU TUCKER. THE ONE THEY CALL THE "SEWING-LIFE ALCHEMIST."
EDWARD'S INTERESTED IN BIOLOGICAL ALCHEMY. I TOLD HIM YOU MIGHT BE ABLE TO SHOW HIM YOUR RESEARCH.
OH, I DON'T MIND...

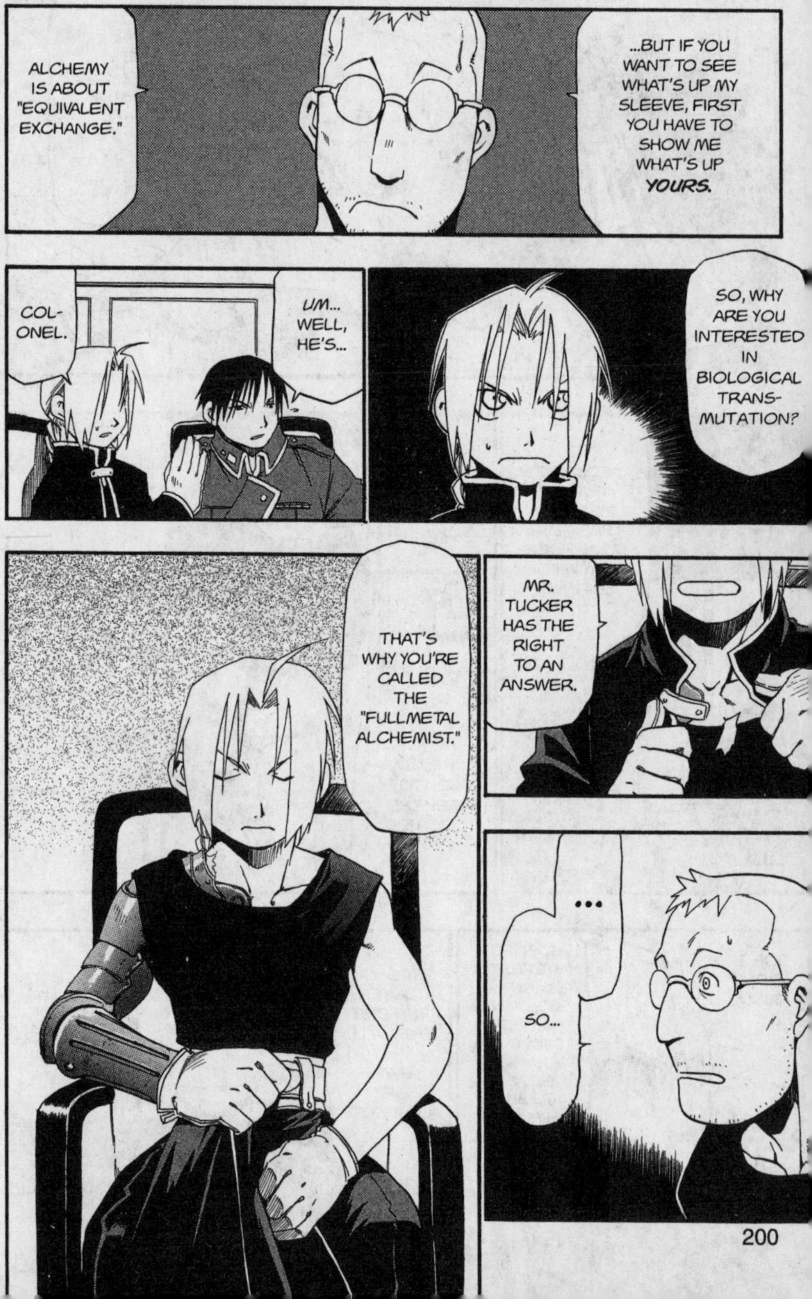
ALCHEMY IS ABOUT "EQUIVALENT EXCHANGE."
...BUT IF YOU WANT TO SEE WHAT'S UP MY SLEEVE, FIRST YOU HAVE TO SHOW ME WHAT'S UP *YOURS.*
SO, WHY ARE YOU INTERESTED IN BIOLOGICAL TRANS-MUTATION?
COL-ONEL.
UM... WELL, HE'S...
MR. TUCKER HAS THE RIGHT TO AN ANSWER.
...
SO...
THAT'S WHY YOU'RE CALLED THE "FULLMETAL ALCHEMIST."

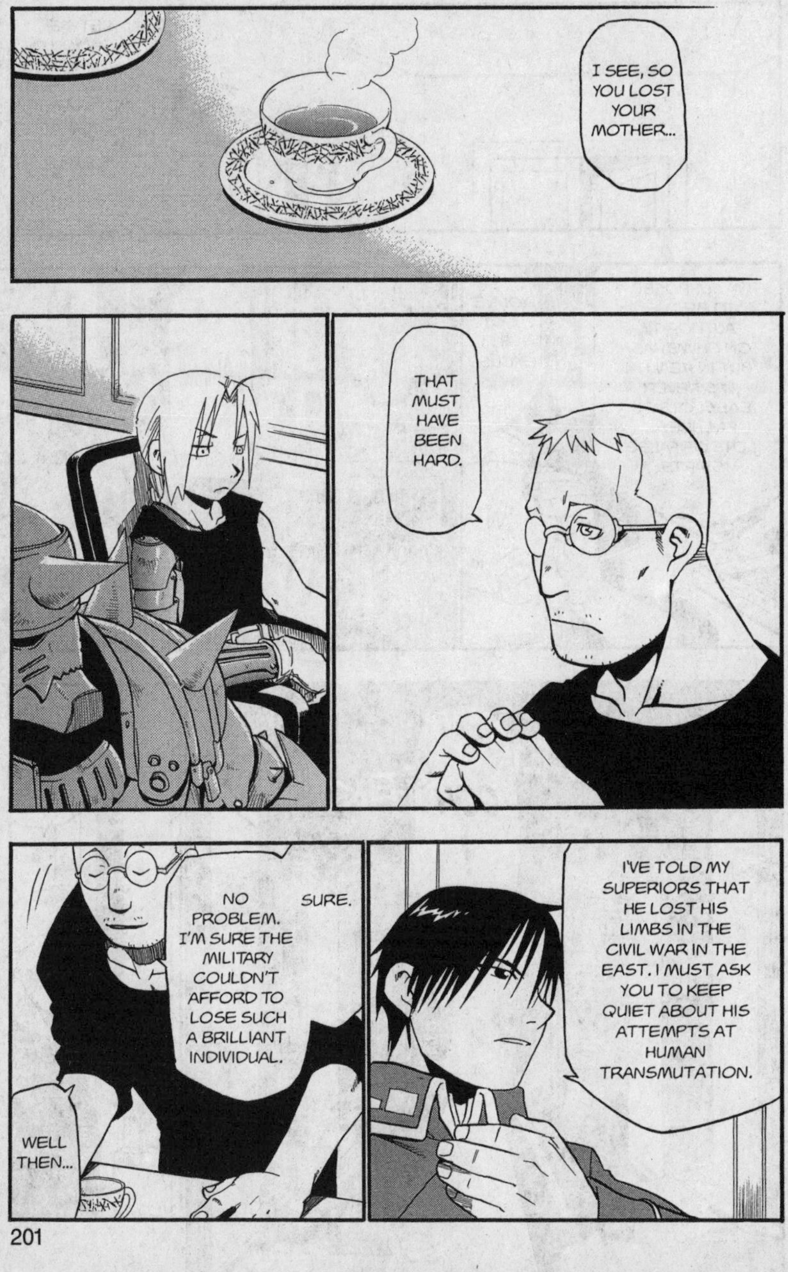
I SEE, SO YOU LOST YOUR MOTHER...
THAT MUST HAVE BEEN HARD.
I'VE TOLD MY SUPERIORS THAT HE LOST HIS LIMBS IN THE CIVIL WAR IN THE EAST. I MUST ASK YOU TO KEEP QUIET ABOUT HIS ATTEMPTS AT HUMAN TRANSMUTATION.
SURE.
NO PROBLEM. I'M SURE THE MILITARY COULDN'T AFFORD TO LOSE SUCH A BRILLIANT INDIVIDUAL.
WELL THEN...

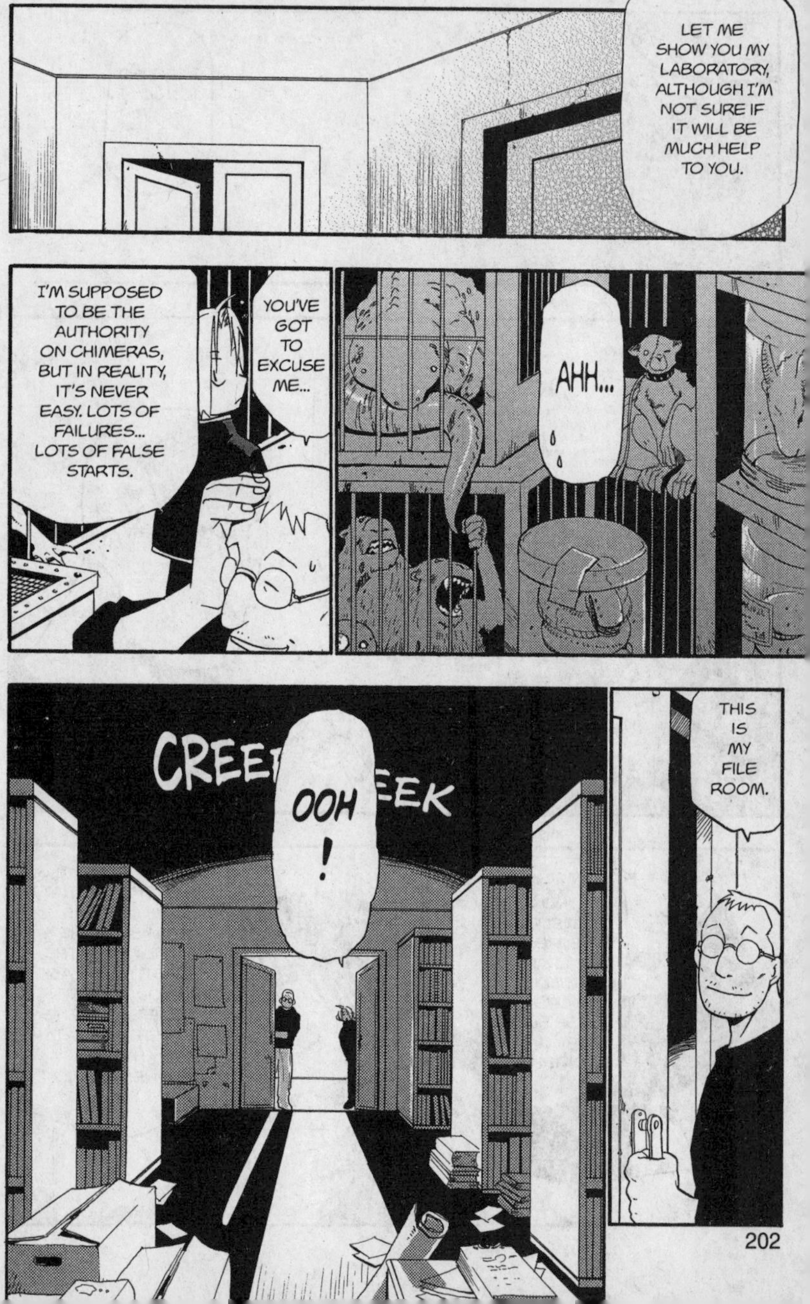
LET ME SHOW YOU MY LABORATORY, ALTHOUGH I'M NOT SURE IF IT WILL BE MUCH HELP TO YOU.
AHH...
YOU'VE GOT TO EXCUSE ME...
I'M SUPPOSED TO BE THE AUTHORITY ON CHIMERAS, BUT IN REALITY, IT'S NEVER EASY. LOTS OF FAILURES... LOTS OF FALSE STARTS.
THIS IS MY FILE ROOM.
CREE
EEK
OOH !

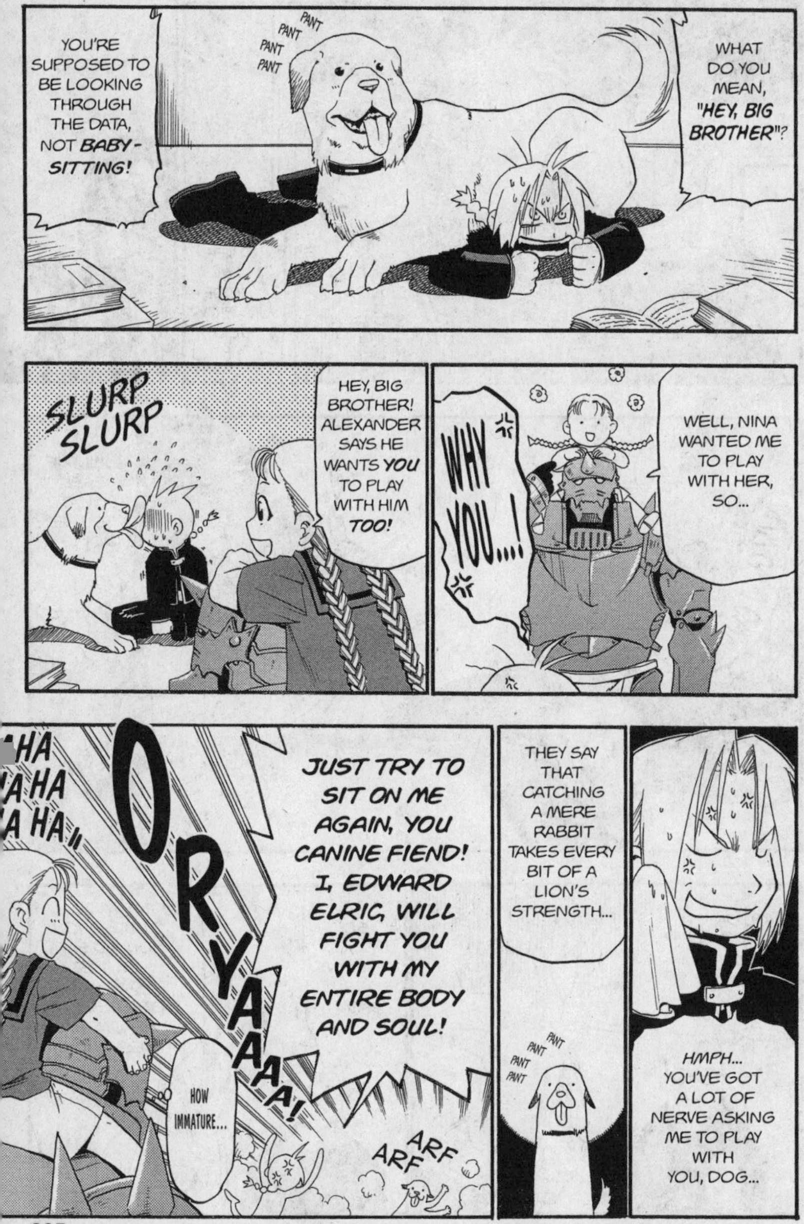
WHAT DO YOU MEAN, "HEY, BIG BROTHER"?
PANT PANT PANT PANT
YOU'RE SUPPOSED TO BE LOOKING THROUGH THE DATA, NOT BABY-SITTING!
WELL, NINA WANTED ME TO PLAY WITH HER, SO...
WHY YOU...!
HEY, BIG BROTHER! ALEXANDER SAYS HE WANTS YOU TO PLAY WITH HIM TOO!
SLURP SLURP
HMPH... YOU'VE GOT A LOT OF NERVE ASKING ME TO PLAY WITH YOU, DOG...
THEY SAY THAT CATCHING A MERE RABBIT TAKES EVERY BIT OF A LION'S STRENGTH...
PANT PANT PANT PANT
JUST TRY TO SIT ON ME AGAIN, YOU CANINE FIEND! I, EDWARD ELRIC, WILL FIGHT YOU WITH MY ENTIRE BODY AND SOUL!
ORYAAAA!
HA HA HA HA HA HA
HOW IMMATURE...
ARF ARF

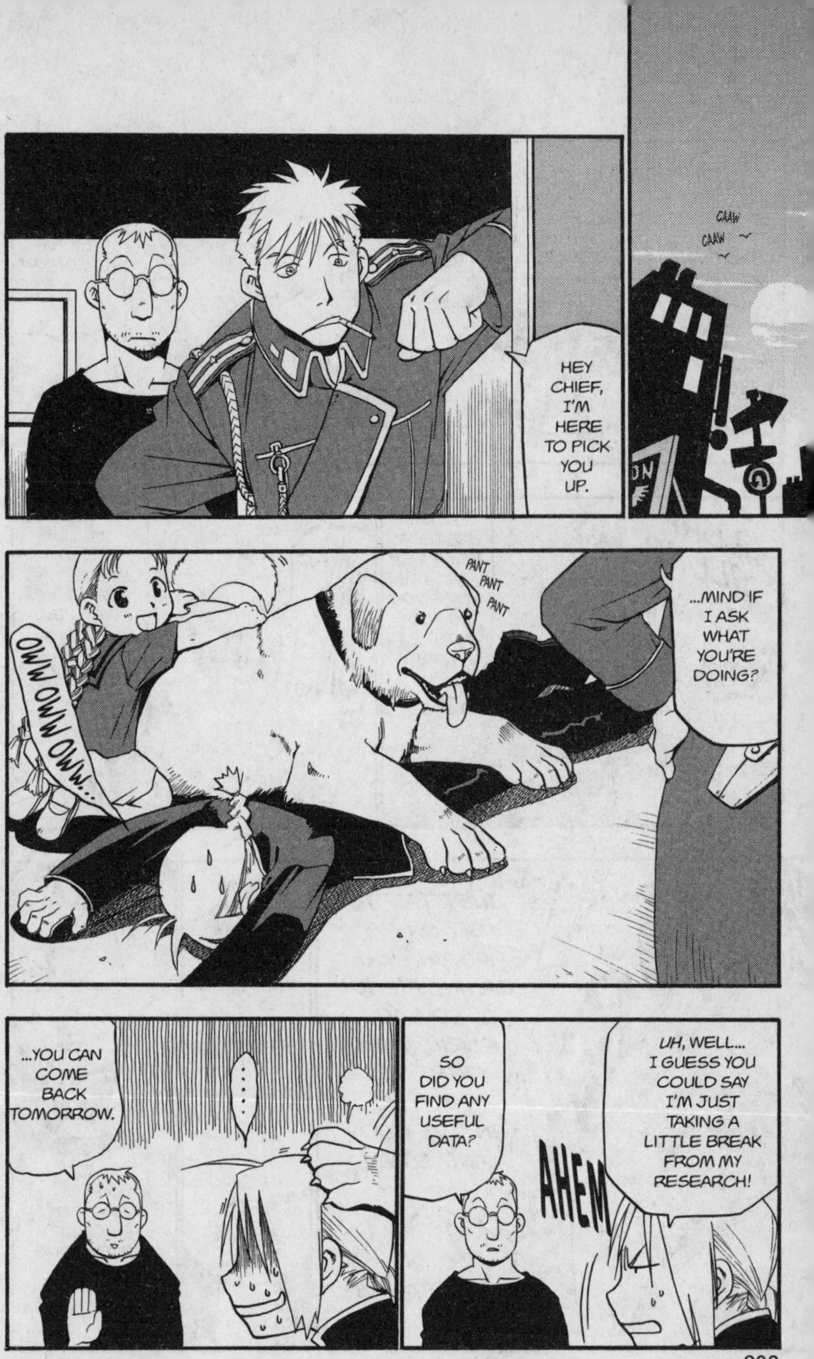
CAAW
CAAW
HEY CHIEF, I'M HERE TO PICK YOU UP.
...MIND IF I ASK WHAT YOU'RE DOING?
PANT PANT PANT
OWW OWW OWW...
UH, WELL... I GUESS YOU COULD SAY I'M JUST TAKING A LITTLE BREAK FROM MY RESEARCH!
AHEM
SO DID YOU FIND ANY USEFUL DATA?
...YOU CAN COME BACK TOMORROW.

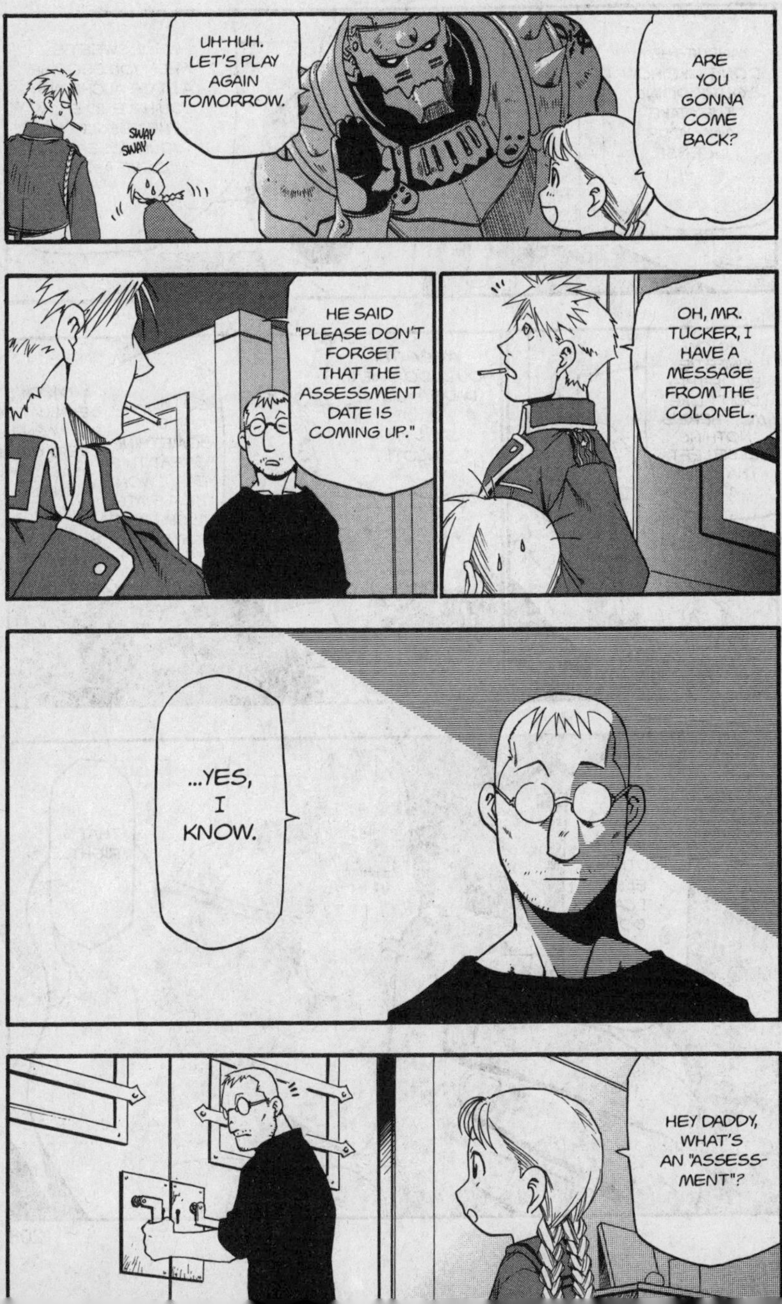
ARE YOU GONNA COME BACK?
UH-HUH. LET'S PLAY AGAIN TOMORROW.
SWAY SWAY
OH, MR. TUCKER, I HAVE A MESSAGE FROM THE COLONEL.
HE SAID "PLEASE DON'T FORGET THAT THE ASSESSMENT DATE IS COMING UP."
...YES, I KNOW.
HEY DADDY, WHAT'S AN "ASSESSMENT"?

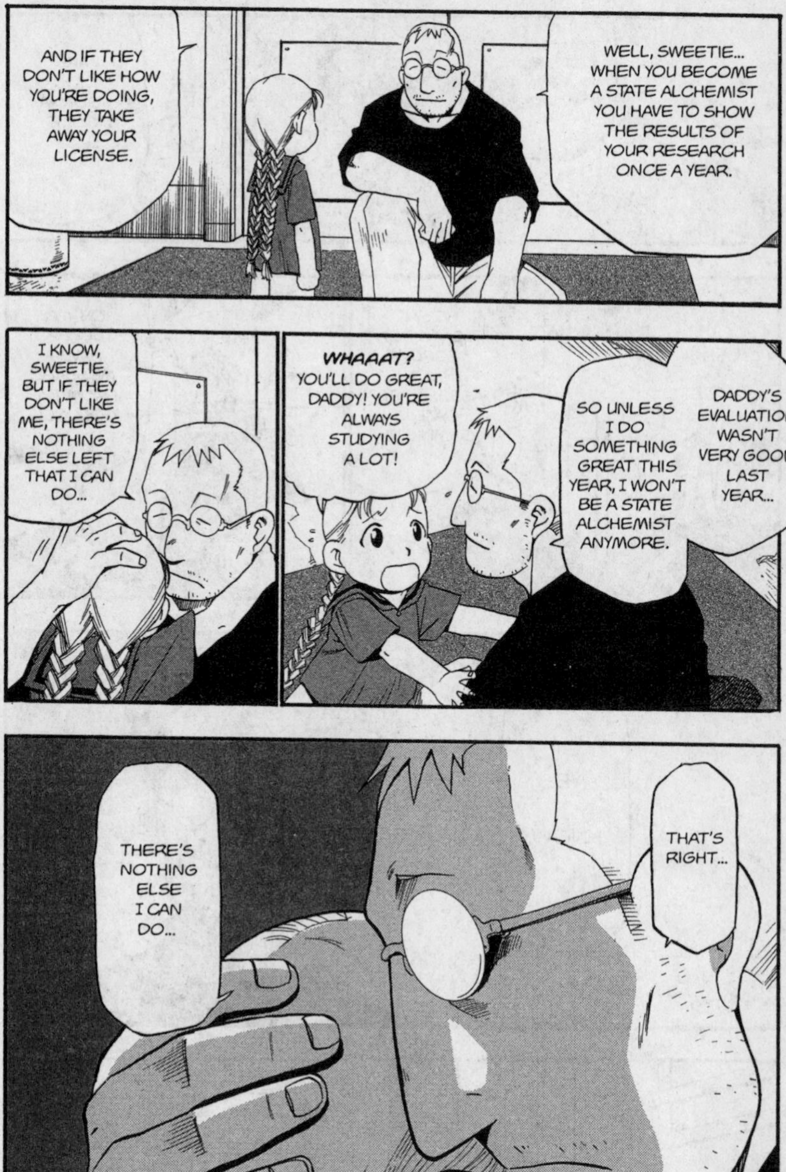
WELL, SWEETIE... WHEN YOU BECOME A STATE ALCHEMIST YOU HAVE TO SHOW THE RESULTS OF YOUR RESEARCH ONCE A YEAR.
AND IF THEY DON'T LIKE HOW YOU'RE DOING, THEY TAKE AWAY YOUR LICENSE.
DADDY'S EVALUATION WASN'T VERY GOOD LAST YEAR...
SO UNLESS I DO SOMETHING GREAT THIS YEAR, I WON'T BE A STATE ALCHEMIST ANYMORE.
WHAAAT? YOU'LL DO GREAT, DADDY! YOU'RE ALWAYS STUDYING A LOT!
I KNOW, SWEETIE. BUT IF THEY DON'T LIKE ME, THERE'S NOTHING ELSE LEFT THAT I CAN DO...
THAT'S RIGHT...
THERE'S NOTHING ELSE I CAN DO...

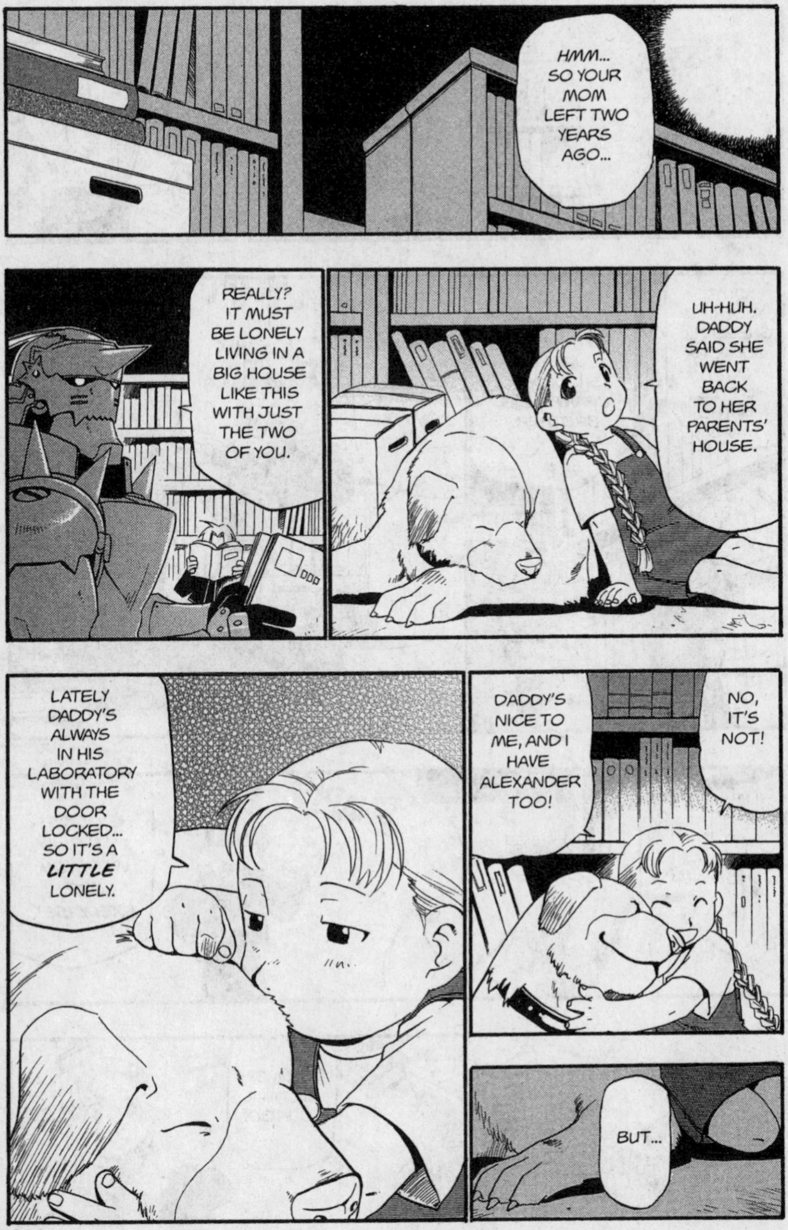
HMM... SO YOUR MOM LEFT TWO YEARS AGO...
UH-HUH. DADDY SAID SHE WENT BACK TO HER PARENTS' HOUSE.
REALLY? IT MUST BE LONELY LIVING IN A BIG HOUSE LIKE THIS WITH JUST THE TWO OF YOU.
NO, IT'S NOT!
DADDY'S NICE TO ME, AND I HAVE ALEXANDER TOO!
BUT...
LATELY DADDY'S ALWAYS IN HIS LABORATORY WITH THE DOOR LOCKED... SO IT'S A *LITTLE* LONELY.

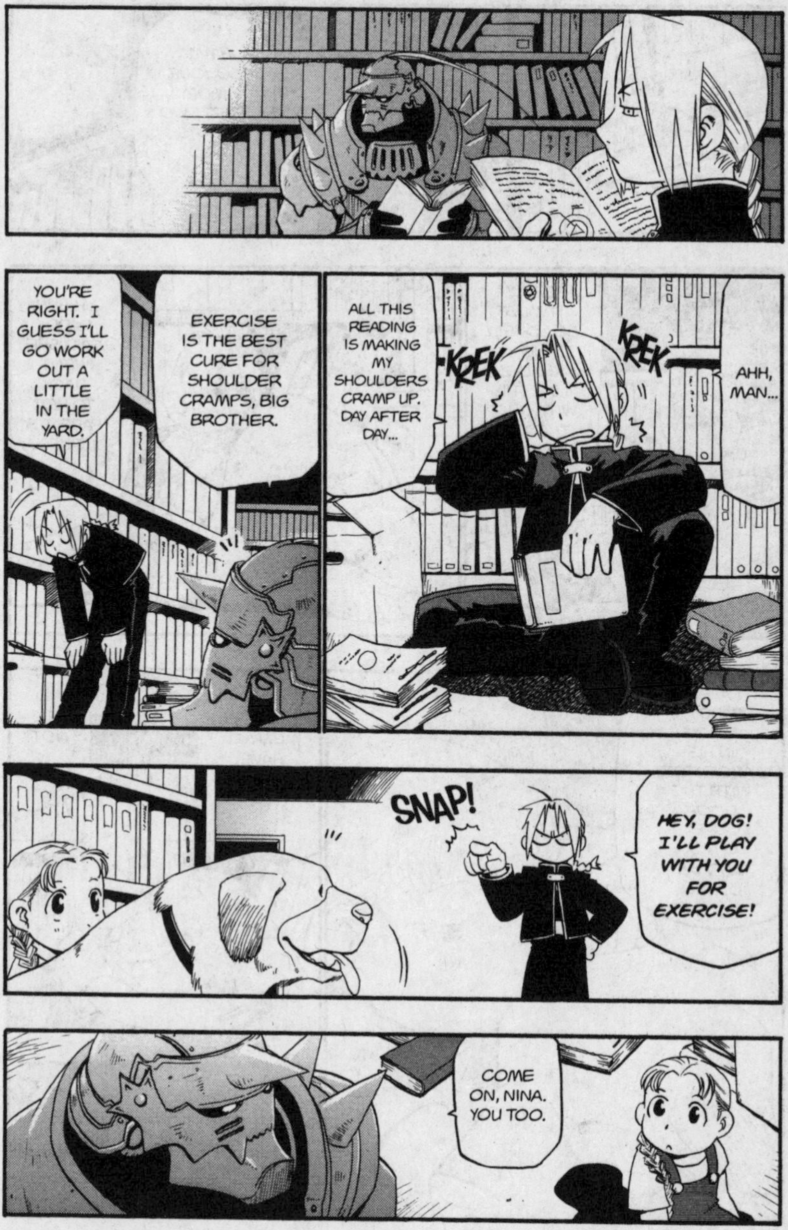
KREK
AHH, MAN...
KREK
ALL THIS READING IS MAKING MY SHOULDERS CRAMP UP. DAY AFTER DAY...
EXERCISE IS THE BEST CURE FOR SHOULDER CRAMPS, BIG BROTHER.
YOU'RE RIGHT. I GUESS I'LL GO WORK OUT A LITTLE IN THE YARD.
HEY, DOG! I'LL PLAY WITH YOU FOR EXERCISE!
SNAP!
COME ON, NINA. YOU TOO.

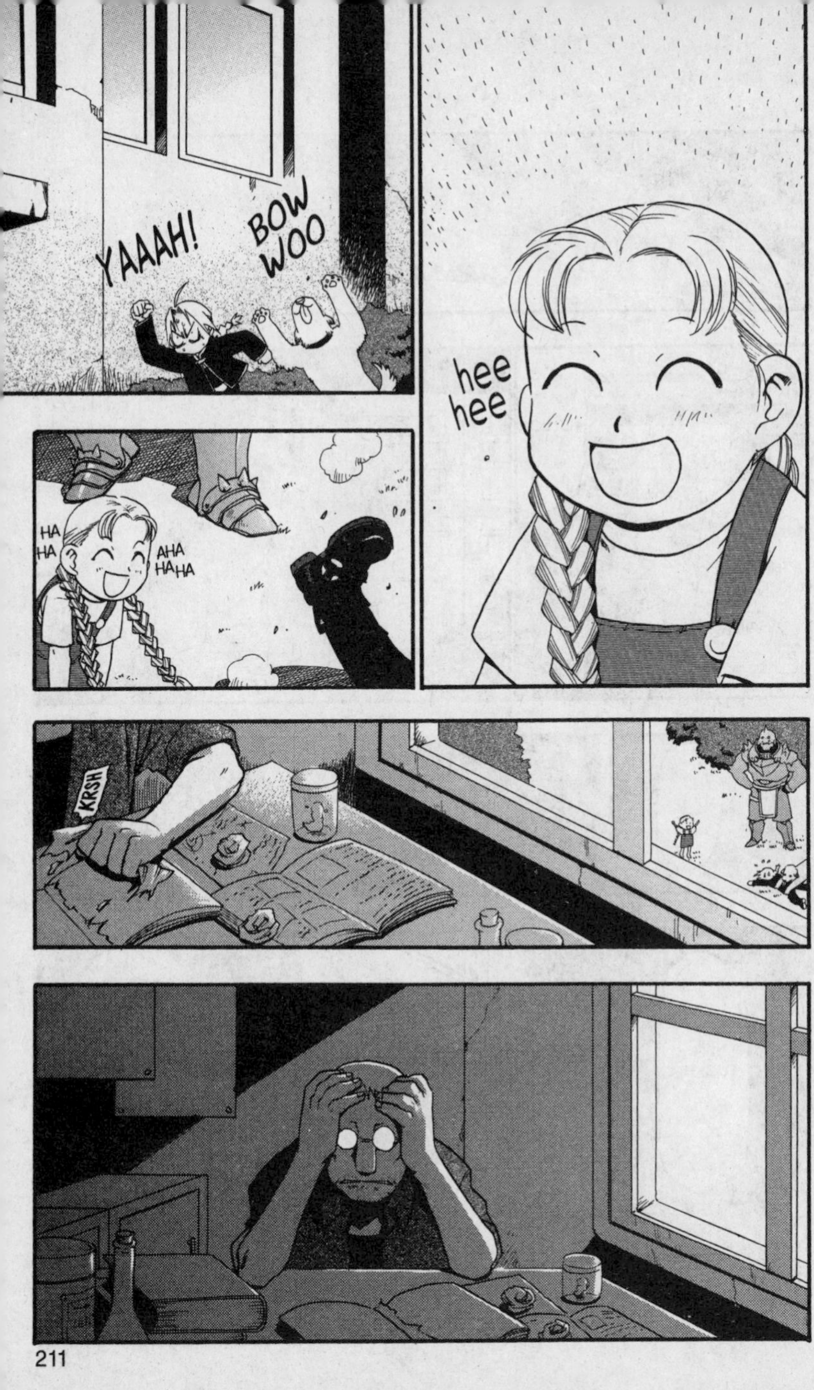
hee hee
BOW WOO
YAAAH!
AHA HAHA
HA HA
KRSH

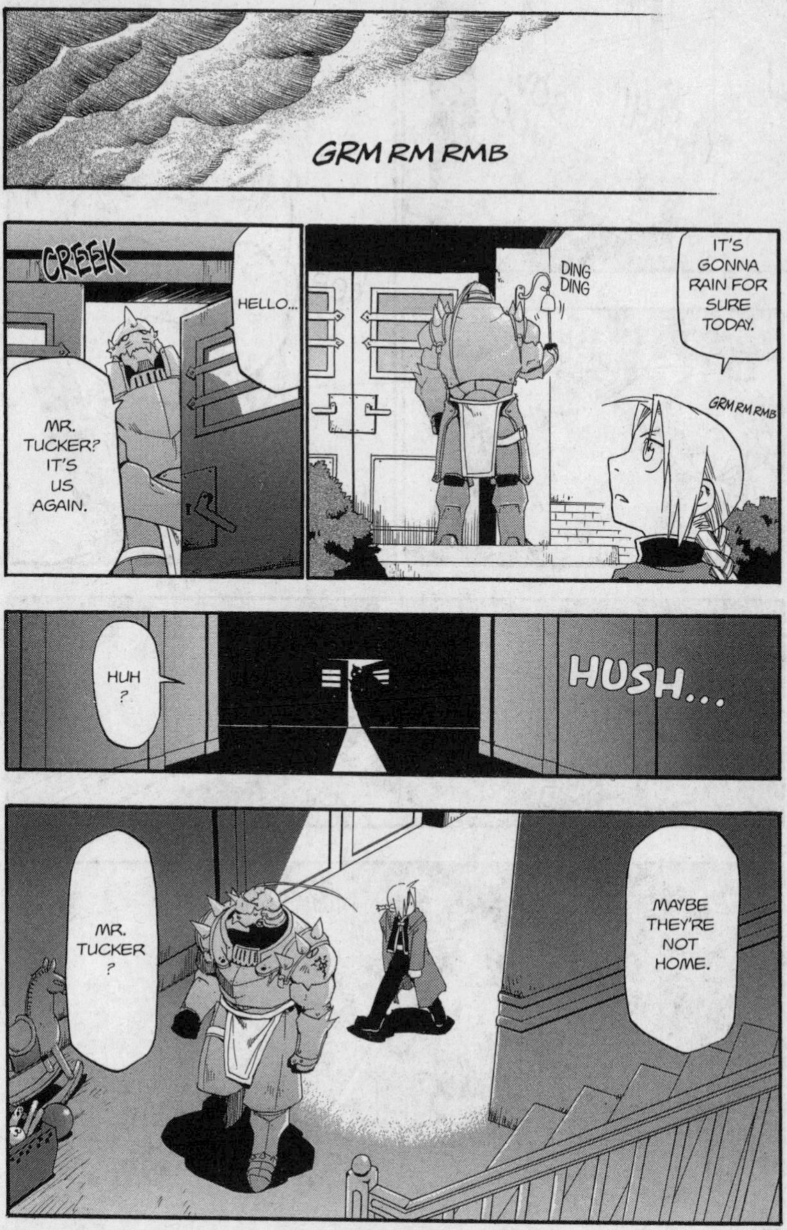
GRM RM RMB
IT'S GONNA RAIN FOR SURE TODAY.
DING DING
GRM RM RMB
CREEK
HELLO...
MR. TUCKER? IT'S US AGAIN.
HUSH...
HUH?
MAYBE THEY'RE NOT HOME.
MR. TUCKER?

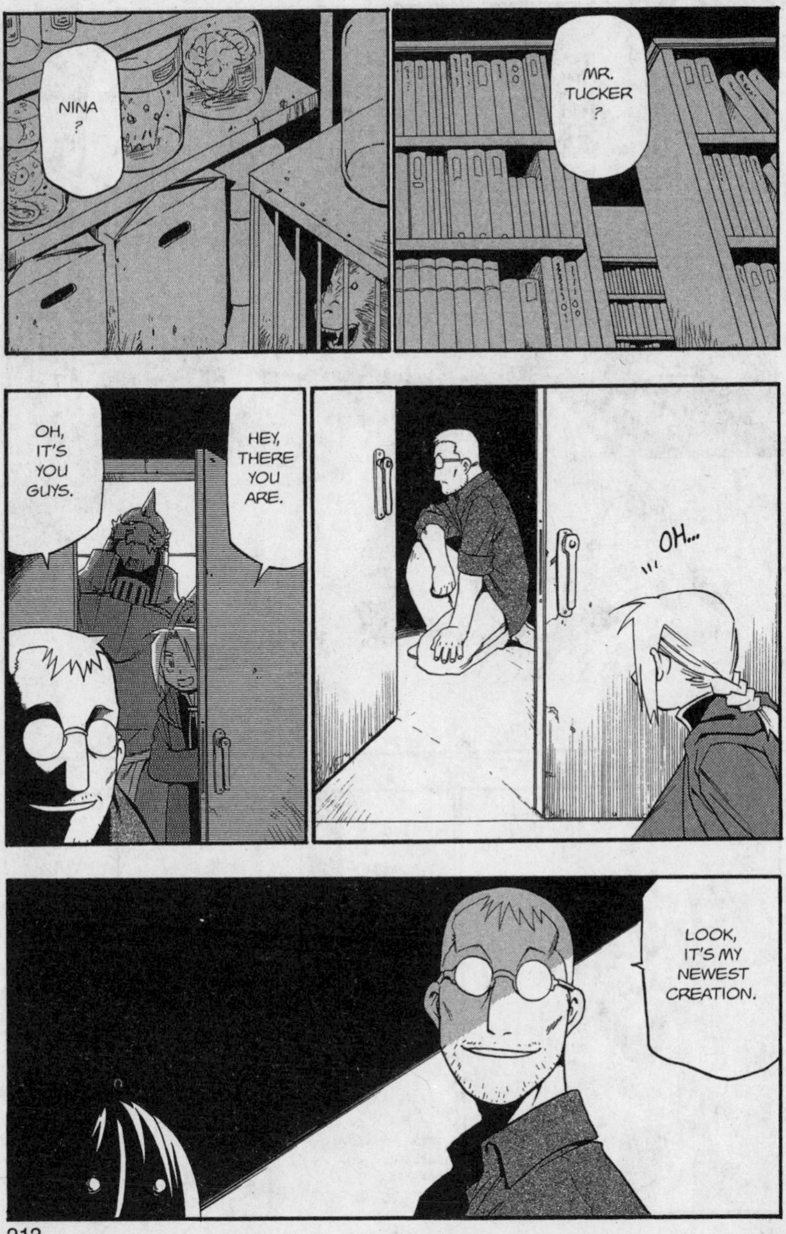
MR. TUCKER ?
NINA ?
OH...
HEY, THERE YOU ARE.
OH, IT'S YOU GUYS.
LOOK, IT'S MY NEWEST CREATION.

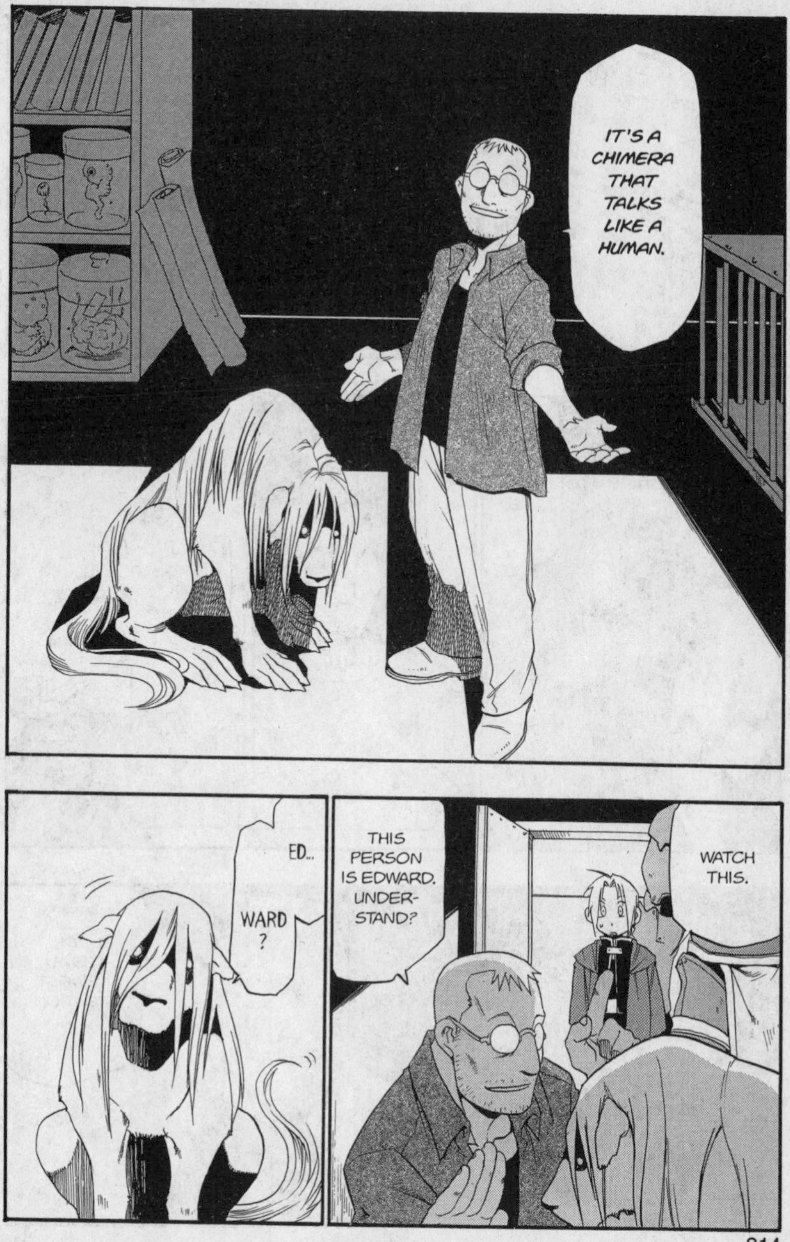
IT'S A CHIMERA THAT TALKS LIKE A HUMAN.
WATCH THIS.
THIS PERSON IS EDWARD. UNDERSTAND?
ED...
WARD?

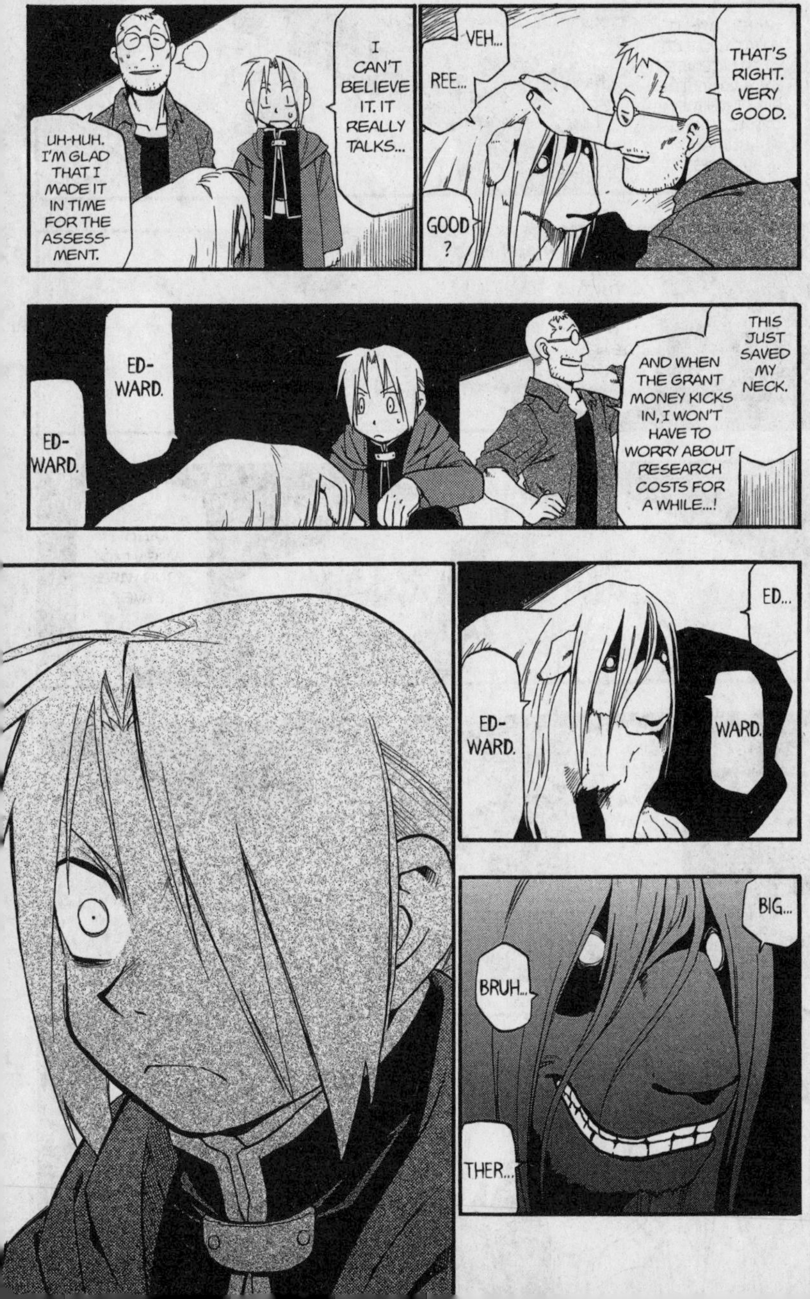
THAT'S RIGHT. VERY GOOD.
VEH...
REE...
GOOD?
I CAN'T BELIEVE IT. IT REALLY TALKS...
UH-HUH. I'M GLAD THAT I MADE IT IN TIME FOR THE ASSESSMENT.
THIS JUST SAVED MY NECK.
AND WHEN THE GRANT MONEY KICKS IN, I WON'T HAVE TO WORRY ABOUT RESEARCH COSTS FOR A WHILE...!
ED-WARD.
ED-WARD.
ED...
WARD.
ED-WARD.
BIG...
BRUH...
THER...

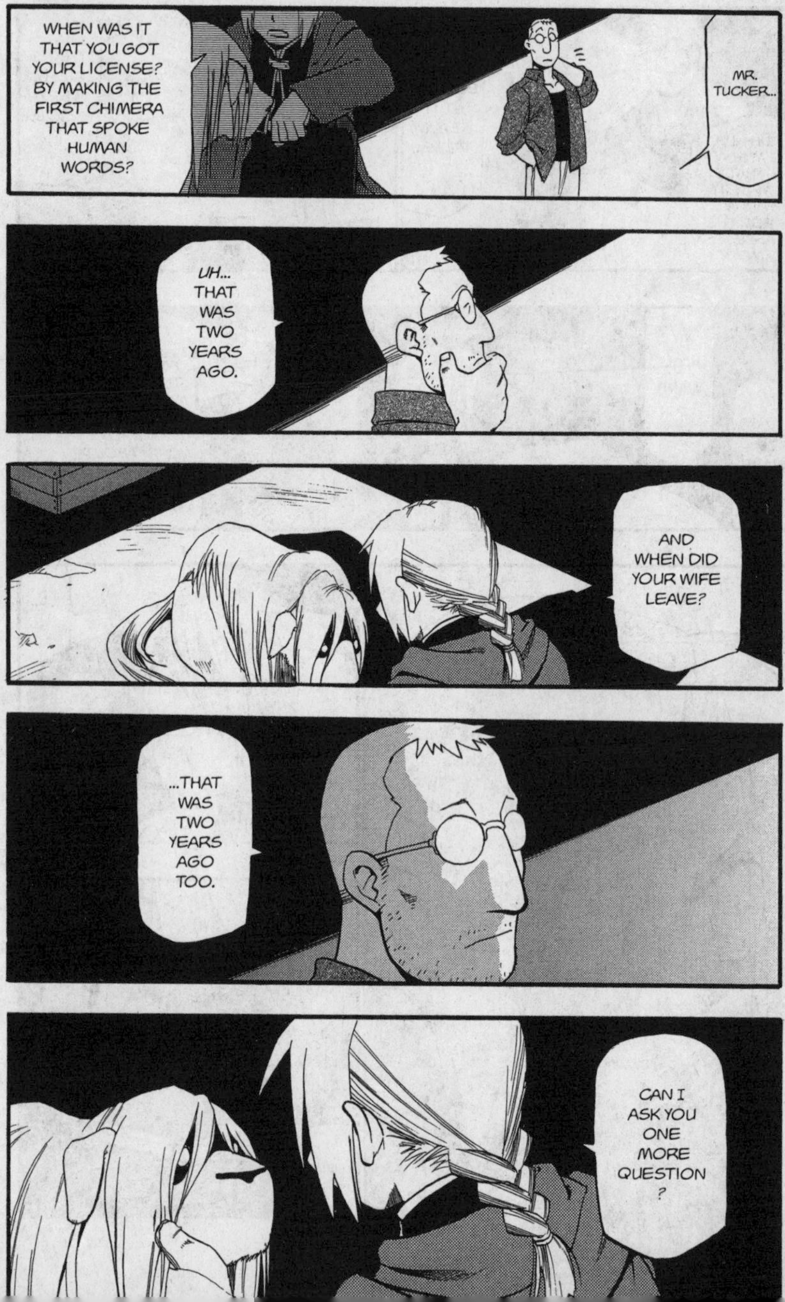
MR. TUCKER..
WHEN WAS IT THAT YOU GOT YOUR LICENSE? BY MAKING THE FIRST CHIMERA THAT SPOKE HUMAN WORDS?
UH... THAT WAS TWO YEARS AGO.
AND WHEN DID YOUR WIFE LEAVE?
...THAT WAS TWO YEARS AGO TOO.
CAN I ASK YOU ONE MORE QUESTION?

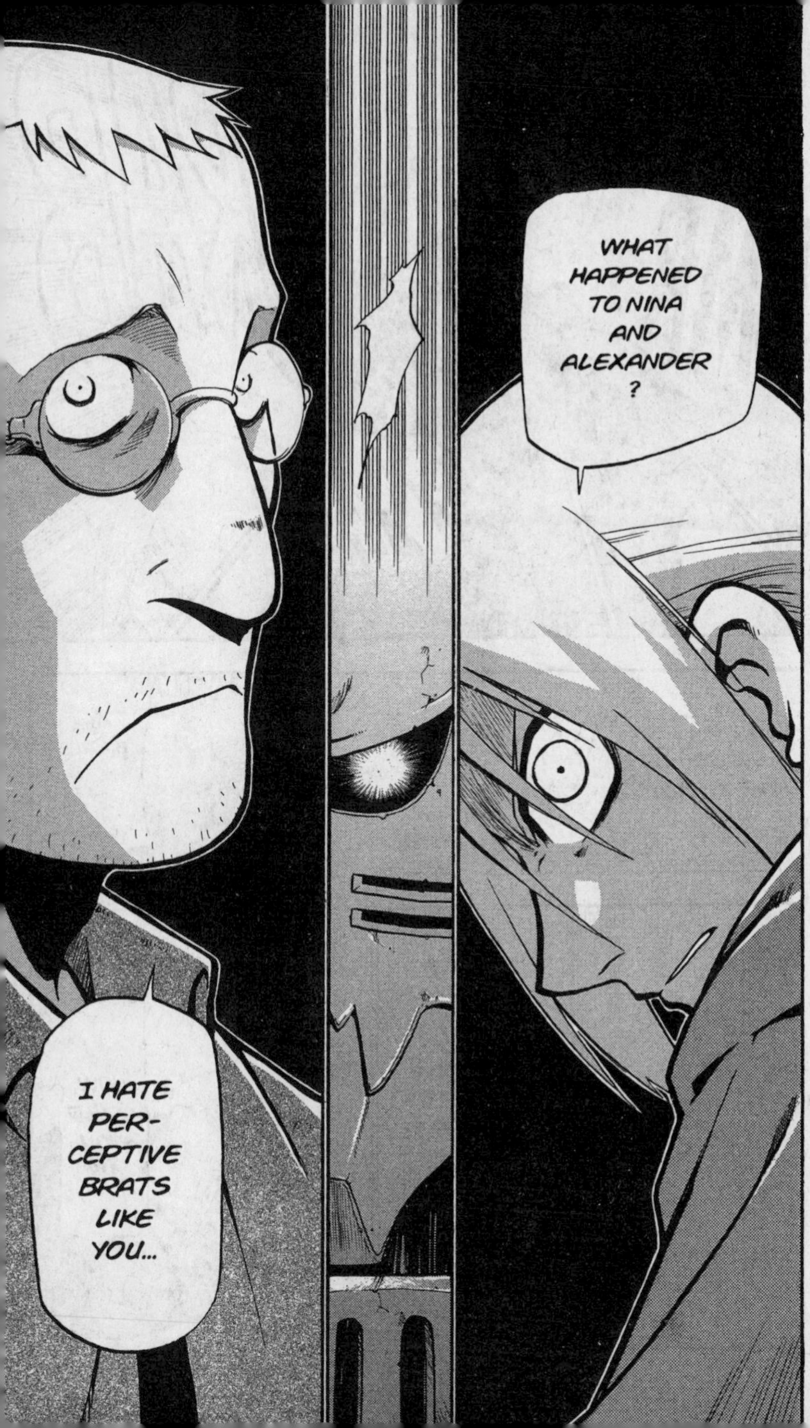
WHAT HAPPENED TO NINA AND ALEXANDER ?
I HATE PER-CEPTIVE BRATS LIKE YOU...

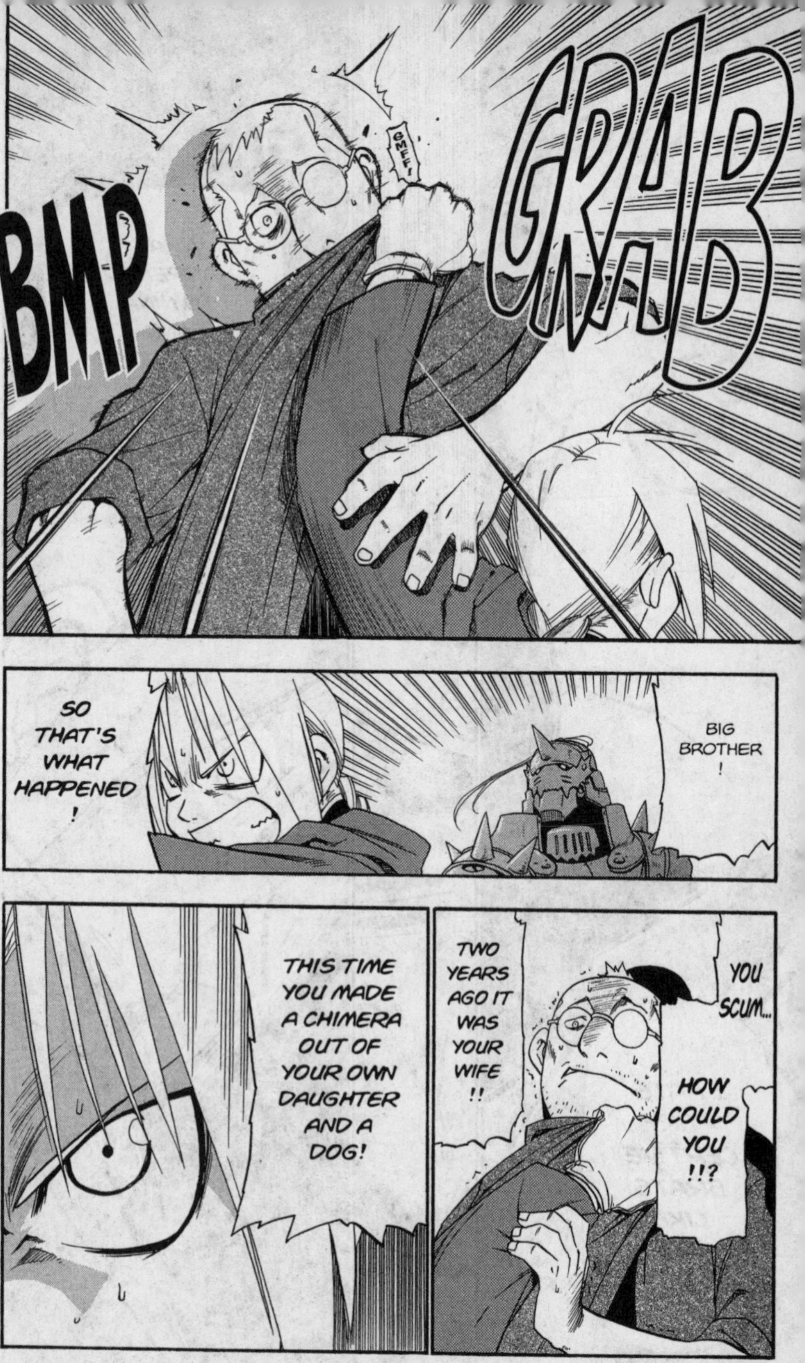
GRAB
GMFF!
BMP
BIG BROTHER!
SO THAT'S WHAT HAPPENED!
YOU SCUM...
TWO YEARS AGO IT WAS YOUR WIFE!!
HOW COULD YOU!!?
THIS TIME YOU MADE A CHIMERA OUT OF YOUR OWN DAUGHTER AND A DOG!

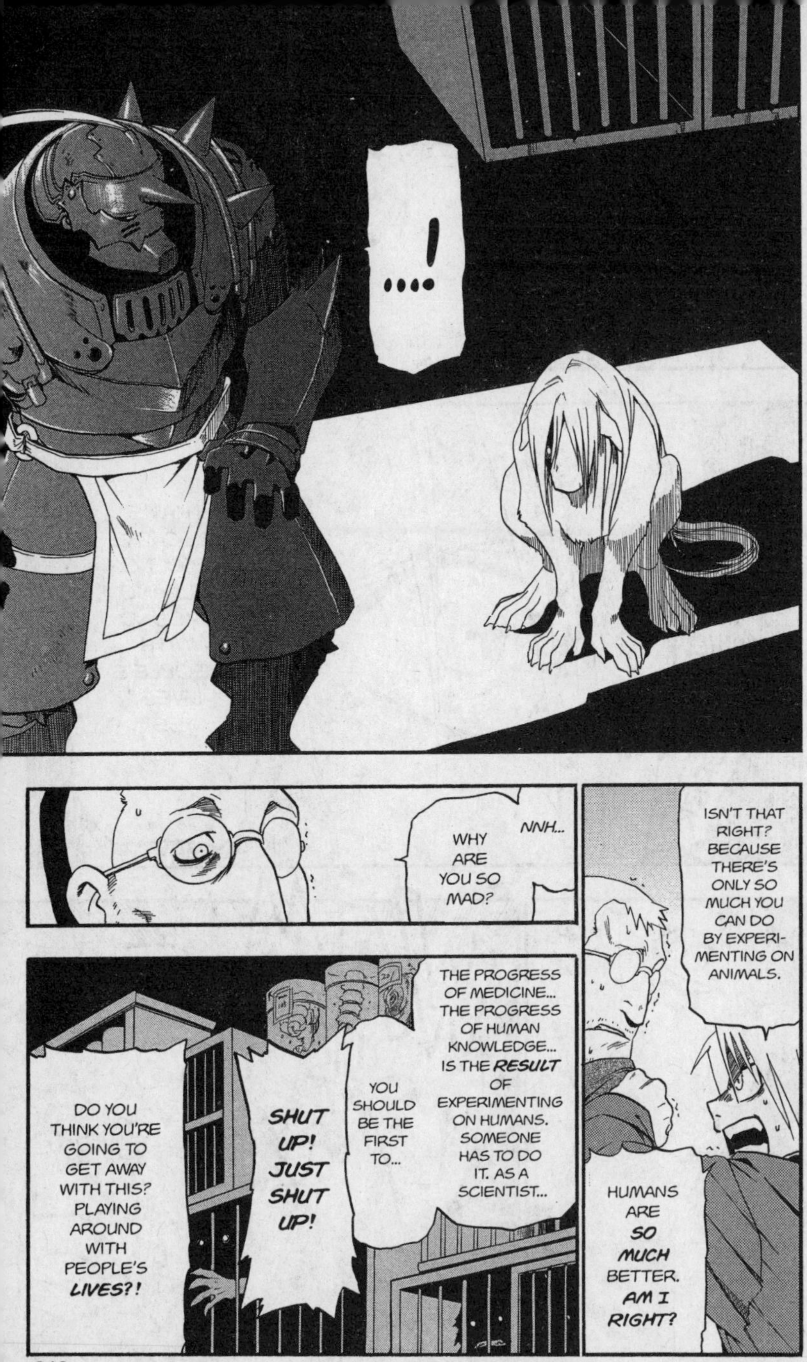
...!
ISN'T THAT RIGHT? BECAUSE THERE'S ONLY SO MUCH YOU CAN DO BY EXPERIMENTING ON ANIMALS.
HUMANS ARE **SO MUCH** BETTER. **AM I RIGHT?**
NNH...
WHY ARE YOU SO MAD?
THE PROGRESS OF MEDICINE... THE PROGRESS OF HUMAN KNOWLEDGE... IS THE ***RESULT*** OF EXPERIMENTING ON HUMANS. SOMEONE HAS TO DO IT. AS A SCIENTIST...
YOU SHOULD BE THE FIRST TO...
SHUT UP! JUST SHUT UP!
DO YOU THINK YOU'RE GOING TO GET AWAY WITH THIS? PLAYING AROUND WITH PEOPLE'S ***LIVES?!***

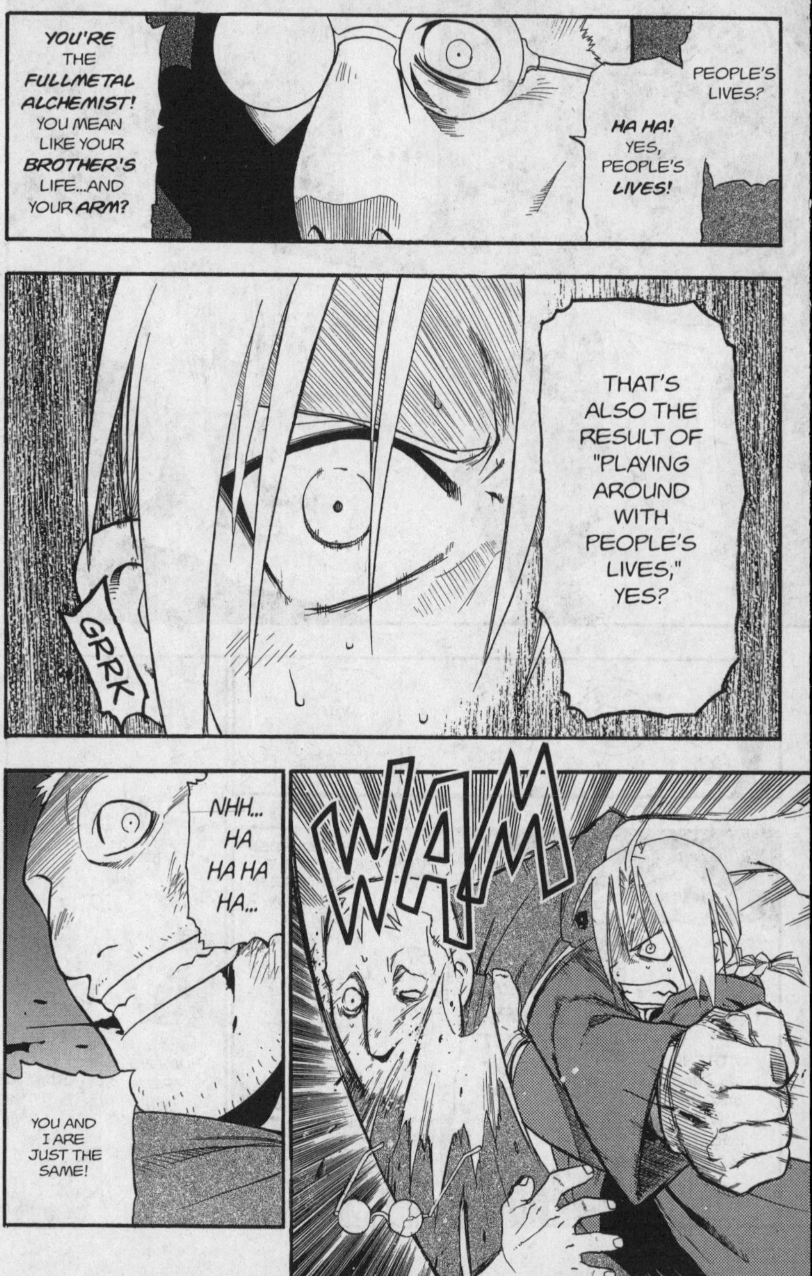
PEOPLE'S LIVES?
HA HA! YES, PEOPLE'S LIVES!
YOU'RE THE FULLMETAL ALCHEMIST! YOU MEAN LIKE YOUR BROTHER'S LIFE...AND YOUR ARM?
THAT'S ALSO THE RESULT OF "PLAYING AROUND WITH PEOPLE'S LIVES," YES?
GRRK
WAM
NHH... HA HA HA HA...
YOU AND I ARE JUST THE SAME!

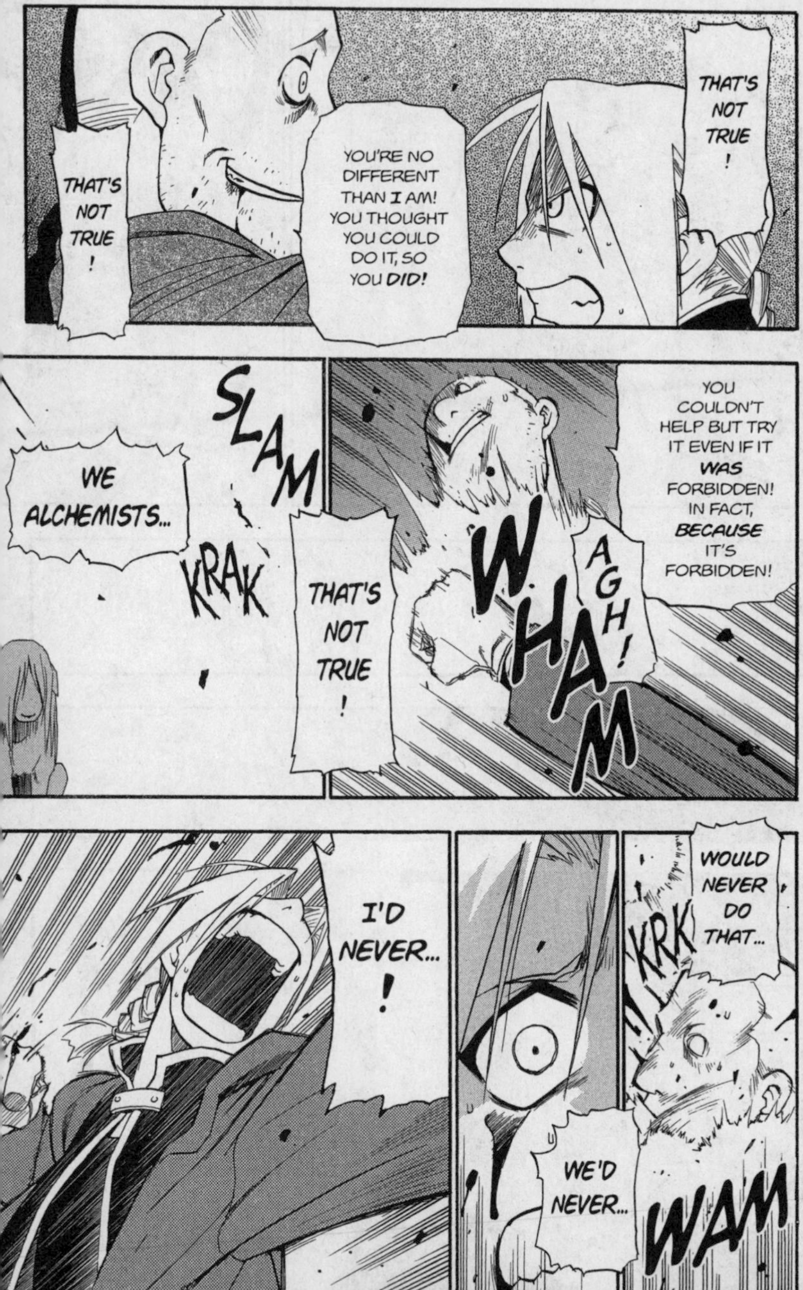
THAT'S NOT TRUE!
YOU'RE NO DIFFERENT THAN I AM! YOU THOUGHT YOU COULD DO IT, SO YOU DID!
THAT'S NOT TRUE!
YOU COULDN'T HELP BUT TRY IT EVEN IF IT WAS FORBIDDEN! IN FACT, BECAUSE IT'S FORBIDDEN!
AGH!
WHAM
SLAM
THAT'S NOT TRUE!
KRAK
WE ALCHEMISTS...
WOULD NEVER DO THAT...
KRK
WE'D NEVER...
WAM
I'D NEVER...!

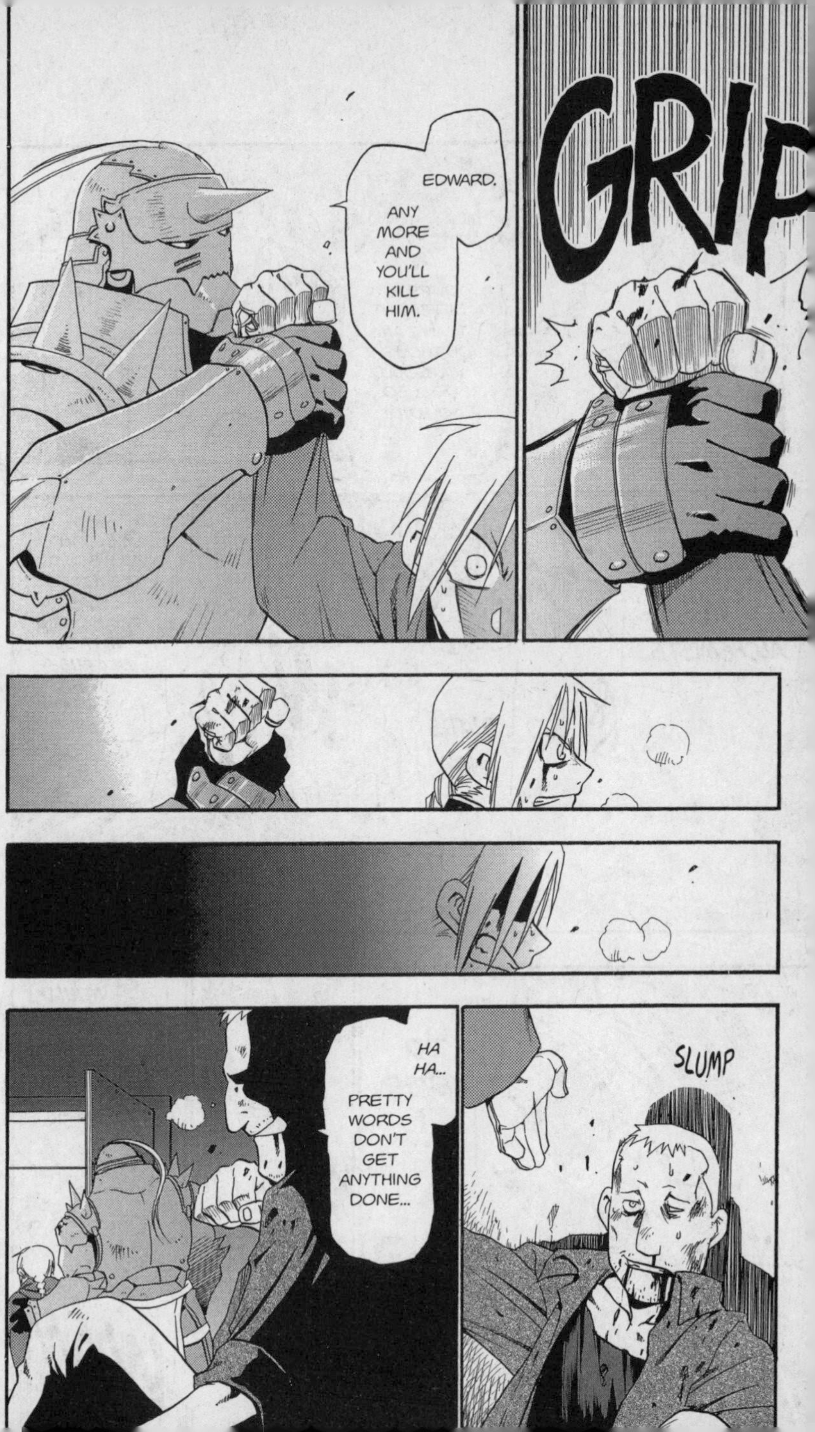
GRIP
EDWARD.
ANY MORE AND YOU'LL KILL HIM.
SLUMP
HA HA...
PRETTY WORDS DON'T GET ANYTHING DONE...

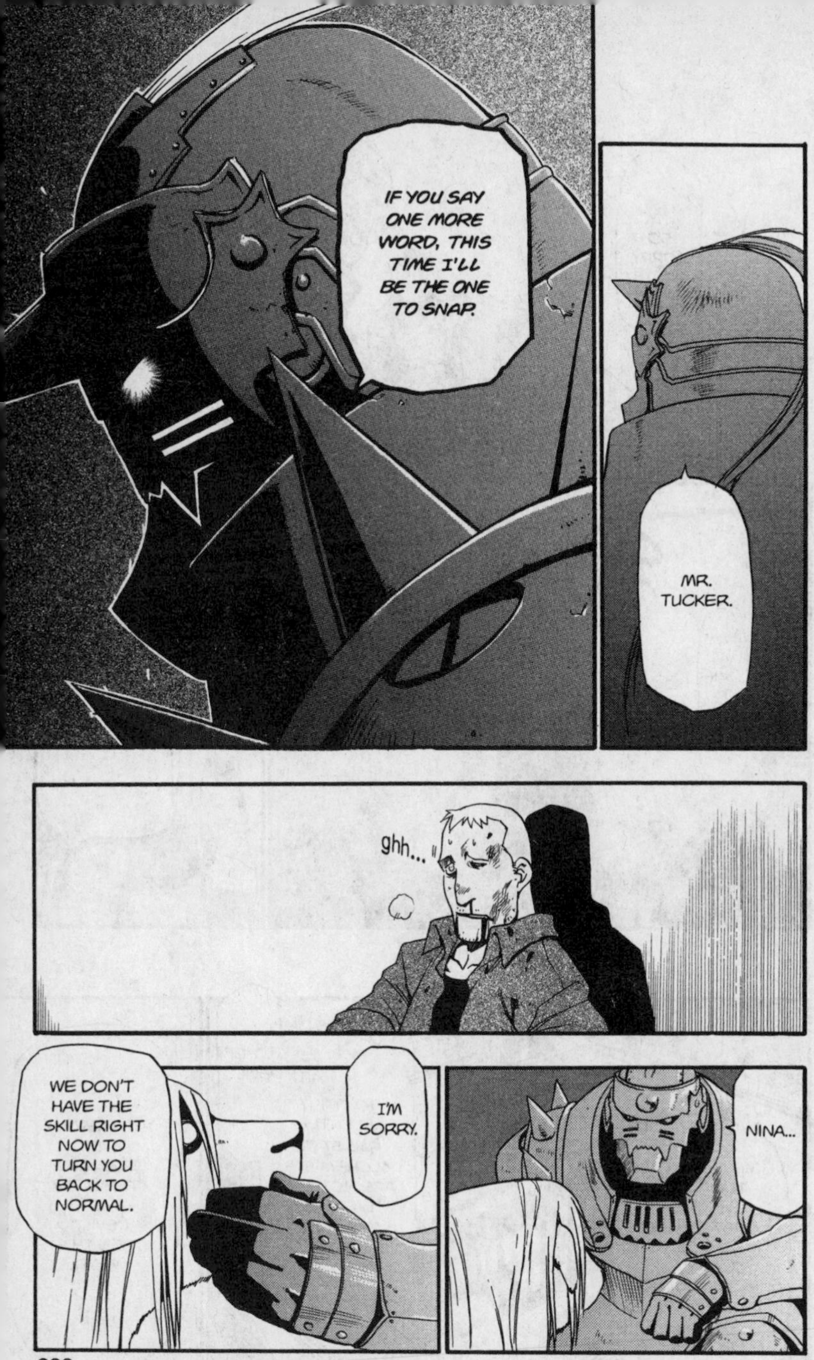
MR. TUCKER.
IF YOU SAY ONE MORE WORD, THIS TIME I'LL BE THE ONE TO SNAP.
ghh...
NINA...
I'M SORRY.
WE DON'T HAVE THE SKILL RIGHT NOW TO TURN YOU BACK TO NORMAL.

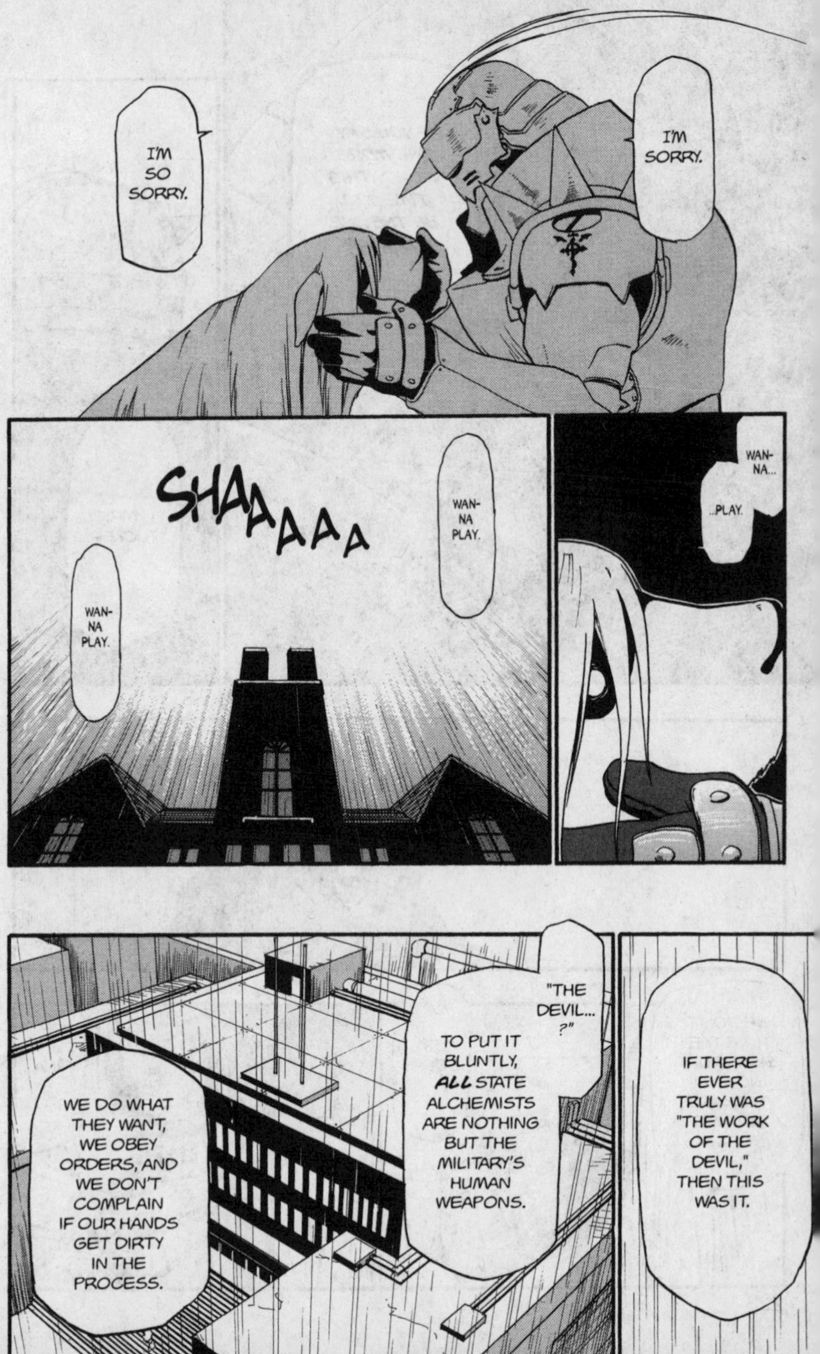
I'M SORRY.
I'M SO SORRY.
WAN-NA...
...PLAY.
WAN-NA PLAY.
SHAAAAAA
WAN-NA PLAY.
IF THERE EVER TRULY WAS "THE WORK OF THE DEVIL," THEN THIS WAS IT.
"THE DEVIL...?"
TO PUT IT BLUNTLY, ALL STATE ALCHEMISTS ARE NOTHING BUT THE MILITARY'S HUMAN WEAPONS.
WE DO WHAT THEY WANT, WE OBEY ORDERS, AND WE DON'T COMPLAIN IF OUR HANDS GET DIRTY IN THE PROCESS.

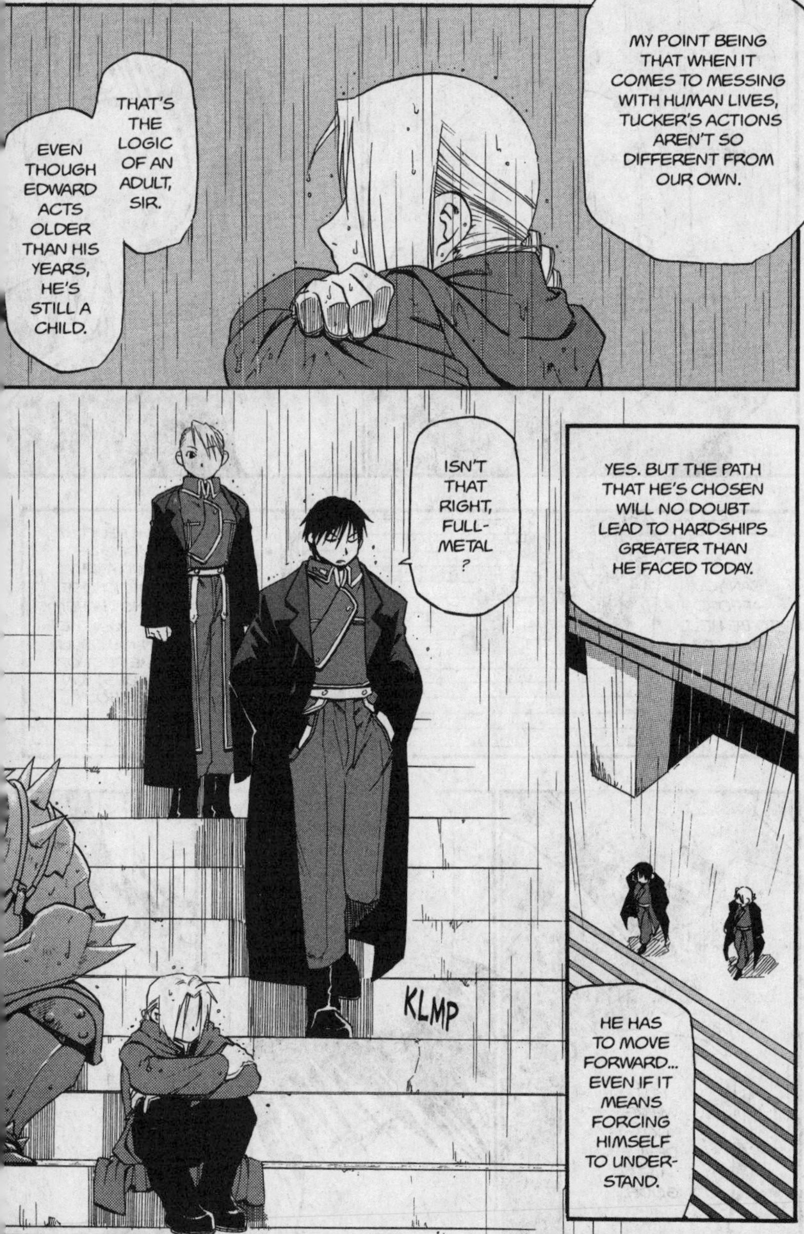
MY POINT BEING THAT WHEN IT COMES TO MESSING WITH HUMAN LIVES, TUCKER'S ACTIONS AREN'T SO DIFFERENT FROM OUR OWN.
THAT'S THE LOGIC OF AN ADULT, SIR.
EVEN THOUGH EDWARD ACTS OLDER THAN HIS YEARS, HE'S STILL A CHILD.
YES. BUT THE PATH THAT HE'S CHOSEN WILL NO DOUBT LEAD TO HARDSHIPS GREATER THAN HE FACED TODAY.
HE HAS TO MOVE FORWARD... EVEN IF IT MEANS FORCING HIMSELF TO UNDER-STAND.
ISN'T THAT RIGHT, FULL-METAL?
KLMP

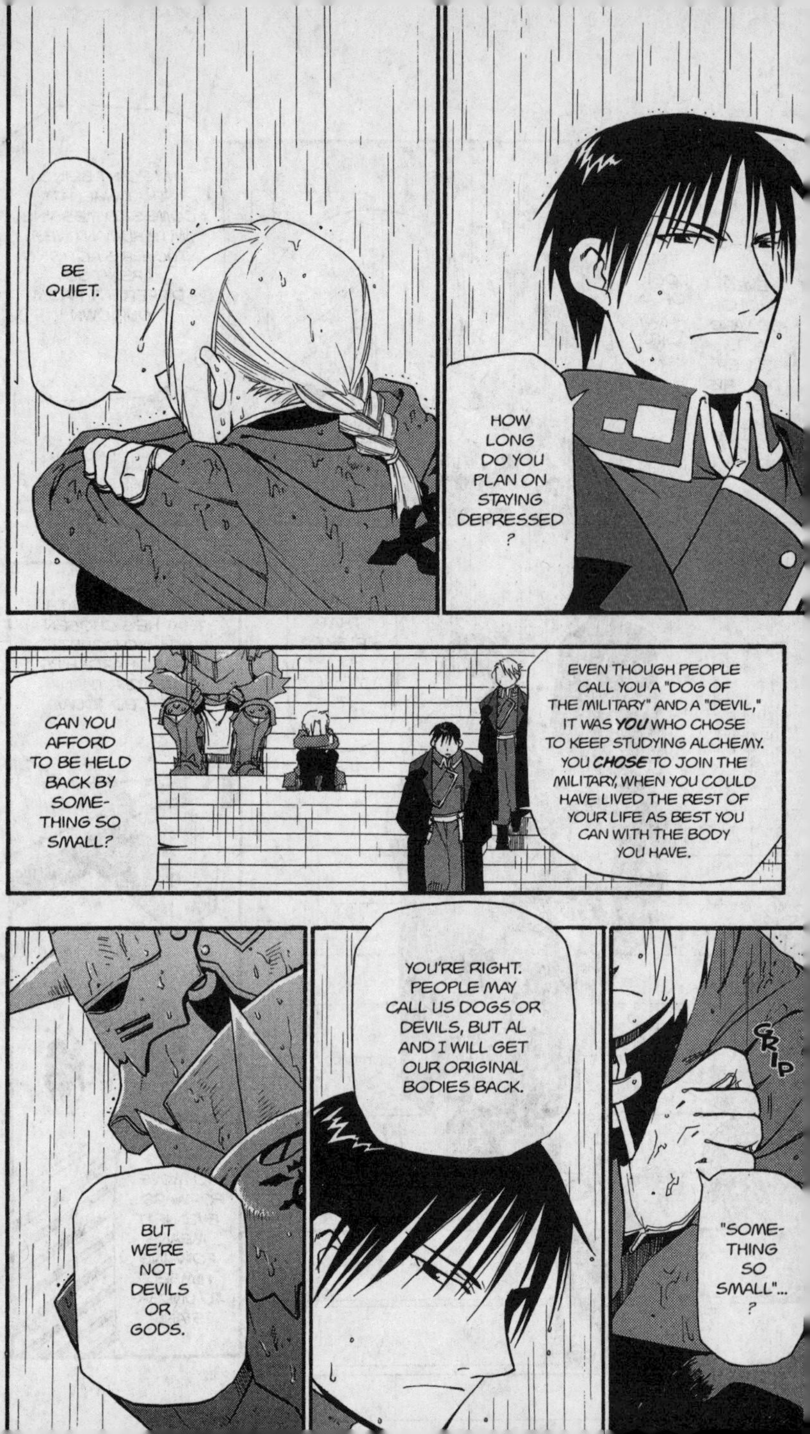
HOW LONG DO YOU PLAN ON STAYING DEPRESSED?
BE QUIET.
EVEN THOUGH PEOPLE CALL YOU A "DOG OF THE MILITARY" AND A "DEVIL," IT WAS YOU WHO CHOSE TO KEEP STUDYING ALCHEMY. YOU CHOSE TO JOIN THE MILITARY, WHEN YOU COULD HAVE LIVED THE REST OF YOUR LIFE AS BEST YOU CAN WITH THE BODY YOU HAVE.
CAN YOU AFFORD TO BE HELD BACK BY SOME-THING SO SMALL?
GRIP
"SOME-THING SO SMALL"...?
YOU'RE RIGHT. PEOPLE MAY CALL US DOGS OR DEVILS, BUT AL AND I WILL GET OUR ORIGINAL BODIES BACK.
BUT WE'RE NOT DEVILS OR GODS.

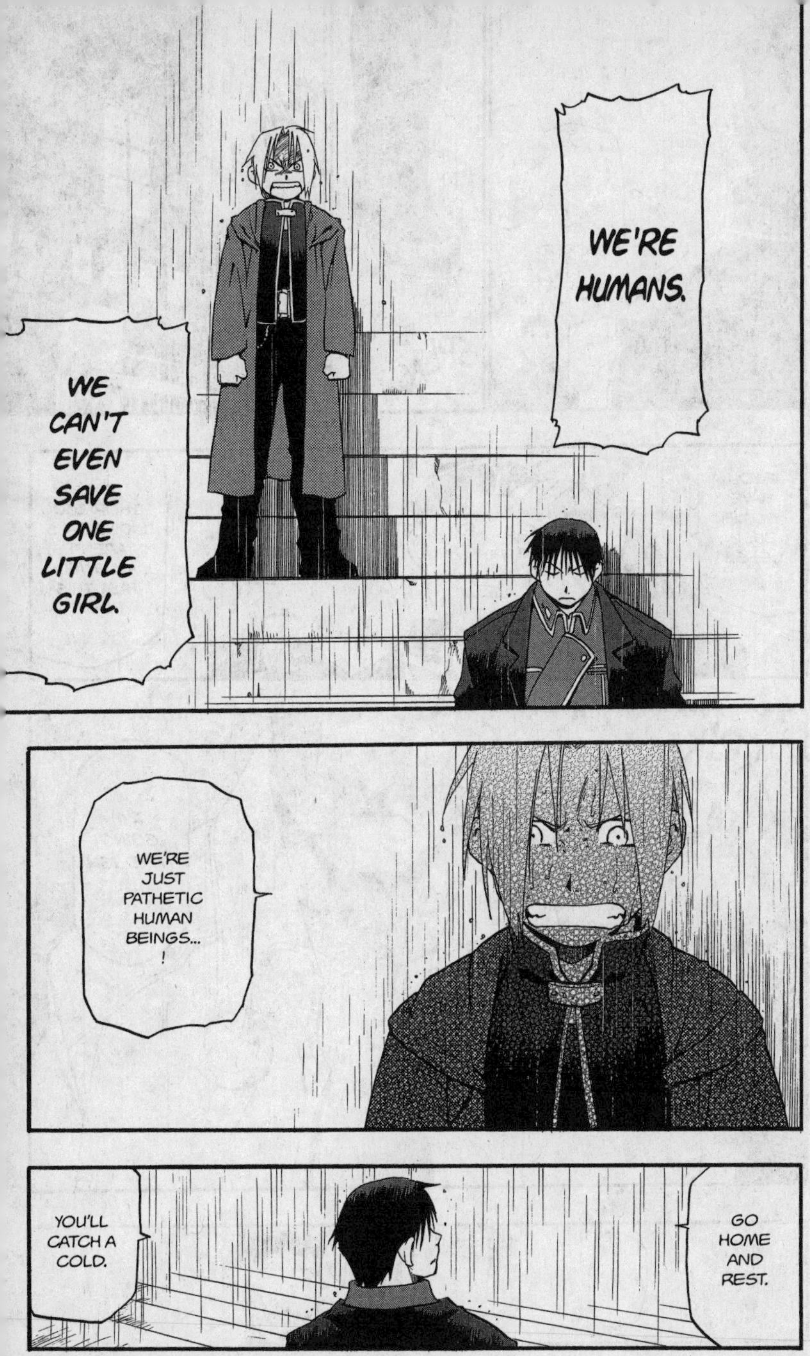
WE'RE HUMANS.
WE CAN'T EVEN SAVE ONE LITTLE GIRL.
WE'RE JUST PATHETIC HUMAN BEINGS... !
GO HOME AND REST.
YOU'LL CATCH A COLD.

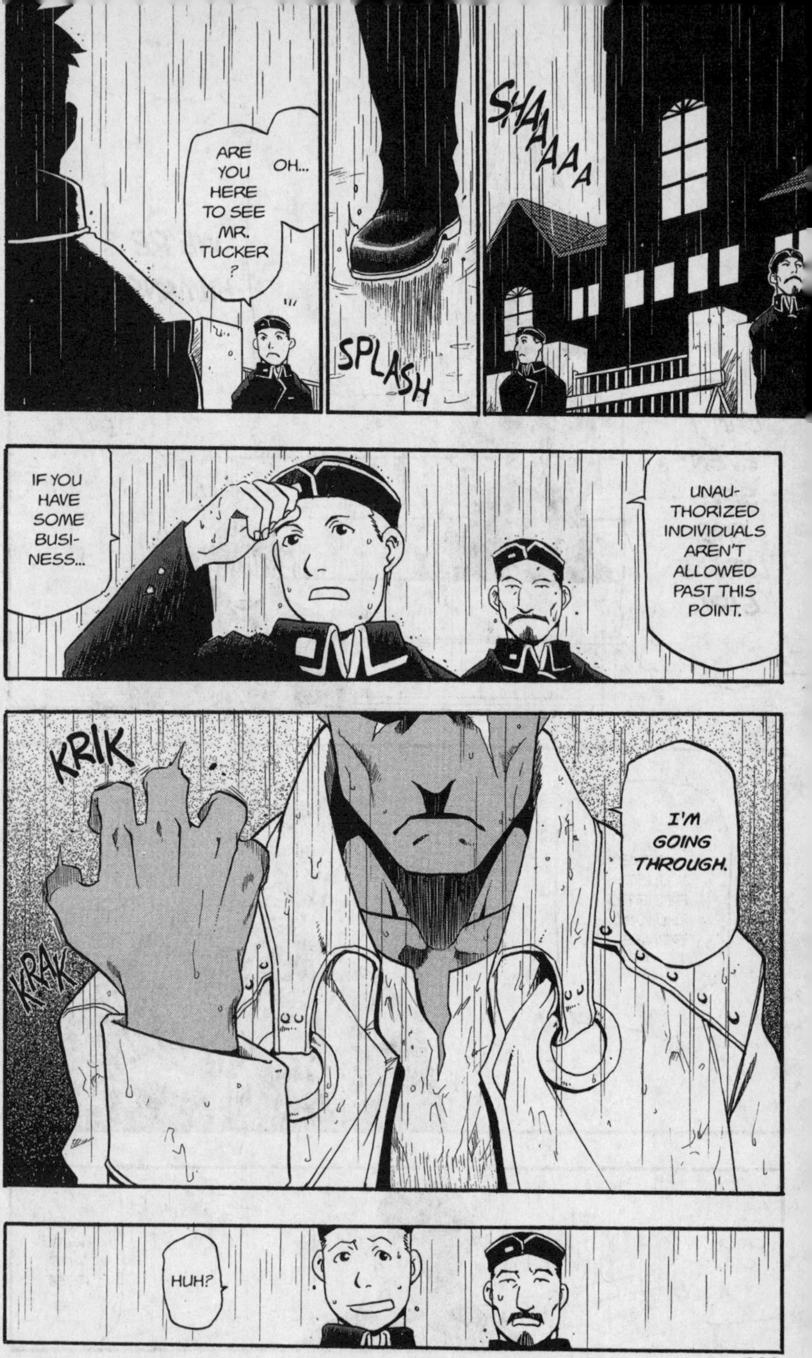
SHAAAAA
SPLASH
OH...
ARE YOU HERE TO SEE MR. TUCKER?
UNAUTHORIZED INDIVIDUALS AREN'T ALLOWED PAST THIS POINT.
IF YOU HAVE SOME BUSINESS...
I'M GOING THROUGH.
KRIK
KRAK
HUH?

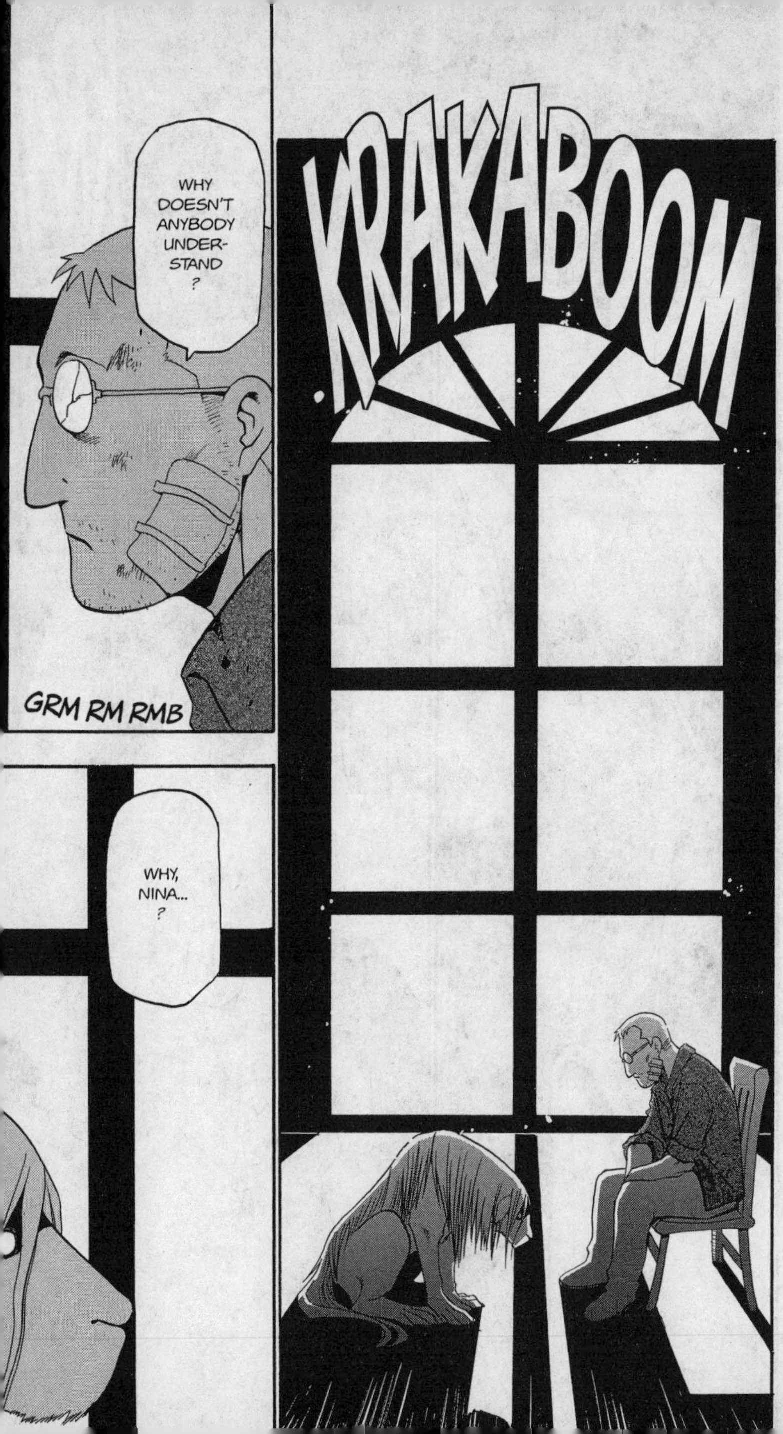
KRAKABOOM
WHY DOESN'T ANYBODY UNDER-STAND?
GRM RM RMB
WHY, NINA...?

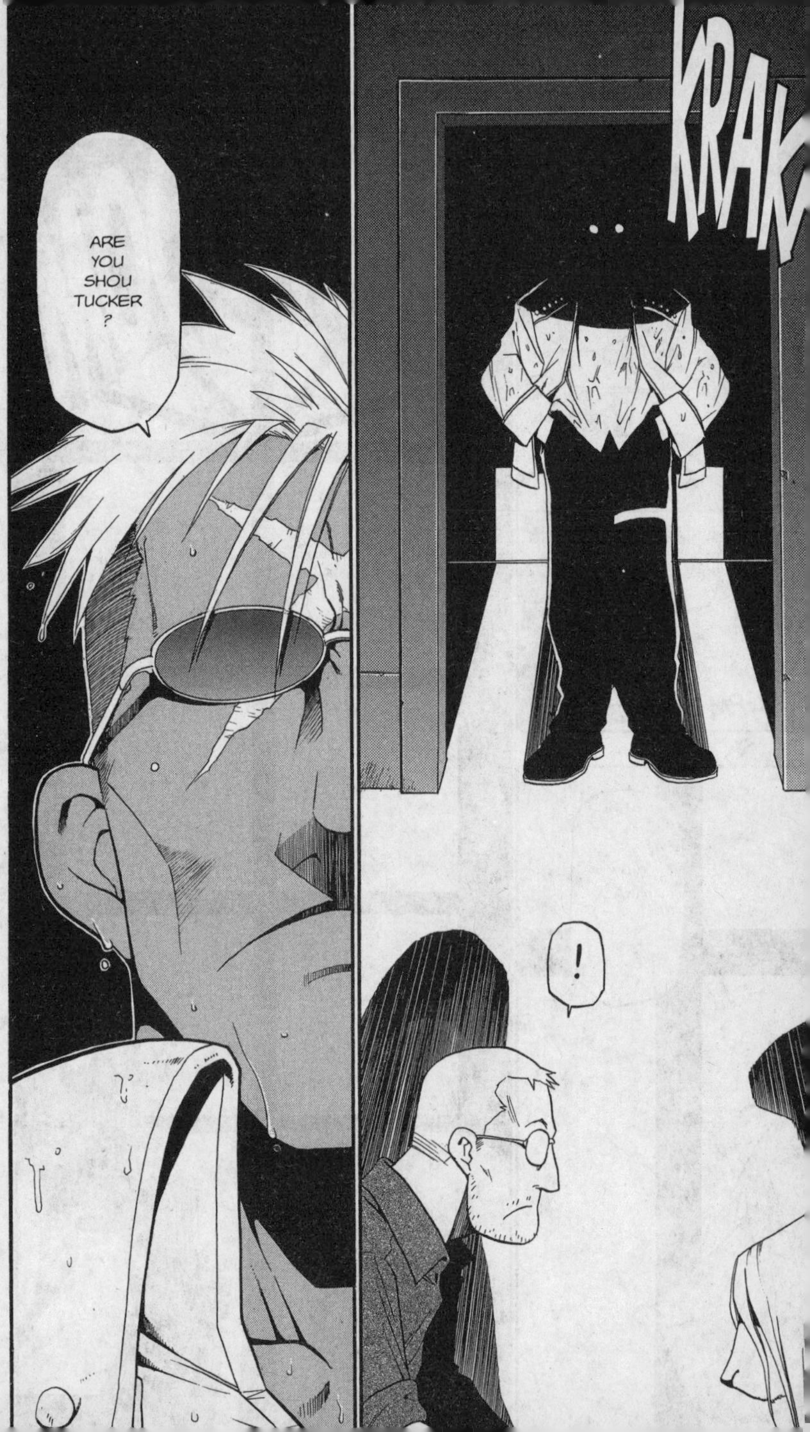
KRAK
!
ARE YOU SHOU TUCKER?

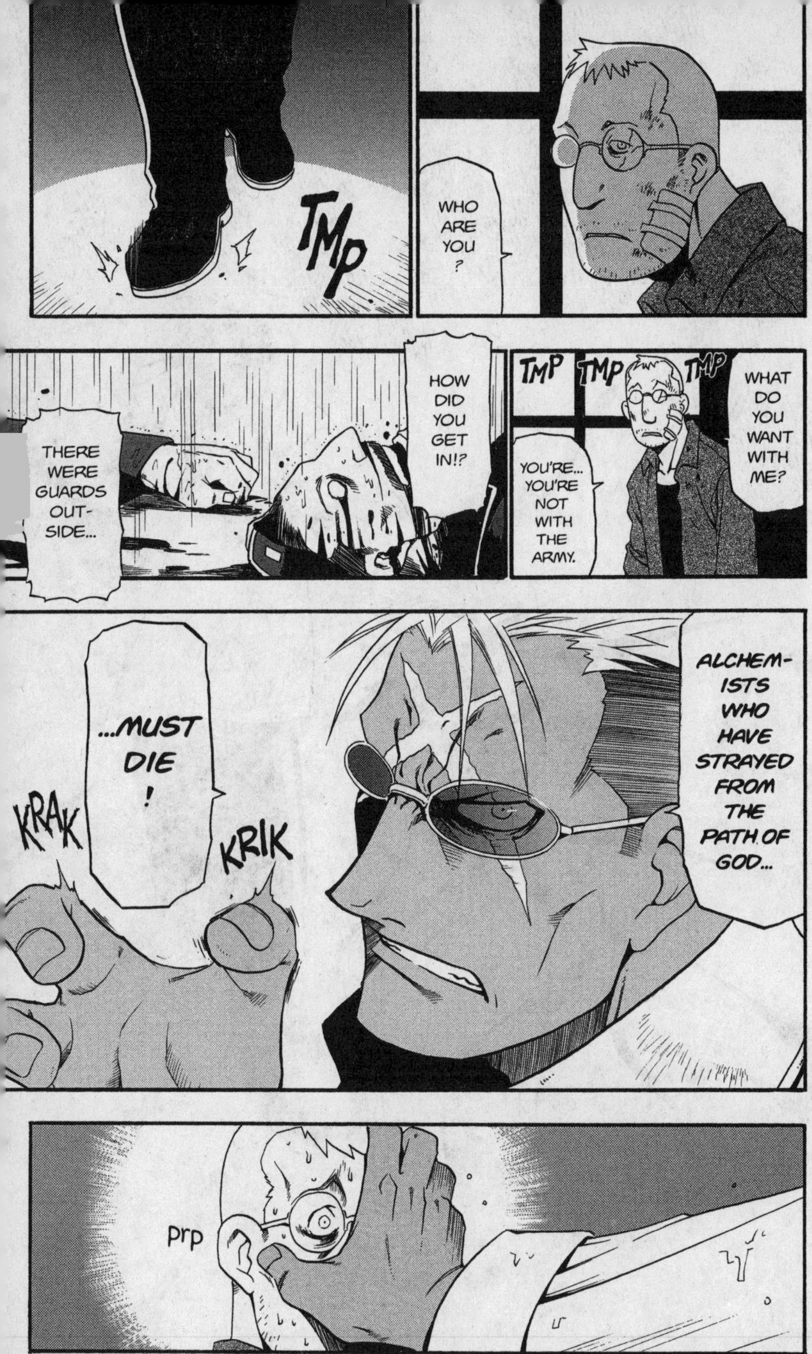
WHO ARE YOU?
TMP
TMP TMP TMP
WHAT DO YOU WANT WITH ME?
YOU'RE... YOU'RE NOT WITH THE ARMY.
HOW DID YOU GET IN!?
THERE WERE GUARDS OUTSIDE...
ALCHEMISTS WHO HAVE STRAYED FROM THE PATH OF GOD...
...MUST DIE!
KRIK
KRAK
prp

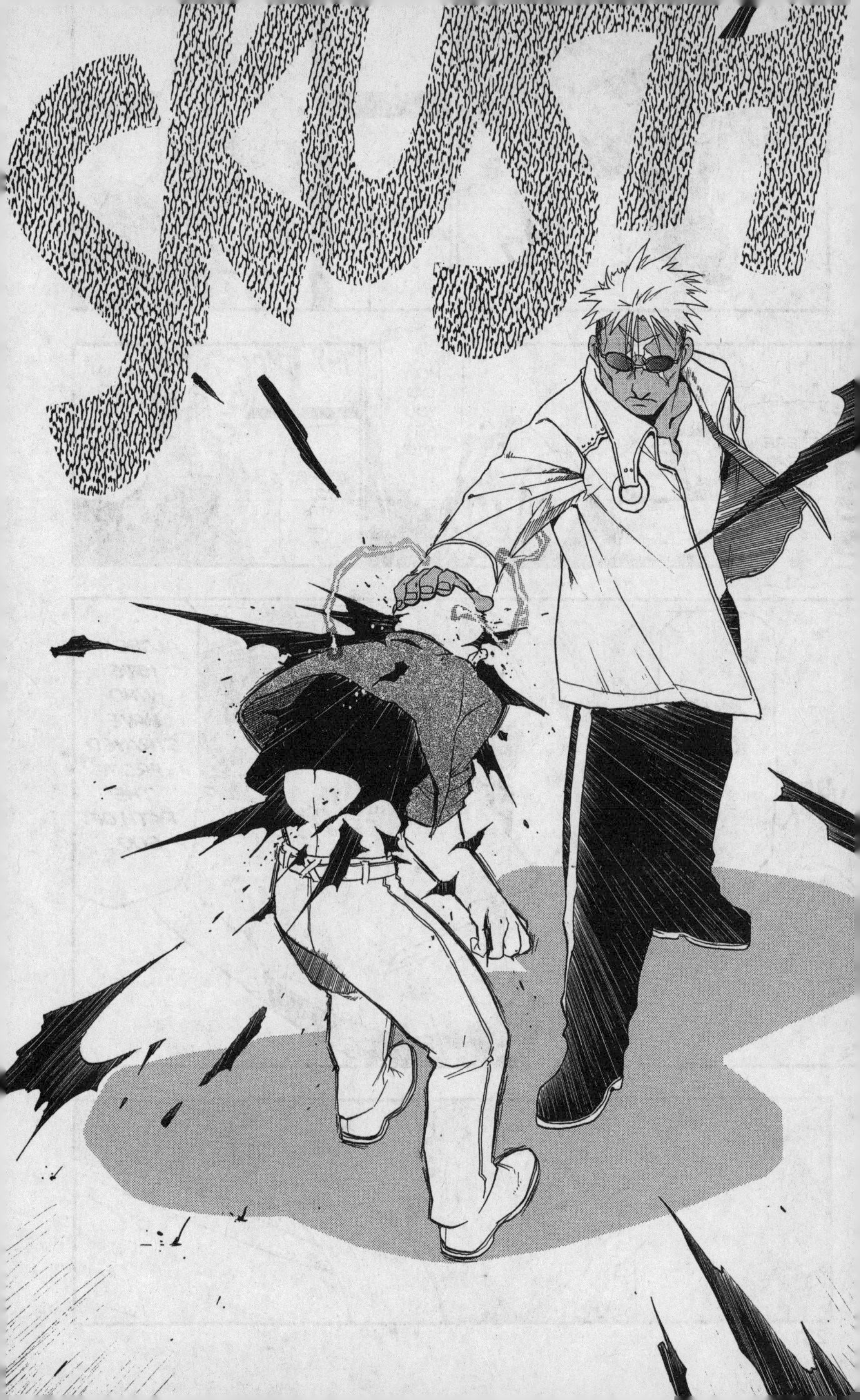
SKUSH

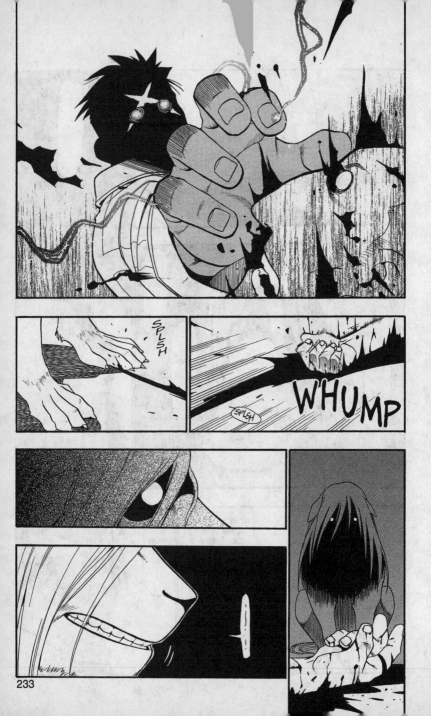

SPLSH

WHUMP

SPLSH

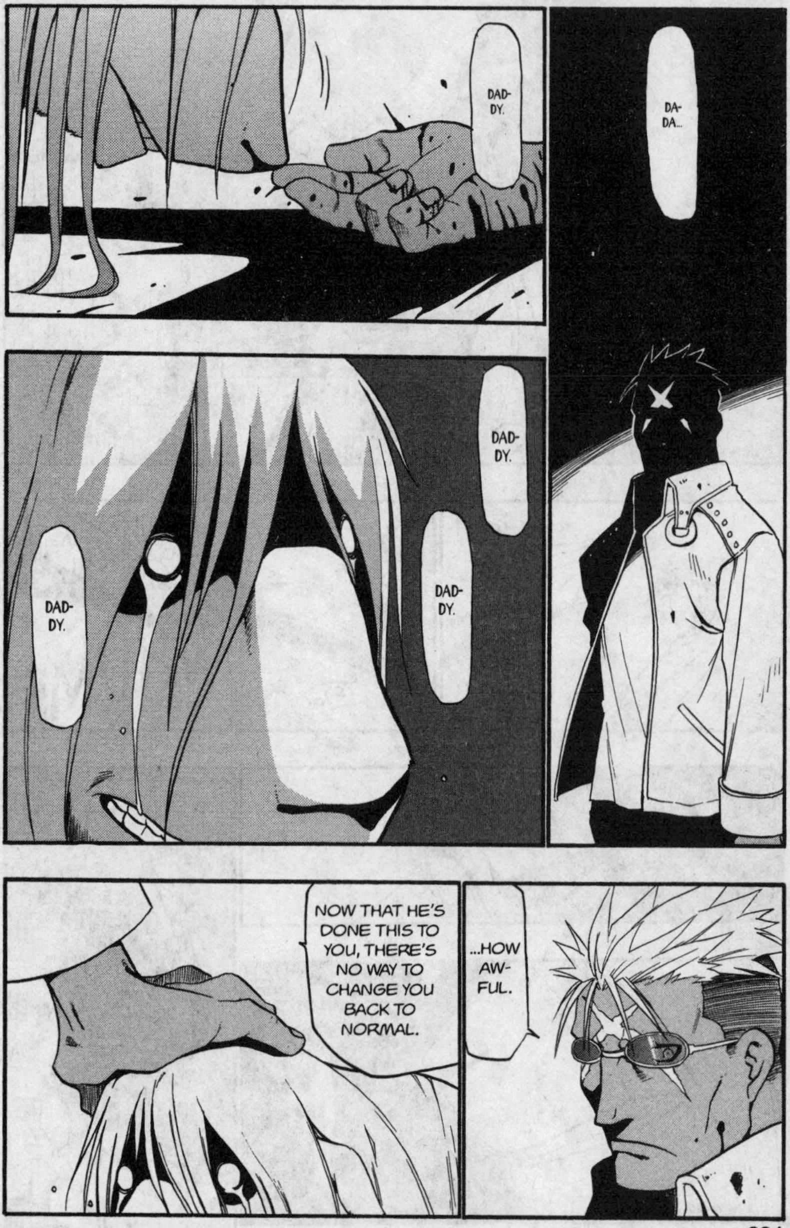
DA-DA...
DADDY.
DADDY.
DADDY.
DADDY.
...HOW AWFUL.
NOW THAT HE'S DONE THIS TO YOU, THERE'S NO WAY TO CHANGE YOU BACK TO NORMAL.

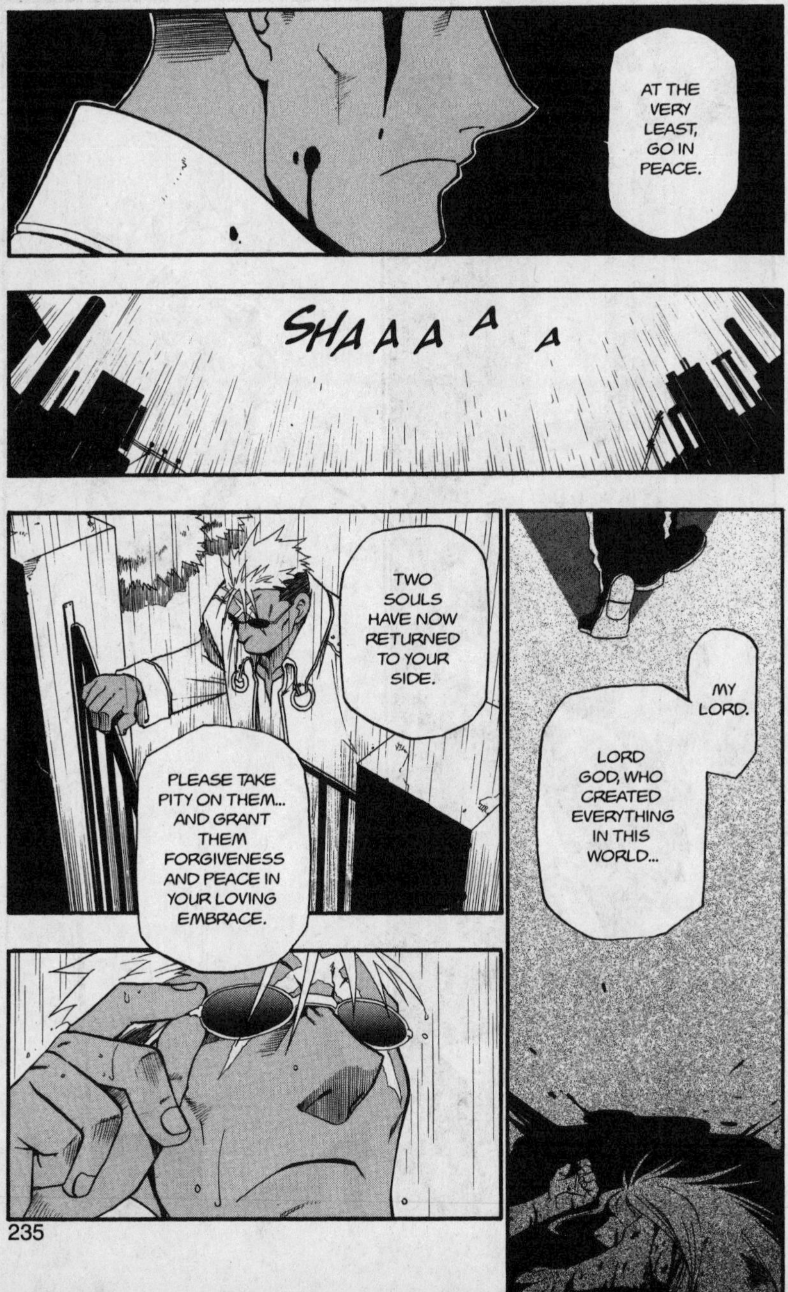
AT THE VERY LEAST, GO IN PEACE.
SHAAAAA
MY LORD.
LORD GOD, WHO CREATED EVERYTHING IN THIS WORLD...
TWO SOULS HAVE NOW RETURNED TO YOUR SIDE.
PLEASE TAKE PITY ON THEM... AND GRANT THEM FORGIVENESS AND PEACE IN YOUR LOVING EMBRACE.

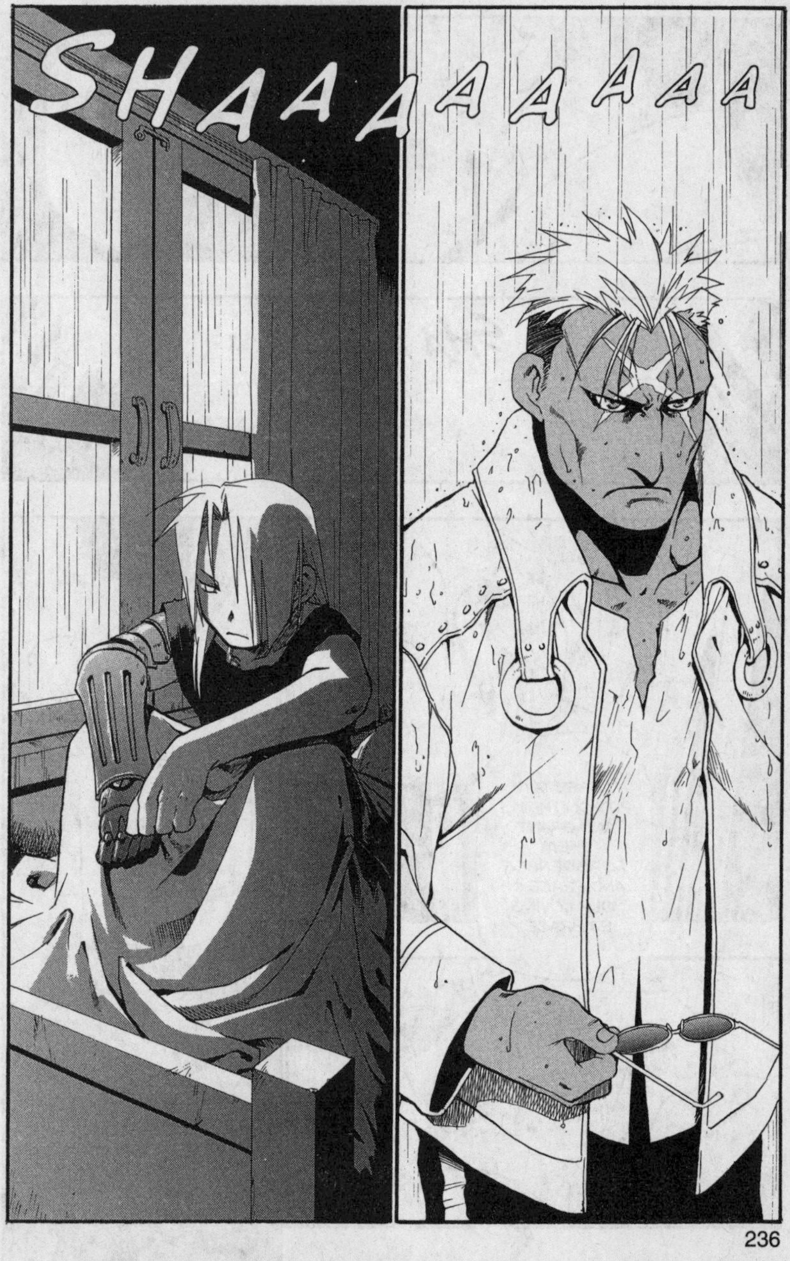
SHAAAAAAAAA

FULLMETAL
ALCHEMIST

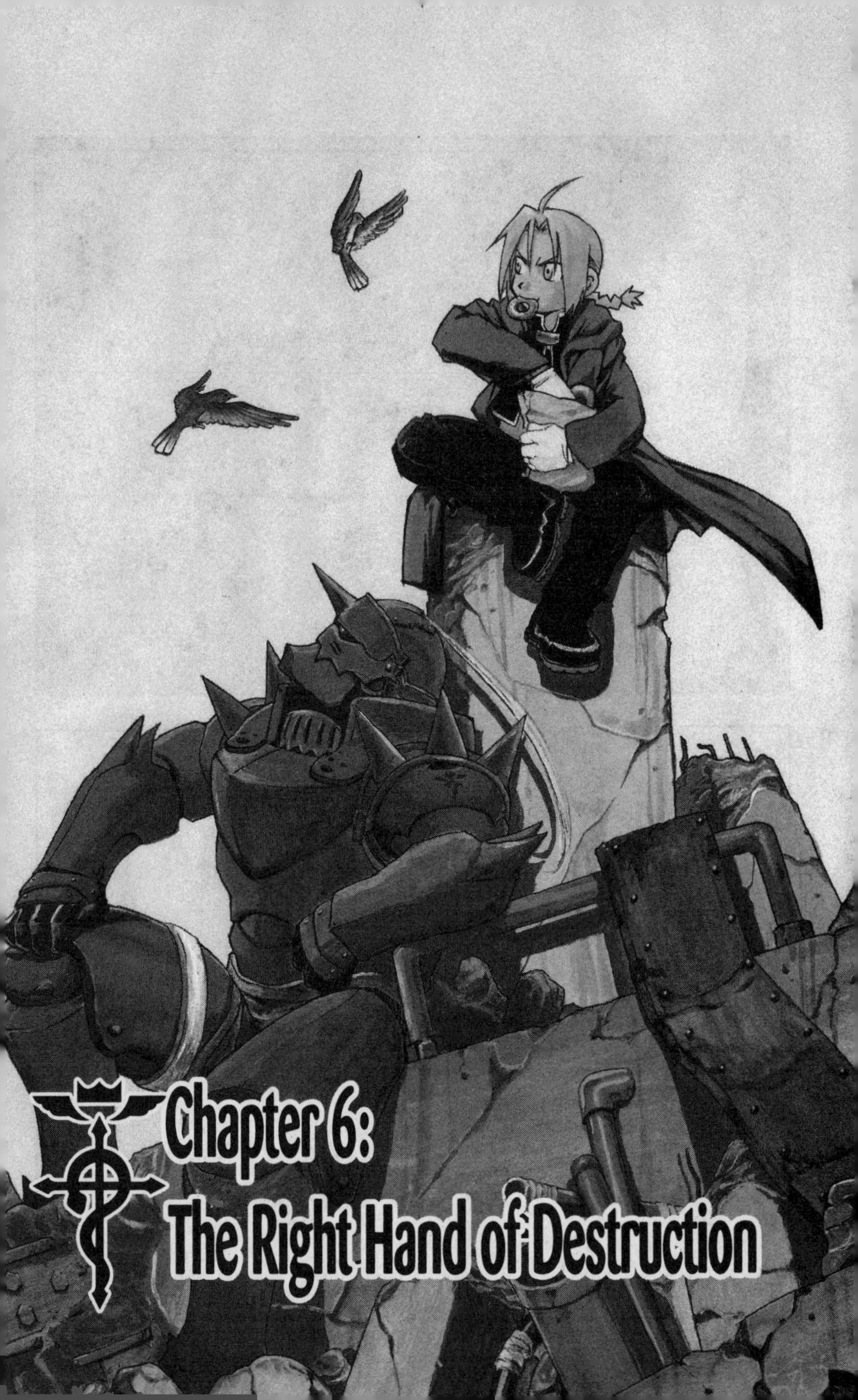

Chapter 6: The Right Hand of Destruction

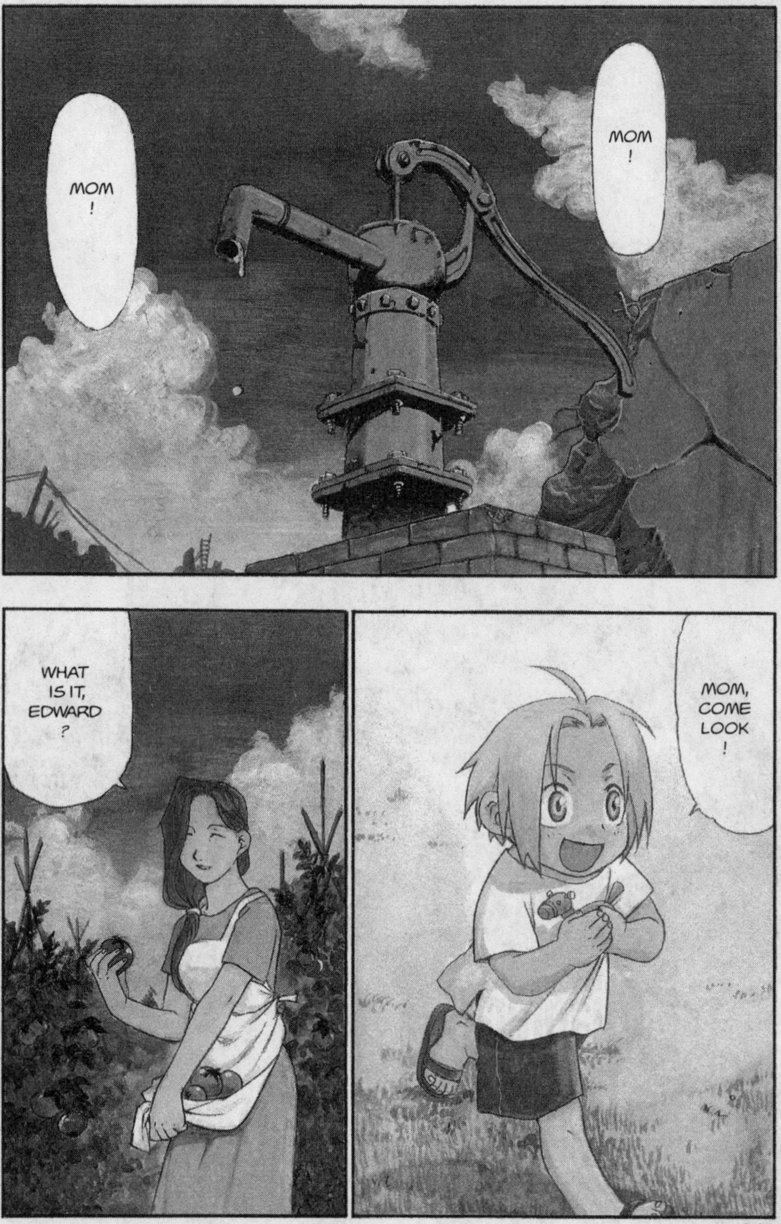
MOM !
MOM !
MOM, COME LOOK !
WHAT IS IT, EDWARD ?

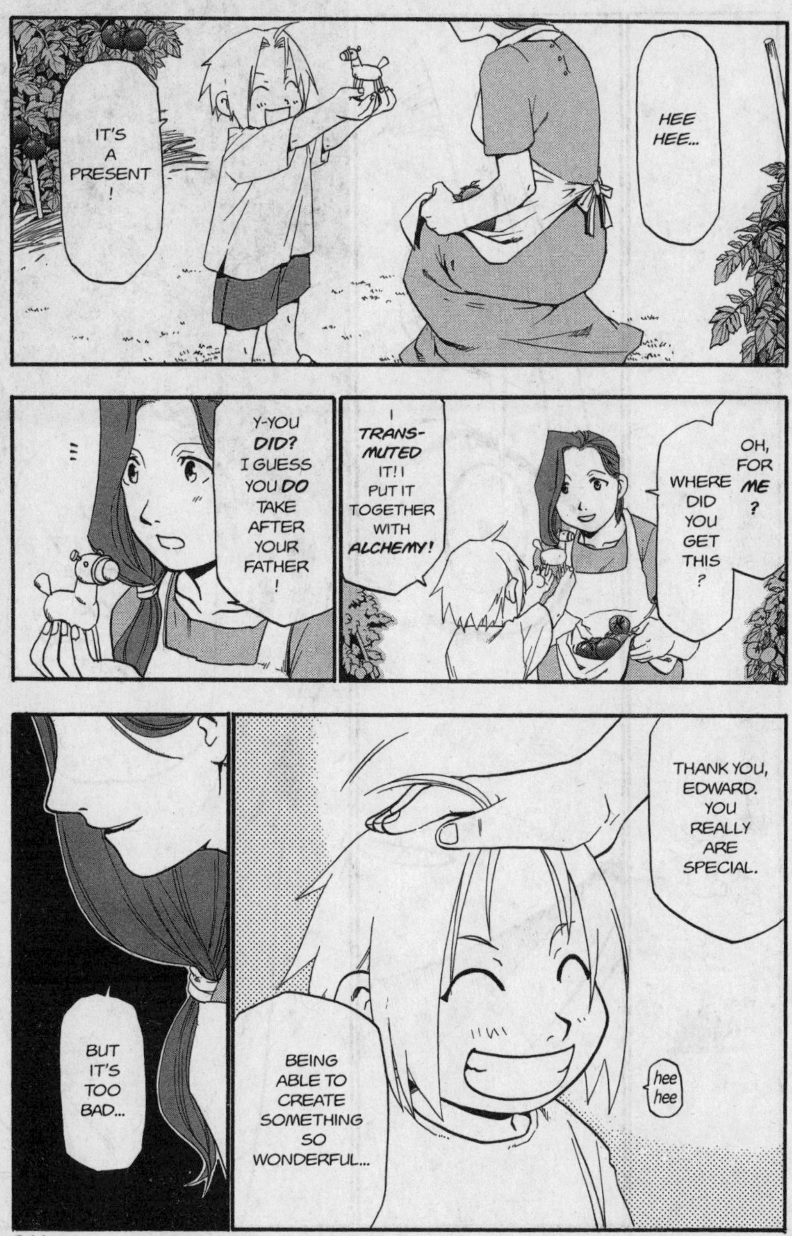
HEE HEE...
IT'S A PRESENT!
OH, FOR ME?
WHERE DID YOU GET THIS?
I TRANSMUTED IT! I PUT IT TOGETHER WITH ALCHEMY!
Y-YOU DID? I GUESS YOU DO TAKE AFTER YOUR FATHER!
THANK YOU, EDWARD. YOU REALLY ARE SPECIAL.
hee hee
BEING ABLE TO CREATE SOMETHING SO WONDERFUL...
BUT IT'S TOO BAD...

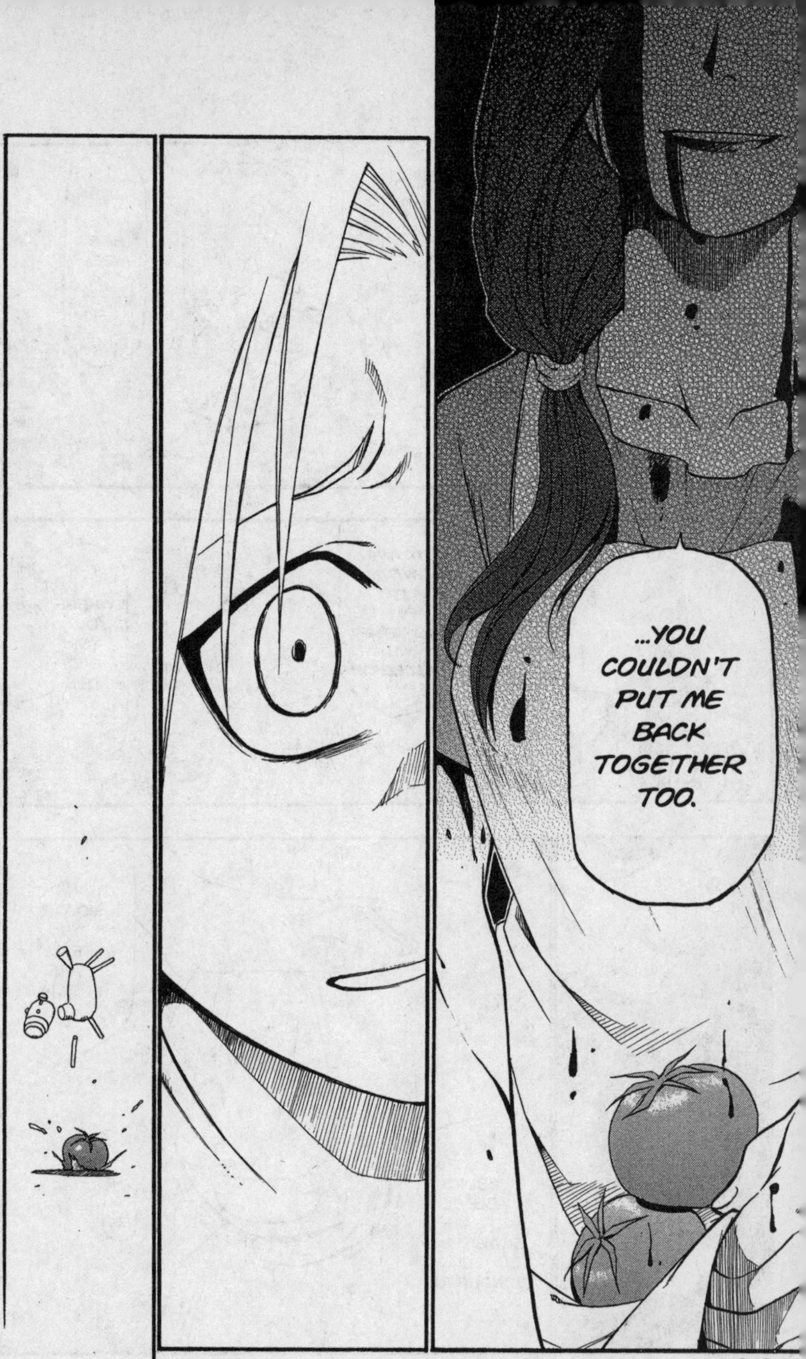
...YOU COULDN'T PUT ME BACK TOGETHER TOO.

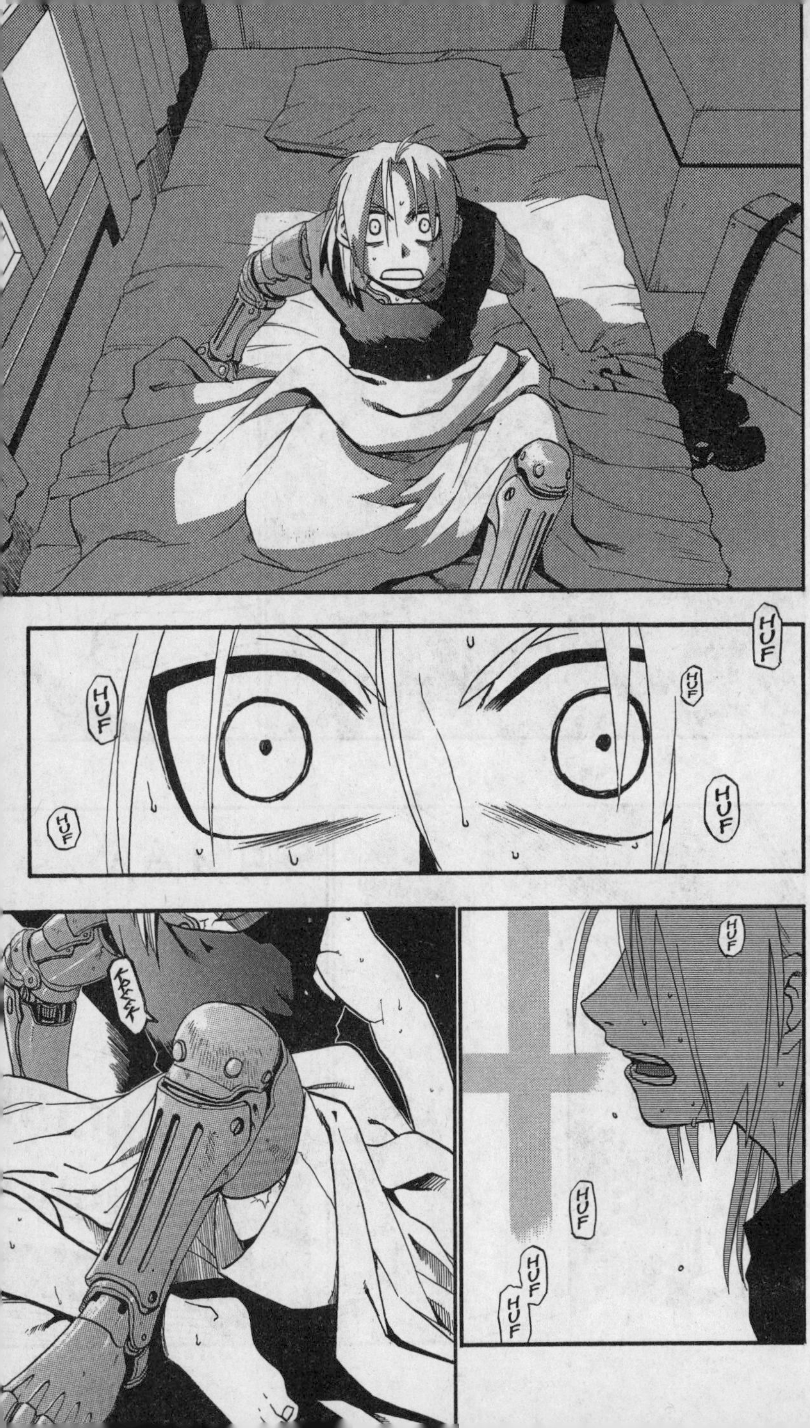
HUF
HUF
HUF
HUF
HUF
HUF
HUF
HUF
HUF
KREEK

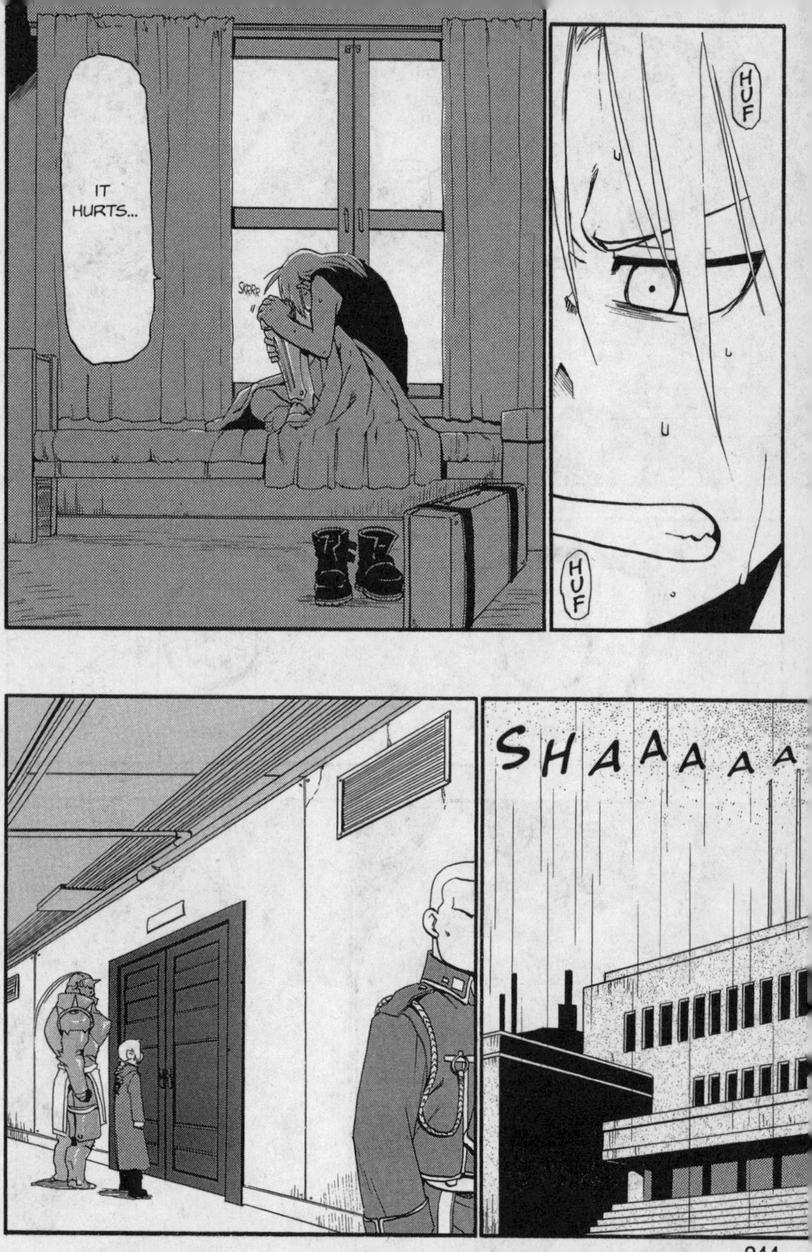
HUF
HUF
SKRRR
IT HURTS...
SHAAAAA

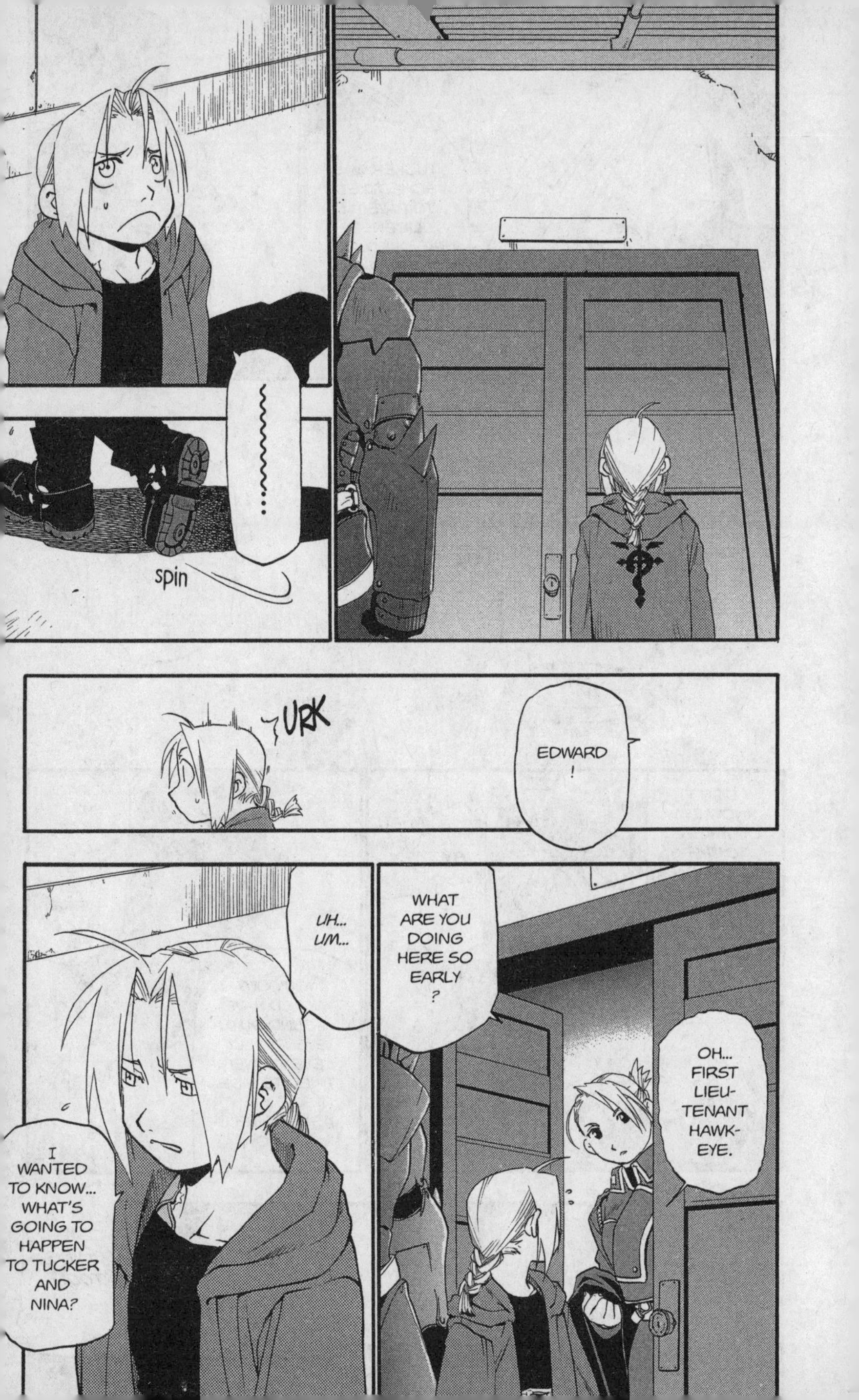
……
spin
EDWARD!
URK
OH... FIRST LIEU-TENANT HAWK-EYE.
WHAT ARE YOU DOING HERE SO EARLY?
UH... UM...
I WANTED TO KNOW... WHAT'S GOING TO HAPPEN TO TUCKER AND NINA?

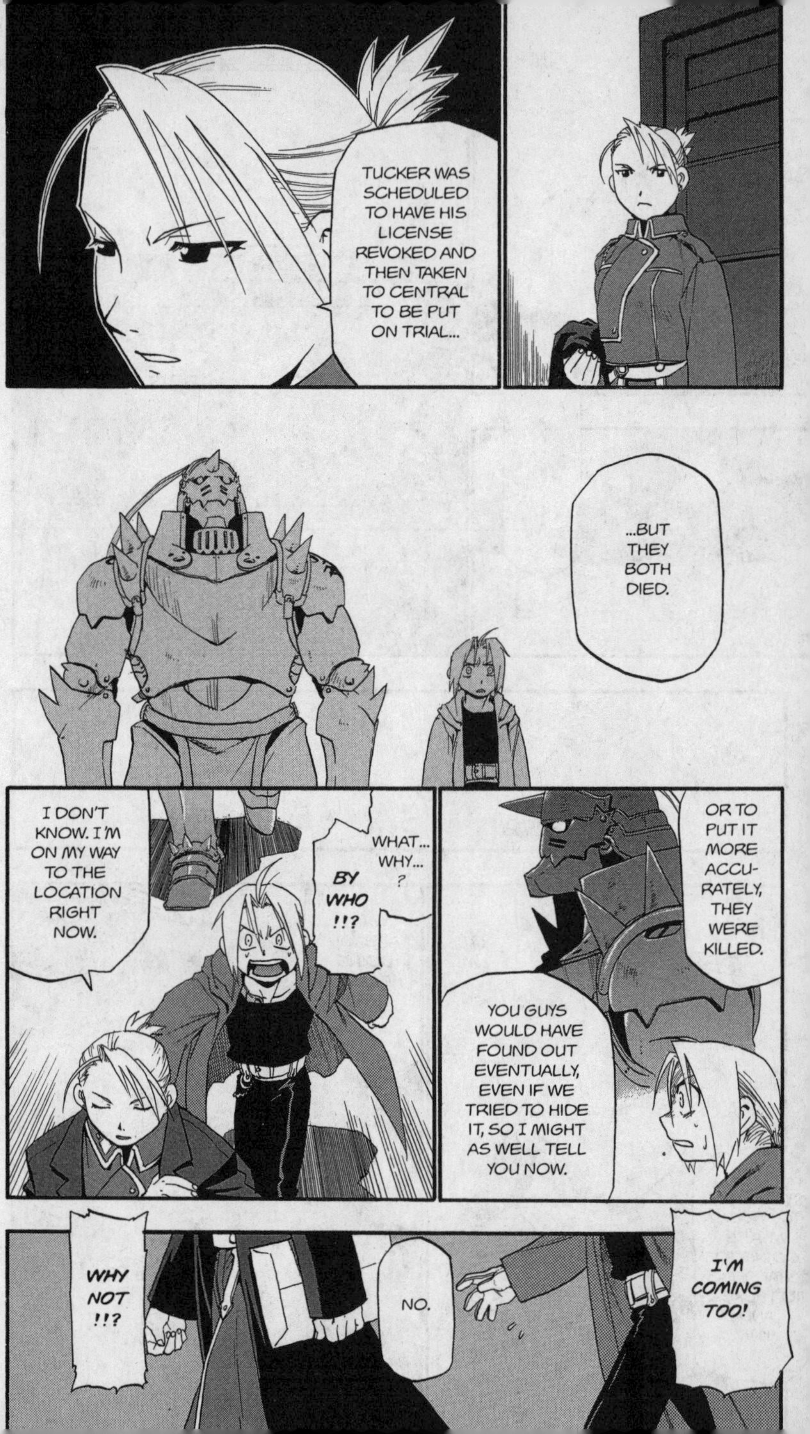
TUCKER WAS SCHEDULED TO HAVE HIS LICENSE REVOKED AND THEN TAKEN TO CENTRAL TO BE PUT ON TRIAL...
...BUT THEY BOTH DIED.
OR TO PUT IT MORE ACCU-RATELY, THEY WERE KILLED.
YOU GUYS WOULD HAVE FOUND OUT EVENTUALLY, EVEN IF WE TRIED TO HIDE IT, SO I MIGHT AS WELL TELL YOU NOW.
WHAT... WHY...?
BY WHO!!?
I DON'T KNOW. I'M ON MY WAY TO THE LOCATION RIGHT NOW.
I'M COMING TOO!
NO.
WHY NOT!!?

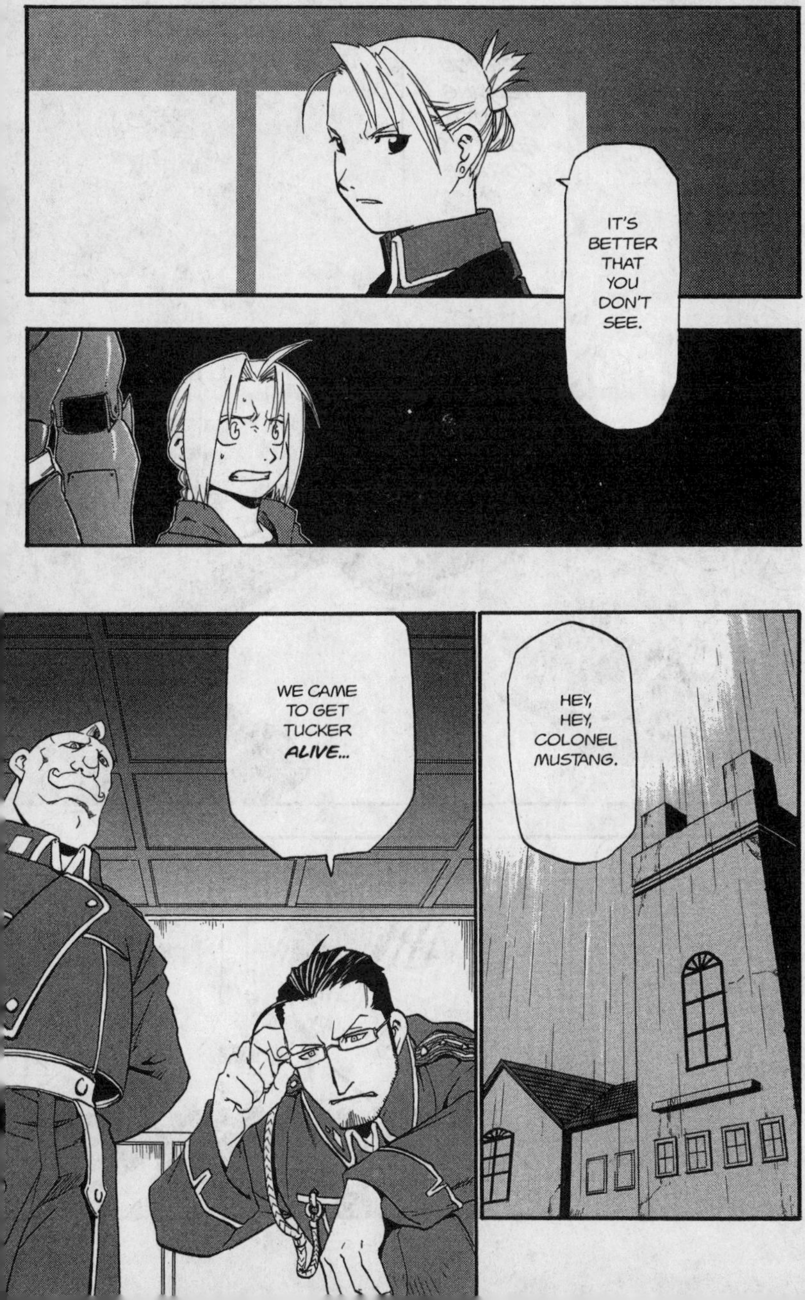
IT'S BETTER THAT YOU DON'T SEE.
HEY, HEY, COLONEL MUSTANG.
WE CAME TO GET TUCKER *ALIVE*...

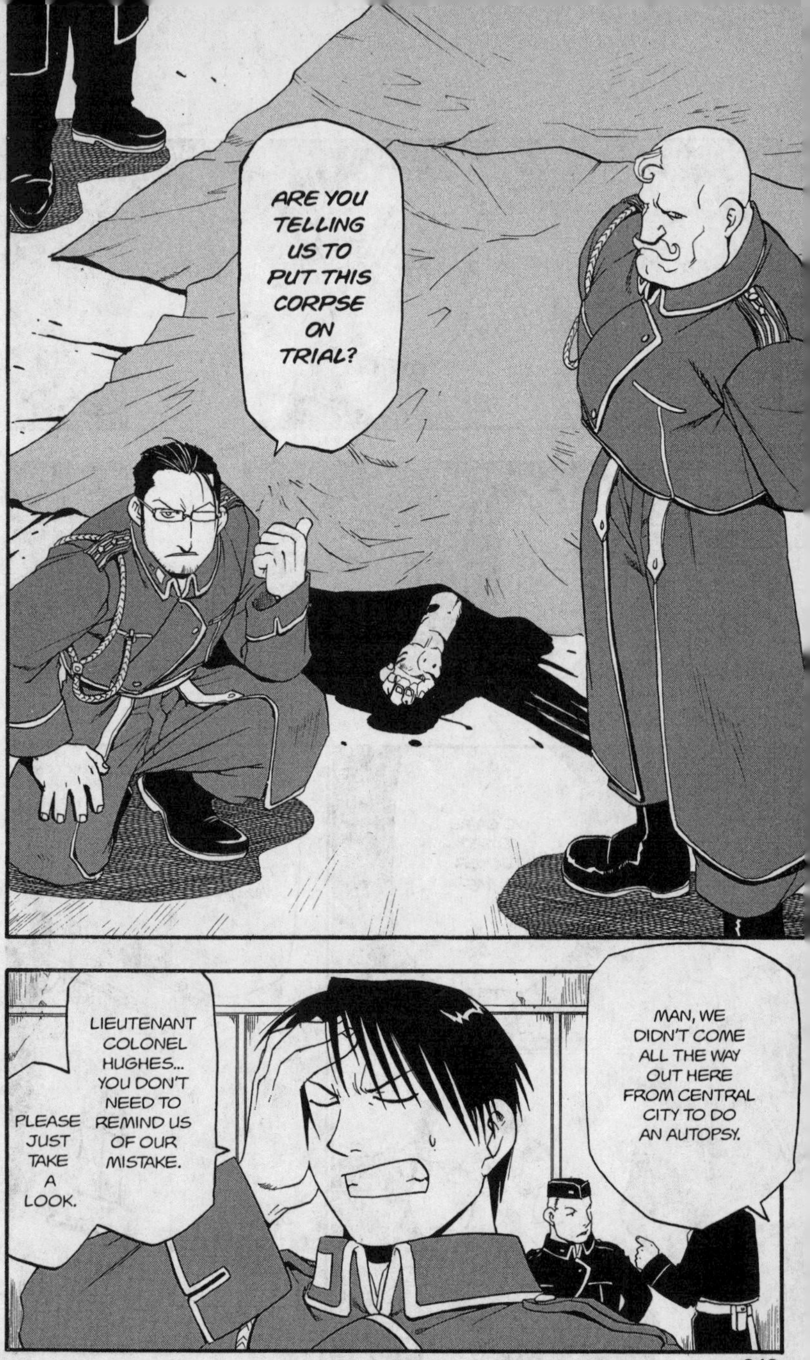
ARE YOU TELLING US TO PUT THIS CORPSE ON TRIAL?
MAN, WE DIDN'T COME ALL THE WAY OUT HERE FROM CENTRAL CITY TO DO AN AUTOPSY.
LIEUTENANT COLONEL HUGHES... YOU DON'T NEED TO REMIND US OF OUR MISTAKE.
PLEASE JUST TAKE A LOOK.

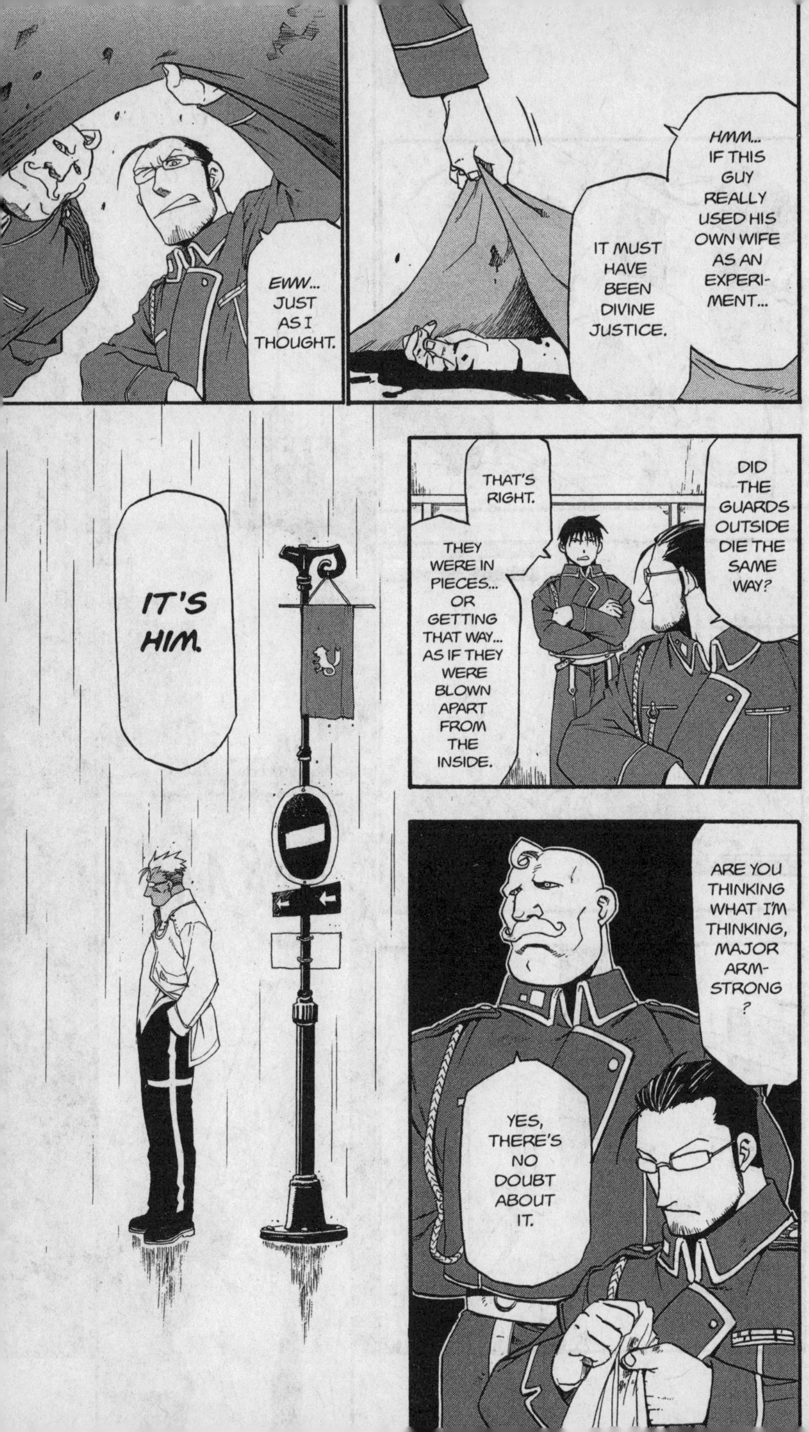
HMM... IF THIS GUY REALLY USED HIS OWN WIFE AS AN EXPERIMENT...
IT MUST HAVE BEEN DIVINE JUSTICE.
EWW... JUST AS I THOUGHT.
DID THE GUARDS OUTSIDE DIE THE SAME WAY?
THAT'S RIGHT.
THEY WERE IN PIECES... OR GETTING THAT WAY... AS IF THEY WERE BLOWN APART FROM THE INSIDE.
ARE YOU THINKING WHAT I'M THINKING, MAJOR ARMSTRONG?
YES, THERE'S NO DOUBT ABOUT IT.
IT'S HIM.

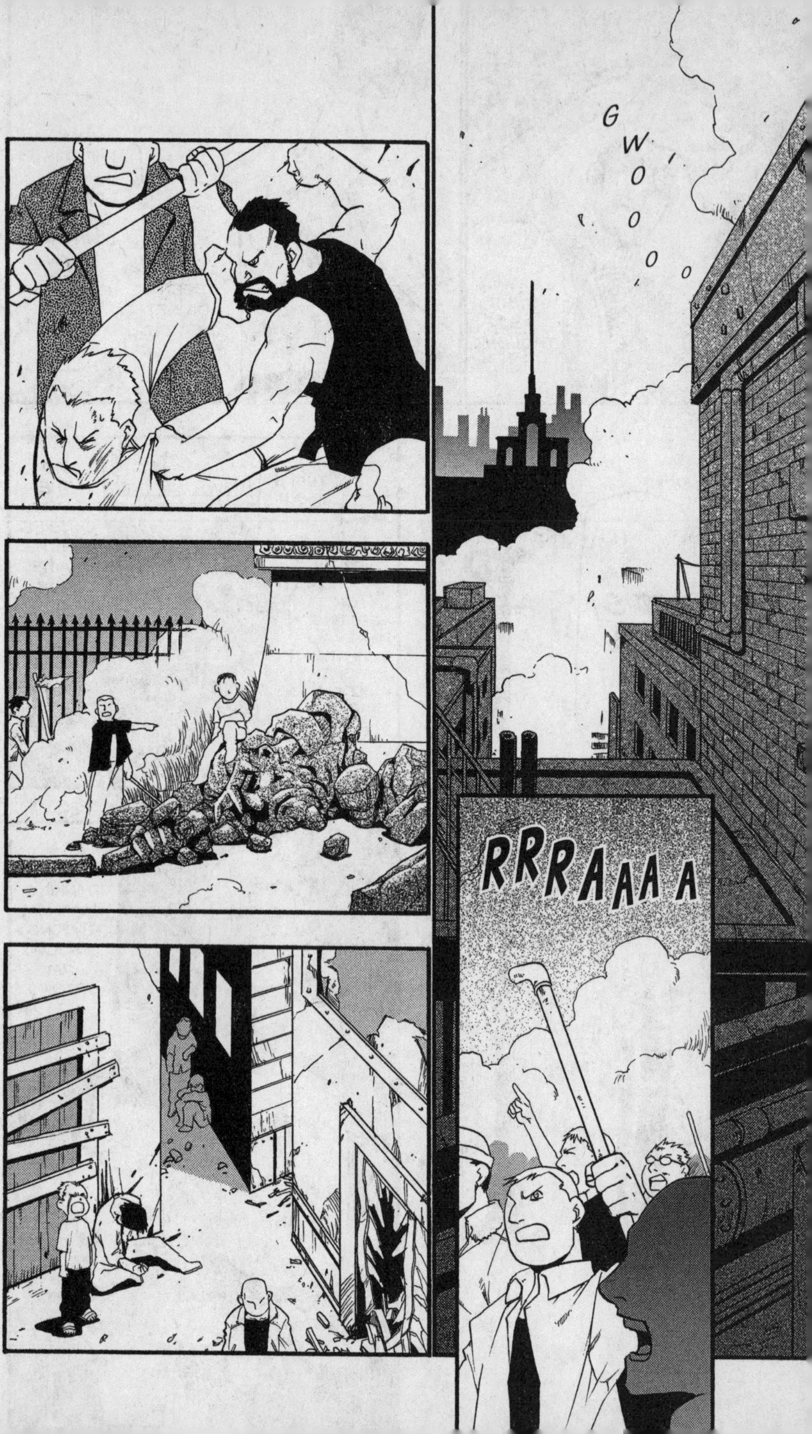
GWOOOOO
RRRAAAA

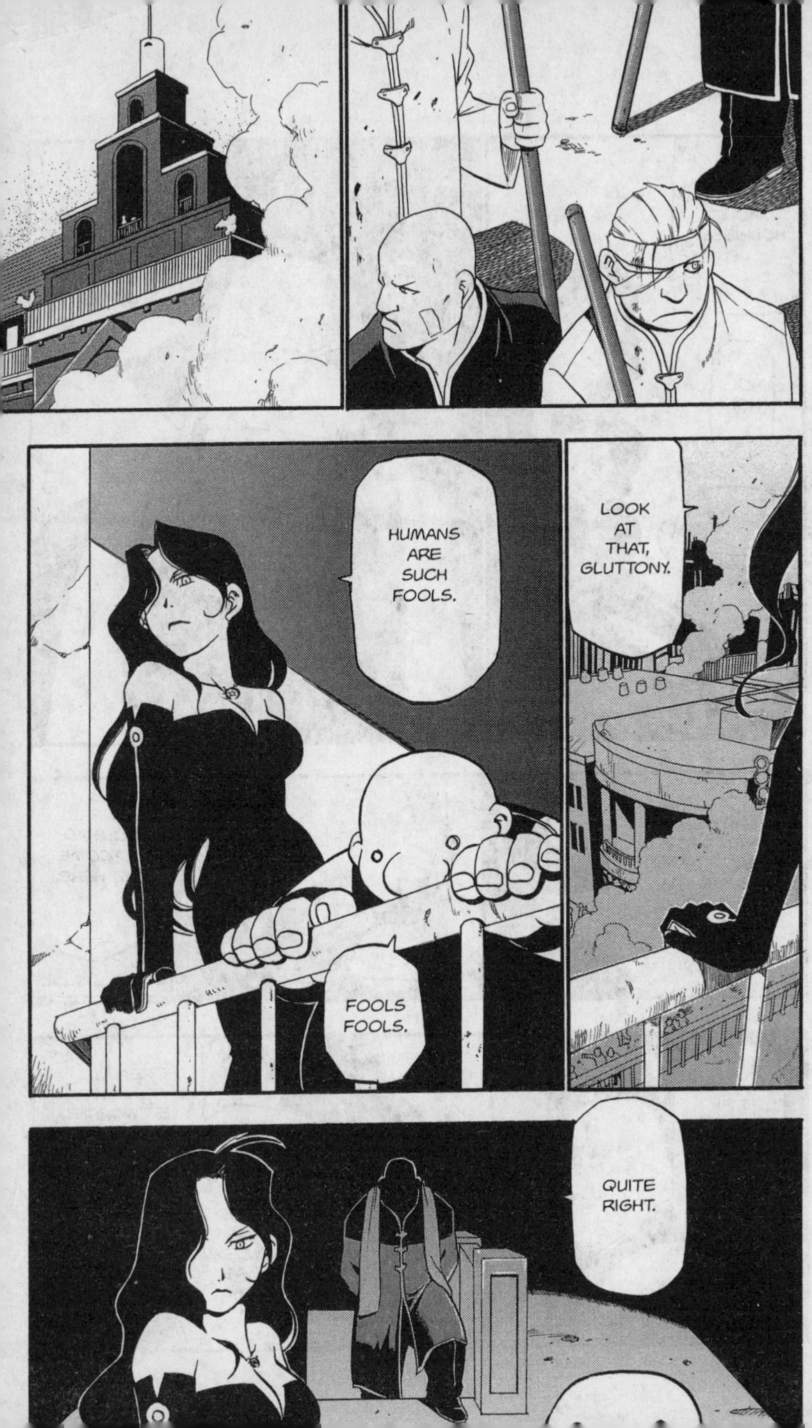
LOOK AT THAT, GLUTTONY.
HUMANS ARE SUCH FOOLS.
FOOLS FOOLS.
QUITE RIGHT.

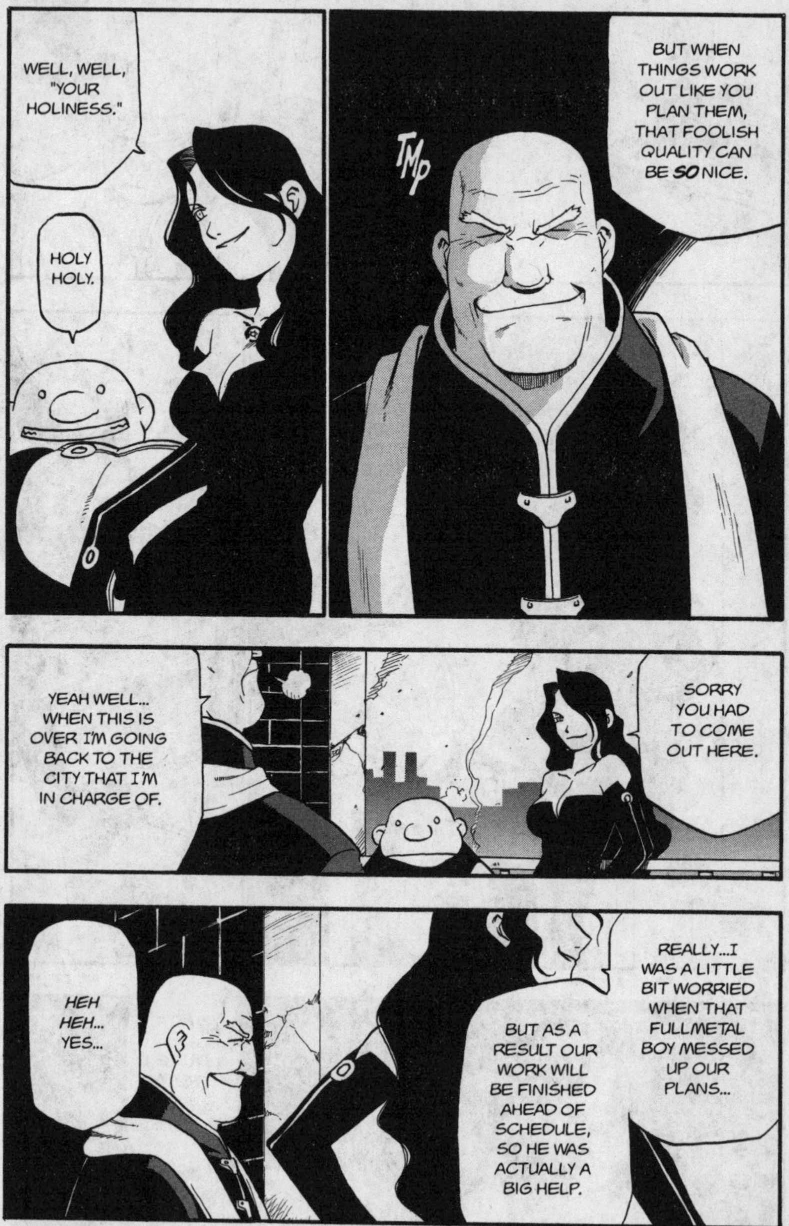
BUT WHEN THINGS WORK OUT LIKE YOU PLAN THEM, THAT FOOLISH QUALITY CAN BE **SO** NICE.
TMP
WELL, WELL, "YOUR HOLINESS."
HOLY HOLY.
SORRY YOU HAD TO COME OUT HERE.
YEAH WELL... WHEN THIS IS OVER I'M GOING BACK TO THE CITY THAT I'M IN CHARGE OF.
REALLY...I WAS A LITTLE BIT WORRIED WHEN THAT FULLMETAL BOY MESSED UP OUR PLANS...
BUT AS A RESULT OUR WORK WILL BE FINISHED AHEAD OF SCHEDULE, SO HE WAS ACTUALLY A BIG HELP.
HEH HEH... YES...

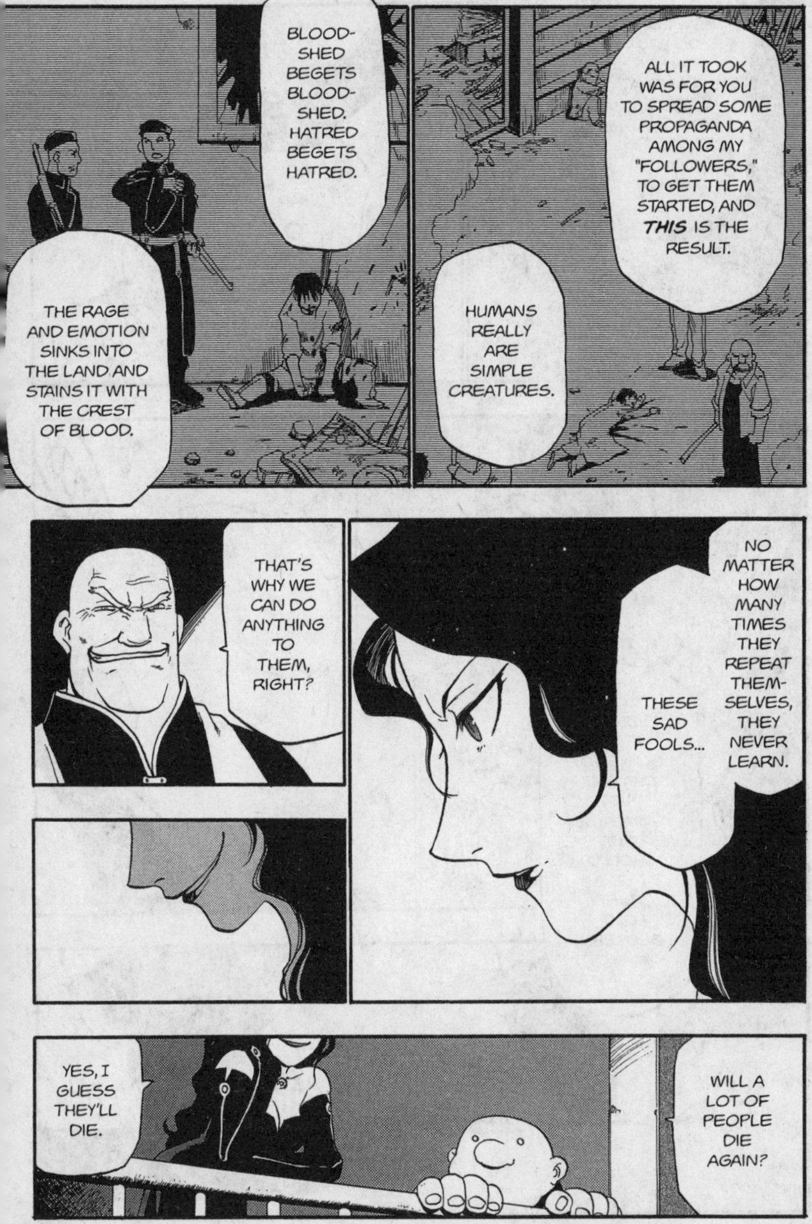
ALL IT TOOK WAS FOR YOU TO SPREAD SOME PROPAGANDA AMONG MY "FOLLOWERS," TO GET THEM STARTED, AND ***THIS*** IS THE RESULT.
HUMANS REALLY ARE SIMPLE CREATURES.
BLOOD-SHED BEGETS BLOOD-SHED. HATRED BEGETS HATRED.
THE RAGE AND EMOTION SINKS INTO THE LAND AND STAINS IT WITH THE CREST OF BLOOD.
NO MATTER HOW MANY TIMES THEY REPEAT THEM-SELVES, THEY NEVER LEARN.
THESE SAD FOOLS...
THAT'S WHY WE CAN DO ANYTHING TO THEM, RIGHT?
WILL A LOT OF PEOPLE DIE AGAIN?
YES, I GUESS THEY'LL DIE.

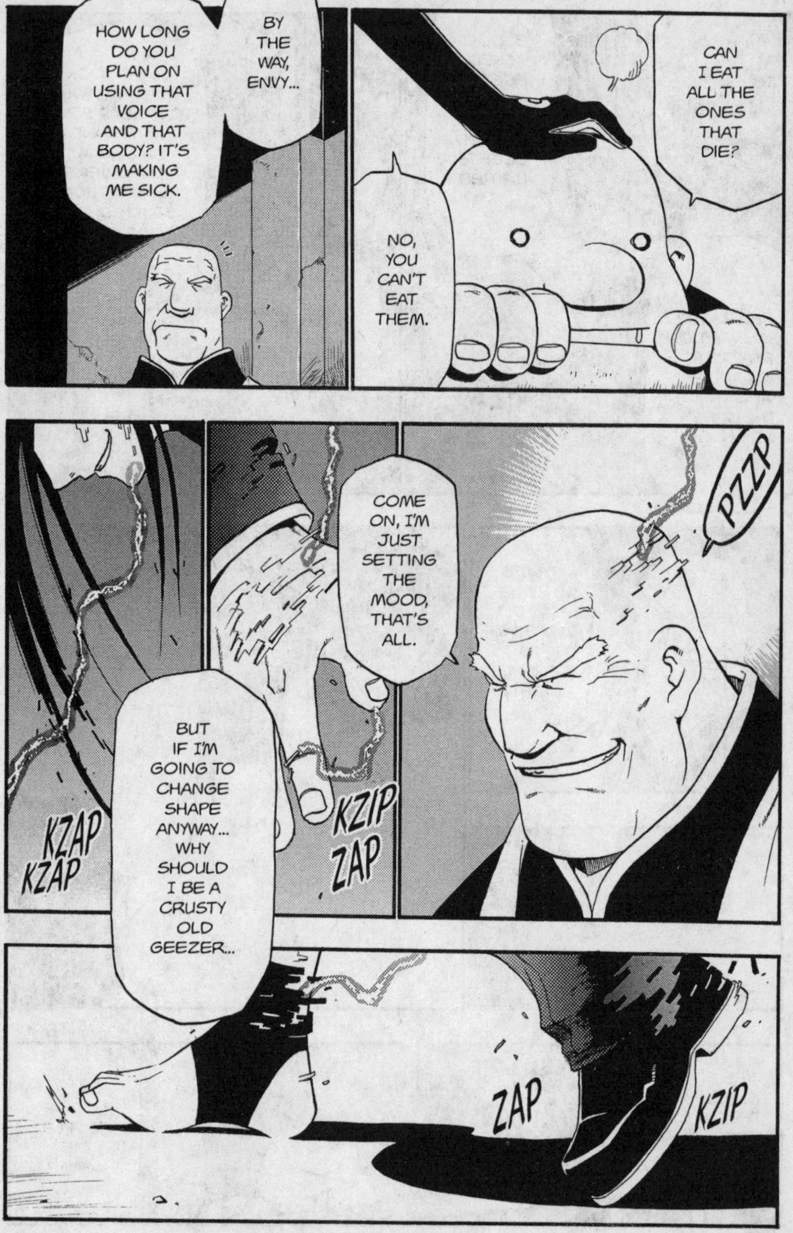
CAN I EAT ALL THE ONES THAT DIE?
NO, YOU CAN'T EAT THEM.
BY THE WAY, ENVY...
HOW LONG DO YOU PLAN ON USING THAT VOICE AND THAT BODY? IT'S MAKING ME SICK.
PZZP
COME ON, I'M JUST SETTING THE MOOD, THAT'S ALL.
KZIP ZAP
KZAP KZAP
BUT IF I'M GOING TO CHANGE SHAPE ANYWAY... WHY SHOULD I BE A CRUSTY OLD GEEZER...
KZIP
ZAP

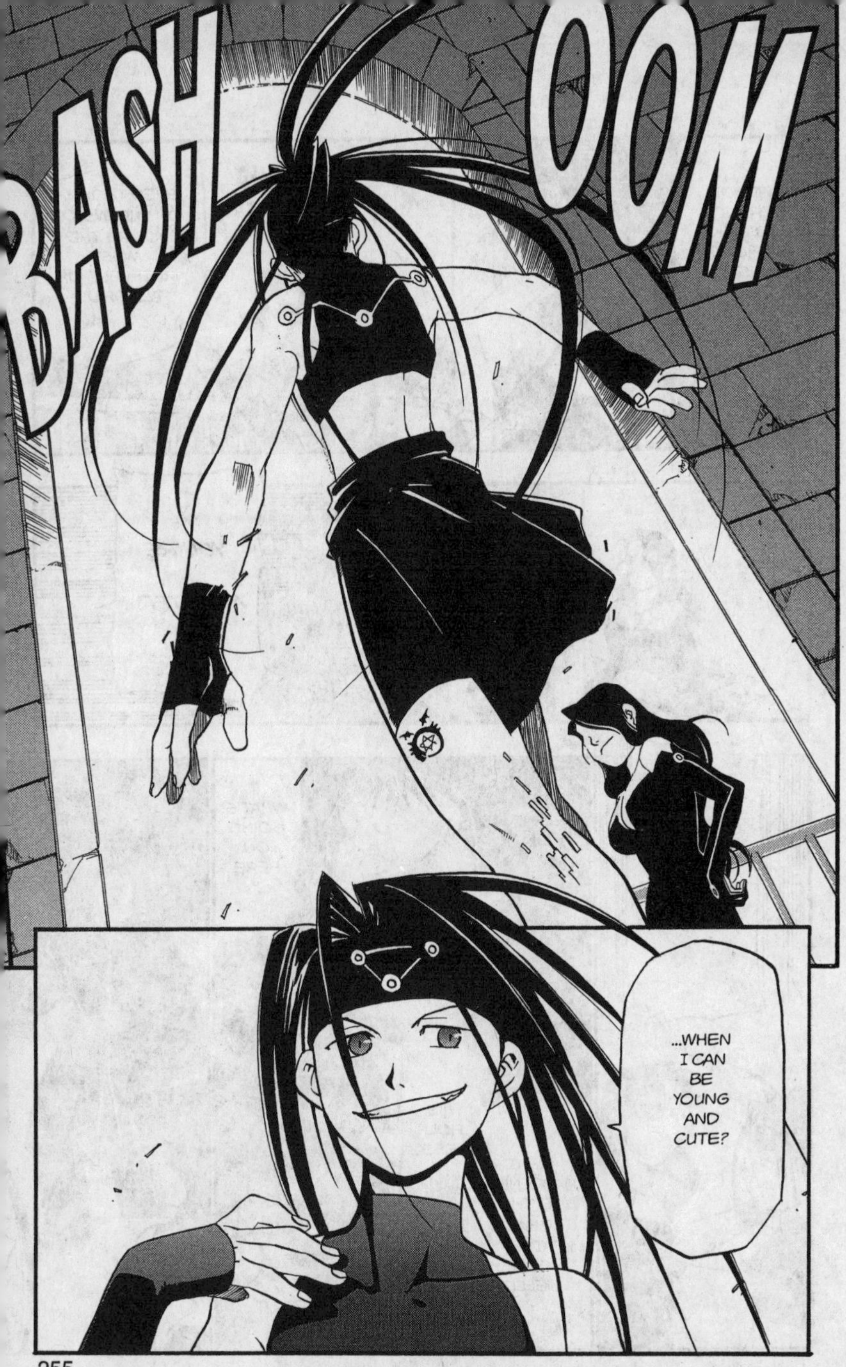
BASH
OOM
...WHEN I CAN BE YOUNG AND CUTE?

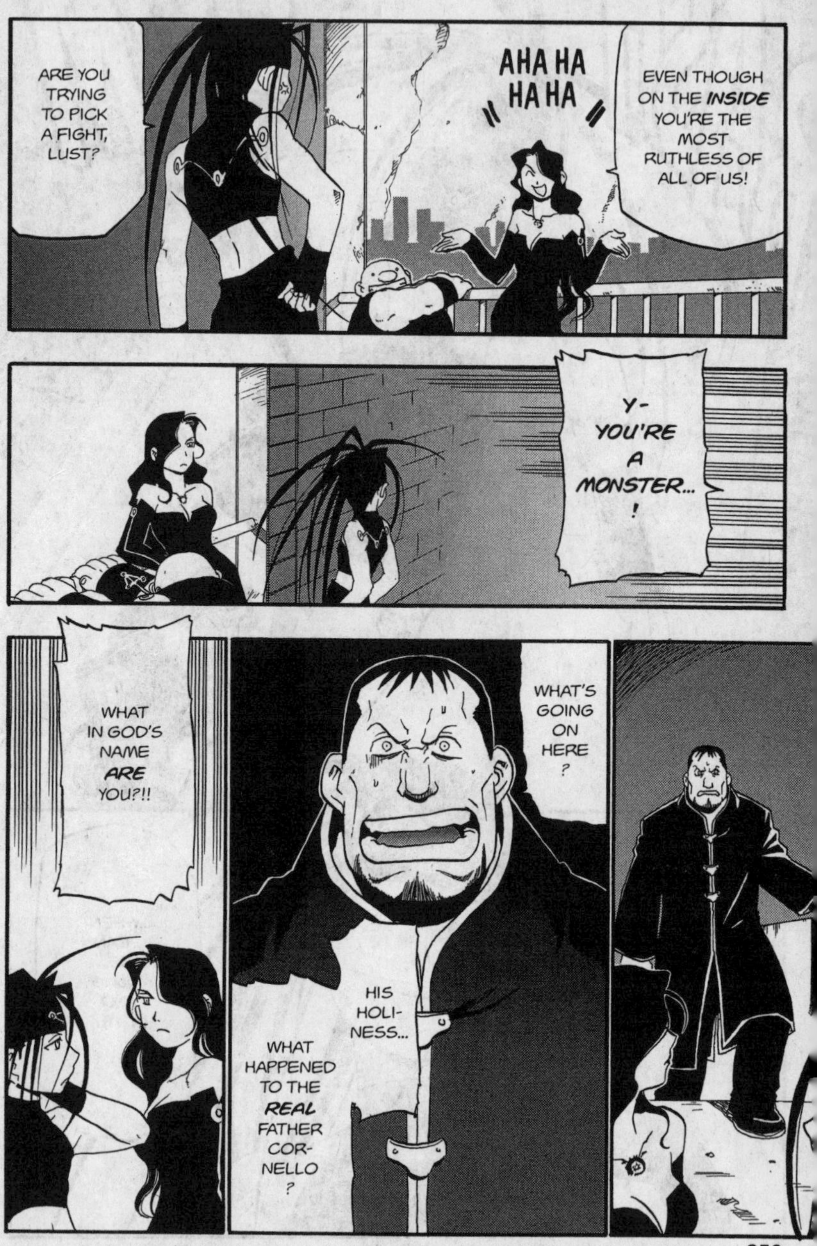
EVEN THOUGH ON THE INSIDE YOU'RE THE MOST RUTHLESS OF ALL OF US!
AHA HA HA HA
ARE YOU TRYING TO PICK A FIGHT, LUST?
Y-YOU'RE A MONSTER...!
WHAT'S GOING ON HERE?
HIS HOLINESS...
WHAT HAPPENED TO THE REAL FATHER CORNELLO?
WHAT IN GOD'S NAME ARE YOU?!!

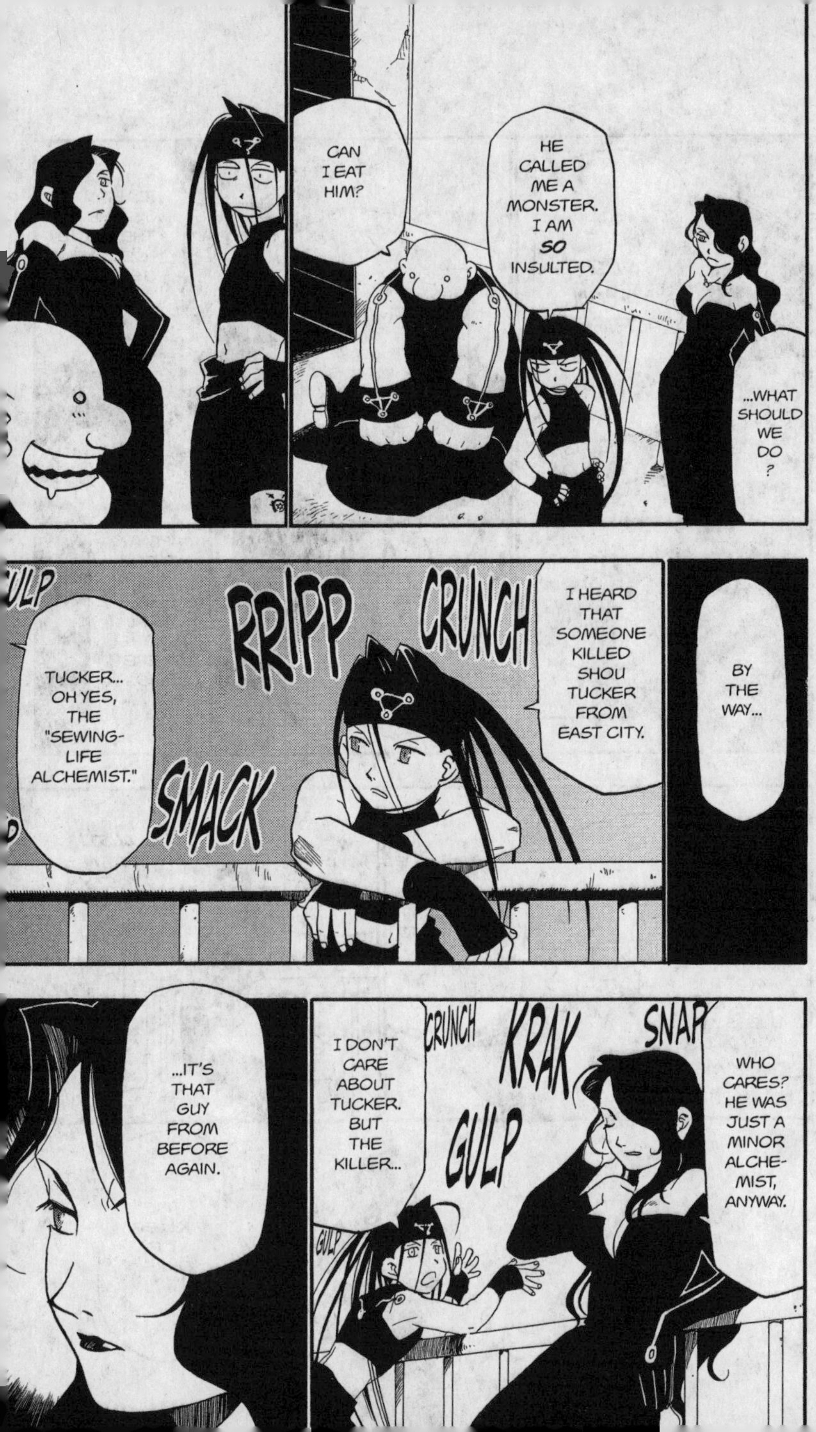
...WHAT SHOULD WE DO?
HE CALLED ME A MONSTER. I AM *SO* INSULTED.
CAN I EAT HIM?
BY THE WAY...
I HEARD THAT SOMEONE KILLED SHOU TUCKER FROM EAST CITY.
CRUNCH
RRIPP
SMACK
ULP
TUCKER... OH YES, THE "SEWING-LIFE ALCHEMIST."
SNAP
WHO CARES? HE WAS JUST A MINOR ALCHE-MIST, ANYWAY.
KRAK
CRUNCH
I DON'T CARE ABOUT TUCKER. BUT THE KILLER...
GULP
GULP
...IT'S THAT GUY FROM BEFORE AGAIN.

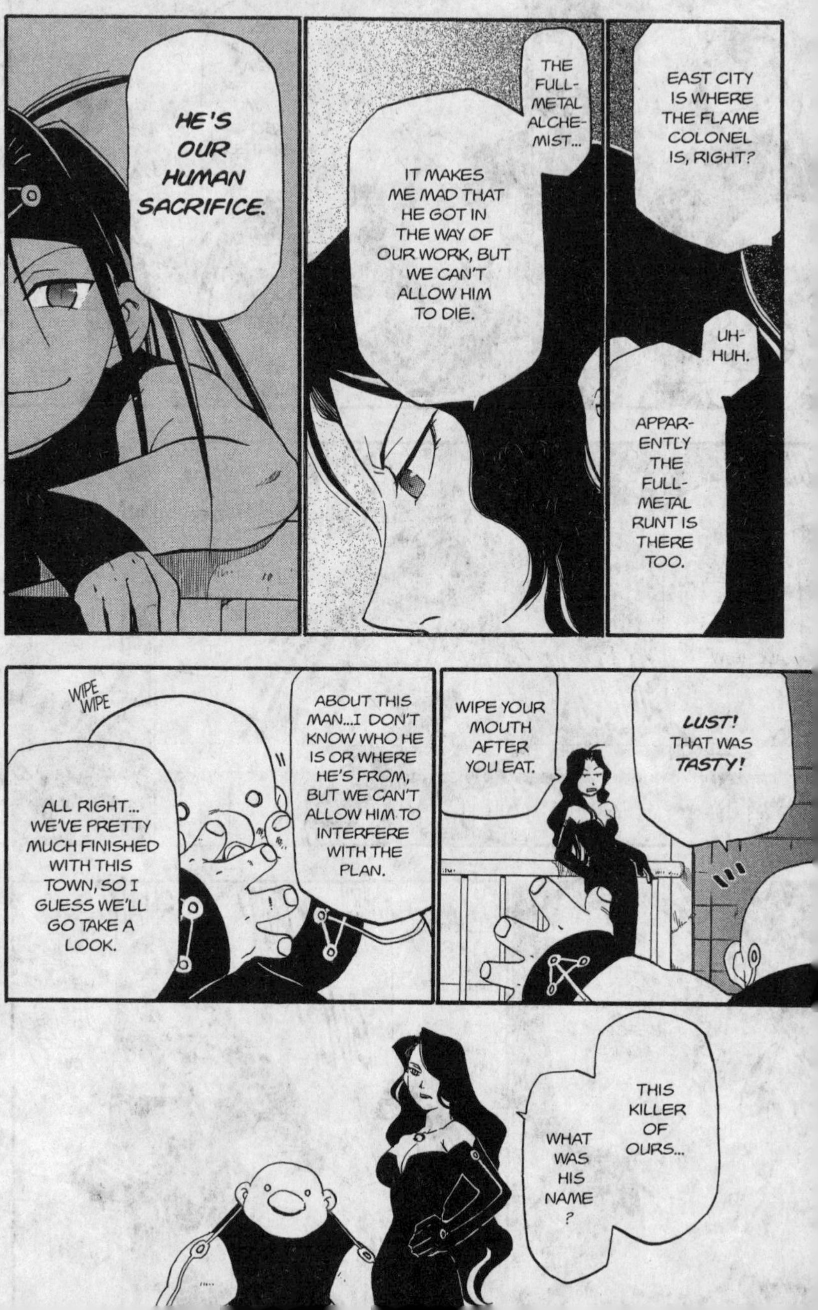
EAST CITY IS WHERE THE FLAME COLONEL IS, RIGHT?
UH-HUH.
APPARENTLY THE FULLMETAL RUNT IS THERE TOO.
THE FULLMETAL ALCHEMIST...
IT MAKES ME MAD THAT HE GOT IN THE WAY OF OUR WORK, BUT WE CAN'T ALLOW HIM TO DIE.
HE'S OUR HUMAN SACRIFICE.
LUST! THAT WAS TASTY!
WIPE YOUR MOUTH AFTER YOU EAT.
ABOUT THIS MAN...I DON'T KNOW WHO HE IS OR WHERE HE'S FROM, BUT WE CAN'T ALLOW HIM TO INTERFERE WITH THE PLAN.
WIPE WIPE
ALL RIGHT... WE'VE PRETTY MUCH FINISHED WITH THIS TOWN, SO I GUESS WE'LL GO TAKE A LOOK.
THIS KILLER OF OURS...
WHAT WAS HIS NAME?

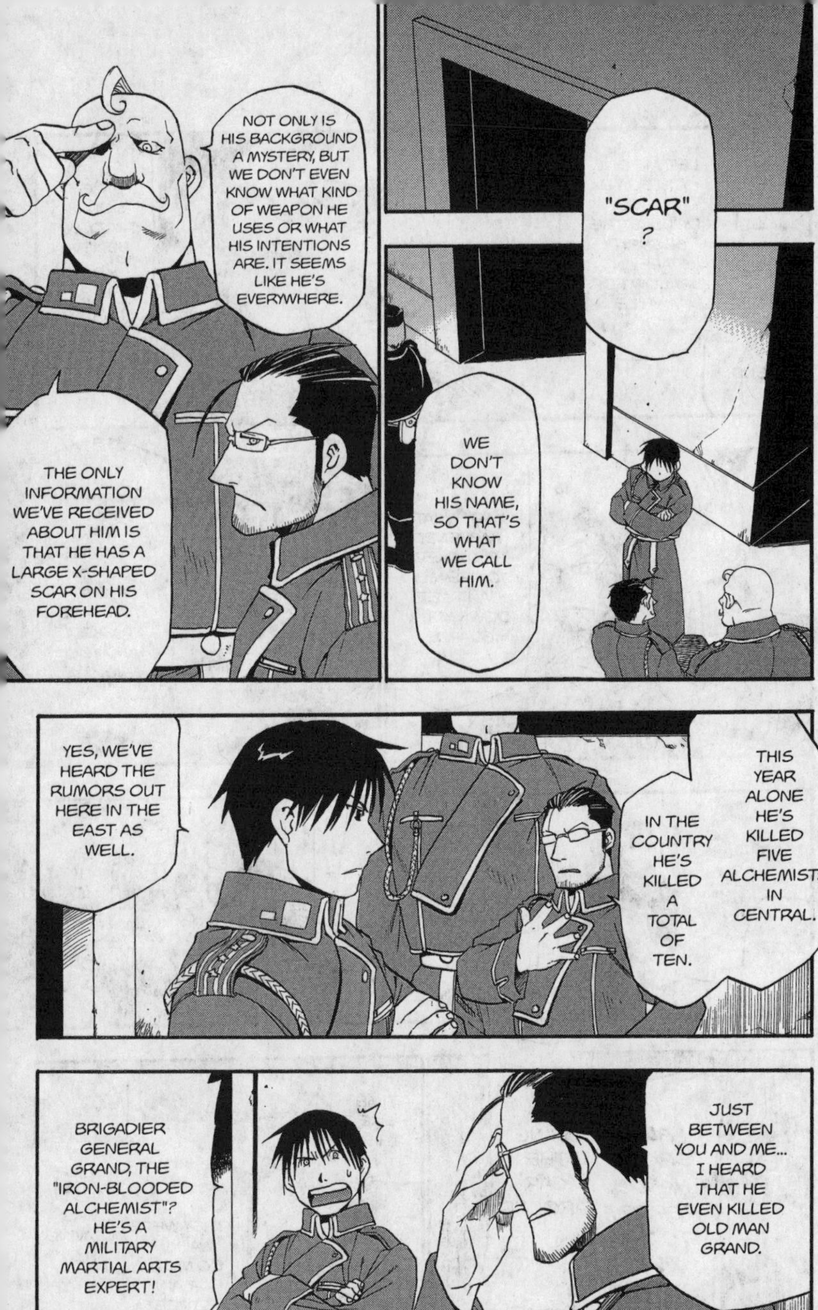
"SCAR"?
WE DON'T KNOW HIS NAME, SO THAT'S WHAT WE CALL HIM.
NOT ONLY IS HIS BACKGROUND A MYSTERY, BUT WE DON'T EVEN KNOW WHAT KIND OF WEAPON HE USES OR WHAT HIS INTENTIONS ARE. IT SEEMS LIKE HE'S EVERYWHERE.
THE ONLY INFORMATION WE'VE RECEIVED ABOUT HIM IS THAT HE HAS A LARGE X-SHAPED SCAR ON HIS FOREHEAD.
THIS YEAR ALONE HE'S KILLED FIVE ALCHEMISTS IN CENTRAL.
IN THE COUNTRY HE'S KILLED A TOTAL OF TEN.
YES, WE'VE HEARD THE RUMORS OUT HERE IN THE EAST AS WELL.
JUST BETWEEN YOU AND ME... I HEARD THAT HE EVEN KILLED OLD MAN GRAND.
BRIGADIER GENERAL GRAND, THE "IRON-BLOODED ALCHEMIST"? HE'S A MILITARY MARTIAL ARTS EXPERT!

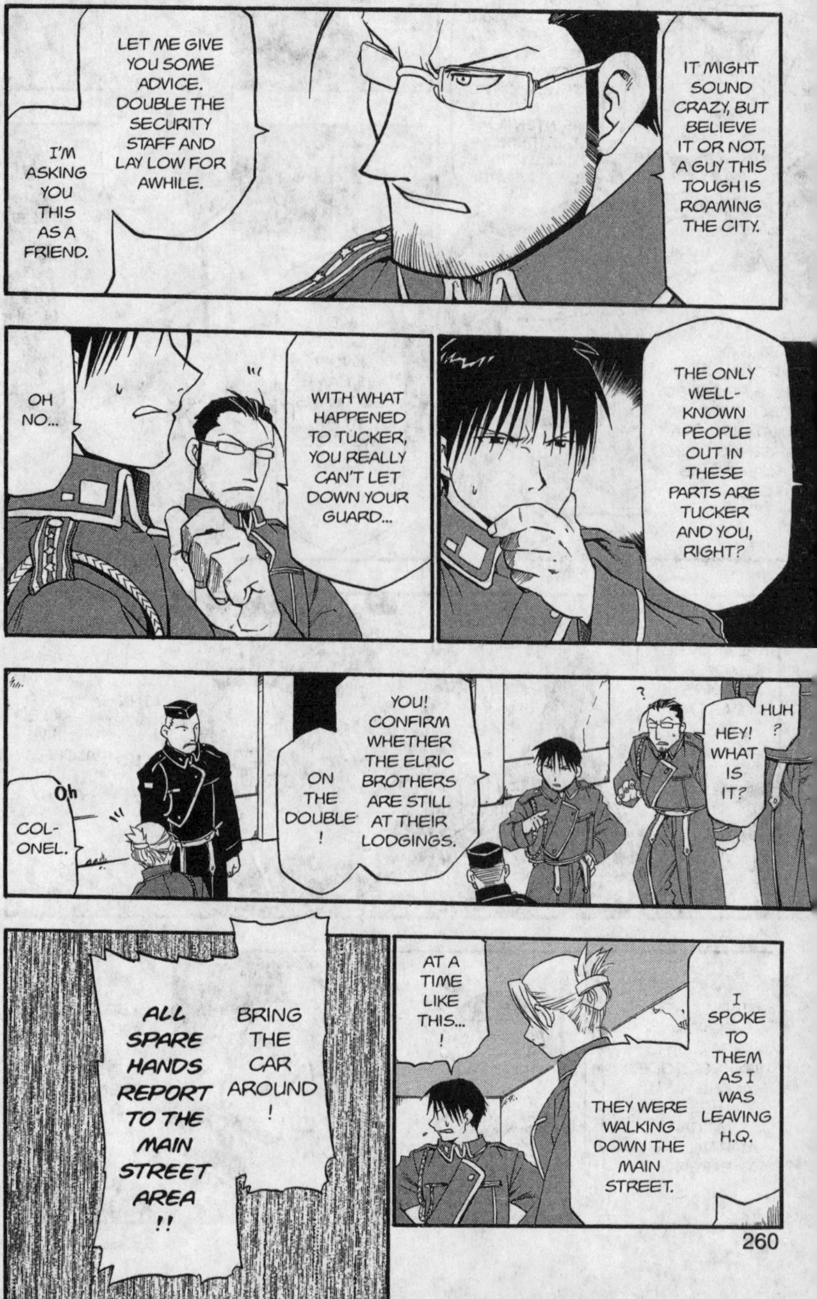
IT MIGHT SOUND CRAZY, BUT BELIEVE IT OR NOT, A GUY THIS TOUGH IS ROAMING THE CITY.
LET ME GIVE YOU SOME ADVICE. DOUBLE THE SECURITY STAFF AND LAY LOW FOR AWHILE.
I'M ASKING YOU THIS AS A FRIEND.
THE ONLY WELL-KNOWN PEOPLE OUT IN THESE PARTS ARE TUCKER AND YOU, RIGHT?
WITH WHAT HAPPENED TO TUCKER, YOU REALLY CAN'T LET DOWN YOUR GUARD...
OH NO...
HUH?
HEY! WHAT IS IT?
YOU! CONFIRM WHETHER THE ELRIC BROTHERS ARE STILL AT THEIR LODGINGS.
ON THE DOUBLE!
Oh
COLONEL.
I SPOKE TO THEM AS I WAS LEAVING H.Q.
THEY WERE WALKING DOWN THE MAIN STREET.
AT A TIME LIKE THIS...!
BRING THE CAR AROUND!
ALL SPARE HANDS REPORT TO THE MAIN STREET AREA!!

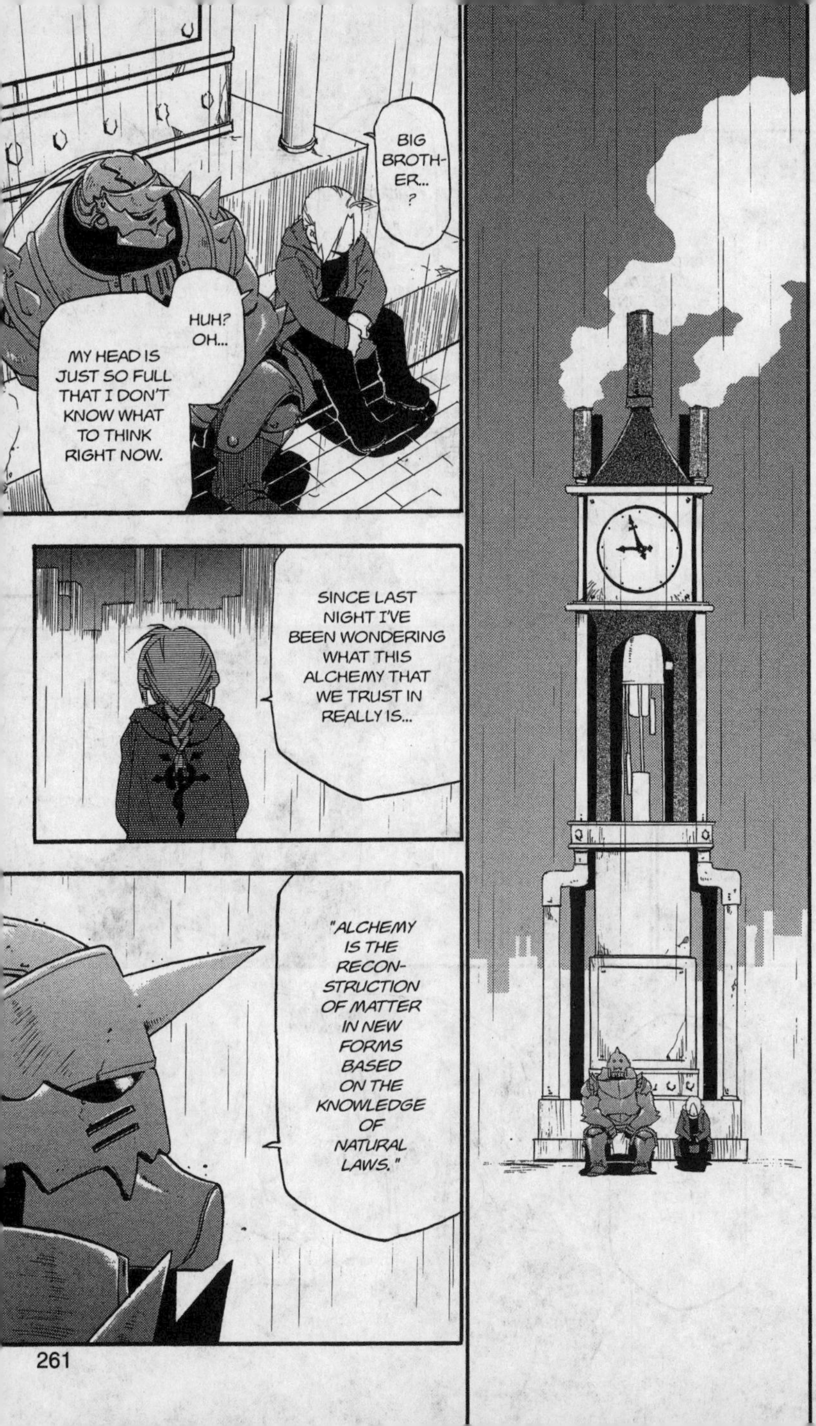
BIG BROTHER-ER...?
HUH? OH...
MY HEAD IS JUST SO FULL THAT I DON'T KNOW WHAT TO THINK RIGHT NOW.
SINCE LAST NIGHT I'VE BEEN WONDERING WHAT THIS ALCHEMY THAT WE TRUST IN REALLY IS...
"ALCHEMY IS THE RECON-STRUCTION OF MATTER IN NEW FORMS BASED ON THE KNOWLEDGE OF NATURAL LAWS."

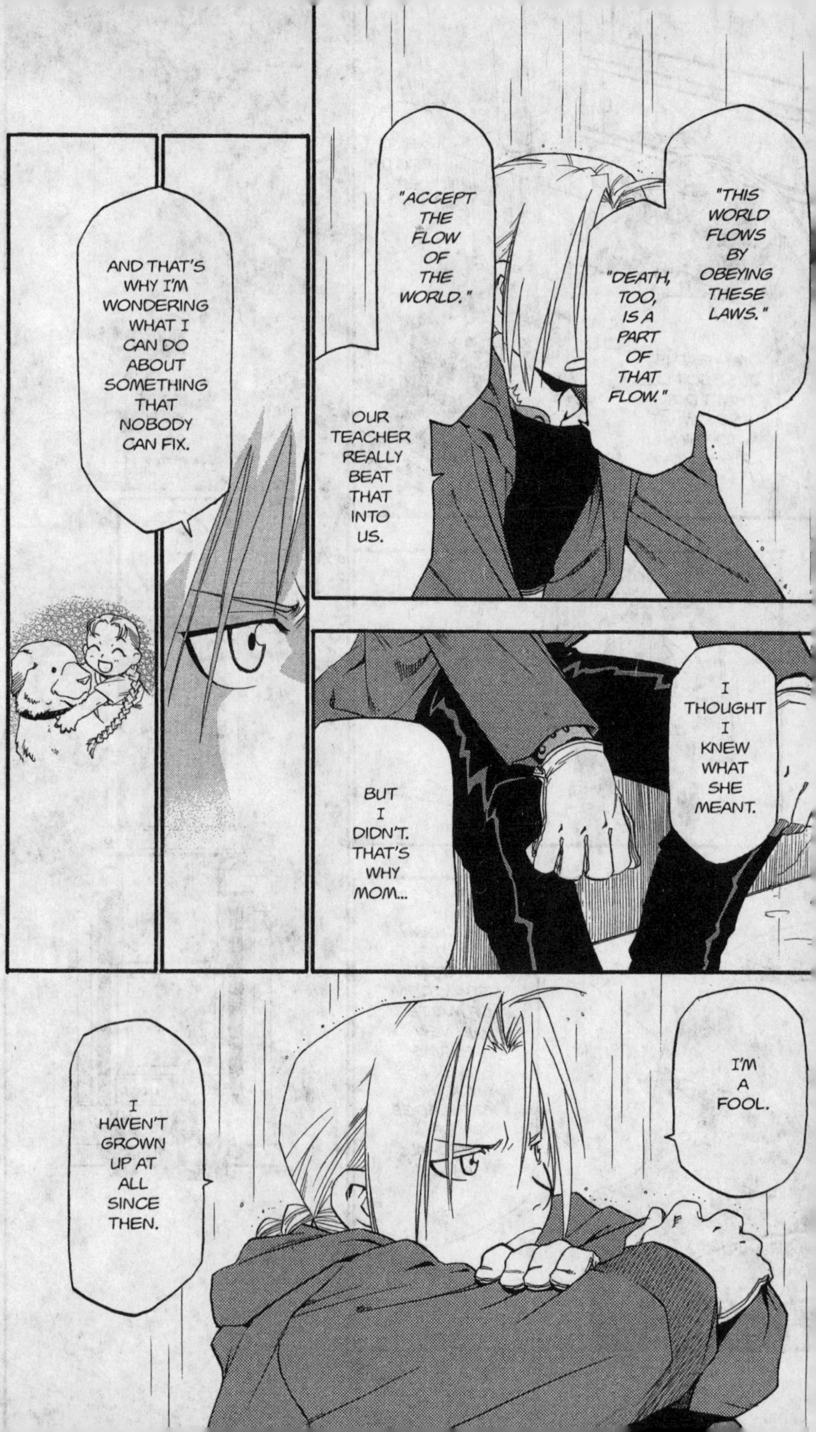
"THIS WORLD FLOWS BY OBEYING THESE LAWS."
"DEATH, TOO, IS A PART OF THAT FLOW."
"ACCEPT THE FLOW OF THE WORLD."
OUR TEACHER REALLY BEAT THAT INTO US.
I THOUGHT I KNEW WHAT SHE MEANT.
BUT I DIDN'T. THAT'S WHY MOM...
AND THAT'S WHY I'M WONDERING WHAT I CAN DO ABOUT SOMETHING THAT NOBODY CAN FIX.
I'M A FOOL.
I HAVEN'T GROWN UP AT ALL SINCE THEN.

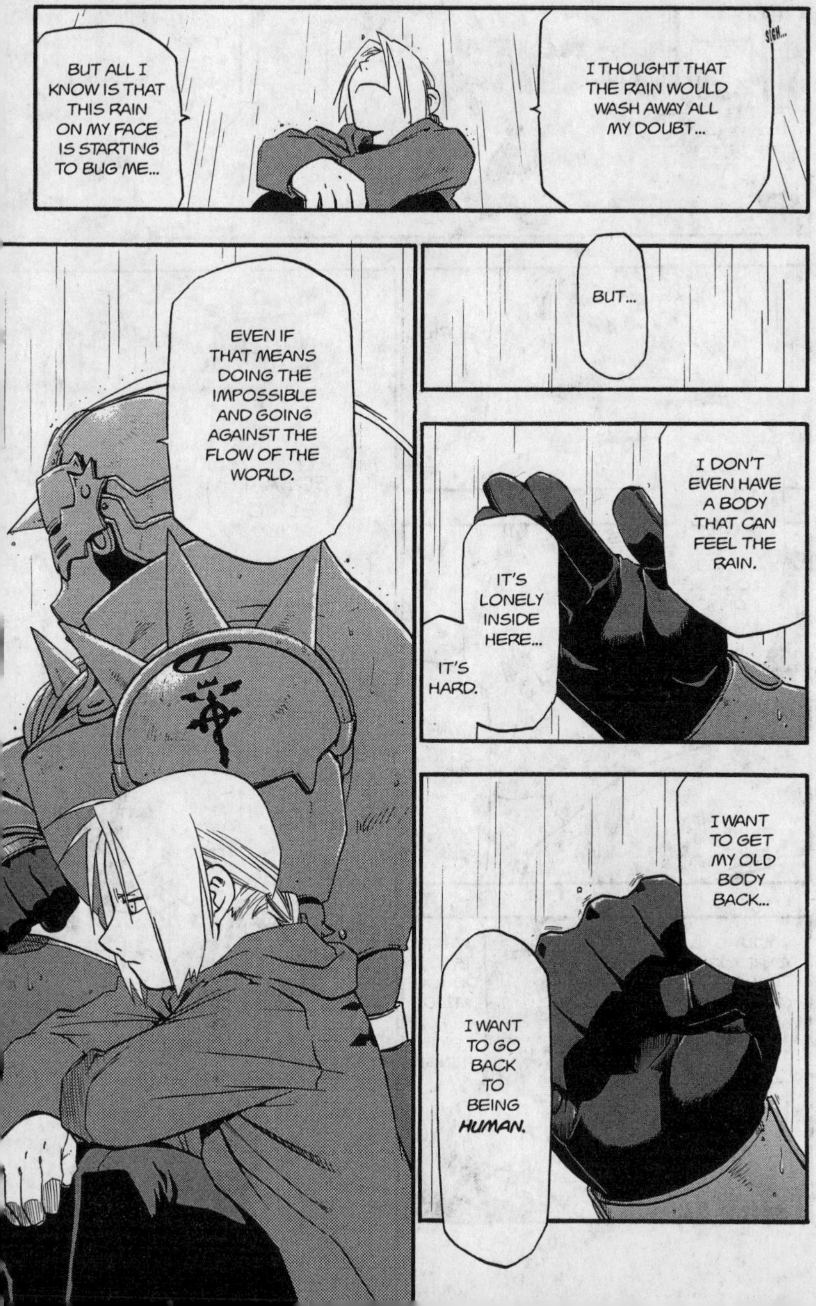
SIGH...
I THOUGHT THAT THE RAIN WOULD WASH AWAY ALL MY DOUBT...
BUT ALL I KNOW IS THAT THIS RAIN ON MY FACE IS STARTING TO BUG ME...
BUT...
I DON'T EVEN HAVE A BODY THAT CAN FEEL THE RAIN.
IT'S LONELY INSIDE HERE...
IT'S HARD.
I WANT TO GET MY OLD BODY BACK...
I WANT TO GO BACK TO BEING ***HUMAN.***
EVEN IF THAT MEANS DOING THE IMPOSSIBLE AND GOING AGAINST THE FLOW OF THE WORLD.

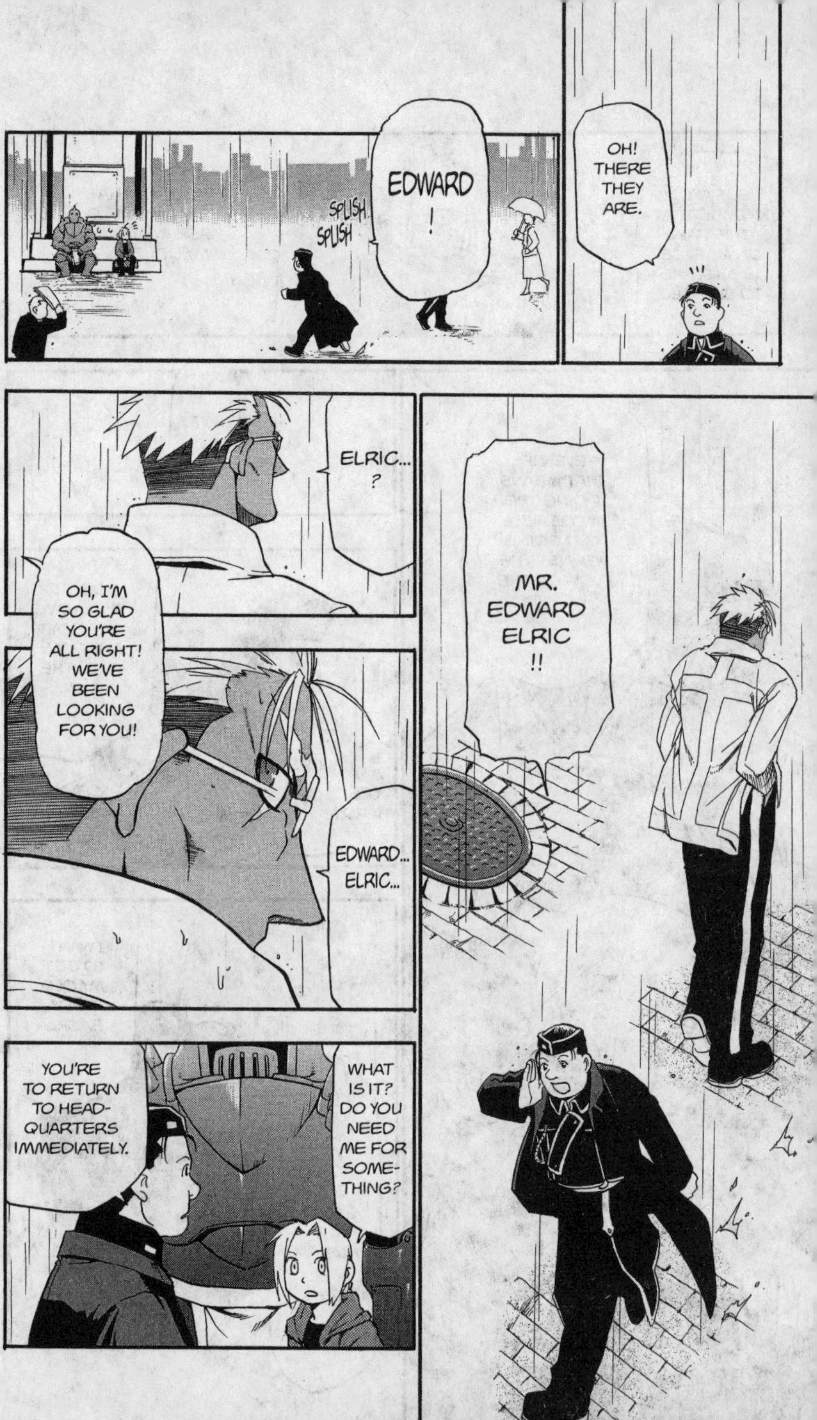
OH! THERE THEY ARE.
EDWARD!
SPLISH SPLISH
MR. EDWARD ELRIC!!
ELRIC...?
OH, I'M SO GLAD YOU'RE ALL RIGHT! WE'VE BEEN LOOKING FOR YOU!
EDWARD... ELRIC...
WHAT IS IT? DO YOU NEED ME FOR SOMETHING?
YOU'RE TO RETURN TO HEADQUARTERS IMMEDIATELY.

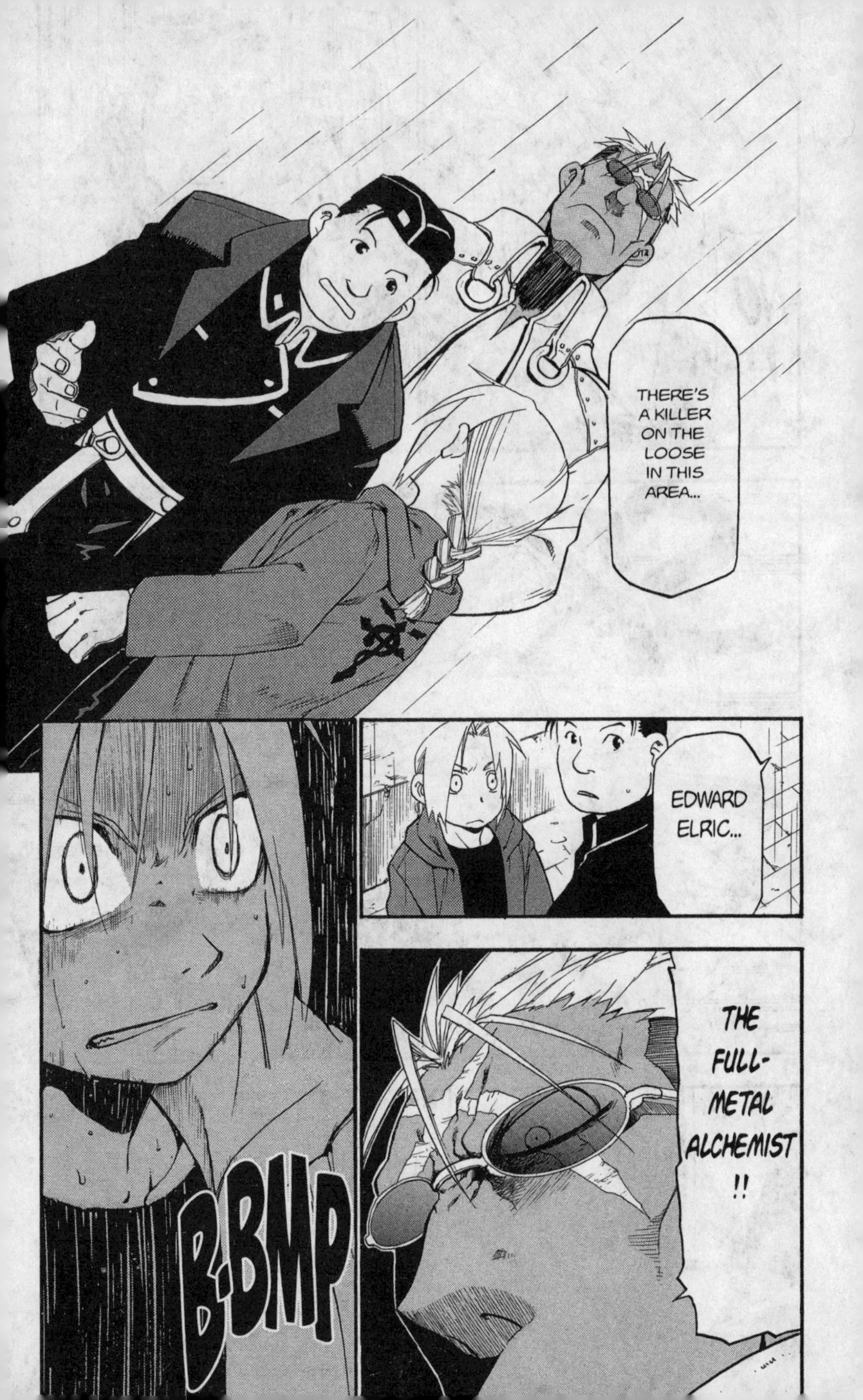
THERE'S A KILLER ON THE LOOSE IN THIS AREA...
EDWARD ELRIC...
THE FULL-METAL ALCHEMIST !!
B-BMP

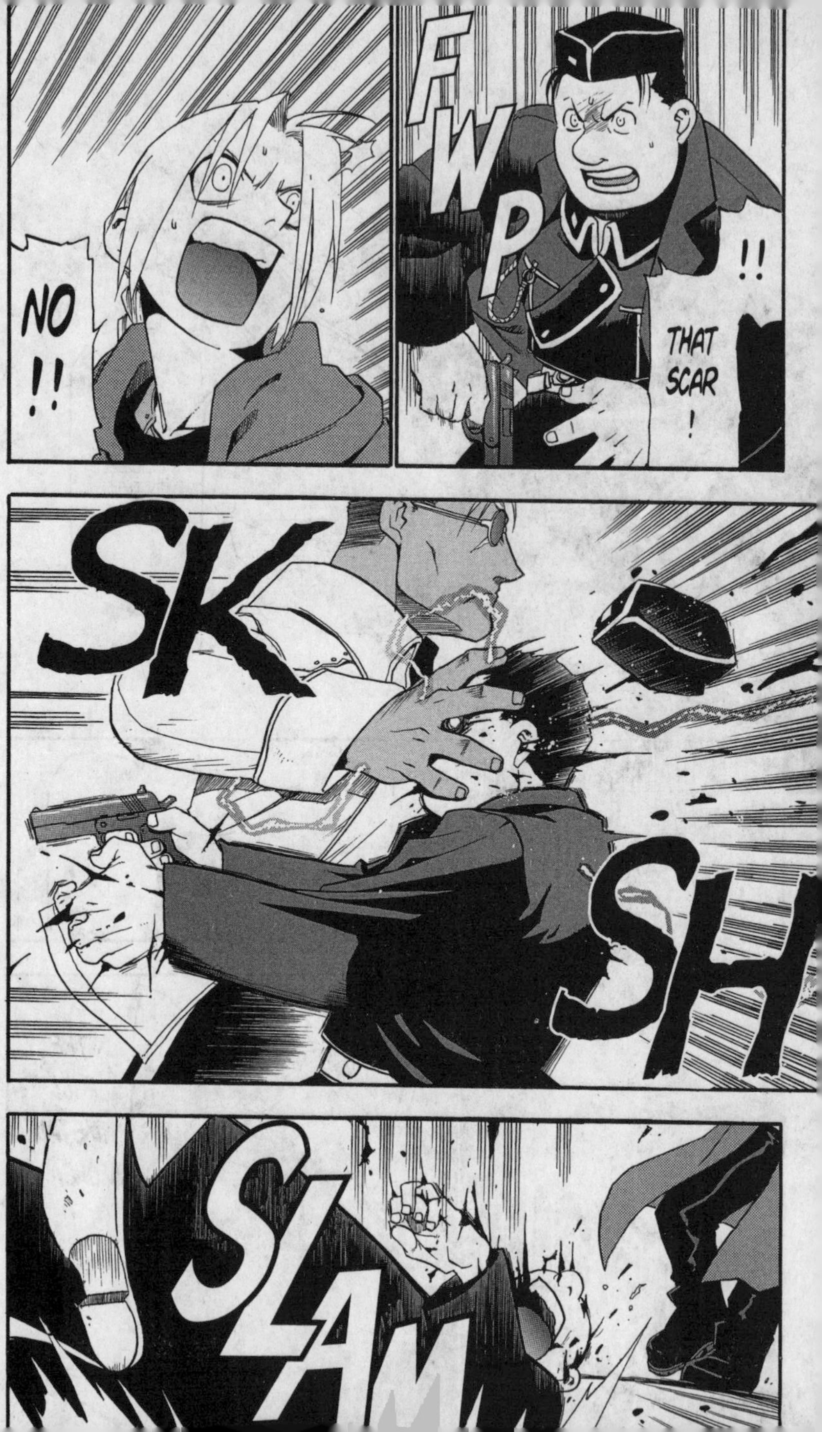
FWP
!!
THAT SCAR !
NO !!
SK
SH
SLAM

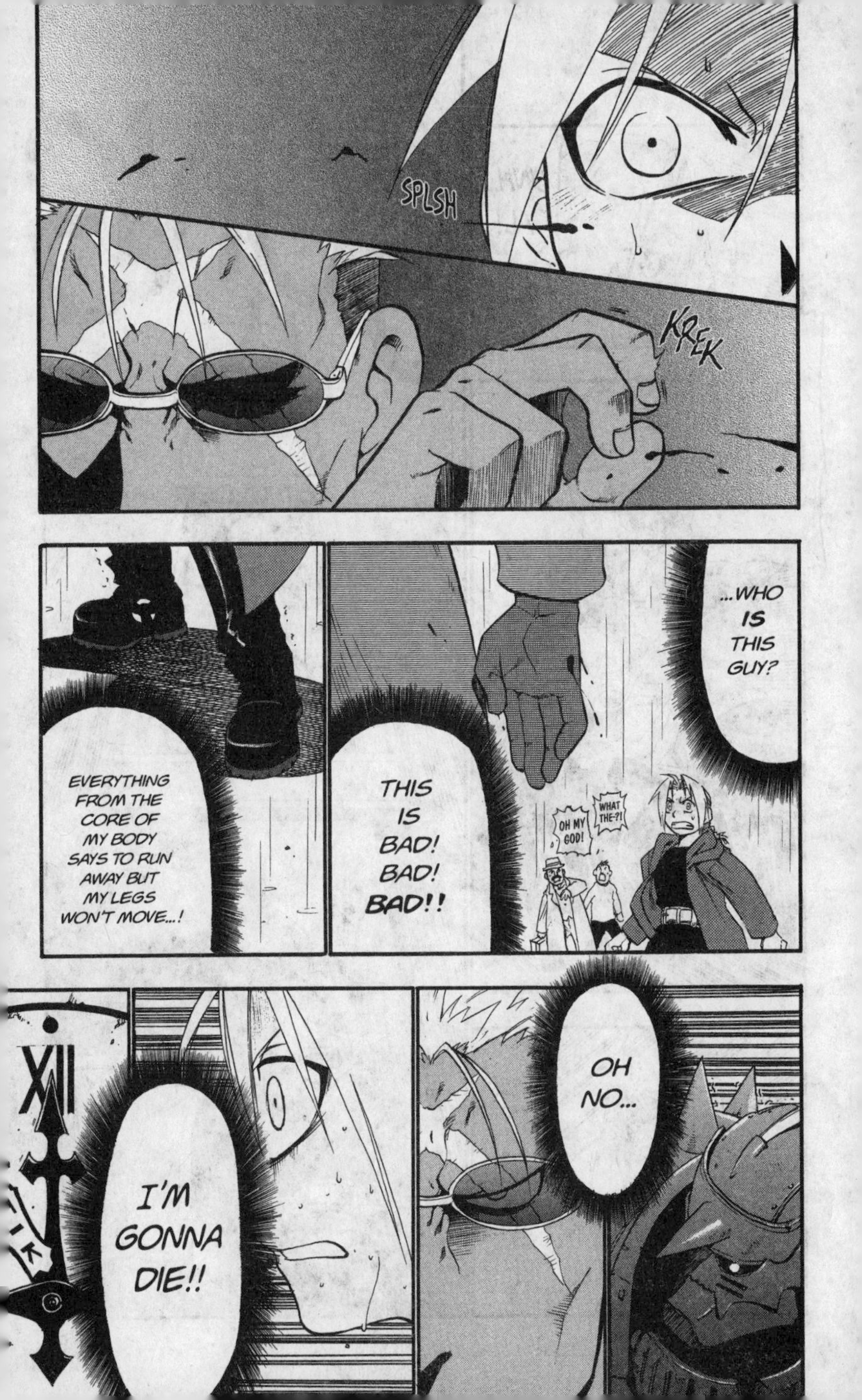
SPLSH
KREK
...WHO IS THIS GUY?
WHAT THE-?!
OH MY GOD!
THIS IS BAD! BAD! BAD!!
EVERYTHING FROM THE CORE OF MY BODY SAYS TO RUN AWAY BUT MY LEGS WON'T MOVE...!
OH NO...
I'M GONNA DIE!!
TIK

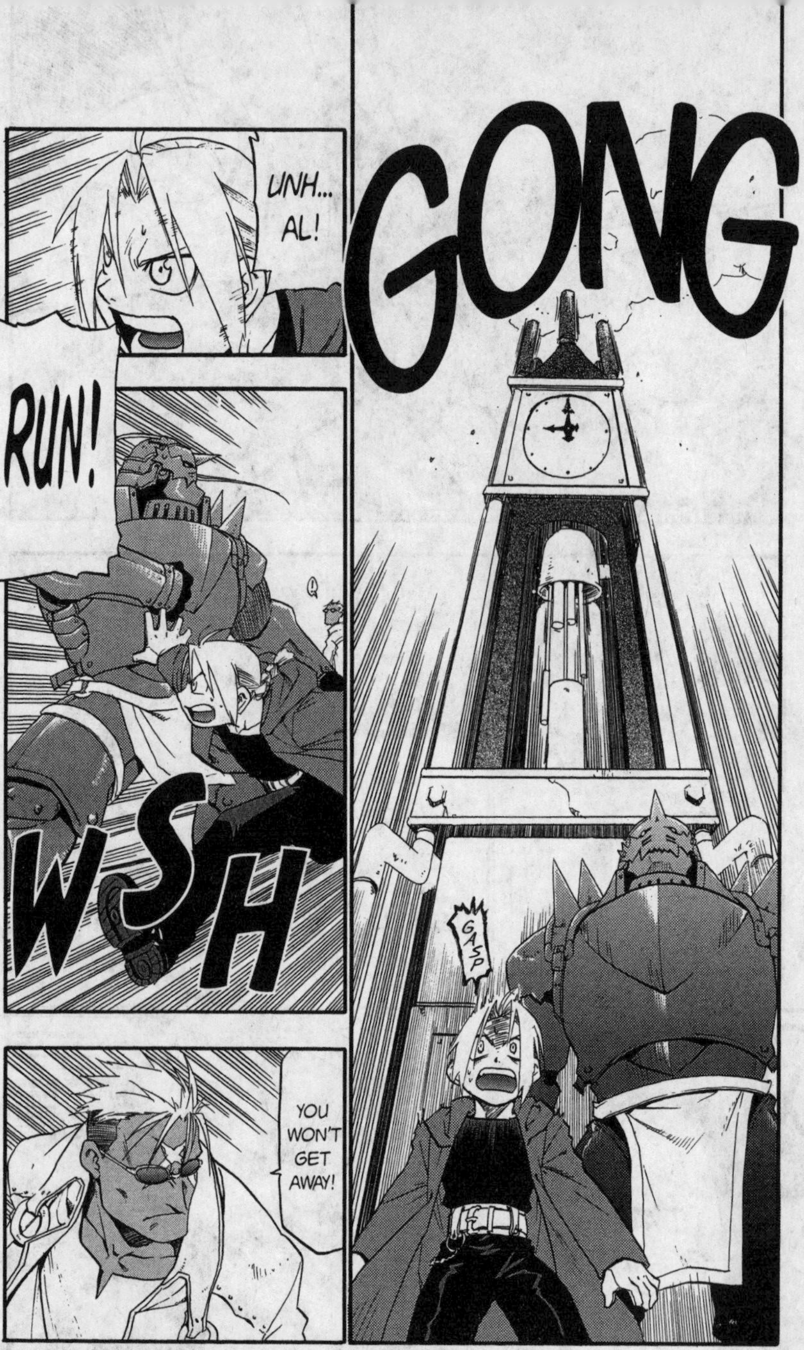
GONG
GASP
UNH... AL!
RUN!
WSH
YOU WON'T GET AWAY!

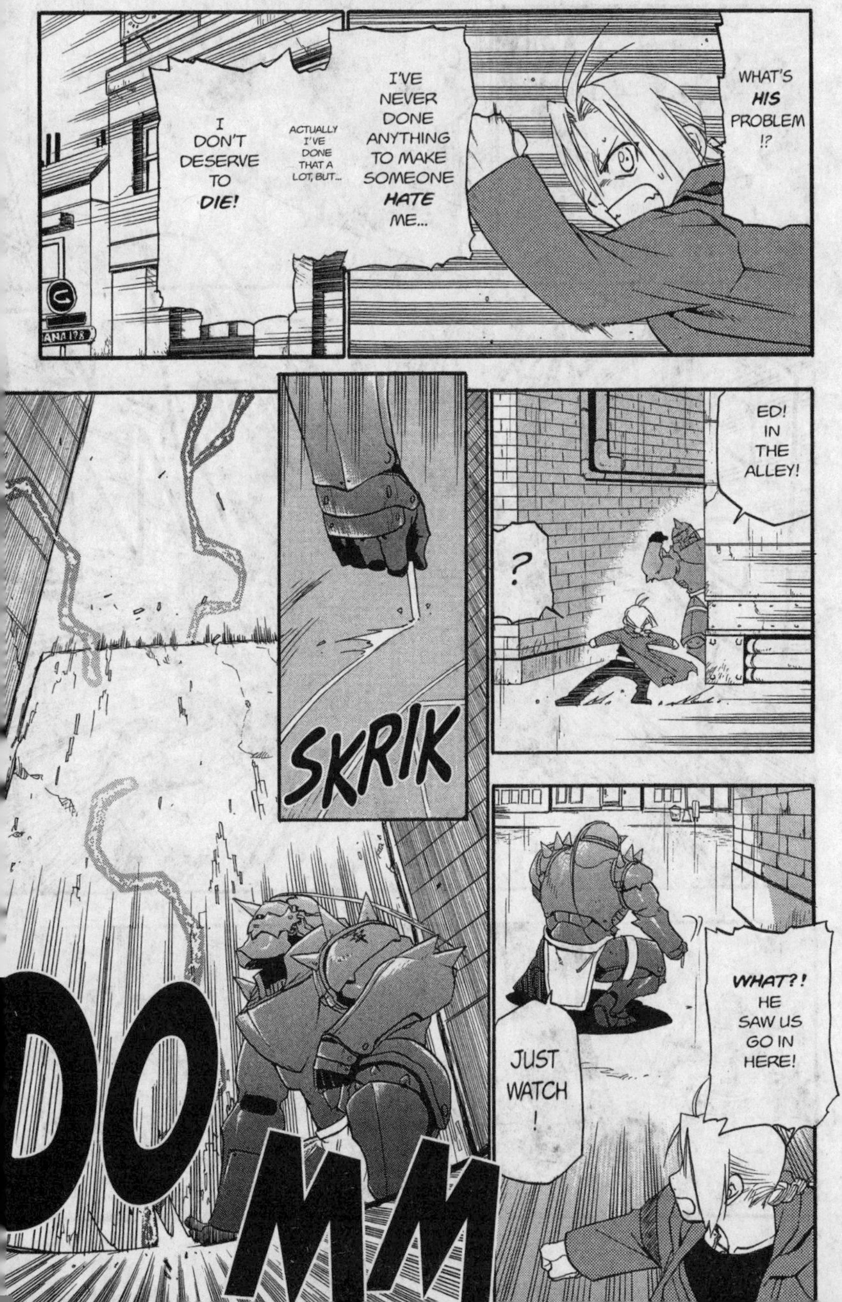
WHAT'S HIS PROBLEM!?
I'VE NEVER DONE ANYTHING TO MAKE SOMEONE HATE ME...
ACTUALLY I'VE DONE THAT A LOT, BUT...
I DON'T DESERVE TO DIE!
ED! IN THE ALLEY!
?
WHAT?! HE SAW US GO IN HERE!
JUST WATCH!
SKRIK
DOMM

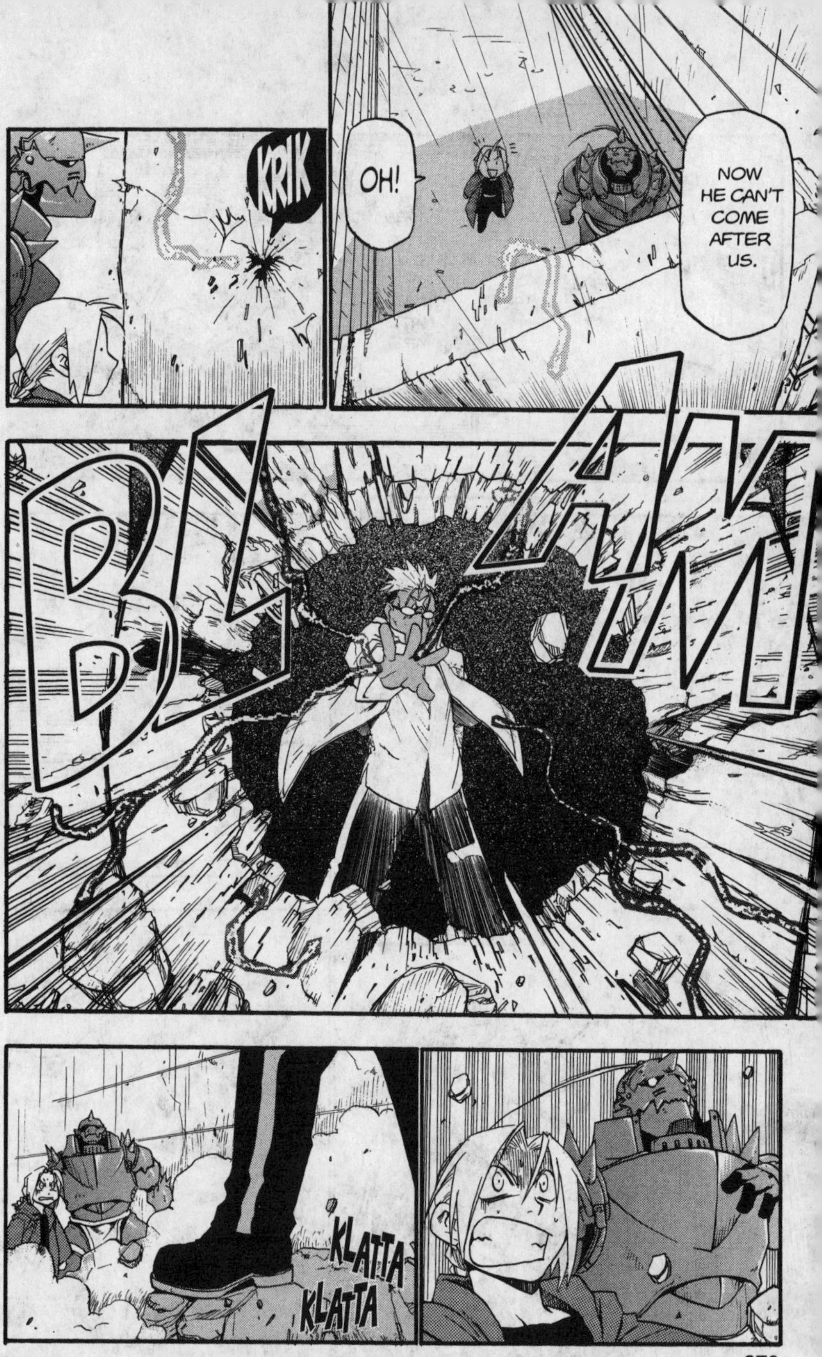
NOW HE CAN'T COME AFTER US.
OH!
KRIK
BLAM
KLATTA
KLATTA

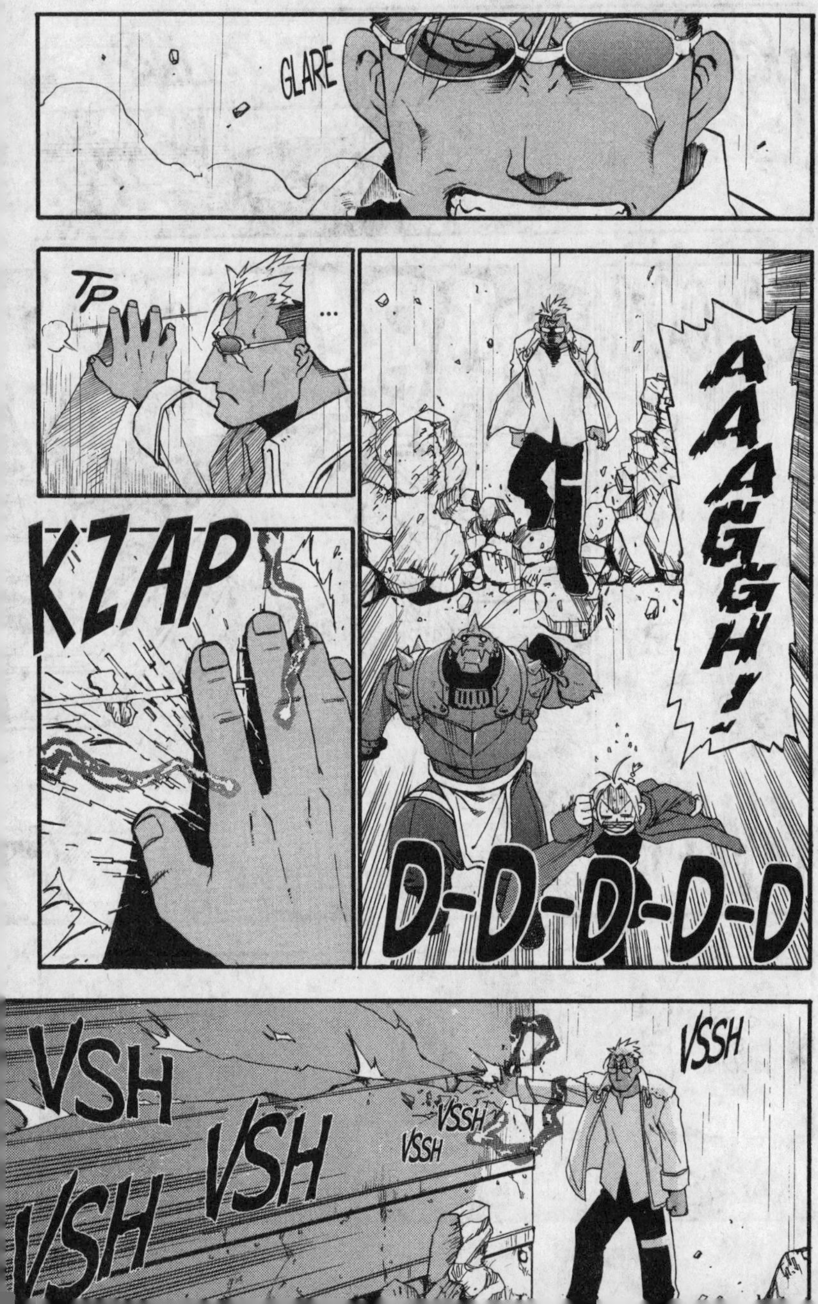
GLARE
AAAGGH!!
D-D-D-D-D-D
TP
...
KZAP
VSSH
VSSH
VSSH
VSH
VSH
VSH

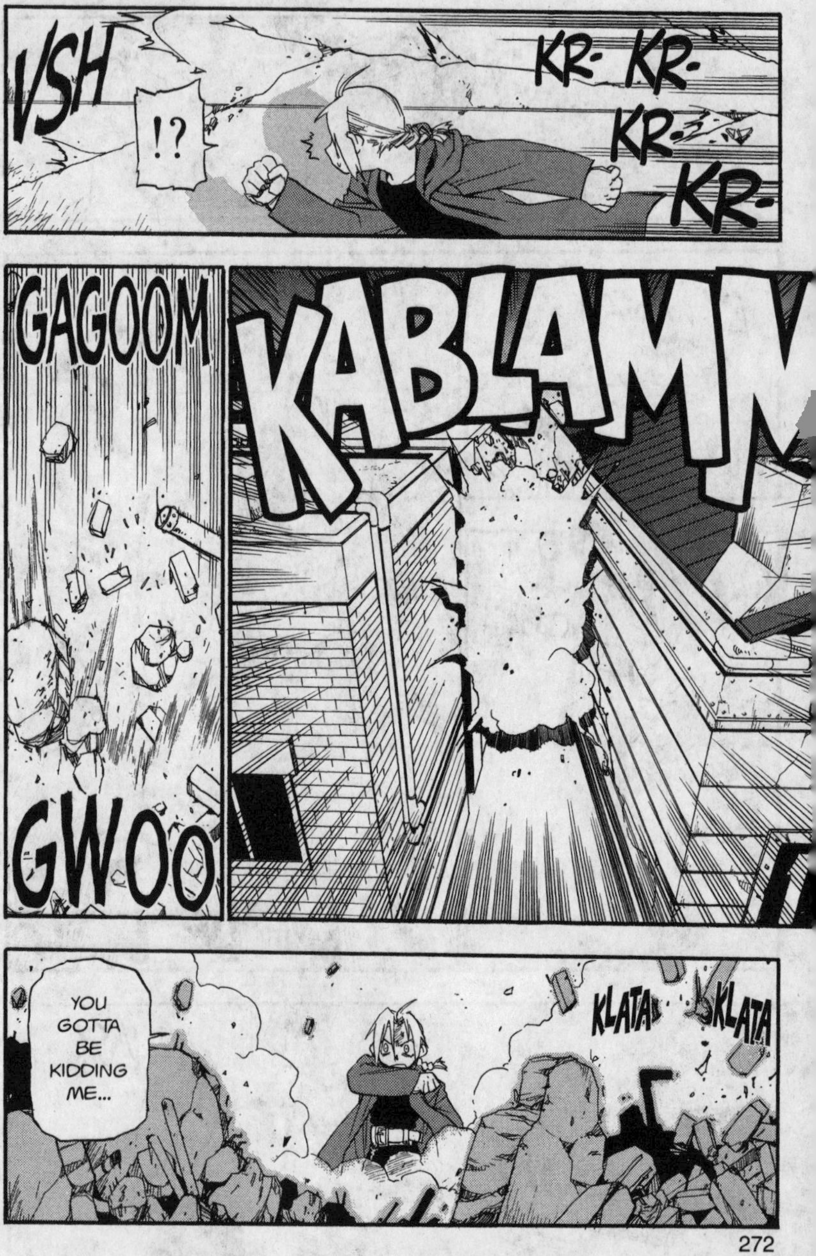
KR- KR-
KR-
KR-
VSH
!?
KABLAM
GAGOOM
GWOO
KLATA KLATA
YOU GOTTA BE KIDDING ME...

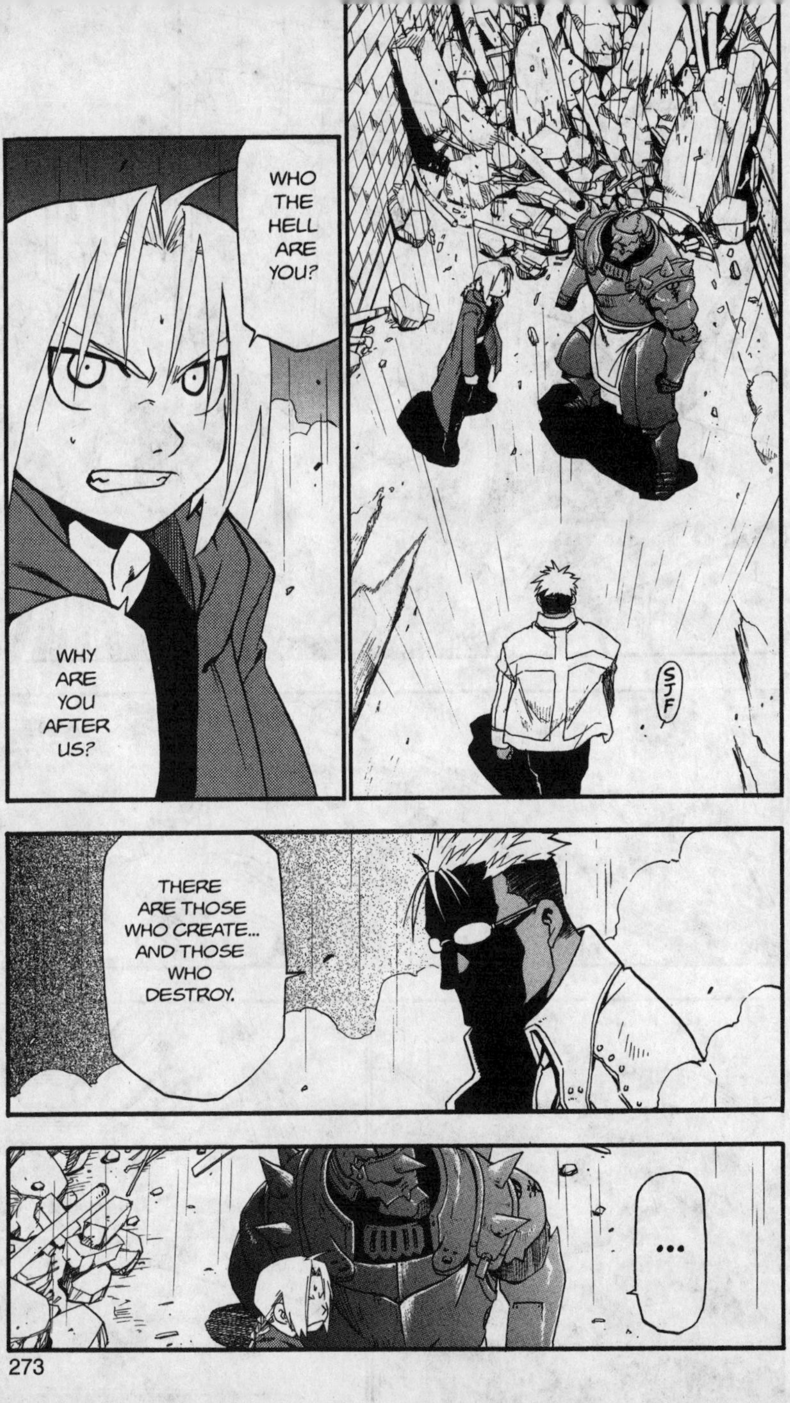
SJF
WHO THE HELL ARE YOU?
WHY ARE YOU AFTER US?
THERE ARE THOSE WHO CREATE... AND THOSE WHO DESTROY.
...

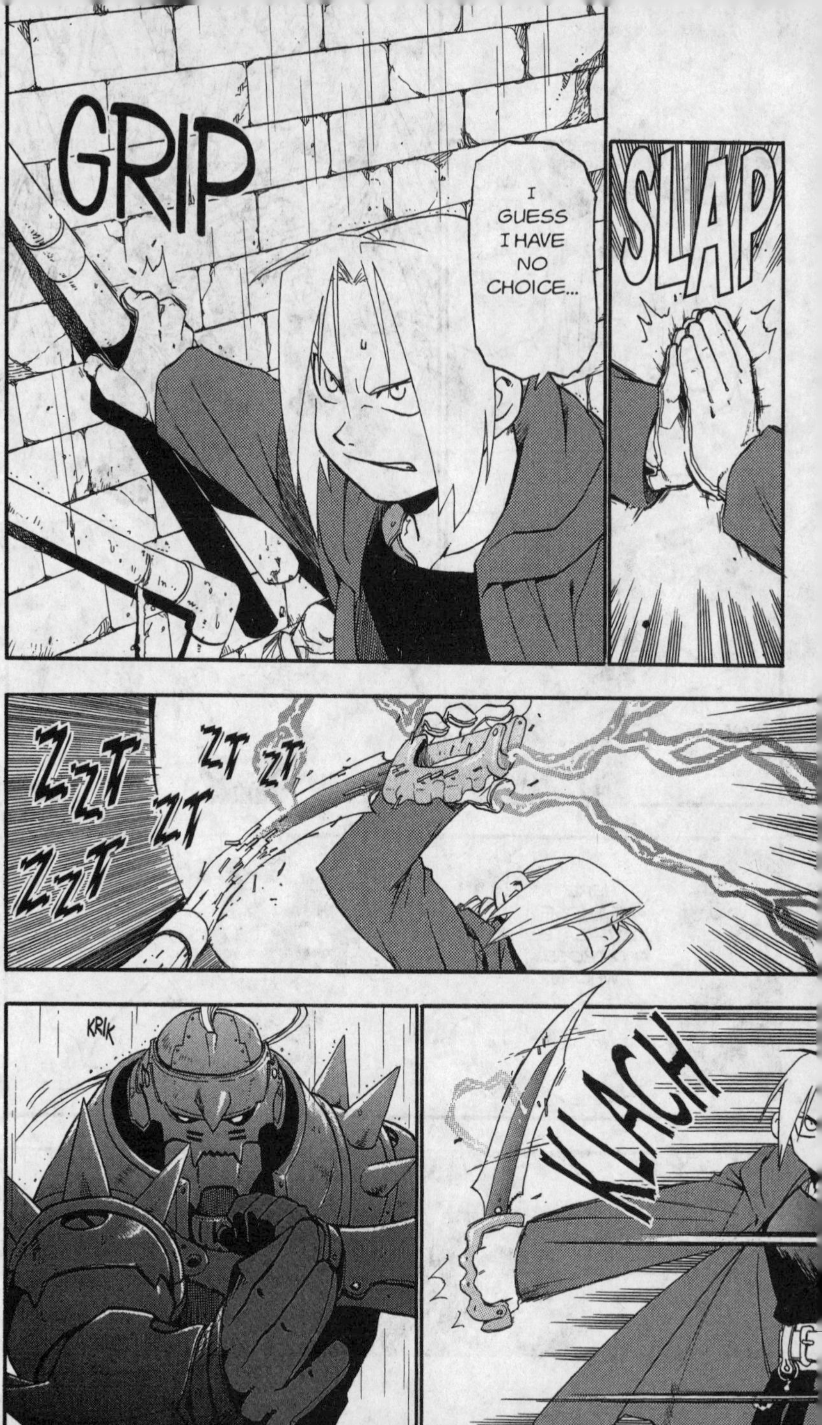
SLAP
GRIP
I GUESS I HAVE NO CHOICE...
ZT
ZT
ZT
ZZT
ZZT
KLACH
KRIK

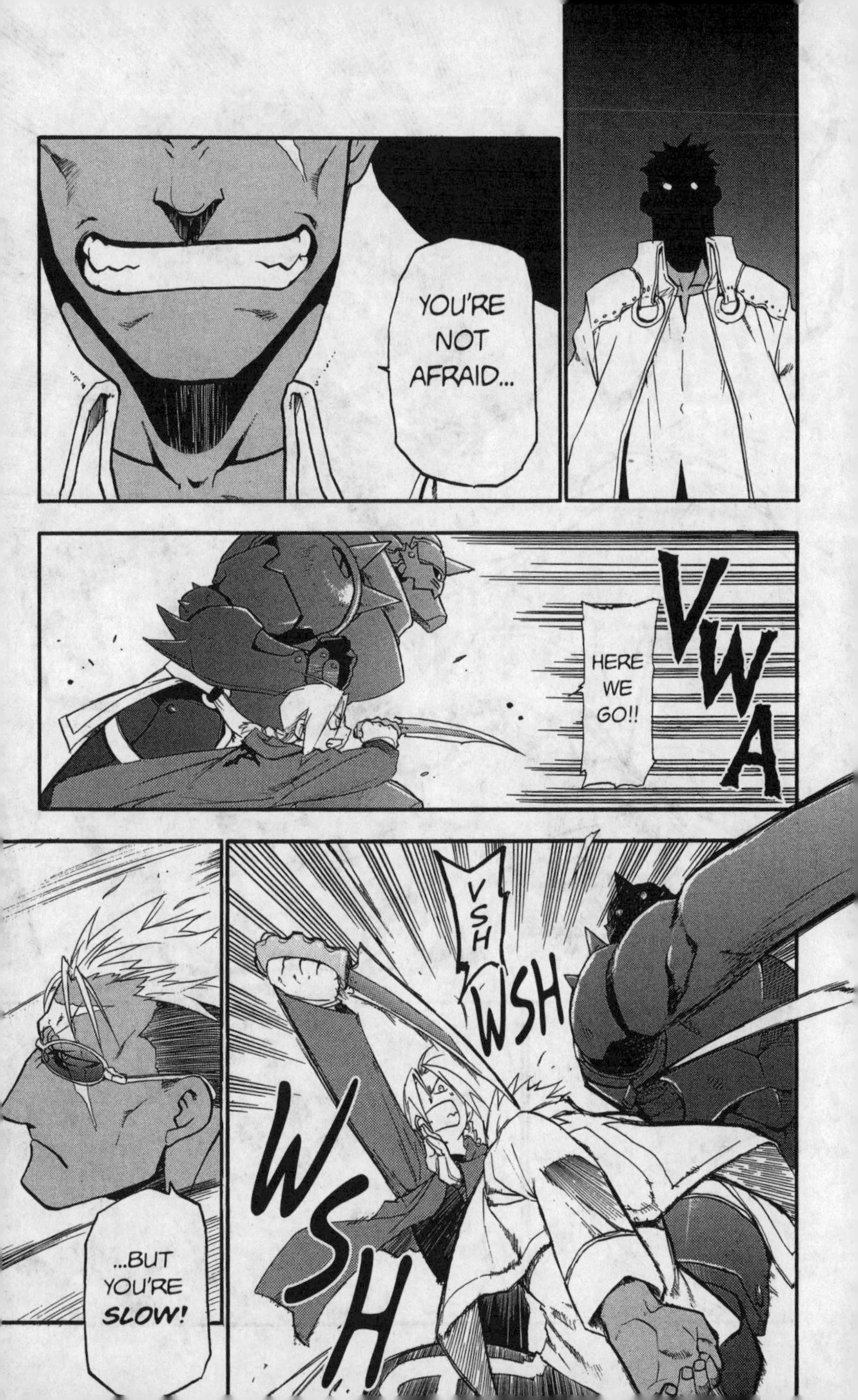
YOU'RE NOT AFRAID...
VWA
HERE WE GO!!
VSH
WSH
WSH
...BUT YOU'RE SLOW!

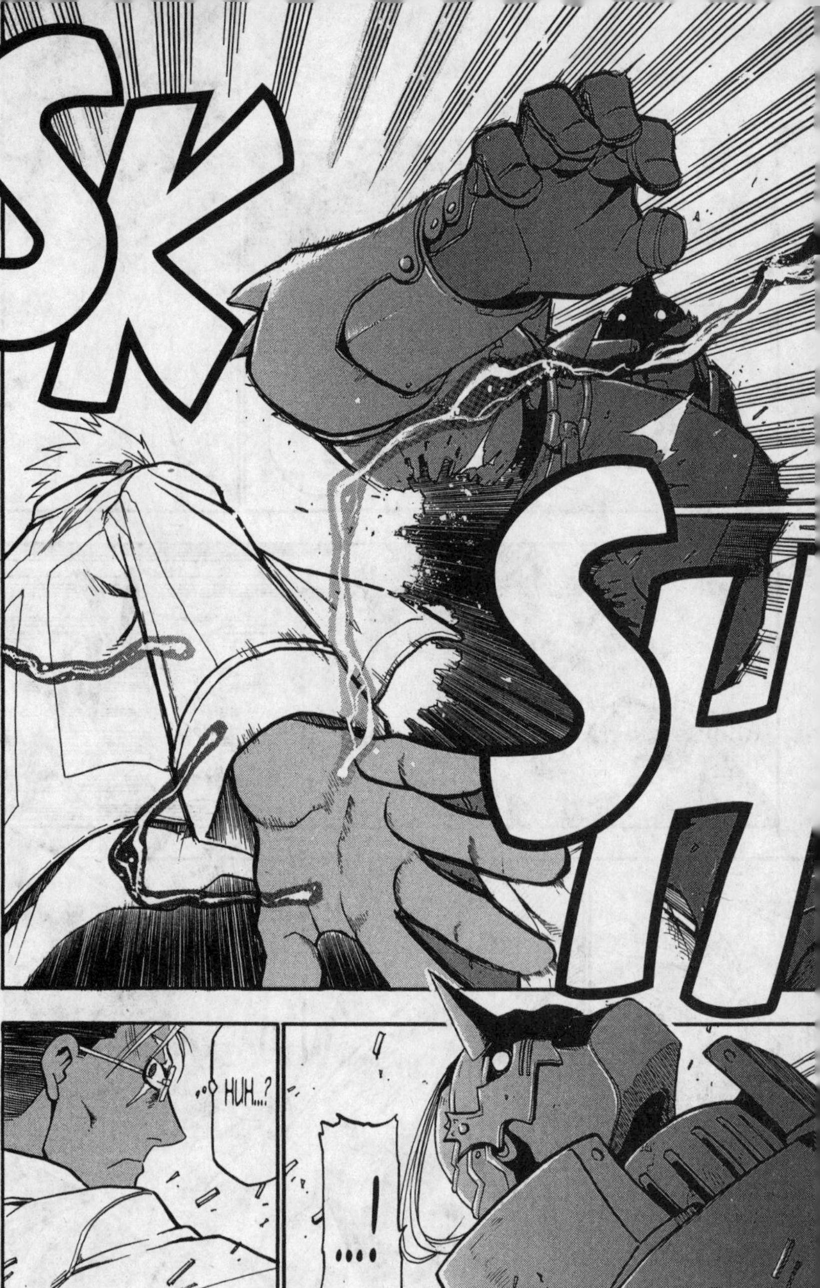
SK
SH
...!
HUH...?

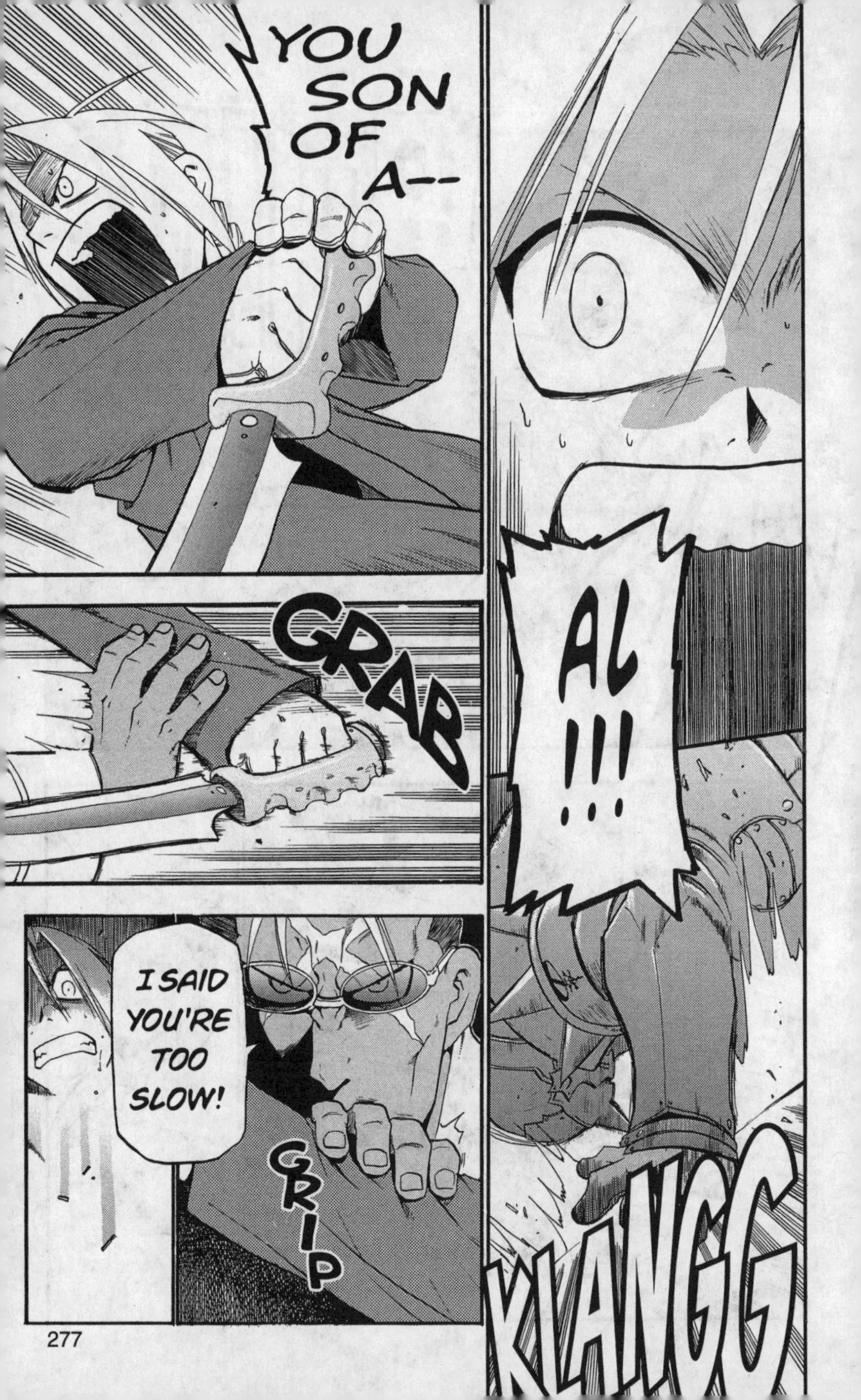
AL!!!
KLANGG
YOU SON OF A--
GRAB
I SAID YOU'RE TOO SLOW!
GRIP

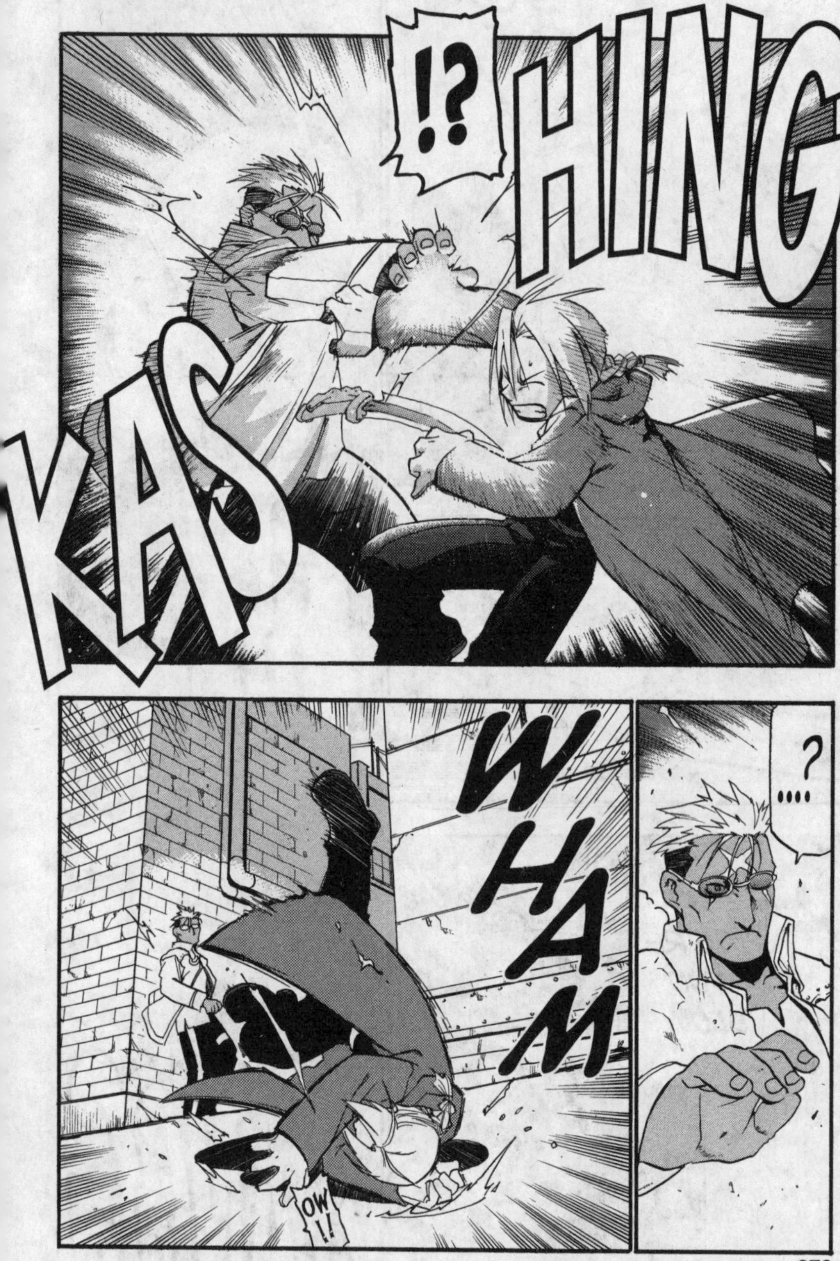
HING
!?
KAS
....?
WHAM
OW!!

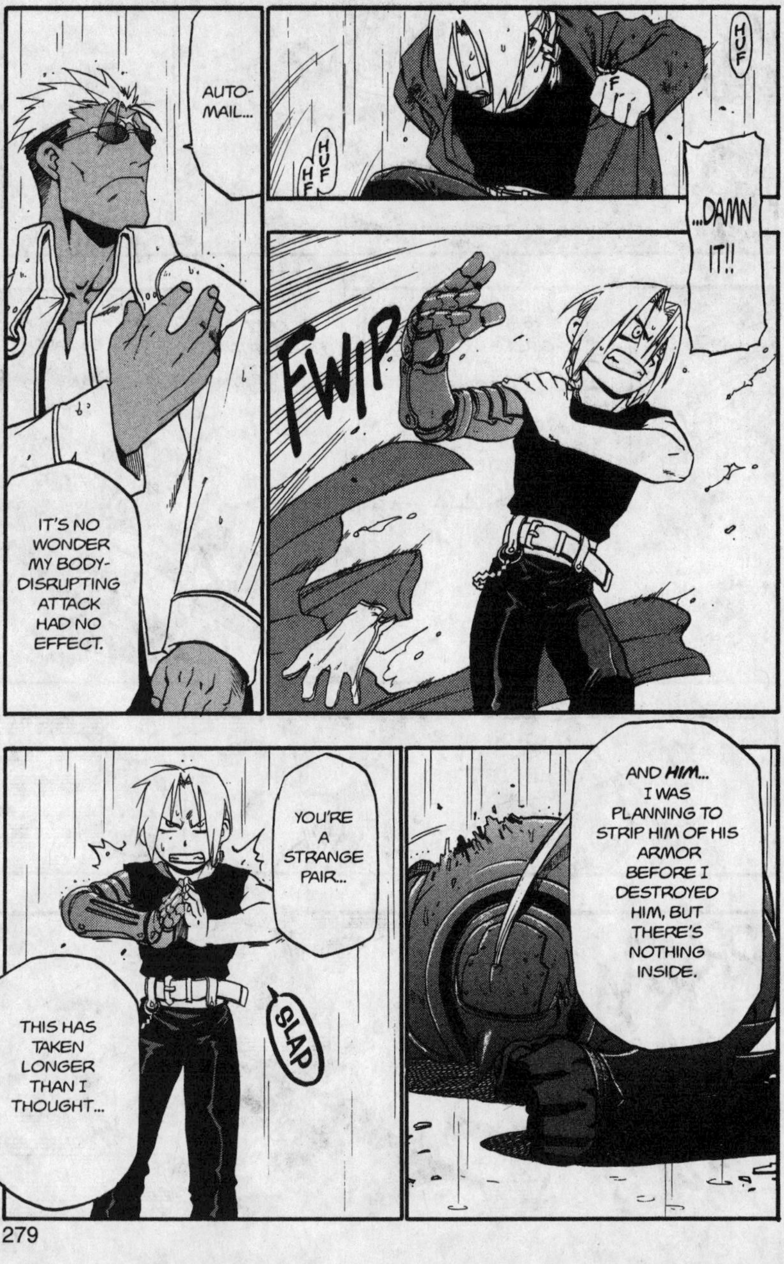
HUF
F
HUF
HF
...DAMN IT!!
FWIP
AUTO-MAIL...
IT'S NO WONDER MY BODY-DISRUPTING ATTACK HAD NO EFFECT.
AND *HIM*... I WAS PLANNING TO STRIP HIM OF HIS ARMOR BEFORE I DESTROYED HIM, BUT THERE'S NOTHING INSIDE.
YOU'RE A STRANGE PAIR...
SLAP
THIS HAS TAKEN LONGER THAN I THOUGHT...

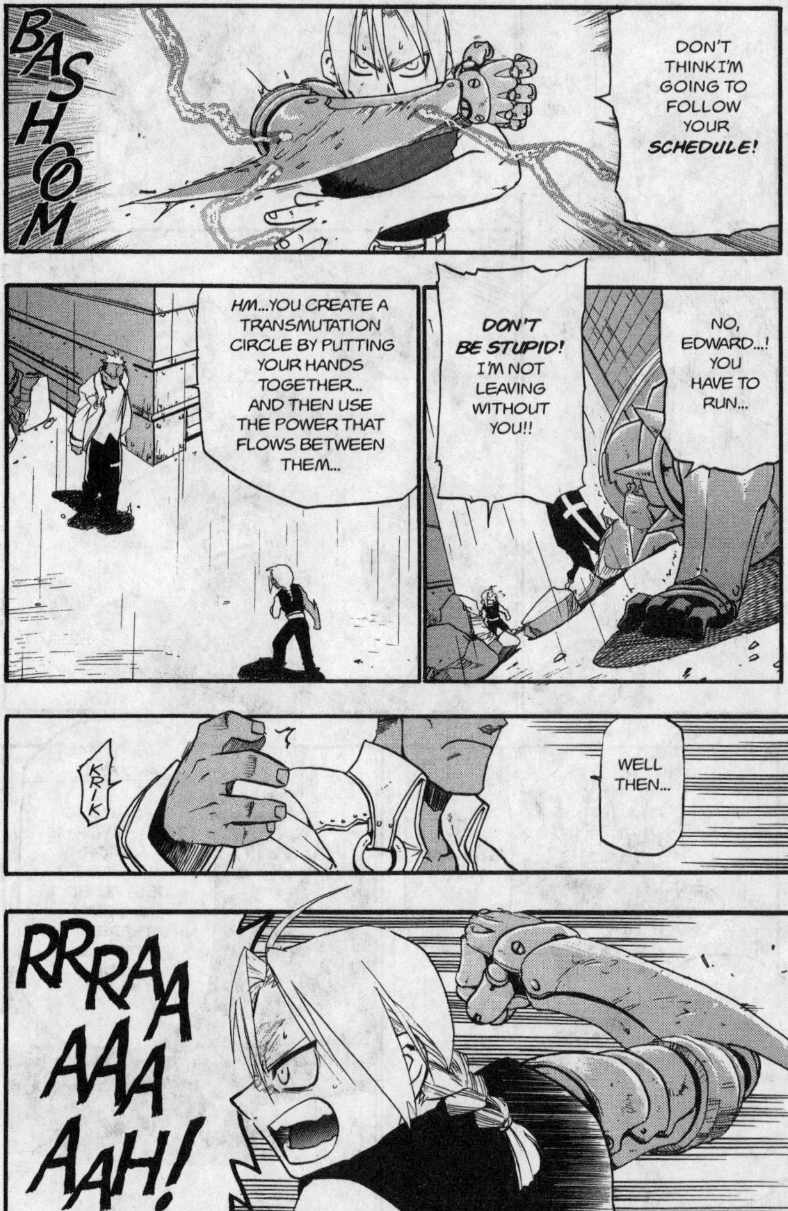
DON'T THINK I'M GOING TO FOLLOW YOUR SCHEDULE!
BASHOOM
NO, EDWARD...! YOU HAVE TO RUN...
DON'T BE STUPID! I'M NOT LEAVING WITHOUT YOU!!
HM...YOU CREATE A TRANSMUTATION CIRCLE BY PUTTING YOUR HANDS TOGETHER... AND THEN USE THE POWER THAT FLOWS BETWEEN THEM...
WELL THEN...
KRIK
RRRAAAAAAAH!

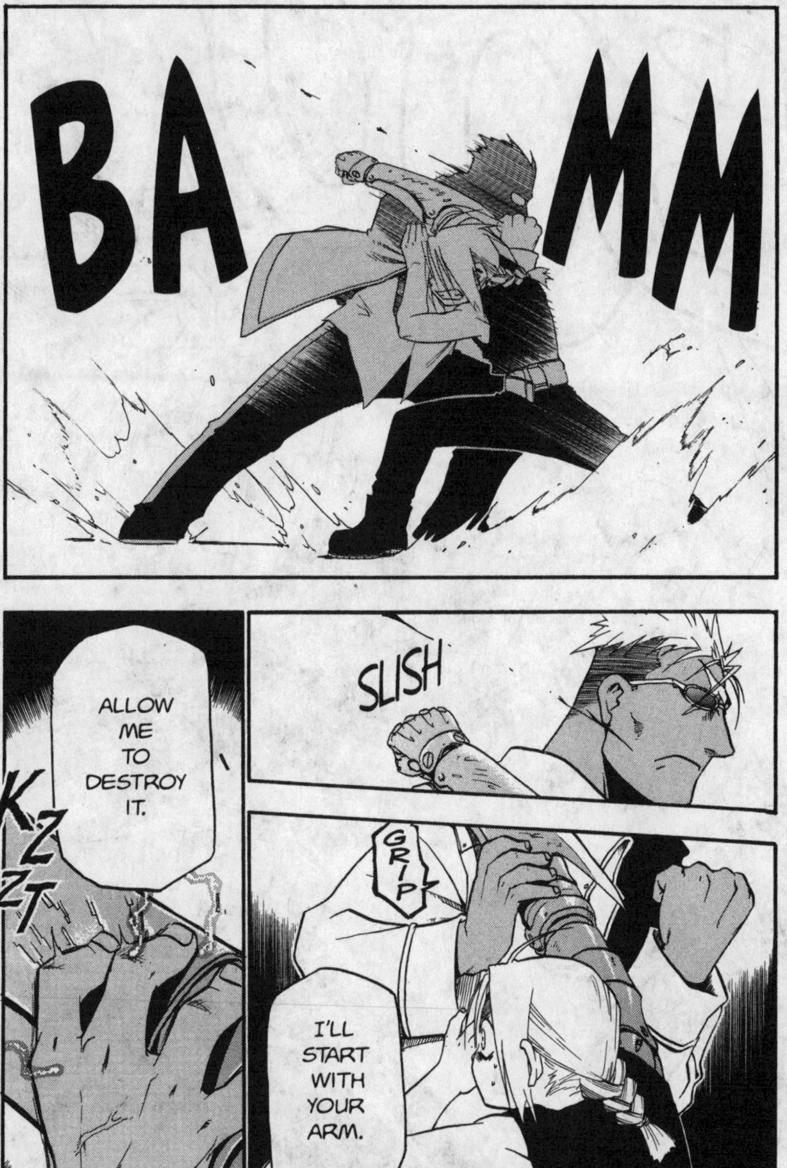
BAMM
SLISH
GRIP
I'LL START WITH YOUR ARM.
ALLOW ME TO DESTROY IT.
KZZT

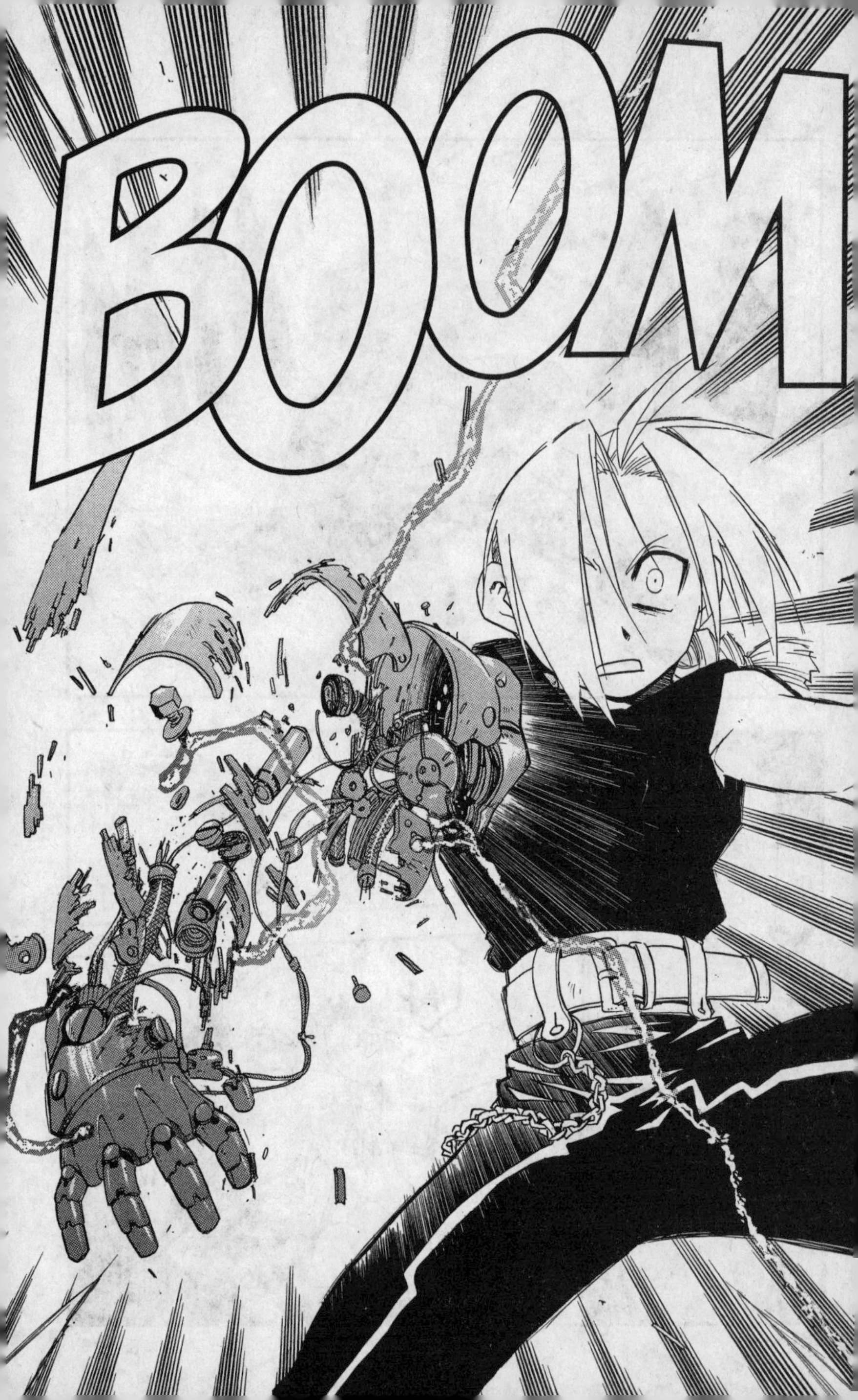
BOOM

FULLMETAL
ALCHEMIST

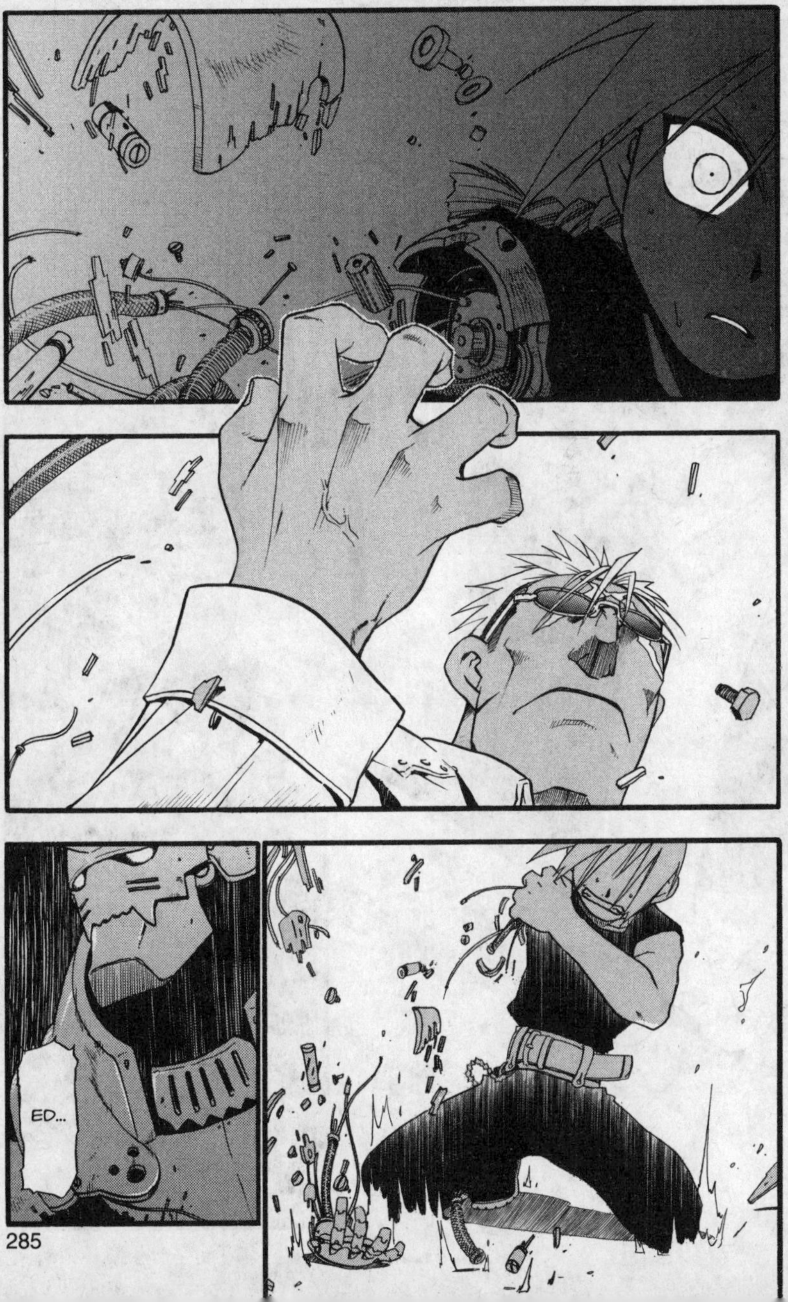
ED...

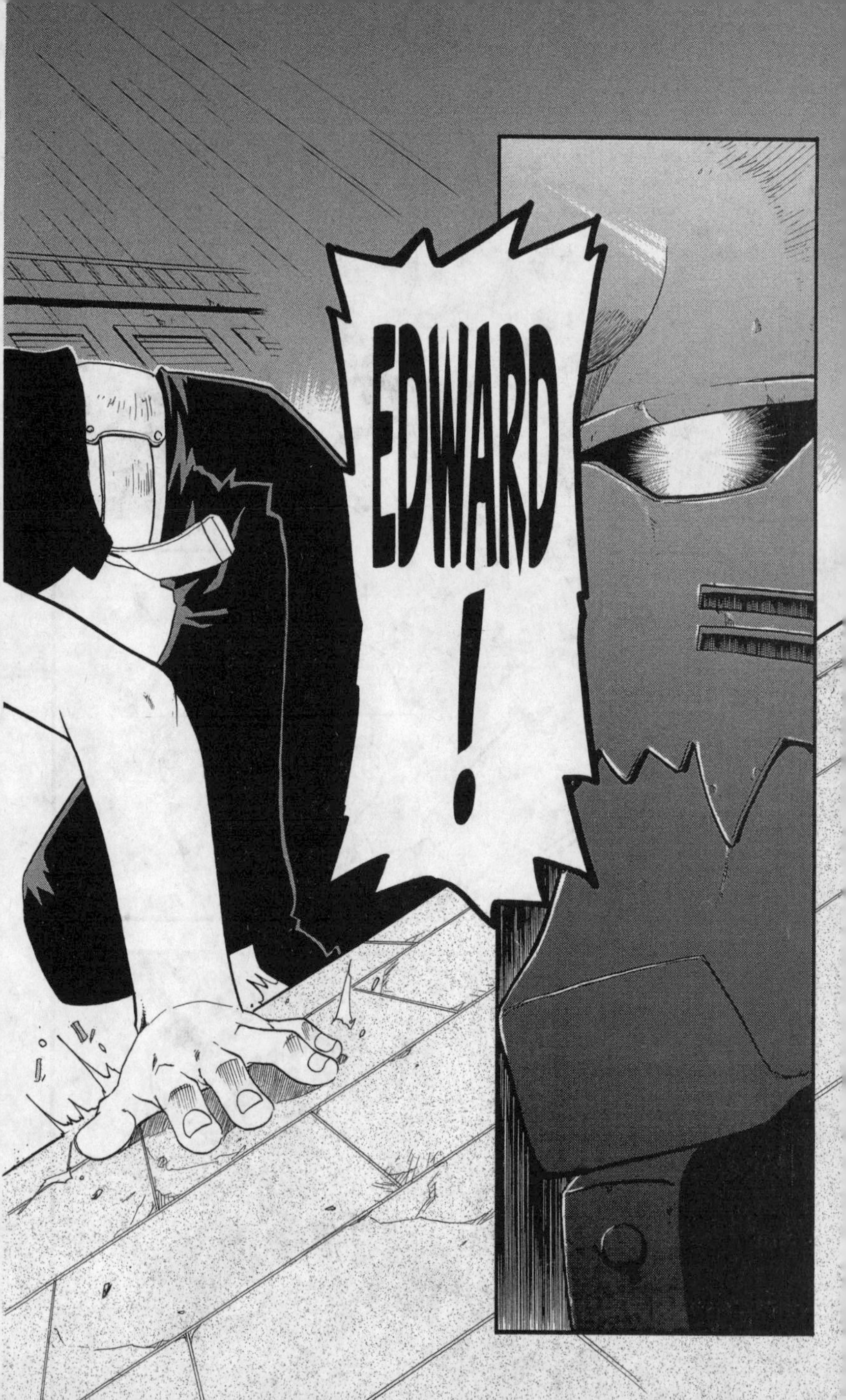
EDWARD!

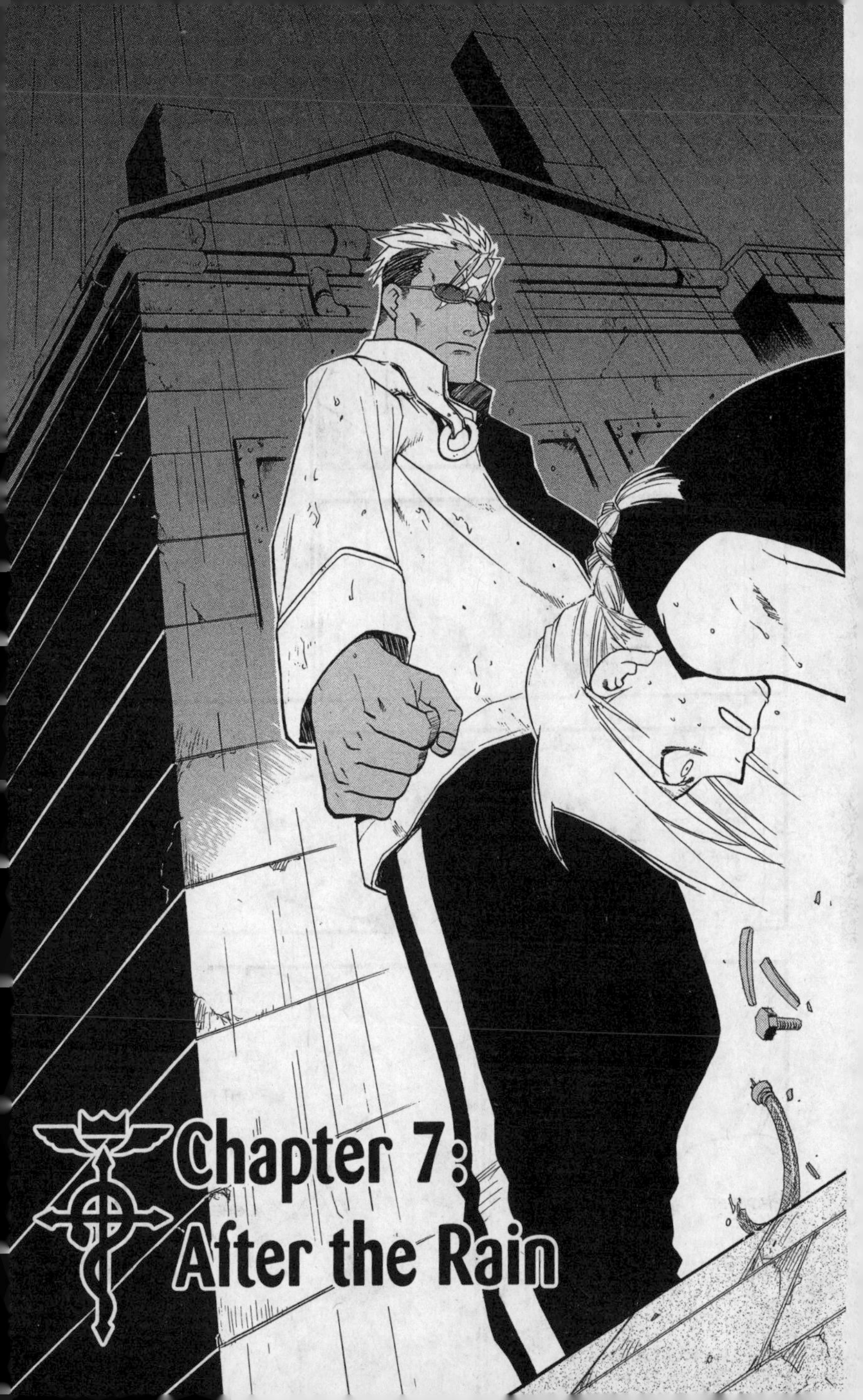
Chapter 7:
After the Rain

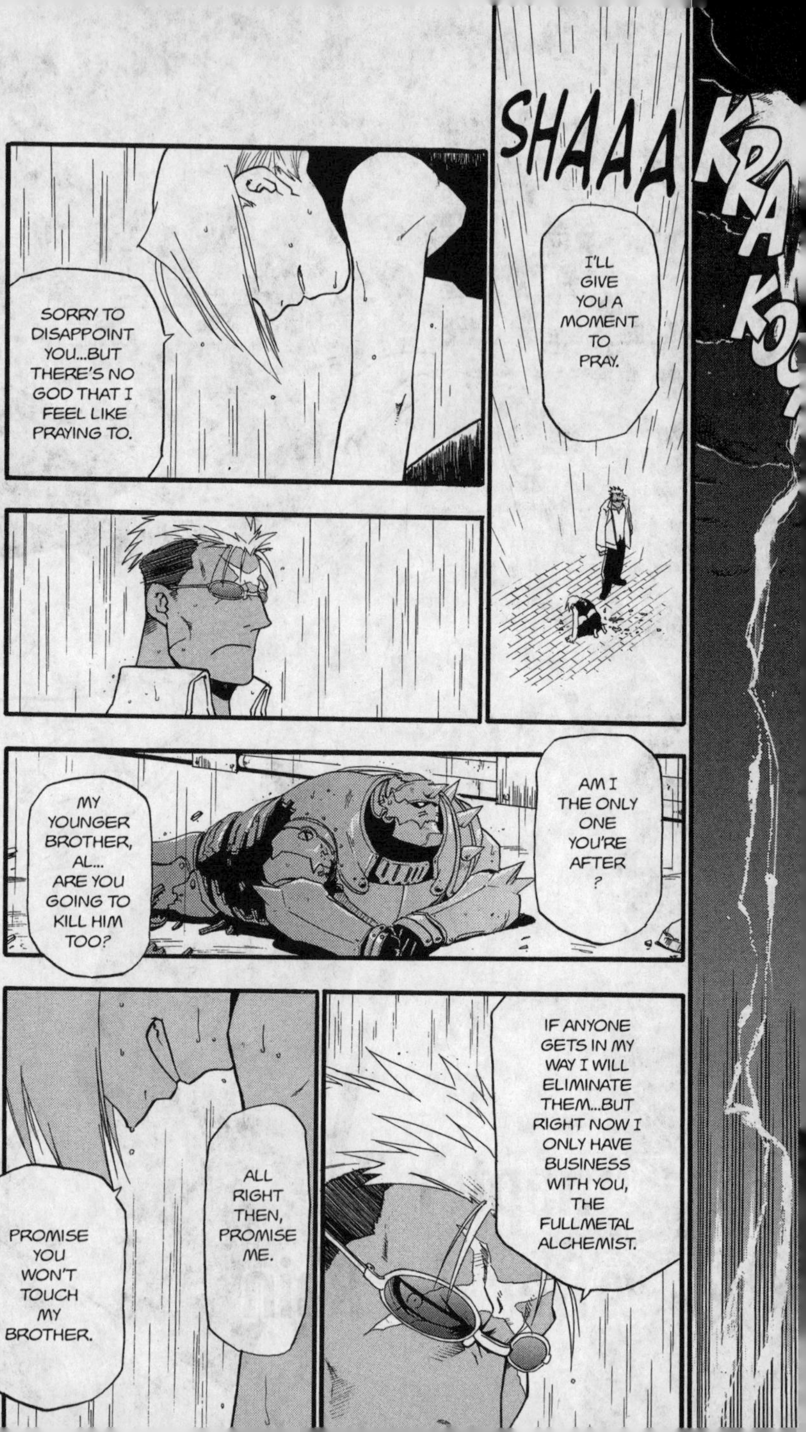
KRAKO
SHAAA
I'LL GIVE YOU A MOMENT TO PRAY.
SORRY TO DISAPPOINT YOU...BUT THERE'S NO GOD THAT I FEEL LIKE PRAYING TO.
AM I THE ONLY ONE YOU'RE AFTER?
MY YOUNGER BROTHER, AL... ARE YOU GOING TO KILL HIM TOO?
IF ANYONE GETS IN MY WAY I WILL ELIMINATE THEM...BUT RIGHT NOW I ONLY HAVE BUSINESS WITH YOU, THE FULLMETAL ALCHEMIST.
ALL RIGHT THEN, PROMISE ME.
PROMISE YOU WON'T TOUCH MY BROTHER.

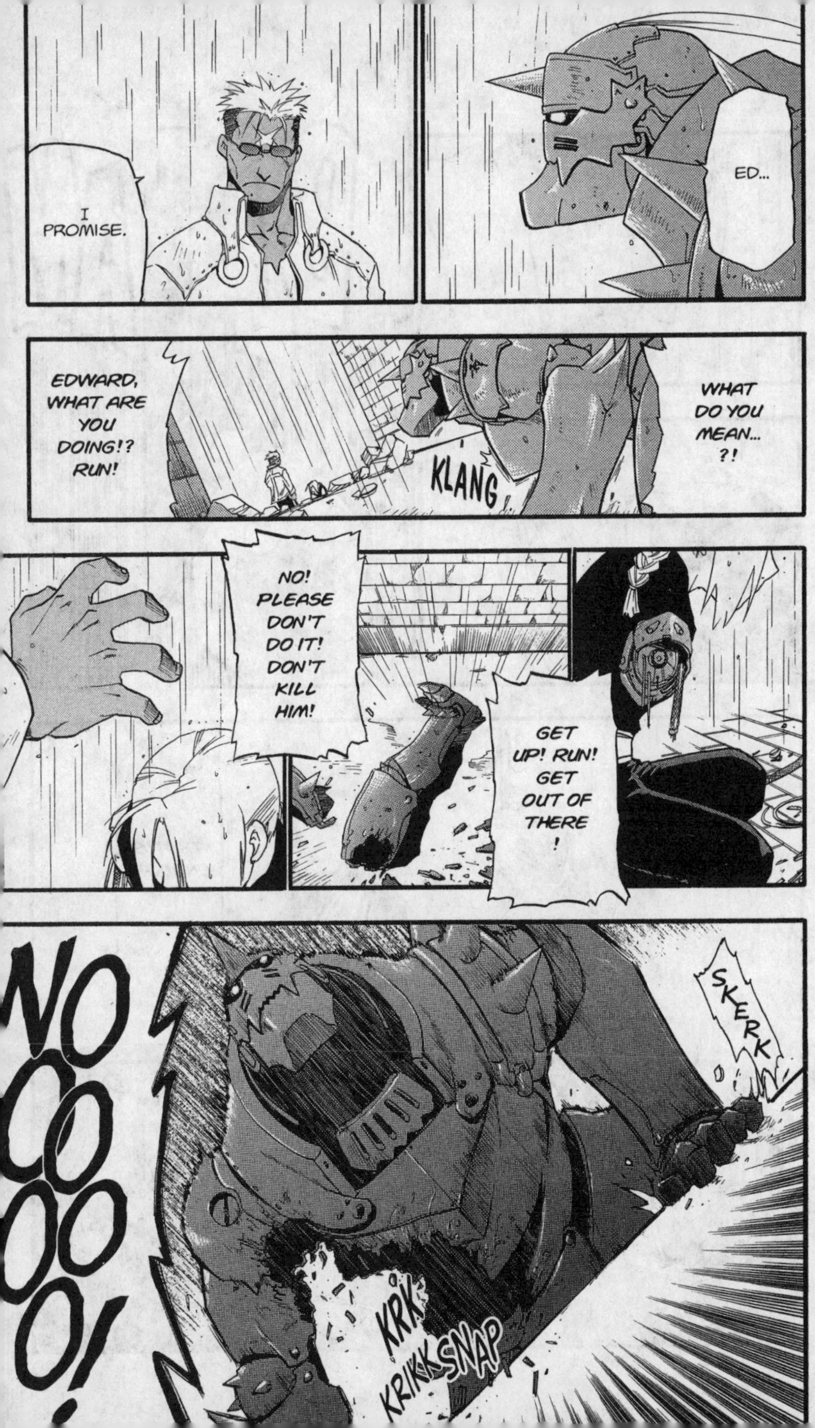
ED...
I PROMISE.
WHAT DO YOU MEAN...?!
KLANG
EDWARD, WHAT ARE YOU DOING!? RUN!
GET UP! RUN! GET OUT OF THERE!
NO! PLEASE DON'T DO IT! DON'T KILL HIM!
SKERK
NOOOOOO!
KRK
KRIKKSNAP

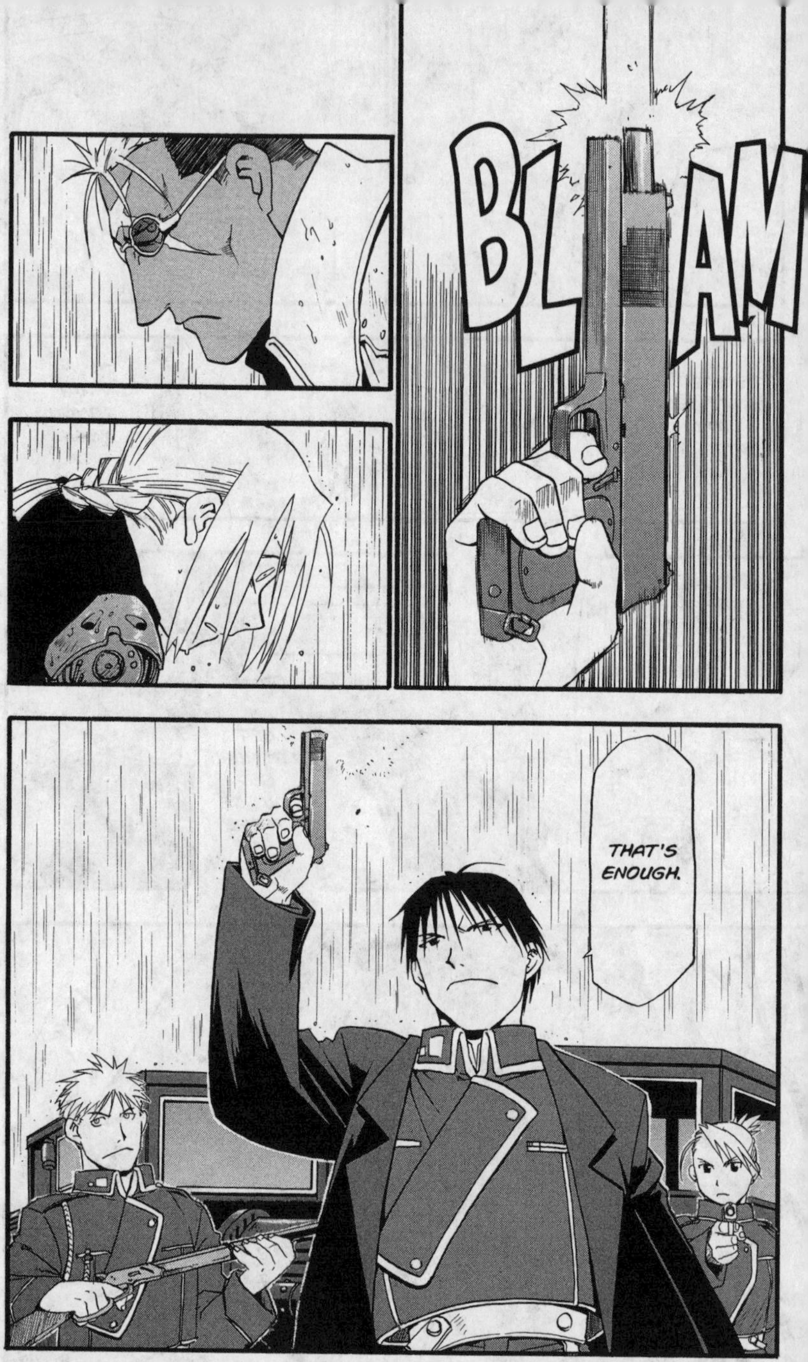
BLAM
THAT'S ENOUGH.

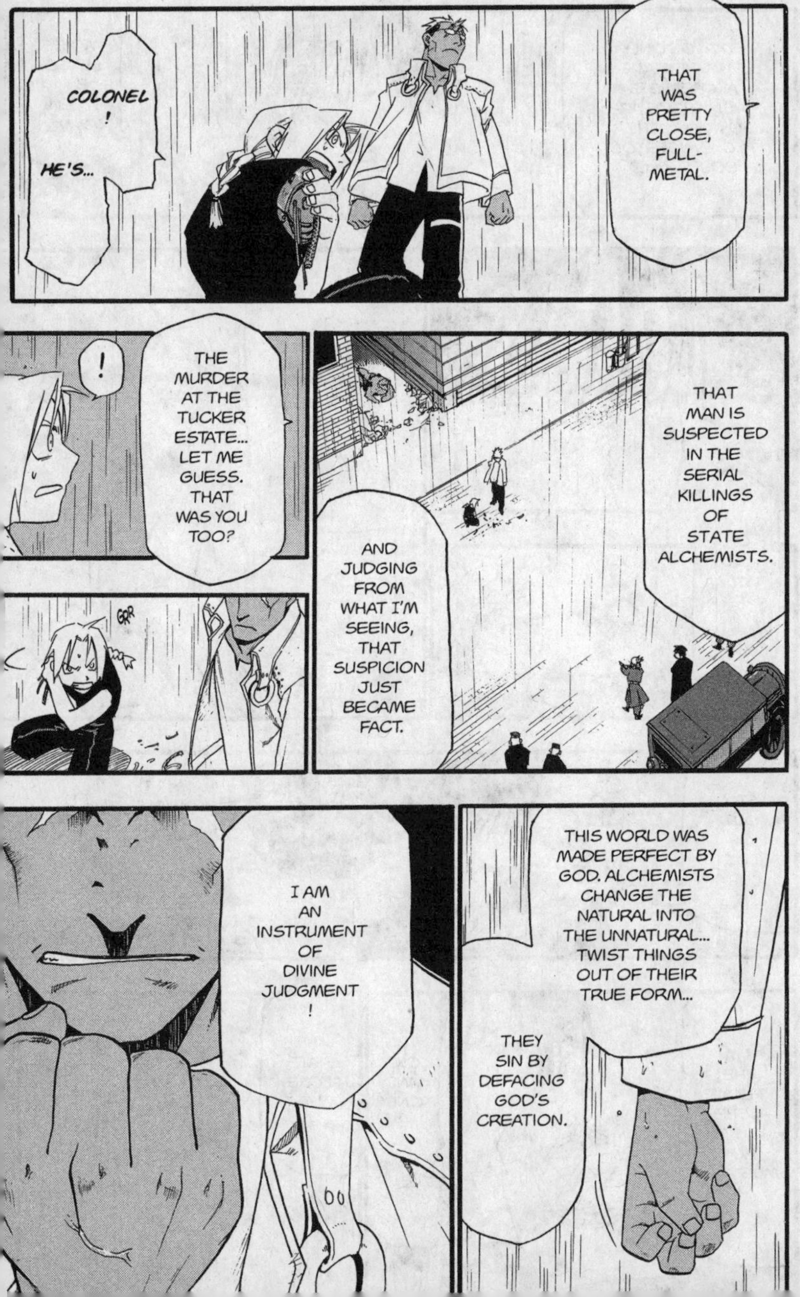
THAT WAS PRETTY CLOSE, FULL-METAL.
COLONEL! HE'S...
THAT MAN IS SUSPECTED IN THE SERIAL KILLINGS OF STATE ALCHEMISTS.
AND JUDGING FROM WHAT I'M SEEING, THAT SUSPICION JUST BECAME FACT.
THE MURDER AT THE TUCKER ESTATE... LET ME GUESS. THAT WAS YOU TOO?
!
GRR
THIS WORLD WAS MADE PERFECT BY GOD. ALCHEMISTS CHANGE THE NATURAL INTO THE UNNATURAL... TWIST THINGS OUT OF THEIR TRUE FORM...
THEY SIN BY DEFACING GOD'S CREATION.
I AM AN INSTRUMENT OF DIVINE JUDGMENT!

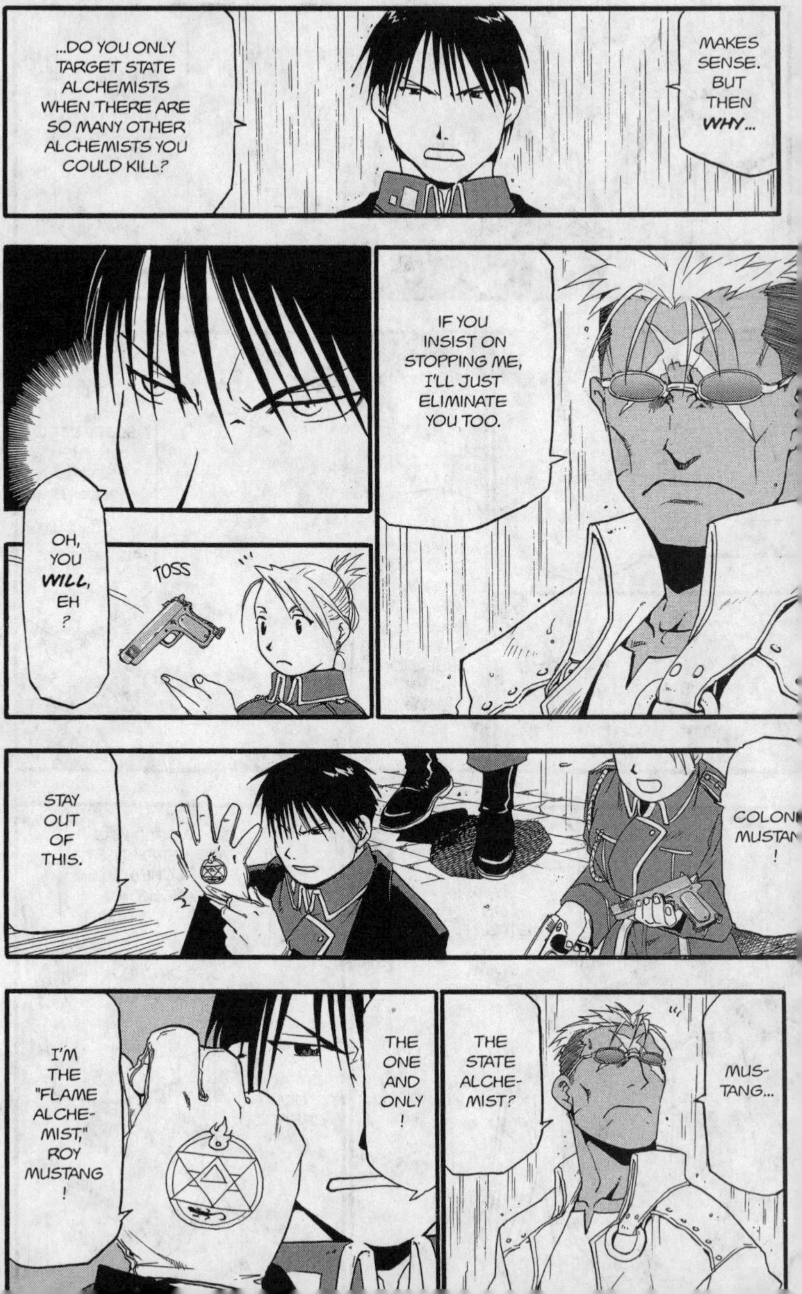
MAKES SENSE. BUT THEN WHY...
...DO YOU ONLY TARGET STATE ALCHEMISTS WHEN THERE ARE SO MANY OTHER ALCHEMISTS YOU COULD KILL?
IF YOU INSIST ON STOPPING ME, I'LL JUST ELIMINATE YOU TOO.
TOSS
OH, YOU WILL, EH?
COLON MUSTAN !
STAY OUT OF THIS.
MUS-TANG...
THE STATE ALCHE-MIST?
THE ONE AND ONLY!
I'M THE "FLAME ALCHE-MIST," ROY MUSTANG!

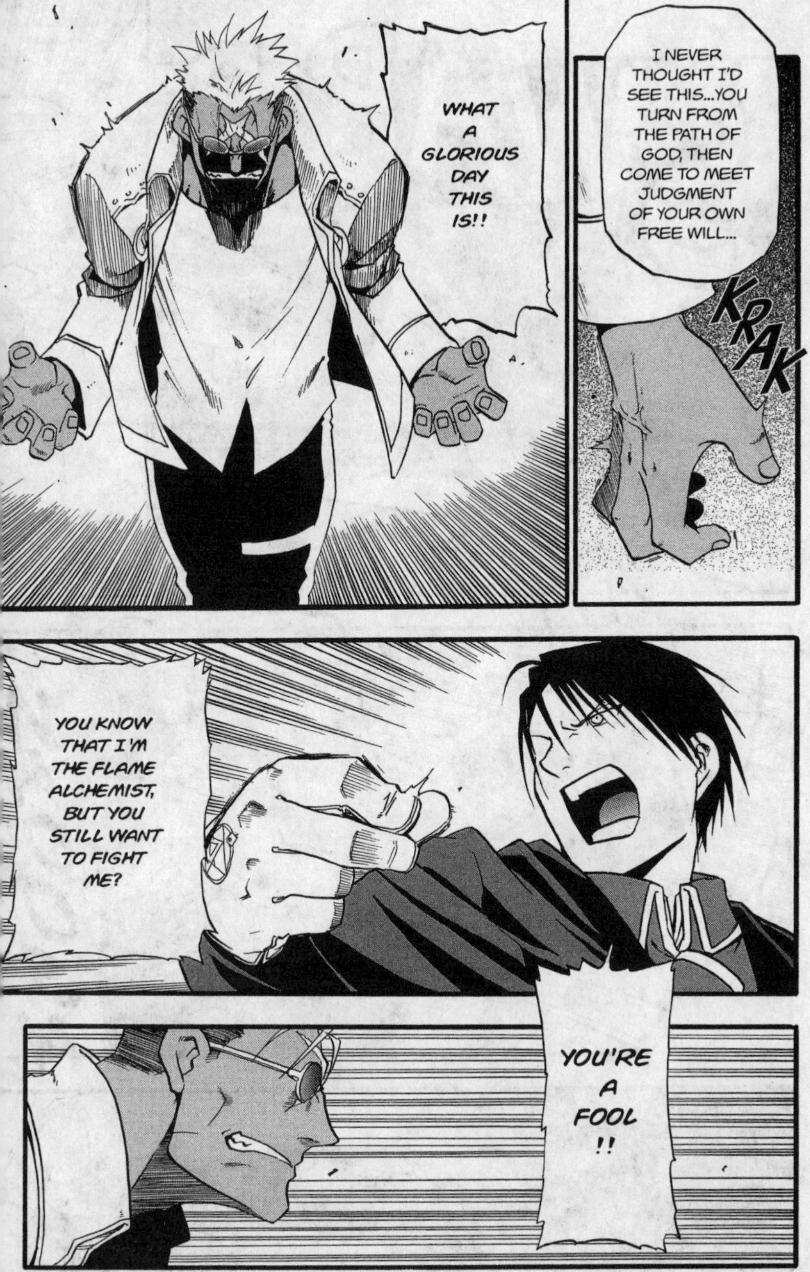
I NEVER THOUGHT I'D SEE THIS...YOU TURN FROM THE PATH OF GOD, THEN COME TO MEET JUDGMENT OF YOUR OWN FREE WILL...
KRAK
WHAT A GLORIOUS DAY THIS IS!!
YOU KNOW THAT I'M THE FLAME ALCHEMIST, BUT YOU STILL WANT TO FIGHT ME?
YOU'RE A FOOL!!

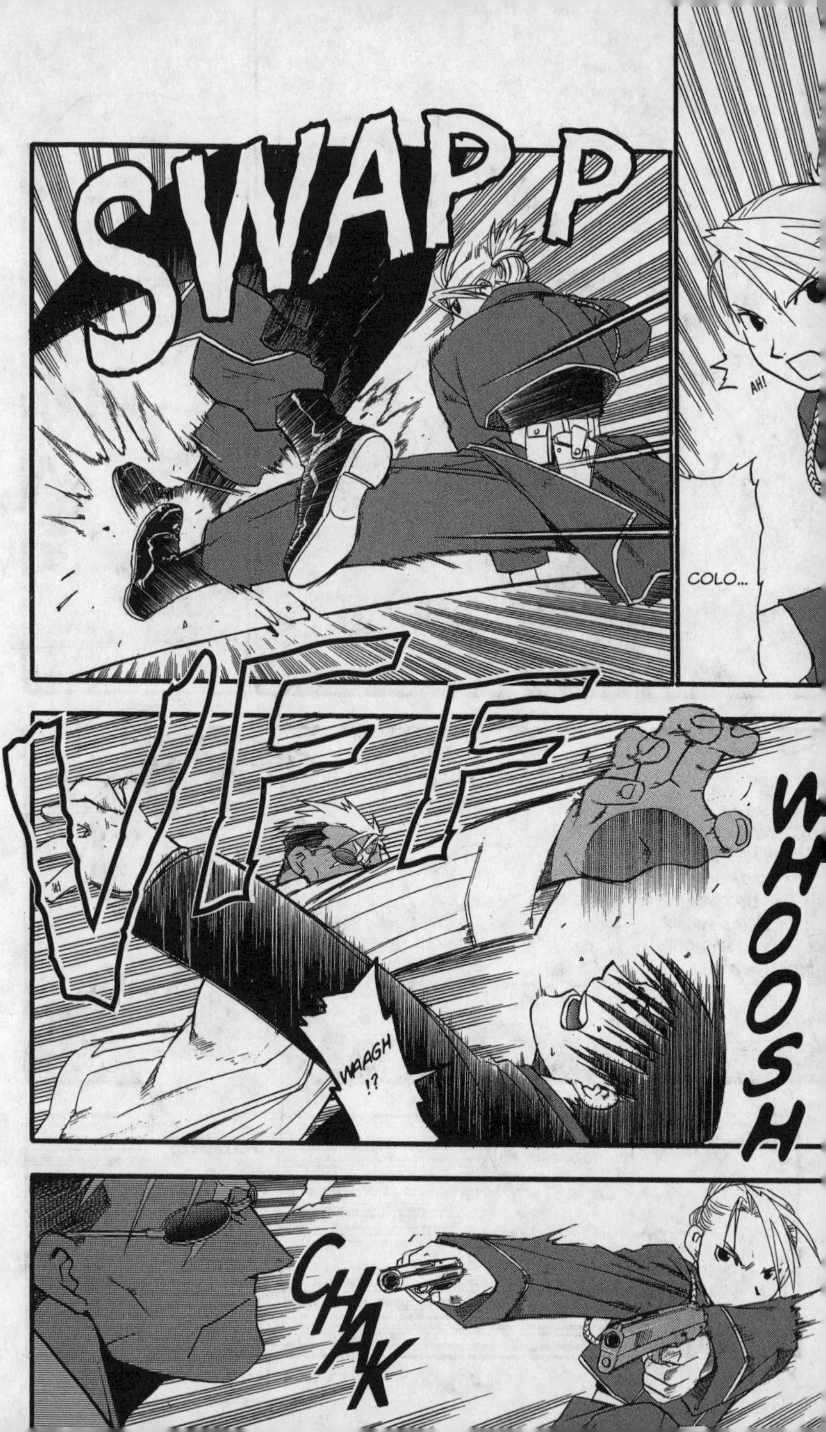
AH!
COLO...
SWAPP
WHOOSH
VFF
WAAGH !?
CHAK

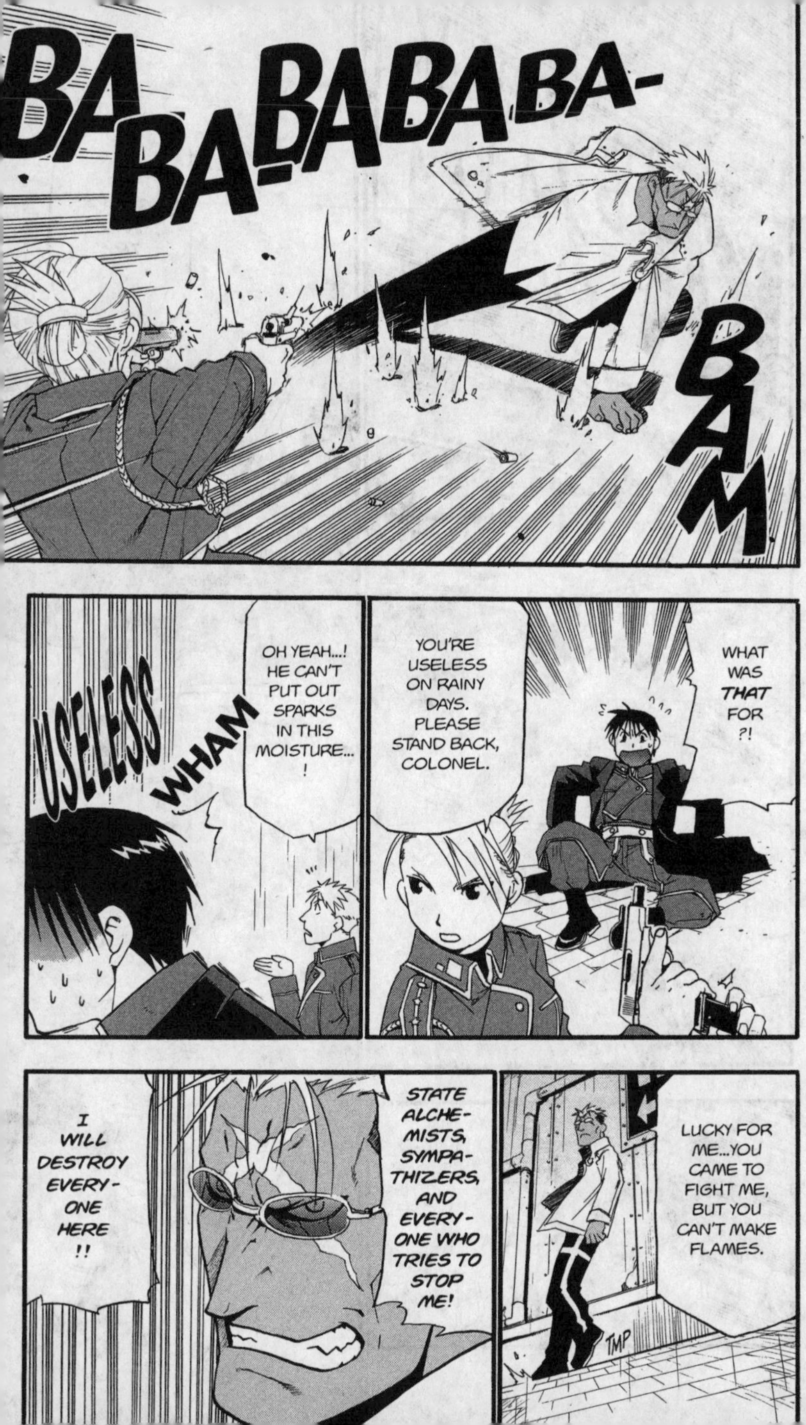
BA BA-BABABABA-
BAM
WHAT WAS *THAT* FOR?!
YOU'RE USELESS ON RAINY DAYS. PLEASE STAND BACK, COLONEL.
OH YEAH...! HE CAN'T PUT OUT SPARKS IN THIS MOISTURE...!
WHAM
USELESS
LUCKY FOR ME...YOU CAME TO FIGHT ME, BUT YOU CAN'T MAKE FLAMES.
TMP
STATE ALCHEMISTS, SYMPATHIZERS, AND EVERYONE WHO TRIES TO STOP ME!
I WILL DESTROY EVERYONE HERE!!

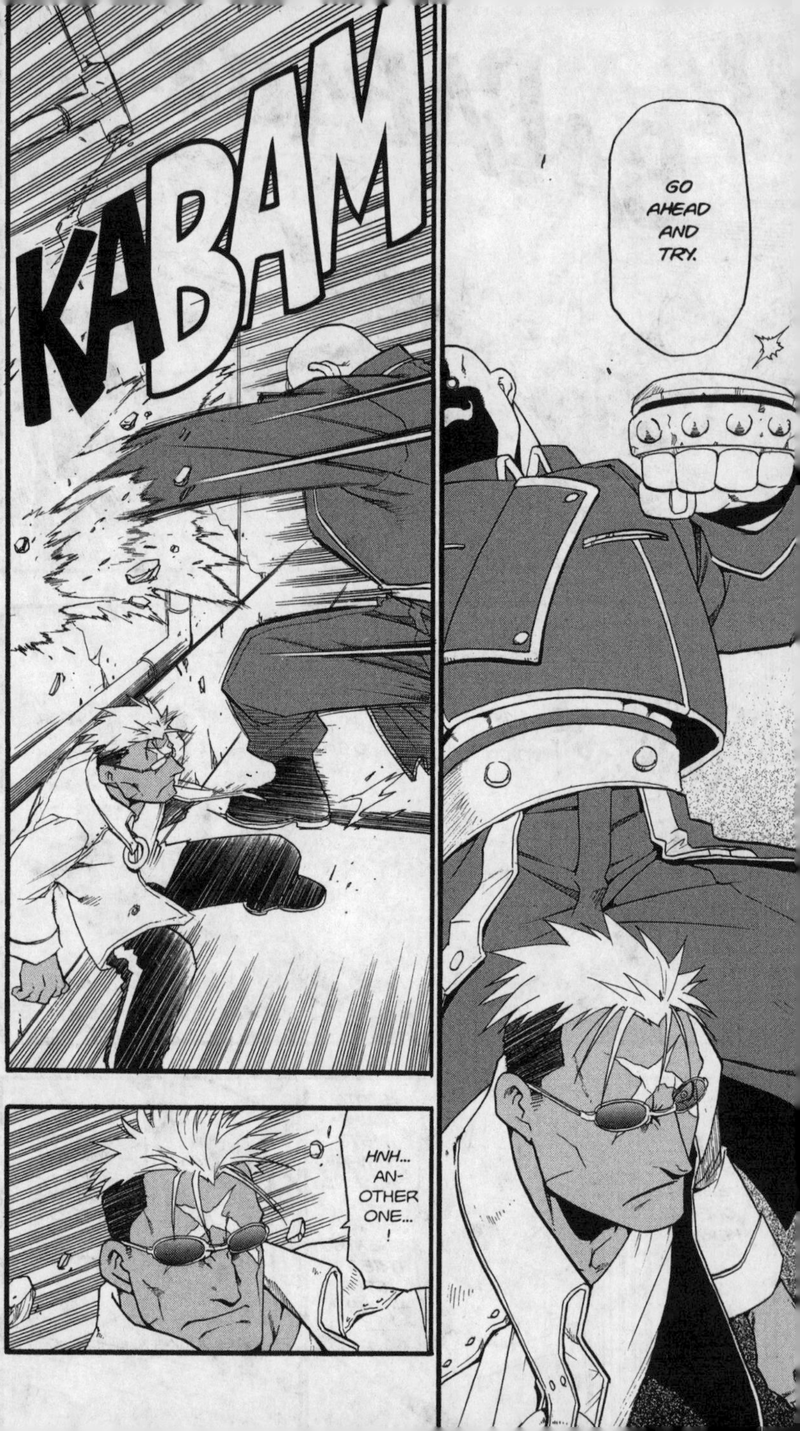
GO AHEAD AND TRY.
KABAM
HNH... AN-OTHER ONE...!

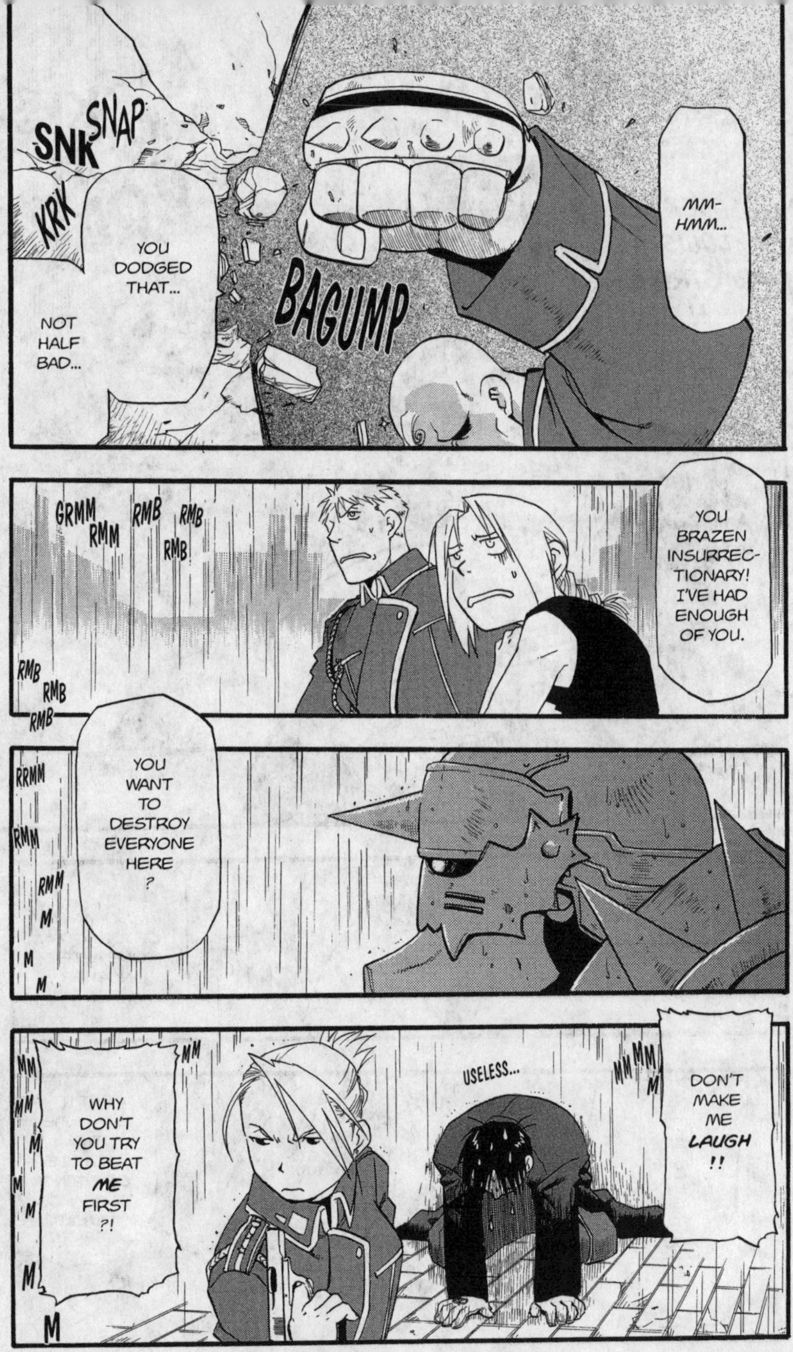
MM-HMM...
SNAP
SNK
KRK
YOU DODGED THAT...
BAGUMP
NOT HALF BAD...
YOU BRAZEN INSURREC-TIONARY! I'VE HAD ENOUGH OF YOU.
RMB RMB
RMB
GRMM RMM
RMB RMB RMB
YOU WANT TO DESTROY EVERYONE HERE?
RRMM RMM RMM M M M
DON'T MAKE ME *LAUGH*!!
MMMM M
USELESS...
MM
WHY DON'T YOU TRY TO BEAT *ME* FIRST?!
MM MM M M M M M

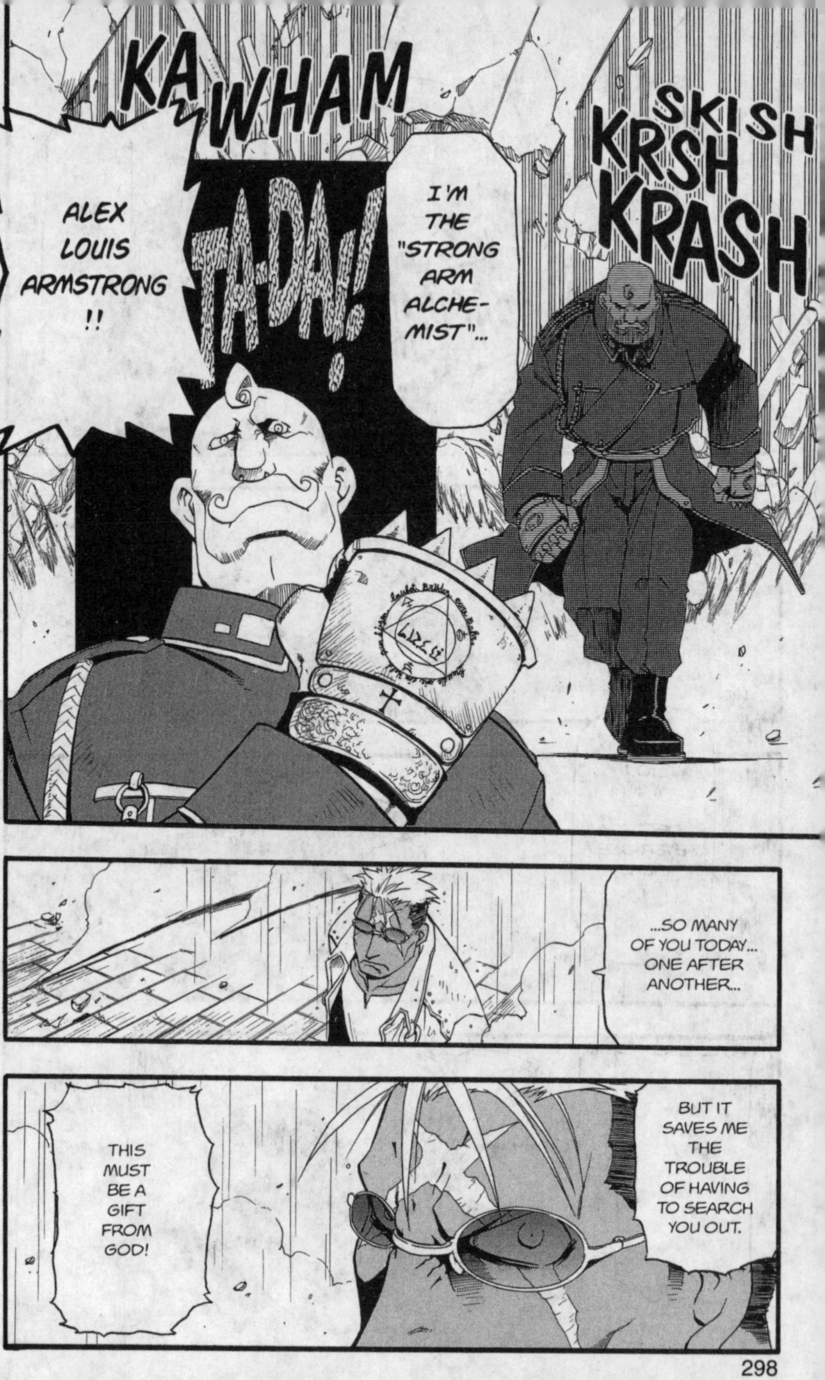
SKISH KRSH KRASH
I'M THE "STRONG ARM ALCHEMIST"...
TA-DA!!
KA WHAM
ALEX LOUIS ARMSTRONG !!
...SO MANY OF YOU TODAY... ONE AFTER ANOTHER...
BUT IT SAVES ME THE TROUBLE OF HAVING TO SEARCH YOU OUT.
THIS MUST BE A GIFT FROM GOD!

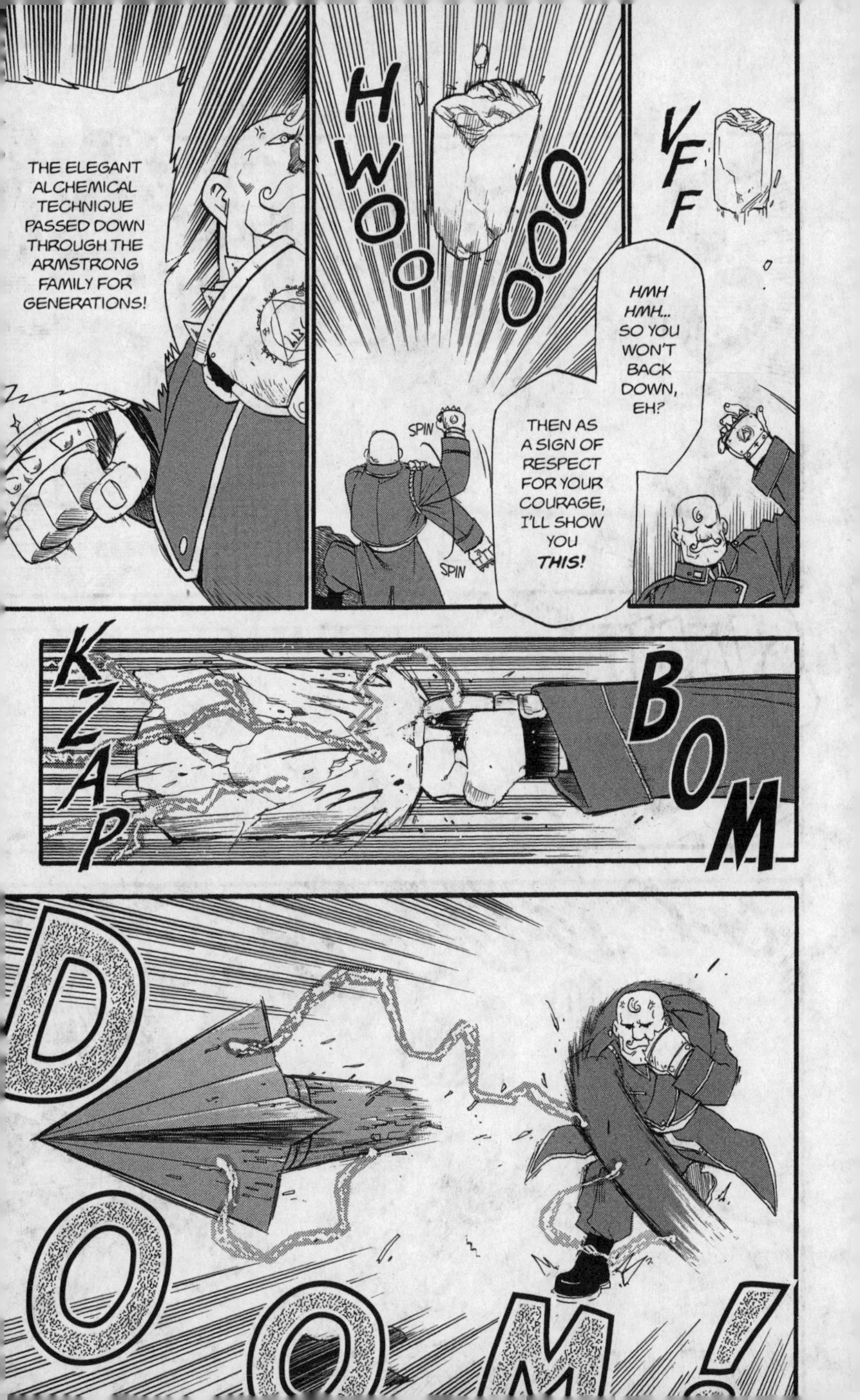
VFF
HMH HMH... SO YOU WON'T BACK DOWN, EH?
THEN AS A SIGN OF RESPECT FOR YOUR COURAGE, I'LL SHOW YOU *THIS!*
HWOOOOOO
SPIN
SPIN
THE ELEGANT ALCHEMICAL TECHNIQUE PASSED DOWN THROUGH THE ARMSTRONG FAMILY FOR GENERATIONS!
BOM
KZAP
DOOM!

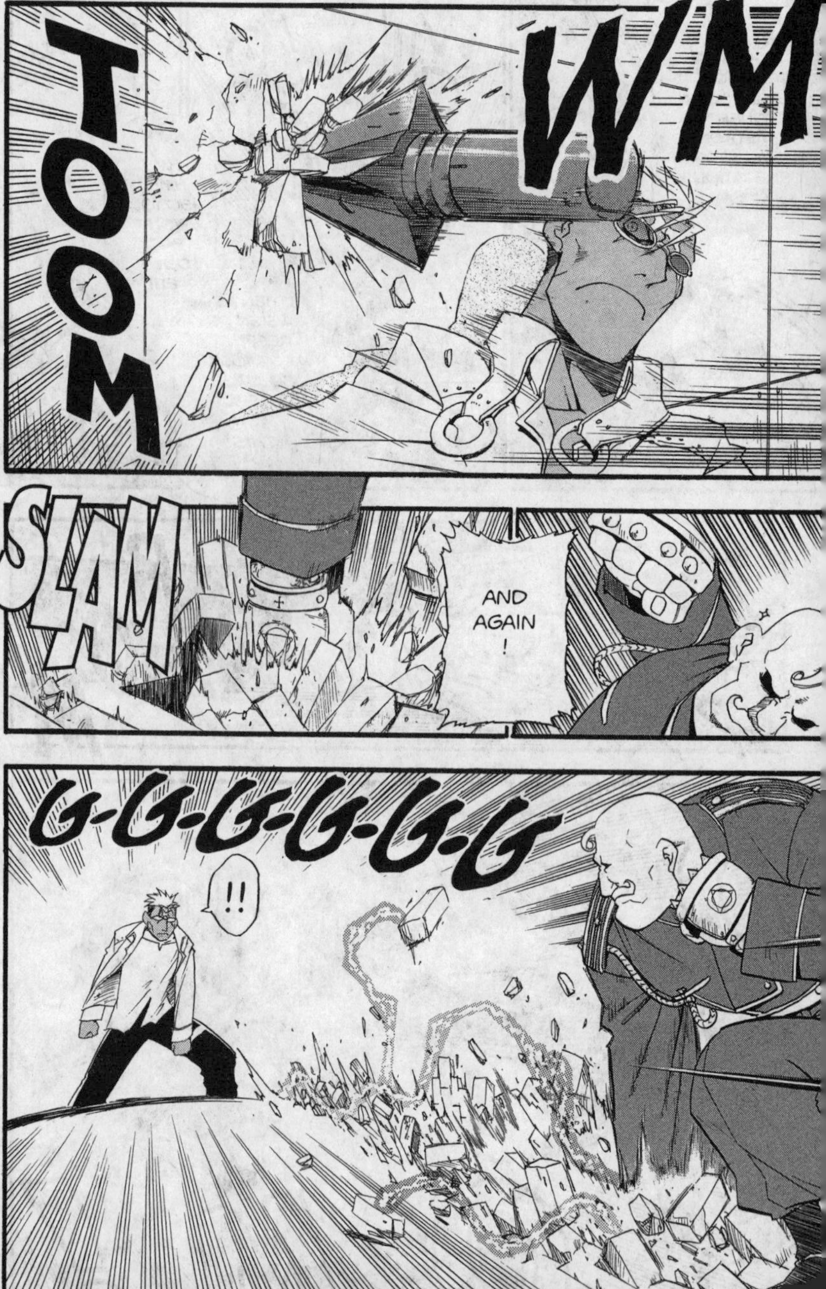
WM
TOOOM
AND AGAIN!
SLAM
G-G-G-G-G-G-G
!!

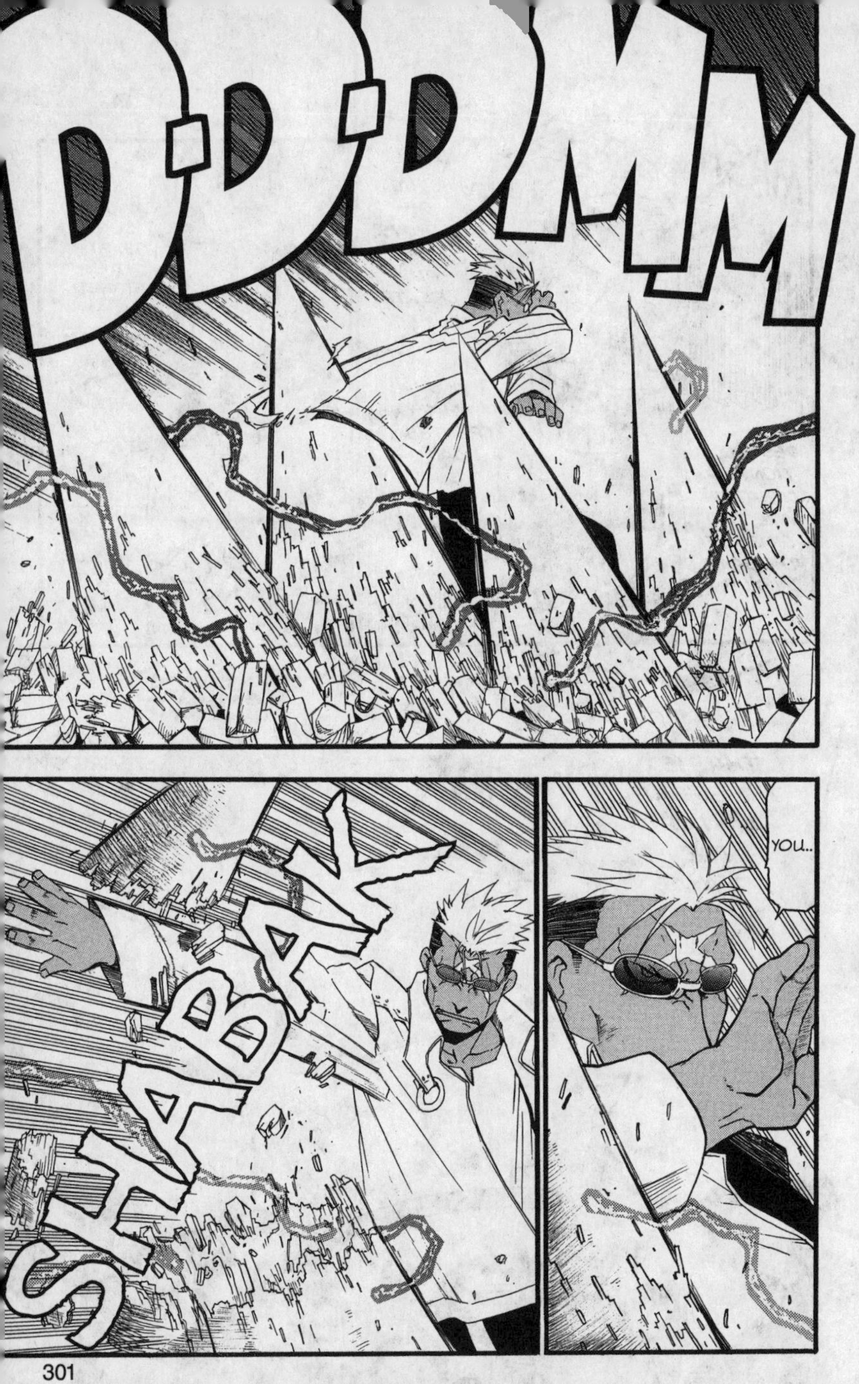
D-D-DMM
YOU...
SHABAK

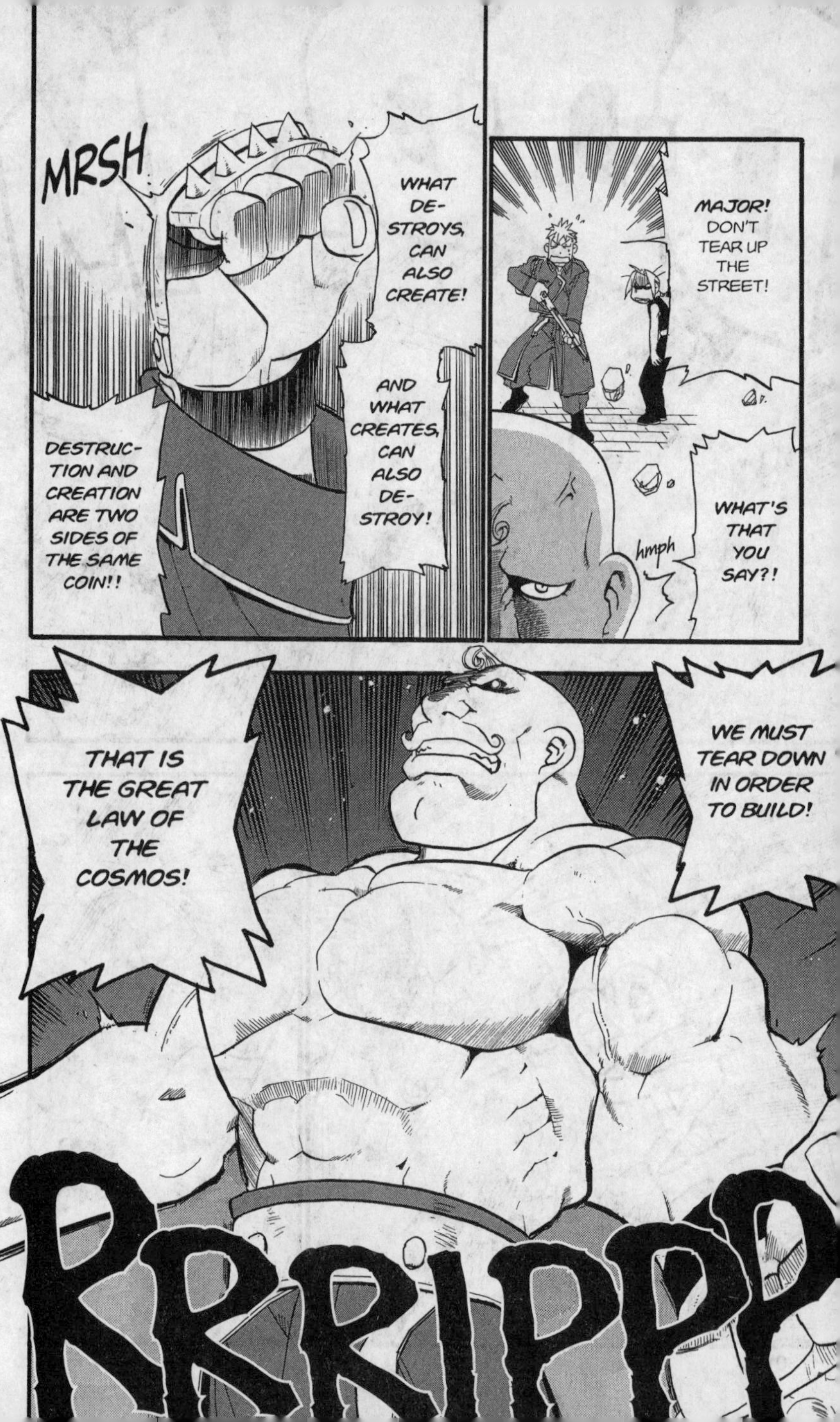
MAJOR! DON'T TEAR UP THE STREET!
WHAT'S THAT YOU SAY?!
hmph
WHAT DESTROYS, CAN ALSO CREATE!
MRSH
AND WHAT CREATES, CAN ALSO DESTROY!
DESTRUCTION AND CREATION ARE TWO SIDES OF THE SAME COIN!!
WE MUST TEAR DOWN IN ORDER TO BUILD!
THAT IS THE GREAT LAW OF THE COSMOS!
RRRIPPP

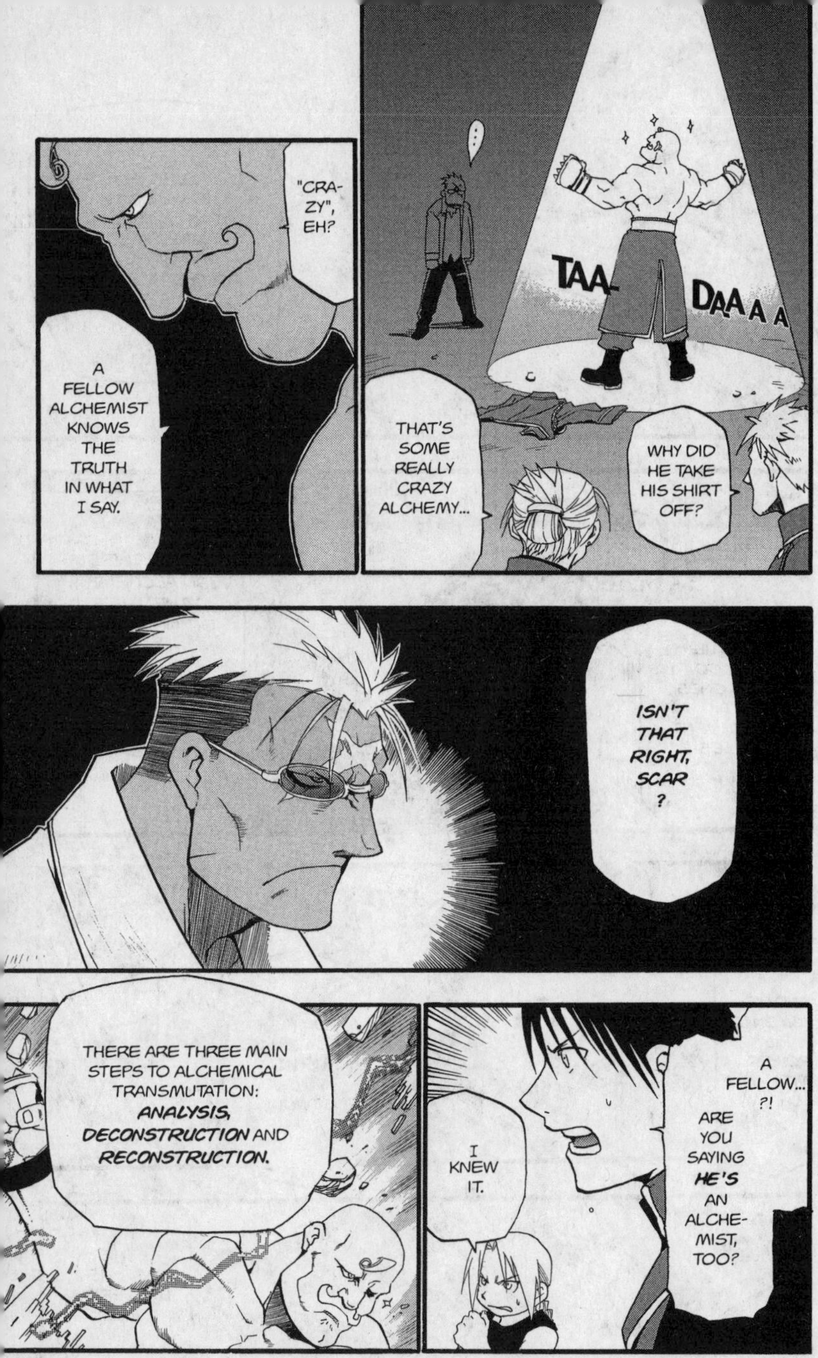
TAA-DAAAA
WHY DID HE TAKE HIS SHIRT OFF?
THAT'S SOME REALLY CRAZY ALCHEMY...
"CRAZY", EH?
A FELLOW ALCHEMIST KNOWS THE TRUTH IN WHAT I SAY.
ISN'T THAT RIGHT, SCAR?
A FELLOW...?! ARE YOU SAYING HE'S AN ALCHEMIST, TOO?
I KNEW IT.
THERE ARE THREE MAIN STEPS TO ALCHEMICAL TRANSMUTATION: ANALYSIS, DECONSTRUCTION AND RECONSTRUCTION.

HE'S RECOVERED BY THIS TIME...

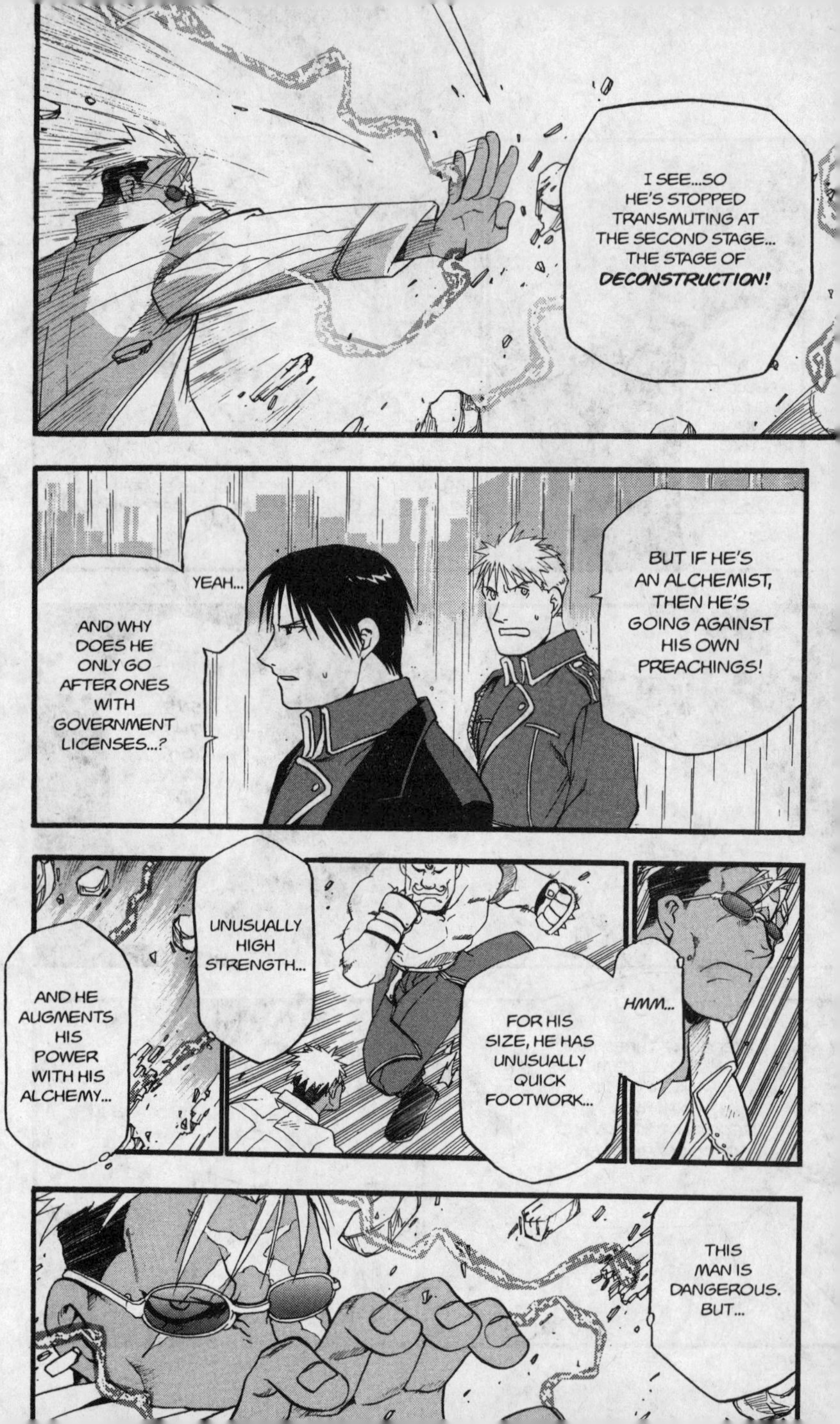
I SEE...SO HE'S STOPPED TRANSMUTING AT THE SECOND STAGE... THE STAGE OF **DECONSTRUCTION!**
BUT IF HE'S AN ALCHEMIST, THEN HE'S GOING AGAINST HIS OWN PREACHINGS!
YEAH...
AND WHY DOES HE ONLY GO AFTER ONES WITH GOVERNMENT LICENSES...?
HMM...
FOR HIS SIZE, HE HAS UNUSUALLY QUICK FOOTWORK...
UNUSUALLY HIGH STRENGTH...
AND HE AUGMENTS HIS POWER WITH HIS ALCHEMY...
THIS MAN IS DANGEROUS. BUT...

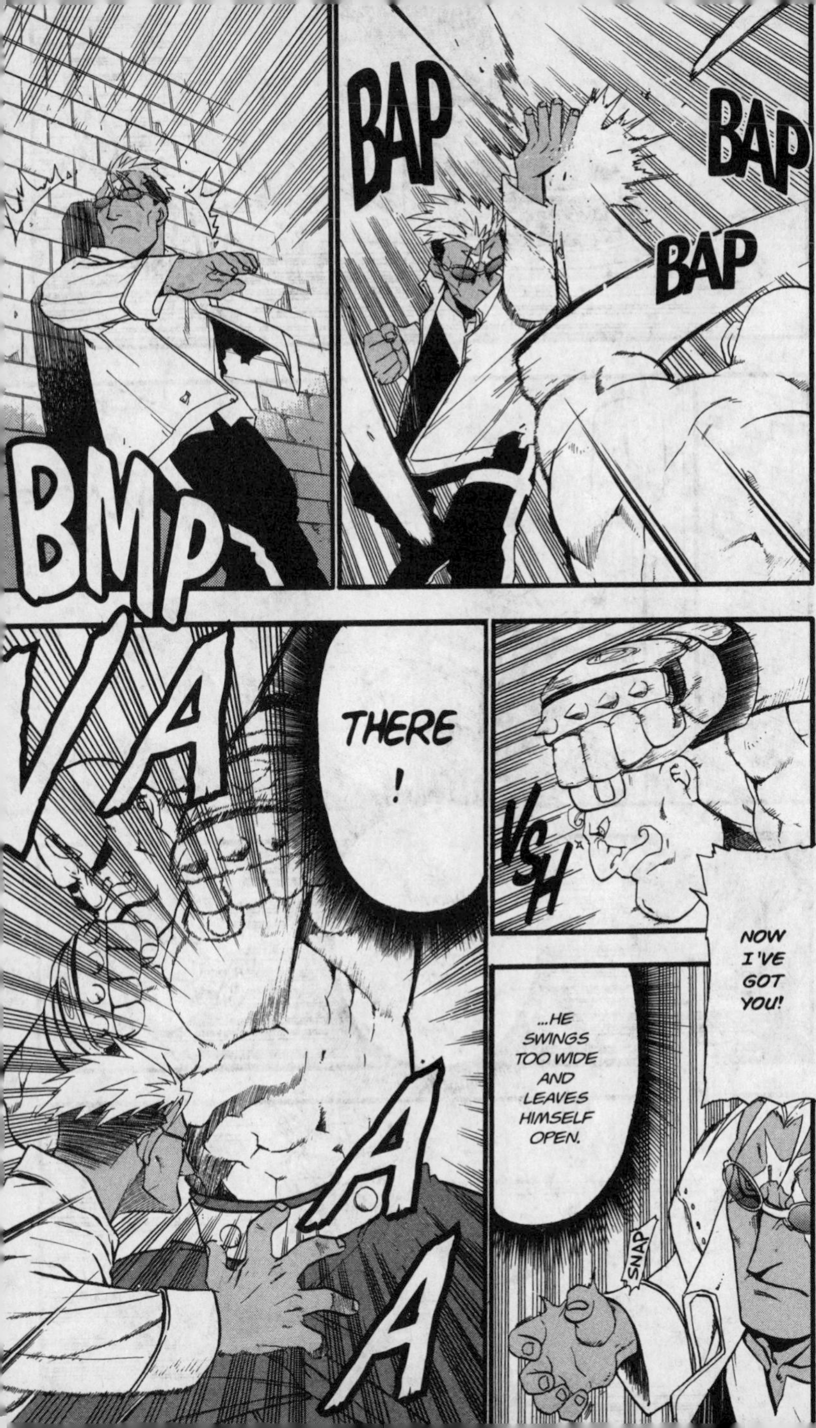
BAP
BAP
BAP
BMP
VSH
NOW I'VE GOT YOU!
...HE SWINGS TOO WIDE AND LEAVES HIMSELF OPEN.
SNAP
VA
THERE!
AA

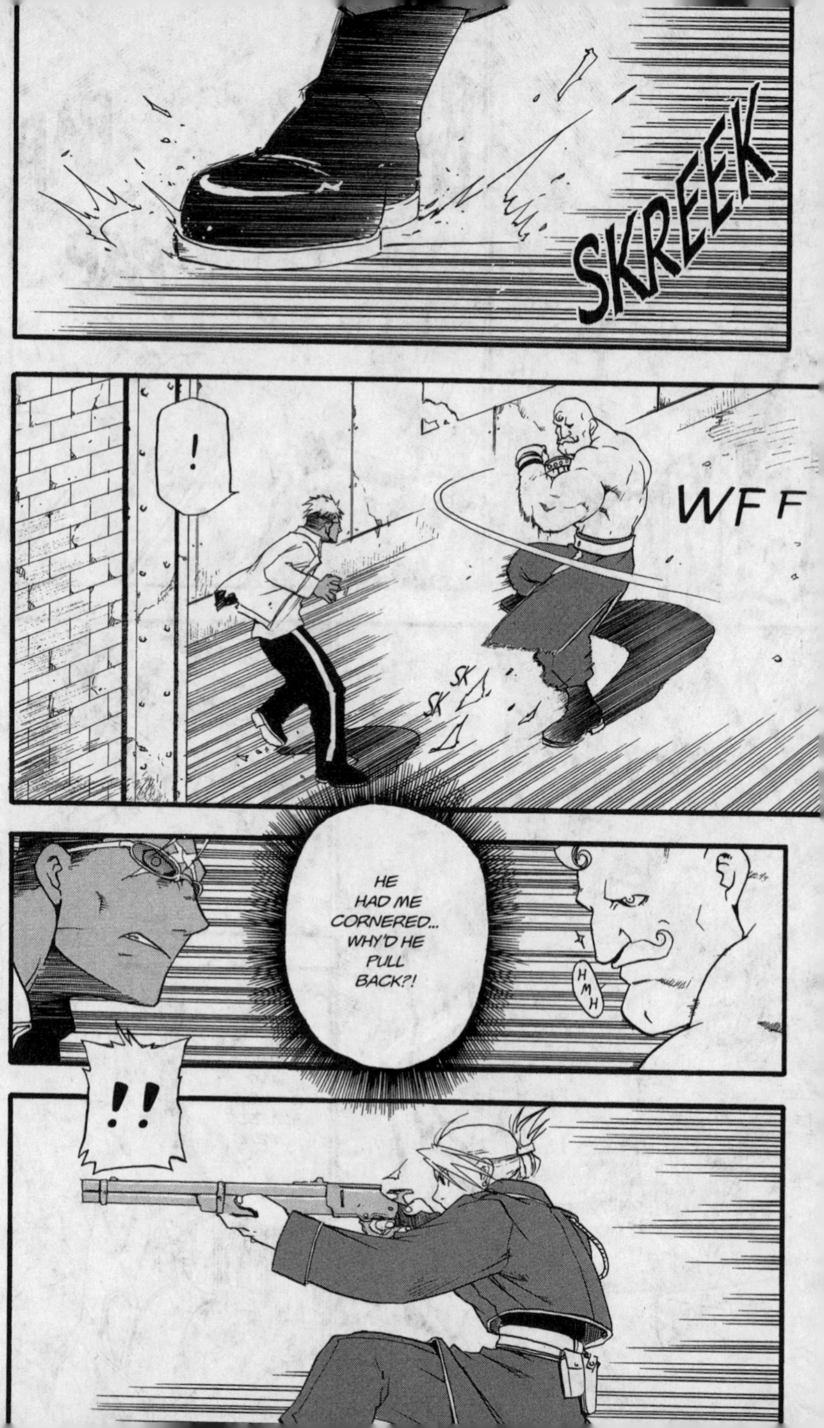
SKREEK
WFF
SK SK
!
H M H
HE HAD ME CORNERED... WHY'D HE PULL BACK?!
!!

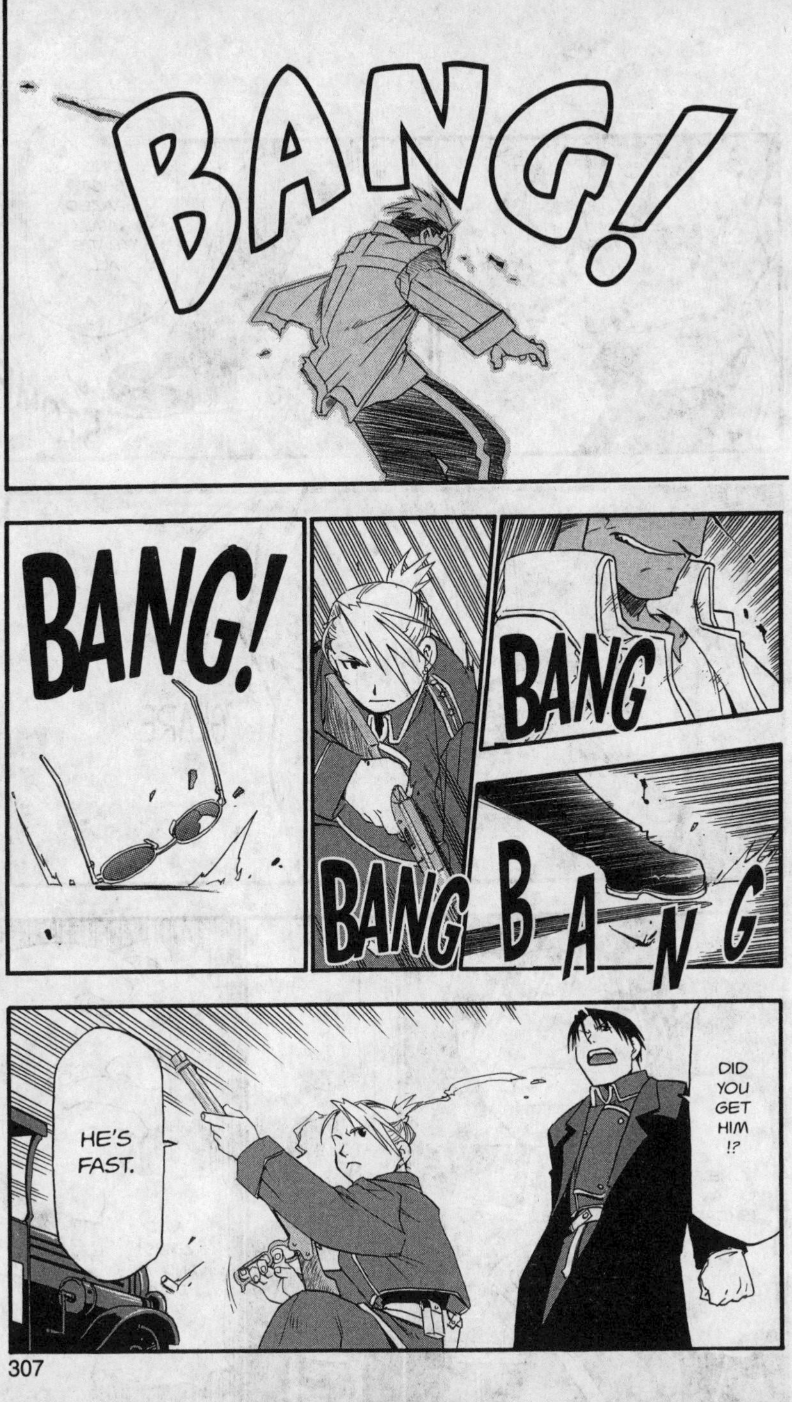
BANG!
BANG
BANG
BANG
BANG!
DID YOU GET HIM !?
HE'S FAST.

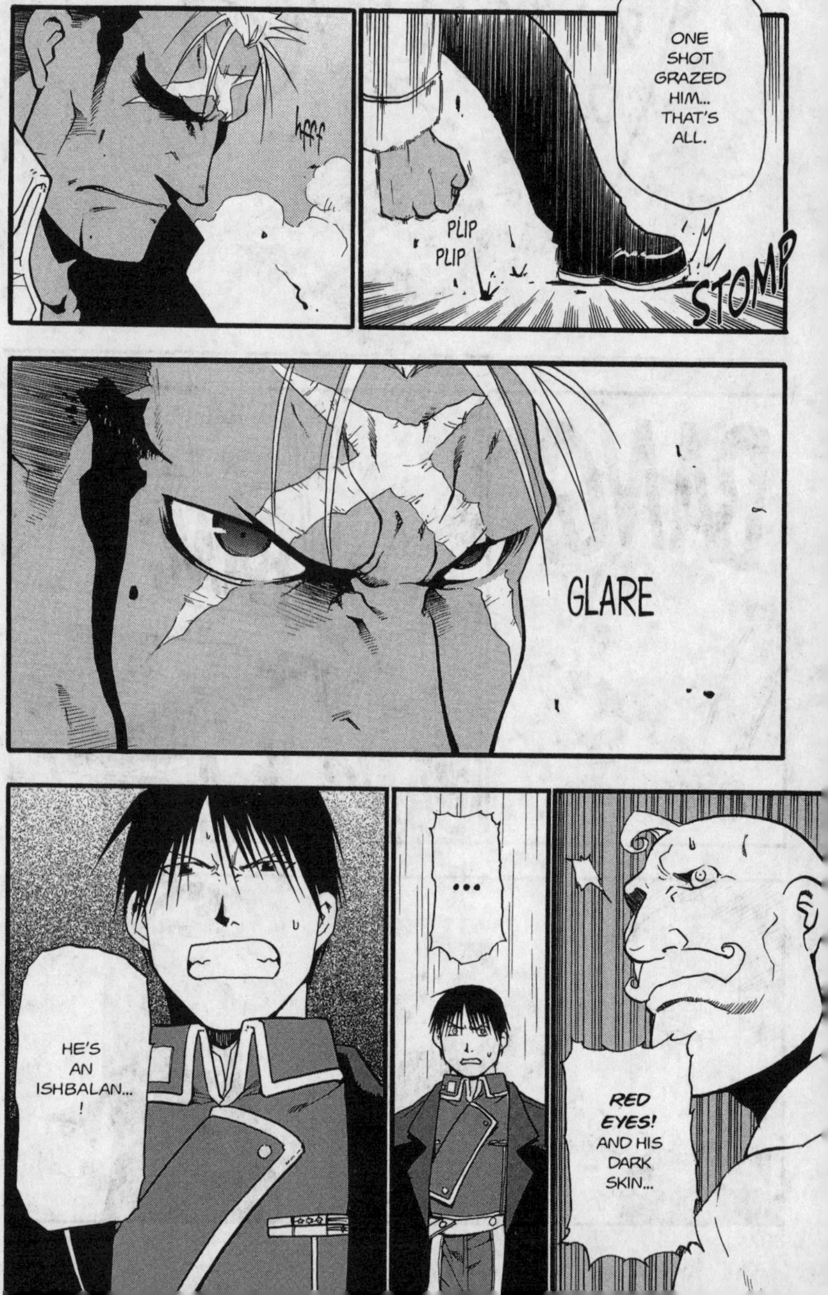
ONE SHOT GRAZED HIM... THAT'S ALL.
PLIP PLIP
STOMP
GLARE
RED EYES! AND HIS DARK SKIN...
...
HE'S AN ISHBALAN... !

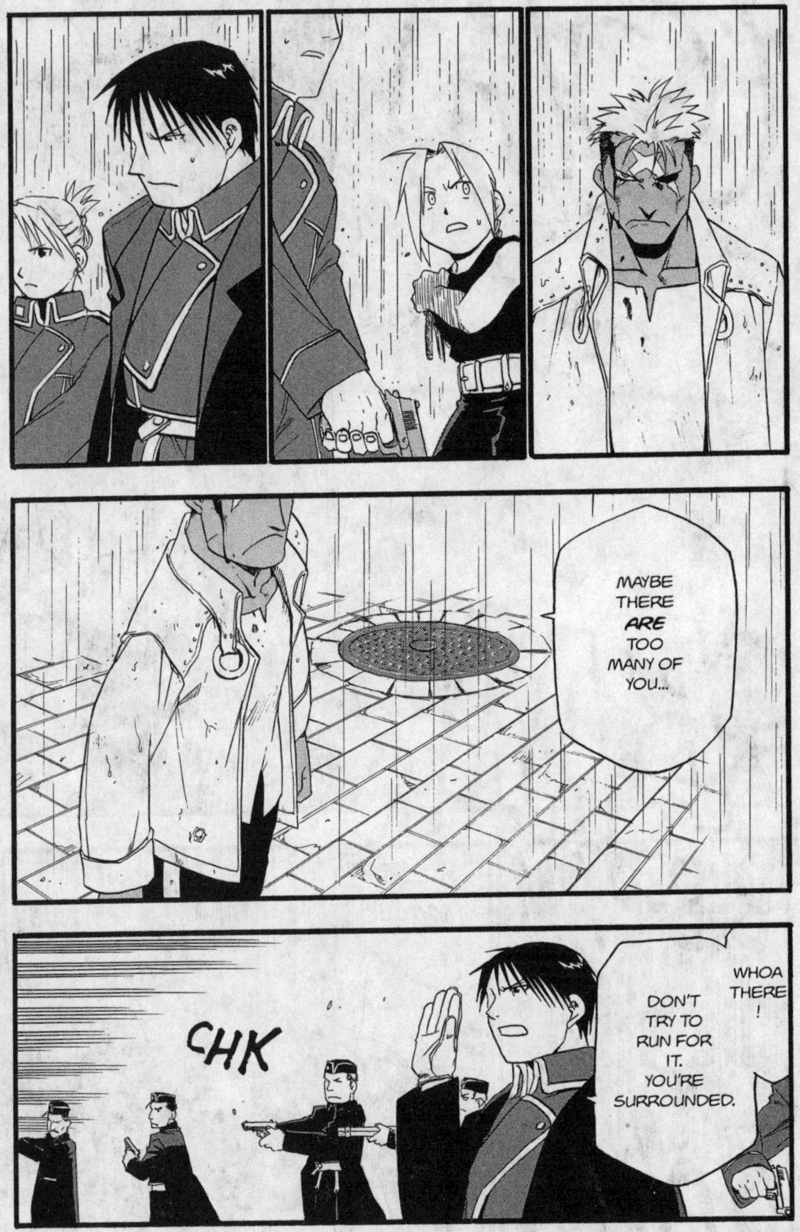
MAYBE THERE ARE TOO MANY OF YOU...
WHOA THERE!
DON'T TRY TO RUN FOR IT. YOU'RE SURROUNDED.
CHK

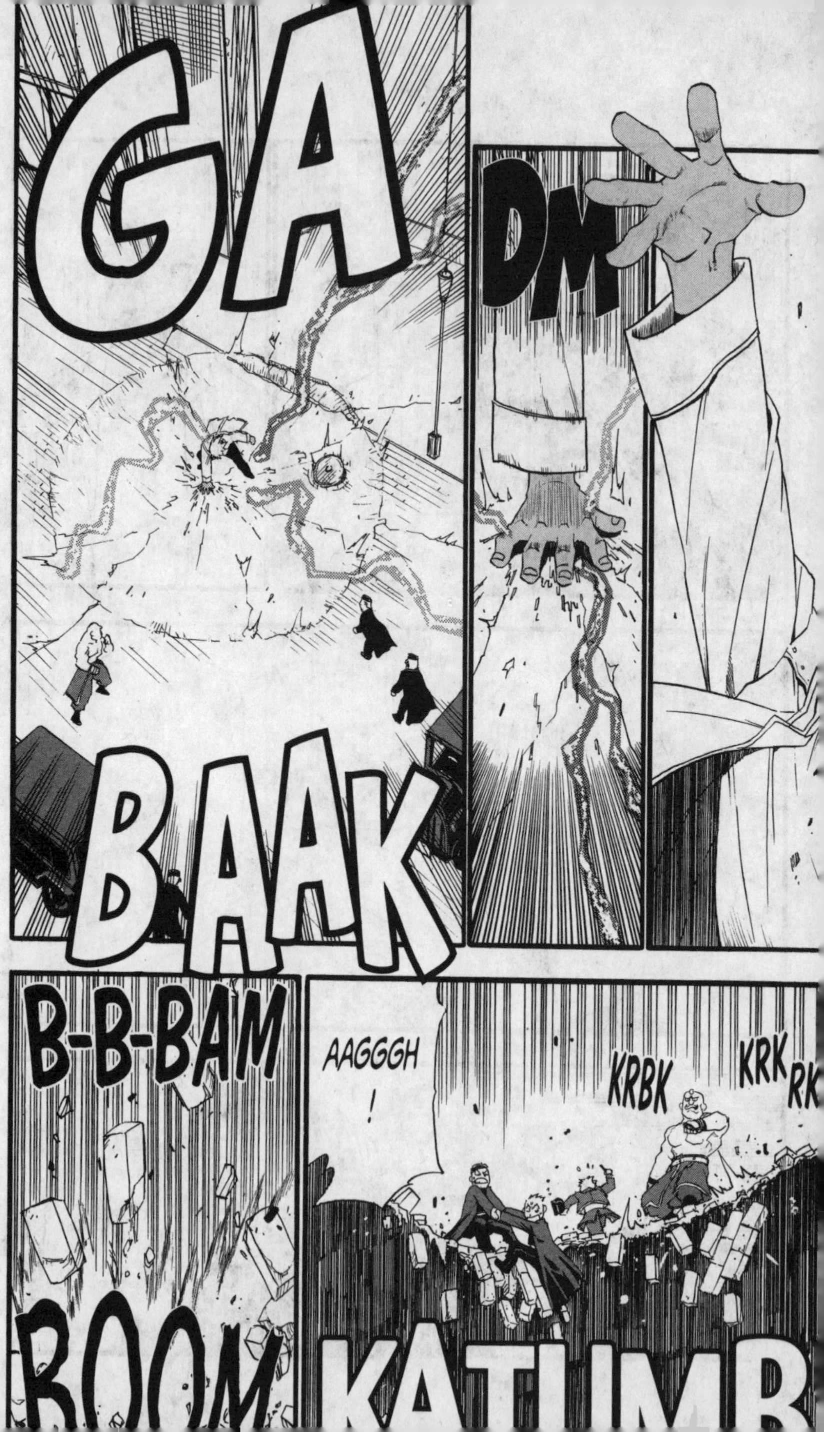
DM
GA
BAAK
KRK RK
KRBK
AAGGGH!
KATUMB
B-B-BAM
BOOM

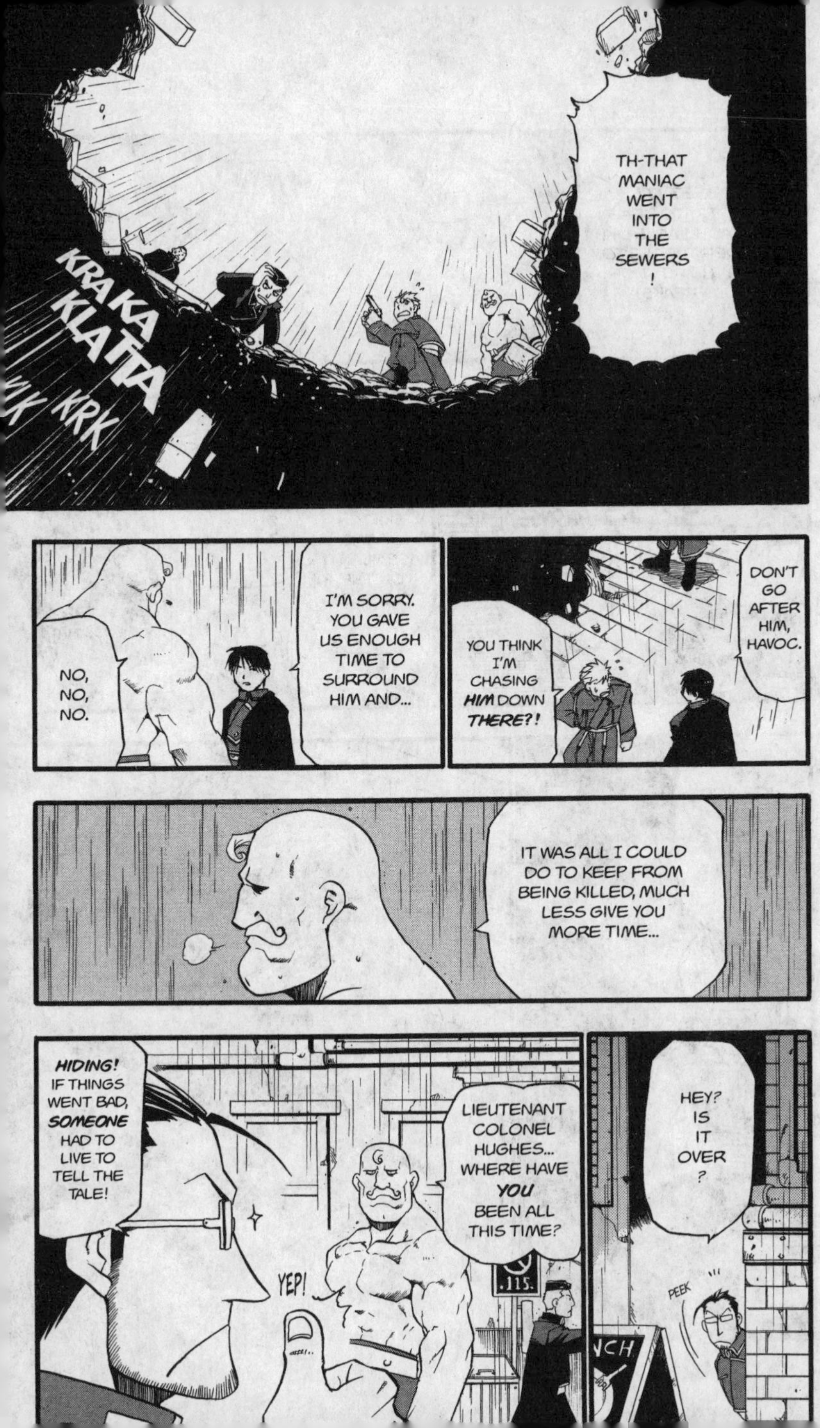
TH-THAT MANIAC WENT INTO THE SEWERS!
KRA KA KLATTA
KRK
DON'T GO AFTER HIM, HAVOC.
YOU THINK I'M CHASING HIM DOWN THERE?!
I'M SORRY. YOU GAVE US ENOUGH TIME TO SURROUND HIM AND...
NO, NO, NO.
IT WAS ALL I COULD DO TO KEEP FROM BEING KILLED, MUCH LESS GIVE YOU MORE TIME...
HEY? IS IT OVER?
PEEK
LIEUTENANT COLONEL HUGHES... WHERE HAVE YOU BEEN ALL THIS TIME?
HIDING! IF THINGS WENT BAD, SOMEONE HAD TO LIVE TO TELL THE TALE!
YEP!

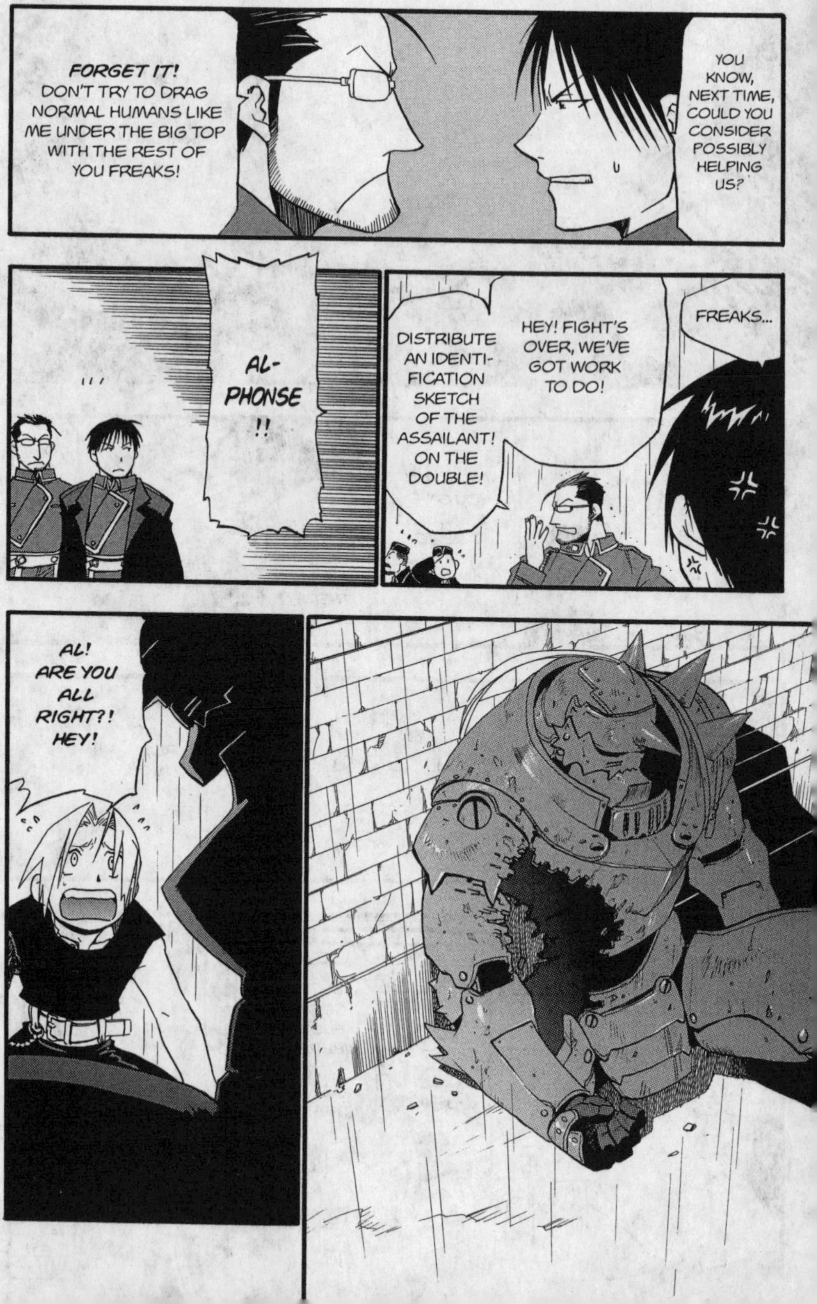
YOU KNOW, NEXT TIME, COULD YOU CONSIDER POSSIBLY HELPING US?
FORGET IT! DON'T TRY TO DRAG NORMAL HUMANS LIKE ME UNDER THE BIG TOP WITH THE REST OF YOU FREAKS!
FREAKS...
HEY! FIGHT'S OVER, WE'VE GOT WORK TO DO!
DISTRIBUTE AN IDENTI-FICATION SKETCH OF THE ASSAILANT! ON THE DOUBLE!
AL-PHONSE!!
AL! ARE YOU ALL RIGHT?! HEY!

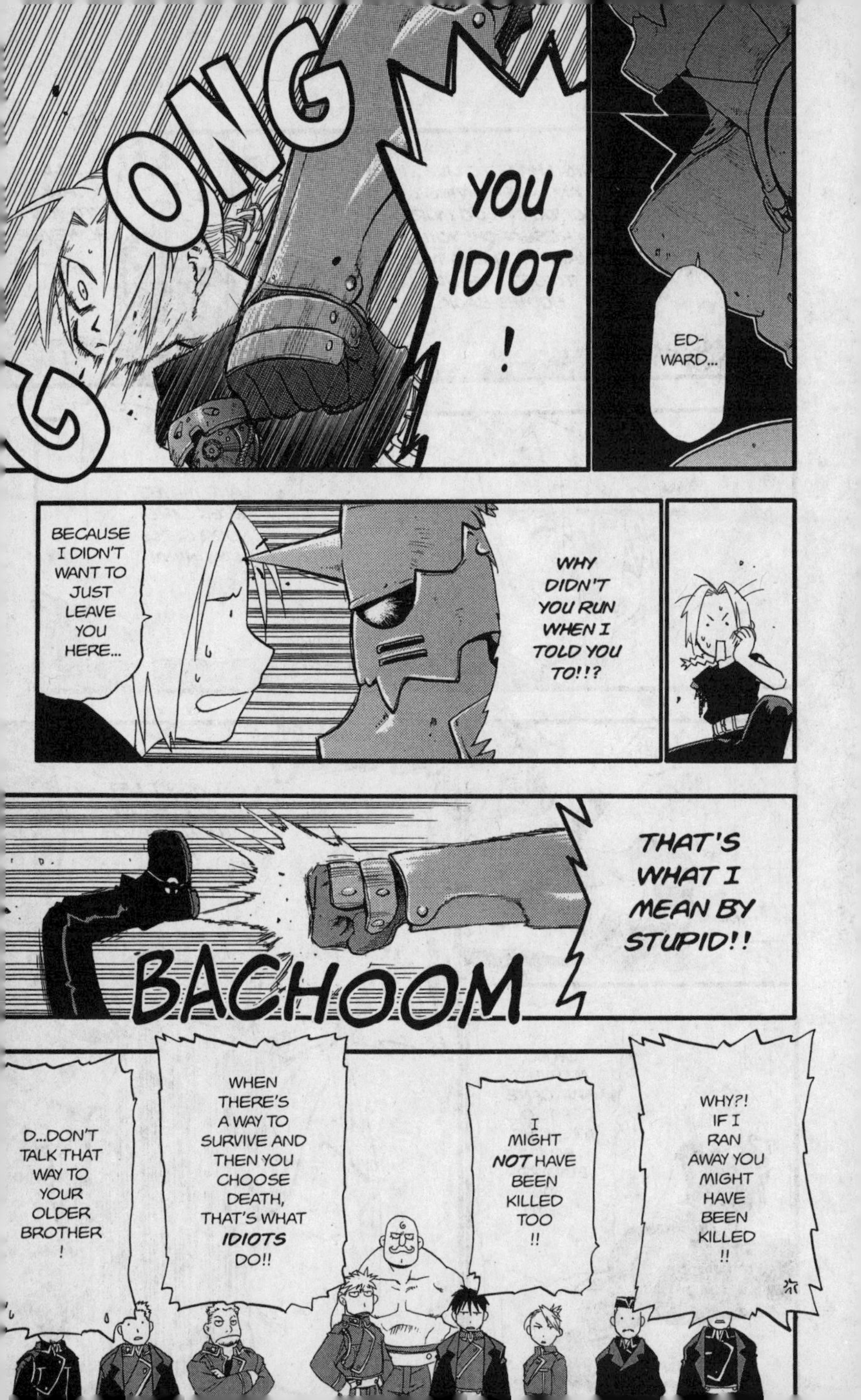
ED-WARD...
GONG
YOU IDIOT!
WHY DIDN'T YOU RUN WHEN I TOLD YOU TO!!?
BECAUSE I DIDN'T WANT TO JUST LEAVE YOU HERE...
THAT'S WHAT I MEAN BY STUPID!!
BACHOOM
WHY?! IF I RAN AWAY YOU MIGHT HAVE BEEN KILLED!!
I MIGHT **NOT** HAVE BEEN KILLED TOO!!
WHEN THERE'S A WAY TO SURVIVE AND THEN YOU CHOOSE DEATH, THAT'S WHAT **IDIOTS** DO!!
D...DON'T TALK THAT WAY TO YOUR OLDER BROTHER!

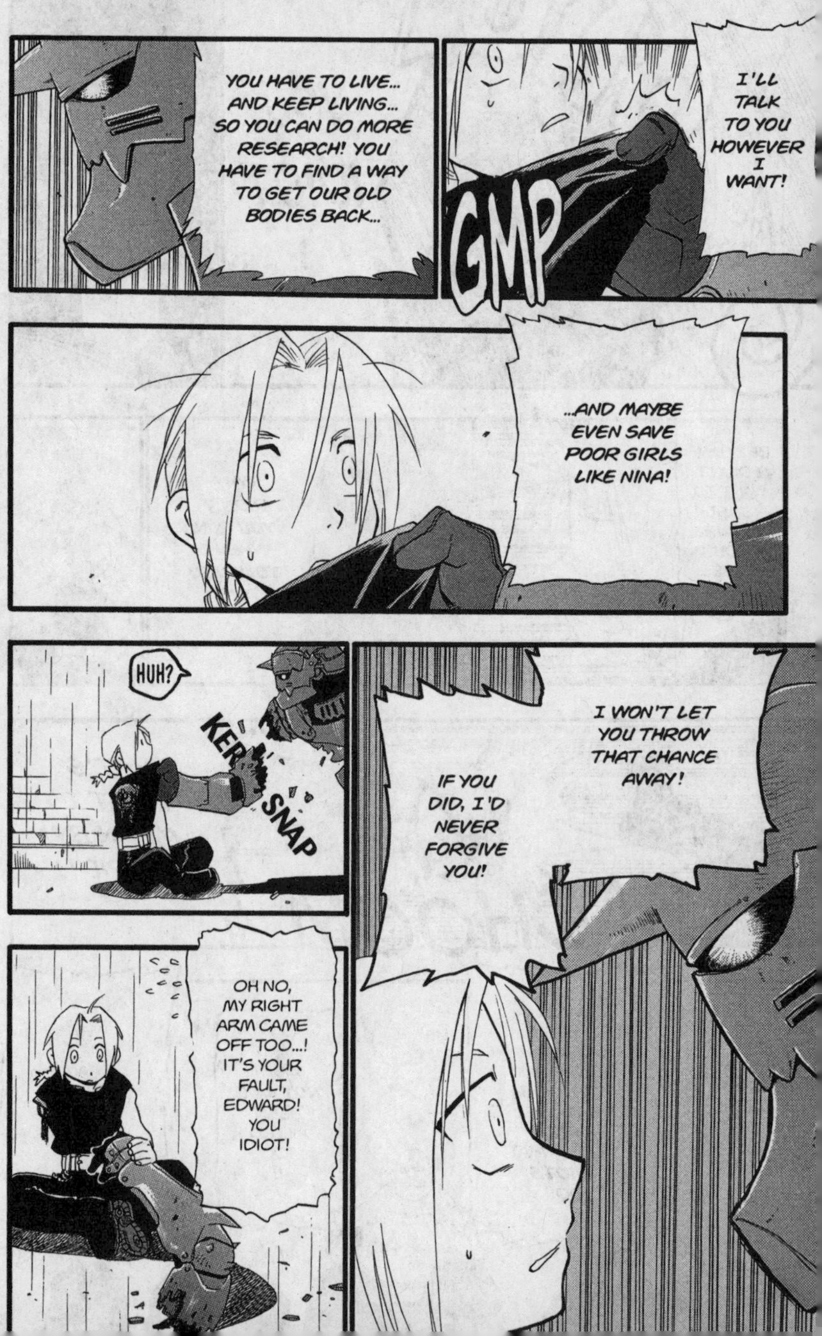
GMP
I'LL TALK TO YOU HOWEVER I WANT!
YOU HAVE TO LIVE... AND KEEP LIVING... SO YOU CAN DO MORE RESEARCH! YOU HAVE TO FIND A WAY TO GET OUR OLD BODIES BACK...
...AND MAYBE EVEN SAVE POOR GIRLS LIKE NINA!
I WON'T LET YOU THROW THAT CHANCE AWAY!
IF YOU DID, I'D NEVER FORGIVE YOU!
HUH?
KER SNAP
OH NO, MY RIGHT ARM CAME OFF TOO...! IT'S YOUR FAULT, EDWARD! YOU IDIOT!

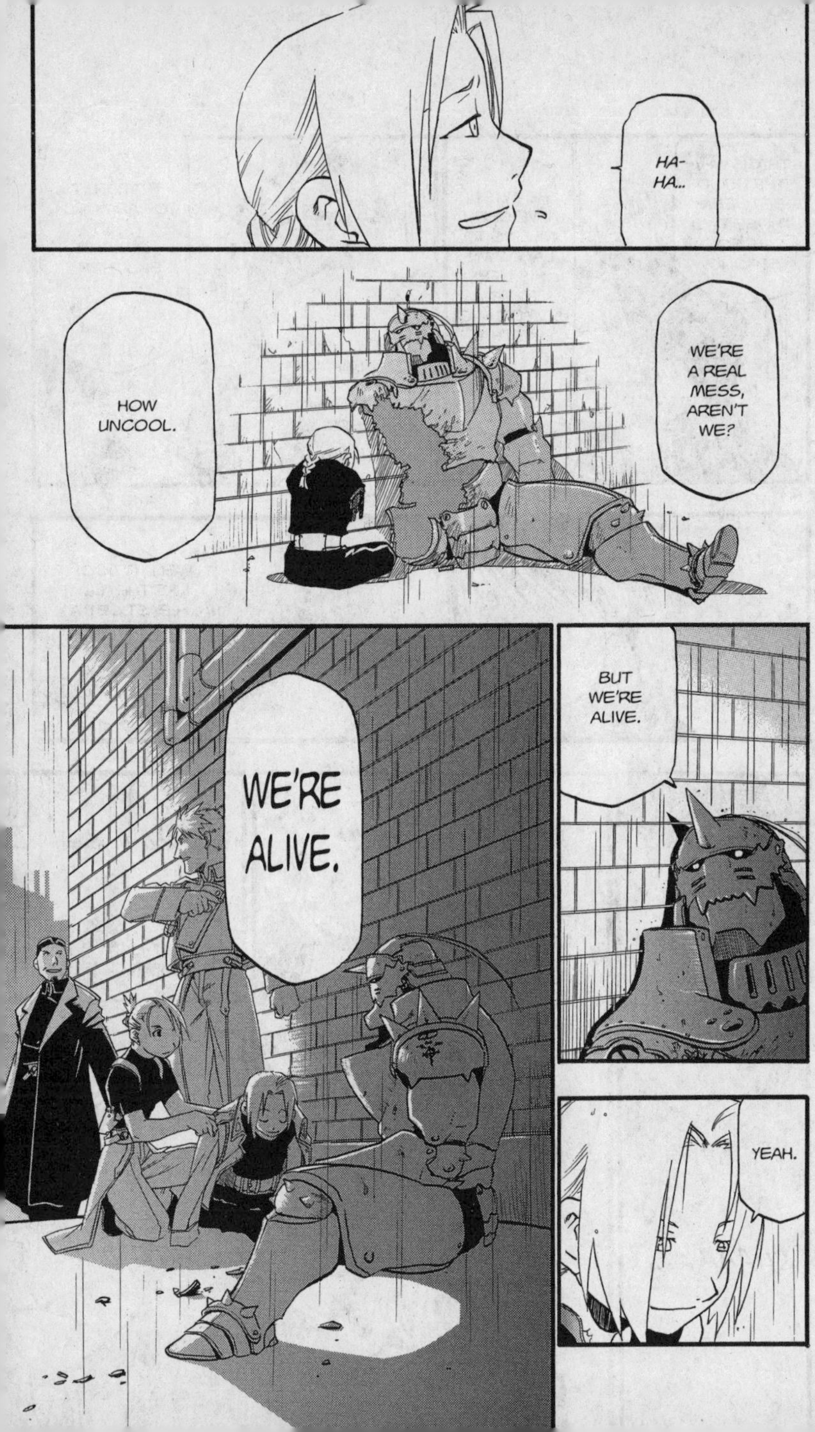
HA-HA...
WE'RE A REAL MESS, AREN'T WE?
HOW UNCOOL.
BUT WE'RE ALIVE.
YEAH.
WE'RE ALIVE.

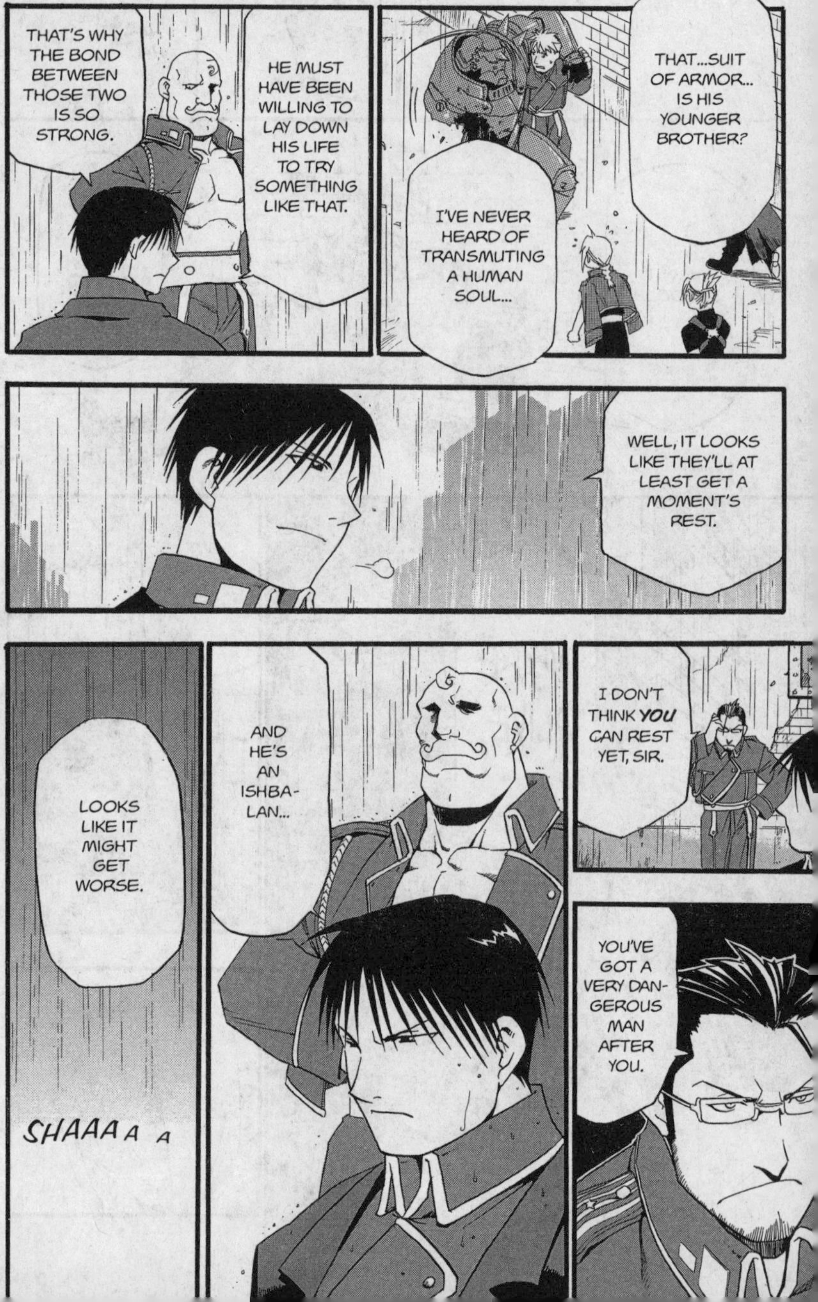
THAT...SUIT OF ARMOR... IS HIS YOUNGER BROTHER?
I'VE NEVER HEARD OF TRANSMUTING A HUMAN SOUL...
HE MUST HAVE BEEN WILLING TO LAY DOWN HIS LIFE TO TRY SOMETHING LIKE THAT.
THAT'S WHY THE BOND BETWEEN THOSE TWO IS SO STRONG.
WELL, IT LOOKS LIKE THEY'LL AT LEAST GET A MOMENT'S REST.
I DON'T THINK ***YOU*** CAN REST YET, SIR.
YOU'VE GOT A VERY DAN-GEROUS MAN AFTER YOU.
AND HE'S AN ISHBA-LAN...
LOOKS LIKE IT MIGHT GET WORSE.
SHAAA A A

THE ISHBALANS ARE A PEOPLE FROM THE EAST, WHO BELIEVE IN ONE GOD, ISHVARA.

EAST CITY
EAST AREA

DUE TO RELIGIOUS DIFFERENCES, THEY'D ALWAYS BEEN IN CONFLICT WITH THE CENTRAL GOVERNMENT...

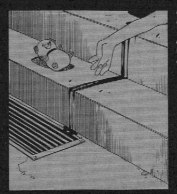

BUT THIRTEEN YEARS AGO, WHEN AN ARMY OFFICER ACCIDENTALLY SHOT AN ISHBALAN CHILD, THE INCIDENT EXPLODED INTO CIVIL WAR.

RIOT LED TO RIOT, AND SOON THE FIRES OF CIVIL WAR SPREAD THROUGHOUT THE ENTIRE EAST AREA. AFTER SEVEN FRUSTRATING YEARS, THE MILITARY COMMANDERS TOOK A NEW TACTIC...

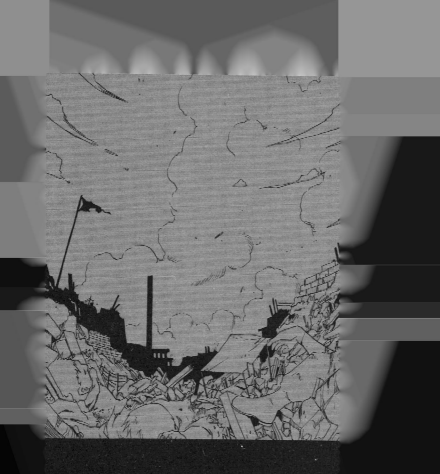

THEY WERE
RECRUITED
AS HUMAN
WEAPONS.
IT WAS AN
OPPORTUNITY
TO TEST THEIR
SUITABILITY
FOR WAR.

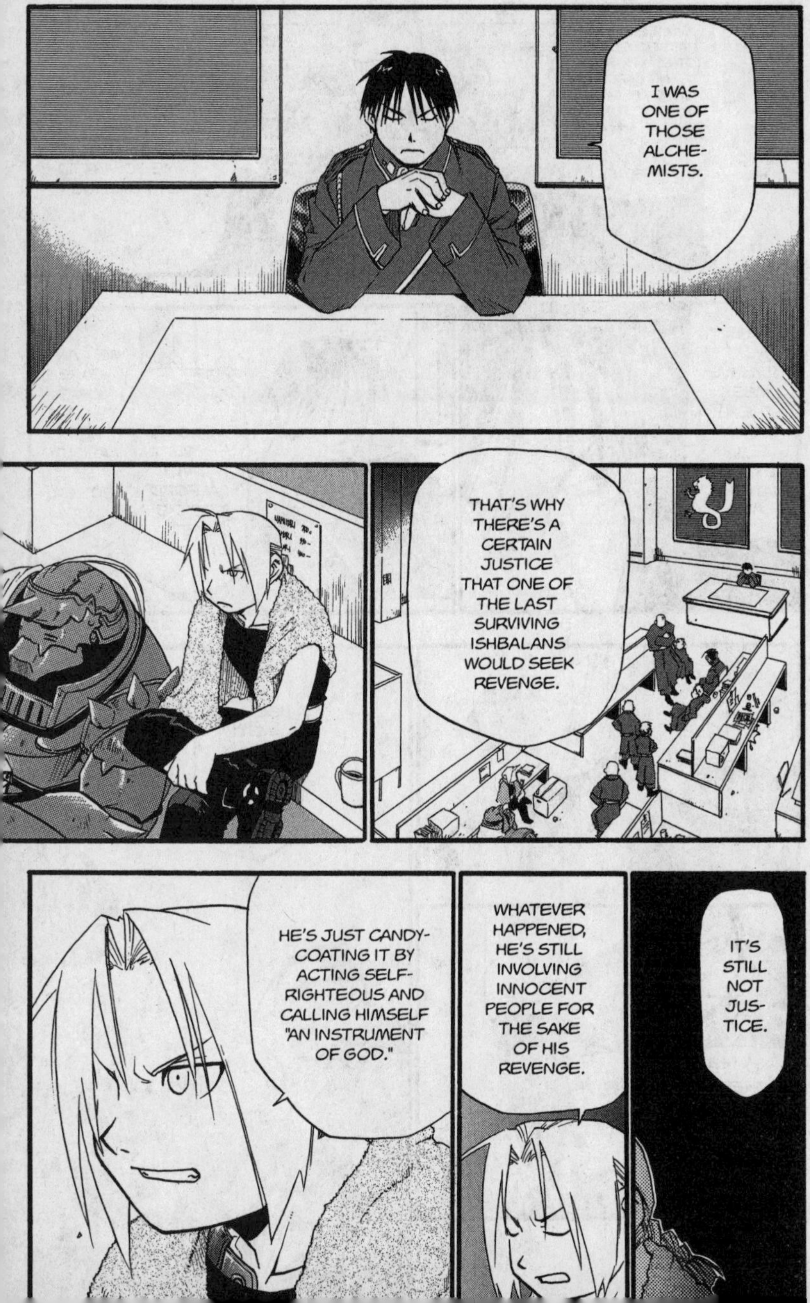
I WAS ONE OF THOSE ALCHEMISTS.
THAT'S WHY THERE'S A CERTAIN JUSTICE THAT ONE OF THE LAST SURVIVING ISHBALANS WOULD SEEK REVENGE.
IT'S STILL NOT JUSTICE.
WHATEVER HAPPENED, HE'S STILL INVOLVING INNOCENT PEOPLE FOR THE SAKE OF HIS REVENGE.
HE'S JUST CANDY-COATING IT BY ACTING SELF-RIGHTEOUS AND CALLING HIMSELF "AN INSTRUMENT OF GOD."

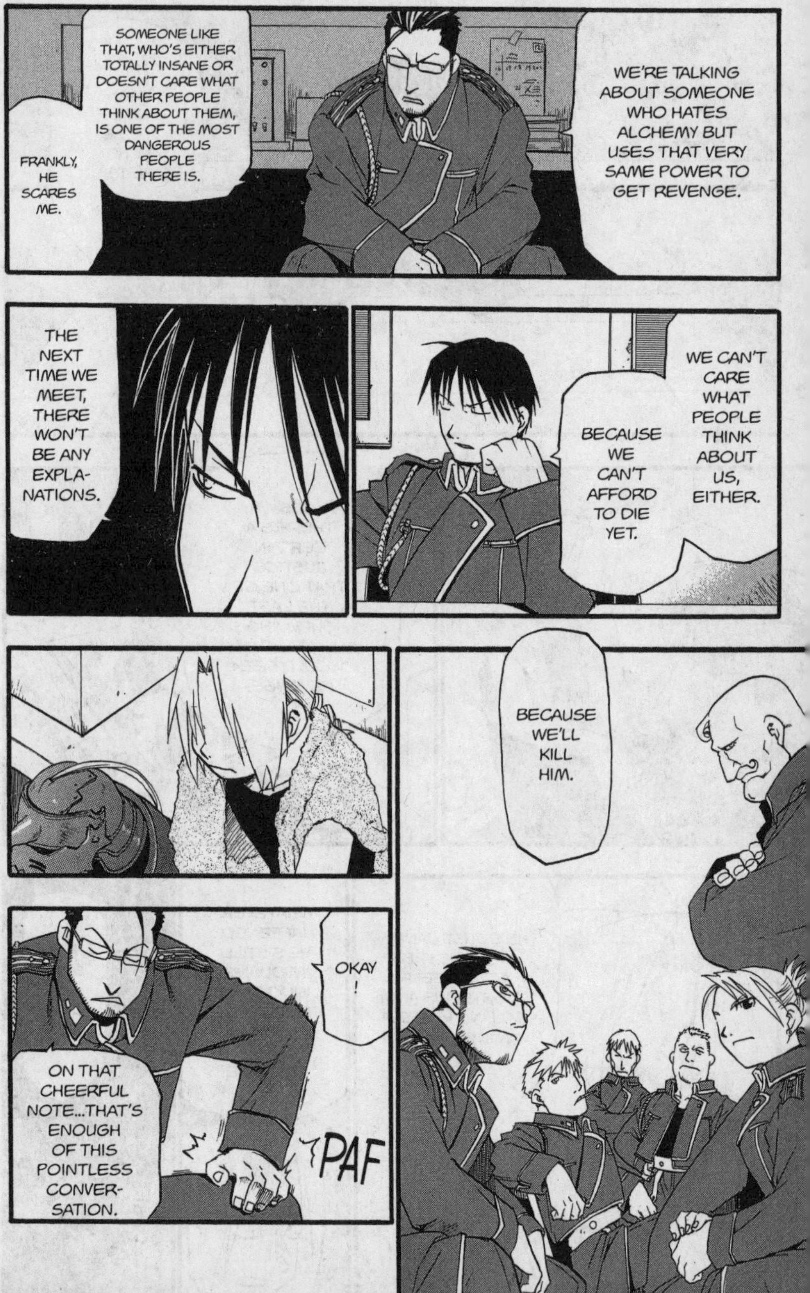
WE'RE TALKING ABOUT SOMEONE WHO HATES ALCHEMY BUT USES THAT VERY SAME POWER TO GET REVENGE.
SOMEONE LIKE THAT, WHO'S EITHER TOTALLY INSANE OR DOESN'T CARE WHAT OTHER PEOPLE THINK ABOUT THEM, IS ONE OF THE MOST DANGEROUS PEOPLE THERE IS.
FRANKLY, HE SCARES ME.
WE CAN'T CARE WHAT PEOPLE THINK ABOUT US, EITHER.
BECAUSE WE CAN'T AFFORD TO DIE YET.
THE NEXT TIME WE MEET, THERE WON'T BE ANY EXPLANATIONS.
BECAUSE WE'LL KILL HIM.
OKAY !
PAF
ON THAT CHEERFUL NOTE...THAT'S ENOUGH OF THIS POINTLESS CONVER-SATION.

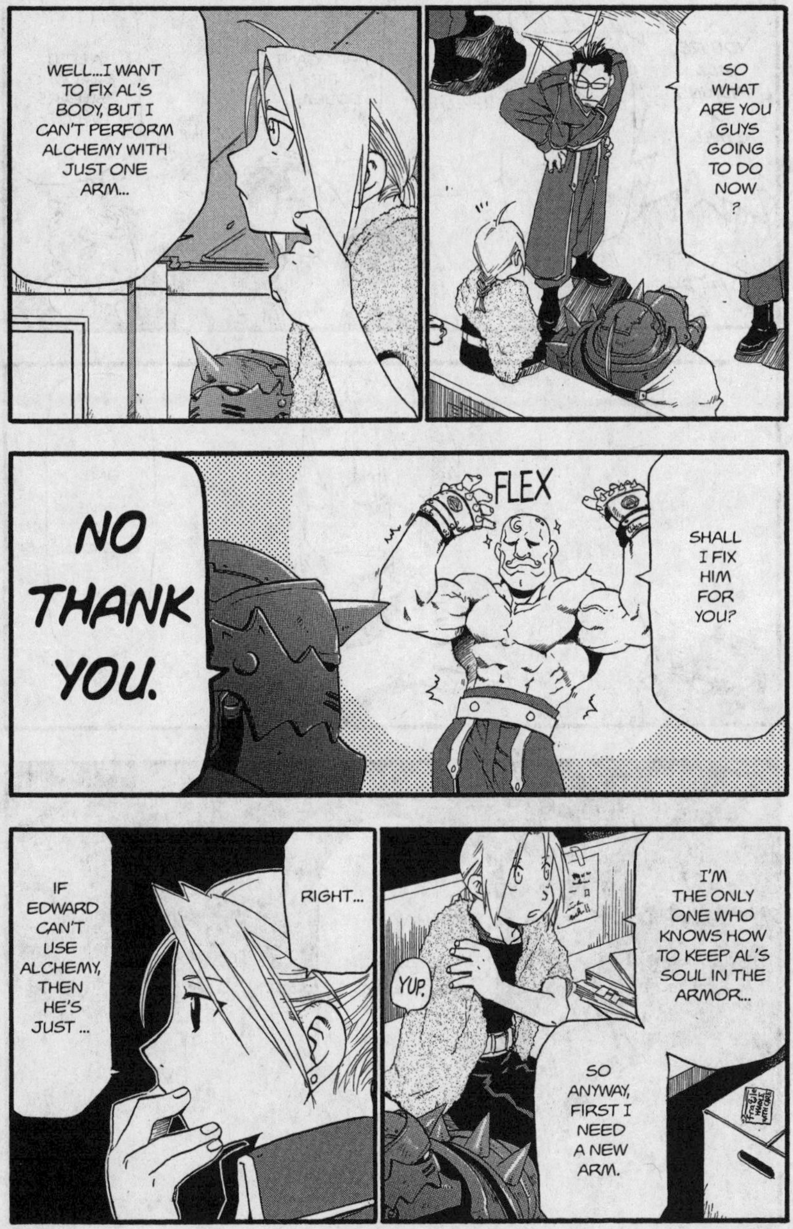
SO WHAT ARE YOU GUYS GOING TO DO NOW?
WELL...I WANT TO FIX AL'S BODY, BUT I CAN'T PERFORM ALCHEMY WITH JUST ONE ARM...
SHALL I FIX HIM FOR YOU?
FLEX
NO THANK YOU.
I'M THE ONLY ONE WHO KNOWS HOW TO KEEP AL'S SOUL IN THE ARMOR...
YUP.
SO ANYWAY, FIRST I NEED A NEW ARM.
RIGHT...
IF EDWARD CAN'T USE ALCHEMY, THEN HE'S JUST ...

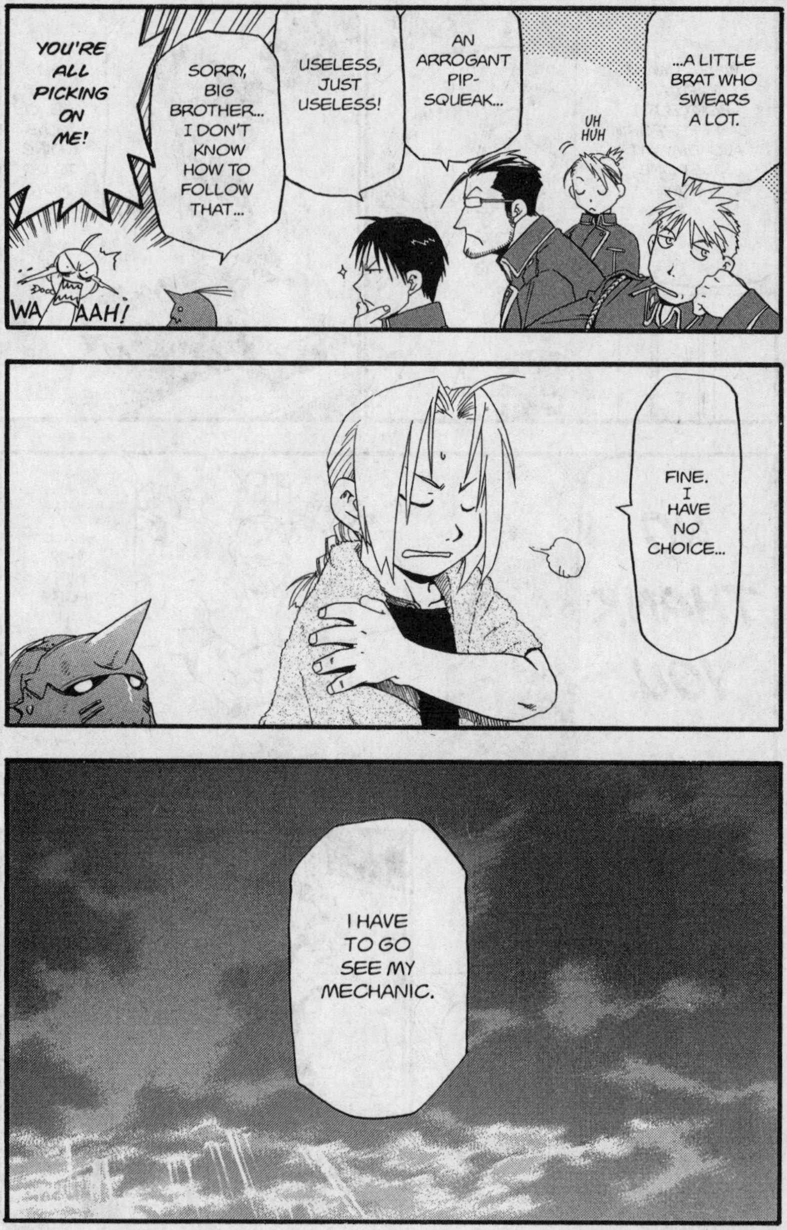
...A LITTLE BRAT WHO SWEARS A LOT.
UH HUH
AN ARROGANT PIP-SQUEAK...
USELESS, JUST USELESS!
SORRY, BIG BROTHER... I DON'T KNOW HOW TO FOLLOW THAT...
YOU'RE ALL PICKING ON ME!
WAAAH!
FINE. I HAVE NO CHOICE...
I HAVE TO GO SEE MY MECHANIC.

FULLMETAL
ALCHEMIST

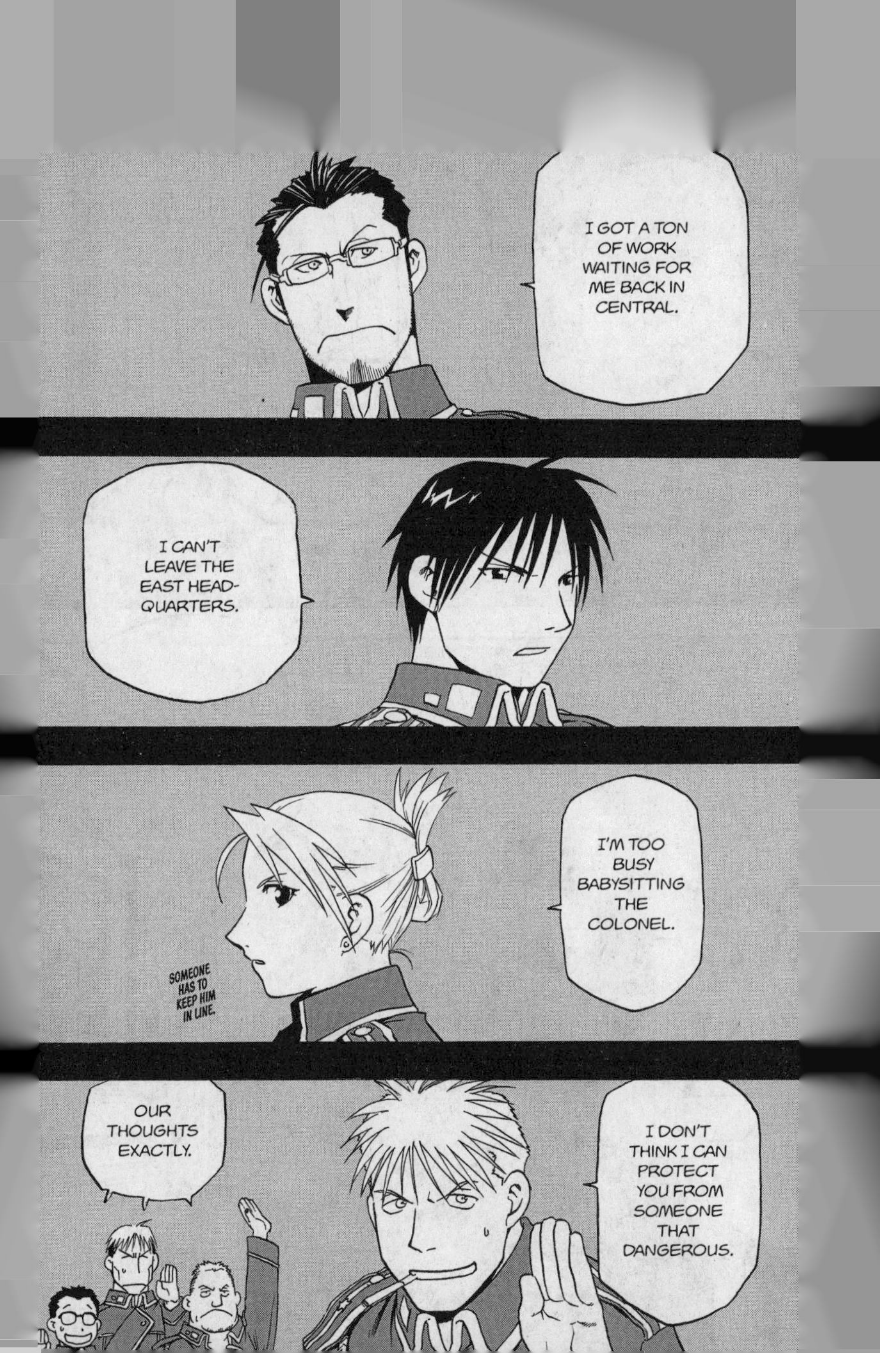
I GOT A TON OF WORK WAITING FOR ME BACK IN CENTRAL.
I CAN'T LEAVE THE EAST HEAD-QUARTERS.
I'M TOO BUSY BABYSITTING THE COLONEL.
SOMEONE HAS TO KEEP HIM IN LINE.
I DON'T THINK I CAN PROTECT YOU FROM SOMEONE THAT DANGEROUS.
OUR THOUGHTS EXACTLY.

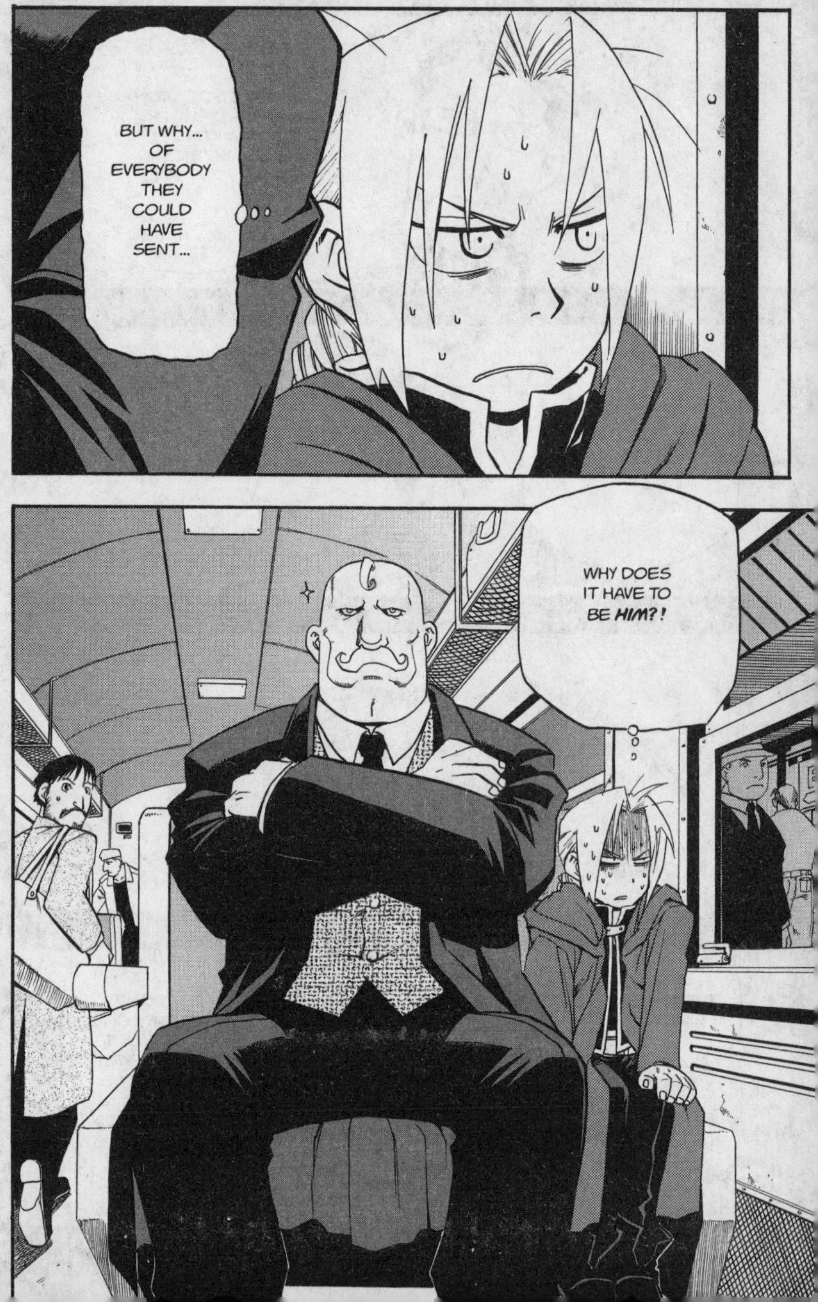
BUT WHY... OF EVERYBODY THEY COULD HAVE SENT...
WHY DOES IT HAVE TO BE *HIM*?!

Chapter 8: The Road of Hope

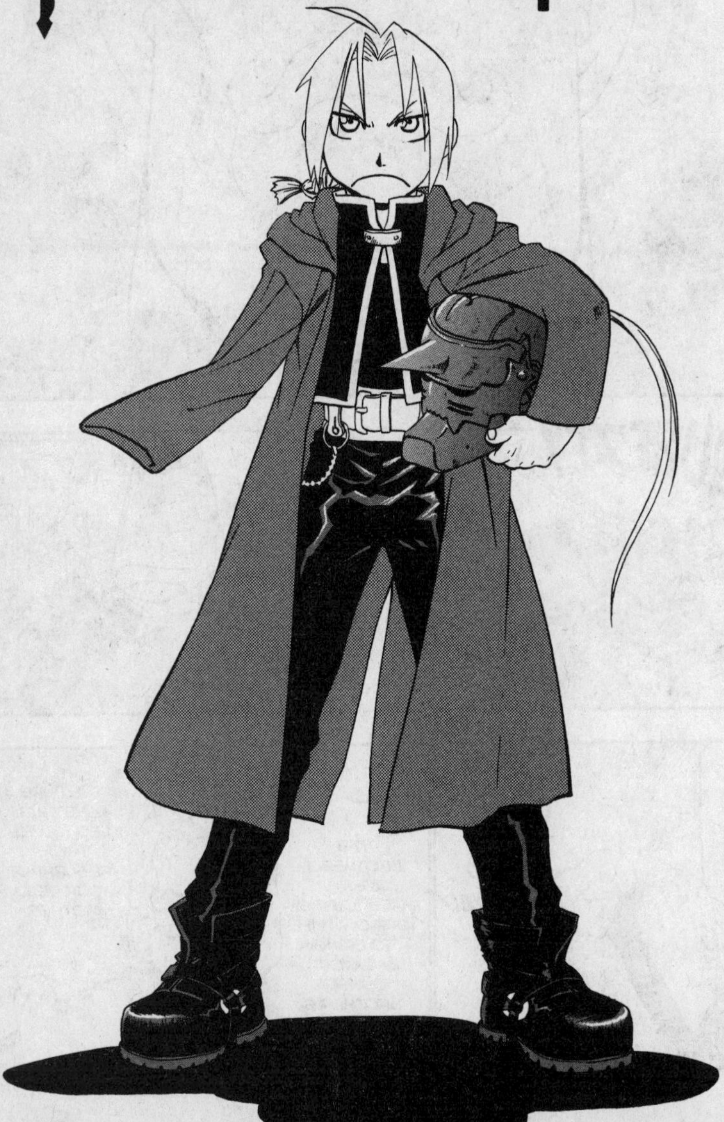

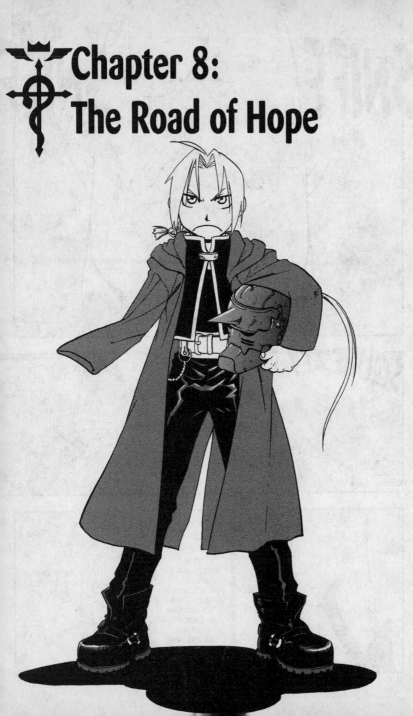

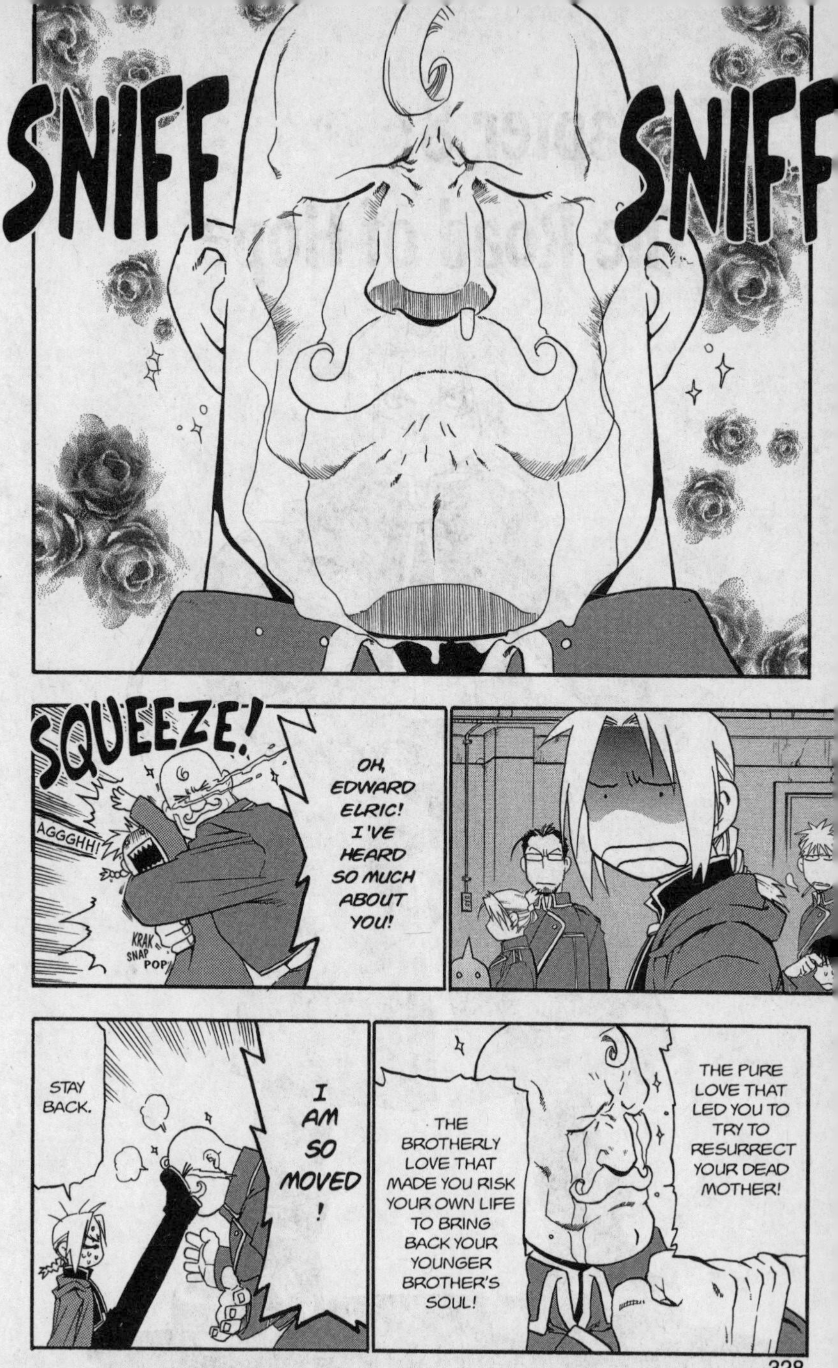
SNIFF
SNIFF
SQUEEZE!
OH, EDWARD ELRIC! I'VE HEARD SO MUCH ABOUT YOU!
AGGGHH!
KRAK
SNAP
POP
THE PURE LOVE THAT LED YOU TO TRY TO RESURRECT YOUR DEAD MOTHER!
THE BROTHERLY LOVE THAT MADE YOU RISK YOUR OWN LIFE TO BRING BACK YOUR YOUNGER BROTHER'S SOUL!
I AM SO MOVED!
STAY BACK.

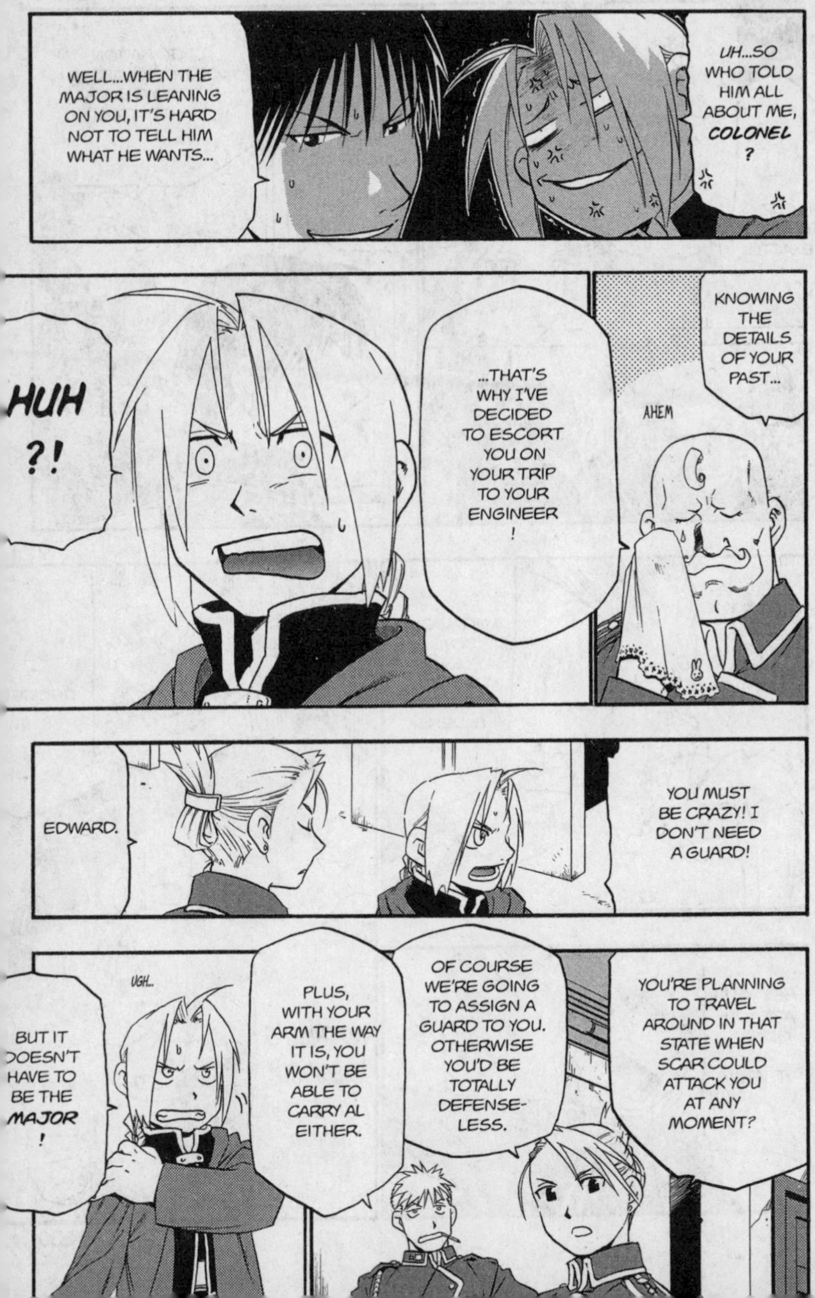
UH...SO WHO TOLD HIM ALL ABOUT ME, COLONEL?
WELL...WHEN THE MAJOR IS LEANING ON YOU, IT'S HARD NOT TO TELL HIM WHAT HE WANTS...
KNOWING THE DETAILS OF YOUR PAST...
AHEM
...THAT'S WHY I'VE DECIDED TO ESCORT YOU ON YOUR TRIP TO YOUR ENGINEER!
HUH?!
YOU MUST BE CRAZY! I DON'T NEED A GUARD!
EDWARD.
YOU'RE PLANNING TO TRAVEL AROUND IN THAT STATE WHEN SCAR COULD ATTACK YOU AT ANY MOMENT?
OF COURSE WE'RE GOING TO ASSIGN A GUARD TO YOU. OTHERWISE YOU'D BE TOTALLY DEFENSE-LESS.
PLUS, WITH YOUR ARM THE WAY IT IS, YOU WON'T BE ABLE TO CARRY AL EITHER.
UGH...
BUT IT DOESN'T HAVE TO BE THE MAJOR!

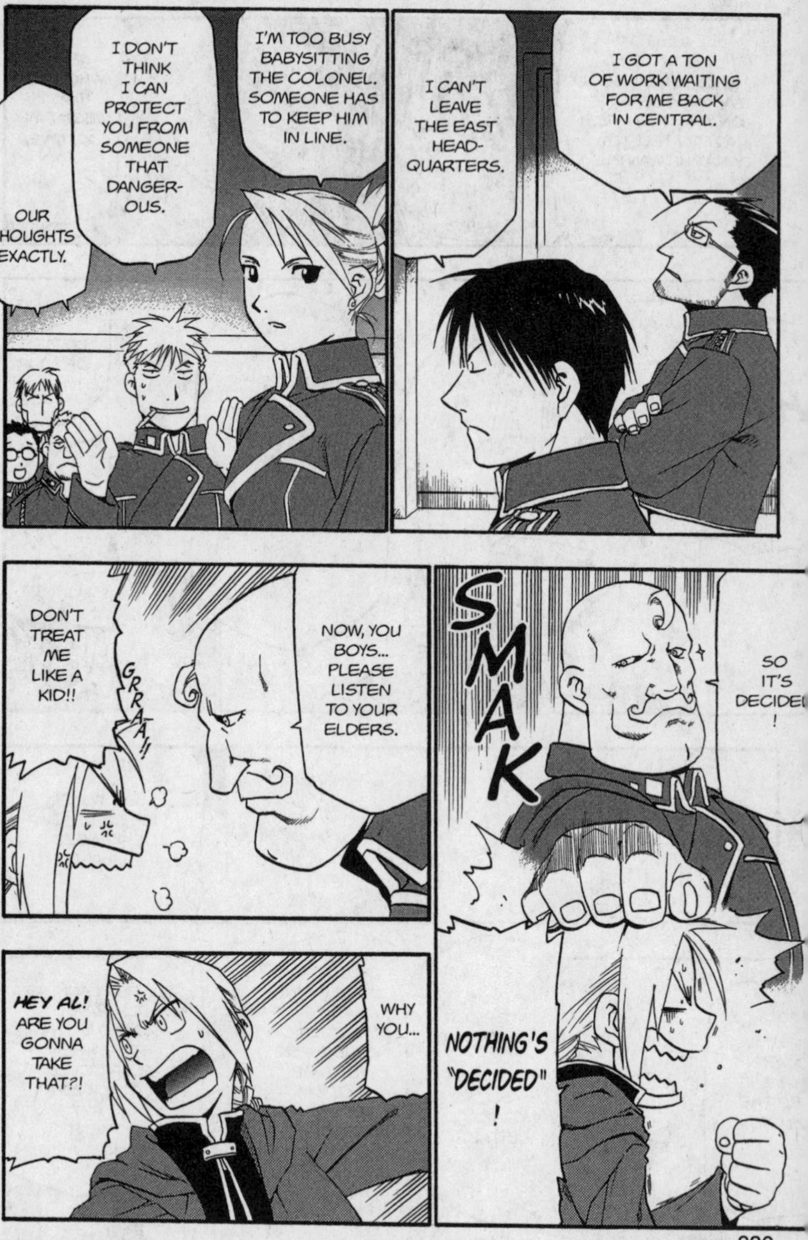

I GOT A TON OF WORK WAITING FOR ME BACK IN CENTRAL.
I CAN'T LEAVE THE EAST HEAD-QUARTERS.
I'M TOO BUSY BABYSITTING THE COLONEL. SOMEONE HAS TO KEEP HIM IN LINE.
I DON'T THINK I CAN PROTECT YOU FROM SOMEONE THAT DANGER-OUS.
OUR THOUGHTS EXACTLY.
SO IT'S DECIDE !
SMAK
NOTHING'S "DECIDED" !
NOW, YOU BOYS... PLEASE LISTEN TO YOUR ELDERS.
DON'T TREAT ME LIKE A KID!!
GRRAA!!
WHY YOU...
HEY AL! ARE YOU GONNA TAKE THAT?!

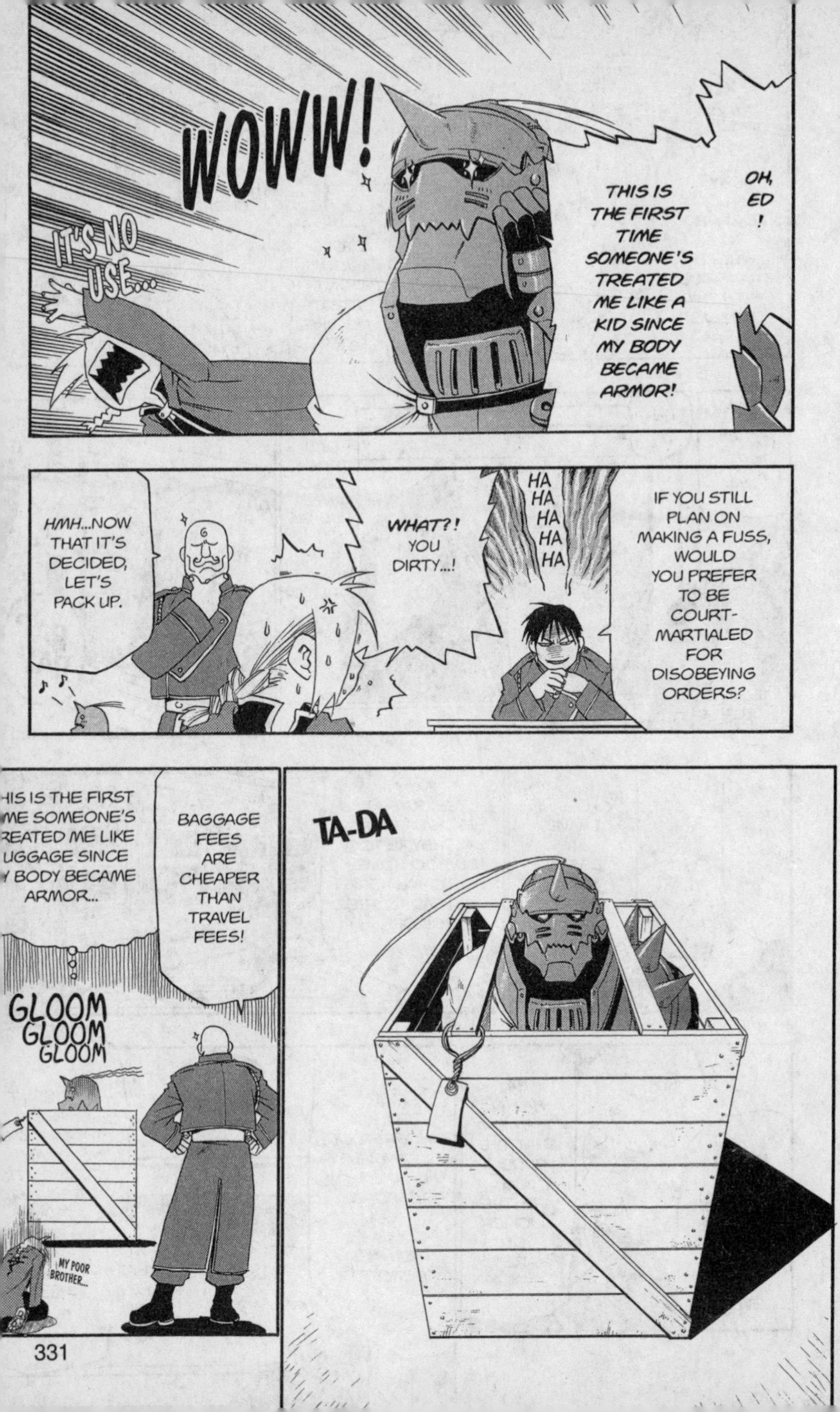
OH, ED!
THIS IS THE FIRST TIME SOMEONE'S TREATED ME LIKE A KID SINCE MY BODY BECAME ARMOR!
WOWW!
IT'S NO USE...
IF YOU STILL PLAN ON MAKING A FUSS, WOULD YOU PREFER TO BE COURT-MARTIALED FOR DISOBEYING ORDERS?
HA HA HA HA HA
WHAT?! YOU DIRTY...!
HMH...NOW THAT IT'S DECIDED, LET'S PACK UP.
TA-DA
BAGGAGE FEES ARE CHEAPER THAN TRAVEL FEES!
HIS IS THE FIRST ME SOMEONE'S REATED ME LIKE UGGAGE SINCE Y BODY BECAME ARMOR...
GLOOM GLOOM GLOOM
MY POOR BROTHER...

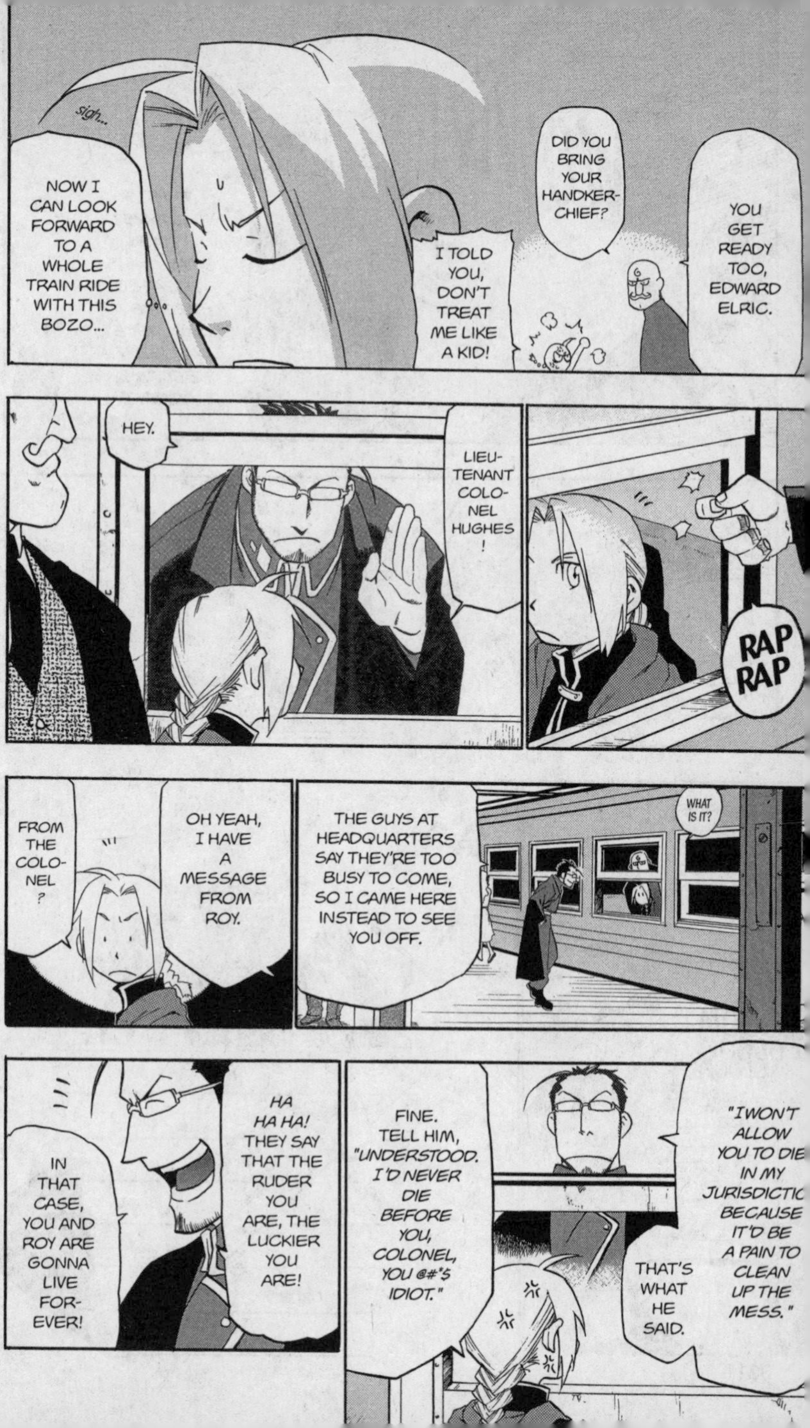
YOU GET READY TOO, EDWARD ELRIC.
DID YOU BRING YOUR HANDKER-CHIEF?
I TOLD YOU, DON'T TREAT ME LIKE A KID!
sigh...
NOW I CAN LOOK FORWARD TO A WHOLE TRAIN RIDE WITH THIS BOZO...
RAP RAP
LIEU-TENANT COLO-NEL HUGHES!
HEY.
WHAT IS IT?
THE GUYS AT HEADQUARTERS SAY THEY'RE TOO BUSY TO COME, SO I CAME HERE INSTEAD TO SEE YOU OFF.
OH YEAH, I HAVE A MESSAGE FROM ROY.
FROM THE COLO-NEL?
"I WON'T ALLOW YOU TO DIE IN MY JURISDICTIO BECAUSE IT'D BE A PAIN TO CLEAN UP THE MESS."
THAT'S WHAT HE SAID.
FINE. TELL HIM, "UNDERSTOOD. I'D NEVER DIE BEFORE YOU, COLONEL, YOU @#*$ IDIOT."
HA HA HA! THEY SAY THAT THE RUDER YOU ARE, THE LUCKIER YOU ARE!
IN THAT CASE, YOU AND ROY ARE GONNA LIVE FOR-EVER!

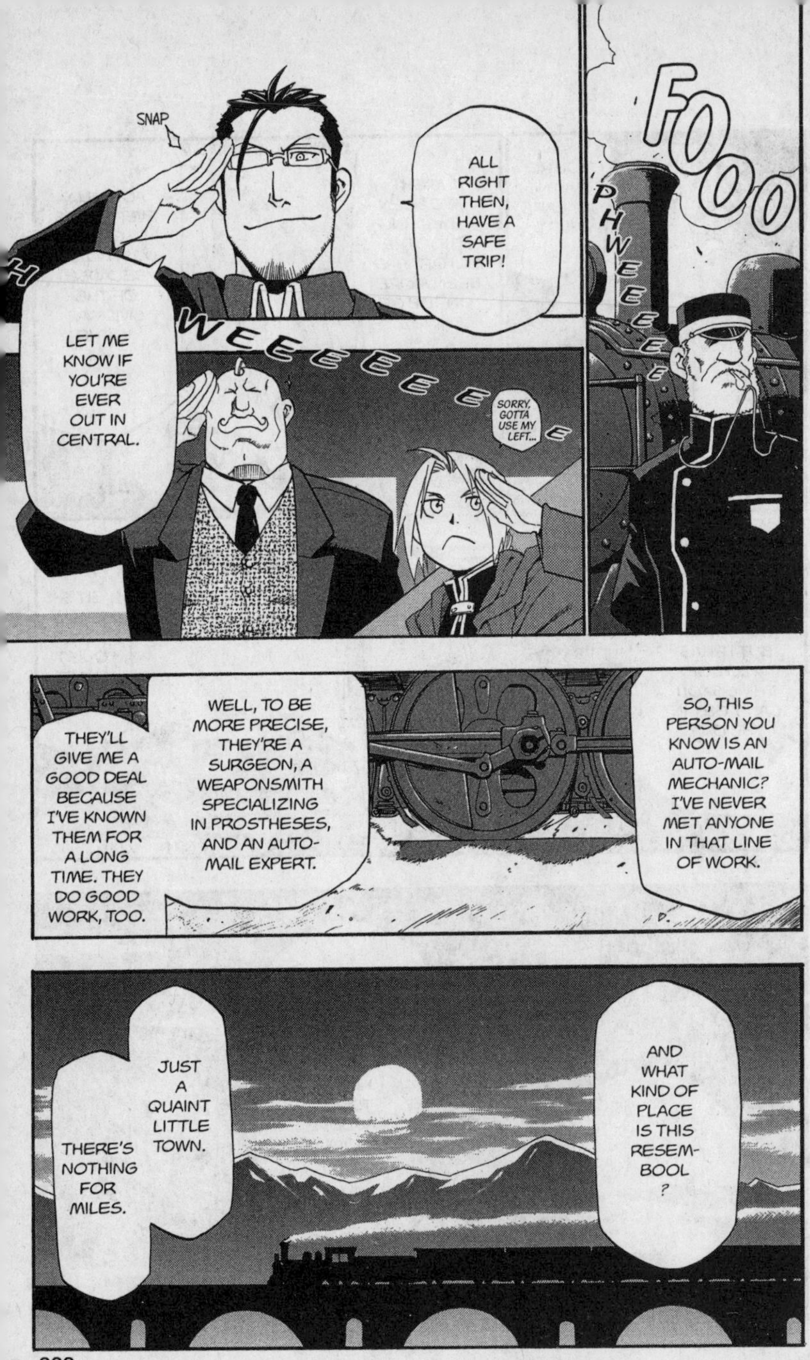
FOOO
PHWEEEEE
SNAP
ALL RIGHT THEN, HAVE A SAFE TRIP!
HWEEEEEEEEEE
LET ME KNOW IF YOU'RE EVER OUT IN CENTRAL.
SORRY, GOTTA USE MY LEFT...
SO, THIS PERSON YOU KNOW IS AN AUTO-MAIL MECHANIC? I'VE NEVER MET ANYONE IN THAT LINE OF WORK.
WELL, TO BE MORE PRECISE, THEY'RE A SURGEON, A WEAPONSMITH SPECIALIZING IN PROSTHESES, AND AN AUTO-MAIL EXPERT.
THEY'LL GIVE ME A GOOD DEAL BECAUSE I'VE KNOWN THEM FOR A LONG TIME. THEY DO GOOD WORK, TOO.
AND WHAT KIND OF PLACE IS THIS RESEMBOOL?
JUST A QUAINT LITTLE TOWN.
THERE'S NOTHING FOR MILES.

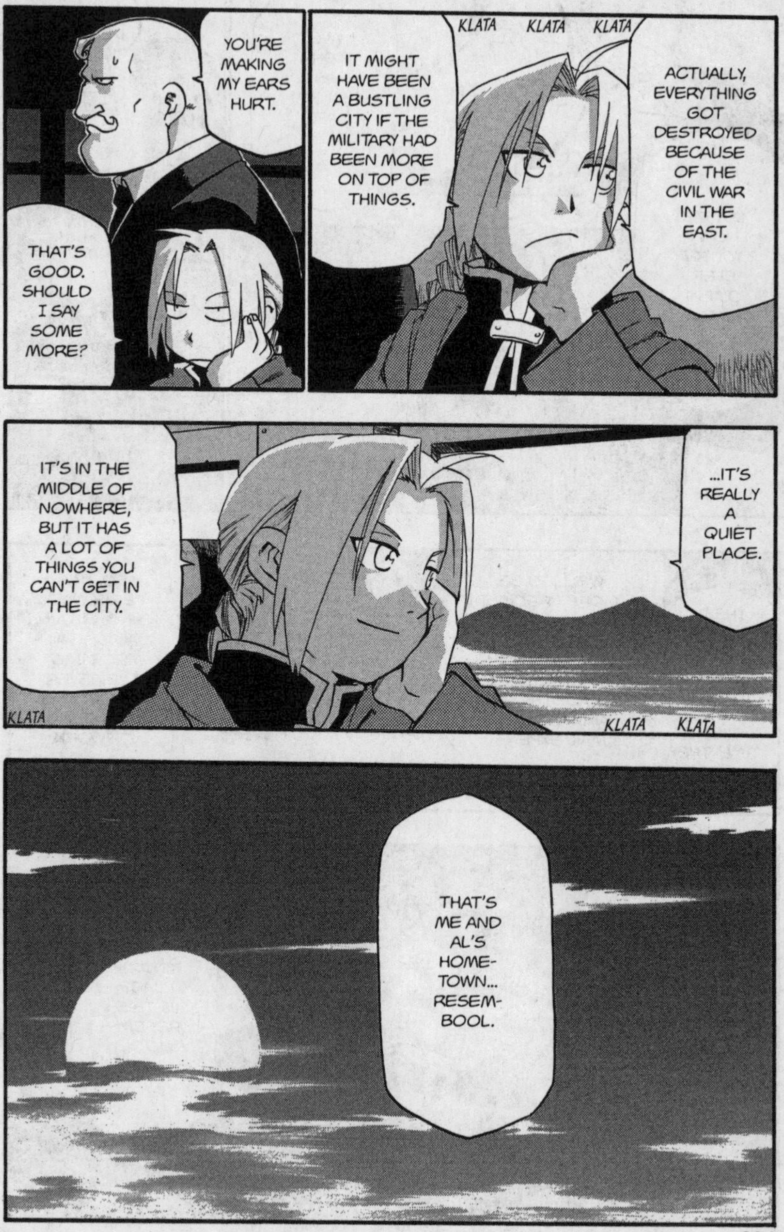
KLATA KLATA KLATA
ACTUALLY, EVERYTHING GOT DESTROYED BECAUSE OF THE CIVIL WAR IN THE EAST.
IT MIGHT HAVE BEEN A BUSTLING CITY IF THE MILITARY HAD BEEN MORE ON TOP OF THINGS.
YOU'RE MAKING MY EARS HURT.
THAT'S GOOD. SHOULD I SAY SOME MORE?
...IT'S REALLY A QUIET PLACE.
IT'S IN THE MIDDLE OF NOWHERE, BUT IT HAS A LOT OF THINGS YOU CAN'T GET IN THE CITY.
KLATA KLATA KLATA
THAT'S ME AND AL'S HOME-TOWN... RESEM-BOOL.

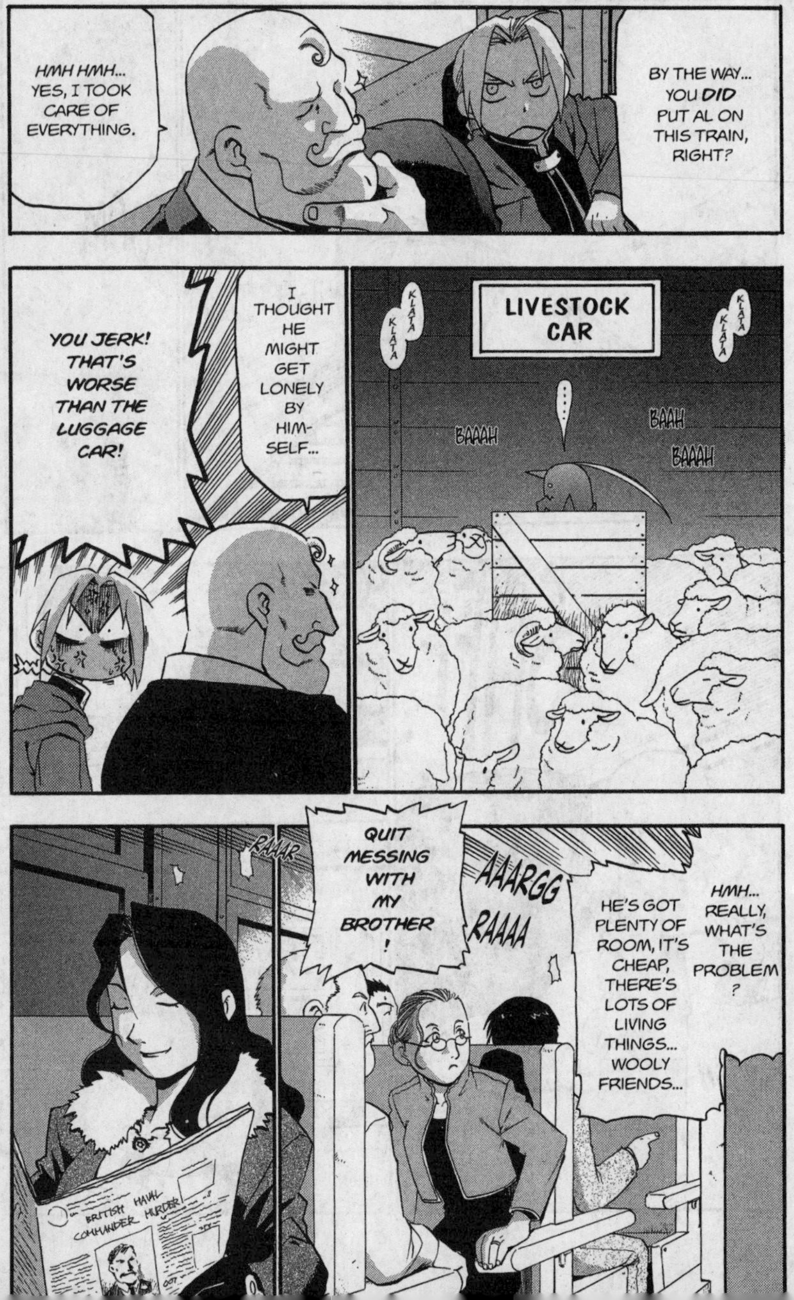
BY THE WAY... YOU DID PUT AL ON THIS TRAIN, RIGHT?
HMH HMH... YES, I TOOK CARE OF EVERYTHING.
LIVESTOCK CAR
KLATA KLATA
KLATA KLATA
...!
BAAH
BAAAH
BAAAH
I THOUGHT HE MIGHT GET LONELY BY HIM-SELF...
YOU JERK! THAT'S WORSE THAN THE LUGGAGE CAR!
HMH... REALLY, WHAT'S THE PROBLEM?
HE'S GOT PLENTY OF ROOM, IT'S CHEAP, THERE'S LOTS OF LIVING THINGS... WOOLY FRIENDS...
AAARGG
RAAAA
QUIT MESSING WITH MY BROTHER!
RAAAR

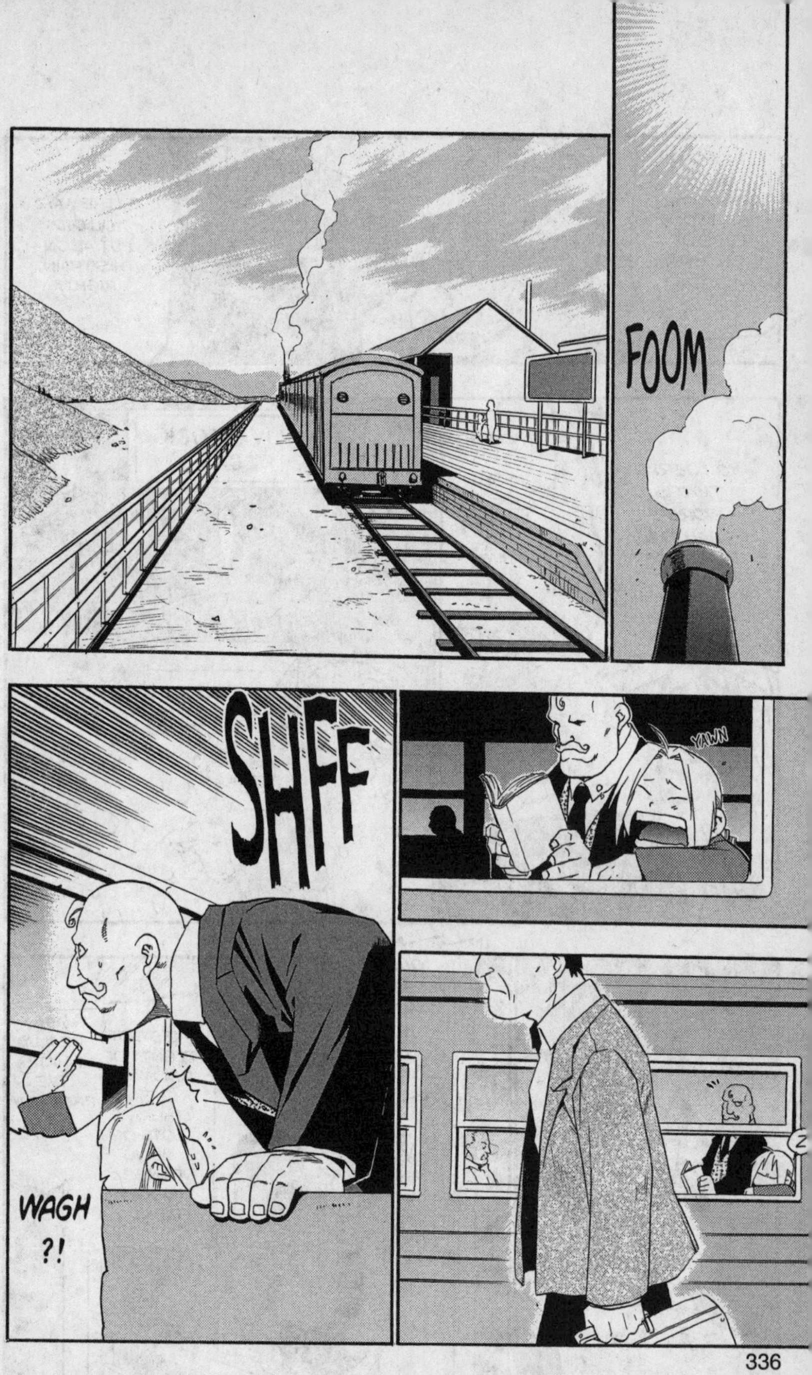
FOOM
YAWN
SHFF
WAGH ?!

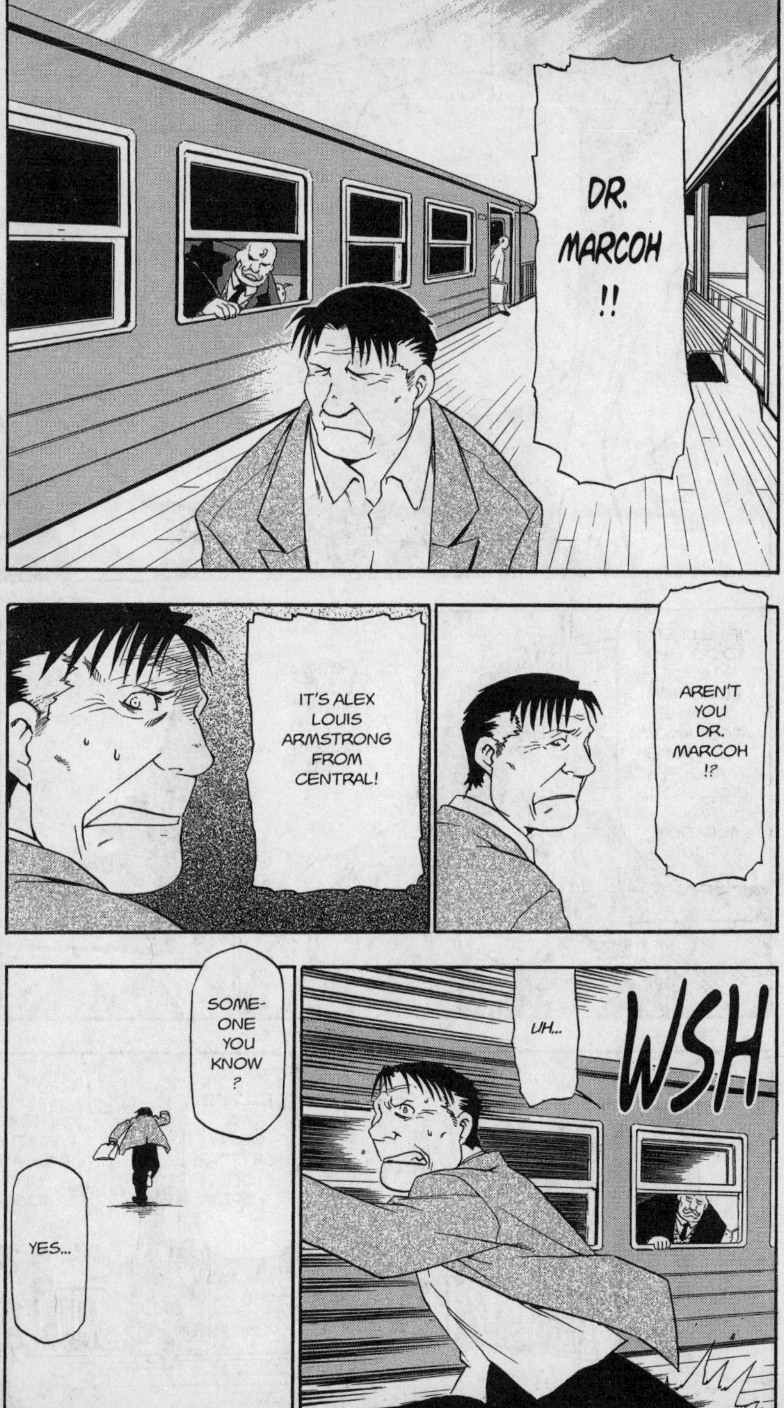
DR. MARCOH !!
AREN'T YOU DR. MARCOH !?
IT'S ALEX LOUIS ARMSTRONG FROM CENTRAL!
UH...
WSH
SOME-ONE YOU KNOW ?
YES...

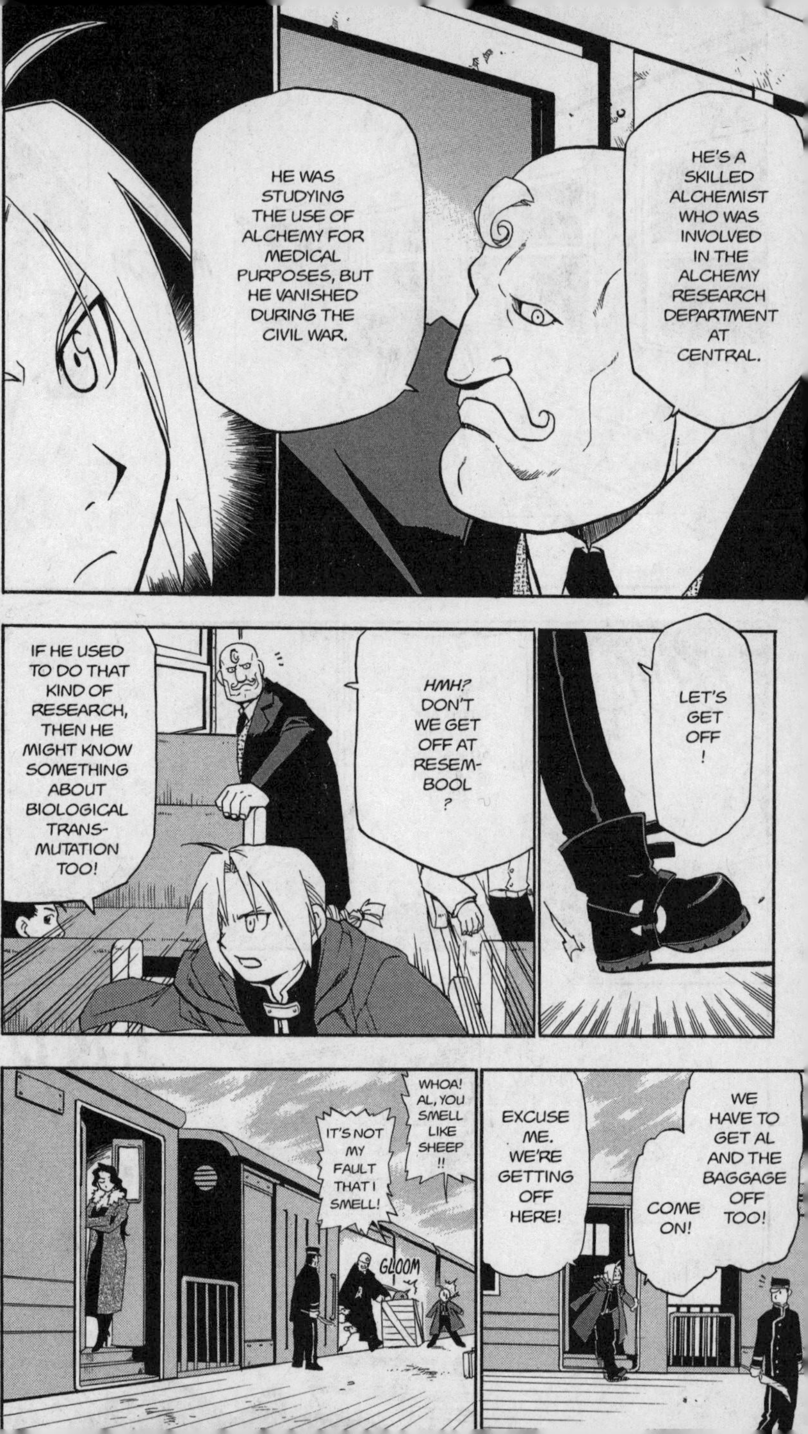
HE'S A SKILLED ALCHEMIST WHO WAS INVOLVED IN THE ALCHEMY RESEARCH DEPARTMENT AT CENTRAL.
HE WAS STUDYING THE USE OF ALCHEMY FOR MEDICAL PURPOSES, BUT HE VANISHED DURING THE CIVIL WAR.
LET'S GET OFF!
HMH? DON'T WE GET OFF AT RESEMBOOL?
IF HE USED TO DO THAT KIND OF RESEARCH, THEN HE MIGHT KNOW SOMETHING ABOUT BIOLOGICAL TRANSMUTATION TOO!
WE HAVE TO GET AL AND THE BAGGAGE OFF TOO!
COME ON!
EXCUSE ME. WE'RE GETTING OFF HERE!
WHOA! AL, YOU SMELL LIKE SHEEP!!
IT'S NOT MY FAULT THAT I SMELL!
GLOOM

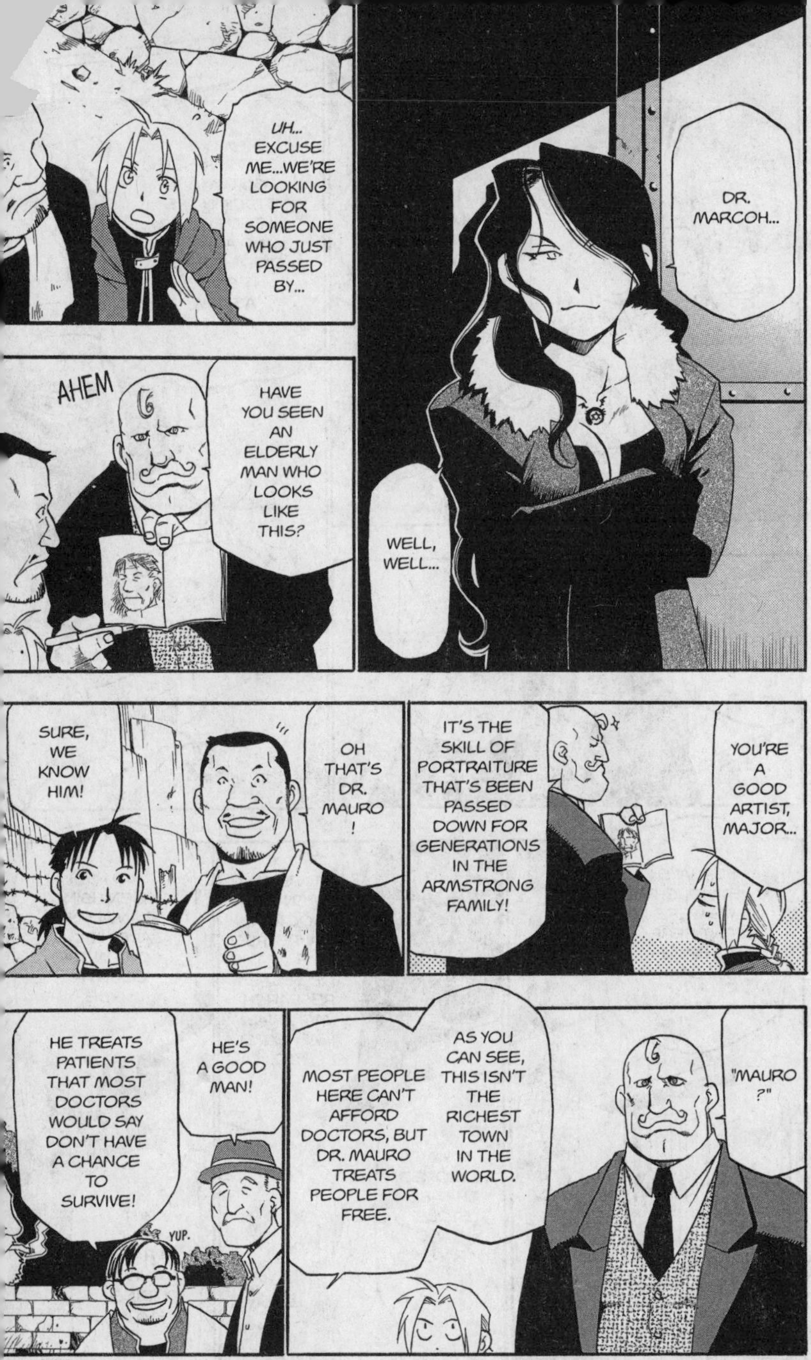
DR. MARCOH...
WELL, WELL...
UH... EXCUSE ME...WE'RE LOOKING FOR SOMEONE WHO JUST PASSED BY...
HAVE YOU SEEN AN ELDERLY MAN WHO LOOKS LIKE THIS?
AHEM
YOU'RE A GOOD ARTIST, MAJOR...
IT'S THE SKILL OF PORTRAITURE THAT'S BEEN PASSED DOWN FOR GENERATIONS IN THE ARMSTRONG FAMILY!
OH THAT'S DR. MAURO!
SURE, WE KNOW HIM!
"MAURO?"
AS YOU CAN SEE, THIS ISN'T THE RICHEST TOWN IN THE WORLD.
MOST PEOPLE HERE CAN'T AFFORD DOCTORS, BUT DR. MAURO TREATS PEOPLE FOR FREE.
HE'S A GOOD MAN!
HE TREATS PATIENTS THAT MOST DOCTORS WOULD SAY DON'T HAVE A CHANCE TO SURVIVE!
YUP.

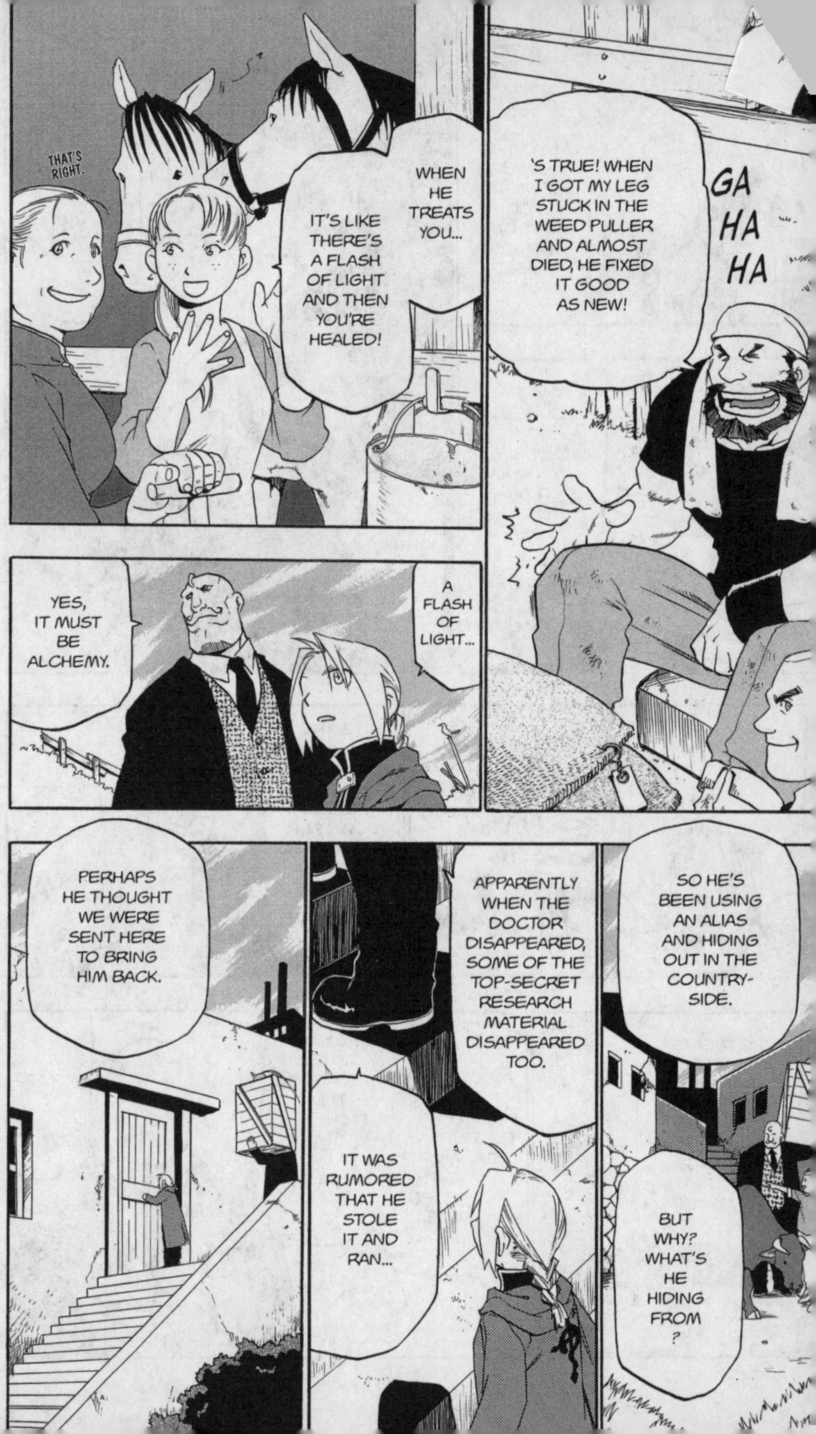
'S TRUE! WHEN I GOT MY LEG STUCK IN THE WEED PULLER AND ALMOST DIED, HE FIXED IT GOOD AS NEW!
GA HA HA
WHEN HE TREATS YOU...
IT'S LIKE THERE'S A FLASH OF LIGHT AND THEN YOU'RE HEALED!
THAT'S RIGHT.
A FLASH OF LIGHT...
YES, IT MUST BE ALCHEMY.
SO HE'S BEEN USING AN ALIAS AND HIDING OUT IN THE COUNTRY-SIDE.
BUT WHY? WHAT'S HE HIDING FROM?
APPARENTLY WHEN THE DOCTOR DISAPPEARED, SOME OF THE TOP-SECRET RESEARCH MATERIAL DISAPPEARED TOO.
IT WAS RUMORED THAT HE STOLE IT AND RAN...
PERHAPS HE THOUGHT WE WERE SENT HERE TO BRING HIM BACK.

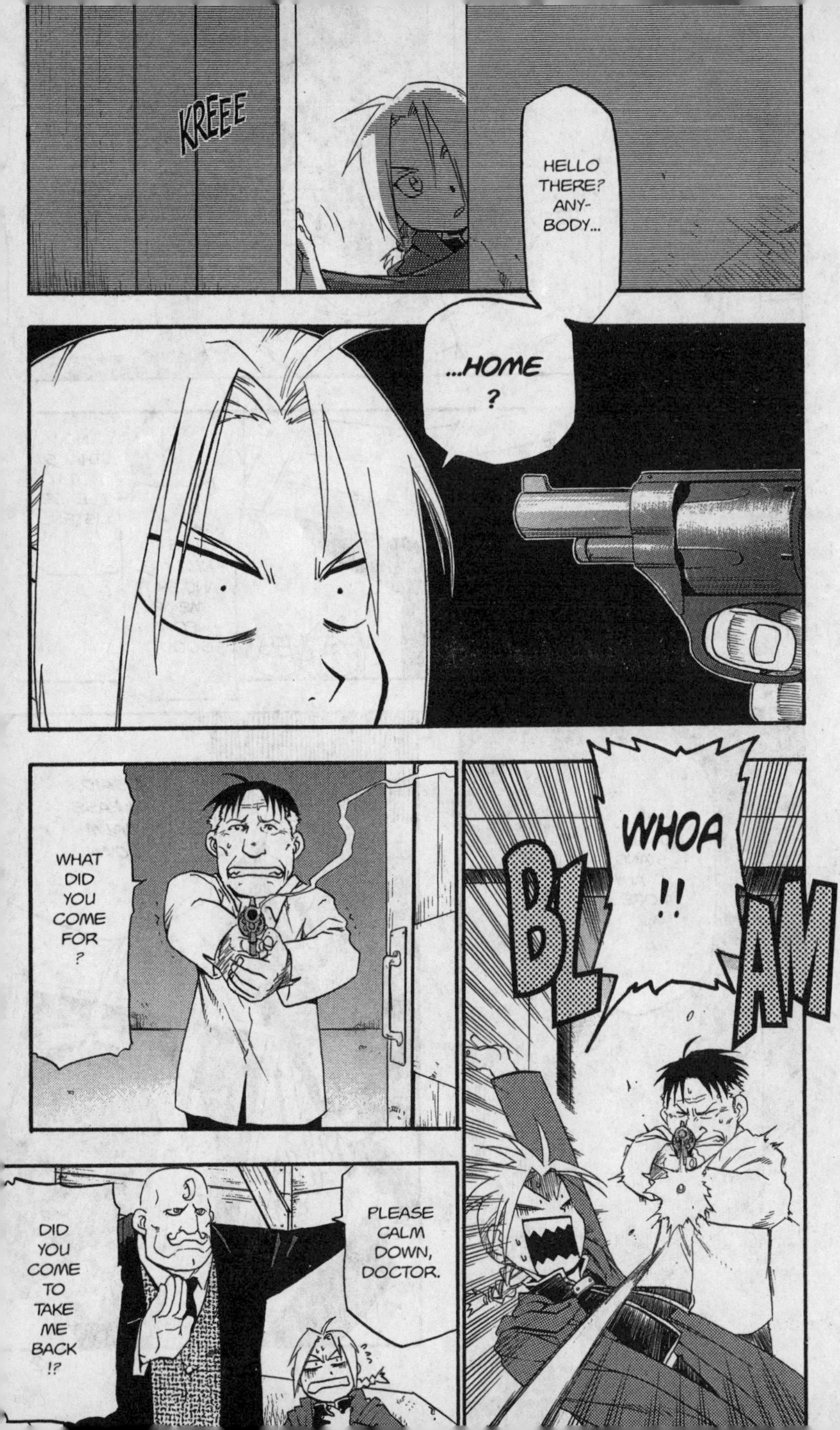
HELLO THERE? ANY-BODY...
KREEE
...HOME ?
WHOA !!
BLAM
WHAT DID YOU COME FOR ?
PLEASE CALM DOWN, DOCTOR.
DID YOU COME TO TAKE ME BACK !?

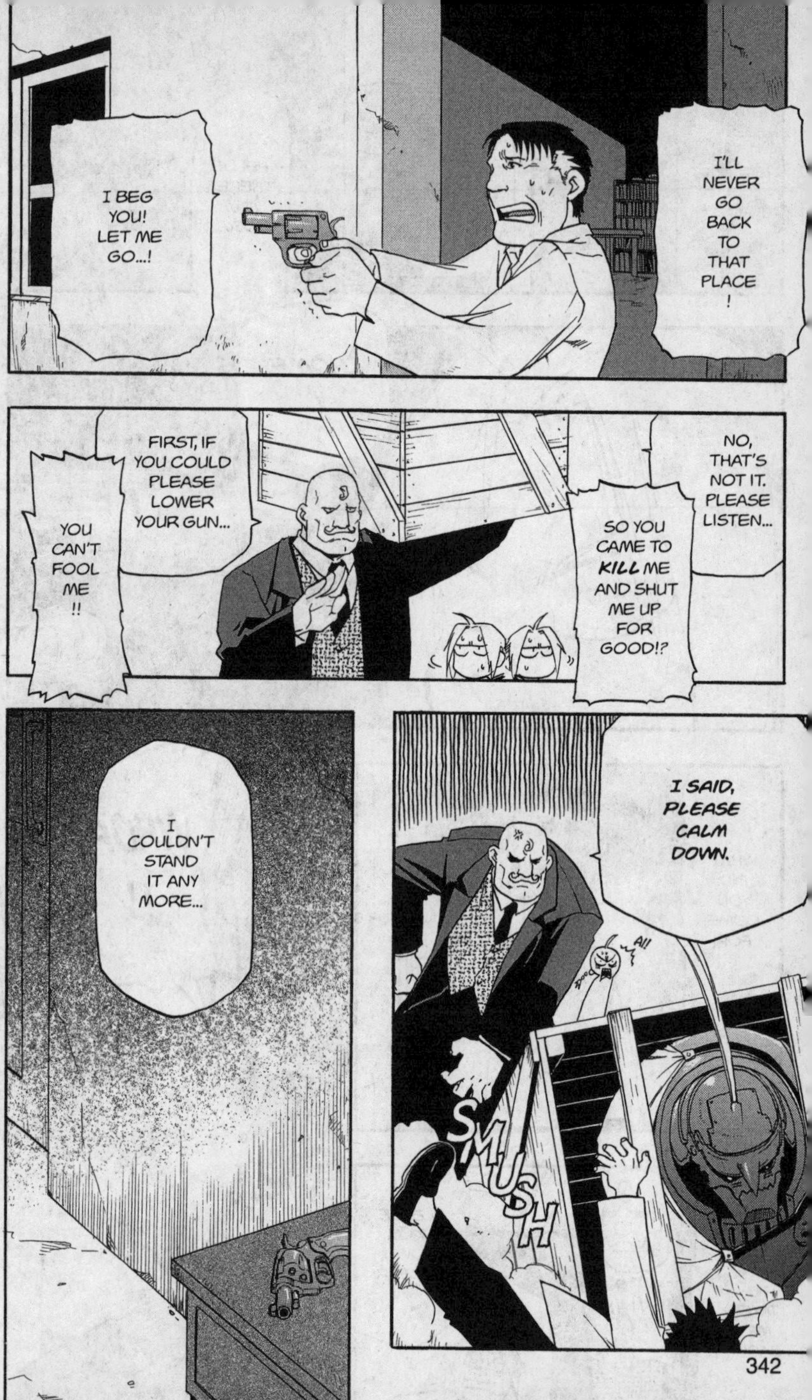
I'LL NEVER GO BACK TO THAT PLACE!
I BEG YOU! LET ME GO...!
NO, THAT'S NOT IT. PLEASE LISTEN...
SO YOU CAME TO KILL ME AND SHUT ME UP FOR GOOD!?
FIRST, IF YOU COULD PLEASE LOWER YOUR GUN...
YOU CAN'T FOOL ME!!
I SAID, PLEASE CALM DOWN.
AI!
SMUSH
I COULDN'T STAND IT ANY MORE...

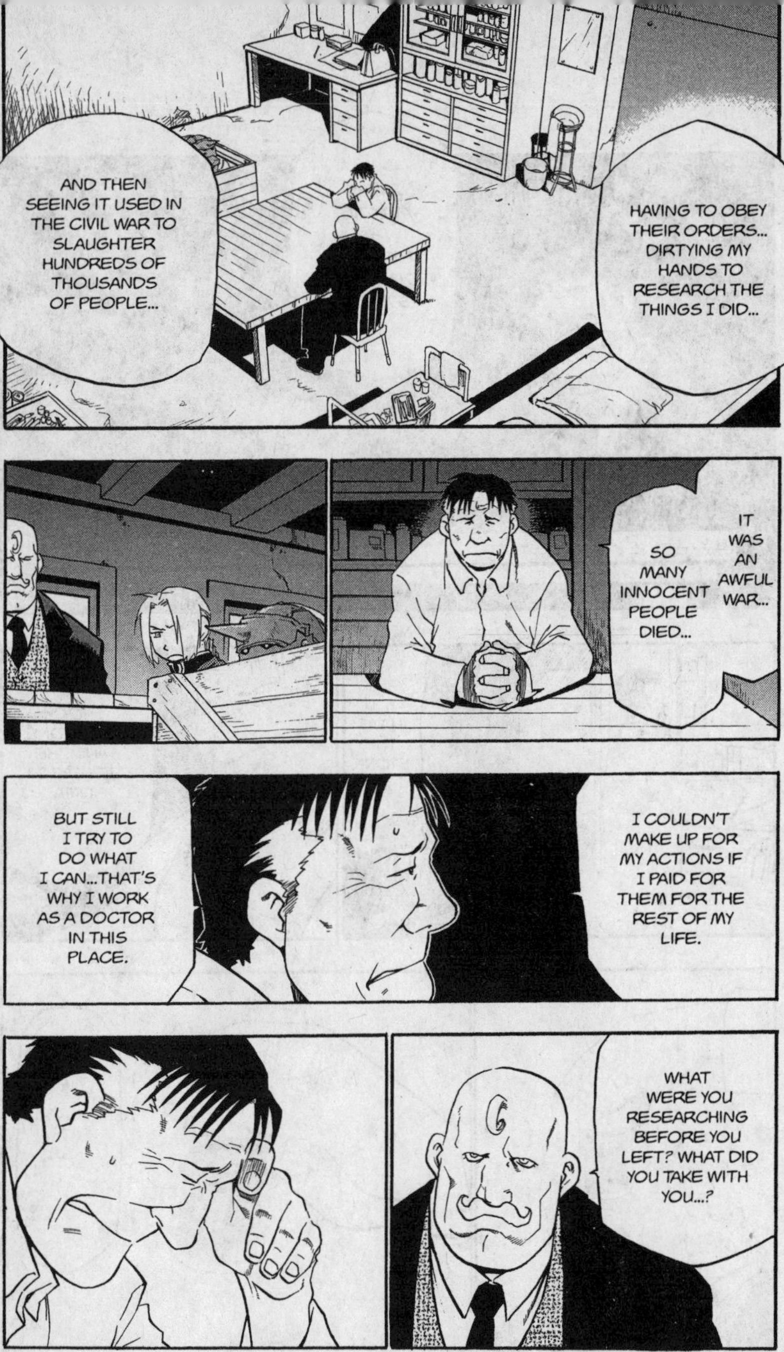
HAVING TO OBEY THEIR ORDERS... DIRTYING MY HANDS TO RESEARCH THE THINGS I DID...
AND THEN SEEING IT USED IN THE CIVIL WAR TO SLAUGHTER HUNDREDS OF THOUSANDS OF PEOPLE...
IT WAS AN AWFUL WAR...
SO MANY INNOCENT PEOPLE DIED...
I COULDN'T MAKE UP FOR MY ACTIONS IF I PAID FOR THEM FOR THE REST OF MY LIFE.
BUT STILL I TRY TO DO WHAT I CAN...THAT'S WHY I WORK AS A DOCTOR IN THIS PLACE.
WHAT WERE YOU RESEARCHING BEFORE YOU LEFT? WHAT DID YOU TAKE WITH YOU...?

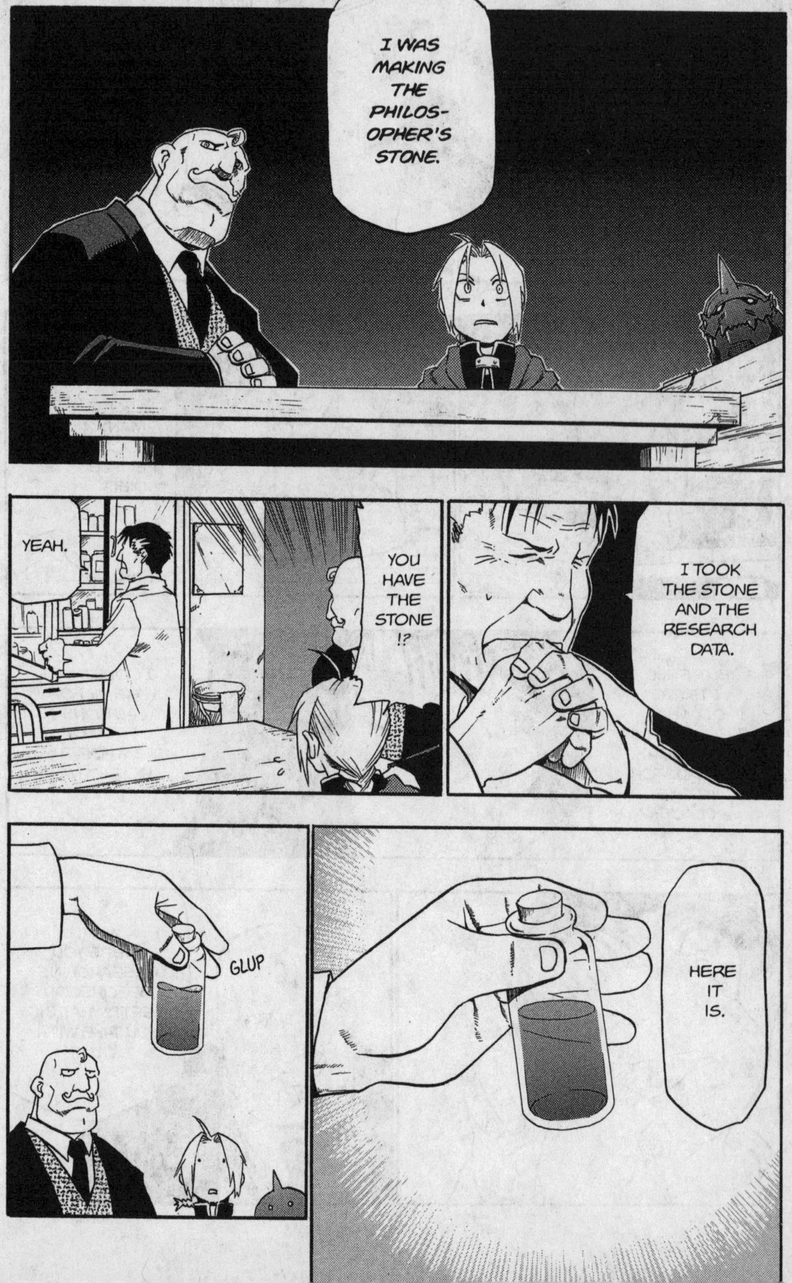
I WAS MAKING THE PHILOS-OPHER'S STONE.
I TOOK THE STONE AND THE RESEARCH DATA.
YOU HAVE THE STONE !?
YEAH.
HERE IT IS.
GLUP

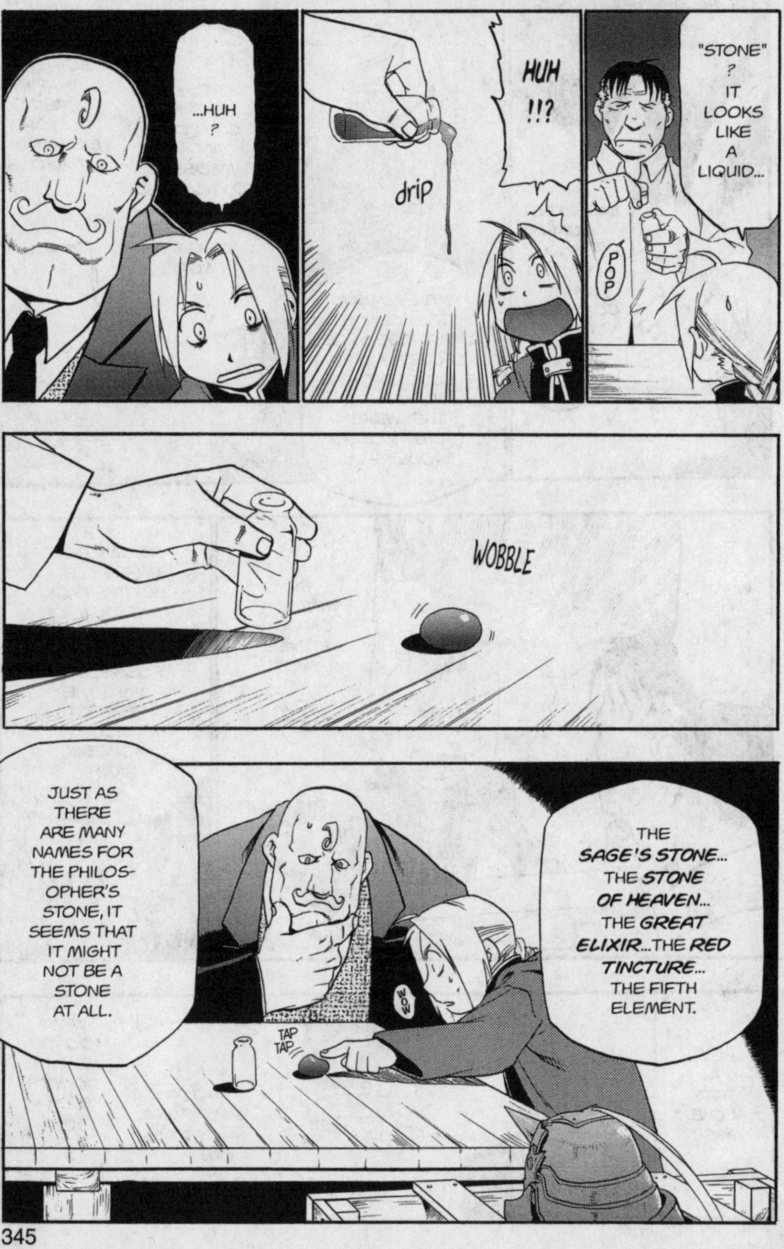
"STONE"? IT LOOKS LIKE A LIQUID...
POP
HUH!!?
drip
...HUH?
WOBBLE
THE SAGE'S STONE... THE STONE OF HEAVEN... THE GREAT ELIXIR...THE RED TINCTURE... THE FIFTH ELEMENT.
WOW
TAP TAP
JUST AS THERE ARE MANY NAMES FOR THE PHILOSOPHER'S STONE, IT SEEMS THAT IT MIGHT NOT BE A STONE AT ALL.

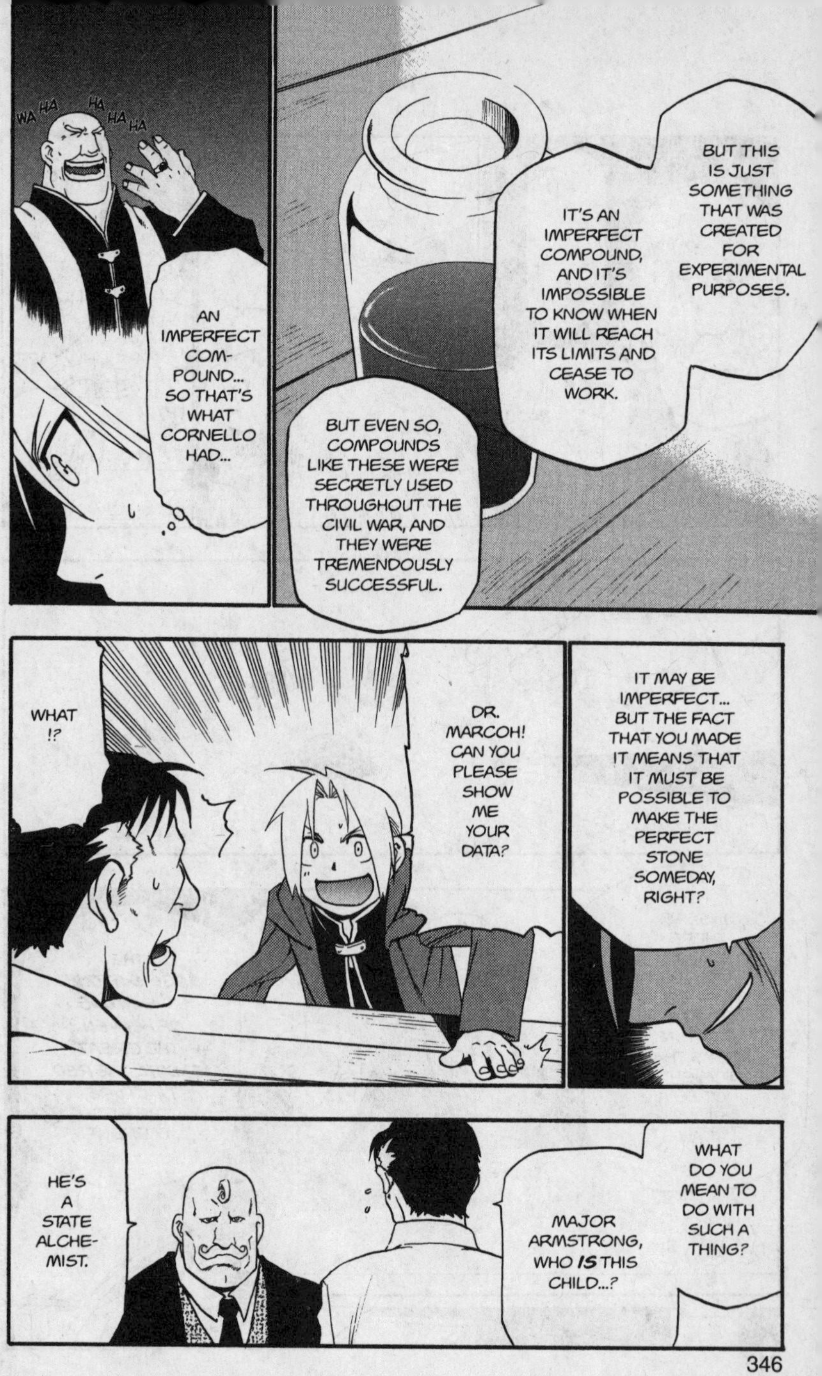
BUT THIS IS JUST SOMETHING THAT WAS CREATED FOR EXPERIMENTAL PURPOSES.
IT'S AN IMPERFECT COMPOUND, AND IT'S IMPOSSIBLE TO KNOW WHEN IT WILL REACH ITS LIMITS AND CEASE TO WORK.
BUT EVEN SO, COMPOUNDS LIKE THESE WERE SECRETLY USED THROUGHOUT THE CIVIL WAR, AND THEY WERE TREMENDOUSLY SUCCESSFUL.
WA HA HA HA HA HA
AN IMPERFECT COM-POUND... SO THAT'S WHAT CORNELLO HAD...
IT MAY BE IMPERFECT... BUT THE FACT THAT YOU MADE IT MEANS THAT IT MUST BE POSSIBLE TO MAKE THE PERFECT STONE SOMEDAY, RIGHT?
DR. MARCOH! CAN YOU PLEASE SHOW ME YOUR DATA?
WHAT !?
WHAT DO YOU MEAN TO DO WITH SUCH A THING?
MAJOR ARMSTRONG, WHO ***IS*** THIS CHILD...?
HE'S A STATE ALCHE-MIST.

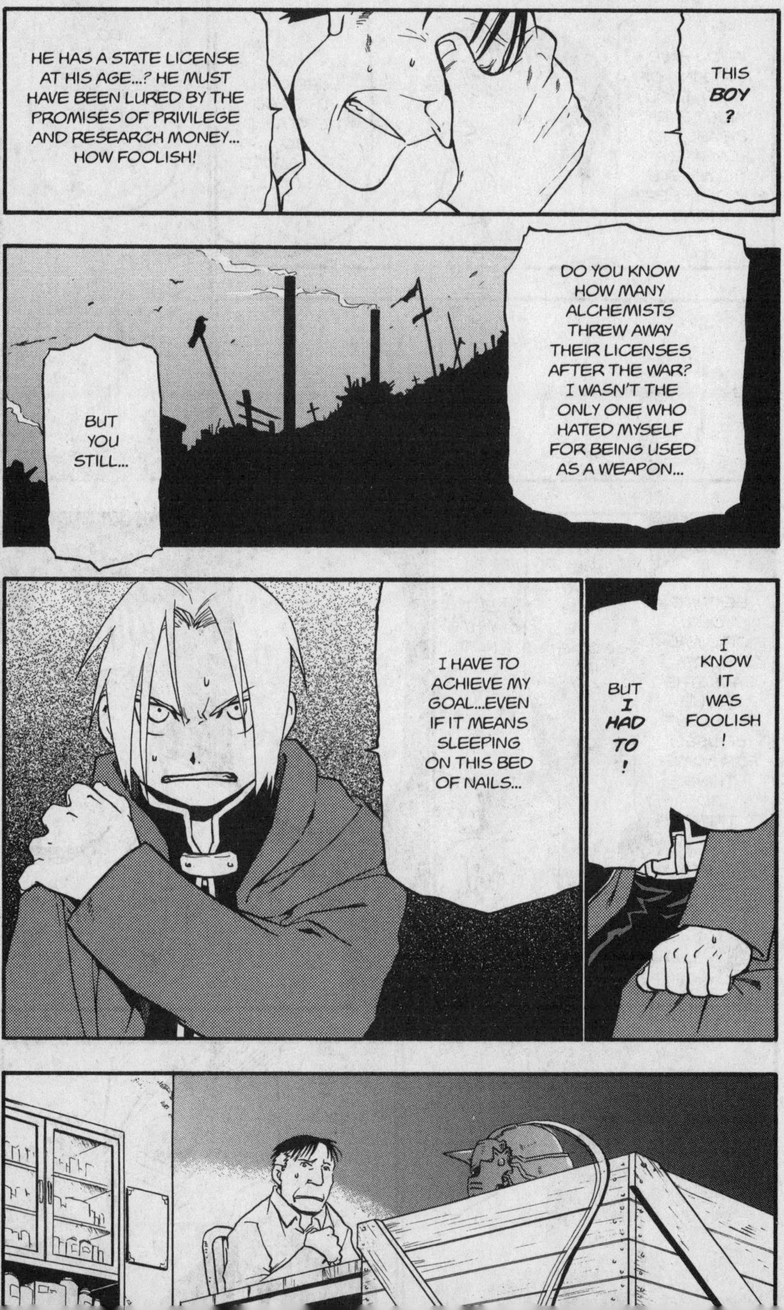
THIS BOY?
HE HAS A STATE LICENSE AT HIS AGE...? HE MUST HAVE BEEN LURED BY THE PROMISES OF PRIVILEGE AND RESEARCH MONEY... HOW FOOLISH!
DO YOU KNOW HOW MANY ALCHEMISTS THREW AWAY THEIR LICENSES AFTER THE WAR? I WASN'T THE ONLY ONE WHO HATED MYSELF FOR BEING USED AS A WEAPON...
BUT YOU STILL...
I KNOW IT WAS FOOLISH!
BUT I HAD TO!
I HAVE TO ACHIEVE MY GOAL...EVEN IF IT MEANS SLEEPING ON THIS BED OF NAILS...

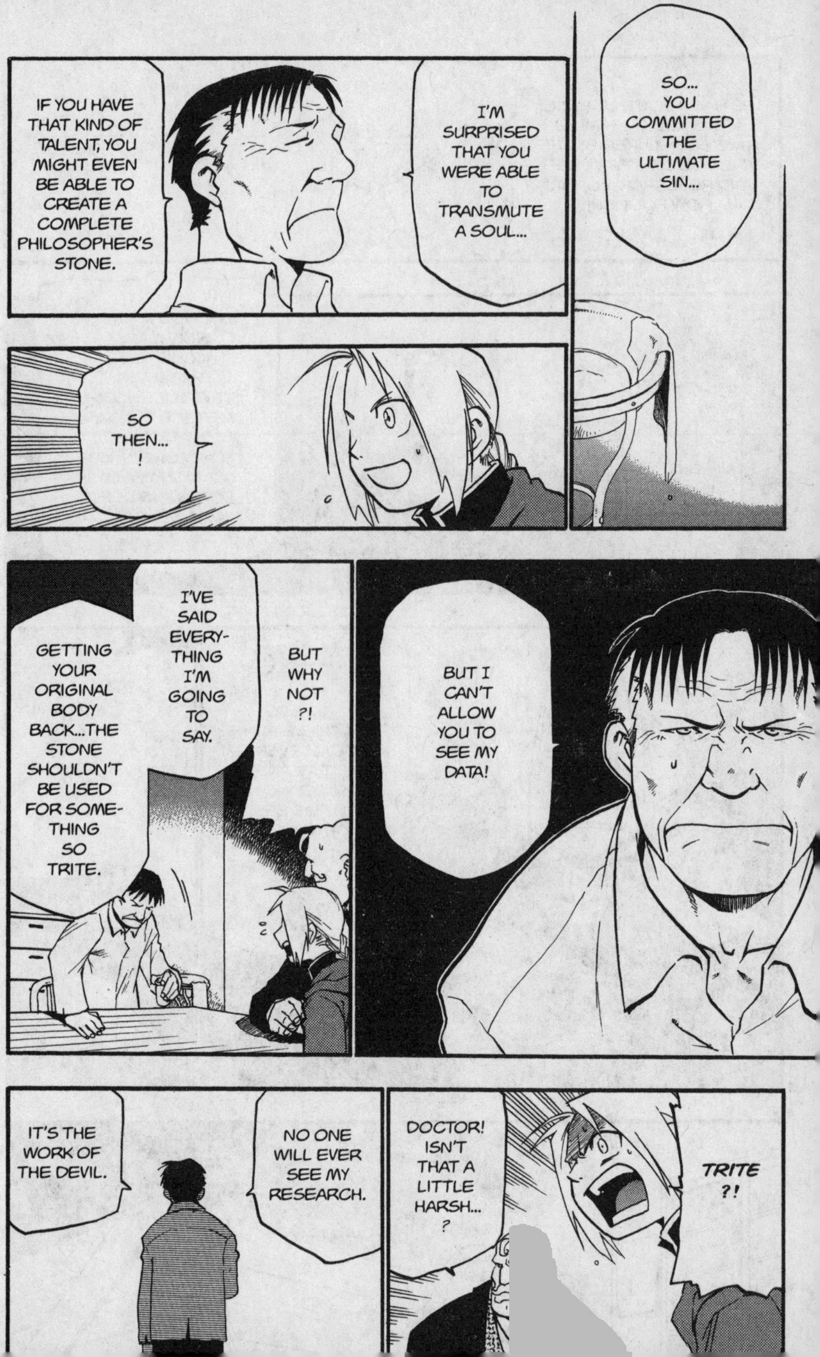
SO... YOU COMMITTED THE ULTIMATE SIN...
I'M SURPRISED THAT YOU WERE ABLE TO TRANSMUTE A SOUL...
IF YOU HAVE THAT KIND OF TALENT, YOU MIGHT EVEN BE ABLE TO CREATE A COMPLETE PHILOSOPHER'S STONE.
SO THEN...!
BUT I CAN'T ALLOW YOU TO SEE MY DATA!
BUT WHY NOT?!
I'VE SAID EVERY-THING I'M GOING TO SAY.
GETTING YOUR ORIGINAL BODY BACK...THE STONE SHOULDN'T BE USED FOR SOME-THING SO TRITE.
TRITE?!
DOCTOR! ISN'T THAT A LITTLE HARSH...?
NO ONE WILL EVER SEE MY RESEARCH.
IT'S THE WORK OF THE DEVIL.

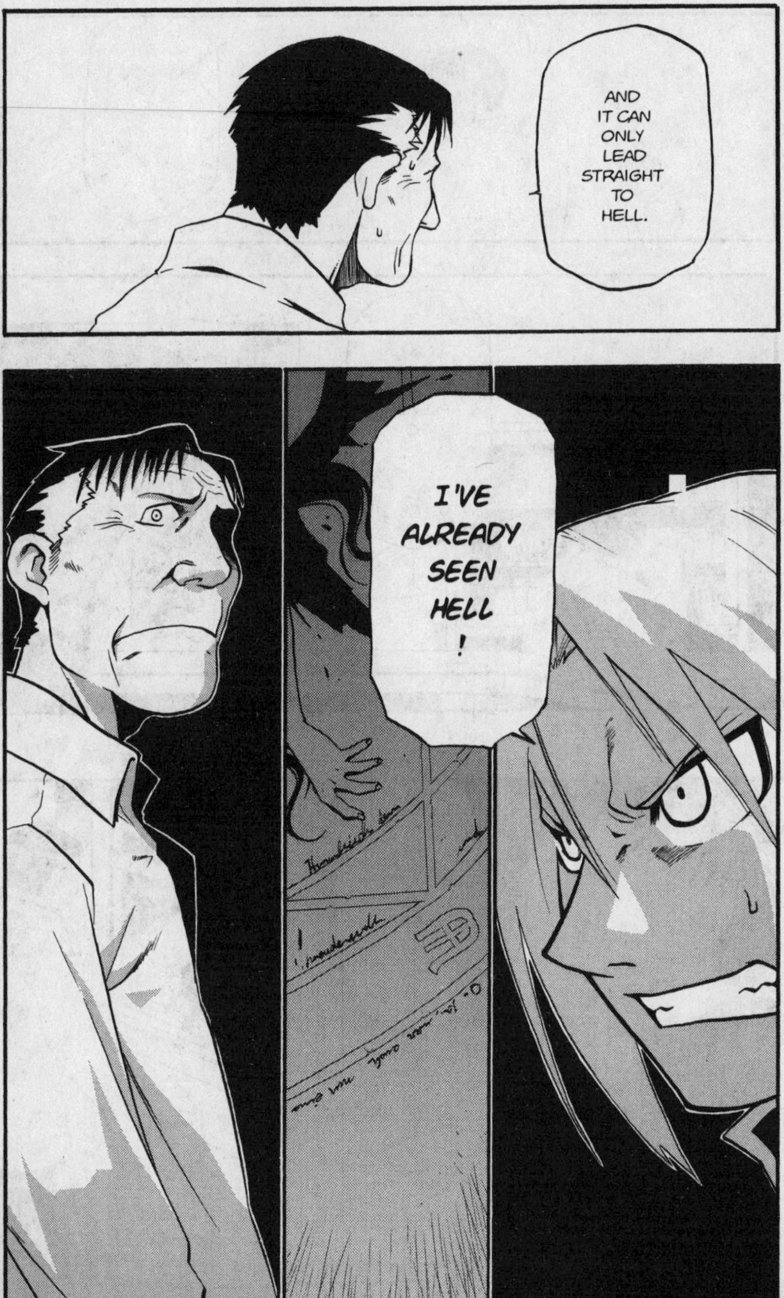
AND IT CAN ONLY LEAD STRAIGHT TO HELL.
I'VE ALREADY SEEN HELL!

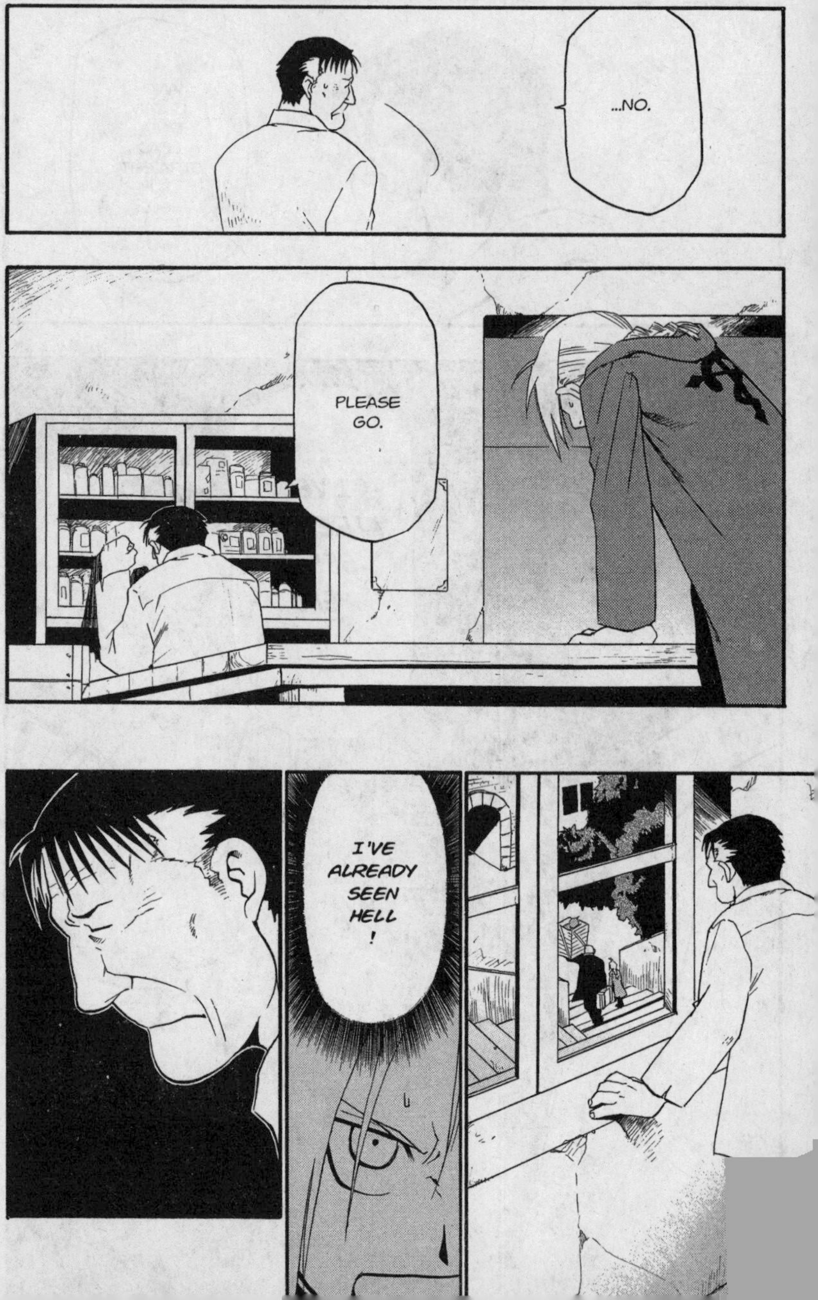
...NO.
PLEASE GO.
I'VE ALREADY SEEN HELL!

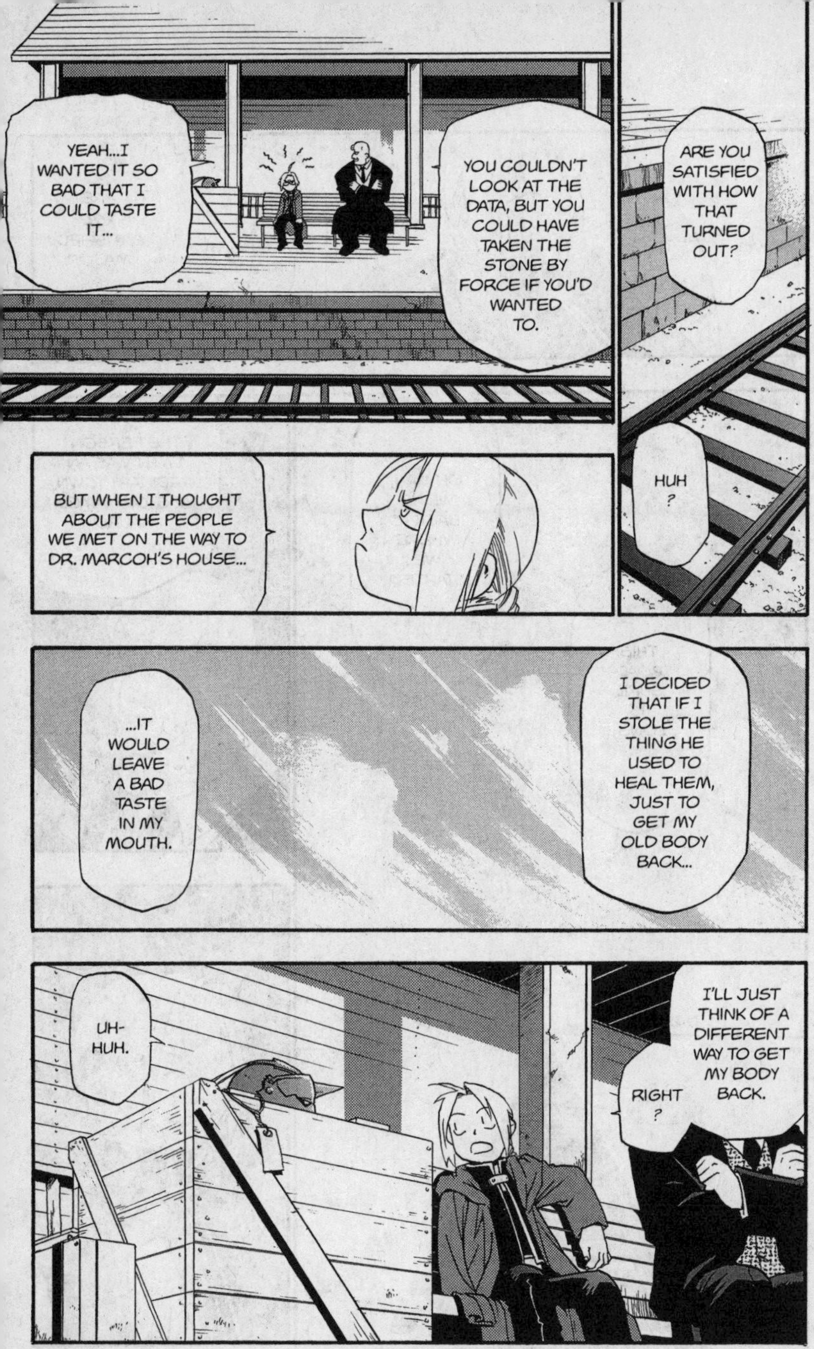
ARE YOU SATISFIED WITH HOW THAT TURNED OUT?
HUH?
YOU COULDN'T LOOK AT THE DATA, BUT YOU COULD HAVE TAKEN THE STONE BY FORCE IF YOU'D WANTED TO.
YEAH...I WANTED IT SO BAD THAT I COULD TASTE IT...
BUT WHEN I THOUGHT ABOUT THE PEOPLE WE MET ON THE WAY TO DR. MARCOH'S HOUSE...
I DECIDED THAT IF I STOLE THE THING HE USED TO HEAL THEM, JUST TO GET MY OLD BODY BACK...
...IT WOULD LEAVE A BAD TASTE IN MY MOUTH.
I'LL JUST THINK OF A DIFFERENT WAY TO GET MY BODY BACK.
RIGHT?
UH-HUH.

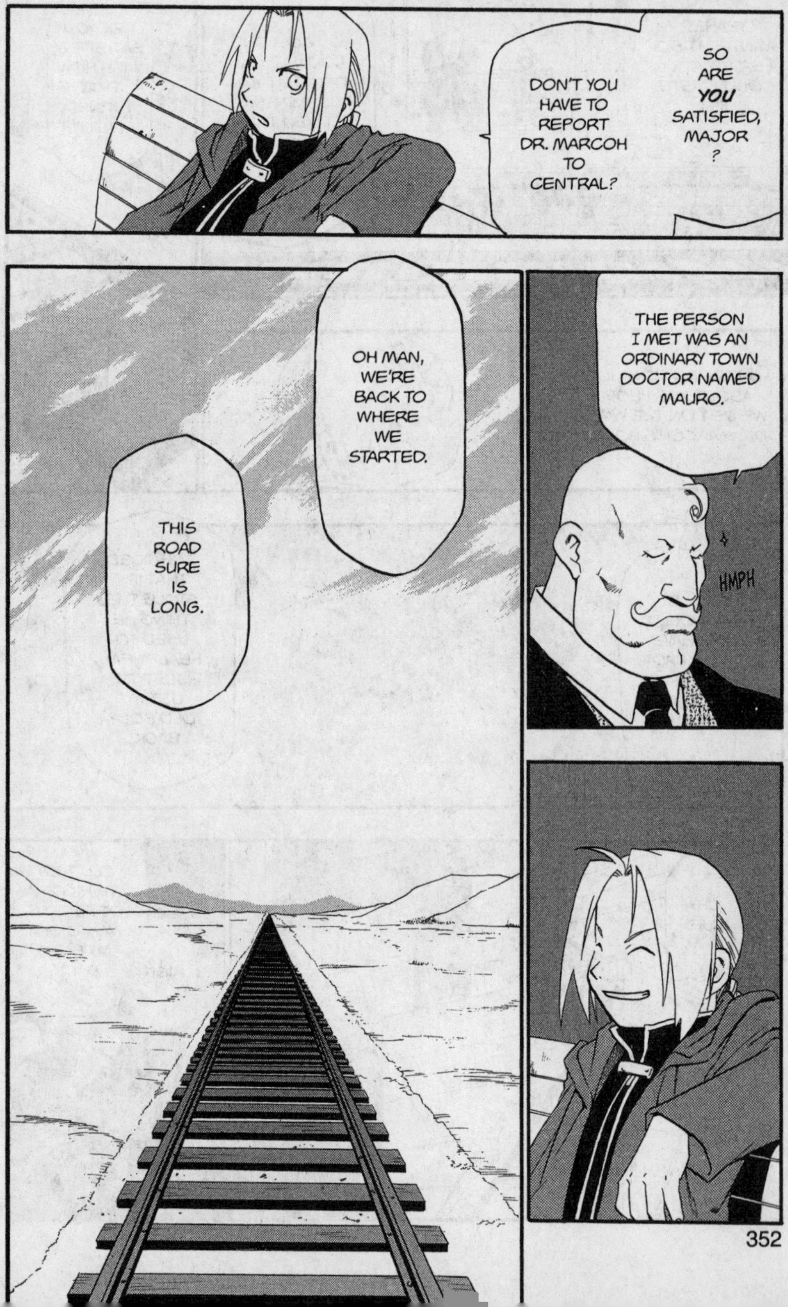
SO ARE YOU SATISFIED, MAJOR?
DON'T YOU HAVE TO REPORT DR. MARCOH TO CENTRAL?
THE PERSON I MET WAS AN ORDINARY TOWN DOCTOR NAMED MAURO.
HMPH
OH MAN, WE'RE BACK TO WHERE WE STARTED.
THIS ROAD SURE IS LONG.

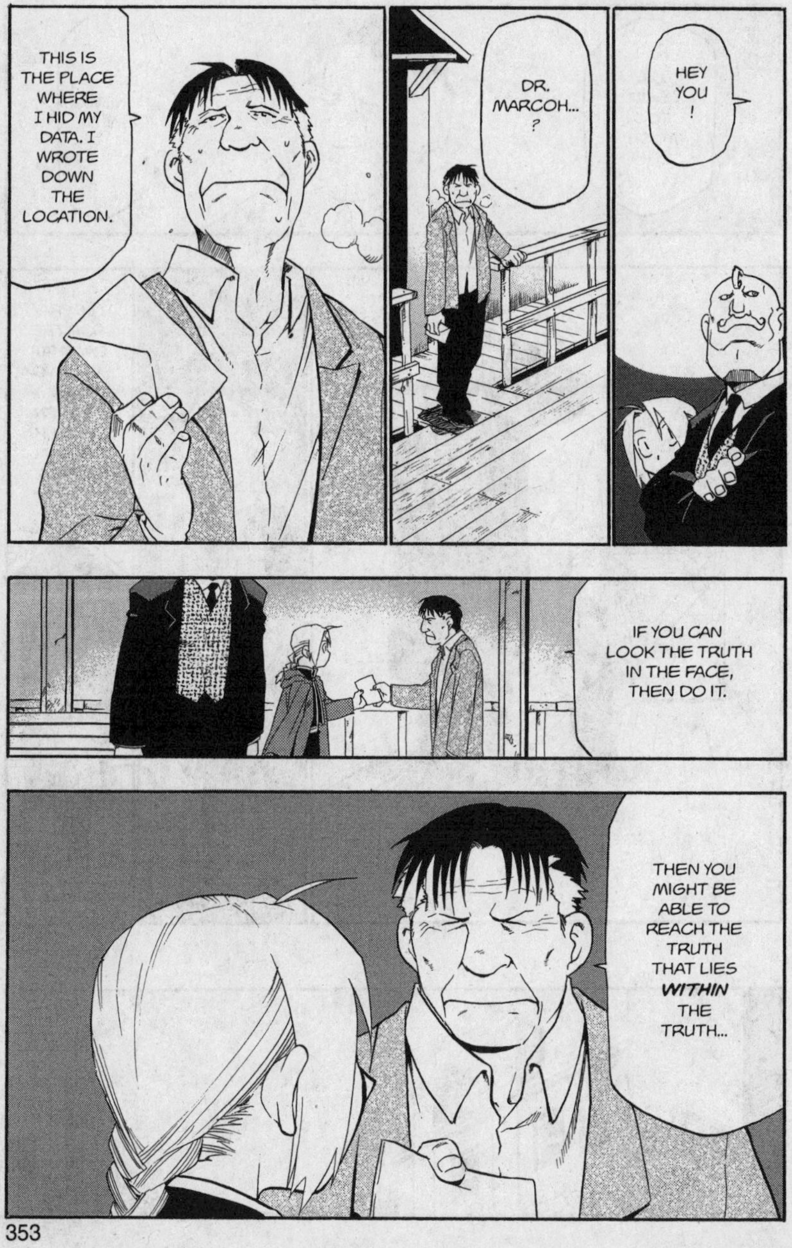
HEY YOU!
DR. MARCOH...?
THIS IS THE PLACE WHERE I HID MY DATA. I WROTE DOWN THE LOCATION.
IF YOU CAN LOOK THE TRUTH IN THE FACE, THEN DO IT.
THEN YOU MIGHT BE ABLE TO REACH THE TRUTH THAT LIES WITHIN THE TRUTH...

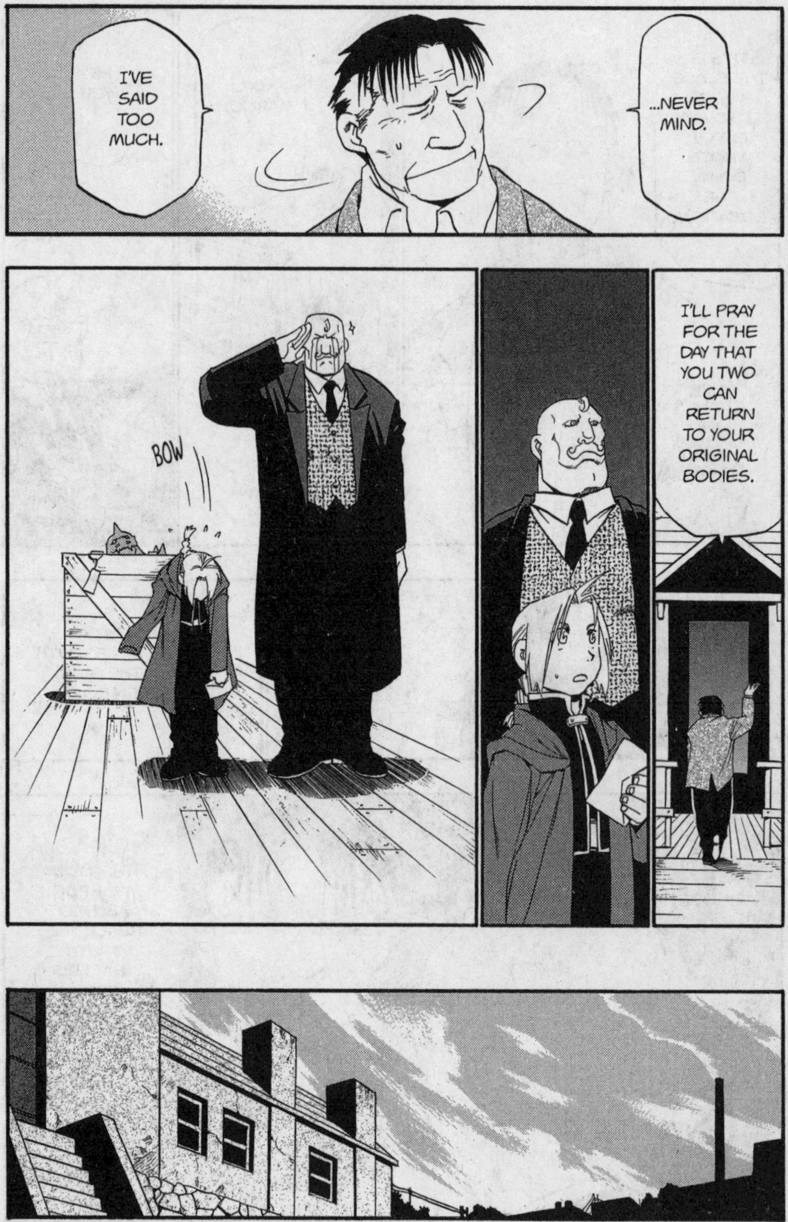
...NEVER MIND.
I'VE SAID TOO MUCH.
I'LL PRAY FOR THE DAY THAT YOU TWO CAN RETURN TO YOUR ORIGINAL BODIES.
BOW

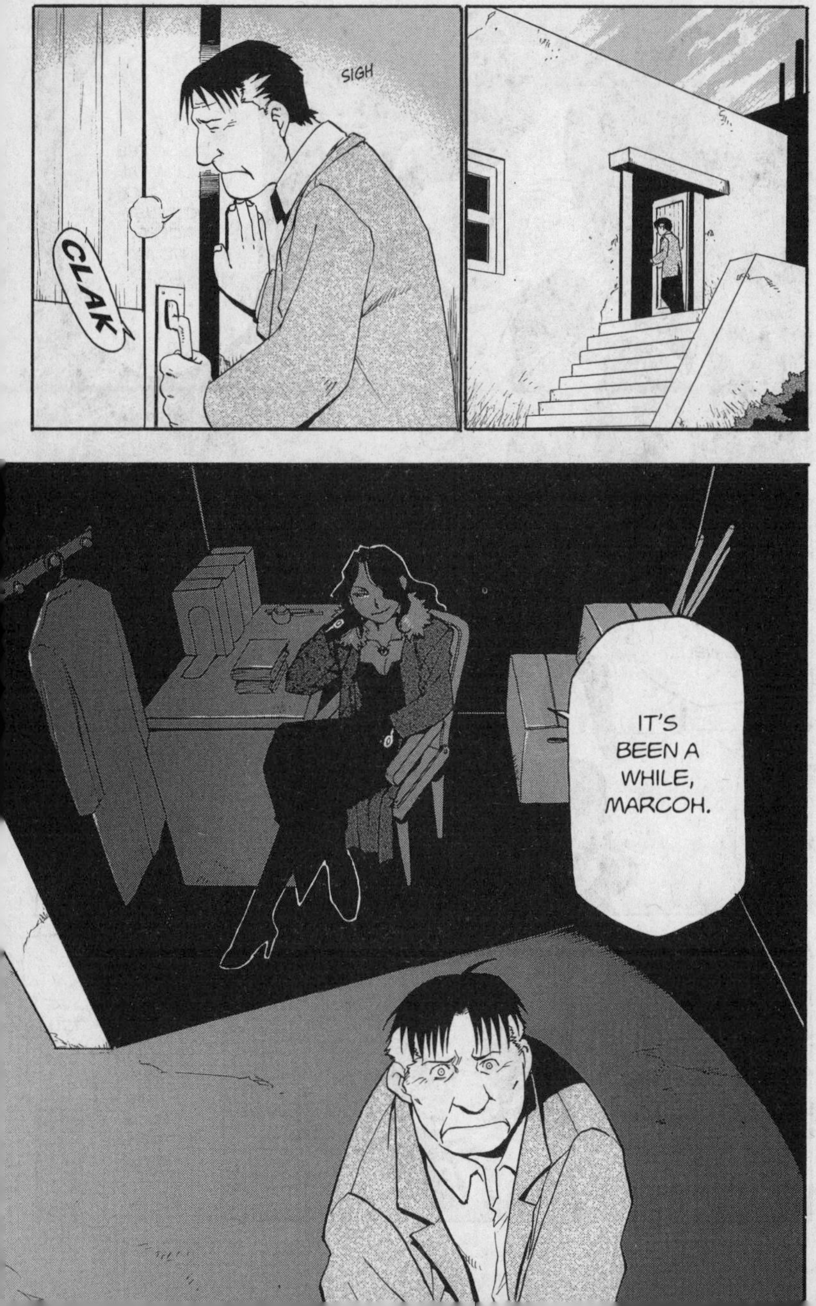
SIGH
CLAK
IT'S BEEN A WHILE, MARCOH.

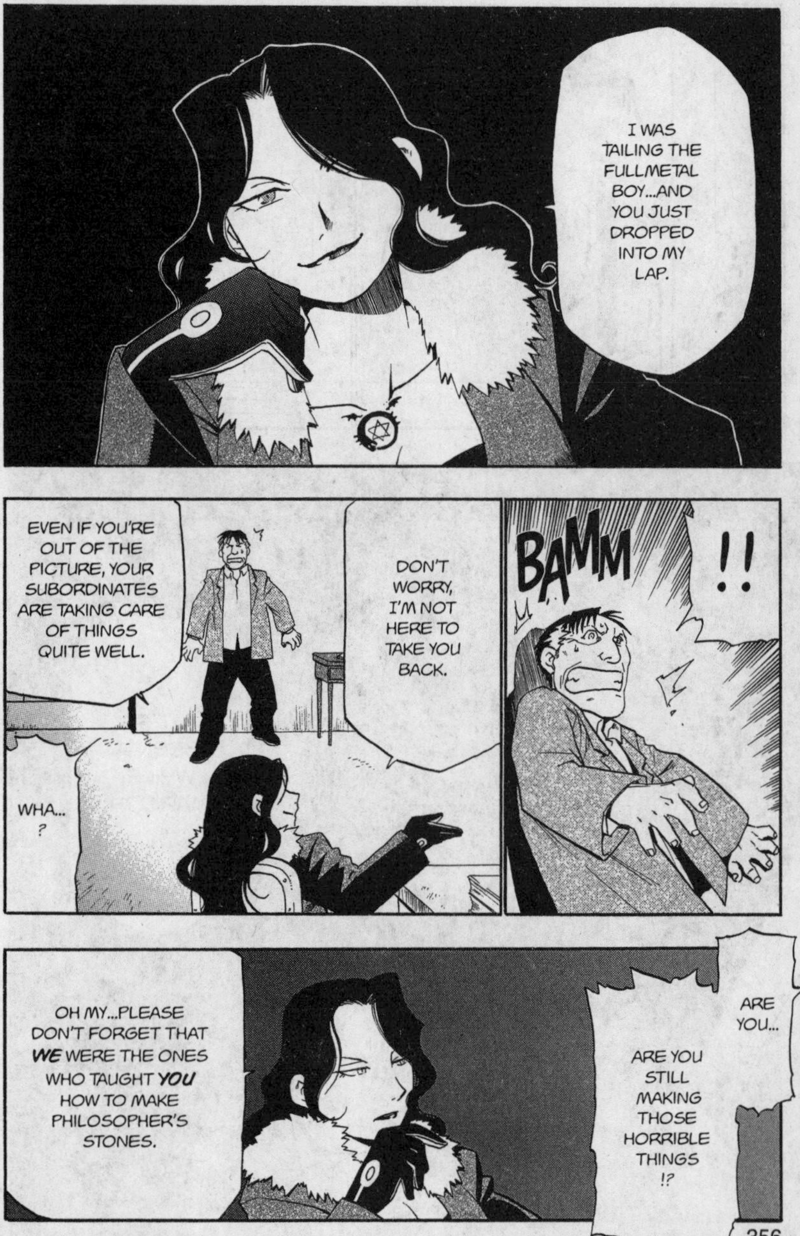
I WAS TAILING THE FULLMETAL BOY...AND YOU JUST DROPPED INTO MY LAP.
BAMM
!!
DON'T WORRY, I'M NOT HERE TO TAKE YOU BACK.
EVEN IF YOU'RE OUT OF THE PICTURE, YOUR SUBORDINATES ARE TAKING CARE OF THINGS QUITE WELL.
WHA... ?
ARE YOU...
ARE YOU STILL MAKING THOSE HORRIBLE THINGS !?
OH MY...PLEASE DON'T FORGET THAT *WE* WERE THE ONES WHO TAUGHT *YOU* HOW TO MAKE PHILOSOPHER'S STONES.

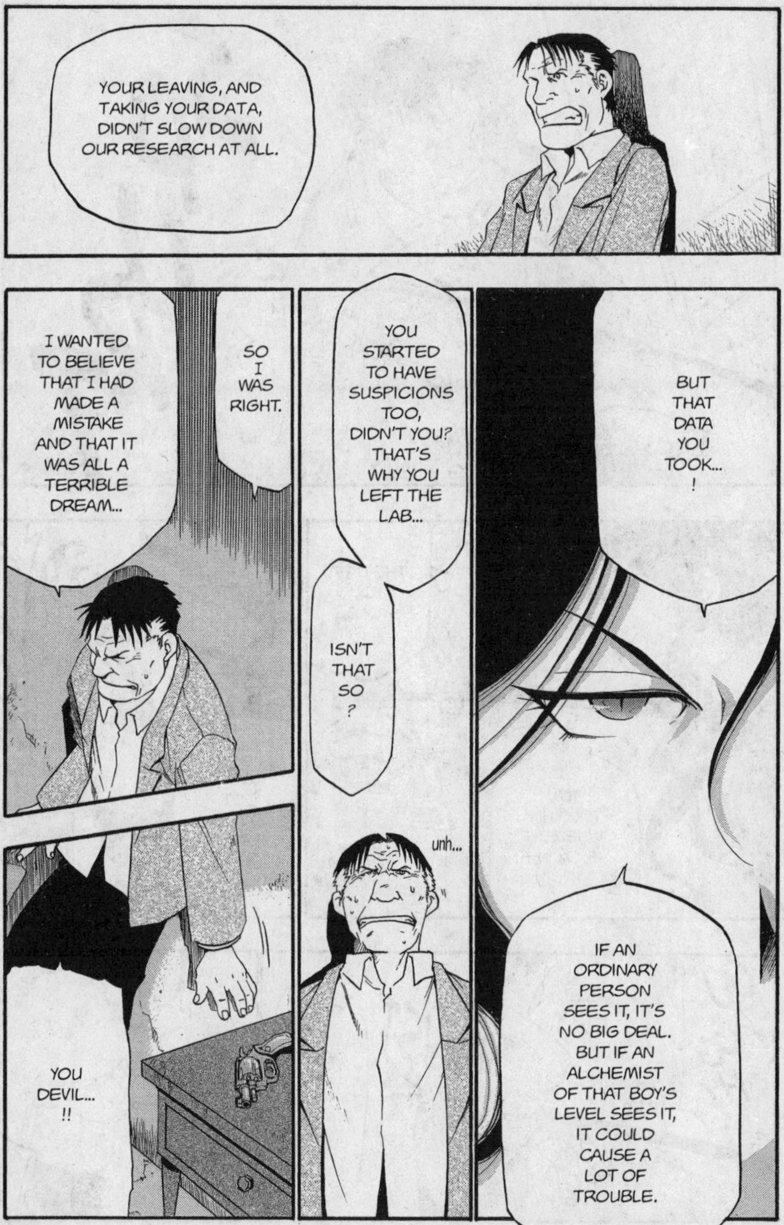
YOUR LEAVING, AND TAKING YOUR DATA, DIDN'T SLOW DOWN OUR RESEARCH AT ALL.
BUT THAT DATA YOU TOOK...!
IF AN ORDINARY PERSON SEES IT, IT'S NO BIG DEAL. BUT IF AN ALCHEMIST OF THAT BOY'S LEVEL SEES IT, IT COULD CAUSE A LOT OF TROUBLE.
YOU STARTED TO HAVE SUSPICIONS TOO, DIDN'T YOU? THAT'S WHY YOU LEFT THE LAB...
ISN'T THAT SO?
unh...
SO I WAS RIGHT.
I WANTED TO BELIEVE THAT I HAD MADE A MISTAKE AND THAT IT WAS ALL A TERRIBLE DREAM...
YOU DEVIL...!!

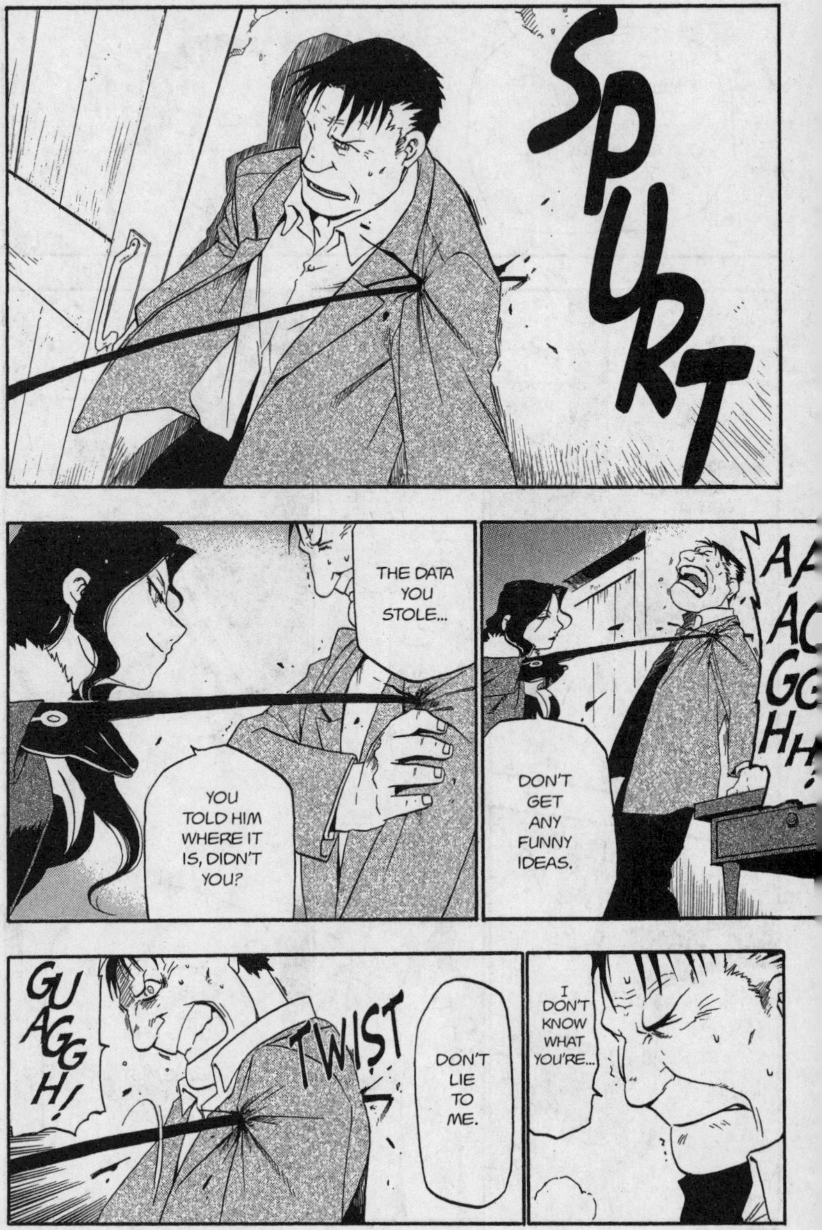
SPURT
DON'T GET ANY FUNNY IDEAS.
THE DATA YOU STOLE...
YOU TOLD HIM WHERE IT IS, DIDN'T YOU?
I DON'T KNOW WHAT YOU'RE...
DON'T LIE TO ME.
TWIST
GUAGGH!

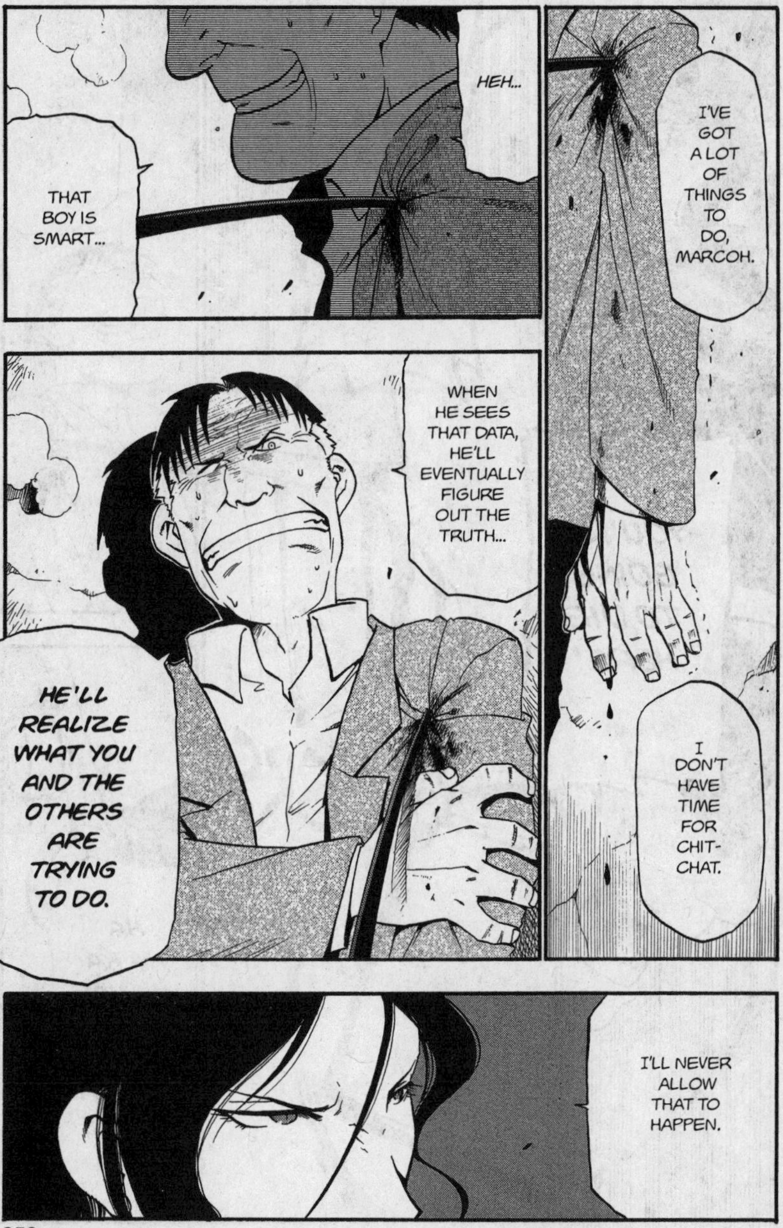
I'VE GOT A LOT OF THINGS TO DO, MARCOH.
I DON'T HAVE TIME FOR CHIT-CHAT.
HEH...
THAT BOY IS SMART...
WHEN HE SEES THAT DATA, HE'LL EVENTUALLY FIGURE OUT THE TRUTH...
HE'LL REALIZE WHAT YOU AND THE OTHERS ARE TRYING TO DO.
I'LL NEVER ALLOW THAT TO HAPPEN.

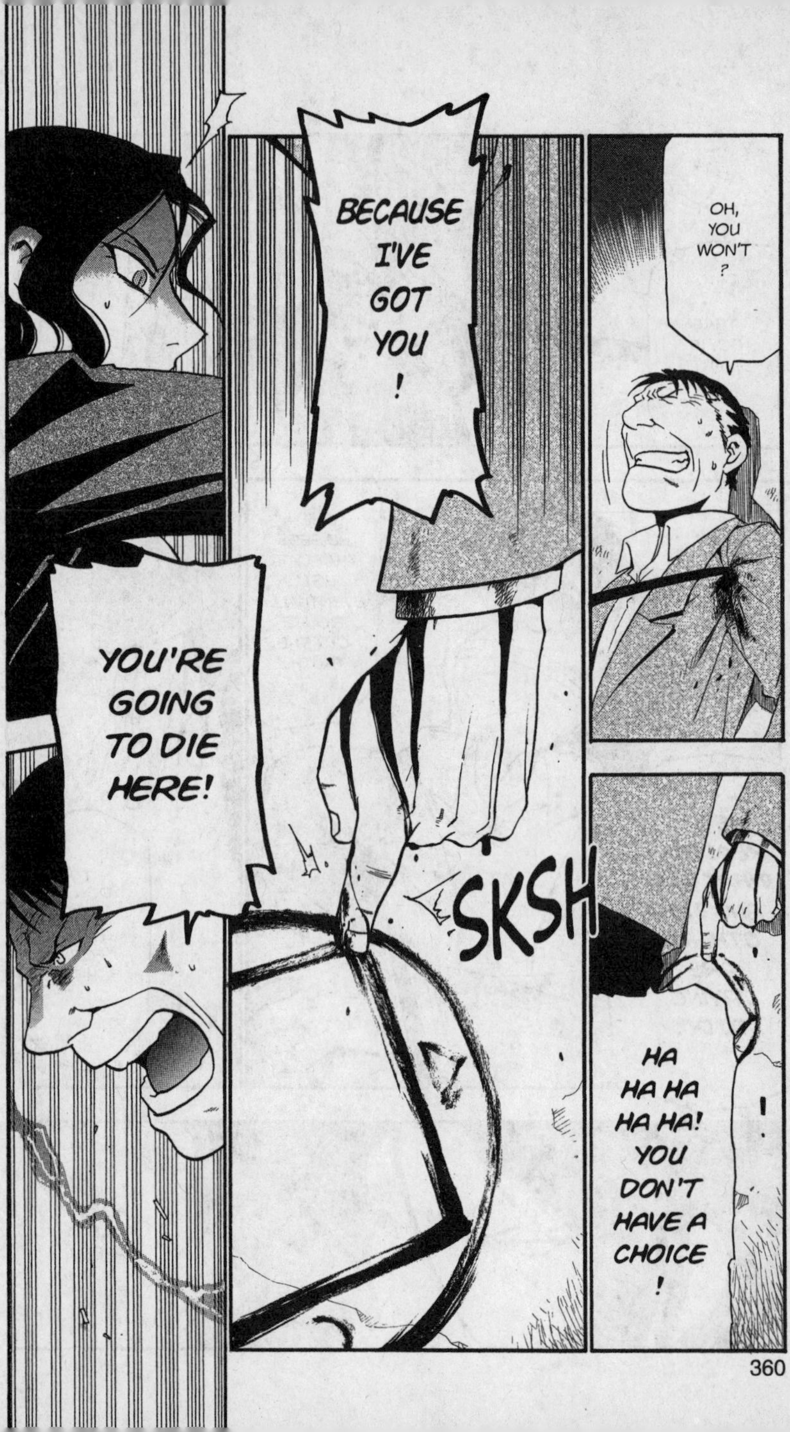
OH, YOU WON'T?
HA HA HA HA HA! YOU DON'T HAVE A CHOICE!
BECAUSE I'VE GOT YOU!
SKSH
YOU'RE GOING TO DIE HERE!

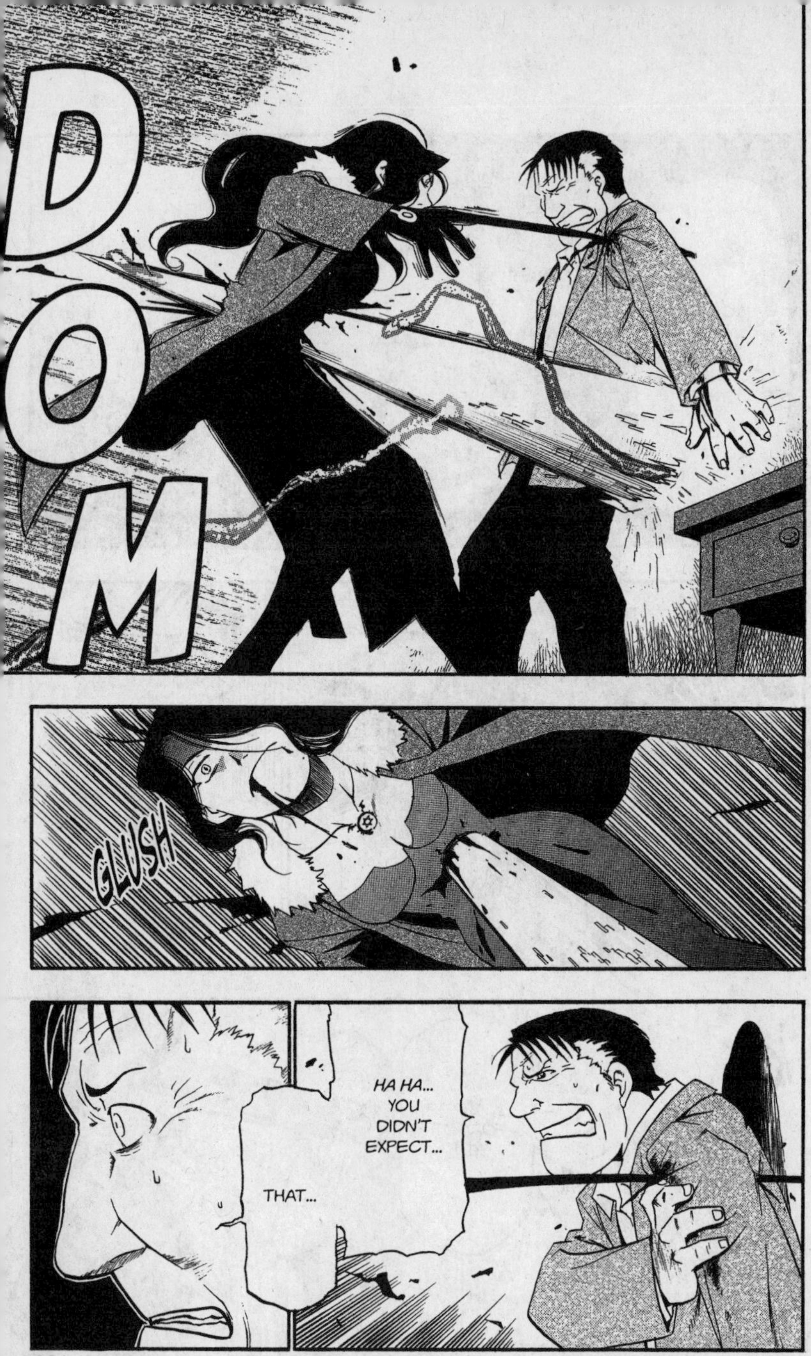
DOM
GLUSH
HA HA... YOU DIDN'T EXPECT...
THAT...

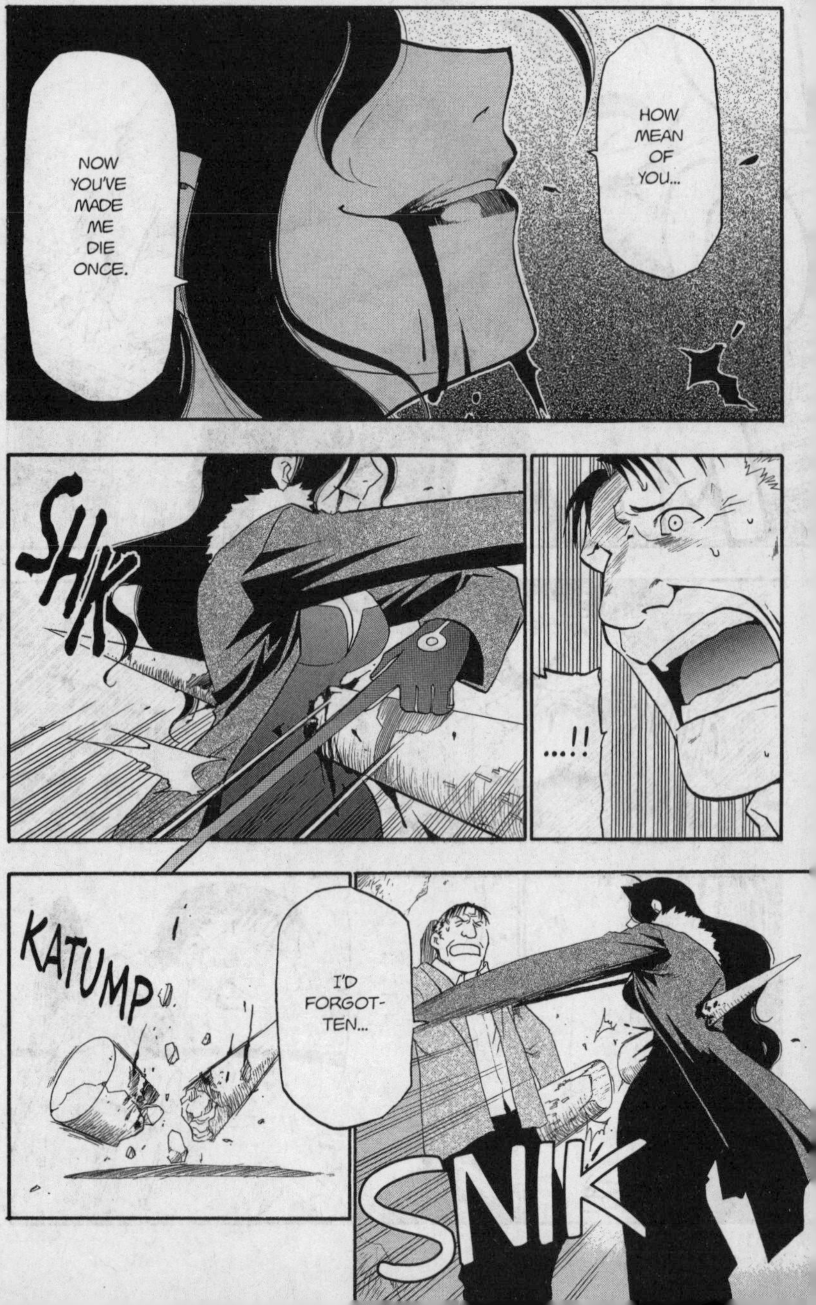
HOW MEAN OF YOU...
NOW YOU'VE MADE ME DIE ONCE.
...!!
SHK
I'D FORGOT-TEN...
SNIK
KATUMP

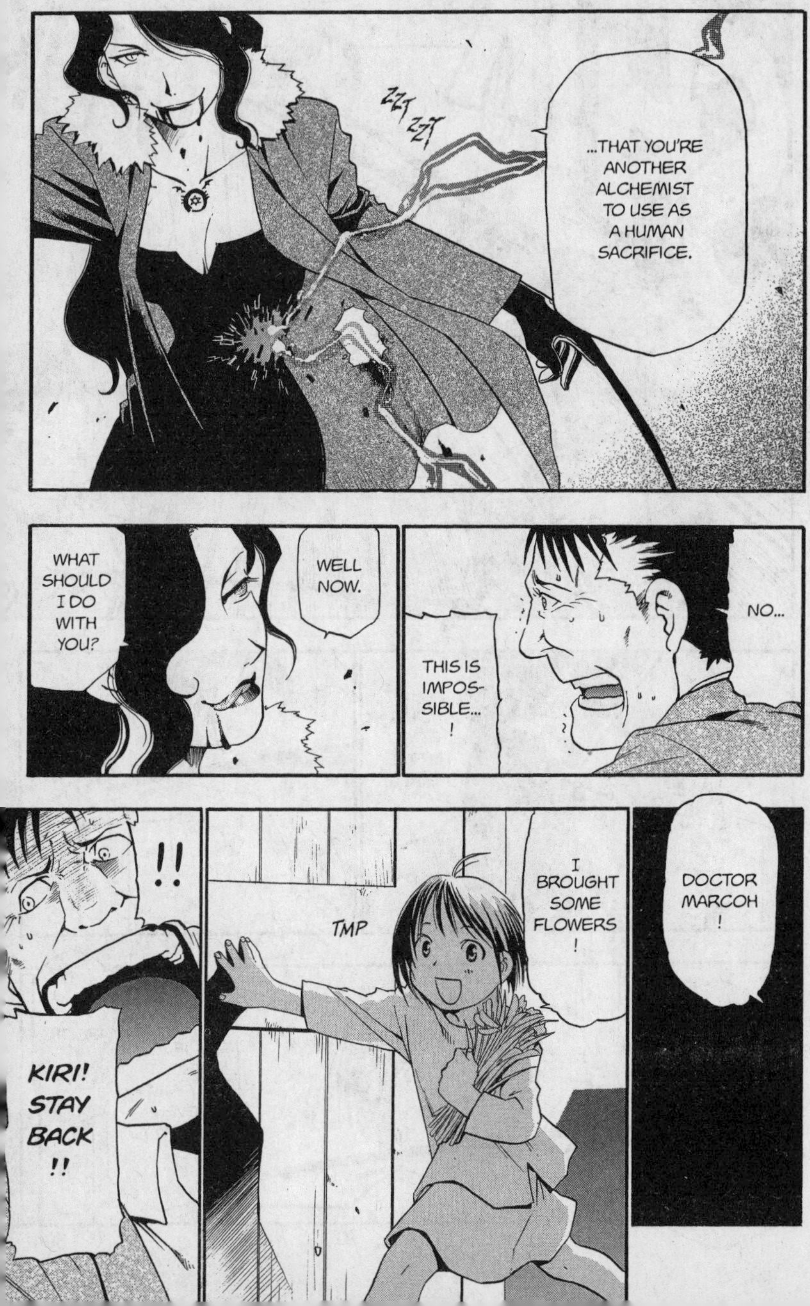
...THAT YOU'RE ANOTHER ALCHEMIST TO USE AS A HUMAN SACRIFICE.
NO...
THIS IS IMPOSSIBLE...!
WELL NOW.
WHAT SHOULD I DO WITH YOU?
DOCTOR MARCOH!
I BROUGHT SOME FLOWERS!
TMP
!!
KIRI! STAY BACK!!

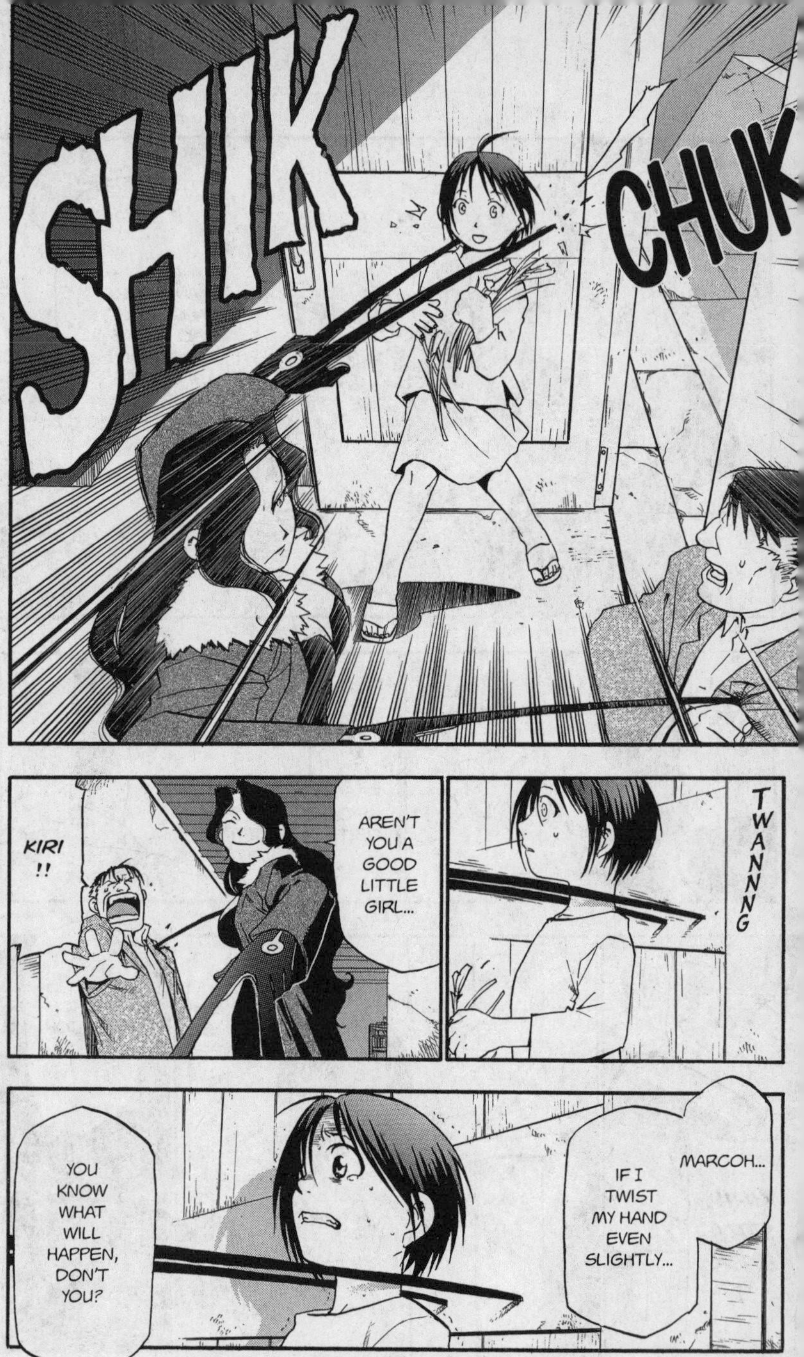
CHUK
SHIK
TWANNNG
AREN'T YOU A GOOD LITTLE GIRL...
KIRI !!
MARCOH...
IF I TWIST MY HAND EVEN SLIGHTLY...
YOU KNOW WHAT WILL HAPPEN, DON'T YOU?

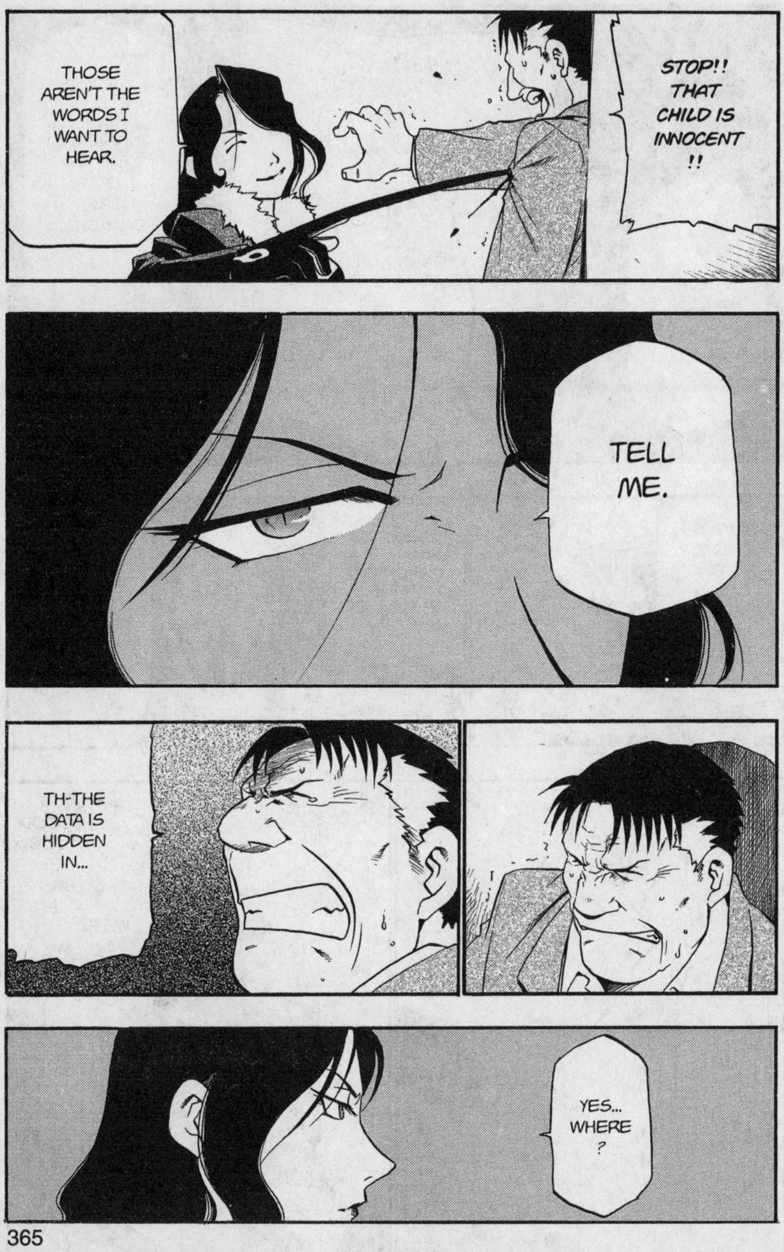
STOP!! THAT CHILD IS INNOCENT!!
THOSE AREN'T THE WORDS I WANT TO HEAR.
TELL ME.
TH-THE DATA IS HIDDEN IN...
YES... WHERE?

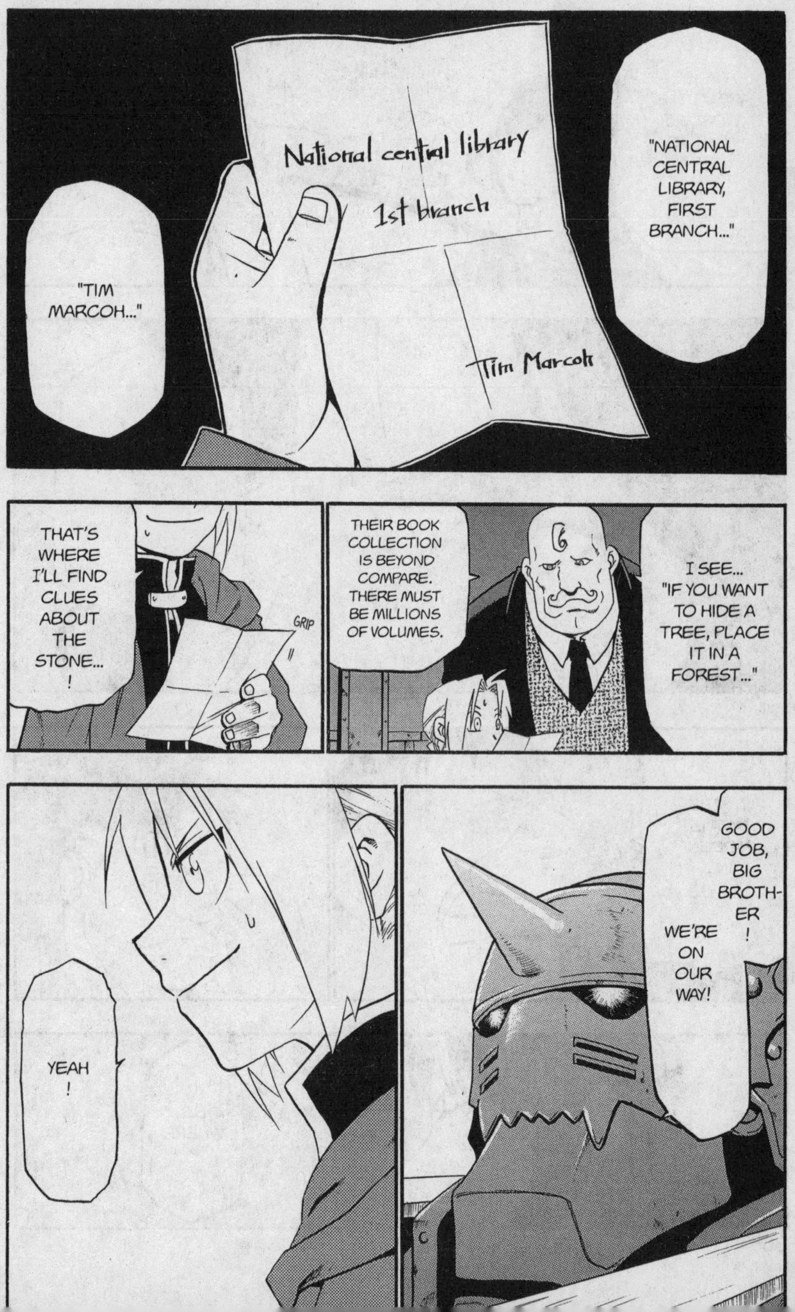
"NATIONAL CENTRAL LIBRARY, FIRST BRANCH..."
National central library
1st branch
Tim Marcoh
"TIM MARCOH..."
I SEE... "IF YOU WANT TO HIDE A TREE, PLACE IT IN A FOREST..."
THEIR BOOK COLLECTION IS BEYOND COMPARE. THERE MUST BE MILLIONS OF VOLUMES.
THAT'S WHERE I'LL FIND CLUES ABOUT THE STONE...!
GRIP
GOOD JOB, BIG BROTH-ER!
WE'RE ON OUR WAY!
YEAH!

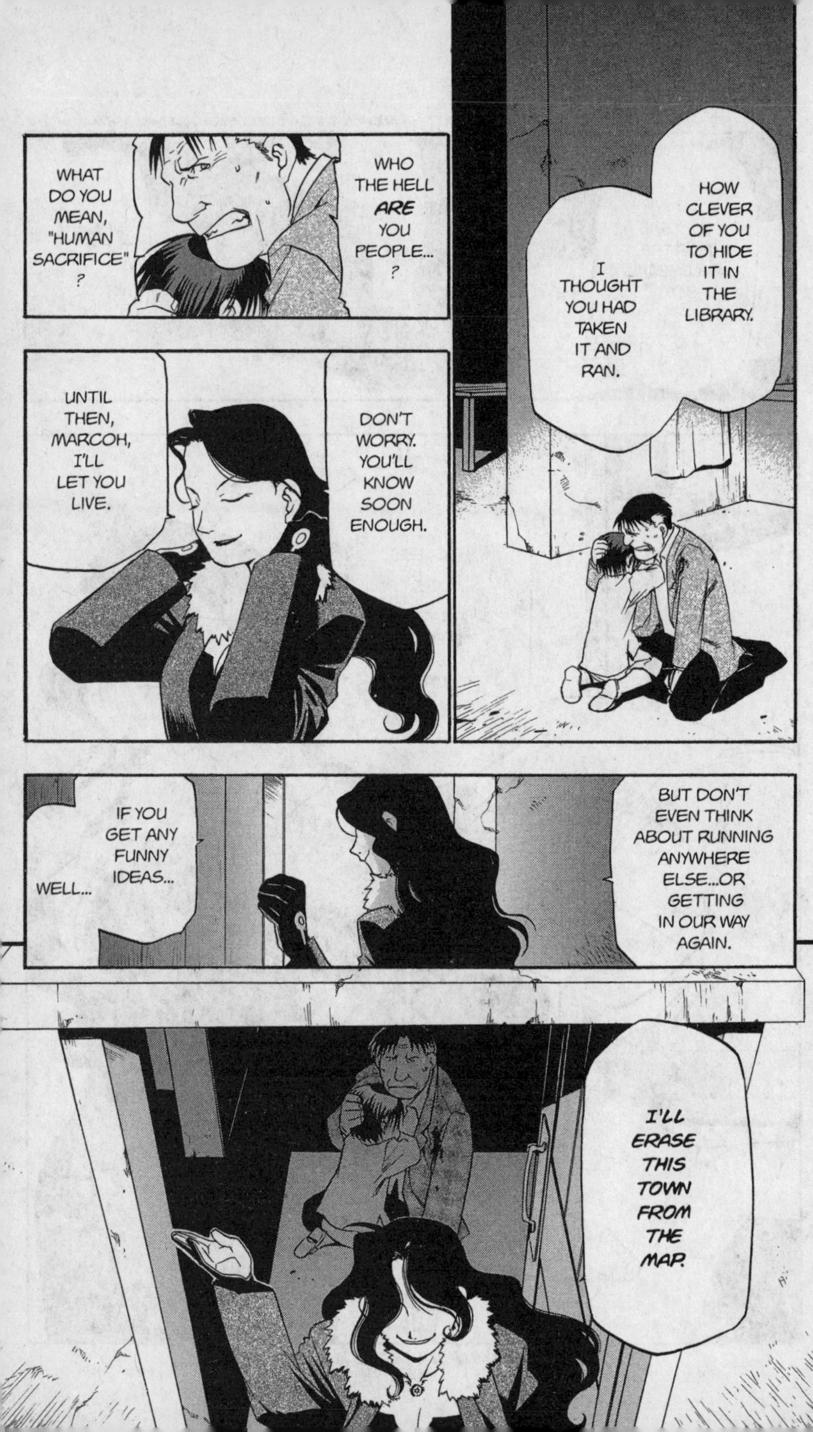
HOW CLEVER OF YOU TO HIDE IT IN THE LIBRARY.
I THOUGHT YOU HAD TAKEN IT AND RAN.
WHO THE HELL *ARE* YOU PEOPLE... ?
WHAT DO YOU MEAN, "HUMAN SACRIFICE" ?
DON'T WORRY. YOU'LL KNOW SOON ENOUGH.
UNTIL THEN, MARCOH, I'LL LET YOU LIVE.
BUT DON'T EVEN THINK ABOUT RUNNING ANYWHERE ELSE...OR GETTING IN OUR WAY AGAIN.
IF YOU GET ANY FUNNY IDEAS...
WELL...
I'LL ERASE THIS TOWN FROM THE MAP.

THIS MANGA WAS ORIGINALLY PRINTED IN MONTHLY ***SHONEN GANGAN****, DECEMBER 2001 THROUGH MARCH 2002.*

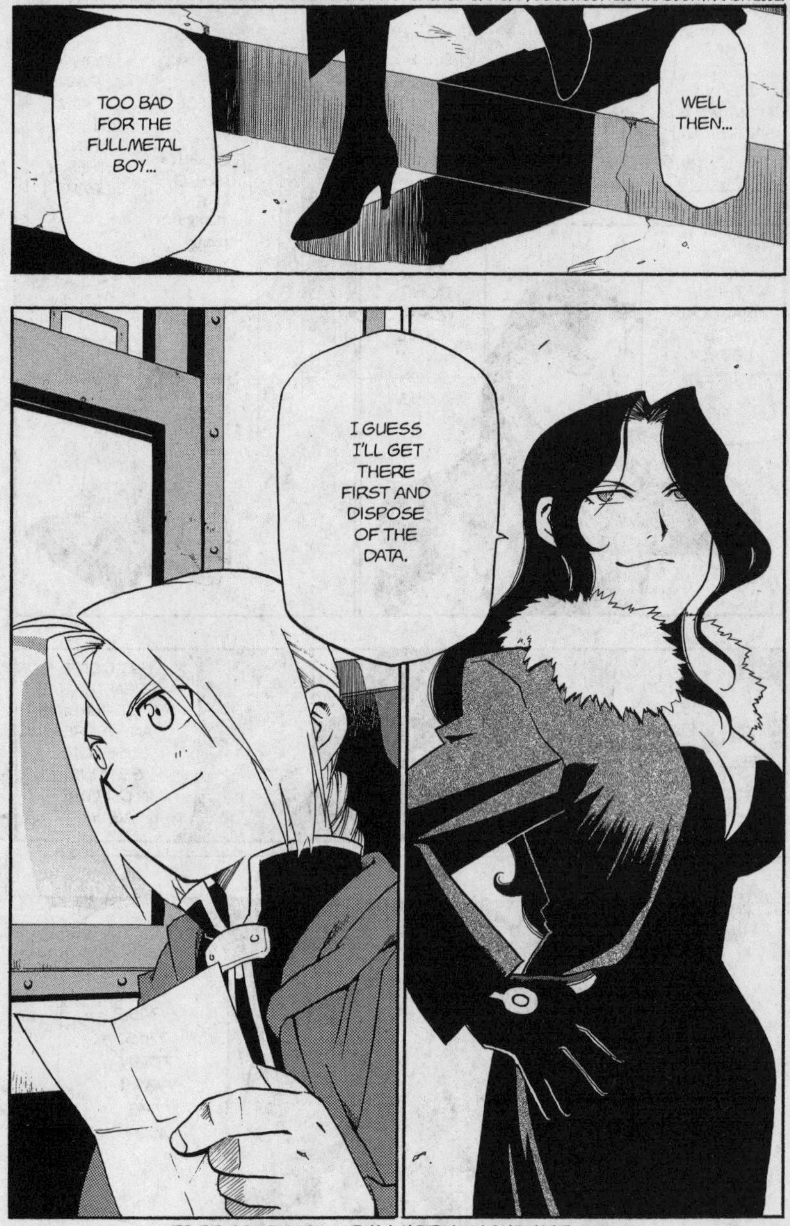
WELL THEN...
TOO BAD FOR THE FULLMETAL BOY...
I GUESS I'LL GET THERE FIRST AND DISPOSE OF THE DATA.

TO BE CONTINUED IN ***FULLMETAL ALCHEMIST*** *VOL. 3...*

EXTRA

A SPECIAL PRESENT FOR GOOD BOYS AND GIRLS!

MAJOR ARMSTRONG
LUCKY CHARM

MIGHTY 大 盛 FLEX

※ Please be extra careful when using it.

POPULARITY EMPIRE

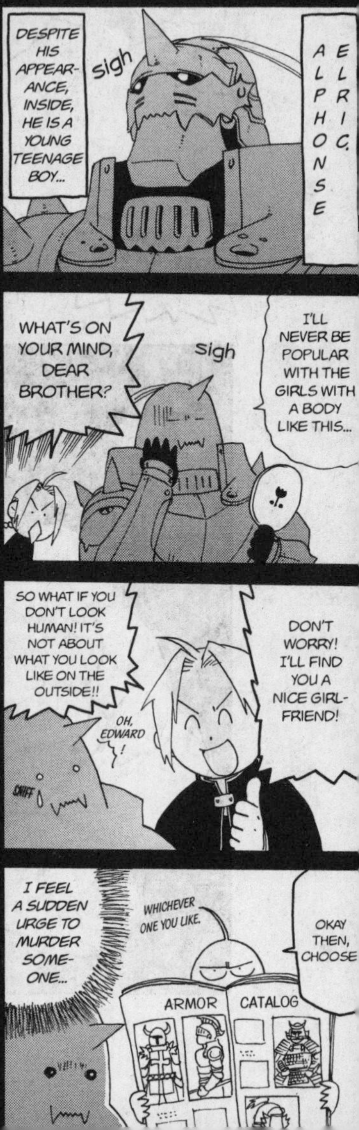
ALPHONSE ELRIC.
Sigh
DESPITE HIS APPEARANCE, INSIDE, HE IS A YOUNG TEENAGE BOY...
I'LL NEVER BE POPULAR WITH THE GIRLS WITH A BODY LIKE THIS...
sigh
WHAT'S ON YOUR MIND, DEAR BROTHER?
DON'T WORRY! I'LL FIND YOU A NICE GIRLFRIEND!
SO WHAT IF YOU DON'T LOOK HUMAN! IT'S NOT ABOUT WHAT YOU LOOK LIKE ON THE OUTSIDE!!
OH, EDWARD!
SNIFF
OKAY THEN, CHOOSE
WHICHEVER ONE YOU LIKE.
ARMOR CATALOG
I FEEL A SUDDEN URGE TO MURDER SOMEONE...

FIRST, DO SOMETHING ABOUT THE LOINCLOTH

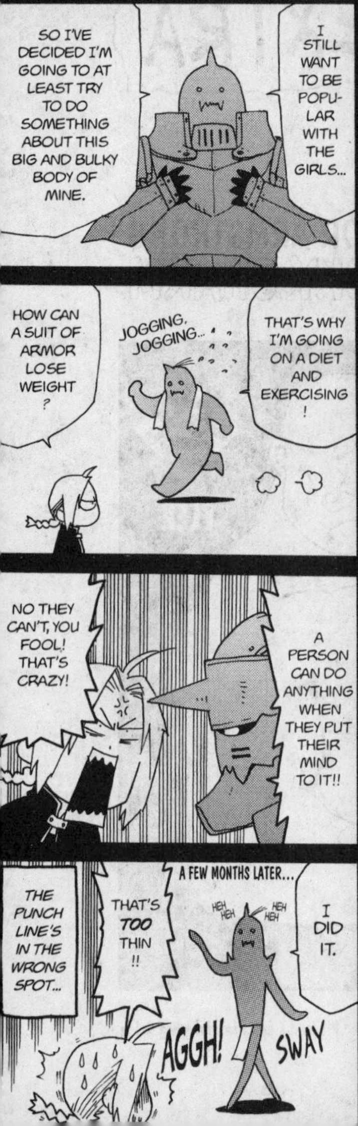
I STILL WANT TO BE POPULAR WITH THE GIRLS...
SO I'VE DECIDED I'M GOING TO AT LEAST TRY TO DO SOMETHING ABOUT THIS BIG AND BULKY BODY OF MINE.
THAT'S WHY I'M GOING ON A DIET AND EXERCISING!
JOGGING, JOGGING...
HOW CAN A SUIT OF ARMOR LOSE WEIGHT?
A PERSON CAN DO ANYTHING WHEN THEY PUT THEIR MIND TO IT!!
NO THEY CAN'T, YOU FOOL! THAT'S CRAZY!
A FEW MONTHS LATER...
I DID IT.
HEH HEH
HEH HEH
SWAY
THAT'S TOO THIN!!
AGGH!
THE PUNCH LINE'S IN THE WRONG SPOT...

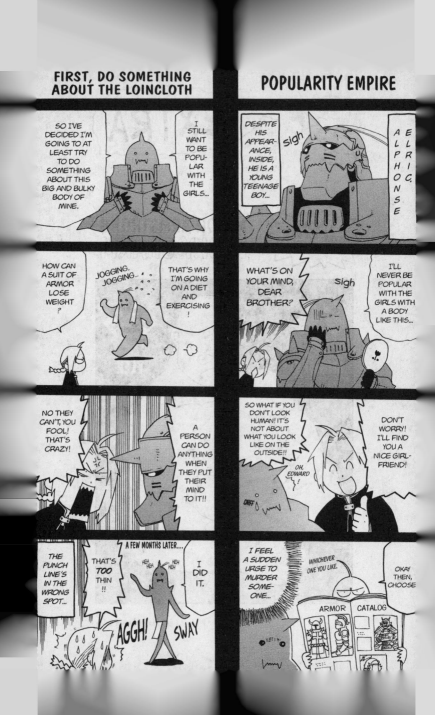

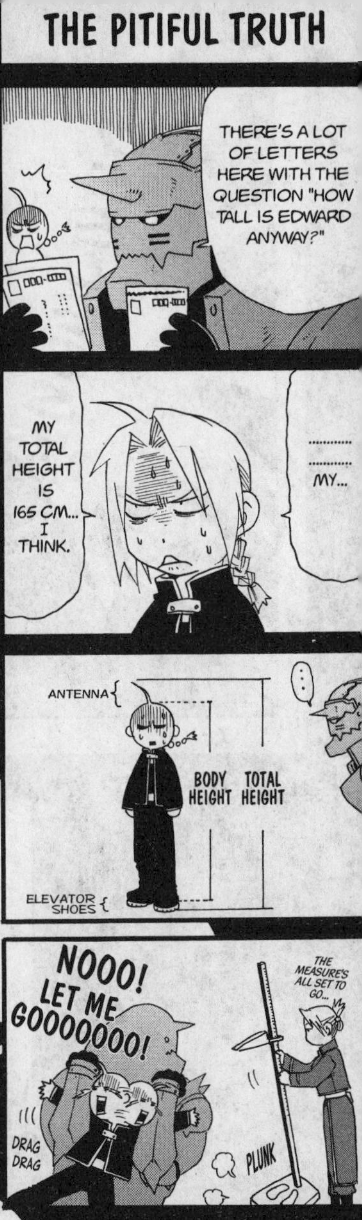
THE PITIFUL TRUTH
THERE'S A LOT OF LETTERS HERE WITH THE QUESTION "HOW TALL IS EDWARD ANYWAY?"
....
..........MY...
MY TOTAL HEIGHT IS 165 CM... I THINK.
ANTENNA
TOTAL HEIGHT
BODY HEIGHT
ELEVATOR SHOES
THE MEASURE'S ALL SET TO GO...
NOOO! LET ME GOOOOOOOO!
DRAG DRAG
PLUNK

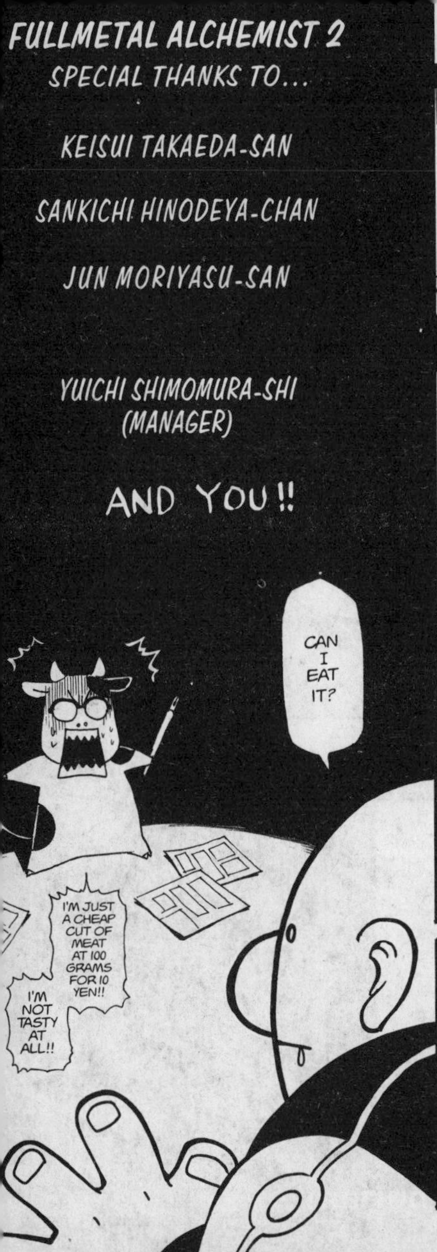
FULLMETAL ALCHEMIST 2
SPECIAL THANKS TO...
KEISUI TAKAEDA-SAN
SANKICHI HINODEYA-CHAN
JUN MORIYASU-SAN
YUICHI SHIMOMURA-SHI (MANAGER)
AND YOU!!
CAN I EAT IT?
I'M JUST A CHEAP CUT OF MEAT AT 100 GRAMS FOR 10 YEN!!
I'M NOT TASTY AT ALL!!

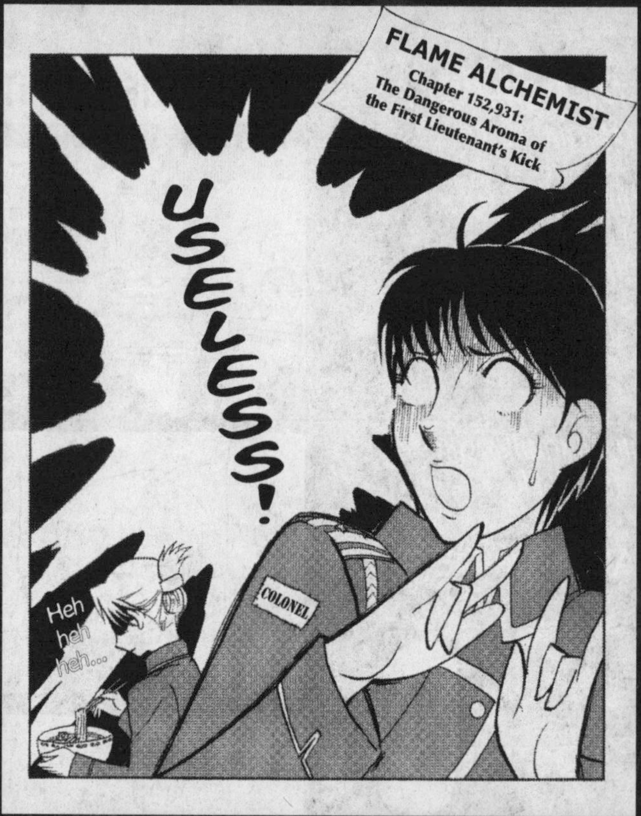
FLAME ALCHEMIST
Chapter 152,931: The Dangerous Aroma of the First Lieutenant's Kick
USELESS!
COLONEL
Heh heh heh...

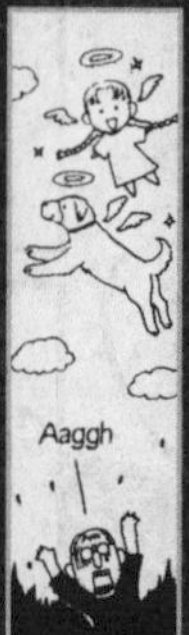
Aaggh
HELL

In Memoriam

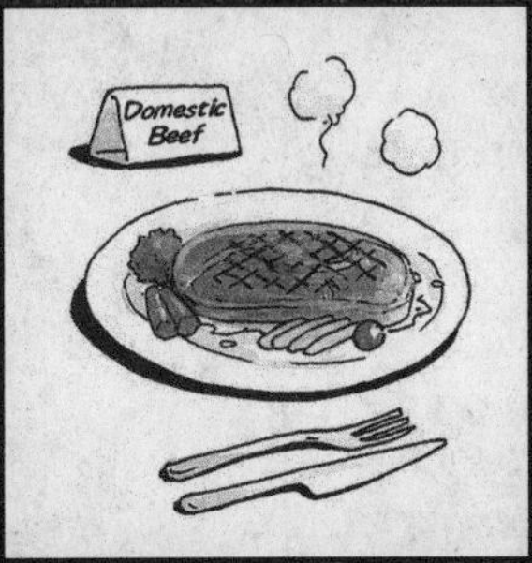
Domestic Beef

"I love to read manga!"

"I love to draw manga so much I don't know what to do!"

"I draw, therefore I am!"

"That's all the proof I need to know that I exist!!!"

—Hiromu Arakawa, 2002

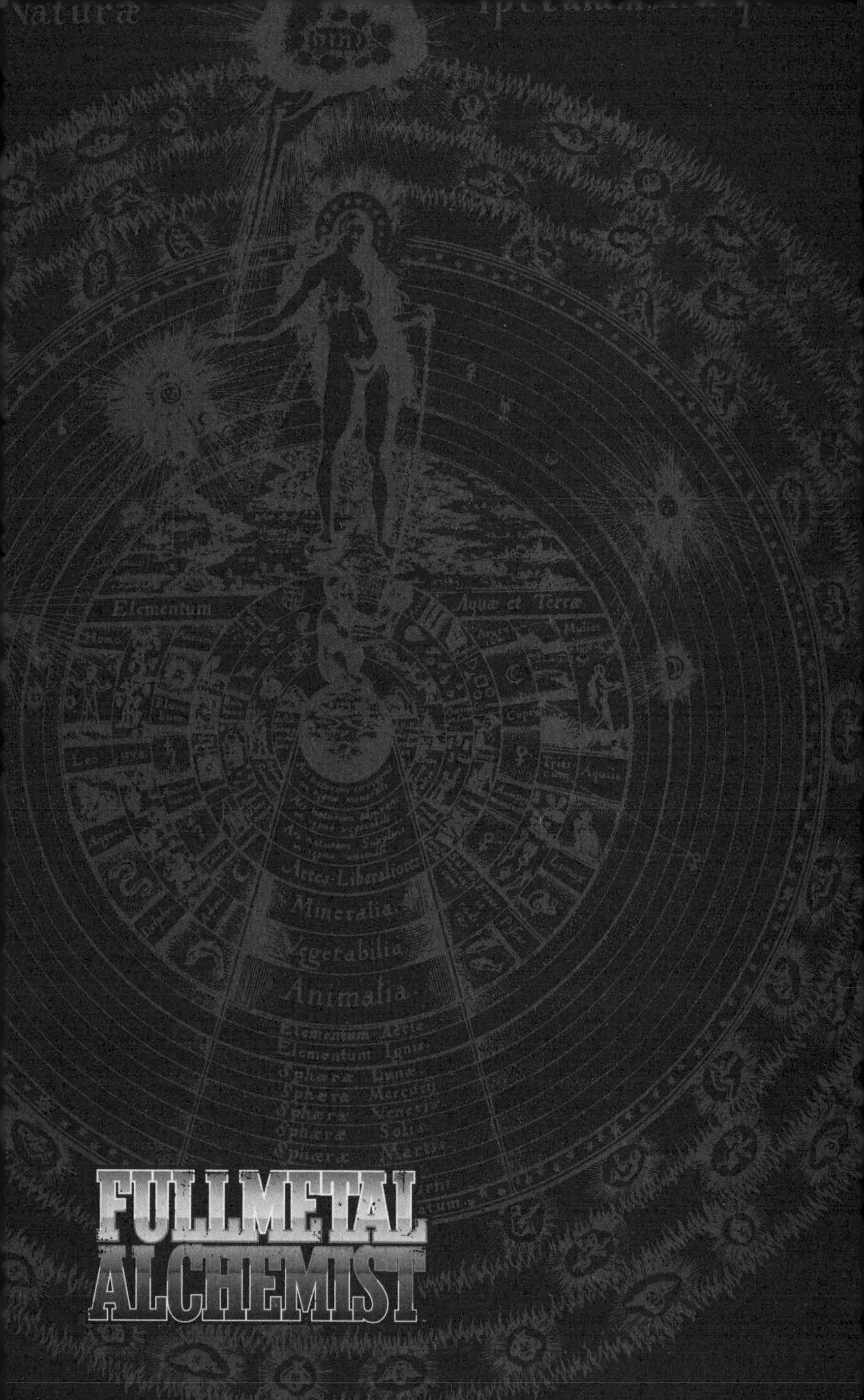
natura
Elementum
Aquæ et Terræ
Artes Liberaliores
Mineralia
Vegetabilia
Animalia
Elementum Aeris
Elementum Ignis
Sphæra Lunæ
Sphæra Mercurii
Sphæra Veneris
Sphæra Solis
Sphæra Martis
FULLMETAL
ALCHEMIST

鋼の錬金術師

FULLMETAL ALCHEMIST

3

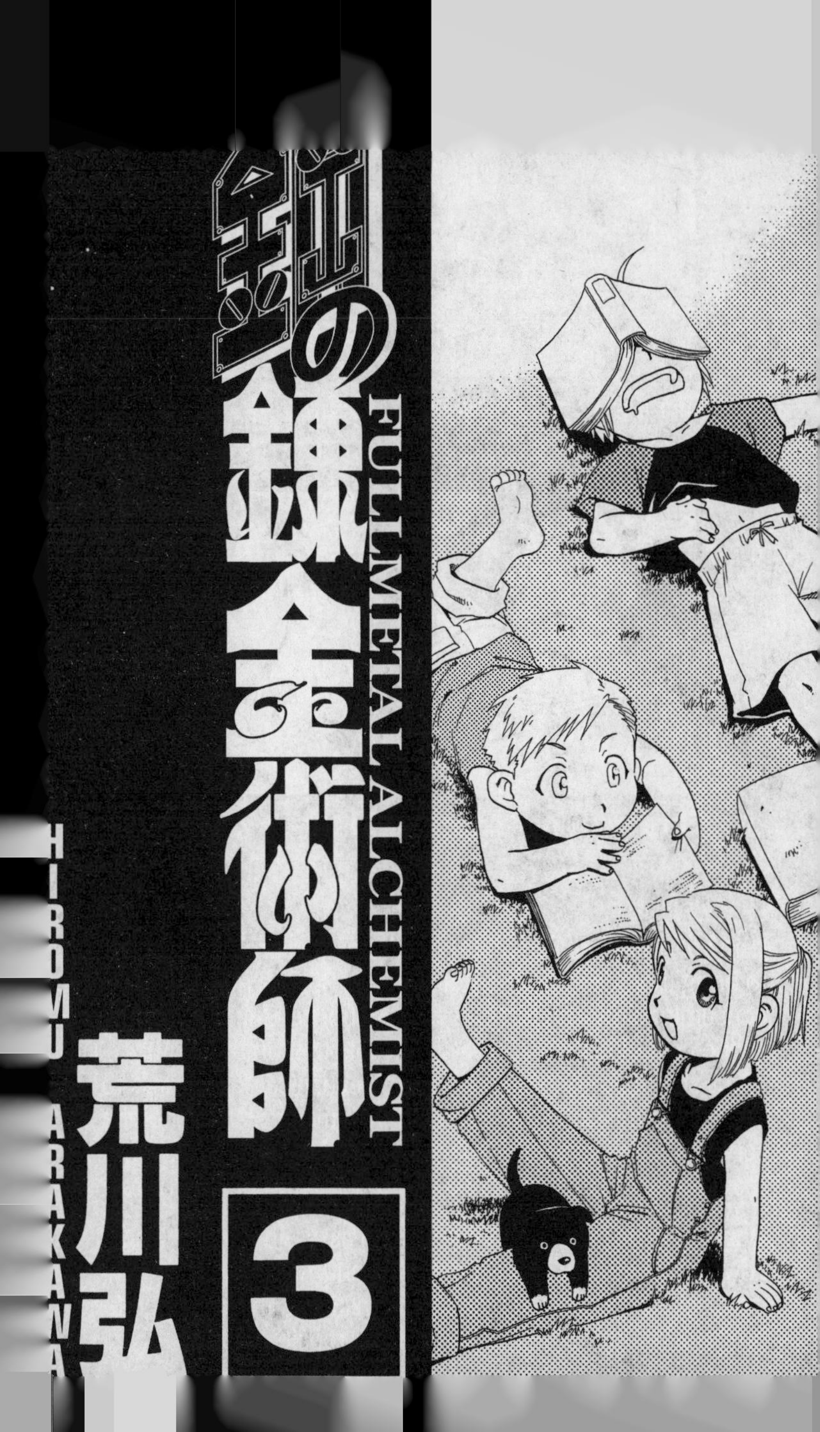

荒川弘

HIROMU ARAKAWA

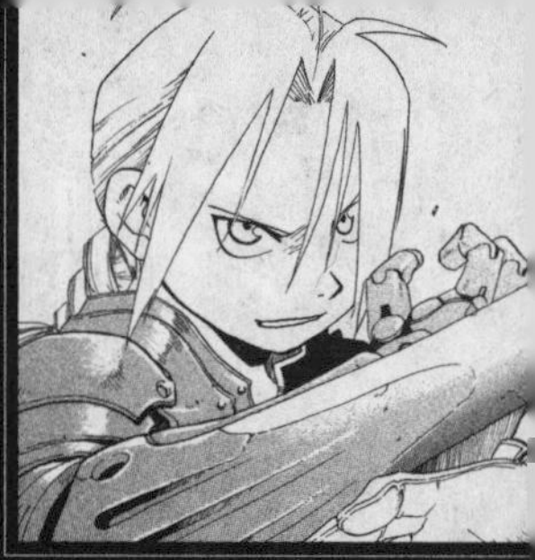

エドワード・エルリック

Edward Elric

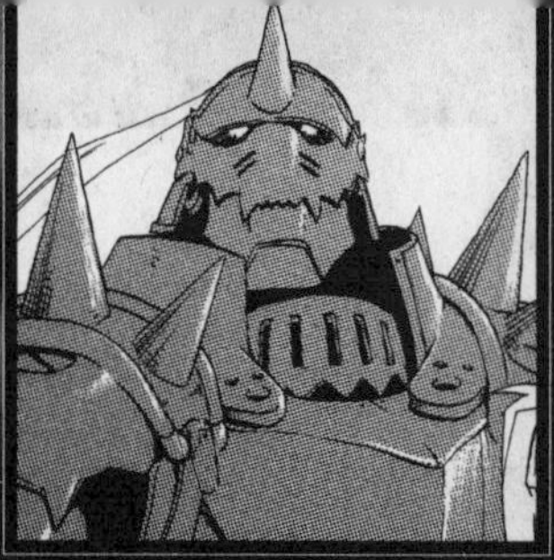

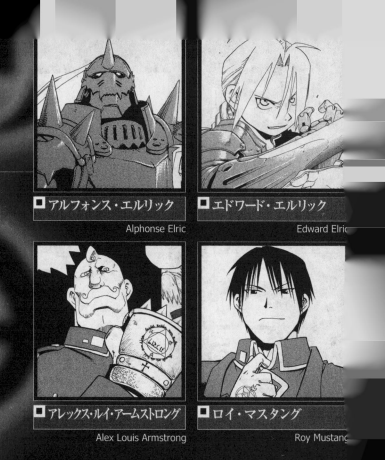

アルフォンス・エルリック

Alphonse Elric

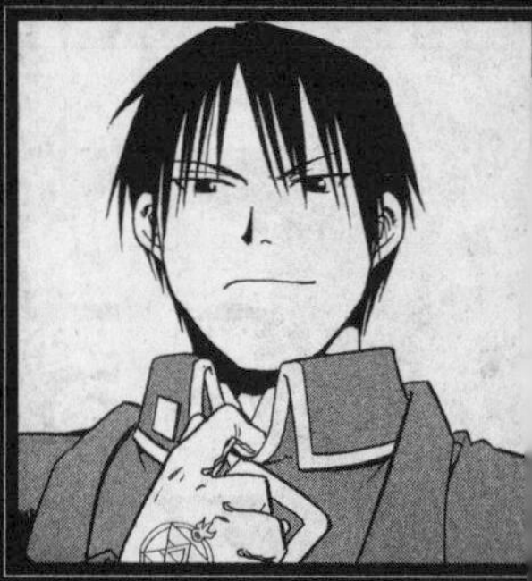

ロイ・マスタング

Roy Mustang

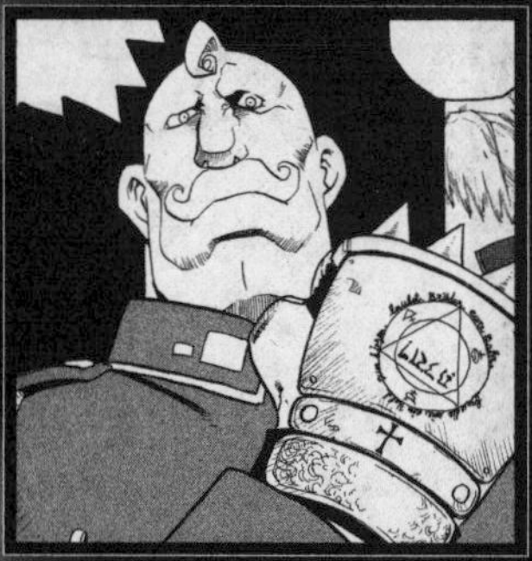

アレックス・ルイ・アームストロング

Alex Louis Armstrong

Using a forbidden alchemical ritual, the Elric brothers attemptec to bring their dead mother back to life. But the ritual went wron consuming Edward Elric's leg and Alphonse Elric's entire body. At the cost of his arm, Edward was able to graft his brother's so into a suit of armor. Equipped with mechanical "auto-mail" to replace his missing limbs, Edward becomes a state alchemist, serving the military on deadly missions. Now, the two brothers roam the world in search of a way to regain what they have lost

During a near-fatal encounter with an assassin named Scar, Edward's auto-mail arm is destroyed and Alphonse is incapacitated. Escorted by Major Armstrong, the damaged Elric brothers return to their hometown for repairs.

鋼の錬金術師
FULLMETAL ALCHEMIST

CHARACTERS
FULLMETAL ALCHEMIST

□ ウィンリィ・ロックベル

Winry Rockbell

□ 傷の男(スカー)

Scar

□ グラトニー

Gluttony

□ ラスト

Lust

OUTLINE
FULLMETAL ALCHEMIST

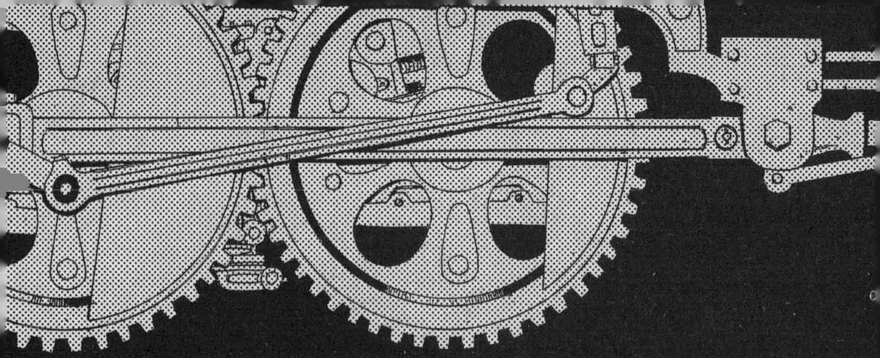

CONTENTS

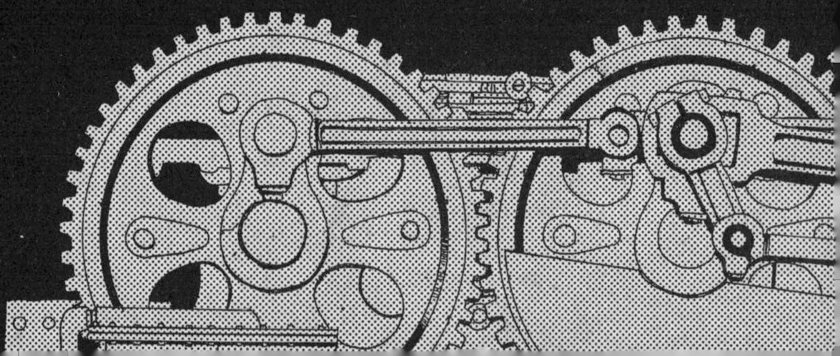

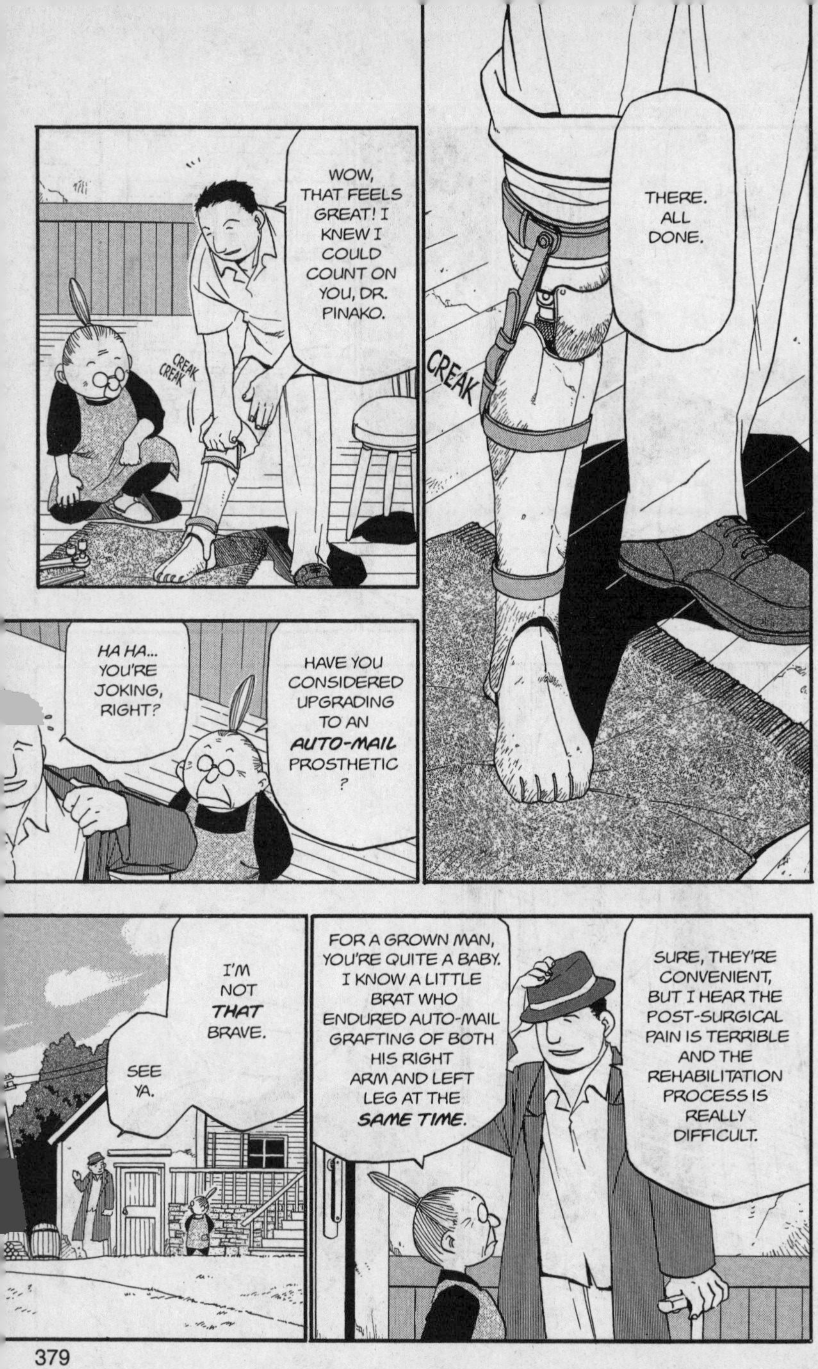
THERE. ALL DONE.
CREAK
WOW, THAT FEELS GREAT! I KNEW I COULD COUNT ON YOU, DR. PINAKO.
CREAK CREAK
HAVE YOU CONSIDERED UPGRADING TO AN AUTO-MAIL PROSTHETIC?
HA HA... YOU'RE JOKING, RIGHT?
SURE, THEY'RE CONVENIENT, BUT I HEAR THE POST-SURGICAL PAIN IS TERRIBLE AND THE REHABILITATION PROCESS IS REALLY DIFFICULT.
FOR A GROWN MAN, YOU'RE QUITE A BABY. I KNOW A LITTLE BRAT WHO ENDURED AUTO-MAIL GRAFTING OF BOTH HIS RIGHT ARM AND LEFT LEG AT THE SAME TIME.
I'M NOT THAT BRAVE.
SEE YA.

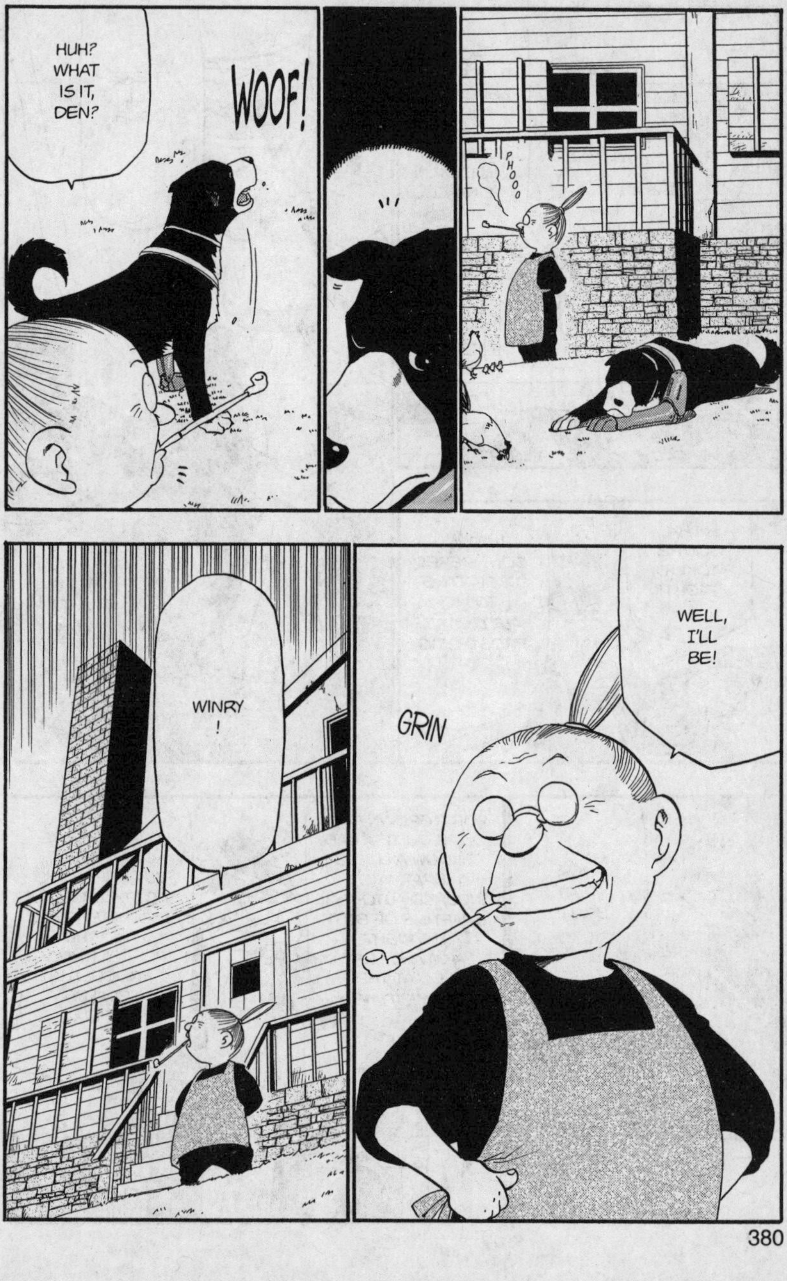
PHOOO
WOOF!
HUH? WHAT IS IT, DEN?
WELL, I'LL BE!
GRIN
WINRY!

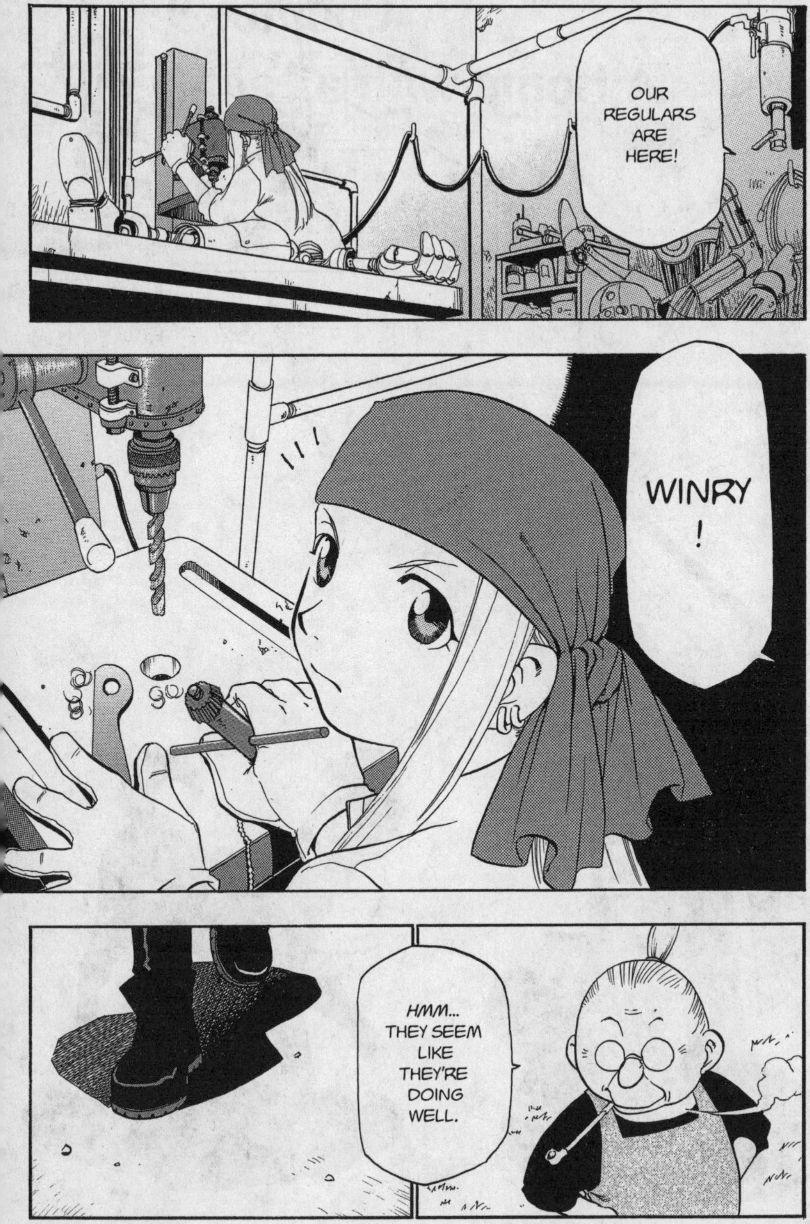
OUR REGULARS ARE HERE!
WINRY !
HMM... THEY SEEM LIKE THEY'RE DOING WELL.

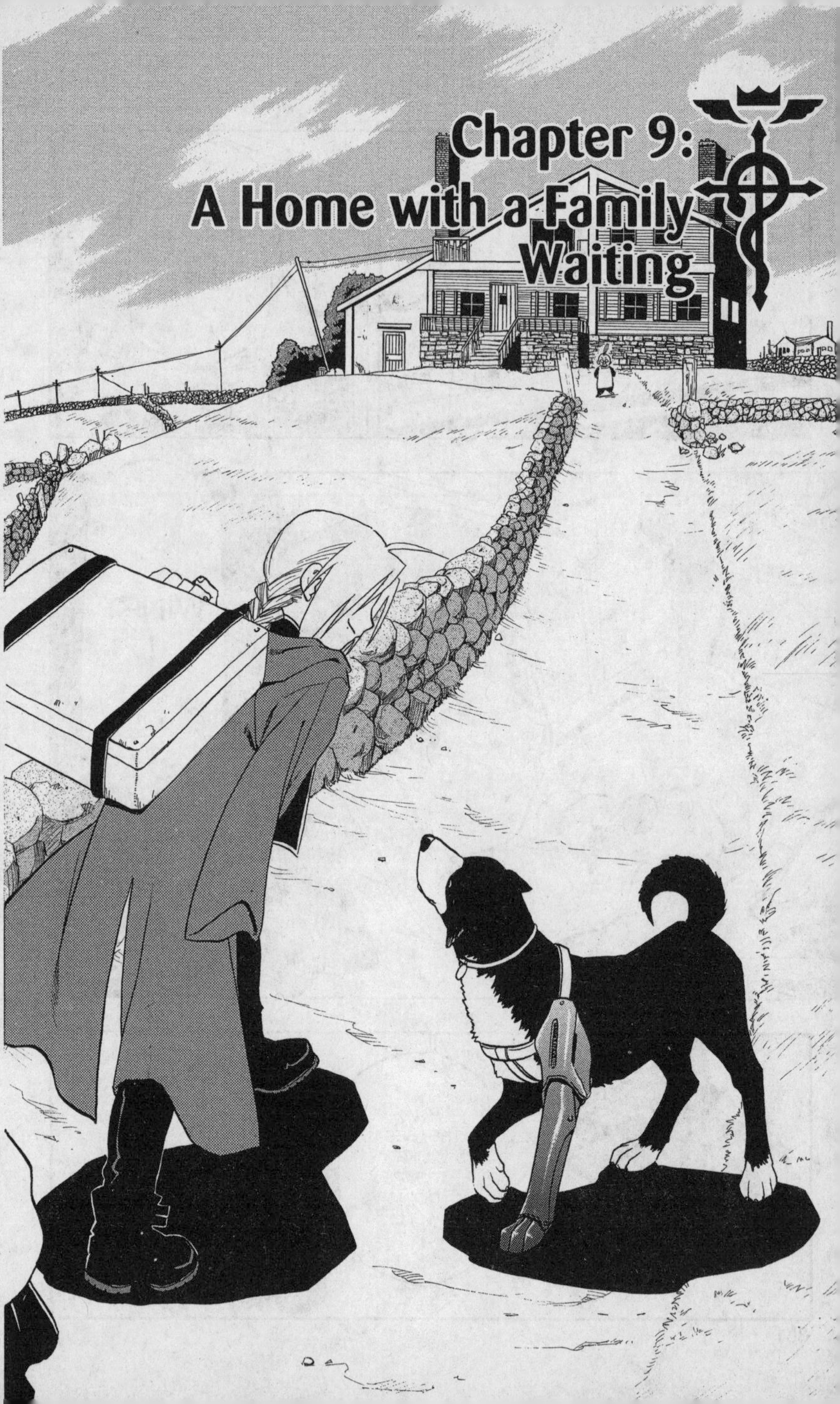
Chapter 9:
A Home with a Family Waiting

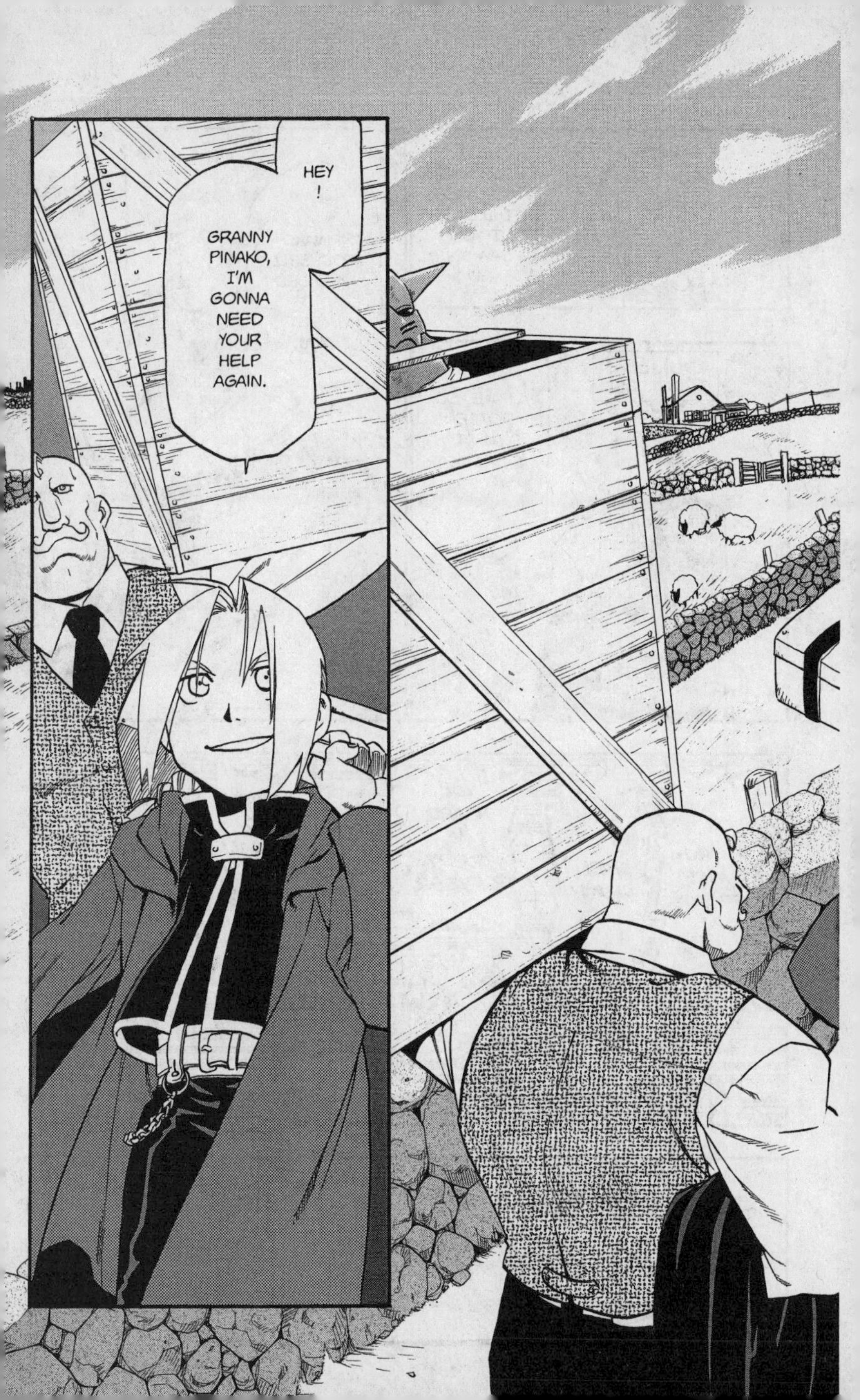
HEY!
GRANNY PINAKO, I'M GONNA NEED YOUR HELP AGAIN.

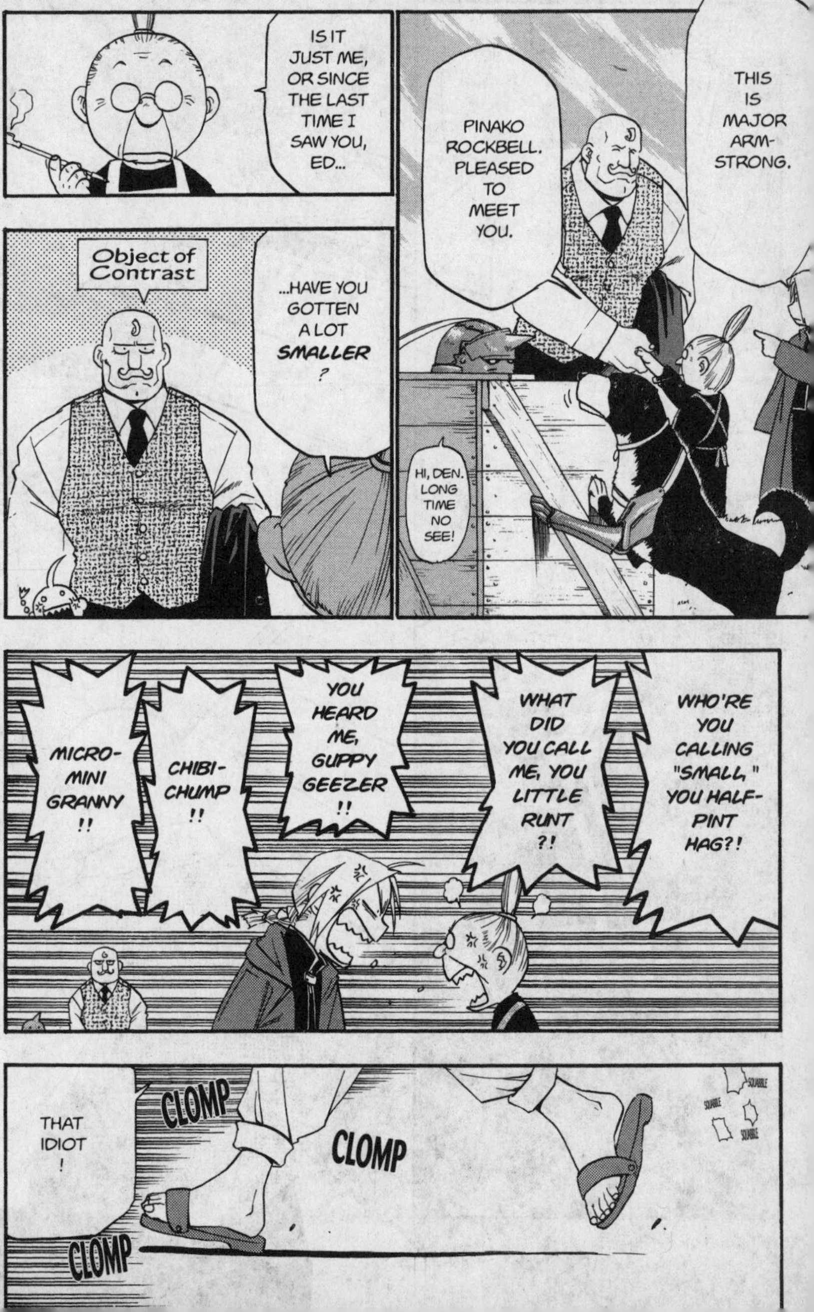
THIS IS MAJOR ARMSTRONG.
PINAKO ROCKBELL. PLEASED TO MEET YOU.
HI, DEN. LONG TIME NO SEE!
IS IT JUST ME, OR SINCE THE LAST TIME I SAW YOU, ED...
Object of Contrast
...HAVE YOU GOTTEN A LOT SMALLER?
WHO'RE YOU CALLING "SMALL," YOU HALF-PINT HAG?!
WHAT DID YOU CALL ME, YOU LITTLE RUNT?!
YOU HEARD ME, GUPPY GEEZER!!
CHIBI-CHUMP!!
MICRO-MINI GRANNY!!
SQUABBLE
SQUABBLE
SQUABBLE
CLOMP
CLOMP
THAT IDIOT!
CLOMP

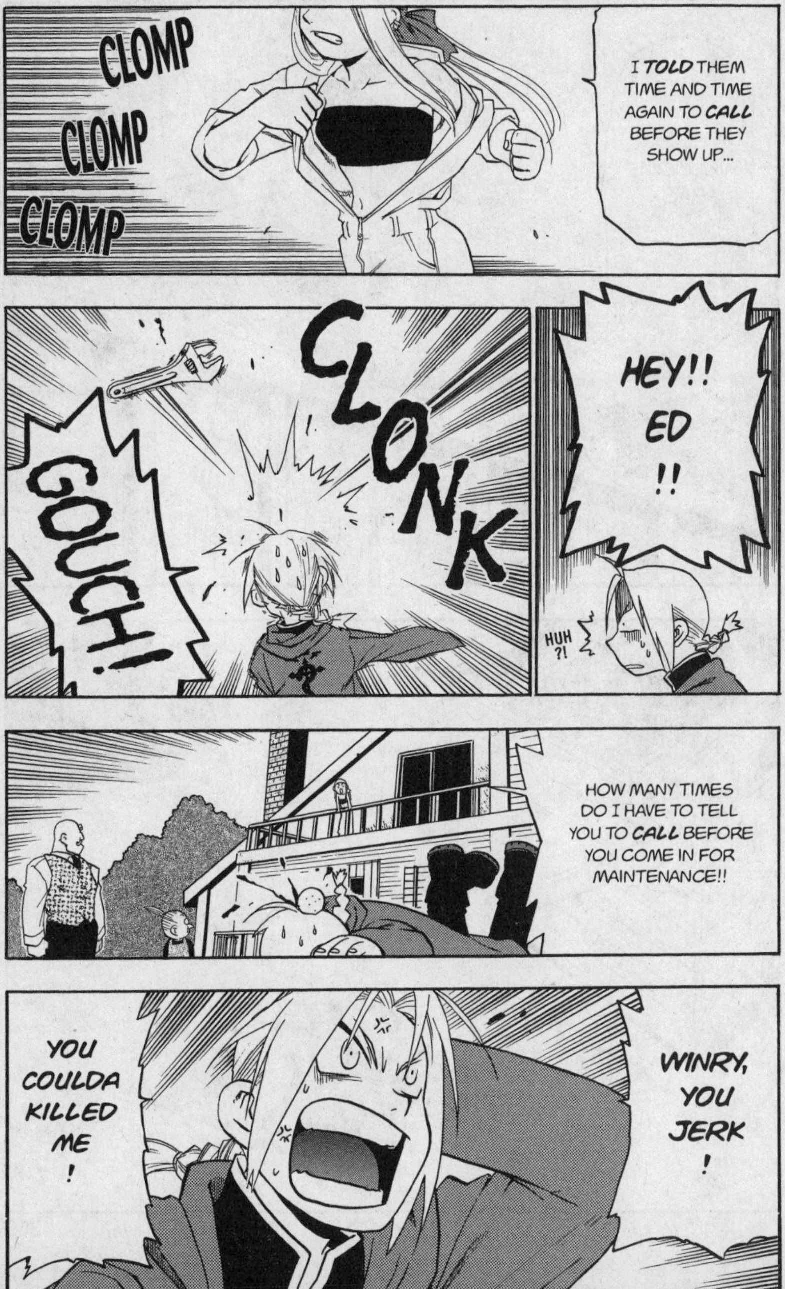
I TOLD THEM TIME AND TIME AGAIN TO CALL BEFORE THEY SHOW UP...
CLOMP
CLOMP
CLOMP
HEY!! ED!!
HUH?!
CLONK
GOUCH!
HOW MANY TIMES DO I HAVE TO TELL YOU TO CALL BEFORE YOU COME IN FOR MAINTENANCE!!
WINRY, YOU JERK!
YOU COULDA KILLED ME!

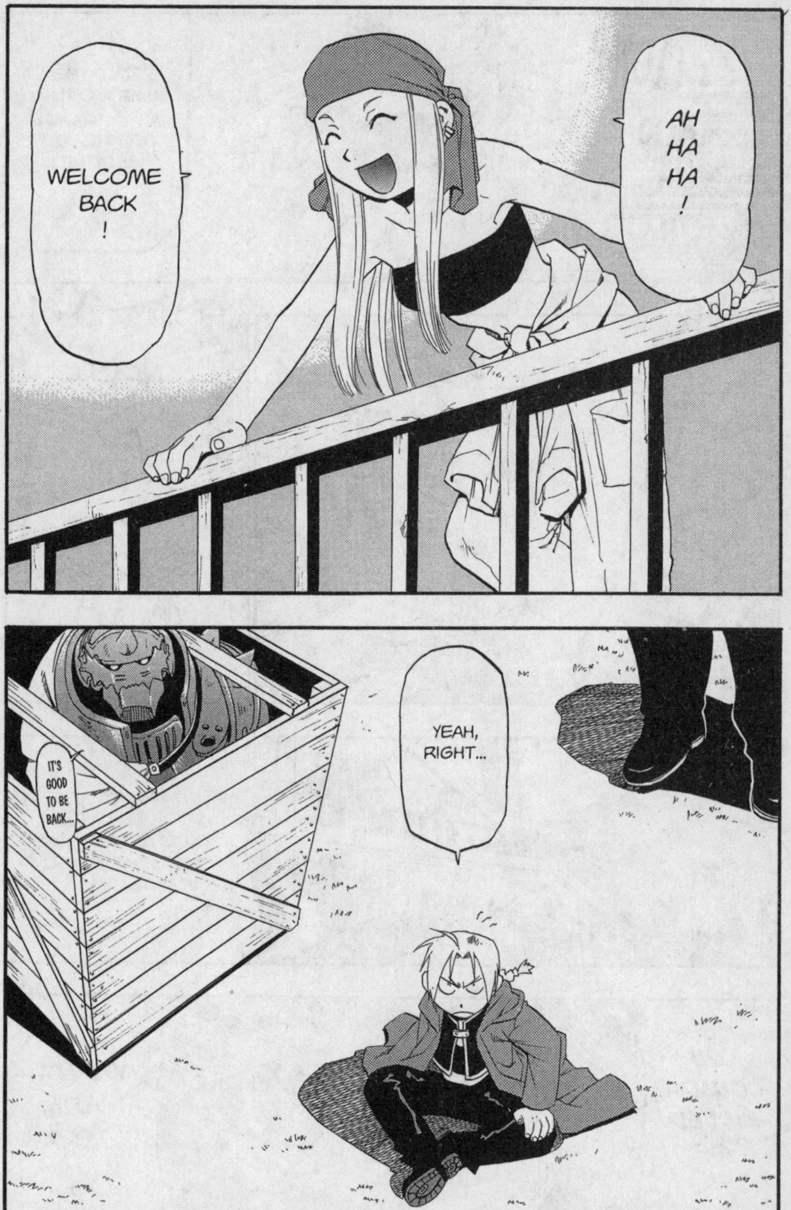
AH HA HA!
WELCOME BACK!
YEAH, RIGHT...
IT'S GOOD TO BE BACK...

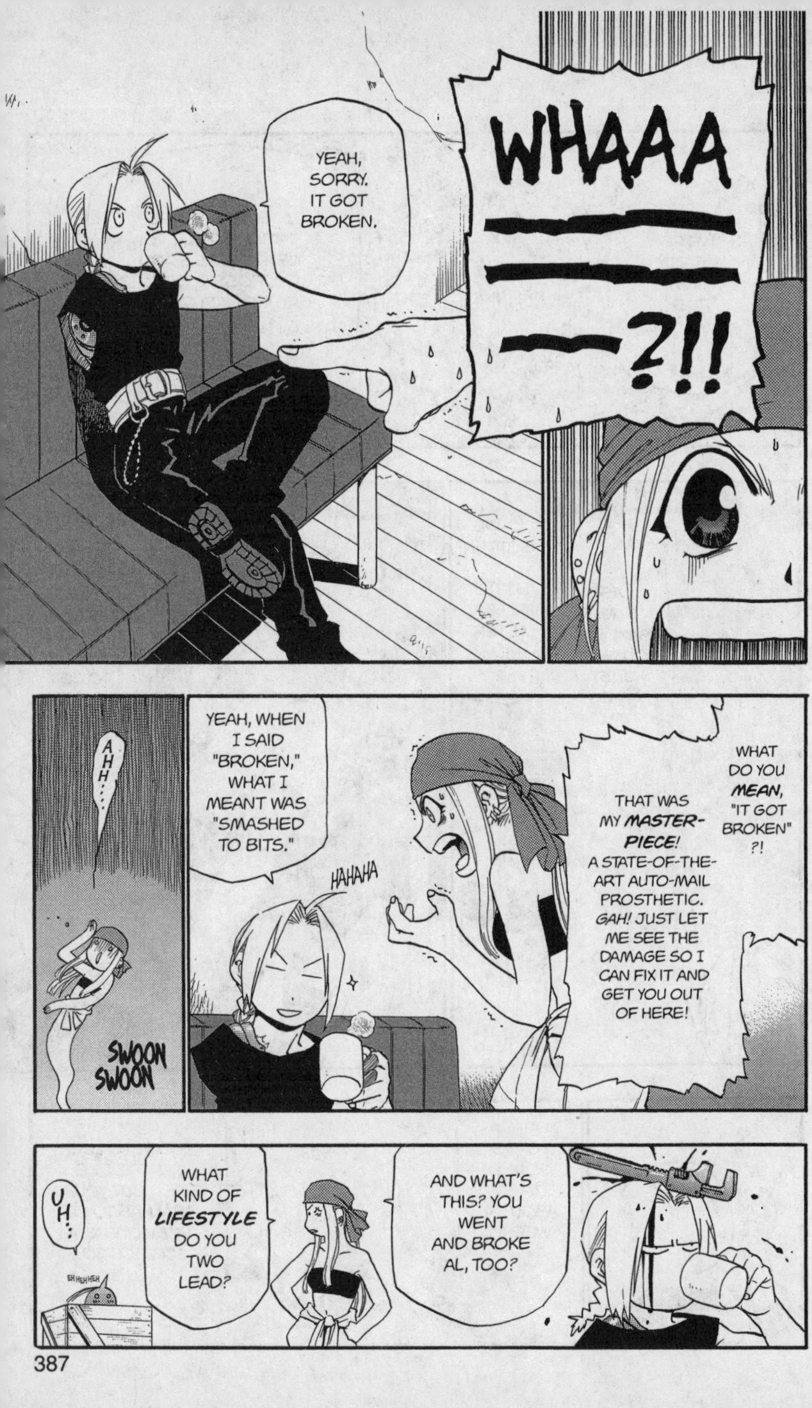
YEAH, SORRY. IT GOT BROKEN.
WHAAAA———?!!
WHAT DO YOU MEAN, "IT GOT BROKEN"?!
THAT WAS MY MASTERPIECE! A STATE-OF-THE-ART AUTO-MAIL PROSTHETIC. GAH! JUST LET ME SEE THE DAMAGE SO I CAN FIX IT AND GET YOU OUT OF HERE!
YEAH, WHEN I SAID "BROKEN," WHAT I MEANT WAS "SMASHED TO BITS."
HAHAHA
AHH...
SWOON SWOON
AND WHAT'S THIS? YOU WENT AND BROKE AL, TOO?
WHAT KIND OF LIFESTYLE DO YOU TWO LEAD?
UH...
EH HEH HEH

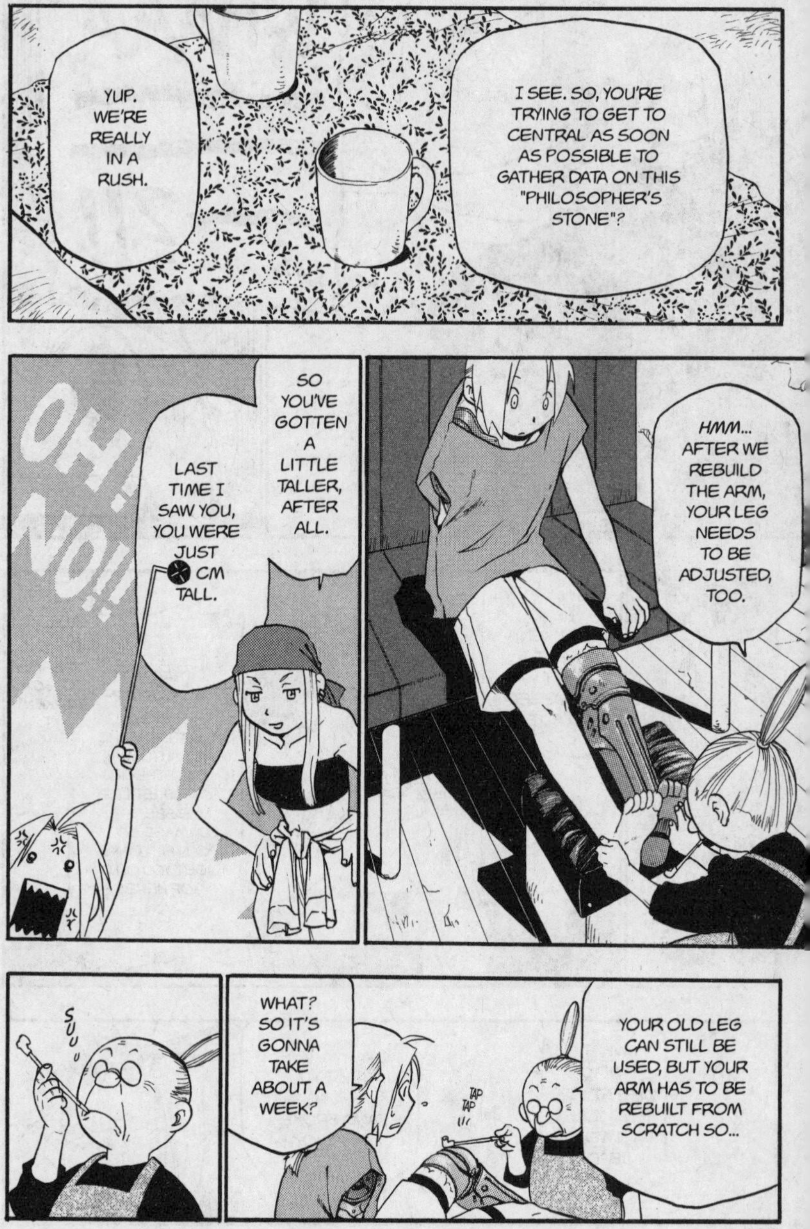
I SEE. SO, YOU'RE TRYING TO GET TO CENTRAL AS SOON AS POSSIBLE TO GATHER DATA ON THIS "PHILOSOPHER'S STONE"?
YUP. WE'RE REALLY IN A RUSH.
HMM... AFTER WE REBUILD THE ARM, YOUR LEG NEEDS TO BE ADJUSTED, TOO.
SO YOU'VE GOTTEN A LITTLE TALLER, AFTER ALL.
LAST TIME I SAW YOU, YOU WERE JUST CM TALL.
OH!! NO!!
YOUR OLD LEG CAN STILL BE USED, BUT YOUR ARM HAS TO BE REBUILT FROM SCRATCH SO...
TAP TAP
WHAT? SO IT'S GONNA TAKE ABOUT A WEEK?
SUUU

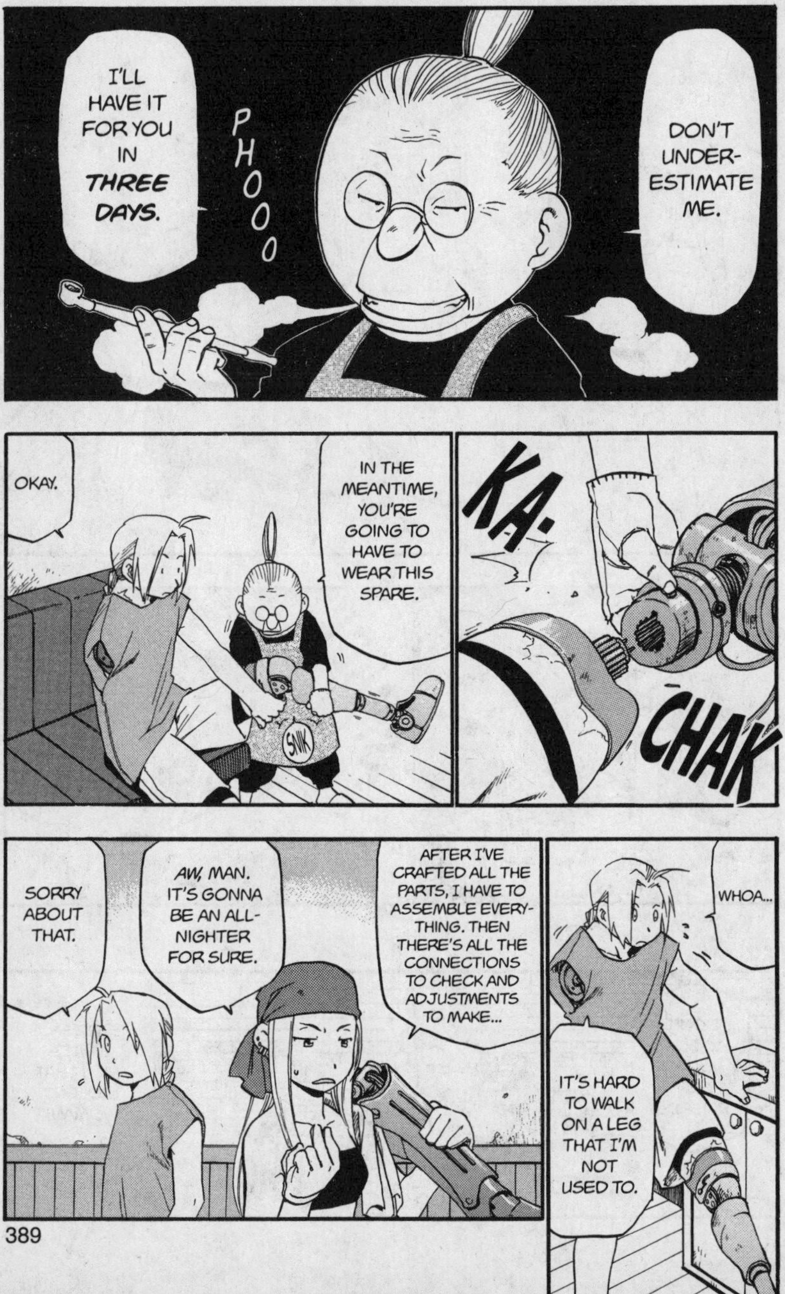
DON'T UNDER-ESTIMATE ME.
PHOOOO
I'LL HAVE IT FOR YOU IN THREE DAYS.
KA-
CHAK
IN THE MEANTIME, YOU'RE GOING TO HAVE TO WEAR THIS SPARE.
SNIK
OKAY.
WHOA...
IT'S HARD TO WALK ON A LEG THAT I'M NOT USED TO.
AFTER I'VE CRAFTED ALL THE PARTS, I HAVE TO ASSEMBLE EVERY-THING. THEN THERE'S ALL THE CONNECTIONS TO CHECK AND ADJUSTMENTS TO MAKE...
AW, MAN. IT'S GONNA BE AN ALL-NIGHTER FOR SURE.
SORRY ABOUT THAT.

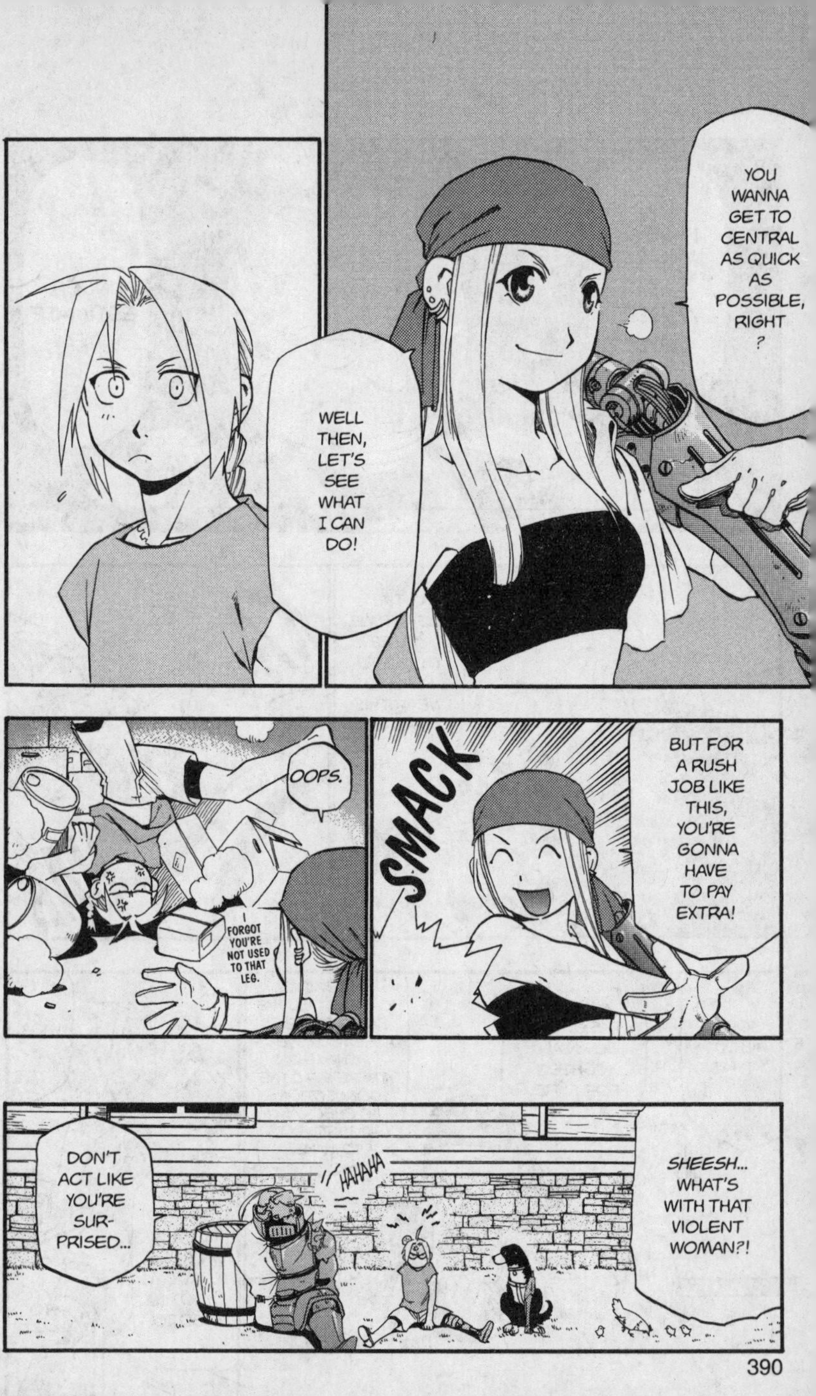
YOU WANNA GET TO CENTRAL AS QUICK AS POSSIBLE, RIGHT?
WELL THEN, LET'S SEE WHAT I CAN DO!
BUT FOR A RUSH JOB LIKE THIS, YOU'RE GONNA HAVE TO PAY EXTRA!
SMACK
OOPS.
I FORGOT YOU'RE NOT USED TO THAT LEG.
SHEESH... WHAT'S WITH THAT VIOLENT WOMAN?!
HAHAHA
DON'T ACT LIKE YOU'RE SURPRISED...

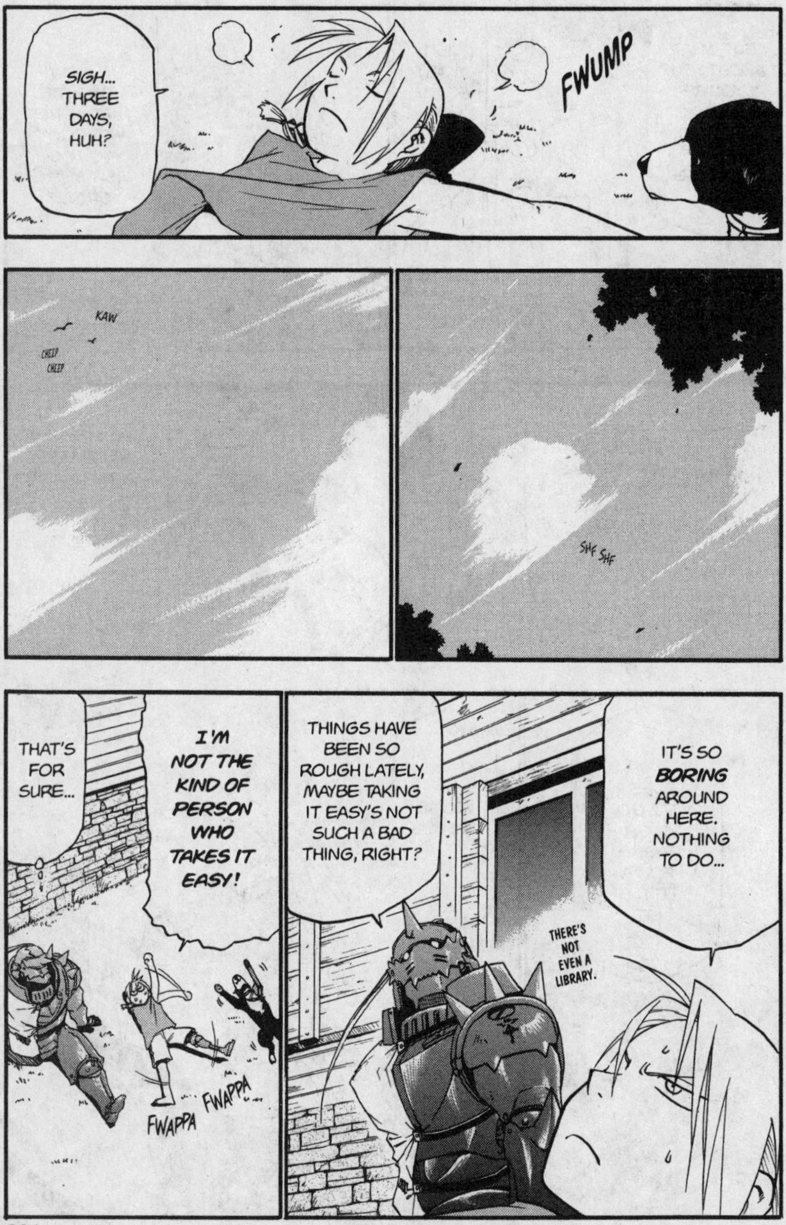
SIGH... THREE DAYS, HUH?
FWUMP
SHF SHF
KAW
CHEEP CHEEP
IT'S SO BORING AROUND HERE. NOTHING TO DO...
THERE'S NOT EVEN A LIBRARY.
THINGS HAVE BEEN SO ROUGH LATELY, MAYBE TAKING IT EASY'S NOT SUCH A BAD THING, RIGHT?
I'M NOT THE KIND OF PERSON WHO TAKES IT EASY!
THAT'S FOR SURE...
FWAPPA
FWAPPA

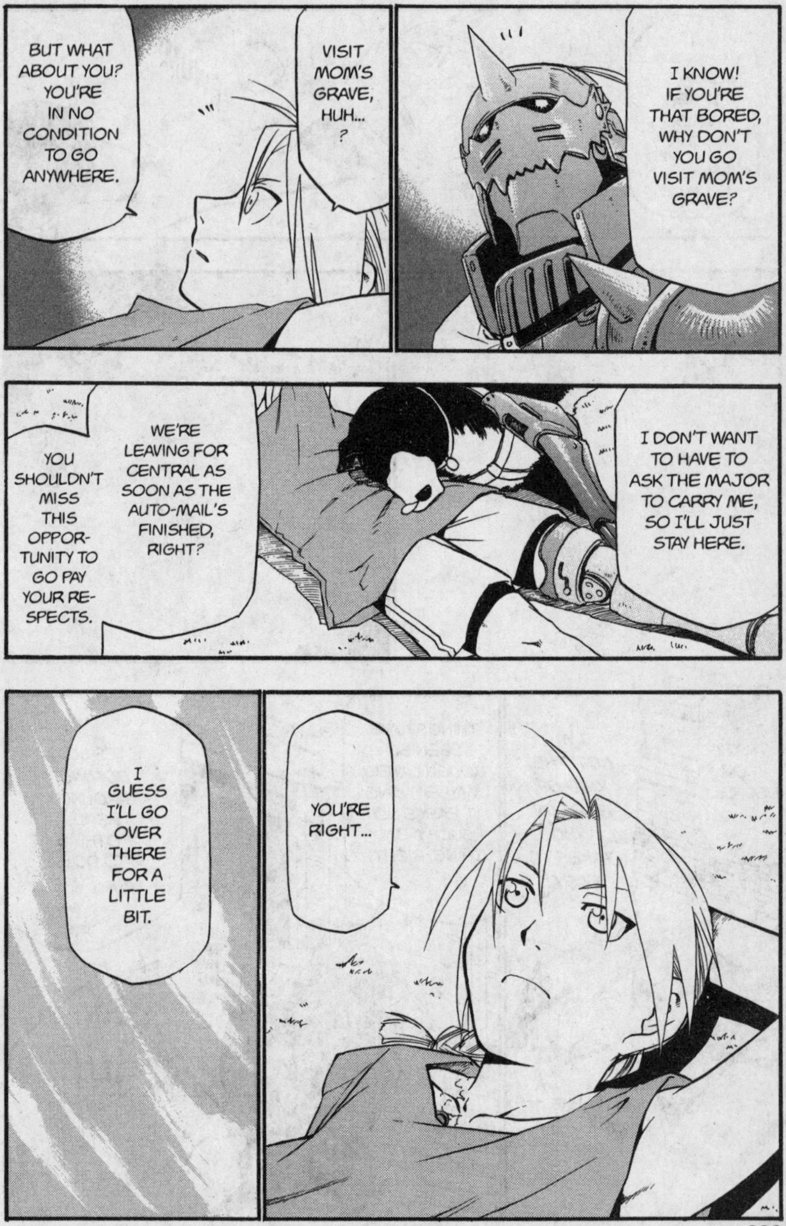
I KNOW! IF YOU'RE THAT BORED, WHY DON'T YOU GO VISIT MOM'S GRAVE?
VISIT MOM'S GRAVE, HUH...?
BUT WHAT ABOUT YOU? YOU'RE IN NO CONDITION TO GO ANYWHERE.
I DON'T WANT TO HAVE TO ASK THE MAJOR TO CARRY ME, SO I'LL JUST STAY HERE.
WE'RE LEAVING FOR CENTRAL AS SOON AS THE AUTO-MAIL'S FINISHED, RIGHT?
YOU SHOULDN'T MISS THIS OPPOR-TUNITY TO GO PAY YOUR RE-SPECTS.
YOU'RE RIGHT...
I GUESS I'LL GO OVER THERE FOR A LITTLE BIT.

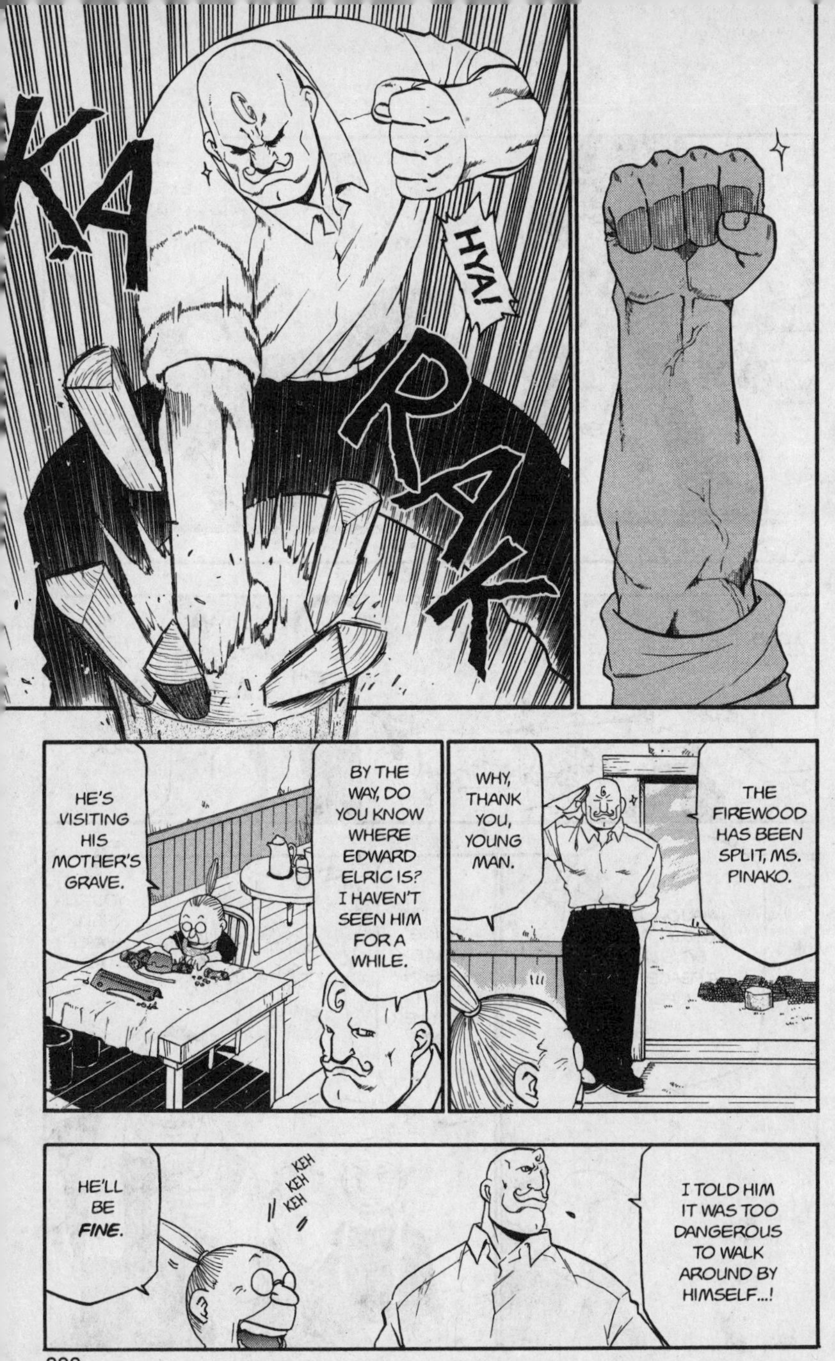
HYA!
KA
RAK
THE FIREWOOD HAS BEEN SPLIT, MS. PINAKO.
WHY, THANK YOU, YOUNG MAN.
BY THE WAY, DO YOU KNOW WHERE EDWARD ELRIC IS? I HAVEN'T SEEN HIM FOR A WHILE.
HE'S VISITING HIS MOTHER'S GRAVE.
I TOLD HIM IT WAS TOO DANGEROUS TO WALK AROUND BY HIMSELF...!
KEH KEH KEH
HE'LL BE *FINE*.

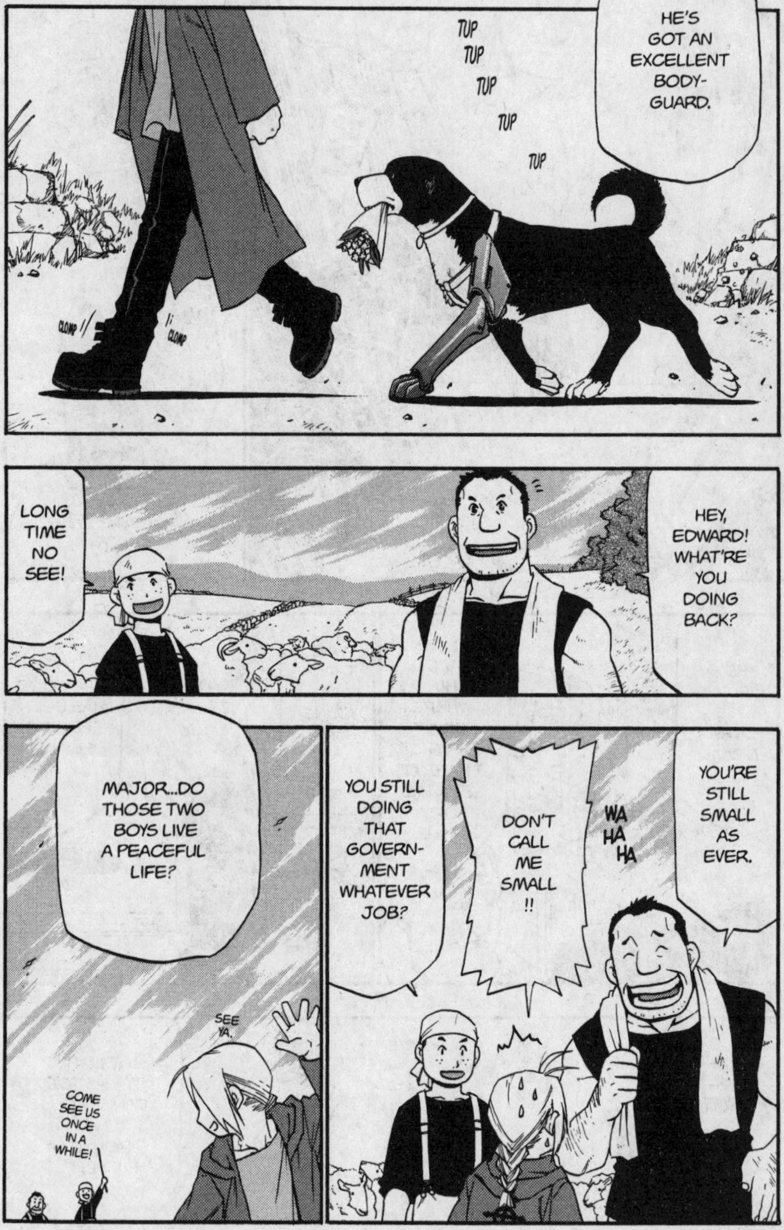
HE'S GOT AN EXCELLENT BODY-GUARD.
TUP TUP TUP TUP TUP
CLOMP CLOMP
HEY, EDWARD! WHAT'RE YOU DOING BACK?
LONG TIME NO SEE!
YOU'RE STILL SMALL AS EVER.
WA HA HA
DON'T CALL ME SMALL!!
YOU STILL DOING THAT GOVERN-MENT WHATEVER JOB?
MAJOR...DO THOSE TWO BOYS LIVE A PEACEFUL LIFE?
SEE YA.
COME SEE US ONCE IN A WHILE!

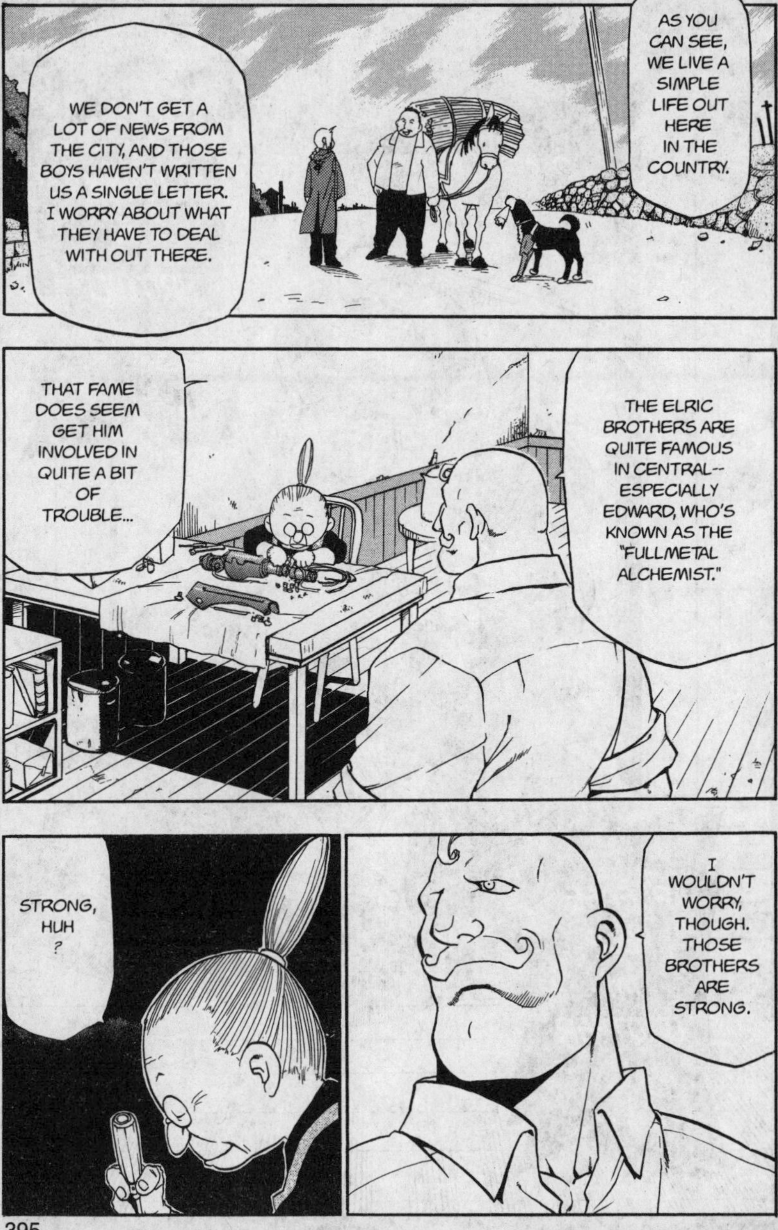
AS YOU CAN SEE, WE LIVE A SIMPLE LIFE OUT HERE IN THE COUNTRY.
WE DON'T GET A LOT OF NEWS FROM THE CITY, AND THOSE BOYS HAVEN'T WRITTEN US A SINGLE LETTER. I WORRY ABOUT WHAT THEY HAVE TO DEAL WITH OUT THERE.
THE ELRIC BROTHERS ARE QUITE FAMOUS IN CENTRAL-- ESPECIALLY EDWARD, WHO'S KNOWN AS THE "FULLMETAL ALCHEMIST."
THAT FAME DOES SEEM GET HIM INVOLVED IN QUITE A BIT OF TROUBLE...
I WOULDN'T WORRY, THOUGH. THOSE BROTHERS ARE STRONG.
STRONG, HUH?

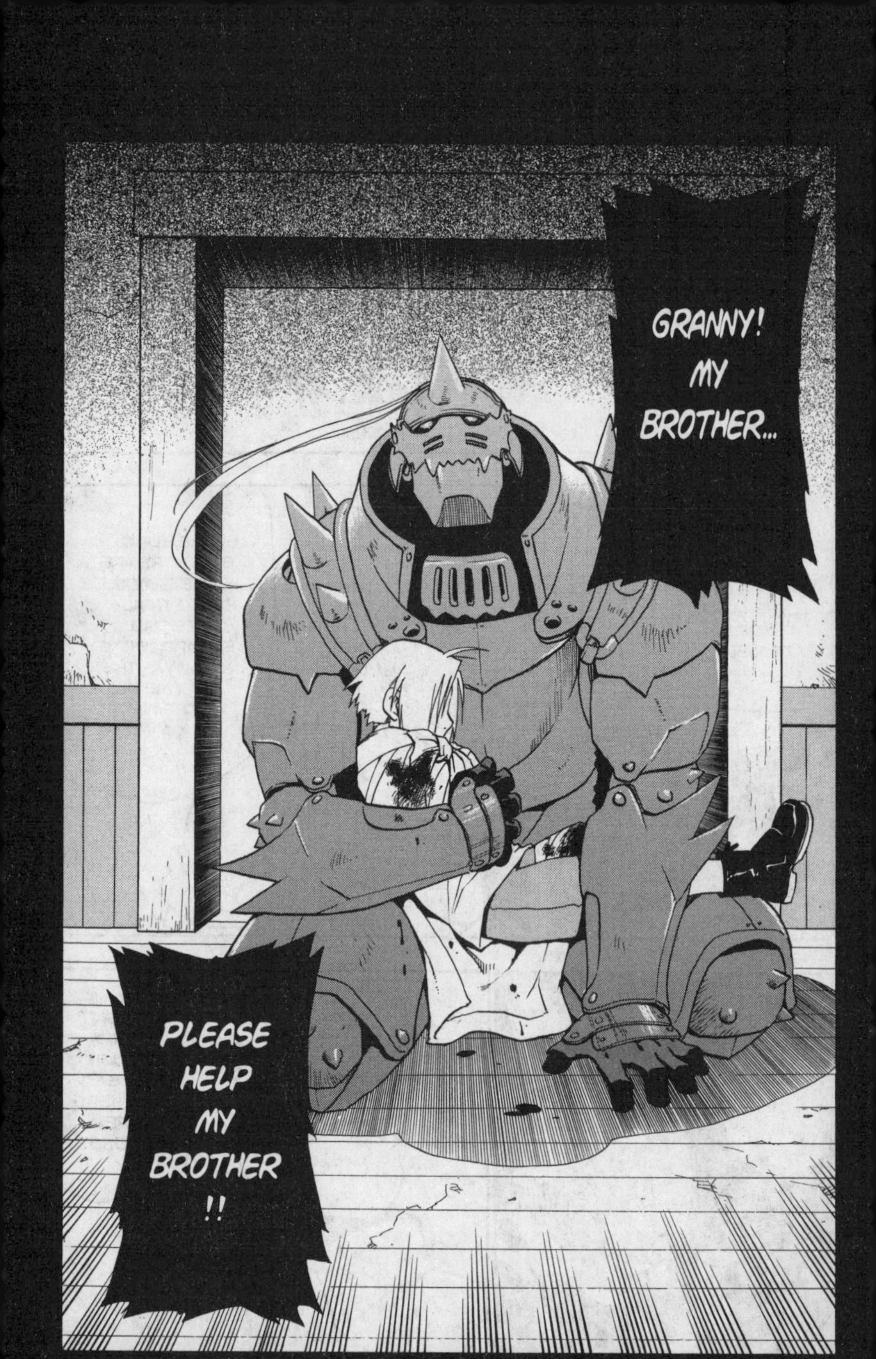
GRANNY! MY BROTHER...
PLEASE HELP MY BROTHER !!

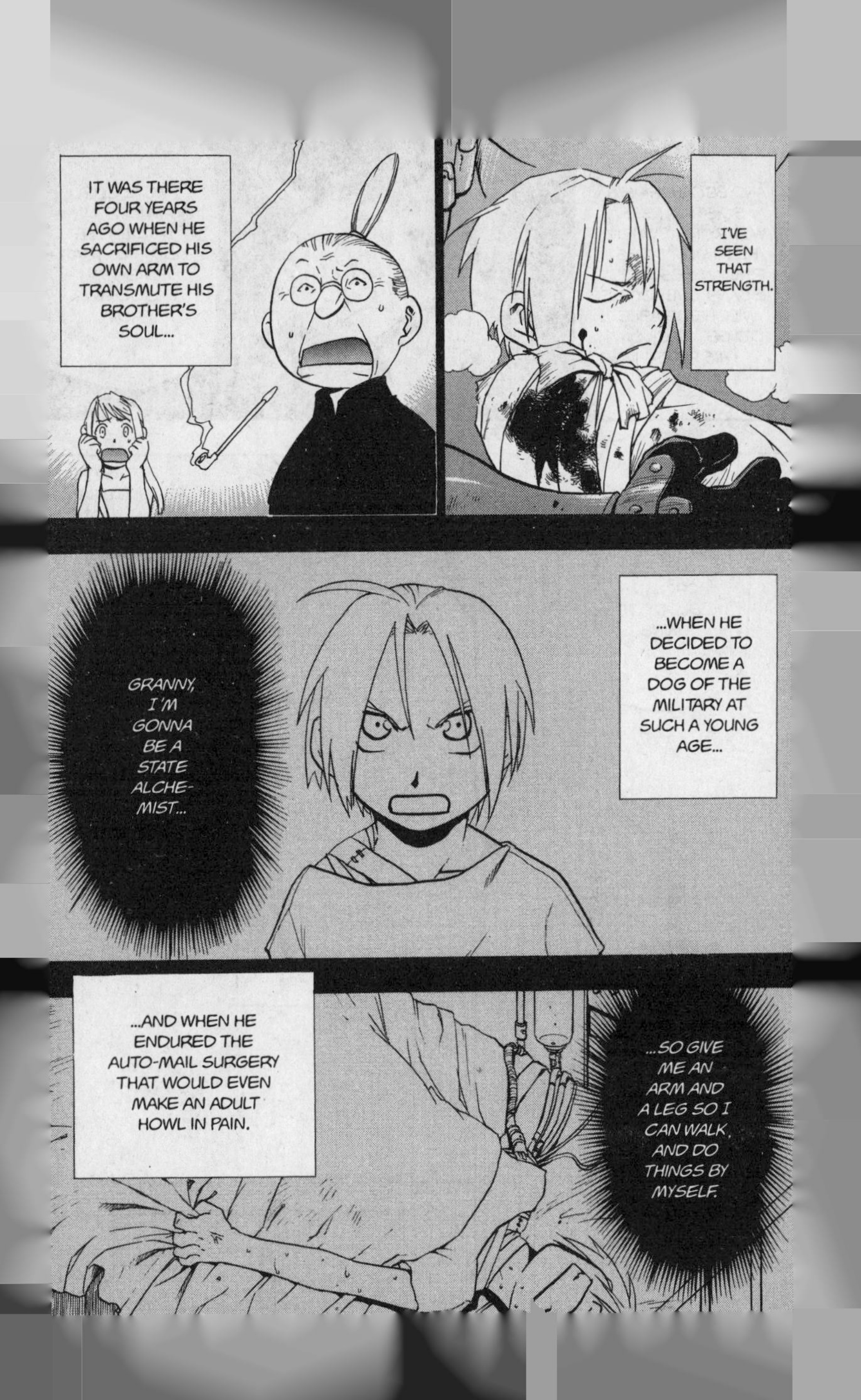
I'VE SEEN THAT STRENGTH.
IT WAS THERE FOUR YEARS AGO WHEN HE SACRIFICED HIS OWN ARM TO TRANSMUTE HIS BROTHER'S SOUL...
...WHEN HE DECIDED TO BECOME A DOG OF THE MILITARY AT SUCH A YOUNG AGE...
GRANNY, I'M GONNA BE A STATE ALCHE-MIST...
...SO GIVE ME AN ARM AND A LEG SO I CAN WALK, AND DO THINGS BY MYSELF.
...AND WHEN HE ENDURED THE AUTO-MAIL SURGERY THAT WOULD EVEN MAKE AN ADULT HOWL IN PAIN.

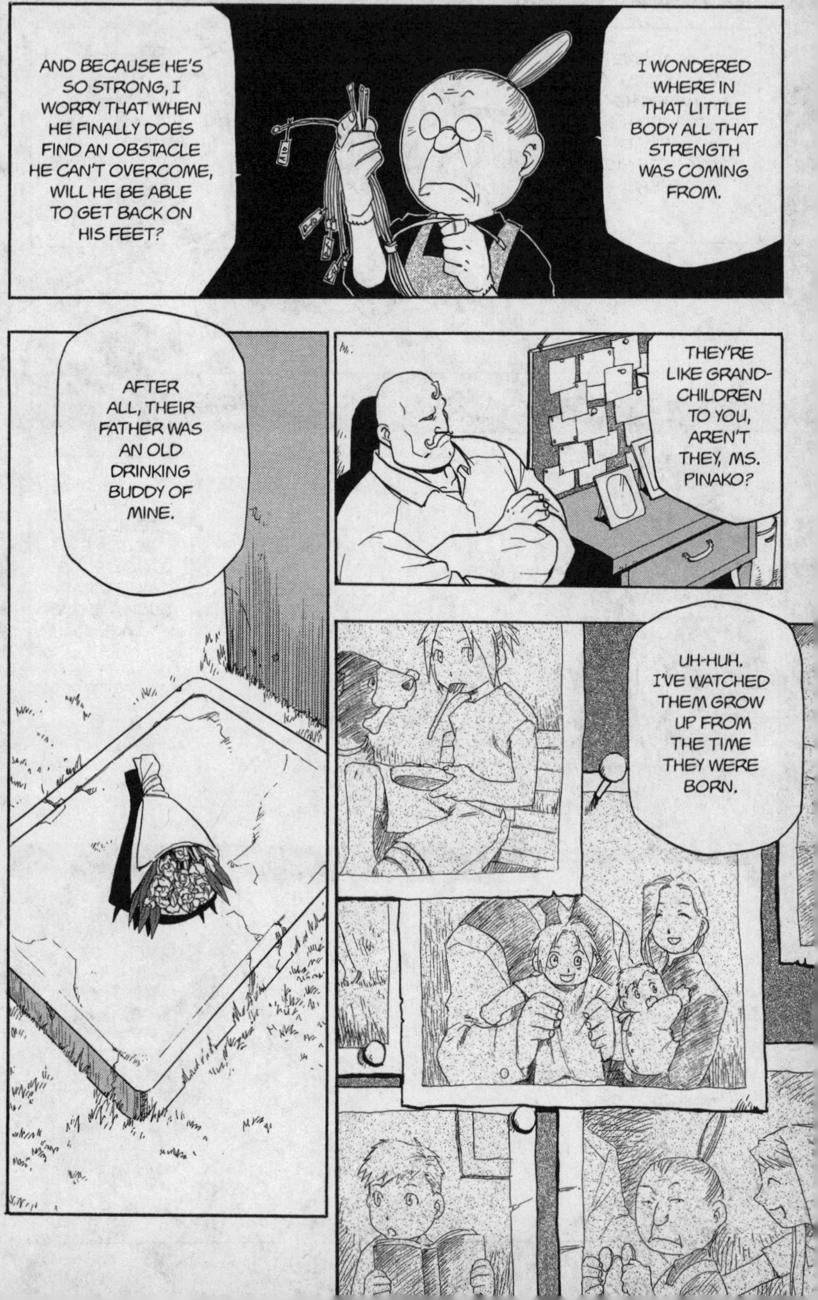
I WONDERED WHERE IN THAT LITTLE BODY ALL THAT STRENGTH WAS COMING FROM.
AND BECAUSE HE'S SO STRONG, I WORRY THAT WHEN HE FINALLY DOES FIND AN OBSTACLE HE CAN'T OVERCOME, WILL HE BE ABLE TO GET BACK ON HIS FEET?
THEY'RE LIKE GRAND-CHILDREN TO YOU, AREN'T THEY, MS. PINAKO?
UH-HUH. I'VE WATCHED THEM GROW UP FROM THE TIME THEY WERE BORN.
AFTER ALL, THEIR FATHER WAS AN OLD DRINKING BUDDY OF MINE.

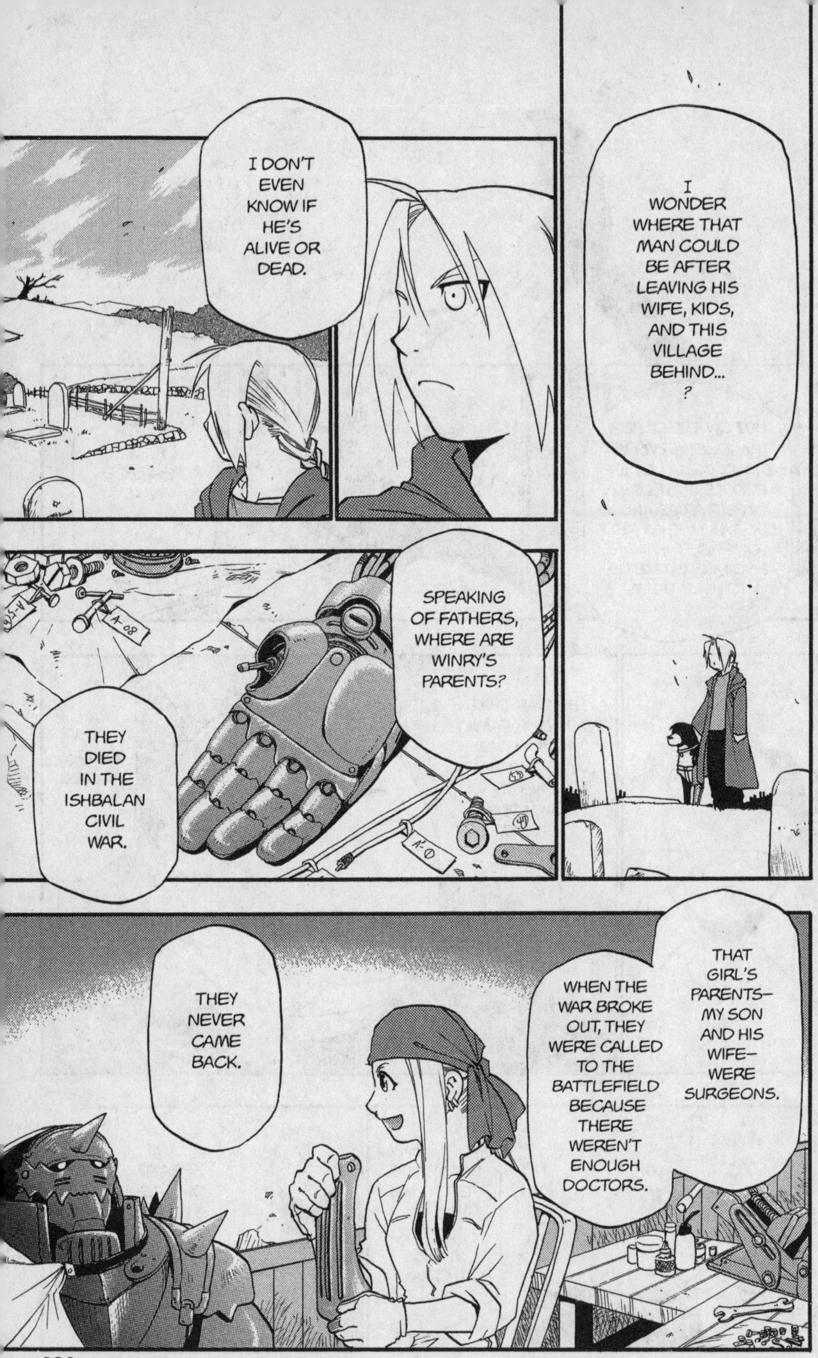
I WONDER WHERE THAT MAN COULD BE AFTER LEAVING HIS WIFE, KIDS, AND THIS VILLAGE BEHIND...?
I DON'T EVEN KNOW IF HE'S ALIVE OR DEAD.
SPEAKING OF FATHERS, WHERE ARE WINRY'S PARENTS?
THEY DIED IN THE ISHBALAN CIVIL WAR.
THAT GIRL'S PARENTS— MY SON AND HIS WIFE— WERE SURGEONS.
WHEN THE WAR BROKE OUT, THEY WERE CALLED TO THE BATTLEFIELD BECAUSE THERE WEREN'T ENOUGH DOCTORS.
THEY NEVER CAME BACK.

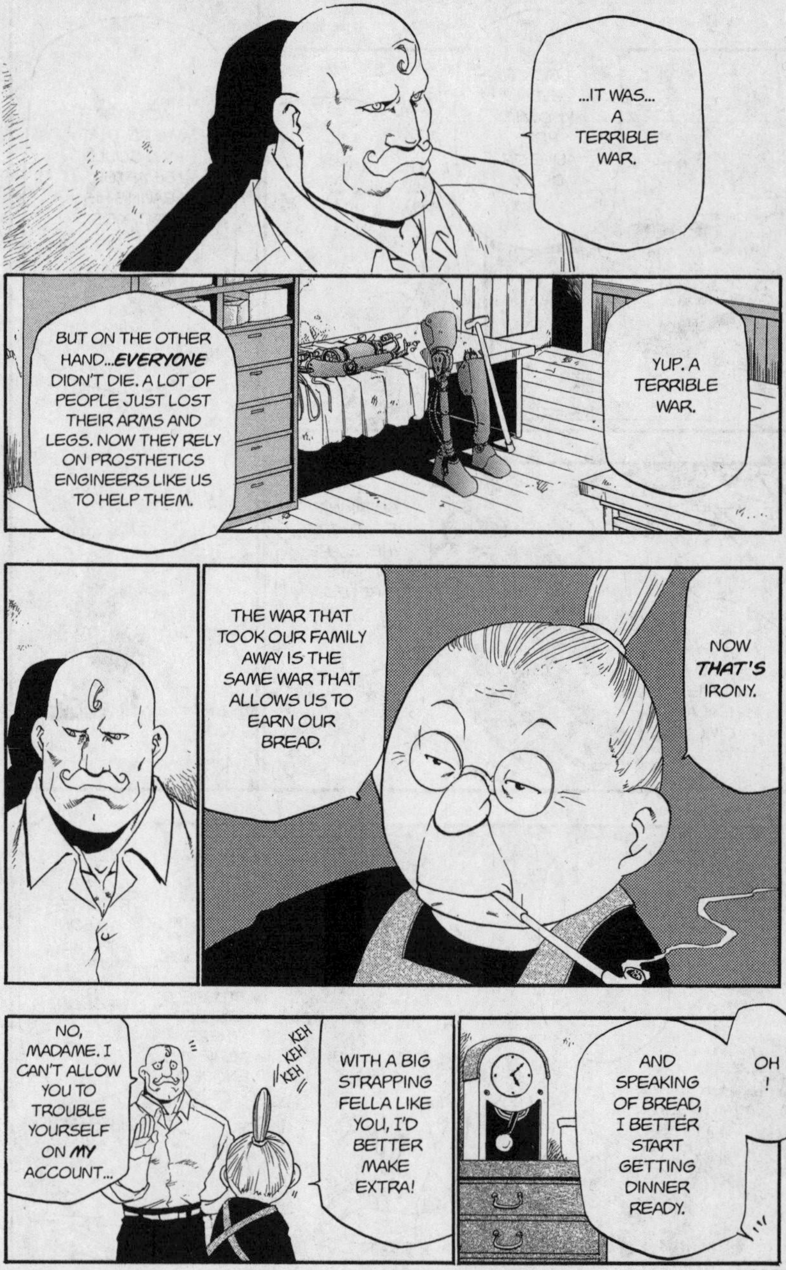
...IT WAS... A TERRIBLE WAR.
YUP. A TERRIBLE WAR.
BUT ON THE OTHER HAND...**EVERYONE** DIDN'T DIE. A LOT OF PEOPLE JUST LOST THEIR ARMS AND LEGS. NOW THEY RELY ON PROSTHETICS ENGINEERS LIKE US TO HELP THEM.
THE WAR THAT TOOK OUR FAMILY AWAY IS THE SAME WAR THAT ALLOWS US TO EARN OUR BREAD.
NOW **THAT'S** IRONY.
OH!
AND SPEAKING OF BREAD, I BETTER START GETTING DINNER READY.
KEH KEH KEH
WITH A BIG STRAPPING FELLA LIKE YOU, I'D BETTER MAKE EXTRA!
NO, MADAME. I CAN'T ALLOW YOU TO TROUBLE YOURSELF ON **MY** ACCOUNT...

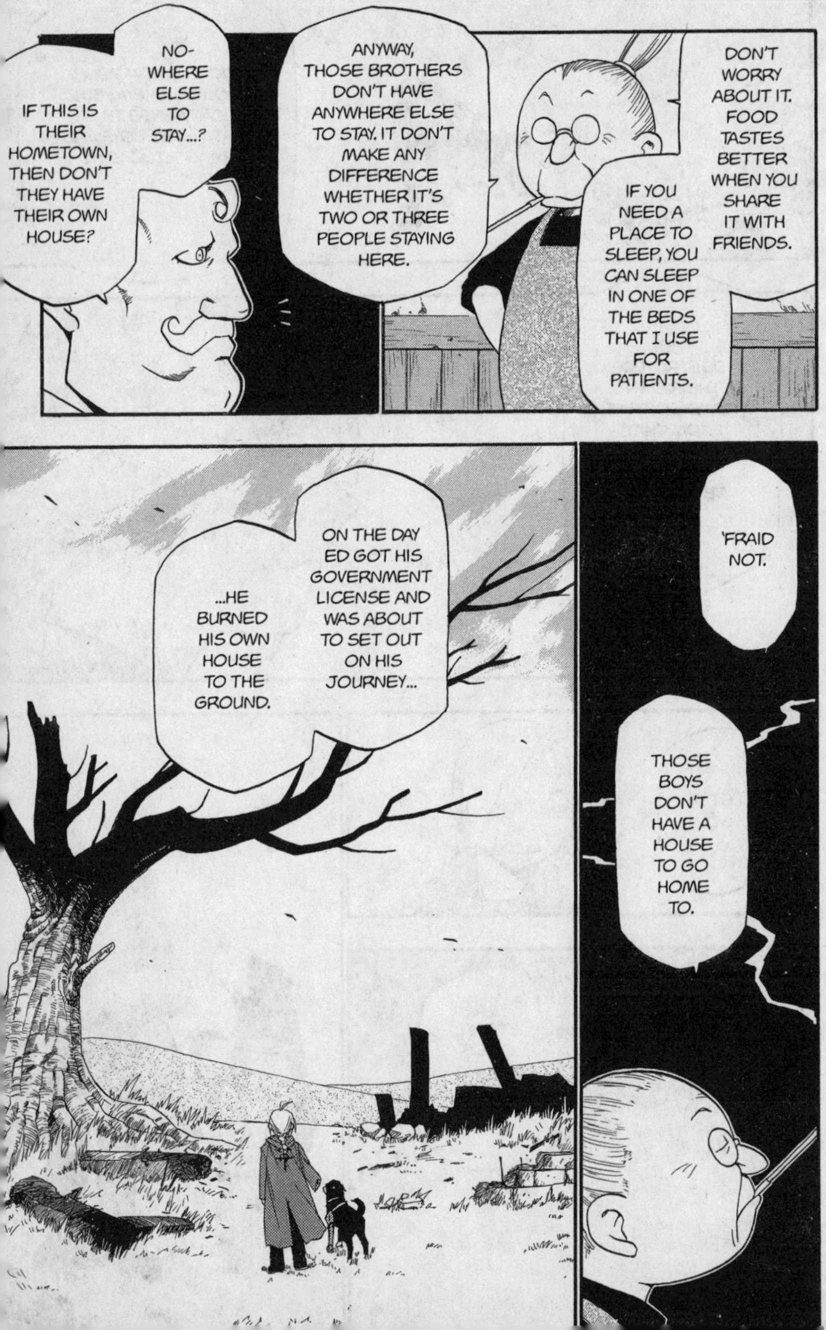
DON'T WORRY ABOUT IT. FOOD TASTES BETTER WHEN YOU SHARE IT WITH FRIENDS.
IF YOU NEED A PLACE TO SLEEP, YOU CAN SLEEP IN ONE OF THE BEDS THAT I USE FOR PATIENTS.
ANYWAY, THOSE BROTHERS DON'T HAVE ANYWHERE ELSE TO STAY. IT DON'T MAKE ANY DIFFERENCE WHETHER IT'S TWO OR THREE PEOPLE STAYING HERE.
NO-WHERE ELSE TO STAY...?
IF THIS IS THEIR HOMETOWN, THEN DON'T THEY HAVE THEIR OWN HOUSE?
'FRAID NOT.
THOSE BOYS DON'T HAVE A HOUSE TO GO HOME TO.
ON THE DAY ED GOT HIS GOVERNMENT LICENSE AND WAS ABOUT TO SET OUT ON HIS JOURNEY...
...HE BURNED HIS OWN HOUSE TO THE GROUND.

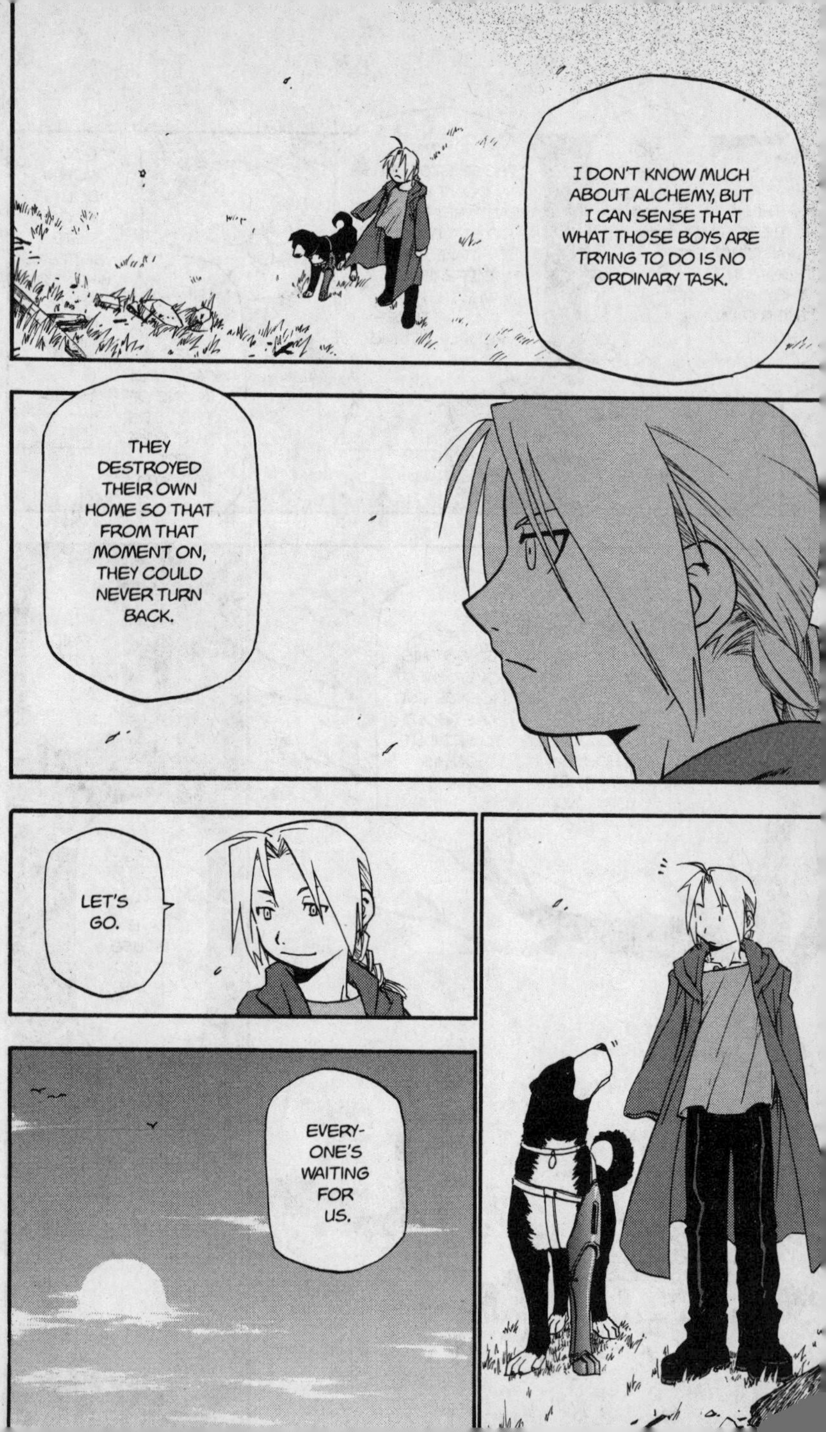
I DON'T KNOW MUCH ABOUT ALCHEMY, BUT I CAN SENSE THAT WHAT THOSE BOYS ARE TRYING TO DO IS NO ORDINARY TASK.
THEY DESTROYED THEIR OWN HOME SO THAT FROM THAT MOMENT ON, THEY COULD NEVER TURN BACK.
LET'S GO.
EVERY-ONE'S WAITING FOR US.

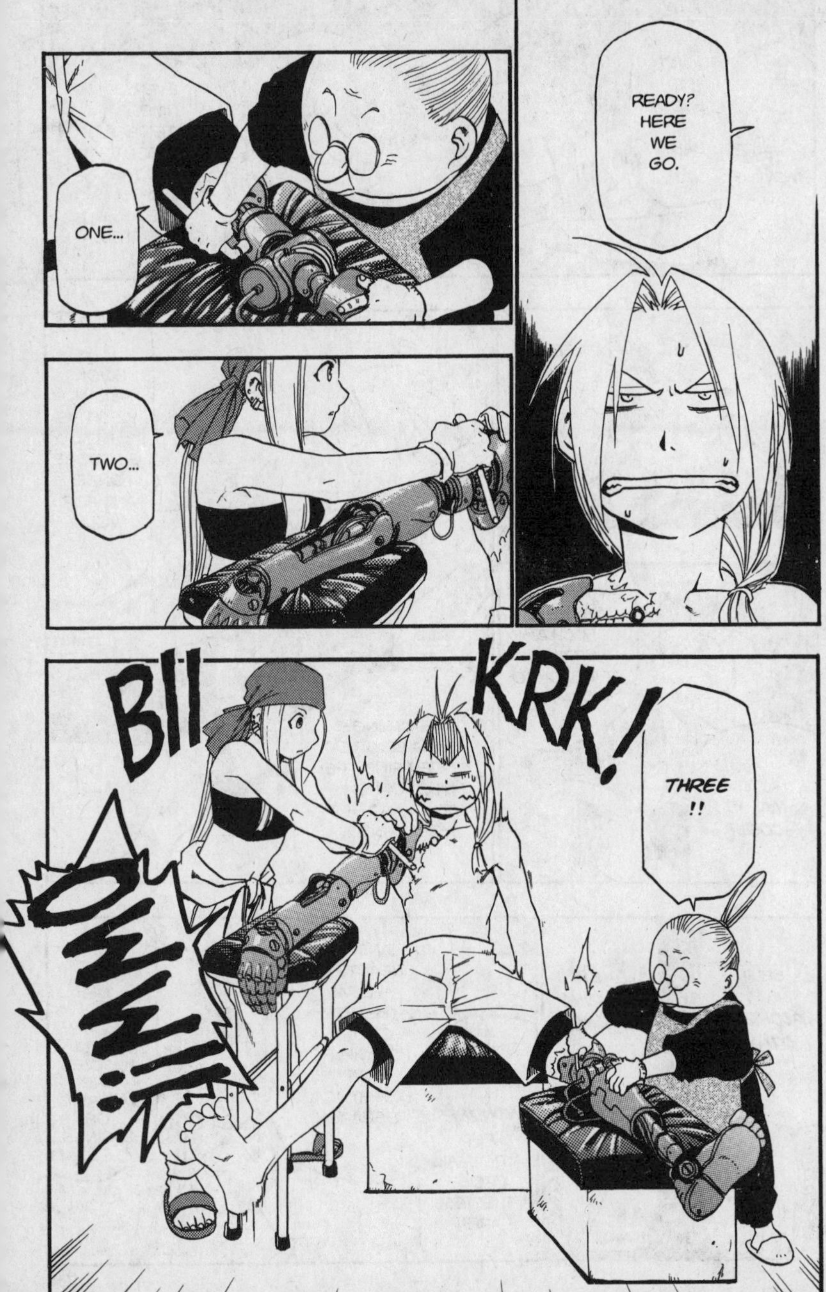
READY? HERE WE GO.
ONE...
TWO...
THREE !!
BII KRK!
OWW!!!

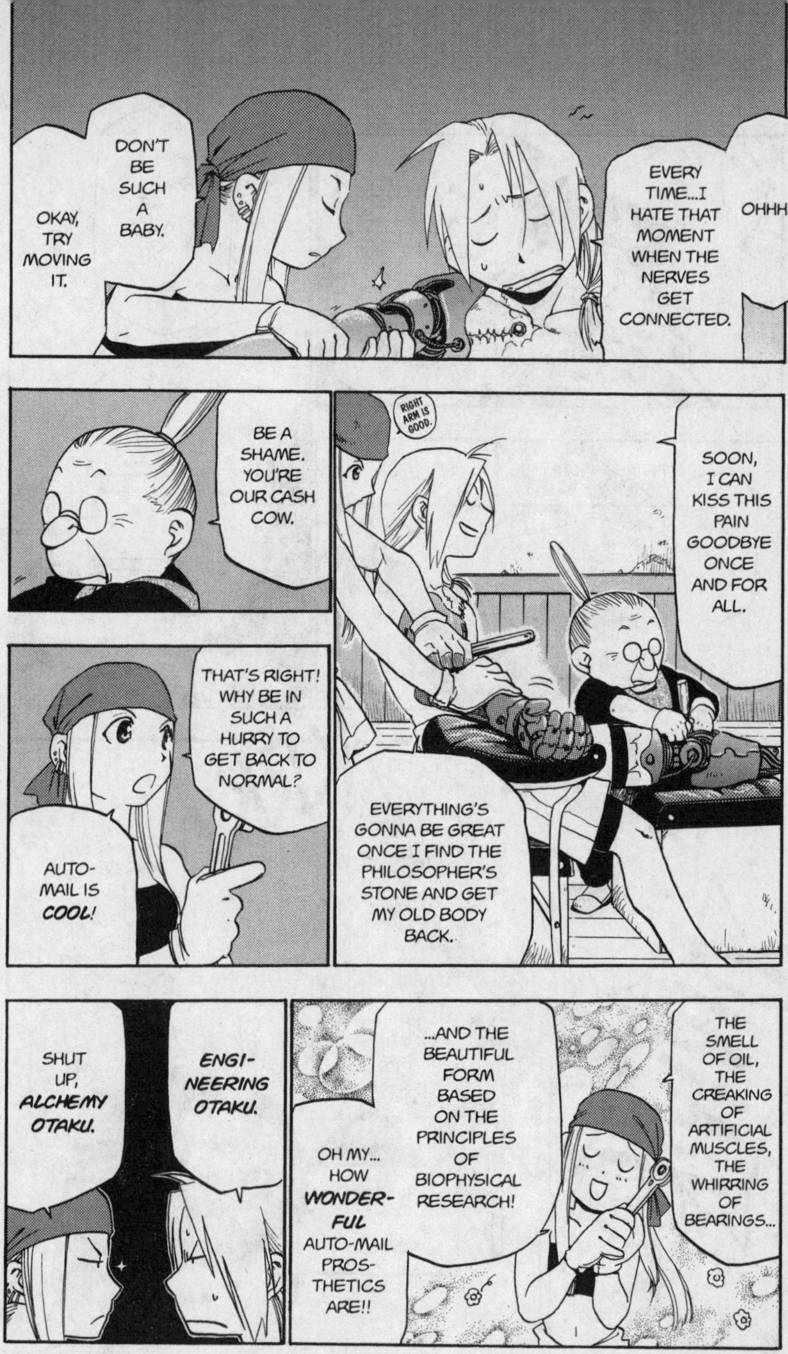

OHHH...
EVERY TIME...I HATE THAT MOMENT WHEN THE NERVES GET CONNECTED.
DON'T BE SUCH A BABY.
OKAY, TRY MOVING IT.
SOON, I CAN KISS THIS PAIN GOODBYE ONCE AND FOR ALL.
RIGHT ARM IS GOOD.
EVERYTHING'S GONNA BE GREAT ONCE I FIND THE PHILOSOPHER'S STONE AND GET MY OLD BODY BACK.
BE A SHAME. YOU'RE OUR CASH COW.
THAT'S RIGHT! WHY BE IN SUCH A HURRY TO GET BACK TO NORMAL?
AUTO-MAIL IS **COOL!**
THE SMELL OF OIL, THE CREAKING OF ARTIFICIAL MUSCLES, THE WHIRRING OF BEARINGS...
...AND THE BEAUTIFUL FORM BASED ON THE PRINCIPLES OF BIOPHYSICAL RESEARCH!
OH MY... HOW **WONDERFUL** AUTO-MAIL PROSTHETICS ARE!!
ENGINEERING OTAKU.
SHUT UP, **ALCHEMY OTAKU.**

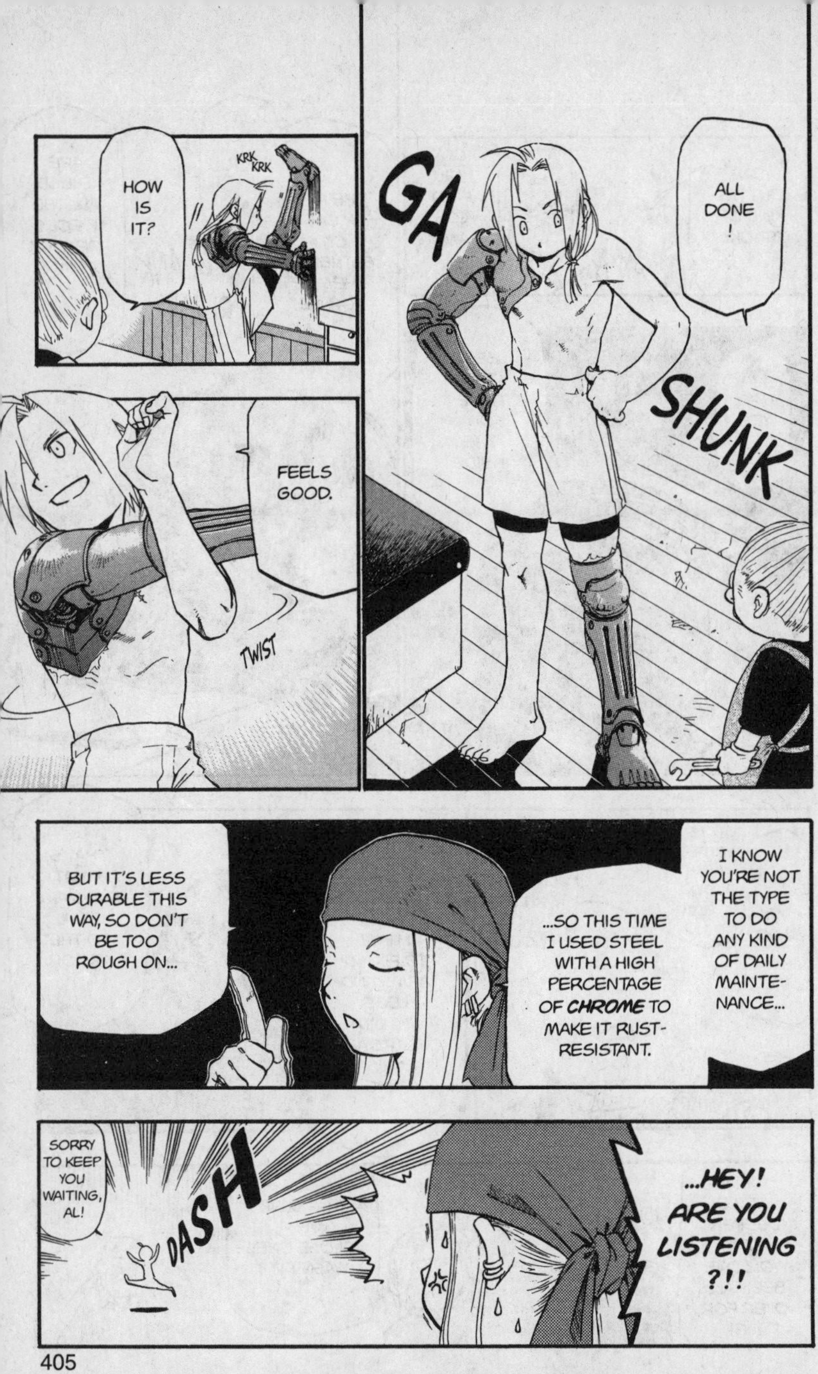
ALL DONE!
GA
SHUNK
HOW IS IT?
KRK KRK
FEELS GOOD.
TWIST
I KNOW YOU'RE NOT THE TYPE TO DO ANY KIND OF DAILY MAINTE-NANCE...
...SO THIS TIME I USED STEEL WITH A HIGH PERCENTAGE OF ***CHROME*** TO MAKE IT RUST-RESISTANT.
BUT IT'S LESS DURABLE THIS WAY, SO DON'T BE TOO ROUGH ON...
...HEY! ARE YOU LISTENING?!!
DASH
SORRY TO KEEP YOU WAITING, AL!

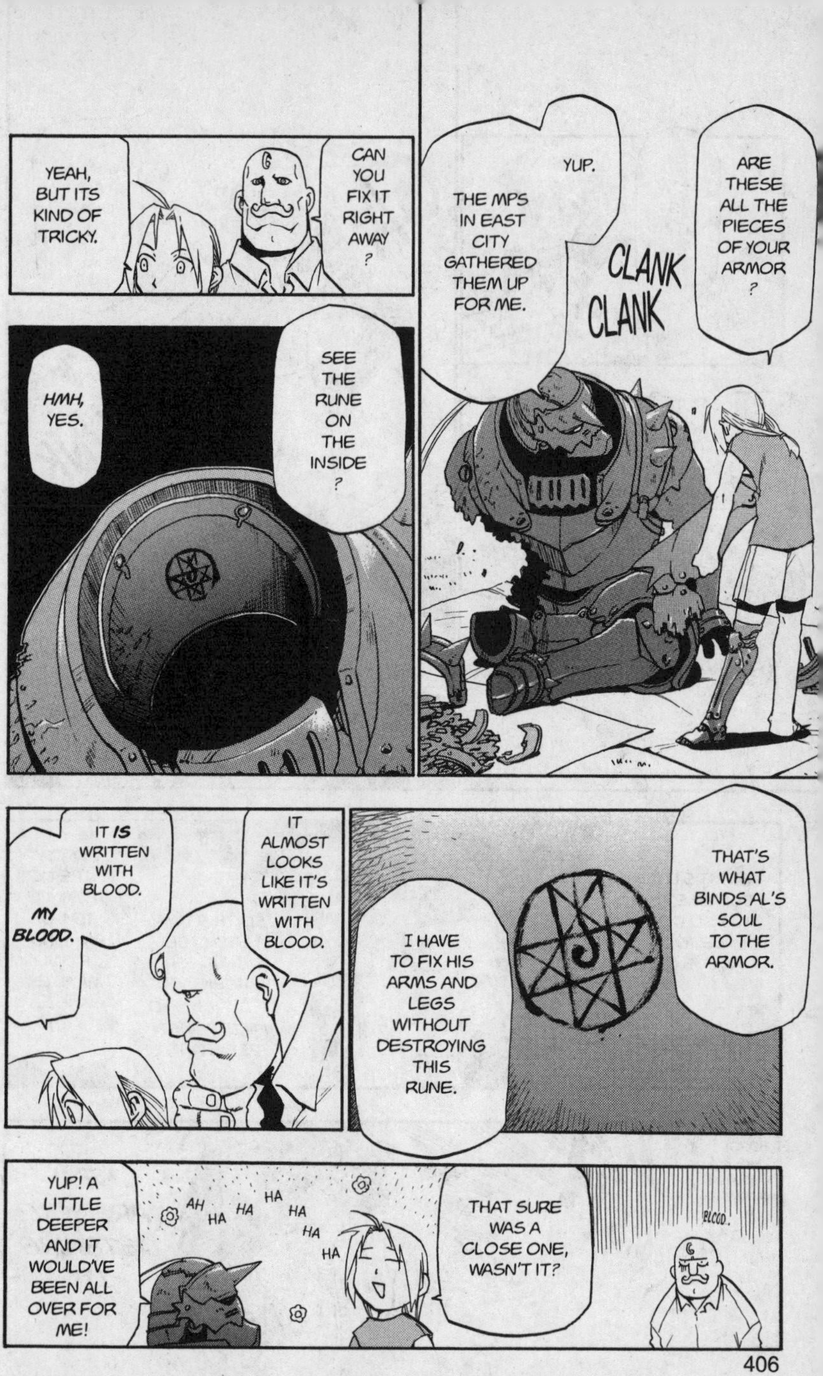
ARE THESE ALL THE PIECES OF YOUR ARMOR?
YUP.
THE MPS IN EAST CITY GATHERED THEM UP FOR ME.
CLANK CLANK
CAN YOU FIX IT RIGHT AWAY?
YEAH, BUT ITS KIND OF TRICKY.
SEE THE RUNE ON THE INSIDE?
HMH, YES.
THAT'S WHAT BINDS AL'S SOUL TO THE ARMOR.
I HAVE TO FIX HIS ARMS AND LEGS WITHOUT DESTROYING THIS RUNE.
IT ALMOST LOOKS LIKE IT'S WRITTEN WITH BLOOD.
IT IS WRITTEN WITH BLOOD.
MY BLOOD.
BLOOD.
THAT SURE WAS A CLOSE ONE, WASN'T IT?
AH HA HA HA HA HA HA
YUP! A LITTLE DEEPER AND IT WOULD'VE BEEN ALL OVER FOR ME!

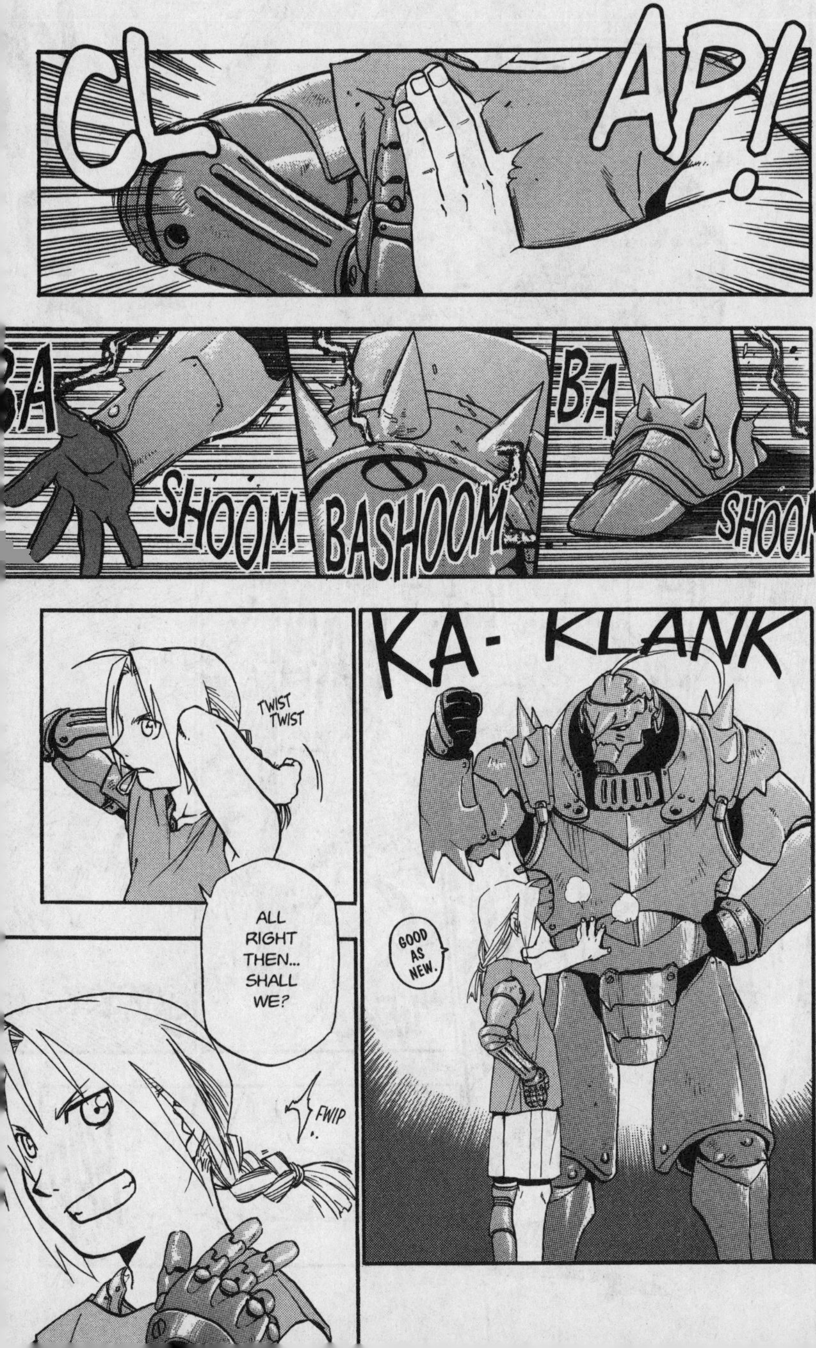
CLAP!
BA SHOOM
BASHOOM
BA SHOOM
KA-KLANK
GOOD AS NEW.
TWIST TWIST
ALL RIGHT THEN... SHALL WE?
FWIP

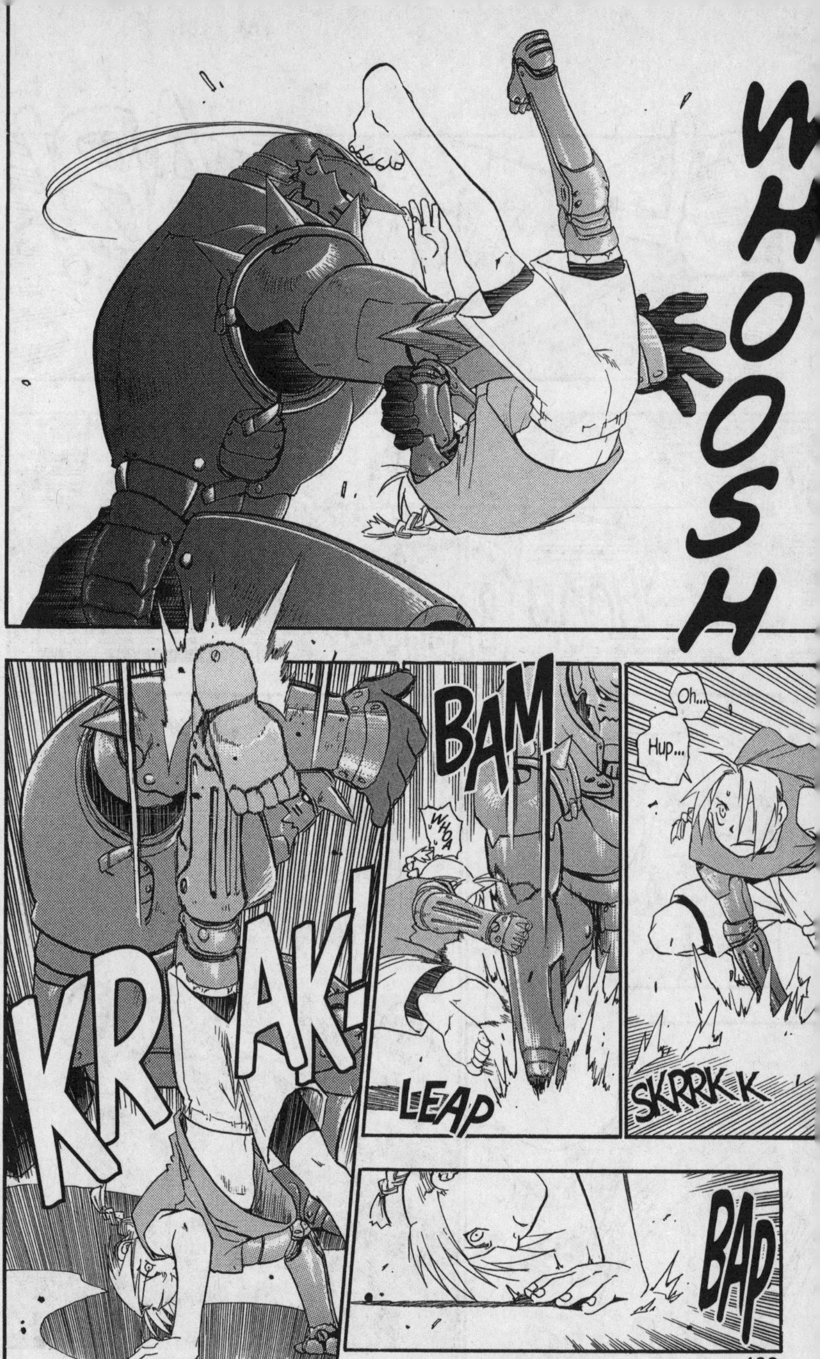
WHOOSH
Oh...
Hup...
SKRRK K
BAM
WHOA
LEAP
BAP
KRAK!

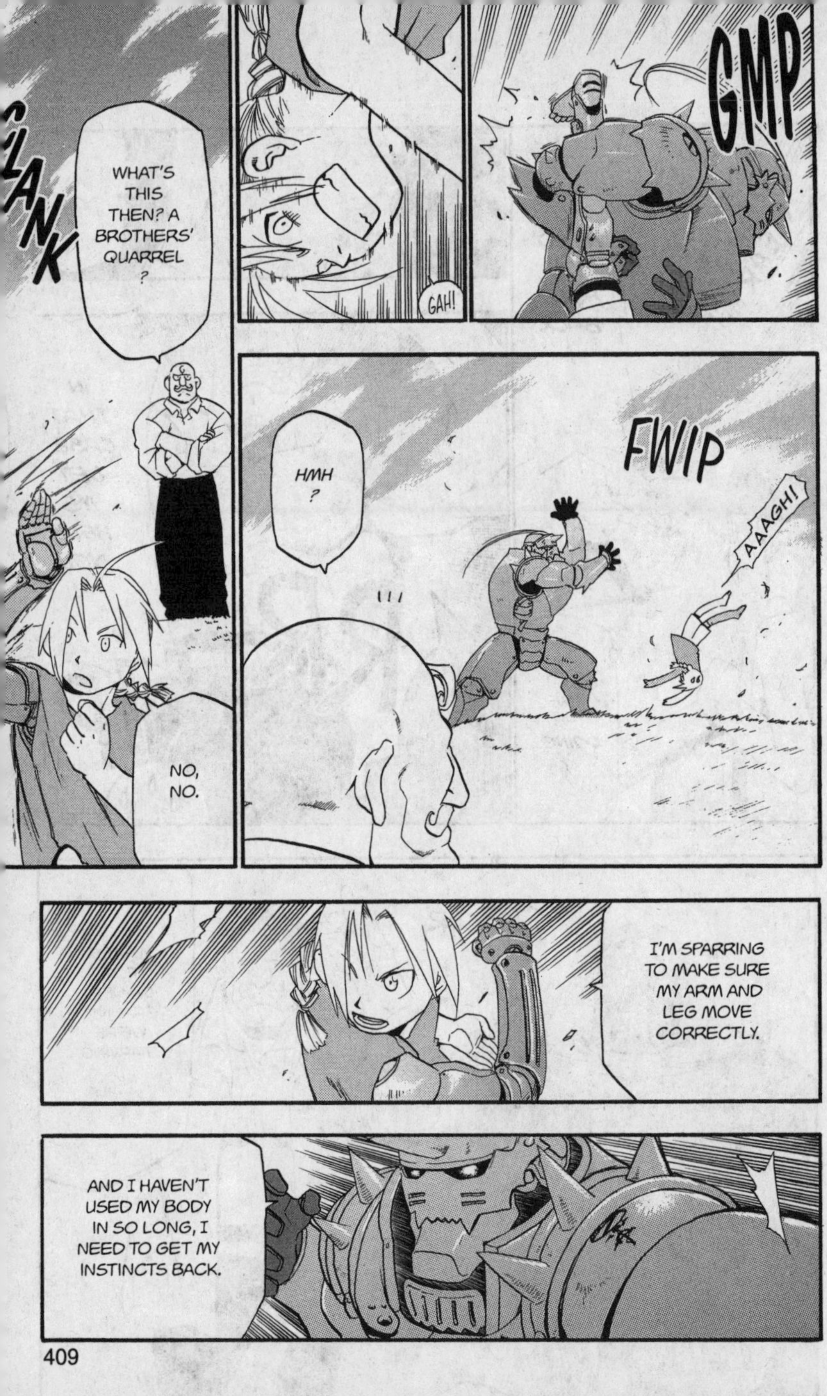
GMP
GAH!
FWIP
AAAGH!
HMH ?
CLANK
WHAT'S THIS THEN? A BROTHERS' QUARREL ?
NO, NO.
I'M SPARRING TO MAKE SURE MY ARM AND LEG MOVE CORRECTLY.
AND I HAVEN'T USED MY BODY IN SO LONG, I NEED TO GET MY INSTINCTS BACK.

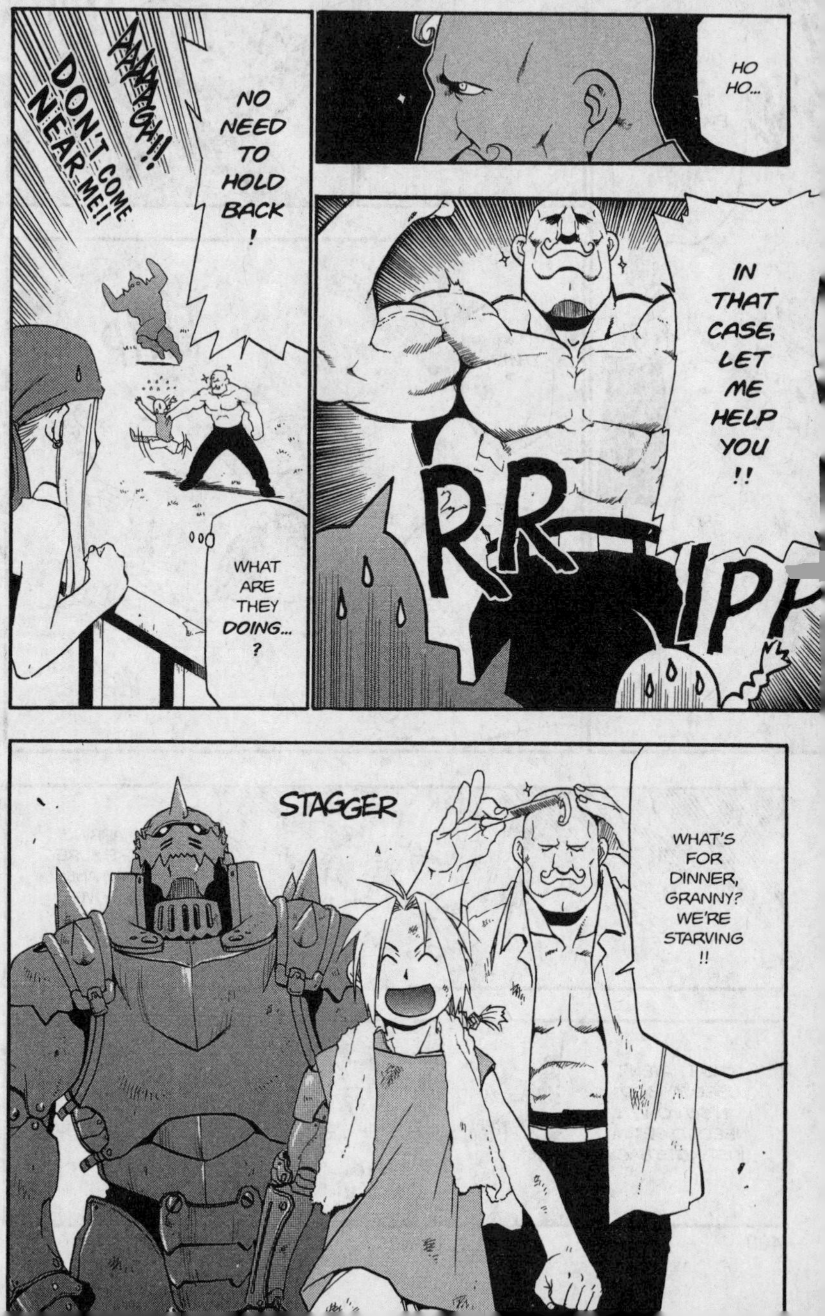
HO HO...
IN THAT CASE, LET ME HELP YOU!!
RR-RIPP
NO NEED TO HOLD BACK!
AAAAAGH!!
DON'T COME NEAR ME!!
WHAT ARE THEY DOING...?
WHAT'S FOR DINNER, GRANNY? WE'RE STARVING!!
STAGGER

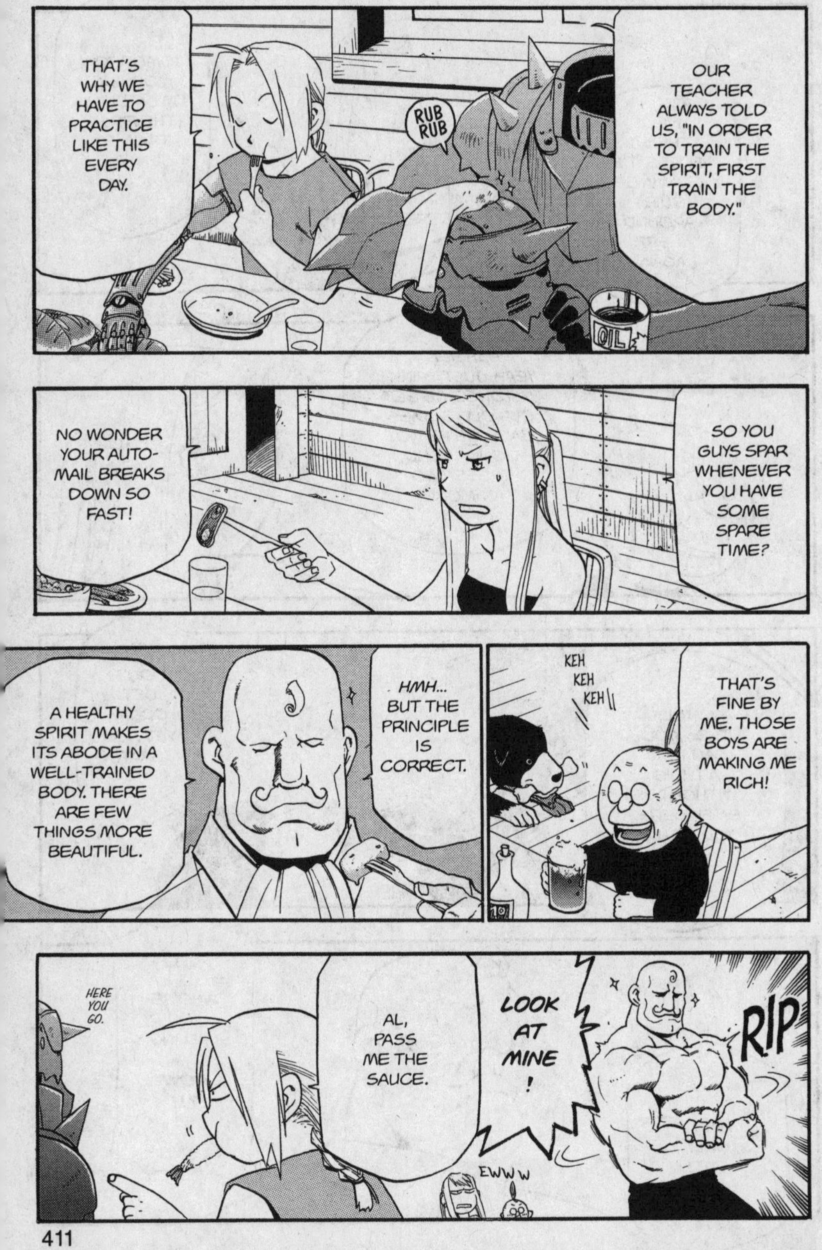
OUR TEACHER ALWAYS TOLD US, "IN ORDER TO TRAIN THE SPIRIT, FIRST TRAIN THE BODY."
RUB RUB
THAT'S WHY WE HAVE TO PRACTICE LIKE THIS EVERY DAY.
OIL
SO YOU GUYS SPAR WHENEVER YOU HAVE SOME SPARE TIME?
NO WONDER YOUR AUTO-MAIL BREAKS DOWN SO FAST!
THAT'S FINE BY ME. THOSE BOYS ARE MAKING ME RICH!
KEH KEH KEH
HMH... BUT THE PRINCIPLE IS CORRECT.
A HEALTHY SPIRIT MAKES ITS ABODE IN A WELL-TRAINED BODY. THERE ARE FEW THINGS MORE BEAUTIFUL.
RIP
LOOK AT MINE!
EWWW
AL, PASS ME THE SAUCE.
HERE YOU GO.

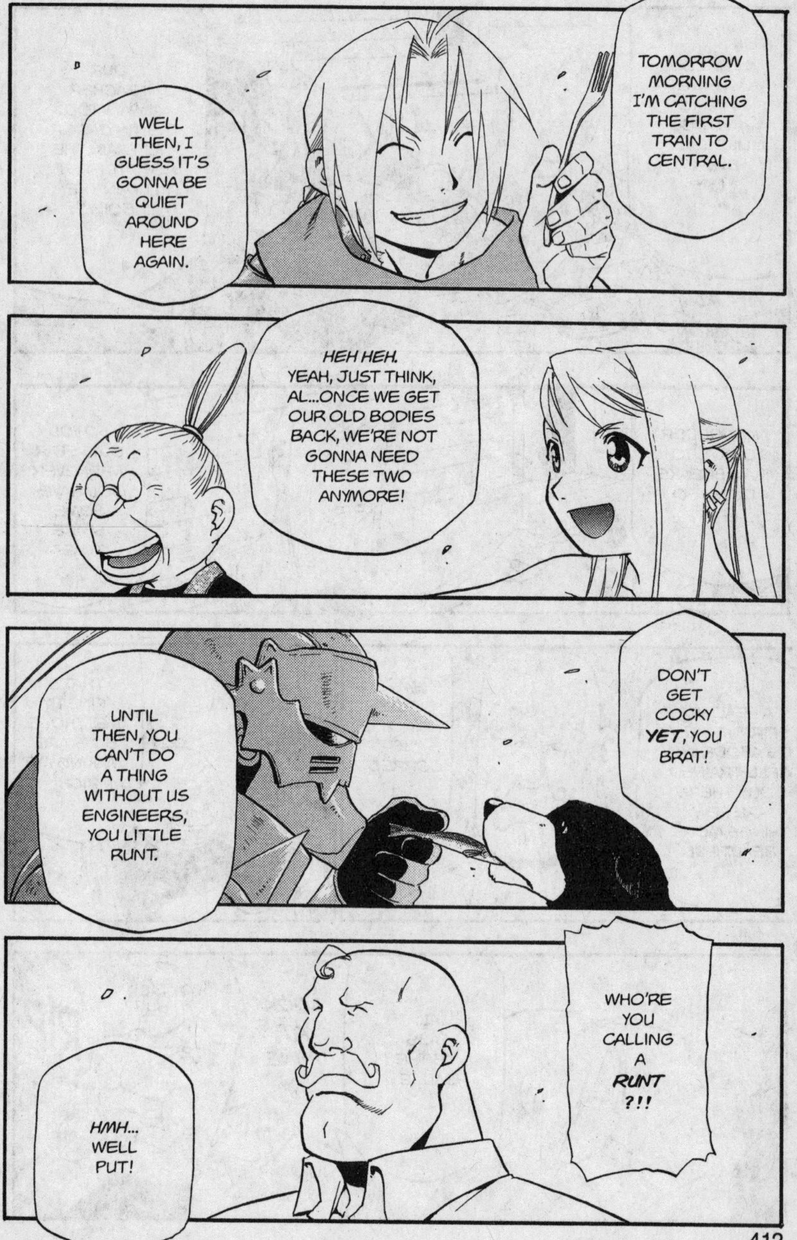
TOMORROW MORNING I'M CATCHING THE FIRST TRAIN TO CENTRAL.
WELL THEN, I GUESS IT'S GONNA BE QUIET AROUND HERE AGAIN.
HEH HEH. YEAH, JUST THINK, AL...ONCE WE GET OUR OLD BODIES BACK, WE'RE NOT GONNA NEED THESE TWO ANYMORE!
DON'T GET COCKY ***YET***, YOU BRAT!
UNTIL THEN, YOU CAN'T DO A THING WITHOUT US ENGINEERS, YOU LITTLE RUNT.
WHO'RE YOU CALLING A ***RUNT*** ?!!
HMH... WELL PUT!

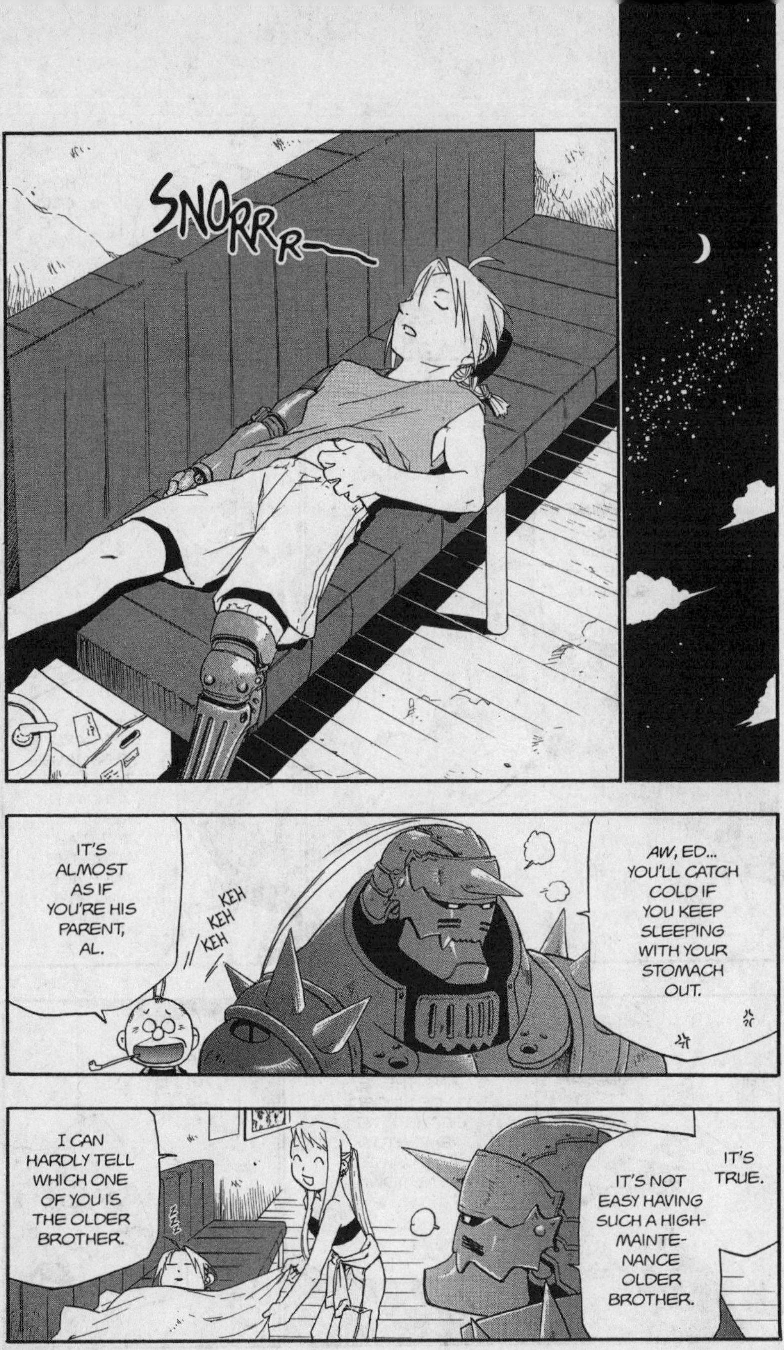
SNORRR
AW, ED... YOU'LL CATCH COLD IF YOU KEEP SLEEPING WITH YOUR STOMACH OUT.
KEH KEH KEH
IT'S ALMOST AS IF YOU'RE HIS PARENT, AL.
IT'S TRUE.
IT'S NOT EASY HAVING SUCH A HIGH-MAINTENANCE OLDER BROTHER.
I CAN HARDLY TELL WHICH ONE OF YOU IS THE OLDER BROTHER.

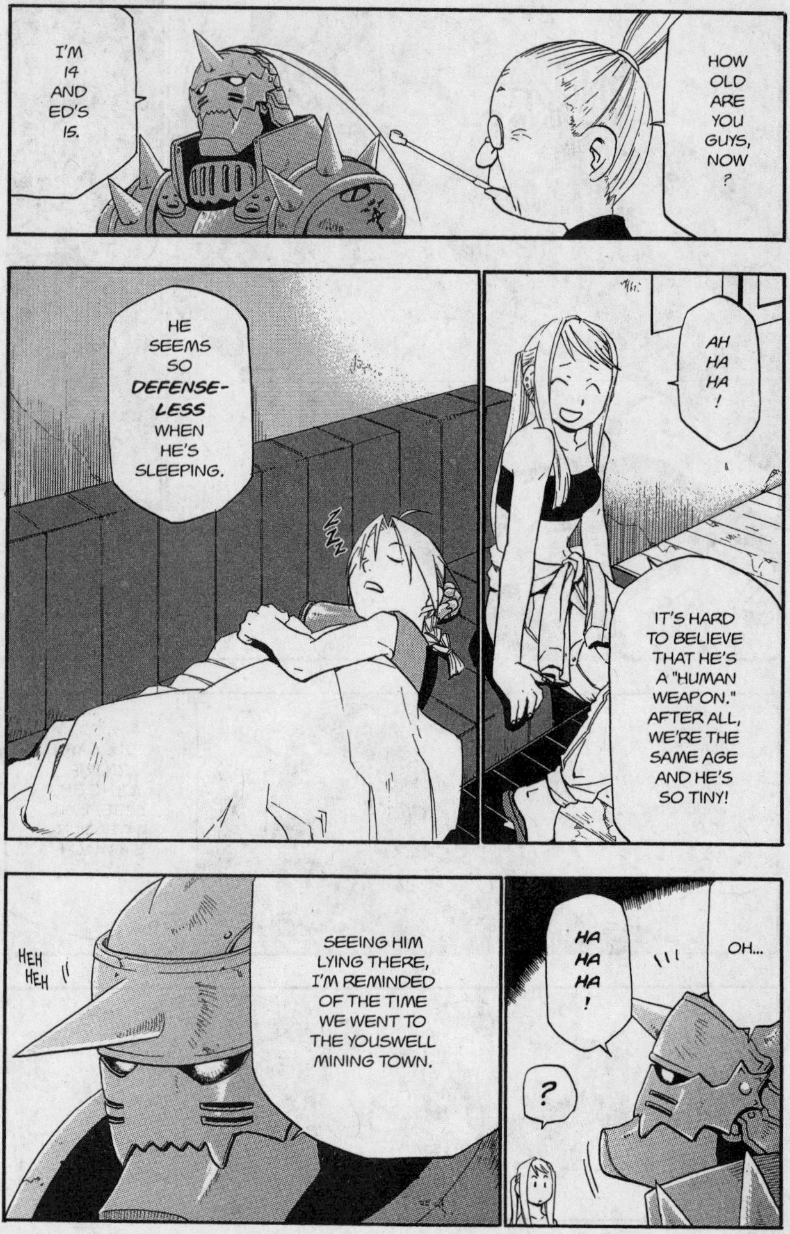
HOW OLD ARE YOU GUYS, NOW?
I'M 14 AND ED'S 15.
AH HA HA!
IT'S HARD TO BELIEVE THAT HE'S A "HUMAN WEAPON." AFTER ALL, WE'RE THE SAME AGE AND HE'S SO TINY!
HE SEEMS SO DEFENSE-LESS WHEN HE'S SLEEPING.
OH...
HA HA HA!
?
HEH HEH
SEEING HIM LYING THERE, I'M REMINDED OF THE TIME WE WENT TO THE YOUSWELL MINING TOWN.

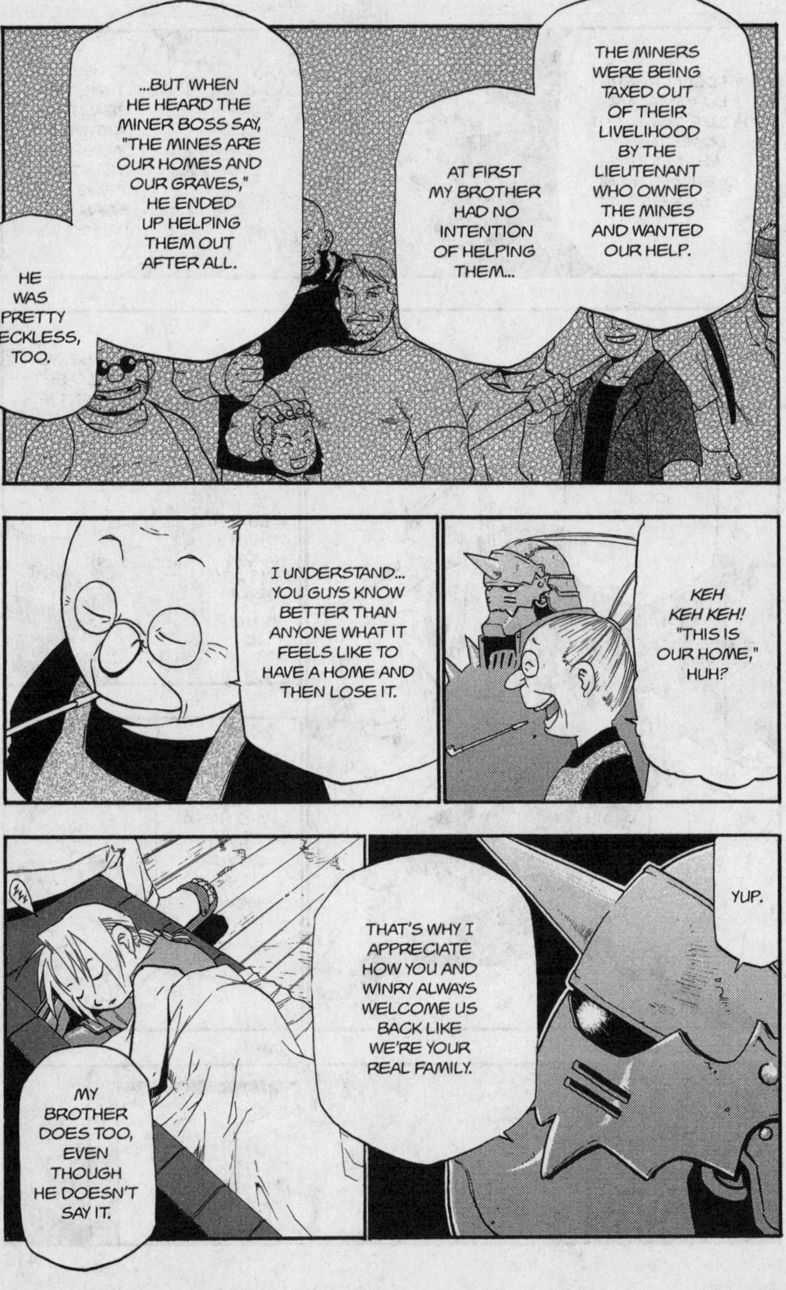
THE MINERS WERE BEING TAXED OUT OF THEIR LIVELIHOOD BY THE LIEUTENANT WHO OWNED THE MINES AND WANTED OUR HELP.
AT FIRST MY BROTHER HAD NO INTENTION OF HELPING THEM...
...BUT WHEN HE HEARD THE MINER BOSS SAY, "THE MINES ARE OUR HOMES AND OUR GRAVES," HE ENDED UP HELPING THEM OUT AFTER ALL.
HE WAS PRETTY RECKLESS, TOO.
KEH KEH KEH! "THIS IS OUR HOME," HUH?
I UNDERSTAND... YOU GUYS KNOW BETTER THAN ANYONE WHAT IT FEELS LIKE TO HAVE A HOME AND THEN LOSE IT.
YUP.
THAT'S WHY I APPRECIATE HOW YOU AND WINRY ALWAYS WELCOME US BACK LIKE WE'RE YOUR REAL FAMILY.
MY BROTHER DOES TOO, EVEN THOUGH HE DOESN'T SAY IT.

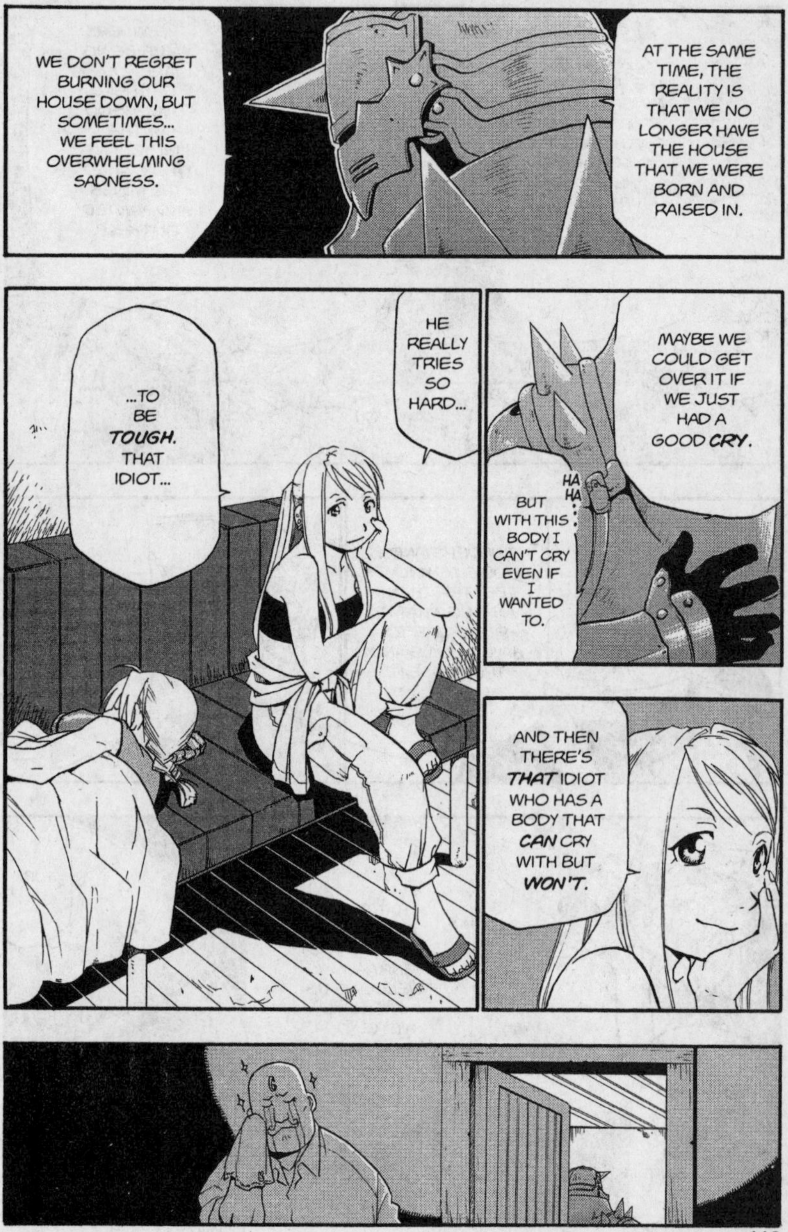
AT THE SAME TIME, THE REALITY IS THAT WE NO LONGER HAVE THE HOUSE THAT WE WERE BORN AND RAISED IN.
WE DON'T REGRET BURNING OUR HOUSE DOWN, BUT SOMETIMES... WE FEEL THIS OVERWHELMING SADNESS.
MAYBE WE COULD GET OVER IT IF WE JUST HAD A GOOD CRY.
HA HA...
BUT WITH THIS BODY I CAN'T CRY EVEN IF I WANTED TO.
AND THEN THERE'S THAT IDIOT WHO HAS A BODY THAT CAN CRY WITH BUT WON'T.
HE REALLY TRIES SO HARD...
...TO BE TOUGH. THAT IDIOT...

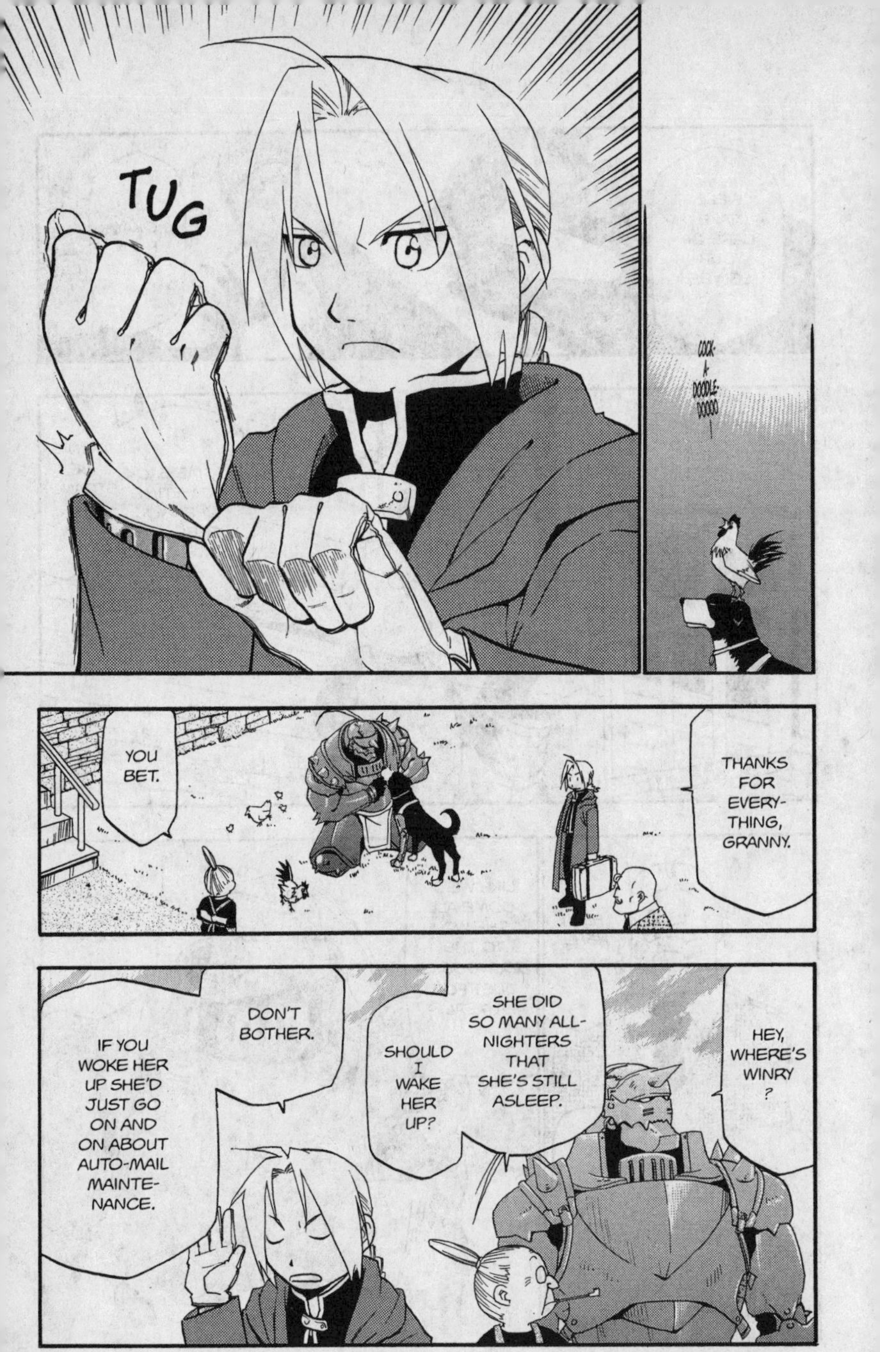

COCK-A-DOODLE-DOOOO!
TUG
THANKS FOR EVERYTHING, GRANNY.
YOU BET.
HEY, WHERE'S WINRY?
SHE DID SO MANY ALL-NIGHTERS THAT SHE'S STILL ASLEEP.
SHOULD I WAKE HER UP?
DON'T BOTHER.
IF YOU WOKE HER UP SHE'D JUST GO ON AND ON ABOUT AUTO-MAIL MAINTENANCE.

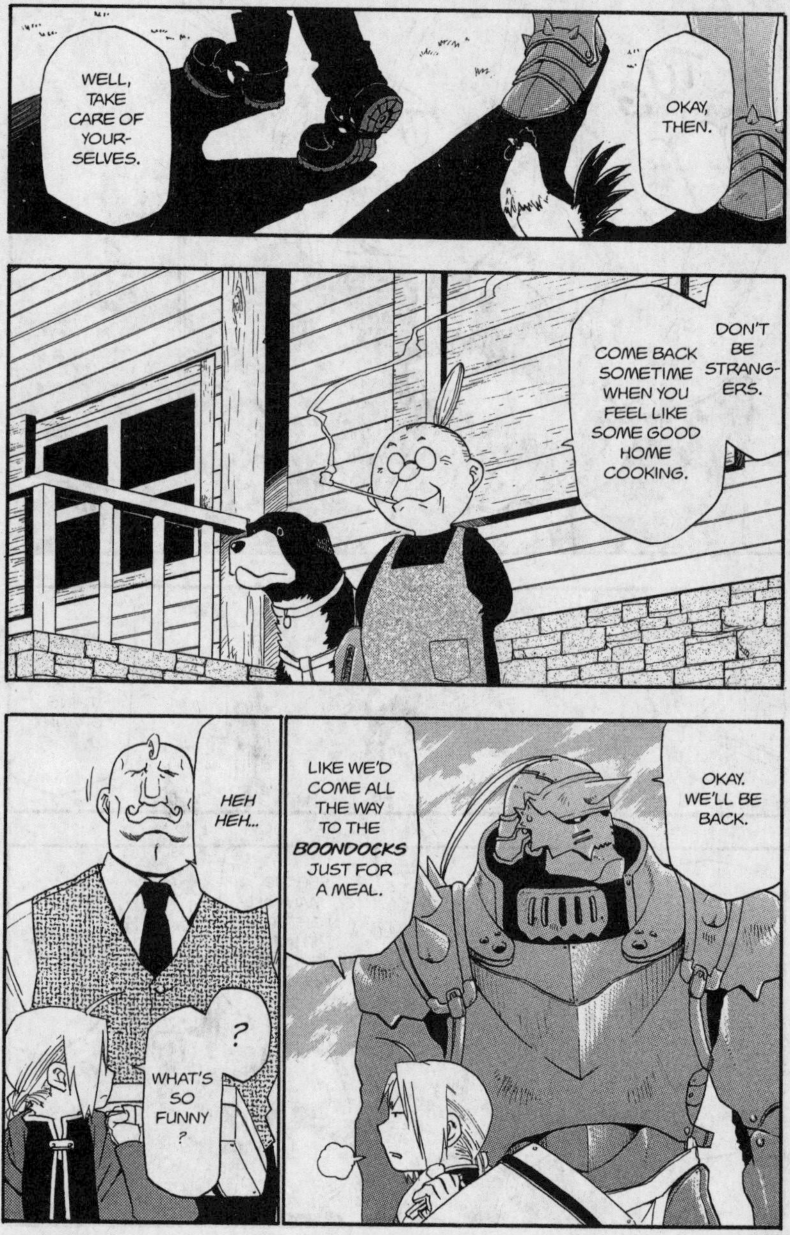
OKAY, THEN.
WELL, TAKE CARE OF YOURSELVES.
DON'T BE STRANGERS.
COME BACK SOMETIME WHEN YOU FEEL LIKE SOME GOOD HOME COOKING.
OKAY. WE'LL BE BACK.
LIKE WE'D COME ALL THE WAY TO THE BOONDOCKS JUST FOR A MEAL.
HEH HEH...
?
WHAT'S SO FUNNY?

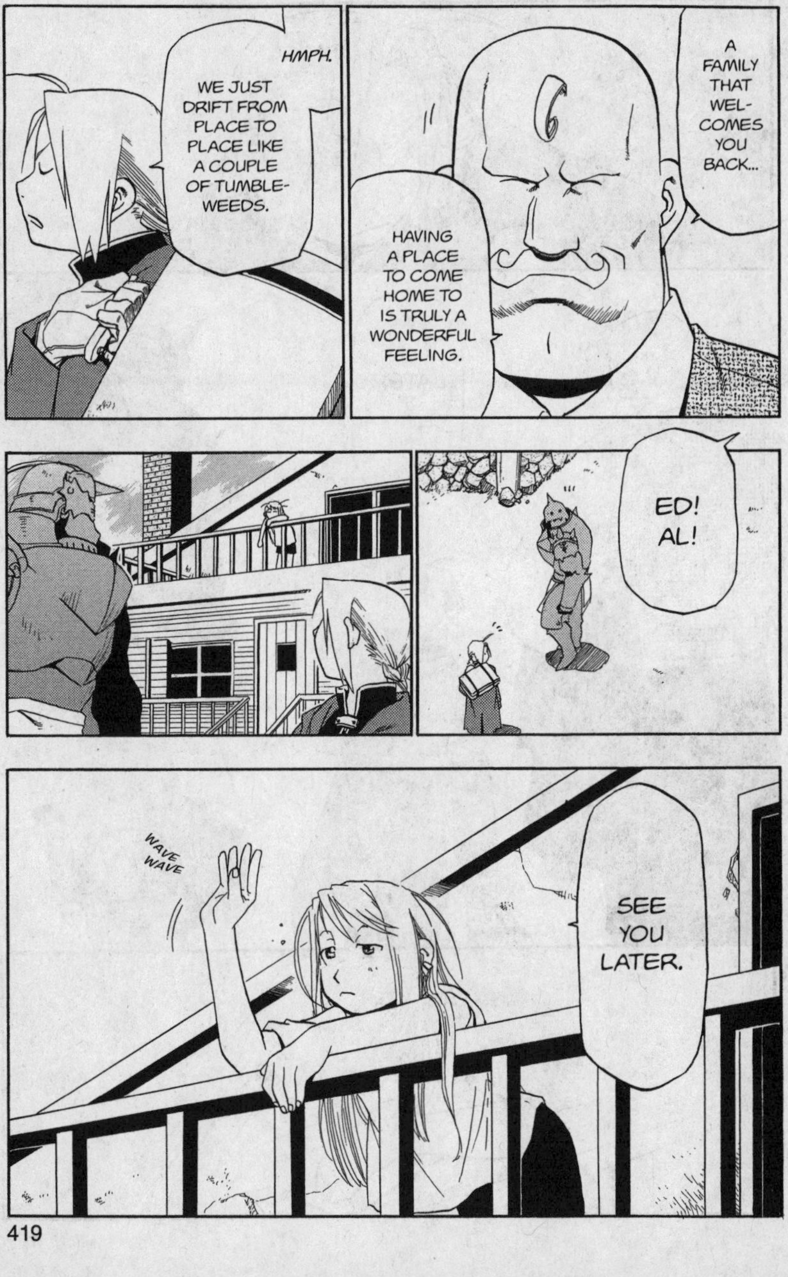

A FAMILY THAT WEL-COMES YOU BACK...
HAVING A PLACE TO COME HOME TO IS TRULY A WONDERFUL FEELING.
HMPH.
WE JUST DRIFT FROM PLACE TO PLACE LIKE A COUPLE OF TUMBLE-WEEDS.
ED! AL!
SEE YOU LATER.
WAVE WAVE

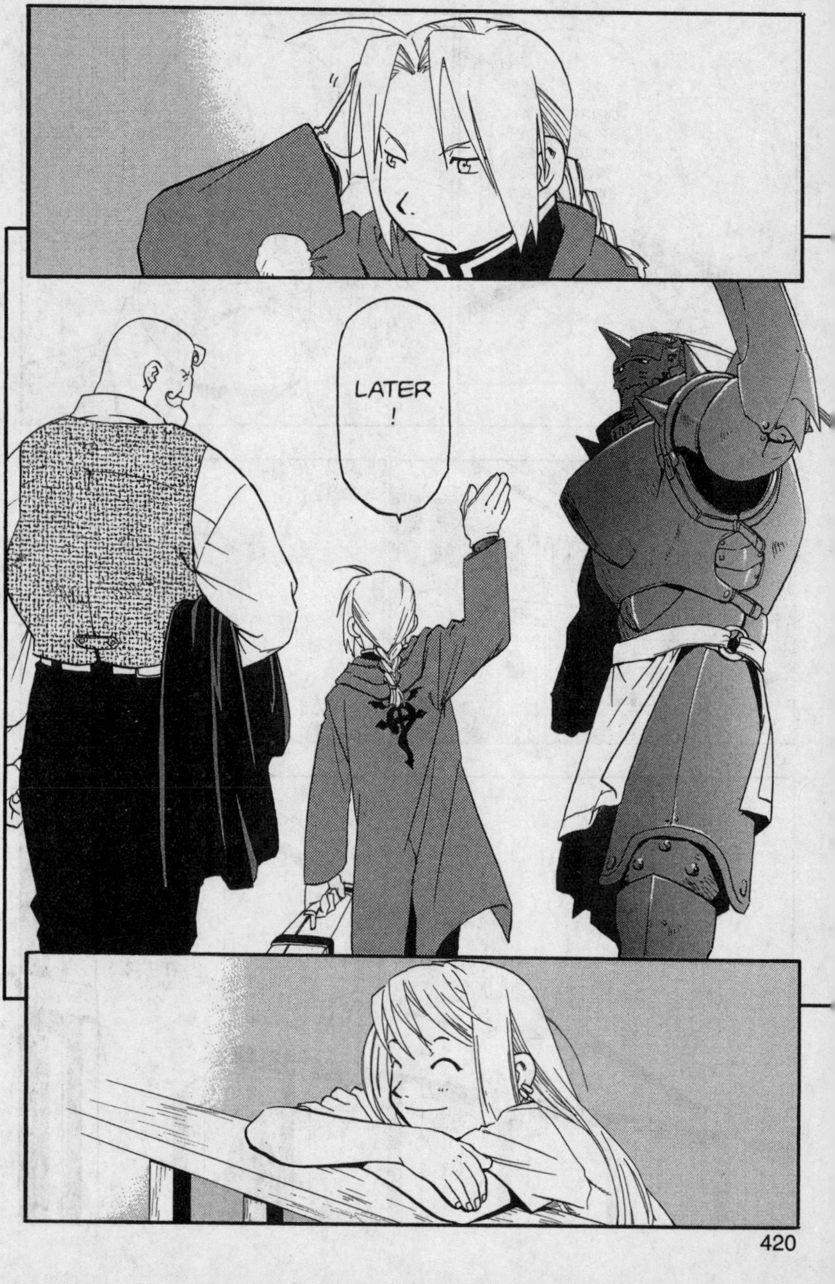
LATER!

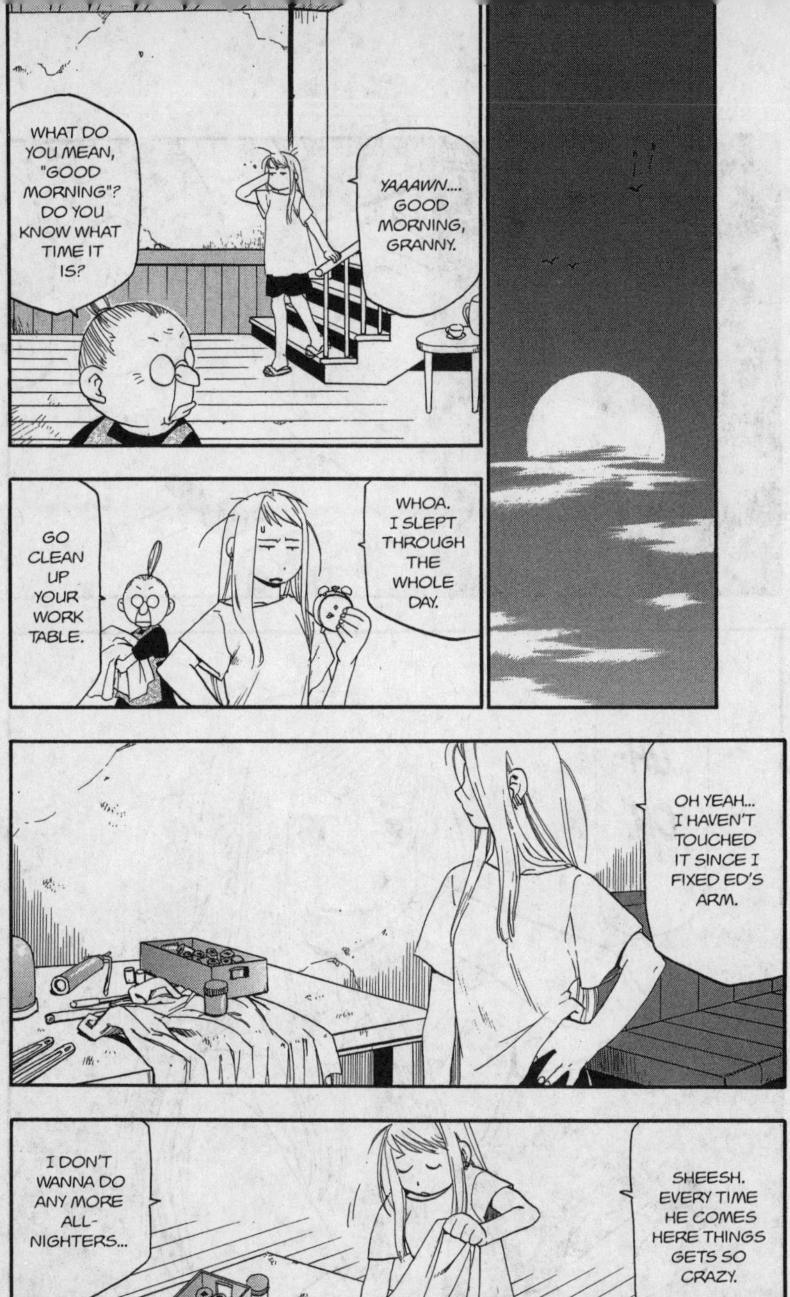
YAAAWN.... GOOD MORNING, GRANNY.
WHAT DO YOU MEAN, "GOOD MORNING"? DO YOU KNOW WHAT TIME IT IS?
WHOA. I SLEPT THROUGH THE WHOLE DAY.
GO CLEAN UP YOUR WORK TABLE.
OH YEAH... I HAVEN'T TOUCHED IT SINCE I FIXED ED'S ARM.
SHEESH. EVERY TIME HE COMES HERE THINGS GETS SO CRAZY.
I DON'T WANNA DO ANY MORE ALL-NIGHTERS...

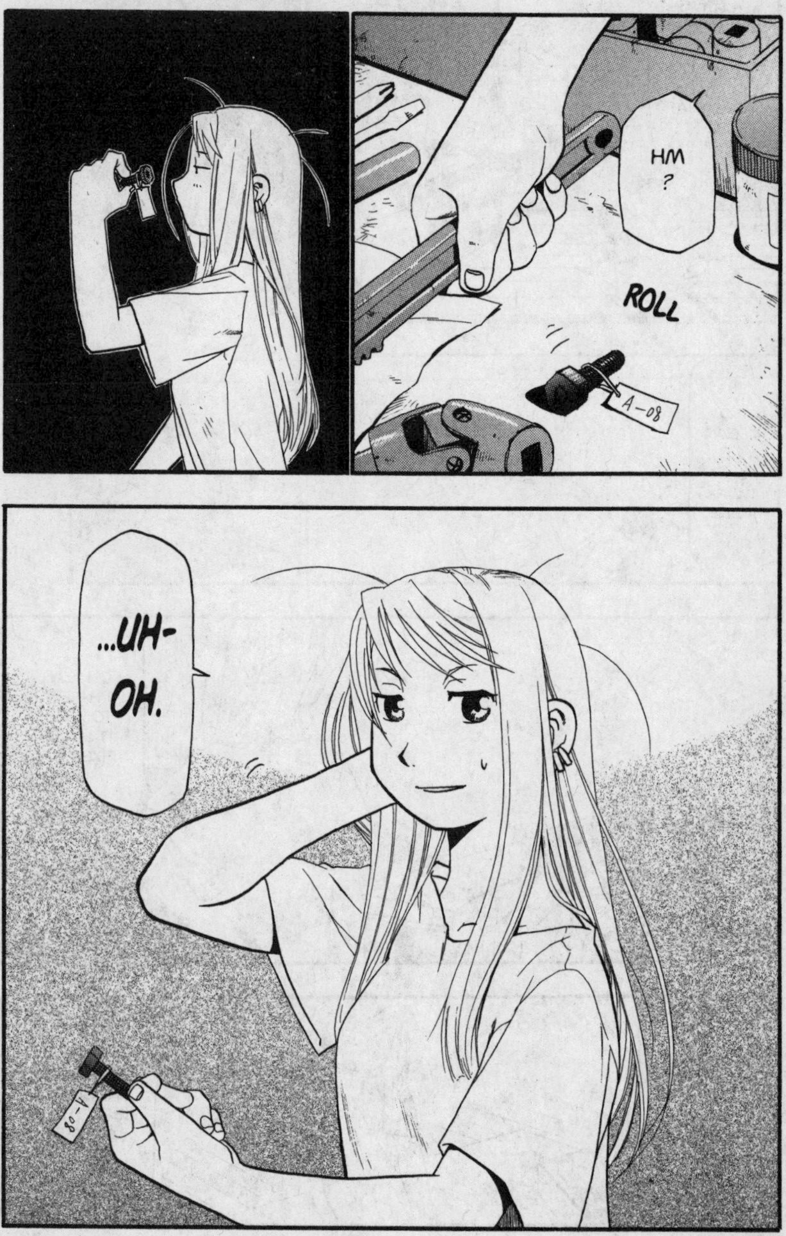
HM ?
ROLL
A-08
...UH-OH.
A-08

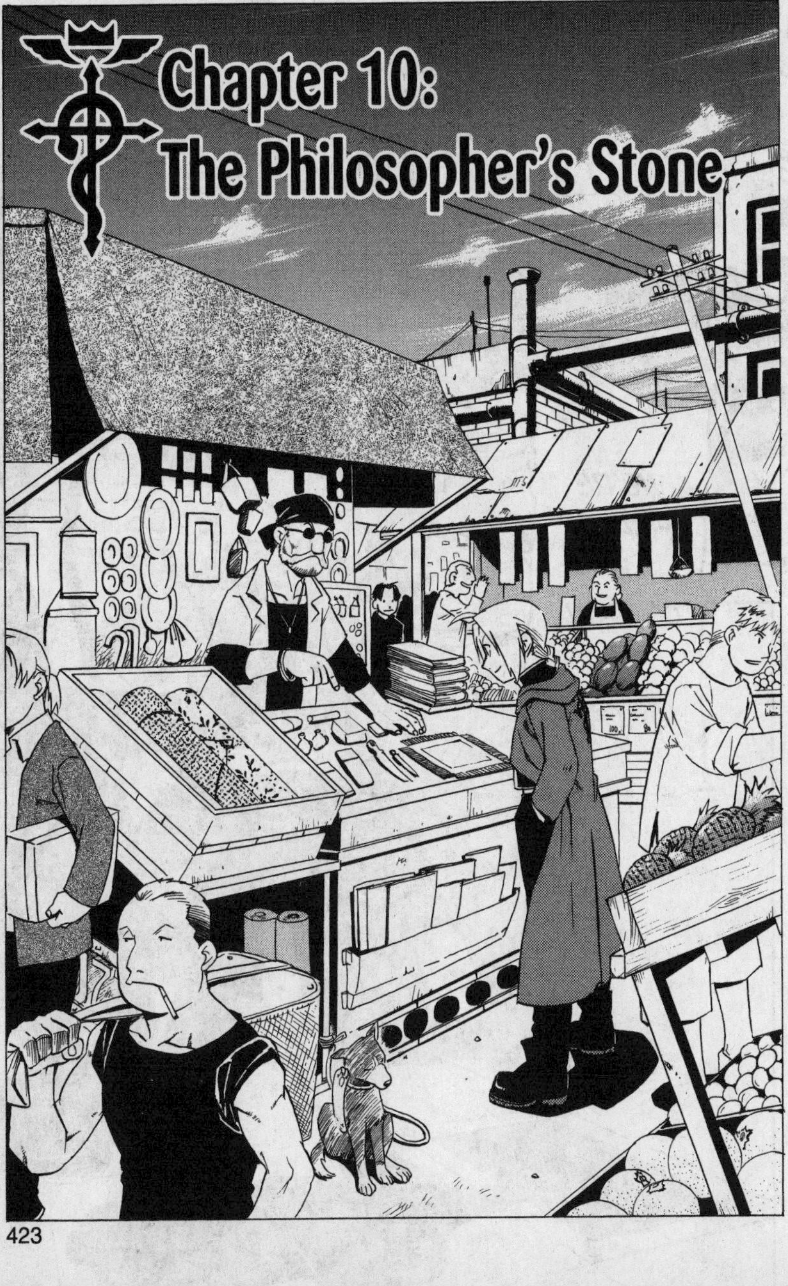
Chapter 10:
The Philosopher's Stone

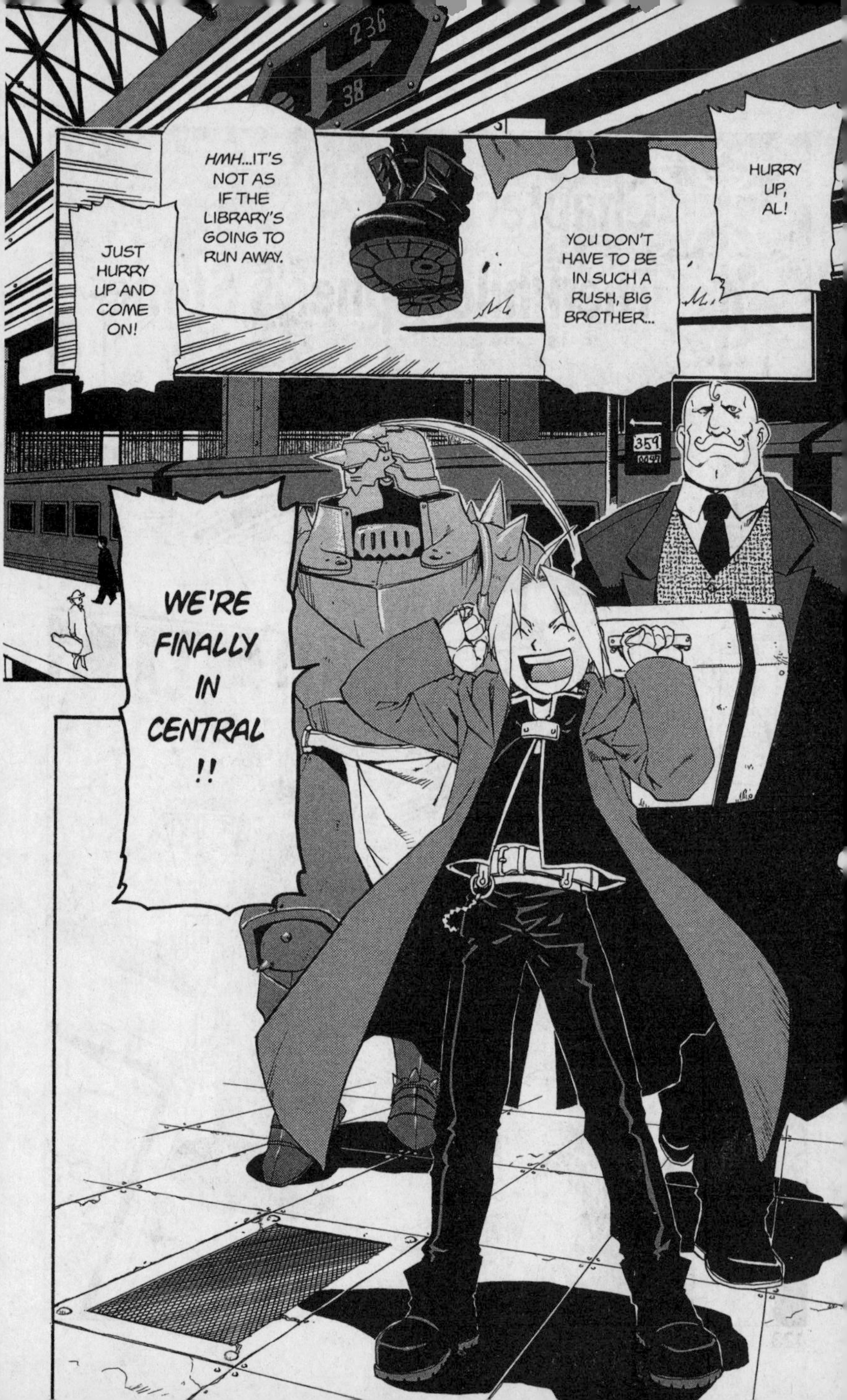
HURRY UP, AL!
YOU DON'T HAVE TO BE IN SUCH A RUSH, BIG BROTHER...
HMH...IT'S NOT AS IF THE LIBRARY'S GOING TO RUN AWAY.
JUST HURRY UP AND COME ON!
WE'RE FINALLY IN CENTRAL!!

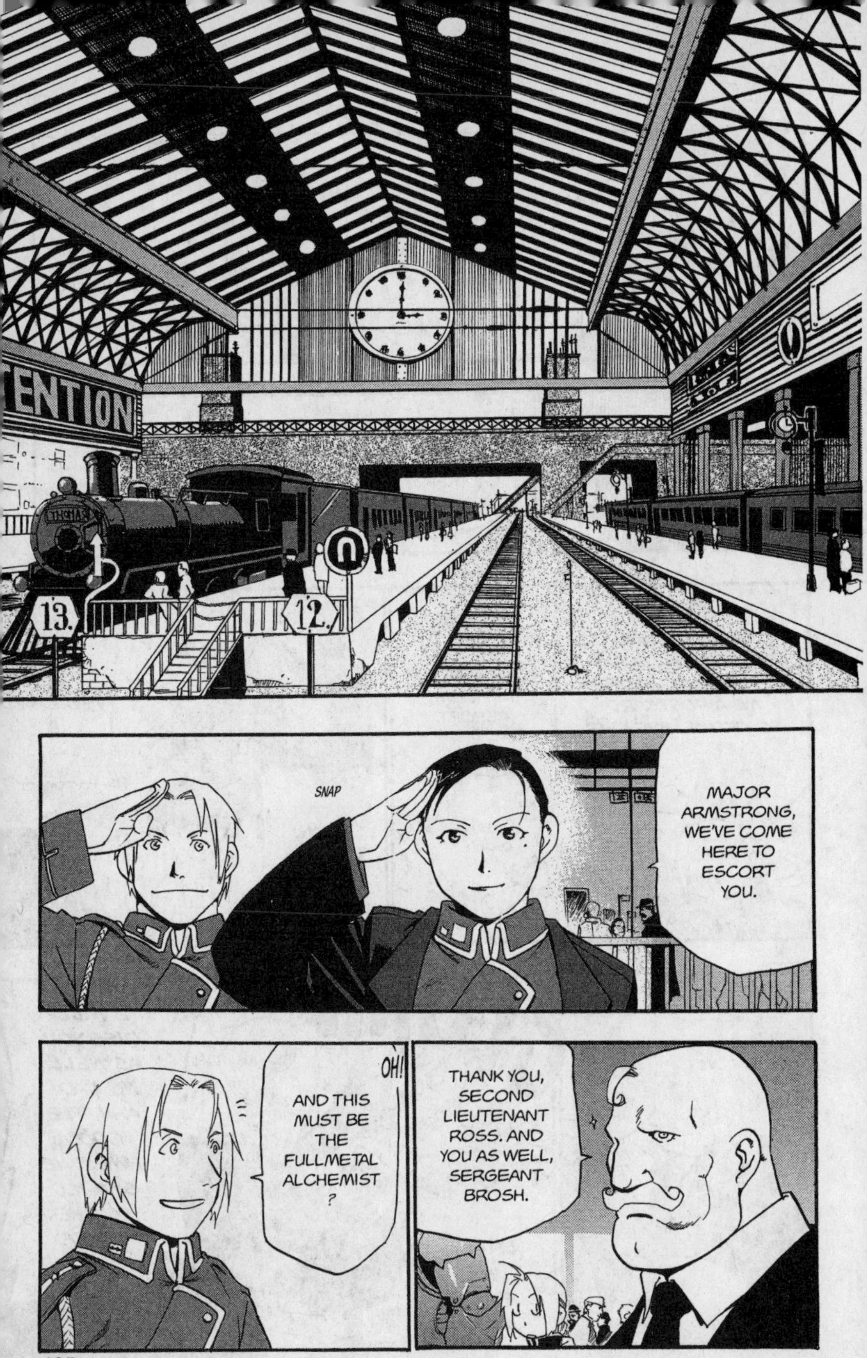
13.
12.
MAJOR ARMSTRONG, WE'VE COME HERE TO ESCORT YOU.
SNAP
THANK YOU, SECOND LIEUTENANT ROSS. AND YOU AS WELL, SERGEANT BROSH.
OH!
AND THIS MUST BE THE FULLMETAL ALCHEMIST?

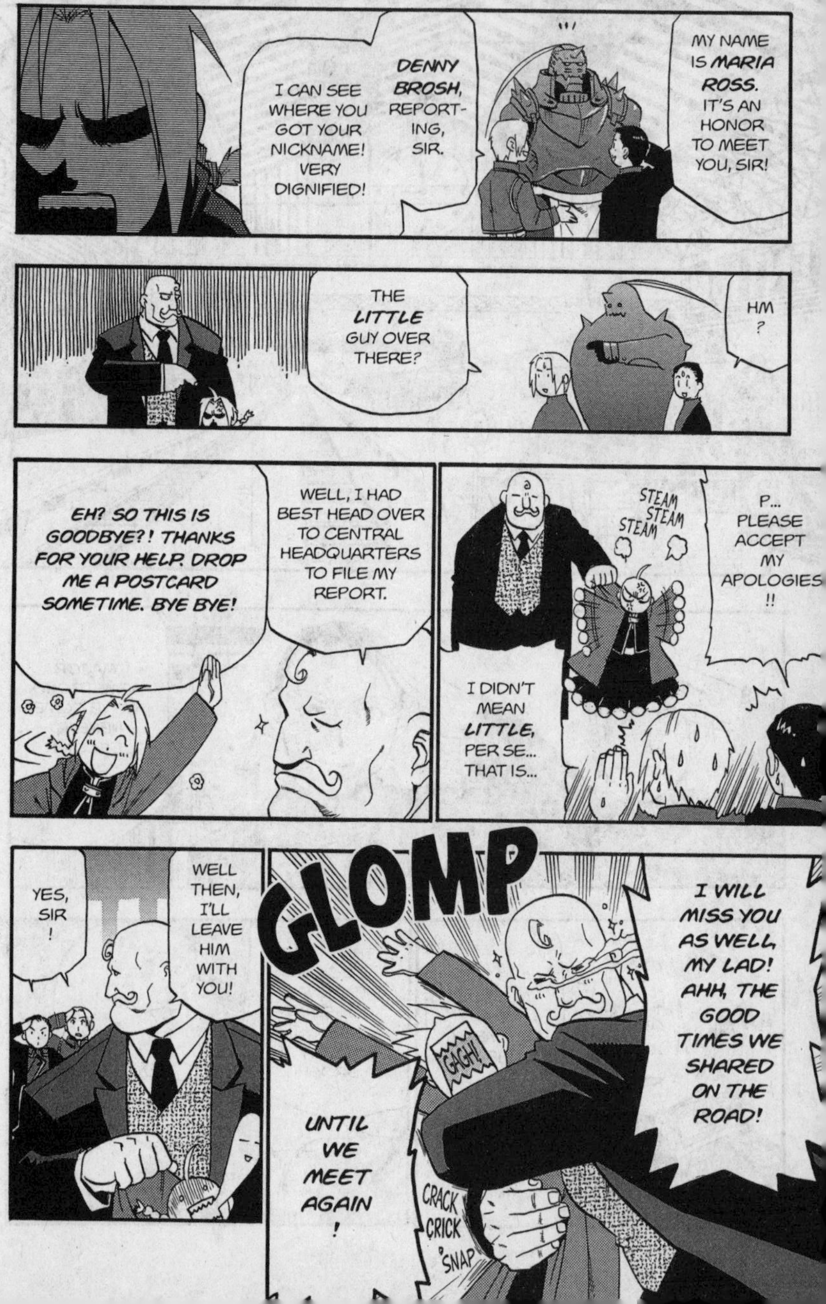
MY NAME IS MARIA ROSS. IT'S AN HONOR TO MEET YOU, SIR!
DENNY BROSH, REPORTING, SIR.
I CAN SEE WHERE YOU GOT YOUR NICKNAME! VERY DIGNIFIED!
HM?
THE LITTLE GUY OVER THERE?
P... PLEASE ACCEPT MY APOLOGIES!!
STEAM STEAM STEAM
I DIDN'T MEAN LITTLE, PER SE... THAT IS...
WELL, I HAD BEST HEAD OVER TO CENTRAL HEADQUARTERS TO FILE MY REPORT.
EH? SO THIS IS GOODBYE?! THANKS FOR YOUR HELP. DROP ME A POSTCARD SOMETIME. BYE BYE!
GLOMP
I WILL MISS YOU AS WELL, MY LAD! AHH, THE GOOD TIMES WE SHARED ON THE ROAD!
GAGH!
UNTIL WE MEET AGAIN!
CRACK CRICK SNAP
WELL THEN, I'LL LEAVE HIM WITH YOU!
YES, SIR!

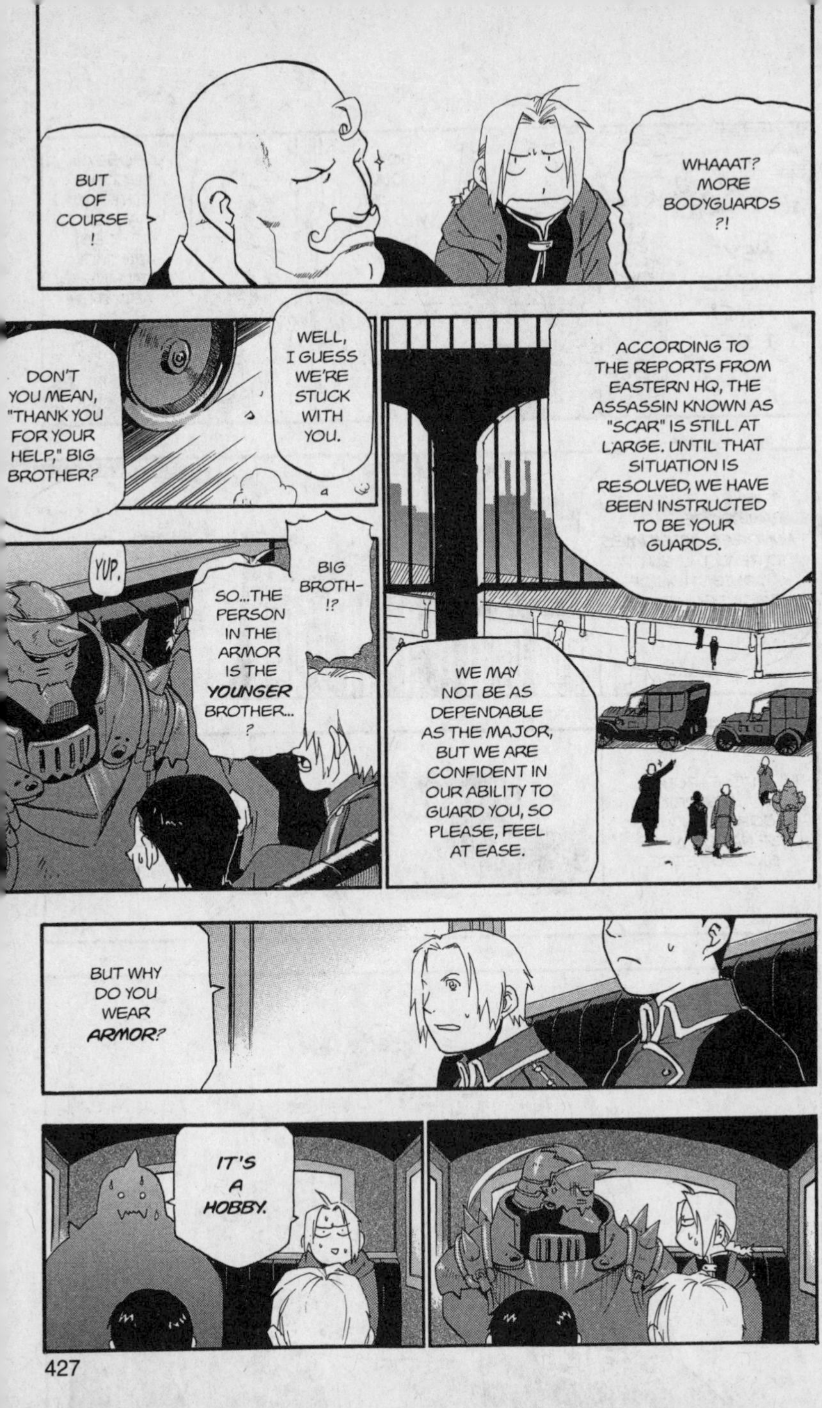
WHAAAT? MORE BODYGUARDS ?!
BUT OF COURSE !
ACCORDING TO THE REPORTS FROM EASTERN HQ, THE ASSASSIN KNOWN AS "SCAR" IS STILL AT LARGE. UNTIL THAT SITUATION IS RESOLVED, WE HAVE BEEN INSTRUCTED TO BE YOUR GUARDS.
WE MAY NOT BE AS DEPENDABLE AS THE MAJOR, BUT WE ARE CONFIDENT IN OUR ABILITY TO GUARD YOU, SO PLEASE, FEEL AT EASE.
WELL, I GUESS WE'RE STUCK WITH YOU.
DON'T YOU MEAN, "THANK YOU FOR YOUR HELP," BIG BROTHER?
BIG BROTH- !?
SO...THE PERSON IN THE ARMOR IS THE YOUNGER BROTHER... ?
YUP.
BUT WHY DO YOU WEAR ARMOR?
IT'S A HOBBY.

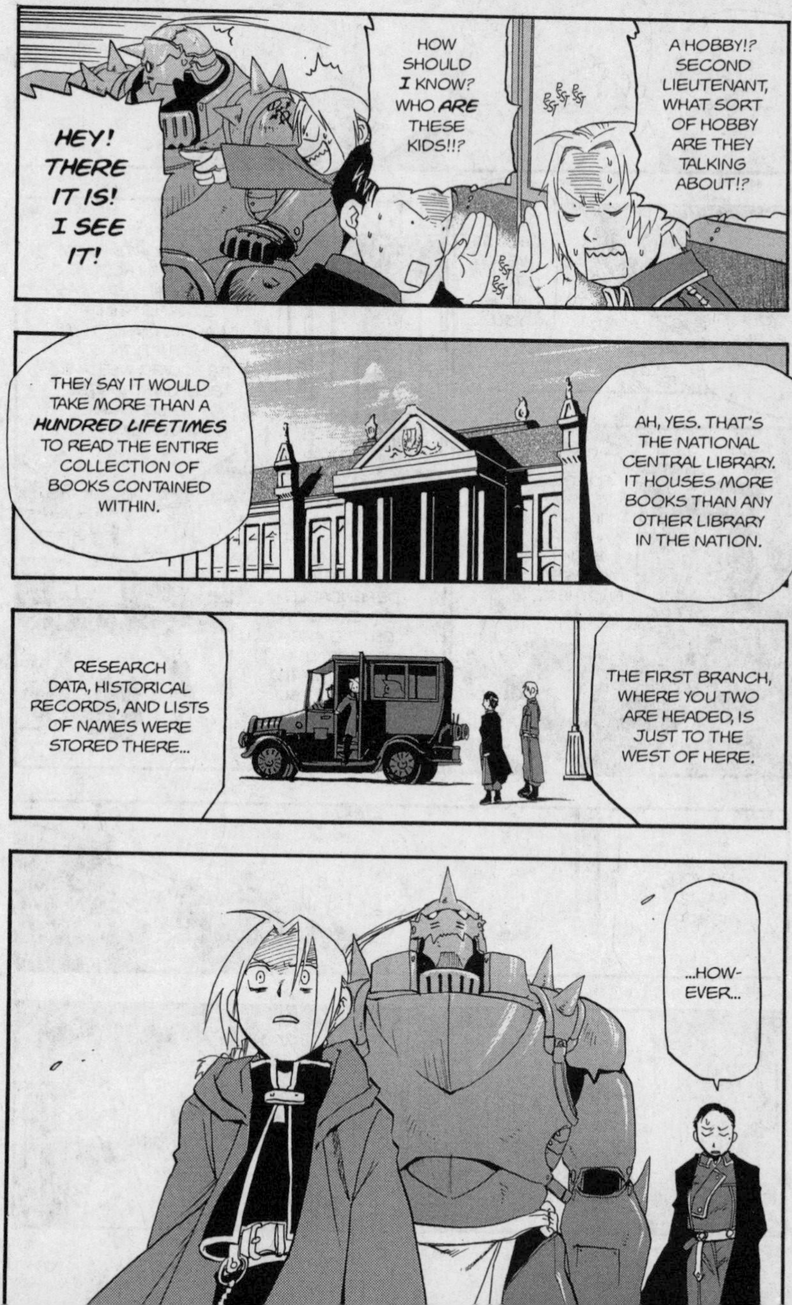
A HOBBY!? SECOND LIEUTENANT, WHAT SORT OF HOBBY ARE THEY TALKING ABOUT!?
PSST PSST
HOW SHOULD I KNOW? WHO ARE THESE KIDS!!?
PSST PSST
HEY! THERE IT IS! I SEE IT!
AH, YES. THAT'S THE NATIONAL CENTRAL LIBRARY. IT HOUSES MORE BOOKS THAN ANY OTHER LIBRARY IN THE NATION.
THEY SAY IT WOULD TAKE MORE THAN A HUNDRED LIFETIMES TO READ THE ENTIRE COLLECTION OF BOOKS CONTAINED WITHIN.
THE FIRST BRANCH, WHERE YOU TWO ARE HEADED, IS JUST TO THE WEST OF HERE.
RESEARCH DATA, HISTORICAL RECORDS, AND LISTS OF NAMES WERE STORED THERE...
...HOW-EVER...

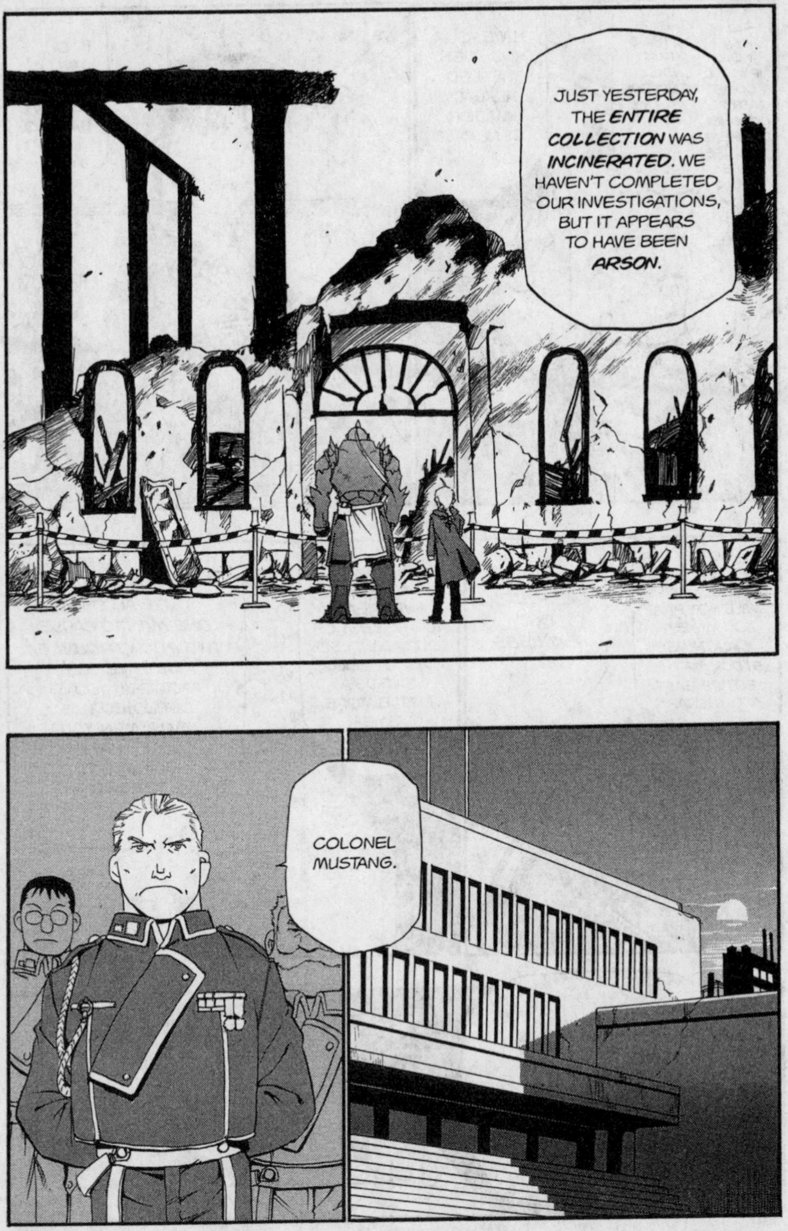
JUST YESTERDAY, THE ENTIRE COLLECTION WAS INCINERATED. WE HAVEN'T COMPLETED OUR INVESTIGATIONS, BUT IT APPEARS TO HAVE BEEN ARSON.
COLONEL MUSTANG.

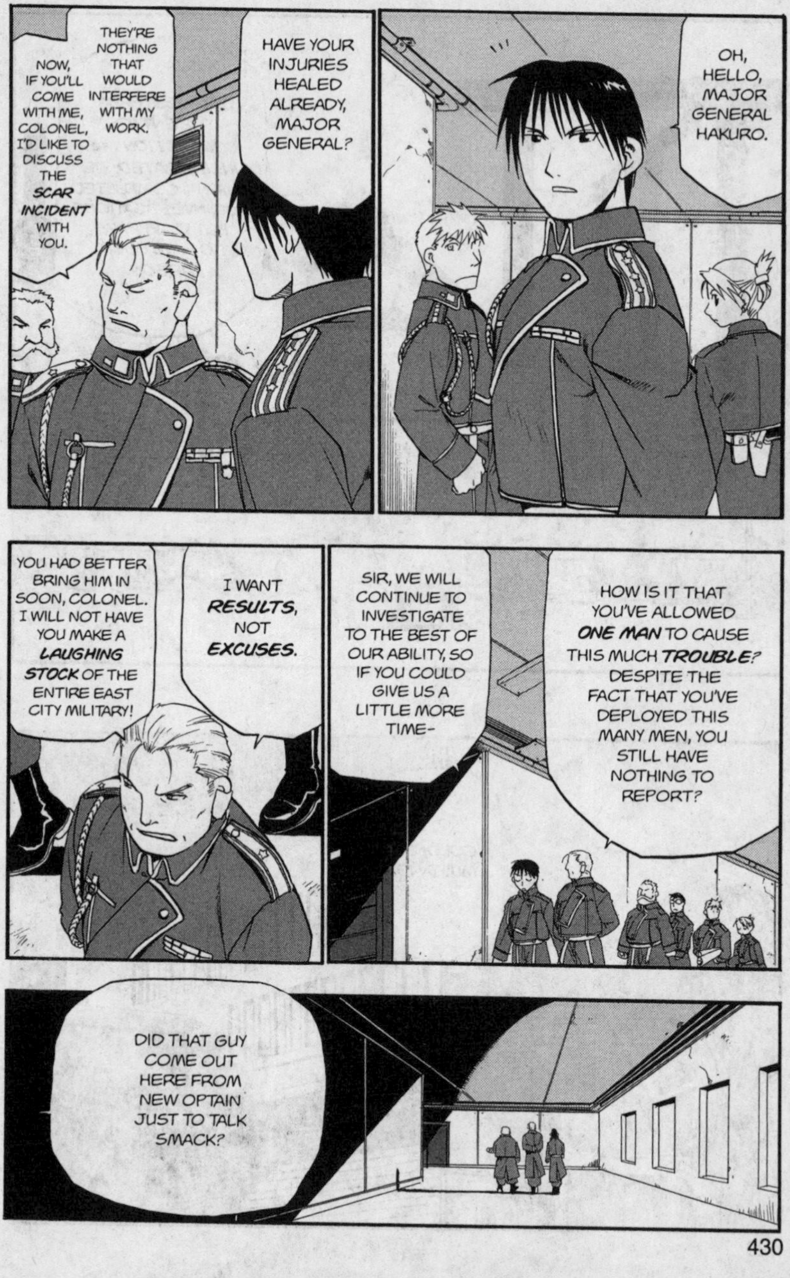
OH, HELLO, MAJOR GENERAL HAKURO.
HAVE YOUR INJURIES HEALED ALREADY, MAJOR GENERAL?
THEY'RE NOTHING THAT WOULD INTERFERE WITH MY WORK.
NOW, IF YOU'LL COME WITH ME, COLONEL, I'D LIKE TO DISCUSS THE SCAR INCIDENT WITH YOU.
HOW IS IT THAT YOU'VE ALLOWED ONE MAN TO CAUSE THIS MUCH TROUBLE? DESPITE THE FACT THAT YOU'VE DEPLOYED THIS MANY MEN, YOU STILL HAVE NOTHING TO REPORT?
SIR, WE WILL CONTINUE TO INVESTIGATE TO THE BEST OF OUR ABILITY, SO IF YOU COULD GIVE US A LITTLE MORE TIME-
I WANT RESULTS, NOT EXCUSES.
YOU HAD BETTER BRING HIM IN SOON, COLONEL. I WILL NOT HAVE YOU MAKE A LAUGHING STOCK OF THE ENTIRE EAST CITY MILITARY!
DID THAT GUY COME OUT HERE FROM NEW OPTAIN JUST TO TALK SMACK?

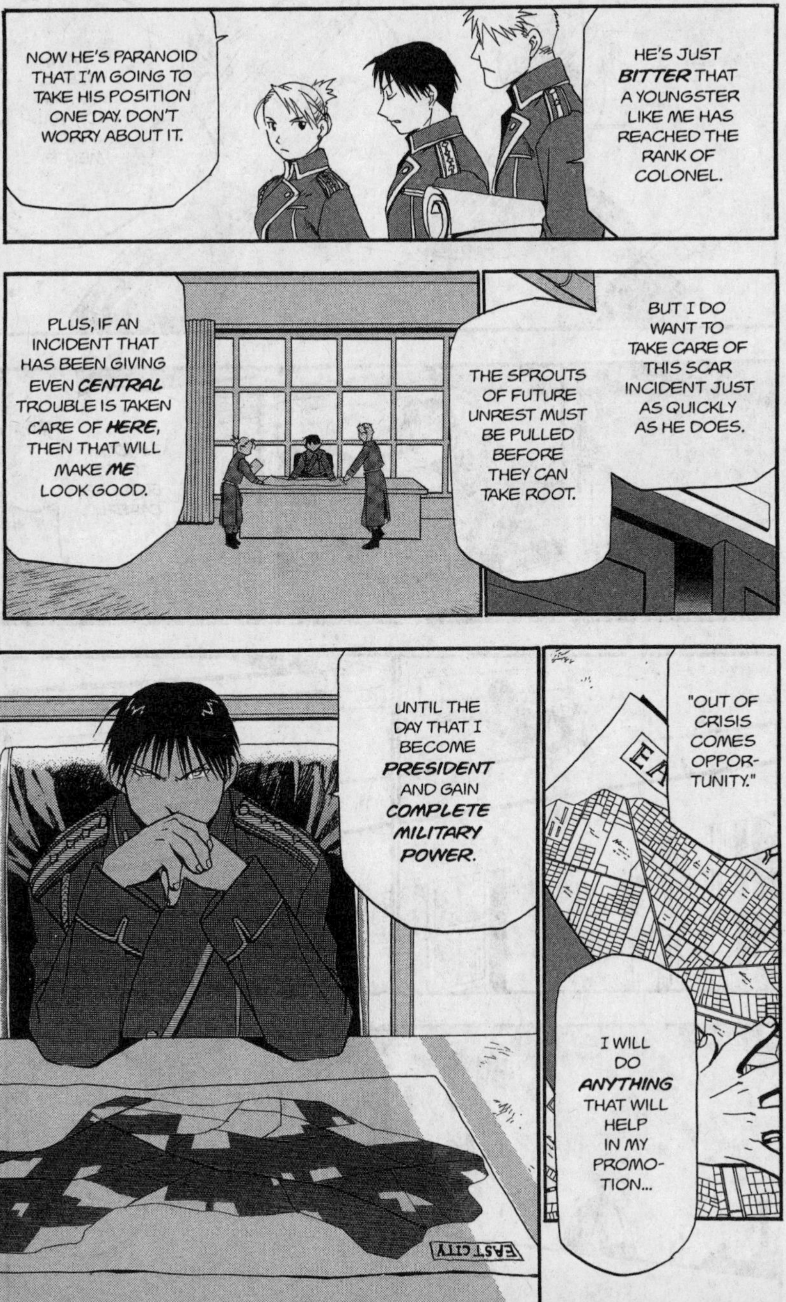
HE'S JUST BITTER THAT A YOUNGSTER LIKE ME HAS REACHED THE RANK OF COLONEL.
NOW HE'S PARANOID THAT I'M GOING TO TAKE HIS POSITION ONE DAY. DON'T WORRY ABOUT IT.
BUT I DO WANT TO TAKE CARE OF THIS SCAR INCIDENT JUST AS QUICKLY AS HE DOES.
THE SPROUTS OF FUTURE UNREST MUST BE PULLED BEFORE THEY CAN TAKE ROOT.
PLUS, IF AN INCIDENT THAT HAS BEEN GIVING EVEN CENTRAL TROUBLE IS TAKEN CARE OF HERE, THEN THAT WILL MAKE ME LOOK GOOD.
"OUT OF CRISIS COMES OPPOR-TUNITY."
I WILL DO ANYTHING THAT WILL HELP IN MY PROMO-TION...
UNTIL THE DAY THAT I BECOME PRESIDENT AND GAIN COMPLETE MILITARY POWER.
EAST CITY

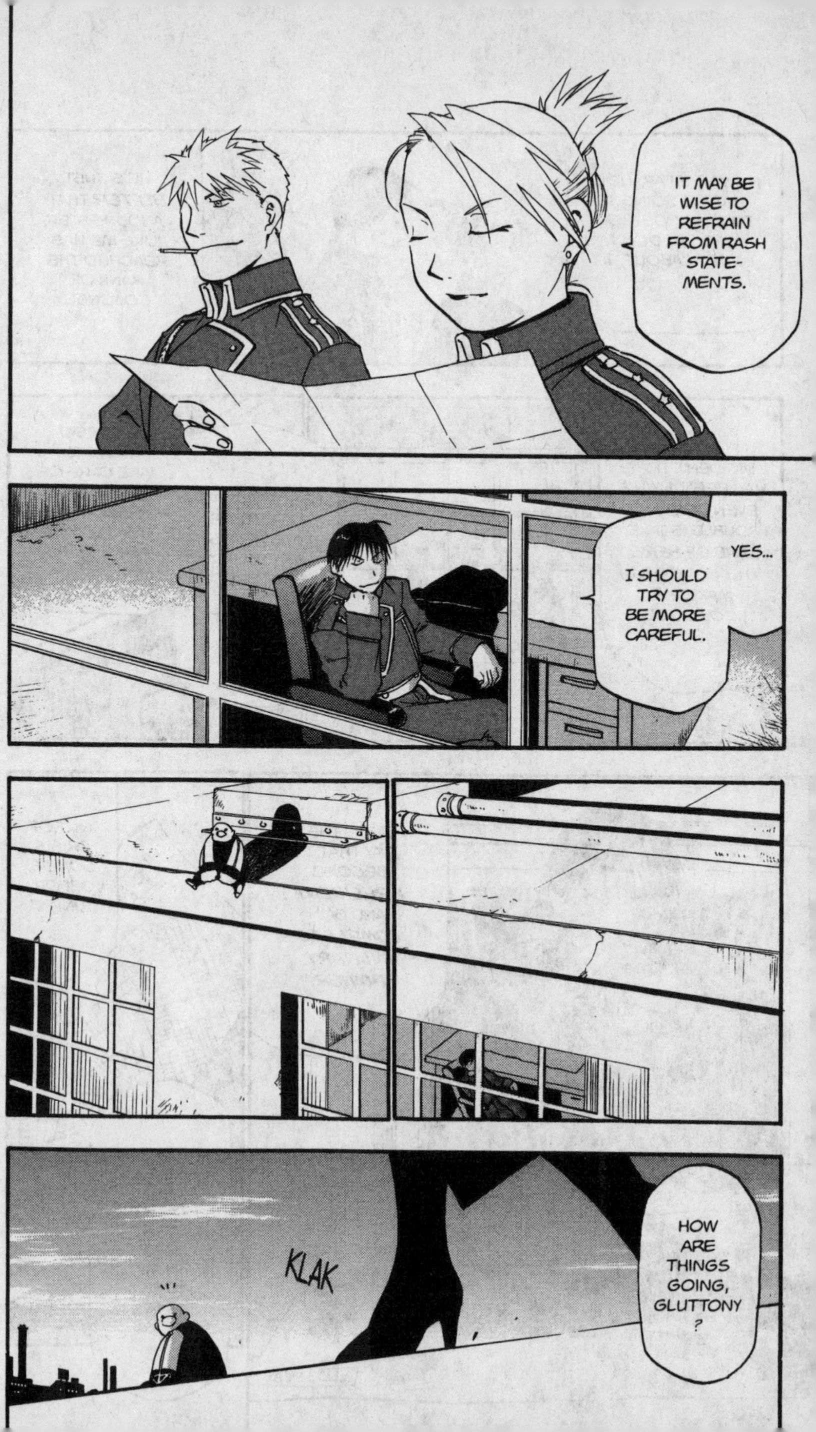
IT MAY BE WISE TO REFRAIN FROM RASH STATE-MENTS.
YES... I SHOULD TRY TO BE MORE CAREFUL.
KLAK
HOW ARE THINGS GOING, GLUTTONY ?

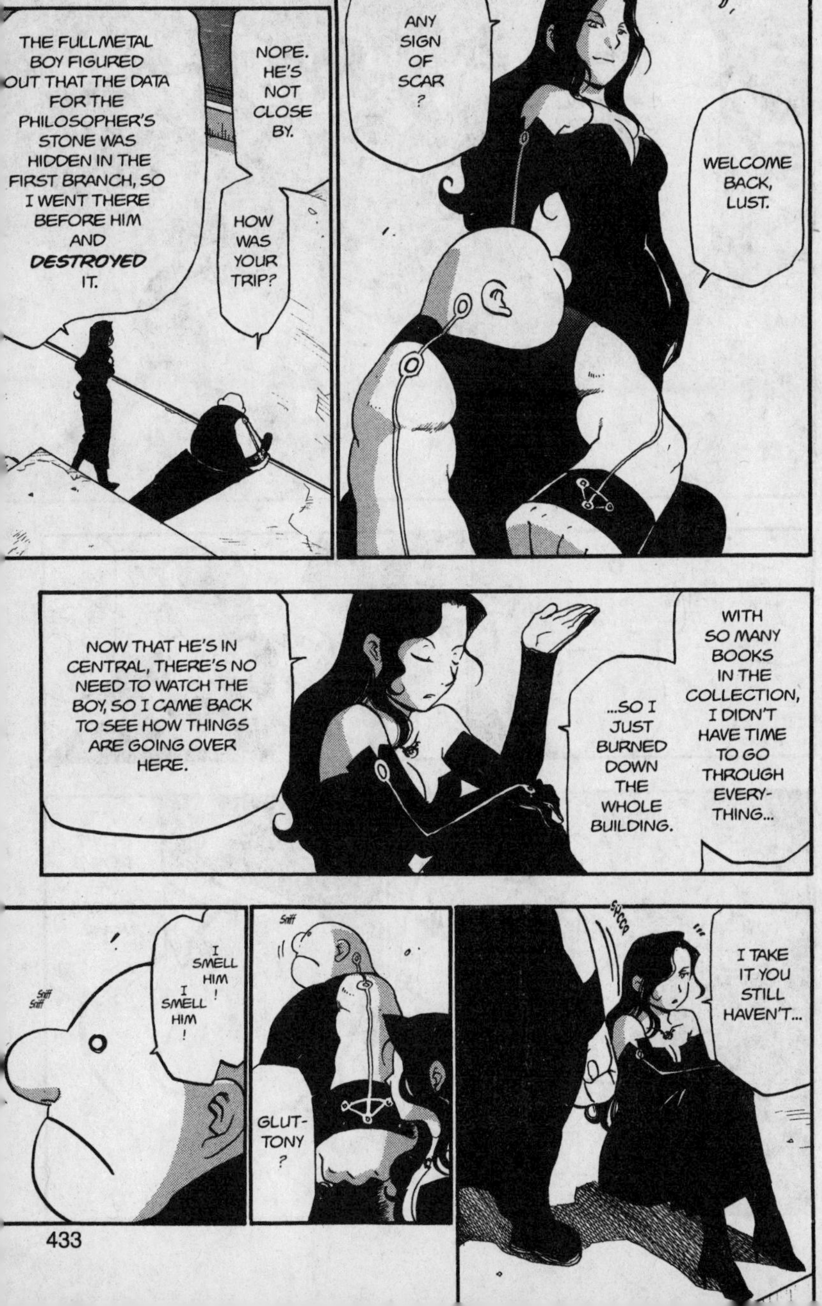
WELCOME BACK, LUST.
ANY SIGN OF SCAR?
NOPE. HE'S NOT CLOSE BY.
HOW WAS YOUR TRIP?
THE FULLMETAL BOY FIGURED OUT THAT THE DATA FOR THE PHILOSOPHER'S STONE WAS HIDDEN IN THE FIRST BRANCH, SO I WENT THERE BEFORE HIM AND DESTROYED IT.
WITH SO MANY BOOKS IN THE COLLECTION, I DIDN'T HAVE TIME TO GO THROUGH EVERYTHING...
...SO I JUST BURNED DOWN THE WHOLE BUILDING.
NOW THAT HE'S IN CENTRAL, THERE'S NO NEED TO WATCH THE BOY, SO I CAME BACK TO SEE HOW THINGS ARE GOING OVER HERE.
I TAKE IT YOU STILL HAVEN'T...
Sniff
GLUTTONY?
Sniff Sniff
I SMELL HIM! I SMELL HIM!

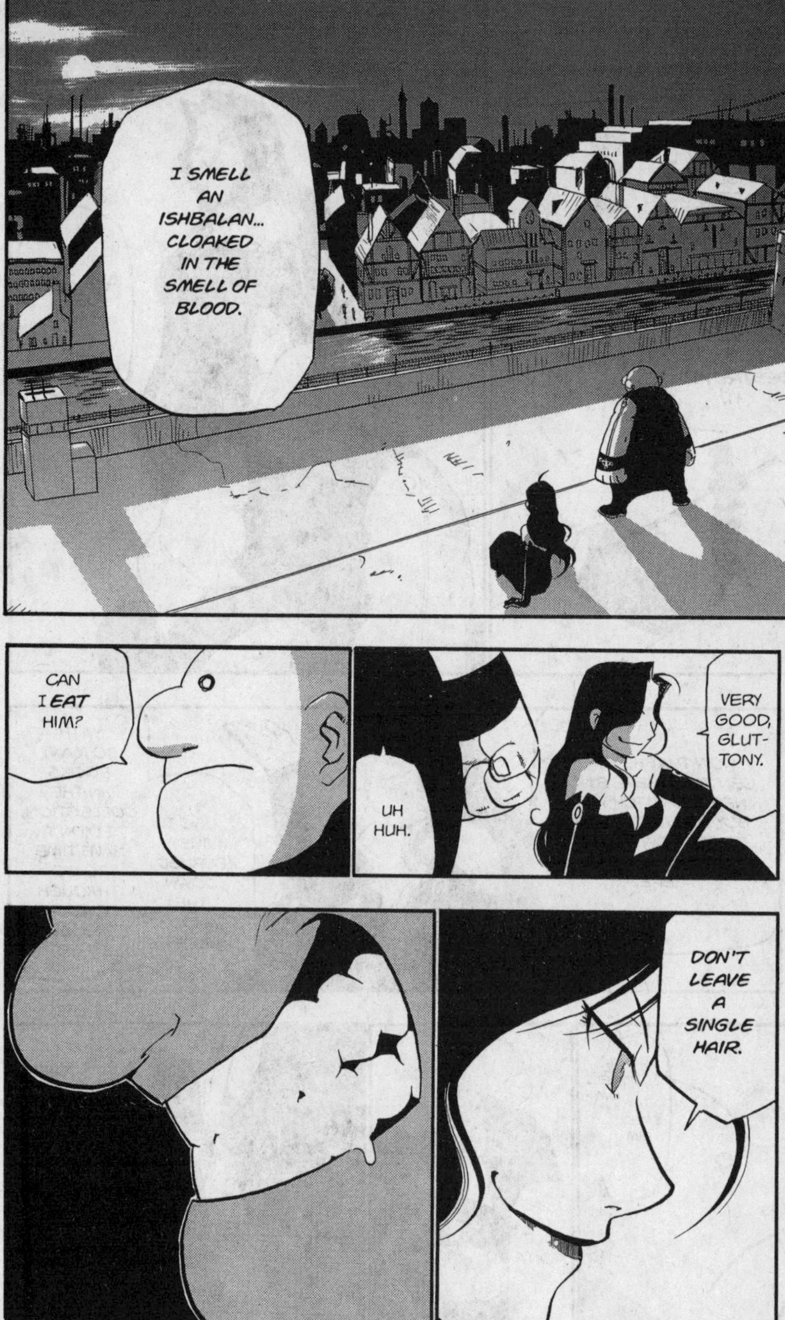
I SMELL AN ISHBALAN... CLOAKED IN THE SMELL OF BLOOD.
VERY GOOD, GLUTTONY.
UH HUH.
CAN I EAT HIM?
DON'T LEAVE A SINGLE HAIR.

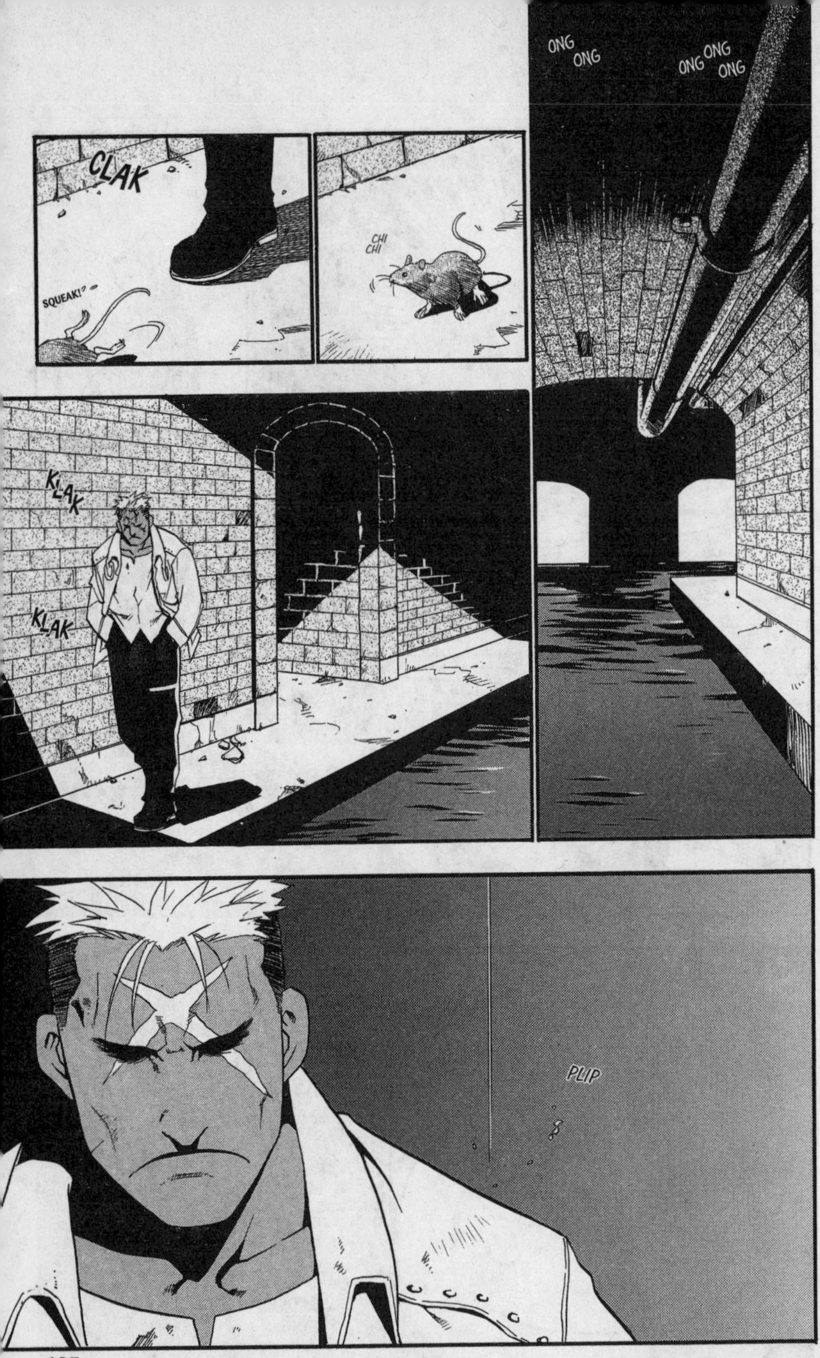
ONG ONG
ONG ONG ONG
CHI CHI
CLAK
SQUEAK!?
KLAK
KLAK
PLIP

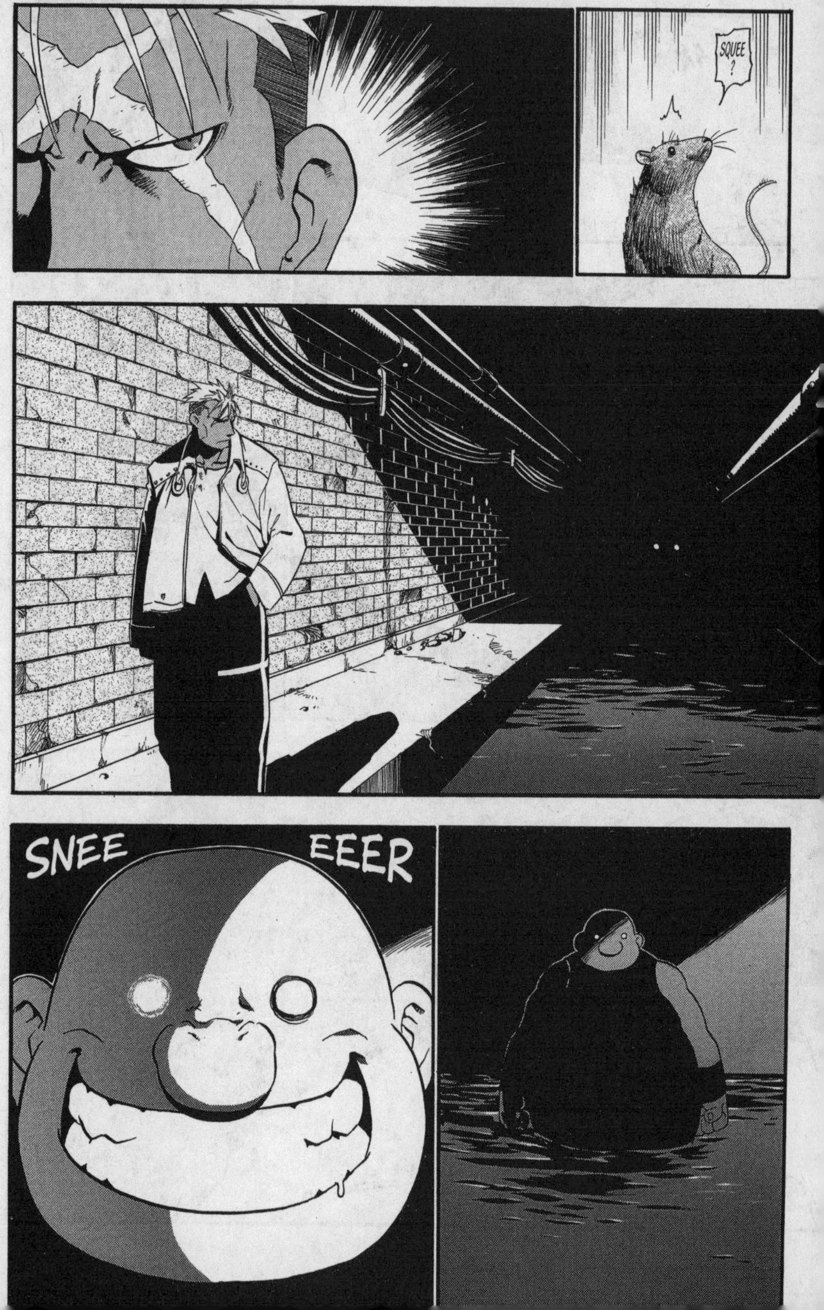
SQUEE ?
SNEE EEER

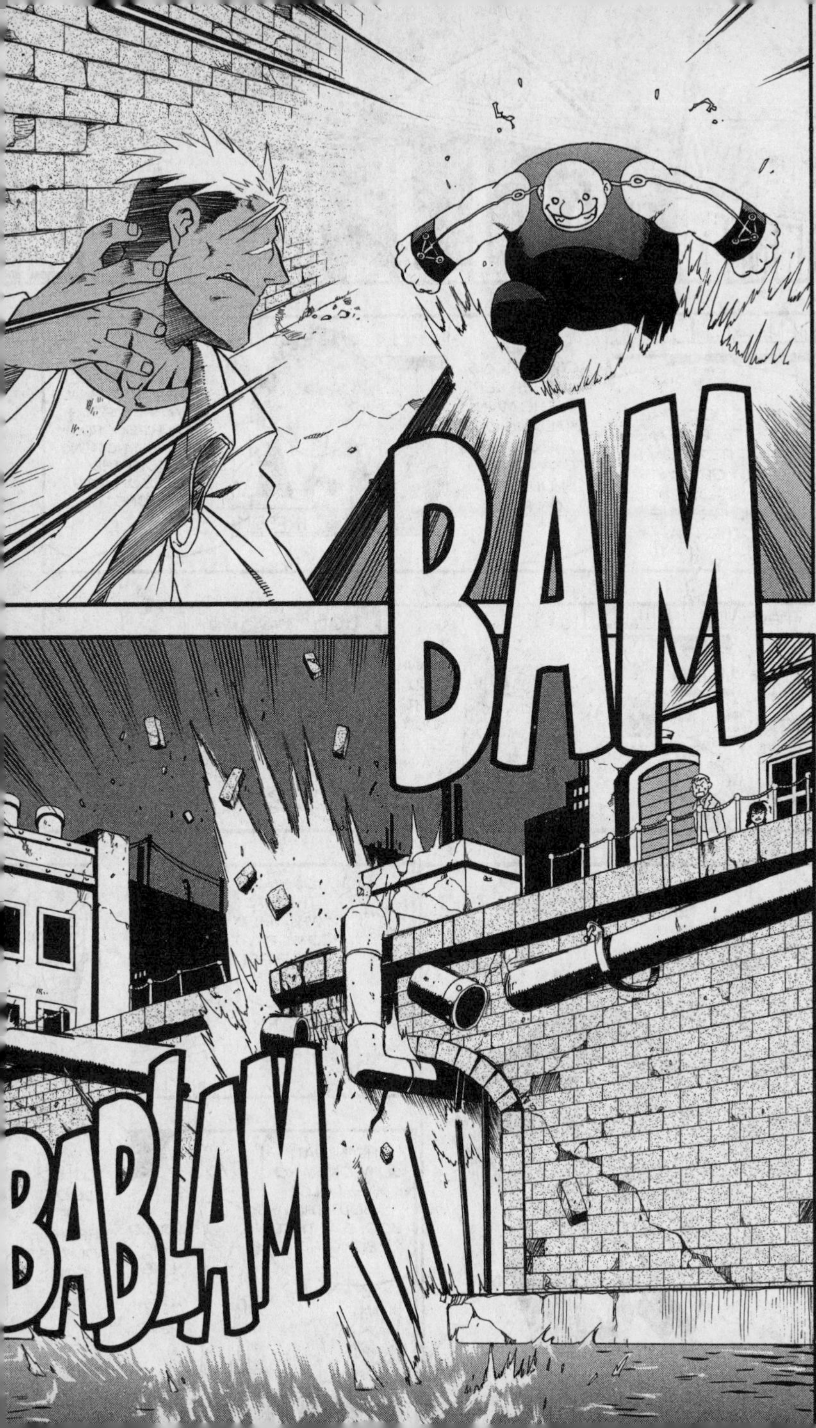
BAM
BABLAM

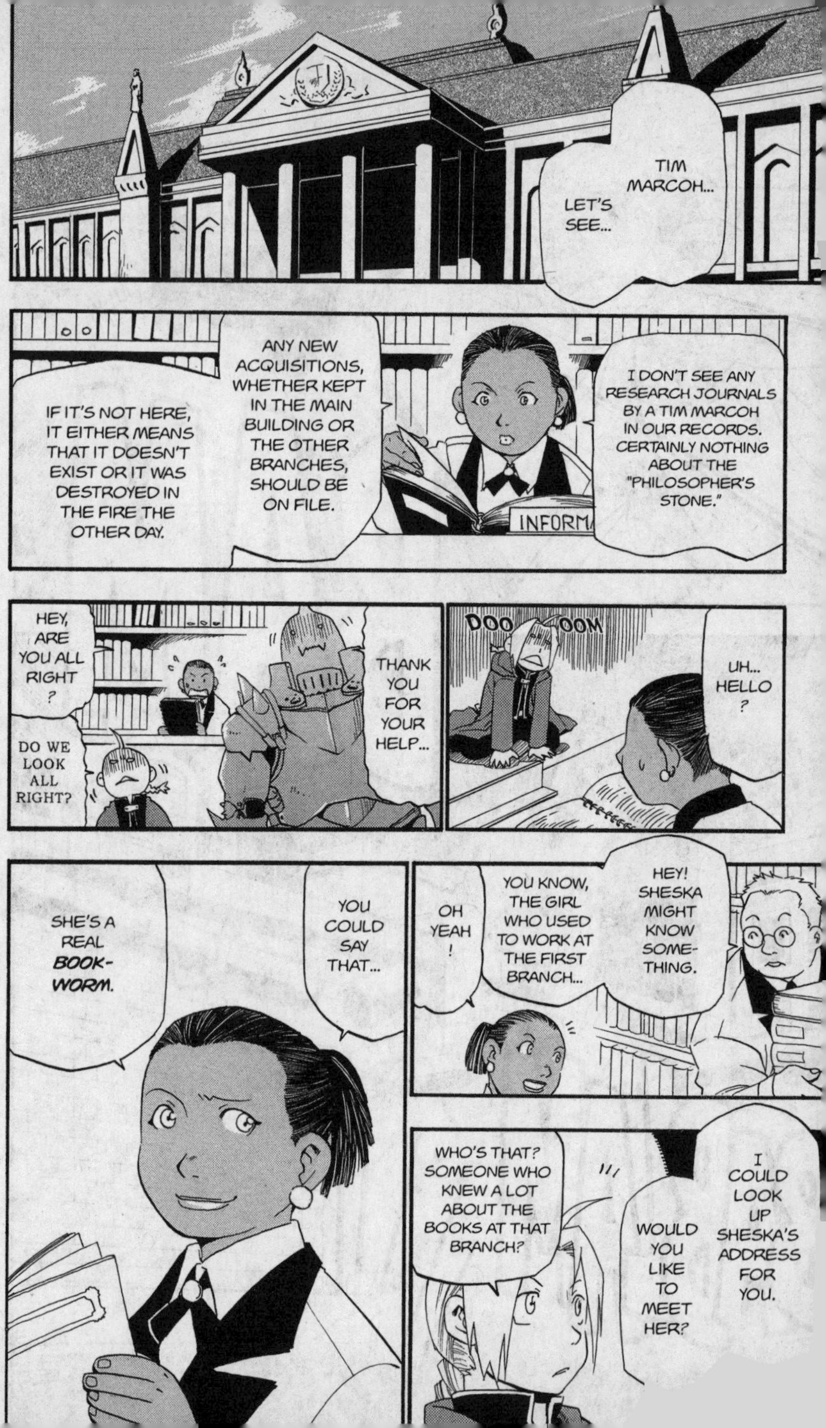
LET'S SEE... TIM MARCOH...
I DON'T SEE ANY RESEARCH JOURNALS BY A TIM MARCOH IN OUR RECORDS. CERTAINLY NOTHING ABOUT THE "PHILOSOPHER'S STONE."
ANY NEW ACQUISITIONS, WHETHER KEPT IN THE MAIN BUILDING OR THE OTHER BRANCHES, SHOULD BE ON FILE.
IF IT'S NOT HERE, IT EITHER MEANS THAT IT DOESN'T EXIST OR IT WAS DESTROYED IN THE FIRE THE OTHER DAY.
INFORM
DOO OOM
UH... HELLO?
THANK YOU FOR YOUR HELP...
HEY, ARE YOU ALL RIGHT?
DO WE LOOK ALL RIGHT?
HEY! SHESKA MIGHT KNOW SOME-THING.
YOU KNOW, THE GIRL WHO USED TO WORK AT THE FIRST BRANCH...
OH YEAH!
I COULD LOOK UP SHESKA'S ADDRESS FOR YOU.
WOULD YOU LIKE TO MEET HER?
WHO'S THAT? SOMEONE WHO KNEW A LOT ABOUT THE BOOKS AT THAT BRANCH?
YOU COULD SAY THAT...
SHE'S A REAL *BOOK-WORM.*

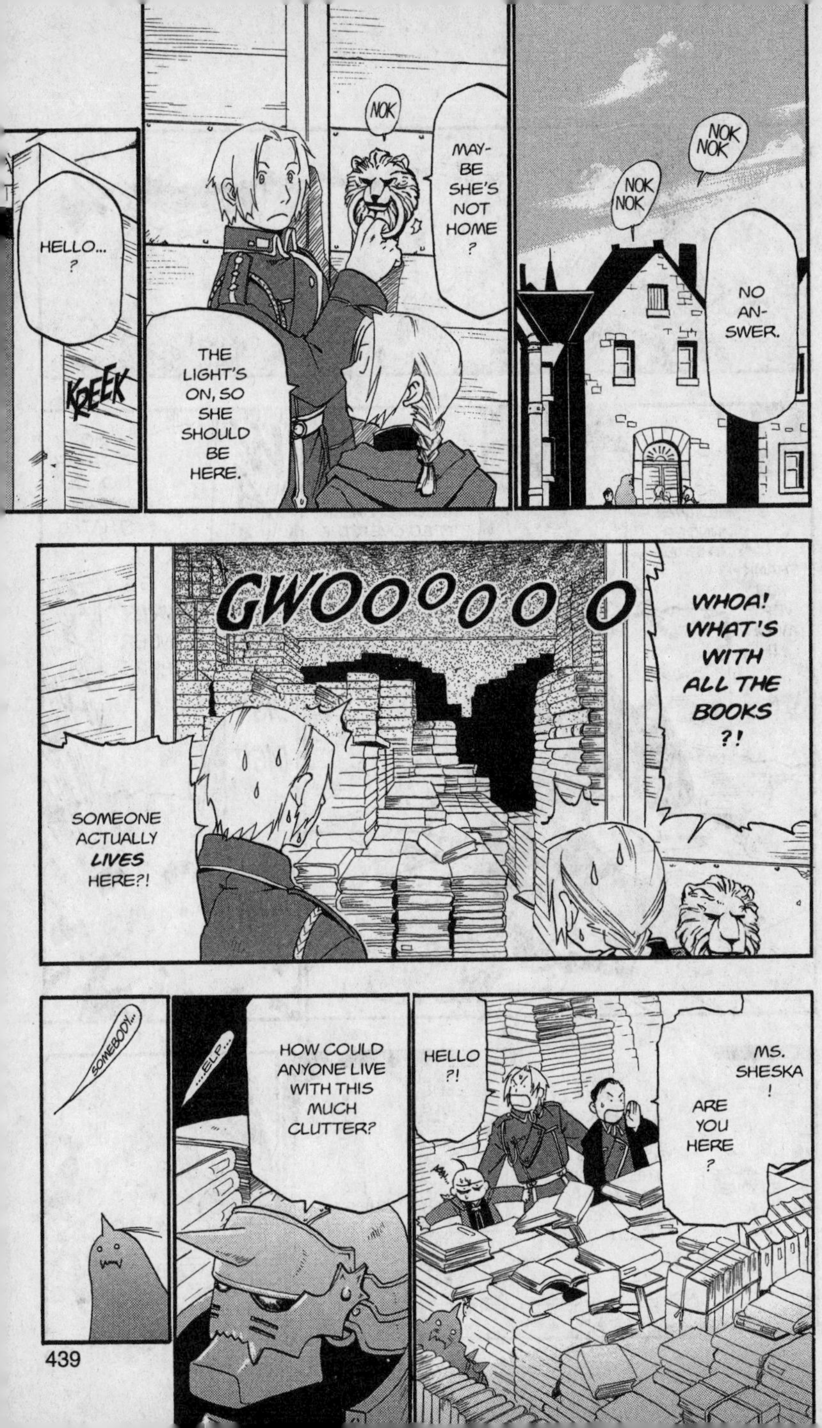
NOK NOK
NOK NOK
NO ANSWER.
NOK
MAYBE SHE'S NOT HOME?
THE LIGHT'S ON, SO SHE SHOULD BE HERE.
HELLO...?
KREEK
GWOOOOOO
WHOA! WHAT'S WITH ALL THE BOOKS?!
SOMEONE ACTUALLY LIVES HERE?!
MS. SHESKA!
ARE YOU HERE?
HELLO?!
HOW COULD ANYONE LIVE WITH THIS MUCH CLUTTER?
...ELP...
SOMEBODY...

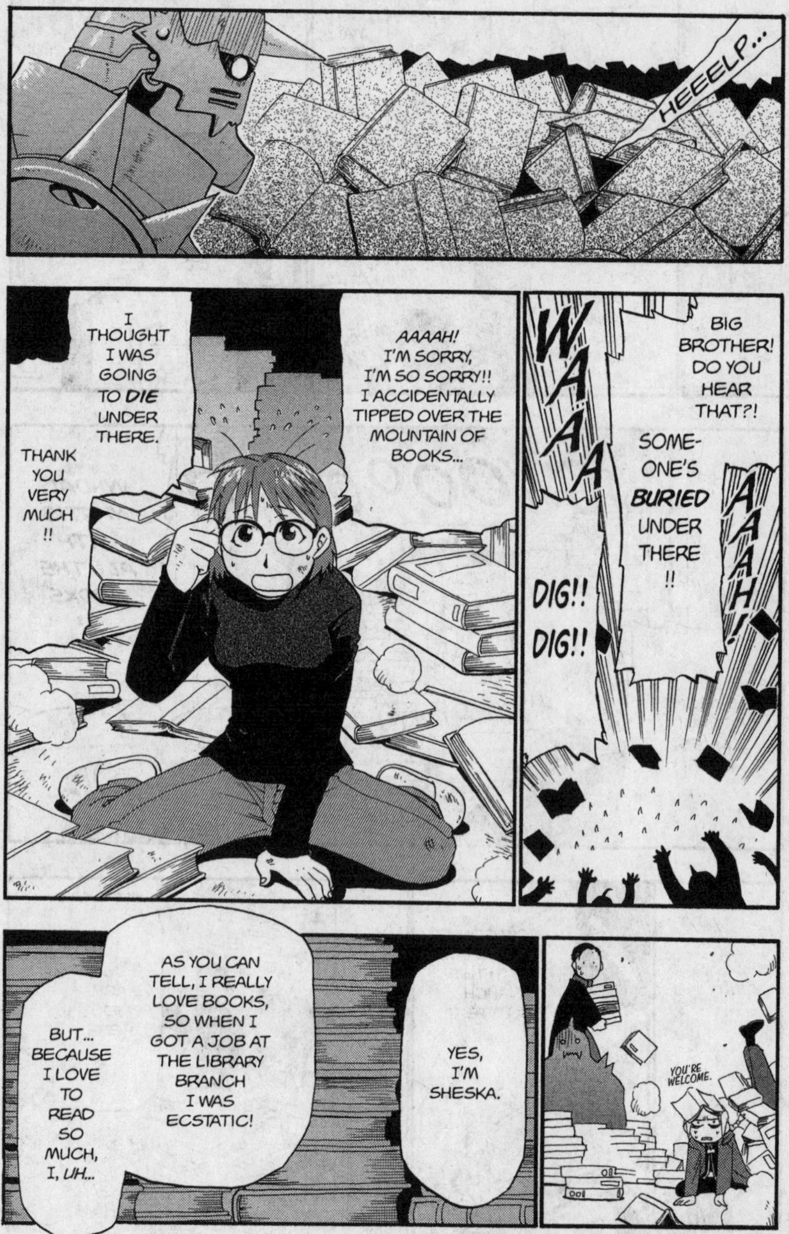
HEEELP...
BIG BROTHER! DO YOU HEAR THAT?!
SOME-ONE'S **BURIED** UNDER THERE!!
WAAA
AAAH!
DIG!! DIG!!
AAAAH! I'M SORRY, I'M SO SORRY!! I ACCIDENTALLY TIPPED OVER THE MOUNTAIN OF BOOKS...
I THOUGHT I WAS GOING TO **DIE** UNDER THERE.
THANK YOU VERY MUCH!!
YOU'RE WELCOME.
YES, I'M SHESKA.
AS YOU CAN TELL, I REALLY LOVE BOOKS, SO WHEN I GOT A JOB AT THE LIBRARY BRANCH I WAS ECSTATIC!
BUT... BECAUSE I LOVE TO READ SO MUCH, I, *UH*...

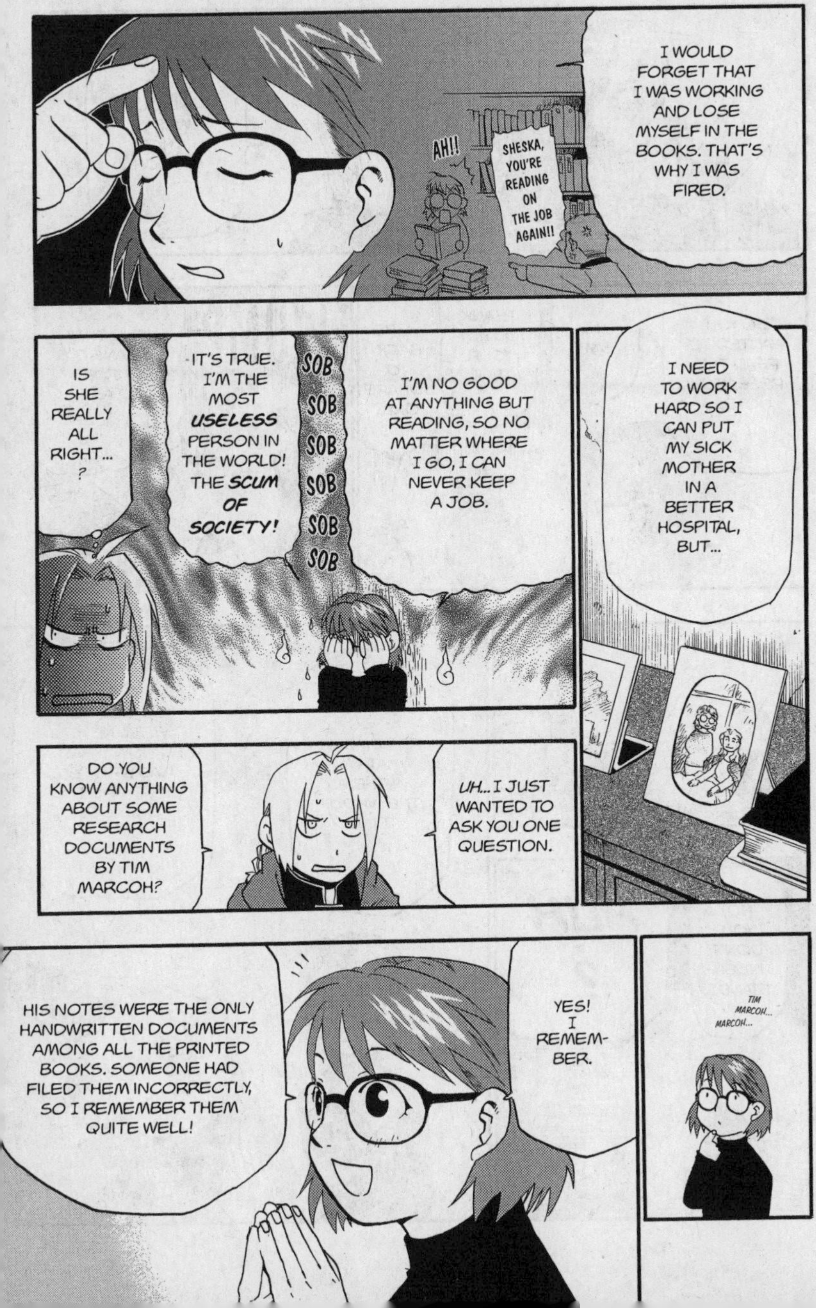
I WOULD FORGET THAT I WAS WORKING AND LOSE MYSELF IN THE BOOKS. THAT'S WHY I WAS FIRED.
SHESKA, YOU'RE READING ON THE JOB AGAIN!!
AH!!
I NEED TO WORK HARD SO I CAN PUT MY SICK MOTHER IN A BETTER HOSPITAL, BUT...
I'M NO GOOD AT ANYTHING BUT READING, SO NO MATTER WHERE I GO, I CAN NEVER KEEP A JOB.
SOB SOB SOB SOB SOB SOB
-IT'S TRUE. I'M THE MOST *USELESS* PERSON IN THE WORLD! THE *SCUM OF SOCIETY!*
IS SHE REALLY ALL RIGHT... ?
UH... I JUST WANTED TO ASK YOU ONE QUESTION.
DO YOU KNOW ANYTHING ABOUT SOME RESEARCH DOCUMENTS BY TIM MARCOH?
TIM MARCOH... MARCOH...
YES! I REMEMBER.
HIS NOTES WERE THE ONLY HANDWRITTEN DOCUMENTS AMONG ALL THE PRINTED BOOKS. SOMEONE HAD FILED THEM INCORRECTLY, SO I REMEMBER THEM QUITE WELL!

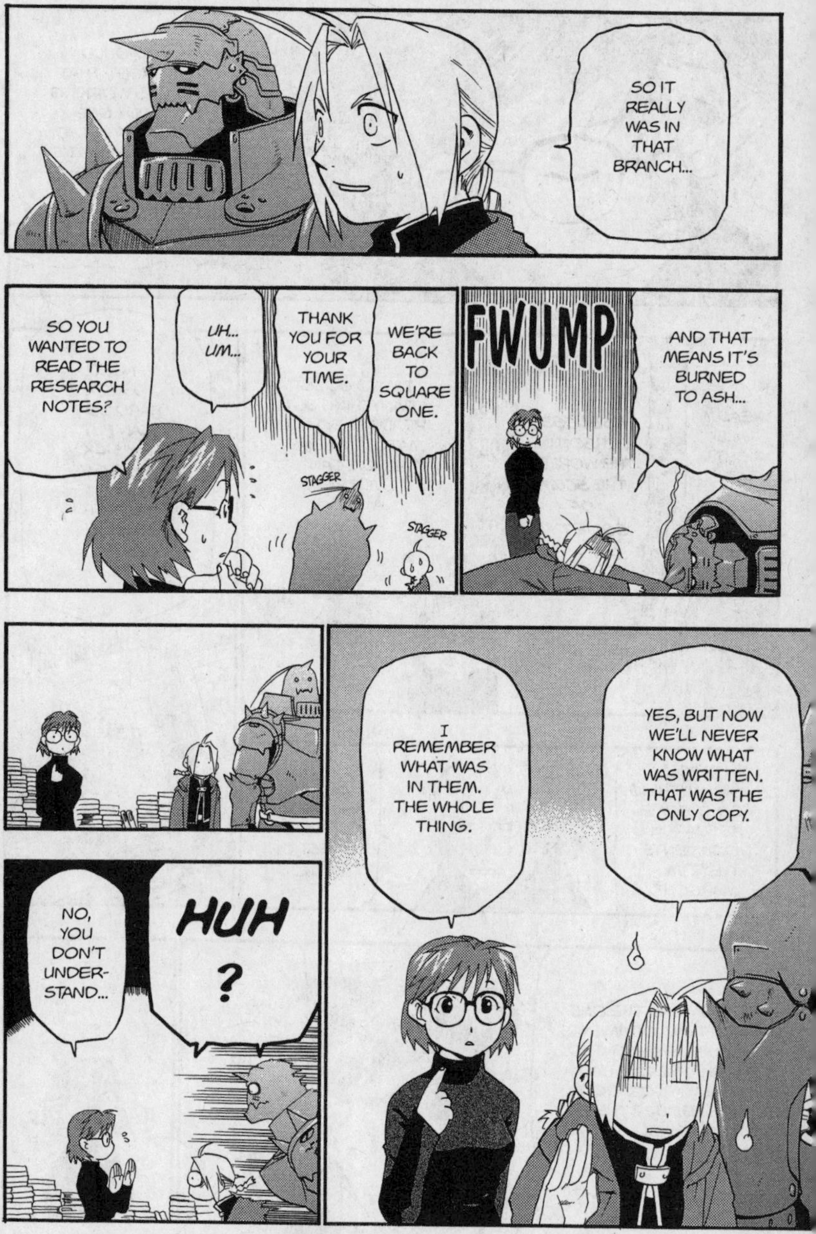
SO IT REALLY WAS IN THAT BRANCH...
FWUMP
AND THAT MEANS IT'S BURNED TO ASH...
WE'RE BACK TO SQUARE ONE.
THANK YOU FOR YOUR TIME.
UH... UM...
SO YOU WANTED TO READ THE RESEARCH NOTES?
STAGGER
STAGGER
YES, BUT NOW WE'LL NEVER KNOW WHAT WAS WRITTEN. THAT WAS THE ONLY COPY.
I REMEMBER WHAT WAS IN THEM. THE WHOLE THING.
HUH ?
NO, YOU DON'T UNDER-STAND...

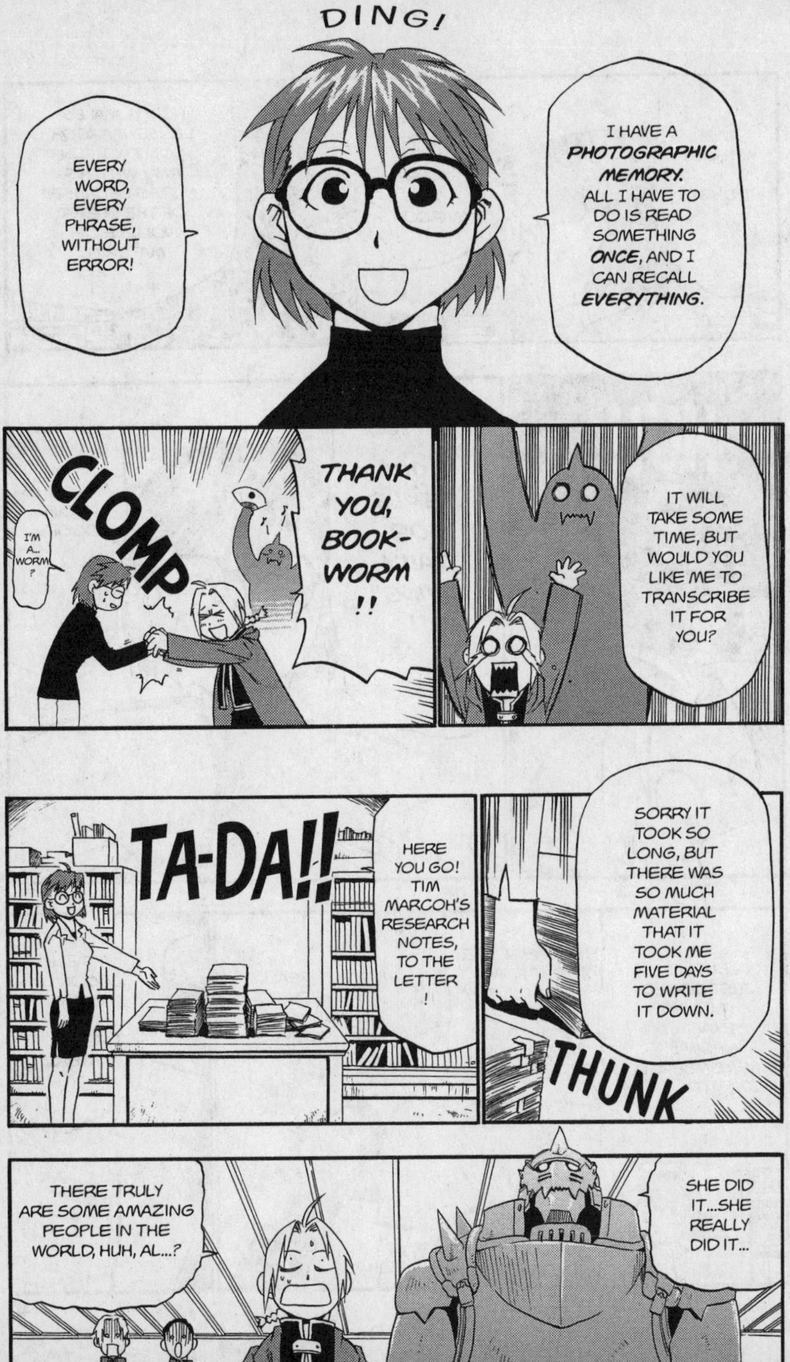
DING!
I HAVE A PHOTOGRAPHIC MEMORY. ALL I HAVE TO DO IS READ SOMETHING ONCE, AND I CAN RECALL EVERYTHING.
EVERY WORD, EVERY PHRASE, WITHOUT ERROR!
IT WILL TAKE SOME TIME, BUT WOULD YOU LIKE ME TO TRANSCRIBE IT FOR YOU?
THANK YOU, BOOK-WORM!!
CLOMP
I'M A... WORM?
SORRY IT TOOK SO LONG, BUT THERE WAS SO MUCH MATERIAL THAT IT TOOK ME FIVE DAYS TO WRITE IT DOWN.
THUNK
TA-DA!!
HERE YOU GO! TIM MARCOH'S RESEARCH NOTES, TO THE LETTER!
SHE DID IT...SHE REALLY DID IT...
THERE TRULY ARE SOME AMAZING PEOPLE IN THE WORLD, HUH, AL...?

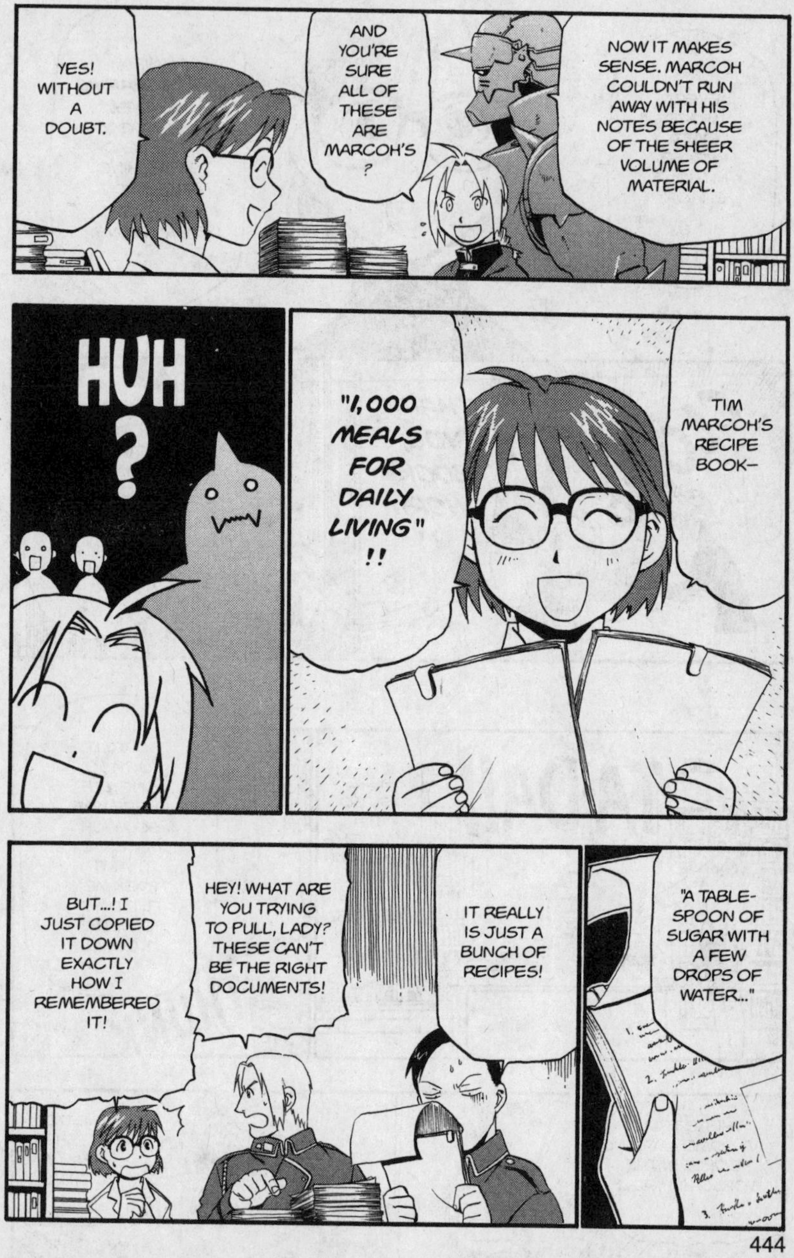
NOW IT MAKES SENSE. MARCOH COULDN'T RUN AWAY WITH HIS NOTES BECAUSE OF THE SHEER VOLUME OF MATERIAL.
AND YOU'RE SURE ALL OF THESE ARE MARCOH'S ?
YES! WITHOUT A DOUBT.
TIM MARCOH'S RECIPE BOOK—
"1,000 MEALS FOR DAILY LIVING" !!
HUH ?
"A TABLE-SPOON OF SUGAR WITH A FEW DROPS OF WATER..."
IT REALLY IS JUST A BUNCH OF RECIPES!
HEY! WHAT ARE YOU TRYING TO PULL, LADY? THESE CAN'T BE THE RIGHT DOCUMENTS!
BUT...! I JUST COPIED IT DOWN EXACTLY HOW I REMEMBERED IT!

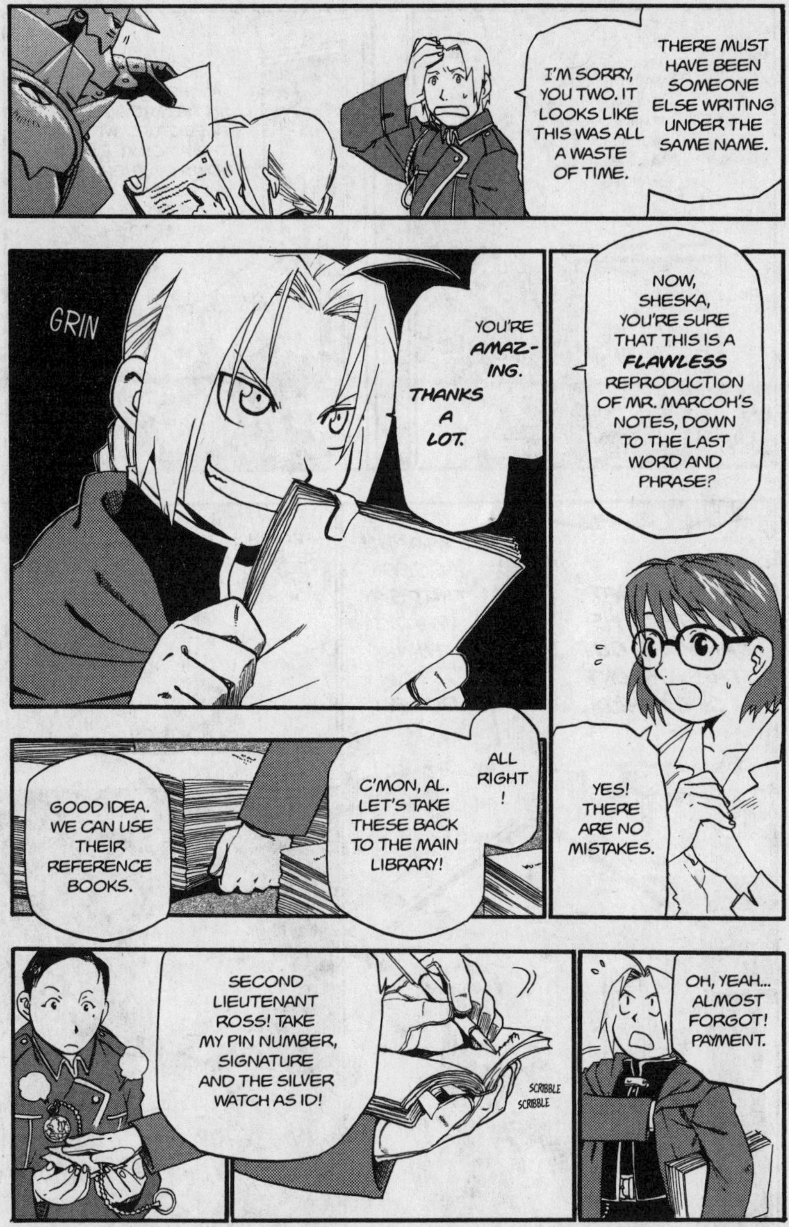
THERE MUST HAVE BEEN SOMEONE ELSE WRITING UNDER THE SAME NAME.
I'M SORRY, YOU TWO. IT LOOKS LIKE THIS WAS ALL A WASTE OF TIME.
NOW, SHESKA, YOU'RE SURE THAT THIS IS A **FLAWLESS** REPRODUCTION OF MR. MARCOH'S NOTES, DOWN TO THE LAST WORD AND PHRASE?
YES! THERE ARE NO MISTAKES.
YOU'RE **AMAZ-ING.**
THANKS A LOT.
GRIN
ALL RIGHT!
C'MON, AL. LET'S TAKE THESE BACK TO THE MAIN LIBRARY!
GOOD IDEA. WE CAN USE THEIR REFERENCE BOOKS.
OH, YEAH... ALMOST FORGOT! PAYMENT.
SECOND LIEUTENANT ROSS! TAKE MY PIN NUMBER, SIGNATURE AND THE SILVER WATCH AS ID!
SCRIBBLE SCRIBBLE

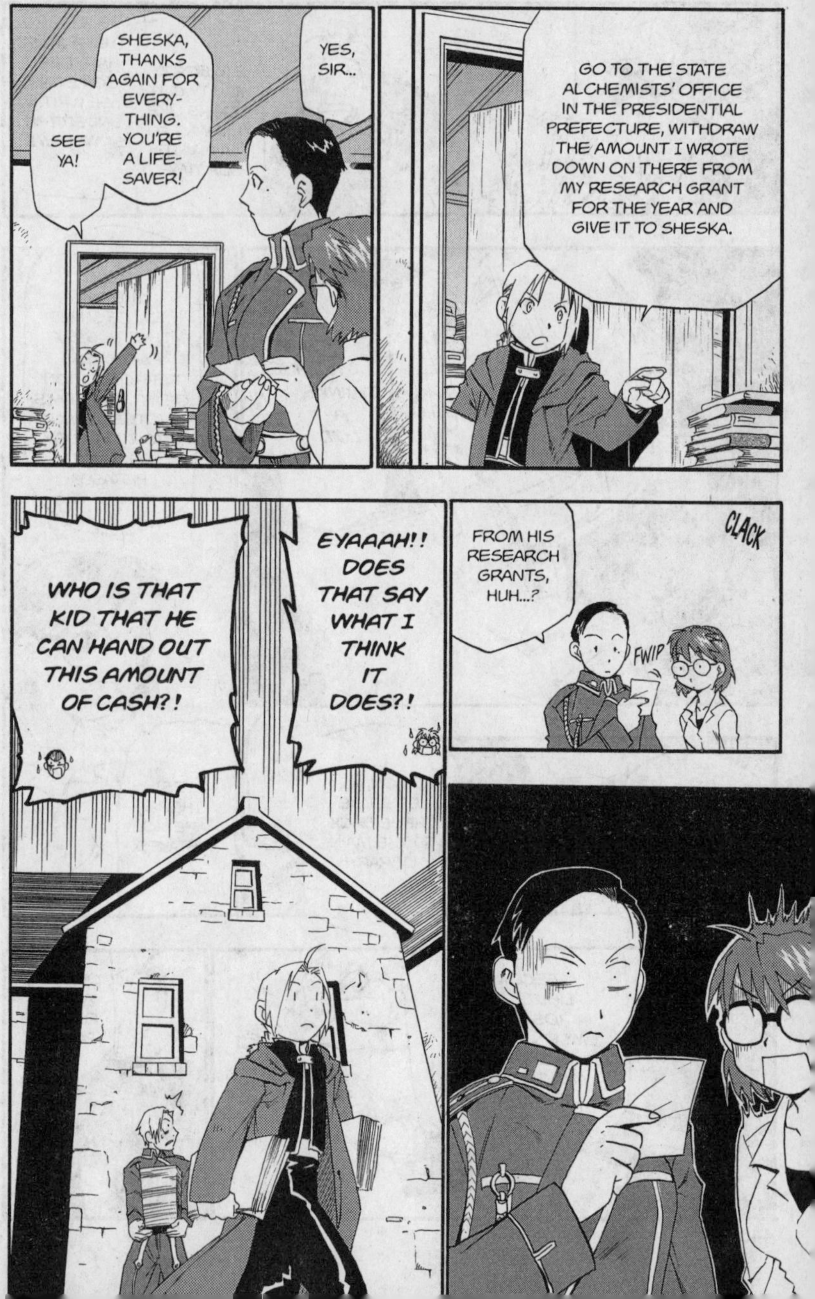
GO TO THE STATE ALCHEMISTS' OFFICE IN THE PRESIDENTIAL PREFECTURE, WITHDRAW THE AMOUNT I WROTE DOWN ON THERE FROM MY RESEARCH GRANT FOR THE YEAR AND GIVE IT TO SHESKA.
YES, SIR...
SHESKA, THANKS AGAIN FOR EVERY-THING. YOU'RE A LIFE-SAVER!
SEE YA!
CLACK
FROM HIS RESEARCH GRANTS, HUH...?
FWIP
EYAAAH!! DOES THAT SAY WHAT I THINK IT DOES?!
WHO IS THAT KID THAT HE CAN HAND OUT THIS AMOUNT OF CASH?!

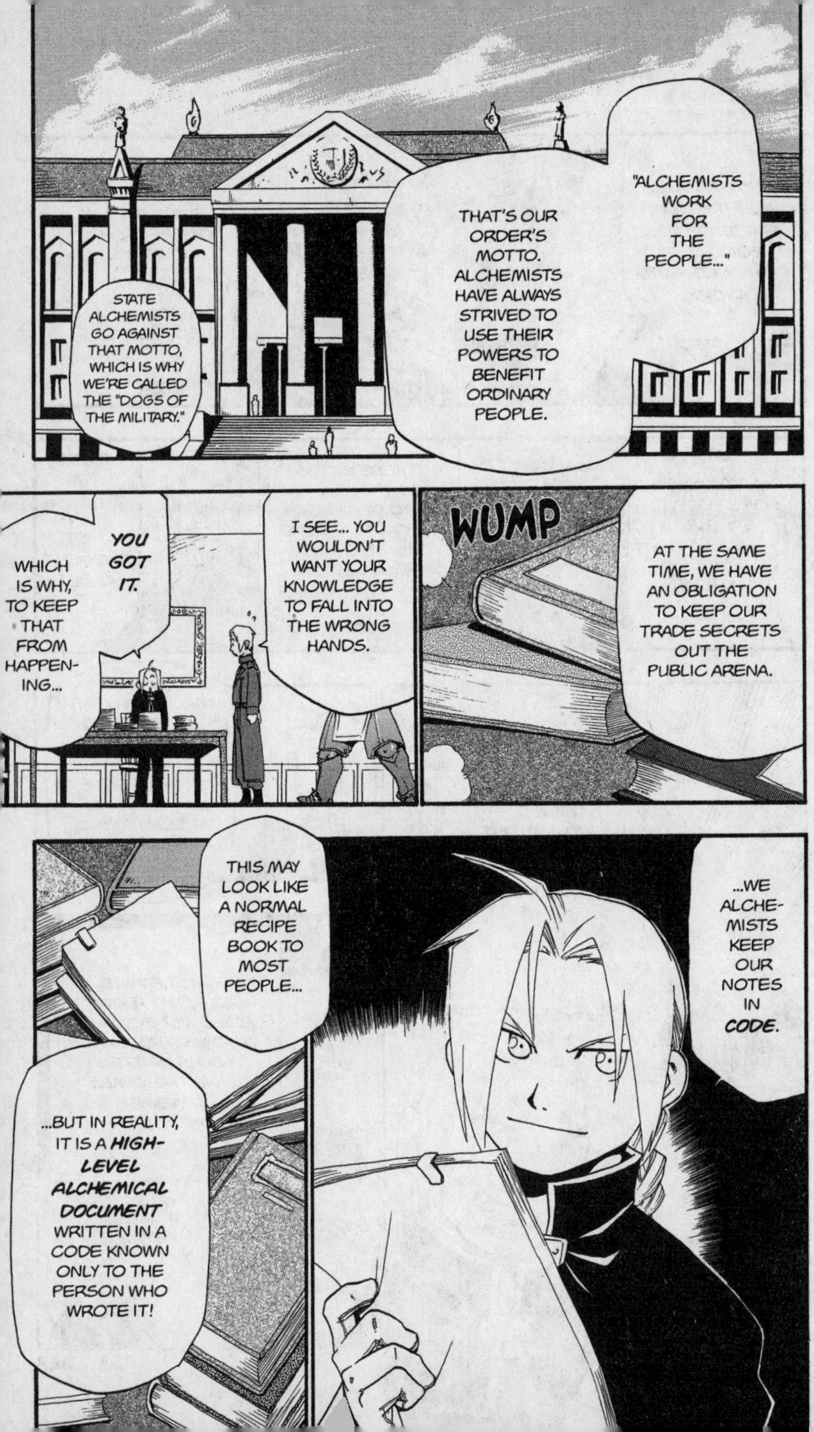
"ALCHEMISTS WORK FOR THE PEOPLE..."
THAT'S OUR ORDER'S MOTTO. ALCHEMISTS HAVE ALWAYS STRIVED TO USE THEIR POWERS TO BENEFIT ORDINARY PEOPLE.
STATE ALCHEMISTS GO AGAINST THAT MOTTO, WHICH IS WHY WE'RE CALLED THE "DOGS OF THE MILITARY."
WUMP
AT THE SAME TIME, WE HAVE AN OBLIGATION TO KEEP OUR TRADE SECRETS OUT THE PUBLIC ARENA.
I SEE... YOU WOULDN'T WANT YOUR KNOWLEDGE TO FALL INTO THE WRONG HANDS.
YOU GOT IT.
WHICH IS WHY, TO KEEP THAT FROM HAPPENING...
...WE ALCHEMISTS KEEP OUR NOTES IN CODE.
THIS MAY LOOK LIKE A NORMAL RECIPE BOOK TO MOST PEOPLE...
...BUT IN REALITY, IT IS A HIGH-LEVEL ALCHEMICAL DOCUMENT WRITTEN IN A CODE KNOWN ONLY TO THE PERSON WHO WROTE IT!

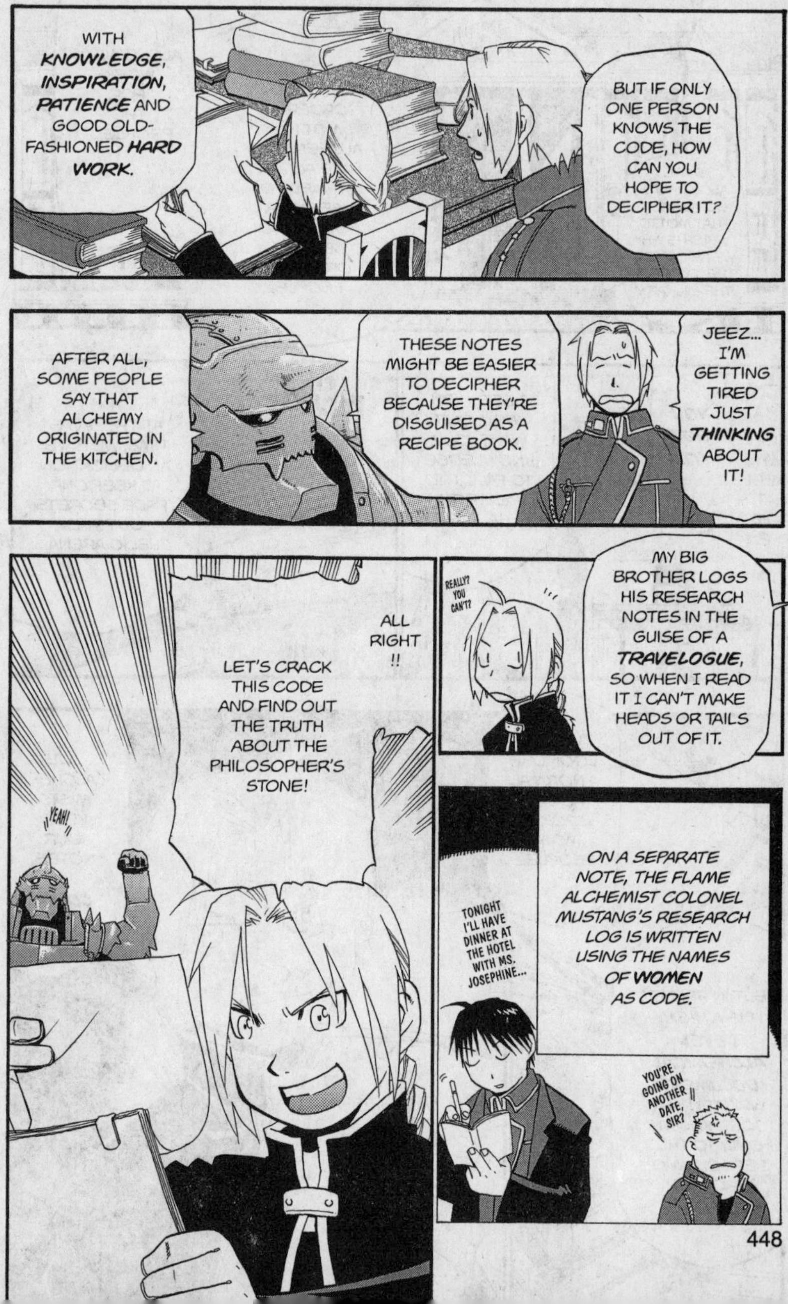
BUT IF ONLY ONE PERSON KNOWS THE CODE, HOW CAN YOU HOPE TO DECIPHER IT?
WITH KNOWLEDGE, INSPIRATION, PATIENCE AND GOOD OLD-FASHIONED HARD WORK.
JEEZ... I'M GETTING TIRED JUST THINKING ABOUT IT!
THESE NOTES MIGHT BE EASIER TO DECIPHER BECAUSE THEY'RE DISGUISED AS A RECIPE BOOK.
AFTER ALL, SOME PEOPLE SAY THAT ALCHEMY ORIGINATED IN THE KITCHEN.
MY BIG BROTHER LOGS HIS RESEARCH NOTES IN THE GUISE OF A TRAVELOGUE, SO WHEN I READ IT I CAN'T MAKE HEADS OR TAILS OUT OF IT.
REALLY? YOU CAN'T?
ON A SEPARATE NOTE, THE FLAME ALCHEMIST COLONEL MUSTANG'S RESEARCH LOG IS WRITTEN USING THE NAMES OF WOMEN AS CODE.
TONIGHT I'LL HAVE DINNER AT THE HOTEL WITH MS. JOSEPHINE...
YOU'RE GOING ON ANOTHER DATE, SIR?
ALL RIGHT !!
LET'S CRACK THIS CODE AND FIND OUT THE TRUTH ABOUT THE PHILOSOPHER'S STONE!
YEAH!

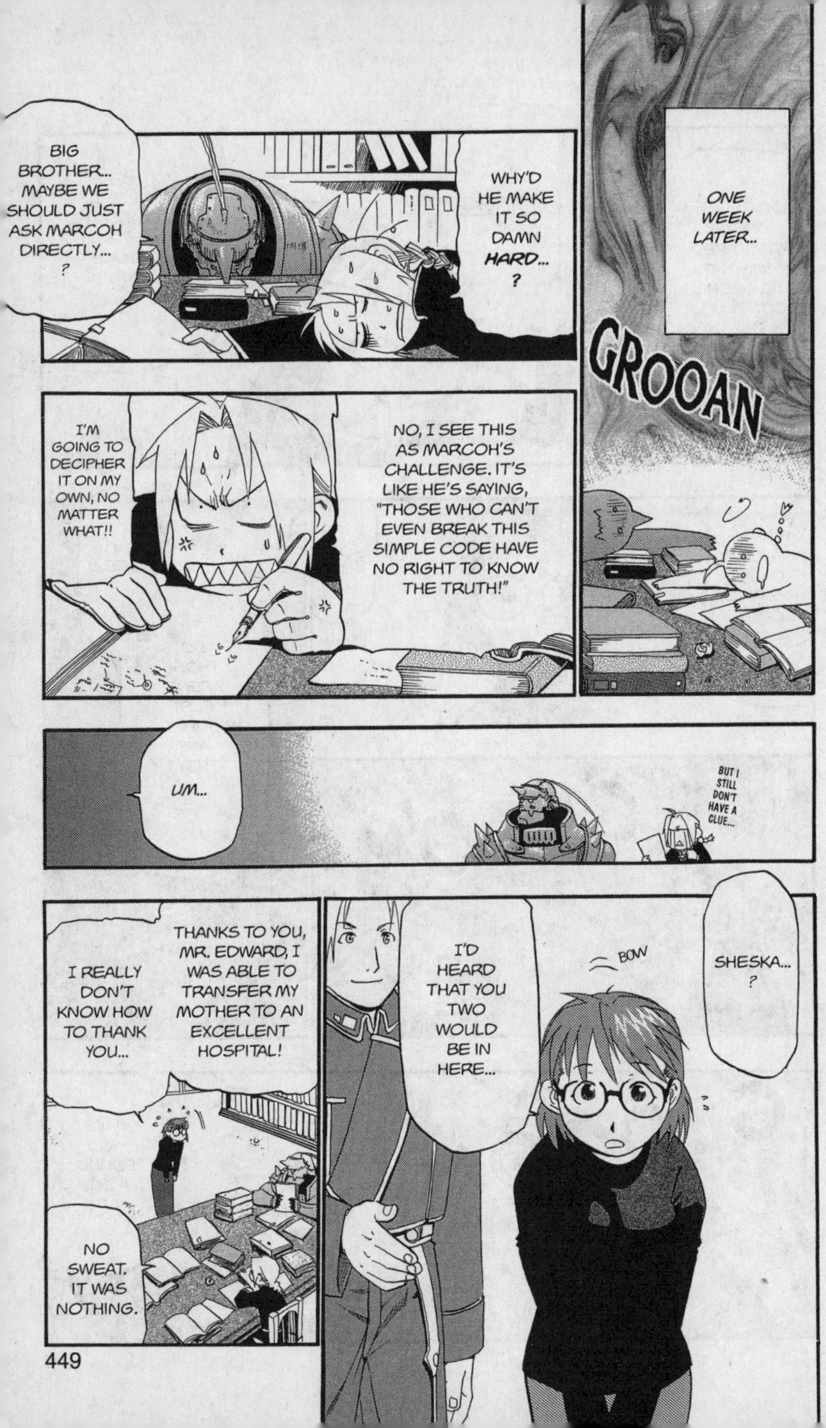
ONE WEEK LATER...
GROOAN
WHY'D HE MAKE IT SO DAMN HARD...?
BIG BROTHER... MAYBE WE SHOULD JUST ASK MARCOH DIRECTLY...?
NO, I SEE THIS AS MARCOH'S CHALLENGE. IT'S LIKE HE'S SAYING, "THOSE WHO CAN'T EVEN BREAK THIS SIMPLE CODE HAVE NO RIGHT TO KNOW THE TRUTH!"
I'M GOING TO DECIPHER IT ON MY OWN, NO MATTER WHAT!!
BUT I STILL DON'T HAVE A CLUE...
UM...
SHESKA...?
BOW
I'D HEARD THAT YOU TWO WOULD BE IN HERE...
THANKS TO YOU, MR. EDWARD, I WAS ABLE TO TRANSFER MY MOTHER TO AN EXCELLENT HOSPITAL!
I REALLY DON'T KNOW HOW TO THANK YOU...
NO SWEAT. IT WAS NOTHING.

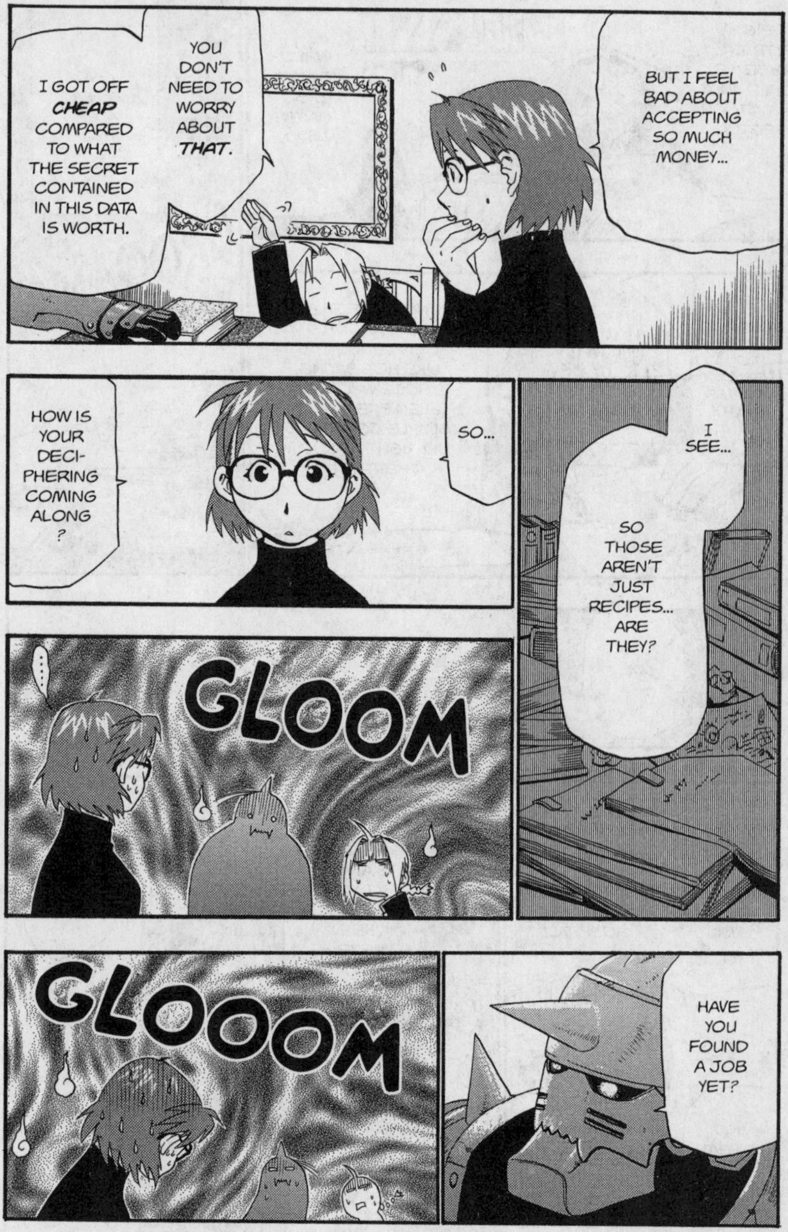
BUT I FEEL BAD ABOUT ACCEPTING SO MUCH MONEY...
YOU DON'T NEED TO WORRY ABOUT ***THAT***.
I GOT OFF ***CHEAP*** COMPARED TO WHAT THE SECRET CONTAINED IN THIS DATA IS WORTH.
I SEE...
SO THOSE AREN'T JUST RECIPES... ARE THEY?
SO...
HOW IS YOUR DECIPHERING COMING ALONG?
...
GLOOM
HAVE YOU FOUND A JOB YET?
GLOOOM

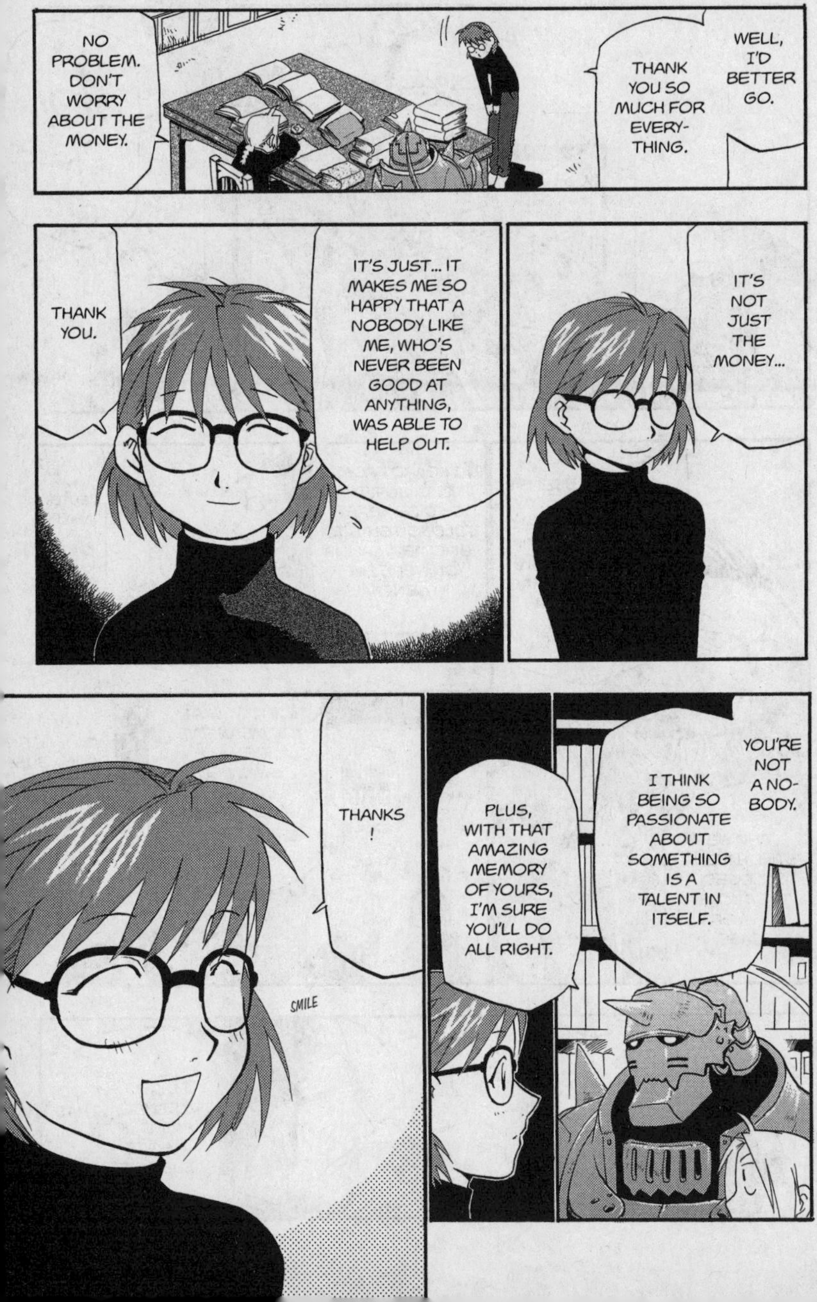
WELL, I'D BETTER GO.
THANK YOU SO MUCH FOR EVERY-THING.
NO PROBLEM. DON'T WORRY ABOUT THE MONEY.
IT'S NOT JUST THE MONEY...
IT'S JUST... IT MAKES ME SO HAPPY THAT A NOBODY LIKE ME, WHO'S NEVER BEEN GOOD AT ANYTHING, WAS ABLE TO HELP OUT.
THANK YOU.
YOU'RE NOT A NO-BODY.
I THINK BEING SO PASSIONATE ABOUT SOMETHING IS A TALENT IN ITSELF.
PLUS, WITH THAT AMAZING MEMORY OF YOURS, I'M SURE YOU'LL DO ALL RIGHT.
THANKS!
SMILE

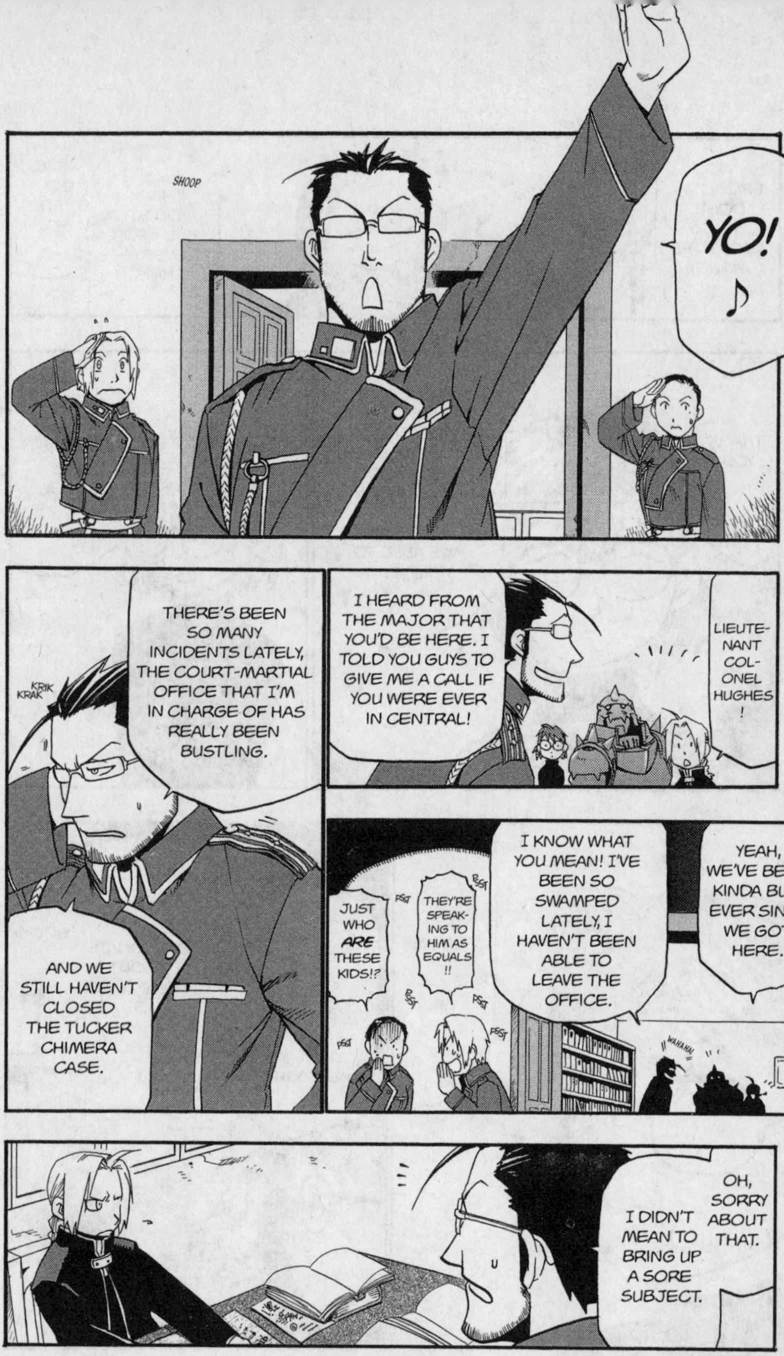
YO! ♪
SHOOP
LIEUTENANT COLONEL HUGHES!
I HEARD FROM THE MAJOR THAT YOU'D BE HERE. I TOLD YOU GUYS TO GIVE ME A CALL IF YOU WERE EVER IN CENTRAL!
YEAH, WE'VE BEEN KINDA BUSY EVER SINCE WE GOT HERE.
I KNOW WHAT YOU MEAN! I'VE BEEN SO SWAMPED LATELY, I HAVEN'T BEEN ABLE TO LEAVE THE OFFICE.
WAHAHA
PSST
THEY'RE SPEAKING TO HIM AS EQUALS!!
JUST WHO ARE THESE KIDS!?
PSST
THERE'S BEEN SO MANY INCIDENTS LATELY, THE COURT-MARTIAL OFFICE THAT I'M IN CHARGE OF HAS REALLY BEEN BUSTLING.
KRIK KRAK
AND WE STILL HAVEN'T CLOSED THE TUCKER CHIMERA CASE.
OH, SORRY ABOUT THAT.
I DIDN'T MEAN TO BRING UP A SORE SUBJECT.

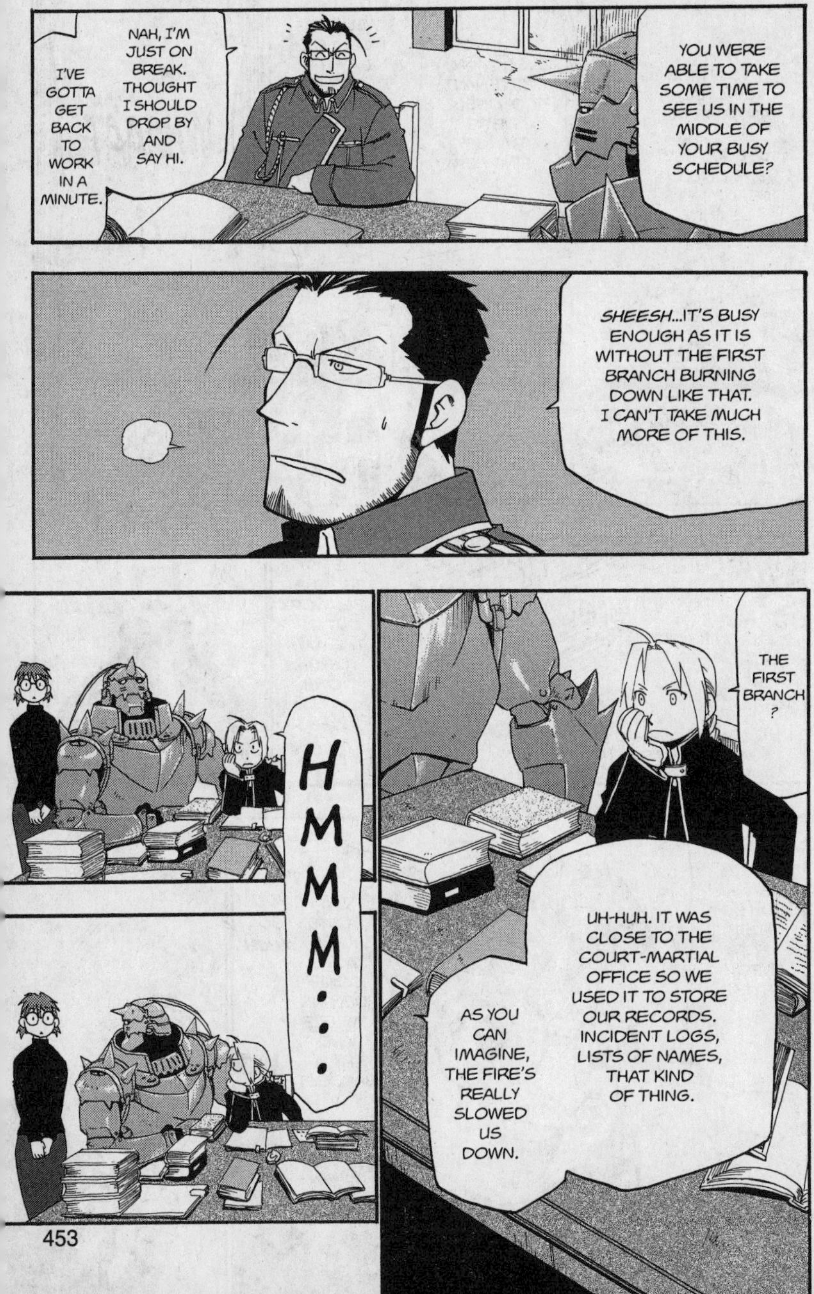
YOU WERE ABLE TO TAKE SOME TIME TO SEE US IN THE MIDDLE OF YOUR BUSY SCHEDULE?
NAH, I'M JUST ON BREAK. THOUGHT I SHOULD DROP BY AND SAY HI.
I'VE GOTTA GET BACK TO WORK IN A MINUTE.
SHEESH...IT'S BUSY ENOUGH AS IT IS WITHOUT THE FIRST BRANCH BURNING DOWN LIKE THAT. I CAN'T TAKE MUCH MORE OF THIS.
THE FIRST BRANCH?
UH-HUH. IT WAS CLOSE TO THE COURT-MARTIAL OFFICE SO WE USED IT TO STORE OUR RECORDS. INCIDENT LOGS, LISTS OF NAMES, THAT KIND OF THING.
AS YOU CAN IMAGINE, THE FIRE'S REALLY SLOWED US DOWN.
HMMM...

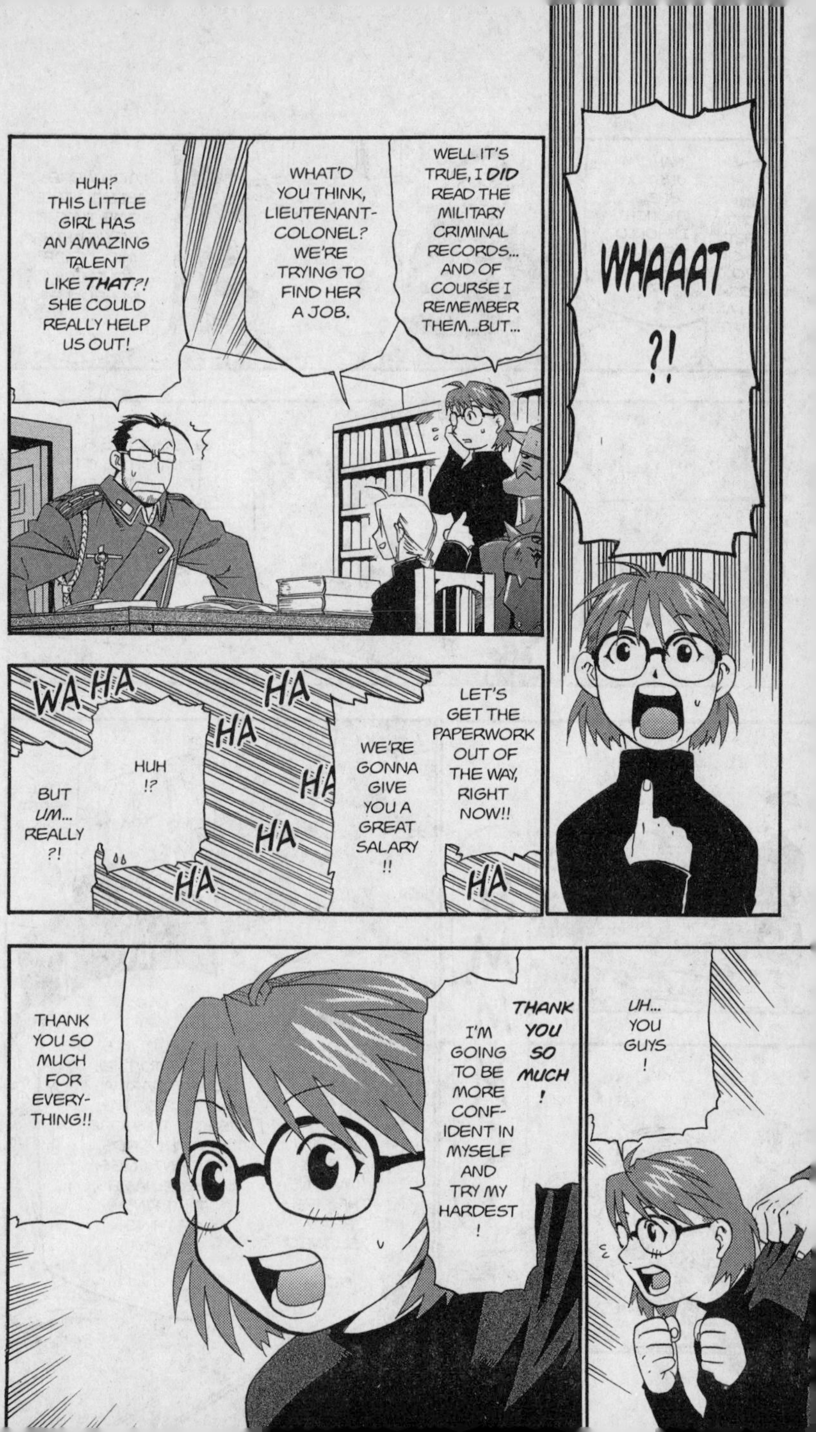
WHAAAT ?!
WELL IT'S TRUE, I DID READ THE MILITARY CRIMINAL RECORDS... AND OF COURSE I REMEMBER THEM...BUT...
WHAT'D YOU THINK, LIEUTENANT-COLONEL? WE'RE TRYING TO FIND HER A JOB.
HUH? THIS LITTLE GIRL HAS AN AMAZING TALENT LIKE THAT?! SHE COULD REALLY HELP US OUT!
LET'S GET THE PAPERWORK OUT OF THE WAY, RIGHT NOW!!
WE'RE GONNA GIVE YOU A GREAT SALARY !!
HA HA HA HA HA HA HA
HUH !?
BUT UM... REALLY ?!
WA HA
UH... YOU GUYS !
THANK YOU SO MUCH !
I'M GOING TO BE MORE CONFIDENT IN MYSELF AND TRY MY HARDEST !
THANK YOU SO MUCH FOR EVERYTHING!!

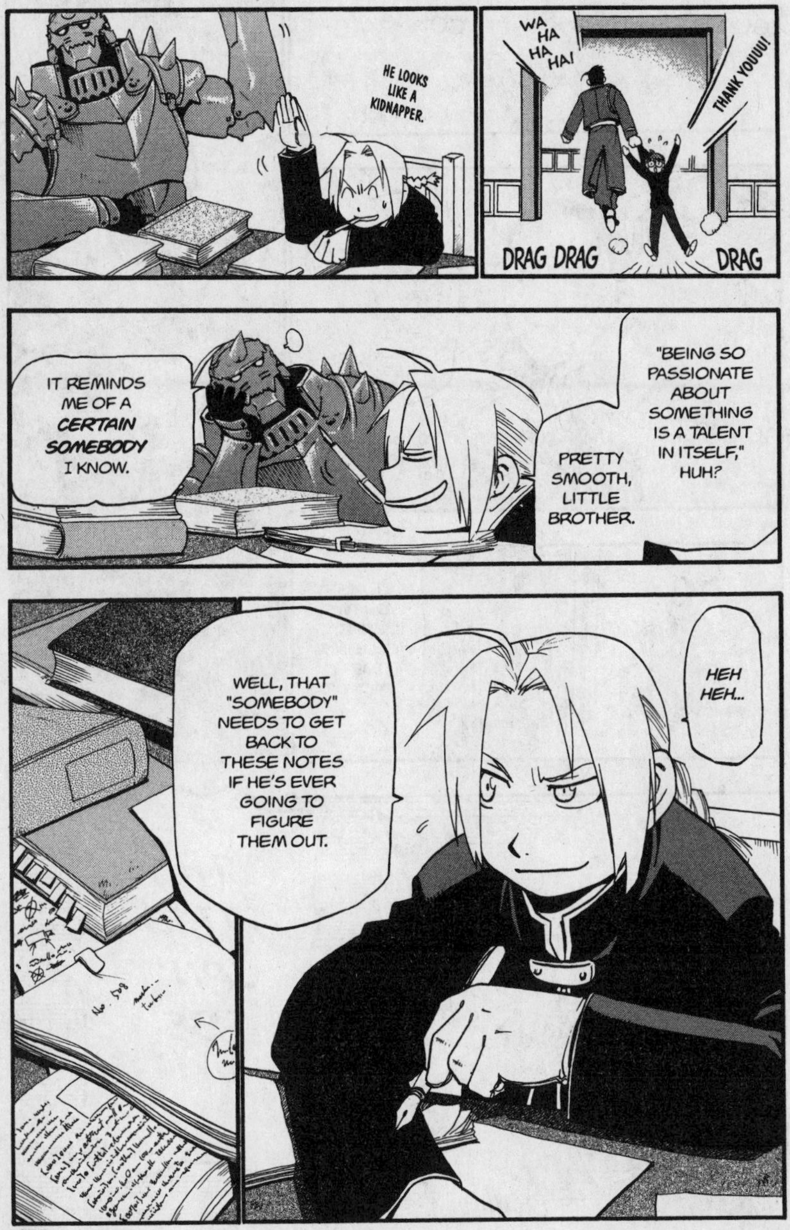
WA HA HA HA!
THANK YOUUU!
DRAG DRAG
DRAG
HE LOOKS LIKE A KIDNAPPER.
"BEING SO PASSIONATE ABOUT SOMETHING IS A TALENT IN ITSELF," HUH?
PRETTY SMOOTH, LITTLE BROTHER.
IT REMINDS ME OF A *CERTAIN SOMEBODY* I KNOW.
HEH HEH...
WELL, THAT "SOMEBODY" NEEDS TO GET BACK TO THESE NOTES IF HE'S EVER GOING TO FIGURE THEM OUT.

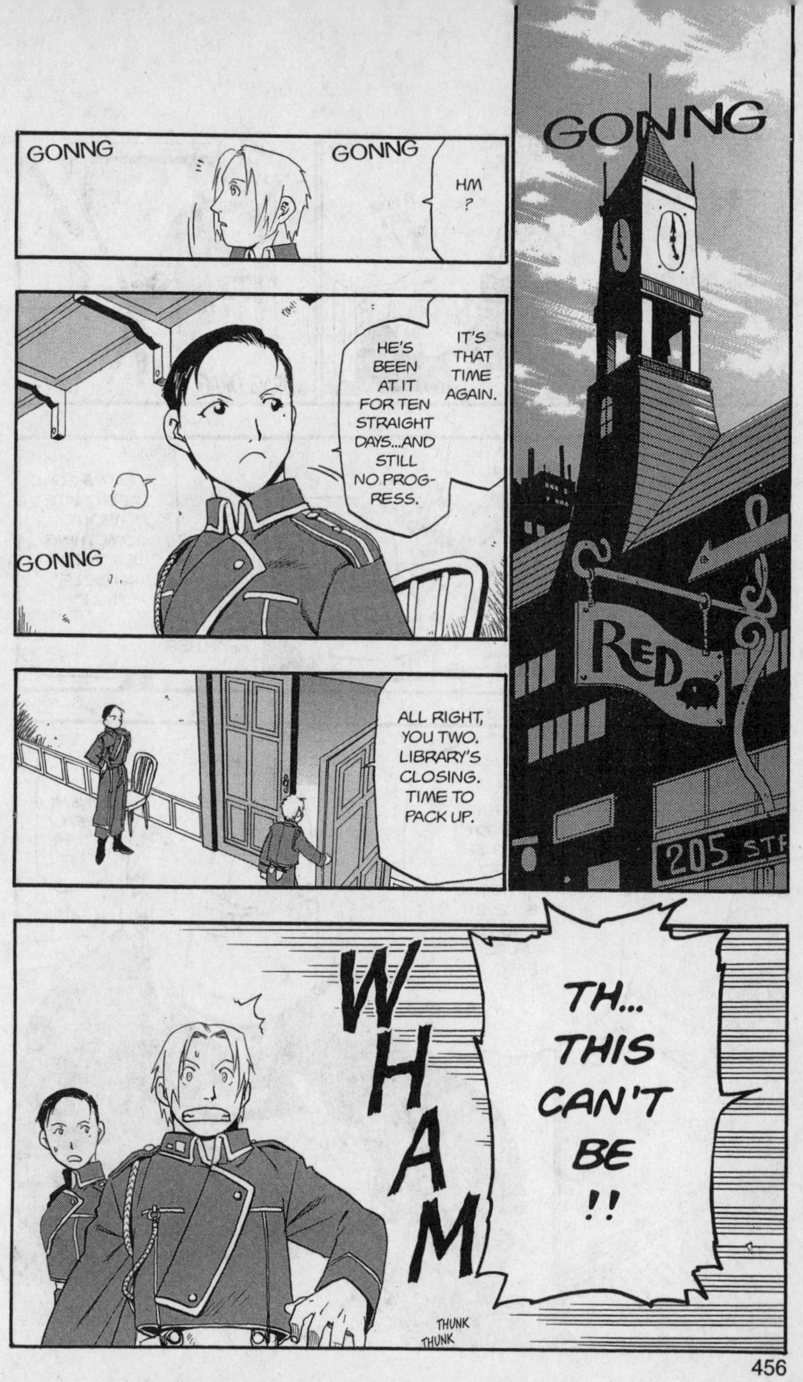
GONNG
RED
205 STR
HM ?
GONNG
GONNG
IT'S THAT TIME AGAIN.
HE'S BEEN AT IT FOR TEN STRAIGHT DAYS...AND STILL NO PROGRESS.
GONNG
ALL RIGHT, YOU TWO. LIBRARY'S CLOSING. TIME TO PACK UP.
TH... THIS CAN'T BE !!
WHAM
THUNK THUNK

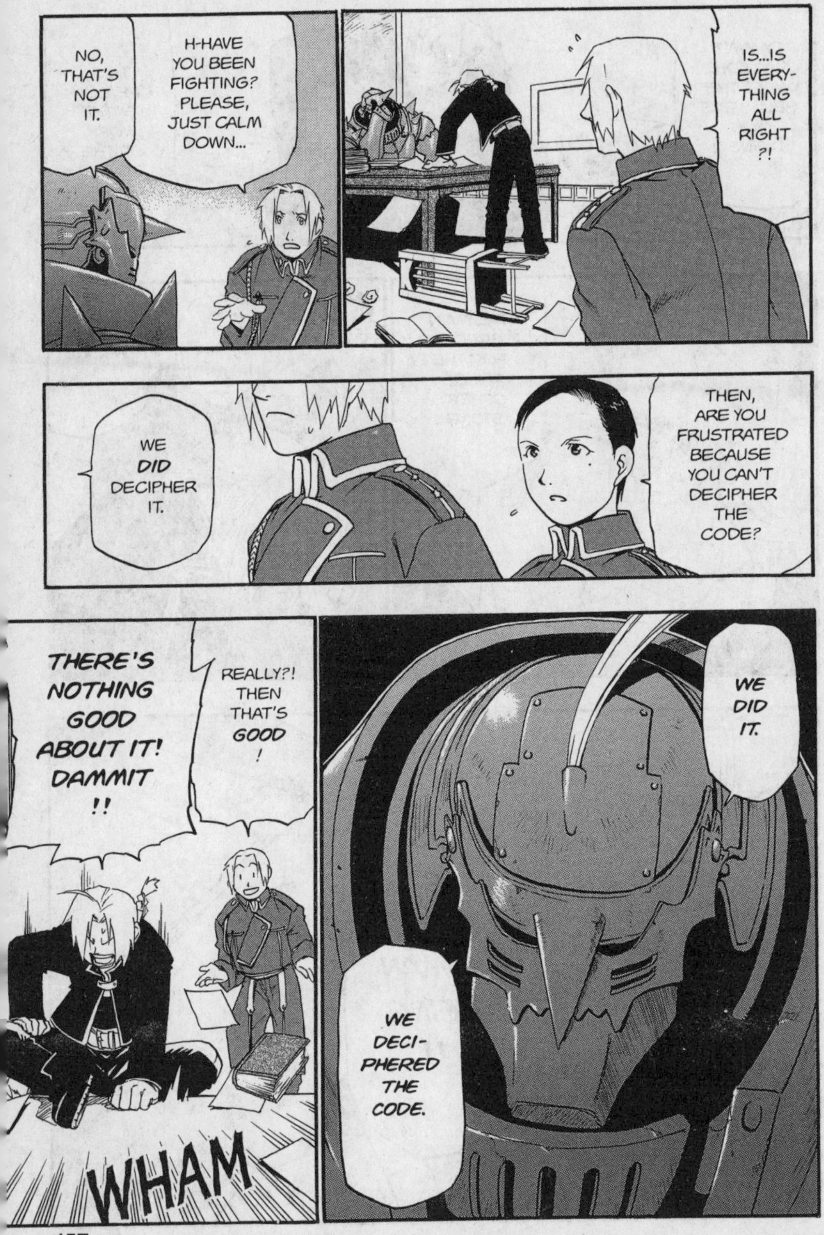
IS...IS EVERYTHING ALL RIGHT?!
H-HAVE YOU BEEN FIGHTING? PLEASE, JUST CALM DOWN...
NO, THAT'S NOT IT.
THEN, ARE YOU FRUSTRATED BECAUSE YOU CAN'T DECIPHER THE CODE?
WE DID DECIPHER IT.
WE DID IT.
WE DECIPHERED THE CODE.
REALLY?! THEN THAT'S GOOD!
THERE'S NOTHING GOOD ABOUT IT! DAMMIT!!
WHAM

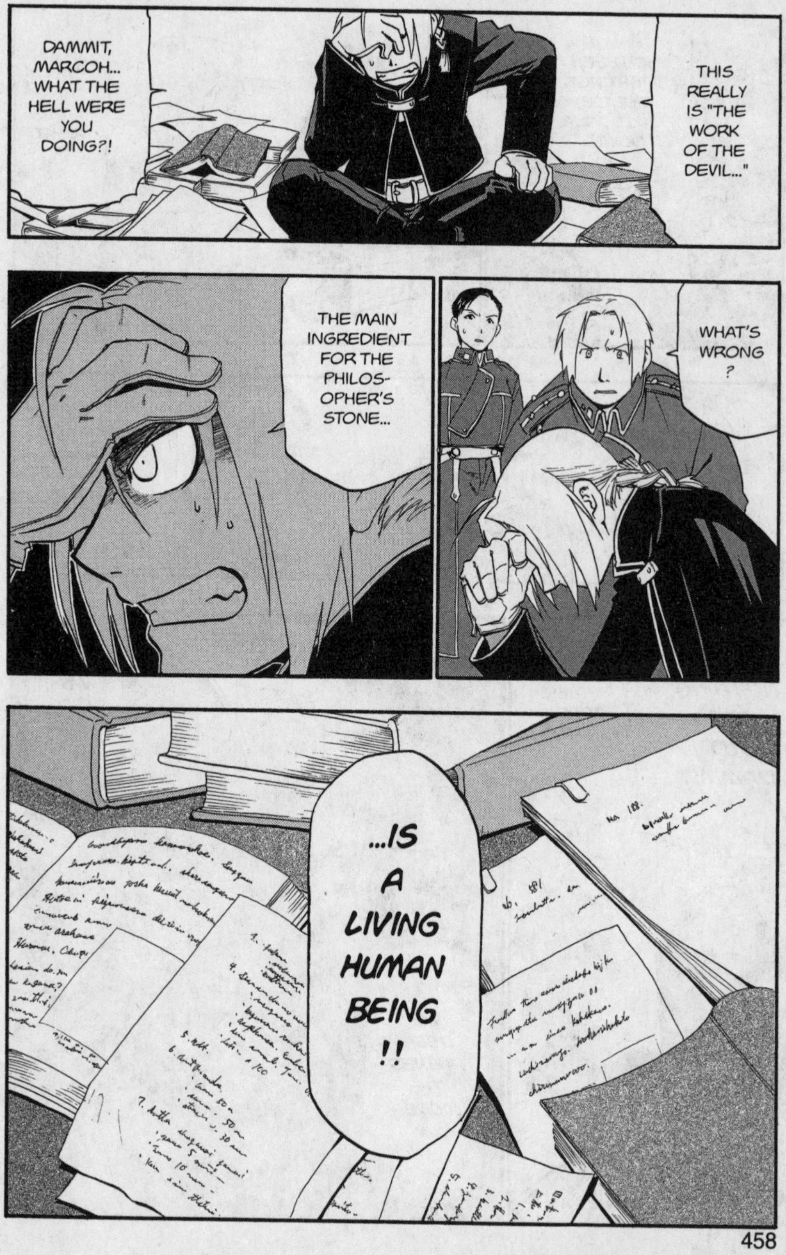

THIS REALLY IS "THE WORK OF THE DEVIL..."
DAMMIT, MARCOH... WHAT THE HELL WERE YOU DOING?!
WHAT'S WRONG?
THE MAIN INGREDIENT FOR THE PHILOS-OPHER'S STONE...
...IS A LIVING HUMAN BEING!!

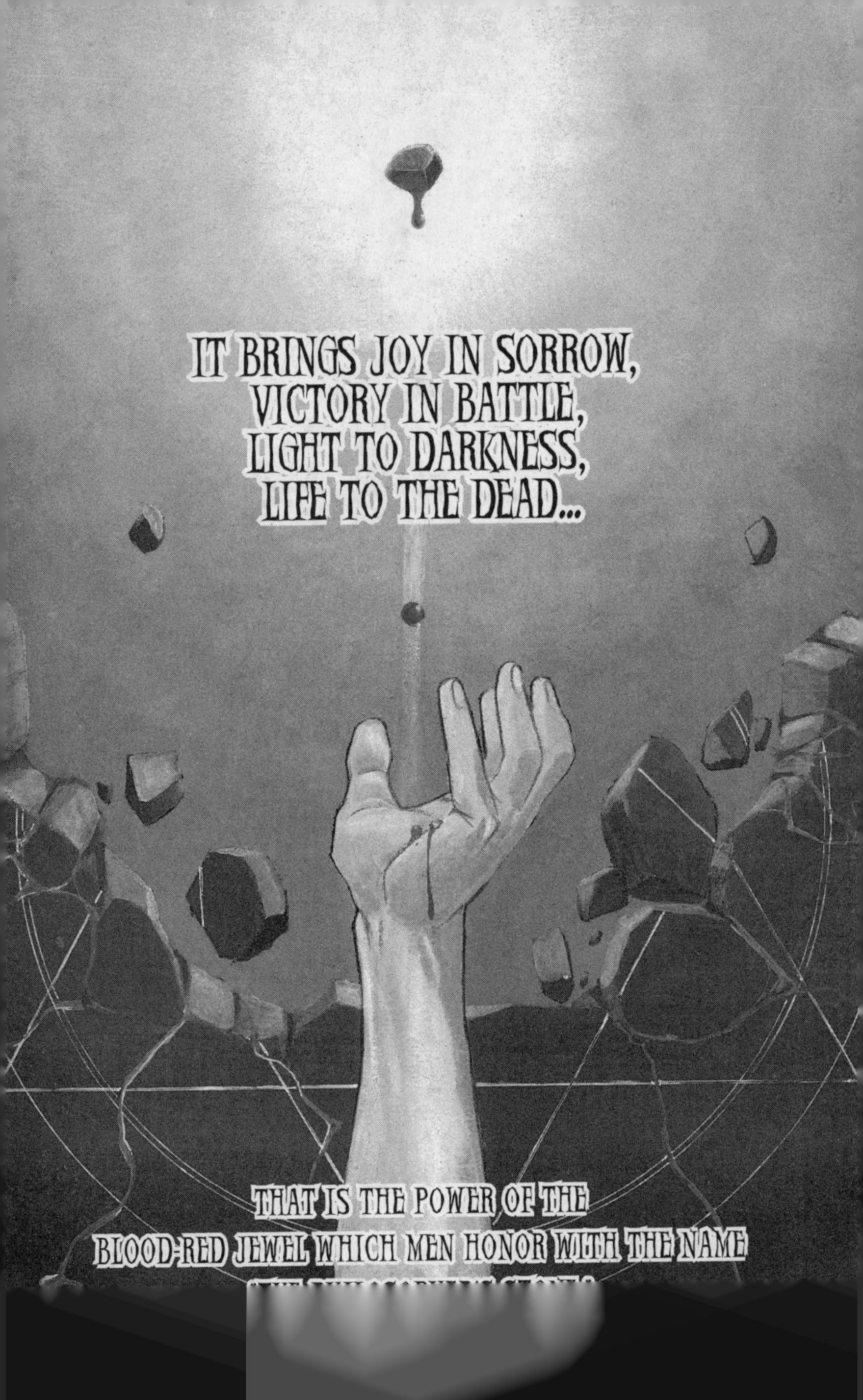
IT BRINGS JOY IN SORROW,
VICTORY IN BATTLE,
LIGHT TO DARKNESS,
LIFE TO THE DEAD...
THAT IS THE POWER OF THE
BLOOD-RED JEWEL WHICH MEN HONOR WITH THE NAME

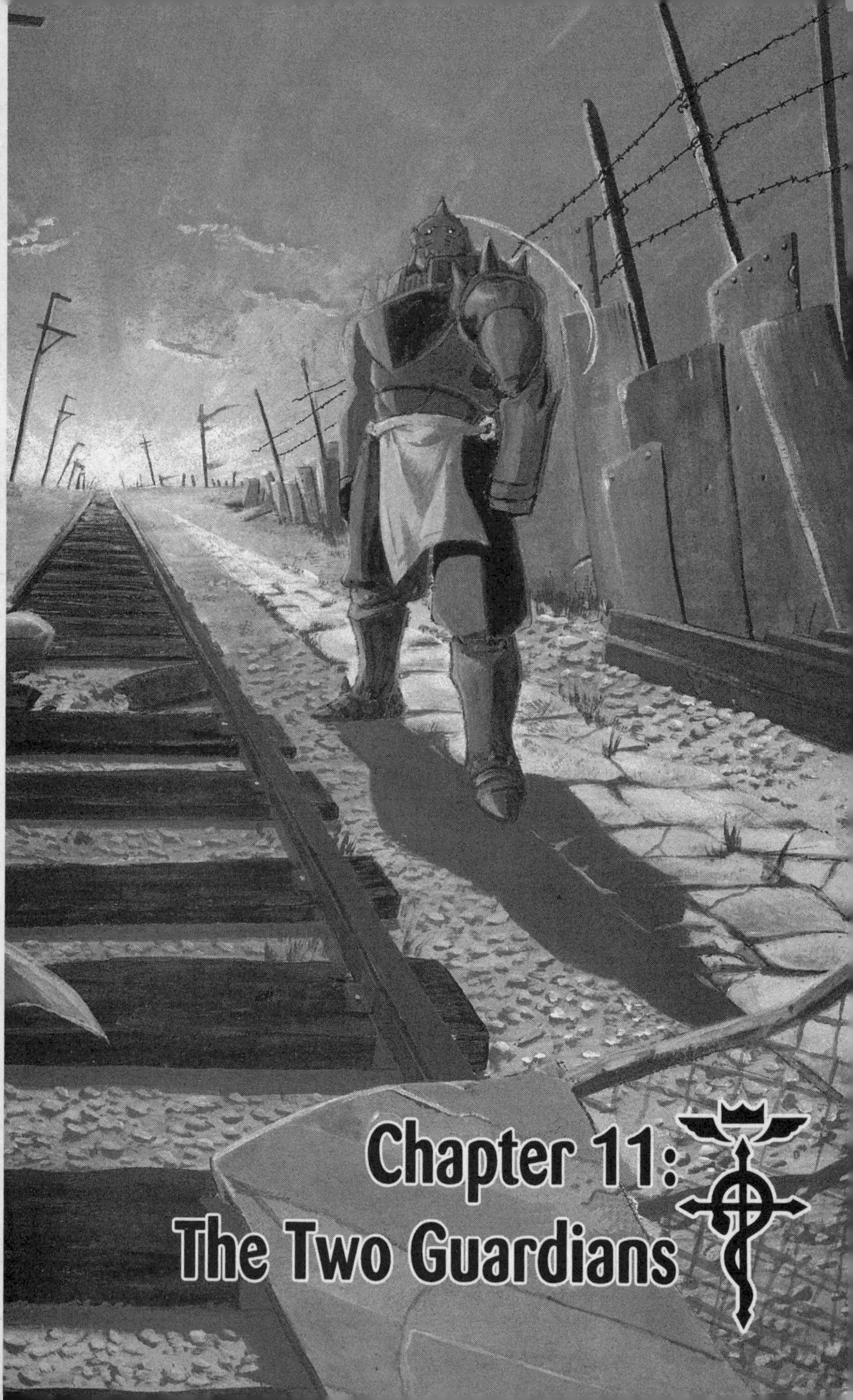
Chapter 11:
The Two Guardians

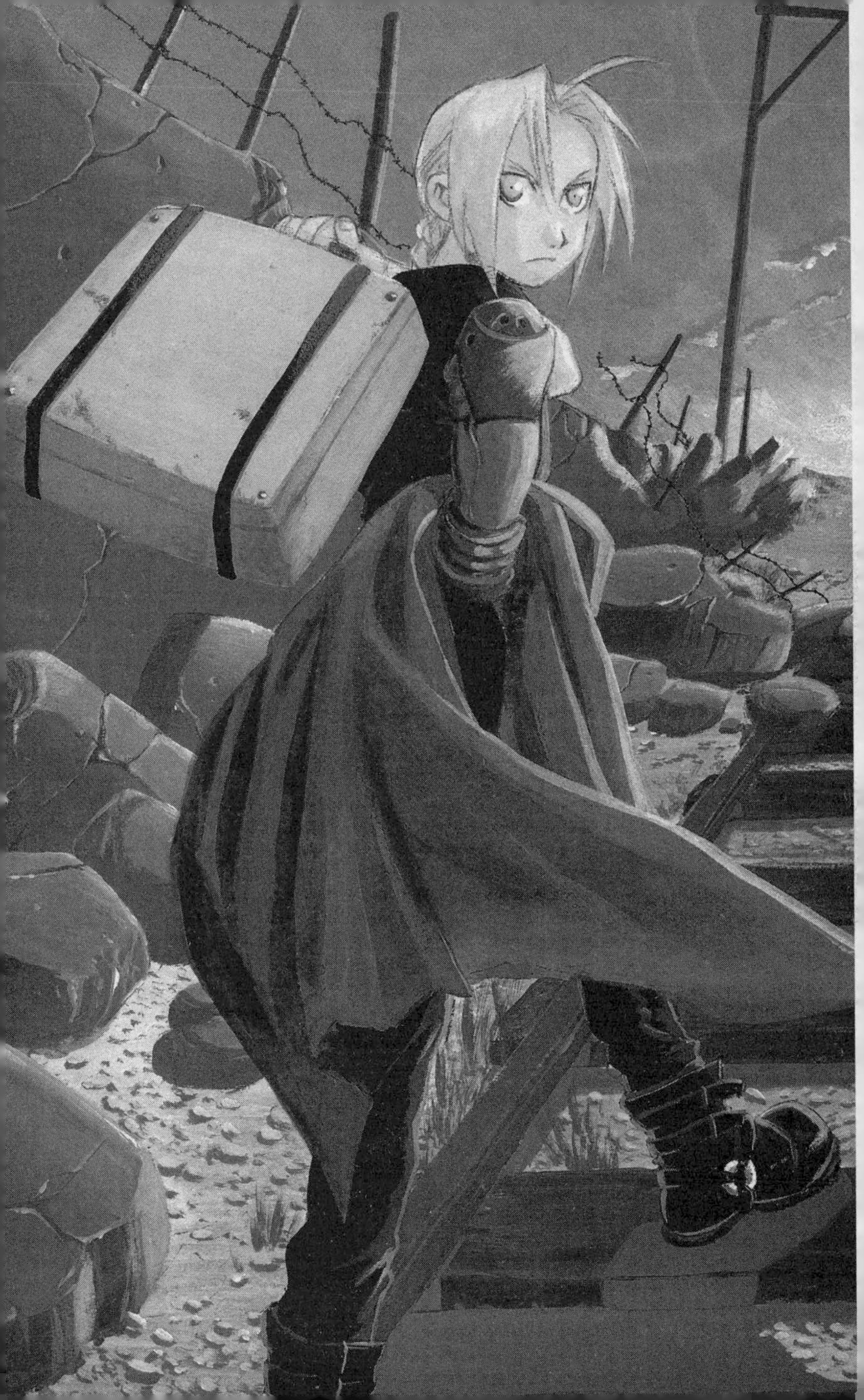

FULLMETAL
ALCHEMIST

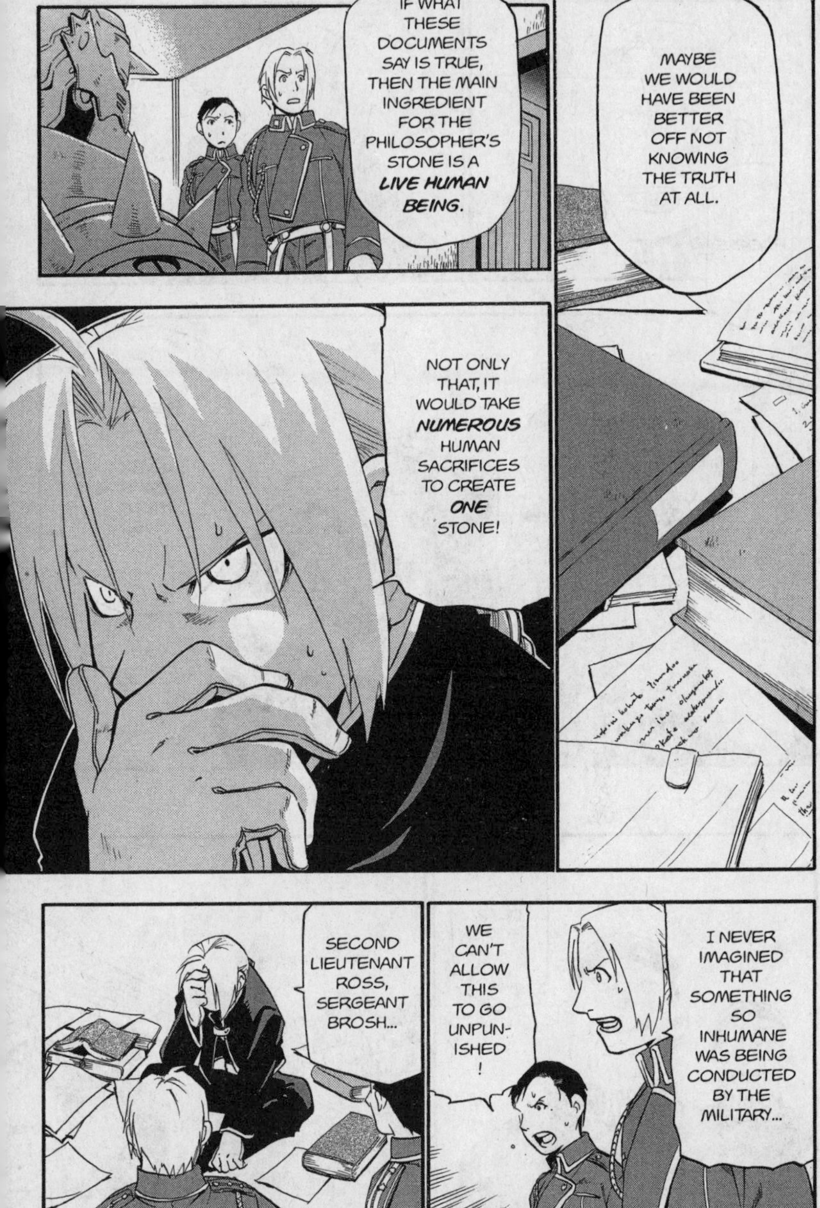
MAYBE WE WOULD HAVE BEEN BETTER OFF NOT KNOWING THE TRUTH AT ALL.
IF WHAT THESE DOCUMENTS SAY IS TRUE, THEN THE MAIN INGREDIENT FOR THE PHILOSOPHER'S STONE IS A **LIVE HUMAN BEING.**
NOT ONLY THAT, IT WOULD TAKE **NUMEROUS** HUMAN SACRIFICES TO CREATE **ONE** STONE!
I NEVER IMAGINED THAT SOMETHING SO INHUMANE WAS BEING CONDUCTED BY THE MILITARY...
WE CAN'T ALLOW THIS TO GO UNPUNISHED!
SECOND LIEUTENANT ROSS, SERGEANT BROSH...

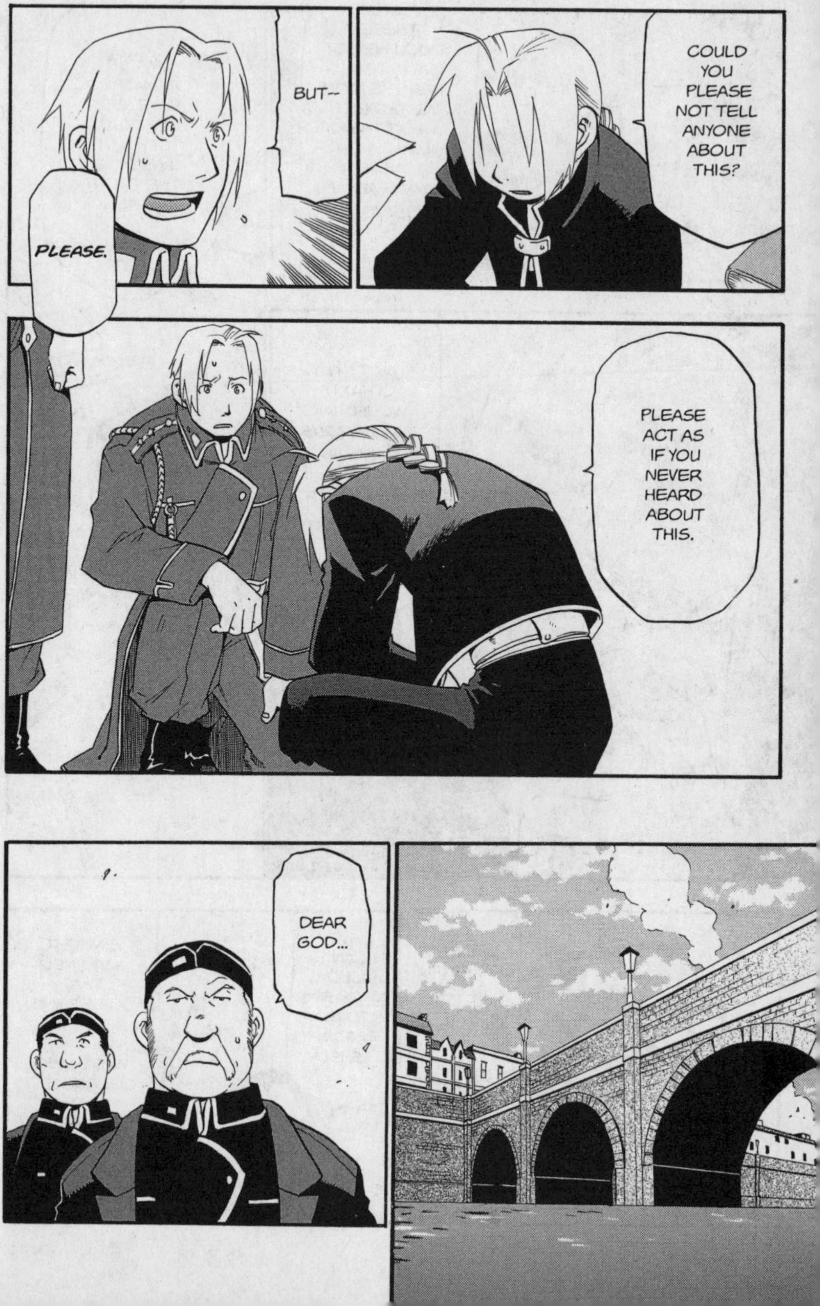
COULD YOU PLEASE NOT TELL ANYONE ABOUT THIS?
BUT--
PLEASE.
PLEASE ACT AS IF YOU NEVER HEARD ABOUT THIS.
DEAR GOD...

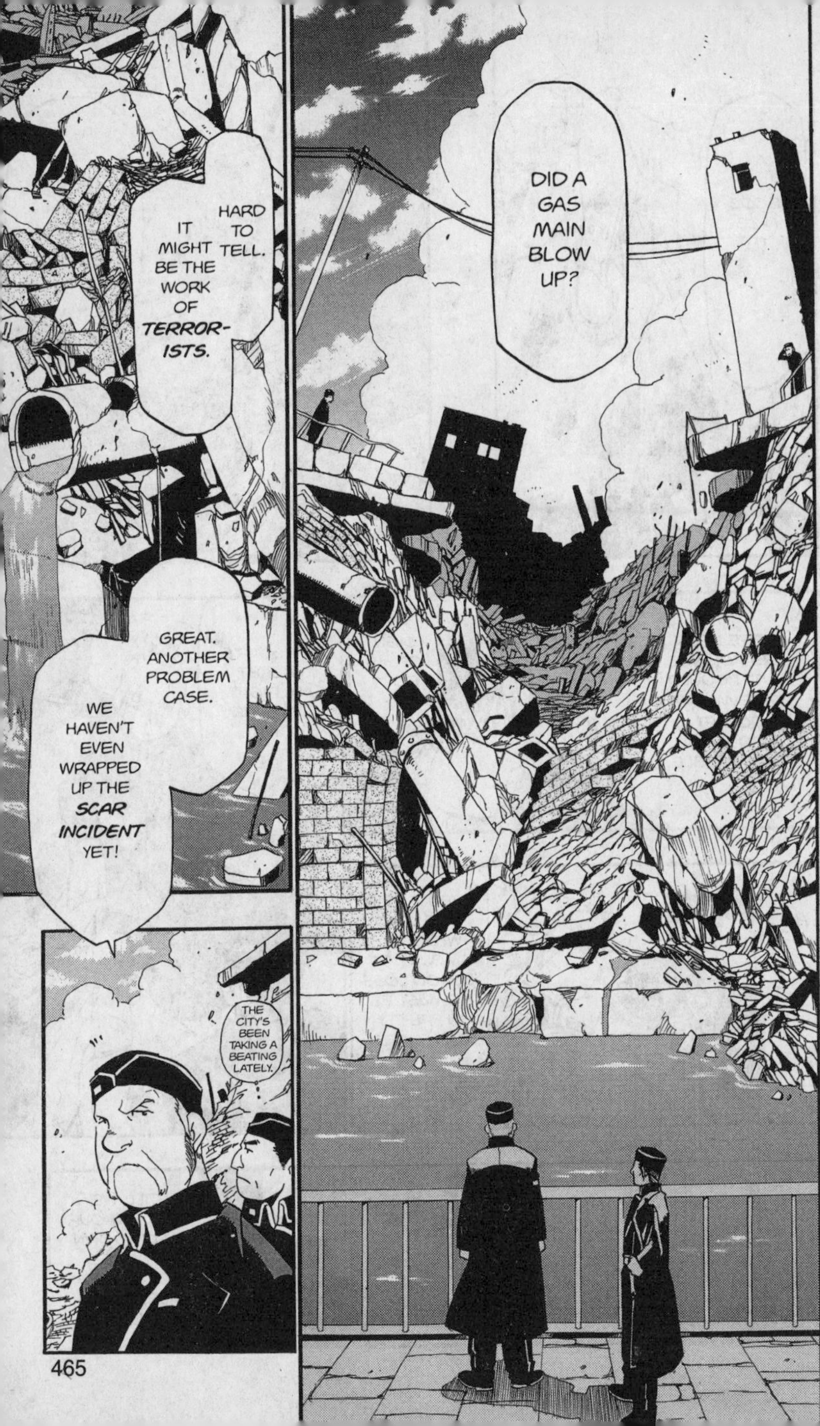
DID A GAS MAIN BLOW UP?
HARD TO TELL.
IT MIGHT BE THE WORK OF TERRORISTS.
GREAT. ANOTHER PROBLEM CASE.
WE HAVEN'T EVEN WRAPPED UP THE SCAR INCIDENT YET!
THE CITY'S BEEN TAKING A BEATING LATELY.

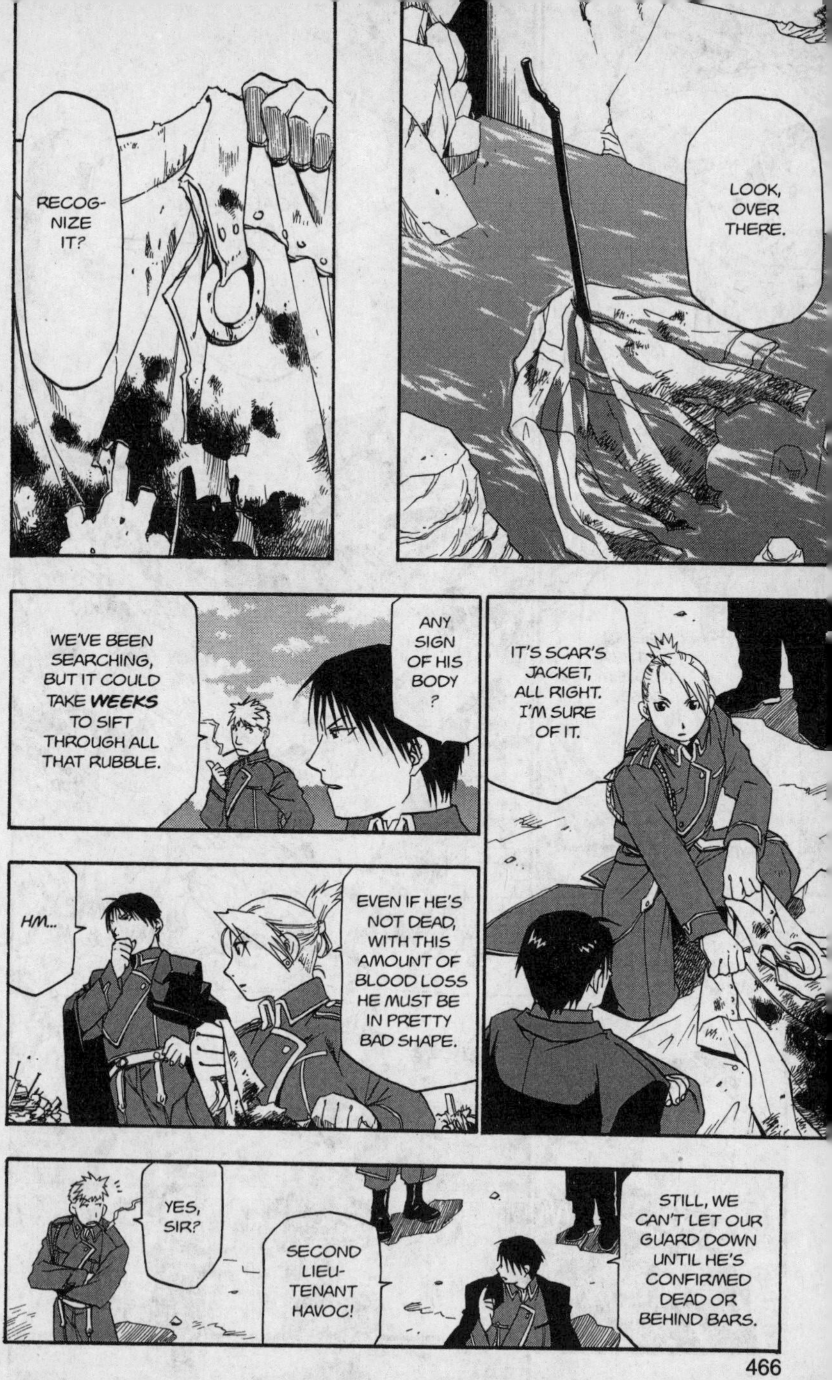
LOOK, OVER THERE.
RECOG-NIZE IT?
IT'S SCAR'S JACKET, ALL RIGHT. I'M SURE OF IT.
ANY SIGN OF HIS BODY?
WE'VE BEEN SEARCHING, BUT IT COULD TAKE **WEEKS** TO SIFT THROUGH ALL THAT RUBBLE.
EVEN IF HE'S NOT DEAD, WITH THIS AMOUNT OF BLOOD LOSS HE MUST BE IN PRETTY BAD SHAPE.
HM...
STILL, WE CAN'T LET OUR GUARD DOWN UNTIL HE'S CONFIRMED DEAD OR BEHIND BARS.
SECOND LIEU-TENANT HAVOC!
YES, SIR?

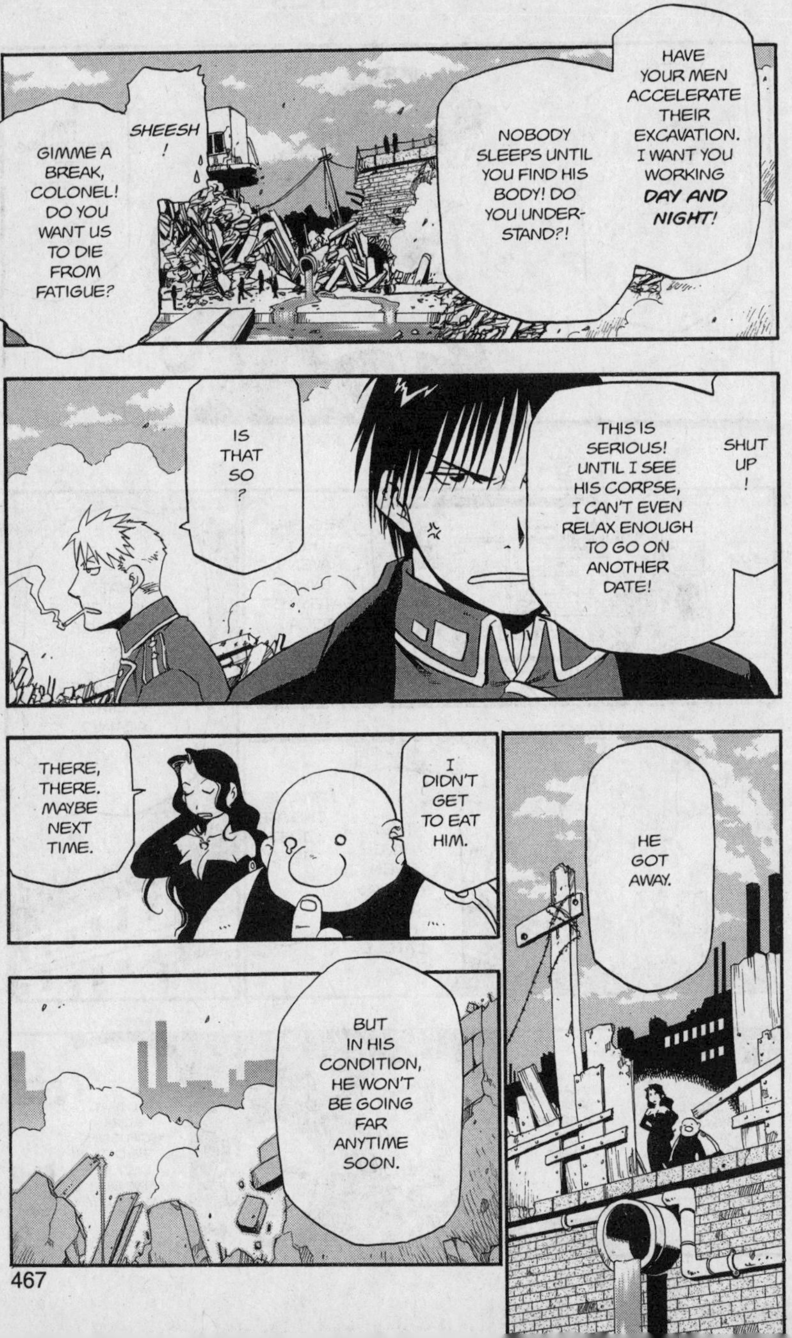
HAVE YOUR MEN ACCELERATE THEIR EXCAVATION. I WANT YOU WORKING **DAY AND NIGHT!**
NOBODY SLEEPS UNTIL YOU FIND HIS BODY! DO YOU UNDERSTAND?!
SHEESH!
GIMME A BREAK, COLONEL! DO YOU WANT US TO DIE FROM FATIGUE?
SHUT UP!
THIS IS SERIOUS! UNTIL I SEE HIS CORPSE, I CAN'T EVEN RELAX ENOUGH TO GO ON ANOTHER DATE!
IS THAT SO?
HE GOT AWAY.
I DIDN'T GET TO EAT HIM.
THERE, THERE. MAYBE NEXT TIME.
BUT IN HIS CONDITION, HE WON'T BE GOING FAR ANYTIME SOON.

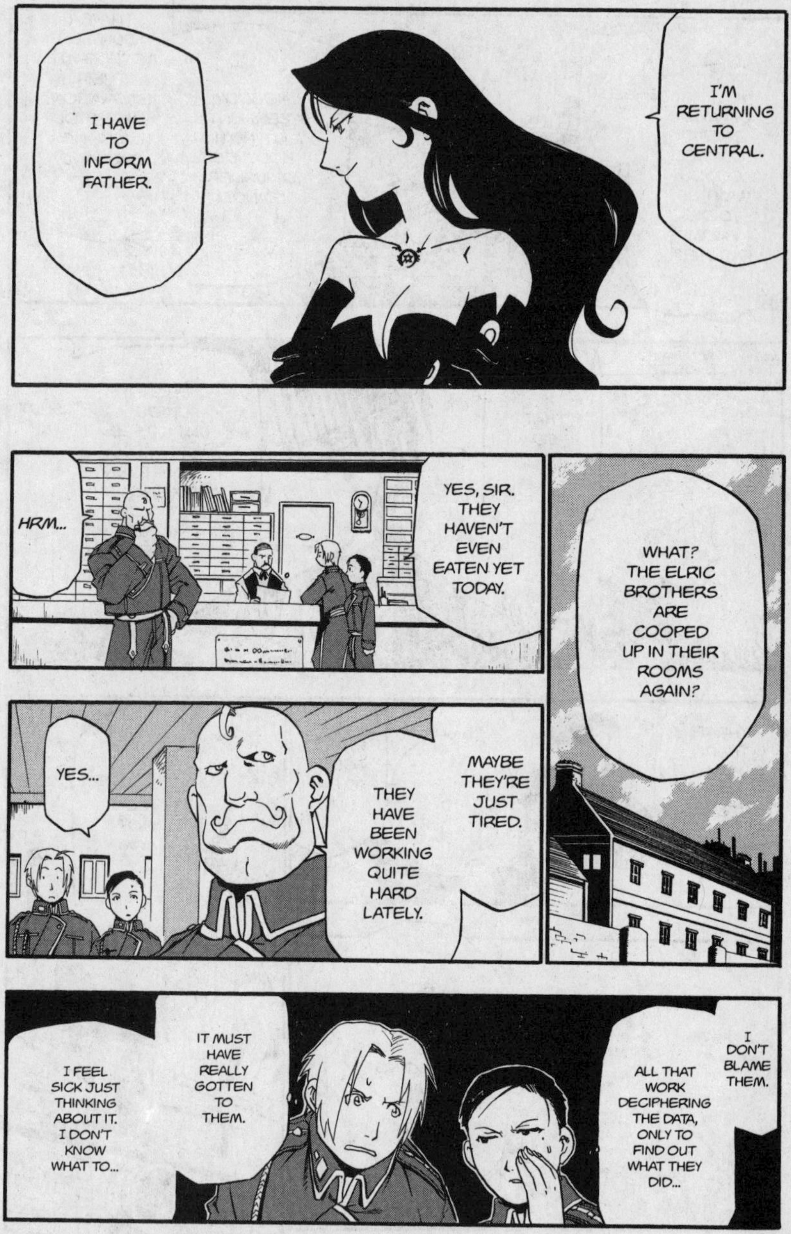
I'M RETURNING TO CENTRAL.
I HAVE TO INFORM FATHER.
WHAT? THE ELRIC BROTHERS ARE COOPED UP IN THEIR ROOMS AGAIN?
YES, SIR. THEY HAVEN'T EVEN EATEN YET TODAY.
HRM...
MAYBE THEY'RE JUST TIRED.
THEY HAVE BEEN WORKING QUITE HARD LATELY.
YES...
I DON'T BLAME THEM.
ALL THAT WORK DECIPHERING THE DATA, ONLY TO FIND OUT WHAT THEY DID...
IT MUST HAVE REALLY GOTTEN TO THEM.
I FEEL SICK JUST THINKING ABOUT IT. I DON'T KNOW WHAT TO...

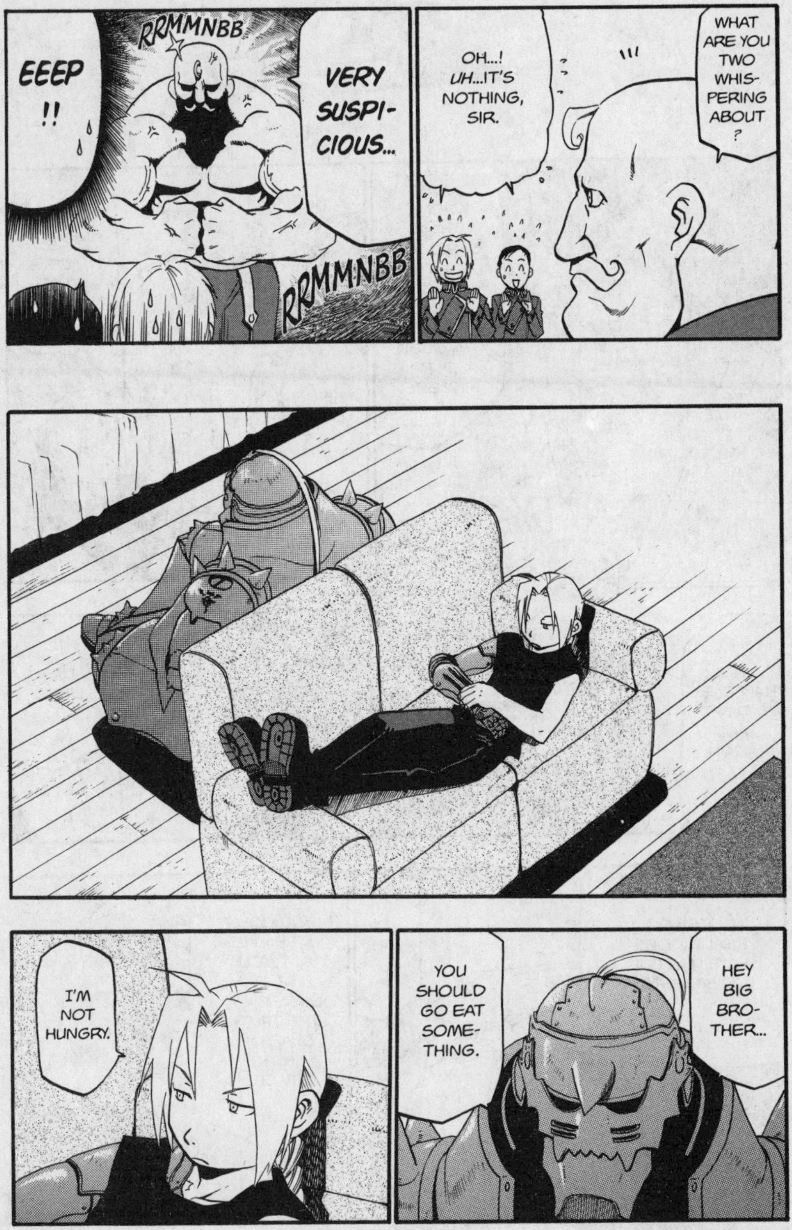
WHAT ARE YOU TWO WHISPERING ABOUT?
OH...! UH...IT'S NOTHING, SIR.
VERY SUSPICIOUS...
RRMMNBB
EEEP !!
RRMMNBB
HEY BIG BROTHER...
YOU SHOULD GO EAT SOMETHING.
I'M NOT HUNGRY.

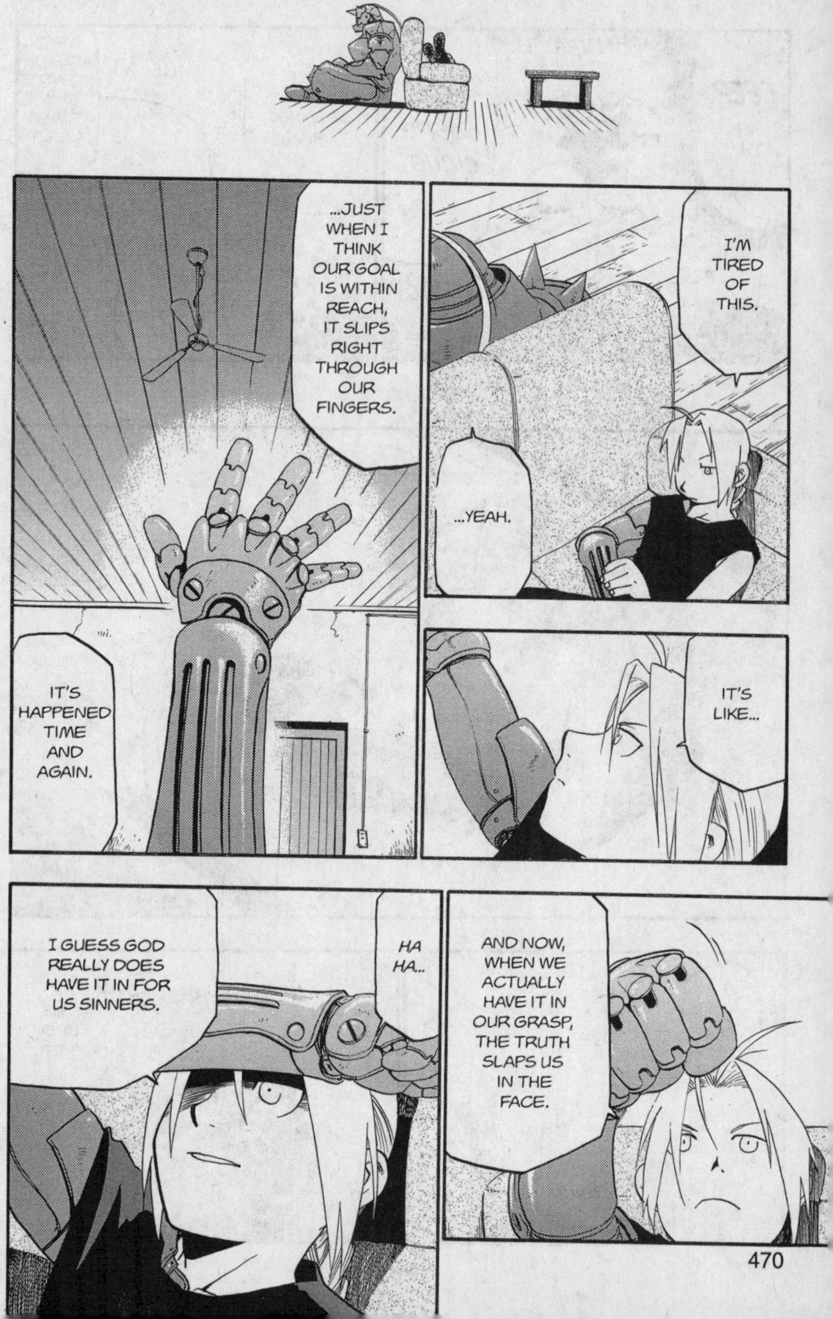
I'M TIRED OF THIS.
...YEAH.
IT'S LIKE...
...JUST WHEN I THINK OUR GOAL IS WITHIN REACH, IT SLIPS RIGHT THROUGH OUR FINGERS.
IT'S HAPPENED TIME AND AGAIN.
AND NOW, WHEN WE ACTUALLY HAVE IT IN OUR GRASP, THE TRUTH SLAPS US IN THE FACE.
HA HA...
I GUESS GOD REALLY DOES HAVE IT IN FOR US SINNERS.

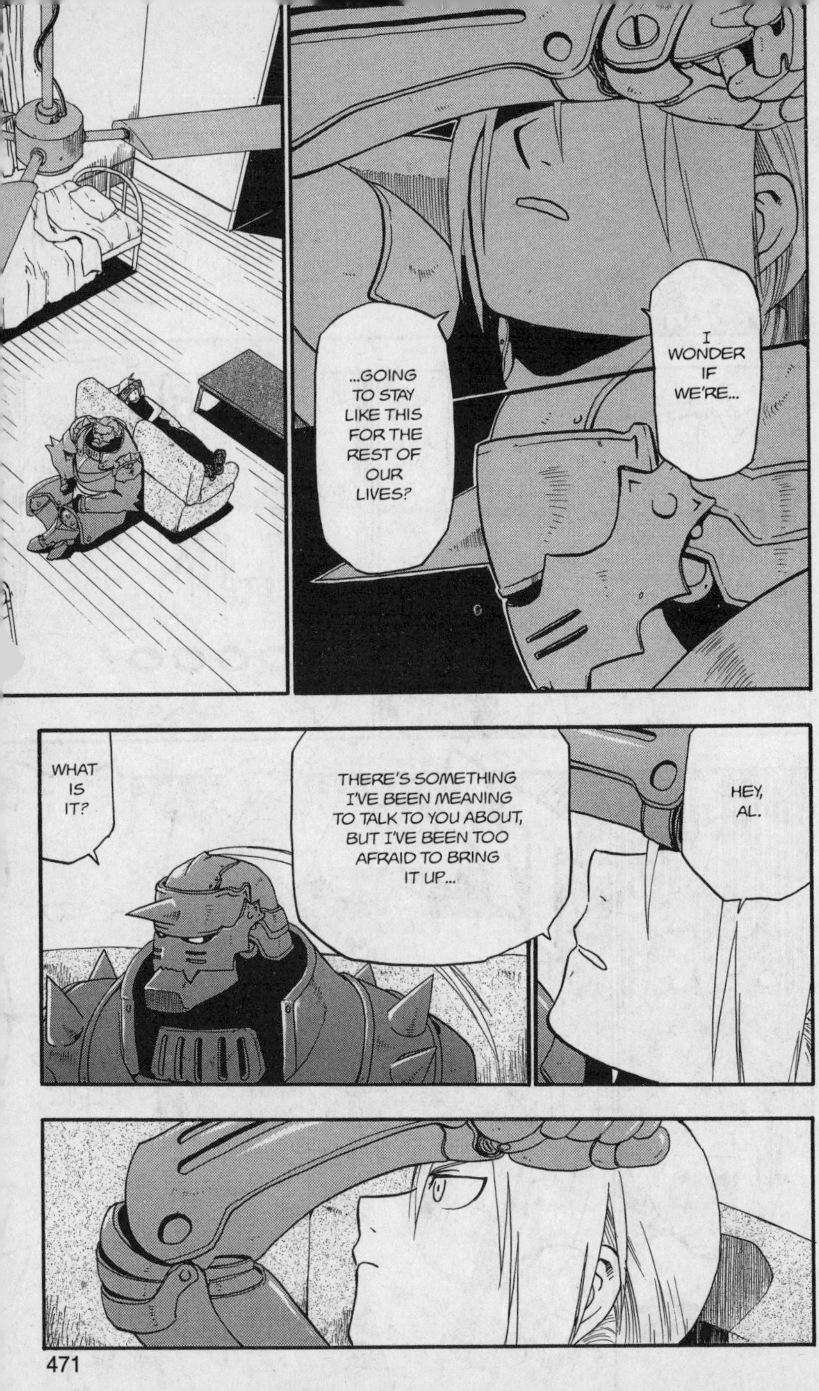
I WONDER IF WE'RE...
...GOING TO STAY LIKE THIS FOR THE REST OF OUR LIVES?
HEY, AL.
WHAT IS IT?
THERE'S SOMETHING I'VE BEEN MEANING TO TALK TO YOU ABOUT, BUT I'VE BEEN TOO AFRAID TO BRING IT UP...

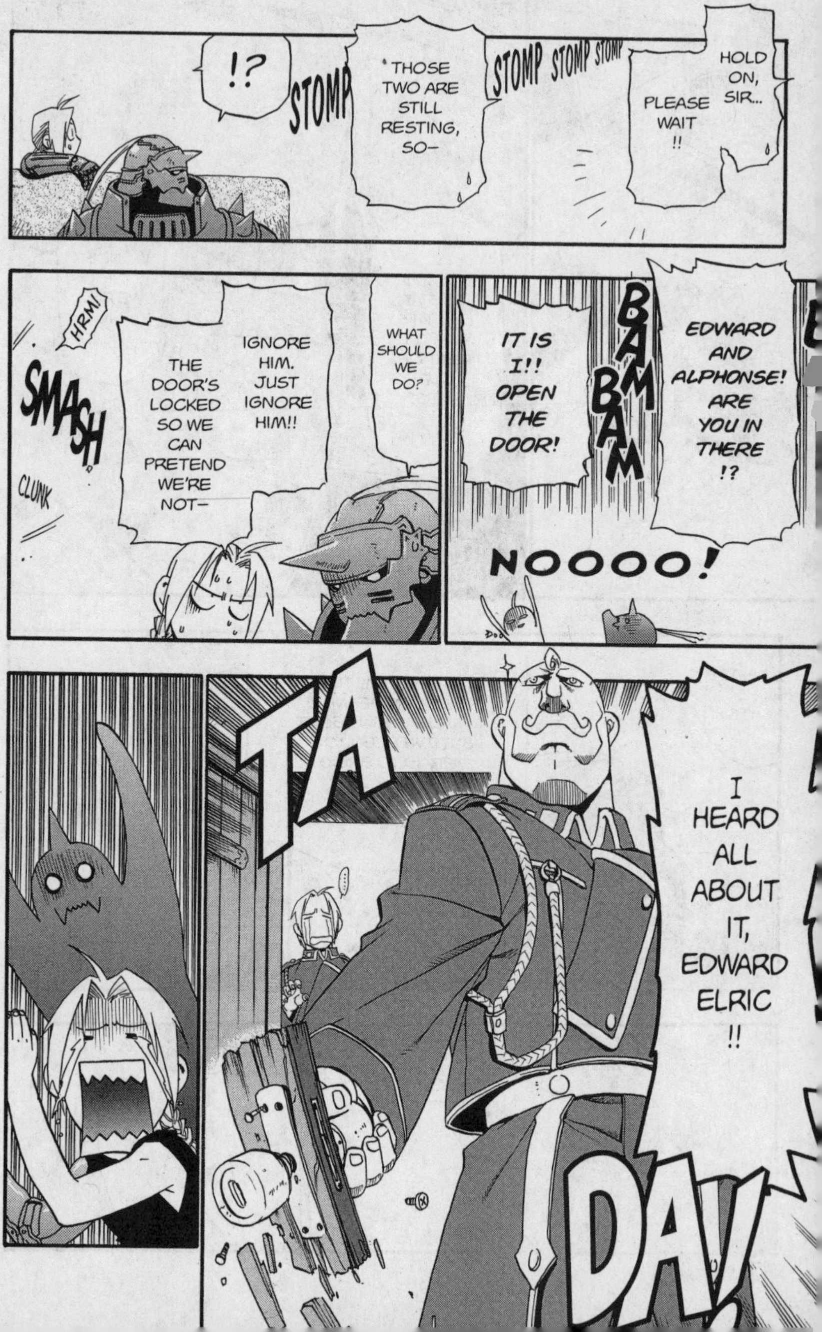
HOLD ON, SIR...
PLEASE WAIT !!
STOMP STOMP STOMP
THOSE TWO ARE STILL RESTING, SO—
STOMP
!?
EDWARD AND ALPHONSE! ARE YOU IN THERE !?
BAM BAM
IT IS I!! OPEN THE DOOR!
NOOOO!
WHAT SHOULD WE DO?
IGNORE HIM. JUST IGNORE HIM!!
THE DOOR'S LOCKED SO WE CAN PRETEND WE'RE NOT—
HRM!
SMASH
CLUNK
I HEARD ALL ABOUT IT, EDWARD ELRIC !!
TA
DA!

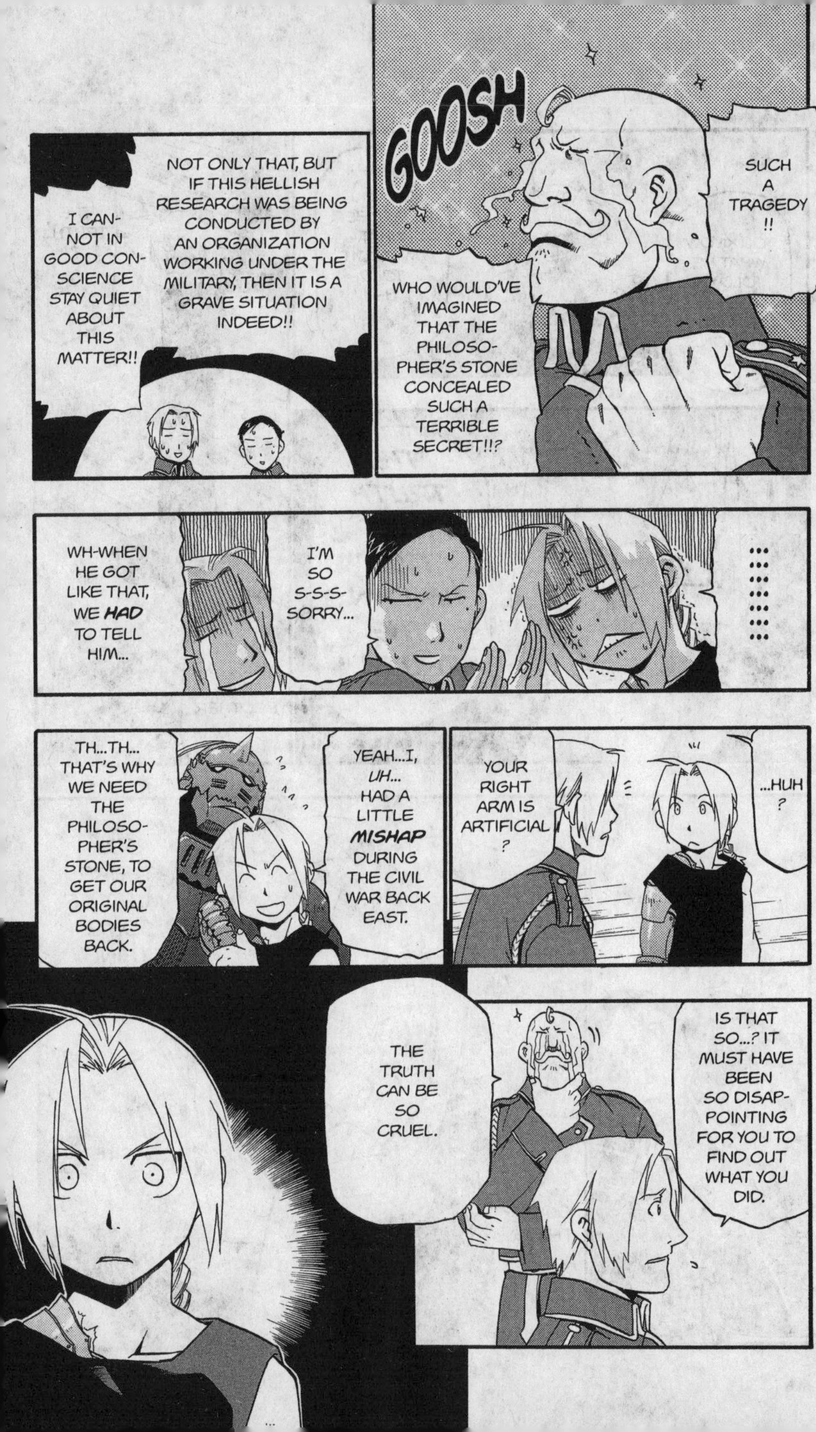
GOOSH
SUCH A TRAGEDY!!
WHO WOULD'VE IMAGINED THAT THE PHILOSOPHER'S STONE CONCEALED SUCH A TERRIBLE SECRET!!?
NOT ONLY THAT, BUT IF THIS HELLISH RESEARCH WAS BEING CONDUCTED BY AN ORGANIZATION WORKING UNDER THE MILITARY, THEN IT IS A GRAVE SITUATION INDEED!!
I CANNOT IN GOOD CONSCIENCE STAY QUIET ABOUT THIS MATTER!!
......
I'M SO S-S-S-SORRY...
WH-WHEN HE GOT LIKE THAT, WE HAD TO TELL HIM...
...HUH?
YOUR RIGHT ARM IS ARTIFICIAL?
YEAH...I, UH... HAD A LITTLE MISHAP DURING THE CIVIL WAR BACK EAST.
TH...TH... THAT'S WHY WE NEED THE PHILOSOPHER'S STONE, TO GET OUR ORIGINAL BODIES BACK.
IS THAT SO...? IT MUST HAVE BEEN SO DISAPPOINTING FOR YOU TO FIND OUT WHAT YOU DID.
THE TRUTH CAN BE SO CRUEL.

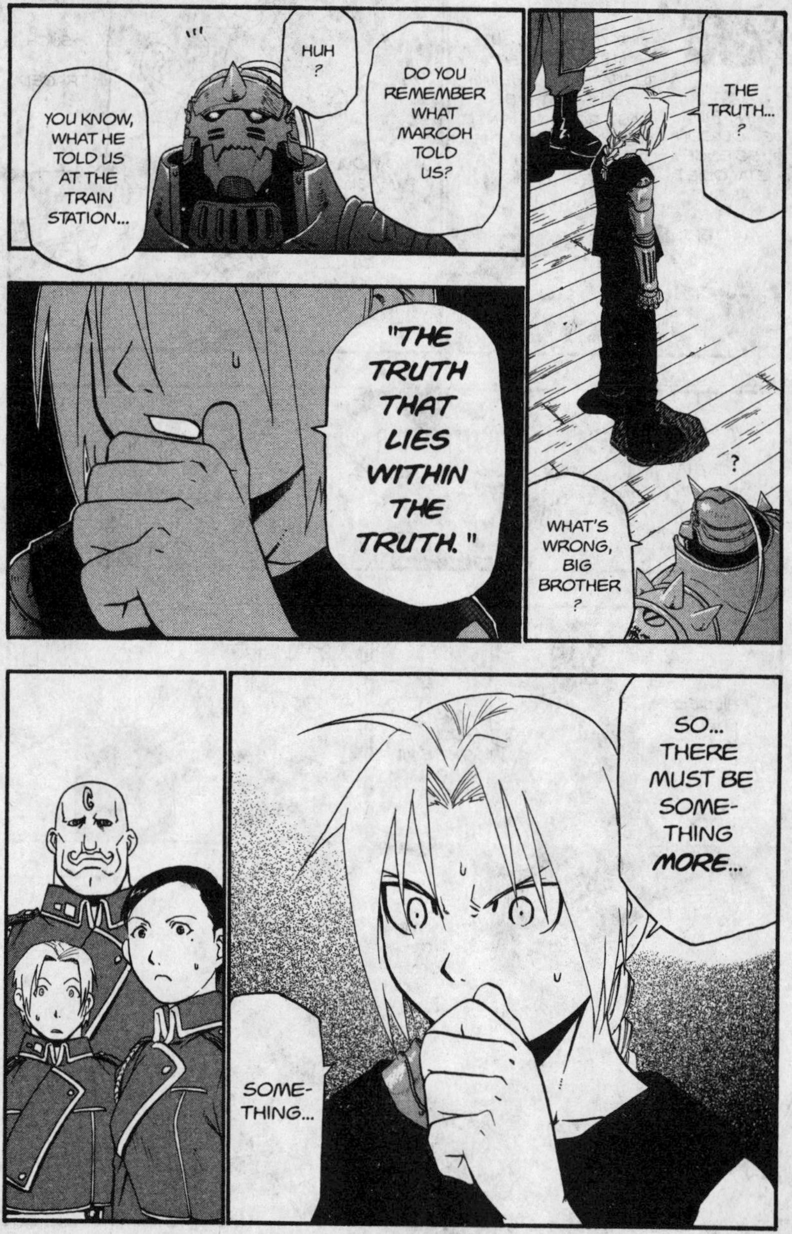
THE TRUTH...?
WHAT'S WRONG, BIG BROTHER?
HUH?
DO YOU REMEMBER WHAT MARCOH TOLD US?
YOU KNOW, WHAT HE TOLD US AT THE TRAIN STATION...
"THE TRUTH THAT LIES WITHIN THE TRUTH."
SO... THERE MUST BE SOME-THING MORE...
SOME-THING...

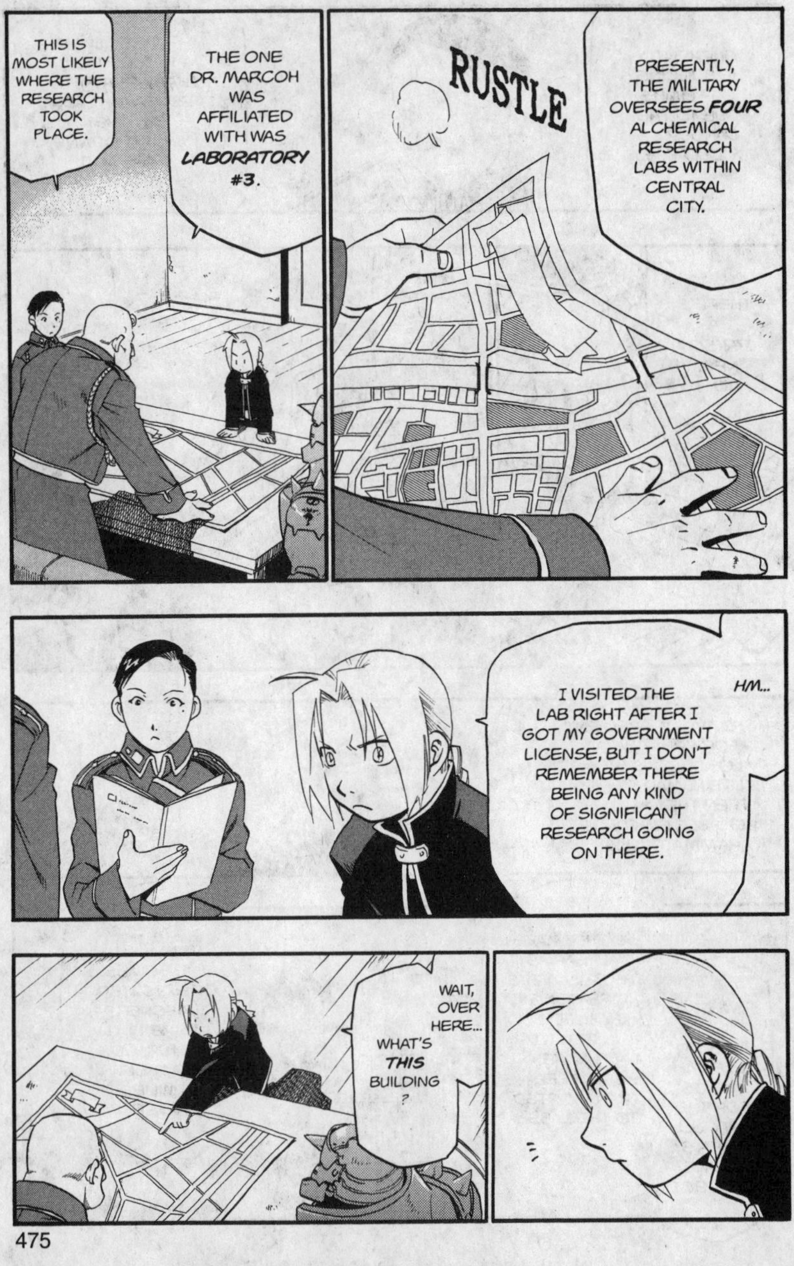
RUSTLE
PRESENTLY, THE MILITARY OVERSEES FOUR ALCHEMICAL RESEARCH LABS WITHIN CENTRAL CITY.
THE ONE DR. MARCOH WAS AFFILIATED WITH WAS LABORATORY #3.
THIS IS MOST LIKELY WHERE THE RESEARCH TOOK PLACE.
HM...
I VISITED THE LAB RIGHT AFTER I GOT MY GOVERNMENT LICENSE, BUT I DON'T REMEMBER THERE BEING ANY KIND OF SIGNIFICANT RESEARCH GOING ON THERE.
WAIT, OVER HERE... WHAT'S THIS BUILDING?

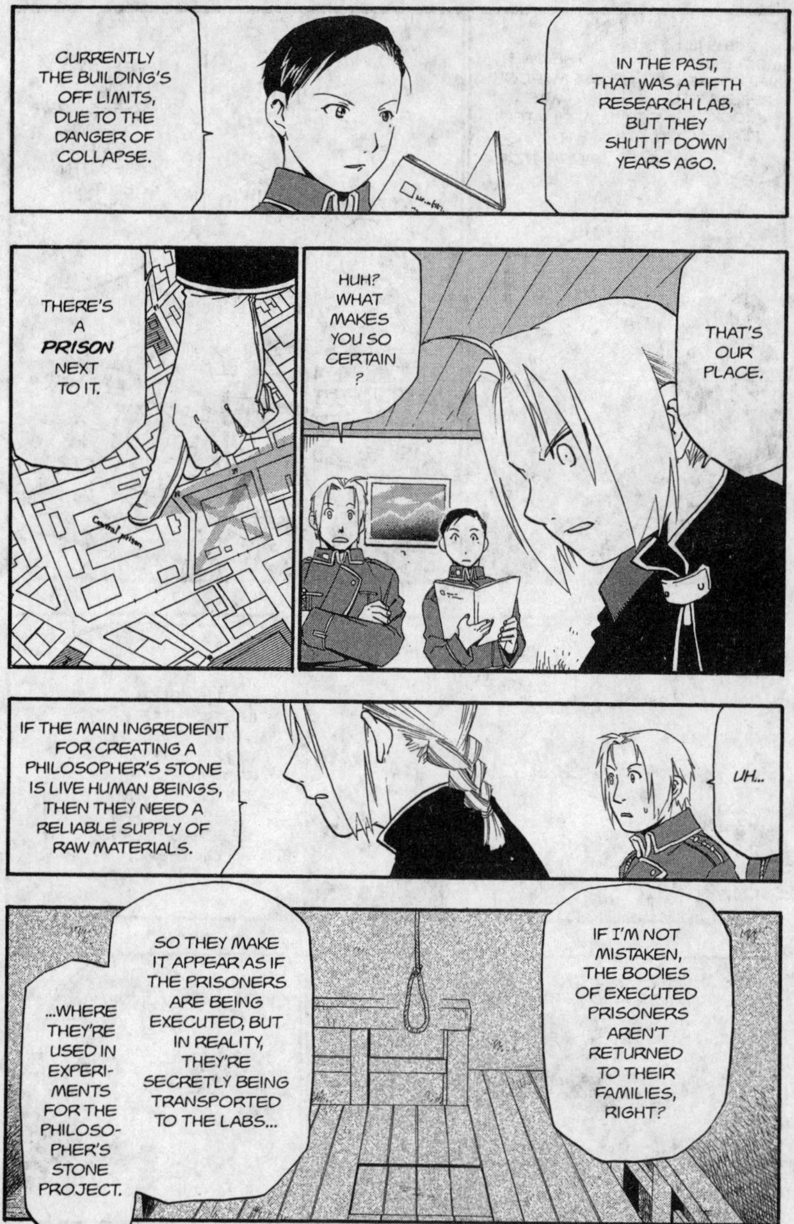
IN THE PAST, THAT WAS A FIFTH RESEARCH LAB, BUT THEY SHUT IT DOWN YEARS AGO.
CURRENTLY THE BUILDING'S OFF LIMITS, DUE TO THE DANGER OF COLLAPSE.
THAT'S OUR PLACE.
HUH? WHAT MAKES YOU SO CERTAIN?
THERE'S A **PRISON** NEXT TO IT.
Central prison
UH...
IF THE MAIN INGREDIENT FOR CREATING A PHILOSOPHER'S STONE IS LIVE HUMAN BEINGS, THEN THEY NEED A RELIABLE SUPPLY OF RAW MATERIALS.
IF I'M NOT MISTAKEN, THE BODIES OF EXECUTED PRISONERS AREN'T RETURNED TO THEIR FAMILIES, RIGHT?
SO THEY MAKE IT APPEAR AS IF THE PRISONERS ARE BEING EXECUTED, BUT IN REALITY, THEY'RE SECRETLY BEING TRANSPORTED TO THE LABS...
...WHERE THEY'RE USED IN EXPERIMENTS FOR THE PHILOSOPHER'S STONE PROJECT.

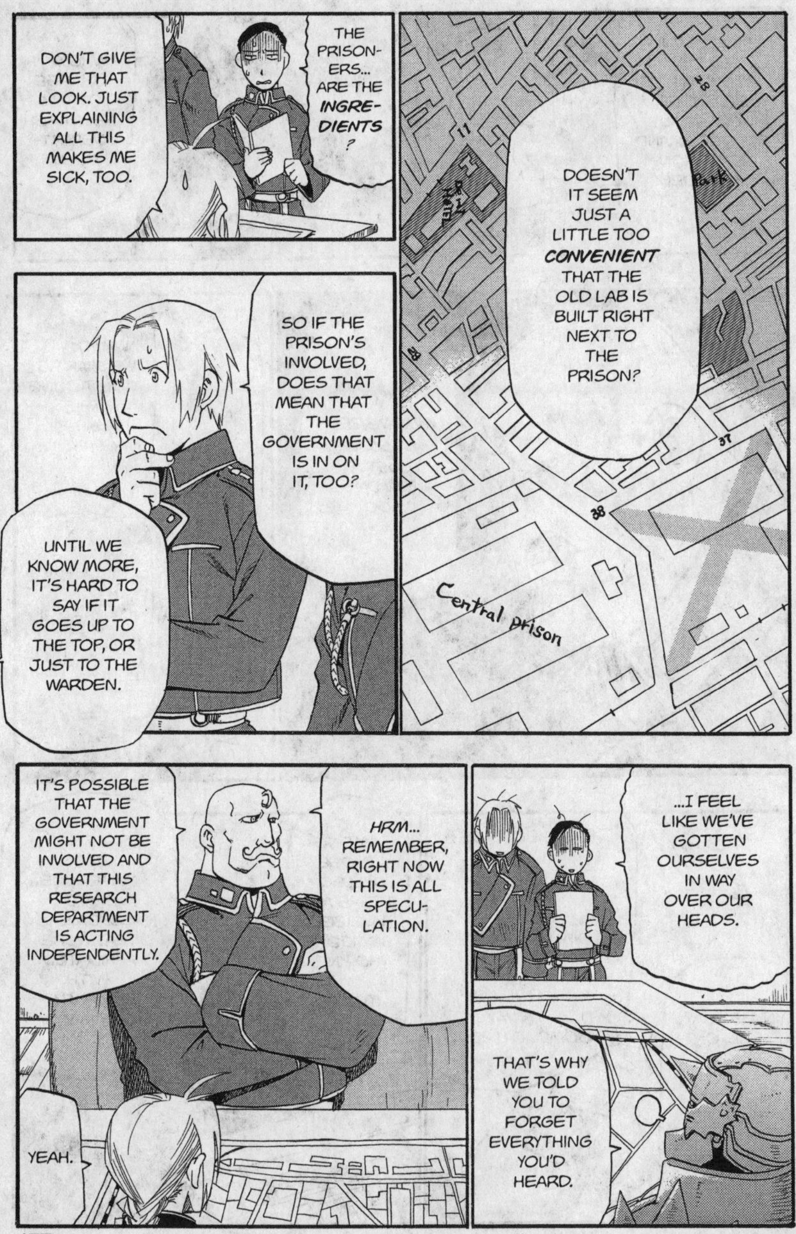
DOESN'T IT SEEM JUST A LITTLE TOO **CONVENIENT** THAT THE OLD LAB IS BUILT RIGHT NEXT TO THE PRISON?
Park
Central prison
THE PRISONERS... ARE THE ***INGREDIENTS***?
DON'T GIVE ME THAT LOOK. JUST EXPLAINING ALL THIS MAKES ME SICK, TOO.
SO IF THE PRISON'S INVOLVED, DOES THAT MEAN THAT THE GOVERNMENT IS IN ON IT, TOO?
UNTIL WE KNOW MORE, IT'S HARD TO SAY IF IT GOES UP TO THE TOP, OR JUST TO THE WARDEN.
...I FEEL LIKE WE'VE GOTTEN OURSELVES IN WAY OVER OUR HEADS.
THAT'S WHY WE TOLD YOU TO FORGET EVERYTHING YOU'D HEARD.
HRM... REMEMBER, RIGHT NOW THIS IS ALL SPECULATION.
IT'S POSSIBLE THAT THE GOVERNMENT MIGHT NOT BE INVOLVED AND THAT THIS RESEARCH DEPARTMENT IS ACTING INDEPENDENTLY.
YEAH.

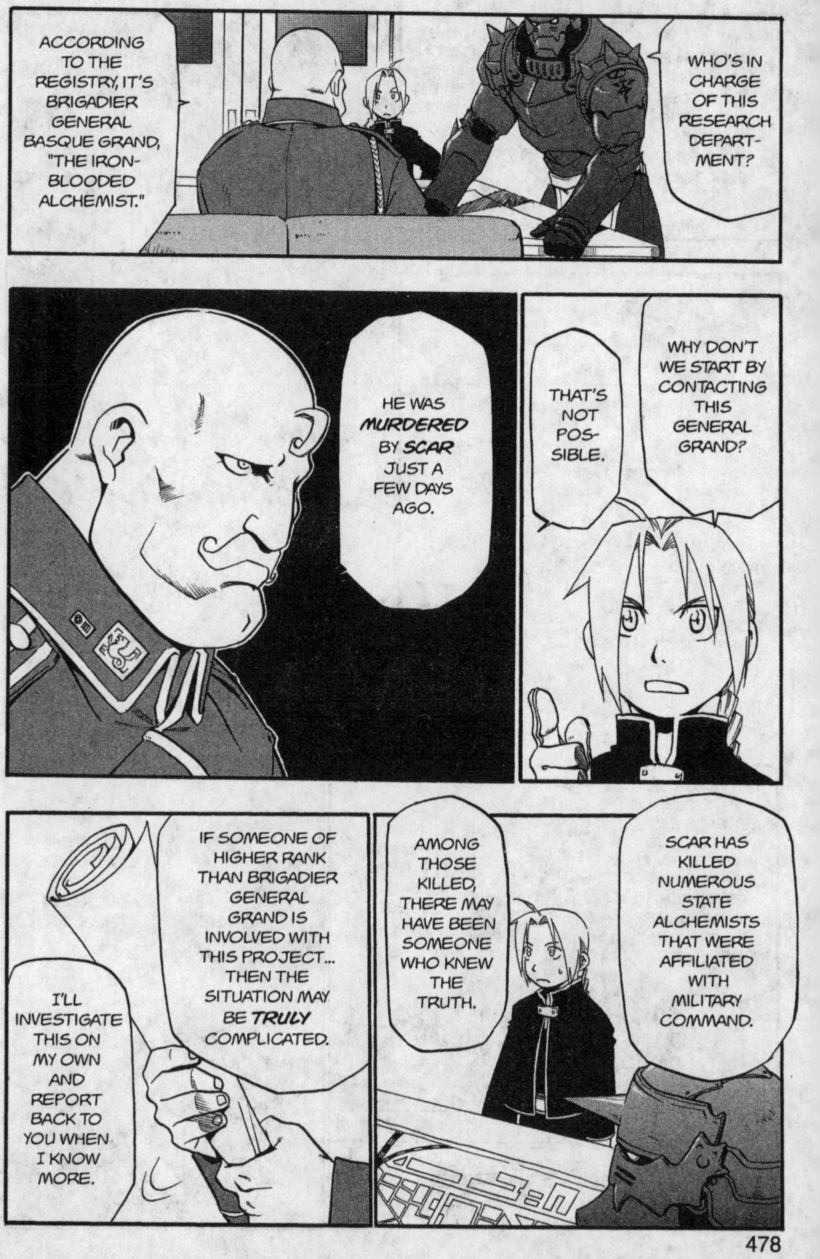

WHO'S IN CHARGE OF THIS RESEARCH DEPARTMENT?
ACCORDING TO THE REGISTRY, IT'S BRIGADIER GENERAL BASQUE GRAND, "THE IRON-BLOODED ALCHEMIST."
WHY DON'T WE START BY CONTACTING THIS GENERAL GRAND?
THAT'S NOT POSSIBLE.
HE WAS ***MURDERED*** BY ***SCAR*** JUST A FEW DAYS AGO.
SCAR HAS KILLED NUMEROUS STATE ALCHEMISTS THAT WERE AFFILIATED WITH MILITARY COMMAND.
AMONG THOSE KILLED, THERE MAY HAVE BEEN SOMEONE WHO KNEW THE TRUTH.
IF SOMEONE OF HIGHER RANK THAN BRIGADIER GENERAL GRAND IS INVOLVED WITH THIS PROJECT... THEN THE SITUATION MAY BE ***TRULY*** COMPLICATED.
I'LL INVESTIGATE THIS ON MY OWN AND REPORT BACK TO YOU WHEN I KNOW MORE.

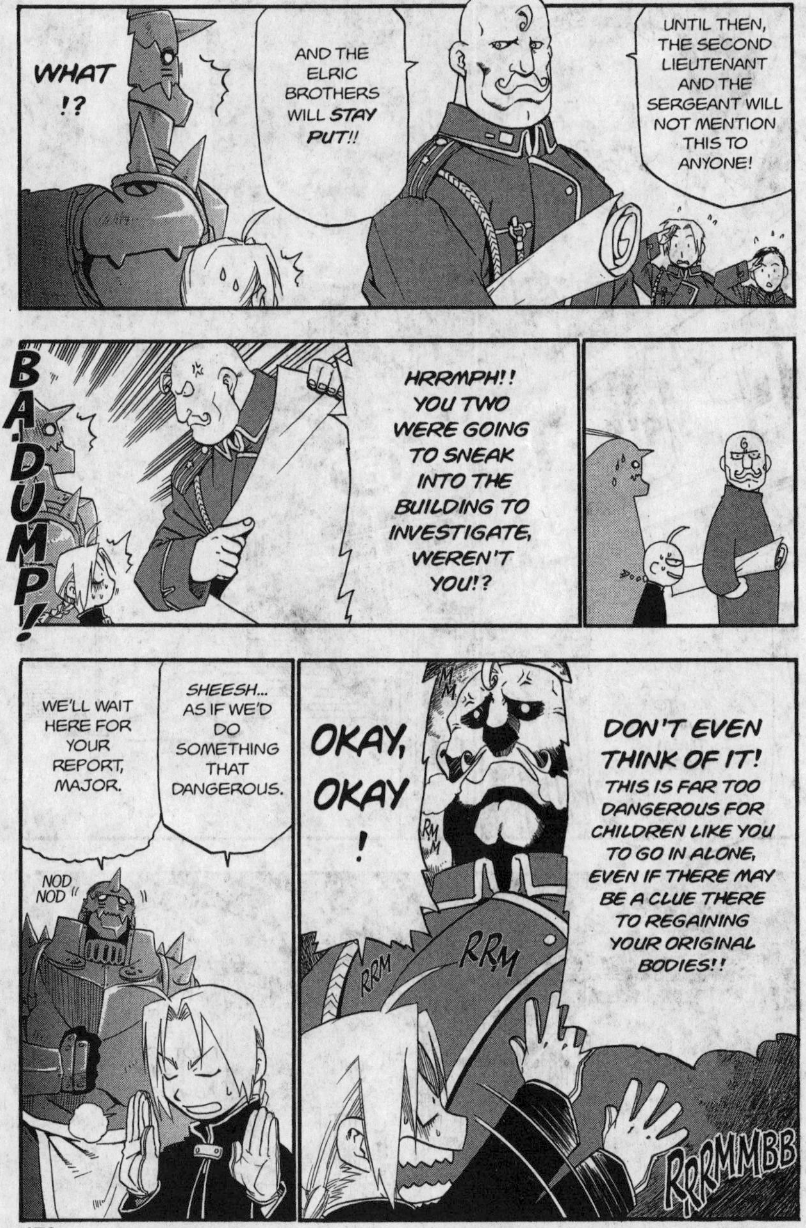
UNTIL THEN, THE SECOND LIEUTENANT AND THE SERGEANT WILL NOT MENTION THIS TO ANYONE!
AND THE ELRIC BROTHERS WILL STAY PUT!!
WHAT!?
HRRMPH!! YOU TWO WERE GOING TO SNEAK INTO THE BUILDING TO INVESTIGATE, WEREN'T YOU!?
BA-DUMP!
DON'T EVEN THINK OF IT! THIS IS FAR TOO DANGEROUS FOR CHILDREN LIKE YOU TO GO IN ALONE, EVEN IF THERE MAY BE A CLUE THERE TO REGAINING YOUR ORIGINAL BODIES!!
MM
RRM
RRM
RRM
OKAY, OKAY!
RRRMMBB
SHEESH... AS IF WE'D DO SOMETHING THAT DANGEROUS.
WE'LL WAIT HERE FOR YOUR REPORT, MAJOR.
NOD NOD

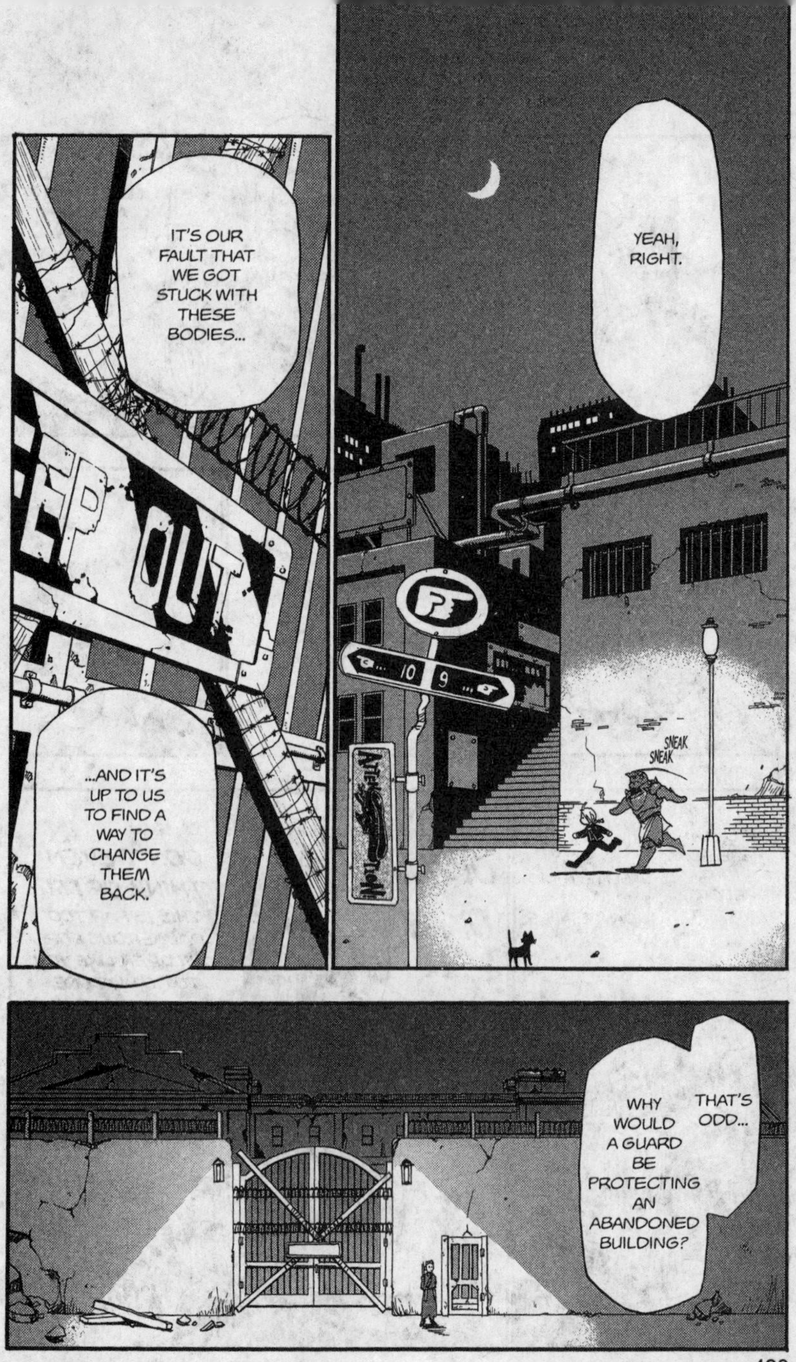
YEAH, RIGHT.
SNEAK SNEAK
IT'S OUR FAULT THAT WE GOT STUCK WITH THESE BODIES...
EP OUT
...AND IT'S UP TO US TO FIND A WAY TO CHANGE THEM BACK.
THAT'S ODD...
WHY WOULD A GUARD BE PROTECTING AN ABANDONED BUILDING?

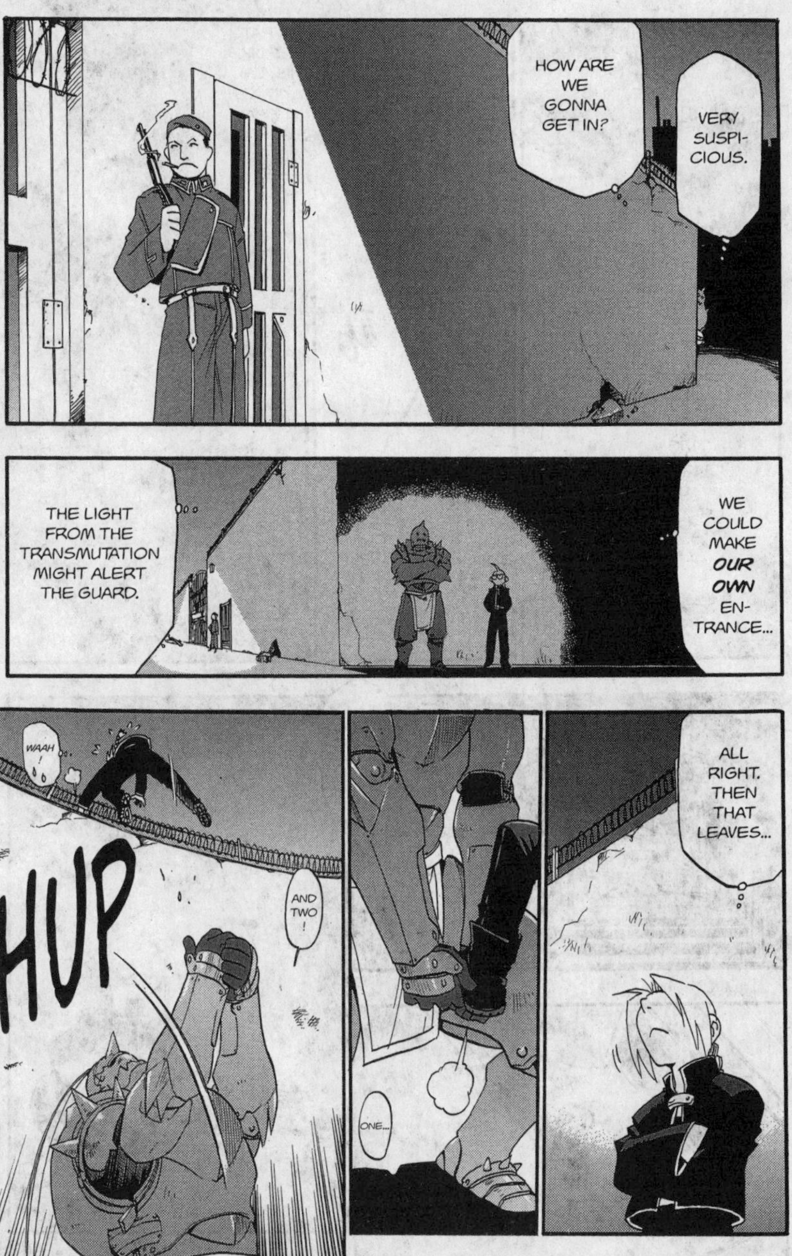
VERY SUSPI-CIOUS.
HOW ARE WE GONNA GET IN?
WE COULD MAKE OUR OWN EN-TRANCE...
THE LIGHT FROM THE TRANSMUTATION MIGHT ALERT THE GUARD.
ALL RIGHT. THEN THAT LEAVES...
ONE...
AND TWO!
WAAH!
HUP

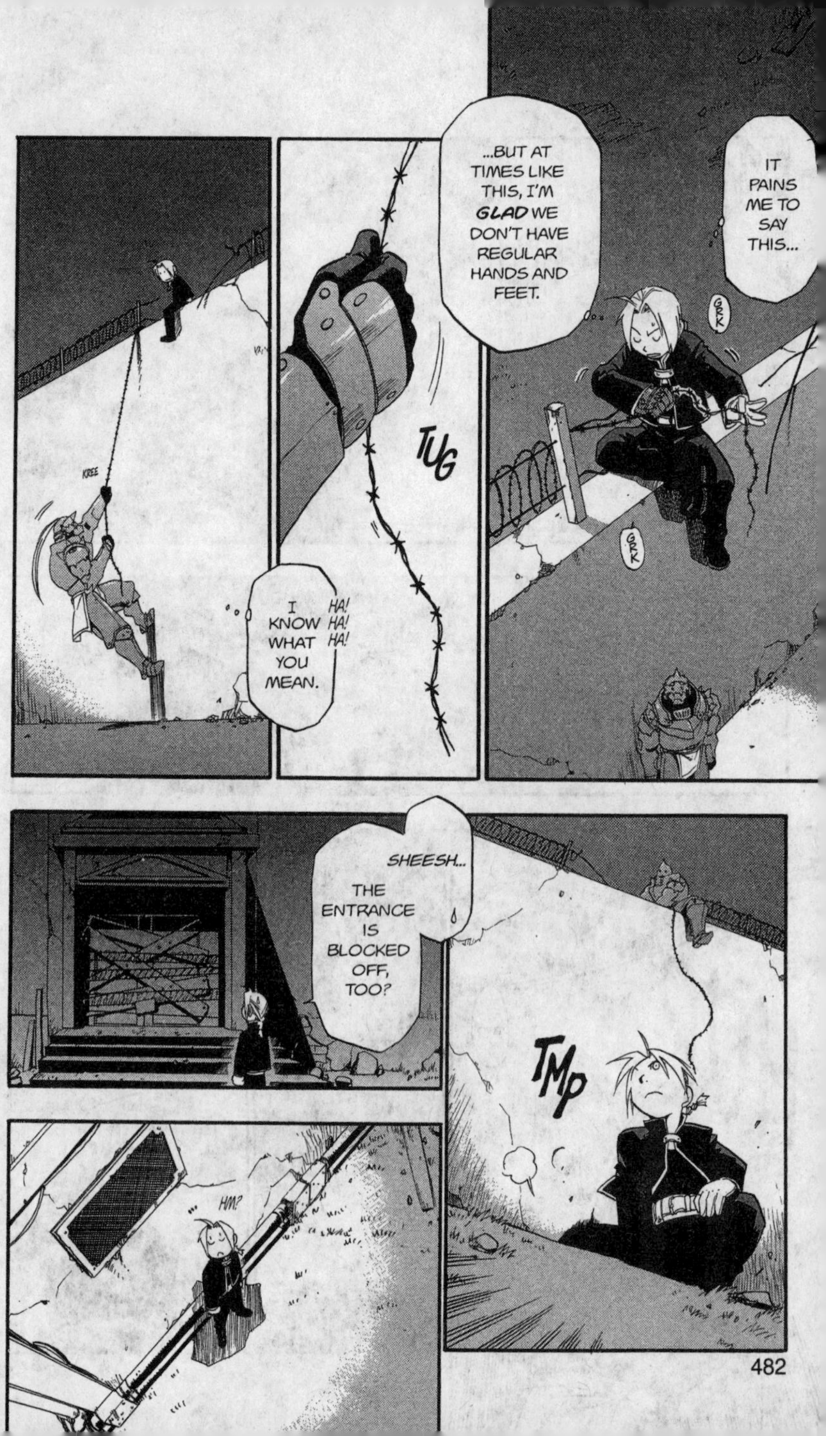
IT PAINS ME TO SAY THIS...
...BUT AT TIMES LIKE THIS, I'M GLAD WE DON'T HAVE REGULAR HANDS AND FEET.
GRK
GRK
TUG
I KNOW WHAT YOU MEAN.
HA! HA! HA!
KREE
TMP
SHEESH... THE ENTRANCE IS BLOCKED OFF, TOO?
HM?

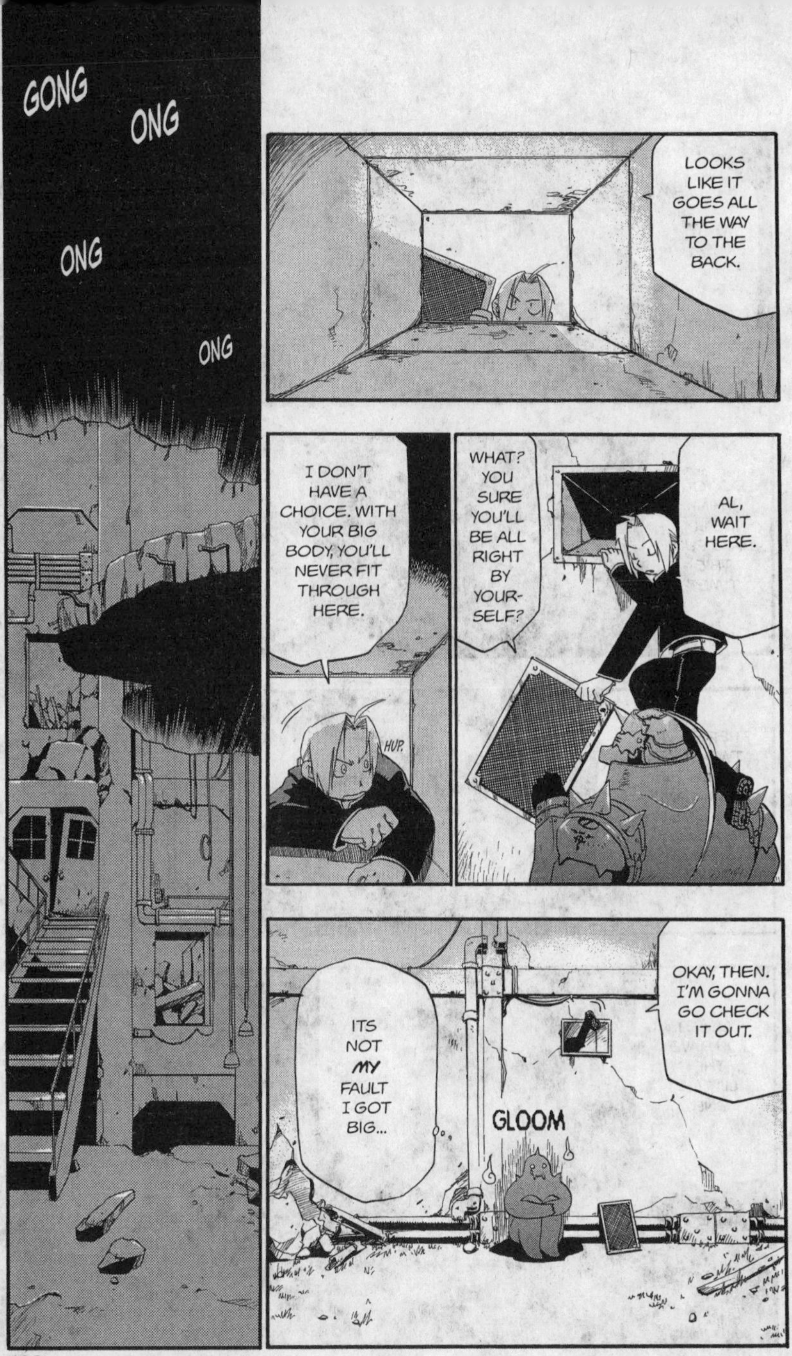
LOOKS LIKE IT GOES ALL THE WAY TO THE BACK.
AL, WAIT HERE.
WHAT? YOU SURE YOU'LL BE ALL RIGHT BY YOURSELF?
I DON'T HAVE A CHOICE. WITH YOUR BIG BODY, YOU'LL NEVER FIT THROUGH HERE.
HUP.
OKAY, THEN. I'M GONNA GO CHECK IT OUT.
ITS NOT MY FAULT I GOT BIG...
GLOOM
GONG
ONG
ONG
ONG

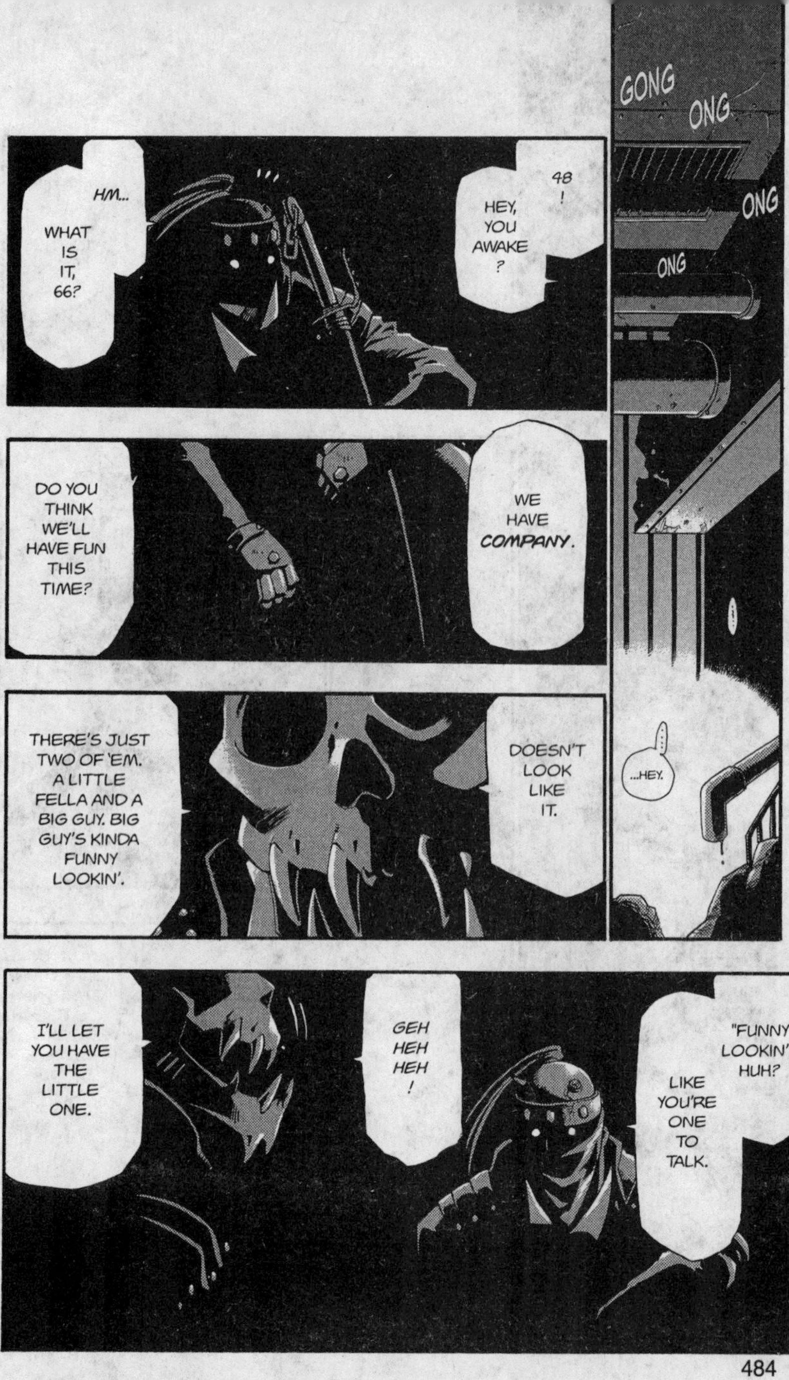
GONG
ONG
ONG
ONG
!
...HEY.
48! HEY, YOU AWAKE?
HM... WHAT IS IT, 66?
WE HAVE **COMPANY**.
DO YOU THINK WE'LL HAVE FUN THIS TIME?
DOESN'T LOOK LIKE IT.
THERE'S JUST TWO OF 'EM. A LITTLE FELLA AND A BIG GUY. BIG GUY'S KINDA FUNNY LOOKIN'.
"FUNNY LOOKIN'," HUH?
LIKE YOU'RE ONE TO TALK.
GEH HEH HEH!
I'LL LET YOU HAVE THE LITTLE ONE.

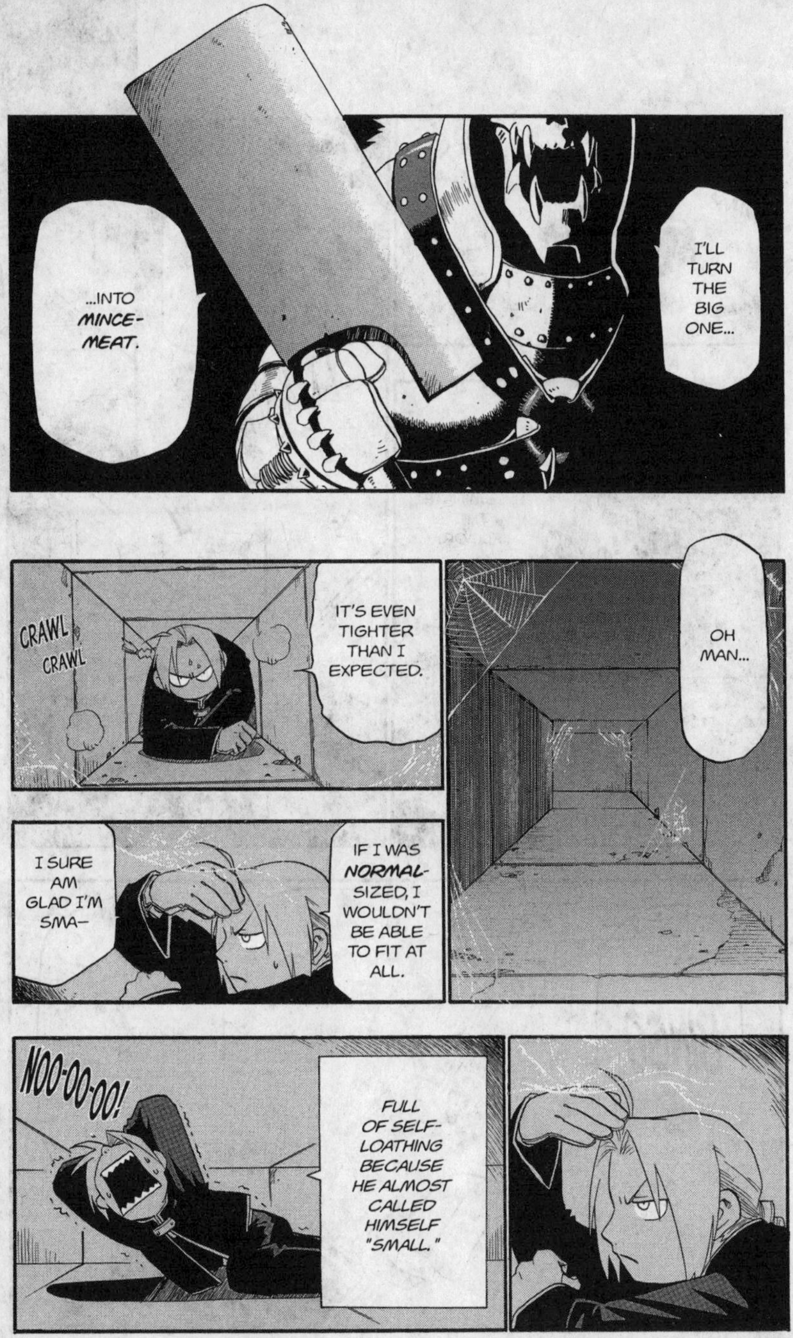
I'LL TURN THE BIG ONE...
...INTO MINCE-MEAT.
OH MAN...
CRAWL CRAWL
IT'S EVEN TIGHTER THAN I EXPECTED.
IF I WAS NORMAL-SIZED, I WOULDN'T BE ABLE TO FIT AT ALL.
I SURE AM GLAD I'M SMA—
FULL OF SELF-LOATHING BECAUSE HE ALMOST CALLED HIMSELF "SMALL."
NOO-OO-OO!

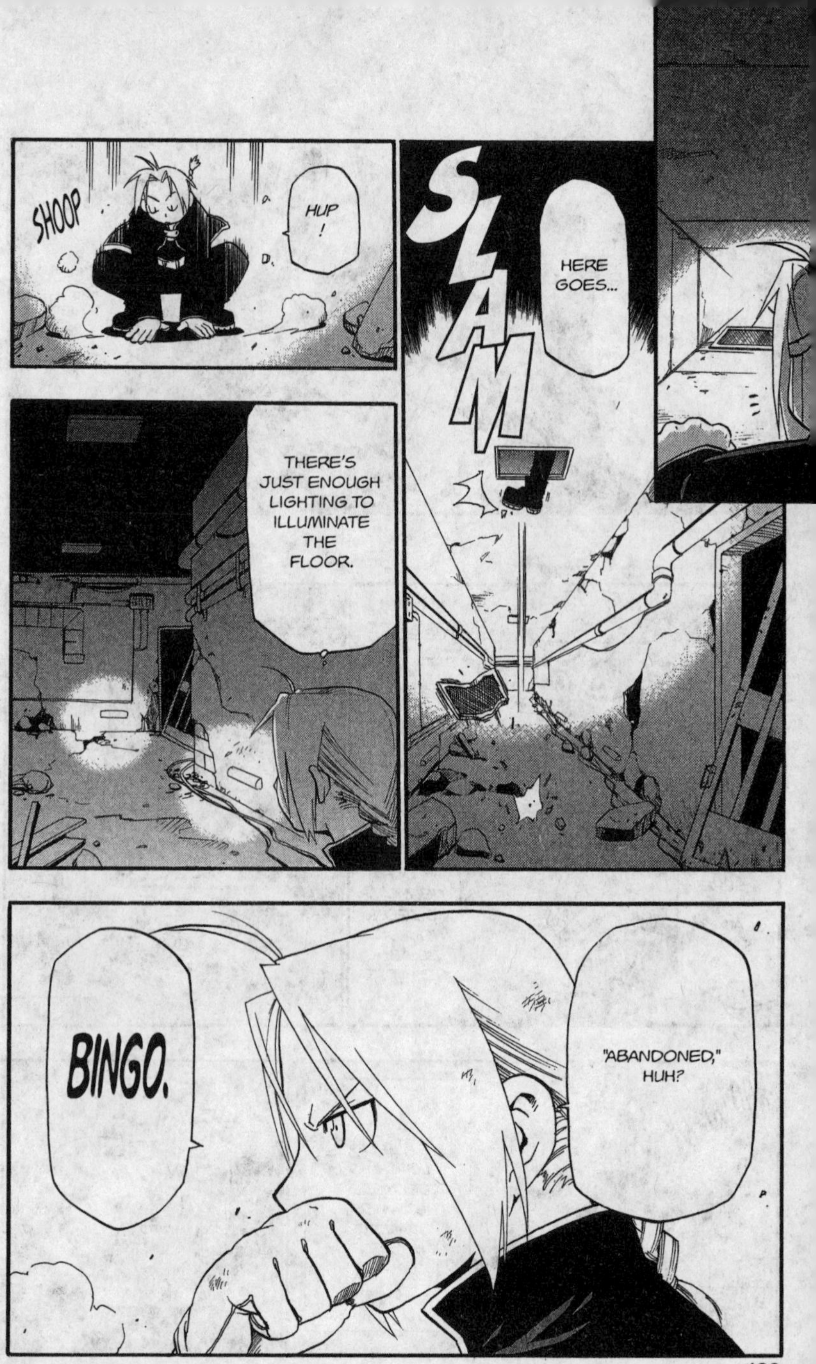
HERE GOES...
SLAM
SHOOP
HUP!
THERE'S JUST ENOUGH LIGHTING TO ILLUMINATE THE FLOOR.
"ABANDONED," HUH?
BINGO.

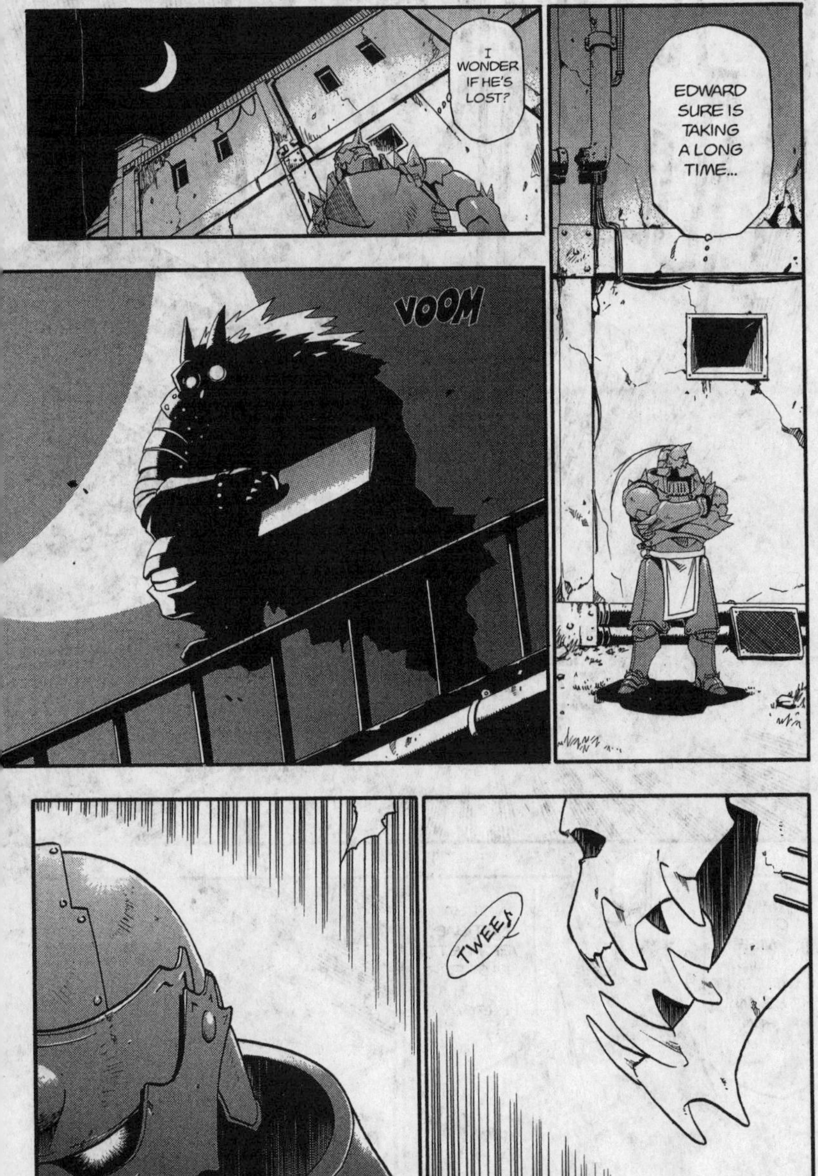
EDWARD SURE IS TAKING A LONG TIME...
I WONDER IF HE'S LOST?
VOOM
TWEE♪

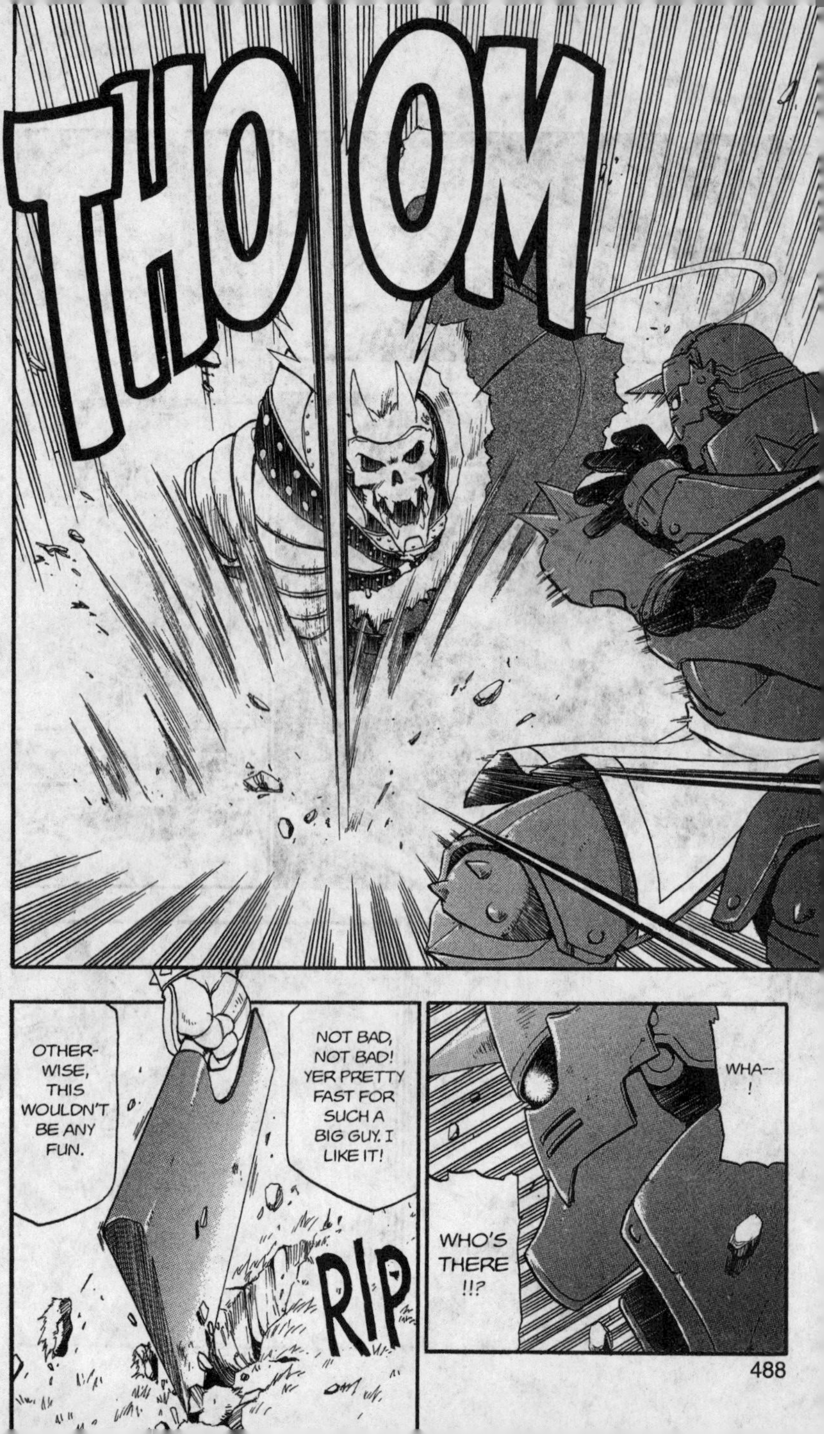
THOOM
WHA--!
WHO'S THERE!!?
NOT BAD, NOT BAD! YER PRETTY FAST FOR SUCH A BIG GUY. I LIKE IT!
OTHER-WISE, THIS WOULDN'T BE ANY FUN.
RIP

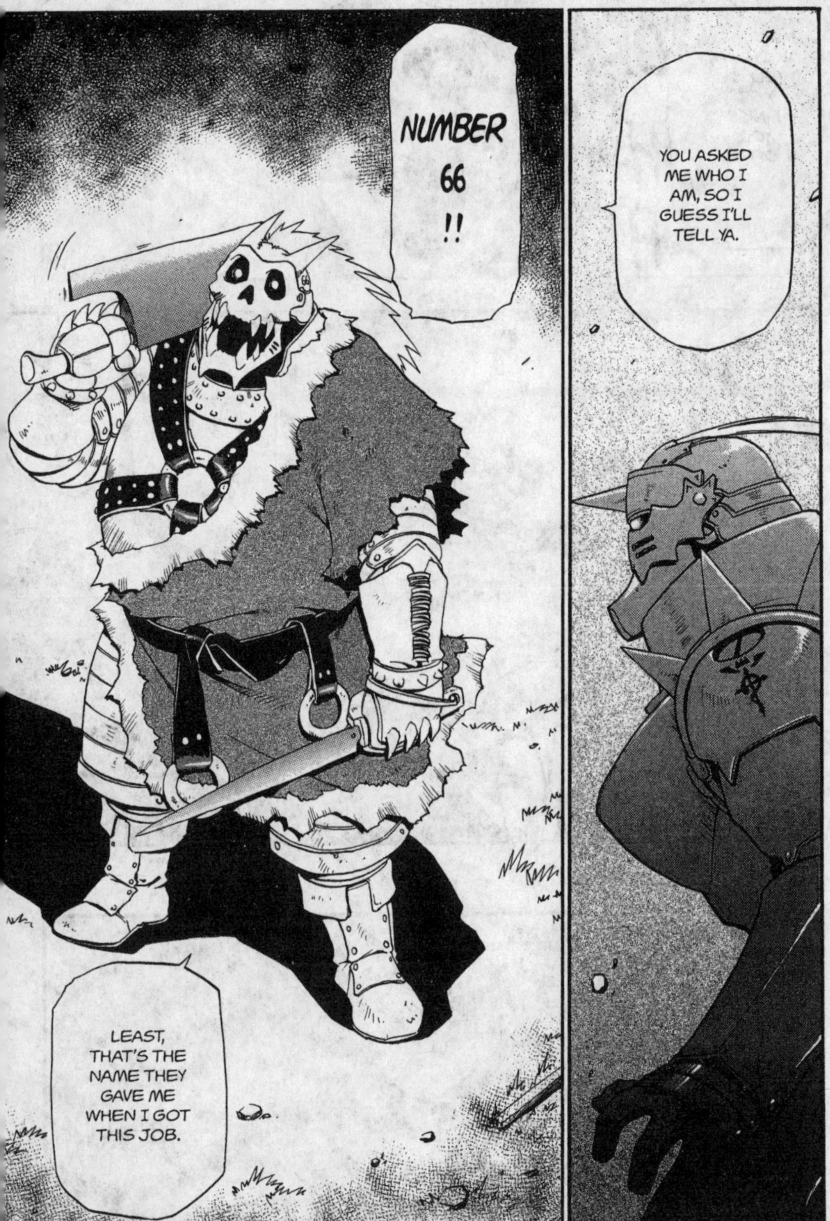
YOU ASKED ME WHO I AM, SO I GUESS I'LL TELL YA.
NUMBER 66 !!
LEAST, THAT'S THE NAME THEY GAVE ME WHEN I GOT THIS JOB.

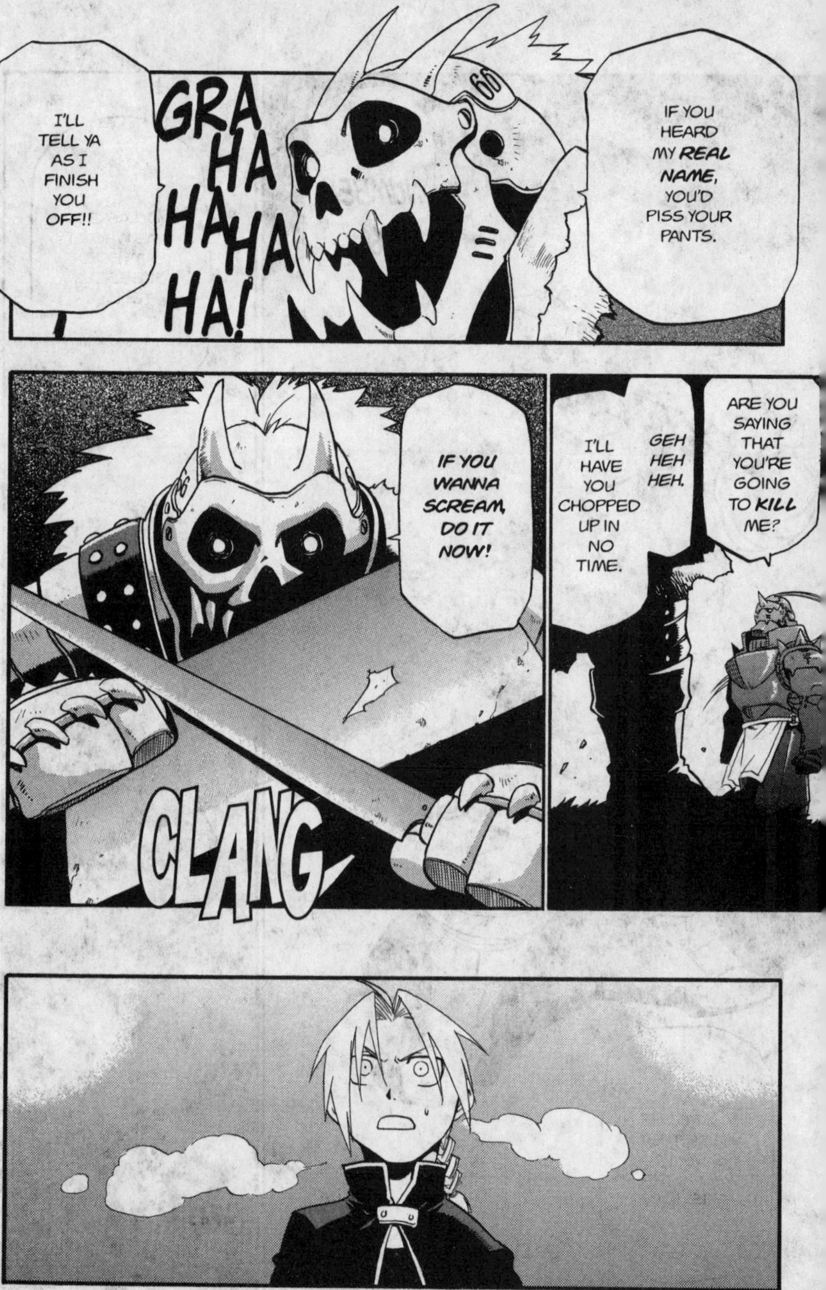
IF YOU HEARD MY **REAL NAME**, YOU'D PISS YOUR PANTS.
GRA HA HA HA HA HA!
I'LL TELL YA AS I FINISH YOU OFF!!
ARE YOU SAYING THAT YOU'RE GOING TO **KILL** ME?
GEH HEH HEH.
I'LL HAVE YOU CHOPPED UP IN NO TIME.
IF YOU WANNA SCREAM, DO IT NOW!
CLANG

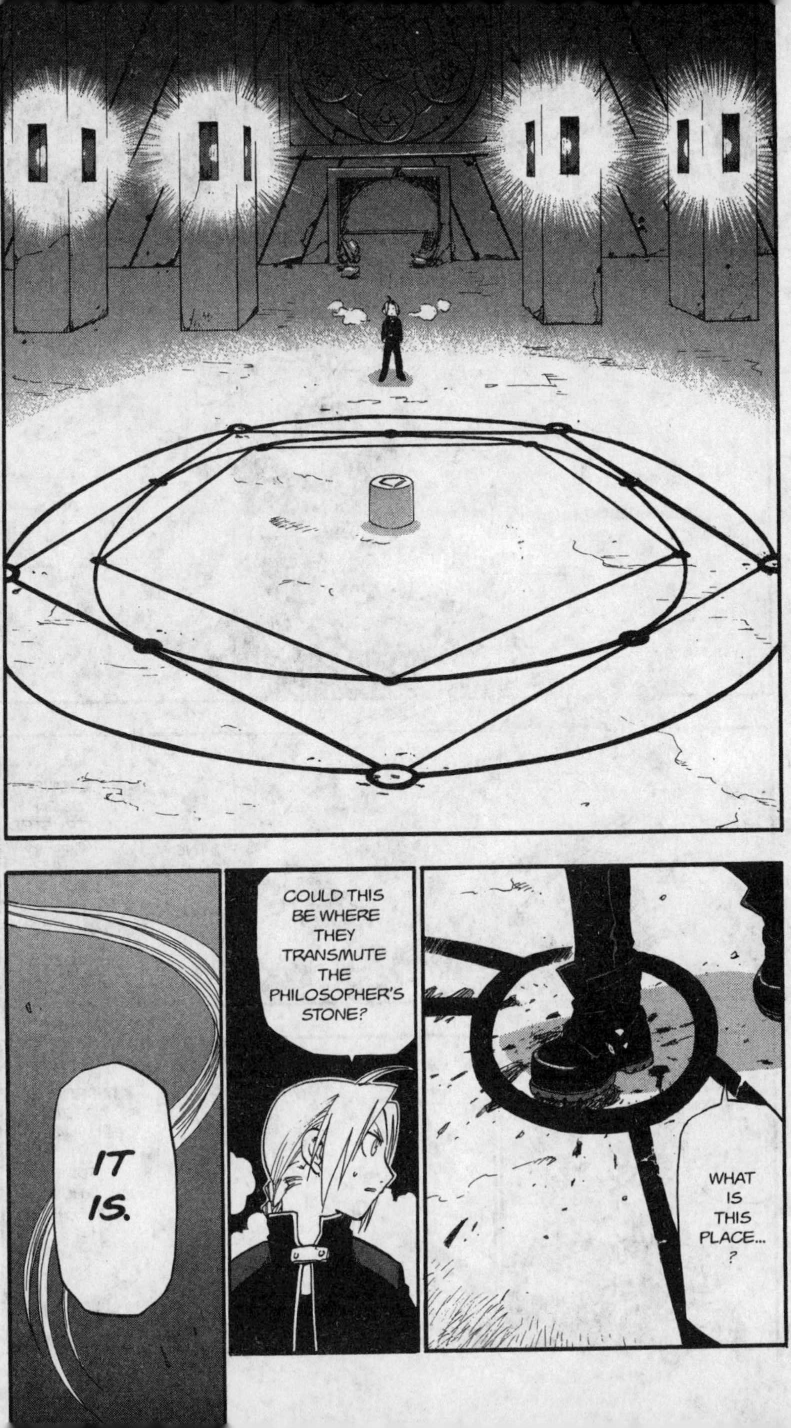
WHAT IS THIS PLACE...?
COULD THIS BE WHERE THEY TRANSMUTE THE PHILOSOPHER'S STONE?
IT IS.

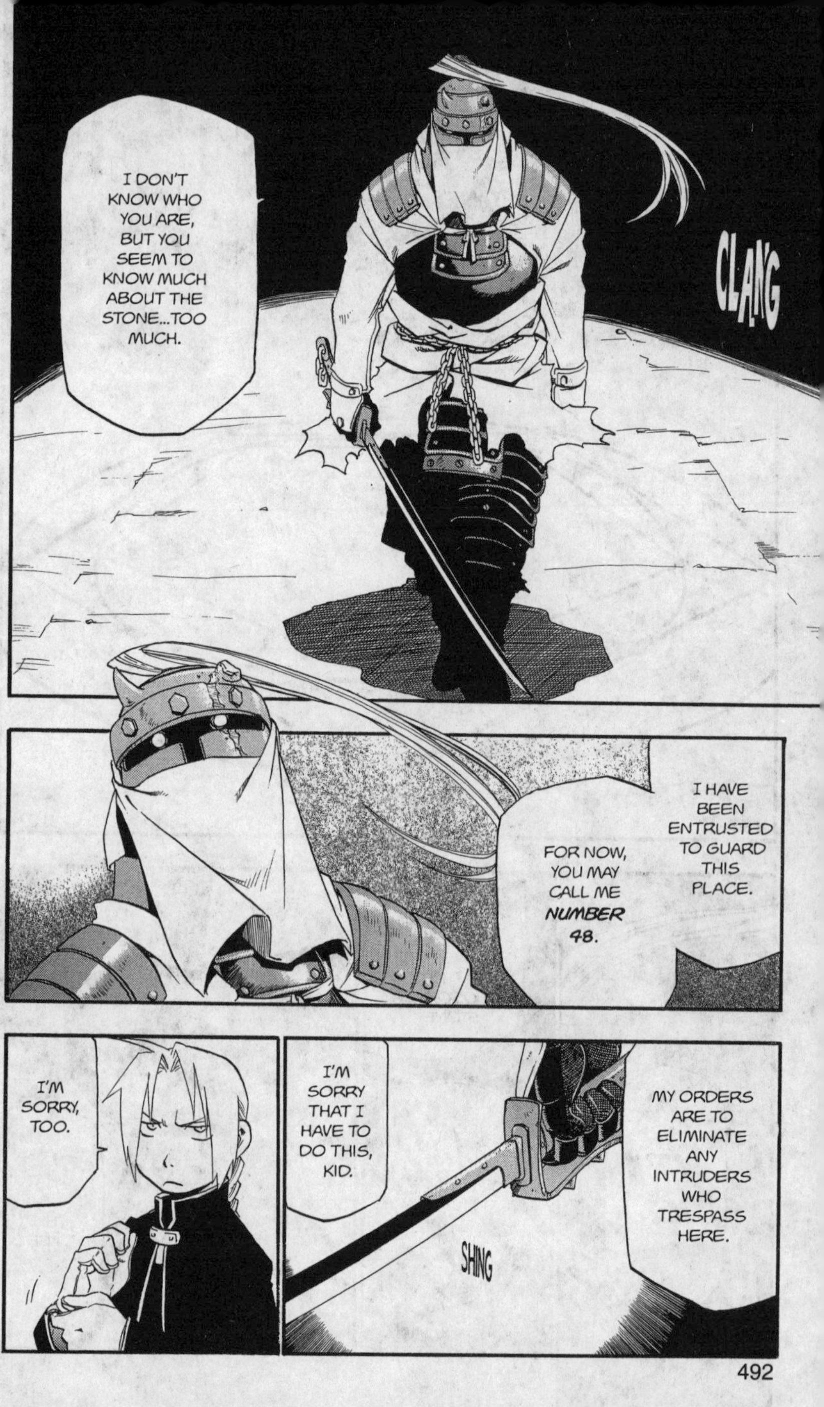
I DON'T KNOW WHO YOU ARE, BUT YOU SEEM TO KNOW MUCH ABOUT THE STONE...TOO MUCH.
CLANG
I HAVE BEEN ENTRUSTED TO GUARD THIS PLACE.
FOR NOW, YOU MAY CALL ME **NUMBER** 48.
MY ORDERS ARE TO ELIMINATE ANY INTRUDERS WHO TRESPASS HERE.
I'M SORRY THAT I HAVE TO DO THIS, KID.
SHING
I'M SORRY, TOO.

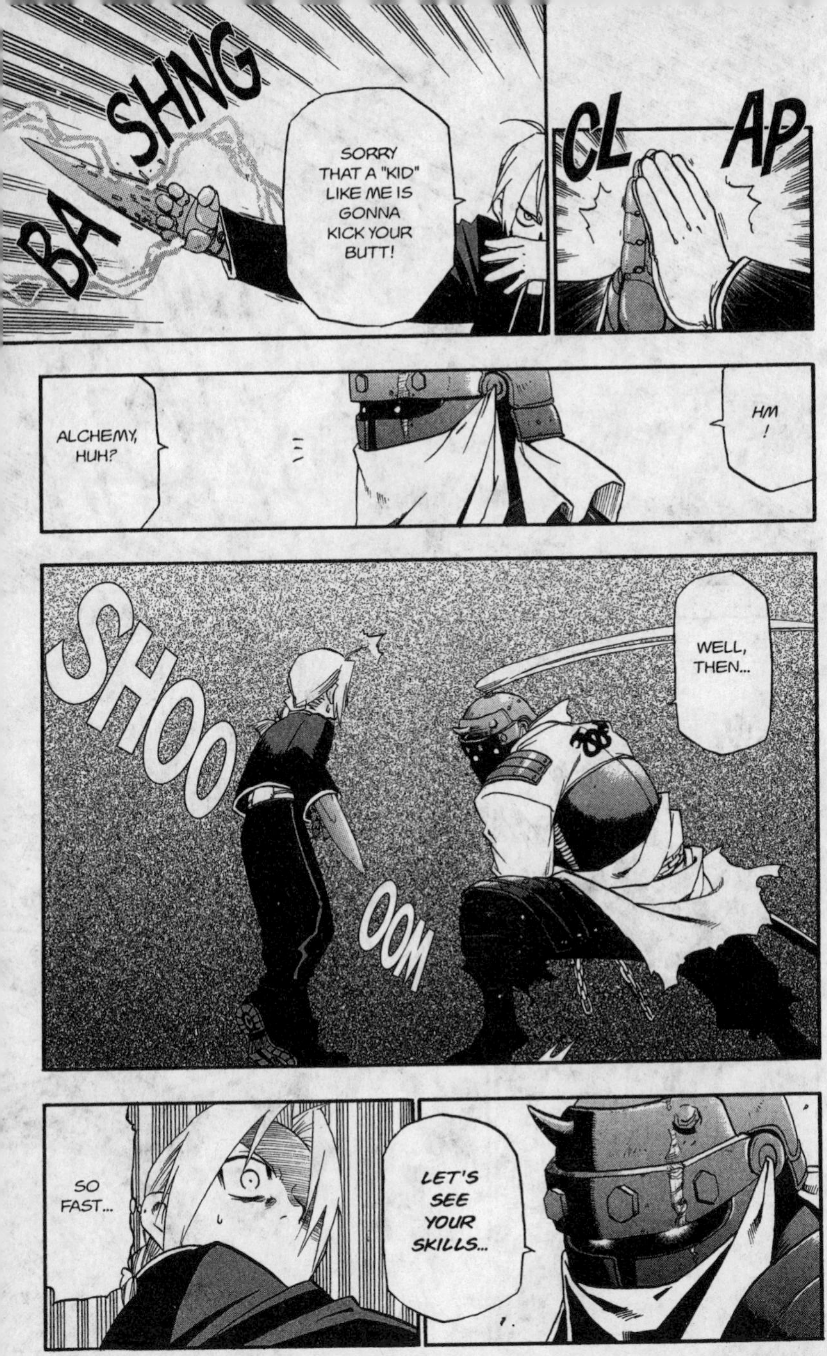
CL AP
BA SHNG
SORRY THAT A "KID" LIKE ME IS GONNA KICK YOUR BUTT!
HM!
ALCHEMY, HUH?
WELL, THEN...
SHOO
OOM
LET'S SEE YOUR SKILLS...
SO FAST...

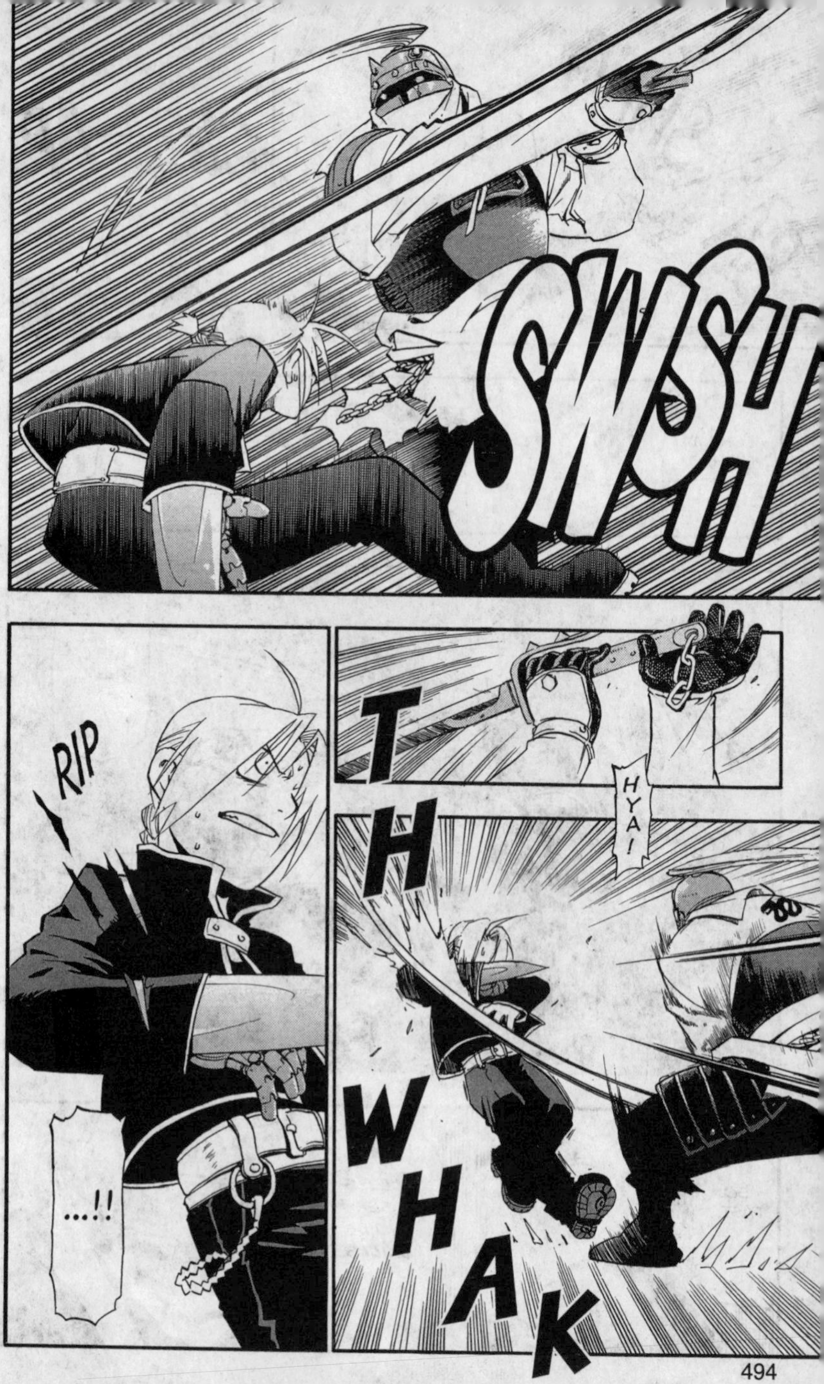
SWSH
THWHAK
HYA!
RIP
...!!

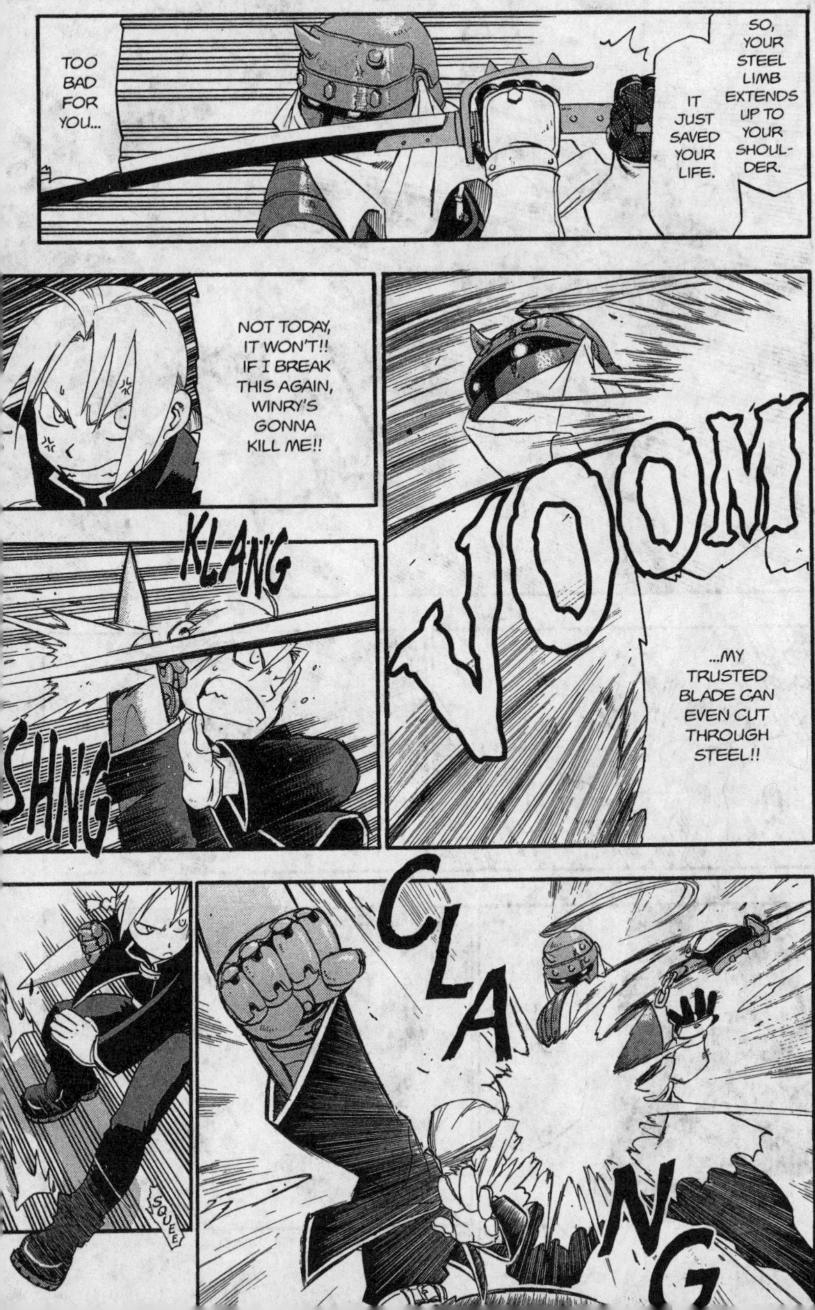
SO, YOUR STEEL LIMB EXTENDS UP TO YOUR SHOULDER.
IT JUST SAVED YOUR LIFE.
TOO BAD FOR YOU...
VOOM
...MY TRUSTED BLADE CAN EVEN CUT THROUGH STEEL!!
NOT TODAY, IT WON'T!! IF I BREAK THIS AGAIN, WINRY'S GONNA KILL ME!!
KLANG
SHNG
CLANG
SQUEE

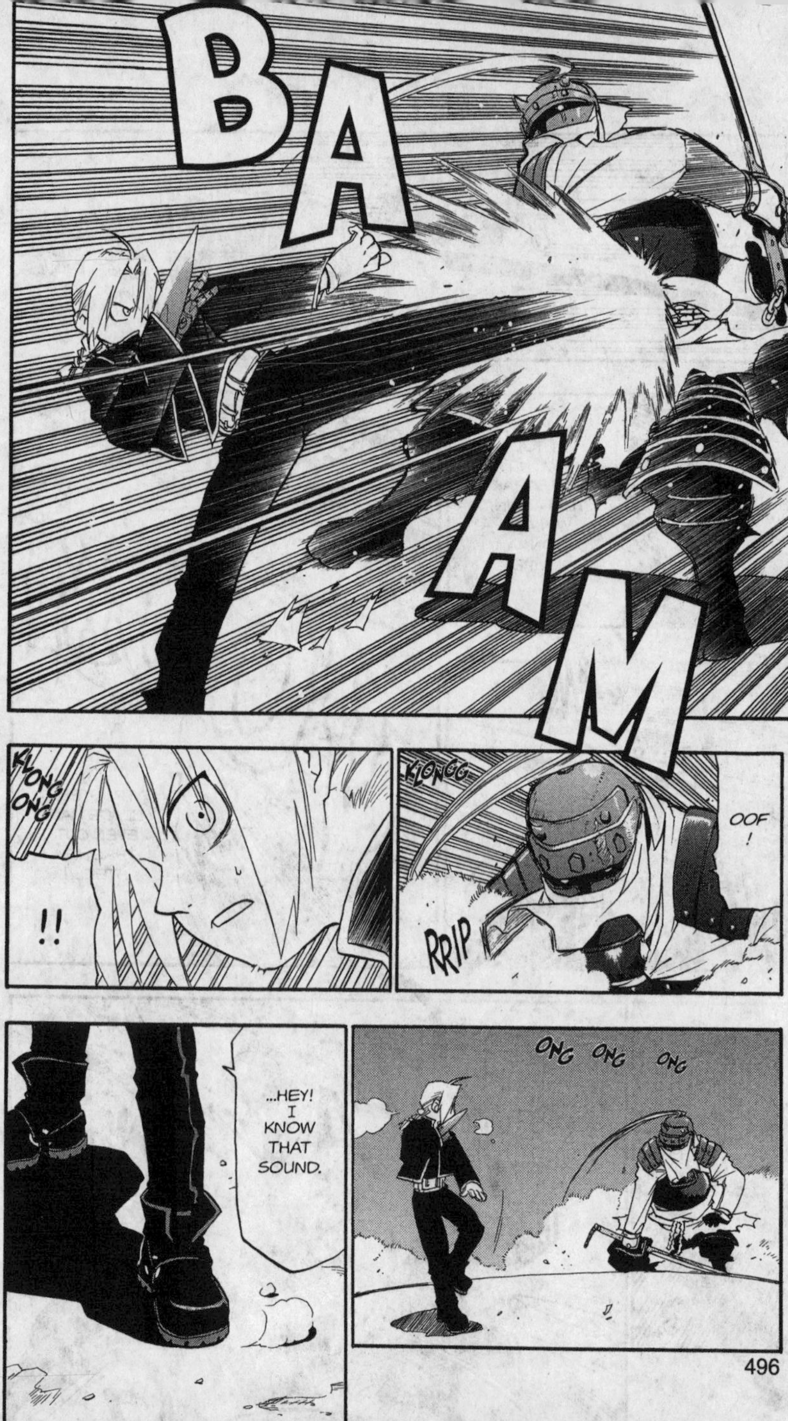
BA
AM
KLONGG
OOF!
RRIP
KLONG ONG ONG
!!
ONG ONG ONG
...HEY! I KNOW THAT SOUND.

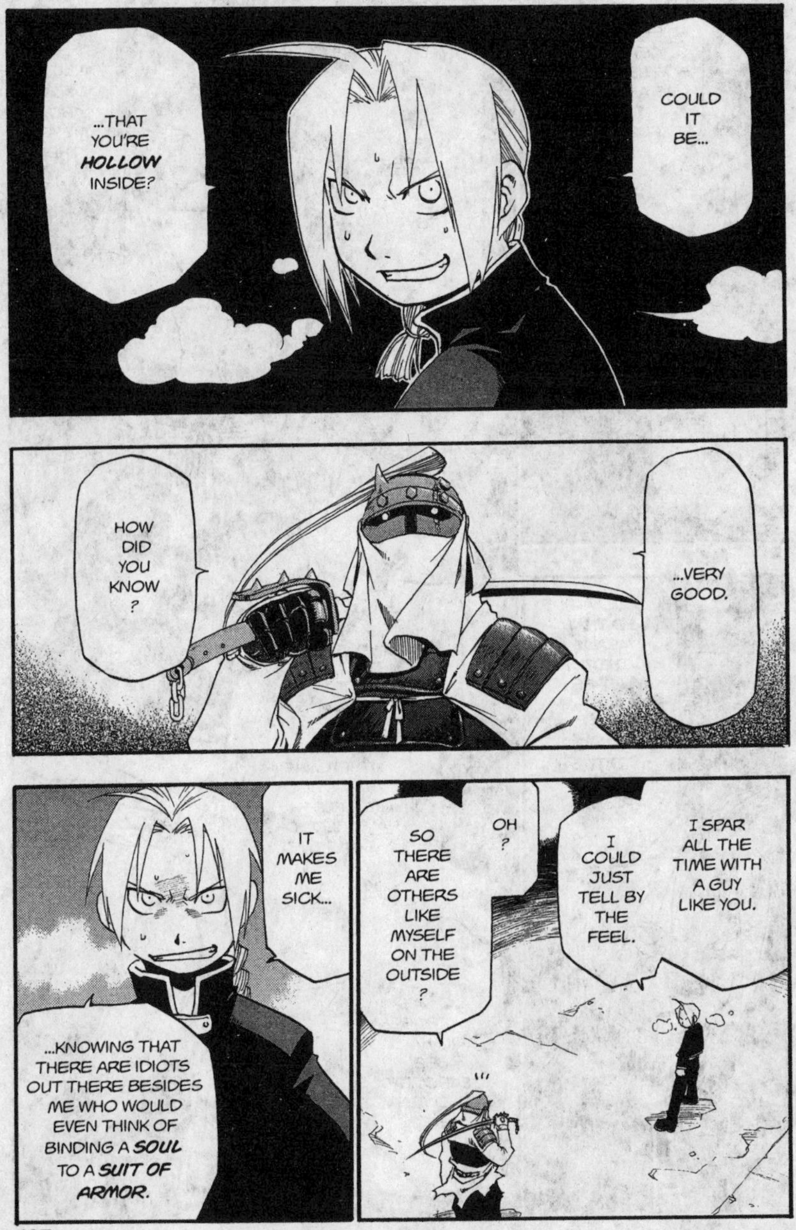
COULD IT BE...
...THAT YOU'RE HOLLOW INSIDE?
...VERY GOOD.
HOW DID YOU KNOW?
I SPAR ALL THE TIME WITH A GUY LIKE YOU.
I COULD JUST TELL BY THE FEEL.
OH?
SO THERE ARE OTHERS LIKE MYSELF ON THE OUTSIDE?
IT MAKES ME SICK...
...KNOWING THAT THERE ARE IDIOTS OUT THERE BESIDES ME WHO WOULD EVEN THINK OF BINDING A SOUL TO A SUIT OF ARMOR.

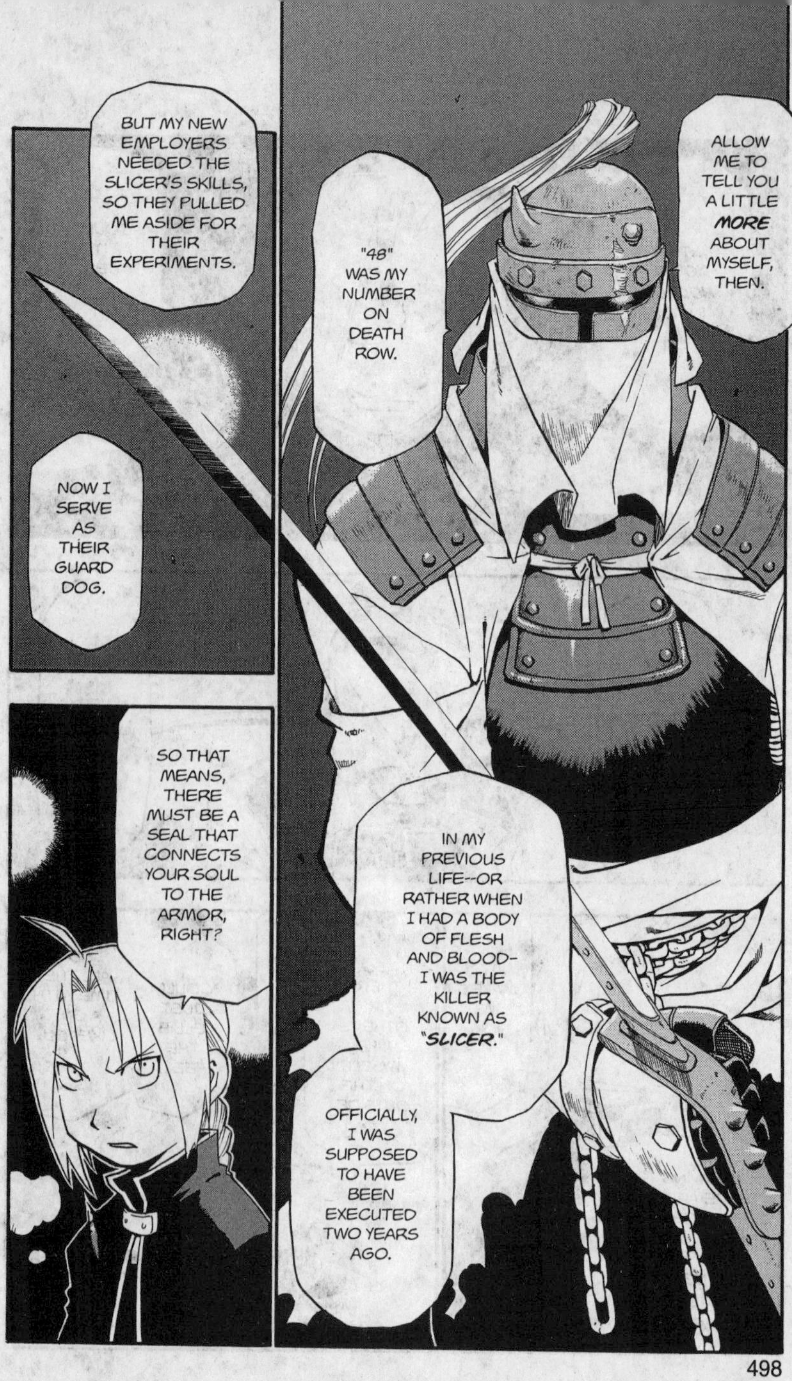
ALLOW ME TO TELL YOU A LITTLE MORE ABOUT MYSELF, THEN.
"48" WAS MY NUMBER ON DEATH ROW.
IN MY PREVIOUS LIFE--OR RATHER WHEN I HAD A BODY OF FLESH AND BLOOD-I WAS THE KILLER KNOWN AS "SLICER."
OFFICIALLY, I WAS SUPPOSED TO HAVE BEEN EXECUTED TWO YEARS AGO.
BUT MY NEW EMPLOYERS NEEDED THE SLICER'S SKILLS, SO THEY PULLED ME ASIDE FOR THEIR EXPERIMENTS.
NOW I SERVE AS THEIR GUARD DOG.
SO THAT MEANS, THERE MUST BE A SEAL THAT CONNECTS YOUR SOUL TO THE ARMOR, RIGHT?

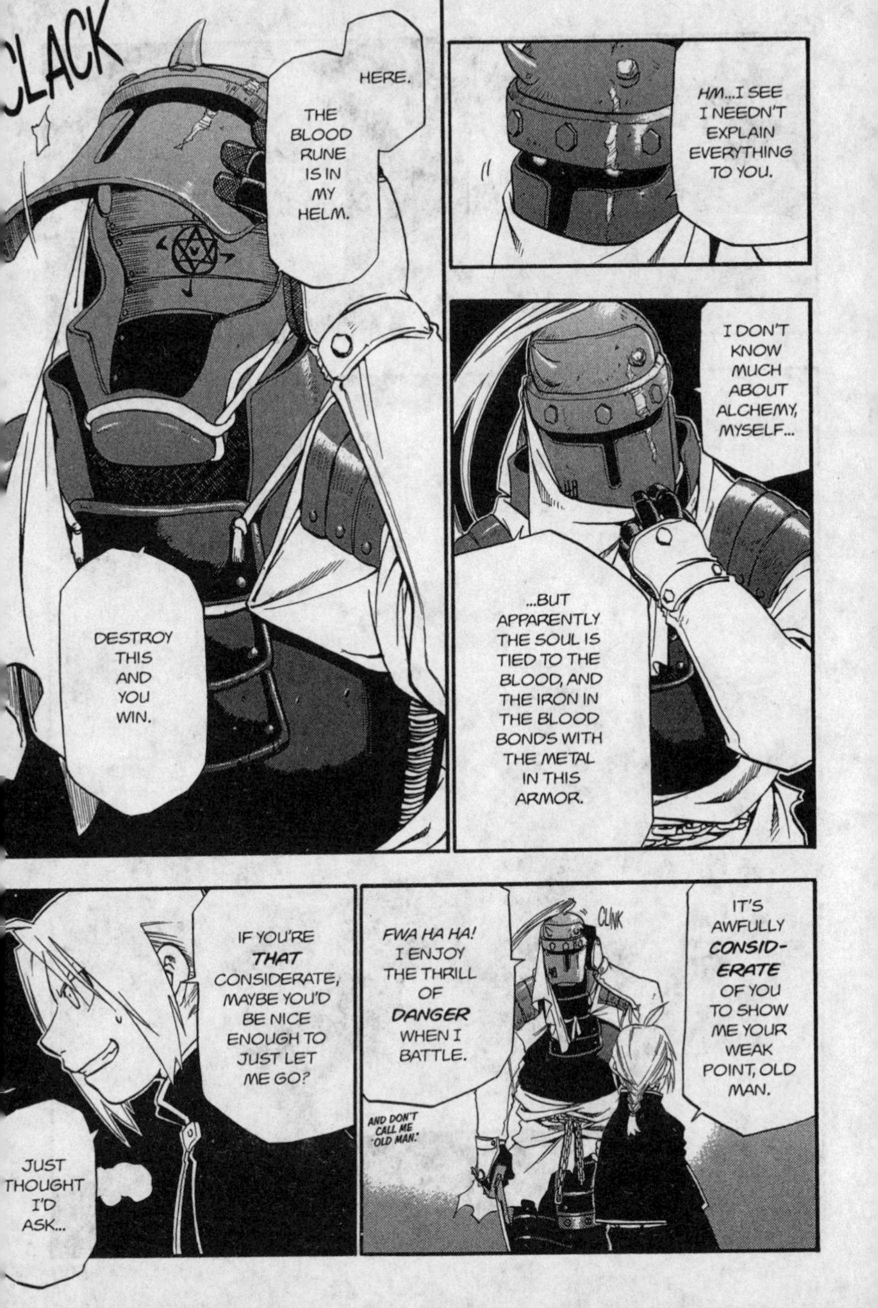
HM...I SEE I NEEDN'T EXPLAIN EVERYTHING TO YOU.
I DON'T KNOW MUCH ABOUT ALCHEMY, MYSELF...
...BUT APPARENTLY THE SOUL IS TIED TO THE BLOOD, AND THE IRON IN THE BLOOD BONDS WITH THE METAL IN THIS ARMOR.
CLACK
HERE.
THE BLOOD RUNE IS IN MY HELM.
DESTROY THIS AND YOU WIN.
IT'S AWFULLY CONSIDERATE OF YOU TO SHOW ME YOUR WEAK POINT, OLD MAN.
CLINK
FWA HA HA! I ENJOY THE THRILL OF DANGER WHEN I BATTLE.
AND DON'T CALL ME "OLD MAN."
IF YOU'RE THAT CONSIDERATE, MAYBE YOU'D BE NICE ENOUGH TO JUST LET ME GO?
JUST THOUGHT I'D ASK...

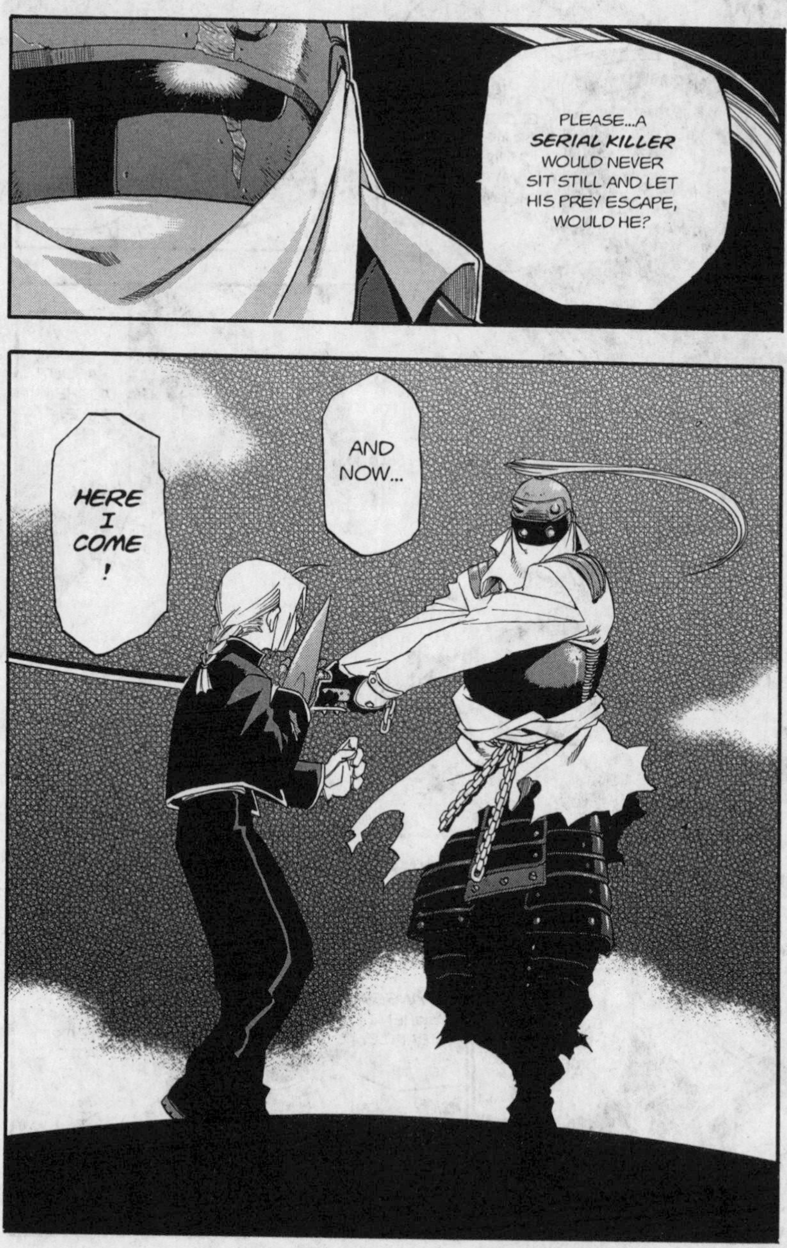
PLEASE...A SERIAL KILLER WOULD NEVER SIT STILL AND LET HIS PREY ESCAPE, WOULD HE?
AND NOW...
HERE I COME!

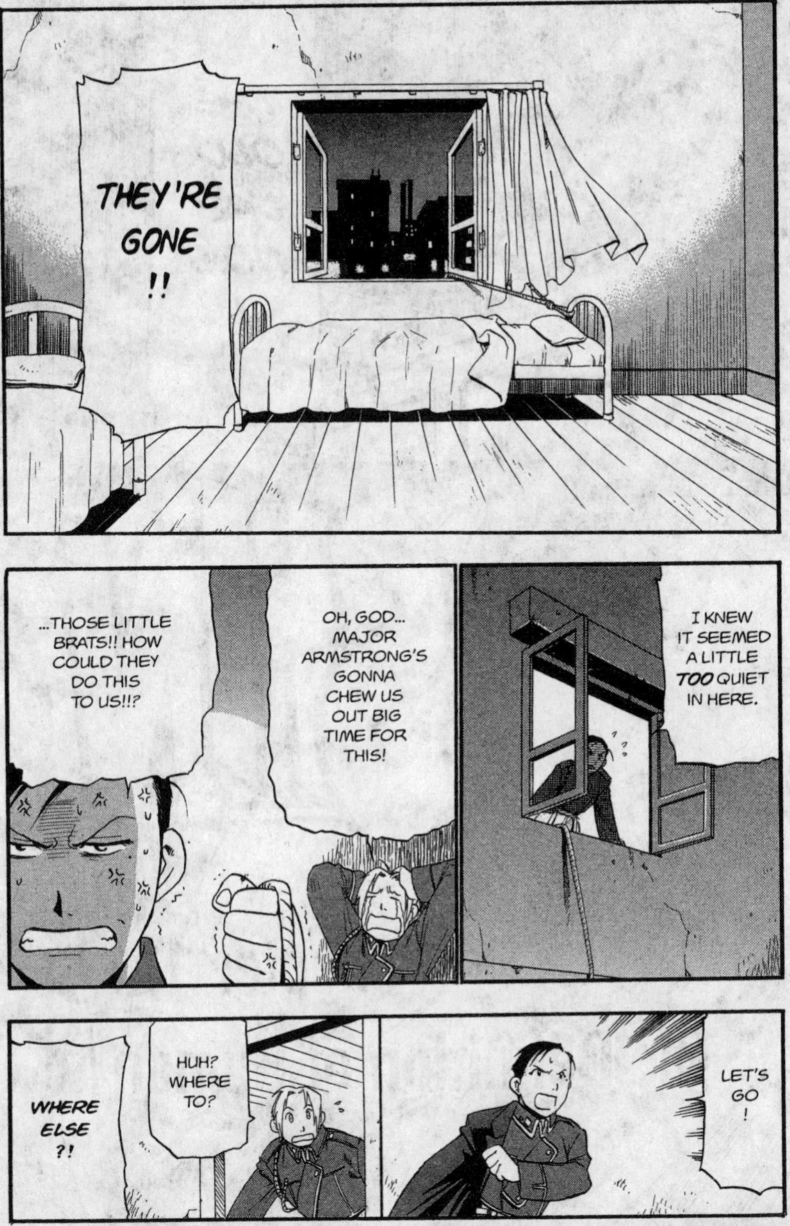
THEY'RE GONE !!
I KNEW IT SEEMED A LITTLE TOO QUIET IN HERE.
OH, GOD... MAJOR ARMSTRONG'S GONNA CHEW US OUT BIG TIME FOR THIS!
...THOSE LITTLE BRATS!! HOW COULD THEY DO THIS TO US!!?
LET'S GO!
HUH? WHERE TO?
WHERE ELSE?!

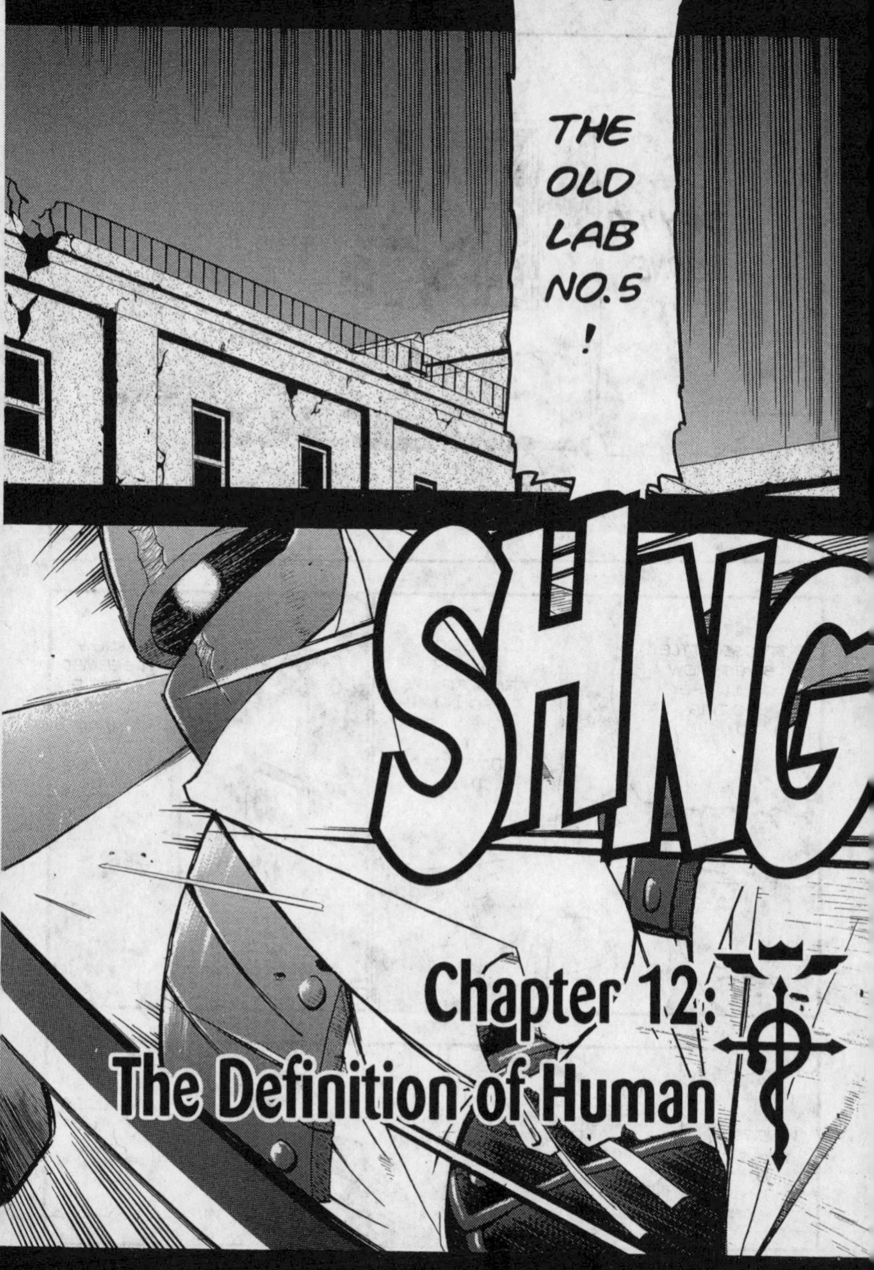
THE OLD LAB NO.5 !
SHNG
Chapter 12:
The Definition of Human

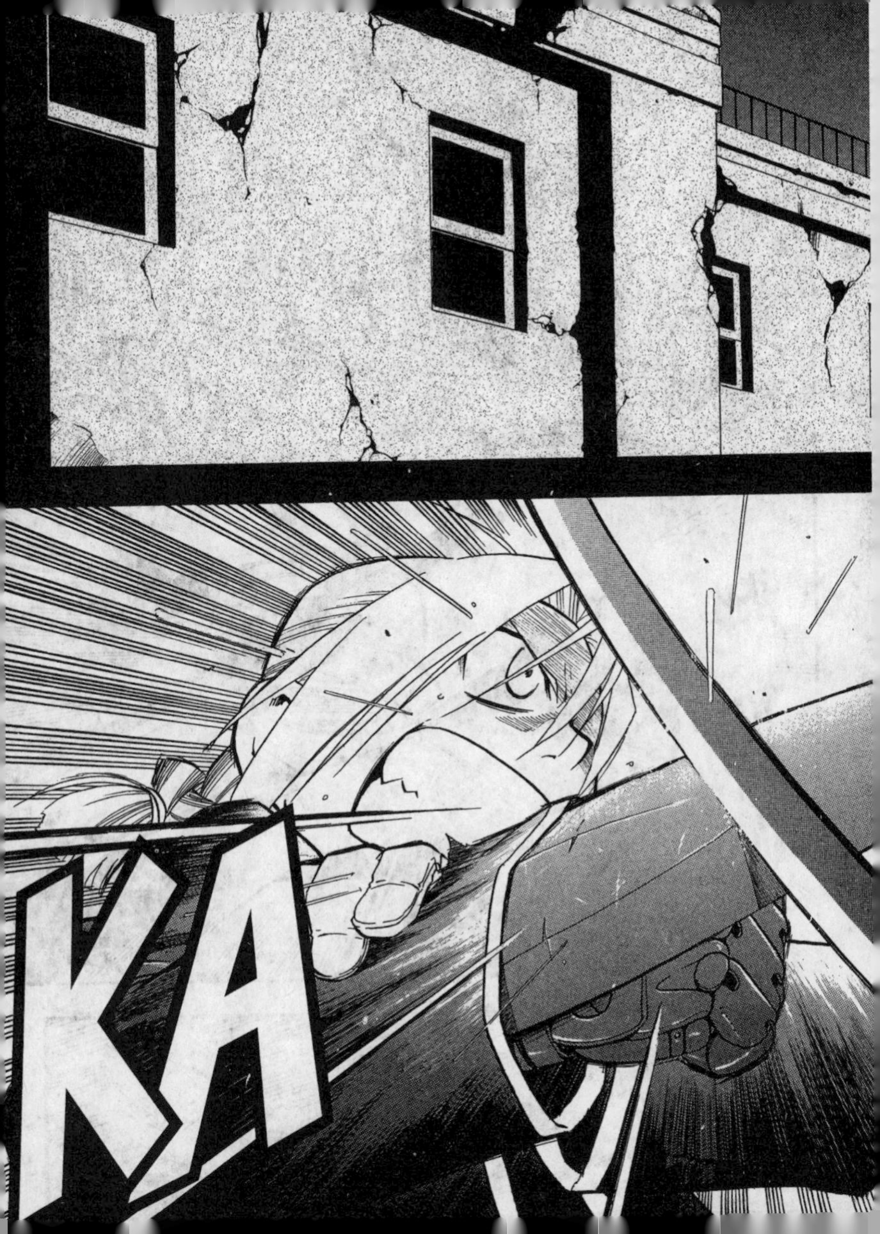
KA

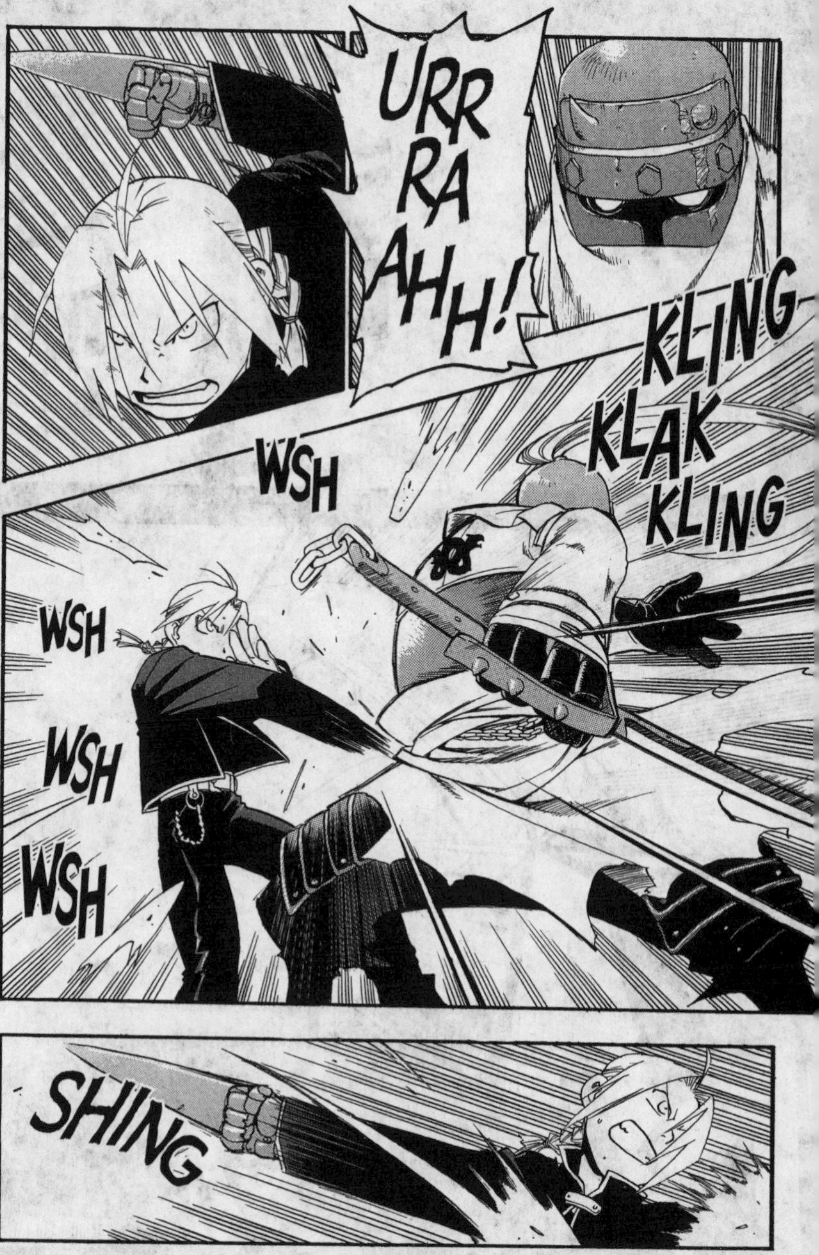
URRRAAHH!
KLING
KLAK
KLING
WSH
WSH
WSH
WSH
SHING

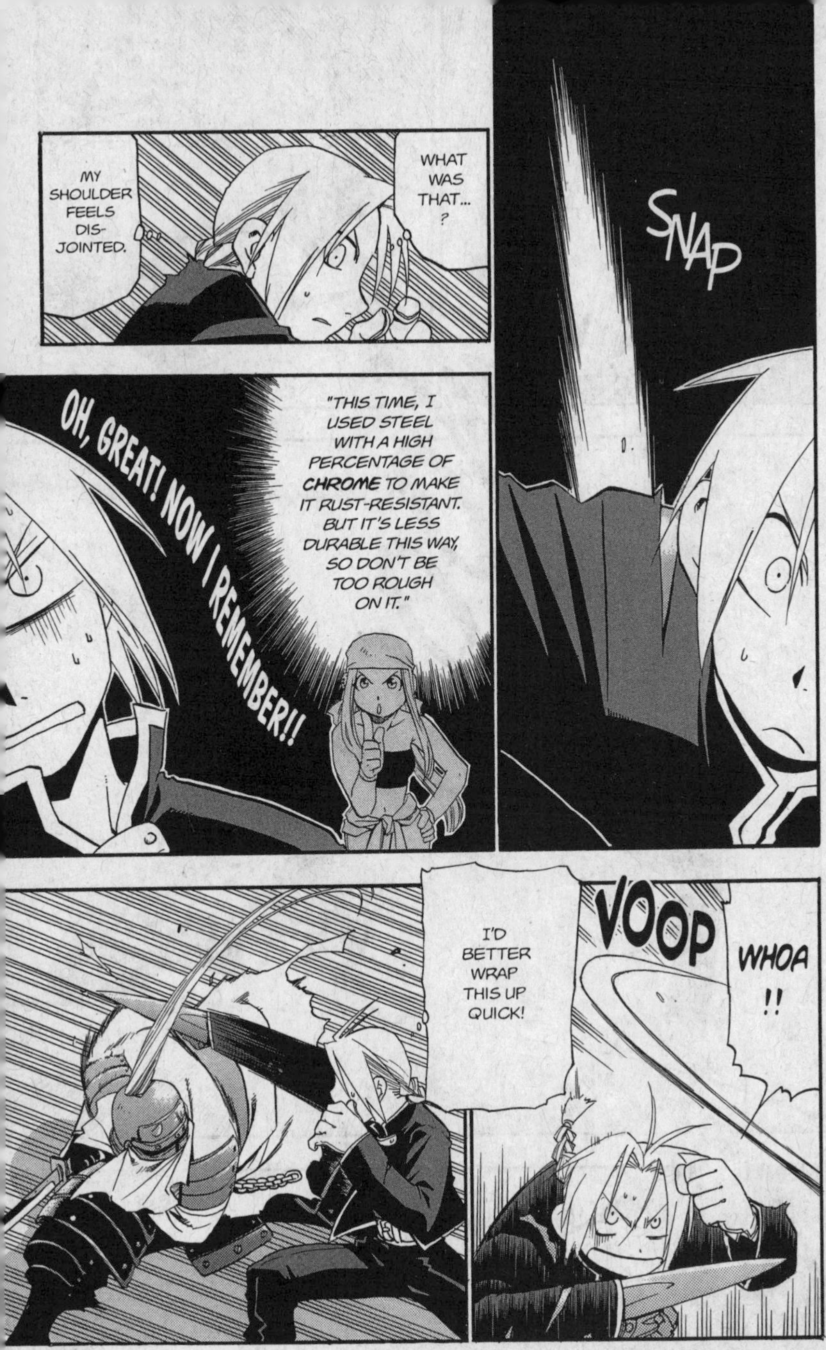
SNAP
WHAT WAS THAT... ?
MY SHOULDER FEELS DIS-JOINTED.
"THIS TIME, I USED STEEL WITH A HIGH PERCENTAGE OF CHROME TO MAKE IT RUST-RESISTANT. BUT IT'S LESS DURABLE THIS WAY, SO DON'T BE TOO ROUGH ON IT."
OH, GREAT! NOW I REMEMBER!!
VOOP
WHOA !!
I'D BETTER WRAP THIS UP QUICK!

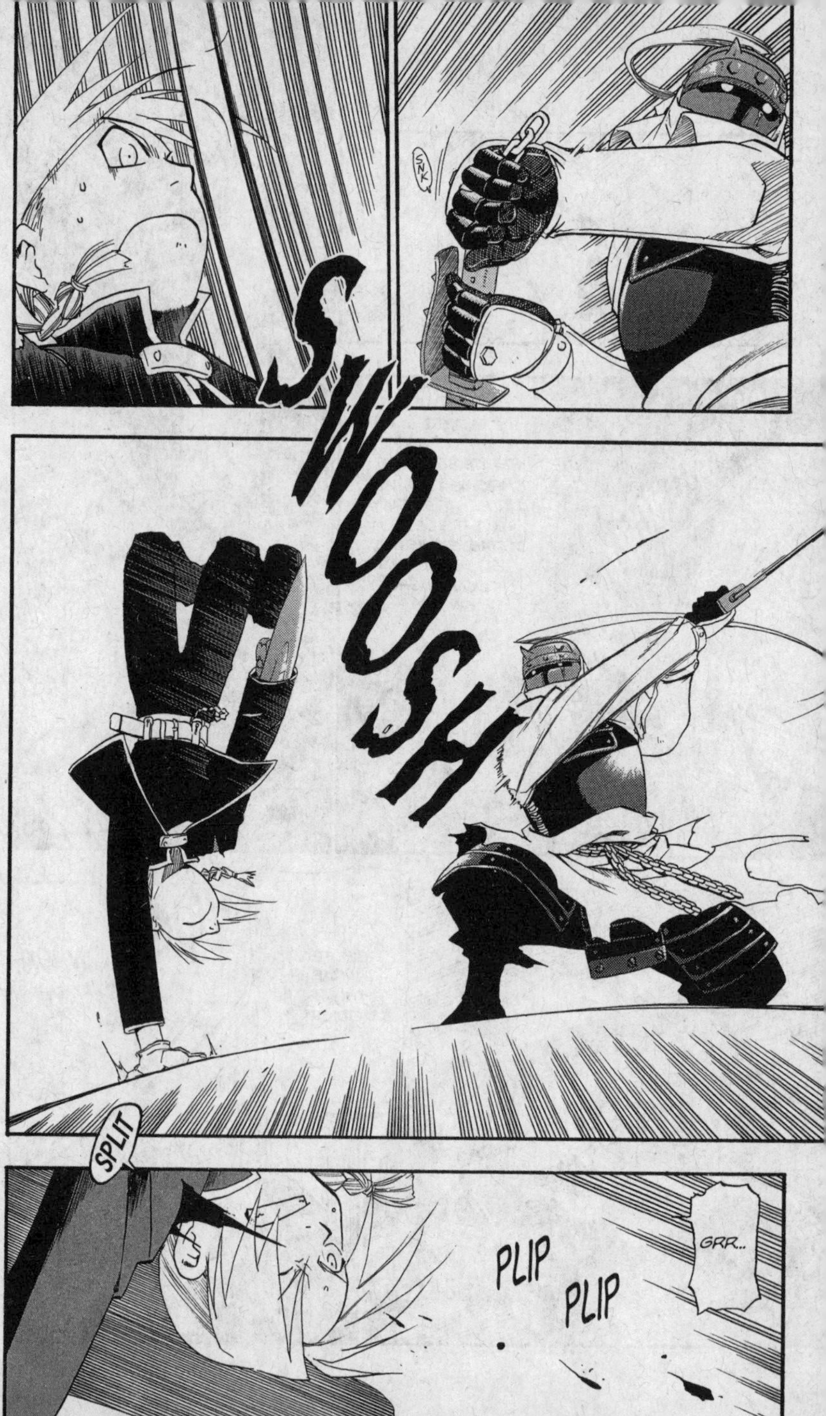
SNK
SWOOSH
GRR...
PLIP
PLIP
SPLIT

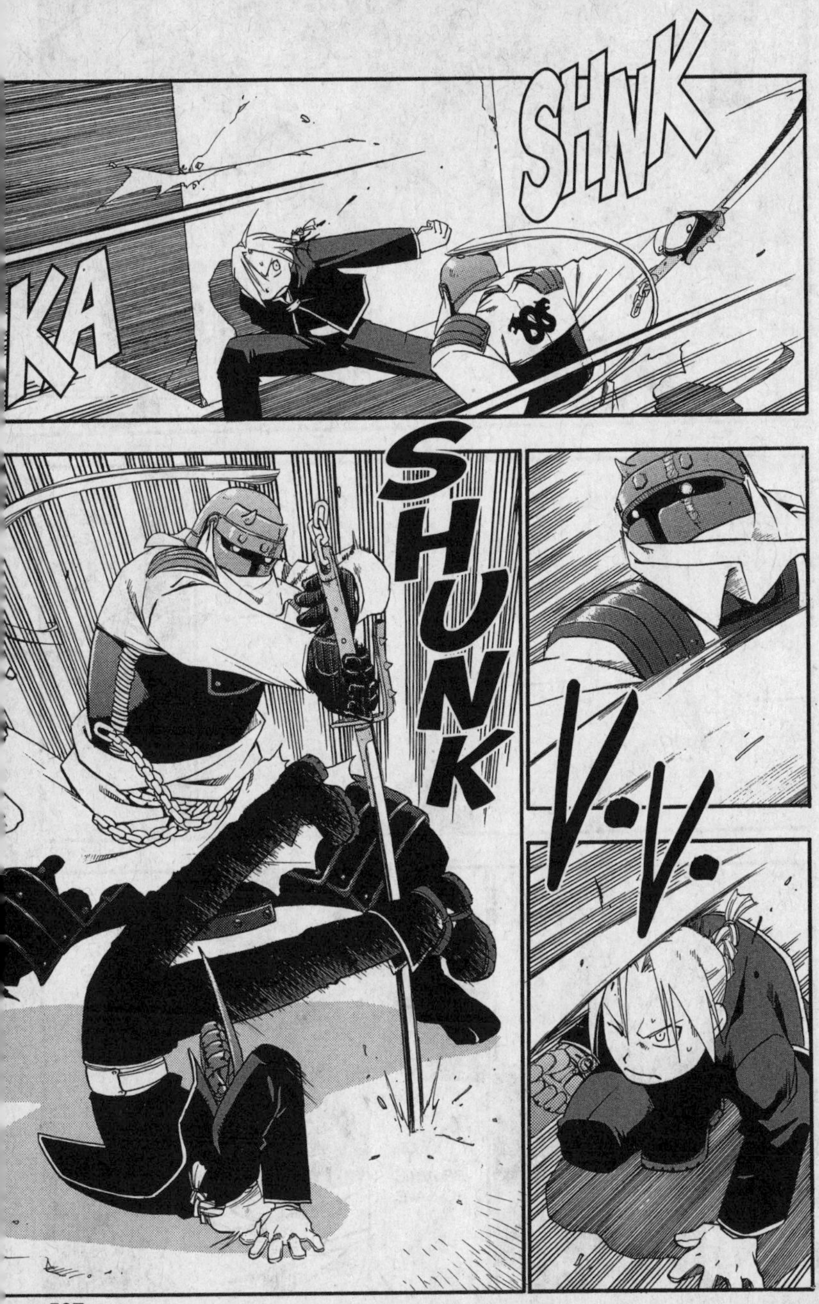
SHNK
KA
V·V·
SHUNK

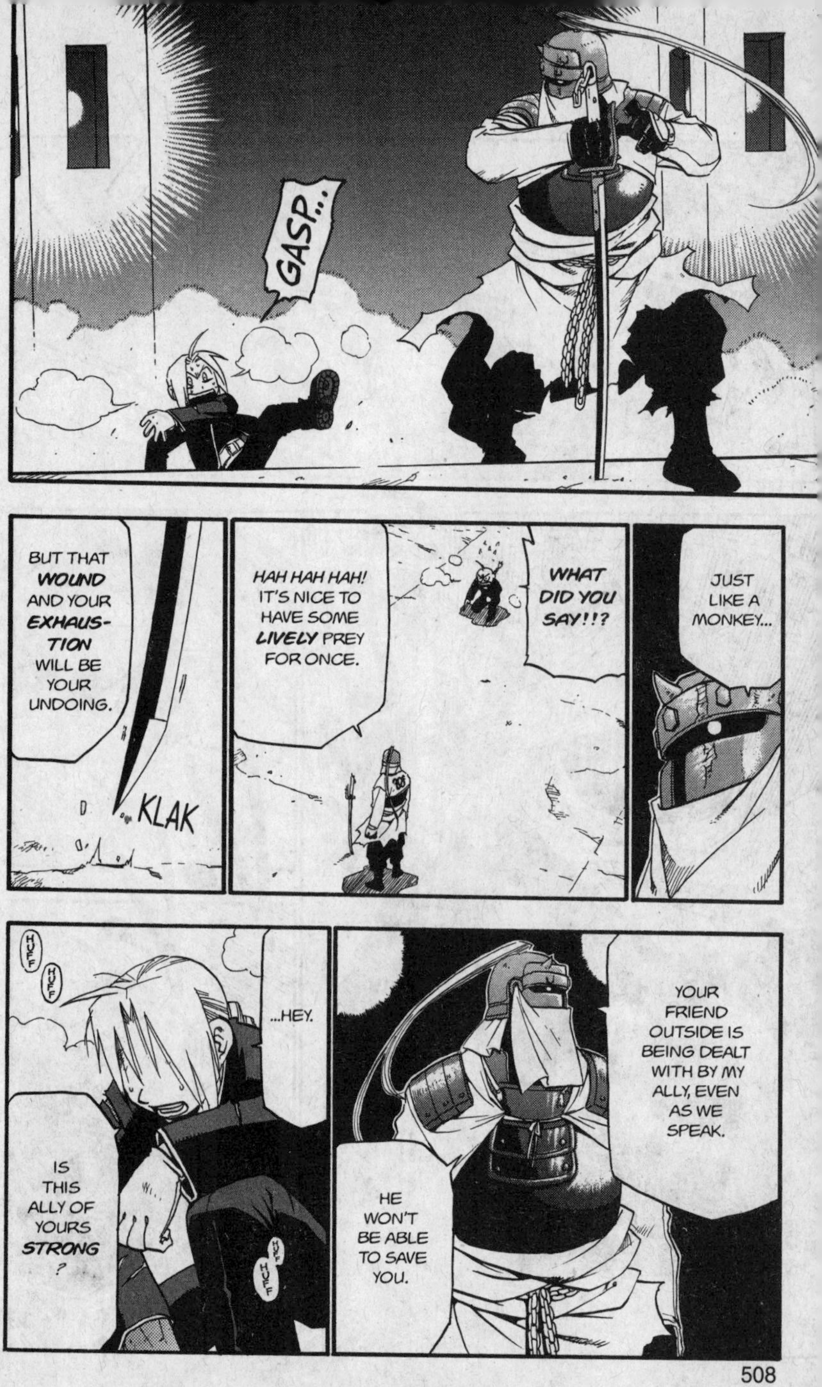
GASP...
JUST LIKE A MONKEY...
WHAT DID YOU SAY!!?
HAH HAH HAH! IT'S NICE TO HAVE SOME LIVELY PREY FOR ONCE.
BUT THAT WOUND AND YOUR EXHAUSTION WILL BE YOUR UNDOING.
KLAK
YOUR FRIEND OUTSIDE IS BEING DEALT WITH BY MY ALLY, EVEN AS WE SPEAK.
HE WON'T BE ABLE TO SAVE YOU.
HUFF
HUFF
...HEY.
IS THIS ALLY OF YOURS STRONG?
HUFF
HUFF

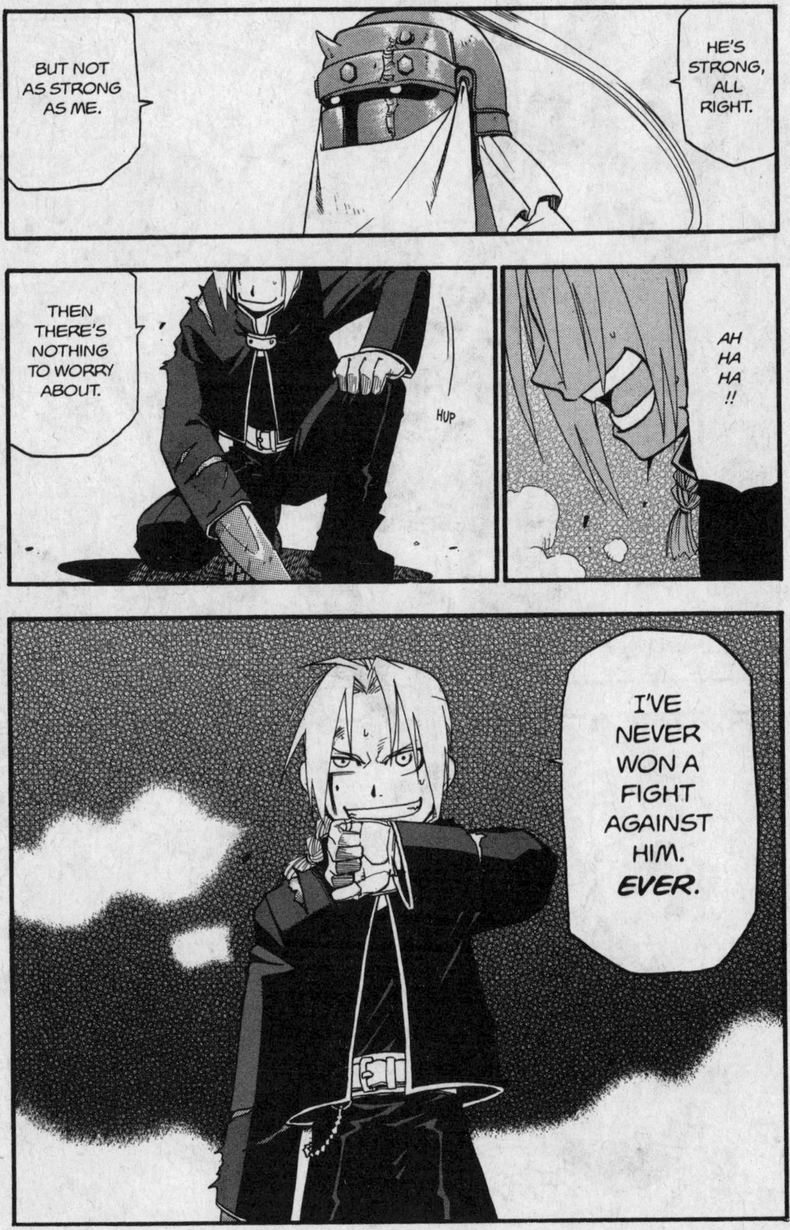
HE'S STRONG, ALL RIGHT.
BUT NOT AS STRONG AS ME.
AH HA HA!!
THEN THERE'S NOTHING TO WORRY ABOUT.
HUP
I'VE NEVER WON A FIGHT AGAINST HIM. *EVER.*

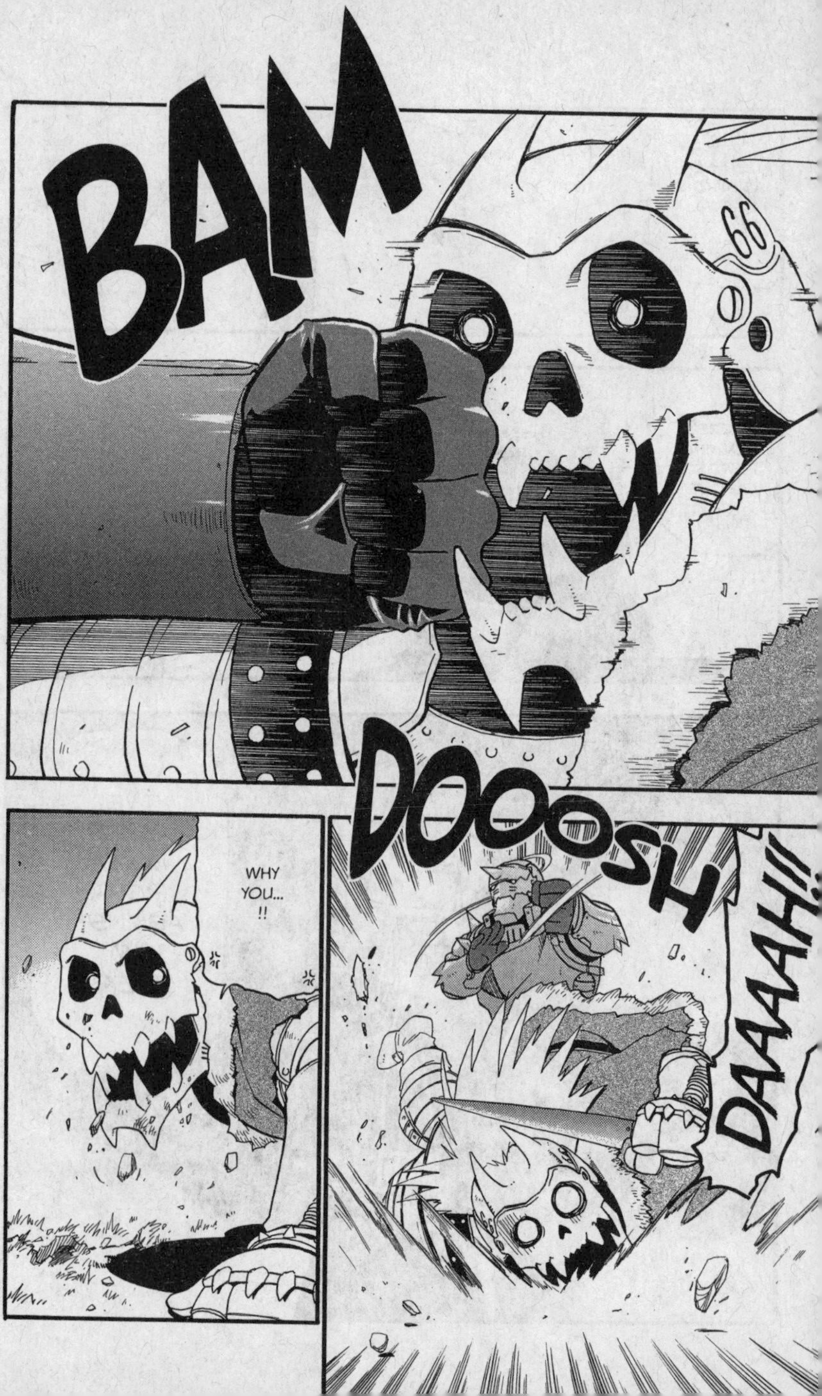
BAM
DOOOSH
DAAAH!!
WHY YOU... !!

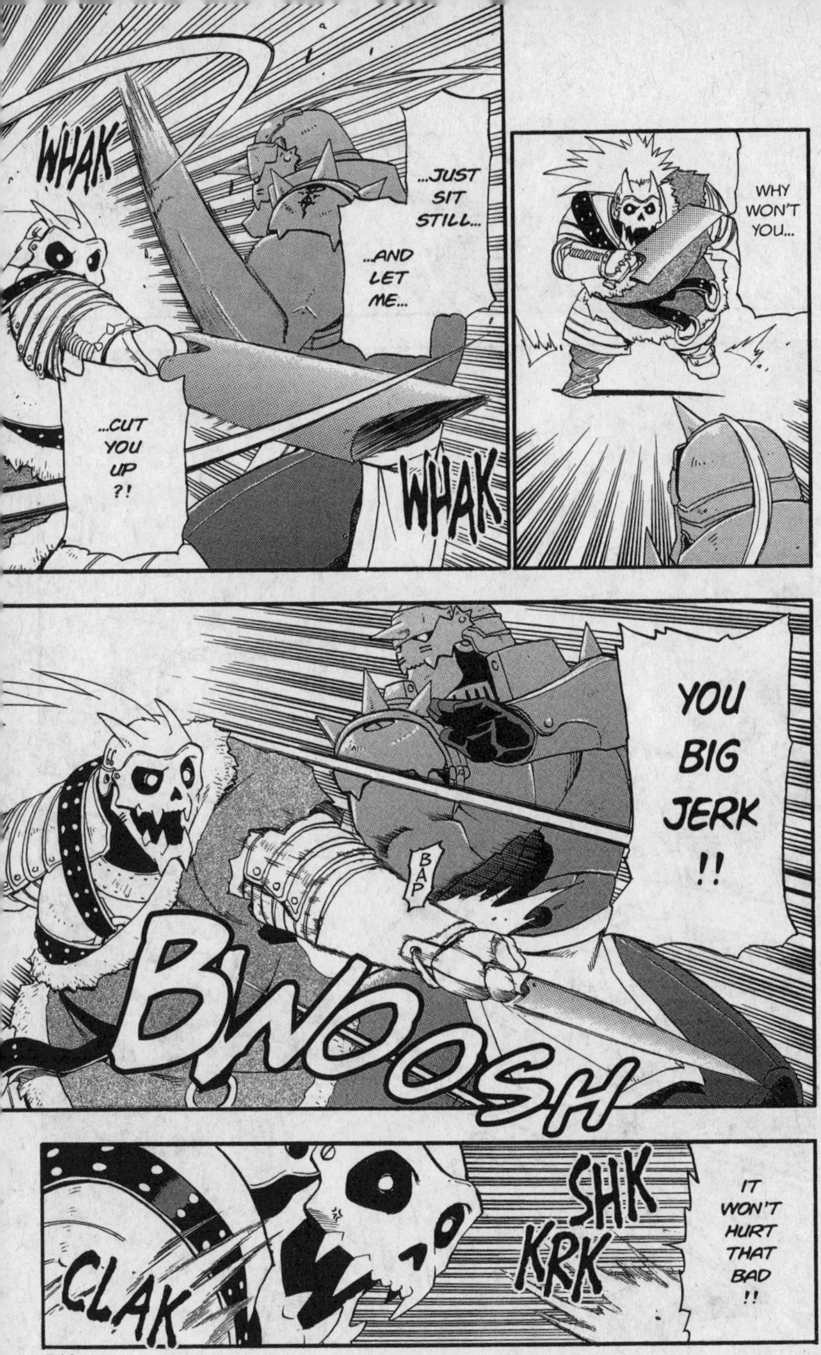
WHY WON'T YOU...
WHAK
...JUST SIT STILL...
...AND LET ME...
...CUT YOU UP ?!
WHAK
YOU BIG JERK !!
BAP
BWOOSH
IT WON'T HURT THAT BAD !!
SHK
KRK
CLAK

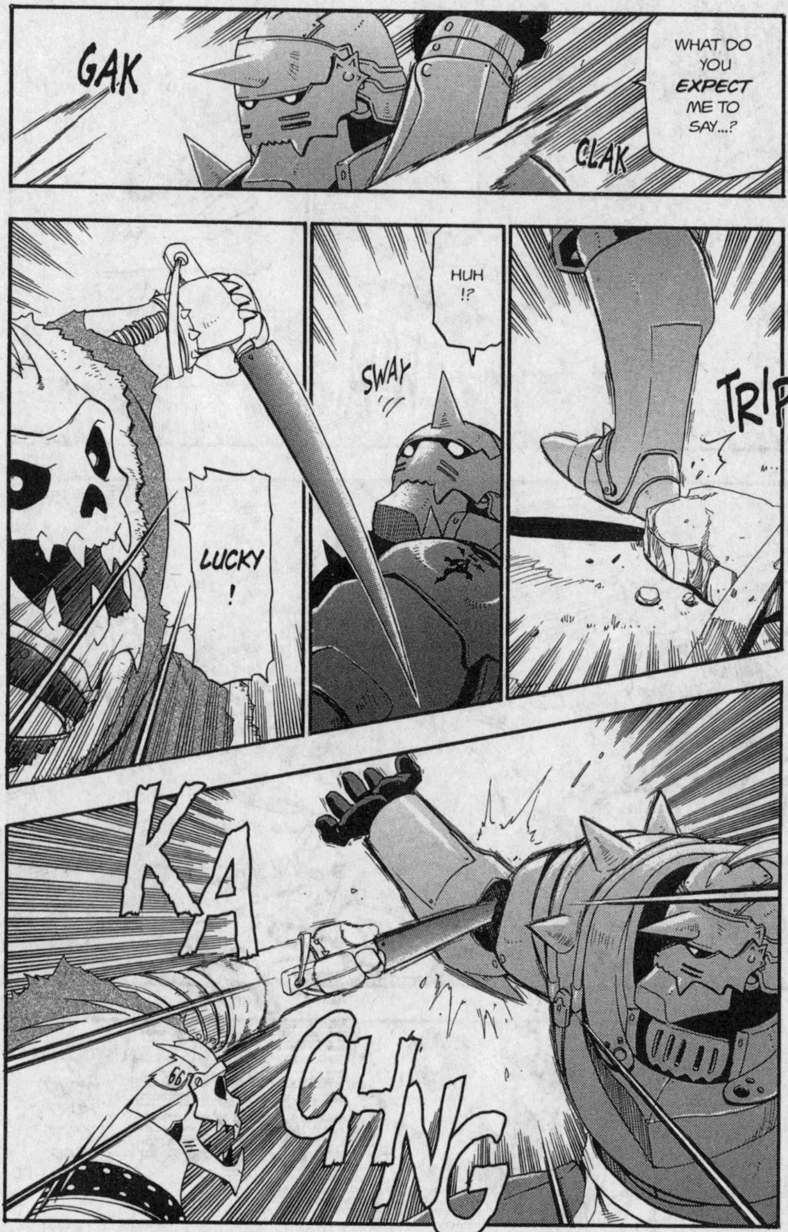
WHAT DO YOU EXPECT ME TO SAY...?
GAK
CLAK
TRIP
HUH !?
SWAY
LUCKY !
KA
CHING

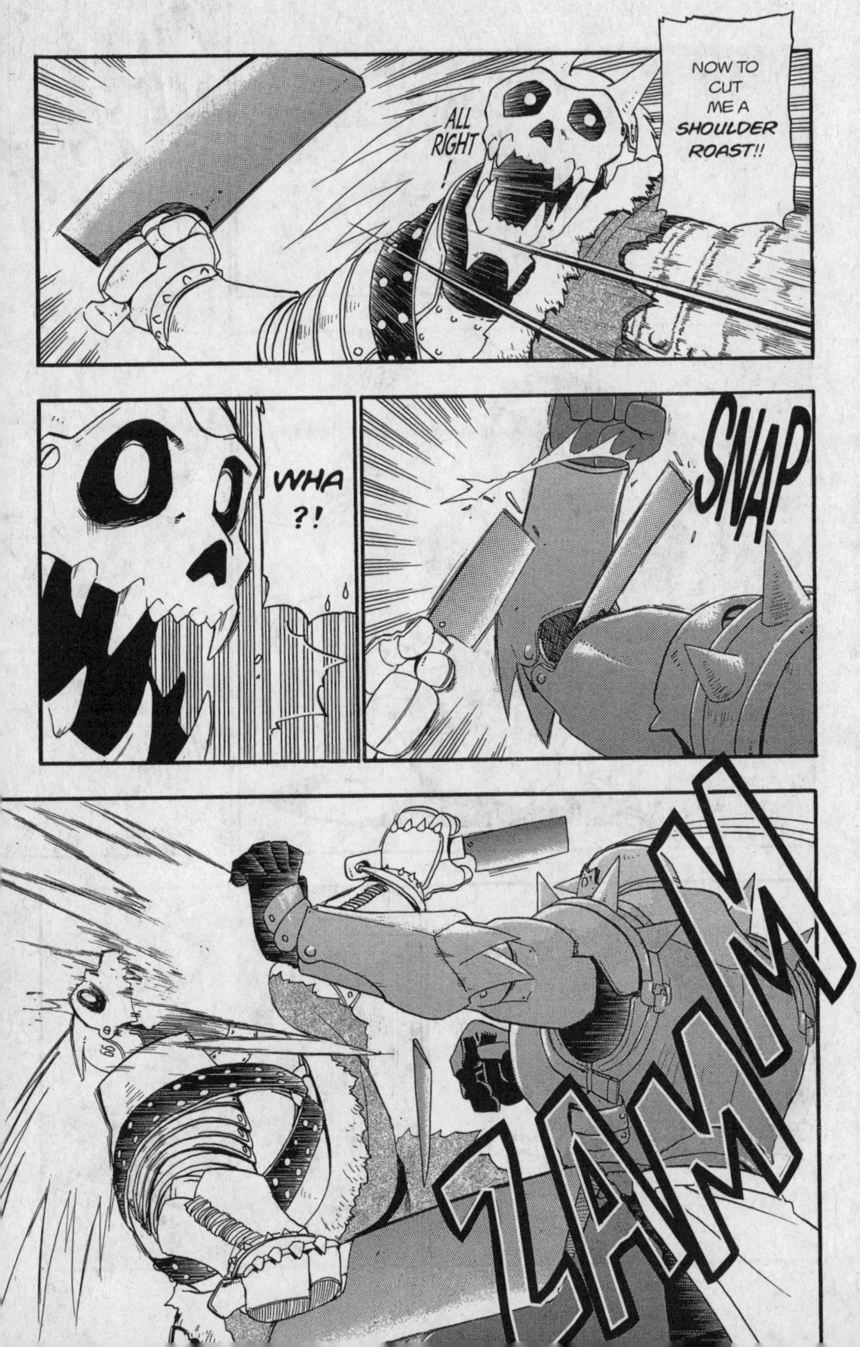
NOW TO CUT ME A **SHOULDER ROAST!!**
ALL RIGHT!
SNAP
WHA?!
ZAMM

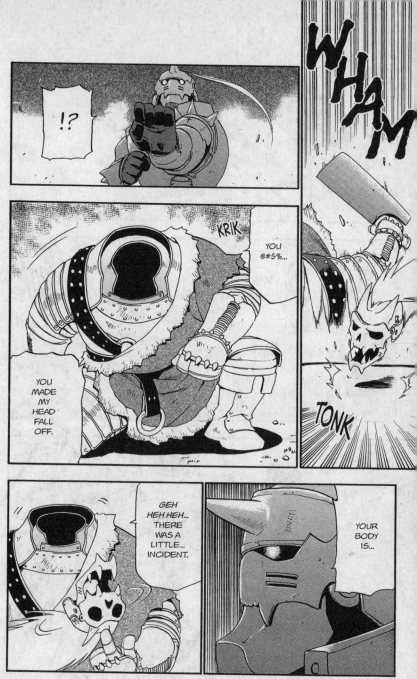

WHAM

!?

KRIK

YOU @#5%...

YOU MADE MY HEAD FALL OFF.

TONK

GEH HEH HEH... THERE WAS A LITTLE... INCIDENT.

YOUR BODY IS...

514

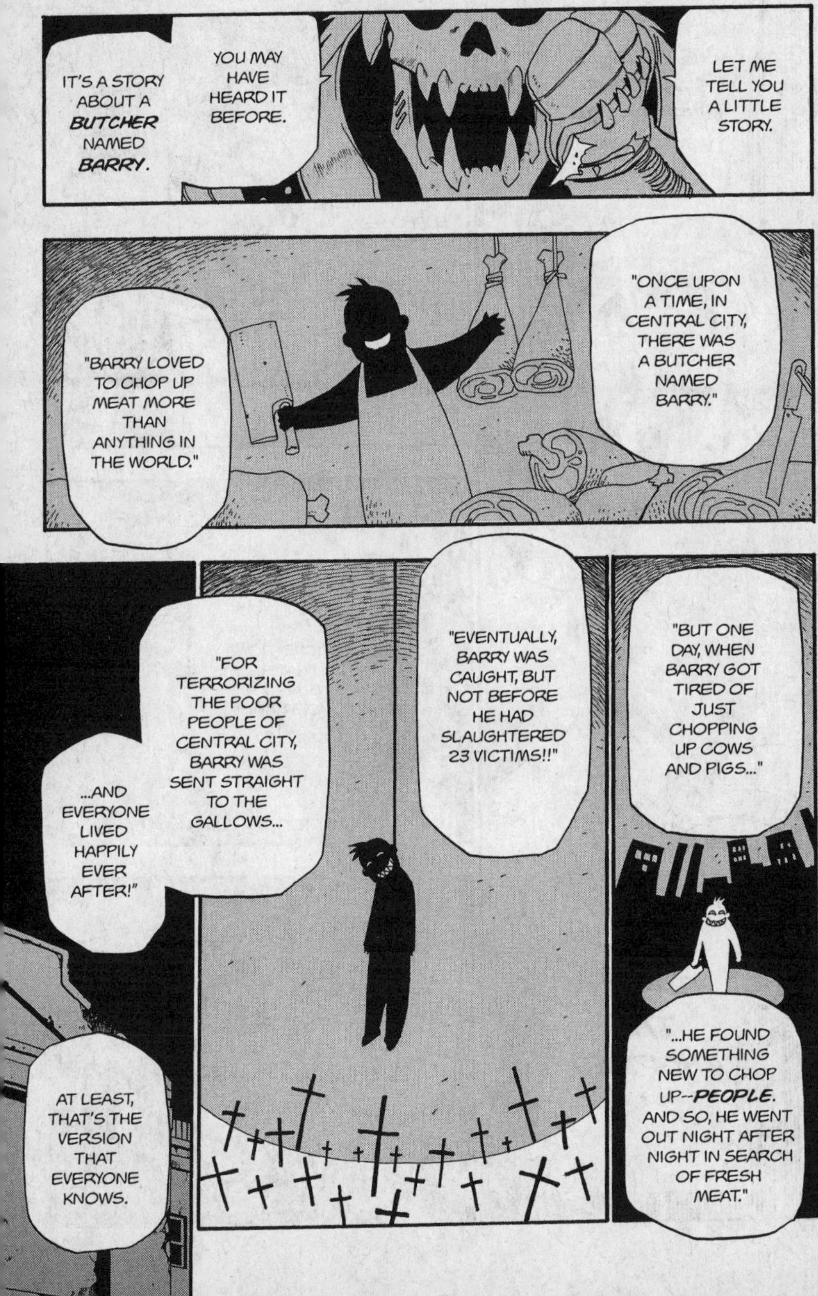
LET ME TELL YOU A LITTLE STORY.
YOU MAY HAVE HEARD IT BEFORE.
IT'S A STORY ABOUT A BUTCHER NAMED BARRY.
"ONCE UPON A TIME, IN CENTRAL CITY, THERE WAS A BUTCHER NAMED BARRY."
"BARRY LOVED TO CHOP UP MEAT MORE THAN ANYTHING IN THE WORLD."
"BUT ONE DAY, WHEN BARRY GOT TIRED OF JUST CHOPPING UP COWS AND PIGS..."
"...HE FOUND SOMETHING NEW TO CHOP UP--PEOPLE. AND SO, HE WENT OUT NIGHT AFTER NIGHT IN SEARCH OF FRESH MEAT."
"EVENTUALLY, BARRY WAS CAUGHT, BUT NOT BEFORE HE HAD SLAUGHTERED 23 VICTIMS!!"
"FOR TERRORIZING THE POOR PEOPLE OF CENTRAL CITY, BARRY WAS SENT STRAIGHT TO THE GALLOWS...
...AND EVERYONE LIVED HAPPILY EVER AFTER!"
AT LEAST, THAT'S THE VERSION THAT EVERYONE KNOWS.

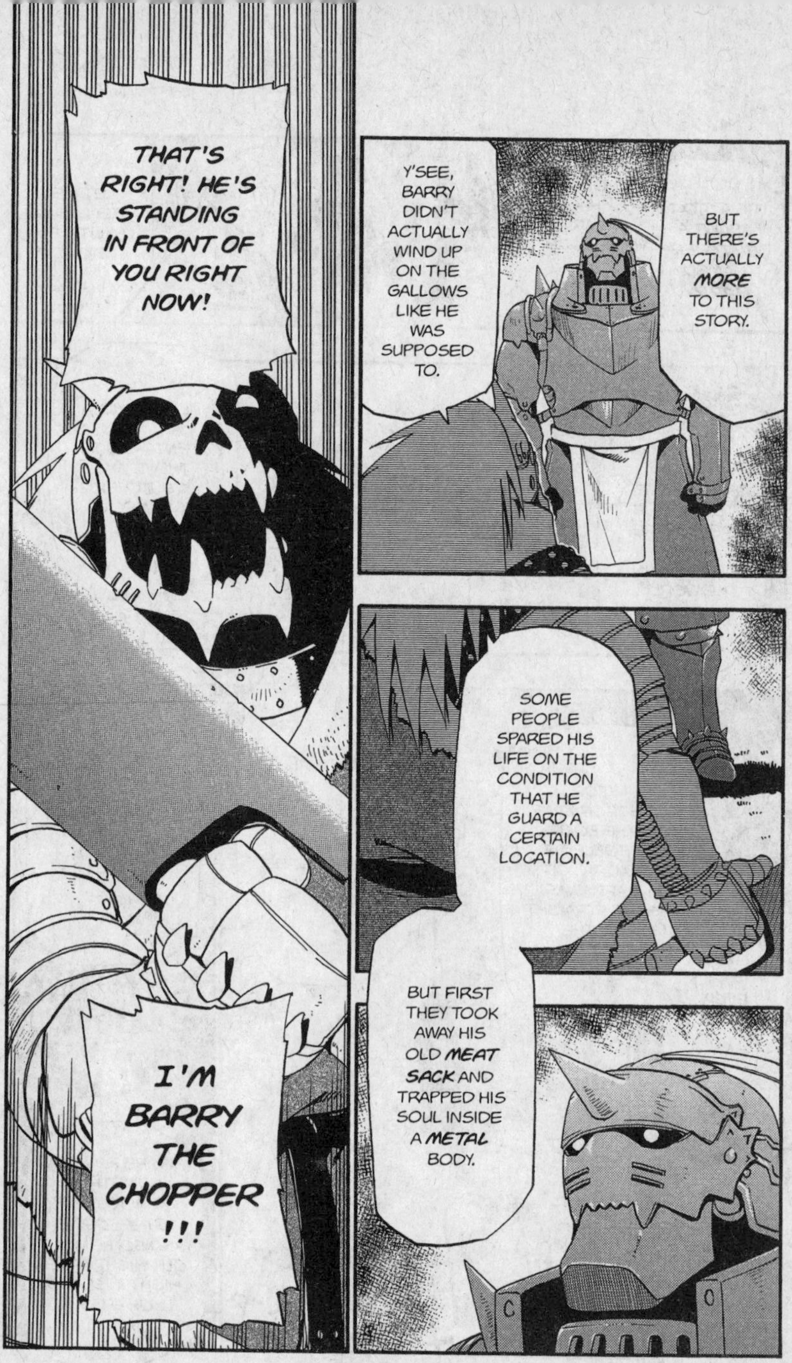
BUT THERE'S ACTUALLY MORE TO THIS STORY.
Y'SEE, BARRY DIDN'T ACTUALLY WIND UP ON THE GALLOWS LIKE HE WAS SUPPOSED TO.
SOME PEOPLE SPARED HIS LIFE ON THE CONDITION THAT HE GUARD A CERTAIN LOCATION.
BUT FIRST THEY TOOK AWAY HIS OLD MEAT SACK AND TRAPPED HIS SOUL INSIDE A METAL BODY.
THAT'S RIGHT! HE'S STANDING IN FRONT OF YOU RIGHT NOW!
I'M BARRY THE CHOPPER !!!

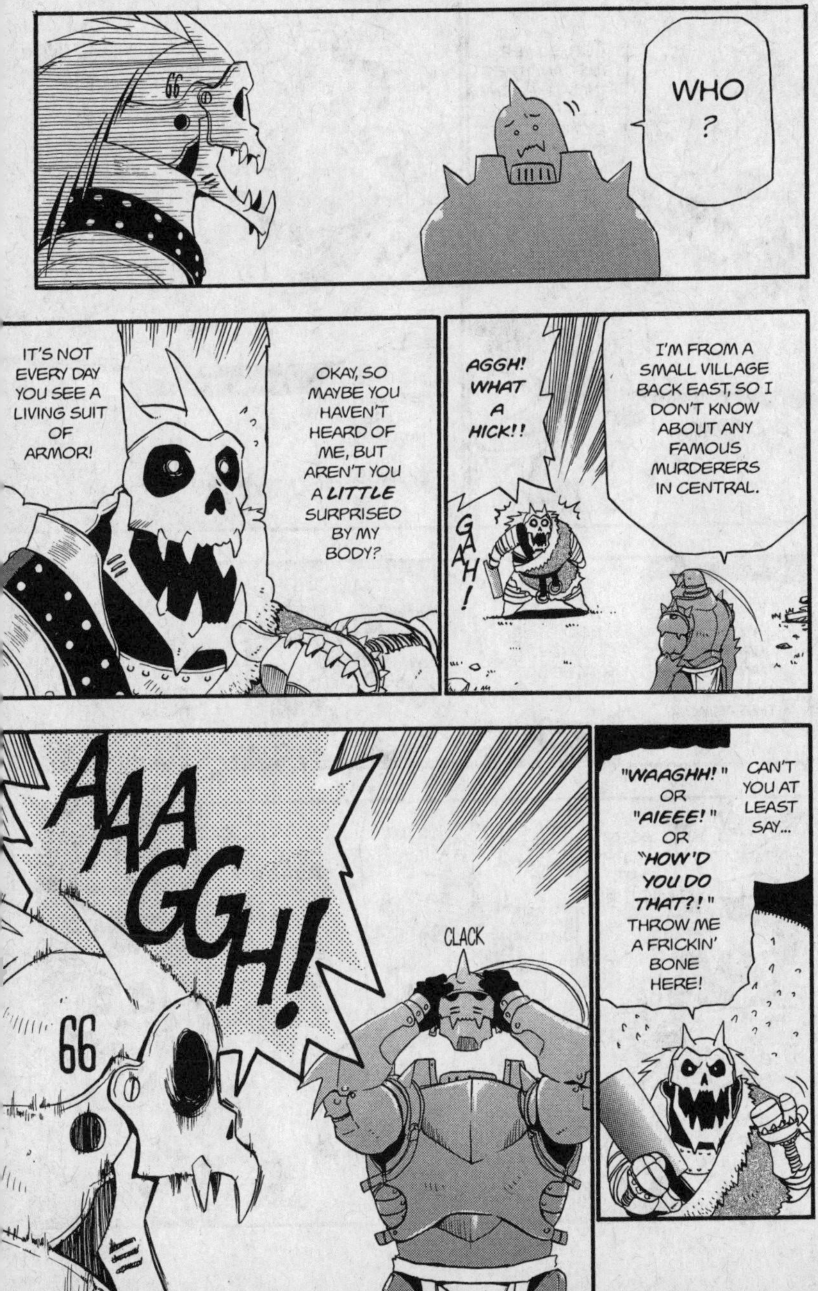
WHO?
I'M FROM A SMALL VILLAGE BACK EAST, SO I DON'T KNOW ABOUT ANY FAMOUS MURDERERS IN CENTRAL.
AGGH! WHAT A HICK!!
GAAH!
OKAY, SO MAYBE YOU HAVEN'T HEARD OF ME, BUT AREN'T YOU A LITTLE SURPRISED BY MY BODY?
IT'S NOT EVERY DAY YOU SEE A LIVING SUIT OF ARMOR!
CAN'T YOU AT LEAST SAY...
"WAAGHH!" OR "AIEEE!" OR "HOW'D YOU DO THAT?!" THROW ME A FRICKIN' BONE HERE!
AAAGGH!
CLACK

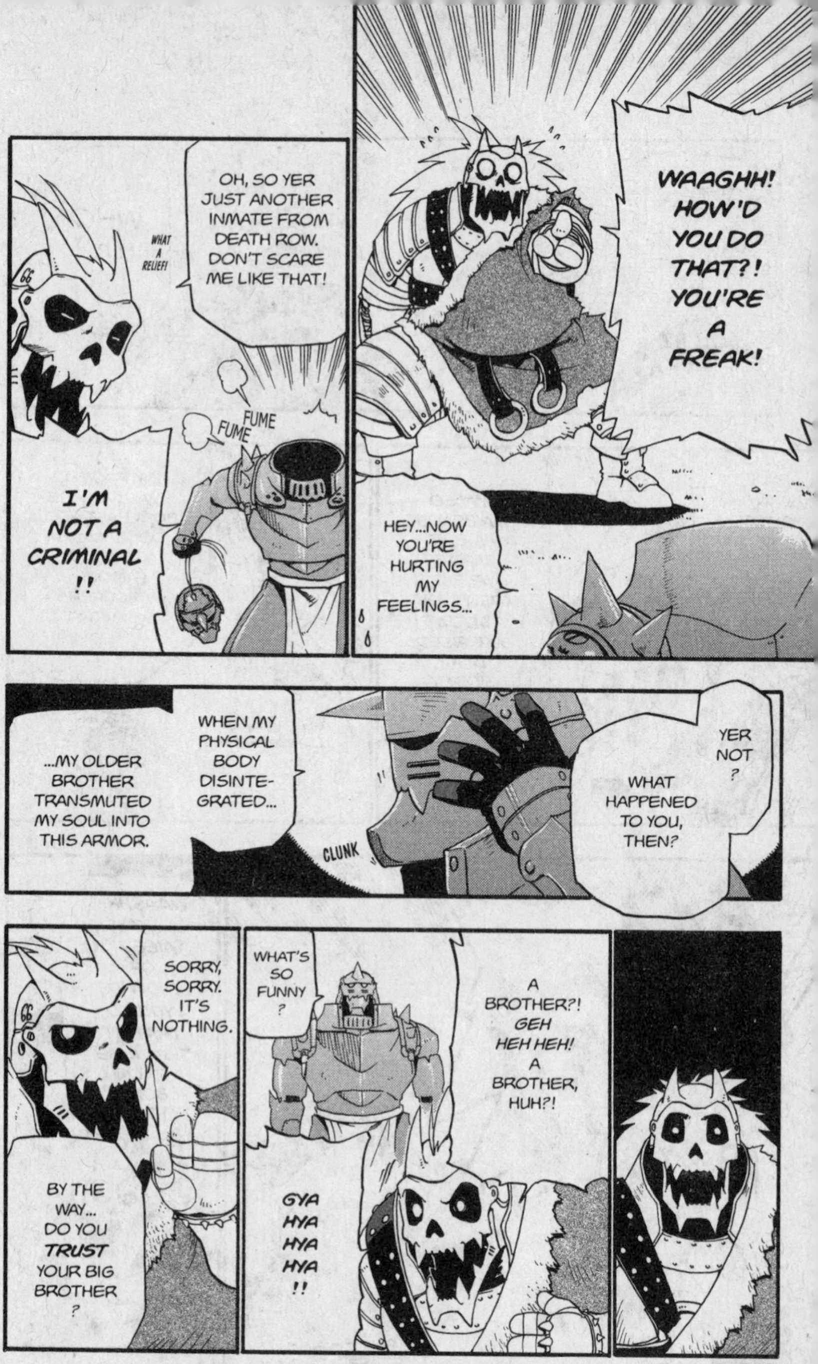
WAAGHH! HOW'D YOU DO THAT?! YOU'RE A FREAK!
HEY...NOW YOU'RE HURTING MY FEELINGS...
OH, SO YER JUST ANOTHER INMATE FROM DEATH ROW. DON'T SCARE ME LIKE THAT!
WHAT A RELIEF!
FUME FUME
I'M NOT A CRIMINAL!!
YER NOT?
WHAT HAPPENED TO YOU, THEN?
CLUNK
WHEN MY PHYSICAL BODY DISINTEGRATED...
...MY OLDER BROTHER TRANSMUTED MY SOUL INTO THIS ARMOR.
A BROTHER?! GEH HEH HEH! A BROTHER, HUH?!
WHAT'S SO FUNNY?
GYA HYA HYA HYA!!
SORRY, SORRY. IT'S NOTHING.
BY THE WAY... DO YOU TRUST YOUR BIG BROTHER?

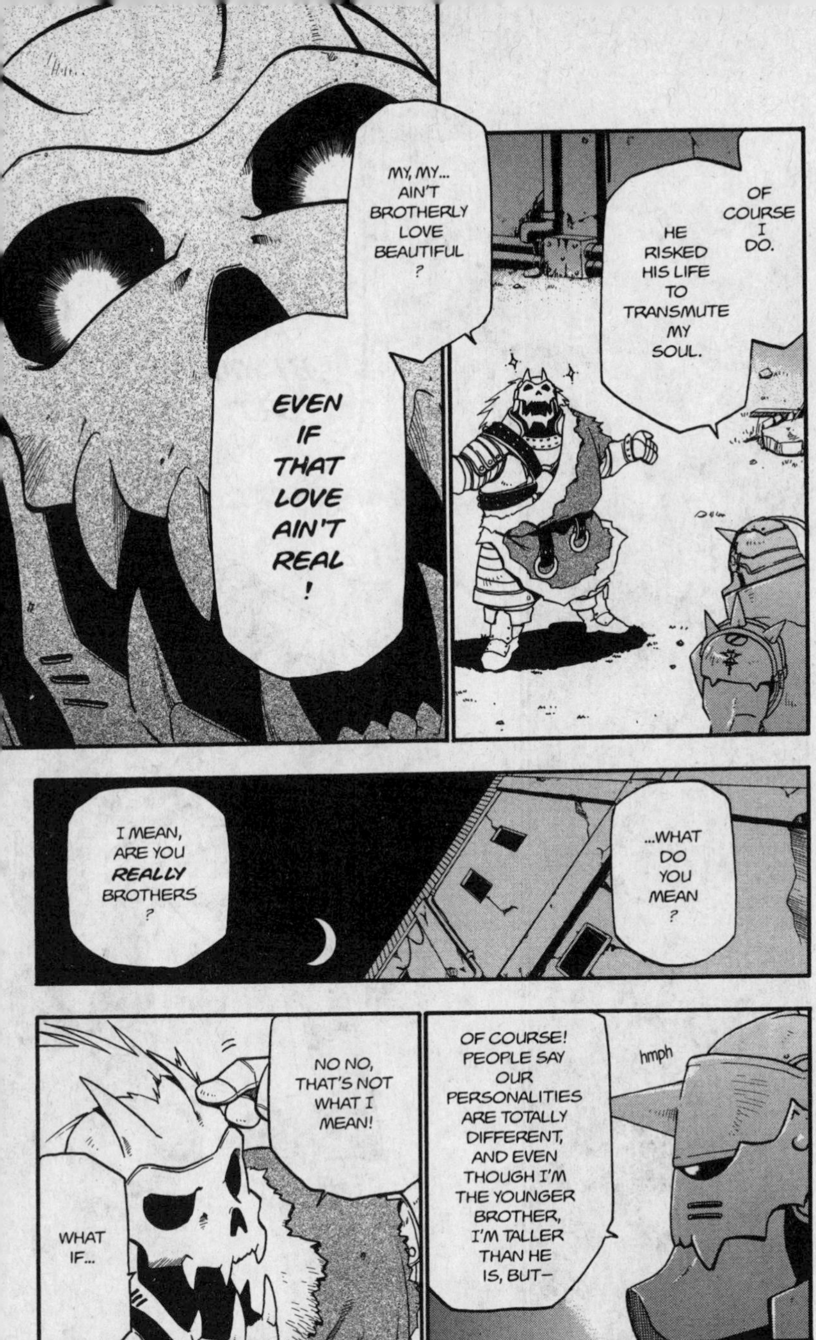
OF COURSE I DO.
HE RISKED HIS LIFE TO TRANSMUTE MY SOUL.
MY, MY... AIN'T BROTHERLY LOVE BEAUTIFUL?
EVEN IF THAT LOVE AIN'T REAL!
...WHAT DO YOU MEAN?
I MEAN, ARE YOU REALLY BROTHERS?
hmph
OF COURSE! PEOPLE SAY OUR PERSONALITIES ARE TOTALLY DIFFERENT, AND EVEN THOUGH I'M THE YOUNGER BROTHER, I'M TALLER THAN HE IS, BUT—
NO NO, THAT'S NOT WHAT I MEAN!
WHAT IF...

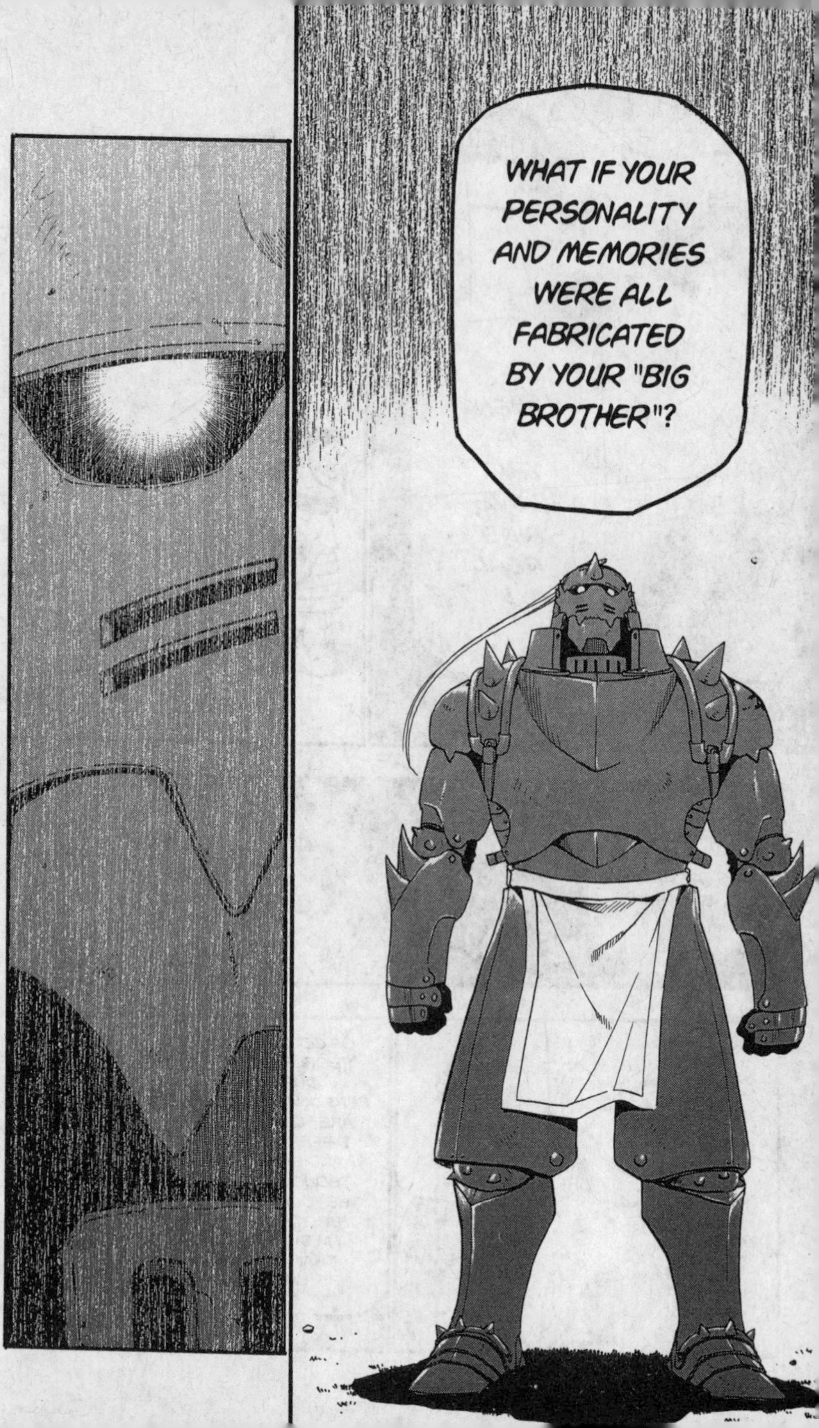
WHAT IF YOUR PERSONALITY AND MEMORIES WERE ALL FABRICATED BY YOUR "BIG BROTHER"?

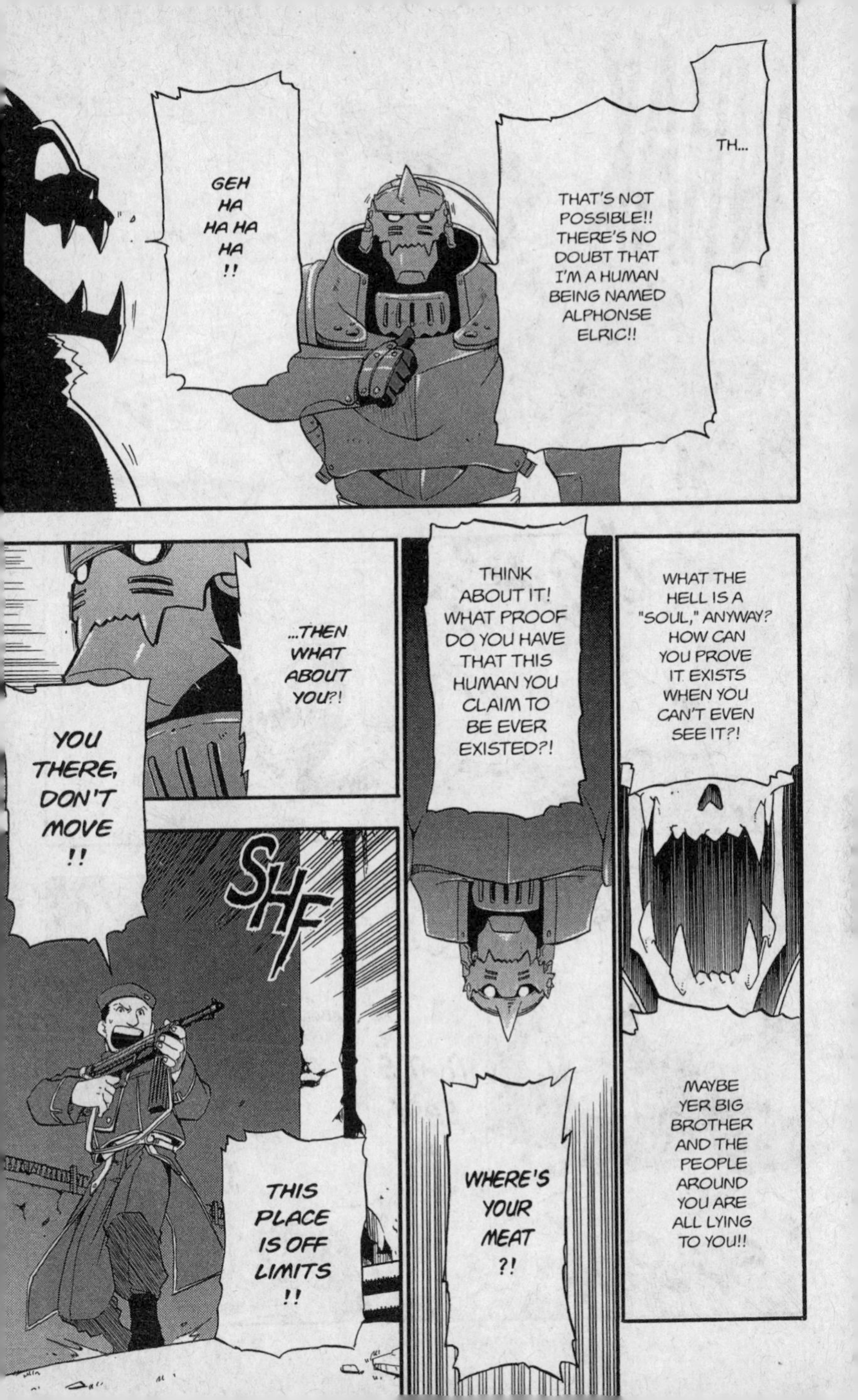
TH...
THAT'S NOT POSSIBLE!! THERE'S NO DOUBT THAT I'M A HUMAN BEING NAMED ALPHONSE ELRIC!!
GEH HA HA HA HA!!
WHAT THE HELL IS A "SOUL," ANYWAY? HOW CAN YOU PROVE IT EXISTS WHEN YOU CAN'T EVEN SEE IT?!
MAYBE YER BIG BROTHER AND THE PEOPLE AROUND YOU ARE ALL LYING TO YOU!!
THINK ABOUT IT! WHAT PROOF DO YOU HAVE THAT THIS HUMAN YOU CLAIM TO BE EVER EXISTED?!
WHERE'S YOUR MEAT?!
...THEN WHAT ABOUT YOU?!
YOU THERE, DON'T MOVE!!
SHF
THIS PLACE IS OFF LIMITS!!

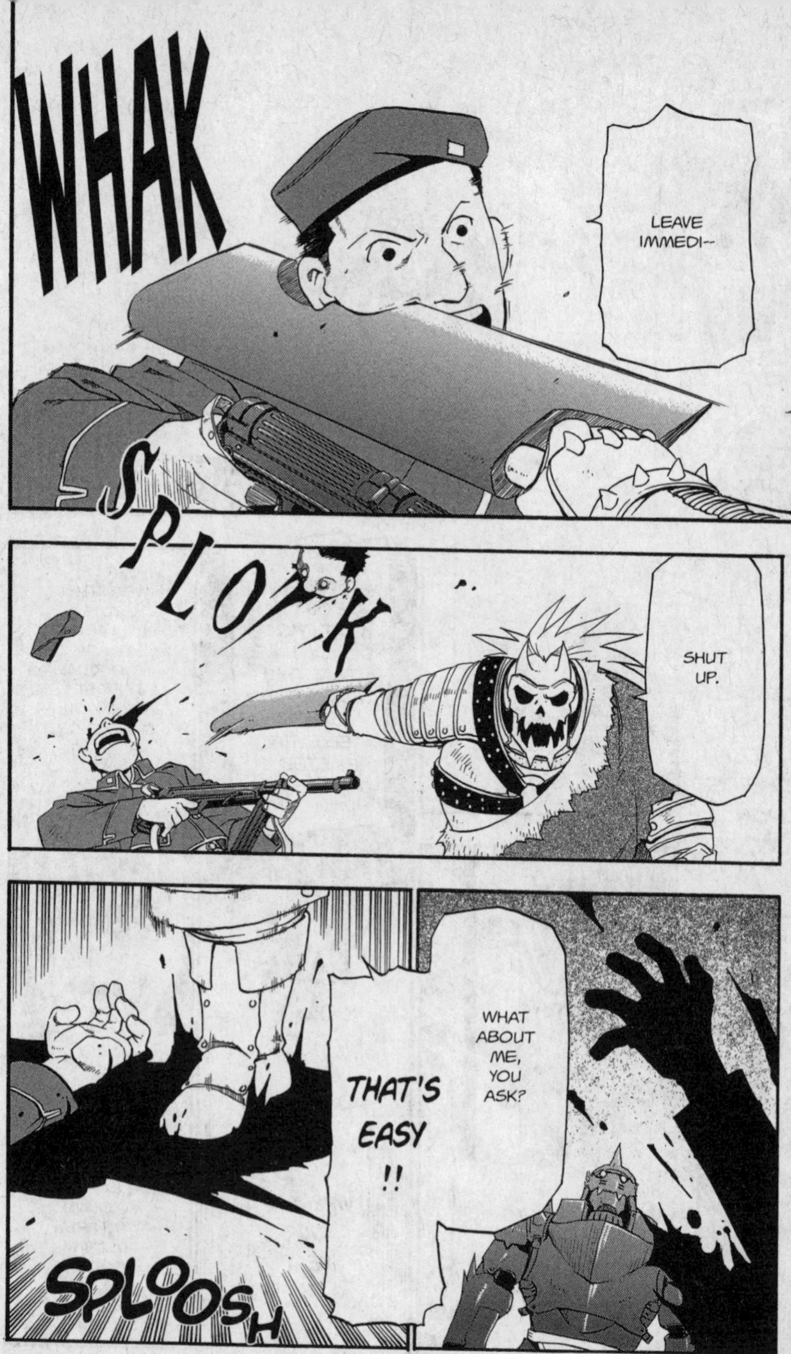
WHAK
LEAVE IMMEDI--
SPLOK
SHUT UP.
WHAT ABOUT ME, YOU ASK?
THAT'S EASY!!
SPLOOSH

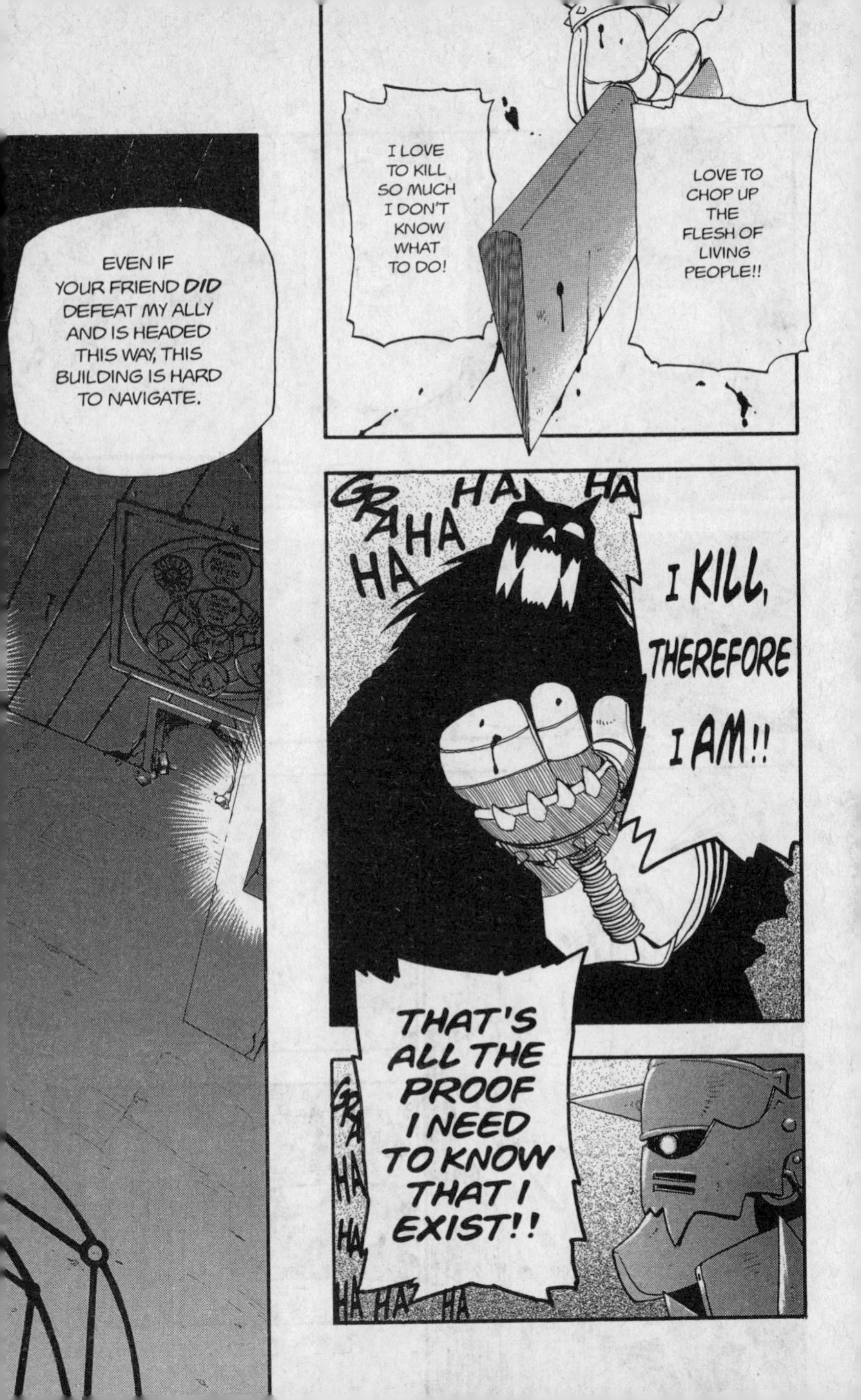
I LOVE TO KILL SO MUCH I DON'T KNOW WHAT TO DO!
LOVE TO CHOP UP THE FLESH OF LIVING PEOPLE!!
HA HA
GRAHA HA HA
I KILL, THEREFORE I AM!!
THAT'S ALL THE PROOF I NEED TO KNOW THAT I EXIST!!
GRAHA HA HA
HA HA HA
EVEN IF YOUR FRIEND ***DID*** DEFEAT MY ALLY AND IS HEADED THIS WAY, THIS BUILDING IS HARD TO NAVIGATE.

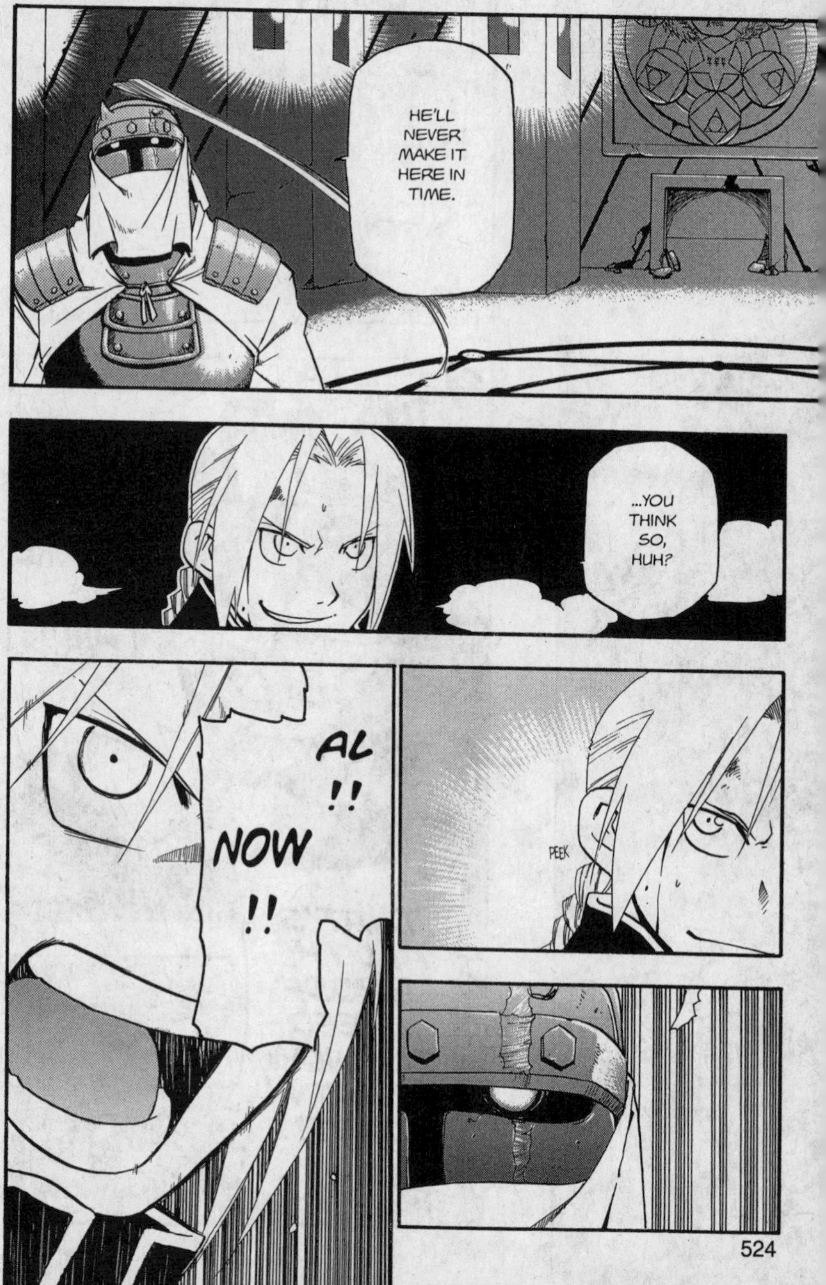
HE'LL NEVER MAKE IT HERE IN TIME.
...YOU THINK SO, HUH?
PEEK
AL!!
NOW!!

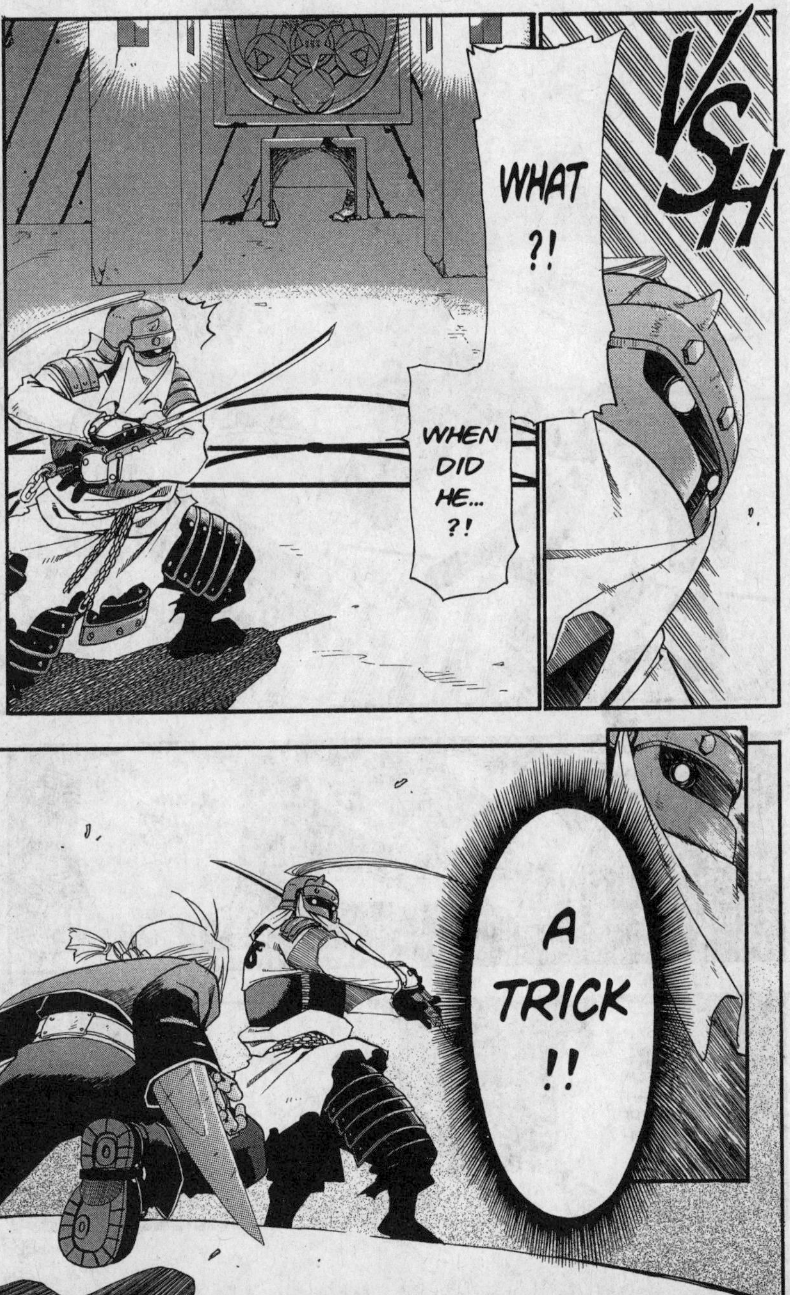
VSH
WHAT ?!
WHEN DID HE... ?!
A TRICK !!

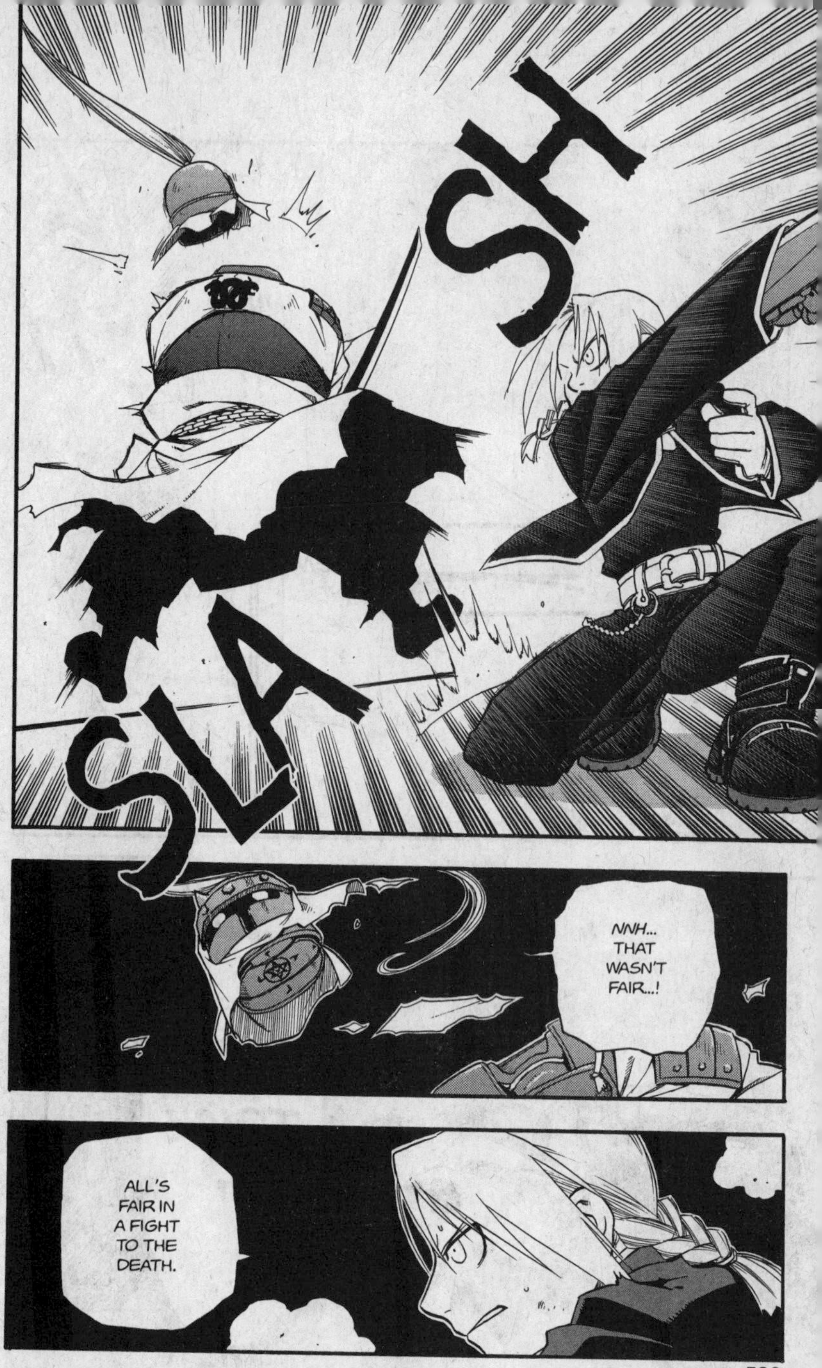
SLASH
NNH... THAT WASN'T FAIR...!
ALL'S FAIR IN A FIGHT TO THE DEATH.

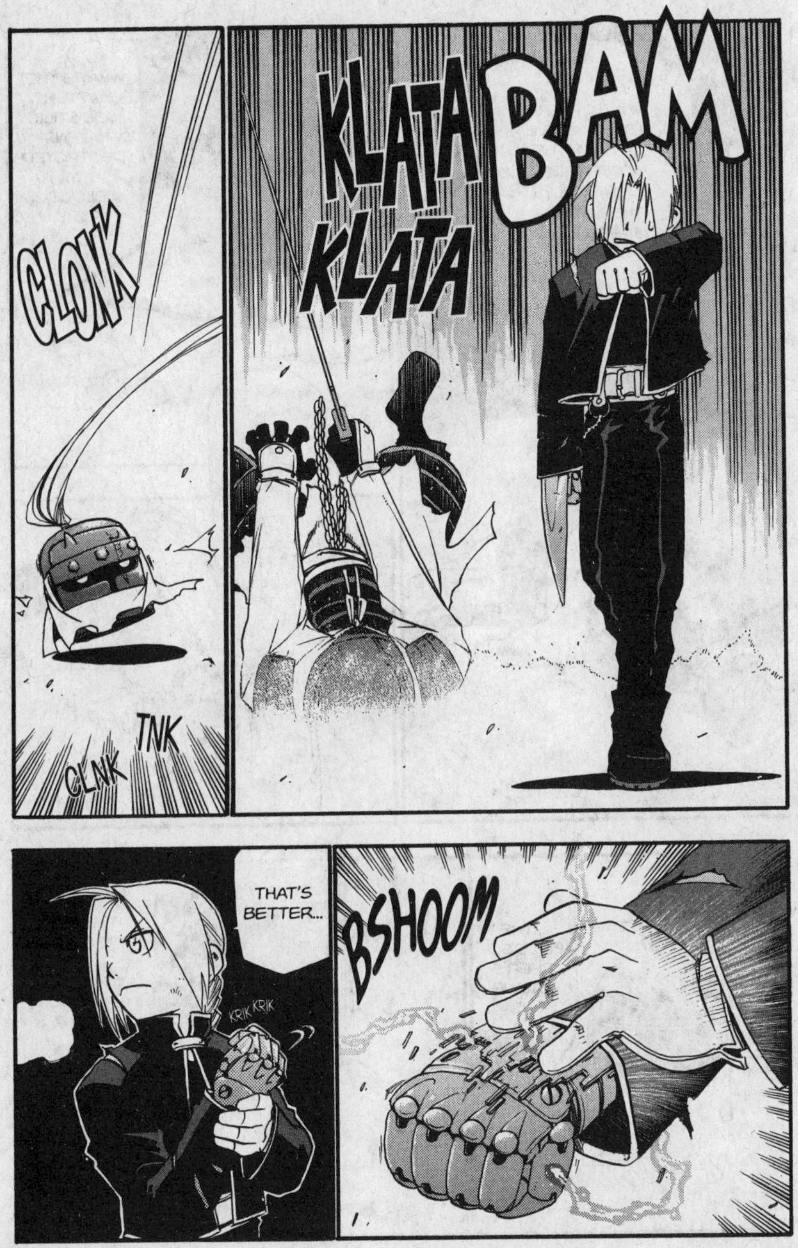
KLATA
KLATA
BAM
CLONK
TNK
CLNK
BSHOOM
THAT'S BETTER...
KRIK KRIK

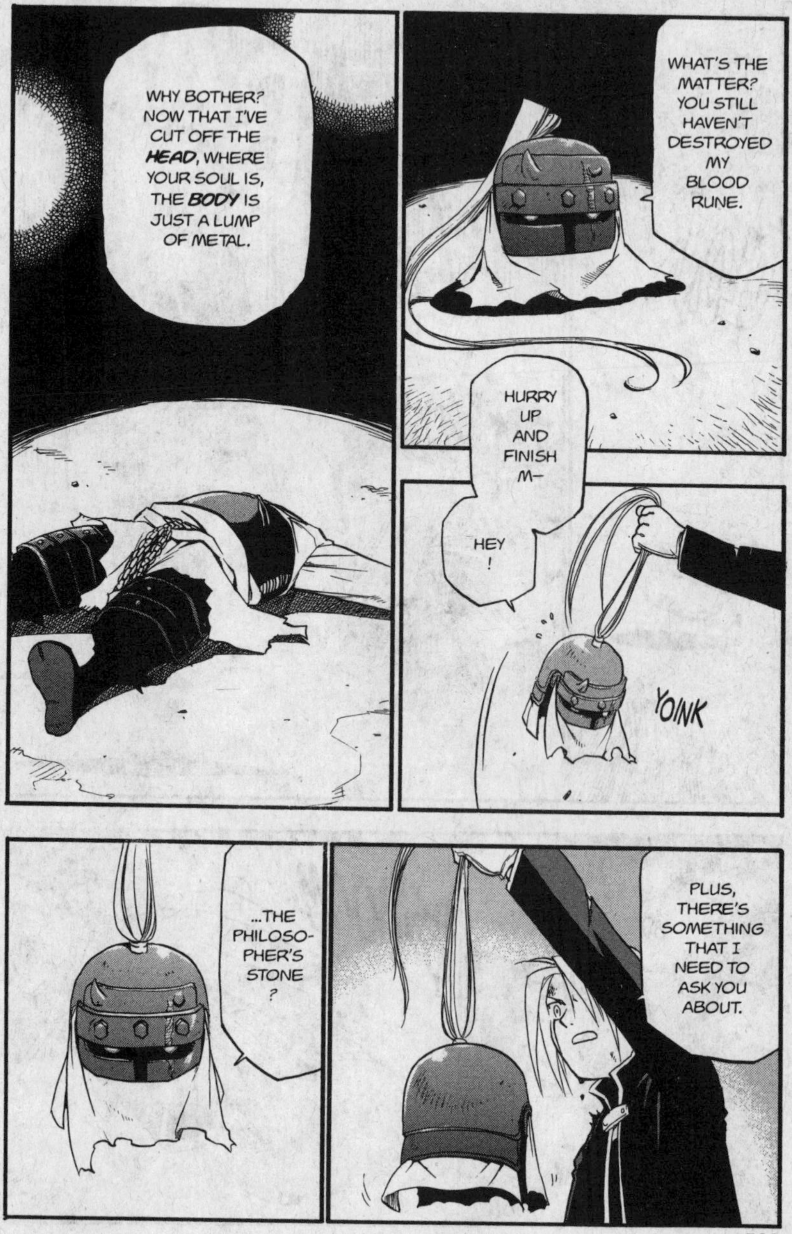
WHAT'S THE MATTER? YOU STILL HAVEN'T DESTROYED MY BLOOD RUNE.
HURRY UP AND FINISH M—
HEY!
YOINK
WHY BOTHER? NOW THAT I'VE CUT OFF THE HEAD, WHERE YOUR SOUL IS, THE BODY IS JUST A LUMP OF METAL.
PLUS, THERE'S SOMETHING THAT I NEED TO ASK YOU ABOUT.
...THE PHILOSOPHER'S STONE?

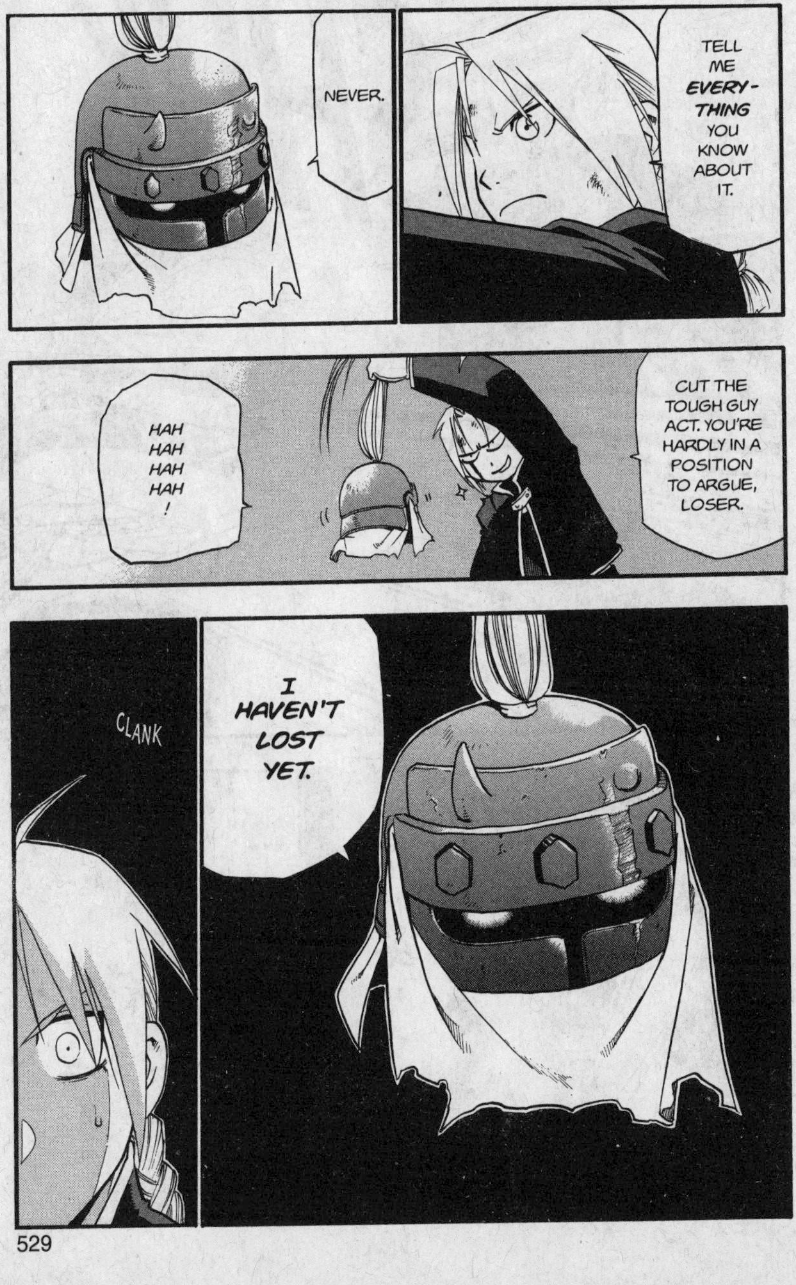
TELL ME EVERY-THING YOU KNOW ABOUT IT.
NEVER.
CUT THE TOUGH GUY ACT. YOU'RE HARDLY IN A POSITION TO ARGUE, LOSER.
HAH HAH HAH HAH!
I HAVEN'T LOST YET.
CLANK

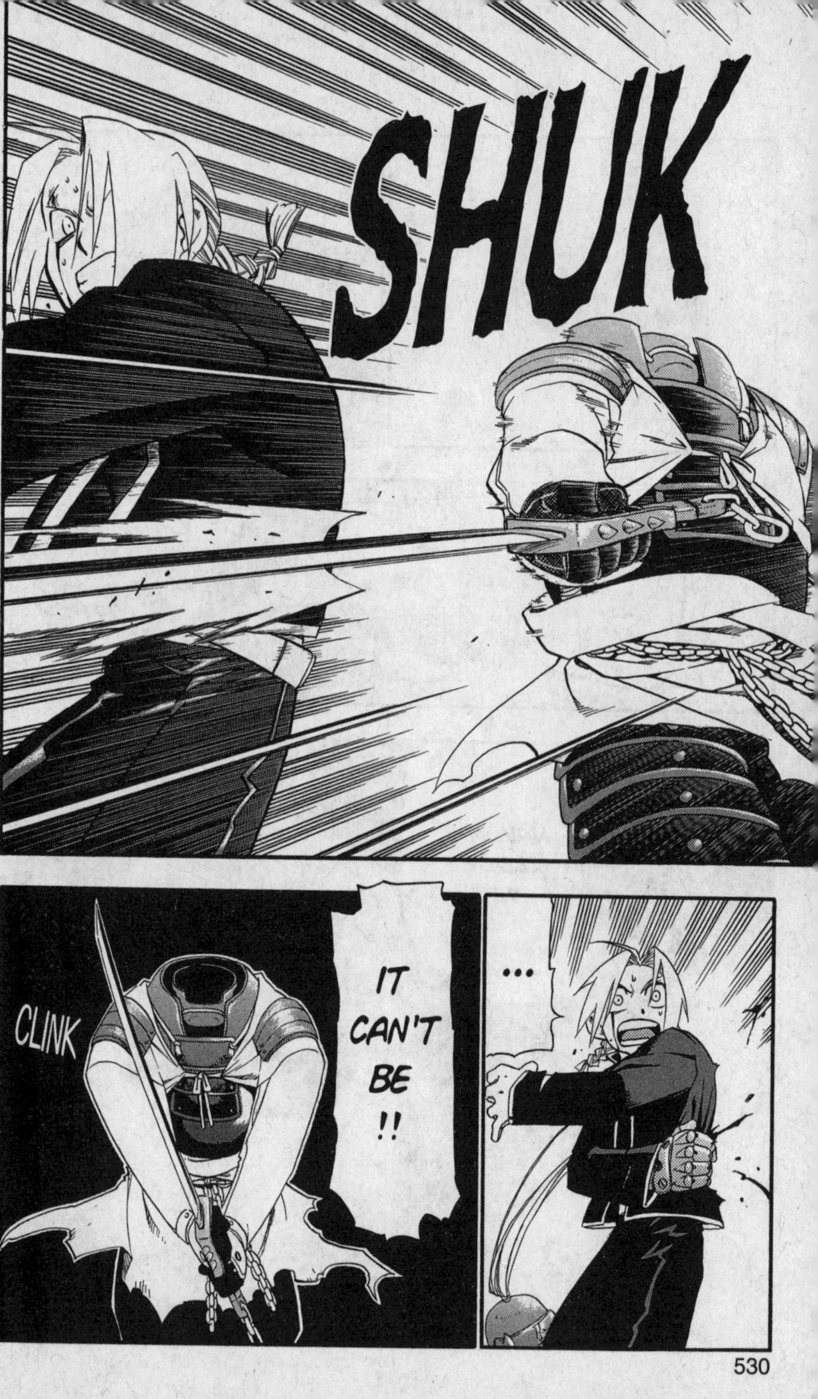
SHUK
...
IT CAN'T BE !!
CLINK

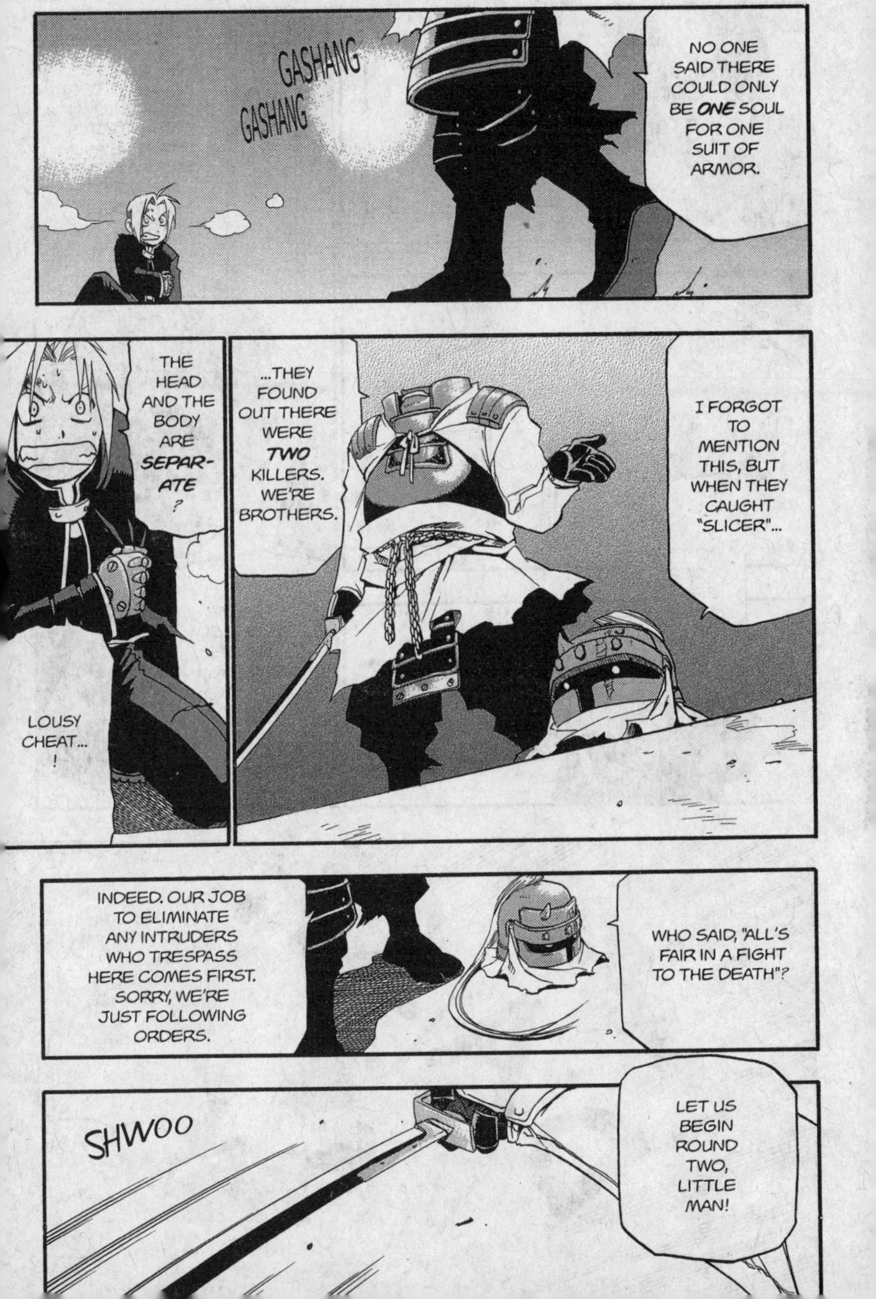
NO ONE SAID THERE COULD ONLY BE ONE SOUL FOR ONE SUIT OF ARMOR.
GASHANG
GASHANG
I FORGOT TO MENTION THIS, BUT WHEN THEY CAUGHT "SLICER"...
...THEY FOUND OUT THERE WERE TWO KILLERS. WE'RE BROTHERS.
THE HEAD AND THE BODY ARE SEPARATE?
LOUSY CHEAT...!
WHO SAID, "ALL'S FAIR IN A FIGHT TO THE DEATH"?
INDEED. OUR JOB TO ELIMINATE ANY INTRUDERS WHO TRESPASS HERE COMES FIRST. SORRY, WE'RE JUST FOLLOWING ORDERS.
LET US BEGIN ROUND TWO, LITTLE MAN!
SHWOO

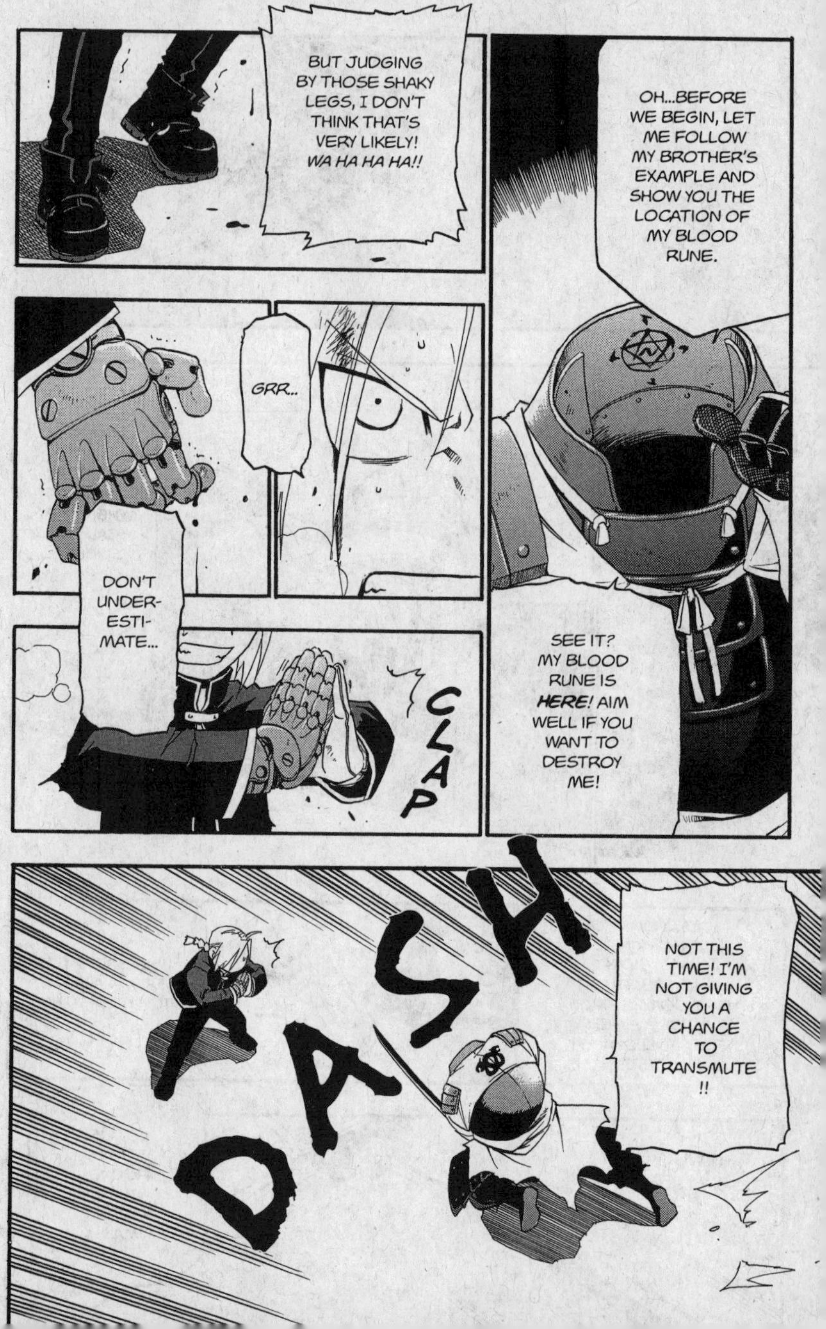
OH...BEFORE WE BEGIN, LET ME FOLLOW MY BROTHER'S EXAMPLE AND SHOW YOU THE LOCATION OF MY BLOOD RUNE.
SEE IT? MY BLOOD RUNE IS *HERE!* AIM WELL IF YOU WANT TO DESTROY ME!
BUT JUDGING BY THOSE SHAKY LEGS, I DON'T THINK THAT'S VERY LIKELY! *WA HA HA HA!!*
GRR...
DON'T UNDER-ESTI-MATE...
CLAP
NOT THIS TIME! I'M NOT GIVING YOU A CHANCE TO TRANSMUTE !!
DASH

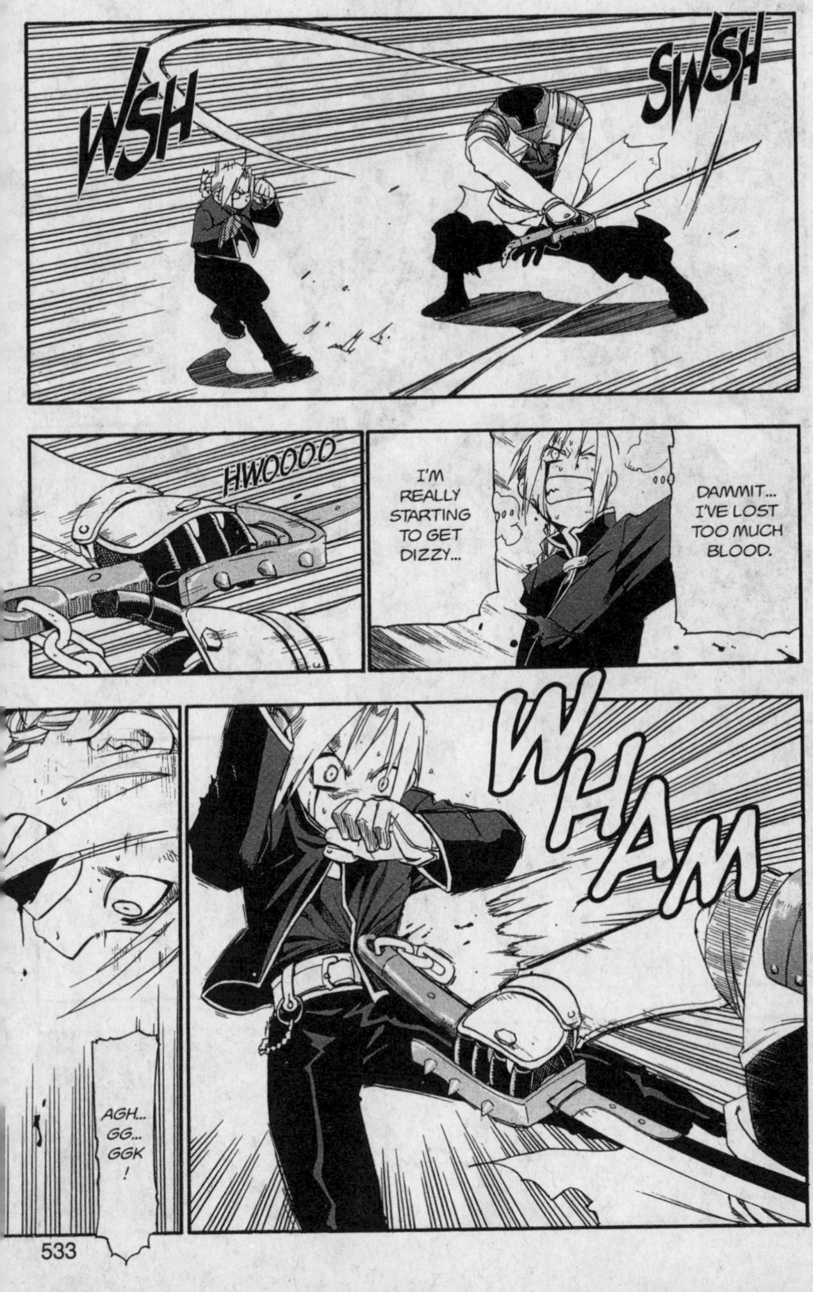
SWSH
WSH
DAMMIT... I'VE LOST TOO MUCH BLOOD.
I'M REALLY STARTING TO GET DIZZY...
HWOOOO
WHAM
AGH... GG... GGK!

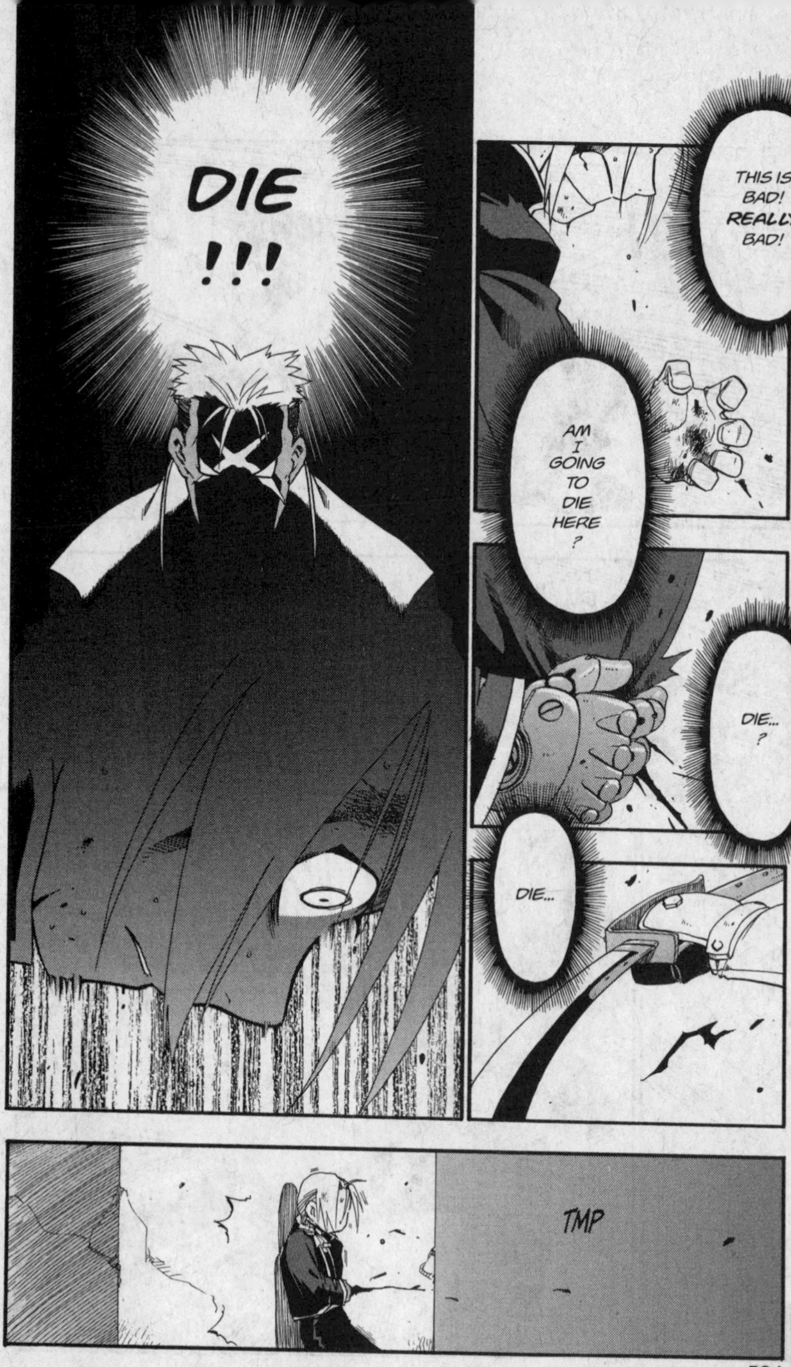
THIS IS BAD! REALLY BAD!
AM I GOING TO DIE HERE?
DIE... ?
DIE...
DIE !!!
TMP

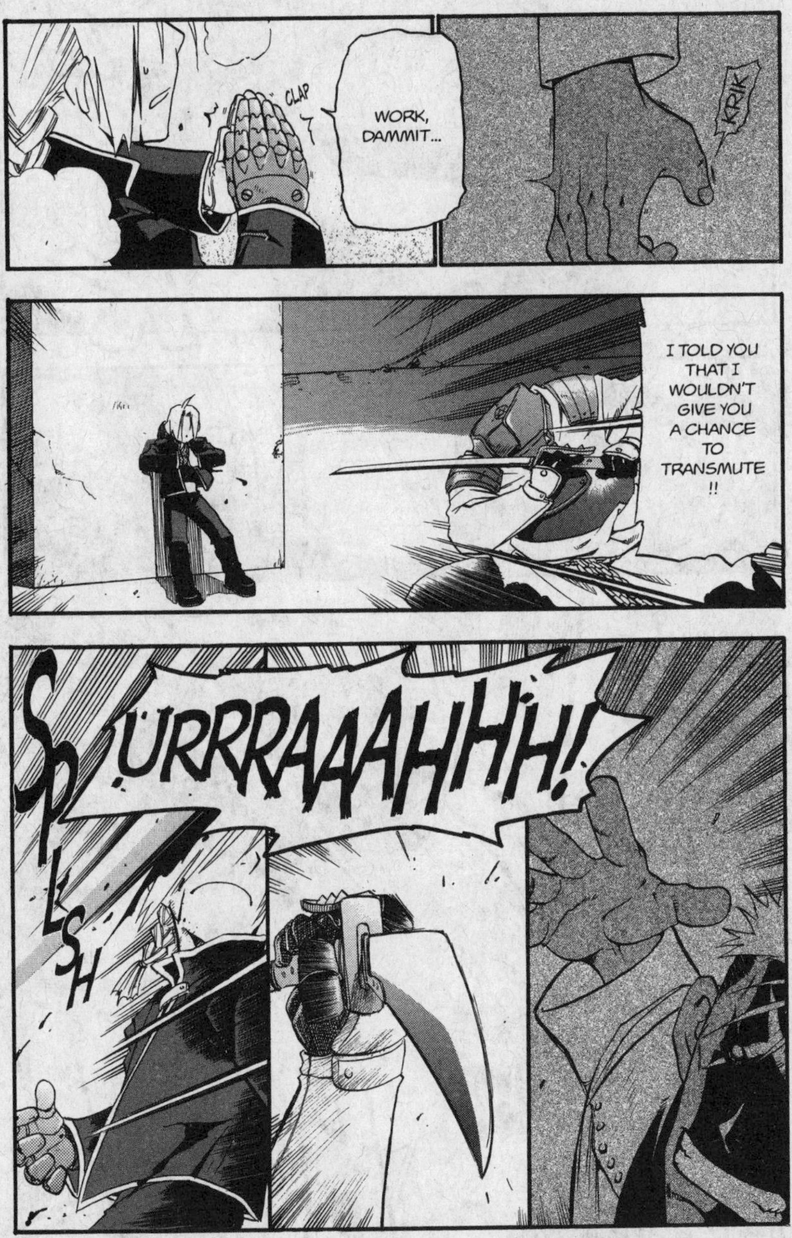
KRIK
CLAP
WORK, DAMMIT...
I TOLD YOU THAT I WOULDN'T GIVE YOU A CHANCE TO TRANSMUTE !!
URRRAAAHHH!
SPLSH

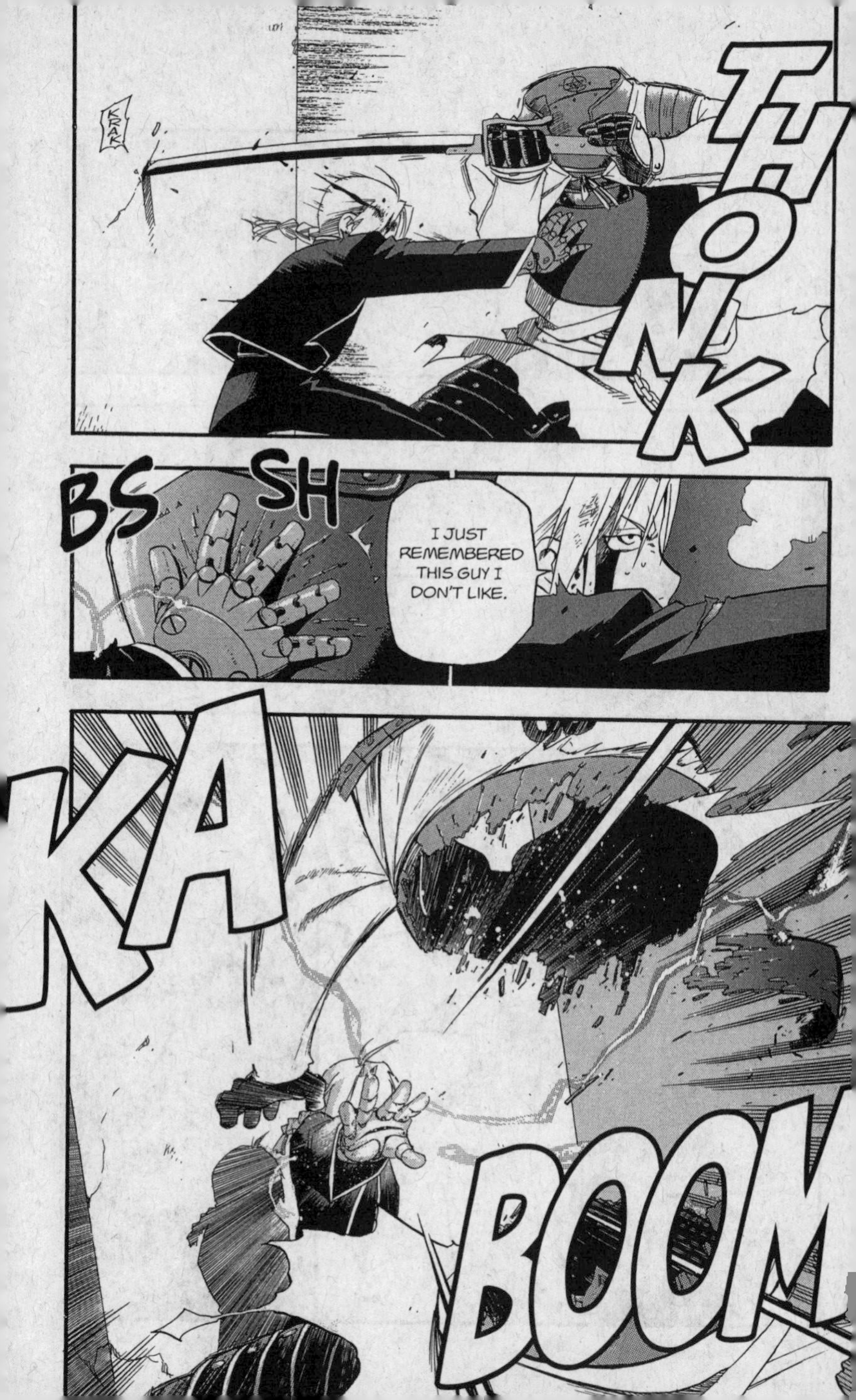
THONK
KRAK
BSSH
I JUST REMEMBERED THIS GUY I DON'T LIKE.
KA BOOM

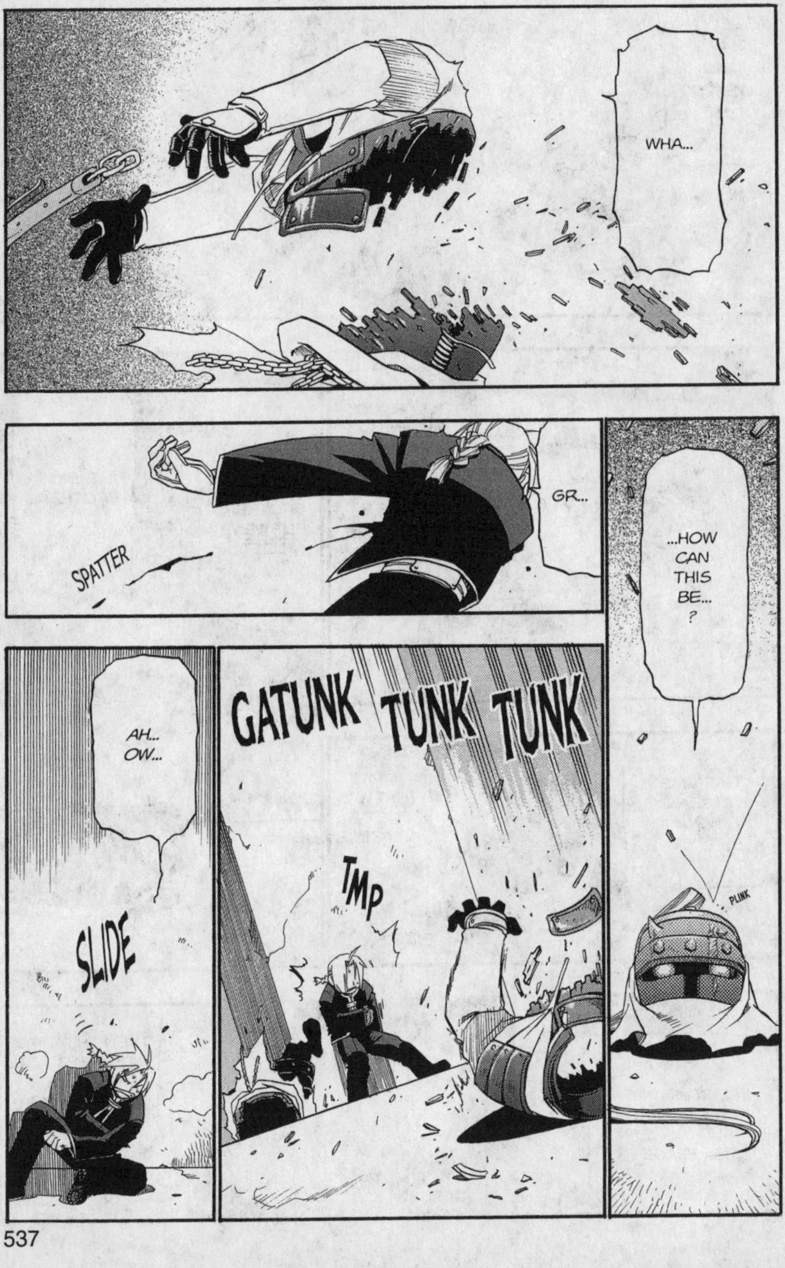
WHA...
...HOW CAN THIS BE...?
PLINK
GR...
SPATTER
GATUNK TUNK TUNK
TMP
AH... OW...
SLIDE

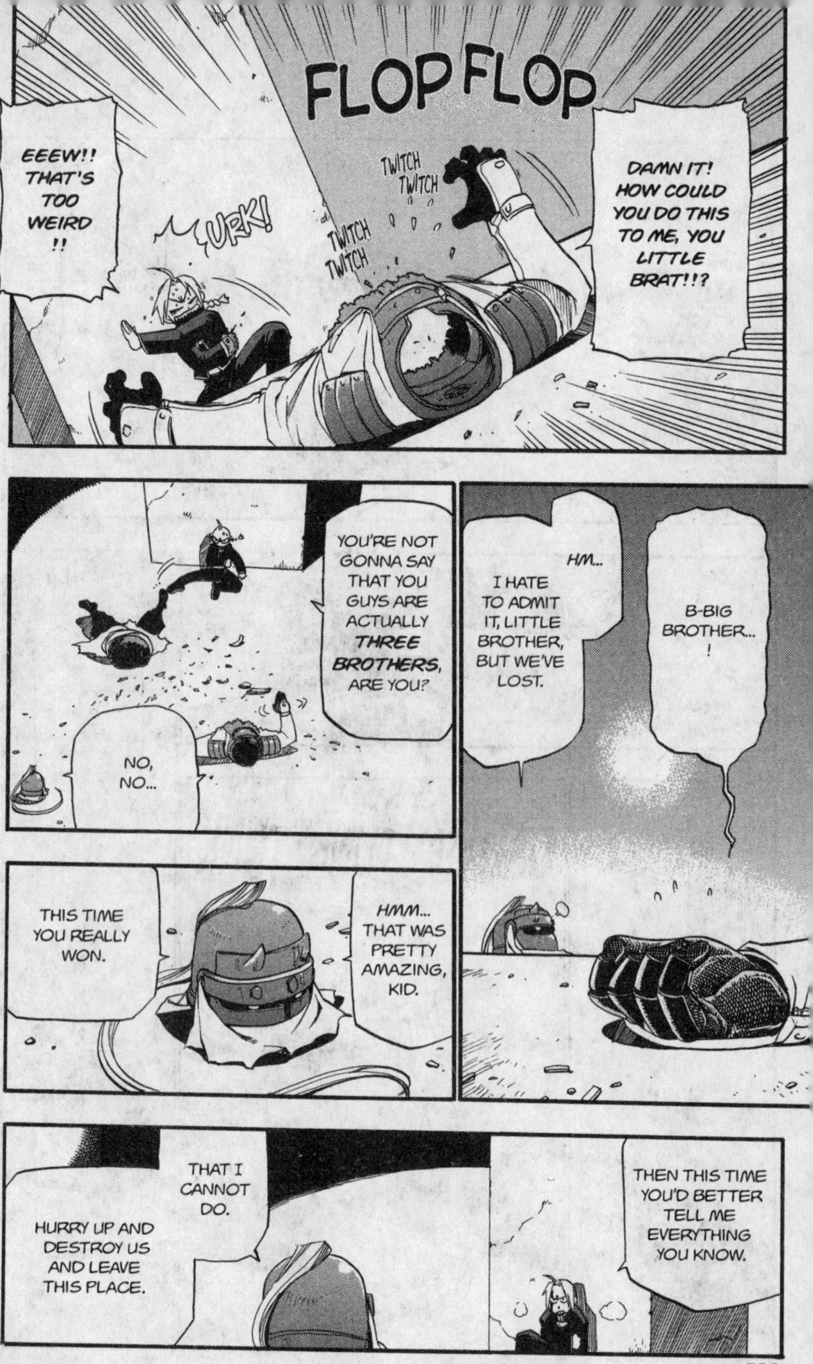
FLOP FLOP
DAMN IT! HOW COULD YOU DO THIS TO ME, YOU LITTLE BRAT!!?
TWITCH TWITCH
EEEW!! THAT'S TOO WEIRD !!
URK!
TWITCH TWITCH
B-BIG BROTHER... !
HM... I HATE TO ADMIT IT, LITTLE BROTHER, BUT WE'VE LOST.
YOU'RE NOT GONNA SAY THAT YOU GUYS ARE ACTUALLY THREE BROTHERS, ARE YOU?
NO, NO...
HMM... THAT WAS PRETTY AMAZING, KID.
THIS TIME YOU REALLY WON.
THEN THIS TIME YOU'D BETTER TELL ME EVERYTHING YOU KNOW.
THAT I CANNOT DO.
HURRY UP AND DESTROY US AND LEAVE THIS PLACE.

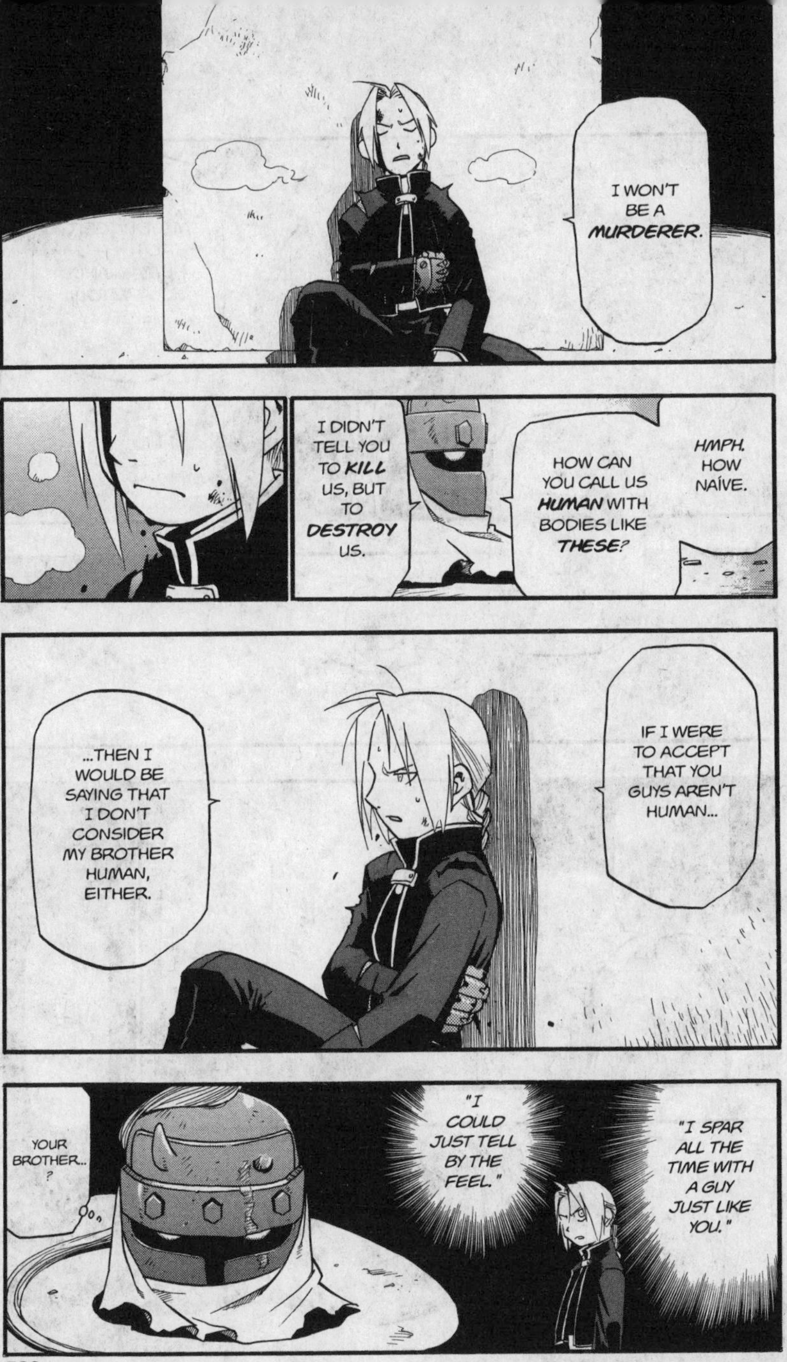
I WON'T BE A MURDERER.
HMPH. HOW NAÏVE.
HOW CAN YOU CALL US HUMAN WITH BODIES LIKE THESE?
I DIDN'T TELL YOU TO KILL US, BUT TO DESTROY US.
IF I WERE TO ACCEPT THAT YOU GUYS AREN'T HUMAN...
...THEN I WOULD BE SAYING THAT I DON'T CONSIDER MY BROTHER HUMAN, EITHER.
"I SPAR ALL THE TIME WITH A GUY JUST LIKE YOU."
"I COULD JUST TELL BY THE FEEL."
YOUR BROTHER...?

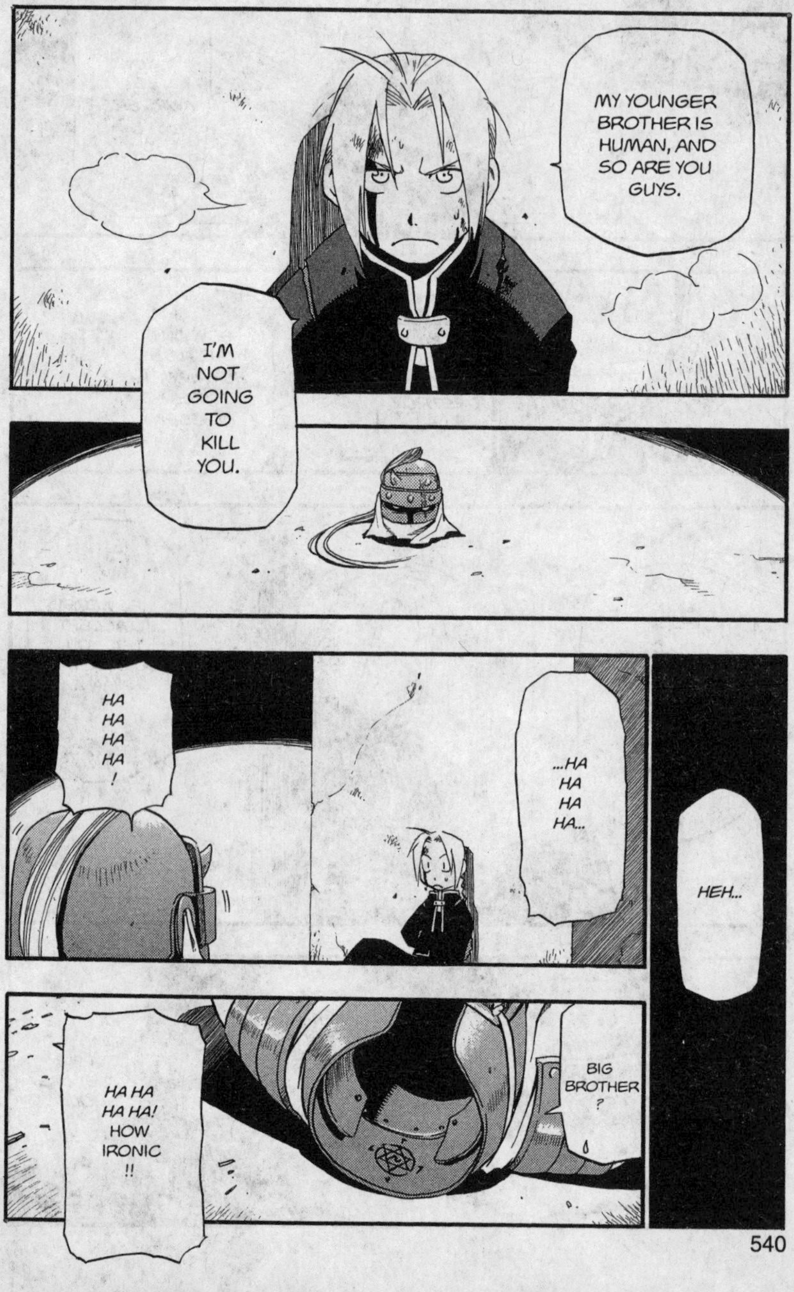

MY YOUNGER BROTHER IS HUMAN, AND SO ARE YOU GUYS.
I'M NOT GOING TO KILL YOU.
HEH...
...HA HA HA HA...
HA HA HA HA!
BIG BROTHER?
HA HA HA HA! HOW IRONIC!!

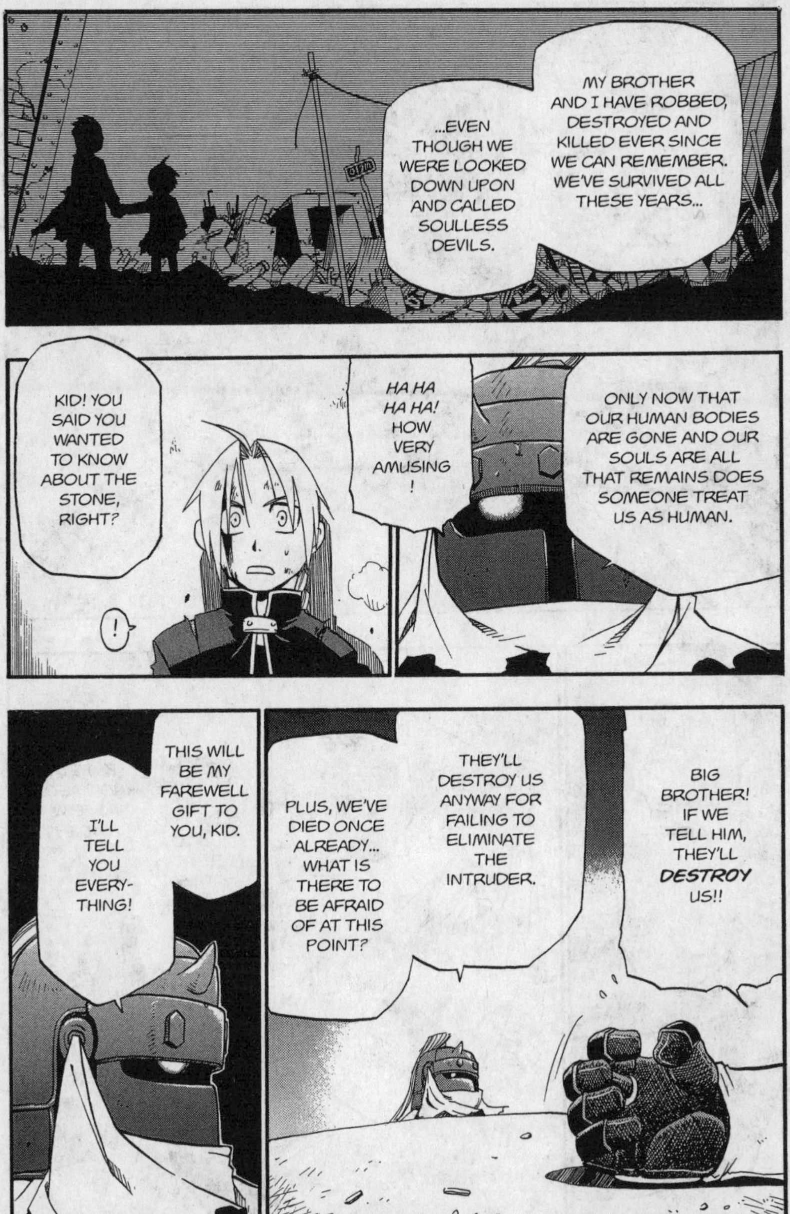
MY BROTHER AND I HAVE ROBBED, DESTROYED AND KILLED EVER SINCE WE CAN REMEMBER. WE'VE SURVIVED ALL THESE YEARS...
...EVEN THOUGH WE WERE LOOKED DOWN UPON AND CALLED SOULLESS DEVILS.
ONLY NOW THAT OUR HUMAN BODIES ARE GONE AND OUR SOULS ARE ALL THAT REMAINS DOES SOMEONE TREAT US AS HUMAN.
HA HA HA HA! HOW VERY AMUSING!
KID! YOU SAID YOU WANTED TO KNOW ABOUT THE STONE, RIGHT?
!
BIG BROTHER! IF WE TELL HIM, THEY'LL DESTROY US!!
THEY'LL DESTROY US ANYWAY FOR FAILING TO ELIMINATE THE INTRUDER.
PLUS, WE'VE DIED ONCE ALREADY... WHAT IS THERE TO BE AFRAID OF AT THIS POINT?
THIS WILL BE MY FAREWELL GIFT TO YOU, KID.
I'LL TELL YOU EVERY-THING!

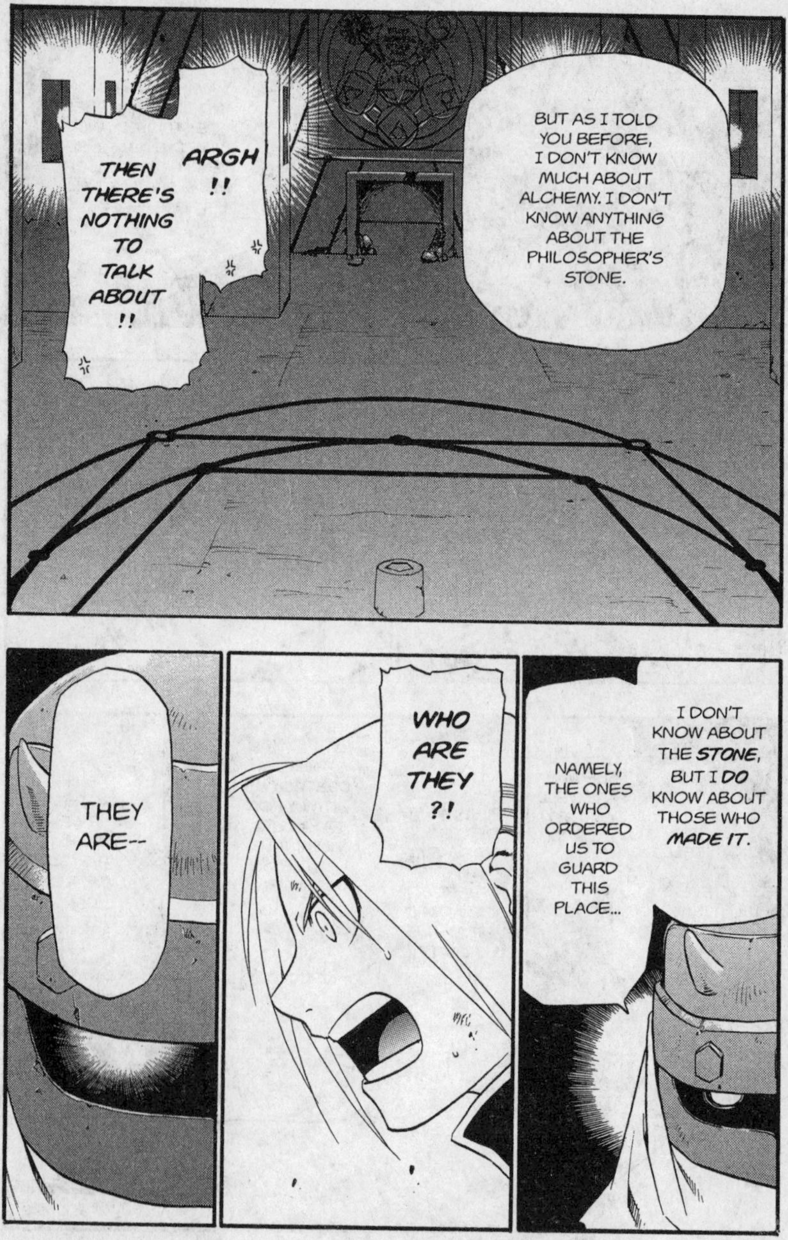
BUT AS I TOLD YOU BEFORE, I DON'T KNOW MUCH ABOUT ALCHEMY. I DON'T KNOW ANYTHING ABOUT THE PHILOSOPHER'S STONE.
ARGH!!
THEN THERE'S NOTHING TO TALK ABOUT!!
I DON'T KNOW ABOUT THE STONE, BUT I DO KNOW ABOUT THOSE WHO MADE IT.
NAMELY, THE ONES WHO ORDERED US TO GUARD THIS PLACE...
WHO ARE THEY?!
THEY ARE--

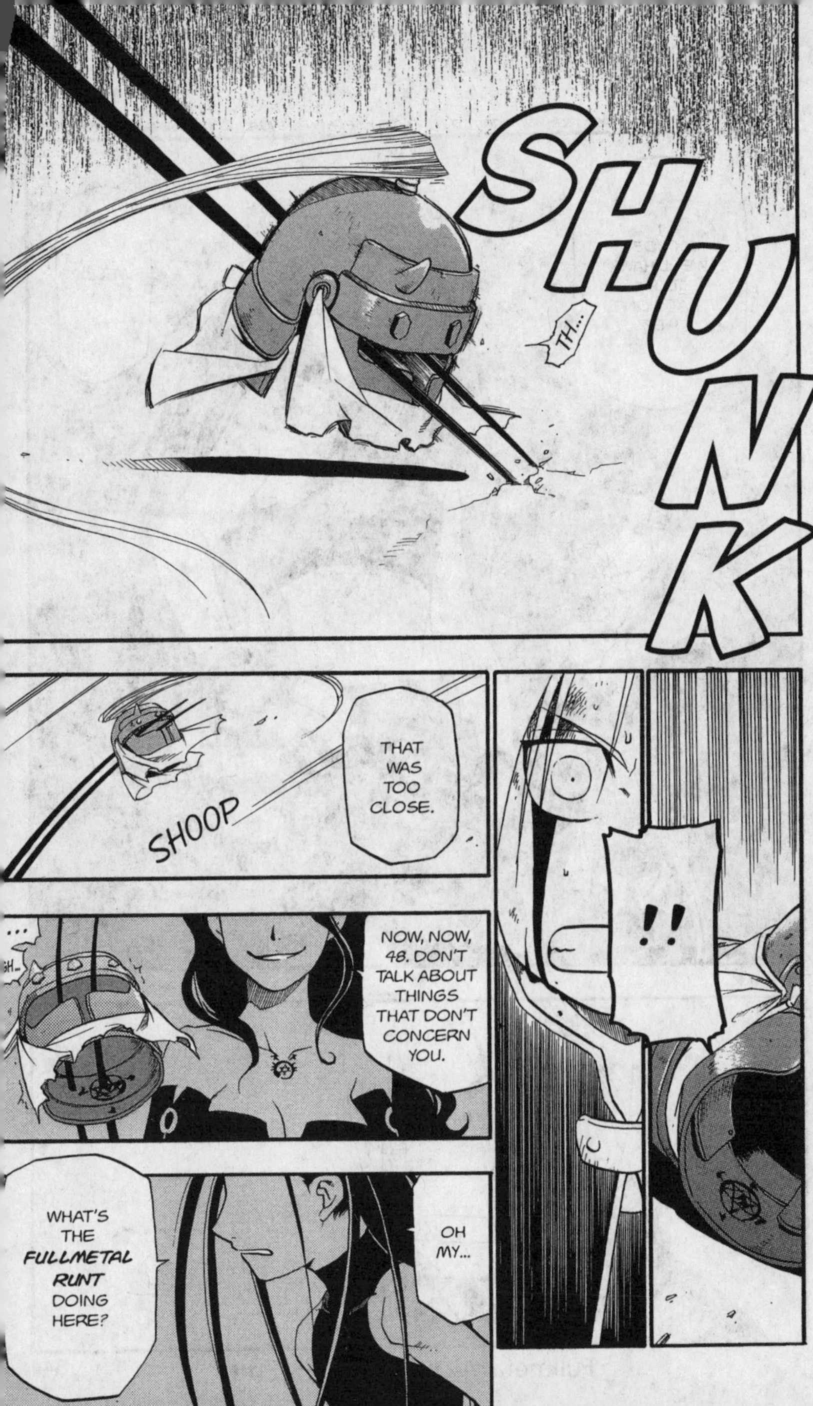
SHUNK
TH...
!!
SHOOP
THAT WAS TOO CLOSE.
...
NOW, NOW, 48. DON'T TALK ABOUT THINGS THAT DON'T CONCERN YOU.
OH MY...
WHAT'S THE *FULLMETAL RUNT* DOING HERE?

*THIS MANGA WAS ORIGINALLY PRINTED IN MONTHLY **SHONEN GANGAN**, APRIL 2002 THROUGH JULY 2002.*

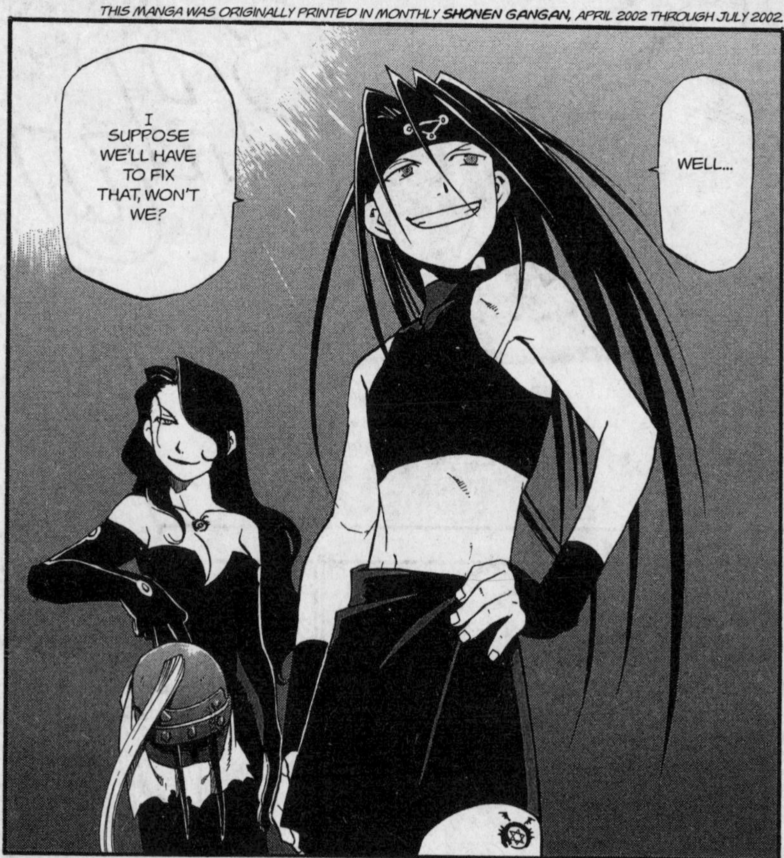
WELL...
I SUPPOSE WE'LL HAVE TO FIX THAT, WON'T WE?

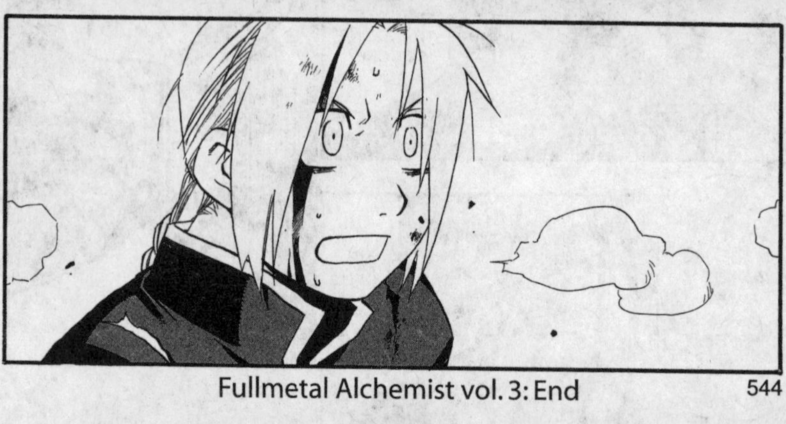

Fullmetal Alchemist vol. 3: End

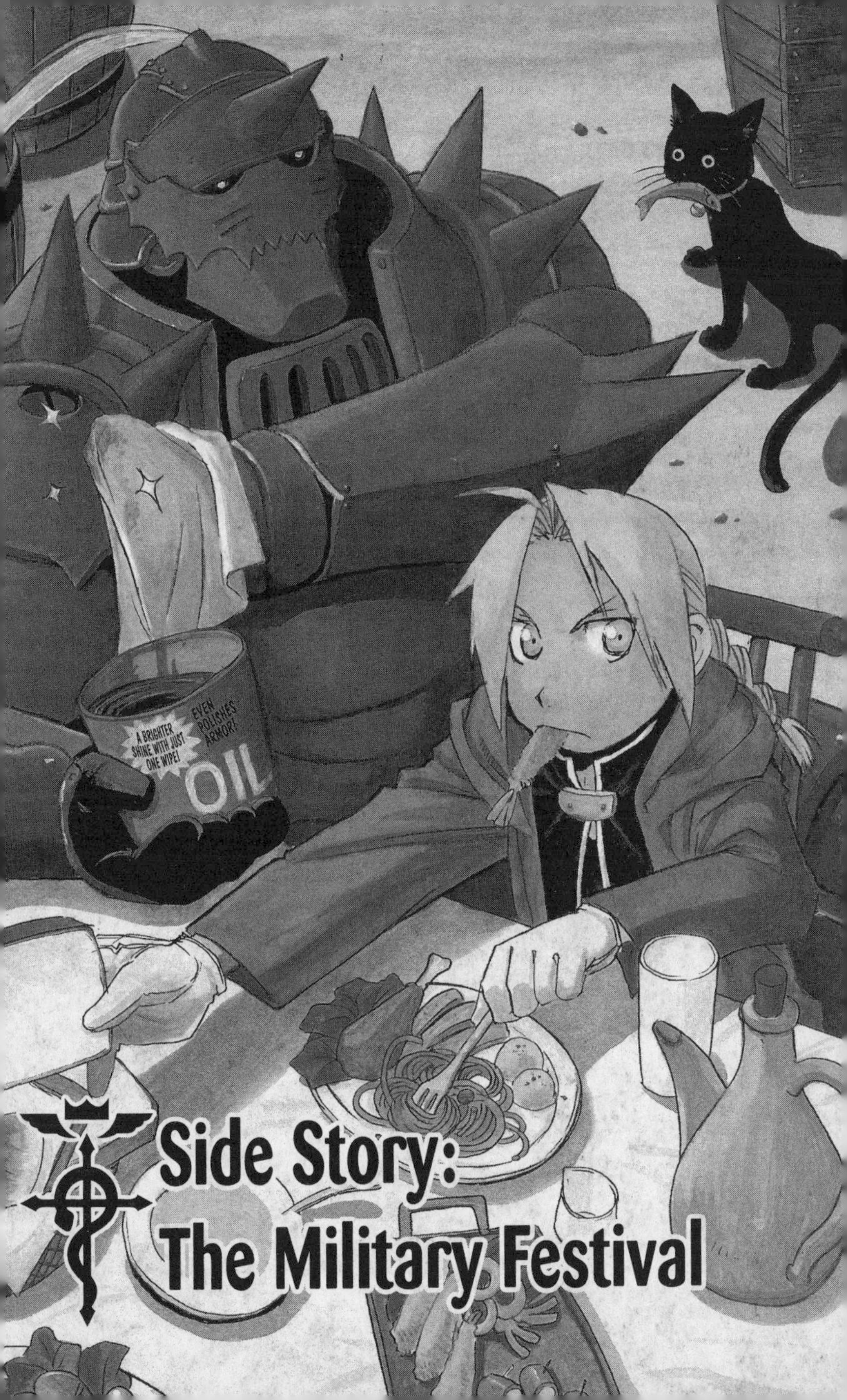
EVEN POLISHES ARMOR!
A BRIGHTER SHINE WITH JUST ONE WIPE!
OIL

Side Story: The Military Festival

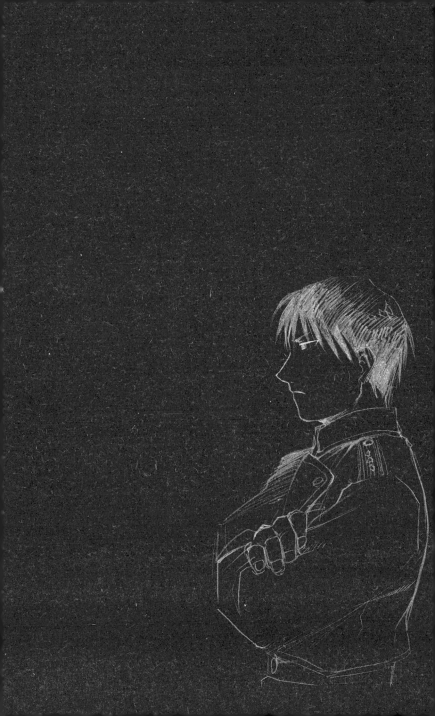

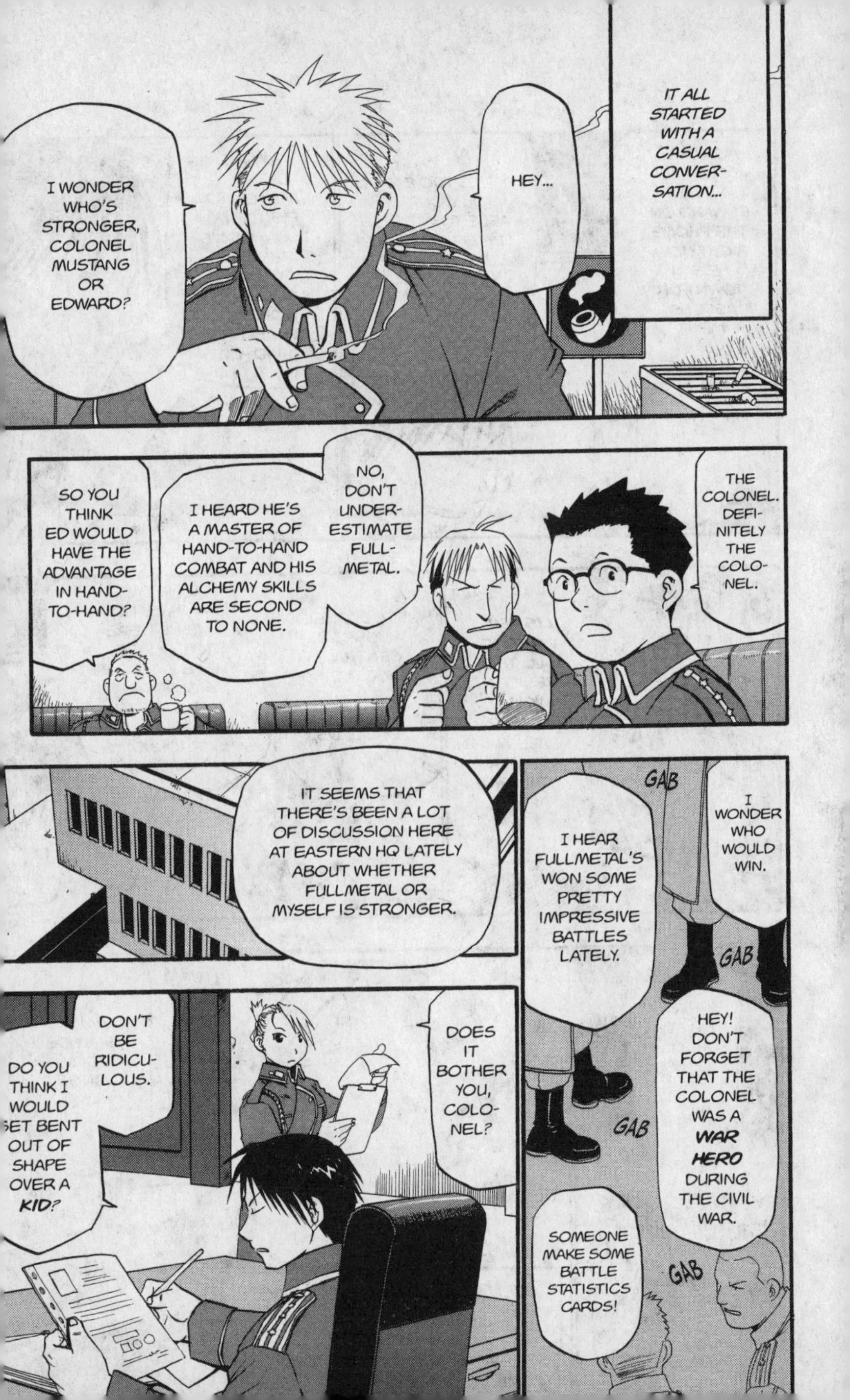
IT ALL STARTED WITH A CASUAL CONVERSATION...
HEY...
I WONDER WHO'S STRONGER, COLONEL MUSTANG OR EDWARD?
THE COLONEL. DEFINITELY THE COLONEL.
NO, DON'T UNDERESTIMATE FULLMETAL.
I HEARD HE'S A MASTER OF HAND-TO-HAND COMBAT AND HIS ALCHEMY SKILLS ARE SECOND TO NONE.
SO YOU THINK ED WOULD HAVE THE ADVANTAGE IN HAND-TO-HAND?
GAB
I WONDER WHO WOULD WIN.
I HEAR FULLMETAL'S WON SOME PRETTY IMPRESSIVE BATTLES LATELY.
GAB
HEY! DON'T FORGET THAT THE COLONEL WAS A **WAR HERO** DURING THE CIVIL WAR.
GAB
SOMEONE MAKE SOME BATTLE STATISTICS CARDS!
GAB
IT SEEMS THAT THERE'S BEEN A LOT OF DISCUSSION HERE AT EASTERN HQ LATELY ABOUT WHETHER FULLMETAL OR MYSELF IS STRONGER.
DOES IT BOTHER YOU, COLONEL?
DON'T BE RIDICULOUS.
DO YOU THINK I WOULD ET BENT OUT OF SHAPE OVER A ***KID***?

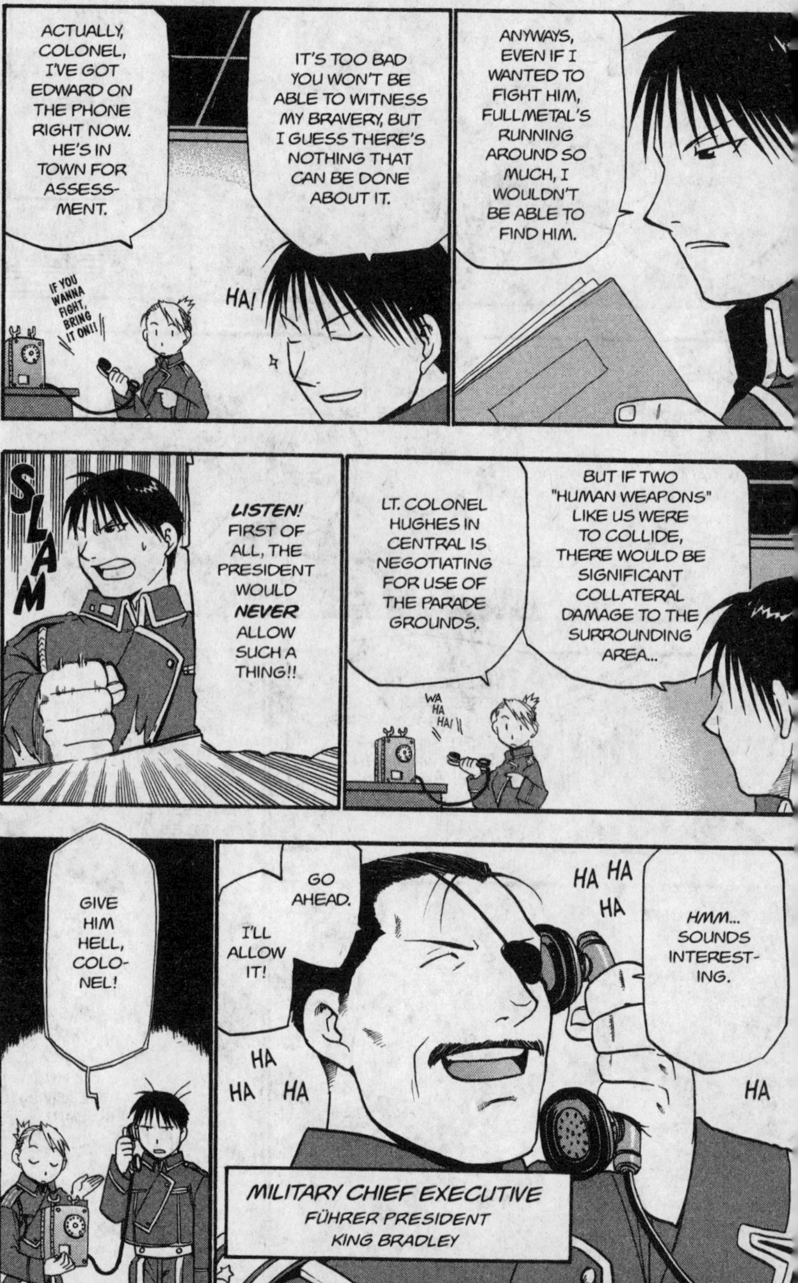
ANYWAYS, EVEN IF I WANTED TO FIGHT HIM, FULLMETAL'S RUNNING AROUND SO MUCH, I WOULDN'T BE ABLE TO FIND HIM.
IT'S TOO BAD YOU WON'T BE ABLE TO WITNESS MY BRAVERY, BUT I GUESS THERE'S NOTHING THAT CAN BE DONE ABOUT IT.
HA!
ACTUALLY, COLONEL, I'VE GOT EDWARD ON THE PHONE RIGHT NOW. HE'S IN TOWN FOR ASSESS-MENT.
IF YOU WANNA FIGHT, BRING IT ON!!
BUT IF TWO "HUMAN WEAPONS" LIKE US WERE TO COLLIDE, THERE WOULD BE SIGNIFICANT COLLATERAL DAMAGE TO THE SURROUNDING AREA...
LT. COLONEL HUGHES IN CENTRAL IS NEGOTIATING FOR USE OF THE PARADE GROUNDS.
WA HA HA!
SLAM
LISTEN! FIRST OF ALL, THE PRESIDENT WOULD *NEVER* ALLOW SUCH A THING!!
HMM... SOUNDS INTEREST-ING.
HA HA HA
GO AHEAD.
I'LL ALLOW IT!
HA HA HA
HA
MILITARY CHIEF EXECUTIVE
FÜHRER PRESIDENT
KING BRADLEY
GIVE HIM HELL, COLO-NEL!

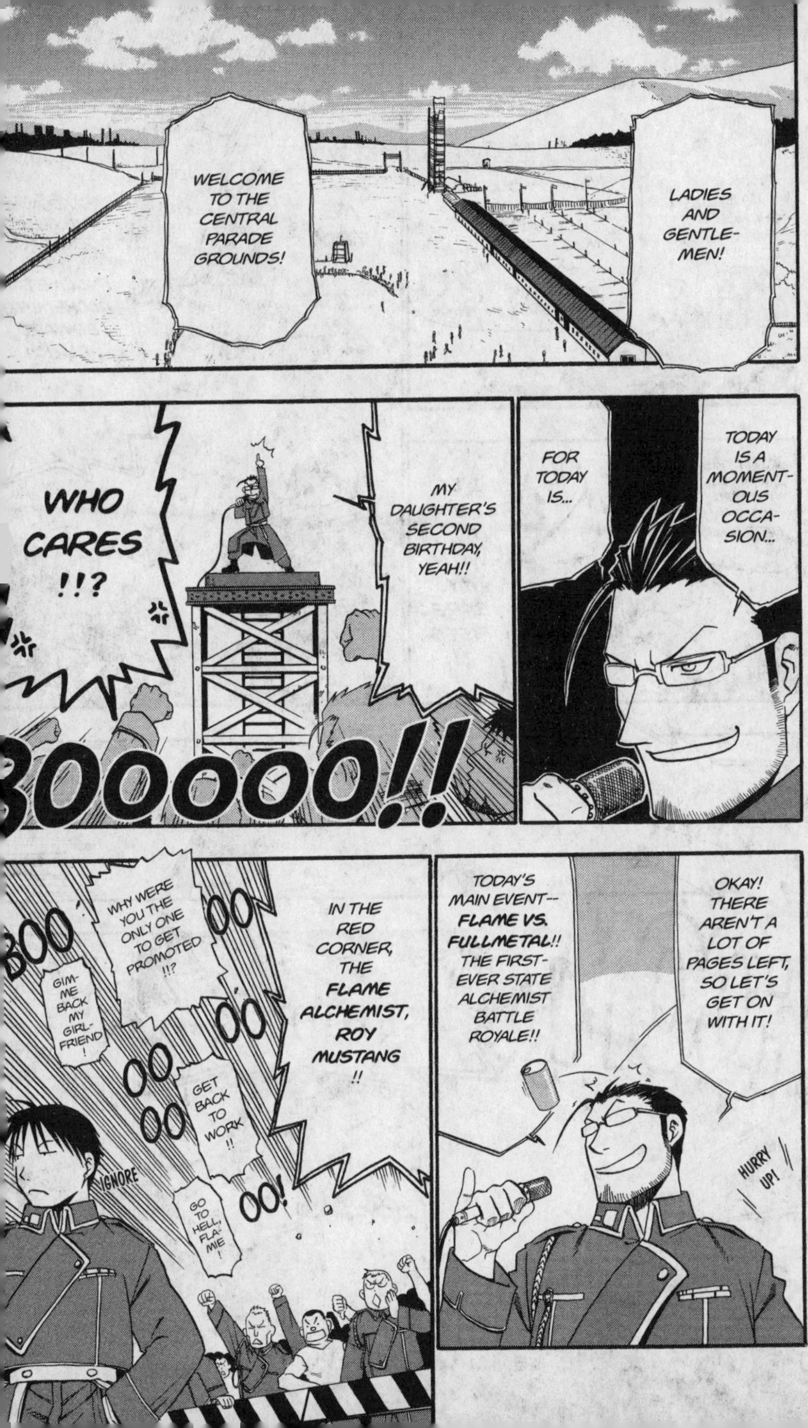
LADIES AND GENTLE-MEN!
WELCOME TO THE CENTRAL PARADE GROUNDS!
TODAY IS A MOMENT-OUS OCCA-SION...
FOR TODAY IS...
MY DAUGHTER'S SECOND BIRTHDAY, YEAH!!
WHO CARES!!?
BOOOOO!!
OKAY! THERE AREN'T A LOT OF PAGES LEFT, SO LET'S GET ON WITH IT!
TODAY'S MAIN EVENT-- **FLAME VS. FULLMETAL!!** THE FIRST-EVER STATE ALCHEMIST BATTLE ROYALE!!
HURRY UP!
IN THE RED CORNER, THE **FLAME ALCHEMIST, ROY MUSTANG**!!
WHY WERE YOU THE ONLY ONE TO GET PROMOTED!!?
GIMME BACK MY GIRL-FRIEND!
GET BACK TO WORK!!
GO TO HELL, FLAMIE!
IGNORE
BOOOOOOOOOOO!

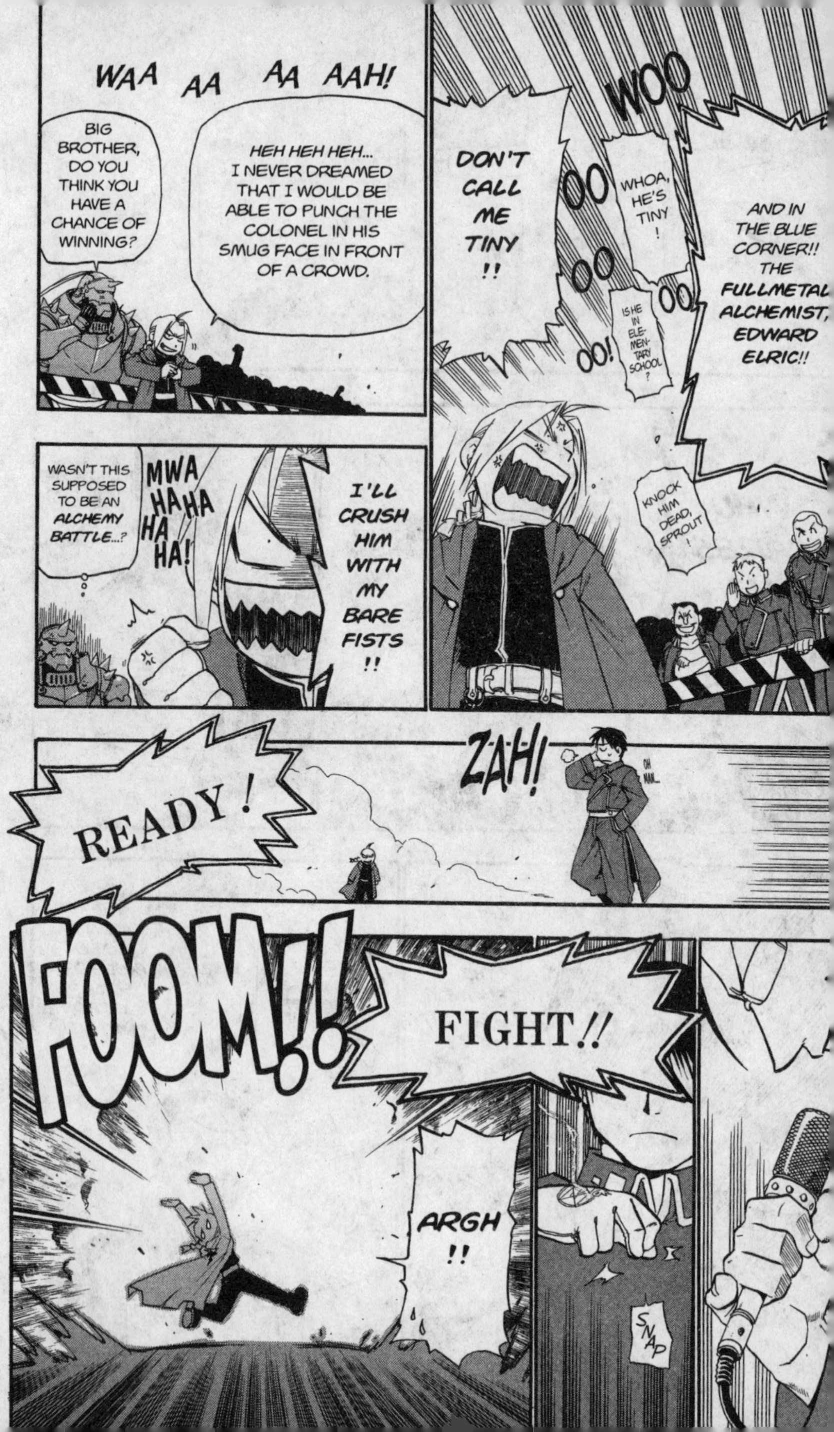
AND IN THE BLUE CORNER!! THE FULLMETAL ALCHEMIST, EDWARD ELRIC!!
WOO OO OO OO OO!
WHOA, HE'S TINY!
IS HE IN ELEMENTARY SCHOOL?
DON'T CALL ME TINY!!
KNOCK HIM DEAD, SPROUT!
WAA AA AA AAH!
HEH HEH HEH... I NEVER DREAMED THAT I WOULD BE ABLE TO PUNCH THE COLONEL IN HIS SMUG FACE IN FRONT OF A CROWD.
BIG BROTHER, DO YOU THINK YOU HAVE A CHANCE OF WINNING?
I'LL CRUSH HIM WITH MY BARE FISTS!!
MWA HA HA HA HA HA!
WASN'T THIS SUPPOSED TO BE AN ALCHEMY BATTLE...?
OH MAN...
ZAH!
READY!
FIGHT!!
SNAP
ARGH!!
FOOM!!

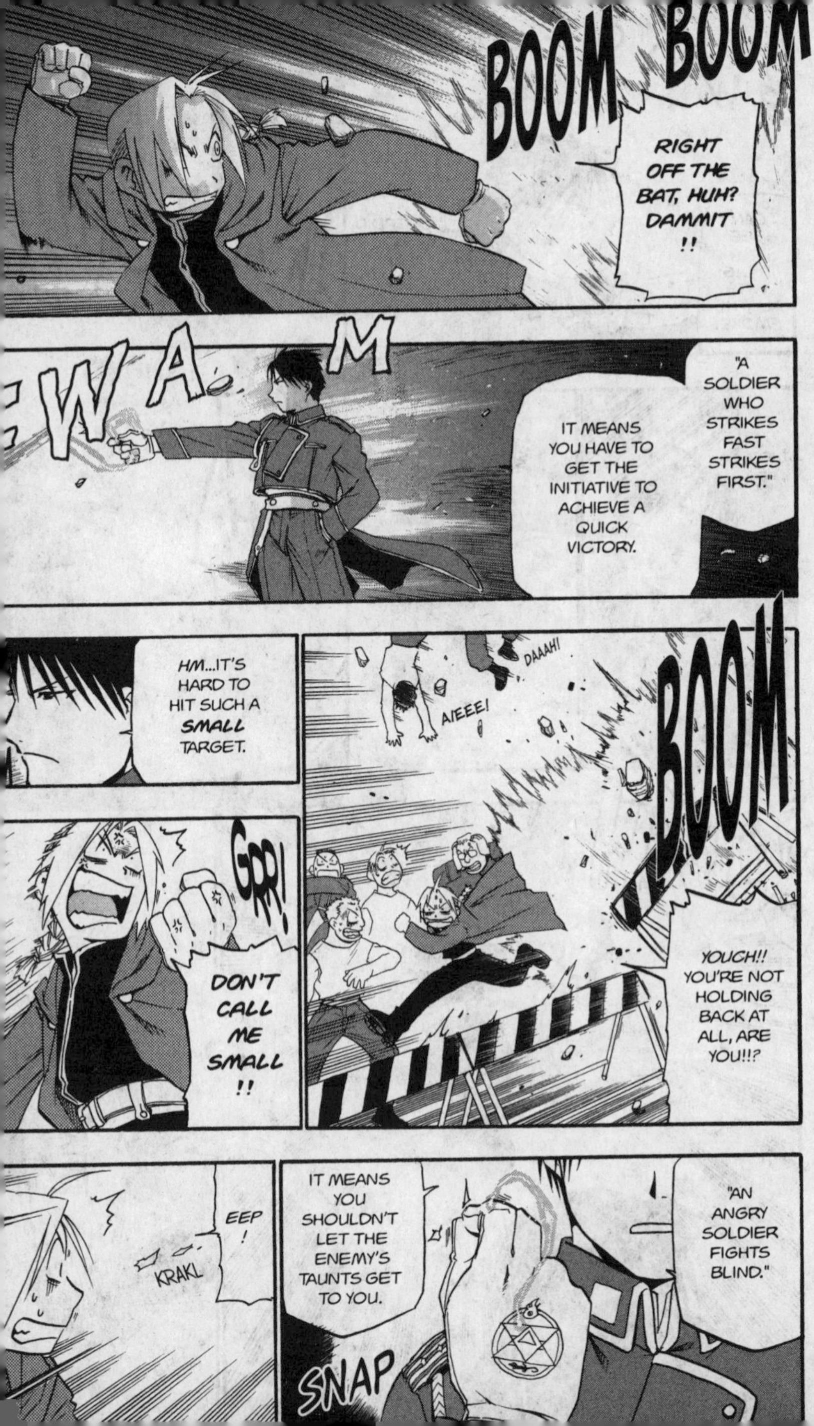
BOOM BOOM
RIGHT OFF THE BAT, HUH? DAMMIT !!
"A SOLDIER WHO STRIKES FAST STRIKES FIRST."
IT MEANS YOU HAVE TO GET THE INITIATIVE TO ACHIEVE A QUICK VICTORY.
WAM
DAAAH!
AIEEE!
BOOM
YOUCH!! YOU'RE NOT HOLDING BACK AT ALL, ARE YOU!!?
HM...IT'S HARD TO HIT SUCH A SMALL TARGET.
GRR!
DON'T CALL ME SMALL !!
"AN ANGRY SOLDIER FIGHTS BLIND."
IT MEANS YOU SHOULDN'T LET THE ENEMY'S TAUNTS GET TO YOU.
SNAP
EEP!
KRAKL

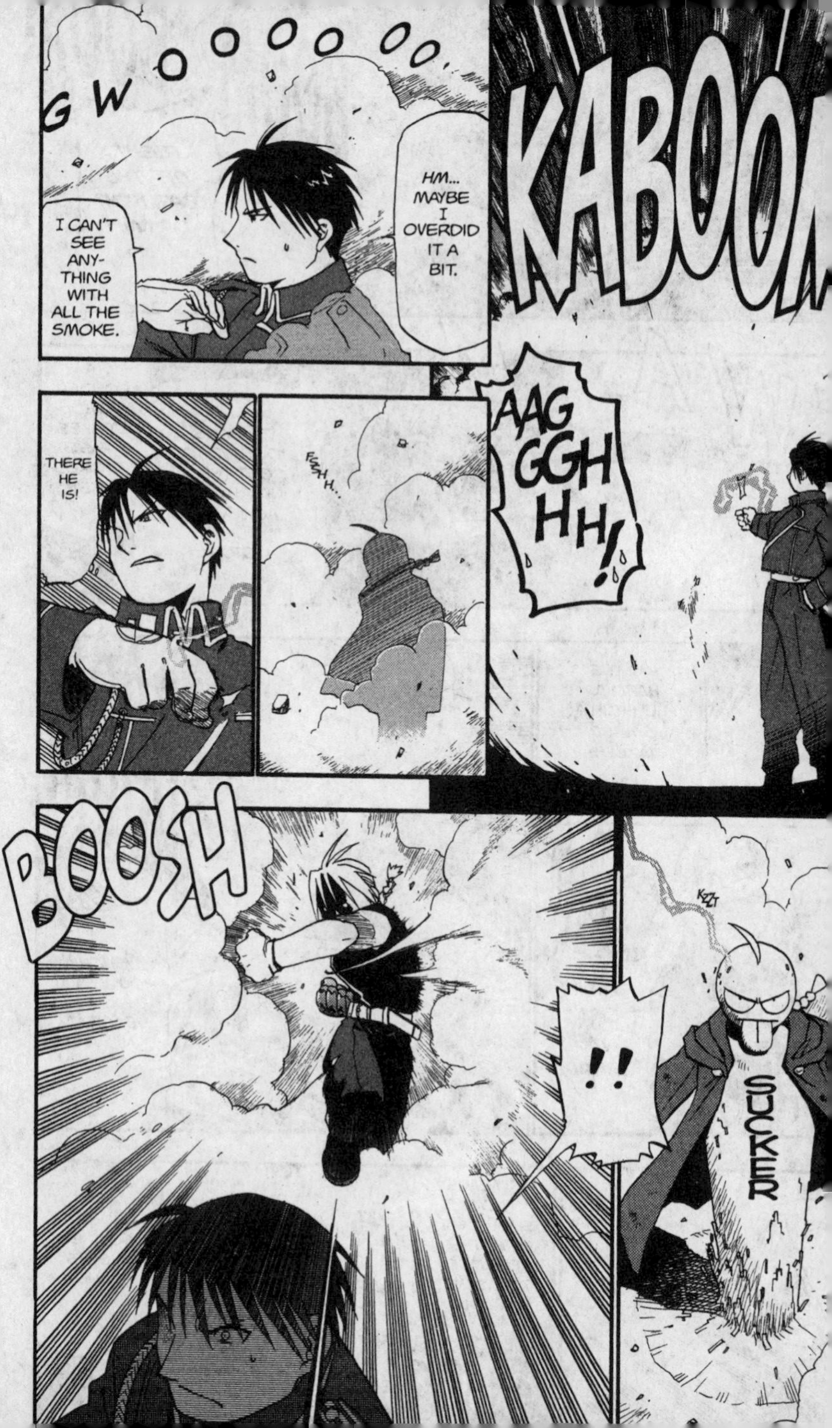

KABOOM
AAGGGHHH!
GWOOOOOO
HM... MAYBE I OVERDID IT A BIT.
I CAN'T SEE ANYTHING WITH ALL THE SMOKE.
FSSHH...
THERE HE IS!
KZZT
SUCKER
BOOSH
!!

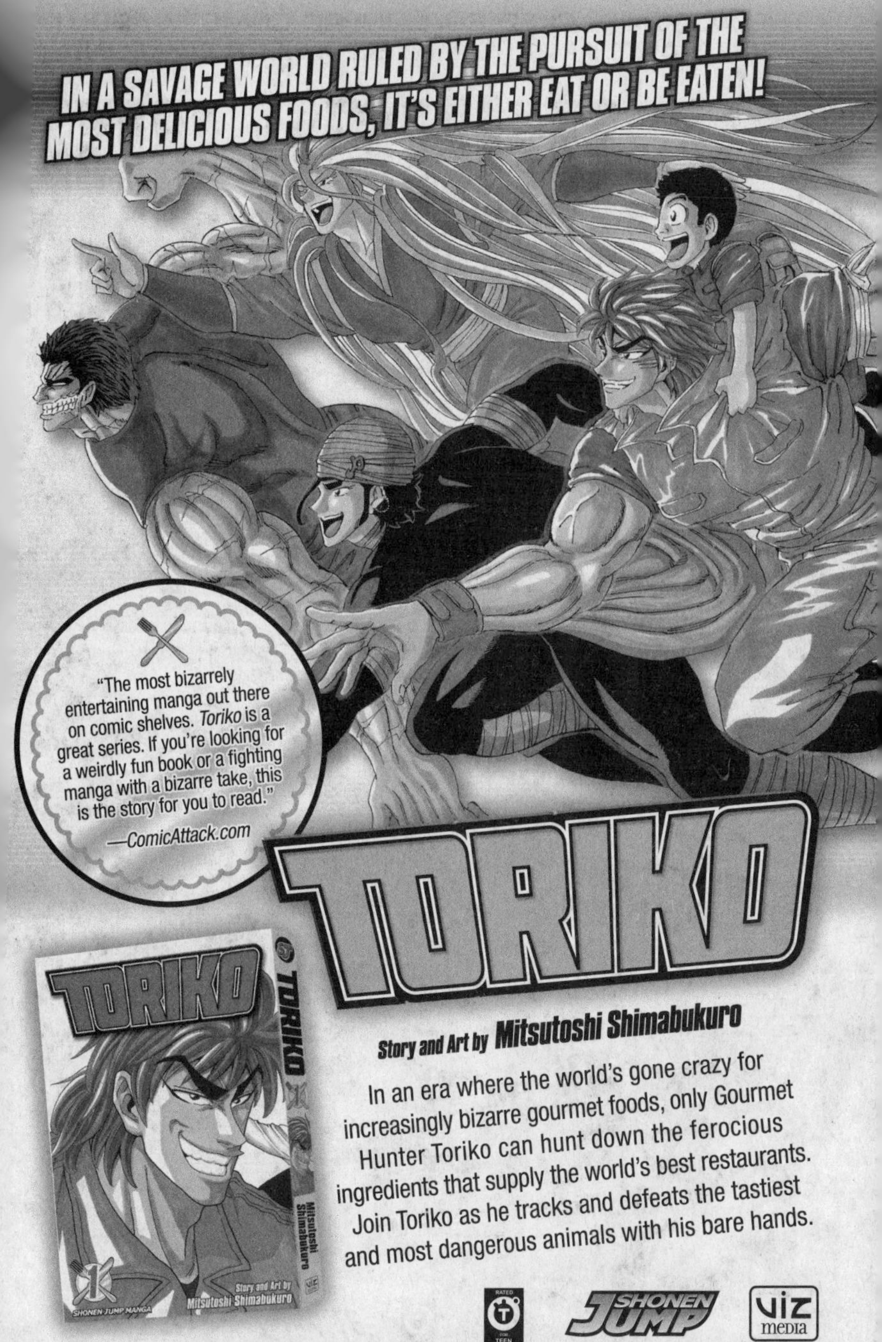
IN A SAVAGE WORLD RULED BY THE PURSUIT OF THE MOST DELICIOUS FOODS, IT'S EITHER EAT OR BE EATEN!
"The most bizarrely entertaining manga out there on comic shelves. Toriko is a great series. If you're looking for a weirdly fun book or a fighting manga with a bizarre take, this is the story for you to read."
—ComicAttack.com
TORIKO
Story and Art by Mitsutoshi Shimabukuro
In an era where the world's gone crazy for increasingly bizarre gourmet foods, only Gourmet Hunter Toriko can hunt down the ferocious ingredients that supply the world's best restaurants. Join Toriko as he tracks and defeats the tastiest and most dangerous animals with his bare hands.
TORIKO
SHONEN JUMP MANGA
Story and Art by Mitsutoshi Shimabukuro
RATED T FOR TEEN
ratings.viz.com
SHONEN JUMP
www.shonenjump.com
VIZ media
www.viz.com

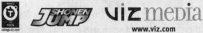

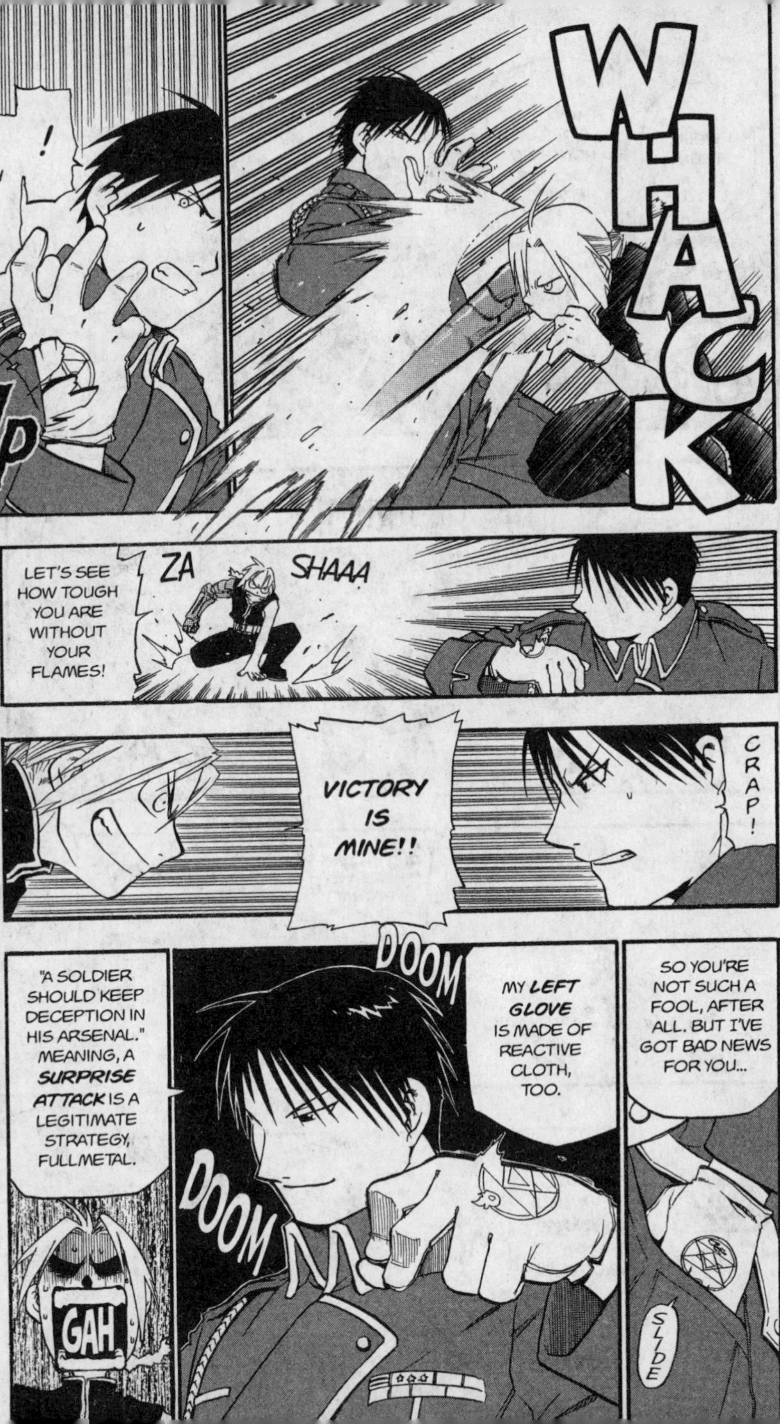
WHACK
!
ZA SHAAA
LET'S SEE HOW TOUGH YOU ARE WITHOUT YOUR FLAMES!
CRAP!
VICTORY IS MINE!!
SO YOU'RE NOT SUCH A FOOL, AFTER ALL. BUT I'VE GOT BAD NEWS FOR YOU...
SLIDE
DOOM
MY LEFT GLOVE IS MADE OF REACTIVE CLOTH, TOO.
DOOM
"A SOLDIER SHOULD KEEP DECEPTION IN HIS ARSENAL." MEANING, A SURPRISE ATTACK IS A LEGITIMATE STRATEGY, FULLMETAL.
GAH

THIS MANGA WAS ORIGINALLY PRINTED IN GANGAN POWERED, SPRING 2002

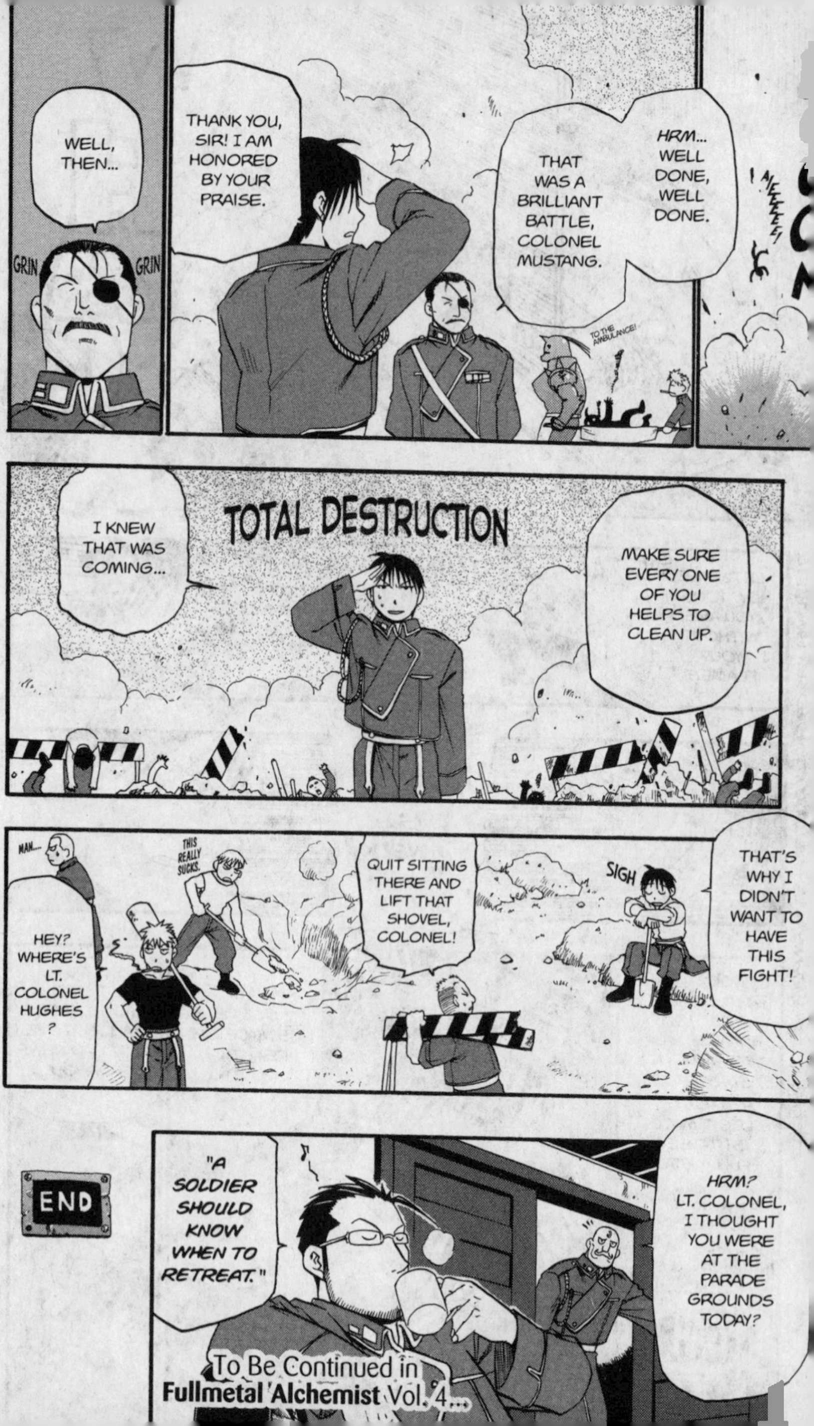
AIEEEEE!
HRM... WELL DONE, WELL DONE.
THAT WAS A BRILLIANT BATTLE, COLONEL MUSTANG.
TO THE AMBULANCE!
THANK YOU, SIR! I AM HONORED BY YOUR PRAISE.
WELL, THEN...
GRIN
GRIN
MAKE SURE EVERY ONE OF YOU HELPS TO CLEAN UP.
TOTAL DESTRUCTION
I KNEW THAT WAS COMING...
THAT'S WHY I DIDN'T WANT TO HAVE THIS FIGHT!
SIGH
QUIT SITTING THERE AND LIFT THAT SHOVEL, COLONEL!
THIS REALLY SUCKS.
HEY? WHERE'S LT. COLONEL HUGHES?
MAN....
HRM? LT. COLONEL, I THOUGHT YOU WERE AT THE PARADE GROUNDS TODAY?
"A SOLDIER SHOULD KNOW WHEN TO RETREAT."
END
To Be Continued in
Fullmetal Alchemist Vol. 4...

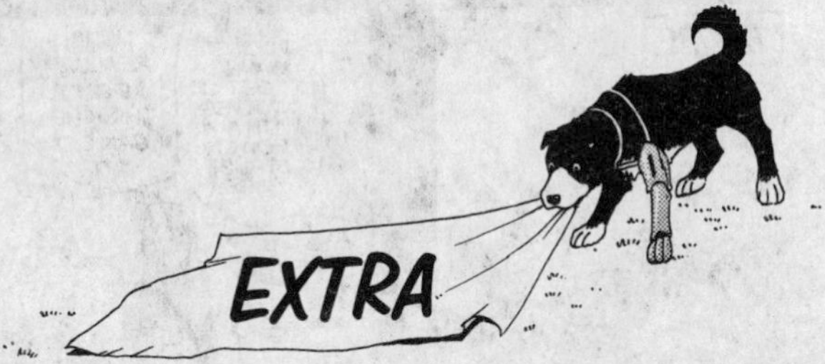
EXTRA

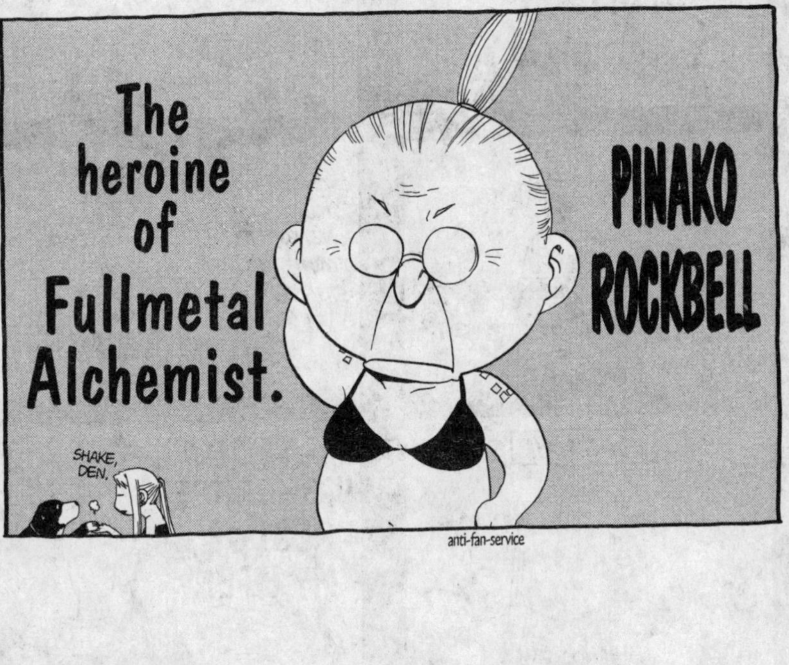
The heroine of Fullmetal Alchemist.
PINAKO ROCKBELL
SHAKE, DEN.

anti-fan-service

THE AMBITIOUS ALCHEMIST

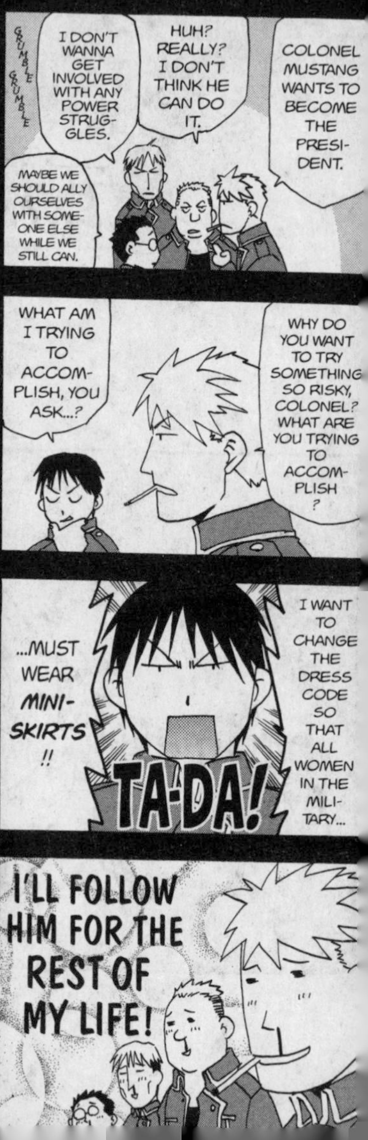
COLONEL MUSTANG WANTS TO BECOME THE PRESIDENT.
HUH? REALLY? I DON'T THINK HE CAN DO IT.
I DON'T WANNA GET INVOLVED WITH ANY POWER STRUGGLES.
GRUMBLE GRUMBLE
MAYBE WE SHOULD ALLY OURSELVES WITH SOMEONE ELSE WHILE WE STILL CAN.
WHY DO YOU WANT TO TRY SOMETHING SO RISKY, COLONEL? WHAT ARE YOU TRYING TO ACCOMPLISH?
WHAT AM I TRYING TO ACCOMPLISH, YOU ASK...?
I WANT TO CHANGE THE DRESS CODE SO THAT ALL WOMEN IN THE MILITARY...
TA-DA!
...MUST WEAR MINI-SKIRTS!!
I'LL FOLLOW HIM FOR THE REST OF MY LIFE!

AL'S BIG HAIRSTYLE STRATEGY

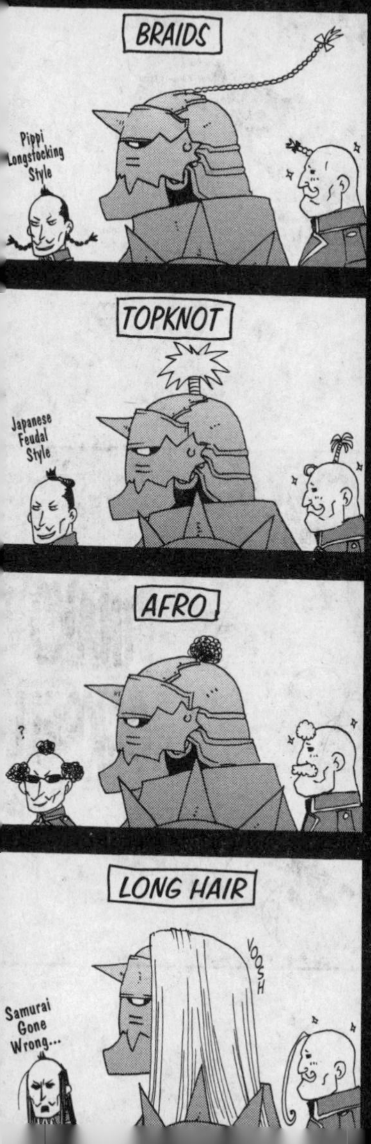
BRAIDS
Pippi Longstocking Style
TOPKNOT
Japanese Feudal Style
AFRO
?
LONG HAIR
VOOSH
Samurai Gone Wrong...

I Made Pinako's Hairstyle like This Just So I Could Do This Joke (Seriously!)

TODAY, WE ARE GOING TO EXPLORE THE MYSTERY BEHIND PINAKO ROCKBELL'S HAIR-STYLE.
FIRST LET'S ZOOM IN.
ZOOM IN CLOS-ER
MUCH, MUCH CLOS-ER
GLOOP...
NATTO!!*
EWWWWWW!

FULLMETAL ALCHEMIST 3

SPECIAL THANKS TO...

KEISUI TAKAEDA-SAN
SANKICHI HINODEYA-CHAN
JUN MORIYASU-SAN
MASANORI-SAN
JUNSHI BABA-SAN
YOICHI KAMITONO-CHAN
NANKAKUREMAN-SAN
NORIKO GUNJO-SAN
HASHIDA-KUN

YUICHI SHIMOMURA-SHI (MANAGER)

AND YOU!!

HAPPY LOAN CO.
MY NAME IS YOKO. PLEASE TAKE ME HOME.

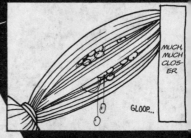